The Complete Cisco
VPN Configuration Guide

Richard Deal

Cisco Press

800 East 96th Street
Indianapolis, Indiana 46240 USA

The Complete Cisco VPN Configuration Guide

Richard Deal

Copyright © 2006 Cisco Systems, Inc.

Published by:
Cisco Press
800 East 96th Street
Indianapolis, IN 46240 USA

Printed in the United States of America   5 6 7 8 9 0

First Printing December 2005

Library of Congress Cataloging-in-Publication Number: 2004105575

ISBN: 1-58705-204-0

Trademark Acknowledgments

All terms mentioned in this book that are known to be trademarks or service marks have been appropriately capitalized. Cisco Press or Cisco Systems, Inc. cannot attest to the accuracy of this information. Use of a term in this book should not be regarded as affecting the validity of any trademark or service mark.

Warning and Disclaimer

This book is designed to provide information about setting up VPNs, on Cisco products, including the IOS routers, VPN 3000 concentrators, PIX and ASA security appliances, VPN Client software, 3002 hardware client, SSL Client, and Microsoft's Windows Client. Every effort has been made to make this book as complete and as accurate as possible, but no warranty or fitness is implied.

The information is provided on an "as is" basis. The author, Cisco Press, and Cisco Systems, Inc. shall have neither liability nor responsibility to any person or entity with respect to any loss or damages arising from the information contained in this book or from the use of the discs or programs that may accompany it.

The opinions expressed in this book belong to the author and are not necessarily those of Cisco Systems, Inc.

Corporate and Government Sales

Cisco Press offers excellent discounts on this book when ordered in quantity for bulk purchases or special sales.

For more information please contact: **U.S. Corporate and Government Sales**   1-800-382-3419
corpsales@pearsontechgroup.com

For sales outside the U.S. please contact: **International Sales**   international@pearsoned.com

Feedback Information

At Cisco Press, our goal is to create in-depth technical books of the highest quality and value. Each book is crafted with care and precision, undergoing rigorous development that involves the unique expertise of members from the professional technical community.

Readers' feedback is a natural continuation of this process. If you have any comments regarding how we could improve the quality of this book, or otherwise alter it to better suit your needs, you can contact us through e-mail at feedback@ciscopress.com. Please make sure to include the book title and ISBN in your message.

We greatly appreciate your assistance.

Publisher	John Wait
Editor-in-Chief	John Kane
Cisco Representative	Anthony Wolfenden
Cisco Press Program Manager	Jeff Brady
Executive Editor	Mary Beth Ray
Production Manager	Patrick Kanouse
Development Editor	Jill Batistick
Project Editor	Rozi Harris
Editorial Assistant	Raina Han
Copy Editor	Ivan Weiss
Technical Editors	Pete Davis, Steve Marcinek, and Mark Newcomb
Book and Cover Designer	Louisa Adair
Composition	Interactive Composition Corporation
Indexer	Keith Cline

CISCO SYSTEMS

Corporate Headquarters
Cisco Systems, Inc.
170 West Tasman Drive
San Jose, CA 95134-1706
USA
www.cisco.com
Tel: 408 526-4000
   800 553-NETS (6387)
Fax: 408 526-4100

European Headquarters
Cisco Systems International BV
Haarlerbergpark
Haarlerbergweg 13-19
1101 CH Amsterdam
The Netherlands
www-europe.cisco.com
Tel: 31 0 20 357 1000
Fax: 31 0 20 357 1100

Americas Headquarters
Cisco Systems, Inc.
170 West Tasman Drive
San Jose, CA 95134-1706
USA
www.cisco.com
Tel: 408 526-7660
Fax: 408 527-0883

Asia Pacific Headquarters
Cisco Systems, Inc.
Capital Tower
168 Robinson Road
#22-01 to #29-01
Singapore 068912
www.cisco.com
Tel: +65 6317 7777
Fax: +65 6317 7799

Cisco Systems has more than 200 offices in the following countries and regions. Addresses, phone numbers, and fax numbers are listed on the
Cisco.com Web site at www.cisco.com/go/offices.

Argentina • Australia • Austria • Belgium • Brazil • Bulgaria • Canada • Chile • China PRC • Colombia • Costa Rica • Croatia • Czech Republic
Denmark • Dubai, UAE • Finland • France • Germany • Greece • Hong Kong SAR • Hungary • India • Indonesia • Ireland • Israel • Italy
Japan • Korea • Luxembourg • Malaysia • Mexico • The Netherlands • New Zealand • Norway • Peru • Philippines • Poland • Portugal
Puerto Rico • Romania • Russia • Saudi Arabia • Scotland • Singapore • Slovakia • Slovenia • South Africa • Spain • Sweden
Switzerland • Taiwan • Thailand • Turkey • Ukraine • United Kingdom • United States • Venezuela • Vietnam • Zimbabwe

About the Author

Richard A. Deal has 20 years of experience in the computing and networking industry including networking, training, systems administration, and programming. In addition to a B.S. in mathematics and computer science from Grove City College; Richard holds many certifications from Cisco. For the past eight years, Richard has operated his own company, The Deal Group Inc.

Besides teaching various Cisco certification courses, Richard has also published many books. Richard recently published *Cisco Router Firewall Security* with Cisco Press, which is on the Cisco CCIE Security reading list. Richard is also the author of the following books: *CCNA Cisco Certified Network Associate Study Guide* (Exam 640-801), *Cisco PIX Firewalls*, and *CCNP BCMSN Exam Cram 2* (642-811).

Richard is actively writing Cisco certification self-preparation tests for Boson (http://www.boson.com) and has written many self-preparation tests for the CCSP certification. Richard currently lives with his wife, Natalya, and his daughter, Emily Alina, in Oviedo, FL, just outside of Orlando.

About the Technical Reviewers

Pete Davis has been working with computers and networks since he was able to walk. By age 15, he was one of the youngest professional network engineers and one of the first employees at an Internet service provider. Pete implemented and maintained the systems and networks behind New England's largest consumer Internet service provider, TIAC (The Internet Access Company). In 1997, Pete joined Shiva Corporation as product specialist. Since 1998, Pete has been with Altiga Networks, a VPN Concentrator manufacturer in Franklin, MA, that was acquired by Cisco Systems on March 29, 2000. As product line manager, Pete is responsible for driving new VPN-related products and features.

Stephen Marcinek, CCIE No. 7225, is a technical trainer for Boson Training, a Cisco Learning Partner. He develops course content and delivers numerous classes in Cisco Networking and Security, from Introductory to CCIE level. Stephen also consults for numerous large organizations. He holds a bachelor's degree from Rutgers University and is a member of Mensa.

Mark Newcomb, CCNP, CCDP, is a retired network security engineer. Mark has more than 20 years of experience in the networking industry, focusing on the financial and medical industries. Mark is a frequent contributor and reviewer for Cisco Press books.

Dedications

This book is dedicated to my family: my wife, Natalya, and my daughter, Emily Alina. Life with you is always filled with joy and happiness. Thank you for making me complete.

Acknowledgments

A real special thanks goes out to the technical editors of this book: Pete Davis, Mark Newcomb, and especially Steve Marcinek. I have personally known Steve for quite some time and can always count on him as a coworker and friend.

A big thank you also goes out to the production team for this book. Raina Han, Brett Bartow, Sheri Cain, Mary Beth Ray, Jim Schachterle, Michelle Grandlin, Jill Batistick, and Rozi Harris have been incredibly professional and a pleasure to work with. I couldn't have asked for a finer team.

This Book Is Safari Enabled

The Safari® Enabled icon on the cover of your favorite technology book means the book is available through Safari Bookshelf. When you buy this book, you get free access to the online edition for 45 days.

Safari Bookshelf is an electronic reference library that lets you easily search thousands of technical books, find code samples, download chapters, and access technical information whenever and wherever you need it.

To gain 45-day Safari Enabled access to this book:

- Go to http://www.ciscopress.com/safarienabled
- Enter the ISBN of this book (shown on the back cover, above the bar code)
- Log in or Sign up (site membership is required to register your book)
- Enter the coupon code I3LK-ZHMM-JPYR-GUM3-LAP4

If you have difficulty registering on Safari Bookshelf or accessing the online edition, please e-mail customer-service@safaribooksonline.com.

Contents at a Glance

Table of Contents

Icons Used in This Book

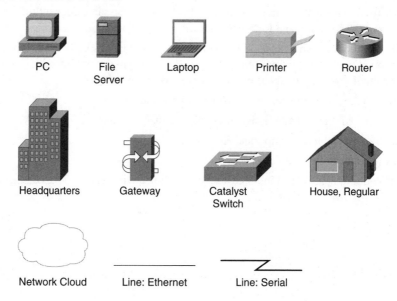

PC

File Server

Laptop

Printer

Router

Headquarters

Gateway

Catalyst Switch

House, Regular

Network Cloud

Line: Ethernet

Line: Serial

Command Syntax Conventions

The conventions used to present command syntax in this book are the same conventions used in the IOS Command Reference. The Command Reference describes these conventions as follows:

- **Boldface** indicates commands and keywords that are entered literally as shown. In actual configuration examples and output (not general command syntax), boldface indicates commands that are input manually by the user (such as a **show** command).
- *Italics* indicate arguments for which you supply actual values.
- Vertical bars (l) separate alternative, mutually exclusive elements.
- Square brackets [ ] indicate optional elements.
- Braces { } indicate a required choice.
- Braces within brackets [{ }] indicate a required choice within an optional element.

Introduction

Cisco has been an important part of the networking industry for many years and will continue to play a key role in company networks. The first router product I worked on, back in 1993, was a Cisco AGS+. I have seen many flavors of the IOS, including the introduction of most of the security features you see today in the Cisco IOS operating system, such as IPsec. Over the past several years, I have seen security becoming a key component in network design. And with more and more companies using the Internet as a business tool today, security is more important than ever, especially the use of VPNs.

Goals and Methods

Four years ago, I realized that there were many certification books to help people pass Cisco security certification exams; however, I found that there were no books of any substance that brought Cisco security features together to be applied in a real-life situation. I continually monitor various Cisco newsgroups and constantly see questions related to how to implement various Cisco security features. This was the foundation of my first security book, *Cisco PIX Firewalls*, with McGraw-Hill/Osborne.

As a security professional, I'm constantly asked questions about designing, implementing, and tuning VPNs that involve Cisco products. Because I constantly see many of the same questions over and over again, I've decided to pull this information together into a guide that encompasses building VPNs with Cisco products. The purpose of this book is to show you how to implement VPNs using the Cisco line of VPN-capable products, including the following:

- IOS Routers
- VPN 3000 Concentrators
- PIX and ASA Security Appliances
- VPN 3002 Hardware Client
- Cisco VPN Client Software
- Cisco SSL VPN Client Software
- Microsoft Client Software

Because this is not a certification book, but a "how to" book, I've included the following methods to help you with the "how to" process:

- Explaining what VPNs are and the technologies commonly used by VPNs
- Discussing the VPN implementation types, including IPsec, L2TP and PPTP, and SSL
- Discussing Cisco VPN-capable products and their features and capabilities
- Configuring the VPN 3000 concentrators for site-to-site, or LAN-to-LAN (L2L), and remote access VPNs
- Configuring the IOS routers for site-to-site and remote access VPNs
- Configuring the PIX and ASA security appliances for site-to-site and remote access VPNs
- Configuring the Cisco VPN Client, Cisco VPN 3002 Hardware Client, Microsoft VPN Windows Client, and the Cisco SSL Client for remote access VPNs
- Troubleshooting common VPN problems on Cisco products

- Supplying many examples, including a detailed case study at the end of the book, to show you how Cisco security features should be implemented

- Introducing you to real-life situations I've had to deal with in implementing and troubleshooting VPNs—every chapter includes a sidebar illustrating my own experiences

Who Should Read This Book?

This book is intended to provide the necessary framework for implementing VPNs on Cisco products. With this goal in mind, this is a "how-to" book. Although other objectives can be achieved from using this book, including preparation for the Cisco CCSP SNRS, SNPA, CSVPN, and SND exams, this book is written with one main goal in mind: implementing VPNs using Cisco VPN-capable products.

This book assumes that you have a basic understanding of the following:

- Cisco routers and the IOS operating system and command-line interface (CLI)
- Cisco PIX and ASA security appliances and the Finesse Operating System (FOS) and its CLI

For the other Cisco products I discuss in this book, such as the VPN 3000 concentrators, I assume you have little or no product knowledge. However, I assume that you do have an intermediate-to-advanced level of knowledge of Cisco products, and at a minimum, you should have the Cisco CCNA certification to understand and make best use of the material in this book.

Because this book focuses on using VPNs to provide secure connectivity between devices or networks, this book will be very useful for any network administrator or engineer who currently must implement VPNs using Cisco products.

How This Book Is Organized

Although this book can be read cover-to-cover, it is designed to be flexible and allow you to move easily between chapters and sections of chapters to cover just the material that you are interested in. However, each part and each chapter in each part builds upon the others. There are six parts to this book, excluding the book's front matter. Each part deals with an important component of VPNs on Cisco products. The following are the topics covered in the chapters of this book:

- **Chapter 1, "Overview of VPNs"**—This chapter contains a brief overview of the kinds of threats that you'll face in moving traffic across unprotected networks, and how VPNs can be used to secure your traffic. The chapter begins with a discussion of three common problems with moving traffic across an unprotected network: eavesdropping, masquerading, and man-in-the-middle attacks. The chapter then covers how a VPN can be used to defeat these attacks. I define what a VPN is, its components, designs, types of VPN implementations, and criteria you should consider when choosing a particular VPN solution.

- **Chapter 2, "VPN Technologies"**—This chapter contains an introduction to the technologies used to implement VPNs. More commonly than not, I'm surprised to see that many network administrators and engineers don't understand the technologies they are using to protect their traffic. Therefore, this chapter will give you an overview of what technologies VPNs commonly use and how these technologies work. This chapter covers keys, encryption, packet authentication, exchanging keys, and authentication methods.

- **Chapter 3, "IPsec"**—This chapter provides an overview of one of the most common VPN implementations: IPsec. Even though this book focuses on choosing VPN devices, configuring them, and troubleshooting them, understanding how a particular VPN is implemented is important to complete the previously mentioned tasks. Of all the VPN implementations I've worked with, IPsec is the most complex; and I've yet to find a book that brings the topic together in an easy-to-read and understandable fashion. Therefore, this chapter will discuss the standards that make up IPsec, the two phases involved in building a secure session, how the connections are built between IPsec peers, and common problems that can cause IPsec sessions to break, including address translation and firewalls, and solutions to these problems.

- **Chapter 4, "PPTP and L2TP"**—This chapter discusses two popular VPN implementations used in Microsoft-centric shops: PPTP and L2TP. I discuss how each of these VPNs are implemented and then compare the two solutions.

- **Chapter 5, "SSL VPNs"**—This chapter covers the use of SSL to implement a VPN solution. I discuss what an SSL VPN is and the three basic methods of implementation: clientless, thin client, and network. I also discuss when SSL VPNs are commonly used and the Cisco SSL solution: WebVPN.

- **Chapter 6, "Concentrator Product Information"**—This chapter introduces the VPN 3000 concentrators, which are commonly used to implement remote access VPNs. The chapter discusses the concentrator models, the modules that can be inserted into their chassis, the features available in various software versions, and an introduction to the CLI and GUI of the concentrators.

- **Chapter 7, "Concentrator Remote Access Connections with IPsec"**—This chapter focuses on terminating IPsec remote access sessions on VPN 3000 concentrators. I begin the chapter by discussing the two methods of controlling remote access: groups and users. I then discuss how to terminate IPsec remote access sessions on the concentrators. I conclude the chapter by discussing a new feature on the concentrators, Network Access Control (NAC), which can be used to force remote access clients to meet certain criteria before allowing them to establish a VPN session.

- **Chapter 8, "Concentrator Remote Access Connections with PPTP, L2TP, and WebVPN"**—This chapter focuses on terminating remote access sessions on VPN 3000 concentrators using PPTP, L2TP, and WebVPN. I begin the chapter by discussing the configuration of PPTP and L2TP on the concentrators. The second half of the chapter discusses the WebVPN (SSL VPN) features of the concentrators, where I cover topics like clientless, thin client, and SSL VPN Client connection. I also cover a new feature with WebVPN called Cisco Secure Desktop (CSD), which enhances security features for WebVPN implementations.

- **Chapter 9, "Concentrator Site-to-Site Connections"**—This chapter focuses on using a VPN 3000 concentrator to terminate L2L sessions. I begin the chapter by discussing some things you need to set up to allow an ISAKMP/IKE Phase 1 connection to be built. I then discuss how to add L2L sessions, which is a simple process. I end the chapter by discussing issues with overlapping addresses when connecting sites together, and how the concentrators can deal with this problem.

- **Chapter 10, "Concentrator Management"**—Unlike in other chapters in this book, I discuss some of the other configuration and administration capabilities of the concentrator here. I discuss the concentrator's bandwidth management feature, which allows it to control the amount of bandwidth a user, group, or L2L session can use; static and dynamic routing capabilities; redundancy features, including Virtual Router Redundancy Protocol (VRRP) and Virtual Cluster Agent (VCA); and the administrative features and screens.

- **Chapter 11, "Verifying and Troubleshooting Concentrator Connections"**—This chapter discusses how to use various tools concentrators have to troubleshoot VPN connection problems, including the Monitoring screens (which include the Live and Filterable Event Logs). The end of the chapter covers common problems you'll experience with remote access VPNs and what to look for on the concentrator to troubleshoot these problems. Problems I'll discuss include ISAKMP/IKE Phase 1 problems, such as policy mismatches and authentication issues, and ISAKMP/IKE Phase 2 problems, such as mismatches in transform sets and protected traffic.

- **Chapter 12, "Cisco VPN Software Client"**—This chapter focuses on using Cisco VPN Client software to establish IPsec remote access sessions to supported server products. I cover the client's features and installation, its GUI interface, creating connections to Easy VPN Servers (VPN gateways), GUI options (including application launcher, Windows login properties, automatic initiation, and its integrated stateful firewall), updating the client, and troubleshooting common problems with the software client.

- **Chapter 13, "Windows Software Client"**—This chapter discusses how to use Microsoft's Windows VPN client to establish PPTP and L2TP/IPsec sessions to a Cisco VPN gateway product. Even though this obviously is not a Cisco product, I discuss the use of Microsoft's client in this book because it is commonly used to establish VPNs to Cisco gateway devices. The chapter discusses the client's configuration, how to configure the VPN 3000 concentrators to accept connections from the Microsoft client, establishing connections from the client, and troubleshooting common client problems.

- **Chapter 14, "3002 Hardware Client"**—This chapter covers the use of the VPN 3002 hardware client for IPsec remote access sessions. This chapter discusses the client's models and features, deployment options, its CLI and GUI, using Quick Configuration to put a simple configuration on the client, authentication and connection options, and administrative tasks, including upgrading the client.

- **Chapter 15, "Router Product Information"**—This chapter covers two main topics: router deployment scenarios for VPNs and Cisco VPN-capable router products. It focuses on the special abilities of routers for VPN solutions: quality of service (QoS), data transport, and routing scalability.

- **Chapter 16, "Router ISKAMP/IKE Phase 1 Connectivity"**—This chapter focuses on ISAKMP/IKE Phase 1 connectivity for Cisco routers when using IPsec. I discuss how to create ISAKMP/IKE Phase 1 policies to protect the management connection, how to configure device authentication, monitoring the management connection, and how to configure a Cisco router as a Certificate Authority (CA).

- **Chapter 17, "Router Site-to-Site Connections"**—This chapter focuses on building L2L IPsec sessions on Cisco IOS routers. I discuss how to configure ISAKMP/IKE Phase 2 parameters (transform sets, crypto ACLs, and crypto maps), viewing and managing your L2L sessions, and issues with L2L sessions. When covering issues, the chapter discusses the details of a particular problem and a feature or features you can use on routers to solve these. Issues covered include migrating to an IPsec VPN solution, filtering IPsec traffic, connections breaking because of address translation and firewall devices, moving multicast and broadcast traffic across an L2L session, simplifying the L2L configuration, providing redundancy for IPsec, and scaling L2L implementations to very large peer numbers using dynamic multipoint VPNs (DMVPNs).

- **Chapter 18, "Router Remote Access Connections"**—This chapter discusses how to use an IOS router for remote access VPN solutions. This chapter discusses how to use the router as an Easy VPN Server and terminate IPsec sessions from clients, how to use the router as a client and terminate IPsec sessions on Easy VPN Servers, how to terminate L2L and remote access sessions on the same router, and how to terminate WebVPN client connections on a router.

- **Chapter 19, "Troubleshooting Router Connections"**—This chapter focuses on troubleshooting IPsec sessions on IOS routers. The first two sections discuss various **show**, **debug**, and **clear** commands you can use to assist you in viewing and troubleshooting ISAKMP/IKE Phase 1 and 2 connections. The chapter then introduces some new troubleshooting features, including IPsec VPN Monitoring, the Invalid SPI recovery feature, and clearing crypto sessions. The chapter ends with an in-depth discussion on fragmentation and the problems it causes for VPNs, and the tools you can use on a router to discover fragmentation problems and to deal with them, including the extended ping command, static MTU settings, TCP maximum segment size (MSS) tuning, and path MTU discovery (PMTUD).

- **Chapter 20, "PIX and ASA Product Information"**—This chapter covers two main topics: PIX and ASA deployment scenarios for VPNs and Cisco PIX and ASA products. This chapter focuses on the special abilities of PIXs and ASAs for VPN solutions: address translation, stateful firewall services, and redundancy.

- **Chapter 21, "PIX and ASA Site-to-Site Connections"**—This chapter discusses how to build IPsec L2L sessions on PIX and ASA security appliances using FOS versions 6.x and 7.x. I begin by discussing how to configure ISAKMP/IKE Phase 1 policies for the management connection and for authentication options. I then proceed to discuss the configuration of the ISAKMP/IKE Phase 2 parameters for the data connections, including transform sets, crypto ACLs, and crypto maps. The end of the chapter illustrates an example using security appliances to terminate L2L sessions.

- **Chapter 22, "PIX and ASA Remote Access Connections"**— This chapter discusses how to build IPsec remote access sessions on PIX and ASA security appliances using FOS 6.x and 7.x. I begin the chapter by discussing how to use a 6.x PIX as an Easy VPN Server to terminate IPsec remote access client sessions. I then discuss how to configure the PIX 501 and 506E as hardware clients to establish IPsec sessions to an Easy VPN Server. The last half of the chapter deals with IPsec remote access configurations using FOS 7.x, where I discuss how to configure the PIX and ASA as an Easy VPN Server. Many new features have been added in FOS 7.0, including tunnel groups, VCA, and WebVPN, which I discuss here.

- **Chapter 23, "Troubleshooting PIX And ASA Connections"**—This chapter discusses troubleshooting IPsec sessions on Cisco PIX and ASA security appliances. I focus on using various **show**, **debug**, and **clear** commands to view and troubleshoot ISAKMP/IKE Phase 1 and 2 connections, including examples of sessions that successfully establish to a peer and those that fail to establish.

- **Chapter 24, "Case Study"**—The last chapter contains a case study, implementing many of the features discussed throughout this book. It will present solutions and explanations to a company's problems for setting up VPN connectivity.

Originally, I had planned on covering a few other topics in this book, such as Security Device Manager (SDM) for IOS routers, Adaptive Security Device Manager (ASDM) for PIX and ASA security appliances, and VPN Router Management Center for Cisco Works VMS; however, because of page constraints, I've had to limit the material to a size that would fit into one book. Therefore, this book focuses on each product's main interface type when I discuss VPN configurations, like the IOS router's CLI. Also, many of the troubleshooting topics I discuss apply to all of the Cisco VPN products; therefore, I've selectively chosen to discuss certain problems in certain chapters, even though these problems are typically common with a particular VPN implementation type, such as IPsec.

Additional Information

Many of the features I discuss in this book are only supported on various software versions on the particular products. To find whether or not a feature is supported on a specific product platform or software version, use the Cisco Feature Navigator at http://www.cisco.com/go/fn. You'll need a CCO account to use this feature.

For a list of product security advisories and notices for Cisco products and software version releases, visit http://www.cisco.com/en/US/products/products_security_advisories_listing.html.

TIP   I highly recommend that you *carefully* view this list before loading a specific software version on your VPN product.

PART I

VPNs

CHAPTER 1

Overview of VPNs

This chapter introduces the concepts of virtual private networks (VPNs) and why they are used. I examine issues with sending traffic across public networks and what VPNs can do to protect this traffic. I introduce connection methods for VPNs, types of VPNs, things to consider when using VPNs, VPN components, VPN designs and issues, examples of VPN implementations, and some issues to consider when choosing a VPN implementation. Further chapters in this book expand on the topics introduced here.

Traffic Issues

VPNs were developed initially to deal with security issues of transmitting clear text data across a network. Clear text data is information that can examined and understood by any person, including the source, destination, and anyone in between. Examples of applications that send traffic in a clear text format are Telnet, file transfers via FTP or TFTP, e-mail using the Post Office Protocol (POP) or Simple Mail Transfer Protocol (SMTP), and many others. Unethical individuals, such as hackers, can take advantage of applications that send clear text data to execute the following types of attacks:

- Eavesdropping
- Masquerading
- Man-in-the-middle

Each type of attack exposes your data and company assets to various risks. The following three sections discuss these attacks in more depth.

Eavesdropping Attacks

The most common type of attack with clear text data is *eavesdropping*. In an eavesdropping attack, a person examines the contents of packets as they are transmitted between two devices. Some types of applications and protocols are susceptible to eavesdropping attacks, including Telnet, POP, HTTP, TFTP, FTP, Simple Management Network Protocol (SNMP), and others.

With all of these applications and protocols, authentication information, like usernames and passwords, is passed, in clear text, between two devices. A hacker can use this information to execute access and other types of attacks.

NOTE   Even though some protocols might send information in clear text, they, in many cases, have a minimal authentication method to verify an individual's identity before allowing that person access to a resource. For example, applications such as Telnet, POP, and SMTP allow for authentication, even though the authentication information is sent in clear text. Actually, these protocols initially were not designed for security, but to solve specific connectivity problems. However, things have changed since these applications were developed in the 1970s, 1980s, and early 1990s, especially with the explosion of Internet usage.

Eavesdropping Tools

Typically, a protocol analyzer is used to examine (sniff) packets. The analyzer can be a hardware-based solution or a PC with a promiscuous network interface card (NIC) and appropriate software. For this kind of attack to work, the attacker must have access to a connection between the actual source and destination devices.

There are two main categories of protocol analyzers: general and attack. A general protocol analyzer captures all packets it sees and typically is used as a diagnostic tool to troubleshoot problems. There are many freeware, software-based protocol analyzers available that perform this function.

An attack protocol analyzer, on the other hand, is an enhanced form of a general protocol analyzer. Attack protocol analyzers look at certain types of applications and protocols for authentication, financial, and security information. An attacker will use this specific information to execute other types of attacks.

Eavesdropping Solutions

Sensitive information includes credit card information, personal information, Social Security numbers, telephone numbers and addresses, usernames and passwords, and proprietary information. Because many protocols and applications are insecure when transmitting sensitive information (they send their information in clear text), protection becomes necessary. One solution is to use one-time passwords (OTP) with token cards. This prevents someone from executing an access attack when using a protocol analyzer to capture password information. However, this solution only protects against password attacks; other types of information transmitted across the clear text connection are not protected.

One of the most common solutions for companies to protect credit card information in an e-commerce environment is to use HTTP with SSL (HTTPS) to encrypt user-sensitive information. Another common solution for corporate and partner access is to implement a VPN with encryption. Encryption scrambles the clear text information into what appears as a random string of characters; only the destination will be able to decipher the information. Encryption can be implemented with one of the two following methods:

- **Link encryption**—The entire frame (such as a PPP or HDLC frame) is encrypted between two devices; this is used on point-to-point connections of directly connected devices.

- **Packet payload encryption**—Only the packet payload is encrypted, which allows this form of encryption to be routed across a Layer-3 network, such as the Internet.

Encryption is commonly used for external connections that traverse public networks; however, for certain types of sensitive data, you might want to encrypt it as it traverses your intranet. Of the two solutions, packet payload encryption is the most common one you'll see used in a VPN solution. The reason packet payload encryption is most common is that in many situations, the data must transfer multiple hops, and thus packet payload encryption is the most scalable: only two devices need to handle the encryption/decryption process and the intermediate devices just route the encrypted packets.

Masquerading Attacks

A masquerading attack is where an individual hides their identity, possibly even assuming someone else's identity. In a networking environment, this is accomplished by changing the source addressing information in packets. In the TCP/IP world, this is commonly referred to as *spoofing*. An attacker using spoofing typically combines this with either a denial of service (DoS) or unauthorized access attack.

Masquerading Tools

Unlike eavesdropping attacks, many types of tools can be used in a masquerading attack. To change the source IP address in a packet, a specialized packet-generating program is needed. This allows the hacker to specify the source address to be used, instead of using the IP address associated with the hacker's PC NIC.

An attacker will typically try to use an authorized external source IP address to bypass any packet filters. Of course, any returning traffic would return to the actual authorized external address instead of to the attacker. To see the returning traffic, the attacker would have to combine this attack with a routing attack, allowing the returning traffic to be redirected to the attacker. To implement a simple DoS attack, the attacker will attempt to use an internal source address that a packet filter might allow through a firewall system.

NOTE   In a Layer-2 network, a hacker could use ARP spoofing to redirect traffic between two
                devices to the hacker's device.

Masquerading Solutions

Of course, using a robust firewall system to restrict the kinds of packets into your network
is a necessity. However, a firewall system will allow traffic from authorized external
systems, even if it happens to be VPN traffic. Therefore, some type of packet authentication
check is required. For example, you need to determine if packets are coming from a valid
source, rather than from an attacker executing a masquerading attack.

The most common solution is to use a packet integrity check system, which is implemented
with a hashing function. Hashing functions allow you to verify the source of transmitted
packets. Because hashing functions use a one-way hash with a shared key, only the devices
that have the key will be able to create and verify the hash values. With VPNs, the most
common hashing functions used are MD5 and SHA.

NOTE   Packet authentication is discussed in the "Packet Integrity" section later in this chapter and
                hashing functions are discussed in Chapter 2, "VPN Technologies."

Man-in-the-Middle Attacks

A man-in-the-middle attack can take on many forms, including the two most common:

- Session replay attacks
- Session hijacking attacks

With a session replay attack, the attacker, sitting between two devices, captures the packets
from the session. The attacker will then try to use the captured packets at a later time by
replaying (resending) them. The attacker's goal is to gain access to the remote system with
the same packets. In some instances, the attacker will change the contents of the packets to
assist in this process.

The diagram in Figure 1-1 illustrates an example. In Step 1, the user sends traffic to the real
server. In Step 2, the attacker intercepts traffic from the user to the real server (assume that
it's a web session). Typically, an attacker would do this either by spoofing DNS replies
with the attacker's source address instead of the real destination's address, which is a form
of a masquerading attack, or by spoofing packets, combined with a rerouting attack. Of
course, if the attacker has access to a link between the source and destination, the attacker
can easily use a protocol analyzer to examine the packets. In this example, assume that
the attacker is using a redirection attack and that all traffic is being sent to the attacker. The
attacker pretends to be the real server and sends responses back to the user PC, possibly

even malicious Java or ActiveX scripts, to capture any user-specific credentials. In this instance, the attacker would redirect the user's original traffic and responses to the real destination, as seen in Step 3.

Figure 1-1 *Session Replay Attack*

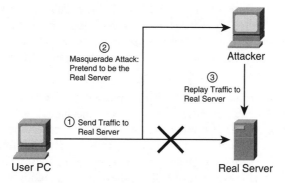

In a session hijacking attack, the attacker will attempt to insert himself into an existing connection and then take over the connection between two devices. Figure 1-2 illustrates a session hijacking attack.

Figure 1-2 *Session Hijacking Attack*

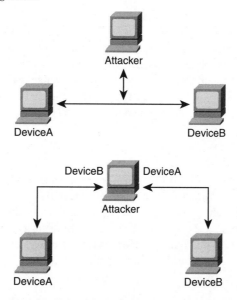

To execute this attack, the attacker will have to perform masquerading, where the attacker is pretending to be the source *and* destination devices. Plus, the attacker must have access to the packets flowing between the source and destination devices. Physically, this looks like the top part of Figure 1-2.

On the other hand, the diagram in the bottom part of Figure 1-2 is more representative of how a session hijacking attack occurs. In this example, when DeviceA sends traffic to DeviceB, the attacker intercepts the traffic and pretends to be DeviceB. He responds back to DeviceA with information similar to what DeviceB would send. From DeviceA's perspective, the device assumes it is really interacting with DeviceB. The attacker uses the same process when interacting with DeviceB. With data flowing back and forth between DeviceA and DeviceB, the attacker will typically perform a data manipulation attack—modifying data between the two devices to pull off the actual session hijacking. The attacker uses this process to learn more information about the two devices, including their security weaknesses.

With protocols such as UDP and ICMP, implementing a session hijacking attack is a simple process for the hacker because there are no real mechanics that define how a connection is maintained. With TCP, this becomes more difficult, especially with TCP's sequencing process. Sequence numbers should be random, making it very difficult for a hacker to guess what a sequence number might be for the next segment. Therefore, hijacking a TCP session can be difficult. However, not all TCP applications use random sequence numbers. In many instances, it is very easy to guess what the sequence number is, based on past numbers seen for an existing connection. A skilled attacker can then insert himself into the existing TCP connection. Of course, this is not a simple process. The hacker will need to perform quite a few steps and use some sophisticated tools to pull off this attack.

Man-in-the-Middle Tools

Attackers will typically use an attack protocol analyzer to capture packets with the two types of attacks described. With a session replay attack, the hacker might even use Java or ActiveX scripts to capture packets from a web server session. With TCP session hijacking attacks, the attacker will need some type of specialized TCP sequence-number-guessing program to successfully intercept and take over an existing TCP connection.

Man-in-the-Middle Solutions

There are several solutions for man-in-the-middle attacks. For instance, to prevent the hijacking of TCP sessions, you could have a firewall system randomize TCP sequence numbers, ensuring that it becomes almost impossible for the attacker to predict future sequence numbers for the session. The Cisco PIX security appliance and other available devices can perform this function. However, an attacker can use other methods, as discussed in the last section, to take over a session.

NOTE   TCP sequence numbers are 32 bits in length, providing over 2 billion possible combinations; randomizing sequence numbers makes it practically impossible to guess the next sequence number in a transmission.

The best solution to this kind of problem is to use a VPN. VPNs provide three tools to combat man-in-the-middle attacks:

- Device authentication
- Packet integrity checking
- Encryption

With device authentication, you can be assured that the device that is sending traffic to you is an authorized device instead of a masquerading device. With packet integrity checking, you can be assured that the packets coming to you are from an authorized source, and haven't been tampered with or are spoofed. And with encryption, you can be assured that a man-in-the-middle device cannot eavesdrop on the actual data your two devices are trying to share with each other. These topics will be discussed more in the "VPN Components" section of this chapter.

VPN Definition

I've mentioned, in the last few sections, that VPNs can be used to deal with certain kinds of attacks. Therefore, the question is: What is a virtual private network (VPN)? Having worked in the computer field for almost twenty years, I am constantly asked to explain various technologies and what they are used for. In security, the most common question I'm asked is "What's a VPN?" I've probably seen all possible explanations of what a VPN is, such as the following:

- It's an encrypted tunnel.
- It uses IPsec, GRE, PPTP, SSL, L2TP, or MPLS (described later in the chapter).
- It encrypts data.
- It protects traffic across the Internet.
- It protects your data from hackers and attacks.

As you can see, many people have different views or perceptions of what a VPN is. For example, if you would search the Internet for the term VPN, you would easily find dozens of different, sometimes similar, sometimes conflicting definitions. For instance, at www.webopedia.com, the definition of a VPN is: "a network that is constructed by using public wires to connect nodes. For example, there are a number of systems that enable you to create networks using the Internet as the medium for transporting data. These systems use encryption and other security mechanisms to ensure that only authorized users can access the network and that the data cannot be intercepted."

VPN Description

To me, webopedia's definition makes it even more confusing as to what a VPN is. To clear up the confusion, I'll discuss what a VPN actually is and the different types of categories a VPN falls under. I'll then discuss some different types of VPN implementations. In its simplest form, a VPN is a connection, typically protected, between two entities that are not necessarily directly connected. The two entities could be directly connected via a point-to-point link, but it is more common to see them separated by more than one hop or network. The term "entities" could refer to either a specific device or a particular network (multiple devices). The connection, in many instances, crosses a public network; however, VPNs easily can be used for internal purposes. And the word "protected" in my definition of a VPN is somewhat open to interpretation. Most people assume that this means encryption (protecting traffic from eavesdropping attacks), or that packets haven't been tampered with (by a man-in-the-middle attack). And these assumptions are typically correct; however, a good VPN solution will deal with most, if not all, of the following issues:

- Protecting data from eavesdropping by using encryption technologies, such as RC-4, DES, 3DES, and AES

- Protecting packets from tampering by using packet integrity hashing functions such as MD5 and SHA

- Protecting against man-in-the-middle attacks by using identity authentication mechanisms, such as pre-shared keys or digital certificates

- Protecting against replay attacks by using sequence numbers when transmitting protected data

- Defining the mechanics of how data is encapsulated and protected, and how protected traffic is transmitted between devices

- Defining what traffic actually needs to be protected

As you can see, a VPN is responsible for all kinds of functions.

NOTE Of course, not every VPN implementation will include all of these components or will not implement them as securely as other methods. How the connection is set up, protected, maintained, and torn down varies on the VPN solution. Therefore, it is very important to use your company's security policy in determining which VPN technology is best for your particular situation. In some instances, it is common to see more than one VPN solution being deployed in the same network.

VPN Connection Modes

Before I discuss the four general types of VPNs and the three VPN categories, I first need to discuss the two basic types of connection modes used to move data between devices:

- Tunnel mode
- Transport mode

If you have worked with Internet Protocol Security (IPsec) before, you are probably familiar with these two terms. Other types of VPNs might use different terminology to describe these two connections modes, but since I grew up with IPsec, I favor its terminology when I typically discuss VPNs.

Both modes define the basic encapsulation process used to move protected data between two entities. I commonly see people use the word "tunnel" to describe this process; however, I don't like to use the word tunnel because it can have other meanings with VPNs. Therefore, I like to use the term "encapsulation" to describe how data is moved between the two VPN entities. The next two sections will discuss these two connection modes.

Transport Mode

A transport mode connection is used between the real source and destination IP addresses of the devices. Figure 1-3 illustrates the use of transport mode. In this example, the network administrator is concerned about sending syslog messages from the corporate office's PIX security appliance to the corporate office's internal syslog server. The network administrator has decided to use a VPN to protect the syslog messages.

Figure 1-3 *VPN Types and Categories*

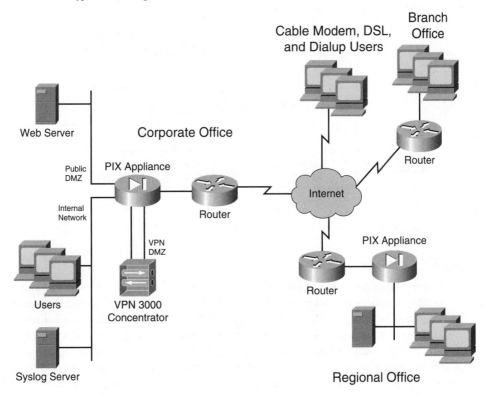

Because this is a VPN connection between the devices actually transmitting data, a transport mode connection is used. In a transport mode connection, the actual user data (the UDP segment containing the syslog information) is encapsulated in a VPN packet.

Figure 1-4 shows an example of the encapsulation process used in transport mode. In this example, the PIX creates a UDP segment with the syslog data. The PIX encapsulates the UDP segment in a VPN packet or segment. The VPN encapsulation would include information that would help the destination validate the protection information (and would decrypt it, if encryption is used). The VPN information is then encapsulated in an IP packet, where the source address is the PIX and the destination is the syslog server.

NOTE   With transport mode, if the VPN-protected packet is examined by an eavesdropping attack, the attacker will know the actual source and destination devices involved in the communication; of course, if you're using encryption as one of the protection methods with the VPN, the attacker will not be able to decipher the actual payload being transported between the VPN devices (in this case, the syslog data).

Figure 1-4   *Transport Mode Encapsulation Method*

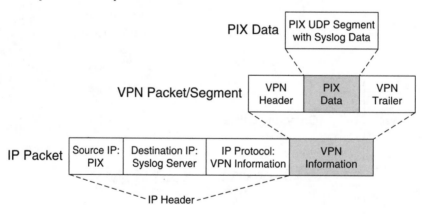

Tunnel Mode

One limitation of transport mode is that it doesn't scale very well because the protection is done on a device-by-device basis. Figure 1-3 illustrates a situation in which transport mode would not be a good VPN connection method. In this example, assume that there are 10 devices at the regional office that need to communicate with 10 devices at the corporate office, and assume further that all 10 devices from one side need to communicate with all 10 devices at the remote side. Given this information, you would need to create nine VPN connections on each device, and with 10 devices on each side, this would total 180 connections! In other words, you would have your work cut out for you when setting up this scenario.

Therefore, if you have many devices at two separated locations that need to talk to each other in a secure fashion, you would use tunnel mode instead of transport mode. In tunnel mode, the actual source and destination devices typically do *not* protect the traffic. Instead, some intermediate device is used to protect the traffic. From the previous example of devices at the corporate office and regional office requiring protection, the two routers at each location could be responsible for the VPN protection. Devices that provide VPN protection on behalf of other devices are commonly called *VPN gateways*.

I'll examine an example to illustrate how tunnel mode works. In this example, the local device would create a normal IP packet and forward this to the local VPN gateway. Assume that the PIX at the regional site (shown previously in Figure 1-3) needs to send a syslog message to the syslog server at the corporate site, where the perimeter routers at the two locations are performing the function of the VPN gateway.

Figure 1-5 shows an example of the encapsulation process used. In the figure, the regional PIX generates a syslog message and encapsulates it in UDP and then in an IP packet, where the source address is the PIX's local address and the destination address is the corporate syslog server's IP address. When the regional router/VPN gateway receives the syslog IP packet from the regional PIX, the VPN gateway encapsulates the packet with VPN protection information, possibly even encrypting the original entire PIX packet. Next, the VPN gateway places this information inside *another* IP packet, where the source address of the packet is the regional office router and the destination address is the corporate office VPN gateway (in this example, the perimeter router). Once the corporate office router receives the protected packet, it verifies the protection and removes it (if you were using encryption to protect the packet, the corporate office VPN gateway would decrypt it). The syslog server then receives the original IP packet, not knowing (or caring) that the packet was protected part of the way from the regional PIX appliance to the syslog server.

Figure 1-5   *Tunnel Mode Encapsulation Method*

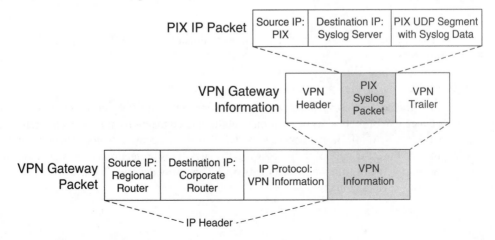

Given this connection mode process, tunnel mode provides these advantages over transport mode:

- **Provides scalability**—You can choose a more appropriate device to perform the protection process, offloading the CPU-intensive protection process.

- **Allows for flexibility**—You will typically not have to make changes to your VPN configuration when you add a new device behind a VPN gateway and you want the traffic from this new device protected.

- **Hides communications**—An attacker performing an eavesdropping attack on the network between the VPN gateway devices knows that traffic is protected between the VPN gateways, but has no way of knowing if the VPN gateways are the real source and destination devices for the transmission, or if the data is being transmitted by some other devices.

- **Uses private addressing**—The real source and destination devices can use public or private addressing because this is being encapsulated in another packet by the VPN gateway devices.

- **Uses existing security policies**—Because devices are using their real IP addresses when communicating with each other, you typically don't have to change any internal security policies you have defined on your firewall and packet-filtering devices.

VPN Types

A VPN type describes, generally speaking, the type of entities that are involved with the actual VPN connection. There are four general VPN types:

- Site-to-Site VPNs
- Remote Access VPNs
- Firewall VPNs
- User-to-User VPNs

I'll use Figure 1-3 in the following sections to illustrate the four VPN types.

Site-to-Site VPNs

A site-to-site VPN uses a tunnel mode connection between VPN gateways to protect traffic between two or more sites or locations. Site-to-site connections are commonly referred to as LAN-to-LAN (L2L) connections. With L2L VPNs, a central device at each location provides the protection of traffic between the sites. This protection process, and thus the transport network sitting between the two VPN gateway devices, is transparent to the end-user devices at the two sites.

As to what kind of device can play the role of a VPN gateway, with Cisco, you have the following items to choose from:

- VPN 3000 series concentrators
- IOS-based routers with VPN software
- PIX and ASA security appliances

In Figure 1-3, to set up a protected connection between the regional office and the corporate office, you could use the following configuration:

- At the corporate office the VPN gateway could be the perimeter router, the PIX, or the VPN concentrator.
- At the regional office, the VPN gateway could be either the perimeter router or the PIX.

NOTE   Cisco generally recommends that you use routers for VPN L2L solutions; however, this is a *very* general statement and many factors have to be considered before making this decision. As you will see throughout this book, each type of device has both advantages and disadvantages. For example, here are some basic advantages one type of Cisco product has over another:

- **IOS router**—Has advanced QOS, GRE tunneling, routing, and scalable and advanced VPN L2L capabilities.

- **Cisco VPN 3000 concentrator**—Is easy to set up and troubleshoot.

- **PIX Security Appliance firewall**—Has advanced firewall and security features, including stateful filtering, application filtering, and advanced address translation capabilities.

Remote Access VPNs

Remote access VPNs typically are used for low-bandwidth or broadband connections between a single-user device, such as a PC or small-office-home-office (SOHO), a hardware client (a Cisco VPN 3002 hardware client, small-end PIX appliance or small-end IOS-based router), and a VPN gateway device. Remote access VPNs typically use tunnel more for their connections. At first this sounds strange, given that one device is a VPN gateway and the other is not. However, if you think about how a transport mode connection works where the protected data is transmitted between the real source and destination devices, a remote access connection doesn't quite fit into this mold. With remote access, the traffic needs to be protected from the source to some intermediate device, which verifies the protected information (and decrypts it if it was encrypted). The real destination will receive the unprotected information. For this to work, tunnel mode is used.

With remote access, the VPN endpoint, or client, that connects to the VPN gateway will need *two* IP addresses: one for its NIC and one for an internal address, which is sometimes referred to as a virtual or logical address or assigned IP address.

Figure 1-6 to illustrates an example of a remote access connection. In this example, a cable modem user from home is using a PC to connect to the corporate office through a VPN gateway, say the VPN 3000 concentrator. The ISP uses DHCP to assign an IP address to the user's NIC on the home PC. A second address is needed for communication to devices at the corporate office that need to be protected; this is the internal address, which can sometimes be assigned by the user manually, or, more commonly, acquired from the VPN gateway during the setup of the VPN session. Usually the IP address comes from a central site DHCP server or a locally defined address pool. When the remote access client wants to send information to a device behind the VPN gateway at the corporate office, such as the web server, the remote access client creates an IP packet where the source IP address is the internal address, and the destination IP address is the device at the corporate office network. This packet is then encapsulated and protected with VPN information, and then an outer IP header is added. In the outer IP header, the source address is the remote access user's ISP-assigned NIC address and the destination address is the VPN gateway. The VPN gateway, upon receiving the protected packet, will verify the protection, decrypt the encapsulated packet, if necessary, and forward the encapsulated IP packet to the internal corporate device.

Because the internal address is protected (that is, you're using tunnel mode), you can easily make the remote access client look like it is an extension of the corporate office network. For example, if the corporate office is using the address space of 172.16.0.0/16, as shown in Figure 1-6, you could have the client use an internal address from a pool, say 172.16.254.0/24, to make the client appear that it is connected to the 172.16.0.0/16 network. From a device at the corporate office's perspective, it appears that the remote access client is directly attached to the 172.16.0.0/16 network; however, in reality, the client can be many hops away from the corporate office, as demonstrated in Figure 1-6.

NOTE   Cisco recommends that you use Cisco VPN 3000 series concentrators as the VPN gateway product for remote access connections. When comparing the 3000 series concentrators to Cisco routers or PIX or ASA security appliances for remote access VPN gateway solutions, it is much, much easier to set up and troubleshoot remote access connectivity on the concentrators than on the other two products. However, if I only had a small number of users who needed remote access connectivity, and I already had either a PIX or ASA appliance or IOS router installed at the corporate office, I would use the existing equipment instead of purchasing a 3000 concentrator. Once the number of users started going above a dozen or so, I would seriously consider the purchase of a concentrator. The only other time I would consider a router over a concentrator for remote access would be if I needed advanced QoS capabilities that the concentrator lacks.

Figure 1-6   *Remote Access Example*

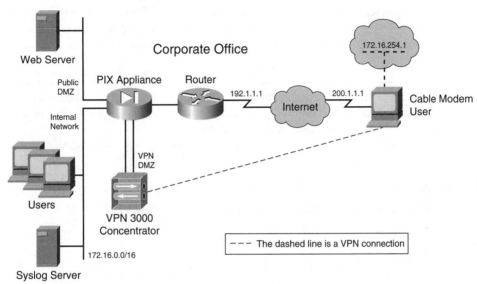

Firewall VPNs

A firewall VPN is basically an L2L or remote access VPN enhanced with additional security and firewall functions. Firewall VPNs typically are used when one side of the VPN connection needs enhanced security and firewall functions based on their company's security policy, and they manage or own the security solution that is currently in place in their network.

Some of these security or firewall functions performed by a firewall VPN include the following:

- Stateful filtering
- Application layer filtering
- Advanced address translation policies
- Addressing issues with problematic protocols such as multimedia and voice

Other than the functions in the preceding list, a firewall VPN has the same characteristics as an L2L or remote access VPN. From my perspective, I don't like the classification of a firewall VPN as a separate VPN type; however, Cisco commonly uses this term when discussing VPN types. If you are deploying Cisco equipment to implement a firewall VPN, the VPN gateway device typically would be a PIX or ASA security appliance.

User-to-User VPNs

A user-to-user VPN type is basically a transport mode VPN connection between two devices. The two devices can be a PIX appliance and a syslog server, a router and a TFTP server, a user using Telnet to access a Cisco router, or many other connection pairings.

NOTE   Cisco doesn't officially consider user-to-user as a VPN type, but since I commonly use this to protect specific kinds of traffic between specific devices, I've included this type to round out the VPN types you'll see in the real world.

VPN Categories

There are three basic VPN categories that describe where a VPN is used:

- Intranet
- Extranet
- Internet

Figure 1-3 to illustrates what these terms describe when used in conjunction with VPNs.

Intranet

An intranet VPN connects resources from the same company across that company's infrastructure. Here are some simple examples of intranet VPN connections:

- Transport mode connections within a company's infrastructure, such as VPNs between two devices (a router sending traffic to a syslog server, a PIX appliance backing up its configuration to a TFTP server, and a user on a PC using Telnet to a Catalyst 3550 switch, to name a few)

- Tunnel mode connections between different locations within a company's infrastructure, such as VPNs between two offices via a private Frame Relay or ATM network

Extranet

An extranet VPN connects resources from one company to another company, such as a business partner. These are typically L2L connections, but can be other types. An example of an extranet could be a company that has outsourced its help desk functions and sets up a VPN to provide a secure connection from its corporate office to the outsourcing company.

Internet

An Internet VPN uses a public network as the backbone to transport VPN traffic between devices. As an example, you might use the Internet, which is a public network, to connect two sites together (L2L connection), or have telecommuters use their local ISPs to set up a VPN connection to the corporate network (remote access connections).

NOTE   Remember that all of the four VPN types are supported by the three VPN categories. As to which you should use, this is based on your access needs and your company's security policy's statements.

VPN Components

Now that you have a basic understanding of what a VPN is, let's discuss the components that make up a traditional VPN. Not every VPN implementation will include any or all of these components. Plus, based on the requirements listed in your security policy, you might not need all of these components. Therefore, you need to examine your security policy to determine which VPN implementation (or implementations) has the necessary components to meet your security policy's requirements.

The following sections will discuss some of the more important components that are typically part of a VPN implementation. Specifically, they will cover the following:

- Authentication
- Encapsulation Method
- Data Encryption
- Packet Integrity
- Key Management
- Non-Repudiation
- Application and Protocol Support
- Address Management

Authentication

One concern you might have is to somehow verify a device's or user's identity before allowing it to establish a VPN connection to your network. There are two general categories of authentication:

- Device
- User

Device Authentication

Device authentication allows you to restrict VPN access to your network based on authentication information that a remote VPN device provides. Typically this is one of the following two types of authentication:

- Pre-shared key or keys
- Digital signature or certificate

Pre-shared keys are typically used in smaller VPN environments. One or more keys is configured and used to authenticate a device's identity. Setting up pre-shared key authentication is very simple. Many administrators prefer its use instead of digital signatures or certificates, which require a lot more work to set up. Pre-shared keys requires you to manually configure a key or keys on each device that will participate with VPN connectivity.

Given the amount of configuration, though, pre-shared keys have one main disadvantage: they don't scale well. For example, assume that you currently have nine sites with a router at each site, where pre-shared keys are used for device authentication and the VPN L2L design is fully meshed between the sites. You add an additional site. This requires you to add nine keys to the router at the new site and set up keying information on the routers at the other nine sites. So adding more sites makes addition and management of authentication keys very complex.

NOTE   The original idea behind the use of pre-shared keys was that a key would be associated with a specific static source IP address; however, this concept did not work for remote access where users can originate their connection from anywhere on the Internet and have dynamic IP addresses. As a result, the concept of group-based pre-shared keys came to life. In this model, a specific pre-shared key would be looked up based on a clear-text group name sent as part of the remote access VPN connection initiation process. Pre-shared keys, in general, suffer from some of the concerns associated with man-in-the-middle attacks as discussed earlier, since one end of the connection can only validate that the other end has the same pre-shared key, not who the other end actually is. The solution to this man-in-the-middle issue is known as *mutual group authentication* and allows the head-end to identify itself with a certificate without requiring a certificate for each of the end users.

Normally digital signatures or, more commonly, digital certificates, are used for device authentication in large VPN deployments. Certificates that are centralized by a common authority, known as a certificate authority (CA), make adding and removing VPN devices a simple process. Any time a device is added to the VPN topology, a new certificate is generated for the device, containing that device's authentication information. This is held by the certificate authority. Other VPN devices can access the certificate authority to validate another device's identity. As you can see, a device doesn't have to locally store other devices' authentication information—this information is centralized by the certificate authority. However, the main drawback of the use of certificates is that the initial setup and deployment of certificate services can be work-intensive.

User Authentication

One issue with device authentication, like pre-shared keys, is that the device authentication information is stored locally on the device. This presents a problem if the device itself is compromised. Normally I'm not concerned about this issue where the device is located in a secure environment, like a data center; however, I am concerned about authentication information stored on insecure devices, such as PCs and laptops. Many VPN implementations, therefore, will add an additional layer of authentication, called user authentication, to verify whether or not a VPN connection is allowed by a user using a specific device. Normally this is employed in remote access VPNs. In some instances, depending on the VPN implementation type (discussed later in the "VPN Implementations" section of this chapter), the VPN might perform both device and user authentication.

With user authentication, the user must supply a username and a password. This password might be a static password or a one-time password (through the use of token cards). As an example, assume that your VPN implementation used both device and user authentication. If someone were to steal one of your employee's laptops, the thief would be able to use the device authentication stored locally on the device, but would have to know the user's name and password to gain access. With token cards, the thief would have to know the user's name, have access to the user's token card, and know the user's PIN (personal identification number). Plus, many VPN implementations allow you to prevent a user from storing user authentication information locally on their desktop. Chapter 2, "VPN Technologies," discusses authentication methods in more depth.

Encapsulation Method

Another component a VPN must define is an encapsulation method: how user information, like data, is to be encapsulated and transported across a network. In other words, what is the actual format of the contents? You can determine this by asking the following questions:

- What fields appear in the VPN header or trailer information?
- In what order do the fields appear?
- What is the size of the fields?

Encapsulation also defines what application(s) or protocol(s) can be placed in the payload of a VPN packet. Some VPN implementations will encapsulate only application layer information, whereas others can encapsulate an entire Layer-3 packet or Layer-2 frame. How information is encapsulated is important because it can affect whether or not the data might experience problems with firewall or address translation devices. This issue is discussed in the "Address Translation and Firewall Issues" section later in this chapter.

Data Encryption

Data encryption is used to solve eavesdropping issues. Data encryption basically takes user data and a key value and runs it through an encryption algorithm, producing what looks like a random string of characters. Only a device with the same key value can decrypt the information. Many encryption algorithms exist, such as DES, 3DES, AES, Blowfish, RSA, IDEA, SEAL, and RC4, to name a few; however, not every VPN implementation supports all encryption algorithms. Typically, two or three algorithms are supported. Encryption algorithms are discussed in more depth in Chapter 2.

Packet Integrity

Encryption is CPU-intensive for a device. An attacker, knowing that you are using a VPN with encryption, might take advantage of this by executing a denial of service (DoS) attack against your VPN device. Basically, the hacker would spoof packets with garbage in them, using an IP address from a trusted VPN source. When your VPN device received the spoofed packets, it would try to decrypt them. Of course, it would not be successful and would throw away the spoofed packets; however, your device would have wasted CPU cycles to perform this process.

Because of possible packet tampering or packet spoofing, some VPN implementations give you the option of performing packet integrity checking, or what some people commonly refer to as *packet authentication*. With packet authentication, a signature is attached to the packet. The signature is created by taking contents from the packet and a shared key and running this information through a hashing function, producing a fixed output, called a digital signature. This signature is then added to the original packet and the new altered packet is sent to the destination. The destination verifies the signature; and if the signature is valid, the destination will decrypt the packet contents. Verifying a hashed signature requires far fewer CPU cycles than does the decryption process.

Two of the more common hashing functions used for packet integrity checking are SHA and MD5. Hashing functions are discussed in more depth in Chapter 2.

Key Management

I've already mentioned three VPN components that use keys: authentication, encryption, and hashing functions. Management of keys becomes important with VPN connections. For instance, how are keys derived? Are they statically configured or randomly generated? How often are keys regenerated to increase security?

For example, assume that your security policy stated that keying material used for encryption and packet integrity checking needed to be changed at least once every eight hours. If you used static keys for different sites, and had 100 sites, you would be spending about an hour each time manually changing keys. Therefore, in most instances, a dynamic key management process is needed. You should carefully evaluate how this is handled when choosing a VPN implementation. Chapter 3, "IPsec," discusses how this is handled with the VPN implementation of the IPsec standard for VPNs.

Non-Repudiation

Repudiation is where you cannot prove that a transaction, like the establishment of a connection, or the purchase of an item, occurred. Non-repudiation is the opposite of this: you can prove that a transaction occurred between two parties. Attackers often attempt to execute repudiation attacks.

In the financial world, non-repudiation is very important. For example, if I were to go to an online store on the Internet, like Amazon.com, and buy a book with my credit card, Amazon would have to be able to prove that it was me buying the book before they could successfully bill my credit card. They would have to gather personal information about me when I filled out my order, like my name, billing address, telephone number, and credit card information, and use this information to verify my identity with my credit card company. And of course, Amazon would keep a record of the transaction: what I had entered, the date and time, and my IP address, to track me down if I was trying to use someone else's credit card fraudulently.

Non-repudiation can be a component of a VPN implementation. In the VPN world, non-repudiation involves two components: authentication and accounting. I've already discussed authentication in the "Authentication" section of this chapter. Accounting is the recording of the VPN session. This could include the identities of the two devices establishing the connection, how long the connection was used, how much information was transmitted across it, what types of information traversed the connection, and so on. This can then be used later to detect access attacks and for management purposes, such as creating baselines and looking for bandwidth issues.

Application and Protocol Support

When choosing a VPN implementation, you'll need to first determine what kinds of traffic need to be protected. For example, if you only have IP traffic in your network, most VPN implementations will be available to you; however, if you need to protect both IP and IPX traffic, the number of VPN implementations available to you quickly dwindles. Likewise, maybe you only need to protect traffic for specific applications, such as web and e-mail traffic. Again, this could affect the choice you make in choosing a VPN solution, like SSL versus PPTP or IPsec. Remember that a VPN implementation might pose restrictions on protocols and applications that can be encapsulated by the VPN, as I discussed earlier in the "Encapsulation Method" section of this chapter.

Address Management

Address management is an issue only with remote access connections. As I mentioned in the "Remote Access" section earlier in the chapter, a remote access client is commonly assigned an internal address. Keeping track of which internal address is assigned to which remote access client can be problematic.

Look at Figure 1-7 as an example of this problem. In this network, the client has two choices for setting up the VPN session: VPN gateway A and VPN gateway B. Perhaps the network administrator has no control over which gateway the remote access user connects to, or perhaps it's random. Let's assume that the client belongs to a group where the pool of addresses assigned to the client is from 172.16.254.0/24. That means that if the client connects to VPN gateway A and is assigned an IP address of 172.16.254.1, VPN gateway B must know somehow that it cannot use this address to assign to a different client. Plus, devices on the internal network somehow need to know that when they want to send traffic to 172.16.254.1, they forward the traffic to VPN gateway A and not B. In addition, if the remote access user would tear down his VPN connection and re-establish the connection to the network, but via VPN gateway B, VPN gateway A would have to know this to update its addressing pool information. VPN gateway A also would need to update its routing information to reach 172.16.254.1.

Figure 1-7   *Remote Access Addressing Example*

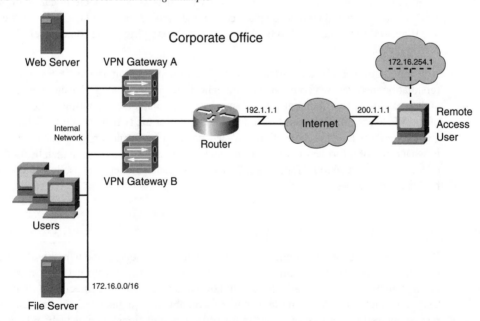

There are actually many ways of solving the address/assignment problem, in addition to the routing problem, for this type of situation. As to the assignment of addresses, a common solution is to use an external DHCP server or an AAA (authentication, authorization, and accounting) server to assign an address to the user. An AAA server assigning addresses is done typically in situations where the client always needs the same address assigned to it; otherwise, either a DHCP server or the VPN gateway will assign the client its IP address. As to the routing issue of internal devices reaching the remote access user, the VPN gateways can create static host routes in their local routing tables and redistribute this information via a dynamic routing protocol. Cisco commonly refers to this process as Reverse Route Injection (RRI) when dealing with IPsec. For devices on the same segment as the VPN gateways, the VPN gateways can use proxy ARP to tell directly connected devices how to correctly reach the remote access clients.

NOTE   When an IP address is assigned from the VPN gateway's local interface subnet (the Internal Network in Figure 1-7), proxy ARP is used. When the assigned IP comes from a non-local subnet, the address must be routed to the VPN gateway for local devices. This can be done using a dynamic routing process. Another option is to add static routes to internal routers for this subnet pointing to the VPN gateway's internal interface; however, this only works if there is only one VPN gateway. When you have two or more gateways, you'll need a dynamic routing process to discover which client is connected to which VPN gateway.

Again, you need to weigh this factor when choosing a VPN implementation. Some VPN implementations might lack address management, or have very poor address management, affecting your choice in a VPN implementation.

VPN Designs

After you have weighed the VPN components necessary for your VPN implementation, you'll need to take a look at the layout of your VPN design: what devices need VPN functionality (servers, routers, firewalls, PCs, and so on), what type of VPN functionality they need, and what connectivity is required. This information will greatly assist you in picking a suitable VPN implementation, and will bring up any design issues and problems you should consider before making a final choice.

The following sections discuss some VPN designs, and some issues to consider when using VPNs in your network. Specifically, the section covers the following:

- Connection types
- Considerations
- Redundancy

Connection Types

From a design perspective, this section will cover the various types of basic connections that VPNs use. These connections include point-to-point, hub-and-spoke, and fully meshed.

Point-to-Point

There are two basic types of VPN point-to-point connections:

- Device-to-device
- Network-to-network

Device-to-Device Connection

A device-to-device VPN connection is a user-to-user VPN type, where only two devices are involved in the VPN. This connection type is usually deployed where only a specific type of traffic between two devices needs to be protected. An example of device-to-device connection includes backing up the configuration file on a Cisco router to a TFTP server, sending SNMPv2 traffic from a managed device, like a Catalyst switch, to an SNMP management server, or sending logging traffic from a PIX security appliance to a syslog server.

One concern of device-to-device connections is that they place an extra burden on the VPN endpoint device. For example, imagine that you have a syslog server that has to handle logging information from 200 devices. In this situation, the syslog server would have to terminate 200 VPN device-to-device connections, which might place an undue burden on it. This is shown in the top part of Figure 1-8.

Network-to-Network Connection

A network-to-network VPN connection would be considered an L2L VPN type. With a network-to-network connection, two VPN gateways provide protection of traffic between two or more networks. One advantage this type of point-to-point connection has over a device-to-device connection is that traffic from more than one device can be protected via the same VPN connection. Plus, you can choose an appropriate VPN gateway device to handle the VPN traffic overhead and processing, offloading this from endpoint clients. The middle part of Figure 1-8 shows a network-to-network connection type.

I'll re-examine the one concern from the last section, in which 200 devices are sending logging messages to a central syslog server. Instead of terminating the VPN connections on the syslog server itself, you could put a VPN gateway device in front of the syslog server and set up remote access connections to the VPN gateway, which would be responsible for processing the VPN traffic from the remote devices. This would be a hybrid point-to-point connection. It is shown in the bottom third of Figure 1-8 (device-to-network).

Figure 1-8   *Device-to-Device and Network-to-Network Connections*

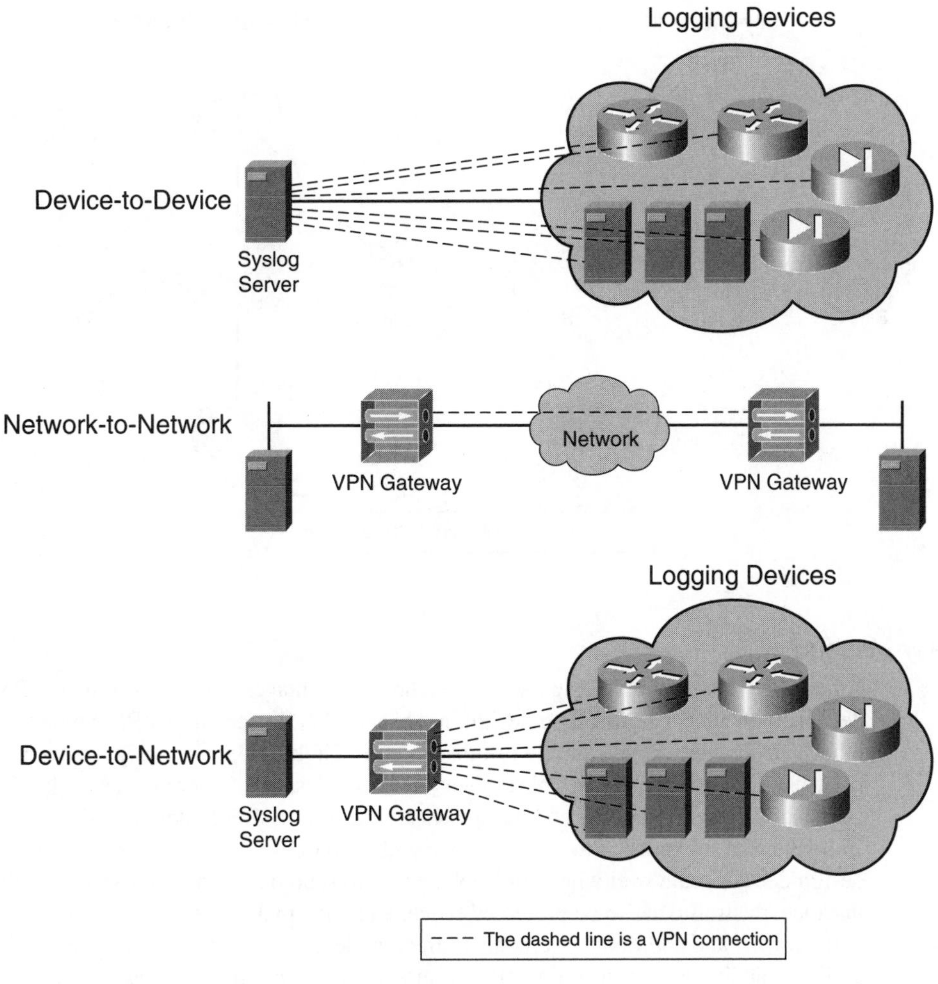

Fully-Meshed

A fully-meshed VPN network has each VPN device or network connecting to each other's VPN device or network. The left-hand part of Figure 1-9 shows an example of a fully-meshed design, connecting multiple networks to each other.

One advantage of this design is that a device or network can send traffic directly across a VPN to a remote destination without having to go through intervening VPN connections. However, the main disadvantage of this solution is scalability. For example, in Figure 1-9, as you add more sites, you're increasing the number of VPN connections on a device at each site. This increases the processing required on the VPN devices and scales poorly.

Figure 1-9 *Fully- and Partially-Meshed VPN Network Designs*

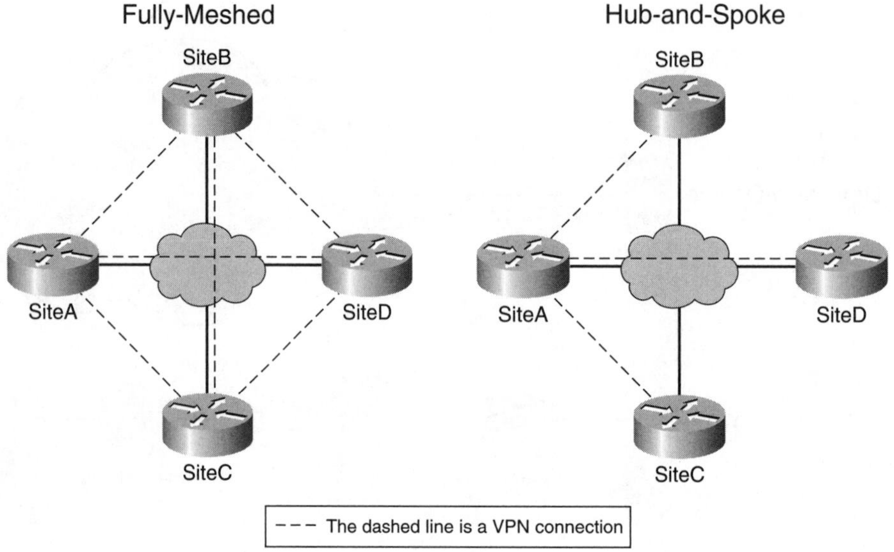

Fully-Meshed   Hub-and-Spoke

--- The dashed line is a VPN connection

Partially-Meshed

A partially-meshed VPN design addresses the disadvantages of a fully-meshed VPN design. With a partially-meshed design, not every VPN device has a VPN connection to other VPN devices. One example of this design is a hub-and-spoke design, shown in the right-hand part of Figure 1-9. This is a very common design in corporate networks. The hub is typically the corporate site and the spokes are the remote office sites. This design works well when the spokes need to communicate with resources located at the hub; however, this design doesn't scale well when one spoke needs to send data to another spoke. In this instance, the traffic has to be protected twice, and must make an extra hop, adding latency to the traffic, and additional overhead on the hub device. You could overcome this issue easily by adding a point-to-point VPN connection between the two spokes that constantly need to communicate with each other.

VPN Considerations

When designing a VPN solution, there are many factors to consider to create a suitable solution for your network. Some of these factors include the following:

- Protected versus unprotected traffic
- Fragmentation
- Application types

- Traffic protection
- Address translation and firewalls

The following sections will cover these factors.

Protected Versus Unprotected Traffic

One of the factors you'll need to consider is whether or not traffic needs to be protected when sent between two devices that have a VPN connection currently set up. Some things to consider are the amount of traffic protected and whether or not it is necessary to protect the information (the security sensitivity of the information).

For example, assume that your VPN device supports VPN processing at 5 Mbps. However, the amount of VPN traffic sent to your device is 6 Mbps. Unfortunately, you'll have a lot of performance problems on your VPN device. To solve this problem, you could set up a feature called "split tunneling," which sends some traffic protected and some in clear text.

In the example of the 1 Mbps performance difference (5 Mbps is the processing limit, but 6 Mbps is received), you would need to evaluate what traffic actually needs to be protected. Perhaps 2 Mbps of this traffic is web traffic and you've decided that it is not necessary to protect this traffic. You could set up a split tunneling policy that would protect all traffic for the VPN connection except for the web traffic. Therefore, your VPN device would have to protect only 4 Mbps, which is manageable by your device's 5 Mbps VPN performance.

TIP   To determine what should and shouldn't be protected, you'll need to examine your company's security policy. For remote access clients, I highly recommend that the client use a client-side software firewall to protect against attacks that are related to the unprotected traffic.

Fragmentation

When I see performance problems with VPN implementations, the first thing I look at are issues with fragmentation. Administrators commonly forget to factor in the overhead that VPNs add to packets, and that fragmentation might occur because of this overhead.

For example, assume that you have a database application sending data across a VPN connection. The devices involved use an MTU size of 1,500 bytes. On average, the data sent use up most of this. On top of this, the VPN adds another 80 bytes of overhead, commonly causing the necessary MTU size to require 1,580 bytes. However, the VPN device supports a maximum of 1,500 bytes for the Ethernet segment to which it is connected. In this instance, the VPN device has to break the original packet into two packets.

Most people would think that this process would introduce some, but not a lot of, overhead to the VPN device; however, in many cases, it will kill the performance of the device because the VPN device now has to protect twice the number of packets!

Therefore, when looking at a particular VPN design and VPN type you'll use, you'll need to consider fragmentation issues. To prevent fragmentation, you'll need to examine the VPN implementation to see the amount of overhead that it will add to packets, and then determine what MTU size the client devices are originally using. You'll either need to implement a dynamic MTU discovery process, such as path MTU discovery (PMTUD), that will adjust the MTU size to an appropriate size to prevent fragmentation, or manually adjust the MTU size. For example, if the MTU size of the client is 1,500 bytes and the VPN overhead is 80 bytes, you'll need to make sure the client devices originating the data have their MTU size decreased to 1,420 bytes. I discuss troubleshooting of fragmentation problems in more depth in Chapter 19, "Troubleshooting Router Connections."

Fragmentation Surprise

I once was hired by a company to help them with their current VPN implementation. They relayed to me that when they put the VPN implementation in place, their performance dropped to unacceptable levels; and when they removed their VPN configuration, the problem disappeared. Their assumption was that the processing required to protect the traffic overwhelmed their 3620 router with a VPN network module (NM) installed. I learned that they were only trying to protect about 2 Mbps of traffic, and that the VPN-NM should have been able to handle this amount of traffic easily. My immediate suspicion was that their problem had nothing to do with the VPN protection function, but with fragmentation. Apparently clients at the site were using an MTU size of 1,500 bytes and most of the data transmitted across the VPN was fairly large; and when you added the overhead of the VPN to this, about 60 percent of their packets were being fragmented, meaning that the 3620 had to not only perform fragmentation and reassembly, it also had to protect traffic of additional fragmented packets. When examining the CPU cycles of the router, sure enough, the problem was related to fragmentation. I had the administrators adjust the clients' MTU size to a smaller value manually, thereby alleviating any fragmentation issues. This made the administrators very happy, because they were worried that they would have to explain to their boss that they had bought an under-powered router and would have to spend more money on a more powerful one.

Application Types

As I mentioned in the first consideration section, "Protected Versus Unprotected Traffic," you might not want to protect certain kinds of traffic based on the amount of traffic you are transmitting. And as I mentioned earlier in this section, you'll need to examine your security policy to determine what types of traffic you don't need to protect.

Some application types actually don't necessarily need protection, like HTTPS and SSH. They don't need protection because a protection function is built into them. Therefore, protecting this traffic again just adds additional processing to your VPN device. Because of this, you might want to exclude this traffic, and other already protected traffic, from traversing your VPN.

Another thing to consider is whether or not the VPN implementation you choose can actually protect the traffic you need it to protect. For example, SSL VPNs protect web traffic (HTTP) very well, but were not really designed to protect other types of traffic, such as SMTP, TFTP, FTP, Telnet, and others. SSL is discussed later in the "VPN Implementations" section. After determining what traffic needs to be protected, you'll need to choose a VPN implementation that will protect this traffic adequately.

Traffic Protection

After you have decided what traffic needs to be protected, you'll need to determine *how* it should be protected. This information should be defined in your company's security policy. For example, if your policy states that you should be implementing encryption and packet integrity checking for sensitive information across public networks, you'll need to determine the encryption algorithm your VPN should use, and the hashing function. In some cases, the more secure solution you implement, the more processing overhead this will add to your VPN device; you'll need to carefully weigh the processing overhead and latency that the VPN feature adds compared to the additional security you'll gain from the feature—there's always a trade-off. For example, for delay-sensitive traffic such as voice and video, you'll probably spend a lot of time picking and testing various VPN protection methods to ensure that you don't experience connectivity problems for your multimedia traffic. For more information on protection types, see Chapter 2.

Address Translation and Firewalls

Some VPN implementations cause problems when trying to transmit their information through address translation or firewall devices. The following sections discuss these two issues, starting with address translation.

Address Translation Issues

With address translation, the address translation device can translate one IP address to another and, possibly, one port number to another. Mapping one IP address to another is commonly referred to as network address translation (NAT); mapping multiple IP addresses to one IP address and differentiating them by different source port numbers is commonly referred to as port address translation (PAT) or address overloading.

I'll use IPsec to illustrate the problems you might have if your VPN traffic must travel through an address translation device. IPsec has two protocols it can use to transmit data between VPN devices: authentication header (AH) and encapsulation security payload or protocol (ESP). Don't worry about the actual details of these protocols, because I'll discuss these in Chapter 3, "IPsec." Here in this current chapter, I'll discuss these protocols only as they relate to address translation.

AH provides only packet integrity checking—it doesn't perform encryption. And with packet integrity checking, a hashed value is created based on almost all of the fields of an IP packet, including the source and destination IP address fields. Imagine that this packet is traveling through a network with an address translation device. When an address translation device performs NAT or PAT on this packet, it would corrupt the packet integrity signature contained in the packet: with NAT, the address translation device changes an address in the IP header, and with PAT, it changes a port number in the TCP or UDP segment header. Therefore, AH breaks when any type of address translation is performed on its packets.

ESP provides both encryption and packet integrity checking; however, how packet integrity checking is computed is different from AH: the outside IP header is *not* included when creating the digital signature for the packet integrity check value; therefore this packet can be processed by an address translation device performing NAT. There is one problem, though, that ESP still has, as does AH. Both of these protocols are Layer-3 protocols. For address translation devices performing PAT, which requires information to be encapsulated in TCP or UDP segments, the address translation device won't be able to deal with AH or ESP packets (they don't have port numbers!); therefore, PAT translation breaks with both protocols.

NOTE   Some address translation devices now have the capability of performing PAT translation on protocols that don't have ports, like ICMP and ESP. However, this is vendor-specific and not always guaranteed to work.

Some VPN implementations deal with this address translation problem by encapsulating the VPN information in a TCP or UDP segment. For AH, this still doesn't work because the AH packet integrity check value would include this information in its computation; however, this would solve both NAT and PAT translation issues with ESP. As you will see with IPsec, Cisco supports three methods for this process, although not all Cisco devices support all of these mechanisms. The three methods are as follows:

- NAT traversal (NAT-T) encapsulates ESP IPsec packets in UDP segments; this is an open standard defined in RFC 3947/3948.

- IPsec over UDP encapsulates ESP IPsec packets in UDP segments; this is proprietary to Cisco.

- IPsec over TCP encapsulates ESP IPsec packets in TCP segments; this is proprietary to Cisco.

I'll discuss these three solutions in more depth in Chapter 3, "IPsec." Remember that VPN implementations might have issues with address translation.

Firewall Issues

VPNs might also have issues with traveling through stateful filtering firewalls. A stateful firewall keeps track of the state of a connection, allowing only returning traffic for outbound connections, by default. The stateful function is based on keeping track of sessions between devices. In most cases, this only includes TCP and UDP sessions. That is because it is very easy to track TCP and UDP sessions by examining the source and destination IP addresses, and the source and destination port numbers—if these values change, the change indicates a different connection.

However, not all types of traffic use a transport layer protocol. Again, I'll use IPsec as an example. When transporting data in IPsec, AH or ESP is used. Both of these protocols are Layer-3 protocols, like TCP and UDP, but don't have upper-layer information such as port numbers. AH and ESP, however, do have a special field in their headers called a security parameter index (SPI). This value is used to uniquely identify VPN connections on a device. A firewall, if properly coded by the vendor, could use this value to differentiate VPN connections when implementing a stateful firewall.

To keep track of different IPsec connections is much more difficult than I have described, however. This is very difficult with IPsec because IPsec doesn't use a single bidirectional connection for the data; instead, two unidirectional connections are used:

- One from the local device to the remote device
- One from the remote device to the local device

Remember that a stateful firewall allows outbound connections and their returning traffic, but typically *denies* connections that originate on the outside, like the second bulleted connection, when directed to internal devices. Special types of inspection have to be coded by the firewall vendor to deal with this scenario. Therefore, not every firewall product will necessarily be able to deal with the VPN implementation you might want to use. You'll need to examine closely the VPN implementation you'll want to use, and determine if address translation or firewall devices will create problems for your VPN.

NOTE   For more information on stateful firewalls, read either of my books entitled *Cisco Router Firewall Security*, published by Cisco Press, or *Cisco PIX Firewalls*, published by McGraw-Hill.

Redundancy

Another important component of a VPN design is redundancy. For example, if you examine the hub-and-spoke network shown at the bottom of Figure 1-9, you'll notice that this example lacks redundancy. For instance, if the hub router would fail in this design, every site would lose connectivity to every other site. Therefore, you'll need to carefully examine your network and implement a suitable redundant design, if necessary.

For solving the hub-and-spoke redundancy example, you might use something like that shown in Figure 1-10. In this design, the hub network (SiteA) has two VPN routers for redundancy, and each VPN spoke router has two VPN connections to SiteA—one to each hub router. Of course, this requires special configuration on each spoke. For example, you'll probably want to ensure that not all spokes use the same hub router as the primary VPN connection; otherwise, you might overload the primary VPN router. Or you might want to actually use both VPN connections from the spoke to the hub, which would require you to configure routing correctly on both the hub and spoke routers to perform load balancing.

Figure 1-10 *Hub-and-Spoke Redundant Design*

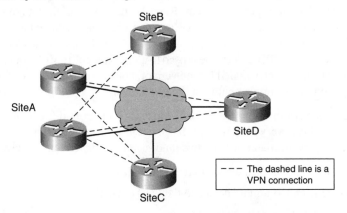

On top of this, you might even need additional redundancy at the spokes, requiring dual routers. Again, this can complicate your design. Plan carefully to ensure that your design functions as desired.

VPN Implementations

Throughout the chapter up to this point, I have repeatedly referred to "VPN implementations," but haven't defined what a VPN implementation actually is. First, let me discuss what a VPN is and what it can encompass. Specifically, the following sections will discuss these popular VPN implementation methods, including how they are implemented, and their basic advantages and disadvantages:

- GRE
- IPsec
- PPTP
- L2TP
- MPLS
- SSL

Other chapters in the book will expand on many of these VPN implementations, so the material you see in the following sections is a basic overview.

GRE

Generic Route Encapsulation (GRE) is a VPN technology originally developed by Cisco and later written up under two Internet Engineering Task Force (IETF) RFCs—1701 and 2784. Cisco developed GRE as an encapsulation method to take a packet from one protocol, encapsulate it in an IP packet, and transport the encapsulated packet across an IP backbone.

Figure 1-11 to illustrates the usefulness of GRE tunneling. In many earlier networks, companies had problems moving traffic between various networking locations where the backbone of the network, or the WAN connection, didn't speak the same protocol. In Figure 1-11, two Novell IPX networks need to communicate with each other. In this example, they are connected via the Internet, which is IP-based. Without GRE, the Novell devices would have to speak both IP and IPX: IPX for access internal services and IP for the remote site's services. Cisco developed GRE specifically for this problem. GRE allows you to take a packet from one protocol, such as IPX, and encapsulate it in an IP packet (where the IP protocol number is 47, representing GRE-encapsulated information).

Figure 1-11 *GRE Example*

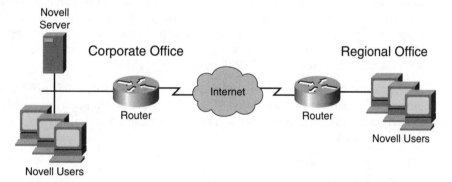

In Figure 1-11, the perimeter routers at the two sites perform this encapsulation/de-encapsulation process. From the Internet's perspective, it only sees IP packets; from the corporate and regional offices' perspectives, they see only IPX packets—which makes everyone happy.

GRE was, and still is, used to connect small pockets of a particular protocol across an IP-based backbone without having to configure the backbone to also run additional protocols. GRE, which is a Layer-3 IP protocol, can encapsulate the following protocols:

- AppleTalk
- Banyan Vines

- Layer-2 bridged traffic
- CLNP
- DECnet
- IP
- IPX

Given its flexibility of encapsulating many protocols, you would think that GRE would be a great VPN solution, at least compared to other VPN solutions with limited protocol support. However, GRE has two main disadvantages:

- From a Cisco-product perspective, GRE works only on Cisco IOS-based routers.
- GRE lacks protection capabilities; in other words, it doesn't perform tasks such as identity authentication, encryption, and packet integrity checking.

Because of these two limitations, GRE is typically not used as a complete VPN solution; however, it can be combined with other solutions, such as IPsec, to create a more robust and scalable VPN deployment.

IPsec

Like GRE, IPsec (short for IP Security) is a Layer-3 protocol. However, there are very few similarities between the two protocols. One advantage of GRE over IPsec is that IPsec only supports TCP/IP protocols—it can't natively transport protocols like IPX or AppleTalk. However, because GRE is an IP protocol, you can deploy a GRE tunnel through an IPsec VPN connection to protect non-TCP/IP traffic.

IPsec is actually a combination of standards defined in IETF RFCs. Where GRE doesn't provide any security, IPsec was designed specifically to deal with moving sensitive data, securely, across an unsecured network. The framework of IPsec deals with the following three main issues:

- Data confidentiality
- Data integrity
- Data authentication

Data confidentiality deals with protecting data from eavesdropping attacks. This is accomplished by using encryption. IPsec supports DES, 3DES, and AES encryption algorithms. Data integrity deals with verifying whether or not packet contents have been tampered with. This is accomplished by using hashing functions such as MD5 and SHA. Data authentication is used to perform packet and device authentication. Hashing functions are used to verify the identity of the device sending the IPsec packets. Device authentication is used to control which remote devices are allowed to establish IPsec connections to a local device. Three types of device authentication are supported: pre-shared keys, RSA encrypted nonces, and RSA signatures (digital certificates). For remote access connections, user authentication is typically employed.

As compared to other VPN implementations, IPsec is the most popular and most widely deployed—not because IPsec is easy to set up and troubleshoot, as you'll see later in this book, but because it is a set of open standards and has been pushed most often by networking vendors when the standards were first ratified. Most networking vendors, when offering a VPN solution, will minimally support IPsec. For example, all of the Cisco devices that support VPN functionality support IPsec. I discuss IPsec in more depth in Chapter 3.

PPTP

The Point-to-Point Tunneling Protocol (PPTP) was originally developed by Microsoft. Its operation is published in RFC 2637. Microsoft developed PPTP to provide a VPN solution for Windows-based systems, such as Windows 95, 98, ME, NT, 2000, and XP. Unlike IPsec, which supports all VPN connection types including site-to-site and remote access, PPTP was developed to allow Windows PC clients secure access to a network access server, such as a Windows remote access server (RAS). Therefore, PPTP is used primarily as a remote access protocol, but it does support site-to-site connectivity.

PPTP is actually a combination of two standards:

- **Point-to-Point Protocol (PPP)**—This standard is used to define the encapsulation process: PPTP encapsulates PPP packets, containing the payload, within an IP packet, which is transported across a network.

- **Microsoft Point-to-Point Encryption (MPPE)**—This standard is used to provide for data confidentiality (encryption) for PPTP.

Unlike IPsec, which only supports TCP/IP protocols, PPTP supports multiple protocols: TCP/IP, IPX, and NetBEUI. Many of the Cisco products, including IOS routers, PIX firewalls, and VPN 3000 concentrators, support PPTP. I'll discuss PPTP in more depth in Chapter 4, "PPTP and L2TP."

L2TP

One problem with using PPTP is that even though the process was defined later in an IETF RFC, PPTP was a semi-open standard. In other words, if you worked in a Microsoft environment, or with vendors that worked closely with Microsoft, deploying PPTP worked well. However, PPTP typically would not work in a mixed-vendor networking environment.

At that time, other vendors also had semi-open VPN types, including Cisco. The Cisco VPN type was called Layer-2 Forwarding (L2F). To provide an alternative solution to IPsec that fit better into smaller Windows PC-based environments, Microsoft, Cisco, and other vendors worked together to develop a VPN standard that would allow all network vendors to produce compatible VPN products.

Basically, L2TP (Layer 2 Tunnel Protocol) is a combination of Cisco L2F and Microsoft's PPTP. L2TP tunnels PPP over a public network, providing services such as data confidentiality. And like GRE, L2TP supports multiple Layer-3 protocols. L2TP incorporates a modified version of Multi-chassis Multilink PPP, which allows a client to stack VPN gateways, making them appear as a single virtual VPN gateway device. L2TP can use MPPE for protection, but like PPTP, this is not as robust as IPsec's protection mechanisms. Because of this, L2TP typically uses IPsec as a protection transport, while still providing some of the same services that Windows environments might need via PPTP.

Cisco no longer supports L2F, but currently supports L2TP on the router, PIX, and concentrator platforms. I'll discuss L2TP in more depth in Chapter 4.

MPLS

Multi-Protocol Label Switching (MPLS) specifies how packets are sent to a destination in an efficient manner, similar to how traffic is managed in a Frame Relay or ATM network, where QoS is supported. MPLS VPNs are sometimes referred to as an enhancement to MPLS; however the term "MPLS VPN" can be very confusing because an MPLS VPN isn't encrypted and the actual data circuit doesn't even traverse a public network such as the Internet!

MPLS circuits are commonly referred to as a VPN. Where IPsec creates a secure connection (tunnel) across a public network, MPLS uses a virtual circuit (VC) across a private network to emulate the VPN function. If you think about the term "virtual private network," a PVC or SVC emulates this type of function in a Frame Relay or ATM network. With MPLS, the tagging information in the MPLS label added to the data provides the segregation function. MPLS can even provide this function in Ethernet backbones. In other words, your traffic is segregated from other people's traffic in the MPLS network. Therefore, your traffic in the carrier's network can be considered "private." Of course, if you're concerned about whether the carrier is eavesdropping on your traffic, an MPLS solution won't solve this problem; you'll have to complement it with another VPN solution, such as IPsec over MPLS.

MPLS is similar to VLAN tagging in Ethernet networks; however, unlike Ethernet VLANs, MPLS supports multiple protocols. In other words, you can use MPLS to tag IP packets, Ethernet frames, IPX packets, and much more. And unlike VLAN tagging, MPLS supports broad QoS abilities. Other than the information discussed in this section, MPLS and MPLS VPNs are beyond the scope of this book.

SSL

Secure Socket Layer (SSL) is an existing technology to encrypt data sent via a web browser connection. Until recently, it was used solely to secure web connections and transactions. However, networking vendors have enhanced SSL to provide SSL-based VPNs. SSL VPNs are used as a remote access VPN solution. One issue with other types of VPNs, such as

IPsec, PPTP, and L2TP/IPsec, is that they require special client software to be installed on the remote access client. This requires special configuration and additional management.

With clientless SSL VPNs, a user uses a web browser as the client software. And because most users have a web browser already installed on their PCs and are very comfortable with web browser applications, there is basically no special client software nor any learning curve involved to use the SSL VPN. SSL VPNs, however, have one limitation: because they are implemented at the application layer, only web-based applications (those via a web browser) can be protected. Other applications, by default, are not protected. In some instances, an SSL VPN vendor can write special code on the SSL VPN gateway device to handle additional applications. But as to what applications are actually supported, this will vary from vendor to vendor. In this instance, a Layer-3 VPN solution, such as IPsec or L2TP/IPsec, would be better because they can protect all traffic from the network layer and above; in other words, these VPNs are not application-specific. SSL VPNs are discussed in more depth in Chapter 5, "SSL VPNs."

VPNs: Choosing a Solution

As you saw in the section, "VPN Implementations," there are actually quite a few VPN solutions to choose from. You should use several criteria in selecting the correct VPN solution for your company's network. It might involve more than one solution, like IPsec and SSL, or IPsec and L2TP/IPsec.

To simplify this process, I evaluate the following criteria when choosing a VPN solution:

- Security
- Implementation, management, and support
- High availability
- Scalability and flexibility
- Cost

The following sections will cover these criteria in more depth.

Security

One of the first things I consider with a VPN solution is security. Toward that end, I ask the following questions:

- What do I need to protect?
- What kind of protection is required?
- How much protection is needed?

As shown in the preceding list, I first need to determine what is to be protected. Do I need to protect traffic for specific applications, such as e-mail, database access, file transfers, and others? Do I need to protect traffic for specific hosts? Do I need to protect traffic for specific network segments? If I only need to protect traffic for specific applications, I would probably first examine SSL VPNs to see if there is a solution available for the particular application or applications that need to be protected. Otherwise, I would look at other VPN solutions.

Second, what kind of protection is necessary? Does the traffic need to be encrypted? Do I need to perform packet integrity checking? How important is it to verify a device's identity? Once I've answered these questions, I can narrow in on a more specific VPN solution. For instance, if I need encryption, I can immediately rule out GRE.

And third, how much protection is needed? For example, if I require encryption to provide data confidentiality, how strong does the encryption process need to be? Can I use DES or must I use a much stronger encryption algorithm, like 3DES? For device authentication, can I use pre-shared keys or should I use digital certificates? Again, I use these questions to narrow my pick to the most appropriate VPN solution.

Implementation, Management, and Support

Most often network administrators forget to factor in implementation, management, and support when choosing a VPN solution. For example, if I compared SSL VPNs to IPsec, I would find that setting up, managing, and troubleshooting SSL VPNs is *much* easier when compared to IPsec.

As an example, you might only need to protect HTTP traffic. Both SSL and IPsec VPNs can do this; however, you'll have to perform a lot more work to implement, manage, and support an IPsec solution than you would an SSL solution, making the SSL a lower-cost, more scalable solution. This difference will become more apparent as you go through the IPsec and SSL components of this book on concentrators, routers, and PIX and ASA security appliances.

High Availability

As I mentioned earlier in the "Redundancy" section of this chapter, redundancy might be a component you desire or need in a VPN implementation. Some VPN implementations support redundancy well and some don't. And when evaluating a redundancy solution, you need to determine the type of redundancy you need (chassis redundancy and/or connection redundancy) and how well your VPN implementation can deal with your type of redundancy. On top of this, a networking vendor might have a special proprietary redundancy feature, like the Cisco Virtual Cluster Agent (VCA), that is not tied to a particular VPN implementation, so you might want to examine redundancy advantages that network vendors offer with their VPN solutions.

Overall, you'll need to be familiar with the advantages and limitations of redundancy solutions. For example, the Cisco VCA feature, discussed in Chapter 10, "Concentrator Management," and Chapter 22, "PIX and ASA Remote Access Connections," is supported only on Cisco 3000 concentrators and ASA security appliances. VCA can be used to load-balance remote access VPN connections; it can't load-balance site-to-site connections.

Scalability and Flexibility

When choosing a VPN implementation, you also need to ensure that the solution you choose is scalable and flexible. The solution needs to be scalable to accommodate the future growth of your network, and flexible to deal with changes that occur within your network.

In other words, if you need to add three more sites to your VPN design, how much work will you have to perform to accommodate this change? How many devices will you have to configure or reconfigure? How much configuration must you perform on these devices? What additional overhead will this place on existing devices? A well-designed solution should resolve these questions. I discuss one Cisco solution for site-to-site connections, called dynamic multipoint VPN (DMVPN), in Chapter 17, "Router Site-to-Site Connections."

Cost

And of course, you can't forget about what a VPN solution will cost your company. Some costs you'll need to evaluate are:

- Hardware devices
- Software products, including remote access clients and management (some vendors charge for remote access client software and some don't—Cisco doesn't charge for their remote access VPN Client for IPsec)
- Network vendor maintenance and support costs
- Personnel and training costs for personnel
- Bandwidth for the VPN traffic and overhead and for normal traffic

In many situations, you'll be using a VPN to replace an existing private WAN, such as Frame Relay, ATM, or dedicated leased circuits. So compare the overall ownership of the private WAN solution to each VPN implementation you might be considering.

Summary

This chapter introduced you to the concept of virtual private networks. As I mentioned in the chapter introduction, I'll expand on many of the topics and issues discussed here in future chapters.

Next up is Chapter 2, "VPN Technologies," where I delve further into technologies used by VPNs to provide protection for data, such as keys, encryption algorithms, hashing functions, and authentication methods.

VPN Technologies

Before I can begin discussing VPN implementations such as Internet Protocol Security (IPsec), Layer 2 Tunnel Protocol (L2TP), Point-to-Point Tunneling Protocol (PPTP), and Secure Socket Layer (SSL), you first need an understanding of the technologies that VPNs can use to provide protection for traffic. I'm sure you have already heard of terms such as keys, DES, 3DES, MD5, pre-shared keys, and the like; however, an in-depth understanding of these protocols, algorithms, functions, and processes will help you determine the pros and cons of VPN technologies. Use this information to pick the optimal VPN implementation based on the type of technologies you'll need to protect your traffic.

I've broken this chapter into five sections: keys, encryption, packet authentication, key exchange, and authentication methods. This chapter will discuss these technologies and how they are related to VPNs, including the advantages and disadvantages of the technologies for a particular category, for example, using a pre-shared key or keys for authentication versus digital certificates.

Keys

We commonly use the term "key" in day-to-day life. One definition of a key is a tool to open a locked door, where something is kept hidden from prying eyes. In the data world, the term "key" has a similar meaning. A key is used to protect information in various ways. For instance, a data key performs a similar function as a password used to protect a user account or a PIN (personal identification number) used with your ATM card to access your bank account. Normally, the longer the key, the more secure the protection it can provide; however, this is not always the case. The following three sections will discuss how keys are used and the two types of keying algorithms: symmetric and asymmetric.

Key Usage

In network security, keys serve a multi-functional process. For example, keys are used for all of these three critical VPN functions:

- Encryption
- Packet integrity checking
- Authentication

There are two basic types of keying solutions:

- Symmetric
- Asymmetric

The following sections will talk more about these two basic types of keying implementations.

Symmetric Keys

Symmetric keys use the same single key to provide a security function to protect information. For example, an encryption algorithm that uses symmetric keys uses the same key to encrypt and decrypt information. Because the same key is used to create and verify the security protection, the algorithm used tends to be fairly simple and thus very efficient. Therefore, symmetric algorithms, like symmetric encryption algorithms, tend to work very quickly.

Because symmetric keying is very efficient and fast, it typically is used in encryption and packet integrity checking. Some encryption algorithms and standards that use symmetric keying are: DES, 3DES, CAST, IDEA, RC-4, RC-6, Skipjack, and AES. MD5 and SHA are examples of hashing functions that use symmetric keying.

One problem, however, with symmetric keying is that the two devices performing protection of data somehow have to get the same key value. For example, if two devices, RouterA and RouterB, are performing DES encryption, and RouterA generates the symmetric key for DES, RouterB also will need this same key to decrypt information that RouterA sends it. There are two basic ways to accomplish this:

- **Pre-sharing keys**— You can pre-share the keys, out-of-band between the two devices.
- **Using a secure connection**— You can use either an existing secure, protected connection to send keys across, or create a new protected connection to send keys across.

This last option is a "catch-22" situation, because to have a secure connection, you need keys; and to share keys, you need a secure connection. Pre-sharing keys doesn't scale very well. Later in the chapter in the "Key Exchange" section I'll discuss ways of sharing keys, dynamically, in a secure fashion between two devices without having to resort to a manual-based pre-sharing method.

Asymmetric Keys

Unlike symmetric keying, where the same key is used to create and verify the protection information, asymmetric keying uses two keys:

- Private keys
- Public keys

The private key is kept secret by the source and is never shared with any other device. The public key is given out to other devices. You can't randomly choose any value for the two keys; instead, a special algorithm is used to create the keys, because they need to have a symbiotic relationship with each other to provide protection.

Asymmetric keys are used for two basic security functions:

- Encryption
- Authentication

The following two sections will discuss each of these functions where asymmetric keying is used; the next two sections will discuss advantages and disadvantages of asymmetric keying, and examples of where asymmetric keying is used.

Asymmetric Keying and Encryption

Asymmetric keys can be used for encrypting data. In such cases, a device first creates a public/private key combination. The device, say RouterA, then gives the public key to a remote peer, like RouterB. RouterB uses the public key to encrypt any data that needs to be sent to RouterA. With asymmetric keying, only the related private key will be able to decrypt the information; therefore, RouterA will use its private key to decrypt it.

Likewise, for RouterA to send data to RouterB, RouterB would generate a separate public/private key pairing and share the public key with RouterA. RouterA then would use this second public key to encrypt data meant for RouterB and RouterB would use the related private key to decrypt it.

As you can see from this example, even if an attacker was eavesdropping and saw the public key being transmitted from RouterA to RouterB or vice versa, it would not do him any good—he would need the private keys to decrypt data, and these are never shared by RouterA or RouterB.

Asymmetric Keying and Authentication

Besides being used for encryption, asymmetric keying also can help perform authentication functions. Figure 2-1 illustrates the use of asymmetric keying for authentication, where RouterA needs to authenticate to RouterB.

As you can see in the figure, the following happens:

1 RouterA generates a public/private key combination.

2 RouterA shares its public key with RouterB.

3 RouterA takes identity information about itself, like its name, and encrypts it with its private key.

4 RouterA sends both the identity information and the encrypted identity information to RouterB.

5 RouterB decrypts the encrypted identity information and compares this with the clear-text identity information that RouterA sent.

6 If RouterB's comparison between the clear-text and decrypted identity information matches, then RouterB can be assured that RouterA did the encryption.

Figure 2-1 *Asymmetric Keys and Authentication*

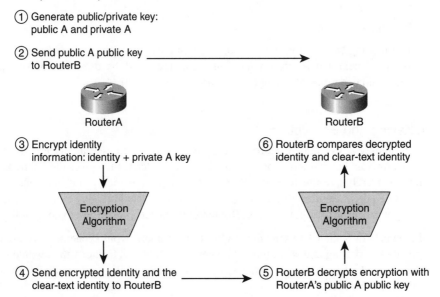

In the example in Figure 2-1, the private key, as in encryption, is never shared (kept private). The public key is shared and used to verify the encrypted identity information, commonly called a *digital signature*, created with the related private key.

One concern with this method of authentication is a man-in-the-middle attack, where someone other than RouterA generates the public/private keys and pretends to be RouterA. This can be overcome by pre-sharing the public key of RouterA, out-of-band, with RouterB. A more scalable approach will be discussed in the "Digital Certificates" section later in this chapter.

Advantages and Disadvantages of Asymmetric Keying

Asymmetric has many advantages over symmetric keying. First, through the use of large prime numbers, the protection process is more secure than with symmetric keys. A prime number is a positive integer not divisible without a remainder by any positive integer excluding itself and one. Two large prime numbers, multiplied together, are used, with an additional input, to generate the public and private keys.

No known method as of today can factor the correct number to break the encryption in a reasonable time, unlike with symmetric keying. For example, if I gave you two very large numbers, like 34,555 and 88,333, and asked you to multiply these numbers together, you could easily figure out the answer: 3,052,346,815. However, if I gave you 3,052,346,815 and asked you to figure out the two numbers that were originally used to come up with this value, you would probably spend the rest of your life trying to find the answer, and would probably be unsuccessful. This is the beauty of asymmetric keying, which is why, first, most asymmetric keying algorithms use this computation process. Second, an attacker needs to know *both* the private and public keys to compromise security, and the private key is *never* shared with any other device.

You would think that given these advantages, most algorithms would use asymmetric keying for security functions. But asymmetric keying is much slower than symmetric keying when performing its security function—in the neighborhood of 1,500 times slower! Therefore, symmetric keys are preferred when encrypting data, since latency and processing is of concern, but asymmetric keys are preferred when performing authentication, where establishing a device's identity is of importance, or for sharing keys, like symmetric keys, across an unprotected network.

Asymmetric Keying Examples

Here are some examples of standards/algorithms that use asymmetric keys:

- **RSA public keying**—This is used for authentication functions to produce digital signatures and to perform encryption. RSA is short for Rivest, Shamir, and Adleman (Ronald Rivest, Adi Shamir, and Len Adleman), who were professors at the Massachusetts Institute of Technology who developed the process. RSA keying is commonly used with digital signatures found on certificates. It supports key lengths of 512, 768, and 1,024 bits, and larger.

- **Digital Signature Algorithm (DSA)**—This is similar to RSA in that it is used to generate signatures for authentication functions, such as certificates; it is typically not used for encryption functions.

- **Diffie-Hellman (DH)**—This is used by the Internet Key Exchange (IKE) protocol in IPsec to exchange keying information and keys securely between IPsec devices. DH is discussed in more depth toward the end of this chapter in the "Diffie-Hellman" section.

- **KEA (Key Exchange Algorithm)**—This is an enhanced version of the DH implementation.

Encryption

Encryption is the process of transforming data in a form which is impossible to decipher without the knowledge of the key or keys used to encrypt it. Depending on the encryption algorithm, either symmetric or asymmetric keys are used. These keys were discussed in the preceding sections of this chapter.

This part of the chapter will cover the following:

- Encryption process
- Encryption algorithms

Encryption Process

The type of keying used affects how encryption is performed. For example, if you use a symmetric keying algorithm, data is encrypted and decrypted with the same key. However, with an asymmetric keying encryption algorithm, a public key is used to encrypt the data and the corresponding private key is used to decrypt it. We have seen the advantage of asymmetric key algorithms for encryption: you can easily share the public key across a public network and have a remote device use this key to encrypt data sent to you. Even if an attacker sees the public key, it won't do him any good because only the corresponding private key can decrypt the data.

However, because the complexity of the encryption/decryption algorithm makes asymmetric keying with encryption a very slow process, asymmetric keying typically is reserved for identity authentication and key sharing, and symmetric keying is used for data encryption. Because of this, the following sections will focus only on encryption algorithms that use symmetric keys.

NOTE   VPN devices, especially VPN gateways, commonly offload encryption processes to a hardware module to speed up the encryption and decryption of packets.

One main problem with symmetric encryption algorithms, though, is that the same key must be used on the source and destination. Sharing the key can be problematic. If you sent the key across the network to a peer, an eavesdropping attacker could see the key and be able to decrypt your messages. You could pre-share the key, but managing the periodic changing of the key for increased security causes management headaches. The "Key Exchange" section later in the chapter will examine this issue in more depth.

Encryption Algorithms

Many encryption algorithms have been developed that use symmetric keys. These algorithms include the following:

- **Data Encryption Standard (DES)** — DES was developed by the National Institute of Standards and Technology (NIST). It uses a 56-bit key structure, which is the most common implementation, but weak by today's symmetric keying standards.

- **Triple DES (3DES)**—3DES is an enhanced implementation of DES, which basically uses DES three times, with three different keys, on the data that need to be protected. Because it uses three 56-bit keys, DES is commonly referred to as using 168-bit keying structure. 3DES is much stronger than DES, but is slower.

- **Advanced Encryption Standard (AES)**—AES was designed to replace 3DES, providing faster and more secure encryption.

- **CAST**—CAST is similar to DES and uses a 128- or 256-bit key structure. It is less secure than 3DES, but is faster.

- **International Data Encryption Algorithm (IDEA)**—IDEA was developed by the Swiss Institute of Technology. It uses a 128-bit key structure; it falls somewhere between CAST and 3DES for security, but like these two algorithms, it is also definitely not the fastest.

- **RC-6 and RC-4**—RC-6 was developed by RSA labs. It supports variable-length keys of up to 2,040 bits (RC-6). One of the more common RC algorithms is RC-4, which supports 40-bit and 128-bit keys. Some VPNs, such as PPTP support it, as do web browsers that use SSL. RC-4 encryption/de-encryption is actually much faster than 3DES in both software and hardware encryption, but less secure.

- **Skipjack**—Skipjack was developed by the National Security Agency (NSA). It uses an 80-bit key structure.

The following sections will discuss some of the more common algorithms used by VPN implementations.

DES and 3DES Algorithms

DES and 3DES are very popular encryption algorithms used by VPN implementations. DES, originally named Lucifer, was developed at IBM in the early 1970s. The NSA and NIST modified Lucifer, resulting in DES, which is a federal standard defined in FIPS 46-3 and ANSI X9.32.

DES is a block cipher encryption algorithm: it takes a fixed-length block of data and converts it into a fixed-length block of encrypted data of the same size by using a symmetric key. The key's length is 64 bits, but because 8 bits are used for parity, the effective key length is 56 bits. Decryption uses a reverse process on the encrypted data block with the same symmetric key, resulting in the original clear-text block of data.

No easy method has been found to break DES; however, with a brute force approach, guessing the keying information used can be done by trying out 2^{55} possible key values. There are other possible methods of breaking DES encryption, but the brute force approach has proven to be the best option. For example, DES was broken in 1998 by a supercomputer in 56 hours and again broken in 1999 in 22 hours by a network of distributed computers. On top of this, it is possible to build specialized hardware appliances to break DES even more quickly . . . in less than 1 hour!

Because computers were becoming more and more powerful during the 1980s and 1990s, and because DES was proven crackable in a reasonable amount of time, NIST created 3DES in 1999. 3DES is basically an enhanced version of DES. 3DES uses three stages of DES and is more secure. DES is applied three times with three different 56-bit keys, resulting in an effective key length of 168 bits. Whereas no successful attack has ever been documented in cracking 3DES, this enhanced security of DES is sufficient for most current applications. No current amount of computing power exists to use a brute force approach to break 3DES.

NOTE 3DES is generally 168-bit, though it could be effectively 112-bit if the same key was used twice. Some vendors are not using a third unique key, but still call their implementation 3DES. Although 3DES is slower in software, the speed difference is barely noticeable when performed in hardware.

DES and 3DES have the following advantages as encryption algorithms:

- Both use symmetric keying, making them much faster at encryption than asymmetric key encryption algorithms.

- Both are easy to implement in both software and hardware when compared to other encryption algorithms.

Given their advantages, DES and 3DES have the following disadvantages:

- Because both use symmetric keying, sharing the symmetric key (or keys) is a problem when the two devices are separated by a public network. Asymmetric key encryption algorithms do not suffer this problem.

- Newer encryption algorithms have been developed that are much faster and more secure than 3DES, such as AES, RC-6, and Blowfish.

AES Algorithm

Expecting that computing power eventually would catch up with 3DES and make it feasible to break it, NIST replaced DES and 3DES with the Advanced Encryption Standard (AES) in 2002. AES is more secure than 3DES and is expected to have a security lifetime of about 10 to 20 years, based on the past history of the increase of computing power.

Actually, there was competition for which new encryption algorithm would replace 3DES: Twofish or Rijndael. Twofish is an enhanced version of the Blowfish algorithm. It can use keys lengths up to 448 bits, requires a very small amount of memory, and is very fast; however, its cipher structure is very complex, making it difficult to analyze to determine how hard, or easy, it is to break. Rijndael uses key lengths of 128, 192, and 256 bits, and sizes of 128, 192, and 256 bits. It is very flexible and is easy to implement. Rijndael won the competition and is now what we know as AES.

AES is a symmetric block cipher that supports 128-, 192-, and 256-bit key lengths. It consists of four stages in a round, which is repeated 10 times for 128-bit keys, 12 times for 192-bit keys, and 14 times for 256-bit keys. At first you might think this would be more process-intensive when compared to something like 3DES; but because of the efficient way AES was written, it is actually less CPU-intensive. Plus, when using larger key sizes, the number of extra rounds increases by two for each step up in key size. Therefore, there is not a linear process relating to the key size and necessary CPU cycles to perform encryption. Actually, the processing cycles slowly increase as the key size increases, obtaining better security without sacrificing performance. Many VPN implementations, such as IPsec, are moving toward using AES to provide for data encryption functions.

Packet Authentication

Packet authentication is used for two purposes:

- To provide data origin authentication
- To detect packets that have been tampered with

The following sections will discuss how packet authentication works (implementation), examples of functions that are used with packet authentication, the uses of packet authentication, and issues with performing packet authentication.

Packet Authentication Implementation

Hashing functions are used to create a digital signature by taking a variable-length input, such as user data or a packet, along with a key and feeding it into a hashing function. The output is a fixed-length result. If the same input is fed into the hashing function, it will always result in the same output.

Hashing Message Authentication Codes (HMAC) functions are a subset of hashing functions. HMAC functions were developed specifically to deal with authentication issues with data and packets. HMACs use a shared secret symmetric key to create the fixed output, called a digital signature or fingerprint. Generic hashing functions have a drawback: If an eavesdropper can intercept the sent data, he can easily generate his own signature of the data and send this "doctored" information to you. HMAC overcomes this problem by using a shared secret key to create the digital signature; therefore, only the parties that know the key can create and verify the signature for sent data.

| NOTE | With HMAC functions, if the same data and same secret key are used to generate a signature, they will always generate the same signature; if you change the data or the key value, the resulting signature changes. |

Two examples of HMAC functions are MD5 and SHA, which I'll discuss in the following two sub-sections. For now, know that the basic mechanics for HMAC functions are shown in Figure 2-2. Here is an explanation of the steps shown in Figure 2-2:

1 The source takes data that needs to be protected and a key, which is shared with the destination, and runs it through an HMAC function.

2 The output of the HMAC function is a digital signature or fingerprint. In IPsec VPNs, it is also called an Integrity Checksum Value (ICV).

3 The source then takes the data that was originally fed into the HMAC function and sends the data along with the digital signature, to the destination.

4 The destination will use the same process to verify the signature; it takes the data sent by the source, along with the same shared key, and inputs this into the same HMAC function, resulting in a second signature.

5 The destination then compares the source's sent signature to the just-computed signature. If they are the same, the destination recognizes that the only device that could have created the signature was a device with the same key. The HMAC function is a one-way process: it is impossible to reverse-engineer the process by taking the fingerprint and data and coming up with the symmetric key used to create the fingerprint. If the two fingerprints are different, the destination assumes that the data was tampered with (purposefully, like by an attacker, or by accident, like data corruption or address translation) and discards the data.

Figure 2-2 *HMAC Signature Creation and Verification*

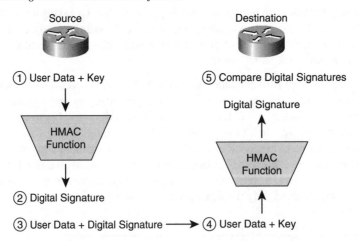

Many VPN implementations use HMAC functions to verify that packet contents haven't been tampered with, such as IPsec's Authentication Header (AH) protocol and the Encapsulation Security Payload (ESP) protocol. The following two sections will discuss two of the most popular HMAC functions: MD5 and SHA.

MD5 HMAC Function

Message Digest 5 (MD5) was developed by Ronald Rivest in 1994. It is specified in IETF RFC 1321. MD5 creates a 128-bit signature (16 bytes in length). It is faster, but less secure, than SHA. MD5 is probably the most popular HMAC function used in the security market today. You can find it being used in PPP's Challenge Handshake Authentication Protocol (CHAP) and routing protocol authentication for routing protocols such as Border Gateway Protocol (BGP), Enhanced Interior Gateway Routing Protocol (EIGRP), Intermediate System-to-Intermediate System (IS-IS), Open Shortest Path First (OSPF), and Routing Information Protocol (RIP) Version 2.

SHA HMAC Function

The Secure Hashing Algorithm (SHA) was developed by NIST and specified in the Secure Hash Standard (SHS FIPS 180). A revision was made to the original HMAC function, called SHA-1, in 1994. It is detailed in the ANSI X9.30 standard. Using SHA-1 in VPNs such as IPsec is described in RFC 2404. SHA-1 creates a 160-bit signature (20 bytes in length). SHA-1 is slower than MD5, but more secure; because its signature is larger, it is stronger against brute force attacks to break the function and discover the shared secret key.

NOTE   In early 2005, certain groups of people have proven that it is possible to create the same signature with different inputs than the original inputs in MD5, creating what is called a *collision*. This can create security issues because it is now possible, in MD5, to create false signatures on a very small scale. Because of this, most vendors support the use of SHA. However, there are reports that the current version of SHA also suffers from this problem. There has not been that much concern about this problem with VPN implementations, but there has with other applications. Because of this possible security issue, work is being developed on SHA-256 and SHA-512, which have much longer signature lengths (256-bit and 512-bit) than MD5 and SHA, making it extremely unlikely, with current computing technology, that collisions can be created purposefully for signatures.

Packet Authentication Uses

As a destination device, how can you verify that packets sent to you are coming from a trusted source which can be verified, versus packets being sent to you from an attacker? HMAC functions can be used for this verification process. We can use packet authentication, through HMAC functions such as MD5 and SHA, to verify that a packet is sent by a trusted source and that it wasn't tampered with while in transit.

As a simple example of using these functions for the verification process, I'll use authentication with a routing protocol. One concern for a router administrator is using a dynamic routing protocol and accepting routing updates from a valid source. You wouldn't want an attacker to corrupt your routing tables by sending your routers false routing information.

With HMAC functions, you can provide this authentication and verification function. With a routing protocol, a router can take routing information that you want to send to a neighboring router, along with an HMAC symmetric key, and run this through an HMAC function, producing a packet signature. The original routing information and packet signature are sent to the neighboring router. The neighboring router then takes the sent routing information and the shared HMAC key and runs them through the same HMAC function. If the computed packet signature matches what the source sent, the neighboring router recognizes that because the same key was used to create and verify the signature, the routing update must be from a trusted source. HMAC functions can provide the same advantage for VPN implementations and for other applications like routing protocol authentication.

Routing Protocol Authentication

In the early 1990s, I once worked on a project to implement and test Internet services that would make documents available to the public for one of the main departments of the state government of Florida. This was before web browsers existed and the applications available to me were FTP and Gopher.

While waiting for a permanent T3 connection from the local carrier (which took almost four months), the networking department of Florida State University (FSU) was kind enough to allow the department to connect to FSU's network for Internet access via a temporary fractional T1 connection. I set up my UNIX server for this access, connected it to FSU's network at about 4 PM, and then went home for the evening. The UNIX server was dual-connected: one connection went to FSU's network and one went to the state government network.

Unfortunately, I had forgotten that RIPv1 was enabled by default on my UNIX server, and both the state government and FSU's network was using RIP. In this instance, the state government was passing my UNIX box a default route, which, in turn, I passed into FSU's network. Unfortunately, a large part of FSU's network, instead of using its default route to reach the Internet, used the state government's default route, breaking FSU's Internet connectivity.

When I arrived to work the next morning, I had a not-so-nice voice mail from the administrator of FSU's network concerning my "default" route. I was red-faced about the problem and immediately disabled routing on my UNIX server to solve the problem. As you can see, without any type of authentication, routing updates can be very easily falsified by rogue devices such as my UNIX server.

One question that I'm commonly asked about VPNs is "Why would you need to perform packet authentication if you're already using encryption?" For example, obviously the only way to decrypt data successfully is if the destination has the encryption key that was used for the initial encryption. Even though that is true, there are still two issues. First, after decrypting the information, you would need to verify that what was decrypted was actually the information sent and not spoofed traffic. Second, a hacker could take advantage of this process by spoofing packets to your device, causing it to waste CPU cycles to decrypt the traffic.

Hashing functions require very few CPU cycles to create and verify the digital signature (hashed output). So they are more efficient. Therefore the following steps typically occur in protecting information between a source and destination in a VPN implementation, as shown in Figure 2-3 and detailed in the following step sequence:

1 The source encrypts the data with the encryption key and an encryption algorithm.

2 The source takes the encrypted data and hash key and feeds them into an HMAC function, resulting in a packet signature.

3 The source sends the encrypted data and the packet signature to the destination.

4 The destination takes the received encrypted data, along with the same hash key, and runs them through the same HMAC function as the source.

5 The destination compares the computed packet signature and the received packet signature.

6 If the just-computed signature matches what the source device sent it, then no packet tampering has occurred, and therefore the destination decrypts the encrypted data using the encryption key; otherwise the destination assumes the packet has been tampered with and discards the data.

Figure 2-3   *Protection Steps*

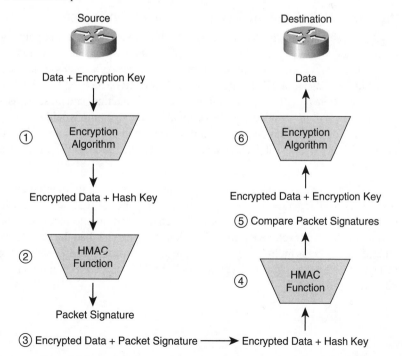

Packet Authentication Issues

There are three main issues with the use of HMAC functions:

- How the shared secret key actually gets shared between the two peers
- The impact that address translation devices have on data signatures created by HMAC functions
- How VPNs implement HMAC functions

The following three sections will discuss each of these issues in more depth.

Sharing the HMAC Secret Key

HMAC functions have more than one problem, including: both devices that share and protect data need the same key. Somehow the symmetric key must be shared for the HMAC function the two devices are using. Of course, if you send the shared key across a public network, the key is susceptible to an eavesdropping attack.

One option is to hard-code the key on both devices; however, this option does doesn't scale well in large networks where a security policy states that keys should be changed periodically. Another option is to use an already encrypted connection across which to share the key. This assumes, though, that an encrypted connection exists between the peers. The "Key Exchange" section later in this chapter will explore this issue in more depth.

Sending Data and HMAC Signatures Through Translation Devices

Another problem with HMAC functions and digital signatures is that your signature could be corrupted by an intermediate device as your data is being sent between two devices. For example, an address translation device performing network address translation (NAT) or port address translation (PAT) alters the headers of IP packets or TCP/UDP segments. If these fields were part of the data fed into the HMAC function, and these fields were changed by the address translation device, the original digital signature would be corrupted, and the destination device would consider that the packet had been tampered with. Also, an intermediate device might place or change quality of service (QoS) information in a packet header.

One solution is to not include all fields in a packet when computing the digital signature with the HMAC function; for example, include only the user data, or certain fields of packet or segment headers that you know won't be changed by an intermediate device. Basically, you would have to exclude all mutable fields, or fields that had the possibility of being altered. These fields include the following in an IP packet: IP address fields, the time-to-live (TTL) field, the type of service (TOS) field, the TCP or UDP port number fields, and possibly other fields.

Using HMAC Functions in VPN Implementations

Even though HMAC functions commonly are used for authentication and integrity checking functions, one issue might arise with certain VPN implementations. I'll use IPsec as an example and one of its security protocols: AH (discussed in more depth in Chapter 3, "IPsec"). AH supports both the MD5 and SHA-1 HMAC functions.

Assume that AH needs to protect 200 bytes of data with SHA-1. SHA-1 creates a 160-bit signature, which is 20 bytes. The addition of the signature adds 10 percent overhead to the data transfer, assuming that the average packet size sent was 200 bytes. In addition, AH can use either MD5 or SHA-1, making the AH packet length variable, because MD5 adds 16 bytes for the signature and AH 20 bytes. IPsec's dilemma was to set the signature field to a fixed 12 bytes, meaning that AH and ESP include only the first 12 bytes no matter whether MD5 or SHA-1 is used.

This is a problem because if you use only part of the hashed output of the signature, there is more of a chance an attacker might find data that produces the same partial hash signature. For example, with MD5's signature being 16 bytes in length, it would take 2^{128} different guesses at messages before finding one that produced the same signature (a collision). If you decided to only use the first 8 bytes of the MD5 signature to reduce the size for efficiency, it might take an attacker 2^{64} guesses; or assuming that the attacker had to go through only half the number of possibilities, then he would have to go through only 2^{63} guesses to find the data that produced the same signature. Because IPsec has AH and ESP using 12 bytes for the signature, it might require the attacker to go through 2^{96} possibilities to find the message.

Also, because IPsec isn't using all the bits of the signature, there is a chance, albeit a small chance, that the data sent might get corrupted. In addition, when the destination received the sent data, the destination might be able to duplicate the same signature and assume the corrupted data was valid. However, given that 12 bytes produces a result of 2^{96} possibilities, it would be extremely rare to run into this situation—you would actually have a better chance of winning the state lottery than finding a corrupted packet that the destination found valid through the process of a truncated signature of 12 bytes—but winning the lottery would definitely be a lot more fun!

CAUTION   Just because a VPN implementation says it supports a particular security function, for example, AH and ESP supporting MD5 and SHA or 3DES using three separate keys, that doesn't mean that it implements these features the way they were intended. In AH's and ESP's case, they truncate the length of MD5 and SHA-1's signatures to a fixed length of 12 bytes, reducing the level of security natively provided by MD5 and SHA-1.

Key Exchange

So far I've talked about all different kinds of keys: symmetric and asymmetric keys, and encryption and HMAC keys. As I mentioned in the last two sections on encryption and packet authentication, which typically use symmetrical keys, the sharing of the protection keys is a security issue. This next section will explore the key-sharing process in more depth and talk about some possible solutions, such as the following:

- Key Sharing Dilemma
- Diffie-Hellman
- Key Refreshing
- Limitations of Key Exchange Methods

Key Sharing Dilemma

A simple example illustrates the issues of sharing keys for symmetric keying algorithms and functions. You have decided to protect financial data between two devices, PeerA and PeerB, and want to encrypt this information using a special symmetric encryption algorithm. PeerA has decided that the encryption key should be "If you can guess this key, you win a lollipop!" Now the issue is to get this key to PeerB so that it can decrypt your financial data successfully. I'll discuss some possible solutions in the following subsections.

Pre-Share the Key

One solution might be to take the key on PeerA and share it, out-of-band, with PeerB. For instance, you could copy the key to a floppy disk or write it down on a piece of paper and then mail this to PeerB. Or you could just call up PeerB and tell him what the key is over the phone. Both of these are referred to "out-of-band" sharing, since the actual key is not shared across the data network.

One downside to pre-sharing keys is that it doesn't scale very well. For example, if you had 100 peers you needed to share keys with, it would take quite a while to perform this process. At a minimum, you would want to change keys every time an employee left the company who knew the pre-shared keys. Also, you would want to change the keys periodically to make your encryption process more secure, just in the off chance your encryption key was compromised. If your security policy stated that you needed to change the encryption key every hour, this solution would not be feasible because of the out-of-band delay involved in getting the keys between the two peers.

Use an Already Encrypted Connection

If you would attempt to share the encryption key in-band with PeerB, like using Telnet to access PeerB, the key would be susceptible to an eavesdropping attack. One solution is to use an already encrypted connection. You could use a secure program to do this, such as SSH; however, SSH requires keys that would have to be exchanged in a secure fashion—a catch-22 situation, because you would need a secure connection to share the SSH keys in the first place.

Encrypt the Key with an Asymmetric Keying Algorithm

I've already (indirectly) discussed one way to solve the symmetric key-sharing issue: use asymmetric encryption. If you recall from the "Asymmetric keys" section, asymmetric keying uses two keys: a public and private key. These keys have a symbiotic relationship with each other and a special algorithm is used to generate these keys. When used for encryption purposes, each peer would generate a public/private key pair. Then each peer would share their public keys with each other. When PeerA would want to send traffic to PeerB, PeerA would use PeerB's public key to encrypt data and then send it to PeerB. PeerB would then use its own private key to decrypt the data.

In our example of financial data, I'll assume that each transfer is 100 MB in size, and this happens every 15 or 20 minutes. This is a large amount of data; asymmetric encryption algorithms are very slow and process-intensive; so they are not desirable when large amounts of data need to be transferred.

However, instead of using asymmetric keying to encrypt the actual financial data, we could, instead, use asymmetric keying to encrypt the *symmetric key*. This allows us to share the symmetric key across an insecure connection, while sending it in an encrypted format.

In the example of the financial data, PeerA has the encryption key; therefore, PeerB creates a public/private key combination and sends its public key to PeerA. PeerA then takes the symmetric key and encrypts it with PeerB's public key. PeerA sends the encrypted symmetric key, "If you can guess this key, you win a lollipop!", to PeerB, which decrypts it with its own private key. Therefore, whenever PeerB receives encrypted financial data from PeerA, it will be able to decrypt the data successfully with the shared symmetric key. The advantage of this approach is that the asymmetric key encryption process occurs only on the symmetric key: the financial data is encrypted using a symmetric encryption algorithm and the shared symmetric key.

Most VPN implementations use a public/private key algorithm in this way to share symmetric keys. In the next section I'll discuss a public/private key implementation that is commonly used by most VPN implementations today.

Diffie-Hellman Algorithm

The public/private key cryptography process was originally credited to Whitfield Diffie, Martin Hellman, and Ralph Merkle in 1976. Their ideas are covered by U.S. patent 4,200,770, which expired in 1994. The process is commonly referred to as Diffie-Hellman (DH).

However, there is evidence to prove that these three actually didn't discover the public/private key cryptography process; rather it was one of two government agencies of the British or the U.S. (National Security Agency) government 10 years before Diffie, Hellman, and Merkle developed a similar process independently. These processes, however, were kept secret from the public; and whereas this information was classified and never published, these three people created the same solution for public use.

Today our concern is not who discovered the process, but how to share symmetric keys in an insecure network. Most networking vendors look at the Public Key Cryptography Standard (PKCS) #3 standard to implement DH.

Simply put, DH is typically not used to encrypt user data, but is, in most cases, used by VPN implementations to share keying information securely, such as DES, 3DES, AES, SHA, MD5 and other symmetric keys, across an insecure public network, like the Internet. DH uses public key cryptography (asymmetric keying) to accomplish this. Therefore, it is commonly referred to as a public key exchange method.

Many VPN implementations, such as IPsec, use DH to share symmetric encryption keys in a secure fashion. For instance, IPsec's RFCs 2401, 2408, and 2412 rely on the use of DH for sharing of keying information for HMAC functions, such as MD5 and SHA, and encryption algorithms, like DES, 3DES, and AES.

Figure 2-4 explains how DH works. DH uses the following six steps to share symmetric keys across an insecure network:

1 Each of the two peers shares information that will help them create their own public/ private key combinations; this is necessary because DH supports varying key sizes, called key *groups*. I'll discuss DH key groups after these numbered steps. Once the key size is known, the two peers create their personal public/private key pair combination. Actually, each creates its private key first, and uses a derivative process to derive the public key from the private key.

2 Each peer shares its public key with the remote peer.

3 Each peer takes *its* personal private key and the *remote* peer's public key and runs them through the DH algorithm.

4 The mathematical beauty of the DH algorithm is that even though different inputs are fed into the algorithm, the *same output results on both sides*: Diffie, Hellman, and Merkle figured out that if you have one pair of values that have a relation, and another pair of values that have a relation, when you exchange one value for another in the different pair, there is still a relationship between the values. I have a degree in mathematics, but coming up with this proof is way beyond my abilities—I'm just glad these three guys made it easier for me to set up secure networks!

5 Because PeerA created the symmetric encryption key for the financial data, PeerA encrypts the data with the output key from the DH algorithm, Secret_key_X, and sends the encrypted symmetric encryption key to PeerB across the network.

6 When PeerB receives the encrypted key, PeerB uses the same derived DH key, Secret_key_X, to decrypt the symmetric key, resulting in "If you can guess this key, you win a lollipop!"; therefore, when PeerA sends financial data to PeerB, PeerB will be able to decrypt it successfully with the symmetric encryption key.

Figure 2-4   *The Diffie-Hellman Process*

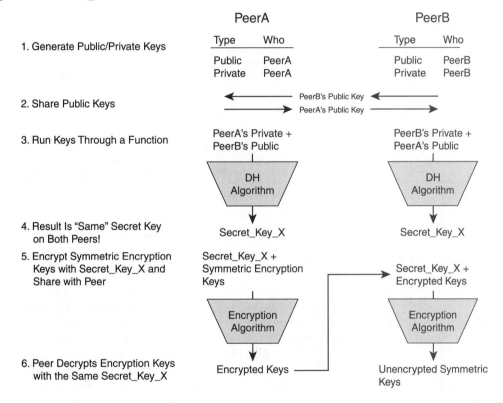

DH uses key groups to define how the shared secret key is actually generated. The key groups define the key length for the public and private keys and the DH algorithm to use in generating the shared secret key.

Table 2-1 has a quick breakdown of the DH key groups. In this table, the first column indicates the name of the key group, denoted by a number. Following this is the length of the keys, and, in the last column, the type of algorithm used to create the shared secret key. DH key groups are commonly referred to with their number, as in DH group 1.

Straight algorithms use a normal computation process, like an equation, to produce a secure key. The longer the bit length is for a straight algorithm, the stronger the resulting secret key. But straight algorithms and keys with long bit lengths are very computational-intensive. For example, a Cisco 7200 router with a VAM card would have no problem processing a straight algorithm using DH group 15; however, a personal digital assistant (PDA) device doesn't have that capacity.

To accommodate devices that have limited processing power, elliptical curve algorithms are used; they can use a smaller key size, but can create a more secure result than a corresponding straight algorithm using the same key size. But because they are also process-intensive, the key sizes are kept small so that limited processing devices can still use them.

Table 2-1 *DH Key Groups*

Key Group	Length	Equation
1	768 bits	Straight algorithm
2	1,024 bits	Straight algorithm
3	155 bits	Elliptical curve algorithm
4	185 bits	Elliptical curve algorithm
5	1,536 bits	Straight algorithm (most secure key group supported by Cisco)
7	163 bits	Elliptical curve algorithm
14	2,048 bits	Straight algorithm
15	3,072 bits	Straight algorithm (most secure key group, but Cisco doesn't support it)

NOTE Remember that if a VPN implementation uses DH, it won't necessarily support all DH groups. For instance, if a Cisco router is using IPsec, it supports only DH groups 1, 2, and 5 (as of the writing of this book); whereas the Cisco VPN 3000 series concentrators support DH groups 1, 2, 5, and 7 for IPsec. Whatever DH groups a device supports for a VPN implementation, in other words, is device- or vendor-specific.

Key Refreshing

Another thing to consider is the management of keys. Periodically, you'll probably want to change your symmetric keys used by encryption algorithms and HMAC functions for a more secure solution. For example, if you had 100 sets of keys, and your security policy stated that you should change the keys once every hour, you definitely would not want to do this manually—this would require multiple full-time people to perform this task 24 hours a day, seven days a week!

Therefore, one of the important features a VPN implementation should support is management of keys: the ability to refresh them periodically in a dynamic, secure, in-band fashion, reducing the amount of physical management to a very small amount of time. For example, DH doesn't specify how to deal with key management functions; however, VPN implementations, such as IPsec, have other components that handle this process.

Limitations of Key Exchange Methods

One strength of asymmetric keying algorithms is that the private key, used to decrypt information, is never sent across the network. And with DH, the derived secret key also never traverses the network. Thus an attacker, even if he is eavesdropping on the public key exchange process and sees the exchanged public key or keys, wouldn't be able to use this to decrypt any transmitted information. In a simple asymmetric algorithm implementation, the eavesdropping attacker would have to know the private key to decrypt information; and in the case of DH, the attacker would have to know of one of the two private keys to decrypt information.

However, DH does have one main weakness: it is susceptible to a man-in-the-middle attack. I'll use the PeerA-to-PeerB example. PeerA needs to encrypt financial data to PeerB. In this example, assume DH is being used for sharing keys. PeerA initiates a connection to PeerB; assume that instead of the real PeerB responding back, a man-in-the-middle attack occurs and the attacker's device responds back. DH, however, assumes that the two devices trust each other. In the PeerA-to-PeerB example, especially if they're separated by a public network, they have no idea if they're interacting with each other, or with some device pretending to be one of the two parties.

In other words, key exchange protocols such as DH deal strictly with one thing: key exchanges. They don't deal with authentication mechanisms. Some other component is required to verify the identities of the two devices to ensure that PeerA doesn't mistakenly send sensitive financial data to a man-in-the-middle device (attacker).

Authentication Methods

Authentication is implemented using digital signatures. Digital signatures are most commonly created by taking some message text, such as information unique to a device or person, along with a key, through a hashing function. The digital signature is like the signature that you would use to sign a check, your fingerprint, or a retinal scan of your eye: it's something unique to you and no one else. Digital signatures are used to implement non-repudiation in VPNs: being able to prove, with certainty, the identity of a device.

The last part of this chapter on VPN technologies will cover authentication methods: how two peers can recognize that when they establish a connection to each other, they are really connecting to the associated peer and not someone pretending to be that peer. In this section I'll explore further how man-in-the-middle attacks occur and the types of authentication you can use to discover and prevent man-in-the-middle attacks.

Man-in-the-Middle Attacks

So that you have a better understanding of a man-in-the-middle attack, I'll use Figure 2-5 to illustrate how this attack occurs. In this example, PeerA wants to send data to PeerB. PeerA does a DNS lookup for PeerB's address, shown in Step 1. However, the attacker also sees the DNS request and sends a reply back to PeerA before the DNS server has a chance, shown in Steps 2 and 3. The IP address that the attacker sends is the attacker's own IP address. PeerA knows no better and assumes that when it uses the IP address in the DNS reply that it is sending traffic to PeerB; however, as shown in Step 4, the traffic actually is directed to the attacker.

Figure 2-5 *Man-in-the-Middle Attack Example*

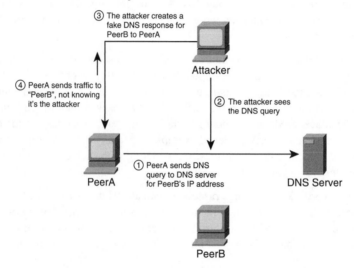

This is a simple example of using spoofing of DNS replies. If the DNS server's reply was received before the attacker's, PeerA would connect to PeerB; however, a sophisticated hacker could use a session hijacking/re-routing attack to redirect traffic sent from PeerA to PeerB to the attacker himself, still pulling off the man-in-the-middle attack. Given this security problem, some type of authentication is required to allow PeerA and PeerB to verify their identities when communicating with each other. The next section will discuss different types of authentication that might solve this problem.

Authentication Solutions

With VPN implementations, you can use two types of authentication to verify a peer's identity:

- Device authentication
- User authentication

Device authentication is used with both site-to-site and remote access VPNs. With device authentication, either keying information is pre-shared to assist with the identification process, or it is acquired and verified when the devices need to communicate with each other via digital certificates. Pre-shared authentication can use either symmetric or asymmetric keys, whereas in-band authentication uses asymmetric keys with digital certificates.

User authentication is used only with remote access. With device authentication, the keying information typically is stored on the device. This can be a concern if the device is broken into or stolen, as could easily happen with a laptop or PC. Therefore, it is very common to see remote access VPNs use two methods of authentication: both device and user. User authentication normally uses pre-shared keys (a static password) or token card services (one-time passwords). The following sections will discuss these methods in more depth.

Device Authentication

All secure VPN implementations I have dealt with at least support device authentication. Device authentication authenticates the devices that are establishing a protected connection; however it does not authenticate the people who want to use the VPN connection. Therefore, device authentication is common in site-to-site VPNs, and is the first method of authentication in remote access VPNs.

Device authentication is most often accomplished using one of the three following methods:

- Pre-shared symmetric keys
- Pre-shared asymmetric keys
- Digital certificates

The following sections will discuss these three methods.

Pre-Shared Symmetric Keys

The most common method of authenticating devices is with pre-shared keys. Of the three methods mentioned in the last section, the configuration of pre-shared symmetric keys is the simplest.

With pre-shared symmetric key authentication, a single key is used to perform the authentication. This key is shared on two peers, out-of-band, before they need to establish a secured connection, and is saved locally on the devices. The authentication process will use an encryption algorithm or HMAC function for authentication.

With the encryption approach, each peer will take some identity information about themselves; for example, their IP address, hostname, serial number, or a combination of these things, along with the pre-shared symmetric key, and run them through an encryption algorithm. Then both sides will send both the original identity information, along with the output of the encryption algorithm, to the other peer. Each peer then takes the received encrypted identification information and decrypts it with the pre-shared symmetric key. If the received clear-text identity information matches the just-decrypted identity information, both peers can feel safe in assuming that the other device is who it says it is, because the encrypted information could be created only with the pre-shared key.

I'll now examine the use of HMAC functions and pre-shared symmetric keys for identity authentication. Each peer will take identity information about themselves, such as their IP address, hostname, serial number, or a combination of these things, along with the pre-shared symmetric key, and run them through an HMAC function. The output is called a digital signature. The signature, along with the input identification information, is sent to the remote peer. The remote peer will take the identification, along with the same pre-shared key, and run them through the same HMAC function. If the just-computed signature matches what the other peer sent, then it can be assumed that the same key was used to create the signature, and thus the peer who is making the connection must be who it says it is, and not an impostor.

Of the two methods, encryption is less likely to be used for identity authentication. Encryption is reversible: one device encrypts and the other decrypts. Because you must send the identity information along with the encryption, this tells an eavesdropping attacker one of the two inputs into the encryption algorithm, making it easier to determine what the encryption key is. HMAC functions, on the other hand, are one-way functions; so even if the hacker sees one of the two inputs into the HMAC function, such as the identity information, it doesn't help him to reverse the signature to determine the symmetric key used to create the signature and thus be able to spoof an identity.

Pre-Shared Asymmetric Keys

With a symmetric key, the same key is used for identification authentication, which is typically less secure than a process that uses two keys, as with asymmetric keys. With asymmetric keys, each side creates a public and private key combination. Each peer then, out-of-band, shares its public key, which is stored locally on the devices, with the remote peer.

For example, assume there are two devices, PeerA and PeerB. PeerA creates two keys, PubA and PrivA, and PeerB creates two keys, PubB and PrivB. Out-of-band, the two peers share their public keys with each other. At this point, PeerA has three keys: PubA, PrivA, and PubB. The same is true of PeerB: PubB, PrivB, and PubA. When performing authentication, a peer takes identity information about itself, along with its personal private key, and encrypts it, creating a signature. The peer then sends the identity information, along with the encrypted information, to the remote peer.

In my ongoing example, PeerA, for instance, takes its own identity information and the PrivA key and encrypts it. This is sent, in-band, to PeerB when the two peers want to establish a connection with each other. PeerB then uses PeerA's public key, PubA, to decrypt the signature and compare it with the sent identity information to verify PeerA's identity. If the identity information matches, PeerB recognizes that the only key that could have encrypted this was the corresponding key of PubA: PrivA.

One popular method of this implementation was developed by RSA Labs, called RSA encrypted nonces. Sometimes IPsec uses this method to perform device authentication between IPsec peers. With RSA encrypted nonces, the RSA public key encryption standard is used, which requires each peer to create a random number, called a nonce, and encrypt it with the other peer's public key. The encrypted nonce is sent to the peer with the corresponding private key, which is used to decrypt the encrypted nonce. The decrypted nonce is then used to compute an HMAC key. This is then used with an HMAC function to provide identity authentication by taking identity information, such as a hostname, and hashing it with the hash key and an HMAC function, resulting in a signature. The peer then shares the identity information and the signature, which can be verified by the remote peer.

TIP	To ensure the best security, each pair of peers should have separate keys—different peer sets, different keys. When using different keys for different peers, this is referred to as *unique* keying, whereas using the same key with multiple peers is referred to as *wildcarding*. Even though unique keying is possible for site-to-site VPNs with static source IP addresses, it is not always possible for remote access users when their source IP address typically is acquired, dynamically, from their connected ISP.

Digital Certificates

Pre-shared keys are easy to configure for a small number of devices; however, for a large number of devices, they don't scale well. For example, you have nine peers pre-configured with pre-shared keys and you've just added a tenth device. You need to set up VPN connections from the other nine devices to the new device (fully meshed). Assume that you are using pre-shared symmetric keys. To ensure security, you would have to create a separate key for each set of peers. On the new device, you would need to configure all nine keys and on the other devices, the respected key to connect to the new device. Likewise, if you decided to implement asymmetric keying for authentication, each peer would need to create a new public/private key pair. On the new device, you would need to configure nine public keys, and on the other devices, the new peer's public key.

As you add more and more devices to your network that need to establish protected connections, the amount of configuration and management required increases exponentially. Therefore, it is uncommon to see the use of pre-shared keys for identity authentication in large VPN implementation solutions.

Pre-shared authentication methods have one problem: you must "pre-share" the keying information that is used for identity authentication. Therefore, a scalable solution should allow you to perform authentication, in-band, without having to pre-share information to each respective peer with which you wish to set up a protected connection.

To help you scale device authentication to a large number of devices and reduce the risk of a man-in-the-middle attack, the following sections of the chapter cover these topics:

- Definition of a digital certificate
- Standards and components
- Certificates: Acquiring them
- Certificates: Using them

Definition of a Digital Certificate

Certificates contain information to assist in the authentication process. Unlike pre-shared key authentication methods, certificates are not pre-shared. Instead, only when devices need to make connections with each other are certificates shared. Therefore, the hardest part is getting certificates on devices—you don't have to configure other peer's certificates on your device.

A digital certificate is similar to an electronic version of a driver's license or passport: it can be used to authenticate a person's (or in this case, a device's) identity. Digital certificates are based on the use of asymmetric (public/private) keys, as are RSA encrypted nonces. You'll actually find many things on a digital certificate, which I discuss in depth in the "X.509 Certificates" section. However, three main things found on a digital certificate are a device's identity information, its public key, and its signature, created with its corresponding private key. Therefore, the necessary information to prove a device's identity is located in one place: its certificate. To authenticate a remote peer, you only need its digital certificate.

Of course, this presents a problem: how can you be sure when someone sends you a certificate that they are who they say they are? In other words, an attacker could generate a certificate and send this to you, pretending to be someone else. How can you detect this kind of masquerading attack?

This is where we draw a line between self-signed certificates and the use of a trusted third party, called a Certificate Authority, to provide a trusted source of certificate information. For example, if two peers generate their own self-signed certificates, you can't really verify the remote device's identity if they're masquerading as someone else. Therefore, a trusted certificate repository is necessary. This repository is called a Certificate Authority (CA). In this situation, the CA is a device trusted by all devices that want to use certificates. Then, when peers want to establish connections to each other and authenticate using certificates, they can use the CA as a trusted party to ensure that a masquerading attack isn't occurring, and that the peers you're connecting to are really who they say they are. I'll discuss CAs in more depth later in the "Certificate Authorities" section.

Standards and Components

Before I can begin discussing how a device gets a certificate and then uses it for authentication, I first need to discuss some of the standards and components used with certificate authentication. There are many standards and components used to implement an authentication scheme that uses certificates. The following sections will cover these in more depth.

Certificate Authorities   A CA performs a similar function to a notary. A notary verifies and validates a person's identity when that person signs a document. For example, to sign a mortgage for a bank, the bank will require that you prove your identity to ensure that they are lending money to the right person. A notary will validate your identity by examining a government identification you have, like a driver's license or passport; comparing not just your picture to what you look like, but also comparing your written signature on the mortgage with the signature on your government ID. The notary also will ensure that your ID is current by looking at the expiration date; because if your ID is expired, there might be some legal issue about your right to sign the document.

CAs perform the notary's role in the digital world. In one example, two peers, PeerA and PeerB, want to share information securely. Both peers generate public and private keys and share their public keys with each other. They can then use the remote peer's public key to encrypt information that is to be sent to the remote peer, and the remote peer can use its own private key to decrypt it. By now you're familiar with this process. However, what if there is an attacker, PeerC, who pretends to be PeerB. How can PeerA feel confident that when it uses the remote peer's public key that it belongs to PeerB, and not to some device, like PeerC, that is masquerading as PeerB?

To solve this issue, CAs use a hierarchical trust. The CA is the most trusted device and is the repository of certificates. All devices that want to communicate with each other in a secure fashion must obtain their certificates from the same trusted source. Then, when two peers from the CA's domain want to establish secure connections, they can use the CA to detect masquerading attacks: CAs can be used to check a device's identity. I'll discuss this process in more depth in the "Using Certificates" section later.

Public Key Infrastructure   The Public Key Infrastructure (PKI) includes the following components: policies, people, software, hardware, and processes needed to create, store, manage, share, and revoke certificates. There are two PKI models used in certificate implementations:

- Central
- Hierarchical

In a design where there is a single CA, this is referred to as a *central* authentication implementation, where all certificates can be created and verified from a single CA. Central CA models commonly are used in small networks where the devices are in the same geographic region.

Of course, in a large-scale deployment of certificates in an enterprise (probably global) network, the two devices that want to establish a secure connection might be using *different* CAs. In other words, there might be a CA in the USA for devices in North and South America, one in England for devices in Europe, one in Asia for devices in Japan and China, one in Australia for devices in the Pacific, and one in Africa for devices in Africa. If the certificates are from different CAs, how can there be a trust relationship between the two peers?

To solve this problem, a higher-level CA is used, with the two lower-level CAs of the two peers being subordinate to the higher-level CA. This is referred to as a hierarchical PKI model. The ability to create and validate certificates is delegated through a hierarchical chain of CAs. At the top of the hierarchy is the root CA, which is the most trusted device. The root CA creates certificates for the subordinate CAs. These CAs implicitly trust the root CA and can use the root CA to verify the identity of other CAs that they need to interact with. Likewise, the subordinate CAs can create certificates for devices, such as routers, PCs, and firewalls. If two devices need to validate each other's certificates, they can go up the chain of authority from a subordinate CA to the root CA, the device everyone trusts (this is done without actually talking directly to the CA in real time, but rather by using an algorithm in conjunction with the root/top-level CA certificates).

Given the two models, central and hierarchical, you'll notice that trust is never between two entities, like two PCs, but the trust is between a device and a CA, or a CA and a root CA. This presents a problem, though, if you're concerned about redundancy. If your CA (central) or root CA (hierarchical) fails, how can devices authenticate with a trusted source?

PKI uses Registration Authorities (RAs) to solve this problem. An RA is a device that can serve as a limited backup of a CA: it can hold existing certificates, but it cannot create or revoke them. Therefore, if a CA fails, devices in the network can still use the RA to validate each others' certificates. But until a failed CA is restored to an operational status, you won't be able to create new certificates, or revoke existing ones.

TIP   Because a CA is the only one that can create new certificates, it is imperative that it is backed up periodically. I even recommend that my customers who are building their own certificate infrastructure have a spare identical server to which they periodically mirror the active CA disk drives, typically using something like Ghost. Then you only have to change the IP addressing of the new CA to match that of the old one, and you're back in the certificate business.

PKCS #10   The Public Key Cryptography Standards (PKCS) was an attempt by RSA Security, Inc. to standardize public key processes not covered by other standards. Of the PKCS standards, two play an important role with certificates: PKCS #10 and #7 (the latter of which is discussed later in the chapter).

PKCS #10 defines the actual information and format that a device needs to include and use when creating and requesting its personal certificate. The CA will then use this information to create the device's personal certificate, commonly called an *identity* certificate. The identity information that is sent in the PKCS #10 certificate request can include the following:

- **Common Name or Distinguished Name (CN or DN)**—This is the name or identity of the device; this is required.

- **Organizational Unit (OU) or Department**—This is the department the device is located in; this is optional.

- **Organization (O)**—This is the name of the company the device is located in; this is optional.

- **Locality (L)**—This is the city the device is located in; this is optional.

- **State Province (SP)**—This is the state or province the device is located in; this is optional.

- **Country**—This is the country the device is located in; this is optional.

- **Subject Alternative Name (FQDN)**—This is the Fully Qualified Domain Name (FQDN) of the device; this is optional.

- **Subject Alternative Name (E-mail Address)**—This is the e-mail address of the person responsible for the device; this is optional.

- **Key Size**—This is the key size used to create the public/private key pair, which is typically either 512 bits in length, 768 bits, 1,024 bits, 2,048 bits, or even higher; this is required and usually defaults to 512 bits.

Note   1,024- and 2,048-bit keys for certificates are fairly common today. Unfortunately, some more security-conscious companies want certificates with 4,096-bit keys, but not all Cisco devices support this key size. To create a 4,096-bit key requires a hardware encryption accelerator, and not all hardware encryption cards or modules support 4,096-bit or higher key lengths.

- **Public key**—This is the device's public key that other devices can use to verify this device's identity; this is required.

- **Challenge Password**—This can be used by the CA to validate a device's request for a certificate and to revoke the certificate if this becomes necessary; this value is dependent on whether or not the CA is configured for challenges.

The preceding information is then signed by the device's private key and then the above information, along with the signature, is used to generate a certificate request. The device takes the PKCS #10 information and places it into an ASN.1 message format, which is then sent to the CA. The resulting information can be sent to the CA using either of the following two ways:

- **In-band**—The PKCS #10 information is sent directly across the network to the CA; if the CA is set up to generate a certificate automatically, it will do so and send this back to the requestor. The standard that defines this process is the Simple Certificate Enrollment Protocol (SCEP), which is discussed later in the "Simple Certificate Enrollment Protocol (SCEP)" section.

- **Out-of-band**—The PKCS #10 information is placed on a floppy or CD-ROM or in an e-mail message and sent to the administrator of the CA.

The PKCS #10 information is used by the CA to create the digital certificate for the requesting device.

X.509v3 Certificates   When a CA receives the PKCS #10 information, it will validate the request by the challenge, if implemented on the CA, in addition to decrypting the device's signature with the included public key. Assuming that the PKCS #10 information can be validated by both methods, or at least the latter, the CA can generate a certificate for the device.

The most common standard for creating certificates is the ITU-T X.509 standard. The X.500 system actually has never been fully developed by ITU-T, including X.509; IETF has taken the ITU-T standard and narrowed its definition for use in device authentication. This is specified in RFC 3280; however, most people commonly refer to this certificate implementation as X.509v3.

NOTE   There are two types of certificates: root and identity. The CA itself needs a certificate, and each device that wants to perform device authentication. The root certificate represents the CA, and the identity certificates represent the devices within the CA's domain. In a domain, each certificate will have a unique serial number, to verify if a certificate is still valid or has been revoked.

The CA, when issuing an identity certificate, will bind a public key to a particular certificate field, like the DN or Alternative Name (e-mail address or FQDN). Each certificate will contain the following information:

- **Information supplied by the CA**—Identity of the CA who issued the certificate, a serial number unique within the CA's domain, the beginning and ending validity dates, the public key of the CA, the signature HMAC algorithm used by the CA to sign the certificate, and the location of the Certificate Revocation List (CRL); the CRL is discussed in the "Certificate Revocation List" section.

- **Information from the device's PKCS #10 information**—The device's name and optionally other information included from the PKCS #10 information.

The CA then generates a random symmetric key and takes this key, the information from the device's PKCS #10, and information the CA supplied and runs all of this through an HMAC function. The CA then encrypts the HMAC symmetric key with its private key. The CA then places the signature hash value (the just created HMAC signature), the encrypted HMAC symmetric key, and the HMAC function used to create the HMAC signature on the device's identity certificate.

It is important to include the HMAC function on the certificate so that someone else can use the same function to verify the HMAC signature with the same HMAC symmetric key. This is shown in Figure 2-6. A device can use the CA's public key to decrypt the HMAC symmetric key and the device can then feed the certificate and HMAC key through the HMAC function to verify that the certificate is authentic. This process is shown in Figure 2-7. Given that the information on the certificate (such as the serial number) and the random HMAC symmetric key are different, every identity certificate will have a unique HMAC signature.

Figure 2-6   *Certificate Signature Creation*

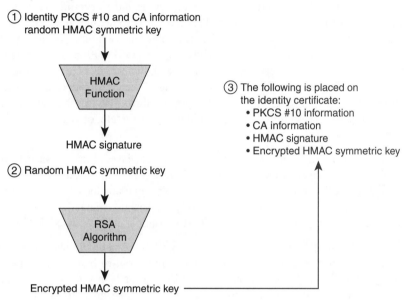

Figure 2-7   *Certificate Signature Validation*

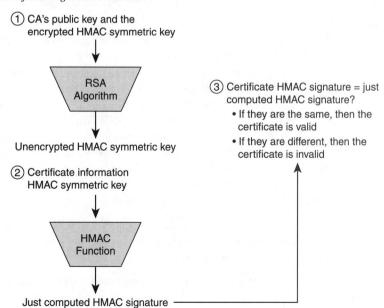

The CA's public key is not located on the identity certificate. In the "Certificates: Acquiring Them" section I'll show how the device acquires the CA's public key so that it can decrypt the hashed signature key to verify the authenticity of any certificate created by the CA.

PKCS #7   PKCS #7 is an RSA standard for signing and encrypting the identity certificate, which will then be sent to the device. This process is sometimes referred to as *enveloping*. The information (the X.509v3 certificate) is encrypted with the public key of the device for which the certificate is intended. The encrypted information, a file, is then sent by the CA to the device, which can then decrypt it with the device's corresponding private key. This allows the device to detect any tampering of the certificate or a man-in-the-middle attack. PKCS #7 has one interesting feature: it allows you to send multiple certificates in one request; for example, a root and identity certificate, or two or more identity certificates.

There are many ways the CA can envelop, or encode, the certificate besides using PKCS #7. Here is a list of the common file formats: .DER or .CER, .PEM (base-64), .P7B or .P7C (PKCS #7), .PFX or .P12 (PKCS #12). This file (containing the device's encrypted identity certificate) then needs to be sent, in-band or out-of-band, to the requesting device, which, in turn, needs to install the certificate locally (for example, in its flash, NVRAM, or disk drive).

Simple Certificate Enrollment Protocol (SCEP)   As I mentioned, the encoded identity certificate can be sent out-of-band or in-band. In the out-of-band approach, the device generates its PKCS #10 information and mails or e-mails this file to the CA administrator. The CA administrator then creates an X.509 identity certificate from this information and encodes it into a file, like the .P7C or .CER file, which would then be mailed or e-mailed back to the device. This process is not very scalable, especially if you have hundreds or thousands of devices that need identity certificates.

A more scalable approach is to use an in-band solution to acquire certificates. The Simple Certificate Enrollment Protocol (SCEP) uses PKCS #10 and #7 to request and acquire an identity certificate from a CA using an in-band process across an IP network. To use SCEP, the CA must be set up with the SCEP protocol. SCEP uses HTTP to share information between devices; you would have to configure the URL on the device to access the SCEP process on the CA. With SCEP, once you enter your PKCS #10 information and send it, via HTTP, to the CA, the CA will either manually or automatically generate a certificate for you and send this back, in a PKCS #7 format, via HTTP. This whole process can be completed in a handful of minutes compared to the out-of-band approach, making SCEP a more desirable option when you need to install certificates on many devices. In the "Acquiring Certificates" section we'll discuss the SCEP process in more depth.

Certificate Revocation Lists   A Certificate Revocation List (CRL) is a list of certificates that have been revoked by the CA. There are many reasons why you might need to revoke a certificate, including these common ones:

- The private key that the device uses for authentication with its identity certificate has been compromised.

- The identity certificate has been compromised.

- The device is no longer being used, and therefore the identity certificate is not needed.
- The identity certificate has expired and the device needs a new identity certificate.
- The security policy has changed, requiring longer (or shorter) keys for signature functions, thus requiring new public/private keys, a new signature, and a new identity certificate.

To ensure that not just anyone can revoke a certificate, a couple of methods are used to prove a person's identity when they call up the administrator of the CA to revoke a certificate: you don't want anyone to call up and be able to revoke certificates. Therefore the CA needs some method of verifying your identity. Of course, if the administrator personally knows you, then this is not an issue. But if you're using a public CA service, such as Verisign, they'll want some information. This is typically the original challenge password you could optionally enter in the PKCS #10 information when creating the certificate information for the CA. When you give the challenge password to the administrator, he'll verify it with what you originally sent via PKCS #10. If the challenge passwords match, the CA can feel comfortable about your identity and revoke your certificate; otherwise the administrator of the CA will assume that this might be a possible DoS attempt by an attacker and not revoke your certificate. An attacker might try to pretend to be you when talking to the CA administrator and cause the administrator to revoke your certificate. This would be bad for you, because if you would try to use this certificate for authentication functions, your device authentication would fail.

One of the concerns when using certificates for authentication is that when your device receives a certificate from a peer, how does your device know that the certificate is still valid and hasn't been revoked by the CA? This is especially important if the certificate or the keying information associated with the certificate has somehow been compromised. In this situation, the administrator of the CA can revoke the certificate. The list of revoked certificates is stored in the CRL, which contains a list of serial numbers of revoked certificates.

Of course, one easy way of dealing with this is that every time you authenticate to the peer, you download the peer's certificate from the peer and the CA. This can be a time-consuming process if done every hour. In other words, there is a delay in performing the re-authentication, and possibly rebuilding the VPN connection, every hour, which might affect traffic flow between the two devices.

Therefore, it is common that devices *cache* the peer's certificate locally in RAM. Again, the problem here is that if the certificate is revoked, your device somehow has to figure this out. This is where CRLs play a role. Your device can have the CRL cached locally and periodically check to ensure that it has the most up-to-date list of revoked certificates. Then, when your device needs to authenticate to a remote peer, and you have the remote peer's certificate in your local cache, you can just look up the serial number on the cached certificate and compare this to the list of serial numbers on the CRL. If there's a match, the peer's certificate has been revoked and you should re-request the peer's certificate from the peer and the CA; otherwise, you can use the existing certificate of the peer you have cached locally. If you are unsuccessful in obtaining a peer's new certificate, after being revoked, your device will reject the connection attempt.

To obtain the CRL, the device has to know the location, on the network, where this can be found. The most common place is to examine the CA's certificate (the root certificate) or the RA's certificate. The location will be specified in a URL-style syntax on these certificates. This reference is commonly referred to as a *CRL distribution point* (CRL DP). If you're not using SCEP, you would have to download the CRL manually and install it on your device.

SCEP can automatically download the CRL. The most common methods of downloading the CRL are HTTP, HTTPS, and Lightweight Directory Access Protocol (LDAP), but other methods might be supported, such as FTP. The most common methods I have seen are HTTP and LDAP. The supported download method or methods are all dependent on the CA product that is being used in the network and how it is configured. For example, if you are using HTTP to download the CRL, your device initiates an HTTP GET request to the server that has the CRL. If the certificate services are set up with LDAP, your device will have to perform an LDAP query to the LDAP service containing the CRL, which might require an additional authentication process. I'll discuss the use of CRLs in more depth in the "Using Certificates" section.

CAUTION   The CRL list will grow indefinitely until it is safe to dispose of the CRL (at the end of the maximum certificate lifetime). In a large CA environment, this file could become gigantic, taking forever to download and taking up too much space in the local device's cache. To forestall this, a new process was developed, called Online Certificate Status Protocol (OCSP).OCSP is discussed in more depth in the "Using Certificates" section.

Acquiring Certificates

Now that you have a basic understanding of some of the components used with certificates, I'll discuss, in more depth, how certificates are obtained and used. First, I'll discuss how a device can obtain certificates and then how they are used for authentication functions.

To authenticate with certificates, all peers that wish to authenticate will need to obtain an identity certificate. This could be a self-generated, self-signed certificate, but there is still an issue of proving one's identity because the device might not be considered a trusted source. Therefore, most VPN implementations will use a CA as the trusted source. You'll need to obtain both a root and identity certificate from the CA. There are two approaches a device can use to accomplish this:

*   File-based enrollment (out-of-band)
*   Network-based enrollment (in-band, uses SCEP)

File-Based Enrollment   The file-based approach is more labor-intensive, but is common in situations where the CA device is a public CA; you're buying a certificate from a third-party company. This is common where the two peers come from two different networks and they want a neutral, trusted third party, like Verisign or Baltimore Technologies (which sell certificates).

To obtain a certificate, your device will need to create some information and package it into a PKCS #10 format and send this off to the CA. Your device will need to create a public/private key and will use the private key to sign the PKCS #10 information. In other words, the device uses the private key to create a signature from the PKCS #10 information and then the PKCS #10 information and the new signature are sent to the CA (actually, the signature is part of the PKCS #10 information the CA will receive). This was discussed earlier in the "PKCS #10" section.

The CA administrator receives the PKCS #10 information from a device and typically copies and pastes that information into its CA product. The CA software will then validate the device's signature in the PKCS #10 information with the device's included public key. Assuming that the signature can be validated, the CA can proceed to create an identity certificate.

The CA uses some of its own information, and some information from the device's PKCS #10 information, to generate an identity certificate. The CA will sign this certificate using its private key. This was discussed earlier in the "X.509 v3 Certificates" section. The certificates will then be encoded using one of two types: DER/CER (raw binary) or PEM (binary-64). You will need to notify the CA if your device supports only one of the two types, so that the CA administrator can use the correct encoding scheme. Optionally, the CA can use the PKCS #7 format method, which allows the CA to encapsulate both certificates in the same file. This would be similar to what ZIP allows you to do (put many files into one). Normally this method is not used in the file-based method.

The CA will then send two certificates to the device: the CA's certificate (root) and the device's new certificate (identity). These two certificates could be mailed to the administrator of the requesting device or electronically transmitted (like e-mail). These two certificates will need to be loaded onto the device.

NOTE	Please note that if your CA is configured to use RAs for backup, your CA also will send you the RA certificates. Also, if you'll be authenticating to devices in a different CA domain than what your device is using, your device will need a root and identity certificate from each domain with which it will be authenticating connections.

CAUTION	Upon receiving both certificates, it is very important that you, as an administrator, verify the authenticity of the root's certificate. This is to ensure that a man-in-the-middle attack hasn't taken place and someone has replaced the root certificate with a fake one. This is important because the device inherently will trust the root certificate and use it to validate all other certificates it receives. Therefore, you will need to verify the signature on the root certificate in an out-of-band means, like calling the CA administrator and verifying the contents of the root certificate you're about to install.

The order of the installation of the two certificates on the device is very important: the *root* certificate must be installed *first*, and the *identity* certificate *second*. This is because all other certificates your device receives from this CA (from the same domain) will be validated using this stored root certificate. There are three items the device can check to determine the validity of any root certificate:

1 Is the CA's signature on the certificate valid; in other words, can it be validated with the CA's public key on the root certificate?

2 Is the current time between the beginning and ending times listed on the certificate (has the certificate expired)?

3 If CRLs are being used, is the certificate's serial number *not* found on the CRL?

If your device can answer "yes" to all three of these answers, then the certificate is considered valid. If the device answers "no" to even one of the questions, the certificate is considered invalid and won't be used, causing authentication to fail. CRLs, in many instances, are optional; so the third step might not be performed if CRL checking is not enabled on the device. After installing the root certificate, you then need to install any RA certificates, and last, the device's identity certificate.

Assuming the root, identity, and RA certificates (if supported), are valid, you are ready to proceed using certificates for authenticating to other devices in the same domain of your CA.

TIP Because the beginning and ending validity dates are used to determine if a certificate is valid, it is very important that your device have the correct time (or fairly close to being correct). Therefore, I recommend that you use an internal NTP time source (master clock) to synchronize your devices that use certificates for authentication. Be sure to use NTPv3 and configure NTPv3's authentication, which uses a pre-shared key with an MD5 hashing function to validate any timing information you received from the NTP server.

Network-Based Enrollment   As I mentioned in the "Simple Certificate Enrollment Protocol (SCEP)" section earlier, the file-based (out-of-band) approach to obtain certificates is not very scalable. Therefore, if you're installing your own CA product, such as Microsoft's Certificate Server product (part of Microsoft Windows Server 2000 and 2003 Server and Advanced Server editions), then you'll probably use the network-based approach, that is, SCEP, to install certificates on your networking devices.

With SCEP enrollment, you will need to configure your device to interact with the CA. You will need to configure the name of the CA, which is probably a Fully Qualified Domain Name (FQDN), and the URL to interact with the CA via SCEP. The URL will use HTTP as a transport. Each CA product will use a different URL based on the back-end program that handles the SCEP process. For example, Microsoft's CA product would use the following URL:

```
http://FQDN_or_IP_address_of_CA_server/certsrv/mscep/mscep.dll
```

Other vendors' products will use a different URL.

There are two approaches your device can use with SCEP to obtain an identity certificate:

- Request and download the root certificate (and, possibly, RA certificates), then request and download the identity certificate. Both operations use PKCS #7.

- Simultaneously request and download both the root (and, possibly, RA certificates) and identity certificates, using PKCS #7 to encode both of them in the same message.

Which method your device uses depends on how the software is written for your VPN device. For example, the Cisco VPN 3000 concentrators, IOS routers, and PIX and ASA security appliances use the former approach, but the Cisco VPN software client (Versions 3.x and 4.x) uses the latter. In the following explanation of using SCEP to obtain an identity certificate, I'll assume that your device uses the latter approach, because the two processes are similar.

As in the file-based enrollment process, your device will need to create a public and private key. Then it will need to create some identity information, like a Common Name, and package it into a PKCS #10 format. One item that is typically configured is a challenge password. The challenge password can be used by the CA to validate the device's identity before granting a certificate. One concern, from the CA administrator's perspective, is that he wants to control who's actually allowed to be given a certificate; and as a CA administrator, you don't want to give just anyone a certificate. Therefore, you can use two approaches to control the certificate granting process:

- Challenge passwords
- Manual verification

The CA can be configured with a challenge password (symmetric pre-shared key) for a device. When the device wants to obtain a certificate, the device must enter the password associated with it that the CA administrator generates for the device. This can sometimes be tied to some other identity information, like the device's IP address or hostname. Therefore, for the device to successfully request a certificate, it must supply the same challenge password and, possibly, identity information.

In many instances the challenge password is a one-time password: it can be used only once to request a certificate. Using the challenge approach for certificate request authentication allows you to request and automatically receive a certificate without manual intervention from the CA administrator.

The challenge password serves a second purpose: it can be used to restrict the revocation of the certificate. In this instance, if someone wanted to revoke your device's certificate, they would need to know the challenge password your device initially used to obtain the certificate. Therefore, you should guard the challenge password carefully.

The CA can be configured to not automatically create a certificate for a device requesting it via SCEP; instead, the administrator of the CA would have to log into the CA, manually verify the request, and then grant or reject the request. In this situation, the device will poll the CA periodically until the certificate request is either granted or rejected.

In either of the two verification approaches, the CA will respond with one of three replies:

- **Success**—The CA responds with the certificate(s) to the device.
- **Failure**—The CA rejects the request, perhaps because of authentication issues (an incorrect challenge password) or SCEP interaction problems (your device and the CA are having SCEP compatibility issues).
- **Pending**—the CA is set up for manual approval; in this case, the CA administrator will have to log in manually and grant or reject the certificate request.

When in a pending state, your device should re-contact the CA periodically to determine if the request was granted. Once granted, your device will request the root certificate, possibly the RA certificate(s), and its own identity certificate. Using PKCS #7, the CA can package all these certificates in one message and send them to your device. When your device receives them, it will install the root certificate first, the RA certificates (if any), and then your identity certificate. Your device will then use the root certificate to validate the RA and identity certificates.

CAUTION   As in the file-based enrollment process, it is very important that you verify the authenticity of the root certificate because your device implicitly trusts it and uses it to validate all other certificates within the same CA domain. Contact the CA administrator and do this out-of-band, like with a phone call.

Using Certificates

Once a device has a root and identity certificate, it can begin using them in the authentication process when establishing a VPN session to a remote peer. Thankfully, using certificates is actually much easier than obtaining them. There are three basic items a device will verify when performing the certificate authentication with a remote peer:

- Is the peer's identity certificate signed by a trusted CA and can this signature be verified with the locally stored public key on the root's (CA's) certificate?
- Is the certificate still within the beginning and ending validation time period?
- Is the certificate *not* listed on the CRL?

If the device can verify all of these and answer "yes" to each of these questions, then the device can be assured of the remote peer's identity and the authentication phase will pass. Checking CRLs, in many devices' implementations, is sometimes optional.

Here are the basic steps involved in the authentication process:

1 When peers make initial contact with each other, they will share their identity certificates.

2 Optionally the peers can contact the CA to obtain the other peer's certificate. One concern is that the certificate the peer sent to us might have been revoked; one method of verifying this is to query the CA for the remote peer's identity certificate and then validate it. The other option is to use a CRL, if these are set up by the CA and enabled on the peer.

3 If Step 2 is performed, then the device will validate the signature on the identity certificate received from the CA with the public key the CA has on its locally stored root certificate. If you recall from the "X.509 v3 Certificates" section, the CA used an HMAC function on the device's PKCS #10 and CA's information that will be used on the certificate. The signature hash value, a symmetric key, is then encrypted with the CA's personal private key, and this signature appears on the device's identity certificate. The CA's public key can be used to verify the CA's signature. To verify this, the device decrypts the HMAC key with the CA's public key and then uses the HMAC key to verify the integrity of the identity certificate (that it hasn't been altered). The peer takes the certificate and HMAC key and runs it through the HMAC function, which is defined on the certificate. If the resulting HMAC signature that results matches the HMAC signature on the certificate, the device can be assured of the authenticity of the signature. This process was shown previously in Figure 2-7.

4 The two peers will validate the identity certificate they received from their peer with the locally stored root certificate; they do this by using the CA's public key to decrypt the CA's signature and to obtain the HMAC symmetric key, and then use the identity certificate, HMAC symmetric key, and HMAC function to verify the HMAC signature on the certificate.

5 Assuming that the CA's signature can be verified on the identity certificate, the second check the device will perform is to compare its time to beginning and ending validation times on the identity certificate. If the device's time falls between the range

of these two values, the second check passes; otherwise, the validation fails, and thus authentication fails. Because time plays an important role in the certificate validation process, I highly recommend that you use NTPv3 with authentication to synchronize your device's time with an internal, trusted time source. This was discussed in the "Certificates: Acquiring Them" section.

6 The use of CRLs is optional and dependent on the device's configuration. If CRL checking is enabled, the device will look for the peer's certificate's serial number in the CRL. If the serial number is found, the certificate is considered invalid and authentication fails; if the serial number is not found, the authentication succeeds because this is the last check for authenticity of the certificate.

Once the authentication passes, the VPN implementation can proceed in its communication of establishing a connection or connections to transmit user traffic.

CAUTION   If your network is constantly adding and removing certificates, I would highly recommend that you use CRLs to check for certificates that are no longer valid. However, one downside of requiring CRLs is that an attacker can use this to his advantage by creating a DoS attack, denying VPN devices from being able to access the CRL and downloading it. And if the CRL is required, and the device can't access it, then authentication of the peer will fail. With some networking devices, like the Cisco VPN 3000 series concentrators, you have the ability to define multiple locations as to where the CRL is stored; however, in other products, you might not have that flexibility. Another solution is to locally cache the CRL.

CRLs also can be quite lengthy, especially those associated with a Public CA like Verisign; and if your device only needs to check if one certificate has been revoked, a CRL is not a very efficient process. Therefore, the Online Certificate Status Protocol (OSCP) was defined in 1999 and was replaced by the Simple Certificate Validation Protocol (SCVP) in 2003. These protocols allow a device to request CRL information about a particular device instead of asking for the entire CRL. One limitation of these protocols, however, is that not all VPN implementations or VPN products will necessarily support them. For example, OCSP is not presently supported by the VPN 3000 Concentrator or PIX and ASA security appliances, but is supported in the newer IOS versions for routers.

User Authentication

Most remote access VPNs use two forms of authentication:

* Device authentication
* User authentication

The following two sections will discuss how device and user authentication are commonly implemented in remote access VPNs.

Remote Access and Device Authentication

Most VPN implementations will use either pre-shared symmetric keys or certificates for device authentication. However, many VPN implementations add an additional feature to their remote access VPN implementations: the ability to put users into groups. By using this function, the VPN implementation can apply the same policies to the members of the group. For example, you might have a programming group and a sales group. You could assign different policies to these groups, such as access restrictions, based on their specific needs in your network. Therefore, the user device must provide some information concerning the group that it belongs to or wants to be associated with.

Pre-shared keys for device authentication in remote access VPNs are sometimes referred to as group keys because the user device supplies both a group name and the pre-shared key for the group. This is a derivation of the device pre-shared key method. With group pre-shared keys, each group would have a unique pre-shared key. And for a user to authenticate its device, its device would have to supply the correct group name and corresponding pre-shared key to authenticate to the network and have the correct policies applied to it. Sometimes this is referred to as *wildcard keying*, because all users in the group use the same key to authenticate their devices.

Certificates present a different issue. When performing device authentication with certificates, the device could supply the group it belongs to and the certificate. However, the more common approach is for the VPN implementation to use a field on the certificate to represent the group name; therefore, the user device doesn't have to supply this information, nor could the user try to access another group, because this is controlled by his installed identity certificate. In most VPN implementations, the OU (department) field is used, but this is vendor-specific. For instance, Cisco VPN gateway products allow you to define which field or fields are used for the group name value for remote access users.

Remote Access and User Authentication

Remote access connections raise one concern: the device authentication information is normally stored locally on a device, for example, a user's PC or laptop. If the user's laptop is stolen, or their PC is hacked into, the device authentication is now known to the outside party and can be used to successfully authenticate to your network.

On top of this, all people in the group, when using pre-shared keys, need to know the same key for the group: the more people that know the key, the less secure the solution becomes. And when people leave the group, you should change the key; but if the group membership is constantly changing, updating the key can become a hassle (in this case, the best solution is to use certificates for device authentication).

Therefore, because of the two issues I mentioned, remote access connections will typically combine device authentication with user authentication. User authentication allows a VPN implementation to prompt a user with a username and password that are unique to the user. In IPsec, XAUTH is an example of an implementation that provides user authentication for VPNs. Many VPN implementations do not allow the user to save this information on a PC or laptop; therefore, if your PC or laptop is broken into or stolen, this won't help someone break into your network via a remote access VPN session: the thief would only know the group name and password or have access to the device's certificate; he would still need to know the user name and password to successfully authenticate and bring up the VPN session.

And for network administrators that are concerned about using a static password for user accounts, many VPN implementations allow the use of one-time password (OTP) solutions, like token cards. With OTP, every time a user authenticates, a different password is used, making it practically impossible for an attacker to be able to guess a valid password for a user's account.

CAUTION   One last thing I would like to point out is that you should also be concerned, as a remote access user, when authenticating to a VPN gateway at your corporate site. There is a small chance that a man-in-the-middle attack, using masquerading, could occur and the man-in-the-middle could learn the group name and group pre-shared key you use (if you're using pre-shared keys) and your username and password. If you're concerned about this kind of attack, you should use certificates for device authentication and your user accounts should use an OTP solution, like token cards.

Another option is to use *mutual group authentication*. Mutual group authentication is asymmetrical, where each side uses a different method to authenticate the other while establishing a secure tunnel to form the basis for group authentication of a remote access session. In this method, authentication happens in two steps: in the first step, the VPN gateway authenticates itself using a certificate; in the second step, the actual authentication of the user by the gateway occurs. Since this approach does not use pre-shared keys for authentication, it provides better security than group authentication with pre-shared keys, because it is not vulnerable to a man-in-the-middle attack. The availability of this feature, though, is vendor-specific, and not all VPN products support this feature.

I'm also concerned if a user is set up for split-tunneling, where clear text traffic is allowed to the user's device, the corporate security policy should dictate that the user's device minimally have a software firewall configured, in addition to anti-virus and possibly anti-spyware software, installed on the desktop. I've even seen some companies require remote access users to have Cisco Security Agent (CSA) software installed, which is an enhanced host IDS solution. This product allows you to lock down access to many components, like directories and files, on a PC.

Summary

This chapter showed you the basics of VPN technologies. Understanding the technologies that VPNs use to protect information is useful when attempting to understand how a VPN implements its protection methods. A VPN implementation will use many of the technologies discussed in this chapter.

Next is Chapter 3, "IPsec," where I introduce the interworkings of the IPsec standard for VPNs. Many of the things I discussed in this chapter are used by IPsec to implement protected connections between networks or devices.

CHAPTER 3

IPsec

IP Security, or IPsec for short, is a framework of standards that provides the following key security features at the network layer between two peer devices:

- Data confidentiality
- Data integrity
- Data authentication
- Anti-replay detection
- Peer authentication

The Internet Engineering Task Force (IETF) defines the standards for IPsec in various RFCs. Because it provides network layer protection between devices or networks, and because it is an open standard, it is commonly used in today's networks that use IPv4 and IPv6.

This chapter will explore many of the standards that IPsec uses to provide a secure transport for communication. I'll first cover the standards used, and then discuss how these standards are implemented by IPsec in the "ISAKMP/IKE Phase 1" and "ISAKMP/IKE Phase 2" sections. As you will see in the chapter, vendors (such as Cisco), have a tendency to *enhance* the standards to overcome problems that IPsec can experience in data networks. Cisco, for example, has added many features to enhance both LAN-to-LAN (L2L) and remote access sessions. I'll discuss many of these features at the end of this chapter.

IPsec Standards

There are many different ways of implementing VPNs, as discussed in Chapter 1. For example, you could use an SSL VPN solution to protect data between two devices; however, the main limitation of SSL VPNs is that they primarily provide application layer protection, which typically is limited to web browser-based connections, and specific applications the vendor has written code for, to tunnel through the SSL VPN. Their advantage, however, is that they can use an existing web browser on the user's desktop.

IPsec, on the other hand, provides protection at the network layer; therefore, any IP traffic can be protected between peer devices. But IPsec is intrusive on the client (remote access) side; typically you need additional software installed on your device to provide the network-layer protection.

NOTE   Depending on the vendor's gateway product, you might be able use the Microsoft
L2TP/IPsec VPN client, which is pre-installed on Microsoft Windows 2000 and XP
desktops.

IPsec's framework is defined in RFC 2401; however, the implementation of IPsec is defined
across quite a few different RFCs. As I mentioned in the chapter introduction, IPsec
provides the following services:

- **Data confidentiality**—This is done via encryption to protect data from eavesdropping
  attacks; supported encryption algorithms include DES, 3DES, and AES.

- **Data integrity and authentication**—This is done via HMAC functions to verify that
  packets haven't been tampered with and are being received from a valid peer; in other
  words, to prevent a man-in-the-middle or session hijacking attack. Supported HMAC
  functions include MD5 and SHA-1.

- **Anti-replay detection**—This is done by including encrypted sequence numbers in
  data packets to ensure that a replay attack doesn't occur from a man-in-the-middle
  device.

- **Peer authentication**—This is done to ensure that before data is transmitted between
  peers, the peers are "who they say they are." Device authentication is supported with
  symmetric pre-shared keys, asymmetric pre-shared keys, and digital certificates.
  remote access connections also support user authentication using XAUTH, short for
  extended authentication.

The two main groupings of standards that IPsec uses are:

- **ISAKMP/IKE/Oakley/SKEME**—These standards are used to set up a secure
  management connection, determine keying information for encryption, and use
  signatures for authentication of the management connection. This connection is used
  so the two IPsec peers can share IPsec messages with each other.

- **AH and ESP**—These standards are used to provide protection for user data. They can
  provide for confidentiality (only ESP), data integrity, data origin authentication, and
  anti-replay services. I like to refer to these connections as *data* connections.

The following sections will provide an overview of the RFCs used by IPsec, including the
standards mentioned in the above bullets. Specifically, they cover the following:

- IETF RFCs
- IPsec Connections
- Basic Process of Building Connections

IETF RFCs

IPsec is a framework of standards defined in IETF RFCs. This section provides a quick overview of these RFCs:

- **RFC 2401**—This RFC defines the role that IPsec plays and an overview as to how it works.

- **RFC 2402**—This RFC is one of two that defines how user data is protected. It defines the Authentication Header (AH) protocol and can authenticate and verify the integrity of packets.

- **RFC 2403**—This RFC defines the use of MD5 as an HMAC function in IPsec data connections.

- **RFC 2404**—This RFC defines the use of SHA-1 as an HMAC function in IPsec data connections.

- **RFC 2405**—This RFC defines the use of DES as an encryption algorithm for data connections.

- **RFC 2406**—This RFC defines the Encapsulation Security Payload (ESP) protocol to provide for confidentiality, packet authentication, and packet integrity for data connections.

- **RFC 2407**—This RFC defines the framework for building a protected connection using IPsec: Internet Security Association and Key Management Protocol (ISAKMP).

- **RFC 2408**—This RFC defines how ISAKMP is used to build secure connections.

- **RFC 2409**—This RFC defines the Internet Key Exchange (IKE) protocol, which is used to negotiate and authenticate keying information to protect connections.

- **RFC 2410**—This RFC allows the use of a "null" encryption algorithm with ESP, allowing the use of ESP without performing encryption.

- **RFC 2411**—This RFC provides a road map for adding new encryption algorithms and HMAC functions to IPsec.

Other RFCs are defined for IPsec, but these are the main and original ones, so the remaining subsections will focus on the RFCs listed above. The actual RFCs can be found on IETF's web site (www.ietf.org).

RFC 2401

RFC 2401 defines the framework of IPsec for both IPv4 and IPv6. It specifies the services for IP layer protection of one or more paths between two devices, which could be two end-stations, two VPN gateways, or an end-station and a VPN gateway. Because IPsec functions at the network layer, it protects traffic at Layer-3 and higher, including protocols such as TCP, UDP, ICMP, and tunneled IP packets, like GRE. The services IPsec provides for are access control, connectionless integrity, rejection of replayed packets, confidentiality, and data origin authentication.

IPsec uses two protocols to provide for data security: AH, defined in RFC 2402, and ESP, defined in RFC 2406. AH provides connectionless integrity, data origin authentication, and anti-replay services. ESP provides the same services, and also confidentiality via encryption, which is its main function. AH and ESP can be used individually to provide for protection, or they can be used in combination. Both support transport and tunnel mode protection. In transport mode, the upper layer protocols are protected, whereas in tunnel mode, an entire tunneled IP packet is protected. These modes are discussed in more depth later in the chapter in the "Connection Modes" section.

IPsec is flexible in that you can choose the protocols and types of protection to be used, custom-tailoring it to fit your specific environment or situation. You control what traffic is to be protected (for example, Telnet and HTTP traffic) and how it should be protected (for example, AH or ESP, MD5, 3DES, and so on).

NOTE   Protecting packets based on IP addresses or applications is vendor- or product-specific. For example, Cisco routers, and PIX and ASA security appliances, allow you to define this granularity on an application-by-application basis, but the VPN 3000 concentrators allow you to define these policies on only an address-by-address basis.

Because some of these security services require keys, such as HMAC functions and encryption algorithms, IPsec defines a set of processes for dynamically creating keying information that peers will use. The Internet Key Exchange (IKE) protocol, discussed in the "RFC 2409" section, defines the mechanics for both dynamic and manual distribution key methods. Even though all vendors today use IKE, IPsec allows for other dynamic key distribution techniques, such as Kerberos's Key Distribution Center and SKIP.

RFC 2402

RFC 2402 defines how to provide for connectionless packet integrity and data origin authentication for IP packets with the AH protocol, which is assigned an IP protocol number of 51. AH can also, optionally, detect and prevent packet replay attacks. AH provides for packet authentication services for most of the IP packet header, and for the upper-layer protocol. This is accomplished using an HMAC function.

Because some IP fields are mutable, they are not included in the input of the HMAC function. Mutable fields are fields that can change in transit, such as the time-to-live (TTL) and type-of-service (TOS) fields. AH is discussed in more depth in the "Security Protocols" section later in the chapter.

RFC 2403

AH and ESP can both provide data authentication and data integrity services. To implement these, HMAC functions are used. RFC 2104 defines the properties of an HMAC function, and RFC 1321 describes MD5. RFC 2403 describes how the MD5 HMAC function can be used by AH and ESP.

The data authentication and integrity services provided by AH and ESP take most of, or at least part of, the packet contents and a shared symmetric key, and run them through the HMAC-MD5 algorithm to provide a signature. This signature, along with the user data, is sent to the remote system. The remote system will verify the integrity of the packet with the same inputted data and the same symmetric key.

RFC 1321 describes the implementation of MD5, where the generated signature is 128 bits in length. IPsec uses RFC 2104 to truncate the digital signature to 96 bits. I described this possible process by a VPN implementation in Chapter 2, "VPN Technologies." One might think that by truncating the signature, it would be easier to forge a signature; however, the possibility of this is less likely than you winning your state lottery, mathematically speaking. The length of 96 bits was chosen because it is the length described in RFC 2402 for AH and meets the necessary security requirements outlined in RFC 2104.

RFC 2404

Like its sister (RFC 2403), RFC 2404 describes the use of an HMAC function for IPsec; in this instance, it's SHA-1. SHA-1 can be used by AH and ESP to provide for data authentication and data integrity services. Like RFC 2403, RFC 2404 truncates the digital signature. In SHA-1's case, it is truncated from 160 bits to 96 bits. The truncation process allows an easier implementation of AH and ESP because the signature field is the same length whether MD5 or SHA-1 is used.

NOTE   Of the two HMAC functions, SHA-1 is more secure, but is more process-intensive. Because HMAC functions are used to add a signature to every packet, you might want to consider the overhead that this might have if you choose SHA-1, which is more secure.

RFC 2405

RFC 2405 describes the use of the DES cipher algorithm as an encryption algorithm for ESP. Other encryption algorithms are supported by IPsec today, including 3DES and AES (128-bit, 192-bit, and 256-bit cipher blocks).

TIP   Because DES is breakable with today's computing power, and because 3DES is very computationally intensive in software, I recommend that you use AES to provide for confidentiality services in IPsec. Even though performing 3DES and AES encryption in hardware requires about the same amount of processing, AES is still a more secure protocol.

RFC 2406

The ESP protocol is defined in RFC 2046. It can be used stand-alone or in conjunction with AH. ESP's main service is to provide confidentiality through the use of encryption. Optionally, it can perform data origin authentication, connectionless data integrity, and anti-replay services.

Because AH doesn't provide for data confidentiality, ESP is more commonly used. One limitation of ESP, though, is that AH provides for a more secure solution with data origin authentication and integrity services than ESP. I'll discuss this in more depth later in the chapter in the "Security Protocols" section.

RFC 2407

RFC 2407 defines a framework for the management of protected connections, commonly called *security associations*, with the Internet Security Association and Key Management (ISAKMP) protocol. ISAKMP defines:

- How devices communicate with each other via IPsec
- The different kinds of communications and acknowledgments (responses)
- How IPsec communications are packaged into an understandable format

This RFC focuses on an overview of this process.

NOTE   A Security Association (SA) contains all of the information necessary for implementing the security services for a connection, such as the use of AH or ESP, the connection mode (tunnel or transport), the HMAC functions and encryption algorithms, the keys to use for these functions and algorithms, the lifetime of the SA, and many other items.

RFC 2408

RFC 2408 actually explains the mechanics of the interaction between two IPsec devices—establishing, negotiating, modifying, and deleting security associations—in other words, how two peers *talk* to each other about using IPsec. ISAKMP is responsible for defining the payload (format of information) for exchanging keying and authentication information; however, this is a basic framework definition. ISAKMP actually doesn't define the mechanics for these processes, which allows the possibility for IPsec to use several methods for these processes. As you will see in RFC 2409, IKE is the component used today to implement keying and authentication services.

ISAKMP centralizes the management of SAs and thus reduces the amount of duplicated functionality with each security protocol. In other words, AH, ESP, and other IPsec protocols do not have to play a role in the negotiation process between peers. With IPsec, ISAKMP plays this centralized role and thereby reduces the setup time for establishing a connection by negotiating all services at one time.

RFC 2409

RFC 2409 defines the Internet Key Exchange (IKE) protocol, which is a hybrid protocol. IKE is responsible for negotiating, creating, and refreshing keying information to protect IPsec connections. ISAKMP defines the framework for this, but IKE defines the actual mechanics for the process. We refer to IKE as a hybrid protocol because it uses a subset of the mechanics from the Oakley and SKEME protocols. In other words, it doesn't use the complete processes defined by Oakley and SKEME, and therefore isn't 100 percent compatible with them. But IKE borrows some of their mechanics to deal with keying issues with IPsec.

Oakley uses a hybrid Diffie-Hellman process to create session keys on peer devices, implementing a unique feature called *Perfect Forward Secrecy* (PFS) — the ability to create a shared secret key on two devices without having to "share" the actual key across the network between the two peers. Diffie-Hellman implements a similar process, which was discussed in Chapter 2. ISAKMP supports a subset of the Oakley key exchange modes and is implemented through the use of Diffie-Hellman.

Where Oakley and SKEME define modes for the actual exchange process, ISAKMP and IKE use phases. IKE operates much like the Oakley and SKEME mode process. With IKE, different exchanges occur in two separate phases. Phase 1 is where the two peers build a secure *management* connection between themselves. No data actually traverses this connection; instead, it is used for IPsec communication, including the negotiation of the secure data connections that are built in Phase 2. The "ISAKMP/IKE Phase 1" and "ISAKMP/IKE Phase 2" sections cover these two phases in more depth.

NOTE   In the industry, I commonly see people incorrectly use the terms ISAKMP, Oakley, SKEME, and IKE when referring to IPsec. Sometimes people will use an individual term to describe the process that is performed by all of these standards. Throughout the book, I'll use ISAKMP/IKE to refer to these standards.

RFC 2410

RFC 2410 allows ESP to not use confidentiality, that is, encryption, when protecting data connections. This is commonly referred to as "NULL encryption." In most cases, ESP is used because it has encryption, but for certain applications, encryption might not be necessary and AH might not be suitable; therefore, you can use ESP for data origin authentication, packet integrity checking, and anti-replay detection.

RFC 2411

The main goal of RFC 2411 is to help reduce the possible number of RFCs that might be created in the future to support new technologies that can be applied to IPsec to enhance security for a network. It focuses mainly on specifying guidelines in how new encryption algorithms and HMAC functions can be integrated into IPsec's AH and ESP protocols, and into key management protocol enhancements.

IPsec Connections

Now that you have had an introduction to some of the standards used by IPsec, let's take a look at the communication process to share data securely between two IPsec peers. Two peers will go through five basic steps during the lifetime of sharing data securely:

1   Something needs to trigger the IPsec process. This is typically caused by one peer needing to send traffic destined to a destination peer that needs to be protected. Of course, an administrator or user could start this process manually from one of the two IPsec peers.

2   If no VPN connection exists, IPsec will use ISAKMP/IKE Phase 1 to build a secure management connection. This management connection is used so that the two peers can communicate with each other securely, via IPsec, and can build secure data connections. Please note that this connection is *not* used to transmit any user data, such as files or e-mail messages. I like to refer to these Phase 1 connections as *management* connections because no user data traverses them.

3   Across the secure management connection, the two IPsec peers will negotiate the security parameters that are used to build the secure data connections; these secure data connections are used to transmit user data, such as files, Telnets, e-mail messages, video, and voice. I like to refer to these connections as *data* connections because the users' actual data traverses these connections.

4   Once the data connections are built, the IPsec devices can use them to share user data securely. If HMAC functions are used by the source to create signatures, the destination verifies these for data integrity and authentication; plus, if the data is encrypted by the source, the destination will decrypt the data.

5   Both the management and data connections have a lifetime associated with them. This ensures that keying information is regenerated to provide for better security in case someone is trying to break your security keys. Once the lifetime of a connection is reached, it is torn down. Of course, if you still need to send data, the connection will be rebuilt dynamically.

NOTE   Cisco, and many other networking vendors, sometimes tend to use IPsec terms poorly to describe Phase 1 and Phase 2. For example, some vendors commonly use the term "ISAKMP" to describe Phase 1 and "IPsec" to describe Phase 2. I've never really liked the use of these terms because more than one standard is used in Phase 1, and IPsec, used by most people in the industry, refers to the grouping of all standards for the VPN, including ISAKMP and IKE! Therefore, when I teach classes on IPsec, I like refer to the ISAKMP/IKE Phase 1 connections as IPsec *management* connections and the ISAKMP/IKE Phase 2 connection as IPsec *data* connections because these definitions make more sense.

A security association (SA) basically groups all of the necessary security components to successfully communicate with an IPsec peer. In other words, once all the parameters have been negotiated and the keying information is generated, the peers have an SA they can use to communicate with each other securely.

There are many components involved in protecting both management and data connections. For example, some of the components you'll find in an SA are:

- The encryption algorithm and symmetric key used
- The HMAC function and the symmetric key used
- The lifetime of the connection
- Diffie-Hellman key group usage
- For management connections: the type of device authentication to use
- For data connections: the security protocol to use (AH and/or ESP)
- The identifier for a connection: for data connections, this is referred to as a security parameter index (SPI) value
- For data connections: The traffic that should be protected to the associated IPsec peer

There are many more components to an SA, but the above are the main ones.

Looking at the preceding five steps in building an IPsec session to a remote peer, it seems that IPsec is a simple process; however, I've summarized the basic steps that take place. In reality, there are *a lot* of things occurring by various IPsec standards to implement these five basic steps. For example, to set up and maintain secure connections with a remote peer, minimally, the following will have to be done:

1 You'll need to determine what traffic should be protected. Sometimes this is done statically and sometimes dynamically. For instance, on a site-to-site session on a Cisco router or PIX, you can configure this with a crypto access control list (crypto ACL). For a site-to-site connection on a 3000 series concentrator, this is commonly done with network lists. For remote access sessions, this policy is defined on the VPN gateway the client is making a connection to.

2 You'll need to determine how the management connection is protected by asking the following questions (note that there might be many other items if the IPsec VPN is remote access):

— How should device authentication be performed?

— Which encryption algorithm and HMAC function should be used?

— Which mode should be used: main or aggressive?

— Which Diffie-Hellman key group should be used?

— What is the lifetime of the connection?

3 You'll need to determine how the data connections are to be protected:

— Which security protocol is used: AH and/or ESP?

— For ESP, what encryption algorithm and/or HMAC function is used?

— For AH, what HMAC function is used?

— For AH and ESP, what mode will they operate in: tunnel or transport?

— What are the lifetimes of the data connections?

— Should the management connection be used for sharing keying material or should Diffie-Hellman be used instead (referred to as perfect forward secrecy)?

4 The IPsec devices will need to keep track of all of this information to enforce the manually configured or negotiated security policies.

As you can see from this list, IPsec is not a simple process no matter what kind of device you'll be using. Because of this complexity, I want to ensure that you know all of the proper steps IPsec goes through in setting up an IPsec session between peers: this will greatly assist you when IPsec sessions fail and you must troubleshoot the problem or problems.

IPsec Intricacies

When I was first exposed to IPsec a handful of years ago, I was completely confused about how to set it up. I was setting up a "simple" site-to-site session between two Cisco 7500 routers. I used a configuration example from the Cisco site to assist in the setup, since I knew, at that time, very little about IPsec. Of course, when I finished the configuration and tried to bring up the session, it wouldn't come up. It took me two days to troubleshoot the problem to an address translation issue, which caused IPsec to break. Back then, I didn't have the luxury of using features like IPsec over UDP or NAT-T. It took me another five days to get public addresses for both routers and make them exceptions to the address translation process. From this experience, I sat down and started reading a lot about IPsec and its implementation, because I knew I would have to do this many more times in the future. And when I teach Cisco VPN material in various Cisco courses, I stress the importance of understanding how IPsec works, because it is a complicated process. By going through how an IPsec session is established, you'll have a better understanding on how to configure IPsec on Cisco devices, and how to troubleshoot problems with peers that fail to bring up an IPsec session.

Basic Process of Building Connections

I believe it is very important to understand how IPsec works when you decide to use it as a VPN implementation. Cisco offers a lot of tools, such as Security Device Manager (SDM) for the routers, the PIX Device Manager (PDM) for the PIXs (pre-7.0), and the Adaptive

Security Device Manager (ASDM) for PIXs and ASAs running 7.0 that support configuration wizards, greatly simplifying the setup of IPsec VPNs. However, not everything in these tools is wizard-based for setting up VPN sessions, and not every session will work the first time you set it up. Moreover, some IPsec features on Cisco devices might require you to configure or troubleshoot them from a CLI. Therefore, having an intimate understanding of the workings of IPsec is essential.

There are two possible processes that will take place in building an IPsec session, depending on whether it's a site-to-site or remote access IPsec session. For a site-to-site session, the following process will be performed:

1 One VPN gateway peer initiates a session to the remote VPN gateway peer.

2 ISAKMP/IKE Phase 1 begins when the peers negotiate how the management connection will be protected.

3 Diffie-Hellman is used to share the keys securely for encryption algorithms and HMAC functions of the management connection.

4 Device authentication is performed across the secure management connection.

5 ISAKMP/IKE Phase 1 ends and Phase 2 begins: the peers negotiate the parameters and the keying information to protect the data connections (this is done across the secure management connection or, optionally, by using Diffie-Hellman again).

6 The data connections are established and Phase 2 ends: the VPN gateways can now protect user traffic across the data connections.

7 Eventually the management and data connections will expire and will have to be rebuilt.

Remote access VPN connections are more complicated than site-to-site connections because you might want to perform user authentication and push session policies from the VPN gateway to the client. This is complicated, because vendors might use proprietary methods to implement some of these steps. I'll focus only on Cisco implementation, because this is a book on Cisco VPNs.

Here is the process that will occur with Cisco remote access IPsec VPNs:

1 The remote access client initiates a connection to the remote VPN gateway.

2 IKE Phase 1 begins when the client and VPN gateway negotiate how the management connection will be protected.

3 Diffie-Hellman is used to share the keys securely for encryption algorithms and HMAC functions for the management connection.

4 Device authentication is performed across the secure management connection.

5 Optionally, user authentication is performed. With IPsec, this is done with the XAUTH standard. With XAUTH, the VPN gateway will challenge the user for a username and password.

6 Most IPsec remote access implementations by vendors will then push policy information to the client. In the Cisco realm, this is commonly referred to as either *IKE Mode Config* or *IKE Client Config*. This process is done in a somewhat proprietary fashion by each vendor; so, for example, a non-Cisco client might not understand the information being pushed to it by a Cisco VPN gateway. With Cisco implementation, the client can be assigned an internal IP address, a domain name, DNS and WINS server addresses, split tunneling policies, firewall policies, and other connection policies.

7 Optionally (in Cisco remote access VPNs), reverse route injection (RRI) can take place. This is where the client can optionally advertise routing information, via the IPsec management connection, to the VPN gateway. The VPN gateway can advertise this routing information to the internal network.

8 ISAKMP/IKE Phase 1 ends and Phase 2 begins: the client and VPN gateway negotiate the parameters and the keying information to protect the data connections (this is done across the secure management connection).

Note   IKE Mode Config and other assorted Cisco-proprietary protocols or processes used for building and maintaining remote access IPsec sessions are referred to as "Easy VPN."

---

9 The data connections are established and Phase 2 ends: the VPN gateways can now protect user traffic across the data connections.

10 Eventually the lifetimes associated with the management and data connections will expire and these connections will have to be rebuilt.

ISAKMP/IKE Phase 1

As you saw in the list in the preceding section, some of the same steps are performed in both the site-to-site and remote access IPsec setup; however, remote access has quite a few additional steps. In this current section, I'll expand on the IPsec setup steps and cover them in more depth.

ISAKMP and IKE work together to establish secure connectivity between two devices. ISAKMP defines the message format, the mechanics for a key exchange protocol, and the negotiation process to build connections. ISAKMP, however (as already mentioned), doesn't define how keys are created, shared, or managed for protecting the secure connections; IKE is responsible for this.

To help you understand the actual details of how an ISAKMP/IKE Phase 1 management connection is established, this part of the chapter covers the following:

- The Management Connection
- Key Exchange Protocol: Diffie-Hellman
- Device Authentication
- Remote Access Additional Steps

The Management Connection

The management connection is established in Phase 1. This connection uses UDP on port 500 for communication. It is a bidirectional connection, and both peers can use it to share IPsec messages with each other.

NOTE   The ISAKMP/IKE connection uses UDP. The source and destination port are 500; however, I have seen some vendors use a random source port number greater than 1,023 instead of 500.

No matter if the session is a site-to-site or remote access session, three things will occur during ISAKMP/IKE Phase 1:

1 The peers will negotiate how the management connection will be protected.
2 The peers will use Diffie-Hellman to share keying information to protect the management connection.
3 The peers will authenticate each other before ISAKMP/IKE Phase 2 can proceed.

ISAKMP/IKE Phase 1 is basically responsible for setting up the secure management connection. However, there are two modes for performing these three steps:

- Main
- Aggressive

The following two sections will cover these two modes, followed by a section that discusses how you can specify the policies that will be used to protect the management connection.

Main Mode

Main mode performs three two-way exchanges totaling six packets. The three exchanges are the three steps listed in the last section: negotiate the security policy to use for the management connection, use DH to encrypt the keys for the encryption algorithm and HMAC function negotiated in Step 1, and perform device authentication using either pre-shared keys, RSA encrypted nonces, or RSA signatures (digital certificates).

Main mode has one advantage: the device authentication step occurs across the secure management connection, because this connection was built in the first two steps. Therefore, any identity information that the two peers need to send to each other is protected from eavesdropping attacks. This is the Cisco default mode for site-to-site sessions and for remote access connections that use certificates for device authentication.

Aggressive Mode

In aggressive mode, two exchanges take place. The first exchange contains a list of possible policies to use to protect the management connection, the public key from the public/private key combination created by DH, identity information, and verification of the identity information (for example, a signature). All of this is squeezed into one packet. The second exchange is an acknowledgment of the receipt of the first packet, sharing the encrypted keys (done by DH), and whether or not the management connection has been established successfully.

Aggressive mode has one main advantage over main mode: it is quicker in establishing the secure management connection. However, its downside is that any identity information is sent in clear text; so if someone was eavesdropping on the transmission, they could see the actual identity information used to create the signature for device authentication. This shouldn't be a security issue, but if you are concerned about this, you can always use main mode.

As I mentioned in the last section, main mode is the default mode for Cisco VPNs with one exception: Aggressive mode is the default mode with the Cisco remote access VPN if the devices will be using group pre-shared keys for device authentication.

ISAKMP/IKE Transforms

One of the first things the two peers must do in ISAKMP/IKE Phase 1 is to negotiate how the management connection will be protected. This is done by defining transforms. A transform is a list of security measures that should be used to protect a connection. With ISAKMP/IKE Phase 1, the transform is sometimes called an *IKE or ISAKMP policy* or *proposal*.

Here are some of the things you would find in a Phase 1 transform:

- The encryption algorithm to use: DES, 3DES, or AES.
- The HMAC function to use: MD5 or SHA-1.
- The type of device authentication: pre-shared keys, RSA encrypted nonces, or RSA signatures (certificates).
- The Diffie-Hellman key group: Cisco only supports 1, 2, 5, and 7, where 7 is only supported on the Cisco 3000 concentrators and PIX and ASA security appliances running 7.0.
- The lifetime of the management connection.

Collectively, these items are referred to as a transform set. Your device might need more than one transform set. For instance, if you need to connect to two different IPsec peers, each with different encryption abilities, like DES and 3DES, you might want to have different transforms so that you can take advantage of using 3DES to the one peer and DES for the other.

Your device would then send its entire list of ISAKMP/IKE transforms to the remote peer. The order in which the transforms are sent (listed or prioritized) is important because of the matching process that the remote peer will use. For example, if your device is initiating the connection to the remote peer, your device will send a list of transforms and the remote peer will compare your list with its own to find a match. It will start with the first one in your list and compare it to the first one in its list. If there is a match, then that's the transform used; otherwise, the remote peer will compare your first transform to its second one. The remote peer will compare your first one to its entire list and if it doesn't find a match, it will then start with your second transform and compare that transform to its list . . . and so on and so forth. Therefore, it is the peer initiating the connection that somewhat controls which transform is chosen.

Figure 3-1 shows an example of this process. In this example, RouterA initiates a connection to RouterB (Step 1). RouterB compares the list of transforms sent from RouterA. In Step 2, RouterB compares its first transform to the first one from RouterA. Because there is no match, RouterB then compares its second transform to RouterA's first transform (Step 3). In this instance, there is a match, so the two peers use this transform.

Figure 3-1   *ISAKMP/IKE Transform Negotiation*

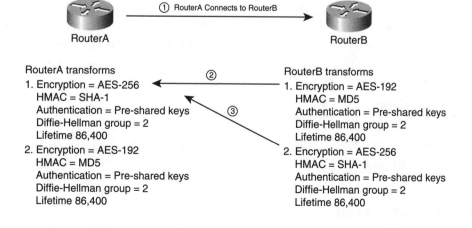

NOTE If a matching ISAKMP/IKE management transform is not found between the two peers, the management connection will not be established and IPsec will fail. The one exception to this is that the lifetime values for the proposals do not have to match; if they don't match, the peers are supposed to use the lower lifetime value between them. However, I have noticed that some vendors in the marketplace don't follow this IPsec guideline; therefore, you might also have to match the lifetime values on both peers. With Cisco products, they will use whichever lifetime is lower for a transform if all other parameters in a transform match.

Key Exchange Protocol: Diffie-Hellman

Once the peers negotiate the protection policy to use for the management connection in Phase 1, DH is used to create a shared secret key. ISAKMP and IKE actually don't define a process to share keying material securely across an insecure network; instead, they use DH for this purpose.

The DH process was discussed in Chapter 2, "VPN Technologies." As a quick review, note that both peers generate a public/private key combination and share their public keys with each other. They take their private key and the remote peer's public key and run this through a function, resulting in a secret key, where the secret key is the same on the two peers. If you recall from Chapter 2, the great feature of this process is that if someone is eavesdropping on the exchange process, they'll see only the public keys, which won't do them any good in deriving the secret key. The eavesdropper also would need to know one of the two private keys to do this, and the private keys are never shared with anyone else.

The resulting secret key is then used to encrypt any additional keying material for the proposed management connection, like the encryption algorithm key and the HMAC function key. The DH key group is used to affect the strength of this encryption process. There are many DH key groups that can be used. The Cisco products support the following:

- **Group 1**—768-bit
- **Group 2**—1,024-bit
- **Group 5**—1,536-bit

The Cisco 3000 series concentrators and PIX and ASA security appliances (in 7.0) also support Group 7 keys.

Device Authentication

One issue with DH is that you are performing an exchange with an "unknown quantity." Therefore, before any other communication occurs, you'll want to authenticate the remote peer's identity. With aggressive mode in Phase 1, the negotiation, DH, and identity check occurs in one large step; however, with main mode, the setup process takes three steps.

In the third step of main mode, the device authentication check takes place, using the secured connection that was established when DH shared the encryption and HMAC keys. The advantage of this approach is that any authentication material for the two peers is sent across the protected management connection.

In either case, though, identity validation is an important part of IPsec. There are three basic methods of performing device authentication in IPsec:

- Symmetric pre-shared keys (commonly called *pre-shared keys*)
- Asymmetric pre-shared keys (commonly called *RSA encrypted nonces*)
- Digital certificates (commonly called *RSA signatures*)

The method that is to be used has already been negotiated with the peers when they shared their ISAKMP/IKE Phase 1 transforms. These methods were already discussed in Chapter 2. Not every device supports the three methods of authentication. For example, when looking at the Cisco product line, only Cisco IOS routers support all three. Other Cisco products support only two: pre-shared symmetric keys and digital certificates.

Also note that remote access connections support a special type of pre-shared key, called a group pre-shared key. With remote access connections, users are grouped together to simplify the process of applying similar policies to similar users. Therefore, the group to which the users belong has a single pre-shared key. When a remote access client performs device authentication, the client device must send both the name of the group and the pre-shared key of the group, assuming pre-shared keys were negotiated successfully in Step 1.

CAUTION   One concern about using pre-shared keys with remote access is that all users in the group must know the same pre-shared key. This can be a security concern. One option of dealing with this security issue is to use digital certificates instead of pre-shared keys. A less secure, but alternate, solution is to perform an additional authentication requiring the user to enter something unique about himself, like a username and password. A third option is to use mutual group authentication, which requires that certificates be installed on the VPN gateways, but not the remote access clients, alleviating the need to implement a full-blown PKI certificate solution. Mutual group authentication was discussed in Chapter 2.

Remote Access Additional Steps

Up to this point, all IPsec sessions go through the process described in the previous sections. And with site-to-site sessions, this would be the end of Phase 1, and Phase 2 would begin. However, with remote access sessions, IPsec vendors typically add some additional steps to help customers more easily manage their IPsec implementation. In this book I'll focus only on the additional processes Cisco uses with their remote access

VPN implementation. All of these additional steps I describe here occur in ISAKMP/IKE Phase 1 after device authentication.

The Cisco VPN product performs three additional steps in Phase 1 for client sessions:

1 Performs user authentication (XAUTH)

2 Applies the group policy to the user (IKE Mode/Client Config)

3 Learns routing information from the client (reverse route injection)

The following sections will discuss these three additional remote access steps.

User Authentication with XAUTH

Device authentication allows both the VPN gateway and remote access clients to authenticate each other. One concern with remote access IPsec VPNs is controlling who can use this authenticated VPN. For example, in the last section I mentioned one issue with device authentication and pre-shared keys—all users in the group need to know the same key to authenticate to the group and have access to its policies and privileges. Obviously, this might pose many security risks. If a user's PC or laptop was stolen or hacked, and the pre-shared key is stored on the hard drive, the thief could use this to freely gain secure access to your network. You could change the pre-shared key in this instance, but if there were a few hundred users in the same group, *all of the users* would have to make this change. In addition, the membership of the group might be dynamic, with people leaving and joining the group on a frequent basis. Therefore, management of the pre-shared key is of concern.

IPsec has an add-on standard that was designed to deal with this problem: XAUTH. XAUTH is in an RFC draft state with IETF. It is a VPN gateway enhancement that allows you to authenticate the user using the client device (user authentication). With XAUTH, the VPN gateway prompts the user for a username and password. This allows the VPN gateway to authenticate the user using the device. Various methods can be deployed to store the user's authentication credentials. Some common methods include:

• An internal database on the VPN gateway itself

• On an external device, such as an AAA server, a directory server or a token card server

As mentioned earlier, one concern is that many people might know the pre-shared key of the group. To solve this problem, you could add XAUTH user authentication to enhance the authentication process. Of course, if the user's PC or laptop is stolen, and the user's authentication information is stored on the device, you're right back to the beginning of the problem. To counteract this problem, you could use one of two possible solutions:

• Use a one-time password (OTP) solution, like token cards, where the user's password is unique each time he authenticates: a thief would have to have access to the user's token card and authentication credentials to pass XAUTH.

- Use a vendor solution, like Cisco, which allows the VPN administrator to prevent the user from storing XAUTH information locally: the user must enter this information each time he's authenticated.

Therefore, if the user's laptop or PC was stolen and the device's group pre-shared key was known to the thief, this wouldn't do him any good unless he also knew the user's username and password.

However, of the two choices, the latter approach is significantly less secure, since the user uses the same password. Thus the solution is open to a brute force attack to anyone in possession of the device's pre-shared key or certificate.

NOTE   XAUTH is an add-on enhancement for remote access IPsec VPNs. Just because you're deploying a remote access solution doesn't mean that you have to use XAUTH; however, because of the additional security it adds in authenticating users, I would always include it in my remote access IPsec implementation.

IKE Client/Mode Config

The second step that might occur with remote access VPNs is applying policies to the remote access users by the VPN gateway device. Again, this occurs during ISAKMP/IKE Phase 1 and is vendor-dependent. Cisco commonly calls this step either IKE Mode or Client Config. In this section, I'll focus on the process Cisco uses for IKE Mode Config.

In the Cisco IKE Mode Config, the IPsec gateway device, such as a router, PIX or ASA security appliance, or VPN 3000 concentrator, can assign policies to the client. These policies can include:

- An internal, or logical, IP address for the client
- Connection type: client or network/LAN extension mode
- DNS domain name
- DNS server addresses
- WINS server addresses
- Split tunneling policies
- Firewall policies
- Split DNS policies
- A list of backup IPsec gateways

I'll discuss a few of the items in the above list in the following sections; items like DNS domain names and DNS and WINS server addresses are self-explanatory.

Client's Internal Address

Clients use tunnel mode for the remote access IPsec data connections. If you recall from Chapter 1, the client appears to be connected directly to the corporate network even though the client could be separated from the VPN gateway by many hops. To accomplish this, the client has two IP addresses: one that the ISP assigns it and one that the VPN gateway assigns it.

The client can obtain the internal address via one of the following methods:

- The client defines this address manually (this mode is not supported by Cisco remote access client products)
- The gateway assigns this address

Of the two, the most common solution is to have the VPN gateway assign the internal address to the client. If the gateway assigns the address, the address can be obtained from an internally defined pool on the gateway, from a DHCP server, or from an AAA server. To ensure that the client always gets the same IP address, typically AAA is used. In most situations, a DHCP server is used to dynamically assign addresses to clients.

When the client sends traffic through the tunnel, the tunneled IP packets use the assigned internal address (assigned by the VPN gateway) as the source IP address and a destination address of the device located at the corporate network. This IP packet is encapsulated inside an IPsec packet, where the source IP address is the client's ISP-assigned address and the destination address is the VPN gateway's address. Figure 3-2 shows an example of this process.

Figure 3-2 *Remote Access Client Addressing*

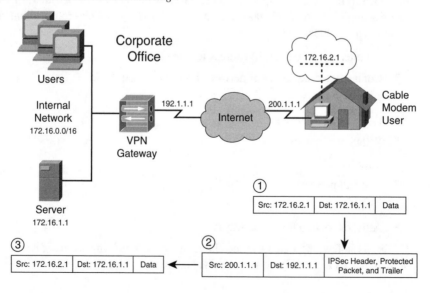

In Figure 3-2, the remote access client is assigned an internal IP address of 172.16.2.1 from the VPN gateway. When the client needs to send traffic to the internal server (172.16.1.1), it creates the packet shown in Step 1. The client, in Step 2, then protects the packet using IPsec (AH and/or ESP) and adds a second IP header to the packet, with the source address of 200.1.1.1 (assigned by the ISP) and a destination address of 192.1.1.1 (the VPN gateway). This packet is sent to the VPN gateway. In Step 3, the VPN gateway validates the IPsec packet and decrypts it, if necessary. Then the internally protected packet, now decrypted, is sent to the internal server. From the internal server's perspective, it appears that the remote access client is directly attached to the 172.16.0.0/16 network.

Client Connection Types

The assumption made in the last section was that the client was a user end-station, like a PC or laptop, when connecting to the corporate network; however, this doesn't necessarily have to be the case. For example, the remote access client could be a small router (Cisco 800, 900, and 1700 series), firewall (Cisco PIX 501 and 506E appliances), or hardware client (Cisco VPN 3002).

There are two types of Cisco remote access connections:

- Client mode
- Network or LAN extension mode

Client Mode   In client mode, the remote access client is assigned an internal IP address by the VPN gateway. However, this presents a problem for a hardware appliance that is the client. In this situation, devices behind the client need to access the tunnel to the corporate network. Cisco solves this problem by having the hardware appliance perform PAT on the inside devices' addresses to the assigned internal address before their traffic is sent across the tunnel. This process is shown in the top part of Figure 3-3, where the hardware appliance at the SOHO is a small-end router. The internal SOHO network segment is 192.168.1.0/24 and this traffic is translated to 172.16.2.1 by the router/client before being tunneled through the IPsec tunnel to the corporate site (172.16.2.1 is the client's internally assigned IP address).

From the corporate site's perspective, the SOHO network actually looks like a single device: 172.16.2.1. Another advantage of client mode is that you can easily use a private address space at the SOHO. Actually, you could use the *same* address space at each SOHO using client mode, since the SOHO's traffic is PATed to a unique internal address assigned by the VPN gateway to the SOHO hardware appliance (the client).

When in client mode, you can either bring up the tunnel manually from the hardware client, or any user traffic behind the hardware client that needs to go to an external network will bring up the tunnel, even if the traffic is not destined to the central office. The tunnel must be brought up for the hardware client to learn the split tunneling policy, which dictates which traffic is tunneled and which traffic is sent to the ISP in clear-text.

Figure 3-3 *Cisco Remote Access Connection Types*

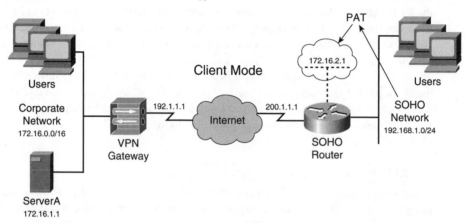

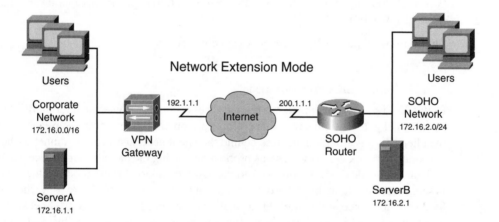

LAN Extension Mode   One limitation of client mode is that the corporate office can't initiate connections to the SOHO devices because the SOHO hardware appliance is using PAT for address translation. To overcome this problem, Cisco developed network extension mode; Cisco sometimes refers to this as LAN extension mode.

Network extension mode simulates a site-to-site session, as shown in the bottom part of Figure 3-3; however, the session is still a remote access session and the SOHO device is treated as a client. Therefore, policies can still be applied to the group that the SOHO device (and the users behind it) belongs to.

In network extension mode, the VPN gateway doesn't assign an IP address to the client and the network segment at the SOHO must be unique throughout the network. The advantage of this approach is that if a device at the corporate site needs to initiate a connection to a SOHO device, the corporate device only would need to know the IP address of the specific

SOHO device. For example, this would be necessary if you were using a voice over IP (VoIP) solution and had phones at both locations or needed to manage devices at the SOHOs. Also, unlike client mode, the hardware client would automatically bring up the remote access session to the VPN gateway, thereby allowing central office traffic to initiate connections to the SOHO devices.

Normally, the network number used at the SOHO in network extension mode is an extension of the address space used at the corporate site. In Figure 3-3, the corporation is using 172.16.0.0/16 and the SOHO is using a subnet of this: 172.16.2.0/24; however, you do not need to follow this process. Just remember that each SOHO site using network extension mode requires unique network numbers.

With Cisco, whether or not a remote access client can use client or network extension mode depends on the following two criteria:

- Only hardware appliances support both modes; software clients only support client mode.

- The use of network extension mode is a policy that sometimes must be enabled on a VPN gateway; otherwise, the hardware appliance might be restricted to using client mode—this is true if the VPN gateway is a VPN 3000 concentrator.

TIP   I'm constantly asked which mode—L2L or remote access—should be used for connectivity from a SOHO or branch office when a hardware appliance is being used. I prefer to set the session up as a remote access session (instead of site-to-site) because I can easily centralize my remote access policies on the VPN gateway and push these down to the clients: hardware and software. Also, if the VPN device at the corporate office is a VPN 3000 concentrator, these typically support more remote access sessions than L2L sessions. When setting it up as a remote access session, if the corporate office needs to initiate connections to the SOHO devices, I'll use network extension mode; otherwise I'll use client mode.

Split Tunneling

As discussed in Chapter 1, split tunneling is the process of sending some traffic across a protected tunnel and some traffic in clear text. In remote access IPsec VPNs, the use of split tunneling is a policy defined on the VPN gateway and pushed to the client. In the Cisco implementation, split tunneling is, by default, disabled on the VPN gateway; therefore, once the IPsec tunnel comes up between the client and gateway, all traffic from the client is sent to the gateway across the protected connection. There is no option on the client to override this behavior. This gives you, the network administrator, control over what traffic should be protected.

In the Cisco implementation, two types of traffic are exceptions to this policy:

- **ARP**—This must be allowed so that the client, if using an Ethernet interface, can learn the MAC addresses of devices so that it can communicate with directly connected devices, such as the ISP's access device.

- **DHCP**—This must be allowed so that the client can obtain an address, typically from the ISP, and renew it once its lease expires.

TIP   Cisco recommends that if you use split tunneling, a firewall solution should be used to protect the client. If the client is a software client, a software firewall should be installed on the client to protect it against clear-text traffic from other sources, which could be attacks against the PC. For hardware appliances, I would either use a low-end PIX as a client, preferably, or a router with the IOS Firewall feature set installed; the 3002, as you will see in Chapter 14, "3002 Hardware Client," lacks the enhanced firewall capabilities of Cisco PIXs and routers.

Firewall Policies

Some remote access VPN implementations support the use of firewall policies. Firewall policies are defined on the VPN gateway and pushed to the client. The Cisco IPsec implementation supports two firewall policies:

- Are You There (AYT)
- Central Policy Protection or Push (CPP)

Both of these policies only apply to the Cisco VPN software client. With AYT, the policy is pushed down to the client and the client software periodically checks for the use of a firewall. If a firewall is not detected, the VPN Client software immediately tears down the IPsec session to the central site. This feature forces a remote access user to use a firewall to establish and maintain IPsec sessions to the VPN gateway.

One limitation of AYT is that it only detects the presence of a firewall. CPP allows you to push down specific filtering policies to the firewall product on the client. For example, you could push down a filter that allows the client to access specific destination addresses, but deny all other access. Both of these features are Cisco features and are not necessarily available in other vendors' IPsec remote access implementations. I'll discuss both of these features in more depth in Chapter 7, "Concentrator Remote Access Connections with IPsec."

NOTE   4.7 of the VPN 3000 concentrators support network admission control (NAC) in conjunction with the Cisco Trust Agent: this allows you to define other access policies, such as the use of anti-virus software on the client. Cisco routers also support NAC.

Split DNS

Another feature a VPN implementation may provide is the use of split DNS. Figure 3-4 illustrates the use of split DNS. In this network the DMZ devices are using private addresses (172.16.254.0/24); however, these devices are being represented with a static translation by the PIX with a global address from 192.1.1.0/24. When the SOHO client boots up and acquires an address from the ISP, it also acquires a DNS address (dynamically or manually). In this example, the DNS server address assigned to the client by the ISP is 200.1.1.254. Normally the client uses this address to resolve names to addresses; however, whenever the remote access client connects to the IPsec gateway, the gateway can also assign a DNS address to the client.

Figure 3-4   *Split DNS Example*

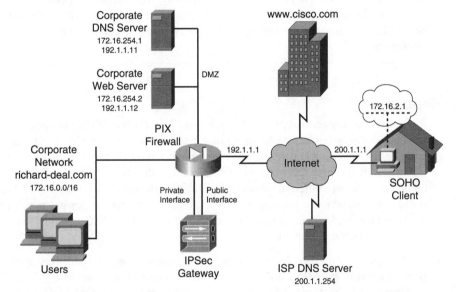

By default, split DNS is *disabled*; therefore, in Figure 3-4, if the SOHO client wanted to reach www.cisco.com, the DNS resolution would be forwarded across the IPsec tunnel to the DNS server (172.16.254.1) at the corporate office: the one assigned by the VPN gateway. However, this can cause problems. For example, let's assume the SOHO client wants to reach the DMZ web server. If the client wanted to reach a web server at the ISP, the DNS query would first go to the DMZ DNS server. The DMZ DNS server would forward this to a root DNS server, which, in turn, would forward this to the ISP DNS server to perform the resolution. In this situation, using the DMZ DNS server to perform all resolutions doesn't make sense.

Split DNS allows you, the IPsec gateway administrator, to control which DNS server the client uses. In this example, the corporate office's domain name is richard-deal.com. You could easily set up split DNS so that any resolution associated with richard-deal.com would be done by 172.16.254.1 and any other resolution would be done by the ISP's DNS server (200.1.1.254). To implement this, during IKE Mode Config, the IPsec gateway would send the list of DNS names to the client. If the client needed to do a DNS lookup for one of these names, it would use the DNS server assigned to it, during IKE Mode Config, by the IPsec gateway. Otherwise, the client would use the ISP's DNS server for name resolution.

NOTE   It is important to point out that in any DNS resolution done to the DNS server address, the VPN gateway supplied to the client is done across the secure data connection built in IKE Phase 2. In split DNS, if the client uses the ISP's DNS server, the DNS request is sent out in clear text directly to the ISP's server. This is basically a modified form of split tunneling. Likewise, split DNS won't work unless you also enable split tunneling, because resolutions for noncorporate devices must be sent clear-text to the ISP's DNS server. Also, split DNS is a Cisco feature that might not be available in other vendors' VPN implementations.

Reverse Route Injection

Remote access connectivity has routing issues. The top part of the network shown in Figure 3-5 illustrates this problem. In this network there are two VPN gateways for redundancy. The SOHO client has been configured and lists both VPN gateways, with VPN GatewayA the primary gateway and VPN GatewayB the backup gateway. The two routers, because they are in a different subnet (172.16.1.0/24) than the SOHO client (172.16.2.0/24), could have a static route pointing to VPN GatewayA; however, if this gateway were to go down and the client would connect to the backup gateway, VPN GatewayB, this would create a connectivity problem.

Another reachability issue can arise if the remote access client is a hardware appliance and is using network extension mode, like that shown in the bottom part of Figure 3-5. The problem in this situation is how the corporate office knows about the SOHO network, 172.16.3.0/24.

There are several ways of solving remote access routing problems, two of which are:

- Dynamic IP routing protocol
- Reverse Route Injection (RRI)

Using a dynamic routing protocol to solve the reachability issues that I previously mentioned presents problems. First, software clients might not support a routing protocol and therefore can't advertise their local routing information. Second, dynamic routing information that uses broadcasts and multicasts is not supported on IPsec connections. Only unicast traffic is supported. This can be circumvented by setting up a GRE tunnel between the remote access client and the VPN gateway device and sending routing traffic across this; but this assumes that these devices support GRE tunnels. Only Cisco routers and certain implementations of Unix support GRE, so this could pose a problem and might not be a viable solution.

Figure 3-5   *Remote Access and Routing Issues*

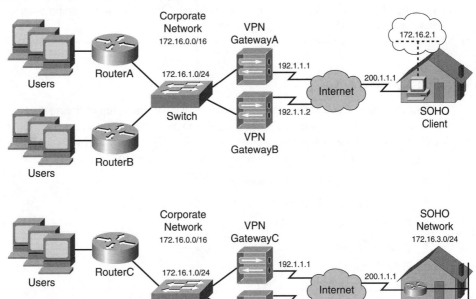

The Cisco RRI provides the best approach for remote access clients. RRI is a Cisco-proprietary enhancement for IPsec. At the end of ISAKMP/IKE Phase 1, the remote access client does one of the following:

- If in client mode, the client is assigned an internal address by the VPN gateway; the VPN gateway will add this as a static route to its local routing table.

- If in network extension mode, the client sends the network number of its inside interface to the VPN gateway via an ISAKMP/IKE Phase 1 message.

On the VPN gateway side, the client or network route is placed in the local routing table as a static route and can be redistributed via a dynamic routing protocol to devices on the corporate network. This solution provides scalability because it doesn't matter which VPN gateway the client connects to, the routing information is updated dynamically and allows internal devices to learn which VPN gateway a remote access software or hardware client is connected to.

NOTE	One limitation of RRI is that only a single route can be advertised to the VPN gateway during ISAKMP/IKE Phase 1 for hardware clients using network extension mode. If the remote access hardware client had more than one network segment behind it, RRI won't solve this problem. In this situation, you would need to use a site-to-site implementation and use a static or dynamic routing process.

ISAKMP/IKE Phase 2

All of the things discussed in the last section only cover the setup of the management connection. No user data actually traverses this management connection; only ISAKMP/IKE messages traverse this management connection. This section will discuss how the protected user data connections are built by covering the following:

- ISAKMP/IKE Phase 2 Components
- Phase 2 Security Protocols
- Phase 2 Connection Modes
- Phase 2 Transforms
- Data Connections

ISAKMP/IKE Phase 2 Components

ISAKMP/IKE Phase 2 only has one mode: Quick mode. Quick mode defines how protected data connections are built between two IPsec peers. Quick mode has two main functions:

- Negotiate the security parameters to protect the data connections.
- Periodically renew the keying information for the data connections (basically rebuilding the connections).

ISAKMP/IKE Phase 2 has one unique characteristic: there are actually *two* unidirectional data connections built between the two peers. For example, PeerA would have a data connection to PeerB and PeerB would have a separate data connection to PeerA. Because these connections are separate connections, the security parameters negotiated could be different between the two peers. For example, the PeerA-to-PeerB connection could use 3DES for encryption, but the PeerB-to-PeerA connection could use DES. However, this is commonly not done: the same security parameters typically are used for both data connections.

The following are policies that need to be determined to configure your devices to build ISAKMP/IKE Phase 2 connections:

- Which data traffic should be protected between the two peers? With site-to-site connections, this is either defined statically or learned dynamically; with remote access connections, this is determined by the split tunneling policy defined on the VPN gateway.

- What security protocol(s) should be used to protect the traffic? The two protocols defined by IPsec are AH and ESP.
- Based on the security protocol(s) selected, how should the data traffic be protected? For example, what HMAC function or encryption algorithm should be used?
- What mode of operation should the security protocols use? The two operation modes are tunnel and transport.
- When refreshing keying information, should the ISAKMP/IKE Phase 1 management be used to share the new keys or should perfect forward secrecy be used instead?
- What's the lifetime of the data connections? This can be based on time expired or amount of data transmitted across the connections.

The following sections will discuss this information in more depth.

Phase 2 Security Protocols

IPsec can use one or two security protocols to protect the data transmitted across the data connections built in ISAKMP/IKE Phase 2:

- AH
- ESP

Table 3-1 provides a brief comparison of the two protocols. The two subsequent sections will cover them in more depth.

Table 3-1   *AH and ESP Comparison*

Security Feature	AH	ESP
Layer-3 IP protocol number	51	50
Provides for data integrity	Yes	Yes
Provides for data authentication	Yes	Yes
Provides for data encryption	No	Yes
Protects against data replay attacks	Yes	Yes
Works with NAT	No	Yes
Works with PAT	No	No[1]
Protects the IP packet	Yes	No
Protects only the data	No	Yes

[1] Many firewall appliances performing PAT use proprietary methods to pass ESP traffic between interfaces. For example, Linksys firewall routers and Cisco PIX and ASA security appliances support this process; however, this feature is vendor-dependent and is implemented using a proprietary method.

AH

AH, defined in RFC 2402, provides three main security functions:

- Data integrity services
- Data authentication
- Protection against data replay attacks

When providing protection of a packet, AH protects the entire packet with the exception of mutable fields, like the TTL and TOS fields in the IP header. AH is an IP protocol like ICMP, TCP, and UDP. It is assigned an IP protocol number of 51. Figure 3-6 shows an example of AH being used to protect an IP packet.

Figure 3-6   *AH Packetization Process*

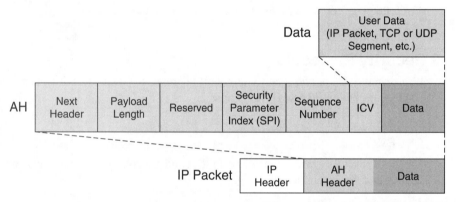

In the figure, if the connection is using tunnel mode, the first IP packet is considered the user data; if the connection is using transport mode, just the transport layer header and payload are considered user data. The "Connection Modes" section discusses these two connection modes in more depth. The user data is appended to an AH header.

Here's a description of the fields found in the AH header:

- **Next header**—This field specifies the protocol of the data being encapsulated (like 6 for TCP or 17 for UDP); these numbers are defined by the IANA.

- **Payload length**—This field defines the length of only the AH header and excludes the outer IP header and the encapsulated data.

- **Reserved**—This field is currently reserved and not used.

- **Security parameter index (SPI)**—This field uniquely identifies the connection to a remote peer with a numerical value; it is a number assigned by the receiving device for the unidirectional connection so that it can differentiate traffic from this connection compared to other connections from this or other peers. This field is 4 bytes in length, allowing for over a billion identifiers for SPI values on a device.

- **Sequence number**—This field specifies a number unique to each packet traversing the data connection and is used to detect replay attacks.

- **Integrity checksum value (ICV)** — This field provides authentication information for the packet; it is the digital signature created from the MD5 or SHA-1 HMAC function. The ICV value is created by taking all of the fields in the complete IP packet (IP packet header, minus the mutable fields, the AH header, minus the ICV field, and the user data), along with the shared HMAC key, and running it through an HMAC function. The peer at the other end can verify the integrity and origin of the packet assuming the remote peer knows about the same HMAC key.

One of the things you've probably noticed is that AH doesn't perform encryption as one of its protection services; therefore, it has limited use when you need to transmit data across public networks. Plus, AH doesn't work with NAT or PAT, for the following reasons:

- PAT needs a TCP or UDP outer header and AH is a Layer-3 protocol.

- NAT changes the source or destination IP addresses; but AH uses these when creating the ICV value.

Therefore AH is commonly used inside a network, typically with connections using transport mode, as between an internal router and a syslog server or a PIX and a TFTP server. I'll discuss address translation issues in more depth later in the "Address Translation Issues" section of this chapter.

ESP

ESP, defined in RFC 2406, provides Layer-3 protection of data. It has an IP protocol number of 50 and offers the same type of services that AH provides, but with two exceptions:

- ESP provides encryption of the user data.

- ESP's data authentication and integrity service include only the ESP header and payload — not the outer IP header. Therefore, if someone were to tamper with the outer IP header, ESP wouldn't detect this (AH could); of course if your ESP traffic is going through a NAT device, this is an advantage.

Figure 3-7 shows the process ESP performs on user data to protect it between two IPsec peers. Depending on whether the connection mode is transport or tunnel, the upper layer data or the first IP packet is padded. The padding is used to reduce the likelihood of an eavesdropper guessing what the payload is based on its length. The length is added to this information, then the next header denotes the contents of the payload — this is the same field used by AH.

Typically the information is then encrypted and an ESP header and, optionally, a trailer, are added. The SPI field serves the same purpose it does with AH: it uniquely identifies each IPsec data connection terminated on a device. The sequence number is used to prevent replay attacks. Optionally, if you have enabled packet authentication, an ICV value is added at the end of the encrypted data. The ICV value is created by taking the ESP header, the encapsulated data, and a key, and running them through an HMAC function (creating a digital signature). An IP header is then added to the front of the ESP header to transport the information to the remote IPsec device.

Figure 3-7 *ESP Packetization Process*

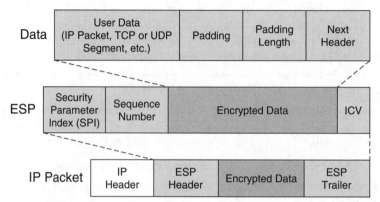

When a remote IPsec peer receives ESP information, it performs the process in reverse. If authentication is used, the ICV value is verified. If valid, the encrypted data is decrypted. This makes sense, because there is no point in wasting extra CPU cycles to decrypt something if it has been tampered with.

NOTE   AH and ESP are not mutually exclusive of one another; they can be used in conjunction with each other because ESP provides encryption and AH provides better protection for data authentication and integrity. However, because AH has problems with intermediate devices changing information in the outer IP header, it is typically not used in public networks.

Phase 2 Connection Modes

As I mentioned in the last two sections, there are two types of modes that AH and ESP can use to transport protected information to a destination:

- Transport mode
- Tunnel mode

In transport mode, the real source and destination of the user data are performing the protection service. It becomes more difficult to manage as you add more and more devices using this connection mode. This mode is commonly used between two devices that need to protect specific information, like TFTP transfers of configuration files or syslog transfers of logging messages.

In tunnel mode, intermediate devices (typically) are performing the protection service for the user data. This connection mode is used for site-to-site and remote access connections. Because the original IP packet is protected and embedded in AH/ESP and an outer IP header is added, the internal IP packet can contain private IP addresses. Plus, if you're using ESP for encryption, the real source and destination of the user data is hidden from eavesdroppers. The main advantage of tunnel mode over transport mode is that the protection service function can be centralized on a small number of devices, reducing the amount of configuration and management required. Both of these modes were discussed in detail in Chapter 1, "Overview of VPNs."

Phase 2 Transforms

A data transform defines *how* the data connections should be protected. If you recall from the "ISAKMP/IKE Transforms" section earlier, to protect the management connection, an ISAKMP/IKE transform or transforms is defined. The same is true of the data connections in ISAKMP/IKE Phase 2. However, management transform sets and data transform sets contain different information. A data transform set contains the following information about how to protect traffic between IPsec peers:

- The security protocol: AH and/or ESP

- The connection mode for the security protocols: tunnel or transport (if you're using both AH and ESP, you must use the same connection mode for both)

- For ESP, encryption information: no encryption algorithm, DES, 3DES, AES-128, AES-192, or AES-256

- The packet authentication and verification HMAC function: MD5 or SHA-1 (with ESP, this is optional)

Data Connections

As mentioned in the "IPsec Connections" section earlier, a security association (SA) groups all of the necessary security components to communicate successfully with an IPsec peer. With data SAs, you'll have one data SA, per direction, per protected pipe. For example, if you were using only ESP for protection between two peers, you'd have two SAs: one for each peer. However, if the peers were using both AH and ESP, you'd have two SAs per peer: one for AH and one for ESP on both peers. Therefore, you can't really look at an SA as a "connection," because you could be using both AH and ESP to provide protection. Both would be separate SAs, but with one single connection to a remote peer. The following two sections will discuss the components of a data SA and how data SAs are negotiated.

Components of a Data SA

Here are the components you'll find in a data SA:

- The security protocol: AH and/or ESP.

- The SPI value for AH and/or ESP (this is assigned by the receiving device for a data connection).

- The connection mode for AH and/or ESP: tunnel or transport (you must use the same mode if using both AH and ESP).

- The lifetime of the SA: the lifetime can be measured in time (seconds) or amount of data transferred (KBs).

- The packet authentication and integrity HMAC function for AH and/or ESP, and the symmetric key(s): MD5 or SHA-1. The symmetric key used here is *different* from the one used in the ISAKMP/IKE Phase 1 management connection; actually a separate key can be used for each data connection.

- The encryption algorithm and symmetric key used if ESP is chosen: null (none), DES, 3DES, AES-128, AES-192, and AES-128. The symmetric key used here is *different* from the one used in the ISAKMP/IKE Phase 1 management connection; actually, there could be different keys for each data connection.

- Perfect Forward Secrecy (PFS) usage: By default, the existing ISAKMP/IKE Phase 1 management connection is used to share the encryption and HMAC symmetric keys; optionally, you can use Diffie-Hellman to do this. DH is more secure than the management connection because of the length of the key structure. For example, 3DES uses 168 bits and DH group 1 is 768 bits. However, the downside of using PFS is that there is more delay in using DH to share the data connection keys than using the existing management connection.

How Data SAs Are Negotiated

Once ISAKMP/IKE Phase 1 completes, the management connection is used for the two peers to communicate to each other with ISAKMP/IKE messages. The negotiation of the ISAKMP/IKE Phase 2 connections is done across the management connection. Each peer shares the following with its remote counterpart:

- The traffic that needs to be protected with the other peer (on Cisco routers and PIX and ASA security appliances, this is commonly called a *crypto ACL*).

- The list of data transforms that can be used to protect the traffic (the order is important because they are processed in the order that they are received—therefore, put the most secure transform at the beginning of the list and the least secure at the end). In a transform, you'll find the following: the security protocol (AH or ESP), the packet authentication and integrity HMAC function, the encryption algorithm, and the connection mode.

- Whether or not PFS should be used. If it is used, the DH key group needs to be negotiated.

- The local IP address that should be used in the outer header of the IP packet.

- The measurement of the lifetime, in seconds and/or KBs.

Let's look at a simple example of how the negotiation process takes place. Assume IPsecA has the following transforms:

1 Transform 1A: AH with MD5, ESP with AES-256, tunnel mode

2 Transform 2A: ESP with MD5, ESP with AES-128, tunnel mode

IPsecB has the following transforms:

1 Transform 1B: ESP with MD5, ESP with AES-128, tunnel mode

2 Transform 2B: ESP with MD5, ESP with 3DES, tunnel mode

Who makes the connection (remember, they're unidirectional) affects how the transforms are processed. The receiving device compares the first transform of the sending device with all of the transforms of the receiving device. If no match is found, the second transform of the sending device is compared with the transforms of the receiving device. This is done in both directions for the two unidirectional connections.

For example, IPsecA, acting as the receiving device, compares Transform 1B to 1A. There isn't a match, so it then compares 1B to 2A. In this case, a matching transform is found and this is used for the unidirectional connection from IPsecB to IPsecA. The same process takes place on IPsecB for the unidirectional connection from IPsecA to IPsecB.

Assuming that there is a matching transform, other things need to be compared or negotiated, such as the traffic that should be protected, the lifetime of the data SAs, and the DH key group to use for PFS, if this is specified and can be negotiated. If this information cannot be negotiated successfully, the data SA setup process fails and no user data can be transmitted between the two IPsec peers.

NOTE   The one thing that doesn't necessarily have to match between the two peers is the lifetime of the data connections. If there is a mismatch in the lifetime, the two IPsec peers should negotiate and use the lower value between them. However, some vendors don't follow this guideline; for those vendors you'll need to also match the lifetime values.

IPsec Traffic and Networks

There are two important issues you might have to deal with concerning the sending and receiving of IPsec traffic:

- Address translation
- Firewalls
- Other IPsec issues

The following three sections will discuss these issues in more depth.

IPsec and Address Translation

Address translation translates addressing and, possibly, port information inside IP, TCP, or UDP headers. My goal here is to not discuss what address translation is; I'm assuming you are already familiar with it. My other Cisco Press book, *Cisco Router Firewall Security*, covers the mechanics of address translation on Cisco routers, if you're not that familiar with the process.

As you already know, there are three IPsec connections between two IPsec peers:

- A management connection, which uses UDP port 500
- Two data connections, which use AH (protocol 51) or ESP (protocol 50)

The following two sections will discuss issues with address translation and IPsec, and possible solutions.

Address Translation Issues

Devices performing address translation typically don't create any issues for the management connection, but can cause problems with the data connections. However, some earlier PAT devices would force all management connections to use UDP port 500 for both the source and destination, which could cause problems for multiple simultaneous connections to the same endpoint through the PAT device; this shouldn't be a problem with most translation devices today, though.

As I mentioned in the "Phase 2 Security Protocols" section, AH breaks completely when any type of address translation is performed on an AH packet. PAT isn't supported because PAT requires an outer TCP or UDP header—and AH is a Layer-3 protocol that lacks this. AH also won't work with NAT because AH includes most of the fields in the entire IP packet in the input of the HMAC function. Therefore, if the source or destination address is changed, this would invalidate the ICV signature by the destination IPsec device.

ESP actually works with NAT, since the outer IP header isn't included in the ICV computation for the digital signature; only the ESP and user data parts are included. However, like AH, ESP doesn't work with PAT because PAT requires the use of TCP or UDP in the outer header and ESP is a Layer-3 protocol that lacks this functionality.

Address Translation Solutions

Given the above issues with address translation, there are some solutions available to you assuming you are willing to forgo the use of AH and stick with only ESP. Remember that ESP will work with NAT, but breaks with PAT. To have ESP interoperate with devices performing PAT, you could insert a TCP or UDP header *between* the outer IP header and the ESP part, as shown in Figure 3-8. By inserting either a TCP or UDP header, you make the address translation device happy and it can perform PAT; plus, because this information is in the outer header, it is not included in the HMAC process to create the digital signature (only the ESP header and user data are included).

Figure 3-8   *ESP Address Translation Solutions*

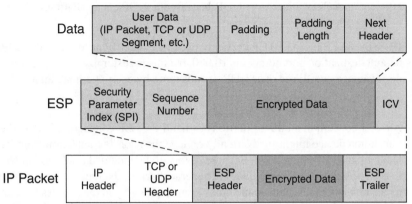

Cisco products have three separate solutions, which are compared in the heading of Table 3-2. Of the three solutions, IPsec over UDP and IPsec over TCP are proprietary to Cisco. With IPsec over UDP, a standard UDP header is always inserted after the outer IP header and before the ESP header. This solves the address translation issue for PAT; however, the device is always performing this process even if no address translation device resides between the two IPsec peers performing PAT. The main problem of the Cisco UDP is that you always have the overhead of the UDP segment even if no address translation is occurring. The default destination port number that Cisco uses for the UDP port is 10,000, but this is customizable. Another limitation is that only Cisco VPN 3000 concentrators and Cisco VPN clients support this feature.

Table 3-2   *Address Translation Solutions*

Comparisons	NAT-T	IPsec over UDP	IPsec over TCP
Standard versus proprietary	RFC	Cisco	Cisco
Encapsulation method	UDP	UDP	TCP
When encapsulation is done	Tested	Always	Always

NAT transversal or traversal (NAT-T) provides an alternative solution with the UDP encapsulation process. Unlike IPsec over UDP, NAT-T is defined by RFC 3947/3948 and thus is an open standard. With NAT-T, a test ESP packet is sent between the two IPsec devices with a standard UDP segment header between the IP outer header and the ESP header. The destination UDP port number must be 4,500.

Note that the UDP header contains a checksum of the header information. This same UDP segment is protected and placed after the UDP header. When the destination receives the NAT-T packet it checks the checksum in the outer and inner UDP headers: if they don't match, an address translation device is performing PAT; otherwise, no address translation device is performing PAT. If the latter is true, then no UDP encapsulation is used; normal

ESP packets are sent, thus reducing the overhead involved. Therefore, NAT-T is more efficient than Cisco IPsec over UDP, because the UDP encapsulation is done only if PAT is being performed on the ESP packet.

IPsec over TCP inserts a TCP header between the outer IP header and the ESP header. The default destination port number is 10,000, but this is customizable. IPsec over TCP has one disadvantage over IPsec over UDP: it adds more bytes of overhead than UDP.

NOTE   Another concern in all three solutions is that if the ESP connection is idle, the address translation device might inadvertently remove the address translation from its table, breaking the ESP connection. Because of this, IETF included a solution in NAT-T's RFCs. In their solution, NAT keepalives are generated across the unidirectional data connections to ensure that the idle data connections' translations stay in the address translation device's address translation table. Cisco also has a proprietary feature called Dead Peer Detection (DPD), or IKE keepalives, that performs this function for the ISAKMP/IKE Phase 1 management connection.

CAUTION   Because ESP is already adding overhead to your IP packet, and you might need to insert a TCP or UDP segment header to get your ESP information through a PAT device, you might experience fragmentation problems. Therefore, you'll need to adjust the MTU of your devices to a smaller value to prevent fragmentation, which can seriously affect delay in your transmissions. I'll discuss this issue more in Part IV, "Clients."

IPsec and Firewalls

There are two basic ways VPN traffic is terminated in your network: on your firewall or on a device behind a firewall. First, in either case, you'll need to permit IPsec traffic into your network. Second, you might experience problems with stateful firewall products and allow returning IPsec traffic back into your network.

The next two sections will discuss both of these issues and how to deal with them when IPsec traffic has to travel to or through a firewall.

Allowing IPsec Traffic into Your Network

Given that IPsec traffic will probably be coming into your network from a public network, there are certain kinds of traffic you'll have to deal with at the perimeter of your network. You'll need to allow some of the following IPsec traffic into your network:

- Management connections: UDP port 500
- Data connections using AH: protocol 51

- Data connections using ESP with no address translation: protocol 50
- Data connections using ESP with NAT-T: UDP port 4,500
- Data connections using ESP with IPsec over UDP: UDP port 10,000 by default, but this can be changed
- Data connections using ESP with IPsec over TCP: TCP port 10,000 by default, but this can be changed and can include multiple ports for different remote peers

You want to be as specific as possible when allowing this traffic into your network to prevent any errant packets from getting through a packet filter.

Using Stateful Firewalls

Another issue can result if you are using a stateful firewall. A stateful firewall is an enhanced version of a packet filtering firewall. Packet filtering firewalls filter only on Layer-3 and Layer-4 information that they find in packet headers; they don't look at anything higher. Stateful firewalls also look at the session layer and keep track of sessions. For example, a stateful firewall would look at an outbound Telnet and know that because this session is allowed out, the returning traffic for that particular Telnet session should be allowed back in.

With TCP, the returning traffic can be inspected easily by the stateful firewall; examining the TCP flags in the TCP header allows the firewall to determine the beginning and end of the TCP session. With IPsec, this can be more problematic in tracking the IPsec connections. First, the management connection uses UDP and all messages are encrypted (with the exception of the first few). Therefore, determining when the connection is finished can be problematic; you don't want to leave the connection in the filtering table forever if it doesn't exist. Most stateful firewalls will use a timer for UDP traffic; if it's idle for more than X number of seconds, the firewall's assumption is that the connection is over, and it is removed from the state table. However, this can still pose a problem with the management connection if an outside peer initiates the connection. Then you would need a filtering rule to allow the inbound traffic.

However, most stateful firewalls *don't* support AH or ESP, which are Layer-3 protocols. A vendor could, for instance, use idle timers to approximate the end of a data connection session, but this could create problems. If the IPsec devices are idle, but still using the connection, and the stateful firewall would remove the connection from its state table, the data connection would fail. Because of this issue, vendors typically require you to use packet filtering rules to allow IPsec data connections into (or out of) your network, or they have a bypass feature that allows all AH and/or ESP packets through the firewall.

Another alternative solution is to use NAT-T or IPsec over UDP and then employ a keepalive function that periodically generates NAT keepalives across the ESP connection. This option was mentioned in the Note at the end of the "Address Translation Solutions" section.

CAUTION   I prefer to be very specific about what traffic is allowed in my firewall, and therefore will use filtering rules to allow IPsec traffic instead of using an IPsec bypass feature. IPsec bypass features allow *all* IPsec traffic to any device. Through the use of filters, you at least can limit what internal devices can use IPsec to external devices.

Other Issues Using IPsec

There are two other issues to discuss before I end this chapter. The first issue deals with detecting dead peers. The second issue deals with a remote access client losing its connection and then trying to reestablish its connection to the same IPsec gateway.

Dead Peer Detection

Dead Peer Detection (DPD) is a fancy name for ISAKMP/IKE keepalives. DPD allows two peers to detect a dead management connection. This is a Cisco-proprietary feature, in an IETF draft state, which allows an IPsec device to discover a dead, or stale, set of IPsec connections.

This feature is important in both site-to-site and remote access implementations where redundancy is required. In other words, for remote access sessions, you need a method that allows a client to discover if the gateway is no longer responding, enabling it to tear down its current session and building a new one to a backup VPN gateway.

Likewise, for the VPN gateway in a remote access implementation, this allows the gateway to detect and remove dead connections, which can affect allowing the addition of new clients based on the license limit in effect on the VPN gateway. For example, the Cisco VPN 3005 concentrator (VPN gateway) supports 100 or 200 IPsec sessions, depending on the version of software running on the product. Dead remote access client sessions count against this license limit, so detecting and removing them is important.

Both of the above features also apply to site-to-site sessions. If your primary IPsec peer dies, you need a method to quickly discover this and build a new IPsec connection to a backup peer. Likewise, site-to-site devices have license limits that restrict the number of IPsec sessions, so removing dead ones is important in an environment that has a large number of IPsec sessions, especially if they're dynamic sessions.

Initial Contact

Initial contact is a Cisco-proprietary feature used in remote access IPsec VPNs. Initial contact is a necessary feature for remote access VPNs, especially where the client uses a dialup connection.

For example, a remote access client dials up to his ISP and establishes an IPsec session to a corporate VPN gateway. Then the client loses his dialup connection and redials, obtaining a different IP address from his last one. This can cause problems with the VPN gateway, because when the client connects again, using the same username and password for XAUTH, the concentrator might deny the connection, seeing that the connection is already "established" from the previously disconnected dialup connection.

DPD can be used to deal with this problem; however, depending on how often keepalives are generated, and how many have to be missed before the connection is considered dead, the user might not be able to reconnect for a few minutes. Therefore, Cisco developed initial contact, which allows the VPN gateway to remove the previously authenticated "dead" connection and reconnect the client by going through ISAKMP/IKE Phase 1 and 2 again.

Summary

This chapter introduced you to an overview of IPsec, including its components and how it implements a secure connectivity solution. Of all of the VPN implementations, IPsec is probably the most complicated one.

Setting up and troubleshooting an IPsec connection is not necessarily a simple process. Therefore, understanding how IPsec works and the types of connections that are built is important when it comes time to troubleshoot connections that won't come up. Whereas this chapter gives you an overview of the IPsec standard and implementation, other chapters will spend more time on the actual configuration and troubleshooting process, because this is different on a product-by-product basis.

Next up is Chapter 4, "PPTP and L2TP," where I discuss an overview of PPTP and L2TP VPN implementations so that you have an understanding as to which VPN implementation, compared to IPsec, makes more sense for your particular network infrastructure. Following this chapter, Chapter 5 will cover the last type of VPN implementation I'll cover in this book: "SSL VPNs."

CHAPTER 4

PPTP and L2TP

Even though IPsec is very popular in the marketplace as far as VPN implementations go, there are many other VPN implementations to choose from. For example, if you come from a Microsoft shop, you probably will be exposed to Microsoft's VPN implementations: the Point-to-Point Tunneling Protocol (PPTP) and the Layer-2 Tunneling Protocol (L2TP). Like IPsec, both of these protocols have been standardized by IETF and ratified into RFCs.

PPTP is a simple-to-implement VPN solution defined in IETF's RFC 2637. It allows for the use of user authentication (before IPsec included this with XAUTH) and the ability to be interoperable with NAT, making it, originally, a preferred remote access solution over IPsec, which lacked these features. IPsec was not designed as a remote access solution, originally lacking features such as user authentication, address assignment, and enforcement of user policies; nor does IPsec support the transport of multiple protocols (only IP is supported) or multicast transmissions. Therefore, PPTP had a lot of support from the user community where secure remote access connectivity was needed.

L2TP is, rather, a merging of two standards: PPTP and the Cisco Layer-2 Forwarding (L2F) protocol. L2TP is defined in IETF's RFCs 2661 and 3438. L2TP can work in conjunction with IPsec to leverage the remote access advantages that L2TP provides, but also the security that IPsec offers. In today's world, you'll typically see Microsoft shops using L2TP over IPsec (L2TP/IPsec) for remote access connectivity. This chapter will be devoted to these protocols, providing an overview of how they work.

PPTP

PPTP originally was developed by Microsoft to provide a secure remote access solution where traffic needed to be transported from a client, across a public network, to a Microsoft server (VPN gateway). One of the interesting items about PPTP's implementation is that it is an extension of the Point-to-Point Protocol (PPP). Because PPTP uses PPP, PPTP can leverage PPP's features. For example, PPTP allows the encapsulation of multiple protocols, such as IP, IPX, and NetBEUI, via the VPN tunnel. Also, PPP supports the use of authentication via PAP, CHAP, and MS-CHAP. PPTP can use this to authenticate devices.

PPTP recently added support for the Extensible Authentication Protocol (EAP) to authenticate users. EAP was designed for wireless networks, but has been incorporated into PPTP. Even though PPP is used in dialup scenarios, PPTP doesn't require the use of dialup to establish remote access connections; you can use dialup or your local LAN connection.

NOTE   If you're in a pure Microsoft shop and using a Windows remote access server (RAS) to terminate remote access connections, you'll typically be using PPTP or L2TP/IPsec for your client connections. PPTP is typically used with the older Microsoft Windows platforms, Windows 95, 98, or ME. For the newer Microsoft platforms, 2000, XP, and 2003, L2TP/IPsec is more commonly used.

Here is a quick review of some of PPTP's features:

- **Compression**—Compression of data is handled by Microsoft's Point-to-Point Compression (MPPC) protocol within the PPP payload. This is supported by both PPTP and L2TP and normally enabled for dialup clients.

- **Encryption**—Encryption of data is handled by Microsoft's Point-to-Point Encryption (MPPE) protocol within the PPP payload. The encryption uses RSA's RC4 encryption algorithm. PPTP uses this method, whereas L2TP uses IPsec, which is more secure. With MPPE, the initial key created during user authentication is used for the encryption algorithm and is regenerated periodically.

- **User authentication**—User authentication is achieved using PPP's authentication methods, such as PAP or CHAP, and others, such as EAP. MPPE support requires the use of MS-CHAPv1 or v2. If you use EAP, you can choose from a wide range of authentication methods, including static passwords and one-time passwords (through the use of token cards).

- **Data delivery**—Data is packetized using PPP, which is then encapsulated in a PPTP/L2TP packet. By using PPP, PPTP can support multiple transport protocols, such as IP, IPX, NetBEUI, and others.

- **Client addressing**—PPTP and L2TP support dynamic addressing of the client using PPP's Network Control Protocol (NCP). As mentioned in the last chapter, the Cisco IKE Mode Config supports a similar function.

To help you understand the inner workings of PPTP, the following sections cover these topics:

- Review of PPP
- PPTP Components
- How PPTP Works
- Issues with the Use of PPTP

PPP Review

Because PPTP leverages the use of PPP, I'll briefly review PPP in this section. PPP originally was designed to transmit data across dialup or point-to-point links. It supports the encapsulation of many Layer-2 and Layer-3 protocols as a transport.

PPP connections will go through four phases when establishing a connection:

1 Link establishment—Phase 1

2 User authentication—Phase 2

3 Callback control—Phase 3

4 Protocol negotiation—Phase 4

The following sections discuss each in turn.

PPTP Phase 1

In phase 1, the Link Control Protocol (LCP) is used to initiate the connection. This includes the negotiation of Layer-2 parameters, such as the use of authentication, compression with MPPC, encryption with MPPE, protocols, and other PPP features—the actual compression or encryption algorithms are negotiated in phase 4.

PPTP Phase 2

In phase 2, the user is authenticated to the server. PPP supports four types of authentication:

- PAP
- CHAP
- MS-CHAPv1
- MS-CHAPv2

The Password Authentication Protocol (PAP) provides clear-text authentication of a user's name and password. This is not secure because it is susceptible to eavesdropping and replay attacks, and therefore is not commonly used. PAP also has a problem with session hijacking.

The Challenge Handshake Authentication Protocol (CHAP), unlike PAP, doesn't send a password between the peers; instead, only the username is sent in clear text. The user's username and password must be listed on the server. The server sends back a random challenge string and a session ID number for the PPP session. Each side takes the challenge, the session ID, and the user's password and runs them through the MD5 HMAC function, producing a digital signature. The user sends the signature to the server, which validates it. Because the password is never sent across the network and a random challenge is used, CHAP protects against replay attacks once the original PPP session is terminated. To increase security, PPP periodically uses CHAP on an existing connection to reduce the likelihood of a session hijacking attack taking place.

An extension of CHAP is the Microsoft Challenge Handshake Authentication Protocol (MS-CHAP). MS-CHAP allows the server to store the digital signature of a user instead of the user's password, providing an additional level of security. MS-CHAP has other enhancements, including password expiration notification, user password changing, additional error codes, and data encryption using MPPE. Therefore, CHAP and MS-CHAP are not compatible with each other. The first implementation of MS-CHAP is referred to as MS-CHAPv1.

Microsoft developed an enhanced version of MS-CHAP called MS-CHAPv2. v2 updated the encrypted authentication process, in which each device needs to authenticate to the other. Through this process, two unidirectional data pipes are established, allowing for a different encryption key for each connection between the peers.

NOTE   The server can store the user's credentials locally, or this can be found on an external server, such as an AAA RADIUS server product.

PPTP Phase 3

Phase 3, an optional phase, provides control of callback functions through the use of the Callback Control Protocol (CBCP). If callback is enabled, once the authentication phase completes, the server disconnects the client and calls the client back based on the phone number the server has in its database for the client. This can be used to provide an extra layer of security, restricting users to use a specific phone to make connections, and reducing the likelihood of access attacks. This phase is performed for dialup clients only.

PPTP Phase 4

In phase 4, the protocols used for the data connection, which were negotiated during phase 1, are invoked. These protocols include IP, IPX, data compression algorithms, encryption algorithms, and others. Once phase 4 completes, data can now be sent across the PPP connection.

PPTP Components

As mentioned in the last section, PPTP uses PPP. However, it doesn't change the PPP protocol; instead, PPP is used to tunnel packets through an IP backbone. PPTP is based on a client-server architecture for remote access connectivity involving two entities:

- The client is commonly referred to as a PPTP Access Concentrator (PAC). The term "concentrator" can be misleading, because in the Cisco world it is commonly used to refer to a device terminating remote access sessions; however, with PPTP, this function can be split between two devices, a PC and a server. Originally this was done to offload the encryption process on a more appropriate device (a concentrator);

however, you can easily combine the two processes (PPP and protection) into a single device, like a PC. The PAC is responsible for establishing a secure connection to a server and tunneling data, via PPP packets, to the server.

- The server is a PPTP Network Server (PNS). The server is responsible for terminating the tunnel from the PAC; it takes the tunneled protected PPP packets, verifies the protection, decrypts the packets, and forwards the encapsulated PPP payload information—for example, an IP packet— to the destination.

The PAC is responsible for initiating a connection to the PNS, using LCP for negotiation, and participating with the PPP authentication process. The PNS is responsible for authenticating the PAC, handling PPP Multilink for channel aggregation and bundle management, terminating the NCP protocols, and routing or bridging the PAC's encapsulated traffic to other locations. The use of multilink is unusual in this situation because it allows the use of multiple PACs to transmit the same data stream to a single PNS.

NOTE   Please note that I use the word "entities" to describe the PAC and PNS, and not "devices." This is because the PAC and PNS describe roles to be played and don't necessarily have to reside in the device initiating or receiving connections. From this perspective, you could view it as an IPsec site-to-site connection or an IPsec remote access network extension mode connection, where the PAC performs the role of the client and PNS performs the role of the gateway.

Two connections are built between the PAC and the PNS:

- A control connection used for call control and management functions. This control connection uses TCP and therefore, both the PAC and PNS must support TCP/IP; however, other protocols can be transported across the data connection.

- A data connection that uses an extended version of the Generic Route Encapsulation (GRE) protocol (this is IP protocol 47). This protocol provides for delivery, flow control, and congestion management of the tunneled PPP packets. The flow control and congestion management implemented for the extended version of GRE are simple in nature; they allow for the efficient use of available bandwidth while avoiding any unnecessary data transmissions because of buffer overruns. PPTP doesn't define the actual algorithms that should be used for these processes, but does define that this information is communicated between the PAC and PNS.

How PPTP Works

This section will provide an overview of how PPTP works. PPTP is a connection-oriented protocol in which the PAC and PNS maintain a state for their connection. This session is created when the PAC initiates a PPP connection to the PNS. Two connections are built for the session: a control connection and a data connection. Once the session is established, the PAC and PNS can use GRE across the data connection to transmit user traffic. Generically, the data connection is called a tunnel.

The following sections will cover these two connections in more depth, and also will cover how a PPTP session is established and used.

Control Connection

The control connection is responsible for establishing, maintaining, and tearing down the data tunnel. It uses TCP as a transport to carry this information with a destination port number of 1,723. This connection can be established either from the PNS or the PAC.

There are two basic types of PPTP messages that can be used in the control connection:

- Control
- Management (this is currently not defined in the RFC)

A magic cookie is included in each control message. It is used to ensure that the sender and receiver are synchronized on the TCP connection. If there is a loss of synchronicity between the PAC and PNS, the TCP connection terminates immediately.

Setting Up the Control Connection

The setup of the control connection encompasses the exchange of two initial messages:

- Start-Control-Connection-Request
- Start-Control-Connection-Reply

The initiator sends the first message while the receiver responds with the second one. Table 4-1 describes the results that can be included in the reply message. Besides initiating the connection, these messages allow the PAC to share capability information with the PNS. Each PNS/PAC pair requires a separate control connection.

Table 4-1   *Start-Control-Connection-Reply Results*

Code	Description
1	Control connection successfully established
2	General error
3	Control connection already exists
4	The requestor is not authorized to establish a control connection to the receiver
5	The requestor's protocol version is not supported

Because both the PNS and PAC can initiate a control connection, there is a possibility of a collision if both try to do it simultaneously; only one control connection can exist between the PAC and PNS. A collision occurs when both the PAC and PNS simultaneously send Start-Control-Connection-Request messages. In this situation, the initiator with the highest IP address (compared as a 32-bit number) is used and the other control connection is immediately terminated.

Because there are different control versions, there is a possibility that one peer has a higher version than the other. In this case, one of two things will occur on the receiver:

- If the receiver's version is higher or the same, it will use the lower version of the sender and send back a Start-Control-Connection-Reply message and continue with the building of the connection.

- If the receiver's version is lower and it cannot support the requested version, it will send a Start-Control-Connection-Reply message and terminate the TCP connection; at this point, it is up to the sender to use a compatible version with the receiver when re-initiating the connection.

Maintaining the Control Connection

Keepalives are used on the control connection to ensure that connectivity exists between the PAC and PNS, and that any failure of either two devices can be quickly detected. There are two types of keepalive messages for the control connection:

- Echo-Request
- Echo-Reply

Both the PAC and PNS can initiate keepalives. Keepalive messages are generated if no type of control message is received from a peer in 60 seconds. If a PAC/PNS doesn't receive an Echo-Reply in response to its request, the control connection will be terminated.

Terminating the Control Connection

The control connection is also responsible for terminating any data connections and for the control connection itself. To terminate the control connection, two messages are used:

- Stop-Control-Connection-Request
- Stop-Control-Connection-Reply

Both the PAC and PNS can initiate the teardown process of the control connection. Whenever the control connection is terminated, any data (user) connections are also terminated automatically. Table 4-2 lists some reasons why the control connection might be terminated. The next section covers the data (tunnel) connection.

Table 4-2 *Stop-Control-Connection-Request Reasons*

Code	Description
1	General teardown request
2	The peer's version of the protocol can't be supported
3	The sender of the request message is being shut down

NOTE   If an invalid or misconfigured control message is received, the correct information should be logged and the control connection is automatically terminated and rebuilt to recover from the error.

Tunnel Connection

The tunnel carries all user session PPP packets. GRE is used as the transport protocol for the PPP packets. The control connection determines the actual rate and buffering parameters to use to ensure that the PAC/PNS do not create flow-control problems. Other parameters that need to be negotiated are the PAC address assignment, the encryption algorithm to use, and the use of compression, if any. The following sections will discuss how the user's data is encapsulated and transported across the tunnel.

Setting Up the Tunnel Connection

Once the Start-Control-Connection-Request and Start-Connection-Reply messages have been exchanged for the control connection, the setup of the tunnel (data) connection is next. The following messages are possibly involved in this process:

- Outgoing-Call-Request
- Outgoing-Call-Reply
- Incoming-Call-Request
- Incoming-Call-Reply
- Incoming-Call-Connected

NOTE   I don't like the use of the term "call" in these messages, since most people would equate it with the use of telephone calls. Remember that PPP is being used here, which is normally a dialup solution, so a lot of PPP's implementation and nomenclature are found here when dealing with PPP and PPTP. The term "session" would be a more precise term, or perhaps "tunnel" in the loosest sense.

Outgoing calls are messages generated by the PNS to the PAC, telling the PAC to establish a tunnel to the PNS. This connection also provides information concerning the regulation of data transmitted across the tunnel from the PAC to the PNS, such as windowing information. The outgoing reply is sent from the PAC to the PNS, with the possible results in the reply listed in Table 4-3. An interesting point about the information for the result codes is that many of these are related to telephony, which is where PPP is typically used. For most situations, only codes 1, 2, 6, and 7 are used because the PAC functionality is built directly into the actual client instead of an intermediate device.

Table 4-3 *Outgoing-Call-Reply Results*

Code	Brief Description	Detailed Description
1	Connected	The tunnel is established with no errors
2	General error	The tunnel could not be established based on the error value in the error code field
3	No carrier	The tunnel could not be established because no carrier was detected
4	Busy	A busy signal was detected, causing the tunnel to fail
5	No dial tone	The outgoing call failed because no dial tone was detected
6	Time-out	The PAC didn't establish the tunnel within the required amount of time
7	Do not accept	The outgoing call was administratively denied

TIP According to the RFC, the outgoing call request is made from the PNS to the PAC; however, my experience with Microsoft's implementation is that it is the reverse: The PAC initiates the outgoing call request to the PNS. A key, called a caller ID value, is placed in the tunnel packet header to indicate which session a PPP packet belongs to because PPP can multiplex traffic across multiple sessions. This value is negotiated during the call setup process on the control connection.

The Incoming-Call-Request message is sent by the PAC to the PNS to indicate that an inbound call is to be established from the PAC to the PNS. This message allows the PNS to obtain information about the call before it is answered or accepted. The Incoming-Call-Reply message is sent from the PNS to the PAC, replying to the acceptance or denial of the connection request. This message can also contain flow control information the PAC should use in tunnel communications to the PNS. Table 4-4 shows the possible results from the PNS.

Table 4-4   *Incoming-Call-Reply Results*

Code	Description
1	The PAC should answer the incoming call
2	The incoming call can't be established based on the error value in the Error Code field
3	The PAC should not accept the incoming call

The Incoming-Call-Connected message is sent from the PAC to the PNS in response to the reply. Therefore, incoming calls use a three-way handshake: request, reply, and connected.

Encapsulating the Payload

GRE is used to carry the PPP packets between the PAC and PNS. Figure 4-1 shows an example of a PPTP packet. As you can see, the PPP packet is encapsulated in a GRE packet, which, in turn, is encapsulated in an IP packet. The PPP packet contains the actual user data which is some protocol packet such as IP, IPX, or another type.

Figure 4-1   *PPTP Tunnel Packet*

The GRE header used to encapsulate the PPP packet is not a standard GRE header, but has been enhanced slightly for PPTP. The main difference between the standard GRE header and the PPTP GRE header is that the PPTP GRE header has a new acknowledgment number field, which is used to determine whether or not a GRE packet(s) has been received by the tunnel endpoint. This GRE acknowledgment process has nothing to do with the actual user data packets; instead, it is used to determine packet rates for packets transmitted via the tunnel. In other words, PPTP uses a sliding window protocol for flow control of the tunneled packets by using the sequence and acknowledgment fields. The window size can be changed dynamically throughout the tunnel's lifetime. PPTP will not retransmit packets that are lost or that arrive outside the window time frame: this is the responsibility of the source device.

Maintaining the Tunnel Connection

The tunnel connection parameters, such as windowing, are negotiated when the tunnel connection is built. Likewise, the parameters can be changed for the tunnel based on current network conditions. The PAC and PNS use a Set-Link-Info message to share tunnel operation parameters. Typically, the PNS sends this message to the PAC to indicate any tunnel/PPP configuration changes.

Tearing Down a Tunnel Connection

When a tunnel connection is no longer needed, it is torn down by the PPTP devices. Two messages are exchanged to handle the teardown process:

- Call-Clear-Request
- Call-Disconnect-Notify

Both the PAC and PNS can initiate a teardown of the tunnel connection. The Call-Clear-Request message is sent from the requestor, signaling that the tunnel connection is being cleared (torn down). The receiver responds with a Call-Disconnect-Notify message, indicating the status of the tunnel clear request.

Example PPTP Connection

Now that I've explained the basic process and messages used to set up a PPTP connection, I'll go through a simple example of a PPTP connection being built, maintained, and then torn down in the following sections.

Here's a brief overview of the setup of a typical PPTP session:

1 The PAC connects to the PNS using TCP on port 1723.

2 The PAC sends a Start-Control-Connection-Request message.

3 The PNS responds with a Start-Control-Connection-Reply message.

4 The PAC sends an Outgoing-Call-Request message, including a caller ID to identify the PAC for the tunnel, to request a tunnel connection from the PNS.

5 The PNS responds with an Outgoing-Call-Reply message to the PAC and selects its own caller ID for the tunnel.

6 The PAC sends a Set-Link-Info message, specifying the PPP options it wants to use for the tunnel.

7 Once the tunnel is up, other Set-Link-Info messages can be shared to change parameters such as window size.

If no messages are received on the control connection for 60 seconds, the PNS (typically) will send Echo-Request messages to the PAC; and assuming the PAC is reachable, the PAC will respond with an Echo-Reply message. These messages are used to ensure that the tunnel endpoints are still alive and reachable.

Eventually the tunnel connection is torn down. Some common reasons for tearing down a tunnel (and control connection) include:

- Reachability problems have been found.
- An error condition exists.
- The PAC or PNS is shutting down.
- The tunnel is no longer needed.

Here is an example of a PAC terminating its PPTP session to a PNS:

1 The PAC first sends a Set-Link-Info message with the configuration parameters of the tunnel and then sends an LCP termination request to the PNS, indicating that the PPP session should be closed.

2 In response, the PNS first sends a Set-Link-Info message with the configuration parameters of the tunnel and then sends an LCP acknowledgement to the LCP termination request.

3 The PAC sends a Clear-Call-Request message to its associated PAC.

4 The PNS responds back with a Call-Disconnected-Notify message to the PAC. At this point the tunnel is terminated.

5 The PAC sends a Stop-Control-Connection-Request message to the PNS.

6 The PNS responds with a Stop-Control-Connection-Reply message. At this point, the TCP control connection has been terminated and the PPTP session no longer exists between the PAC and PNS.

Issues with the Use of PPTP

As in any VPN implementation, you'll have to deal with certain issues for PPTP to perform optimally and with minimal problems. Here are some common issues you'll need to deal with:

- Fragmentation problems
- Security concerns
- Address translation issues

The following sections will address these issues.

Fragmentation Problems

The MTU of the PPP information that is encapsulated in GRE is 1,532 bytes. On top of this, you have the GRE and the IP headers. The GRE header is 16 bytes in length and the IP header is between 20 and 60 bytes, depending on whether or not the IP Options field is used. Therefore, the total length of a PPTP tunneled packet could be 1,608 bytes. And this doesn't even count the outer Layer-2 header. If Ethernet II was used, you would need to add an additional 20 bytes, totaling 1,628. Of course, if it was a dialup connection, you would have to consider the overhead of the PPP data-link protocol to transport the PPTP information between the client and ISP access server.

Because most devices use an MTU size of 1,500 bytes, this can cause these devices to have to fragment each PPTP packet across two frames. This is a very undesirable result, because not only is encryption being done by PPTP, but now there is fragmentation of the protected packets, and the destination has to reassemble the fragments into complete packets and then decrypt them.

More than 60 percent of the throughput problems I've dealt with concerning VPNs have dealt with fragmentation problems. Therefore, you'll definitely want to adjust your PAC's and PNS's MTU size to a better size. Many vendors suggest 1,300 bytes to play it safe; but you could probably increase this to 1,320 or 1,340 and be okay. However, you will definitely want to monitor your PPTP connection to ensure that fragmentation is not occurring.

Security Concerns

There are three security concerns you should consider when using PPTP:

- Session hijacking and data manipulation of the control connection
- No protection for the IP, GRE, and PPP header information
- Weak encryption

There is no security protection for the TCP control connection used by PPTP: the messages sent between the PAC and PNS have no authentication or data integrity check. Therefore, it is susceptible to data manipulation and session hijacking attacks. For example, an attacker could create fake control messages or alter valid ones while the messages are in transit between the PAC and PNS. Likewise, an attacker could execute a session hijacking attack, taking over the control connection and pretending to be the PAC, PNS, or both.

Another security concern is that the IP, GRE, and PPP header information is not protected in the tunnel connection. Therefore it is possible for an attacker to eavesdrop on the tunnel connection and modify these, or hijack the session (as is the case with the control connection).

CAUTION   Be aware that only the PPP payload is encrypted with PPTP: any other information, such as the control connection and the headers of the tunnel connection, are *not* protected. Plus, MPPE supports RC-40 and RC-128 for encryption, both of which are known to be vulnerable.

Address Translation Issues

Address translation can pose a problem with the use of PPTP. There are two general types of translation: NAT and PAT. NAT poses no problems for both the control and tunnel connections because the headers in these are not protected by an HMAC function, and NAT changes only source or destination IP addresses.

However, PAT can create problems. Because the control connection uses TCP, and the TCP header isn't protected, the control connection easily can be established through an address translation device performing PAT. The same cannot be said about the tunnel connection. Because the tunnel connection uses GRE, a Layer-3 protocol, and GRE doesn't have port numbers, PAT doesn't work.

Some vendors have implemented proprietary solutions to get around this problem. Most vendors will use the caller ID field in the GRE header to denote different connections.

However, if more than one device was using the same caller ID in the tunnel header, the address translation device would have to translate the caller ID values to ensure uniqueness. This performs a similar function to what PAT does with TCP or UDP port numbers. Remember that not all address translation devices support this function, and your PPTP connections might break when going through address translation devices.

NOTE PPTP isn't used much anymore because of security concerns regarding MS-CHAPv1 and MS-CHAPv2 being needed as part of the MPPE generation process; moreover, its two encryption algorithms are known to be vulnerable.

The Simplicity of PPTP

One of my favorite VPN implementations is PPTP. It's not my favorite because it's more secure; on the contrary, VPN implementations such as IPsec, L2TP/IPsec, and SSL are more secure. However, of all of the VPN implementations I discuss in this book, PPTP is the easiest to set up and troubleshoot. If you recall my sidebar discussion from Chapter 3, "IPsec," my first experience with IPsec was a hair-pulling one. With PPTP, I was able to set up a similar remote access VPN implementation with no problems; and any problems I experienced were easy to diagnose and fix. Plus, the PPTP software is included with both the Microsoft client (older Windows platforms) and RAS solutions, simplifying your deployment; you don't have to buy additional expensive hardware to implement it.

However, my main complaint about PPTP and L2TP/IPsec is that they both lack a lot of the remote access functionality that Cisco proprietary IPsec remote access features provide, like IKE Mode Config and reverse route injection. The more control I have over a client's VPN connection, the safer I feel. The trade-off, though, is that IPsec is, of course, much more difficult to set up and troubleshoot. Another complaint is that if you're using a purely Microsoft environment with a RAS performing the PPTP or L2TP/IPsec server function, the Microsoft solution scales poorly. And my last, most major complaint is that its encryption is weak by today's standards: RC-4 40-bit and 128-bit encryption can be cracked.

L2TP

L2TP is a combination of PPTP and L2F. It is defined in RFCs 2661 and 3438. L2TP took the best of both PPTP and L2F and integrated them into a single protocol. Like PPTP, L2TP uses PPP to encapsulate user data, allowing the multiple protocols to be sent across a tunnel. L2TP, like PPTP, extends the PPP protocol. As an additional security enhancement, L2TP can be placed in the payload of an IPsec packet, combining the security advantages of IPsec and the benefits of user authentication, tunnel address assignment and configuration, and multiple protocol support with PPP. This combination is commonly referred to as L2TP over IPsec or L2TP/IPsec. The remainder of this chapter is devoted to an overview of L2TP, how it is implemented, and the advantages it has over PPTP.

L2TP Overview

L2TP, like PPTP, encapsulates data in PPP frames and transmits these frames across an IP backbone. Unlike PPTP, L2TP uses UDP as an encapsulation method for both tunnel maintenance and user data. Whereas PPTP uses MPPE for encryption (this is negotiated via PPP), L2TP relies on a more secure solution: L2TP packets are protected by IPsec's ESP using transport mode. Even though you can use L2TP without IPsec, the main issue with this approach is that L2TP itself doesn't perform encryption and therefore needs to rely on something else. Therefore, most L2TP implementation will include the use of IPsec.

TIP	The only time I would use L2TP without IPsec was if I was trying to troubleshoot a connection where I didn't know if the problem was IPsec-related or L2TP-related; by removing IPsec from the equation, I could focus on just the L2TP VPN component.

L2TP is a remote access solution. It consists of two devices: a client and a server. Tunnel maintenance and the tunnel data used between these two devices use the same packet structure, simplifying L2TP's implementation.

Until IPsec introduced XAUTH for user authentication, the only standards-based method of performing user authentication was PPTP and then L2TP. And even now, XAUTH is still in an IETF-RFC draft state, so one vendor's implementation might not be compatible with another's. One of the main concerns with remote access VPNs is who actually is using the device to obtain connectivity. Certificates and pre-shared key information typically are stored on the client; therefore, if someone gains access to the client device, or steals the client device, authentication is defeated. Authenticating the user who is actually using the device is important, which is why many VPN implementations authenticate the users themselves. L2TP allows for many types of user authentication including legacy methods such as PAP, CHAP or MS-CHAP, and current authentication services such as EAP (and its derivatives).

As I mentioned in the last chapter, Cisco uses a proprietary method of assigning addressing and policy information to remote access clients during IKE Mode Config in IPsec. L2TP has standardized this process by using DHCP to handle address assignment. DHCP supports standardized features such as address assignment, failover, address pool management, and even address authentication.

NOTE	If you work in a Microsoft-only shop, your VPN implementation of choice will be L2TP/IPsec. Microsoft pushes this standard heavily over PPTP or IPsec. As mentioned in the last chapter, many vendors enhance IPsec for remote access connectivity, including Cisco. This can create vendor interoperability problems if you want to use one vendor's solution for the client side and another for the server side. By using L2TP/IPsec for remote access VPNs, you can feel fairly safe that no matter what vendor you're using for the client or server, they should be compatible with each other.

L2TP Operation

This section provides an overview of the components of L2TP and how it works. I'll quickly review IPsec, because L2TP relies on this standard to provide for data encryption and protection, and then discuss the L2TP components and the encapsulation they use.

Setting up an L2TP tunnel consists of two steps to tunnel PPP user frames for a session:

1 Establish a control connection for the tunnel.

2 Establish a session to transmit user data across the tunnel.

The following sections will discuss the components that are used to accomplish these two steps.

IPsec Review

As mentioned in the last chapter, IPsec is a Layer-3 protocol that can protect IP packets at Layer-3 and higher. Besides defining data protection processes such as data integrity and authentication with HMAC functions, and data confidentiality with encryption algorithms, IPsec also defines the format of packets (fields) and how the packets are transported (tunnel and transport mode). Tunnel mode is used for site-to-site and remote access connections, whereas transport mode is used for specific point-to-point connections. In tunnel mode, IPsec protects the entire original packet.

Even given its wide acceptance and use, IPsec does have its limitations:

- IPsec only works with TCP/IP; other protocols will not work unless they are tunneled using GRE.

- Parameters are negotiated between the two peers; a mismatch in the parameters typically causes the connection to abort.

- Because IPsec functions at the network layer, all higher-layer protocols and applications have to accept the policies applied to the IPsec connection between two devices; there is no granular process of treating the upper layers differently from each other.

NOTE	Even though AH is also supported with L2TP/IPsec, it is not commonly used because of address translation issues. These issues were discussed in Chapter 3, "IPsec."

Tunnel Types

With L2TP, there are two tunnel types:

- **Voluntary**—The user's PC and the server are the endpoints of the tunnel.
- **Compulsory**—The user's PC is not the endpoint of the tunnel; instead, some other device in front of the user's PC, such as an access server, acts as the tunnel endpoint (this would be similar to using a hardware client instead of a software client).

With a voluntary tunnel, the remote access client runs the L2TP/IPsec software and creates the VPN connection to a server. This works in situations where the user is either using a dialup connection to reach the server or is using its LAN NIC.

With a compulsory tunnel, another device, on behalf of the user, is responsible for setting up the tunnel. The device that initiates the tunnel is commonly called an L2TP Access Concentrator (LAC); in PPTP, this is called a Front End Process (FEP). The server is commonly called an L2TP Network Server (LNS). Because the client is required to use the tunnel created by the LAC/FEP, the tunnel is called "compulsory."

NOTE	Please note that the L2TP FEP is not an IBM FEP for mainframes, but is used to terminate L2TP tunnel connections. Whoever came up with this term for L2TP should have picked a different one, since this can confuse networking people who have been in the field for a long time.
	Also, in voluntary mode, the LAC functionality is built into the software of the user's PC.

Normally, LAC/FEPs are used in situations where a company doesn't want to handle L2TP functionality on its users' desktops, but wants to contract the L2TP VPN client-side out to an ISP. The users will use dialup or PPPoE to establish a PPP connection to the ISP. The ISP device will be a LAC/FEP and the ISP will be responsible for tunneling the PPP traffic to the corporate office's LNS. An example of this is shown in Figure 4-2.

Figure 4-2 *L2TP Compulsory Tunnel*

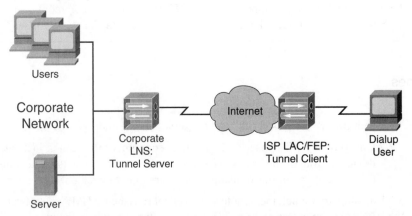

The LAC/FEP typically has the capability of tunneling traffic to a particular destination based on either the phone number the user dials or the username of the user. Based on either of these two methods, the ISP will know which LNS tunnel connection to use (in the case where the ISP is providing this service to multiple customers). The first user that dials into the ISP will cause the LAC/FEP to bring up the tunnel to the LNS at the user's corporate office. All other dialup clients for this corporation connecting to the same LAC/FEP will use the same tunnel. Once all users have disconnected their dialup connections from the ISP, the LAC/FEP will terminate the tunnel to the corporate office LNS.

NOTE   As you can see from this explanation, compulsory tunnel mode extends the PPP termination points from the user's desktop all the way through to the LNS, even though the user's initial PPP connection is terminated on the LAC.

IPsec Tunnel

Because L2TP uses IPsec as a transport, IPsec connectivity must first be established between the LAC and LNS. First, an ISAKMP/IKE management connection must be built; second, an ESP transport mode data connection must be built. L2TP information is then encapsulated in the ESP payload, as shown in Figure 4-3.

Given that IPsec is used as a transport, you'll need to configure ISAKMP/IKE phase 1 and 2 for your LAC and LNS. This was discussed in Chapter 3, "IPsec." Of course, because L2TP is handling remote access policy functions, you wouldn't have to worry about XAUTH, IKE Mode Config, and RRI.

Figure 4-3 *L2TP Encapsulation*

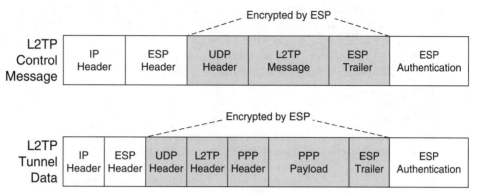

L2TP Control Messages

As mentioned in the first half of the chapter, PPTP uses two connections: a TCP connection for control functions and a GRE connection for tunneling user data. L2TP uses a simpler approach: a single connection is used to transmit both control information and user data. This connection uses UDP and both the LAC and LNS use port 1,701 for the source and destination port numbers.

A typical L2TP control packet is shown in the top part of Figure 4-3. ESP, in transport mode, is used by IPsec to share L2TP messages and user data between devices. When the LAC and LNS need to build, maintain, or tear down a tunnel connection, the ESP IPsec Phase 2 data connection is used. Notice that the UDP header with a source and destination port number of 1,701, the L2TP message, and the ESP trailer are encrypted by ESP and that optionally, ESP authentication can be used to verify the origin of the packet and that the ESP components of the IP packet haven't been tampered with.

With PPTP, a TCP connection is used to exchange control messages. TCP ensures a reliable delivery of PPTP control messages. Because L2TP relies on UDP for delivery of control messages, L2TP uses an additional process to ensure the delivery of control messages. Within an L2TP control message there is a Next-Received field. This field serves a similar function as the Acknowledgment field in a TCP header. Another field, Next-Sent, serves a similar function as the Sequence Number field in a TCP header. These fields can be used for sequencing and flow control of control messages and tunneled packets; however, any out-of-sequence control messages received are automatically dropped.

L2TP uses, for the most part, the same control messages that PPTP uses. Table 4-5 contains a list of these messages; this is not an all-inclusive list, but lists the most common ones. As you can see from the description of the messages, L2TP is connection-oriented; the LNS and LAC maintain state information for each control and tunnel call. Also, each session between an LAC and LNS will have a unique Tunnel-ID. This ID value is used to differentiate different tunnel connections between the LNS and different LACs. When the tunnel is a compulsory tunnel, each user session through the tunnel is assigned a unique Call-ID (Session-ID) value. This is used to differentiate the different users (PPP sessions) that are using the LAC to connect to the LNS through the tunnel. In the case of where the user's PC contains the LAC function, this will be a single session value; however, if the user is connecting to a LAC, which, in turn, provides the L2TP/IPsec connection to the LNS, each user's PPP session will have a different session value.

Table 4-5   *L2TP Control Messages*

Message	Description
Start-Control-Connection-Request	The L2TP client sends this to the server to establish the control connection; this also includes the Tunnel-ID value that will be used to uniquely identify the session; this message can also be used to indicate a version mismatch, requiring a re-initiation of the connection.
Start-Control-Connection-Reply	The L2TP server sends this message in reply to a Start-Control-Connection-Request message.
Start-Control-Connection-Connected	The L2TP client sends this to the L2TP server after receiving the Start-Control-Connection-Reply, indicating that the tunnel was successfully established.
Outgoing-Call-Request	The L2TP client sends this to create the data tunnel. It also includes a Call-ID, which is used to keep track of each session within the tunnel—this situation would occur in compulsory tunnel mode where many dialup clients are using the same LAC. The Call-ID value is commonly referred to as a Session-ID value.
Outgoing-Call-Reply	The L2TP server acknowledges the receipt of the Outgoing-Call-Request message; after receiving this, the L2TP client responds with a Start-Control-Connection-Connected message.
Set-Link-Info	This is used by the L2TP client and server to negotiate or change the PPP connection parameters.
Hello	This is used by the L2TP client and server as a keepalive mechanism. When a hello is sent, an acknowledgment is expected from the other device; if it isn't acknowledged within a period of time, the tunnel is terminated.
WAN-Error-Notify	This is sent by the L2TP server to all L2TP clients, indicating an error condition on its PPP interface.
Call-Disconnect-Notify	Both the L2TP client and server can generate this message, indicating that a connection within a tunnel (Call-ID) is being terminated.
Stop-Control-Connection-Notification	Both the L2TP client and server can generate this message, indicating that the entire L2TP tunnel is to be torn down.

L2TP User Data Tunnel

As mentioned in the last section, the same connection is used by the control and data functions for L2TP. The bottom part of Figure 4-3 shows the encapsulation method used for user traffic across an L2TP/IPsec connection. You'll notice that the user data is encompassed in a PPP packet, and then an L2TP and UDP header (source and destination ports of 1,701) are added. This, in turn, is encapsulated in an ESP packet and protected.

When an L2TP/IPsec packet is received by the destination, the IP header is first removed and the digital signature in the ICV trailer of the ESP packet is validated (assuming that packet authentication is used). If the signature is valid, then the L2TP contents are decrypted. The UDP header is processed and the L2TP packet is forwarded to the L2TP process on the device. L2TP looks at both the Tunnel-ID and Call-ID values to determine the specific L2TP tunnel that will handle the packet. Once the tunnel is determined, the PPP header is used to identify the type of payload information in the PPP payload and forward this encapsulated information, such as an IP packet, to the proper protocol stack for further processing.

NOTE Because IPsec is used as the transport, you'll face the same kinds of problems with firewalls and address translation devices when using L2TP/IPsec. These issues and solutions were discussed in Chapter 3.

CAUTION For compulsory tunnel connections, the actual dialup client could negotiate MPPE (encryption) with the ISP LAC. In most cases this is probably not desirable. If you use this option, the LNS will have to decrypt *two* things: the ESP packet and the PPP payload. Therefore, this option is not recommended.

L2TP/IPsec Versus PPTP

In this section I'll compare L2TP and PPTP so that you have a better understanding of the advantages and disadvantages of the two protocols for remote access solutions. I'll first examine some basic differences between the two protocols and then examine the advantages that each protocol has.

Protocol Differences

There are quite a few differences between PPTP and L2TP/IPsec. However, I'll only focus on three of them:

- Encryption process
- Encryption algorithms
- User authentication

With PPTP, only the PPP payload is encrypted; the outer header is sent in clear text. L2TP/IPsec, on the other hand, encrypts the entire L2TP message (control or data). PPTP uses MPPE to encrypt the PPP payload. MPPE uses RSA's RC-4 encryption algorithm, which supports 40-, 56-, and 128-bit encryption keys (only the first and last are typically implemented for PPTP). L2TP/IPsec supports DES (56-bit keys), 3DES (168-bit keys), and AES (128-, 192-, and 256-bit keys) encryption algorithms.

It has been proven that RC-4 can be cracked. The same applies to DES with IPsec; however, this has not been proven with 3DES and AES, making them a more secure encryption choice.

With PPTP, user authentication is accomplished using only PPP's authentication method. L2TP supports this, in addition to device authentication supported by IPsec, such as pre-shared keys or digital certificates (RSA signatures).

PPTP Advantages

Here are some advantages that PPTP has over L2TP/IPsec:

- PPTP is a much simpler protocol than L2TP/IPsec and is thus easier to set up and troubleshoot.
- PPTP can also be used with Windows 95 systems and higher. L2TP is supported only on Windows 2000, XP, and 2003 systems.

Note	Microsoft has released a third-party client for 95, 98, and NT for L2TP/IPsec support, which is free, whereas originally L2TP/IPsec was supported only for 2000, XP, and 2003.

- PPTP clients and servers can be placed between NAT devices, and, possibly, PAT devices, if the PAT device maps caller-ID values for different devices. L2TP/IPsec also works with NAT, but breaks with PAT unless NAT-T, IPsec over TCP, or some other vendor-proprietary method is used. The IPsec methods require special configuration on the IPsec devices, whereas this is not true with PPTP.

L2TP/IPsec Advantages

Here are some advantages that L2TP/IPsec has over PPTP:

- IPsec supports stronger authentication through the use of certificates or EAP than PPP's PAP/CHAP/MS-CHAP.
- IPsec can provide for data authentication, data integrity, data confidentiality, and replay protection, whereas PPTP only provides for data confidentiality.
- IPsec encrypts the entire PPP packet in all cases. PPTP doesn't encrypt the initial LCP negotiation; therefore, it is more susceptible to session hijacking or session replay attacks.

Summary

This chapter showed you the basics of L2TP and PPTP VPNs. Both have their roots in Microsoft's VPN initiative. PPTP was Microsoft's first VPN implementation, and mostly was an enhanced version of PPP. However, PPTP lacked many security features and thus was combined with the Cisco L2F into L2TP.

Because L2TP doesn't provide for security services such as confidentiality and packet authentication and validation, IPsec is used as a transport. I'll discuss more about how to implement L2TP/IPsec and PPTP remote access VPNs in Chapter 8, "Concentrator Remote Access Connections with PPTP, L2TP, and WebVPN" and Chapter 13, "Windows VPN Client."

Next up is Chapter 5, "SSL VPNs," in which I discuss SSL and its use in implementing VPNs.

CHAPTER 5

SSL VPNs

Chapter 3 discussed IPsec VPNs, and Chapter 4 discussed PPTP and L2TP VPNs. All three of these VPN implementations provide network layer protection; they can protect traffic from the network layer and higher. However, one of their downsides is that they require special software to be installed on the client device, and possible user training on how to use the software.

Some companies want a solution that is more simple to use and more easy to maintain than the three I just mentioned. Secure Socket Layer (SSL) began as a protocol to protect web (HTTP) traffic between an end-user device and a web server. Normally, it is used to provide protection for online purchases and identity information at e-commerce sites such as Cisco Press and Cisco. However, many network vendors are leveraging SSL's capabilities and using SSL to implement VPN solutions. One main advantage that SSL VPNs have over the other three is that SSL VPNs require no VPN software, by default, to be installed on the user's desktop; a currently installed web browser is used. Using a web browser allows a user to access a central site securely from both corporate and non-corporate PCs. The remainder of this chapter will focus on the use of SSL for VPN implementations.

SSL Overview

SSL is an emerging VPN implementation in the marketplace. It was designed for remote access solutions and does not provide site-to-site connections. SSL VPNs provide secure access primarily to web-based applications. Because SSL uses a web browser, users typically do not have to load any special client software on their desktops.

SSL VPNs operate at the session layer of the OSI Reference Model. And because the client is a web browser, only those applications that support a web browser, by default, will work with a VPN solution. Therefore, applications such as Telnet, FTP, SMTP, POP3, multimedia, IP telephony, remote desktop control, and others don't work with SSL VPNs because they don't use a web browser for their front-end user interface. Of course, many vendors use either Java or ActiveX to enhance SSL VPNs by supporting non-HTTP applications, POP3 and SMTP e-mail clients, and Microsoft Windows file and print sharing. For example, the Cisco SSL VPN implementation supports non-web-based applications such as Citrix, Windows Terminal Services, and many others. Plus, some vendors use Java or ActiveX to deliver other SSL VPN components, such as additional security functions for removing any traces from the PC of a user's activity after the SSL VPN has been terminated, in addition to others. Cisco refers to their SSL VPN implementation as *WebVPN*.

NOTE   Be aware that each networking vendor has a list of non-HTTP applications that it supports. Therefore, you should scrutinize a vendor's SSL VPN offering carefully and compare this to your users' needs before choosing between different SSL VPN vendors. In some cases, a vendor might even offer full tunneling of network-level traffic via an SSL VPN, making the solution more similar to the capabilities of a Layer-3 VPN implementation such as IPsec.

SSL Client Implementations

A main reason that network administrators like the appeal that SSL VPN implementations offer is that SSL VPNs don't require any special kind of VPN client software to be pre-installed on the user's desktop. Of course, the user does need some software, like an SSL-enabled web browser, typically with either Java or ActiveX enabled; and the user probably already has these things installed from an initial desktop installation.

There are three general types of SSL client implementations:

- Clientless
- Thin client
- Network client

Because only a web browser is required on the user's desktop, the SSL VPN client is commonly referred to as "clientless" (not quite true, of course) or "webified." Therefore, SSL VPNs are sometimes called clientless VPNs or Web VPNs when only a web browser is used for the SSL VPN. The main drawback of a clientless VPN is that only web-based traffic can be protected.

A thin client typically is Java or ActiveX software downloaded via the SSL VPN to the user's desktop. It allows a small subset of non-web applications to be transported across the SSL VPN. The process of transporting non-web applications across an SSL VPN is sometimes referred to as "port forwarding." The initial Cisco WebVPN implementation supported this feature.

For network-based access, an SSL client is required to be installed on the user's desktop; however, this typically is downloaded dynamically to the user's desktop when he establishes the initial SSL VPN to the central site. With network-based access, most network-layer traffic can be protected by the SSL VPN, which is similar to what other network-based VPN implementations do. Because an SSL client needs to be installed to provide network-level protection, the user must have administrative rights on the PC he is using; without administrative rights, the user will be restricted to a thin client or clientless connection, depending on the vendor's SSL VPN implementation.

TIP	Because the network-based SSL client typically requires the user to have administrative rights to install and use the client, a thin client might be a better solution, because a thin client can be developed with Java or ActiveX code that can be downloaded to the web browser during the initial SSL VPN connection. However, the number of non-web applications supported will be limited. For thin client support, I would definitely scrutinize the non-web applications a vendor supports before choosing a solution.

SSL Protection

In the next few sections I'll discuss some of the features of SSL VPNs: how they provide protection for traffic, methods of authentication and encryption, and content access control. If you recall from Chapter 3, "IPsec," and Chapter 4, "PPTP and L2TP," these VPN implementations provide network-layer (Layer-3) protection. IPsec provides protection for all kinds of IP traffic, whereas the other two, because they use PPP, can provide protection for multiple network-layer protocols.

SSL VPNs don't necessarily provide network-layer protection of data, as IPsec, PPTP, and L2TP do. Clientless SSL VPNs provide session layer protection (Layer-5) for a web-based application that uses a web browser. Therefore, its use in protecting traffic is somewhat limited; for application traffic to be protected, somehow the user's access to the application must be through a web browser. Of course, any HTTP-type connection can easily be protected because the user uses a web browser for this type of function; but this can present problems for other types of applications, such as Telnet, POP3, SMTP, SNMP, ping, traceroute, FTP, IP telephony, Citrix, Oracle's SQL*net, file and print sharing via Windows or Unix, any many, many others. SSL VPN vendors typically have to write special code in either Java or ActiveX for their VPN gateways to allow non-browser applications to actually use the SSL VPN connection between the user's desktop and the SSL VPN gateway device. This code is typically downloaded dynamically from the SSL VPN gateway to the user's desktop when the user brings up the SSL VPN connection.

I'm constantly asked about the difference between IPsec and SSL VPNs. My answer is always that:

- IPsec provides protection for IP packets and protocols transmitted between networks or hosts.
- SSL VPNs provide protection for users' access to services and applications on a network.

I'll use Figure 5-1 to illustrate the basic difference in the protection that IPsec and SSL VPNs provide for remote access connections.

Figure 5-1 *IPsec and SSL VPN Implementations*

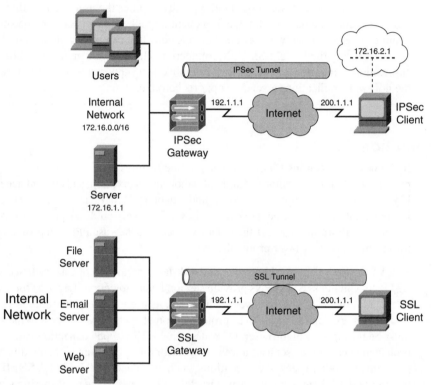

The top part of Figure 5-1 shows an IPsec remote access VPN. In this example, the IPsec remote access client is an *extension* of the network on the left-hand side. The remote access client has two addresses: one for communicating to the IPsec gateway and one for communicating to the internal devices (internal address). As you can see from this example, the client's internal address is associated with the internal network and therefore, from the internal network's perspective, it appears that the client is directly connected to this network.

An SSL clientless VPN implementation example is shown in the bottom part of Figure 5-1. In this example, notice that the SSL client doesn't have two addresses and therefore, from the corporate office's perspective, appears to be *external* to the network. On top of this, only certain applications are supported for this vendor's implementation: web access, webified e-mail server access, and file and print sharing access. The last two applications are vendor-specific and typically require a thin or network-based client; for example, Cisco supports Lotus Notes and port-forwarding of a limited number of non-web applications such as Telnet with their thin client. In the next three sections I'll discuss how SSL VPNs can provide protection and control over your users' traffic.

NOTE   It's worth noting that the lines between SSL VPNs and network-based solutions, such as IPsec, are blurring. Many SSL VPN vendors are adding network-based support to their implementation; however, this process has a downside. An SSL client either has to be pre-installed on a user's desktop (typically done when the user doesn't have administrative rights on the PC) or dynamically installed when the user brings up the SSL VPN connection.

SSL Authentication

Like other VPN implementations, SSL VPNs offer authentication and access control features. If you recall from Chapter 3, IPsec can perform both device and user authentication. Device authentication is handled using pre-shared keys, RSA encrypted nonces, or RSA signatures (digital certificates). User authentication is handled using XAUTH.

In Chapter 4, "PPTP and L2TP," I discussed how these two protocols support authentication: PPTP uses PPP's PAP, CHAP, MS-CHAP, or EAP for user authentication, whereas L2TP/IPsec supports both device and user authentication. L2TP/IPsec supports the same device authentication as IPsec and the same user authentication as PPTP.

SSL VPN implementations typically support two methods of authentication:

- Digital certificates
- Username and passwords (or tokens)

Digital certificates are used to perform device authentication. Some vendors would group both of the above bullets under user authentication; however, I would disagree with this grouping because the certificate is obtained once and stored on the device—it's not something the user must enter dynamically during the authentication process.

SSL certificates contain information about the user, device, or organization that uses them, including a public key and an encrypted digital signature. The public key can decrypt the information in the signature and use the unencrypted key to validate the integrity of the certificate. Remember that SSL certificates can be:

- Self-generated
- Created by a CA and installed on a device

CAUTION   If you are concerned about the security surrounding authentication functions, I would not use self-generated certificates, because anyone can create them! Instead, I would use a third-party trust system with a CA acting as the trusted third party. Another issue with SSL is that by default, only the server-end (the SSL VPN gateway) has to authenticate to the user; you definitely will want to implement two-way authentication when using certificates. Even though digital certificate authentication of user devices is possible, it is not very common today. The most common authentication deployment solution today is to use a CA to create certificates for SSL VPN gateways and to combine this with user authentication, where the password is either static or a one-time password (OTP) via a token card.

SSL Encryption

Netscape originally developed SSL to encrypt traffic between two devices. SSL's latest version is version 3 (SSLv3), which was released in 1996. SSL supports RC4, DES, and 3DES encryption. Later, IETF created a draft standard based on SSL, called Transport Layer Security (TLS). TLS 1.0 (TLSv1) is defined in RFC 2246.

Here are some other RFCs for TLS:

- RFC 2712 adds 40-bit encryption to TLS.
- RFC 2817 allows secured and unsecured traffic over an HTTPS connection (port 443) for TLS.
- RFC 2828 allows HTTP over TLS to operate on a different server port than 443.
- RFC 3268 adds AES to TLS's support for encryption algorithms, which also include RC2, RC4, IDEA, DES, and 3DES.

Both SSL and TLS are supported in most web browser products today, including Microsoft Internet Explorer and Netscape Navigator; of the two, TLS provides for stronger security and encryption.

NOTE   Throughout this chapter and the rest of the book, whenever I refer to SSL VPNs, I'm also including TLS.

SSL Content Control

One advantage of clientless/thin client SSL VPNs is that you have more granular access over the applications than a user can use on the SSL connection, because for many of these applications, you must configure them on your SSL gateway device to allow access to them. Therefore, if you're interested in controlling access to either specific applications or specific web sites, an SSL VPN is a better solution than a Layer-3 VPN implementation that allows all traffic across the VPN by default. Of course, you could always configure a packet filter for the Layer-3 VPN remote access client, but this can be a management headache in a large network with a large number of remote access clients with different access needs.

SSL VPNs allow a more granular access control method. The SSL VPN client initially opens a web page to the VPN gateway. The web page has a list of links for the user to access other locations. In this sense, the VPN gateway acts as a proxy device. You, the administrator, control what appears on the SSL gateway's initial web page and, therefore, control what resources behind the SSL gateway users can access. Some vendors' solutions go into even more depth than this when it comes to access control; with some products, you can even implement content-based filtering.

NOTE   The Cisco SSL VPN implementation does not support content filtering; however, you can easily use one of the other content filtering solutions to accomplish this task.

SSL Components

Now that I've talked briefly about what SSL VPNs are, let's talk about the two components in an SSL VPN implementation:

- SSL Client
- SSL Gateway

The next two sections will discuss these components.

SSL Client

When choosing a VPN implementation for a VPN solution, one question asked is: "Should I use a solution with a client or one that is clientless?" One original eye-catching thing about clientless and thin client SSL VPNs is that they use a standard web browser rather than having to install VPN client software on each remote access user's desktop. However, the choice is not as simple as this sounds.

Web- and Non-Web-Based Applications

SSL VPNs are best suited if your user's applications are, for the most part, web browser-based. If you have a mixture of applications where many of them are not web browser-based, the SSL VPN solution might not be able to support one, some, or all of these applications.

Non-web browser-based applications have to be webified to work with a clientless or thin client SSL VPN. Every vendor that I've dealt with concerning thin client Web VPNs has used either Java or ActiveX code on their SSL VPN gateway to tunnel non-web browser-based applications across the SSL tunnel: this can be done via a thin client or a network client. The applications supported for a thin client or the protocols supported for a network client are vendor-dependent.

Another issue with this process is that a thin client will have to download Java or ActiveX code for each non-web browser-based application it wants to use, such as Windows Terminal Server, Citrix, and others. Moreover, these applets and controls might conflict with the client's web browser security policy concerning the downloading and execution of applets and scripts. For example, some companies automatically have web browsers block all unsigned Java and ActiveX code, assuming that these might be Trojan horse attacks. Therefore, you might have to have your users change this policy on their desktops to allow unsigned applets and controls, which is a security risk in and of itself. To alleviate this problem, all SSL VPN vendors will sign their Java or ActiveX code to allow them to function correctly, in most instances.

Generally, the Java or ActiveX code that is downloaded to the user's desktop is not specific to an application. It provides access to many different protocols or ports over a single application, such as a web browser. The main question about the code that is downloaded is whether it implements a thin or network client implementation.

Given these problems, this is where a Layer-3 VPN implementation, such as IPsec, shines, because Layer-3 VPN implementations can protect all application layer traffic for a particular protocol. In other words, once you've decided that you need to protect all network-layer traffic, the strongest benefits of SSL VPNs begin to vanish in favor of a traditional Layer-3 VPN solution like IPsec, PPTP, or L2TP/IPsec.

SSL Client Security

One major concern about SSL VPNs using a clientless or thin client implementation is that not all traffic to and from the client is protected, thereby leaving the client open to attack: in other words, unlike an IPsec client that might require all traffic to be tunneled (split tunneling is disabled), a user's web browser will allow a user to access any web site on the Internet. With an SSL VPN, only tunneled traffic can be protected. If a user's desktop is compromised, the attacker has a secure connection to your company.

Therefore, if you decide to use a clientless or thin client SSL VPN implementation, your security policy should contain a statement requiring all SSL remote access clients to have, at a minimum, personal software firewalls installed, and more preferably host IDS software, such as Cisco Host IPS or Cisco Security Agent (CSA).

SSL network clients typically add security enhancements to deal with some of these problems. For example, Cisco Secure Desktop (CSD), available on the Cisco 3000 VPN concentrators running 4.7, allows you to require a personal firewall or antivirus software to be installed before the SSL session can be established successfully. Of course, making these requirements will work only when the corporation has rights to access the user's desktop; for users making connections from non-corporate PCs, implementing these safeguards typically is not possible (like at an airport kiosk or an Internet café).

Some vendors' SSL implementations include some safeguards like the following:

- Upon SSL tunnel termination, the SSL client deletes all traces of the SSL tunnel activity, such as cached credentials and web pages, temporary files, and cookies. Incidental tunnel terminations can be detected through the use of idle timeouts or keepalives. For example, CSD encrypts all data created during the duration of the SSL session and ensures that it is non-recoverable at the end of the session.

- The VPN gateway can run an applet or control to check for the existence and operation of a firewall, anti-virus, or anti-spyware software. Cisco implements this with CSD.

- The VPN gateway can implement access control rules to control what applications, and operations within those applications, are allowed.

All of these enhancements, though, are vendor-dependent.

The same security issues can be said to apply to Layer-3 VPN implementations with software clients; however, many of them have the ability to control the traffic that is protected (split tunneling) and some have enhanced features to enforce the use of firewalls. If you're concerned about exposing a user's desktop to outside threats, you could disable split tunneling, requiring all traffic to be sent protected to the VPN gateway. Some vendors' Layer-3 VPN clients even include firewall solutions, such as the Cisco VPN Client, Check Point's VPN-1, and WatchGuard's Mobile User VPN clients.

Brief Overview of SSL Clients

Your choice when dealing with clients comes down to two sets of issues:

- With SSL VPNs, you'll probably have to customize the VPN gateway to support additional non-web browser applications, if this is at all possible; however, the upside is that your users probably will need minimal training, if any, to use a Web VPN solution because they already should be familiar with the use of a web browser. Plus, any necessary software to implement this function for port forwarding of non-web applications or network-based protection typically is downloaded dynamically from the SSL gateway to the user's desktop when the SSL VPN connection is initiated. Optionally, a Layer-3 SSL client can be downloaded and installed on the user's desktop, but this requires administrative rights on the desktop.

- With Layer-3 VPN implementations, such as IPsec, you must install and maintain a software client on each user's desktop. This will require additional training for your users on how to use the VPN client software. The advantage of Layer-3 VPN clients is that users can use their native applications without any special configuration by the VPN software. Of course, if you're concerned about putting a client on a user's desktop and having to manage this, you could always opt for a hardware client solution, which is, for the most part, transparent to the user, or a network-based SSL solution, which typically will be able to protect most of the user's traffic, but might not support split-tunneling policies. In the latter case, you wouldn't be able to protect all traffic to and from the user's PC.

Gateway

One of the key components to consider when choosing a VPN implementation is the product you'll use as a VPN gateway—this seemingly simple choice can make the implementation process a nightmare or an easy process. For example, if you'll be implementing an IPsec VPN, here are some of the criteria to consider when choosing a gateway product:

- Assigning addressing and policy information to the remote access clients; the more options, the more flexible the solution

- Flexibility in defining protected and unprotected traffic (split tunneling)

- Handling routing issues with reaching remote access clients connected to different VPN gateways

- Implementing access control policies for the remote access users

SSL VPNs have different requirements than a Layer-3 VPN implementation. For example, you don't need to assign any addresses to SSL clientless or thin clients, and routing shouldn't be a problem because the client is known via one address, which typically is a public address. With SSL VPNs, you should be asking the following questions concerning SSL gateway products:

- Can you integrate authentication functions with directory services to simplify access control, providing a single-login function?

- What non-web-based applications can be tunneled through the SSL VPN?

- Can you filter access content, for example, what web sites a user can access or what content they can download?

When to Use SSL VPNs

Now that you have a basic understanding of the operation and use of SSL VPNs, I'll discuss when SSL VPNs make sense. Normally, I would consider using clientless SSL VPNs when some or all of the following are true:

- Users use a web browser to access and interact with their applications.

- Users need to access only a very limited number of company resources and not a wide range of hosts and services.

- As an administrator, you have very little or no control over the user's desktop and the software that is or isn't installed on it.

- Users need only occasional access to the network, where sometimes this access is not from their PC but a public device such as an unmanaged PC (PC at an Internet café or an airport or library kiosk).

If you have a small number of non-web applications, in addition to web applications, that you want to protect to a central site, using a thin client SSL VPN would be a good solution; however, you'll need to ensure that for the non-web applications you want to tunnel, the list of vendors you're examining support these.

If you're interested in reducing the amount of management you'll need to perform on a user's desktop but want to be able to protect network-level traffic to the corporate site, I might consider a network SSL VPN. One main disadvantage of this solution, though, is that you might not be able to implement any type of split tunneling policies, and thus the user might be able to access resources from his PC in clear text.

The following two sections discuss the advantages and disadvantages of SSL VPNs, followed by a quick comparison between SSL VPNs and IPsec VPNs.

Advantages of SSL VPNs

SSL VPNs are ideal for those users who use web browsers on a daily basis for interacting with a company's applications. Here is a brief list of the advantages of SSL VPNs:

- No additional software typically needs to be installed on the users' desktops.

- You can access applications securely from anywhere; you only need a device with a web browser.

- A wide variety of web browsers are usually supported.

- Little training is required for your users.

- Users typically can be authenticated by several methods, including static passwords, certificates, directory services, and token card solutions. With directory services, a single login process authenticates the user to the SSL gateway in addition to authenticating to the directory service.

- SSL VPNs work with address translation because SSL/TLS uses TCP, and only the TCP payload is protected. Because SSL provides protection for the payload in the TCP segment, and not the outer TCP segment header, SSL VPN traffic can traverse NAT or PAT devices. This is one headache of most Layer-3 VPN implementations; their data tunnels typically are Layer-3 tunnels. Sometimes NAT works for Layer-3 VPNs, but PAT breaks the tunnel connection. Of course, as I mentioned in Chapters 3 and 4, there are ways of getting around this problem for Layer-3 VPN solutions; however, these add more overhead and make the Layer-3 VPN solution less efficient than a clientless SSL VPN. However, if you'll be using a thin or network client, the amount of overhead to tunnel traffic is comparable to IPsec.

Disadvantages of SSL VPNs

Given their advantages, SSL VPNs do have their limitations and disadvantages. This section will explore a few of them. Web applications use TCP port 80 for their connections. Encrypted web connections (SSL/TLS) also use TCP, but on a different port: 443. By using TCP, SSL has these two advantages:

- It can detect message replay attacks.

- Its protection is the TCP payload, and therefore SSL VPN traffic can traverse a NAT or PAT device.

SSL uses the TCP sequence numbers to detect and drop message replay attacks. Even though it can perform this function, Layer-3 VPNs, like IPsec, actually do this better. IPsec performs this process at Layer-3 while SSL does it at Layer-4. Therefore, IPsec is more efficient since it can detect replay attacks at Layer-3.

TCP has another limiting factor: it is more affected by denial of service (DoS) attacks. For example, with IPsec's management connection, which uses UDP, it is fairly easy to deflect these attacks by examining the digital signature in the UDP packet. However, with SSL and

TCP it's worse, because a TCP SYN flood attack would fill up the TCP session table on the device and bring a device to a screeching halt. Therefore, you might want to consider implementing a solution that can detect and defeat TCP-based DoS attacks. Here are some Cisco solutions that can provide these services:

- Cisco routers with TCP Intercept
- Cisco routers with the IOS Firewall Feature set's Context-Based Access Control
- Cisco PIX and ASA security appliances with FloodGuard

SSL Versus IPsec

Given their advantages and disadvantages, I'll quickly compare SSL VPNs with IPsec so that you have a better understanding as to when to use each solution. Table 5-1 compares these two VPN implementations. This is not to say that your company must choose one over the other; both implementations have strengths and weaknesses. The two can be used in combination to solve specific security problems in your network.

The main advantage of clientless SSL VPNs is that users can use *any* machine with a web browser installed. For thin clients or network clients, Java/ActiveX will need to be installed to access the corporate network securely; this probably has already been done for the user to successfully navigate many web sites on the Internet. Because a PC typically has both a web browser and Java or ActiveX installed, SSL VPNs are ideal for mobile users who might be using different devices at different locations to gain access to your network, for example, another company's PC or an airport kiosk. For the traveling salesperson accessing the corporate network from non-corporate devices, SSL VPNs are ideal.

The downside of clientless or thin client SSL VPNs is that they support only a limited number of applications. Therefore, for users who need secure access to these services, or for users who always will be accessing the company's network from a fixed device, IPsec or, possibly, network client SSL VPNs, would be a better fit (IPsec is typically a better option). And of course, if you have both types of users with these different needs, one set can use an SSL solution and the other an IPsec one! This could be applied to the same user, depending upon where the user is connecting from. As I've pointed out to many customers who have queried me on this topic, it's not that one solution is right or wrong, or better or worse than the other . . . a company's specific situation will determine whether one, the other, or both are used to provide for secure connectivity.

NOTE I'd like to point out that IPv6 standard actually includes IPsec as part of its implementation. Even though it's part of the IPv6 implementation, IPsec is optional. However, because it is a component directly built into IPv6, and if IPv6 would eventually be deployed down to the user desktop, SSL (and SSL VPNs) would no longer be necessary.

Table 5-1   *SSL and IPsec Comparison*

Component	SSL	IPsec
Connectivity	SSL only supports remote access	IPsec supports both site-to-site and remote access
Device authentication	SSL supports digital certificates	IPsec supports pre-shared keys, RSA encrypted nonces, and digital certificates
User authentication	SSL supports user authentication	IPsec supports user authentication through XAUTH unless it's L2TP/IPsec, in which case it's L2TP that is responsible for user authentication
Protection	SSL protects only the TCP payload and is thus susceptible to certain kinds of attacks	IPsec can protect the user's data in a transport connection or an entire IP packet in tunnel mode
Encryption	SSL/TLS support RC2, RC4, IDEA, DES, 3DES, and AES; however most web browsers only support RC4, DES, and 3DES	IPsec supports DES, 3DES, and AES
Message integrity	SSL supports none except that provided by TCP	IPsec supports MD5 and SHA-1 HMAC functions
Implementation requirements	SSL requires a web browser with Java/ActiveX installed for thin and network clients; because a web browser is used, most user operating systems will be supported	IPsec requires an IPsec client installed or built into the operating system and configured on each user's desktop; because a special client must be installed, only operating systems supported by the vendor can use IPsec
Transparency	SSL has no problem with a session traversing an address translation device (NAT and/or PAT)	IPsec has problems with AH traversing through any type of address translation device and ESP traversing a PAT device; however, IPsec is more likely to be denied by a firewall than a TCP port 443 (SSL) connection

continues

Table 5-1 *SSL and IPsec Comparison (Continued)*

Component	SSL	IPsec
ISP issues	Because SSL is commonly used on the Internet, ISPs don't block this kind of traffic	Some ISPs block IPsec traffic and require users to pay an additional fee to use IPsec; you can get around this problem by encapsulating IPsec data in either a TCP or UDP segment, but this adds overhead to the transmission; this assumes that this process doesn't break the ISP's acceptable use policy (AUP)

My Experiences with SSL VPNs

I've had mixed success with SSL VPN implementations. Most SSL VPN implementations offered by vendors are still in their infancy stage and therefore some types of non-web browser-based applications or protocols will work and some won't—even if the vendor says they're supposed to work. For example, I once had an SSL vendor say that they supported Citrix through a port forwarding function. I bought two SSL gateways from them specifically for this function; however, once I installed them, for the life of me, I could never get the Citrix connectivity to work through the SSL VPN. I contacted their support team and they told me that since they had added this feature, it was hit-and-miss about it working. Apparently there were a lot of bugs in the software that they needed to weed out. Of course I returned the two SSL VPN gateways and got my customer's money back. From this and other SSL VPN experiences, I've learned that if a customer needs a specific application to work with SSL VPNs, I'll have the vendor actually prove it with a test unit before investing a lot of time, effort, and money into the process.

Cisco WebVPN Solution

Because the implementation of an SSL VPN typically is unique on a vendor-by-vendor basis, I won't go into the particulars as to how each different SSL VPN vendor implements SSL VPNs. However, since this book focuses on VPNs and Cisco products, this is a good chapter to introduce how Cisco implements SSL VPNs in their *WebVPN* solution. The remainder of this chapter will focus on the Cisco WebVPN solution. This part of the chapter will provide a brief overview, whereas Chapter 8, "Concentrator Remote Access Connections, with PPTP, L2TP, and WebVPN" will discuss how to set them up on Cisco VPN 3000 series concentrators. Chapter 18, "Router remote Access Connections," discusses setup on Cisco routers.

VPN 3000 Series Concentrators

The VPN 3000 concentrators were originally the only Cisco product that supported WebVPN functionality for remote access; Cisco has added WebVPN to the ASA security appliances and the IOS-based routers. The VPN 3000 concentrators also support IPsec, PPTP, and L2TP/IPsec VPNs for site-to-site and remote access connections. As you will see in the next chapter, Cisco has a wide range of 3000 series hardware platforms to choose from. The 3000 series concentrators also support many types of authentication for remote access users (like WebVPN users), including static usernames and passwords, AAA RADIUS, Microsoft NT Domain, Microsoft Active Directory, RSA SDI (token cards), and X.509 digital certificates.

The Cisco WebVPN implementation was introduced in Version 4.1 of the 3000 series software. This implementation was enhanced with the acquisition of Twingo in March of 2004 and added to the 4.7 software, where this feature is referred to as Cisco Secure Desktop (CSD). Cisco integrated Twingo's technology into the 4.7 software to provide for enhanced services, such as technology to reliably eliminate all traces of sensitive data from the user's device after the SSL VPN terminates. This includes clearing out history and temporary files, caches, cookies, e-mail attachments, and other downloaded data. This feature is important where a user is using a public device for the secure access.

WebVPN Operation

The operation of WebVPN is straightforward. The user initiates an SSL connection to the public interface of the 3000 series concentrator: in the web browser address field, the URL would look something like this:

```
https://IP_address_of_concentrator
```

The digital certificate of the concentrator must be accepted by the client if the WebVPN server's certificate is self-signed; otherwise, if a CA is used and the WebVPN server obtains its certificate from a CA, the user's web browser will accept the server's certificate automatically. If digital certificate authentication is enabled for user devices, the WebVPN gateway validates the user's certificate. At this point, a system integrity scan can be accomplished using CSD. CSD can determine if the remote system is a corporate-owned asset based on information included on a user's certificate, a file/hash value, or a particular register entry. After this, CSD can then verify that the user's desktop meets any personal firewall or anti-virus policy defined on the WebVPN server. Once the SSL VPN is established and the virtual desktop starts (assuming it's a network-based SSL VPN), CSD ensures that all data for the duration of the session is encrypted and protected from being left on the system once the SSL VPN is terminated or times out.

NOTE   The use of CSD assumes that the user is initiating the SSL VPN from a corporate-owned PC; otherwise, a clientless SSL VPN solution normally will be used where the use of CSD will probably not work (CSD requires many administrative rights the user will probably not have on a non-corporate PC).

If using a clientless SSL VPN, an initial login page is then presented to the user. At this point the user is actually using the WebVPN tunnel; however, users first must authenticate their identities by supplying a username and password. This information is either validated on the concentrator itself or on an external security server (these were discussed in the "VPN 3000 Series Concentrators" section). Once authenticated, the user is presented with an access page.

How the administrator sets up WebVPN on the concentrator will determine what options the user will see on this page when the user's SSL VPN is clientless or a thin client. Cisco supports four categories of access:

- Web browsing
- Network browsing and file management
- Using applications (port forwarding)
- Using e-mail

All of these are customizable and controlled by the network administrator; therefore, if you don't want users to get access to a particular web server or application, don't list it on this page. The following sections will cover these access features briefly.

NOTE   Using the SSL VPN Client, which is the Cisco version of a network SSL client, network-based protection is provided; thus you won't see a web page that lists hyperlinks to use in order to access resources. However, with a clientless or thin client solution, the process described above is true.

Web Access

The look and feel of the web access feature of clientless or thin client WebVPN will be different from what your users are used to with normal web browser functions. Normally, a user would type the URL in the address bar of a web browser to access a site; if your users would do this, they would not be sending traffic across the VPN. Instead, access to sites is done from the main access page of the concentrator. To access other sites, you, as an administrator, can permit one of the following (depending on whether or not the concentrator's administrator has enabled them):

- The user can enter a URL in the "Enter Web Address (URL)" field.
- The administrator can create a hyperlink on the access page and the user can click on this to access a site.

When using this method, the concentrator is acting as a web proxy; any access from a web page brought up via one of these two methods is being proxied by the concentrator. One feature of the concentrator is that the administrator controls the user's access. The administrator does this by controlling the content that appears on the access page, and by setting up blocks for particular sites.

NOTE	Web browser proxy is also supported by Internet Explorer (IE) in 4.1.6 of the concentrator software, allowing IE to use a web proxy at the corporate office (behind the WebVPN server) directly as a proxy agent.

The SSL VPN Client, which implements network-based protection, installs a virtual user desktop on the user's PC. Within this virtual desktop, any application that sends data traverses the WebVPN. If the user wants to use a web browser, he would use it as he normally would: the only difference is that the web traffic would traverse the SSL VPN. This process makes the SSL VPN more transparent to the user than the clientless or thin client approach. You can implement a very limited form of split tunneling by allowing the user to access a non-SSL VPN Client desktop (the default desktop). If this is allowed, any traffic from the non-SSL VPN Client desktop will not traverse the SSL VPN tunnel. The user can then jump back and forth between the two desktops depending on whether he needs to access corporate resources (the virtual desktop) or Internet resources (the default user's desktop). However, as an administrator of the WebVPN server, you have control over this process.

Network Browsing and File Management Access

The network browsing and file management access allows a user to access Windows network and file resources through the VPN tunnel. For file access in a clientless or thin client implementation, the files and network drives must be configured to allow remote access. There are two basic ways that a user can access files on the company's network:

- The user can enter a file share in the "Network Path" field using a format of "*server\\share*."

- The administrator can create a hyperlink on the access page and the user can click on this to access a file share.

Again, the concentrator is acting as a proxy and the network administrator can lock down the type of access allowed by the user. Also, when a user accesses a share, he can perform the following operations (assuming that he has these privileges on the file server):

- Move up a folder in the directory structure
- Copy a file to or from the server
- Create a new folder
- Delete a file
- Rename a file

Given the preceding capabilities of a clientless or thin client WebVPN session, accessing a Windows resource is *not* the same as remotely attaching to a server and using Windows Explorer to interface with the directory structure and files on the remote server, as would be the case if the user was using the SSL VPN client in a network-based WebVPN session.

Application Access and Port Forwarding

WebVPN's application access and port forwarding feature allows remote users to use non-web-based applications over SSL with a thin client. The following applications have been officially tested by Cisco:

- Lotus Notes
- Outlook, Outlook Express, and Outlook Web Access (OWA)
- Perforce
- Sametime Instant Messaging
- Secure FTP
- SSH
- Telnet
- Windows Terminal Services
- XDDTS

Other applications might work, but they haven't been officially tested by Cisco.

To use port forwarding, the user must start up port forwarding on the WebVPN server's access page by clicking a hyperlink. This process causes a Java applet to be downloaded and executed on the PC. The Cisco implementation of this process requires that the user install Sun's Java Runtime Environment (JRE) 1.4 or higher. If JRE is not installed, the first time a user attempts to perform port forwarding, a pop-up window tells the user where to download JRE.

The Java applet will modify the user's Windows host file to perform a proxy for the connection. For example, if a user wanted to telnet to a server called "server1.richard-deal.com," the Java applet would have to modify the local host's file and put a static resolution for server1.richard-deal.com that would have an address of 127.0.0.2 (a loopback address). If there was a second server, for example, "server2.richard-deal.com," the Java applet would have to create a second static resolution entry with an IP address of 127.0.0.3, and so on.

Now a user can't just create his own port forwarding rules. These are actually created on the concentrator. So on the WebVPN server, you, the administrator, would define the server1.richard-deal.com and server2.richard-deal.com entries and the Java applet would update the user's host file when the user started port forwarding on the concentrator's access page. With this process, when a user would telnet to server1.richard-deal.com, the resolution would point to the user's PC itself on a port number that the Java applet was listening to. The Java applet would then redirect the connection across the WebVPN connection to the concentrator. The WebVPN gateway would act as a proxy and change the IP address and port back to what they should be to reach the remote server.

There are two problems with this approach: you must define the non-web applications to be proxied manually, and the applications that can be proxied are limited. Because of this, in version 4.7 of the Cisco 3000 VPN concentrator software, Cisco introduced their SSL VPN network client, the SSL VPN Client. This client allows all traffic within the user's protected desktop to be protected.

E-mail Client Access

WebVPN allows users to use their native e-mail applications to access e-mail at the corporate office through the WebVPN connection (clientless or thin client) to the concentrator. E-mail client access should work using one of these three methods:

- E-mail proxy using port forwarding
- Web e-mail (using a web browser)—this is set up as a URL in the web access part of the concentrator's access page
- E-mail proxy for e-mail clients using POP3S, IMAP4S, and SMTPS; these protocols provide encrypted e-mail connections directly between the e-mail client and server

I've already discussed the first two items in the "Application Access and Port Forwarding" and "Web Access" sections earlier. Now I'll focus on the last bullet point.

The third option is somewhat unique to the Cisco WebVPN solution. Up to this point, all con-nections used a single HTTPS connection between the user desktop and the concentrator; and the WebVPN server would proxy the traffic to and from this connection. With the third option, the e-mail client actually uses the native secure port connection to access the e-mail server via a proxy, where the proxy is the WebVPN gateway. You'll need to perform two tasks to complete this successfully:

1 Configure the WebVPN gateway to proxy connections to the actual e-mail server.

2 Set up the user's e-mail client to point to the proxy (WebVPN gateway).

This configuration is similar to setting up a web proxy with Internet Explorer or some other web browser.

NOTE   Of course, if you are using the SSL VPN Client, you don't need to do any of this: from the protected virtual desktop, have the users bring up their e-mail clients normally, and this traffic will be tunneled automatically across the SSL VPN.

Summary

This chapter introduced you to SSL VPNs. As you have seen, clientless, thin client, and network client SSL VPNs don't provide a complete VPN solution, but solve specific problems related to secure connectivity. However, network client solutions come close to providing a solution like IPsec remote access solutions. SSL VPNs are great when most of a user's access to the corporate Internet is via a web browser, but when many non-web browser-based applications are being used by the user, a Layer-3 VPN implementation, like IPsec, is probably a better choice for a solution.

Next up is Part II, "Concentrators," where I show you how to use the Cisco 3000 series concentrators as VPN gateway solutions. I'll discuss how to use them for both remote access and site-to-site connectivity, and how to troubleshoot VPN connections that terminate on them.

Concentrators

CHAPTER 6

Concentrator Product Information

Cisco offers a wide range of VPN products, including routers, PIX and ASA security appliances, VPN hardware appliances (concentrators), and software and hardware clients. With this wide range of choices, Cisco provides a VPN solution that can fit any network or market. VPN implementations supported by these products include IPsec, L2TP over IPsec, PPTP, and WebVPN.

A few years back Cisco introduced a concept called "Easy VPN." Easy VPN's premise was to make it easy to set up remote access connections. When I examine the client functionality of Cisco client products throughout this book, you'll see that setting them up as clients is a very simple process—thus the term "easy" in Easy VPN. Easy VPN allows administrators to deploy complicated VPN technologies without the configuration headaches associated with them.

Two components of Easy VPN are as follows:

- **Easy VPN Server**—Products that support the server functions include the VPN 3000 concentrators, IOS routers, and PIX and ASA security appliances.

- **Easy VPN Remote** (sometimes referred to as Client)—Products that support client functions include SOHO IOS routers, SOHO PIX firewalls, the Cisco VPN 3002 hardware client, and the Cisco VPN software client.

This chapter will focus on one set of Easy VPN components: Cisco 3000 series concentrators. Specifically, it will cover:

- Concentrator Models
- Concentrator Modules
- Concentrator Features
- Concentrator Access Introduction

Concentrator Models

The Cisco VPN 3000 series concentrators, commonly referred to as VPN hardware appliances, originally were built by Altiga. Cisco acquired Altiga in 2000. These concentrators were built primarily to handle large numbers of remote access sessions, but they also support site-to-site connectivity.

Of all of the Cisco VPN offerings, the Cisco VPN 3000 series concentrators provide the most flexible and scalable remote access solution: IPsec, L2TP over IPsec, PPTP, and WebVPN VPN implementations are supported. And Cisco has added many enhanced features to their concentrators to meet their customers' remote access needs. Cisco currently sells six different models of the 3000 series:

- **3005**—small branch office
- **3015**—small branch office
- **3020**—medium branch office or small company
- **3030**—small company or medium corporation
- **3060**—medium or enterprise corporation
- **3080**—enterprise corporation or ISP

The 3005 can perform VPN functions only in software, whereas the other concentrators support Scalable Encryption Process (SEP) modules that can perform VPN functions in hardware. SEP modules are upgradeable and can be added easily to increase capacity and throughput. All of the concentrators are software-upgradeable and have a Motorola PowerPC processor, NVRAM (this is where critical system parameters are stored, such as management passwords), and Flash memory for files. The following sections will cover the different concentrator models.

NOTE   Cisco doesn't charge their customers for using the Cisco VPN client software; instead, limits are placed on the Easy VPN server side. In other words, the Easy VPN server product you buy will affect how many simultaneous clients (or users) you can terminate on it.

3005 Concentrator

The 3005 is for small businesses with a small-bandwidth Internet connection. The 3005 supports up to 4 Mbps VPN performance, so it's ideal for sites that have a T1, cable modem, or DSL connection. You can have up to 200 IPsec remote access sessions terminated on the 3005 or 50 WebVPN sessions with Version 4.7 of the operating system installed.

The 3005 is not hardware-upgradeable, but you can upgrade the software. The 3005 does only software-based encryption and supports a single power supply. Figure 6-1 shows the rear of the 3005 chassis. It has two autosensing 10/100BaseTX Ethernet interfaces. The left-hand interface is a private interface, connected to the internal network, and the right-hand interface is the public interface, connected to the external network. The only item of interest on the front of the 3005 chassis is a system LED; hence, the front of the chassis is not shown in the diagram.

Figure 6-1   *3005 Chassis*

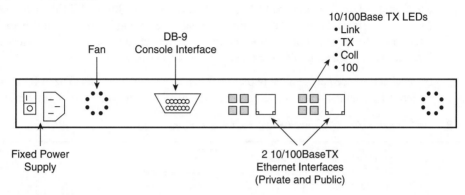

3015 Concentrator

Like the 3005, the 3015 is for small businesses that have a small-bandwidth Internet connection. Unlike the 3005, however, the 3015 is hardware-upgradeable; therefore, it should be targeted for locations that expect growth (the number of remote access users will increase). By default, it doesn't contain any SEP modules; however, you can add these easily.

Without any SEP modules, the 3015 supports 4 Mbps of VPN throughput by performing encryption in software. It can support up to 100 IPsec remote access sessions or 75 WebVPN sessions. Figure 6-2 shows the rear of the chassis for the 3015 (this is the same chassis used by the 3020, 3030, 3060, and 3080 concentrators). The 3015 can be upgraded to a 3030 or 3060 by adding one or two SEP modules, respectively.

Figure 6-2   *3015, 3020, 3030, 3060, and 3080 Chassis Rear*

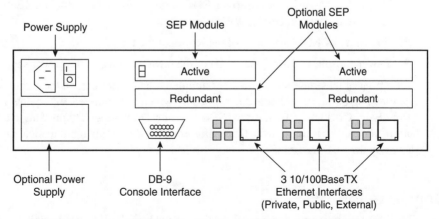

You'll notice some differences between the 3015 and 3005 chassis. First, the 3015 is a 2-unit height chassis, unlike the 3005, which is a 1-unit height chassis. Second, the 3015 has one modular power supply, but you can also install an additional one. Third, the 3015

has four slots for SEP modules; however, on the 3015, no SEP modules ship with the concentrator. Fourth, below the SEP modules are three 10/100BaseTX Ethernet interfaces (from left to right): Private, Public, and External. The private interface connects to the internal network, the public interface connects to the outside world, and the external interface connects to a DMZ or another company's network.

Another difference between the two chassis can be seen on the front. The 3005 only has a system LED, but the other concentrators, as shown in Figure 6-3, have many LEDs:

Figure 6-3   *3015, 3020, 3030, 3060, and 3080 Partial Chassis Front*

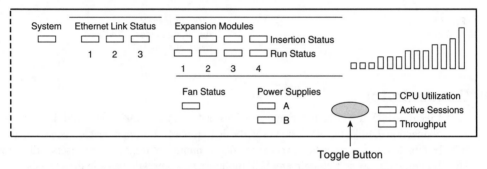

Here's a brief description of the LEDs:

- **System LED**—status of hardware diagnostics and whether or not the operating system has completed loading
- **Ethernet Link Status LEDs**—status for all 3 Ethernet interfaces
- **Expansion Module Insertion Status LEDs**—indicates whether or not an SEP module is installed in a slot
- **Expansion Module Run Status LEDs**—indicates whether or not an SEP module is an active module processing VPN traffic
- **Fan Status LED**—the status of the RPMs of the fans
- **Power Supplies LEDs**—the status of the power voltage of the power supplies

At the front of these chassis is one other unique item: a meter bar, on the right-hand side. The meaning of the meter bar is determined by which of the three LEDs below it is currently lit: CPU Utilization, Active Sessions, and Throughput. By pressing the Toggle button, you can cycle through the three different LEDs, affecting the statistical information shown by the LED meter bar.

3020 Concentrator

The 3020 concentrator is targeted at medium-sized branch offices and small companies. It supports 50 Mbps VPN throughput and can support up to 750 IPsec remote access sessions or 200 WebVPN sessions. It ships with a single SEP module. The 3020 cannot be hardware-upgraded, but as with the 3005, you can upgrade its software. Therefore, the 3020 is targeted for locations that expect little growth in the number of remote access users or VPN throughput.

3030 Concentrator

The 3030 is targeted at small companies and medium-sized corporations. It supports 50 Mbps VPN throughput and can support 1,500 simultaneous IPsec remote access sessions or 500 WebVPN sessions. Because of its VPN throughput, it is ideal for sites that have T3 connections. It ships with a single SEP module. You can upgrade it to a 3060 by buying a second SEP module. Therefore, it is a good choice if you expect growth at the location where the 3030 will be deployed.

3060 Concentrator

The 3060 is targeted at medium-sized or enterprise corporations. It supports 100 Mbps VPN throughput, and can support 5,000 simultaneous IPsec remote access sessions or 500 WebVPN sessions. It ships with two SEP modules. Unfortunately, the 3060 cannot be field-upgraded to a 3080; therefore, it is best used in a location where you don't expect to exceed the 3060's specifications.

NOTE   Once enhanced feature of the concentrators is that they support load balancing—each member of the cluster will handle VPN sessions; therefore, you don't necessarily have to buy a new, higher-end concentrator, if your current concentrator cannot handle the current number of simultaneous remote access sessions—you can buy a more suitable concentrator model to handle the additional connections and cluster it with your current concentrator.

3080 Concentrator

The 3080 is targeted at large enterprise corporations or ISPs. Like the 3060, it supports 100 Mbps VPN throughput. It can support up to 10,000 simultaneous IPsec remote access sessions or 500 WebVPN sessions. It ships with four SEP modules. The 3080 is the only concentrator that, by default, ships with two power supplies and four SEP modules.

Comparison of Concentrator Models

Now that you have a basic idea of the different 3000 series concentrators that Cisco sells, I'll pull all of this information into a table that more easily shows the differences between the various models. Table 6-1 shows a comparison between the different 3000 VPN concentrators. This table is based on the concentrators running 4.7 code (earlier code releases restricted the amount of RAM to a lower number with some of the concentrators).

Table 6-1 *3000 Series Concentrators Comparison*

Model	Total Simultaneous Remote Access Sessions	Total Simultaneous Site-to-Site Sessions	Total Simultaneous WebVPN Sessions	VPN Throughput (Encryption) in Mbps	RAM in MB
3005	200	100	50	4 (SW[1])	64
3015	100	100	75	4 (SW[1])	128
3020	750	250	200	50 (HW[1])	256
3030	1,500	500	500	50 (HW[1])	256
3060	5,000	1,000	500	100 (HW[1])	512
3080	10,000	1,000	500	100 (HW[1])	512

[1] SW indicates that VPN encryption is done in software. HW indicates that it is done in hardware with the SEP module(s).

There are a few important items to point out concerning the information in Table 6-1:

- The 3005 can support 200 remote access connections in Version 4.1; in Version 4.0 and earlier, it can only support 100 because at that time, only 32 MB of RAM could be installed and used.

- The column labeled "Total Simultaneous Remote Access Sessions" really encompasses *both* remote access and site-to-site sessions.

- An IPsec session includes the management (ISAKMP/IKE Phase 1) and two data (ISAKMP/IKE Phase 2) connections.

- Cisco considers a WebVPN session a client retrieving a web page over a 60-second period; not the total number of simultaneous SSL sessions the concentrator has to remote clients.

- The maximum number of sessions (and throughput) is based on the assumption that the concentrator has the maximum amount of memory installed and is using SEP-E modules (for the concentrators that support them); the next section discusses the different types of SEP modules available for the 3000 series concentrators.

Concentrator Modules

The 3015, 3020, 3030, 3060, and 3080 support modular slots for additional cards. Currently, the only two cards that you can put into these slots are SEP-2 and SEP-E modules. SEP modules perform VPN functions, such as encryption, in hardware.

When Cisco acquired Altiga, there were three cards you could put in these slots: an SEP module (Version 1), a T1 module, or an E1 module. Cisco no longer sells these cards: only the SEP-2 and SEP-E modules are available.

SEP Modules

The SEP-2 modules will perform encryption for DES and 3DES only. The SEP-E module has replaced the SEP-2 module. It allows the concentrator to perform DES, 3DES, *and* AES encryption. To perform AES encryption in hardware, the concentrator also needs to be running at least Version 4.0 of the software.

You cannot use both SEP-2 and SEP-E modules in the same chassis. If you have a concentrator that has both, the SEP-2 modules are disabled automatically and only the SEP-E module(s) will be active.

To determine the kind of SEP module you have installed, you can either log in to the concentrator to see the type of module (the **Monitor > System Status** screen) or you can examine the module itself. In the lower right corner of the SEP card's cover plate will be a label with one of these pieces of information:

- SEP 200U indicates an SEP-2 module
- SEP-E indicates an SEP-E module

CAUTION   The SEP modules are *not* hot-swappable; failing to turn off and unplug the concentrator when inserting or removing an SEP module can destroy the box and possibly cause electrocution.

SEP Operation

Each SEP module supports between 1,500 and 5,000 simultaneous remote access sessions, depending on the 3000 series model the module is plugged into. Placement of the SEP modules in the chassis of the concentrator is important. Referring back to Figure 6-2, the top two slots, by default, are the active slots. They process VPN sessions. The slot beneath a top slot provides redundancy for the slot above it. Redundancy is top-down, as follows:

- If a top SEP module fails and there is an SEP module installed beneath it, no VPN sessions are lost because the bottom module has a replication of all VPN information of the module above it.
- If you have only two SEP modules in the chassis and they are installed in the top two slots, sessions will be split between the two modules. If one of the modules fails all VPN sessions are dropped. Site-to-site sessions will be rebuilt to the other SEP module automatically; however, remote access users will have to reinitiate their VPN session manually (unless their client supports the auto-initiation feature).

Concentrator Features

Cisco 3000 series concentrators support features that provide high performance, scalability, enhanced security, high availability, and many other benefits. Here's a brief list of features:

- High performance is provided by SEP modules for hardware-based encryption.

- Scalability is provided by the Cisco Virtual Cluster Agent (VCA) load balancing technology and a modular design with four SEP slots.

- Enhanced security is provided by internal and external (AAA RADIUS, Microsoft's NT Domain and Active Directory, and RSA's SDI) user authentication, firewall policies, user and group management features, and detailed logging.

- High availability is provided by redundant SEPs, redundant chassis failover with VCA or VRRP, and SNMP management and monitoring.

- VPN implementations include WebVPN, IPsec, PPTP, L2TP, L2TP over IPsec, and these features: NAT-T, IPsec over UDP, and IPsec over TCP.

- VPN remote access policy features include (by group or user) filtering, idle and maximum session timeouts, time of day access control, authorization profiles, firewall policies, split tunneling, client and network extension modes, addressing pools, and different authentication methods per group.

- VPN technologies supported include ESP; GRE (for PPTP only); DES, 3DES, and AES; MD5 and SHA-1; MPPE with 40- or 128-bit RC4; ISAKMP and IKE; DH groups 1, 2, 5, and 7; SCEP; and X.509 digital certificates.

- Routing protocols supported include RIP v1 and v2, OSPF, RRI, static routing, and network auto discovery (NAD).

- The concentrators are compatible with the following remote access clients: WebVPN via a web browser or the Cisco SSL VPN Client; Cisco VPN Client for IPsec on Windows 98, ME, NT 4.0, 2000, XP, Linux for Intel, Solaris for UltraSparc, and MAC OS X 10.x; Microsoft's PPTP/MPPE/MPPC client with MS-CHAP or EAP; Microsoft's L2TP over IPsec for Windows 98, ME, NT 4.0, 2000, and XP.

- Management features include access via the console port, Telnet, SSHv1, HTTP, and HTTPS; authentication, authorization, and accounting of administrators through AAA TACACS+; access control of management sessions, logging via the console, a logging buffer, syslog, SNMP, and e-mail; automatic backup of logs via FTP; address translation with NAT and PAT; and packet filtering.

The following sections will discuss some important features that were introduced in newer versions of the concentrator's software. The Cisco 3.0 code release is the first major update of the software since Cisco acquired Altiga. Because this was a handful of years ago, I'll start with 3.5 and work my way up with the new features.

Why I prefer Cisco concentrators

I have worked with many VPN gateway products in my time, including all of the Cisco products—routers, PIXs and ASAs, and concentrators. And out of all the VPN gateway products I've ever dealt with, Cisco VPN 3000 series concentrators are my favorite for remote access solutions. From a feature perspective, there's nothing else in the marketplace in a single chassis that offers all of the features that Cisco has bundled with their concentrators. When it comes to configuration, the GUI interface is very intuitive and *much* easier to use than a CLI like Cisco routers and PIXs (the concentrator does support a menu-based CLI). And when it comes to troubleshooting VPN connections, the logging functions of the concentrator far surpass anything else I've used. The logging output is customizable to 13 different levels and the output is written, for the most part, in layman's terms, making troubleshooting a simple process.

Version 3.5 Features

I'll start with version 3.5 and its sub-versions first. In this and the following sections, I'll mention features only as they relate to the major version, like 3.5, instead of the specific release in which they became available, like 3.5.6.

In 3.5 and its sub-versions, the following features were developed:

- The personal firewall is a feature added to the Cisco VPN client software—it's a DLL from Zone Labs that functions as a simple stateful firewall for the software client. This firewall is referred to as the Cisco Integrated Client (CIC) firewall.

- The Are You There (AYT) feature is a policy defined on the concentrator and pushed to the Cisco VPN software client during IKE Mode Config. It causes the software client to poll the existence and operation of a supported firewall on the client. If one is not found and is not operating, the software client will drop any VPN session to the concentrator.

- The backup server feature for IPsec allows you to define up to ten Easy VPN Servers as backup gateways for Cisco 3002 clients.

- External user authentication with RADIUS as the authentication option now supports the function of a user changing an NT Domain password when it is about to expire.

- Interactive Unit Authentication and Individual User Authentication are authentication policies defined on the concentrator and pushed to hardware clients. Instead of storing the username and password on the hardware client, with interactive unit authentication, a user behind the hardware client is prompted for the user authentication information, and the hardware client uses this for user authentication functions; once the tunnel is up, any user behind the hardware client can use the tunnel. Individual user authentication has the hardware client prompt *each* user for a username and password and lets only authenticated users access the tunnel to the concentrator.

- IPsec over TCP allows client connections to use TCP as a transport for IPsec ESP packets to pass through address translation devices and firewalls.

- RRI allows a client to advertise its internal address (in client mode) or the network number of its private/inside interface (in network extension mode) to the VPN gateway in ISAKMP/IKE Phase 1. The concentrator can advertise these static routes via RIP or OSPF.

- SCEP allows you to acquire certificates in-band from a CA.

- Statistics on statistic screens on the concentrator can be reset (set to 0) for temporary monitoring and then restored back to the current statistical values.

- XML can be used to upload or download data files from the concentrator's Flash memory.

Version 3.6 Features

The following are features added to the concentrator in the 3.6 versions of software:

- Use of network extension mode by hardware clients can be controlled on a group-by-group basis on the concentrator.

- The bandwidth management feature allows you to apply simple bandwidth policies to the concentrator's interfaces and to groups of users or site-to-site sessions. There are two bandwidth management policies:

  — Bandwidth policing: Policing limits traffic to a specified traffic rate; traffic exceeding this rate is dropped.

  — Bandwidth reservation: Bandwidth reservation allows you to reserve a minimum amount of bandwidth for a user.

- The DHCP relay feature allows wireless clients to obtain their network configuration information *before* the tunnel is established. With this feature, the concentrator forwards DHCP requests from clients (typically wireless) to a DHCP server.

- The DHCP Intercept feature allows the concentrator to reply directly to Microsoft client DHCP inform messages for L2TP/IPsec clients.

- NAT-T uses a discovery process to determine if address translation is being performed between the client and concentrator. If so, the devices will wrap the ESP packets in UDP; otherwise, ESP packets are sent out normally. NAT-T is also supported for site-to-site connections.

- AES allows encryption to be performed with fewer processing cycles than 3DES and provides better security. In 3.6, AES is only supported in software—4.0 with the SEP-Es can perform AES in hardware.

- DH group 5 was added (group 1, 2, 5, and 7 DH keys are supported).

- CRLs can be obtained via HTTP. You also have the ability to specify backup CRL distribution points in case the CRL location listed on the CA's certificate is not reachable. Plus, the concentrator can cache CRLs in RAM locally instead of downloading them each time it needs them.

- Split DNS allows a client to use the corporate DNS server for corporate DNS resolutions and the ISP DNS server for other resolutions; this policy, along with the list of corporate domain names and corporate DNS servers, are defined on the concentrator and pushed to the client during IKE mode config.

- Dynamic DNS allows the concentrator to take the hostname found in a DHCP request and send this, along with the client's DHCP address, to a Dynamic DNS server, which will update the DNS resolution for the client on a DNS server.

- L2TP over IPsec can now use EAP/TLS and EAP/SDI for user authentication of Microsoft's VPN clients.

- You can change the MTU size from 68–1,500 bytes on the Ethernet interfaces. This might be necessary for the public interface where VPN sessions are being terminated and VPN overhead is causing fragmented packets. You can also define IPsec fragmentation policies concerning what should happen if packets need to be fragmented.

- You can use Secure Copy (SCP) to back up concentrator files to an SCP server.

- You can create a filter and apply it to a site-to-site session. You can also define address translation policies for site-to-site sessions when there are overlapping addresses at the two sites.

- You can now see the operating system and version of the remote access client that connects to the concentrator.

- If you used digital certificates before Version 3.6, you had to use the Organizational Unit (OU) field, sometimes called Department, to represent the name of the group that the user belongs to. In 3.6 you can use distinguished name (DN) group matching, where you can define rules about what is used on a certificate and how this is mapped to a particular group.

- The backup server feature now supports the Cisco VPN software client.

Version 4.0 Features

The following are features added to the concentrator in the 4.0 versions of software:

- The 3020 concentrator was introduced in this version of software.

- You can now install 64 MB of RAM in the 3005s, which allows it to support up to 200 remote access sessions. You can also install up to 512 MB of RAM in the 3060s and 3080s. (See Table 6-1 for more information.)

- The SEP-E module was introduced, allowing supported concentrators to perform DES, 3DES, and AES encryption in hardware.

- If using CiscoSecure ACS (CSACS) RADIUS for remote access user authentications, you can download predefined ACLs and apply them to a user's remote access session instead of defining the filters locally on the concentrator.

- You can specify backup peers for site-to-site sessions.

- Remote access users can now be authenticated using Active Directory/Kerberos for user authentication of remote access sessions.

- The Sygate Personal Firewall, Personal Firewall Pro, and Security agent were added to the AYT feature.

- You can change the dead peer detection (DPD) timeout value to detect dead IPsec remote access client or site-to-site sessions.

Version 4.1 Features

The following are features added to the concentrator in the 4.1 versions of software:

- The main enhancement of 4.1 is WebVPN: clientless and thin client. Not all functionality for WebVPN was introduced with the first sub-version; many features, such as Internet Explorer Proxy, were added in later sub-versions of 4.1.

- You can now define a period of time for when an internal address assigned to a remote access client such as IPsec is released, until it is returned to the address pool to be used by someone else. Also, the concentrator will do an ARP for an internal address to ensure that it's not being used, before assigning it to a remote access client.

- The Cisco VPN 4.6 software client was introduced. The concentrator now has the ability to update the software client automatically; previously, only the 3002 supported automatic updates.

- You can restrict remote access sessions by forcing users to use supported client types and software versions; this applies to Easy VPN clients.

Version 4.7 Features

Version 4.7 was a major update to the concentrators, in which many features were added. The two main ones are the SSL VPN Client and the Cisco Secure Desktop (CSD). The following are some of the features added to the concentrator in the 4.7 versions of software:

- The SSL VPN Client is a major enhancement to WebVPN, allowing the protection of network-layer traffic and above from the user's desktop to the concentrator. The SSL VPN Client installs a virtual desktop on the user's PC and all applications and protocols initiated from the virtual desktop are protected by an SSL VPN.

- CSD was introduced for WebVPN. It can be combined with network access control (NAC) and AYT to define policies that restrict client connections: clients have to meet prerequisites, such as having antivirus software, personal firewall software, and Windows service updates installed. CSD is used with the SSL VPN Client. Another security of CSD is that it looks for a key-stroke-logging program, such as a Trojan horse, at the beginning and during the SSL VPN session—if one is found, the user is prompted to take action to remove it. CSD also removes all data involved with the SSL VPN session, such as downloaded temporary files and cookies, once the SSL VPN terminates through a Department of Defense (DoD) sanitization algorithm.

- Terminal support for Citrix was introduced for WebVPN port forwarding (thin client).

NOTE   I'll discuss how to configure most of the features that I've talked about here in later chapters on the concentrator, software client, and hardware client configuration.

Introduction to Accessing a Concentrator

Now that I've covered the different 3000 models and provided a brief overview of the features of the concentrators, I'll give a quick overview on how to access a concentrator and navigate through its screens. The remaining chapters in Parts II and III will cover the specifics of how to set up remote access (IPsec, PPTP, L2TP/IPsec, and WebVPN) and site-to-site sessions that terminate on the VPN 3000 concentrators.

You can access the concentrator out-of-band by using its console port. The console port is a DB-9 interface. When using a terminal package, such as HyperTerminal or TeraTerm, set its communications properties to the following:

- 9600 baud
- 8 data bits
- 1 stop bit
- No parity
- Hardware flow control or no flow control

In-band management is supported with the following protocols:

- Telnet
- SSH
- HTTP or HTTPS
- FTP
- TFTP
- SCP

The concentrators support two types of management interfaces: character-based interface, commonly called a command-line interface (CLI), and graphical user interface (GUI). The following sections will discuss these two interfaces.

Command-Line Interface

When you receive a concentrator from the factory, it has no configuration on it; therefore, you need to use the menu-driven CLI to put a basic configuration on it. Once you have, at the minimum, an IP address on the private interface of the concentrator, administrators typically use a web browser from there on out to manage it.

To help you understand the initial access to the CLI, and additional tasks you can perform from the CLI, the following sections cover these topics:

- Bootup Process
- Initial Configuration
- CLI Menu Access
- Password Recovery

Bootup Process

To see the bootup process of the VPN 3000 concentrator, you need to use its console, as shown in Example 6-1.

Example 6-1 *Concentrator Bootup Process*

```
Boot-ROM Initializing...
Boot configured 32Mb of RAM.
...
Loading image .........
Verifying image checksum ..........
Active image loaded and verified...
Starting loaded image...
Starting power-up diagnostics...
...
pSH+ Copyright (c) Integrated Systems, Inc., 1992.
Cisco Systems, Inc./VPN 3000 Concentrator Version 4.1.7.A Oct 18 2004 18:51:42
Features:
Initializing VPN 3000 Concentrator ...
Waiting for CAPI initialization to complete...
Initialization Complete...Waiting for Network...

Login:
```

Otherwise, you can access the CLI remotely via Telnet or SSH.

Initial Configuration

When you boot up the concentrator for the first time, you'll need to use a username of *admin* and a password of *admin* to log in to the concentrator at the *Login:* prompt. At this point, the concentrator will lead you through a quick-configuration mode script to put a base configuration on it. Typically, I answer only enough questions to put an IP address on the private interface; once this is done, I stop the quick configuration script from the CLI and proceed to using the GUI with a web browser. Example 6-2 displays how to answer enough questions for the quick configuration process to put an IP address on the concentrator's private interface:

Example 6-2 *Concentrator CLI Partial Quick Configuration Process*

```
Login: admin
Password: admin
                 Welcome to
                Cisco Systems
        VPN 3000 Concentrator Series
           Command Line Interface
Copyright © 1998-2004 Cisco Systems, Inc.

 -- : Set the time on your device. The correct time is very important,
 -- : so that logging and accounting entries are accurate.
 -- : Enter the system time in the following format:
 -- :        HH:MM:SS.  Example  21:30:00  for 9:30 PM
> Time
Quick -> [ 10:25:46 ] 10:27:00

 -- : Enter the date in the following format.
 -- : MM/DD/YYYY  Example 06/12/1999  for June 12th 1999.
> Date
Quick -> [ 11/11/2004 ]

 -- :  Set the time zone on your device. The correct time zone is very
 -- :  important so that logging and accounting entries are accurate.
 -- :  Enter the time zone using the hour offset from GMT:
 -- :  -12 : Kwajalein   -11 : Samoa      -10 : Hawaii       -9 : Alaska
 -- :   -8 : PST          -7 : MST         -6 : CST          -5 : EST
 -- :   -4 : Atlantic     -3 : Brasilia  -3.5 : Newfoundland  -1 : Mid-Atlantic
 -- :   -1 : Azores        0 : GMT         +1 : Paris         +2 : Cairo
 -- :   +3 : Kuwait      +3.5 : Tehran     +4 : Abu Dhabi    +4.5 : Kabul
 -- :   +5 : Karachi     +5.5 : Calcutta +5.75 : Kathmandu    +6 : Almaty
 -- : +6.5 : Rangoon      +7 : Bangkok     +8 : Singapore     +9 : Tokyo
 -- : +9.5 : Adelaide    +10 : Sydney     +11 : Solomon Is.  +12 : Marshall Is.
> Time Zone
Quick -> [ 0] -5

1) Enable Daylight Savings Time Support
2) Disable Daylight Savings Time Support
Quick -> [ 1 ]
```

continues

Example 6-2 *Concentrator CLI Partial Quick Configuration Process (Continued)*

```
This table shows current IP addresses.
   Intf          Status         IP Address/Subnet Mask          MAC Address
   - - - - - - - - - - - - - - - - - - - - - - - - - - - - - - - - - - - - - - - - - - - - -
Ether1-Pri|Not Configured|       0.0.0.0/0.0.0.0          |
Ether2-Pub|Not Configured|       0.0.0.0/0.0.0.0          |
   - - - - - - - - - - - - - - - - - - - - - - - - - - - - - - - - - - - - - - - - - - - - -
DNS Server(s): DNS Server Not Configured
DNS Domain Name:
Default Gateway: Default Gateway Not Configured
** An address is required for the private interface. **

> Enter IP Address
Quick Ethernet 1 -> [ 0.0.0.0 ] 192.168.101.99
Waiting for Network Initialization...
> Enter Subnet Mask
Quick Ethernet 1 -> [ 255.255.255.0 ]

1) Ethernet Speed 10 Mbps
2) Ethernet Speed 100 Mbps
3) Ethernet Speed 10/100 Mbps Auto Detect
Quick Ethernet 1 -> [ 3 ]

1) Enter Duplex - Half/Full/Auto
2) Enter Duplex - Full Duplex
3) Enter Duplex - Half Duplex
Quick Ethernet 1 -> [ 1 ]

> MTU (68 - 1500)
Quick Ethernet 1 -> [ 1500 ]

1) Modify Ethernet 1 IP Address (Private)
2) Modify Ethernet 2 IP Address (Public)
3) Save changes to Config file
4) Continue
5) Exit
Quick -> 3

1) Modify Ethernet 1 IP Address (Private)
2) Modify Ethernet 2 IP Address (Public)
3) Save changes to Config file
4) Continue
5) Exit
Quick -> 5

Done
Login:
```

In this example, I first logged in to the admin account. During the quick configuration process, many of the parameters have default values listed in brackets ("[ ]"). To accept a default value, just press ENTER on a blank line. In this example, I changed the time, the time zone offset, and the IP address on the private interface. At this point I saved the configuration and then exited the quick configuration script. From this point, I can use a web browser to manage the concentrator.

NOTE   Please note that when you make changes to a concentrator, they are *not* automatically saved to Flash memory. You must manually save your changes; however, when you do make a change, it immediately becomes active in the concentrator's RAM.

CLI Menu Access

From this point onward, if you would log in to the concentrator to access the CLI, you would see a menu like that in Example 6-3:

Example 6-3 *CLI main menu*

```
1) Configuration
2) Administration
3) Monitoring
4) Save changes to Config file
5) Help Information
6) Exit
Main ->
```

Within any menu option, you can enter the letter "h" to take you back to the main menu. This option does not work when you are prompted to enter a value for a concentrator configuration parameter.

Password Recovery

Typically, the only time you would access the concentrator's CLI after putting an initial configuration on it would be for:

- Troubleshooting problems where you can't use a web browser.
- Breaking into the concentrator because you don't have the password for the admin account.
- Changing the NVRAM on the concentrator, or replacing an old concentrator with a new one: the password for the admin account is not stored in the configuration file in Flash memory, but is stored separately in NVRAM.

To perform the password recovery procedure, you need to use the console port of the concentrator (this is true of any Cisco product). To do so, reboot the concentrator and when you see the message "Starting power-up diagnostics . . .", press CNTRL-c or send a break signal, depending on your terminal emulation program. You'll see the output shown in Example 6-4.

Example 6-4 *Password recovery procedure*

```
Boot-ROM Initializing...
Boot configured 32Mb of RAM.
...
Loading image .........
Verifying image checksum ..........
Active image loaded and verified...
Starting loaded image...
Starting power-up diagnostics...
...
CNTRL-C
Main Menu Options
----------------
 1 - Reset Administrator Accounts
 Q - Quit Main Menu
```

Choose Option 1 to reset the password for the administrator accounts.

NOTE   The account concentrator's configurations—names and passwords—are not stored in the concentrator's configuration file in Flash memory; instead, these are stored in NVRAM. The only way to reset these is to use the procedure in Example 6-4. Also, if you have an Altiga concentrator running an earlier version than 2.5.1, you'll have to contact TAC to get instructions for the password recovery process.

Graphical User Interface

After you have configured an IP address on the concentrator's private interface, you can access it from your desktop using a web browser. One component of the GUI, the Live Event Log, uses Java, and therefore your browser should have Java enabled; otherwise, there's no real restriction on the brand of browser that you want to use. Throughout this book, I'll be using Internet Explorer 6.0 with SP1. Also, the concentrator I'm using is a 3005 running 4.1.7A and the first release of 4.7.

In the following sections, I explain:

- HTTP Access
- Quick Configuration
- Main Menu

HTTP Access

To gain access to the concentrator's private interface, in your web browser's address text box, enter:

http://*private_IP_address_of_concentrator*

When you do this, you should see a login screen like that in Figure 6-4. Enter a user name and password to log in to the concentrator.

Figure 6-4   *Concentrator Login Screen*

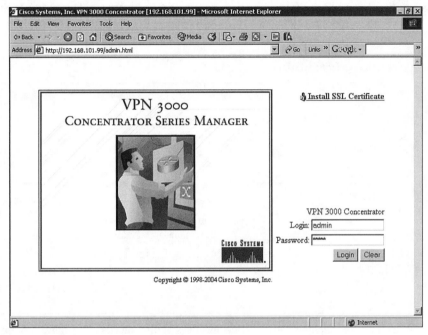

Quick Configuration

If you didn't complete quick configuration from the CLI, the first time you log in to the concentrator via the admin account, you'll see the screen shown in Figure 6-5. From here, you can continue the quick configuration process or abort it and go to the concentrator's main menu.

Figure 6-5   *Quick Configuration: Start*

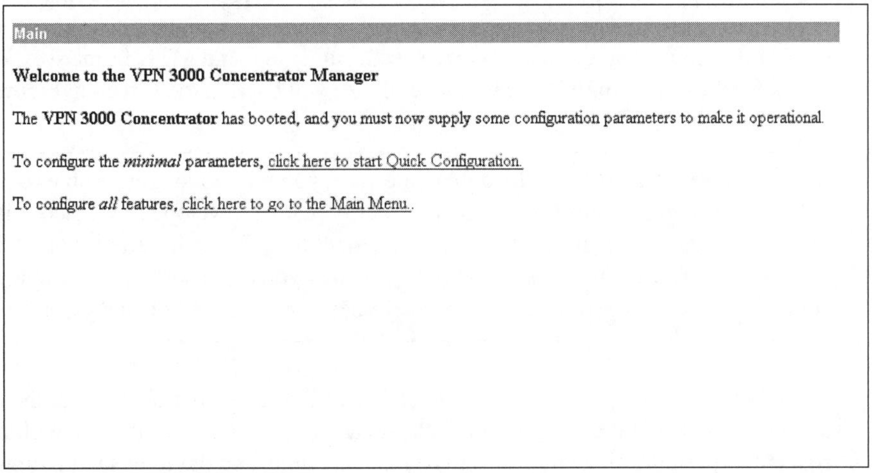

Figure 6-6 shows the first quick configuration screen. From this screen you can see the configuration and statuses of the interfaces on the concentrator. This example shows a 3005 concentrator (only two interfaces). To change the configuration on an interface, click the name of the interface under the "Interface" column.

Figure 6-6 *Quick Configuration: Interfaces*

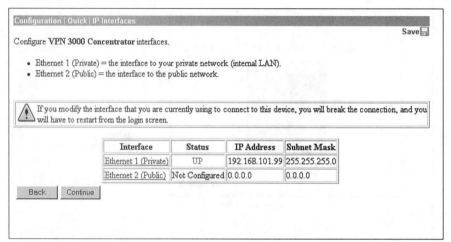

When I clicked the name of the concentrator's public interface in Figure 6-6, my screen then resembled Figure 6-7 (it will look slightly different in 4.7). For the public interface, you can specify that the interface acquires its IP address from a DHCP server (directly connected to a cable modem, for example) or statically configure it. I've chosen the latter option in this example.

Below the addressing section, you can define a filter for the interface. There are already some default filters defined on the concentrator, including one for the public interface. This is currently applied to the interface. Filters function like ACLs on Cisco routers or PIX or ASA security appliances—they're simple packet filters. The public filter already allows for VPN connections. You can also change speed, duplexing, and MTU frame size. When you are done, click the "Apply" button; this will take you back to the screen in Figure 6-6.

NOTE If you remove the filter from the public interface, you will no longer be able to terminate VPN sessions on this interface. This is a security feature developed by Cisco. Likewise, I highly recommend that if you'll be using a default filter for an interface, you go in and remove any unnecessary rules that allow traffic that you don't want: for example, if you're not using PPTP, then remove the associated rules from your public and other filters.

From the screen in Figure 6-7, you can click the "Continue" button. You are then taken to the screen shown in Figure 6-8. In the "System Name" field, enter the name of the concentrator. Below this you can change the date, time, and daylight saving time configuration. Below these parameters, you can enter a primary DNS server, a domain name, and a default gateway address for the concentrator—this is typically a next-hop address off of the public interface. If your concentrator is a DHCP client, the concentrator will learn this when acquiring its address information.

Figure 6-7   *Quick Configuration: Public Interface*

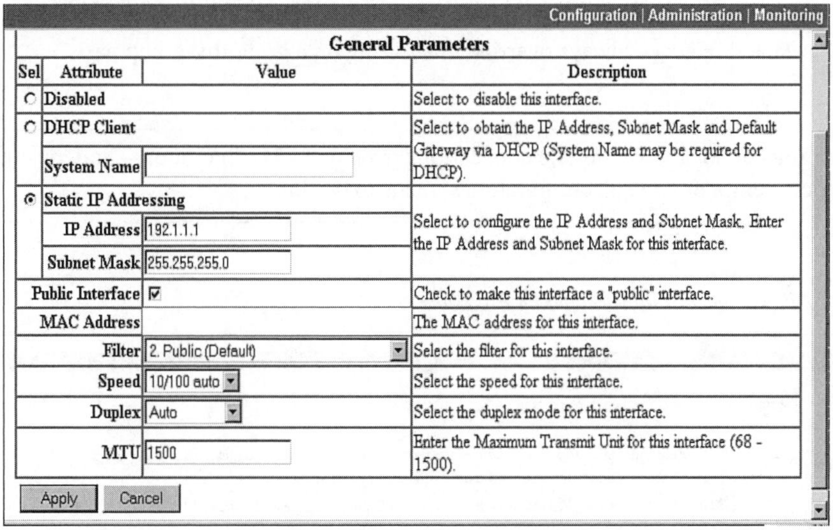

NOTE   If you'll be using certificates, your concentrator needs a system name and domain name—these two parameters are fed into the RSA algorithm to generate a public/private key pair; if you don't define these values here, you can define them from the concentrator's main menu system.

Figure 6-8   *Quick Configuration: System Information*

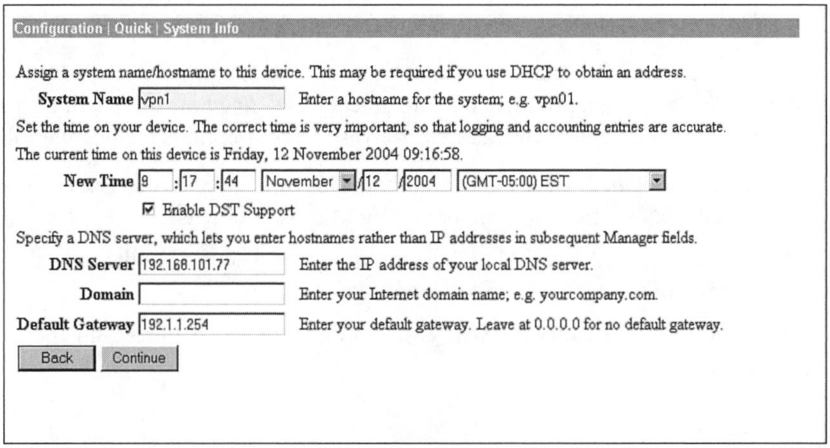

You can click the "Continue" button to continue to the next screen, which is shown in Figure 6-9. Figure 6-9 allows you to select which remote access tunneling protocols will be enabled for your users. By default all protocols are enabled; however, you can selectively disable ones you don't want or need. Please note that you can enable or disable these protocols for remote access from the main configuration screens of the concentrator. However, if you know that your remote access users will be using only one tunneling protocol, such as IPsec, you can disable the rest, forcing your users to use the one you selected. You can always override this setting on a group-by-group basis.

NOTE   You cannot add site-to-site connections from quick configuration—you must use the concentrator's main configuration screens to do this.

Figure 6-9   *Quick Configuration: Tunneling Protocols*

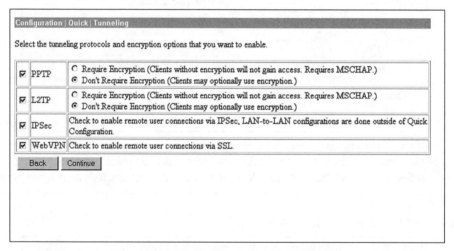

Click the "Continue" button to continue to the next screen, which is the address assignment screen (shown in Figure 6-10). This screen lets you define how users will be assigned their addresses (such as the internal address for IPsec). Your options include the following:

- **Client Specified**—The client configures his own address (this is not supported by the Cisco VPN Client, but is supported by Microsoft clients).

- **Per user**—An AAA RADIUS server assigns the address to the user; the server is defined in the next step of quick configuration.

- **DHCP**—You specify the DHCP server that will be used to assign clients their addresses.

- **Configured Pool**—With this option, you define a global address pool on the concentrator, and all remote access clients can use this pool; this includes the beginning and ending addresses in the pool, and the subnet mask. The last option is the one I chose in Figure 6-10.

NOTE   My personal preference is not to assign a global pool, but to have different pools for each group of remote access users; for example, one for marketing, one for programmers, and one for engineers. By using this approach, it is easier to implement filtering policies on Layer-3 addressing information. The concentrators give you this ability from the group area of the configuration section from the main access page, but not Quick configuration.

Figure 6-10 *Quick Configuration: Address Assignment*

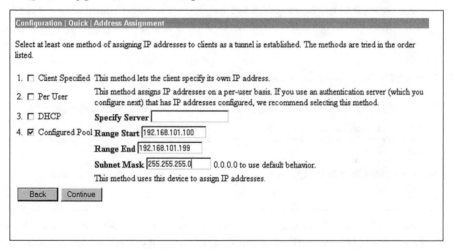

You can click the "Continue" button to continue to the next screen, shown in Figure 6-11. This is the authentication screen. This screen defines how remote access clients will be authenticated. You have the following options to choose from to determine where the user's login credentials are stored:

- **Internal Server**—The concentrator itself
- **RADIUS**—External AAA server using RADIUS as a communications protocol
- **NT Domain**—External NT Domain controller
- **Kerberos/Active Directory**—Windows 2003 server authentication
- **SDI**—RSA Security's SecurID server

In this example, I left the "Server Type" parameter as the default: Internal Server. If you chose an external authentication method, you'd need to specify access parameters for the server. For example, if you chose RADIUS, you'd enter information such as the RADIUS server's IP address and the key used to encrypt passwords in the payload of RADIUS messages; for NT Domain, you'd enter the IP address and name of the domain controller; for Kerberos/Active Directory, you'd enter the IP address and realm of the AD server; and for SDI, you'd enter the IP address and version number of the SDI server.

NOTE The VPN 3000 concentrators support a maximum combination of 1,000 users and groups defined locally on the concentrator (this number varies by platform). Therefore, to get the maximum number of supported users on the 3030, 3060, and 3080 concentrators, you'll need to define the users on an external authentication server and have the concentrator look up the user's access credentials on the external server. The goal of Cisco is to encourage people to use external authentication servers for large, scalable deployments. Plus, if you use one of the Windows options, this can serve as a single login process to the Windows network and to the concentrator for remote access. Most non-Windows-centric companies typically use an AAA RADIUS server such as Cisco Secure Access Control Server (CSACS). Cisco also allows you to use different authentication methods on a group-by-group basis.

Figure 6-11 *Quick Configuration: Authentication*

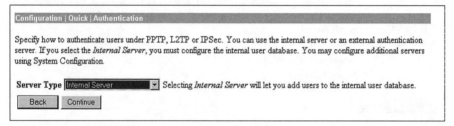

You can click the "Continue" button to continue to the next screen, which is shown in Figure 6-12. This is the IPsec group screen. Here you can add a remote access group for IPsec, along with its pre-shared key. This isn't necessary, though, since you cannot configure the properties of the group here. Therefore, you can skip this step and perform this later from the main configuration screens.

NOTE In 4.0 and earlier versions, quick configuration would prompt you to add remote access users before the IPsec group screen; however, this process had a downside: the users were not associated with the group you added during quick configuration, but with the global group. In 4.1, there is no option in quick configuration to add users—this must be done from the main configuration screens.

You can click the "Continue" button to continue to the next screen, shown in Figure 6-13. This is the WebVPN screen, which is new for quick configuration in 4.1. You'll only see this screen if you selected the "WebVPN" check box on the screen in Figure 6-9. Here you specify the types of proxies the concentrator will perform. I only selected HTTPS proxying; if you select one of the others, you'll need to specify the e-mail server the concentrator is proxying for.

Figure 6-12 *Quick Configuration: IPsec Group*

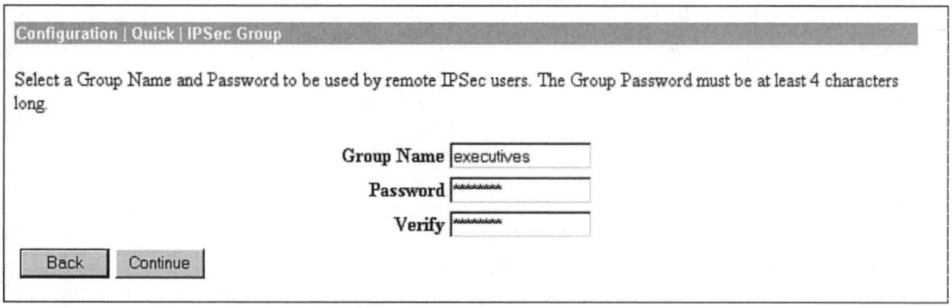

Figure 6-13 *Quick Configuration: WebVPN*

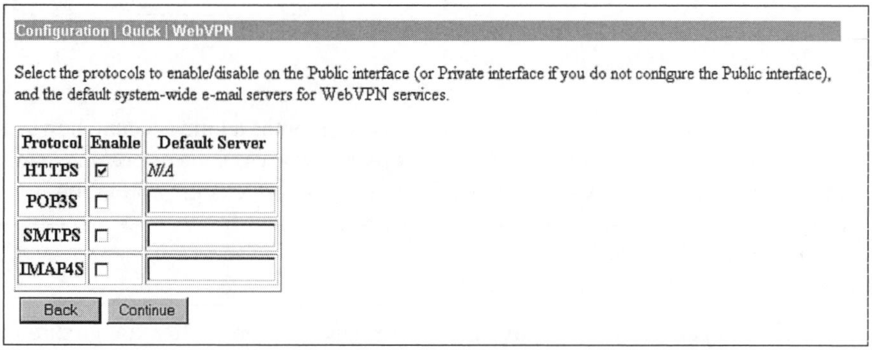

Click the "Continue" button to continue to the next screen, shown in Figure 6-14. This is the WebVPN home page screen. The information you enter on this screen will be shown to the users after they authenticate via WebVPN (SSL). At the top you can enter a title and a login banner. Below this, you can enter up to four hyperlinks that will appear on this page. Optionally, you can have a URL text box appear on the WebVPN access page that allows users to enter their own URLs—select the check box at the bottom for this option. Again, you'll only see this screen if you selected the "WebVPN" check box on the screen in Figure 6-9.

Click the "Continue" button to continue to the next screen, shown in Figure 6-15. This last screen of the quick configuration process allows you to change the password for the admin account. I highly stress that you should change the password to something *different* than "admin." Once you are done, you can click the "Continue" button. This will take you to the main access screen of the concentrator. If you need to change something, click the "Back" button at the bottom to go back one screen at a time. By default, your configuration is *not* saved when you leave quick configuration—you'll need to do this manually. I discuss this process in the next section.

Figure 6-14 *Quick Configuration: WebVPN Home Page*

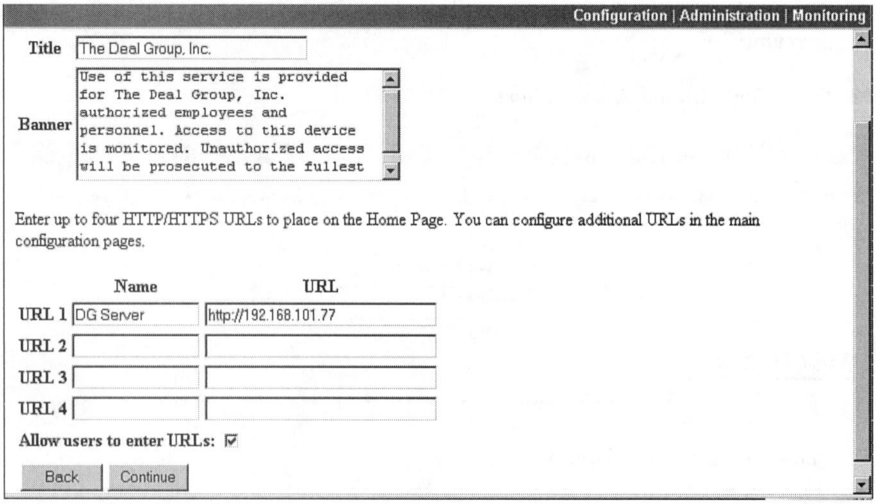

CAUTION Cisco does not require you to change the password for the admin account; however, I highly stress, again, the importance of changing this password as soon as possible, since this account and password are commonly found in password cracking programs.

NOTE Quick configuration occurs only once on the concentrators—after you go through it, you must use the main configuration screens to make any additions, modifications, or deletions to your configuration. Please note that quick configuration only puts a very *minimal* configuration on the concentrator—there are a lot of other things you'll still need to configure on your concentrator.

Figure 6-15 *Quick Configuration: Administrator Password*

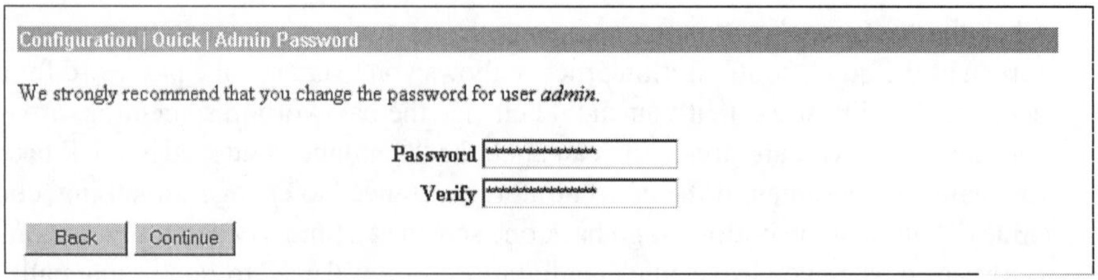

Main Menu

After completing quick configuration, or every time after this process when logging in to the concentrator, you'll be taken to the screen shown in Figure 6-16.

Figure 6-16 *Concentrator's Main Access Page*

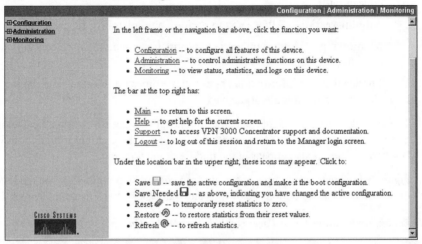

The screen in Figure 6-16 is broken into three sections:

- Top of the page
- Left side
- Middle of the page

At the top of the page there are four hyperlinks:

- **Main**—Takes you to this screen no matter where you are at in the concentrator.
- **Help**—Pulls up help concerning the concentrator screen you currently are on.
- **Support**—Takes you to a support screen where you can access documentation on the Cisco web site or e-mail TAC.
- **Logout**—Will gracefully log you out of the concentrator.

This information also appears in the middle of the main page.

TIP   I highly recommend that you log out of the concentrator gracefully by clicking the **Logout** hyperlink. I've experienced a bug in a couple of older releases of the concentrator software where if you closed down the web browser window without logging out, the concentrator assumed you were still logged in. There is a limit of five administrative login sessions allowed; once this limit is reached, no more login sessions are permitted. The only way to fix this was to log in via the console and remove the ghost sessions or reboot the concentrator.

Below the first row of hyperlinks you can see which account you're using to log in to the concentrator. In this example it's "admin." And below this is a second row of hyperlinks. These will take you to the three main areas of the concentrator:

- **Configuration**—Allows you to make changes that affect the VPN operations of the concentrator.

- **Administration**—Allows you to perform administrative functions.

- **Monitoring**—Allows you to view information concerning the concentrator and its operation.

You'll notice that this information appears three times on the screen: at the top, at the left-hand side, and in the middle of the page.

The left side is an expandable selector of concentrator access options: by clicking a particular hyperlink, like "Configuration," you'll see the configuration options expand below this. They'll also appear in the middle of the window.

Figure 6-17 shows an example of this where I clicked "Configuration" on the left-hand side of the screen. You see options below this and the same options listed in the middle window.

Figure 6-17 *Concentrator's Main Access Page: Left Side Expandable Options*

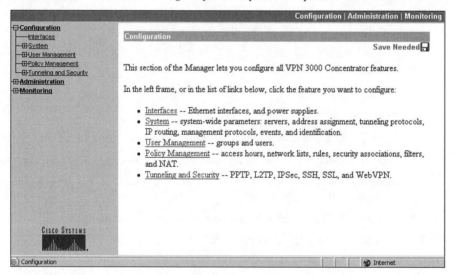

The middle window is where you change configuration options and parameters. At the top is a light-blue shaded bar. This bar tells you what you clicked to get this screen. In Figure 6-17, it displays "Configuration," denoting that I clicked "Configuration" from a previous screen. I like to refer to this bar as the "locator" bar. How information appears in the middle of the screen is different from screen to screen.

The last part of the main access screen I want to discuss is the icons you might see appearing below the locator bar in the upper right-hand corner. The bottom of Figure 6-16 gives a description of these icons:

- **Save**—The current configuration of the concentrator is the same that is stored in Flash memory. This icon appears on configuration screens.

- **Save Needed**—The current configuration is different from that in Flash memory. Click on this icon to save the configuration to Flash. This icon appears on configuration screens. You can see this in Figure 6-17, indicating that the currently running configuration has not yet been saved to Flash.

- **Reset**—This option temporarily resets statistics to zero. This icon appears on monitoring screens.

- **Restore**—This option restores statistics back to their reset values. This icon appears on monitoring screens.

- **Refresh**—This option updates the statistics on the screen. This icon appears on monitoring screens.

NOTE   Remember that the concentrator does *not* automatically save its configuration file to Flash memory—you must do this by clicking the **Save Needed** icon, which looks like a blue floppy diskette. This icon will not appear on Monitoring screens.

Summary

This chapter introduced you to Cisco VPN 3000 series concentrators. I discussed and compared the various models that Cisco sells, and introduced you to the two configuration interfaces the concentrator offers: CLI and GUI. Now that you have a basic understanding of how to interact with the concentrator, the next set of chapters in this part will focus on configuring remote access and site-to-site sessions, managing the concentrator, and troubleshooting connections.

Next up is Chapter 7, "Concentrator Remote Access Connections with IPsec," where I show you how to set up a concentrator to accept remote access connections that use IPsec. Remote acccess solutions using PPTP, L2TP, and WebVPN will be discussed in Chapter 8, "Concentrator Remote Access Connections with PPTP, L2TP, and WebVPN."

Concentrator Remote Access Connections with IPsec

The last chapter introduced the VPN 3000 concentrators, including a basic overview of their CLI and GUI interfaces. This chapter will focus solely on using a concentrator to terminate remote access sessions. Cisco concentrators support these remote access VPN implementations:

- IPsec
- PPTP
- L2TP over IPsec
- WebVPN

The remainder of this chapter will focus on the configuration of the concentrator to support IPsec remote access VPN implementations, including basic monitoring of connections and controlling remote access connectivity to the concentrator through groups, users, and network access control (NAC). Chapter 8 will discuss the latter VPN implementations on the VPN 3000 concentrators. I'll discuss detailed troubleshooting of VPN connections in Chapter 11, "Verifying and Troubleshooting Concentrator Connections," and the setup of the remote access clients in Part III, "Clients."

Controlling Remote Access Sessions to the Concentrator

Before I begin discussing how to terminate remote access sessions on a concentrator, I first need to discuss two basic means for controlling remote access to the concentrator:

- Groups
- Users

The following two sections will discuss these two concepts.

Group Configuration

Groups are used to simplify the application of remote access policies to your remote access users. If users have similar policies, you can create a single group with the associated policies and then place the right users into that group. With this process, you only have to create the policies once, but you can apply the policies to many users.

Cisco supports two types of groups:

- Base or Global
- Specific

The following two sections will discuss these two group types.

Base Group

The base group, commonly called the global group, is used for one primary purpose: to define remote access policies that are common to all specific groups and users. In other words, users typically are not associated with the global group. As an example, perhaps you have a policy that says all remote access users can use IPsec only to establish a tunnel to your concentrator. You have 20 specific groups this policy needs to be applied to. This policy is defined at the group level. However, it makes no sense to have to apply this policy to each of the groups individually. This is the main purpose of the base group: to apply a single policy that will affect all groups on the concentrator.

To access the base group's configuration, go to **Configuration > User Management > Base Group**. From here, you'll see the screen shown in Figure 7-1. At the top of the screen are tabs that take you into different configuration areas for the group policies. In Figure 7-1, the default tab, General, is in the foreground. You can click a tab to take you to different areas. I'll discuss each of these tabs, and their configuration parameters, throughout the rest of this chapter and the next. The one exception to this is the HW Client tab, which I'll discuss in Chapter 14, "3002 Hardware Client."

Figure 7-1 *Global Group Screen*

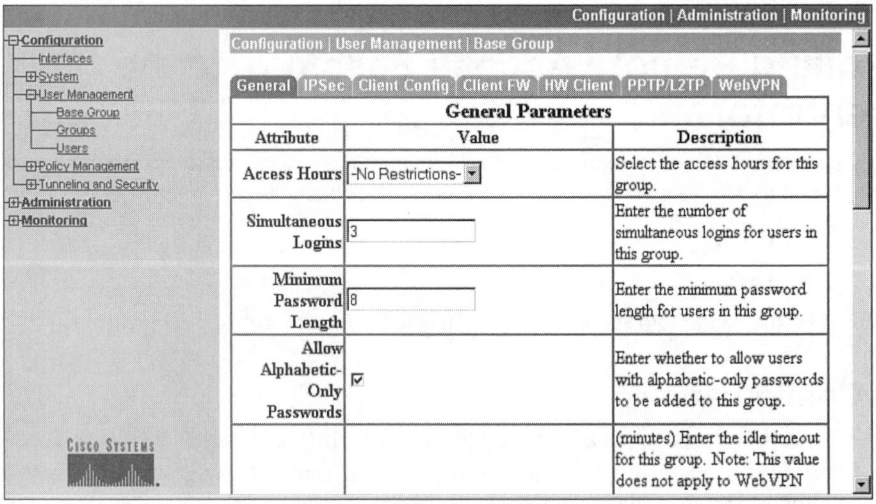

TIP	If you have many groups with similar policies, configure the base group with these policies first, and then create your specific groups. Your specific groups will inherit the properties of the base group, and then you can override any necessary policy configurations on a group-by-group basis.

Specific Groups

Of course, the base group's policy definitions might not be suited to each user or group of users. Therefore, Cisco concentrators let you create specific groups where you can override the policies defined in the base group on a policy-by-policy basis. To create, delete, or modify a group, go to **Configuration > User Management > Groups**. The bottom part of this screen is shown in Figure 7-2. In the middle of the screen is the listing of groups (in this example, no groups exist on the concentrator). To the left and right of the list of groups are buttons you can click to affect an action. For example, if you click the **Add Group** button, you can add a group and configure its remote access policies. For any other button, you first must select a group by clicking its name and then clicking the correct button. Many of these buttons are discussed later in this chapter, and some of the others, such as Client Update and Bandwidth Assignment, are discussed in Chapter 10, "Concentrator Management."

Figure 7-2   *Specific Group Screen*

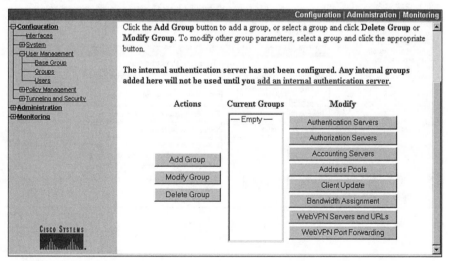

Identity Tab

When you either are adding a new group (clicking the **Add Group** button) or modifying an existing group (clicking the **Modify Group** button), you are taken to the screen shown in Figure 7-3. In this example, I'm adding a new group. You'll notice that the tab in the foreground is the Identity tab. Here you can define:

- The name of the group—I called this group "MyUsers."

- The password for the group (used for device pre-shared key authentication)—The password is hidden with asterisks automatically as you type it in (you must type it in twice for verification purposes).

- How authentication for the group is to be done—This can be selected using either "Internal," where the users are defined on the concentrator, or "External," where the users are defined on an external server (like a RADIUS or NT Domain server). I'll discuss how to set up external authentication later in the chapter in the "External Authentication" section.

As you can see, there's not much to change under this tab.

Figure 7-3 *Group Configuration: Identity Tab*

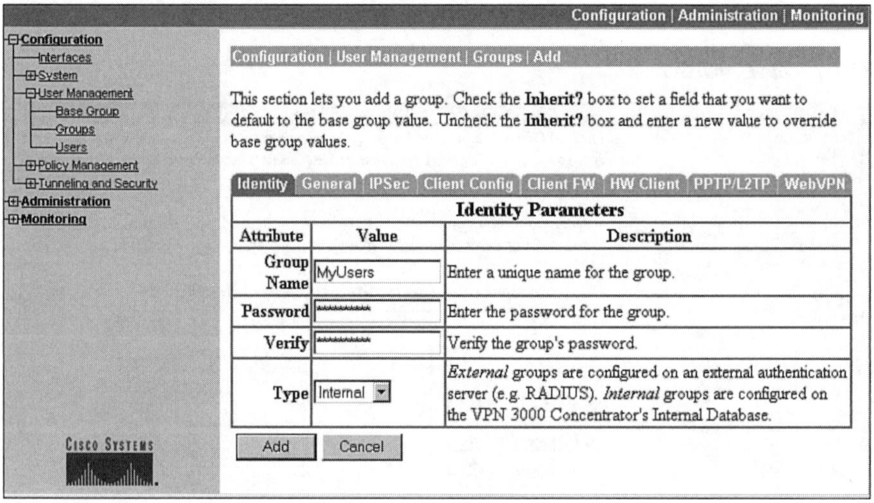

NOTE   At the bottom of the screen, if you click the **Apply** or **Add** button, it activates your changes and takes you back to the group listing screen; however, if you need to make changes where the parameters are located under different tabs for the group, clicking a different tab button will preserve your changes on your current screen. Before leaving the group configuration section, though, click the **Apply** button at the bottom to activate changes made under all of the group tabs. If you don't want to activate any of your changes within the group, click the **Cancel** tab to abort your changes.

General Tab

If you click the **General** tab, you are taken to the screen shown in Figure 7-4. Only the top part of the screen is shown here. The screen is divided into four columns:

- **Attribute**—This is the name of the parameter.
- **Value**—This is the value assigned to the parameter.
- **Inherit?**—This defines whether the parameter is inherited from the base group or not.
- **Description**—This gives a brief description as to what the attribute (parameter) is used for.

These columns, with the exception of the "Inherit?" column, are self-explanatory; so I'll discuss the "Inherit?" column in more depth. All the parameters that you see on the General tab and the other tabs to the right of this tab, like Client FW and WebVPN, have an "Inherit?" check box to the right of each parameter. When this is selected (checked), the concentrator obtains the setting of the parameter from the base group. Anytime you change a parameter, the check mark is removed from the "Inherit?" check box automatically and the concentrator uses whatever value you specify for the parameter.

TIP   If you've changed a specific parameter for a group and want to change it back to what the base group has defined, click the check box to the right of the parameter labeled "Inherit?" and then click the **Apply** button at the bottom of the screen. This changes the parameter's value back to the base group's defined value. You can verify this change easily by going back into the group and selecting the proper tab to see the base group value for the parameter.

Also, make sure that the "Inherit?" check box is unchecked anytime you change a parameter from the base group's configuration—this should happen automatically, but I've seen a couple of instances in various software versions where this doesn't occur for certain parameters.

Figure 7-4 *Group Configuration:* General *Tab*

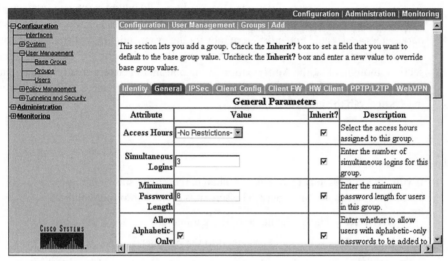

The General tab allows you to define general properties of the group. These properties are defined in Table 7-1. Most of the parameters and their configurations are self-explanatory.

Table 7-1 *General Tab Parameters*

Attribute	Explanation
Access Hours	You can restrict when a remote access user can connect. Your options include: No-Restrictions, Never (no access is allowed by any member of the group), and Business Hours (9AM–5PM, Monday–Friday).
Simultaneous Logins	You can restrict the number of remote access sessions a single internally authenticated user can establish: the default is 3.
Minimum Password Length	You can set the minimum number of characters that a user's password needs to have. This can range from 1–32, where 8 is the default. This parameter is for internally defined users only.
Allow Alphabetic-Only Passwords	You can allow users to use alphabetic-only passwords (contain only letters); I highly recommend that you *uncheck* this option. This parameter is for internally defined users only.

Table 7-1   *General Tab Parameters (Continued)*

Attribute	Explanation
Idle Timeout	You can define the timeout period for an idle remote access user session; this can range from 0 (no limit) to 10,800 minutes, with 30 minutes being the default. For WebVPN users, if the *Idle Timeout* is set to 0, the *Default Idle Timeout* value defined on the **Configuration > Tunneling and Security > WebVPN > HTTP/HTTPS Proxy** screen is used. For WebVPN users, I highly recommend that you set a short idle timeout because when a user's browser is set to disable or prevent the use of cookies, the users don't actually connect, but they still are listed on the **Administration > Administer Sessions** or **Monitoring > Sessions** screens, which can be misleading to an administrator. Also, if you set the *Simultaneous Logins* parameter to 1, and this condition occurs, the user won't be able to connect again until the ghost session idles out. By setting a low idle timeout value, a WebVPN user's cookies are deleted quickly, allowing that user to reconnect in a shorter period. Also, this parameter does not apply to users behind hardware clients, like the VPN 3002; but it does apply to the hardware clients themselves.
Maximum Connect Time	You can define the maximum number of minutes the user is allowed for a remote access session. Once this limit is reached, the user's session is dropped by the concentrator. This value can range from 0 (no limit, which is the default) to 2,147,483,647 minutes (which is more than 4,000 years!)
Filter	You can define a filter that is applied to the user's VPN session. This filter can be used to restrict a user's access to resources. I discuss how to create a filter in the "Client FW Tab" section later in the chapter.
Primary and Secondary DNS	You can define a primary and secondary DNS server to assign to the client. This overrides the client's assigned DNS server settings unless you have set up split DNS.
Primary and Secondary WINS	You can define a primary and secondary WINS server to assign to the client. This overrides the client's assigned WINS server settings.
SEP Card Assignment	You can specify which SEP module, in a dual-SEP module concentrator, a group should be assigned to. Cisco highly recommends that you don't use this process for load balancing, but that you use Virtual Cluster Agent (VCA) instead; VCA is discussed in Chapter 10, "Concentrator Management." If you recall from the last chapter, SEP modules perform encryption processes in hardware.

continues

Table 7-1   *General Tab Parameters (Continued)*

Attribute	Explanation
Tunneling Protocols	You can specify which remote access VPN implementations members of the group can use. The Quick Configuration properties you defined show here, by default (these are applied to the base group). You can specify none, one, or all of the following: IPsec, PPTP, L2TP, L2TP over IPsec, and WebVPN. Please note that if you don't select one or more protocols, no user is allowed remote access connectivity for the group. For example, if you want users to use only IPsec, make sure the check box to the left of IPsec is checked and the rest are unchecked. Please note that for a specific group, you can only select IPsec or L2TP over IPsec—the same group cannot have both of these activated.
Strip Realm	You can define whether or not realm information is stripped from the sent username. For example, some users send something like richard@ntdomain as their username when authenticating to a domain controller. Some external authentication servers don't understand the realm part (the "@" sign and the information following it), so the concentrator can strip the realm information off before sending just the user information to the external authentication server.
DHCP Network Scope	You can define the network scope that the DHCP server should use when assigning an address to the remote access client. Specify a network number here. If you enter 0.0.0.0 as the address, the network number of the concentrator's private interface is used. I discuss the use of DHCP to assign addresses to clients in the "Address Assignment" section later in the chapter.

The Identity and General tabs apply to any type of remote access VPN implementation that the concentrator supports. The other tabs typically are specific to a particular VPN implementation. I'll discuss the other tabs later in this chapter.

TIP   Remember that the concentrator doesn't save its changes automatically. Click the **Save Needed** icon at the top right of a Configuration or Administration screen to save your changes.

External Authentication

One limitation of all Cisco's concentrators is that they support up to a combination of only 1,000 local groups or users. So if you purchase a 3080 concentrator that supports 10,000 remote access sessions, the only way the 3080 will support this number of users is to use an external authentication server. In Chapter 6, "Concentrator Product Information," I discussed the external authentication methods that the concentrators support for remote access users:

- RADIUS
- NT Domain
- SDI
- Kerberos/Active Directory

The following sections will discuss how to specify the use of an external server for authenticating remote access users.

Authentication Server Creation

To specify the use of an external authentication server(s), first go to the Group configuration screen: **Configuration > User Management > Groups**. This screen was shown previously in Figure 7-2. From here, select the group that will be using external user authentication and click the **Authentication Servers** button. This screen is shown in Figure 7-5.

Figure 7-5   *Group External Authentication Screen*

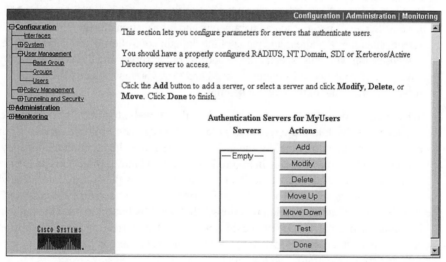

Click the **Add** button to add an external authentication server. When you click the **Add** button, the screen in Figure 7-6 is shown. The default authentication server type is RADIUS. But you also can choose NT Domain, SDI, and Kerberos/Active Directory.

Figure 7-6 *Adding a RADIUS External Authentication Server*

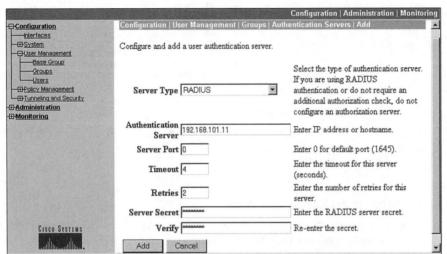

For RADIUS external authentication, enter the IP address of the server in the "Authentication Server" text box and the encryption key used to encrypt password payload information in the "Server Secret" text boxes. The other information is optional. If you choose NT Domain for the "Server Type," the screen parameters and information change. From the updated screen, enter the IP address and name of the domain controller. If you choose SDI external authentication, you must specify the IP address of the server and the version of software on the server. If you choose Kerberos/Active Directory, you must specify the IP address of the server and the name of the realm it belongs to.

When you are done adding your server, click the **Done** button at the bottom of the screen; this takes you back to the screen in Figure 7-5. You can add multiple servers, of the same external authentication type, for the group so as to add authentication redundancy. One additional button on the screen in Figure 7-5 is the Test button. Once you add a server, select it by clicking it and then click the **Test** button; this causes the concentrator to send a test message to the server. You'll be prompted for a remote access username and password to verify that the external authentication functions. Click the **OK** button to send the authentication information to the server. If you see this message, "Authentication Error: No response from server," then either you've misconfigured the server, or there is a connectivity problem between the concentrator and the server.

When you add multiple servers, the first server you add becomes the primary external authentication server for the group (you can have up to 10 authentication servers). You can click a server and click the **Move Up** and **Move Down** buttons to re-prioritize the list of external authentication servers, affecting which server becomes the primary one for the group. The server at the top of the list is the primary server. Click the **Done** button when you are done with the Authentication Servers screen, taking you back to the Groups screen.

NOTE If you define only one external authentication server, and it is not reachable by the concentrator, the user's authentication will fail; therefore, you should have redundant external authentication servers defined, at different locations within your network.

Authorization Servers

From the Groups screen, there are two additional buttons below the Authentication button that deal with external authentication servers:

- Authorization Servers
- Accounting Servers

NOTE The use of authorization and accounting servers is optional, but if you want to use them, you also must specify an authentication server; in other words, external authorization and accounting rely on the use of external authentication. Also, the authentication, authorization, and accounting functions can all be located on *one* external server or they can be spread across *multiple* external servers.

One limitation of defining only authentication servers is that the external authentication server is used only to authenticate the remote access users—check the users' usernames and passwords. You already might have defined many of the group's policies, such as access hours, primary DNS server, login banner, or filter, on an external server; and you want to use this information instead of re-configuring it on the concentrator. This information can be used by a group if you add an external authorization server(s).

To add an authorization server, go to the Group configuration screen: **Configuration > User Management > Groups**. This screen was shown previously in Figure 7-2. From here, select the group that will be using external user authentication and click the **Authorization Servers** button. The screen presented to you is almost the same as that shown previously in Figure 7-5; however, this screen allows you to add/delete/modify authorization servers only. Click the **Add** button to add an external authentication server. When you do this, you'll see the screen shown in Figure 7-7.

Figure 7-7 *Adding a RADIUS External Authorization Server*

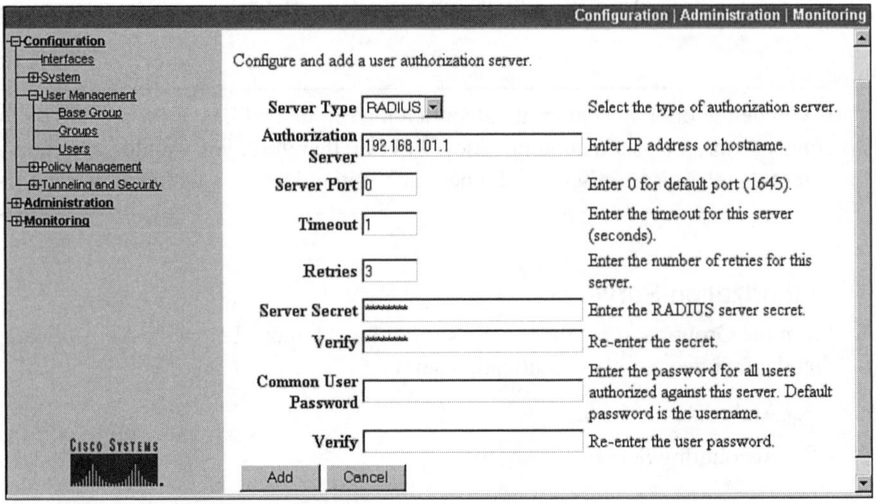

Only two external authorization server types are supported: RADIUS and LDAP. The default is RADIUS, and the RADIUS parameters are shown in Figure 7-7. You must specify the IP address of the RADIUS server in the "Authorization Server" field. The RADIUS server port defaults to 1,645; if you are using an implementation of RADIUS where the server port is 1,812, you'll need to specify this for the "Server Port" parameter. You'll also need to specify the secret key to encrypt payload password information. The "Common User Password" field is a password the RADIUS server needs, but doesn't use; for this reason, Cisco defaults the password to that of the username (this has nothing to do with authentication functions). When you're done, click the **Add** button at the bottom. You can create up to 10 authorization servers per group (of the same external server type). Like authentication servers, you can sort the order of the authorization servers and test connectivity to them.

For a RADIUS authorization server to interoperate correctly with your concentrator, one of the following must be true:

- If the RADIUS server is Cisco Secure ACS, the authorization attributes already are integrated into the concentrator and you need to do nothing further.

- If the RADIUS server is FUNK RADIUS, you must obtain the authorization attribute file from Cisco called cisco3k.dct, which contains the authorization attributes; authorization attributes define message codes used for the server and concentrator to interact with each other. Place this file in Flash memory in the concentrator (I discuss how to do this in Chapter 10, "Concentrator Management").

- For any other RADIUS server product, you must define the attributes *manually* and place the definitions in the concentrator's Flash memory. This process is beyond the scope of this book.

There are over 50 RADIUS authorization attributes the concentrator understands.

If you choose "LDAP" as the *Server Type*, the screen changes to something different than what you saw in Figure 7-7. With LDAP, you must enter the following information:

- **Server Type**—LDAP.
- **Authorization Server**—Server's IP address.
- **Login DN**—The name of the directory object, containing the authorization information that the concentrator will access.
- **Password and Verify**—The password for the login DN.
- **Base DN**—The location of the LDAP hierarchy where the concentrator should begin searching for the authorization information; it's entered in a format like OU=MyUsers, O=cisco.
- **Search Scope**—One-level search searches one level below the base DN, whereas a subtree search searches all levels below the base DN.
- **Naming Attributes**—The list of relative distinguished name attributes that uniquely identify an entry on the LDAP server, like Common name (cn), Organizational Unit (OU), and User ID (uid), to name a few.

When you're done, click the **Add** button at the bottom of the screen.

Accounting Servers

Accounting servers are used to keep a record of a user's authentication and authorization interactions with the VPN 3000 concentrator; by default, this kind of information is not stored on an external server unless you define one or more accounting servers.

To add an accounting server, go to the Group configuration screen: **Configuration > User Management > Groups**. This screen was shown previously in Figure 7-2. From here, select the group that you want to record accounting for (external authentication or authorization) and click the **Accounting Servers** button. The screen presented to you is almost the same as that shown previously in Figure 7-5; however, this screen allows you to add/delete/ modify accounting servers only. Click the **Add** button to add an external authentication server. When you do this, you'll see the screen shown in Figure 7-8.

NOTE	Before you define an external accounting server, first you must define an external authentication server. Also, only RADIUS is supported for accounting functions.

Figure 7-8 *Adding a RADIUS External Accounting Server*

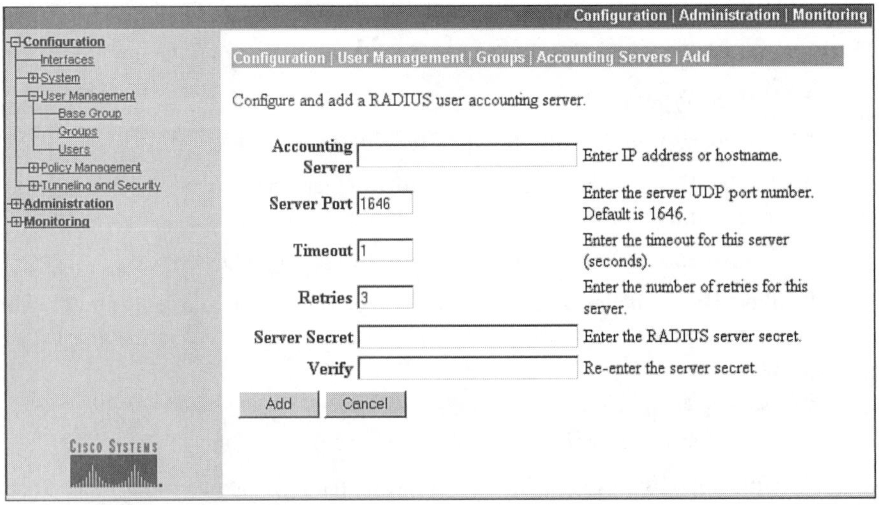

For RADIUS accounting, you must specify the IP address of the RADIUS server in the *Accounting Server* field and the *Server Secret* password used to encrypt password information sent between the concentrator and RADIUS server. The other information is optional. The only other parameter you might change is the *Server Port* field, where the RADIUS server's UDP port defaults to 1,646; some RADIUS implementations use 1,813 for the port. When you're done, click the **Add** button at the bottom of the screen. You can add up to 10 accounting servers, sort them in the proper processing order, and even test connectivity to them (just as you could with the authentication and authorization servers).

Group Configuration

Once you have defined your authentication, authorization, and/or accounting server(s), you need to specify that the group will use the external authentication servers. You do this by choosing **Configuration > User Management > Groups**, selecting the group by clicking it, and then clicking the **Modify Group** button. From the Identity tab, use the pull-down selector to change the authentication *Type* from "Internal" to "External" (see Figure 7-3) and click the **Apply** button. Once you have done this, any user associated with this group will use the defined external authentication, authorization, or accounting servers you have defined.

External Authentication, Authorization, and Accounting

Authentication, authorization, and accounting are commonly known as "AAA," or Triple-A. Only RADIUS supports all three components. In my experience with the concentrators, I mostly stick with an AAA server for an external server type. I prefer Cisco Secure ACS not because it's a good product and it comes from Cisco, but the last thing I want to do is to configure authorization attributes, which can be messy, on a non-Cisco product.

One nice feature of most RADIUS server implementations is that the actual authentication function can be passed off to another source. For example, Cisco Secure ACS can look up a user's authentication credentials on a token card server, like SDI, on a Novell NDS directory tree, on a Windows domain controller, on a Windows Active Directory tree, or on any ODBC-compliant database.

Therefore, if I want to use a single-login process through Microsoft Windows, and I have more than 1,000 users I need to support, I'll use Cisco Secure ACS as my RADIUS server and interface my concentrator with it. Then I'll configure the Cisco Secure ACS server to look up the authentication information on a Windows server, which authenticates the user to Windows, authenticates the user to the Cisco Secure ACS server, and authenticates the user to the concentrator—all in one authentication process! Therefore, I prefer to use Cisco Secure ACS with RADIUS over any other external server type the concentrator supports.

This is a common technique; however, you might run into problems if the administrator of the concentrator is not the administrator of the external source, such as a Windows domain. In this case, both administrators need to work together to ensure that security is implemented properly. Without this discussion between the two administrators, you are likely to find out that the concentrator admin is relying on the Windows admin (external database source) and vice versa.

Address Assignment

In Chapter 6, "Concentrator Product Information," I discussed the use of Quick Configuration; during Quick Configuration, one of the items asked is how addresses will be assigned to remote access clients. To change how addresses are assigned to remote access clients globally, go to **Configuration > System > Address Management > Address Assignment**. On this screen, there are four possible methods that can be used, as shown in Figure 7-9:

- **Use Client Address**—Use the address the client has manually assigned to itself; this doesn't apply to Cisco Easy VPN Remotes (clients), but to other types of clients, like Microsoft's Windows Client.

- **Use Address from Authentication Server**—Use the address the authentication server, like RADIUS, assigns to the client.

- **Use DHCP**—Use the address from a DHCP server to assign to the client.

- **Use Address Pools**—Have the concentrator use a global or group address pool to assign an address to the client.

The first two don't require any additional configuration on the concentrator, whereas the latter two do. Also, different groups can use different addressing methods. The next two sections will discuss the last two options in the above bullet points.

Figure 7-9 *Global Address Assignment Configuration*

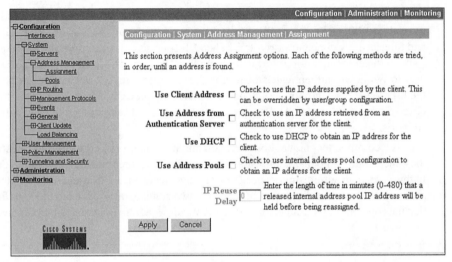

DHCP Address Assignment

If you choose the *Use DHCP* option, a DHCP server will assign an address to the remote access client. For this to function correctly, you must go to the **Configuration > System > Servers > DHCP** screen first. Click the **Add** button to add a DHCP server. From the new screen, you need to enter only the IP address of the DHCP server and then click the **Add** button at the bottom. If you add multiple servers, the first server listed in Figure 7-10 becomes the primary DHCP server—you can use the **Move Up** and **Move Down** buttons to re-prioritize the list.

Once you have added your DHCP servers, go to **Configuration > System > IP Routing > DHCP Parameters**. This screen is shown in Figure 7-11. This screen allows you to define your global DHCP configuration parameters. At a minimum, you must select the *Enabled* check box. The *Lease Timeout* parameter has the concentrator, on behalf of the remote access client, renew the address registration when this time period is reached. The *Timeout Period* is used when you've configured multiple DHCP servers. When the first DHCP server doesn't respond within this time period, the concentrator will contact the second DHCP server for a remote client's address.

Figure 7-10 *DHCP Server Listing*

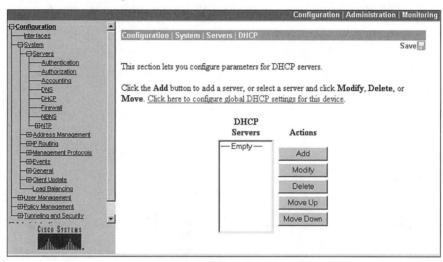

Figure 7-11 *DHCP Parameters*

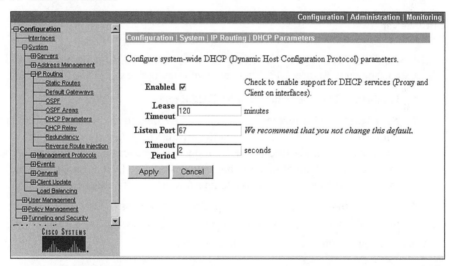

One optional DHCP setting is DHCP relay. DHCP relay is used in an environment where the concentrator is used for internal access of wireless clients, where the wireless clients are using a VPN to connect to the corporate network, as shown in Figure 7-12. However, the wireless clients typically use DHCP to acquire an IP address for their wireless NIC. When the wireless client sends a DHCP request to the public or external interface of the concentrator, the concentrator forwards the request to one or more DHCP servers in the private network. Basically, the concentrator is relaying DHCP messages between the client and server. The advantage of DHCP relay is that you don't have to set up the concentrator as a DHCP server; you have an internal DHCP server perform this process.

Figure 7-12 *DHCP Relay Example*

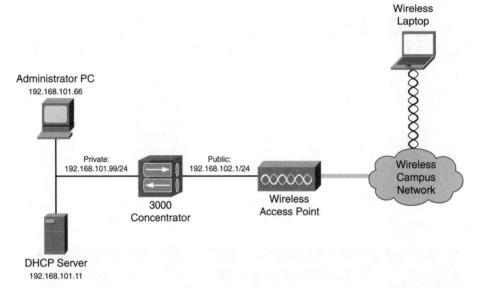

To set up DHCP relay, go to **Configuration > System > IP Routing > DHCP Relay**. This screen is shown in Figure 7-13. There are two relay options:

- **Enabled**—This check box enables DHCP relay.

- **Broadcast to all interfaces**—The client's DHCP request, when received on the public interface, is broadcasted out the private and external interface; if it is received on the external interface, the DHCP request is broadcasted out only the private interface. The assumption with this choice is that the DHCP server is on the segment to which the concentrator's private interface is directly attached.

- **Forward to**—Here you can list a specific host address or network to relay the DHCP request to. You must specify a subnet mask—for a specific host, use 255.255.255.255.

Click the **Apply** button to activate your changes.

NOTE   By default, the concentrator does not permit (blocks) all DHCP messages on its public and external interfaces. To allow DHCP traffic to enter and leave the external or public interface of the concentrator, you must change the filter on its interface by adding two rules to allow inbound and outbound DHCP traffic: *DHCP In* and *DHCP Out*. This process is described in Chapter 10, "Concentrator Management."

Figure 7-13 *DHCP Relay Screen*

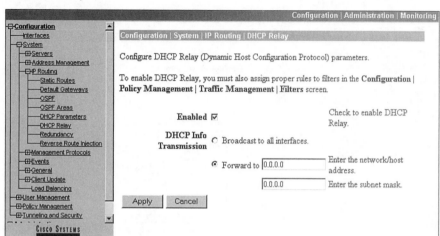

Concentrator Address Pools

Another option you can use for assigning addresses to clients is to define one or more address pools on the concentrator and let the concentrator be responsible for assigning the addresses: Choose *Use Address Pools* on the screen in Figure 7-9 to enable this process. One additional option on this screen is the *IP Reuse Delay* parameter: this parameter, when configured, has the concentrator wait the specified minutes before reusing an address in the address pool.

You can create two types of address pools on your concentrator:

- **Global pool**—This pool(s) is used by all remote access clients if a group pool doesn't exist for a user.

- **Group pools**—This address pool(s) is used by all remote access users associated with the respective group.

When going through Quick Configuration on the concentrator, if you choose the option to have the concentrator assign the addresses, and you specify the addresses in the pool, you have just created a global pool. You can add, change, or delete the global pool configuration by going to **Configuration > System > Address Management > Pools**. This screen lists the global pool or pools you have created on the concentrator. From this screen, click the correct button to make a change. For example, if you want to add a global pool, click the **Add** button. You must enter a starting address, ending address, and a subnet mask for the pool of addresses. Click the **Add** button to add a pool.

The most common way to have the concentrator itself assign internal addresses to clients is on a group-by-group basis. First, create a group from the **Configuration > User Management > Groups** screen, shown previously in Figure 7-2. Once you have done this, click the name of the group and then click the **Address Pools** button. The screen in Figure 7-14 is displayed.

Figure 7-14 *Group Address Pool Listing*

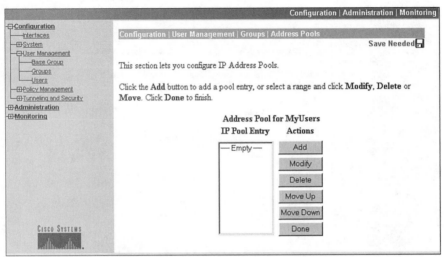

Then click the **Add** button to add an address pool for the group. This screen is shown in Figure 7-15. As in adding a global address pool, the group address pool needs a starting and ending address for the pool and the subnet mask value used for the address pool. Click the **Add** button to add the address pool, which takes you back to the screen in Figure 7-14. If you define multiple pools for a group, you can prioritize their usage by the concentrator by using the **Move Up** and **Move Down** buttons. When you are done adding your pool(s), click the **Done** button at the bottom of Figure 7-14.

Figure 7-15 *Add a Group Address Pool*

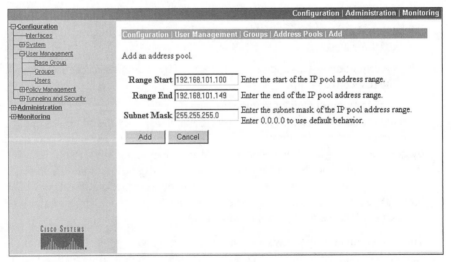

CAUTION	Make sure that when you set up your address pools, these addresses *don't* overlap those that your internal DHCP servers are using; otherwise you'll experience connectivity problems if an inside device is assigned the same address (from a DHCP server) as a VPN client (from the concentrator).

User Configuration

The second method of controlling remote access to the concentrator is through the use of user accounts. Authentication of users can be done externally, as mentioned earlier in the "External Authentication" section, or the users can be defined locally on the concentrator and the concentrator is responsible for the authentication of users. Having the concentrator be responsible for local authentication of users requires you to complete two configuration steps, in any order:

- Specify that the group the users will belong to will use *Internal* authentication.
- Create your users.

Group Setup for Internal Authentication

To specify the use of internal authentication of users, go to the **Configuration > User Management > Groups** screen, shown previously in Figure 7-2. Click the name of a group and click the **Modify** button. This displays the screen shown previously in Figure 7-3. In Figure 7-3, the *Type* of authentication is set to "Internal."

User Setup of Internal Authentication

To add local user accounts to your concentrator, go to **Configuration > User Management > Users**. This screen, shown in Figure 7-16, lists the users that have been added locally to the concentrator.

To add a user, click the **Add** button, which brings you to the screen in Figure 7-17. Like the Group configuration screen, this screen has tabs at the top:

- **Identity**—Defines the name and password for the user, and which group the user belongs to.
- **General**—Defines access restrictions for the user.
- **IPsec**—Defines IPsec properties for the user.
- **PPTP/L2TP**—Defines PPTP and/or L2TP properties for the user.

Figure 7-16 *Local User Account Listing*

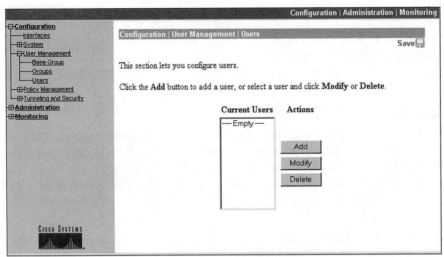

Properties you configure on a user-by-user basis override the group policies the user belongs to. The default tab that is in the foreground when you add or modify a user is the Identity tab, which is shown in Figure 7-17. The first field you must enter is the name of the user. The user's name is case-sensitive and can be up to 64 characters in length. Following this, you must enter the user's password twice. The password can be up to 32 characters in length and also is case-sensitive. Below this is the group that the user belongs to—use this drop-down selector to place the user into the correct group. Last, you can assign an IP address and subnet mask to the user instead of using a dynamic approach as with local address pools, DHCP, or an AAA server. This might be necessary if a particular user always needs to be assigned the same IP address.

Figure 7-17 *Local User Account Creation*

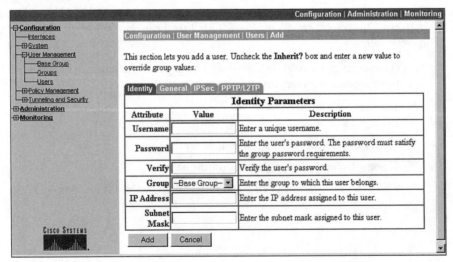

The General tab is similar to the same tab found in the Group configuration screen. This tab allows you to define access restrictions, including access hours, simultaneous logins, idle timeout, maximum connect time, a filter, and the allowed VPN tunneling protocols. These configurations override the group configuration that the user belongs to. I'll discuss the other two tabs later in this chapter and the next chapter.

NOTE   Remember that a concentrator has a limit to the maximum number of groups, users, and L2L sessions it can locally support (L2L sessions are treated as groups). The combination of these cannot exceed the concentrator's L2L session maximum value. For example, on a 3060 or 3080, they support a combination of only 1,000 local groups, users, and L2L sessions. Also, one limitation of local user accounts is that if you have two concentrators, you must *manually* replicate the user accounts across the two concentrators—there is no automatic synchronization of the configuration between concentrators. Therefore, most administrators will use an external authentication method when more than one concentrator is being used to terminate remote access sessions.

IPsec Remote Access

Now that you have a basic understanding of some of the global tasks you'll perform no matter what type of remote access sessions will be terminating on your concentrator, the remainder of this chapter will focus on the setup of IPsec remote access sessions. If you recall from Chapter 3, "IPsec," IPsec is one standard that defines how to protect traffic between devices. It supports site-to-site and remote access connectivity. For remote access sessions, the following steps are performed to build a tunnel:

1 Negotiate the ISAKMP/IKE Phase 1 transform set.

2 Perform Diffie-Hellman (DH) to come up with the shared secret key, and use this to encrypt the encryption key and HMAC function key to share between the peers.

3 Perform device authentication—concentrators only support pre-shared keys and digital certificates with a CA.

4 Authenticate the user using XAUTH.

5 Apply access policies to the user, such as assigning the user an internal IP address, defining split tunneling and split DNS usage, enforcing a firewall policy, and so on. Cisco commonly calls this step either IKE Mode Config or IKE Client Config.

6 You can use reverse route injection (RRI) to advertise the client's internal addressing information; this is necessary if the following are true:

   — The client could connect to more than one concentrator at the corporate site and local address pools are not being used to assign addressing information to the client.

— The client is a hardware client in network extension mode and needs to advertise the address of its private or inside interface to the corporate office.

One of the issues of IPsec is that for remote access connections, how policies are applied to a client are not defined by the IPsec standard—each IPsec vendor does this differently. Therefore, when I explain how to configure Step 5 later in this chapter, it is specific to the Cisco implementation. Also, I'll cover Step 6 in Chapter 14, "3002 Hardware Client," Chapter 18, "Router Remote Access Connections," and Chapter 22, "PIX and ASA Remote Access Connections." This chapter will focus on the configuration of remote access software clients on the concentrator.

This part of the chapter will discuss:

- Configuring ISAKMP/IKE Phase 1 transform sets (proposals) for the management connection of IPsec clients.

- Defining device authentication.

- Configuring the group's general IPsec policies.

- Configuring the group's IKE Mode Config policies.

- Setting up IPsec client firewall policies.

- Configuring ISAKMP/IKE Phase 2 data transform sets.

ISAKMP/IKE Phase 1: IKE Proposals

The first configuration items I'll explain are how to configure Steps 1 and 2: negotiating the Phase 1 transforms and the use of DH to build the secure management connection. On the concentrator, this is referred to as setting up your "IKE Proposals or Policies." The following two sections will discuss how to set up your IKE proposals.

IKE Proposal Screen

To define and use IKE Phase 1 proposals, go to **Configuration > Tunneling and Security > IPsec > IKE Proposals**. This screen is shown in Figure 7-18. The screen is broken into three columns:

- **Active Proposals**—These are management transform sets that can be used to protect the ISAKMP/IKE Phase 1 management connection between the concentrator and another device, like a remote access client or an L2L peer.

- **Actions**—These are actions that can be performed on a selected management transform set.

- **Inactive Proposals**—These are management transform sets that have been created, but are not being used in the negotiation process between the concentrator and another IPsec device.

NOTE   In Versions 4.0 and earlier of the concentrator software, to reach the IKE Proposal screen, go to **Configuration > System > Tunneling Protocols > IPsec > IKE Proposals**. Also, the term "proposal" when dealing with the concentrator is synonymous with the IKE Phase 1 management transform set.

Figure 7-18 *IKE Proposal Listings*

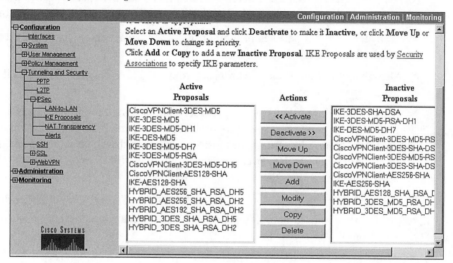

Proposal Names

Each management transform set is given a descriptive name. For example, the first management transform set listed under the *Active Proposals* column is "CiscoVPNClient-3DES-MD5." Based on the Cisco predefined name, it is fairly simple to figure out what the transform is used for: Cisco Easy VPN Remote/Client products with 3DES encryption and MD5 HMAC function. Here is a list of typical uses of transform sets based on Cisco nomenclature:

- Names beginning with "CiscoVPNClient" or "HYBRID" are used by Cisco client products.

- Names ending in "DH7" are used by Certicom's Movian VPN client for PDAs.

- Names beginning with IKE are used for site-to-site or other remote access client products.

NOTE   Certicom's client has been discontinued. There are currently other vendors working on third-party replacement products. One of these vendors is Worldnet21, which recently purchased the Movian source code.

Action Buttons

When you click a proposal name in either column, you can then perform an action on the proposal from the *Action* buttons. Here's a brief explanation of each of these buttons:

- **Activate**—Takes a selected proposal from the *Inactive* column and moves it over to the *Active* column.

- **Deactivate**—Takes a selected proposal from the *Active* column and moves it over to the *Inactive* column.

- **Move Up**—Moves a selected proposal set up in the list of proposals; this is important for the *Active* column because proposals are used in the order listed . . . top-down. Therefore order is important; the most secure entries should be at the top and the least secure at the bottom. However, the ones beginning with "CiscoVPNClient" should appear before the ones that begin with "IKE."

- **Move Down**—Moves a selected set of proposals down in the list of proposals.

- **Add**—Adds a new proposal (you don't have to select any proposal name when adding a new one).

- **Modify**—Modifies a selected proposal.

- **Copy**—Copies a selected proposal; this is useful when you need to create two proposals that are very similar.

- **Delete**—Deletes a selected proposal.

IKE Proposal Components

If you choose to add or modify an IKE proposal, you are taken to the screen shown in Figure 7-19. In this example, I'm adding a new proposal. You must give the proposal a unique name (the name has local significance only). The name can include spaces and is case-sensitive; it can be up to 48 characters in length. Following the name, you need to choose an *Authentication Mode*, which specifies how authentication (device and user) is to be performed.

Figure 7-19 *IKE Proposal Components*

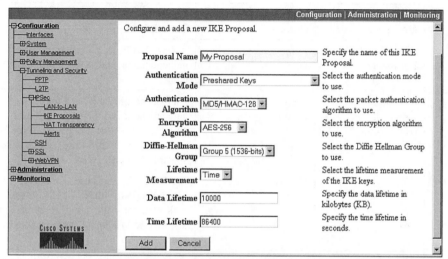

Table 7-2 lists the authentication modes you can specify. Hybrid authentication is new in concentrator software Version 4.1.4 and the VPN Client 4.0.5 software. Remember that the modes that have "XAUTH" or "HYBRID" in them are for IPsec remote access sessions only. Hybrid mode uses certificates to perform device authentication (on the concentrator only) and then the group's pre-shared key to validate a user's access to a group—on the VPN Client, this is referred to as "mutual group authentication."

Table 7-2   *IKE Proposal Authentication Modes*

Authentication Mode	Uses	Description
Pre-shared Keys	Site-to-site and some non-Cisco remote access clients	A pre-shared key is used for device authentication
RSA Digital Certificate	Site-to-site and some non-Cisco remote access clients	An RSA certificate is used for device authentication
DSA Digital Certificate	Site-to-site and some non-Cisco remote access clients	A DSA certificate is used for device authentication (DSA algorithm used to generate keys)
Pre-shared Keys (XAUTH)	Remote access clients	A pre-shared key is used for device authentication, with XAUTH for user authentication
RSA Digital Certificate (XAUTH)	Remote access clients	An RSA certificate is used for device authentication, with XAUTH for user authentication

continues

Table 7-2 *IKE Proposal Authentication Modes (Continued)*

Authentication Mode	Uses	Description
DSA Digital Certificate (XAUTH)	Remote access clients	A DSA certificate is used for device authentication, with XAUTH for user authentication
RSA Digital Certificate (HYBRID)	Cisco remote access clients	An RSA certificate is used for device authentication, with XAUTH for user authentication—the group's pre-shared key also is used to authenticate a user's access to a specific group
DSA Digital Certificate (HYBRID)	Cisco remote access clients	A DSA certificate is used for device authentication, with XAUTH for user authentication—the group's pre-shared key also is used to authenticate a user's access to a specific group
CRACK	Nokia 92xx IP phones	A challenge/response authentication method using cryptographic keys is supported in 4.7 for Nokia phones

Below the *Authentication Mode* parameter, you can choose the HMAC function to use for packet integrity checking: MD5 or SHA-1. Your choices for an encryption algorithm are: DES, 3DES, AES-128, AES-192, and AES-256. For DH groups, the concentrator supports 1, 2, 5, and 7, with 5 being the most secure. The lifetime of the management connection can be measured in time or amount of kilobytes sent across it. Most administrators use time for the measurement, where the default lifetime is 86,400 seconds (1 day) for the management connection.

TIP   In today's world of computers, I would recommend one of the AES algorithms because they are more secure and less computationally intensive than their DES counterparts. Remember that even though SHA-1 is more secure, IPsec uses only 96 bits of the signature, making MD5 and SHA-1 basically equivalent.

If this is a new proposal, click the **Add** button at the bottom; for changes to an existing proposal, click the **Apply** button at the bottom. As you can see, setting up the management transform set is a fairly simple process with the concentrator's web-based interface and drop-down selectors.

NOTE   When you add a new proposal, it will show up in the *Inactive* column; therefore, you'll need to activate it and put it in the proper place in the *Active* column.

ISAKMP/IKE Phase 1: Device Authentication

Once you have set up your IKE proposals, you're now ready to define your authentication information based on what you've specified in your IKE proposal(s). As you saw in the last section, only two basic types of device authentication are supported: pre-shared keys and digital certificates. The next two sections will discuss the use of both of these.

Pre-Shared Keys

Of the two device authentication methods, setting up pre-shared keys is definitely the easiest. You'll need to do this if the authentication mode you chose in your IKE Proposal was either pre-shared keys or HYBRID. Defining a pre-shared key is done on a group-by-group basis. First access the group screen: **Configuration > User Management > Groups**. Next, select a group and click the **Modify** button. Within the Identity tab, as shown previously in Figure 7-3, enter the pre-shared key twice: once in the "Password" field and once in the "Verify" field. Then click the **Apply** button at the bottom to accept your changes.

Digital Certificates

Using certificates on the concentrator for device authentication is much more complex than using pre-shared keys; but it is a more secure method of authentication. Certificates are required if you chose a proposal that included DSA, RSA, or HYBRID. First, you must obtain two certificates for the concentrator: root and identity. Do this using either the file-based or network-based (SCEP) approach. Also, you can configure some parameters related to the use of CRLs and certificate group matching. Last, make sure that you have a corresponding IKE Proposal that specifies the user of certificates for device authentication. The following sections cover the configuration of these steps on the concentrator.

Allowing External Access to the CA

This step might not be necessary; however, let's examine Figure 7-20 to illustrate a problem that you might experience with using a CA. In Figure 7-20, the CA is internal to the network design. This is not a very common implementation; normally, the CA would be placed in a DMZ and a firewall would restrict access to it. However, in my example, the CA is internal and, by default, the concentrator denies HTTP access from the public interface. Therefore, remote access clients won't be able to access the CA to validate other devices' certificates, including the concentrator itself. In this situation, you need to modify the filter on the concentrator's public interface to allow HTTP access inbound and outbound from the CA, assuming that the CA is not located off the private interface of the concentrator. I discuss this process in more depth in Chapter 10, "Concentrator Management."

Figure 7-20 *Internal CA*

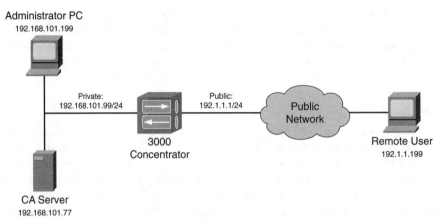

Obtaining a Certificate: File-Based

There are two methods you can use to obtain the root and identity certificates on your concentrator: file-based and network-based. This section will talk about the former. Here are the steps you'll go through:

Step 1   Assign a hostname by going to **Configuration > System > General > Identification**; the hostname is entered into the *System Name* text box. The name must be DNS-friendly.

Step 2   Assign a domain name by going to **Configuration > System > DNS Servers** and entering a domain name in the *Domain* text box. A fully qualified domain name is needed to generate the public/private keys that are used to sign and validate the identity certificate.

Step 3   Go to **Administration > Certificate Management > Enrollment**. Click the **Enroll via PKCS10 Request (Manual)** hyperlink.

Step 4   You now need to enter the PKCS #10 information for the concentrator. This screen is shown in Figure 7-21. The only required field is *Common Name*, where you typically enter the fully qualified DNS name of the concentrator (you can enter a single name, though). The other fields are optional. One field that doesn't appear on the screen shot, but is at the bottom of the screen, is *Key Size*, which allows you to specify the size of the public/private keys to generate. The default is 512 bits, but this can be 768, 1024, and 2048. When finished filling out the PKCS #10 enrollment form, click the **Enroll** button at the bottom of the screen.

Step 5   A web browser window will pop up with the PKCS information that you need to send, out-of-band, to the CA administrator. Figure 7-22 displays the web browser window with the PKCS #10 information. This file also is stored in Flash memory of the concentrator, so if you accidentally close this window, you still can recall the PKCS #10 information. Please note that you need to send the entire contents, including the lines that begin with "---."

Step 6   The CA administrator will send back two certificates (typically out-of-band): the root and your concentrator's new identity certificates. You must install the root certificate first. To install the root certificate, go to **Administration > Certificate Management > Installation**. Click the **Install CA Certificate** hyperlink.

Step 7   Click the **Upload File From Workstation** hyperlink. Click the **Browse** button and find the CA's root certificate on your PC's hard drive. Click the **Install** button to install the root certificate. You'll be returned to the **Administration > Certificate Management** screen. I'll discuss this screen in Step 10.

Step 8   Now you need to install your identity certificate. Go to **Administration > Certificate Management > Installation**. Click the **Install certificate obtained from enrollment** hyperlink. The Enrollment Status screen is displayed, as shown in Figure 7-23. As you can see, the status is "In Progress."

Step 9   Click the **Install** hyperlink. Click the **Upload File From Workstation** hyperlink. Click the **Browse** button and find the concentrator's identity certificate on your PC's hard drive. Click the **Install** button to install the root certificate.

Step 10   You'll be returned to the **Administration > Certificate Management** screen, shown in Figure 7-24. From this screen you can see the root certificate (the *Subject* is "caserver") and the identity certificate (the *Subject* is "vpn3005.richard-deal.com"). To view either certificate, click the **View** hyperlink under the *Actions* column. Figure 7-25 shows the concentrator's identity certificate.

This completes the process for certificate file-based enrollment.

NOTE   The concentrator needs a name and a domain name in order to generate the RSA key pair that will be used to sign and validate the PKCS #10 information.

Figure 7-21 *Certificate PKCS #10 Enrollment*

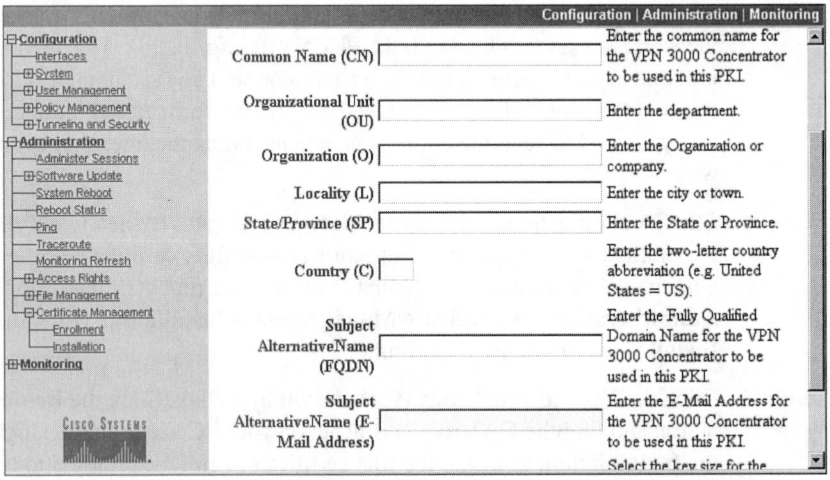

Figure 7-22 *PKCS #10 File*

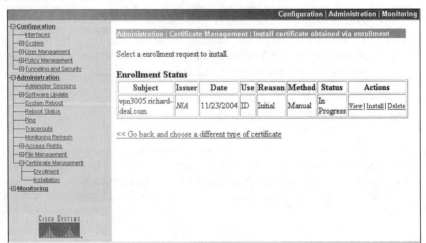

Figure 7-23 *Enrollment Status Screen*

Figure 7-24 *Certificate Management Screen*

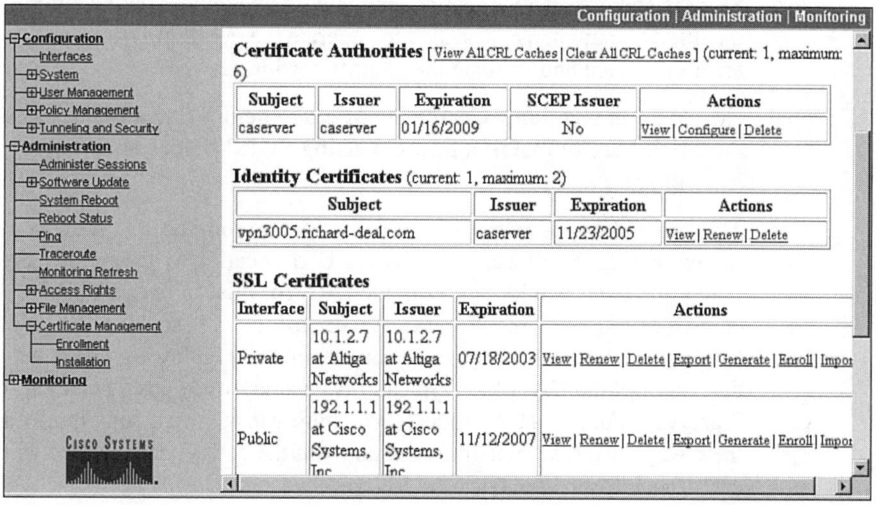

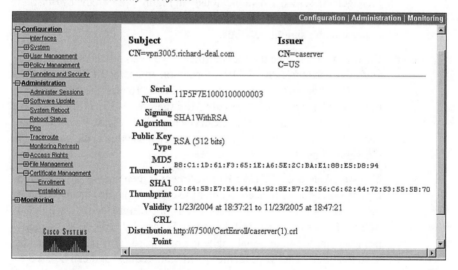

Figure 7-25 *Concentrator's Identity Certificate*

Obtaining a Certificate: Network-Based

The second method you can use to obtain the root and identity certificates is SCEP. Of the two methods, this is definitely easier than the file-based approach. Here are the steps you'll go through:

Step 1   Assign a hostname by going to **Configuration > System > General > Identification**; the hostname is entered into the *System Name* text box. The name must be DNS-friendly.

Step 2 Assign a domain name by going to **Configuration > System > DNS Servers** and entering a domain name in the *Domain* text box. A fully qualified domain name is needed to generate the public/private keys that are used to sign and validate the identity certificate.

Step 3 Go to **Administration > Certificate Management > Enrollment**. Click the **Click here to install a new CA using SCEP before enrolling** hyperlink.

Step 4 This screen lets you retrieve the root certificate from the CA, shown in Figure 7-26. You'll need to enter the URL location to access the CA via SCEP. Each vendor has a unique URL for this. In my case, I'm using a Microsoft Windows 2000 Server for the CA, so the URL is: "http://192.168.101.77/certsrv/mscep/mscep.dll". Following this is the descriptor of the CA, which typically is a name. In my case, I entered "caserver." For some CA products, you must use the name configured on the CA: your CA administrator can tell you the correct name. Once you enter this information, click the **Retrieve** button.

Step 5 If the retrieval process is successful, you should be taken to the Certificate Management screen shown previously in Figure 7-25. In the *Certificate Authorities* section you should see the root certificate, and the *SCEP Issuer* column should say "Yes."

Step 6 Once you've installed the root certificate, you can proceed to generating your concentrator's PKCS #10 information and using SCEP to send this to the CA and to retrieve its identity certificate. To start the process, go to the **Administration > Certificate Management > Enrollment** screen. Click the **Enroll via SCEP at caserver** hyperlink. Please note that your particular situation won't say "caserver," because this is the name of the CA server I used.

Step 7 You are taken to the PKCS #10 enrollment screen shown previously in Figure 7-21. You only need to enter the common name (the name of the concentrator) for the certificate. There is one difference between the SCEP PKCS #10 screen and the one in Figure 7-21: the SCEP screen prompts you for an optional challenge password. This password can be used to authenticate your identity certificate request and can be used to verify your identity when you want to revoke the concentrator's identity certificate. When finished filling out the PKCS #10 enrollment form, click the **Enroll** button at the bottom of the screen.

Step 8 On an updated screen, you should see either "SCEP Status: Poll" or "SCEP Status: Installed," indicating a successful submission to the CA. If it says "Poll," the CA was set up to not automatically grant identity certificates; the CA administrator will have to log in to the CA and grant the certificate request. The concentrator will continue to poll the CA until the CA grants or revokes the certificate request. If it says "Installed," the CA automatically generated a certificate for you.

Step 9   Go to the **Administration > Certificate Management** screen, shown in Figure 7-24, to see the installed certificates. From this screen you can see the root certificate (the *Subject* is "caserver") and the identity certificate (the *Subject* is "vpn3005.richard-deal.com").

This completes the process for certificate network-based enrollment.

Figure 7-26   *CA Location for SCEP Access*

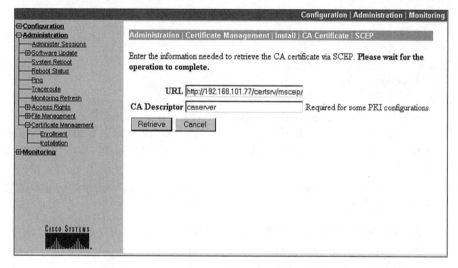

Configuring CRL Parameters

By default, the concentrator does not use certificate revocation lists (CRLs). To enable the use of CRLs, or to customize CRL parameters, go to **Administration > Certificate Management**. This screen was shown previously in Figure 7-25. In the *Certificate Authorities* section, you'll see the root certificates listed. To the far right of the root certificates is a column called *Actions*. To configure CRL options for the associated CA, click the **Configure** button. This will take you to the screen shown in Figure 7-27. At the top of this screen are four tabs:

- *Certificate Acceptance*
- *CRL Retrieval*
- *CRL Protocol*
- *CRL Caching*

Figure 7-27 *CRLs: Certificate Acceptance Tab*

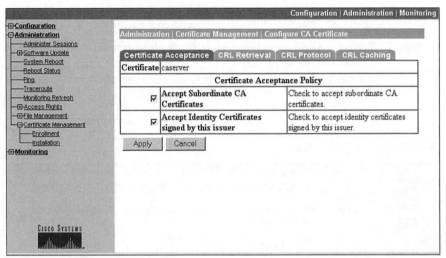

Click the tab to take you to the correct CRL configuration area. The default tab is the Certificate Acceptance tab. Here you can accept subordinate CA certificates if your CA implementation uses a hierarchy, and you also can accept identity certificates assigned by the CA(s).

Clicking the **CRL Retrieval** tab will take you to the screen shown in Figure 7-28. You have the following options:

- You do not want to use CRLs (this is the default).

- You can specify that the concentrator use statically configured CRLs (you specify the URLs for finding the CRL locations).

- You have the concentrator use the CRL listed on the CA's root certificate. If you refer back to Figure 7-25, you'll see the CRL location at the bottom of the root certificate.

- You can have the concentrator use the embedded CRL location on the root certificate; and if this is not reachable, use a static CRL definition(s).

When you are done making your retrieval policy changes within any of the tabs, click the **Apply** button at the bottom of the screen.

Clicking the **CRL Protocol** tab takes you to the screen shown in Figure 7-29. This screen allows you to specify which protocol(s) to use to retrieve the CRL: HTTP or LDAP are supported. For LDAP, you must specify the IP address of the server and authentication information. Below this, you can enter up to five URLs for your static CRL definitions/locations.

Figure 7-28 *CRLs:* CRL Retrieval *Tab*

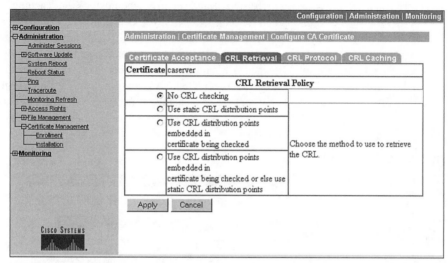

Figure 7-29 *CRLs: CRL Protocol Tab*

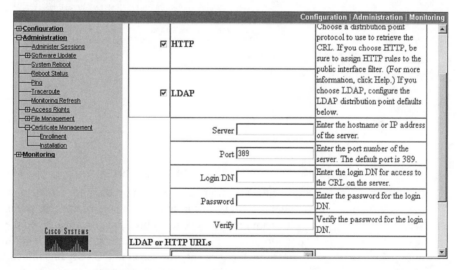

Clicking the **CRL Caching** tab takes you to the screen shown in Figure 7-30. CRL caching is disabled by default, which means that every time the concentrator needs to reference the CRL, the concentrator has to go out to a URL location and download it, which can be time-consuming. You can enable CRL caching by clicking the *Enabled* check box. When enabled, a CRL(s) is cached in RAM on the concentrator. Thus, every time you boot up the concentrator, it must go out and download the CRL(s). You can specify how often the concentrator will download the most current CRL(s), and also validate the date on the CRL.

NOTE	There is a trade-off between performance and security when using CRL caching. The advantage, when caching, is that for lengthy CRLs, you can check the validity of a certificate immediately because you have the CRL in RAM. The disadvantage, however, is that if a certificate has been revoked since the last time your concentrator downloaded the CRL, the concentrator will see the certificate as valid. In most cases, I use caching, but I'll set the refresh time to once every hour or so if the CA is an in-house CA. For external CAs, especially public ones like Verisign, I set up a caching refresh time of typically once a day.

Figure 7-30 *CRLs: CRL Caching Tab*

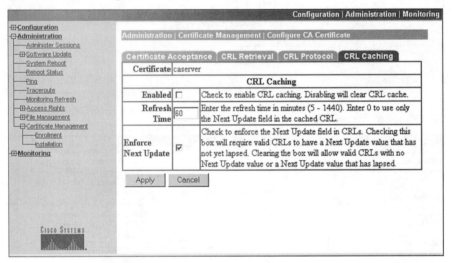

Configuring Certificate Group Matching Parameters

Using a certificate for device authentication can present a problem for remote access connectivity: IPsec doesn't define a way of sharing the group name the user wants to use. With pre-shared keys, this is accomplished by sending both the group name and the key for the group, commonly called *group keying*; but no such method is defined for certificates. Before Version 3.6 of the software, the concentrator used the OU (Organizational Unit), sometimes called the Department, field to represent the name of the group. But this process had limitations: the OU field had to have the correct group name. But what if this was not the case? Or what if a user changed from one group to another? Before 3.6, you would have to reissue a new certificate for the user. Obviously, this is not a flexible solution.

In Version 3.6, the concentrator supports a certificate group matching feature. This feature allows you to look at the values of one or more field on the certificate in order to associate a remote access user to a particular group. To define your group matching policies when certificates are used for device authentication, go to **Configuration > Policy Management >**

Group Matching > Policy, which is shown in Figure 7-31. You have three options:

- Create your own rules as to how matching should occur based on information that appears on a user's identity certificate.

- Use the OU field on the certificate to represent the group name.

- Or, if the above two fail to find a match, put the user in a default group of your choosing.

Figure 7-31 *Certificate Group Matching Policies*

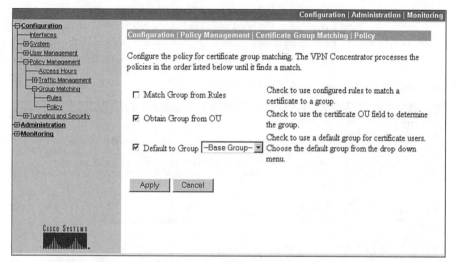

If you enable the first option, you'll need to create your own policy rules for group matching by going to **Configuration > Policy Management > Group Matching > Rules**, shown in Figure 7-32.

Figure 7-32 *Certificate Group Matching Rules Listing*

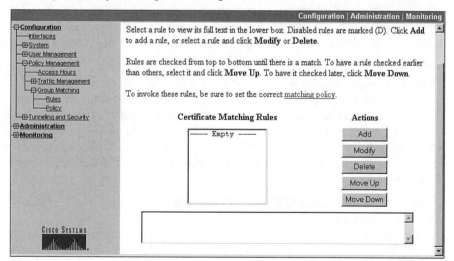

To add a rule, click the **Add** button, which takes you to the screen shown in Figure 7-33. Click the *Enable* check box to enable the rule. Used the *Group* pull-down selector to choose the group that the certificate will be associated with when a match occurs on a rule or rules associated with the group. Below this is a drop-down selector where you either can choose "Subject" (the user) or "Issuer" (the CA); in most cases you'll let it default to "Subject." Next, use the drop-down *Distinguished Name* (DN) selector to choose the field on the certificate that you want to match on. Next choose the *Operator* to match on and then the value that appears in the DN field. To the right of this information (cut from the screen shot) is a button labeled **Append**. Clicking this button will add the match criteria to the section labeled *Matching Criterion* at the bottom. This feature allows you to look at multiple fields on a certificate to determine which group the user belongs to. Click the **Add** button when you're done adding your rule, which takes you back to the screen listed in Figure 7-32.

Figure 7-33 *Certificate Group Matching Rules Creation*

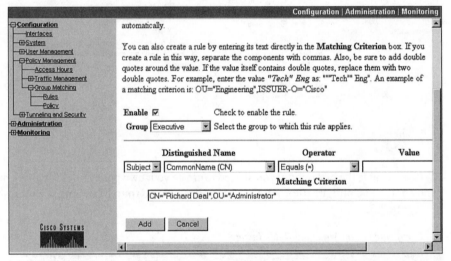

You'll see the rules listed at the bottom of Figure 7-32. The order of the rules is important; because the first match is used by the concentrator when placing a user into a particular group, you can use the **Move Up** and **Move Down** buttons to re-sort the list.

Here's a simple example of the use of group matching. Assume you had a user called "Richard Deal," who showed up as this value in the CN field of his identity certificate. Richard currently belongs to the "Administrator" group, but was promoted to an executive position. Your concentrator is using the OU field for group matching, and Richard has "Administrator" in the OU field. However, now that Richard has been promoted, you want him to be placed in the "Executive" group. You can accomplish this by performing the following:

Step 1 Go to the screen in Figure 7-31 and click the "Match Group from Rules" check box.

Step 2   Go to the screen in Figure 7-32 and click the **Add** button. In Figure 7-33, click the *Enable* check box and select the "Executive" group.

Step 3   Then for the CN, enter "Richard Deal" and click the **Append** button.

Step 4   If there were two Richard Deals, one in the Administrator group and one in the Programming group, you would need to append a second matching criterion like that shown in Figure 7-33: OU=Administrator.

Step 5   When done, click the **Add** button.

This newly created rule will look for two things on an identity certificate: "Richard Deal" in the CN field and Administrator in the OU field. If there is a match, the user of this identity certificate is associated with the Executive group automatically.

TIP   The most common method of associating a user to a particular group when using certificates is to match on the serial number of the certificate, because each certificate, within a CA's scope of domain, has a unique serial number.

Using Certificates

Once you have obtained your concentrator's identity certificate and want to use certificates for device authentication, the use of certificates by IPsec is defined in three places:

- IKE Proposals (this was discussed in the "IKE Proposal Components" section earlier).

- IPsec tab in the group section (this will be discussed in the "ISAKMP/IKE Phase 1: *IPsec* Tab" section next).

- Security Association (this will be discussed in the "ISAKMP/IKE Phase 2: Data SAs" section later).

NOTE   The 3005 supports up to two identity certificates, whereas the other models support up to 20; you need more than one identity certificate if you are using more than one root CA. In this case, you'll need to install a separate root certificate for each root CA and a separate identity certificate (obtained from each individual root CA).

ISAKMP/IKE Phase 1: IPsec Tab

To configure your general IPsec properties for connections, go to either the group or user screen and modify the appropriate value.

Groups IPsec Tab

Most of the general IPsec properties for remote access connections are done from the Groups section under User Management: **Configuration > User Management > Groups**. From here, modify a group and then click the **IPsec** tab. The top part of the screen you'll see is shown in Figure 7-34. Here is a list of parameters you can change on this screen:

- **IPsec SA**—This pull-down selector allows you to choose the name of the data transform you want to use to protect your unidirectional data connections built in Phase 2 (I discuss the configuration of these later in the "ISAKMP/IKE Phase 2: Data SAs" section).

- **IKE Peer Identity Validation**—This pull-down selector allows you to choose whether or not certificates should be used for device authentication in this group. Your options are:
  - **If supported by certificate**—If the client wants to use a certificate and the concentrator has one, use this option.
  - **Required**—All users of this group must use certificates for device authentication.
  - **Do not check**—When using certificates, don't check the user's identity (in other words, ignore the user's certificate for authentication functions); this is used when the identity certificate is missing some information on the certificate that the concentrator might be expecting—use this option if the client will be using pre-shared keys or the HYBRID method of device authentication.

- **IKE Keepalives**—This check box enables or disables IKE keepalives; this is a proprietary Cisco feature that uses the ISAKMP/IKE Phase 1 management connection to send keepalives periodically to ensure that the connection and peer are still operational. IKE keepalives are supported only on Easy VPN devices.

- **Confidence Interval**—This is the number of seconds the concentrator should allow a peer to idle before beginning IKE keepalives. The value can be from 10–300 seconds. For site-to-site sessions, it defaults to 10 seconds; for remote access sessions, it defaults to 300 seconds.

- **Tunnel Type**—This drop-down selector allows you to choose the connection type: "LAN-to-LAN" or "Remote Access." Choose the latter for remote access client sessions (this is the default).

- **Group Lock**—When this check box is checked, the concentrator examines the user's configuration and compares the group name under the user configuration to the group name the user is trying to connect to: if they're different, the user is denied remote access to the concentrator.

- **Authentication**—This drop-down selector allows you to choose the XAUTH authentication method that should be used for the group (in other words, where the user accounts are located—internally or on an external server). These can be: "None,"

"RADIUS," "RADIUS with Expiry," "NT Domain," "SDI," "Kerberos/Active Directory," or "Internal." Use "None" if the group is using L2TP over IPsec or if WebVPN users in the base group are using digital certificates. "RADIUS with Expiry" allows users to change their passwords when they expire: MS-CHAPv2 is used in this process.

- **Authorization Type**—This drop-down selector allows you to choose the authorization method used to authorize users of this group (in other words, where the group policy information is located—internally or on an external server). This value can be: "None" (default), "RADIUS," or "LDAP."

- **Authorization Required**—This check box allows you to make authorization a mandatory process; the default is disabled, making it optional.

- **DN Field**—This drop-down selector allows you to specify for IPsec and WebVPN users using digital certificates for authentication, which field in the certificate should be sent to the authorization server to identify the user. The default is "CN otherwise OU," but you can choose other fields on the certificate to represent the identity of the user. This field is used only if you are using authorization for the group.

- **IPComp**—This drop-down selector allows you to enable LZS compression use by a user. This might be useful for dialup remote access clients where you want to maximize bandwidth efficiency. However, enabling this on both the concentrator and client might affect the CPU utilization of the client; therefore, ensure that users of the group only enable this if they are using dialup for remote access. The default for this parameter is "None" for no compression.

- **Default Pre-shared Key**—This parameter appears only in the Base Group configuration. This is used for clients that don't understand the concepts of groups, like Microsoft's Windows XP/2000 L2TP over IPsec client. These clients send only a pre-shared key value (no group name). The pre-shared key can be up to 32 alphanumeric characters in length.

- **Reauthentication on Rekey**—This check box, when selected, specifies that authentication will take place when the ISAKMP/IKE Phase 1 management connection expires and new keying information needs to be generated. Enabling this slows down the rebuilding process, but provides for better security.

- **Client Type & Version Limiting**—This text box field allows you to specify rules to allow or deny client connections based on their type and software version. Rules are entered as follows:

  ```
  p[ermit]|d[eny] client_type : version
  ```

An example would be "**p vpn 3002 : 4.0***", which would allow any VPN 3002 running any sub-release of Version 4.0. You don't have to use a space between the *client_type*, the colon (":"), and the *version* values. You can enter multiple rules; just put them on separate lines. Rules are processed top-down; if no match is found, the client is denied access for the group automatically. If no rules are defined, there are no restrictions placed on the client type and software version the client uses. This feature needs the client to send the client type and software version information. If they don't, you still can match on this by using "n/a" for the type and version, like this: "p n/a : n/a", which means to permit clients that don't provide a type or version. You are restricted to 255 characters for all of your rules for a group.

- **Mode Configuration**—This check box specifies whether or not IKE Mode/Client Config will take place during ISAKMP/IKE Phase 1 for the group. For non-Cisco clients, it is recommended to unselect this check box, since they don't understand the Cisco IKE Mode/Client Config.

When you are done making changes to a group, click the **Apply** button at the bottom of the screen.

Figure 7-34 *Groups IPsec Tab*

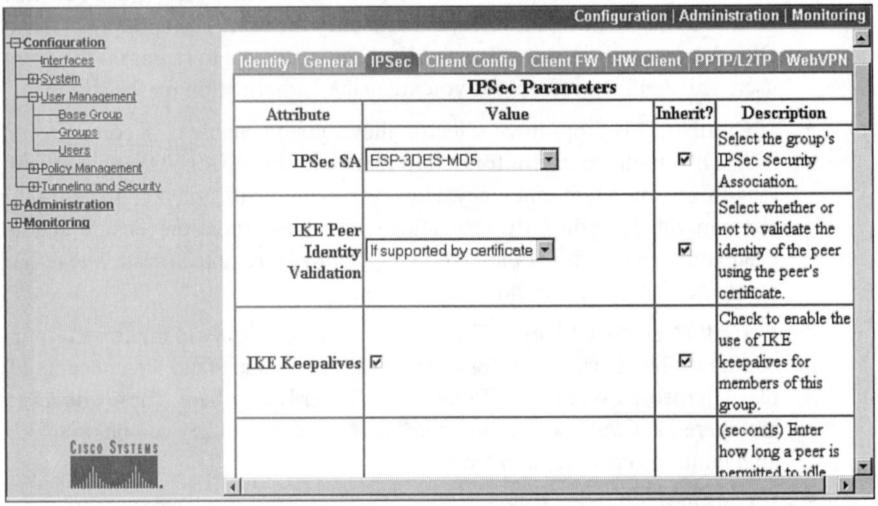

Users IPsec Tab

The user configuration also has an IPsec tab. If you go to **Configuration > User Management > Users**, select a user, and click the **Modify** button, you're taken into the user's configuration. Inside the user's configuration, click the **IPsec** tab. Unlike the same tab under the group configuration, the user's configuration has only two options:

- **IPsec SA**—This pull-down selector chooses the data transform to use to protect the data connections for the user; this overrides the group's configuration.

- **Store Password on Client**—This check box, when selected, allows the user to store his XAUTH password locally on his device. This is unchecked (disabled) by default, and I highly recommend that you keep it this way. This parameter overrides the same group parameter found in the group Mode/Client Config tab.

ISAKMP/IKE Phase 1: Mode/Client Config Tab

If you recall from the beginning of the "IPsec Remote Access" section, Cisco uses IKE Mode or Client Config to assign policies to Cisco Easy VPN Remotes (clients). This process is Cisco-proprietary. By checking the *Mode Config* check box from the group's IPsec tab, the parameters under the Client Config tab are used (in older software versions, it was called the Mode Config tab). This section will cover the configuration options available to you under the group's Client Config tab. The top part of this screen is shown in Figure 7-35. Here are your options:

- **Allow Password Storage on Client**—If this check box is checked, the users can store their XAUTH passwords on their client device; it is unchecked, by default, and I highly recommend that you leave it this way.

- **IPsec over UDP**—See the following section entitled "IPsec Tunneling."

- **IPsec over UDP Port**—See the following section entitled "IPsec Tunneling."

- **IPsec Backup Servers**—The pull-down selector allows you to choose three options for this parameter: "Use the List Below," "Use Client Configured List," and "Disable and Clear Client Configured List." If you choose the first option, you can enter, in the text box beneath it, up to 10 IPsec backup Easy VPN Server addresses; this list is then sent to the client during IKE Client Config. If the client already has a list, it is replaced with this list.

- **Intercept DHCP Configure Message**—This check box, when enabled, allows Microsoft clients to implement split tunneling to the concentrator. For XP clients, the concentrator responds with a DHCP Inform message to the client with the subnet mask, domain name, and a classless static route for the tunnel IP address; for older Microsoft clients, the concentrator responds back with a domain name and subnet mask value.

- **Subnet Mask**—The subnet mask to send to Microsoft clients requesting DHCP options (see the last bullet).

- **IE Proxy Server Policy**—See the following section entitled "IE Proxy."

- **IE Proxy Server**—See the following section entitled "IE Proxy."

- **IE Proxy Server Exception List**—See the following section entitled "IE Proxy."

- **Bypass Proxy Server for Local Addresses**—See the following section entitled "IE Proxy."

- **Banner**—This text box allows you to enter a login in a banner for the group. The banner can be up to 510 characters in length and is displayed to Cisco software VPN Clients, WebVPN users, and the 3002 hardware client only during user authentication.

- **Split Tunneling Policy**—See the following section entitled "Split Tunneling."

- **Split Tunneling Network List**—See the following section entitled "Split Tunneling."

- **Default Domain Name**—This text box allows you to assign a domain name to users who authenticate to this group.

- **Split DNS Names**—See the following section entitled "Split DNS."

The following sections will cover the parameters I did not discuss above, because a more detailed explanation is required for some of the parameter groupings.

Figure 7-35 *Groups Client Config Tab*

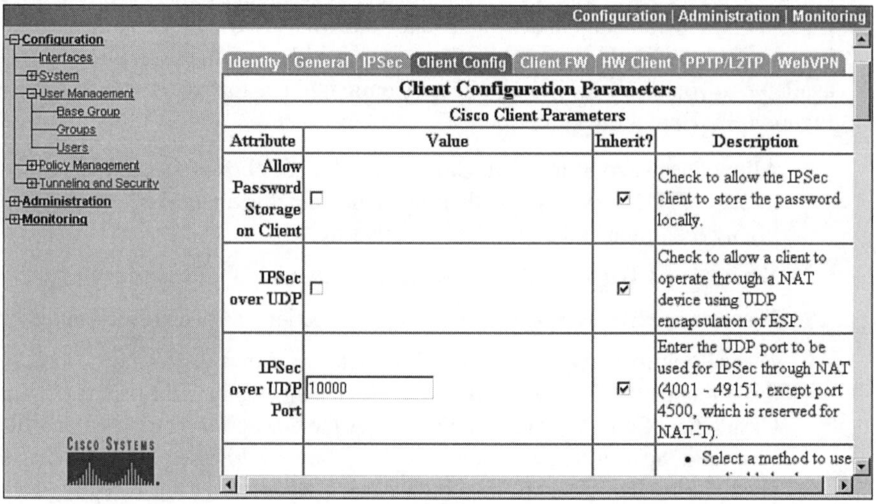

IPsec Tunneling

As mentioned in Chapter 3, "IPsec," encapsulated data with AH doesn't work with any type of address translation; therefore, it normally isn't used with remote access VPNs. This is true of the Cisco Easy VPN: Cisco doesn't support it. ESP works fine with NAT, because ESP's packet integrity protection doesn't include the outer IP header; but because ESP is a layer-3 protocol, ESP doesn't work with PAT. As mentioned in Chapter 3, there are three methods you can use to solve PAT problems with ESP, compared in Table 7-3.

Table 7-3 *IPsec Data Encapsulation Methods*

Encapsulation Method	Standard	Description	Configured
ESP	RFC	Used when no PAT address translation is encountered	N/A
IPsec Over UDP	Cisco-proprietary	Always encapsulates the ESP packet in a UDP header, then adds an outer IP header. This is used when you always know that your remote access client will encounter PAT or a firewall	Group level

Table 7-3   *IPsec Data Encapsulation Methods (Continued)*

Encapsulation Method	Standard	Description	Configured
NAT-Traversal (NAT-T)	RFC	Encapsulates the ESP packet in a UDP header, then adds an outer IP header only when a PAT device is discovered between the client and gateway; a discovery process is used to test for a device performing PAT	Global level
IPsec over TCP	Cisco-proprietary	Always encapsulates IKE and ESP packets in TCP segments, with an IP outer header added; this process is used when you have issues with IPsec over UDP or NAT-T going through a stateful firewall	Global level

The VPN 3000 concentrators can support all four encapsulation methods simultaneously: normal ESP, IPsec over UDP, NAT-T, and IPsec over UDP. If all are enabled, the concentrator looks for a match in this order:

1 ESP

2 IPsec over TCP

3 NAT-T

4 IPsec over UDP

The following sections will explain how to configure these on your concentrator.

IPsec over UDP

IPsec over UDP is configured on a group-by-group basis. To enable it, go into a group (**Configuration > User Management > Groups**) to the Client Config tab. Your two options can be seen in Figure 7-35.

- **IPsec over UDP**—Clicking this check box enables this encapsulation for the group.

- **IPsec over UDP Port**—This is the port number used for the destination UDP port field; it defaults to 10,000, but you can change it to any number from 4,001 to 49,151 except for port 4,500 (which is reserved for NAT-T).

NOTE   If you have a firewall this traffic travels through, you'll need to allow this UDP port (typically 10,000) through the firewall.

NAT-T

Unlike IPsec over UDP, NAT-T is enabled or disabled globally on the concentrator. To access the concentrator's NAT-T parameters, go to **Configuration > Tunneling and Security > IPsec > NAT Transparency**. This screen is shown in Figure 7-36. To enable NAT-T, go to this screen and check the *IPsec over NAT-T* check box.

Figure 7-36 *NAT Transparency Screen*

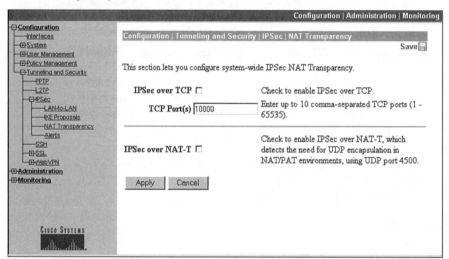

The Cisco 3.6 software version (concentrator and hardware and software clients) and later supports NAT-T. If Cisco remote access clients have both IPsec over UDP and NAT-T enabled, NAT-T is used first, then IPsec over UDP is used if NAT-T is not detected (not enabled) on the concentrator; this is common in ISP environments that drop IPsec traffic like ESP, treating this as a business service: they want money to pass this traffic. By encapsulating ESP in IPsec over UDP or TCP, typically you can get around this problem. Microsoft's L2TP/IPsec client also supports NAT-T and site-to-site sessions also can use it (assuming that the end devices support it).

IPsec over TCP

IPsec over TCP is configured globally on the concentrator. To enable it, go to the screen in Figure 7-36. Click the *IPsec over TCP* check box to enable the process. You can list up to 10 TCP ports, separated by a comma, that clients will use to terminate their TCP-encapsulated ESP connections; the default port number is 10,000.

NOTE   Please note that IPsec over TCP will not work with proxy-based firewalls—only with packet and stateful filtering firewalls.

IE Proxy

The IE Proxy feature allows the remote access client, assuming it's a Cisco software client, to modify Microsoft's Internet Explorer proxy settings. This option is found under the Client Config tab about halfway down the screen, as shown in Figure 7-37.

Figure 7-37 *Groups Client Config Tab: IE Proxy*

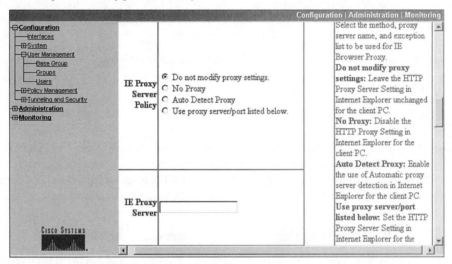

Of the four configuration options you can perform, two are shown in Figure 7-37. The first option, *IE Proxy Server Policy*, allows you to assign the proxy policy to the client. Your options are:

- **Do not modify the proxy settings**—Leave the client's proxy configuration as it is.

- **No proxy**—Disable the proxy setting on the client.

- **Auto detect proxy**—Enable auto proxy server detection in the clients' Internet Explorer web browser; use this configuration if you want the client to learn the proxy on its directly connected network.

- **User proxy server/port listed below**—Use the proxy server and, possibly, port number listed in the *IE Proxy Server* text box below this parameter; this configuration is necessary if you want to force Internet Explorer on the client to use a proxy at the corporate site (across the tunnel) instead of one statically configured or dynamically learned from the local LAN segment.

For the last option, in the *IE Proxy Server* text box, enter the name or IP address of the proxy. If you need to specify a port number, separate the name and port by a colon (":"). Here's a simple example: "**proxy.dealgroup.com:8080**".

Below the above text box (you can't see this in Figure 7-37) is a parameter called *IE Proxy Server Exception List*. This text box allows you to create a list of domain names or IP addresses that are exceptions to the proxy process (they won't use the proxy). You can enter wildcards ("*"), and each exception is listed on a separate line. Here is a simple exception example:

www.*.net
`172.16.*`

In this example, all domain names beginning with "www." and ending in ".net" don't use the proxy and all IP addresses that begin with "172.16." also don't use the proxy. This option typically is used when the web server is at the corporate office and it makes no sense to use the local proxy (split tunneling is enabled).

One more IE Proxy option below this is the *Bypass Proxy Server for Local Addresses* check box. Like the last option, this creates an exception to using a web proxy; in this case, any local address for web access will not involve a proxy.

Split Tunneling

As discussed in Chapter 1, "Overview of VPNs," split tunneling is a VPN process where some traffic is protected when sent from a client, and some is not. For example, if split tunneling is disabled, all traffic must be sent to a VPN gateway from the client. If the client wants to access his ISP's web servers, when split tunneling is disabled, the following sequence occurs:

1 The web traffic is protected by the client and sent to the VPN gateway.

2 The VPN gateway verifies the traffic and decrypts it, forwarding it back out to the Internet to the client's local ISP.

3 The local ISP responds with the web page information to the VPN gateway and the gateway protects this and sends it to the client.

As you can see in this sequence of steps, for the client to access the local ISP's web server, the traffic has to go all the way to the VPN gateway and back, putting a bigger burden on the two IPsec devices.

The split tunneling feature in Cisco products allows you to define the split tunneling policies at the gateway end and push these, during IKE Mode Config, to the client. Split tunneling on the concentrator is set up in the group section under the Client Config tab about two-thirds of the way down the screen, as shown in Figure 7-38. The following subsections will discuss how to set up split tunneling on the concentrator.

Split Tunneling Options

The *Split Tunneling Policy* parameter specifies your tunneling policies. The default is "Tunnel Everything," which means split tunneling is disabled and all of the client's traffic must be sent to the concentrator first, in a protected fashion. You have two additional split tunneling options:

- Allow networks in the list to bypass the tunnel
- Only tunnel networks in the list

Figure 7-38 *Groups Client Config tab: Split Tunneling*

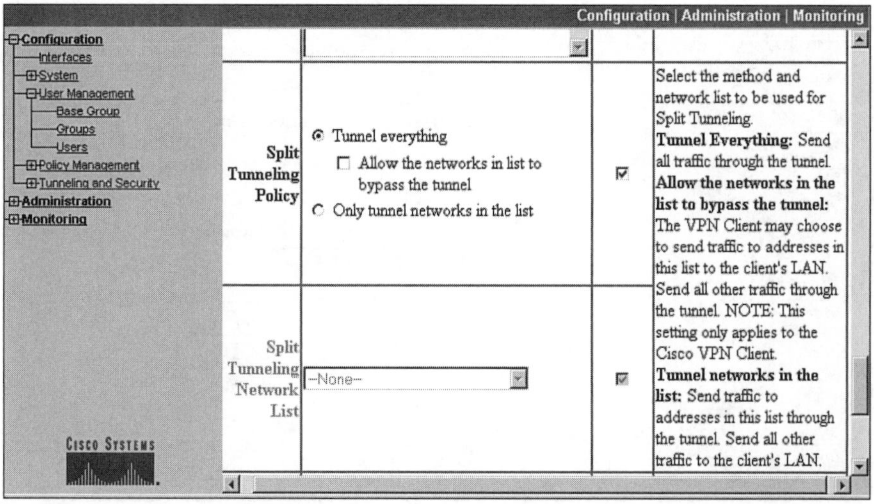

Both of these parameters refer to the pull-down selector called *Split Tunneling Network List* at the bottom of Figure 7-38. The network list contains a list of networks. If you choose the first option, then when the client needs to access these networks, it sends traffic in clear text directly to these networks; otherwise, the client protects the traffic and sends it to the concentrator. This option might be useful in a small office where a handful of networks exist, and you want the client to access them directly in a clear-text fashion; but all other traffic should be protected and sent to the concentrator.

If you choose the latter option, only networks in the list are protected and all other traffic is sent out in clear text directly to the destination. An example of this configuration might require all traffic to be protected when accessing the corporate networks, but all other traffic doesn't have to be protected, like accessing the Internet.

CAUTION   If you enable split tunneling, I highly recommend that for remote access clients, you require them to have a firewall to protect traffic going to and from the clear-text networks; either a software-based firewall or a hardware appliance, like a low-end PIX (501 or 506E).

Network Lists

The network list that defines what is or isn't protected is specified with the drop-down *Split Tunneling Network List* parameter. However, first you need to create a network list before you can select it. To view the existing network lists, go to **Configuration > Policy Management > Traffic Management > Network Lists**, shown in Figure 7-39. There is one default network list, called "VPN Client Local LAN (Default)," which specifies local LAN traffic based on the IP address and subnet mask applied to the remote access client's NIC.

Figure 7-39 *Existing Network Lists*

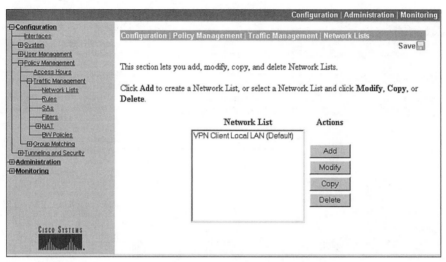

I'll use Figure 7-20 to illustrate a network list example for split tunneling. To add a network list, click the **Add** button in Figure 7-39. You'll see the screen shown in Figure 7-40. At the top of the screen, enter a unique name for the network list. In this example, I used "Corporate Network." In the *Network List* text box, enter your network lists. The format is: *network_number/wildcard_mask*. A wildcard mask is basically an inverted subnet mask. Enter different networks on separate lines. At the bottom of the screen (you can't see it), is a **Generate Local List** button; clicking this button automatically will populate the *Network List* text box with the networks off the concentrator's private interface. For the network shown previously in Figure 7-20, I entered a network list entry of "192.168.101.0/ 0.0.0.255" for the corporate office network. When you are done populating the networks in the *Network List* text box, click the **Add** button at the bottom of the screen. You'll be taken back to the screen in Figure 7-39, where you'll see the name of your new network list.

In my example from Figure 7-20, if you wanted to protect traffic only to the corporate network, and allow the client to send other traffic in clear text, you would go back to the Group's Client Config tab and select *Only tunnel networks in the list*; then use the pull-down *Split Tunneling Network List* selector beneath it to pull up the "Corporate Network" list.

Split DNS

By default, during IKE Mode Config, when the concentrator assigns a DNS server to the client, the client will use this over any other configured or obtained DNS server it has locally. This might cause problems where you want to use both servers depending on the destination that is being resolved. I'll use Figure 7-41 to illustrate split DNS. In this example, I'll assume the corporate office's domain name is richard-deal.com.

Figure 7-40 *Adding a Network List*

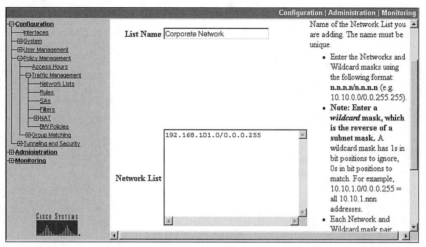

Figure 7-41 *Split DNS Example*

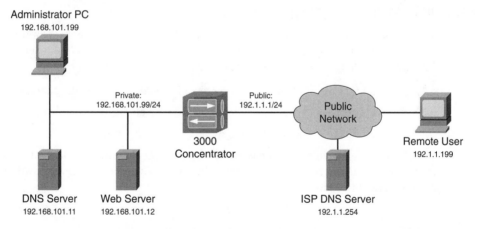

The network administrator wants the remote access clients to use the 192.168.101.11 DNS server when resolving names for the corporate office; but use the ISP's DNS server (192.1.1.254) when resolving any other name. To set this up, go to the Group configuration screen and click the **Client Config** tab; scroll all the way to the bottom of the screen until you see the *Split DNS Names* box (see Figure 7-42). In my example, I entered "richard-deal.com", which indicates that the concentrator-assigned DNS server will be used for name resolution of any name ending in ".richard-deal.com", and any other name will be resolved with the ISP's DNS server. You can put multiple domains in this text box; just separate them by commas (and no spaces). Click the **Apply** button when you're done with the group's configuration changes. Remember that split DNS is used in conjunction with split tunneling: its configuration will not work without split tunneling.

Figure 7-42 *Groups* Client Config *Tab: Split DNS Names*

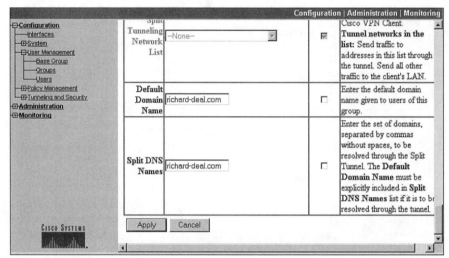

ISAKMP/IKE Phase 1: Client FW Tab

The Client FW tab in the group configuration section allows you to specify a firewall policy for the group. Currently, only the Windows version of the Cisco VPN Client supports this functionality. There are three firewall policies that you can configure:

- **Firewall Setting**—Whether or not a firewall should be used on the client.
- **Firewall Product**—The firewall to be used on the client.
- **Firewall Policy**—The firewall policy the users should use.

The configured firewall policy is pushed down to the client during IKE Mode Config and the Cisco VPN Client software implements the policy. The following sections will discuss each of these three settings.

Firewall Setting

At the top of the Client FW tab you'll find the *Firewall Setting* parameter, as shown in Figure 7-43. This parameter allows you to specify the use of a firewall. Your options are the following radio buttons:

- **No Firewall**—The client is allowed to connect whether or not a firewall is installed and operational (this is the default option).
- **Firewall Required**—The firewall specified by the *Firewall* parameter must be installed and operational on the client. The VPN Client polls the firewall every 30 seconds for its operational status; if the firewall is not operational, the VPN Client terminates any existing IPsec session and prevents further IPsec sessions until the specified firewall is operational.

- **Firewall Optional**—The firewall specified by the *Firewall* parameter is optional on the client. During the IKE Mode Config step, if the VPN Client doesn't detect the specified firewall, a pop-up notification appears, warning the user of the recommended firewall; however, the VPN Client still allows the VPN session to proceed. This option is common when you're migrating users from a no-firewall environment to a required firewall environment.

One of the above three options must be chosen.

NOTE   Currently, there is no way of changing the actual notification message the concentrator sends to the client.

Figure 7-43 *Groups* Client FW *tab: Firewall Setting*

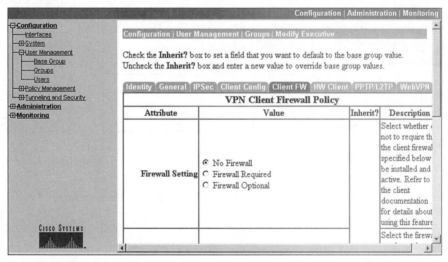

Supported Firewalls

Beneath the *Firewall Setting* parameter is the *Firewall* parameter, shown in Figure 7-44. This drop-down selector allows you to choose a firewall that the VPN Client must or should have installed. Supported firewalls include:

- **Cisco Integrated Client (CIC)**—This is a DLL from Zone Labs that provides a free stateful firewall function for Cisco's VPN Client for Windows software; its default policy is to allow outbound traffic, but deny all inbound traffic with the exception of ARP and DHCP messages.
- Cisco Intrusion Protection Security Agent (CSA).

- Zone Labs' ZoneAlarm, ZoneAlarm Pro, and Integrity.
- NetworkICE's BlackIce Defender/Agent.
- Sygate's Personal Firewall, Personal Firewall Pro, and Security Agent.
- **Custom Firewall**—This feature is used when the VPN Client is running a newer version of code than the concentrator, and thus supports additional firewalls. When this is the case, you choose this option on the concentrator and enter *Vendor ID* and *Product ID* values found on the Cisco web site for the firewall—this relieves you from having to upgrade the concentrator to add the additional firewalls the Cisco VPN Client supports.

Figure 7-44 *Groups Client FW Tab: Firewall Selection*

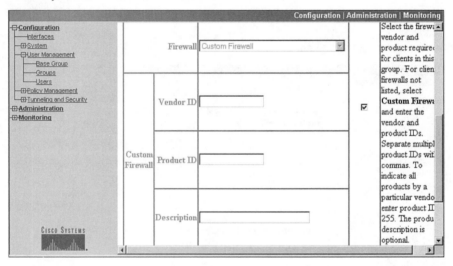

Firewall Policies

The last firewall parameter required is to choose a firewall policy. There are three firewall policies, as shown in Figure 7-45:

- *Policy defined by remote firewall (AYT).*
- *Policy from Server.*
- *Policy Pushed (CPP)*—CPP stands for Central Policy Push or Central Policy Protection.

The AYT (are you there) feature has the software client verify that the specified firewall is operational on the client; however, the actual rules the firewall should use are left up to the user to define. With AYT, the VPN Client software polls the firewall every 30 seconds; if the firewall is disabled by the user, and the policy is "Required," the client terminates the VPN session to the concentrator.

Figure 7-45 *Groups* Client FW *Tab: Firewall Policy*

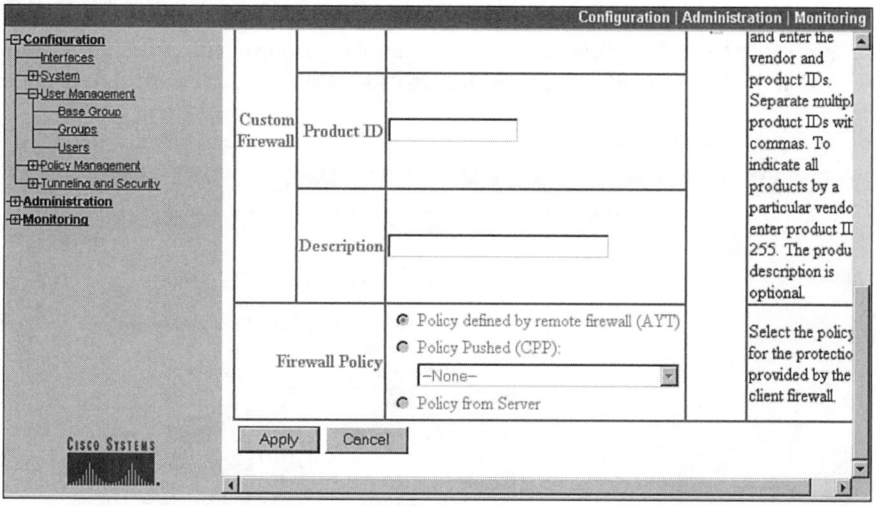

The elements in the last two bullet points of the preceding list allow you to define your own firewall rules, and have them pushed down to the client firewall, and have the client firewall use these rules to enforce filtering decisions. The *Policy from Server* option applies only to users that have Zone Labs Integrity installed. With this firewall product, the users can obtain their firewall filtering rules from a Zone Labs Integrity Server. When choosing this option, you must go to **Configuration > System > Servers > Firewalls** and configure the Integrity server properties:

- IP address(es) of the Integrity Server(s).
- The *Failure Policy*—What should occur if the Integrity Server cannot be reached: permit or deny user access if the Integrity server(s) cannot be reached.
- *Server Port*, which defaults to 5054.
- An option to require the Integrity server to authenticate itself with a client SSL certificate.

Policy Pushed (CPP) allows you to push a firewall filter that you've defined on the concentrator to the VPN Client. When you choose this option, you also must specify the name of the filter on the concentrator that will be pushed down to the client during IKE Mode Config. The VPN Client, upon receiving the filter, will have the firewall use this filter and any locally defined filter to filter traffic entering and leaving the user's PC. Currently, only the CIC and Zone Labs' Zone Alarm products support CPP.

If you choose CPP as your firewall policy, you'll need to perform two things on the concentrator:

1 Create filtering rules that affect traffic coming into and leaving the client.

2 Group the rules together in a filter.

The following two sections discuss both of these items.

Creating Rules

A firewall rule is a statement that defines whether or not a particular type of packet is or is not allowed to come into or leave the client. To view the existing filtering rules, go to **Configuration > Policy Management > Traffic Management > Rules**, which can be seen in Figure 7-46.

Figure 7-46 *Listing of Filtering Rules*

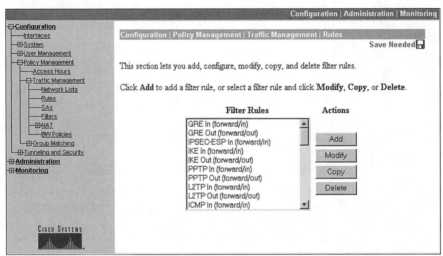

As you can see from this screen, there are a lot of predefined rules on the concentrator; all of these rules are generic in nature: specifying a particular protocol, such as ICMP, or an application, such as HTTP. You can create your own rules by clicking the **Add** button, taking you to the screen in Figure 7-47. This is only a partial screen shot, but you can be very specific about the information in your new filtering rule.

Figure 7-47 *Adding a Filtering Rule*

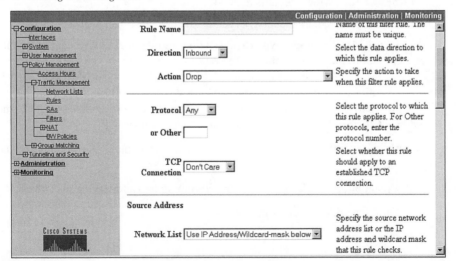

The rule is broken up into sections. At the top, you need to enter a name for the rule. Use a descriptive name that describes what the rule actually does, like "Deny HTTP traffic from 192.168.101.101". Below this is a drop-down selector that allows you to affect the direction of the rule: "inbound" affects traffic coming into the user's computer and "outbound" as traffic leaves the user's computer. Below this is the action the firewall should take when the packet being compared matches the rule:

- *Drop* (this is the default action if you don't override it)
- *Forward*
- *Drop and Log*—drop the packet and create a logging record; use the FILTERDBG event class to find these records in the concentrator's log file (event classes are discussed in more depth in Chapter 10, "Concentrator Management")
- *Forward and Log*
- *Apply IPsec*—this option is for site-to-site sessions only and needs to be associated with a specific site-to-site session (data SA)
- *Apply IPsec and Log*

In my "Deny HTTP traffic from 192.168.101.101" example, you would choose   Drop" or "Drop and Log".

Below the action is the IP protocol that should be examined. There is a drop-down selector where you can choose the name of the protocol, such as ICMP, TCP, UDP, and so on; if the name doesn't appear, you can put in the number of the IP protocol. Use "Any" to match on any IP protocol. For TCP, you specify "Don't care" or "Established" to indicate whether or not you want to include the TCP three-way handshake packets in the filter examination. In my "Deny HTTP traffic from 192.168.101.101", you would choose "TCP" as the IP protocol.

The next two sections are the *Source* and *Destination Address*. Here you can have the rule look at a specific source or destination address(es) in packets entering or leaving the user's computer. In each section, you have the option of specifying a network list for the list of addresses or network numbers. See "Network Lists" earlier in the chapter to see how to define a network list. Or you can specify an IP address or network number with a corresponding wildcard (not subnet) mask for each of these sections. In my "Deny HTTP traffic from 192.168.101.101" example, for the source address you would use 0.0.0.0 and a wildcard mask of 255.255.255.255; for the destination address, you would use 192.168.101.101 and a wildcard mask of 0.0.0.0.

Below the source and destination address sections are three protocol sections: *TCP/UDP source port*, *TCP/UDP destination port*, and *ICMP packet* type. For TCP and UDP packets, you can specify a single source or destination port or a range of ports. There is a pull-down selector to choose the name of the port, or you can enter the number (or range of numbers) for the port. For ICMP, you can be specific about the ICMP message type or range of message types of match. In my "Deny HTTP traffic from 192.168.101.101" example, you would leave the TCP/UDP source port information as is (defaults to all ports) and change the TCP/UDP destination port to "HTTP (80)" with the drop-down selector.

When you are done creating a rule, click the **Add** button at the bottom; this will take you back to the screen in Figure 7-46, where you'll see the name of your new rule.

TIP   I try to be as restrictive as possible with traffic entering and leaving the user's computer when the VPN tunnel is up. For example, many of my filters include rules that block instant messenger communications, peer-to-peer file sharing, and many others which are not business-related, but waste valuable bandwidth. For more information about filtering this kind of traffic using packet filtering rules, see my book entitled *Cisco Router Firewall Security,* published by Cisco Press.

Creating Filters

Once you are done creating your rules, you need to group them together into a filter. A filter is similar to an access control list (ACL) on an IOS router, PIX, or ASA. To create a filter, go to **Configuration > Policy Management > Traffic Management > Filters** (see Figure 7-48) and click the **Add** button. You must give the filter a name, assign a default action if none of the rules in the filter match a packet (drop, drop and log, forward, or forward and log), allow or deny source routing of packets (I would recommend that you deny source routing), allow or deny fragments (in most cases I would deny fragments), and then give an optional description.

Figure 7-48 *Listing of Filters*

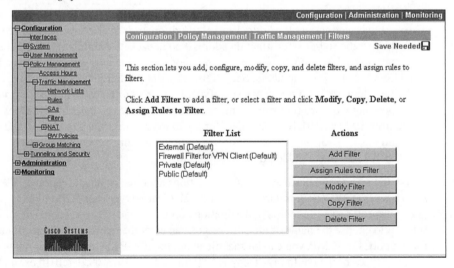

At the bottom of this screen, click the **Add** button to add the filter and to assign rules to the new filter (shown in Figure 7-49).

Figure 7-49 *Assigning Rules to a Filter*

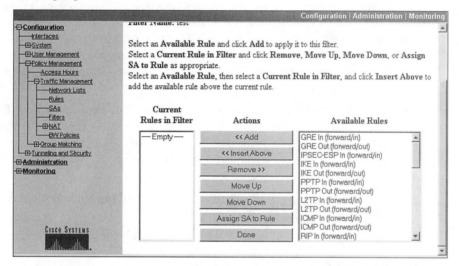

When assigning rules to filters, you'll see three columns on the screen. The left-hand column lists the current rules in the filter. The middle column contains action buttons to perform actions on a selected rule. The right-hand column lists rules you can add to the filter (you must add rules first, otherwise you'll see only the Cisco-defined rules). For example, to add a rule to a filter, in the third column, scroll down to the rule and click it; then click the **Add** button in the *Actions* column to add the rule to the left-hand column (*Current Rules in Filter*). Rules are added to the bottom of the filter, and rules are processed top-down. Therefore, the order of the rules in the left-hand column is important. You can re-sort the rules by clicking a particular rule in the *Current Rules in Filter* column and then clicking the **Move Up** or **Move Down** buttons. The **Assign SA to Rule** button applies only to site-to-site sessions. When you're done manipulating the rules in your filter, click the **Done** button in the middle column, taking you back to Figure 7-48.

You can see some default filters on the screen in Figure 7-48. There is one for the private, public, and external interfaces and one called "Firewall Filter for VPN Client (Default)," which can be used for remote access clients. This latter filter allows outbound traffic from the user's computer, but allows only returning traffic back into the user's computer. From the screen in Figure 7-48, you can manipulate the rules for a filter by clicking a filter and then clicking the **Assign Rules to Filter** button (this takes you to the screen shown previously in Figure 7-49). Remember that firewall filters only affect non-tunneled traffic on the client: you cannot use a firewall filter to filter traffic that will traverse the IPsec tunnel.

ISAKMP/IKE Phase 2: Data SAs

As you can see from the ISAKMP/IKE Phase 1 setup, the concentrator gives you many options to fine-tune your IPsec remote access connectivity. If you're using Cisco products for remote access clients, you probably don't need to worry about setting up the data transform set for ESP; Cisco already has some predefined ones on the concentrator. To see the existing data SA transform sets (or add new ones or modify old ones), go to **Configuration > Policy Management > Traffic Management > SAs**. There are more than half a dozen predefined data SAs. To create a new one, click the **Add** button; to modify an existing one, click the name of the transform set and click the **Modify** button.

Figures 7-50 and 7-51 show an example of modifying a data transform called "ESP-3DES-MD5." This is one of the Cisco default transform sets. As you can see from the name and the screen shots, the name defines how the data connections are protected; however, you can use any name you like. The *Inheritance* parameter below this has two possible values:

- **From Rule**—One tunnel for each rule is created; thus, many hosts specified in the same rule set can use the same tunnel.

- **From Data**—One tunnel for each address pair (within the rule set) is created.

Figure 7-50 *ISAKMP/IKE Phase 2 Data Transforms: Top Screen*

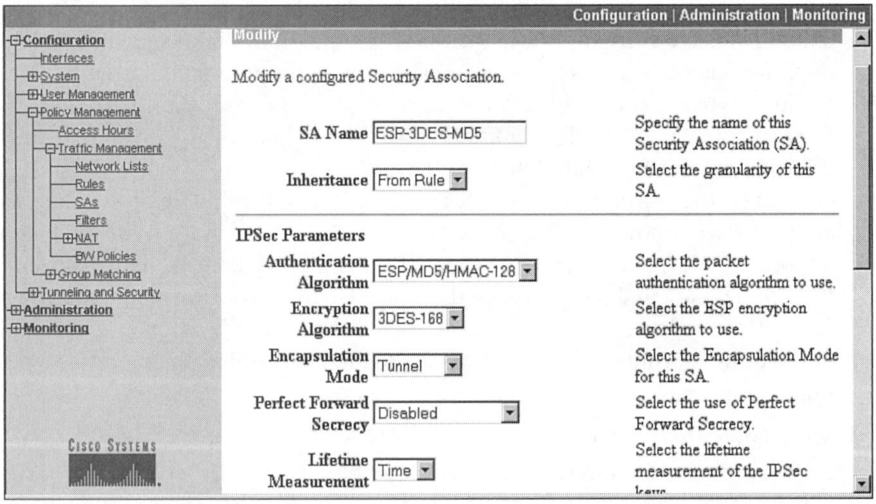

This *Inheritance* parameter defaults to *From Rule*, which is the recommended setting and is only applicable to L2L sessions. *From Data* is more secure because separate address pairs in an L2L session (different internal devices between the two sites) have their own tunnel, and thus their own encryption keys; but this could place a heavy processing burden on the concentrator.

Figure 7-51 *ISAKMP/IKE Phase 2 Data Transforms: Bottom Screen*

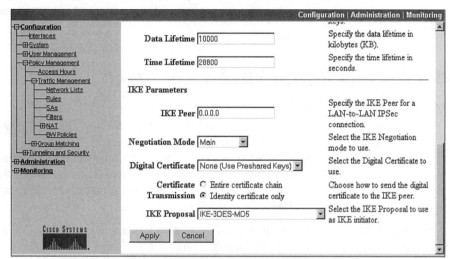

Below the *Inheritance* parameter is the packet HMAC *Authentication Algorithm* in the *IPsec Parameters* section. You can choose either "ESP/MD5/HMAC-128" or "ESP/SHA/HMAC-160." After this is the *Encryption Algorithm* parameter, which can have values of "DES-56," "3DES-168," "AES-128," "AES-192," "AES-256," and "Null" (no encryption). The *Encapsulation Mode* parameter can be either "Tunnel" or "Transport." For remote access and L2L sessions, you need to choose "Tunnel." The *Perfect Forward Secrecy* (PFS) parameter specifies the use of DH to share the data SA's HMAC and encryption keys instead of the ISAKMP/IKE Phase 1 management connection; for Easy VPN, PFS is only recently supported. If enabled, DH groups 1, 2, 5, and 7 are supported. The lifetime of the data connection can be measured in "Time," "Data," "Both," or "None." Below this, you can enter the lifetime in seconds or KBs transferred across the data connection. If you choose "Both," whichever lifetime is reached first causes the data connection to be rebuilt. "None" indicates that unless the data SA is terminated via some other means, it will be disconnected after 86,400 seconds.

The first field in the *IKE Parameters* section is the *IKE Peer*; this is used only for L2L sessions and should be left at 0.0.0.0 (any device) for remote access clients. Next is the *Negotiation Mode* that should be used: "Main" or "Aggressive." If you'll be using digital certificates for device authentication (see the "Using Certificates" section earlier in the chapter), change the *Digital Certificate* parameter from *None* to the actual certificate the concentrator should use when performing device authentication with this data SA. If you specified the use of certificates for device authentication, you'll need to choose a *Certificate Transmission* type:

- **Entire Certificate Chain**—Sent the remote peer the concentrator's identity certificate and all issuing certificates (root CA and subordinate CA certificates).

- **Identity Certificate Only**—This is the default.

Last is the IKE Proposal for ISAKMP/IKE Phase 1 that should be used. Select the Phase 1 transform name from the pull-down selector. When done, click the **Apply** button at the bottom of the screen.

Network Access Control (NAC) for IPsec and L2TP/IPsec Users

In version 4.7, Cisco introduced the Network Access Control (NAC) feature for IPsec and L2TP/IPsec clients. Like the Cisco Secure Desktop (CSD) feature for WebVPN (discussed in the next chapter), NAC for IPsec and L2TP/IPsec provides a method of validating a user's access based on their operating system version and applied service packs, the anti-virus software and applied updates, the personal firewall software and applied updates, and the intrusion protection software and applied updates.

With CSD for WebVPN, the concentrator validates a user's access. With NAC, the concentrator serves as a proxy: the Cisco Trust Agent (CTA) software is installed on a user's PC and sends the required NAC information, using the Extensible Authentication Protocol (EAP), to the concentrator. The concentrator then forwards this information to an AAA server, like Cisco Secure ACS (CSACS), using EAP over RADIUS. The AAA server validates the user's access and sends the reply back to the concentrator, along with any other policy access information, where the concentrator enforces the downloaded policy. With CSD for WebVPN, you have to define all the policies locally on the concentrator, whereas with NAC, these policies are defined on the AAA RADIUS server; because of this, setting up NAC on the concentrator is simpler.

NOTE   The configuration of NAC on CSACS is beyond the scope of this book. Information on configuration NAC on CSACS can be found at http://www.cisco.com/en/US/partner/products/sw/secursw/ps2086/products_user_guide_chapter09186a00802335f1.html.

Global Configuration of NAC for IPsec

To set up the global configuration of NAC, go to **Configuration > Policy Management > Network Admission Control**. There are two options from this screen: *Global Parameters* and *Exception List*. The next two sections will talk about both of these options.

NAC Global Parameters

When you click the **Global Parameters** hyperlink option from the **Configuration > Policy Management > Network Admission Control** screen, you are taken to the screen shown in

Figure 7-52. Here are the parameters you can configure:

- **Retransmission Timer**—Defines how long the concentrator will wait for a NAC response from a device before resending the request. The default is 3 seconds but can range from 1–60.

- **Hold Timer**—Defines how long the concentrator waits before attempting to establish a new association when there is a failed NAC credential validation or the configured number of EAP over UDP (EAPoUDP) retries has been exceeded. The default is 180 seconds but can range from 60–1,440.

- **EAPoUDP Retries**—Defines the number of times the concentrator will retransmit EAP over UDP messages before marking the NAC association as failed, thereby starting the hold timer. The default is 3 times, but this can range from 1–3.

- **EAPoUDP Port**—Defines the EAP over UDP port used for NAC communications; this defaults to 21,862.

- **Clientless Authentication: Enable**—Allows authentication of user devices that aren't using Cisco Trust Agent (perhaps because you're in a migration process and slowly adding CTA to your user's desktops). Once you've enabled this, you need to define a username and password for the *Clientless Authentication: Username* and *Clientless Authentication: Password* parameters. The AAA RADIUS server will use these authentication credentials to validate network access.

Figure 7-52 *NAC Global Parameters Screen*

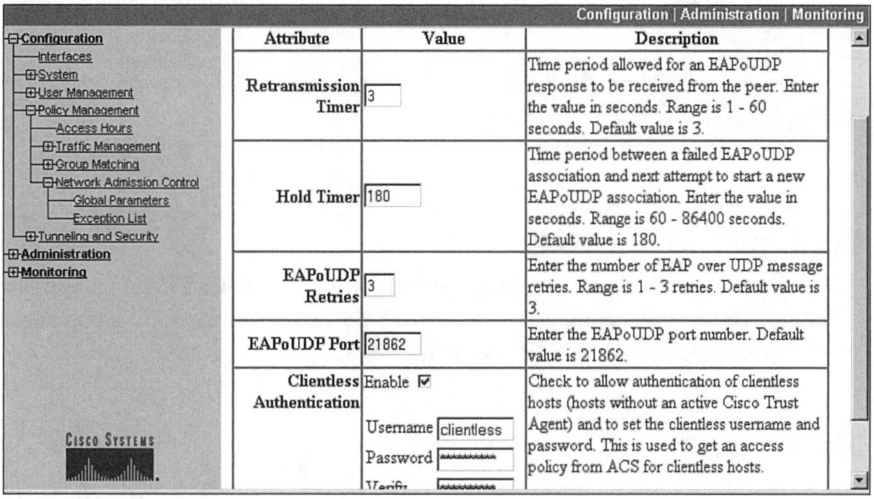

NAC Exception List

Current Cisco NAC architecture doesn't support certain operating systems with their CTA software. You can create exceptions to these operating systems by creating exception list entries by going to the **Configuration > Policy Management > Network Admission Control > Exception List** screen and clicking the **Add** button. This displays the screen in Figure 7-53. Click the *Enable* check box to enable the exception list. In the *Operating System* check box, enter the name of the operating system of the non-CTA devices: you can find the name from the concentrator's **Administration > Administer Sessions** or **Monitoring > Sessions** screen in the *Client Type* column of the *Remote Access Sessions* table. You can apply a filter to the exception list to determine what IP addresses are or are not exempted. You want to make sure that any EAP over UDP traffic is *not* exempted: this should be your first permit rule in your filter. I discussed how to create rules and filters previously in the "Creating Rules" and "Creating Filters" sections.

Figure 7-53 *NAC Exemption Lists*

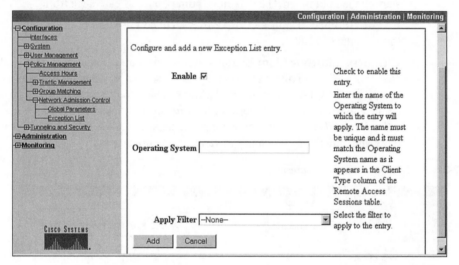

Group Configuration of NAC

After you've defined your global properties for NAC, you need to set up your groups for NAC. This involves defining the AAA RADIUS server and the NAC group attributes. The following two sections will discuss both of these.

AAA RADIUS Server

I've already discussed how to associate an AAA RADIUS server with a group previously in the "Authentication Server Creation" section. However, you might define your NAC properties globally and want to define an AAA RADIUS server once, instead of for each group. To add an AAA RADIUS server globally, go to **Configuration > System > Servers > Authentication Servers** and click the **Add** button. The information found on this screen is the same as described previously in the "Authentication Server Creation" section. Click the **Add** button when done. If the AAA RADIUS server will be performing authorization functions, repeat this process by going to the **Configuration > System > Servers > Authorization Servers** screen, clicking the **Add** button, and re-entering the server information; you can repeat this same process if you want to capture accounting records (**Configuration > System > Servers > Accounting Servers**).

NOTE   The AAA servers you define under **Configuration > System > Servers** are used by the Base Group; if you've added an AAA server and associated to a specific group, the group's configuration will override the global AAA servers defined.

Group NAC Tab

NAC can be configured for both the Base Group and specific groups. The NAC parameters are the same for both: when configured in both places, the specific group settings override the Base Group. To modify the parameters for the Base Group, go to **Configuration > User Management > Base Group** and click the **NAC** tab; this displays the screen in Figure 7-54.

Figure 7-54 *NAC Group Tab*

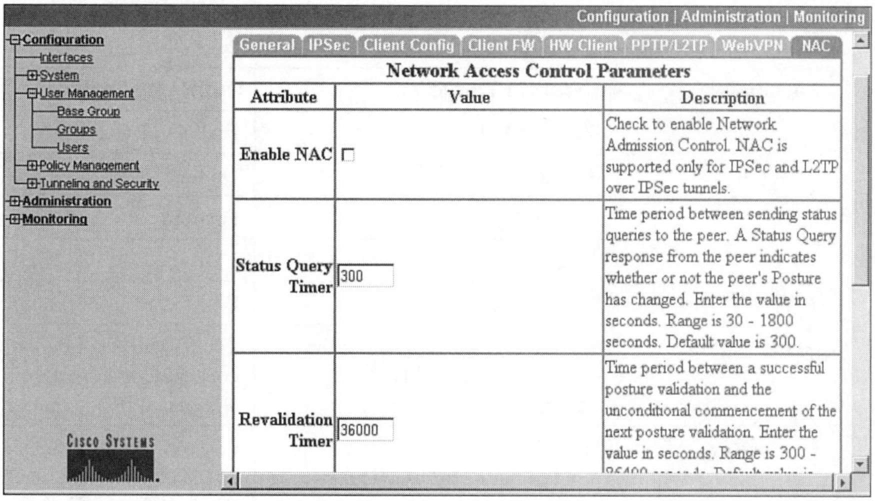

Here are the parameters on this screen:

- **Enable NAC**—This enables NAC: any client not listed in an NAC exemption list for this group will then be validated using NAC before being admitted to the network.

- **Status Query Timer**—Specifies the keepalive to check for any posture changes for clients in the group; the default is 300 seconds but this value can range from 30–1,800 seconds.

- **The Revalidation Timer**—Specifies when the clients must be completely revalidated for admittance to the network; the default is 36,000 seconds, but this can range from 300–86,400 seconds.

- **Default ACL (filter)**—Allows you to choose a filter to use for the user of the group before NAC validation has been completed. This is useful for those clients that fail the admittance test and need to download updated software to become compliant. The filter can allow just this traffic and deny the rest until the client meets the admittance policy. At a minimum, the filter should permit the "EAPoUDP In" and "EAPoUDP Out" rules between the IPsec or L2TP/IPsec client—use the "VPN Client Local LAN (Default)" network list—and the public interface address of the concentrator (or whatever interface the clients will be terminating their IPsec connections on).

NOTE   The 4.7 version of software I used didn't have the "EAPoUDP In" and "EAPoUDP Out" rules predefined, so I had to define them manually. Use the information in Table 7-4 to create these two rules.

Table 7-4   *EAPoUDP In and Out Filtering Rules*

Parameter	Inbound Traffic	Outbound Traffic
Rule Name	EAPoUDP In	EAPoUDP Out
Direction	Inbound	Outbound
Action	Forward	Forward
Protocol	UDP	UDP
TCP/IP Connection	Don't Care	Don't Care
Source Address	0.0.0.0/255.255.255.255 or the "VPN Client Local LAN (Default)" network list	The IP address of the concentrator's interface for terminated IPsec connections
Destination Address	The IP address of the concentrator's interface for terminated IPsec connections	0.0.0.0/255.255.255.255 or the "VPN Client Local LAN (Default)" network list
TCP/UDP Source Port	All	21,862 (or whatever port number you're using)
TCP/UDP Destination Port	21,862 (or whatever port number you're using)	All

Summary

This chapter introduced you to configuring remote access sessions using IPsec. In regard to IPsec, I'll spend more time on how to implement and troubleshoot it on the concentrator when I discuss troubleshooting in Chapter 11, "Verifying and Troubleshooting Concentrator Connections," and the configuration of remote access clients in Part III.

Next up is Chapter 8, "Concentrator Remote Access Connections with PPTP, L2TP, and WebVPN," where I show you how to use your concentrator to terminate remote access sessions from PPTP, L2TP, L2TP/IPsec, and WebVPN clients.

Concentrator Remote Access Connections with PPTP, L2TP, and WebVPN

The last chapter introduced how to configure the VPN 3000 concentrators to accept IPsec remote access sessions. This chapter will focus on using a concentrator to terminate other types of remote access sessions, including:

- PPTP
- L2TP over IPsec
- WebVPN

The remainder of this chapter will focus on the configuration of the concentrator to support these types of remote access VPN implementations. I'll spend more time on implementing PPTP/L2TP connectivity in Chapter 13, "Windows Software Client." Most of this chapter is dedicated to the newest CiscoVPN implementation: SSL. Cisco refers to their SSL VPN implementation as WebVPN. I'll focus on setting up the concentrator to accept clientless connections (just a web browser), thin client connections (port forwarding), and network client connections (SSL VPN Client software).

PPTP and L2TP Remote Access

The configuration of PPTP and L2TP remote access is much simpler than that of IPsec, even if you'll be using L2TP over IPsec; this is because if you're using IPsec with Cisco remote access clients, you have many more IKE Mode Config features than what L2TP over IPsec clients support. The configuration of both of these protocols occurs in two locations on the VPN 3000 concentrator:

- User management
- Global configuration

Most of your configuration is done at the group level; very rarely will you have to change the global (system-wide) properties for PPTP or L2TP. The following three sections will discuss the configuration of these two protocols: group configurations for PPTP and L2TP, global configurations for PPTP, and global configurations for L2TP.

PPTP and L2TP Group Configuration

Most of your configuration for PPTP and L2TP will be done under a group's configuration: **Configuration > User Management > Groups**. In a group within the General tab, (discussed in the last chapter), the *Tunneling Protocols* parameter allows you to specify which tunneling protocols, if any, a group is allowed to use. If you want the group to be able to use PPTP or L2TP, you must select these.

NOTE   If you want to use L2TP over IPsec, the group no longer will be able to perform general IPsec connections to the concentrator.

The remainder of the group's configuration is done under the PPTP/L2TP tab; the top part of this screen is shown in Figure 8-1. The first parameter is the *Use Client Address* parameter, which is disabled. If you want the client to use its own address, make sure you've enabled this option in the **Configuration > System > Address Management > Address** section; this was discussed in the "Address Assignment" section earlier in the last chapter. However, because of various reasons, including security, it is recommended to have the concentrator assign an address to the client.

Figure 8-1   *Group Configuration:* PPTP/L2TP Tab

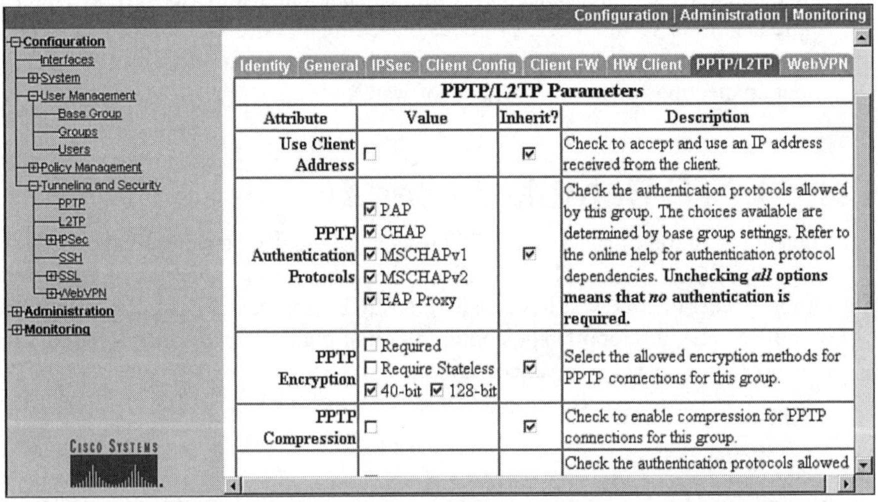

Below this there are two sets of parameters: one set applies to PPTP, which you can see in Figure 8-1, and one set applies to L2TP (you can't see this in Figure 8-1). Here are the parameters:

- **PPTP Authentication Protocols**—These check boxes specify the PPP authentication protocol to use to authenticate the device. These can include: "PAP," "CHAP," "MSCHAPv1," "MSCHAPv2," or "EAP Proxy." If you select "Required" under

PPTP Encryption, you must choose one or both MS-CHAP protocols. Also, EAP is not supported for connections that use encryption. Not selecting at least one authentication protocol means that *no* authentication is required to allow the PPTP connection. You might want to use this to test the connection; but immediately afterward, change it to one or more of the listed options. Because all of the authentication options are check boxes, you can select none, one, or all of them.

- **PPTP Encryption**—These check boxes specify the data encryption to use for the clients. Supported options include "Required," "Require Stateless," "40-bit," or "128-bit." If you choose "Required," the PPTP client must use MPPE and only MS-CHAPv1 and MS-CHAPv2 are supported for authentication. Plus, you also must enable "40-bit" or "128-bit" encryption, which uses the RC-4 encryption algorithm. This option doesn't support NT Domain user authentication. With "Require Stateless," the encryption keys are changed on every packet transmitted. This option is not supported with NT Domain authentication; however, choosing this option might provide better performance in environments where packet loss is to be expected, such as dialup. Since all the encryption options are check boxes, you can select none, one, or all of them.

- **PPTP Compression**—If all your users in the group are using dialup for access, then enabling compression probably will enhance their transmission speeds. MPPC is used. This is disabled by default. Compression is supported only with stateless encryption.

- **L2TP Authentication Protocols**—See *PPTP Authentication Protocols*.

- **L2TP Encryption**—See *PPTP Encryption*.

- **L2TP Compression**—See *PPTP Compression*.

When you are done making your changes to your group, click the **Apply** button at the bottom of the screen to activate them.

NOTE   The *Use Client Address* parameter, *PPTP Authentication Protocols* parameters, and *L2TP Authentication Protocols parameters* can be overridden on a user-by-user basis in the user configuration: **Configuration > User Management > Users**. After selecting a user, you can go to the user's PPTP/L2TP tab to override these parameters for a particular user.

CAUTION   Do not enable compression on the concentrator if you have a mixed group of users: dialup and broadband. The dialup users will notice a boost in speed; however, the broadband throughput will suffer if these users accidentally enable compression. If you have two groups of people—dialup and broadband—I recommend that you put them into two separate groups and enable compression for the dialup group.

PPTP Global Configuration

To configure system-wide PPTP options, go to **Configuration > Tunneling and Security > PPTP**. Here are the global options you can configure:

- **Enabled**—This check box allows you to globally enable or disable PPTP; un-checking it immediately terminates any current PPTP session.

- **Maximum Tunnel Idle Time**—This text box allows you to enter the amount of time to wait, in seconds, before disconnecting a PPTP tunnel that has no active sessions. The default is 5 seconds, but this can range from 5–86,400 seconds.

- **Packet Window Size**—This text box allows you to enter the PPTP packet window size for acknowledgments; the default is 16 packets, but this can range from 0–32 packets.

- **Limit Transmit Window**—This check box allows you to enable the use of windowing to the client's window size; this is disabled by default.

- **Max. Tunnels**—This text box allows you to configure the maximum number of active PPTP tunnels that you want your concentrator to support; please note that you are restricted to a maximum based on the concentrator model the PPTP tunnels terminate on.

- **Max. Sessions/Tunnel**—This text box allows you to configure the maximum number of sessions allowed per tunnel. The default is 0 (no implied limit); and the maximum can be up to the maximum based on the concentrator model.

- **Packet Processing Delay**—This text box allows you to enter the packet processing delay for flow control of PPTP sessions. The number you enter is represented in tenths of a second. The default is 1 (1/10 of a second).

- **Acknowledgment Delay**—This text box allows you to enter the number of milliseconds the concentrator will wait before sending an acknowledgment to a client when there is no returning data to be sent to the client (a packet will have to be sent with only acknowledgment information); the default is 500 milliseconds, but this can range from 0–5,000 milliseconds, where 0 means an immediate acknowledgment response.

- **Acknowledgment Timeout**—This text box allows you to enter the number of seconds the concentrator will wait for a reply before determining that an acknowledgment has been lost. The default is 3 seconds, but this can range from 1–10 seconds.

Click the **Apply** button at the bottom of the screen to save your changes.

L2TP Global Configuration

To configure system-wide L2TP options, go to **Configuration > Tunneling and Security > L2TP**. Here are the global options you can configure:

- **Enabled**—This check box allows you to globally enable or disable L2TP; unchecking it immediately terminates any current L2TP session.

- **Maximum Tunnel Idle Time**—This text box allows you to enter the amount of time to wait, in seconds, before disconnecting an L2TP tunnel that has no active sessions. The default is 5 seconds, but this can range from 5–86,400 seconds.

- **Control Window Size**—This text box allows you to enter the L2TP window size for unacknowledged control channel packets; the default is 4 packets, but this can range from 0–16 packets.

- **Control Retransmit Interval**—This text box allows you to enter the number of seconds to wait before the concentrator retransmits an unacknowledged L2TP tunnel control message; the default is 1 second, but this can range from 1–10.

- **Control Retransmit Limit**—This text box allows you to enter the maximum number of times the concentrator will send L2TP tunnel control packets to a client before assuming the client is dead; the default is 4 times, but this can range from 1–32.

- **Max. Tunnels**—This text box allows you to configure the maximum number of active L2TP tunnels you want your concentrator to support; please note that you are restricted to a maximum based on the concentrator model the PPTP tunnels terminate on.

- **Max. Sessions/Tunnel**—This text box allows you to configure the maximum number of sessions allowed per tunnel. The default is 0 (no implied limit); and the maximum can be up to the maximum based on the concentrator model.

- **Hello Interval**—This text box allows you to enter the hello interval value, which determines when the concentrator sends a hello message after a period of idle time on an L2TP tunnel; the default is 60 seconds, but this can range from 1–3,600 seconds.

Click the **Apply** button at the bottom of the screen to save your changes. In Chapter 13, "Windows Software Client," I'll discuss how to configure Microsoft's client for accessing the concentrator.

NOTE   Cisco highly recommends that you do not change the global properties for PPTP or L2TP sessions without contacting TAC first—the odds are that you'll create more problems than you will solve.

WebVPN Remote Access

The third type of remote access connectivity I will discuss is how to set up the concentrator to accept WebVPN sessions. I discussed SSL VPNs in Chapter 5, along with the Cisco implementation of SSL VPNs: WebVPN.

SSL uses digital certificates for authentication (in most cases this is server-side authentication). By default, the concentrator will create a self-signed SSL server certificate when it boots up. Or, you can install a third-party SSL identity certificate on the concentrator; however, if you choose this option, you also must install certificates on your web browser clients.

If you choose the latter option, you'll need to obtain a certificate for your concentrator, which I explained previously in Chapter 7 in the "Digital Certificates" section.

The remainder of this section will focus on the five areas concerning the setup of WebVPN on the VPN 3000 concentrators:

- HTTPS access
- System-wide WebVPN parameters
- Group WebVPN configuration
- SSL VPN Client (SVC)
- Cisco Secure Desktop (CSD) for WebVPN access

HTTPS Access

One of the first steps you'll need to perform is to make sure that HTTPS access and WebVPN access are allowed to the concentrator. The following two sections will discuss how you allow HTTPS and WebVPN access.

First, you need to make sure that HTTPS access is allowed by your concentrator. There are two areas that you'll need to examine and possibly change:

- HTTPS properties
- WebVPN interface configuration

HTTPS Properties

To access the concentrator's HTTPS properties, go to **Configuration > Tunneling and Security > SSL**. There are two options on this page:

- *HTTPS*
- *Protocols*

If you click the **HTTPS** hyperlink, you'll find three options:

- **Enable HTTPS**—This check box enables or disables HTTPS access; by default it is enabled.
- **HTTPS Port**— This text box allows you to change the TCP port number that HTTPS access will use; this defaults to 443, but you can change it to another number to enhance your security. Please note that IPsec over TCP cannot use a port that WebVPN will be using.
- **Client Authentication**—This check box, when checked, allows the concentrator to verify the client's digital certificate. If you choose this option, you must install certificates manually on all of your client's web browsers as well as on your concentrator. You also must configure an authorization server using RADIUS or LDAP. I discussed

this in the last chapter in the "Authorization Servers" section. Next, in the group configuration's IPsec tab, set *Authentication* to "None" and the *Authorization Type* to either "RADIUS" or "LDAP." Remember that the concentrator will send the contents specified by the *DN Field* parameter in this tab to the authorization server, which typically is the information found in the Common Name (CN) field of the certificate. Instead of using a client-side certificate, you can use usernames and passwords for user authentication. In most implementations I've set up I have not put certificates on the client; however, I have set up WebVPN only in small environments. For a large environment, I would seriously consider the use of certificates.

Click the **Apply** button to accept your changes.

NOTE   There are two important things to point out about the information on this screen. First, if you want to install certificates on both the concentrators and clients, the WebVPN Port Forwarding feature will no longer work. The Port Forwarding feature uses Java for its implementation, and Java doesn't have the ability to access the web browser's certificate for user authentication. Second, when you click the **Apply** button on this screen, even if you haven't made any changes on the screen, the concentrator automatically breaks any web browser management session, forcing you to log back in to the concentrator.

If you click the **Protocols** hyperlink from the **Configuration > Tunneling and Security > SSL** screen, you'll find these options:

- **Encryption Protocols**—These check boxes enable the encryption algorithms that clients can use for SSL connections. If you uncheck all of them, SSL is disabled. You can choose any or all of the following (in order of strength): "3DES-168/SHA," "RC-128/MD5," and "DES-56/SHA." I highly recommend that you don't use RC4-128, because it seriously affects the performance of the WebVPN connection.

- **SSL Version**—This drop-down selector allows you to choose the SSL version that clients must use for WebVPN access. Your options include the following:

    - **"Negotiate SSL V3/TLS V1"**—The concentrator first tries SSLv3 and then TLSv1; this is the default choice because most web browser clients support these.

    - **"Negotiate SSL V3"**—The concentrator tries SSLv3, but will use a less secure access method.

    - **"Negotiate TLS V1"**—The concentrator tries TSLv1, but will use a less secure access method.

    - **"SSL V3 Only"**—Only SSLv3 clients are allowed access.

    - **"TLS V1 Only"**—Only TLSv1 clients are allowed access.

NOTE   If you'll be using the Port Forwarding feature in WebVPN access, you'll need to choose either "Negotiate SSL V3/TLS V1" or "Negotiate SSL V3"; other SSL version options, if chosen, will cause Port Forwarding to break.

WebVPN Interface Configuration

Once you've set up your HTTPS properties, you'll need to allow WebVPN access to the concentrator. The simplest way to accomplish this is to configure the WebVPN properties under the interface for which these remote access sessions will terminate (typically the public interface). To allow WebVPN access, go to **Configuration > Interfaces** and click the hyperlink of the interface name, like **Ethernet 2 (Public)**. Then click the **WebVPN** tab at the top, showing you the screen in Figure 8-2. Here are the parameter options on this screen:

- **Allow Management HTTPS sessions**—When this check box is selected, you can use HTTPS to manage the concentrator from this interface. Enable this option only when the concentrator is at a remote site and you need to manage it from its public interface.

- **Allow WebVPN HTTPS sessions**—You must select this check box to allow WebVPN HTTPS traffic into the concentrator.

- **Redirect HTTP to HTTPS**—This check box allows you to force any incoming HTTP connections to the concentrator's interface to be redirected to using HTTPS. I highly recommend that you enable this for convenience purposes, because many users might forget to include the "s" in "https" in the URL address bar.

- **Allow POP3S sessions**—This check box, when selected, allows the POP3S (secure POP3) to access a configured POP3S proxy behind the concentrator. The default port number for POP3S is 995.

- **Allow IMAP4S sessions**—This check box, when selected, allows the IMAP4S (secure IMAP4) to access a configured IMAP4S proxy behind the concentrator. The default port number for IMAP4 is 993.

- **Allow SMTPS sessions**—This check box, when selected, allows the SMTPS (secure SMTP) to access a configured SMTPS proxy behind the concentrator. The default port number for SMTP is 998.

Using this screen will update the rules in the concentrator's interface filter automatically based on the options you chose here. When you are done, click the **Apply** button at the bottom of the screen to accept your changes.

Figure 8-2 *Interface Configuration: WebVPN Tab*

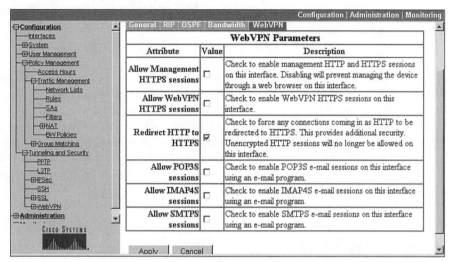

WebVPN Global Configuration

To configure system-wide WebVPN parameters, go to the **Configuration > Tunneling and Security > WebVPN** screen. The following sections will cover the hyperlinks that appear on this page and the configuration options within the hyperlinks.

HTTP/HTTPS Proxy

Clicking the **HTTP/HTTPS Proxy** hyperlink from the **Configuration > Tunneling and Security > WebVPN** screen allows you to set up HTTP and HTTPS proxy services for users. The concentrator can terminate inbound HTTPS connections and forward any HTTP/HTTPS requests to a real proxy server. This process provides better scalability. The HTTP/HTTPS Proxy screen is shown in Figure 8-3. Here are the options on this screen:

- **HTTP Proxy**—This is the IP address of the internal HTTP proxy device (inside server) that the concentrator will forward web requests to; entering an IP address of 0.0.0.0 specifies that no internal proxy is to be used.

- **HTTP Proxy Port**—This is the TCP port number that the internal HTTP proxy is listening on; it defaults to 80.

- **HTTPS Proxy**—This is the IP address of the internal HTTPS proxy device to which the concentrator will forward web requests; entering an IP address of 0.0.0.0 specifies that no internal proxy is to be used.

- **HTTPS Proxy Port**—This is the TCP port number the internal HTTPS proxy is listening on; it defaults to 443.

- **Default Idle Timeout**—This text box allows you to enter the number of minutes that a WebVPN session can be idle before the concentrator terminates it. The default is 30 minutes. The group timeout in **Configuration > User Management** overrides this global timeout value.

TIP   I recommend using a short timeout for the *Default Idle Timeout* parameter. If a user's browser is set to cookies disabled, or the user is prompted for a cookie and denies it, these denied sessions still would appear in the **Administration > Administer Sessions** and **Monitoring > Sessions** screen (they're basically nonexistent or "ghost" sessions), which can be confusing when trying to troubleshoot problems. Using a low idle timeout quickly removes the ghost sessions from the monitoring screens and, more important, from the license limit!

Click the **Apply** button at the bottom to activate your changes.

Figure 8-3   *WebVPN HTTP/HTTPS Proxy*

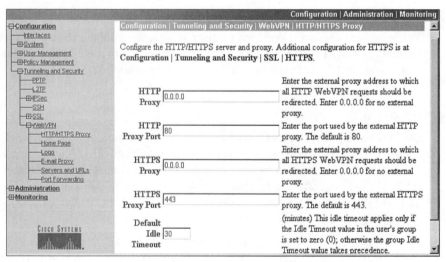

Home Page

Clicking the **Home Page** hyperlink from the **Configuration > Tunneling and Security > WebVPN** screen allows you to configure the web page that the WebVPN users initially will see: the concentrator's home page. This is a web page sitting on a concentrator that you build through the concentrator's GUI interface. The top part of the home page building screen is shown in Figure 8-4. Here are the parameters you can configure that will affect the appearance of your concentrator's home page:

- **Title**—You can enter up to 255 characters, including spaces and the ENTER key, for the title that appears at the top of your screen.

- **Login Message**—This message is displayed above your login credentials; it can be up to 255 characters in length.

- **Logout Message**—This message is displayed when a user terminates a WebVPN session; it can be up to 255 characters in length.

- **Login Prompt**—You can specify up to 16 characters for the username login prompt.

- **Password Prompt**—You can specify up to 16 characters for the password login prompt.

- **Title Bar Color**—You can change the color of the title bar either by entering the name of an RGB color ("red," "green," "blue"), the range of decimal numbers from 0–255 ("x,x,x," where "x" is the decimal color number), or a hexadecimal number representing the RGB color (#000000, where the first two numbers represent red, the second two green, and the third two blue). I commonly use this site to access RGB color coding schemes: http://www.hypersolutions.org/rgb.html. But you can easily do a search for "RGB table" or "RGB color" to find other tables.

- **Title Bar Text**—This is the color of the text in the title bar. Your options are "Black," "White," or "Auto"; choosing "Auto" causes the concentrator to choose the color depending on the color of the *Title Bar Color* parameter.

- **Secondary Bar Color**—This text box allows you to enter the RGB color code for the bar below the title bar.

- **Secondary Bar Text**—This drop-down selector allows you to chose the color of the text appearing in the secondary bar (below the title bar). Your options are the same as with the *Title Bar Text* parameter.

- **Sample Display**—At the bottom is a sample display based on the parameters you entered on this screen (you can't see this in Figure 8-4). Every time you change a color component, this sample coloring section will be updated automatically; this allows you to easily determine if the color schemes you've chosen are easy to comprehend, especially the text coloring.

You can test your changes easily by accessing the concentrator's public IP address externally using HTTPS. Figure 8-5 shows an example of a home page login screen. Before this screen appears, you must accept the concentrator's certificate by clicking the **Yes** button in the pop-up certificate window. Users can be authenticated using RADIUS or via the concentrator. Please note that if you are using Cisco Secure ACS, you can have the ACS server perform the user authentication using other external resources, such as Active Directory, NT Domain, NDS, and others; however, the concentrator itself supports only the two authentication methods I mentioned for WebVPN.

Figure 8-4 *WebVPN Home Page Creation*

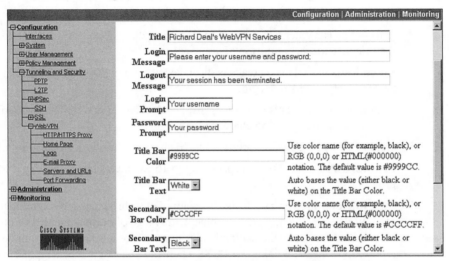

Figure 8-5 *WebVPN Home Page Login Screen Example*

NOTE   If you still want to manage the concentrator on the WebVPN interface, enter the following in your web browser's URL address bar: **http://*concentrator's_IP_address*/access.html**; or you can use **admin.html** at the end. Anything else causes the concentrator to redirect your web browser to the WebVPN login/home page.

Home Page Logo

As you can see in Figure 8-5, you can add a logo to the home page; in this example, it's the Cisco logo. Clicking the **Logo** hyperlink from the **Configuration > Tunneling and Security > WebVPN** screen allows you to configure the logo on the WebVPN home page. Figure 8-6 shows you this configuration screen. Here are the configuration parameters on this screen:

- **No Logo**—Don't put a logo on the WebVPN home page.
- **Use the Cisco Logo**—Use the Cisco logo on the home page.
- **Upload a new logo**—Upload a logo from your hard drive to use on the home page. Click the **Browse** button to find your logos. For logos to display correctly, they shouldn't exceed 100x100 pixels. They also must be in a JPEG, GIF, or PNG format. If you choose this option and click the **Apply** button at the bottom, the screen will be redisplayed, where you'll see a new option: *Use uploaded logo*. As you can see in Figure 8-6, I uploaded a logo—it's not very legible because I exceeded the Cisco 100x100 rule (it's really a picture of a globe).

The top left corners of Figure 8-5 and Figure 8-9 show the Cisco logo on the concentrator's home page.

Figure 8-6   *WebVPN Home Page Logo*

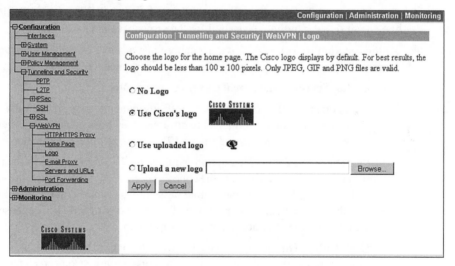

E-mail Proxy

Clicking the **E-mail Proxy** hyperlink from the **Configuration > Tunneling and Security > WebVPN** screen allows you to configure e-mail proxy servers for WebVPN users; this screen is shown in Figure 8-7. The e-mail proxy services supported include POP3S (downloading e-mail), IMAP4S (downloading e-mail), and SMTPS (sending e-mail). Notice that these use an encrypted connection to interact with an e-mail server. Here are the configuration options on the screen:

- **VPN Name Delimiter**—This drop-down selector allows you to choose the delimiter that will be used to differentiate the user's VPN username from the e-mail username.

Delimiters can be ":," "!," "@," "#," or "|." When using the proxy service, the user would need to configure something like *vpn_username:e-mail_username@e-mail_ server_name* for a user account name if the VPN delimiter was ":." Please note that passwords for e-mail proxy users cannot contain the VPN delimiter within their password.

- **Server Delimiter**—This drop-down selector chooses the delimiter that separates the user's e-mail username from the e-mail server's name. Typically this is an "@" but it also can be any of the ones mentioned in the *VPN Delimiter Name* parameter.

- **E-mail Protocol**—Only the three e-mail protocols listed are supported by WebVPN. You must enable access for these protocols on the concentrator in the **Configuration > Interfaces** area, described earlier in the "WebVPN Interface Configuration" section.

- **VPN Concentrator Port**—This text box allows you to change the port number the e-mail proxy server is listening on for protected e-mail connections—both the e-mail server and client must be configured for this port number.

- **Default E-mail Server**—This text box allows you to enter the name or IP address of the e-mail server handling the e-mail for the protocol to the left of it.

- **Authentication Required**—You must choose one or more of the authentication options for your e-mail users using the proxy. These include:

  - **E-Mail Server**—The e-mail server performs authentication.

  - **Concentrator**—The concentrator performs authentication; if the VPN username and e-mail username are different, they both must be specified and separated by the delimiter in the *VPN Name Delimiter* parameter.

  - **Piggyback HTTPS**—This option requires the WebVPN user to have an HTTPS session established to the concentrator already; in this case, the user still must supply a username, but no password is required (authentication already has been done). This option often is used with SMTPS, because most SMTPS servers don't allow users to log in.

  - **Certificate**—The user must have a certificate that the concentrator can validate during the SSL negotiation. The concentrator also needs a root certificate and an identity certificate. This can be the only method of authentication for SMTPS connections, but other proxy connections require at least two methods of authentication, like *E-mail Server* or *Concentrator*. Internet Explorer 6.0 doesn't support this option, but the newest versions of Mozilla, including FireFox, and Netscape Navigator do.

When you are done, click the **Apply** button at the bottom to activate your changes.

Figure 8-7   *WebVPN E-mail Proxy Configuration*

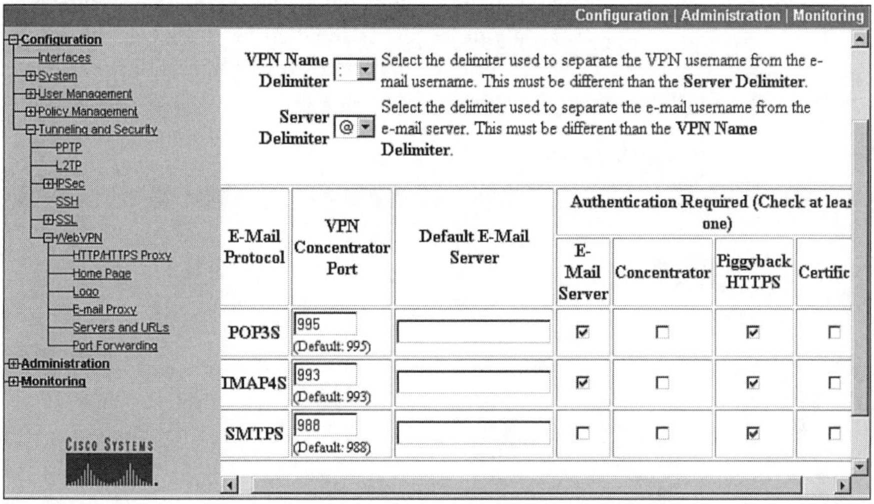

TIP   When using IMAP, a number of sessions can be generated by a user; each of these sessions counts against the simultaneous logins allowed for a user (group configuration in the General tab). To overcome this problem you can increase the number of simultaneous logins allowed per user, have the user close the IMAP application to clear the sessions, or disable the *Piggyback HTTPS* option for IMAP e-mail proxies.

NOTE   You don't have to have the concentrator proxy secure e-mail connections if you feel safe in letting outside users access them directly through the concentrator; however, if you do this, you'll need to add e-mail proxy rules to your public interfaces filter to allow the proxy e-mail traffic. My personal preference is to set up the proxy, because it adds an extra level of security.

Servers and URLs

Clicking the **Servers and URLs** hyperlink from the **Configuration > Tunneling and Security > WebVPN** screen allows you to configure file (CIFS), web (HTTP and HTTPS servers and URLs), and e-mail server proxies for WebVPN users that will appear on the concentrator's home page once a user has authenticated; this screen lists the current entries you've created.

To add a new URL entry, click the **Add** button, which takes you to the screen shown in Figure 8-8. The entries you create here will show up on the WebVPN home page once a user authenticates; however, only these entries show up for users who are not members of a specific group. In other words, this is a generic listing of hyperlinks. You can create hyperlinks for file shares, internal web sites, e-mail proxies, and e-mail servers.

Figure 8-8   *Adding Servers to the Home Page*

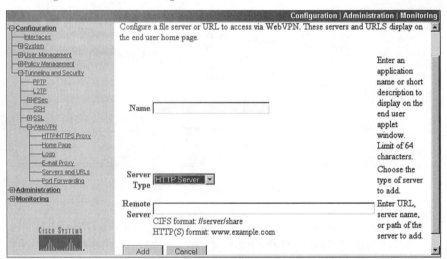

At the top of the screen you need to enter a descriptive name for the hyperlink in the *Name* text box. The *Server Type* hyperlink allows you to choose the type of server: "CIFS" for file servers using NETBIOS names, and "HTTP" or "HTTPS" for web servers. The *Remote Server* field contains the actual URL, DNS name, or network path (CIFS) for the server. For a web server, you would enter something like "www.richard-deal.com"; you can even enter a specific URL like "http://www.richard-deal.com/index.html." For a CIFS file share, it would be something like "//dealserver/sharedfiles" when adding the entry. When done, click the **Add** button to add the hyperlink to the home page.

NOTE   If you are using names for Windows file servers, you'll need to define a WINS server on the concentrator so that the concentrator can resolve the name to an address. To add a WINS server to the concentrator, go to **Configuration > System > Servers > NBNS Servers**. You'll need to enable WINS and can then specify up to three WINS servers for name resolution.

Figure 8-9 shows an example home page of what you see once you have authenticated from the screen in Figure 8-5. At the top right is a set of icons: clicking the **?** icon brings up help;

clicking the icon that looks like a file server brings up a smaller web browser window (this is shown in the bottom right-hand side of the screen); clicking the house icon takes you back to the home page, and clicking the **X** icon logs you out of your WebVPN session.

Figure 8-9   *Example WebVPN Home Page*

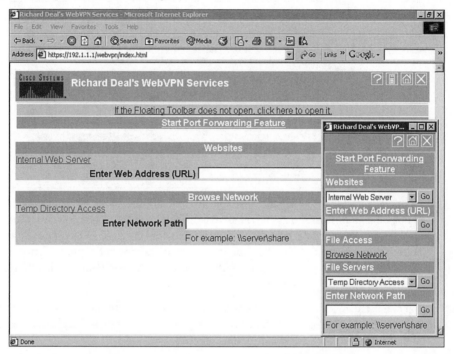

Below the title and icon toolbar at the top of the concentrator's home page are the WebVPN options available to you. The screen is broken into three sections:

- *Start Port Forwarding Feature* (this is discussed in the next section)
- *Web Sites*
- *Browse Networks* (these are file shares)

In this screen, you can see the hyperlink, "Internal Web Server" that I've added through the screen in Figure 8-8. You also can see a file share hyperlink: "Temp Directory Access." Clicking either of these will take you to the respective location (assuming that the directory or file is shared on the server). For Windows file shares, the user might have to authenticate first before being able to access the remote file share. Figure 8-10 shows an example where I clicked the "Temp Directory" file access hyperlink. If you haven't authenticated to the Windows file share already, you'll be prompted to do so; once authenticated, you'll see the screen shown in Figure 8-10.

Figure 8-10   *Network File Access*

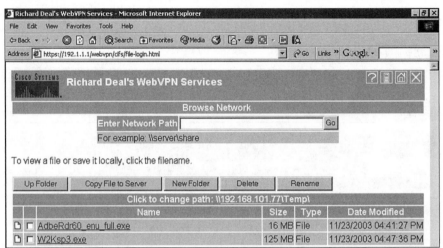

To download a file, just click the file name. To upload a file, click the **Upload** button. When
an upload is in process, do not navigate to a different screen or shut down the web browser
window until the upload is complete—failure to do this can cause an incomplete or corrupted
file to be stored on the server. You can use the other buttons at the top to perform actions
on the file server. As you can see from this screen, interaction with files is different than
when using Microsoft's Windows Explorer program.

You can use the web browser **Back** button to take you back to the WebVPN home page or
you can click the home icon to take you back (see Figure 8-9). I'll discuss the other options
on the WebVPN home page later in this chapter.

NOTE   For WebVPN access to operate correctly, the user's web browser must have cookies
enabled; otherwise, any hyperlinks the user clicks from the home page will open a new
window, prompting the user to log in once again.

All user interaction needs to take place within the WebVPN web browser screens. You'll
need to train your users to *not* enter information in the URL bar in the web browser when
interacting with WebVPN components: everything should be done *within* the web browser
page presented to the user; otherwise, the traffic will not be sent through the SSL VPN
session. By having the user use the hyperlink information within the home page, the
concentrator can proxy the connections.

Port Forwarding

The Cisco WebVPN Port Forwarding feature allows for non-web-based applications to use
the SSL VPN connection (thin client access). If you recall from Chapter 5, "SSL VPNs,"
Cisco has tested the following applications for their thin client implementation: Lotus

Notes, Outlook and Outlook Express, Perforce, Sametime Instant Messaging, Secure FTP (FTP over SSH), SSH, Telnet, Windows Terminal Services, and XDDTS. Other TCP-based applications might work, but Cisco hasn't tested them.

NOTE   Remember that for the client to use the Port Forwarding feature, Sun Microsystems' Java Runtime Environment (JRE) must be installed: Microsoft's Java will *not* work. WebVPN automatically checks to see if JRE is installed on a user's PC; if it isn't, a window pops up and directs the user to a web site where it can be downloaded and installed.

Clicking the **Port Forwarding** hyperlink from the **Configuration > Tunneling and Security > WebVPN** screen allows you to configure TCP-based applications that you want to tunnel through the user's SSL VPN session. You'll be presented with a list of Port Forwarding applications you've already added, if any. Just click the **Add** button to add a new application. This will bring you to the screen in Figure 8-11. Here are the parameters you need to configure:

- **Name**—This will become the name of the port forwarding process you're defining; give it a descriptive name, like "Telnet to the Accounting Server." This name will appear in the list of port forwarding applications within the concentrator's web pages.

- **Local TCP Port**—This is the port number that must be used on the user's PC when making the connection to the application; it should be a number from 1,024 to 65,535 that is *not* going to be used on the user's PC. This number is used by Java to identify the application uniquely on the user's computer.

- **Remote Server**—This is the fully qualified domain name (FQDN) or IP address of the remote server; if you're using DNS mapping, this must be the FQDN of the remote server.

- **Remote TCP Port**—This is the port number of the application that is to be forwarded; for example, if you wanted to enable port forwarding for Telnet, you would enter "23" for this parameter.

When you are done with your Port Forwarding entry, click the **Add** button at the bottom of the screen to add the entry. You can create up to 252 port forwarding entries for your users.

Once you've authenticated as a user for WebVPN and are brought to the screen in Figure 8-9, click the **Start Port Forwarding Feature** hyperlink on the concentrator's home page. A pop-up window states that both secure and unsecured information will appear in the Port Forwarding window; click **OK** to accept this. Next, you must accept two SSL certificates: one for the concentrator and one for Java. After this the window shown in Figure 8-12 will be displayed. This is a display-only window and will require you to train your users on how this information should be used to establish Port Forwarding connections.

Figure 8-11 *Adding Port Forwarding Applications*

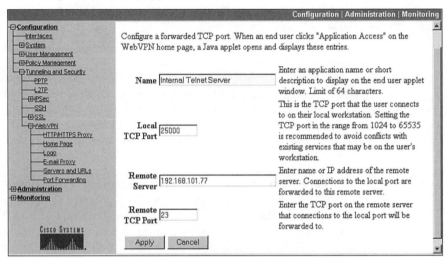

Figure 8-12 *WebVPN Port Forwarding Screen*

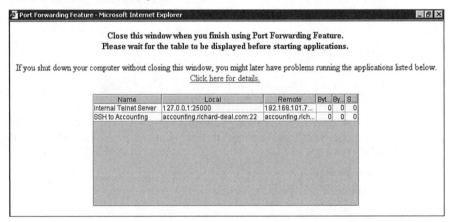

If you used an IP address for the *Remote Server* parameter in Figure 8-11, you'll see something like the first line in the web browser box in Figure 8-12. First you see the name you created, followed by the *Local* information: 127.0.0.1:25000 for a telnet to 192.168.101.77 (this is cut off). Your users, when wanting to telnet to this device, must telnet to 127.0.0.1 and port 25000; by doing this, the Java script will intercept the TCP connection and forward it across the SSL VPN to the actual server (192.168.101.77 on port 23). The Java script is redirecting the connection to the correct server and port.

If you use a hostname to identify a remote server for port forwarding, the WebVPN Java script will back up the user PC's local host file first and then modify it by adding the port forwarding entry. The Windows hosts file is located here: C:\Windows\system32\drivers\

etc\hosts or C:\WINNT\system32\drivers\etc\hosts. Here's an example of a hosts file Java created based on what I set up for the second example in Figure 8-12 (which uses SSH) :

```
127.0.0.3 accounting.richard-deal.com # added by WebVpnPortForward
       at Mon Nov 29 17:58:44 EST 2004
```

In this example, when a user would use SSH to access "accounting.richard-deal.com," the traffic would be directed to the loopback address of "127.0.0.3," which the Java applet would intercept and redirect through the WebVPN session to the concentrator. The concentrator then would redirect the traffic to the actual accounting server. The user *doesn't* have to know about the port to use—this information was already updated, behind the user's back, in the local hosts file.

CAUTION   It is very important that users *correctly exit* the Port Forwarding screen by closing it down—click the **X** in the top right corner of the web browser window; failing to do this can corrupt the user's hosts file by keeping the modified hosts file and not replacing it with the backup file. If the user closes the Port Forwarding screen correctly, Java removes the updated file and replaces it with the backup file (the one before Java made its changes). So, if the user doesn't shut this down correctly, their hosts file will still have the Java information in it. To rectify this, have the user manually delete the "hosts" file and then rename the "hosts.WebVPN" file (in the same directory) to "hosts." If for whatever reason this file doesn't exist, the lines at the beginning of the hosts file (ending in "added by WebVPN...") will need to be removed manually with a text editor. I would send this information out in an e-mail to reduce the amount of time you'll have to spend explaining to your users how to fix this problem. Or you might even want to put a hyperlink on the WebVPN page that points to instructions to do this!

Group Configuration

What I've discussed so far affects all users that access your concentrator via WebVPN. Now I'll discuss how to fine-tune this using base and specific groups. With both, you must enable WebVPN access first by going into the group and clicking the **General** tab. For the *Tunneling Protocols* parameter, you need to make sure the "WebVPN" check box is checked; if this is not done, members of the specific group will not be allowed WebVPN access.

TIP   My recommendation is to disable WebVPN in the base group and then enable it on a specific group-by-group basis, giving you more control over who uses the WebVPN remote access feature.

Because the configuration is almost the same with the base and specific groups, I'll focus only on customizing a specific group's WebVPN access configuration. To make WebVPN changes on a group-by-group basis, go to **Configuration > User Management > Groups**. There are three areas in a specific group where you can enforce WebVPN policies:

- WebVPN tab within a group's configuration
- WebVPN Servers and URLs group button on the group screen
- WebVPN Port Forwarding group button on the group screen

The remaining sections will discuss the configuration of these options.

NOTE   The Cisco clientless WebVPN feature does not use the DNS configuration of the group that a user belongs to; only the concentrator's global DNS settings are used. Remember that the concentrator is acting as a proxy, and thus the concentrator uses its own defined DNS server to perform DNS resolution. The concentrator's DNS server is defined on the **Configuration > System > Servers > DNS Servers** screen. You must click the *Enable* check box and enter the IP address of at least one (but up to three) DNS server(s).

WebVPN Tab

To access the WebVPN tab for a group, from the screen in group screen (**Configuration > User Management > Groups**), click the name of the group, click the **Modify** button, and then click the **WebVPN** tab. The top, middle, and bottom parts of this screen are shown in Figures 8-13, 8-14, and 8-15. The WebVPN tab is broken into three sections: *WebVPN Parameters, Content Filter Parameters,* and *WebVPN ACLs*. Here's an explanation of the parameters found in the three sections.

Figure 8-13   *Group WebVPN Tab: Top Part*

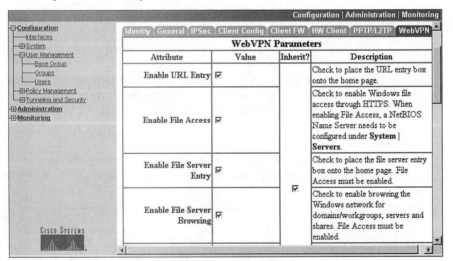

Figure 8-14   *Group WebVPN Tab: Middle Part*

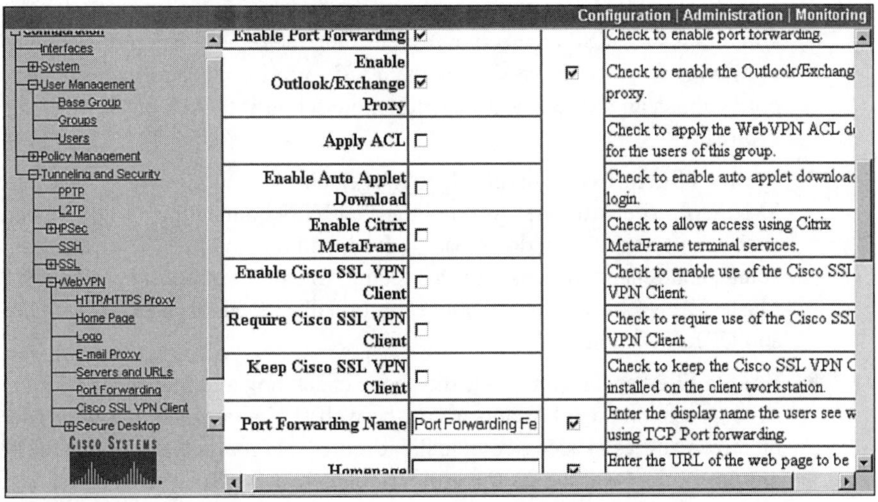

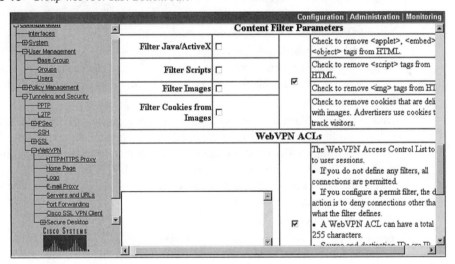

Figure 8-15   *Group WebVPN Tab: Bottom Part*

WebVPN Parameters

The information in the *WebVPN* parameters section affects the kinds of information found on the WebVPN home page shown previously in Figure 8-9. Here are the parameters you can configure:

- **Enable URL Entry**—If you want users to be able to enter their own URLs on the WebVPN home page, check this check box. If you look back to Figure 8-9, you'll see that this has been enabled in the *Websites* section for the group. Please note that the concentrator is acting as a web proxy for the user when the user accesses URLs with this feature. If the user is trying to access a secure, remote site, the concentrator will establish an SSL connection from itself to the remote server on behalf of the user; in the current software version, with an SSL proxy connection, the concentrator will not establish an SSL connection to a remote server if the remote server's certificate is expired.

- **Enable File Access**—This check box, when checked, allows WebVPN users to access SMB/CIFS file structures through the WebVPN connection. When this option is enabled, users can edit, download, upload, and rename files. They also can create, delete, and rename folders. For this feature to work, you must specify a WINS or Master Browser server on the concentrator. I discussed this previously in the "Servers and URLs" section.

- **Enable File Server Entry**—If the above check box and this check box are enabled, a file server entry text box appears on the WebVPN home page, allowing users to enter their own entries to access remote file resources. Figure 8-9 shows that the home page has this option enabled for the group (look below the **Browse Network** hyperlink).

- **Enable File Server Browsing**—If this and the *Enable File Access* check boxes are checked, the **Browse Network** hyperlink appears on the group's WebVPN home page (you can see this in Figure 8-9). When you click this, it functions like the Network Neighborhood on a Windows device.

- **Enable Port Forwarding**—This check box allows the user to use the Port Forwarding feature on the WebVPN home page. As you can see in the top part of Figure 8-9, I've enabled this feature because the *Start Port Forwarding Feature* hyperlink appears.

- **Enable Outlook/Exchange Proxy**—This check box enables the Outlook/Exchange mail forwarding proxy (MAPI). Users get their information about the Outlook/Exchange mail proxy by what you enter in a Java applet; users then launch this applet by clicking the *Application Access* section of the WebVPN home page. To use this feature, the WebVPN user first must make a connection to the Exchange server before making one through WebVPN.

- **Apply ACL**—This check box allows you to apply a WebVPN ACL to the group's access; the ACL itself is defined at the bottom of the *WebVPN* tab. I highly recommend the configuration of ACLs for additional security. Normally I'll allow users access to a small set of services and then deny everything else.

- **Enable Auto Applet Download** (new in 4.7)—This check box allows you to start port forwarding or an Outlook/Exchange Proxy Java applet download when WebVPN users log in.

- **Enable Citrix Metaframe** (new in 4.7)—This check box enables support for Citrix Metaframe. On your Metaframe web software, you must configure it for "Normal Address" mode. You also must install an SSL certificate on the concentrator using an FQDN for the CN in the SSL certificate—using an IP address in this field will not work.

- **Enable Cisco SSL VPN Client** (new in 4.7)—This check box enables the Cisco SSL VPN Client (SVC), which supports a broader range of more complex services not supported across a normal web browser connection. SVC doesn't support WebVPN ACLs, discussed in a later bullet; however, it does support IP-based ACLs, like with the Cisco VPN Client (IPsec). I discuss this in more depth later in the "SSL VPN Client (SVC)" section.

- **Require Cisco SSL VPN Client** (new in 4.7)—This check box, when selected, requires that members of this group use SVC for their WebVPN sessions—the concentrator will verify this upon the client's WebVPN connection attempt. Because SVC is supported for only Windows 2000 and XP systems, don't enable this for a group that contains other client operating systems.

- **Keep Cisco SSL VPN Client** (new in 4.7)—When checked, this allows users to keep the SVC software installed on their computers versus downloading it from the concentrator each time a WebVPN session is made. When not checked (the default), the SVC software is uninstalled each time the client disconnects. If this option is selected and a new SVC client version is installed on the concentrator, the client will download and install it automatically instead of using the currently installed older version.

- **Port Forwarding Name**—This text box allows you to change the name of the hyperlink that appears on the WebVPN home page for the Port Forwarding feature. This defaults to "Port Forwarding Feature."

- **Home Page**—This text box allows you to display a different home page than the one the concentrator builds. This is useful if you want to take your users directly to one web server with a specific web application on it; if users need to access more than one service, I would present the user with the concentrator's home page and add the necessary web links to this page.

CAUTION   If you are concerned about security, especially regarding users accessing remote resources that you have no control over (like Internet web surfing), I would not enable the *Enable URL Entry, Enable File Server Entry, and Enable File Server Browsing* parameters unless you configure ACLs to limit your users' access to internal resources.

Content Filter Parameters

The *Content Filter Parameters* section of the *WebVPN* tab allows you to filter certain kinds of web downloads, including Java/ActiveX applets (remove the "<applet>," "<embed>," and "<object>" tags), scripts (remove the "<script>" tags), images (remove the "<img>"

tags), and cookies delivered with images from HTTP downloads. Here are the parameters you can enable for content filtering of your WebVPN users:

- **Filter Java/ActiveX**—Enabling this might cause some web pages to break.
- **Filter Scripts**—Enabling this might cause some web pages to break.
- **Filter Images**—Enabling this might increase download speeds for your users.
- **Filter Cookies from Images**—Enabling this increases security by preventing web sites from keeping track of your users.

WebVPN ACLs

The last section from the group's WebVPN tab screen, shown at the bottom of Figure 8-15, allows you to configure access control lists (ACLs) to filter users' access to web servers. If you don't configure any WebVPN ACLs, all web access is permitted to your users; however, as soon as you configure one WebVPN ACL, if no match is found in a configured ACL, the user is denied the web access. Therefore, you'll need to configure at least one **permit** statement in an ACL when configuring WebVPN ACLs.

Here's the syntax for creating an ACL that filters protocol information:

```
{permit | deny} {ip | smtp | pop3 | imap4 | http | https | cifs}
          src_address src_wildcard_mask
          dst_address dst_wildcard_mask
```

When creating a protocol ACL, the statement can have a maximum of 255 characters. You start out with an action: either **permit** or **deny**. This is followed by the name of the protocol you want to filter; you must use a protocol from the list of supported ones shown in the above command syntax. Following this are the source and destination addresses and wildcard masks. As you can see, this is a very similar syntax to configuring a named ACL entry on a Cisco IOS router. If you are filtering on a specific device, like 192.1.1.1, you can enter the addressing information as **192.1.1.1 0.0.0.0** or **host 192.1.1.1**; likewise, if you want to match on any address, you can use either **0.0.0.0 255.255.255.255** for the address information (source or destination) or the keyword **any**. Each ACL statement needs to be on a separate line.

You can also do rudimentary URL filtering by using the following syntax:

```
{permit | deny} URL url_definition
```

An example of a URL definition would be **http://www.richard-deal.com**. Any URL style syntax is supported, including HTTP, HTTPS, CIFS, IMAP4S, POP3S, SMTPS, and so on.

Here's a simple ACL configuration:

```
permit URL http://www.richard-deal.com
permit smtp any host 192.168.101.77
permit pop3 any host 192.168.101.77
```

In this example, only URL access to the internal web server (www.richard-deal.com) and e-mail access (SMTP and POP3) to the internal e-mail server (192.168.101.77) are allowed — all other traffic will be dropped for the users' WebVPN sessions.

Once you've completed the configuration of your Web ACLs, be sure to check the *Apply ACL* check box in the *WebVPN Parameters* under the WebVPN tab. After completing the WebVPN tab configuration, click the **Apply** button at the bottom to activate your changes for the group.

NOTE   Remember that a specific group's WebVPN configuration overrides the base group's configuration. Also, if you are using specific groups, each user must be associated with a group. This is accomplished from the **Configuration > User Management > Users** screen discussed previously in the "User Configuration" section in the last chapter.

WebVPN Group Buttons

With the specific groups configuration screen (**Configuration > User Management > Groups**), you have two buttons you can click to add additional URLs and Port Forwarding applications to the selected group that are not available for users that access WebVPN using the base group: the **WebVPN Servers and URLs** and **WebVPN Port Forwarding** buttons. The next two sections will discuss these two group buttons.

WebVPN Servers and URL Button

When you click a group name from the group screen (**Configuration > User Management > Groups**) and click the **WebVPN Servers and URLs** button, you are taken to a screen where you can see the servers and URLs that this group can access through the WebVPN home page. To add a server or URL, click the **Add** button. This takes you to the screen shown previously in Figure 8-6. The difference between the two screens is that the screen from **Configuration > Tunneling and Security > WebVPN > Servers and URLS** and the group screen is that the previous screen adds servers and URLs for only the base group users, and this screen adds servers and URLs for the specific group. In other words, if a user logs in via WebVPN belonging to a specific group, that user will see only the servers and URLs created for the specific group through the group's **WebVPN Servers and URLs** button — the user won't see the base group servers and URLs created from the **Configuration > Tunneling and Security > WebVPN > Servers and URLS** screen.

NOTE   Please note that the group **WebVPN Servers and URLs** button is available only for specific groups; to add servers and URLs for the base group, you need to go to the **Configuration > Tunneling and Security > WebVPN > Servers and URLS** screen.

WebVPN Port Forwarding Button

When you click a group name from the group screen (**Configuration > User Management > Groups**) and click the **WebVPN Port Forwarding button**, you are taken to a screen where you can see the port forwarding applications that only this group can access through the WebVPN home page. To add a server or URL, click the **Add** button. This takes you to the screen shown previously in Figure 8-11. The difference between the two screens is that the screen from **Configuration > Tunneling and Security > WebVPN > Port Forwarding** and this group screen is that the previous screen adds Port Forwarding applications for only the base group users and this screen adds Port Forwarding applications for only the selected specific group. Please see the note in the previous section about the appearance difference on the WebVPN home page concerning the setup of the base group and the specific groups.

SSL VPN Client (SVC)

The SVC client is new in software Version 4.7. SVC works only with Windows 2000 and Windows XP clients. It provides an alternative to using an IPsec VPN client. SVC has one main advantage over a normal HTTPS WebVPN connection: it supports many additional functions, policies, and applications, more than the Cisco clientless and thin client WebVPN implementations. Plus, unlike the IPsec VPN client, SVC is downloaded and installed on the user's desktop automatically, reducing any additional configuration the user has to perform.

To help you with installing and using the SVC, the following sections cover these topics:

- Installing SVC on the Concentrator
- Using the SVC Software
- Non-Administrator Users

Installing SVC on the Concentrator

The SVC software is installed on the concentrator and downloaded by the client during its initial WebVPN connection. To install the SVC software on the concentrator, go to **Configuration > Tunneling and Security > WebVPN > Cisco SSL VPN Client**. Click the **Browse** button to find the client software on your desktop (assuming you've downloaded this from the Cisco site) and then click the **Apply** button to download the SVC software to the concentrator, which stores it locally in Flash memory. The package name you download from Cisco will be something like this: sslclient-win-1.0.0.179.pkg—it's important that you download the file ending in ".pkg" because this is used by the concentrator.

Once installed, if you return to the above screen, you'll see the screen shown in Figure 8-16; here you can see which SVC client version is installed (at the top) and enable (enabled by default), disable, install, or uninstall the SVC client on the concentrator.

Figure 8-16 *SVC Software Screen*

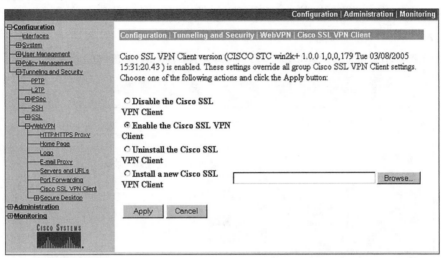

Using the SVC Software

When the user makes the initial connection via HTTPS to the concentrator's public interface, the user will log in normally (see Figure 8-5). Upon successfully logging in, the web browser window will indicate that the SVC software will be installed (see Figure 8-17). The user must accept the SVC certificate by clicking the **Yes** button in the pop-up window. If the concentrator is using a self-signed certificate, you'll receive a couple of warnings regarding this, which the user can click to ignore. If you are concerned about the amount of interaction the user has to perform, install an SSL certificate on concentrator. The SVC software is downloaded and installed on the user's computer automatically. The user is given the option to access the local LAN, and resources behind the VPN 3000 concentrator (a limited form of split tunneling).

NOTE   For the SVC software to be installed on the user's desktop, the user must be logged in with Administrator privileges; otherwise, the install will fail. However, once installed, the use of the software does not require Administrator privileges. Also, for cases where Administrator permissions are not available to the user, an installer helper (stub installer) can be used to install the Administrator piece.

Once a connection has been established, a yellow key icon will appear in the bottom right-hand corner of the Windows taskbar (the bottom right-hand corner of the user's desktop). If you right-click and choose any of the options, the screen in Figure 8-18 appears. The Status tab is in the foreground, displaying protected traffic statistics. The Route Details tab displays what traffic is protected. The About tab displays the SVC software version. To disconnect, either click the **Disconnect** button on the screen in Figure 8-18 or right-click the yellow key icon in the taskbar and choose **Disconnect**. Upon disconnecting, the SVC software is uninstalled from the user's desktop automatically unless you've chosen the *Keep Cisco SSL VPN Client* option under the group WebVPN tab.

Figure 8-17 *Initial SVC User Screen*

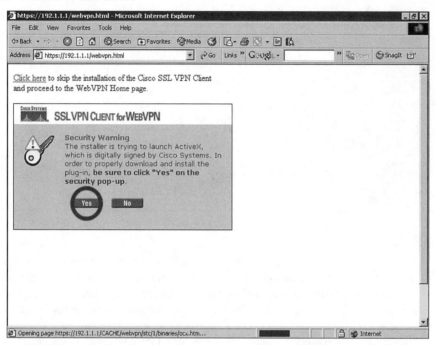

TIP   For users in a group that use dialup for accessing the Internet, I would highly recommend that you choose the *Keep Cisco SSL VPN Client* option, because the downloaded software (SVC) is about 300 KB in size.

Figure 8-18 *SVC Status Window*

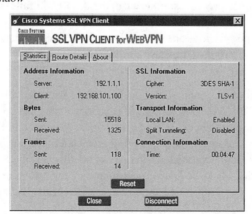

Non-Administrator Users

One limitation of SVC is that for the initial automatic download and install process to work, the users must have Administrator privileges on their 2000 or XP PCs. If they don't, you still can use SVC, but it requires that you give the user a special installation package from Cisco. When you download the SVC software from Cisco, you'll need to look for the file ending in ".zip," like this: sslclient-win-1.0.0.179.zip. Inside this zipped archive are two files: stc.pkg and stcie.exe. Have the user unzip the files and run the stcie.exe file to perform the installation. Some command options may be viewed by executing "stcie.exe /?". This option might be necessary if the user needs to use SVC but is accessing the concentrator from a PC in a controlled environment.

Cisco Secure Desktop for WebVPN Access

Cisco Secure Desktop (CSD) for WebVPN connections was added in Version 4.7. CSD allows you to verify the basic security setup of a PC before it connects to the concentrator, while it is connected, and after it disconnects. This control can include the operating system version installed, including service packs, the installation of antivirus software and its version, the installation of personal firewall software and its version, and the device's IP address.

CSD is responsible for obtaining this information from the client's machine when the client is using WebVPN. The CSD software is installed on the user's computer and will encrypt all CSD queries to and from the concentrator. It isolates the connection information in a Secure Desktop space. Any data downloaded to CSD is encrypted using RC4 or 3DES. Once the client device disconnects from the concentrator, the CSD software automatically erases and overwrites all data obtained from the secured WebVPN session, which meets one of the U.S. Department of Defense standards for security. This includes data downloaded, inserted, or created within the client, such as web browsing information (passwords, auto-completed information, configuration changes, downloaded files, cached browser information, and so on).

CSD is fully supported on Microsoft Windows (2000 and XP) and has limited functionality on Windows 95, 98, ME, MacOS X, and Linux (only the Cache Cleaner). Table 8-1 displays the antivirus products supported by CSD, and Table 8-2 displays the personal firewall products supported by CSD.

Table 8-1 *CSD-Supported Antivirus Packages*

Product	Version
eTrust Antivirus	7.0+
F-Secure Antivirus	2003+
McAfee VirusScan	8.0–9.0 and Enterprise 7.0–8.0
Norton Antivirus for Windows	Professional 2004+ and Corporate 8.0–9.0
Panda Antivirus	Platinum 7.0–8.0 and Titanium 2004

continues

Table 8-1 *CSD-Supported Antivirus Packages (Continued)*

Product	Version
PC-cillin	2003–2004
Trend Micro PC-cillin Internet Security	2004
Microsoft Windows AntiSpyware	Beta v1

Table 8-2 *CSD-Supported Personal Firewall Packages*

Product	Version
Cisco Security Agent (CSA)	4.0+
Internet Connection Firewall	Windows XP–XP SP2
ISS BlackICE PC Protection	3.6
McAfee Personal Firewall	4.0–5.0
Norton Personal Firewall	2003+
Sygate Personal Firewall	5.0–5.5
ZoneAlarm Personal Firewall	4.0–5.0

Installing the Secure Desktop Software on Your Concentrator

The CSD software must be installed on the concentrator and downloaded by the client during its initial WebVPN session connection. To install the CSD software on the concentrator, go to **Configuration > Tunneling and Security > WebVPN > Secure Desktop > Secure Desktop Setup**. Click the **Browse** button to find the CSD client software on your desktop (assuming you've already downloaded this from the Cisco web site). The package name you download from Cisco will be something like this: securedesktop-3.0.1.260-k9.pkg. Then click the **Apply** button to download the software to the concentrator, which stores the CSD software locally in Flash memory. Once CSD is installed, a hyperlink will appear that if you click it, it will take you automatically to the **Configuration > Tunneling and Security > WebVPN > Secure Desktop > Secure Desktop Manager** screen (if you go back to the **Configuration > Tunneling and Security > WebVPN > Secure Desktop > Secure Desktop Setup** screen, you can disable, enable, uninstall, or install the CSD software).

Configuring the Secure Desktop Parameters for Windows

Once the CSD software is installed, you can go to the Secure Desktop Manager screen (**Configuration > Tunneling and Security > WebVPN > Secure Desktop > Secure Desktop Manager**), shown in Figure 8-19, to configure CSD parameters. This is an HTML and JavaScript-based utility that works within your web browser and allows you to build and manage the following components:

- **Locations**—A location from which Microsoft Windows users connect. You can define location settings for these users, like operating system version and VPN feature policies.

Common locations would include Work, Home, and Insecure or Internet, where you can define different policies for different locations. Locations are discussed in more depth in the "Windows Location Settings" and "Windows Location Identification" sections.

- **VPN Feature Policy**—A VPN feature policy can check the following items before allowing access to the network behind the concentrator: SSL VPN Client installation, web browsing, file access, and port forwarding. It also can verify the installation and operation of the operating system and its version, antivirus software, and personal firewall software. VPN Feature Polices are discussed in more depth in the "VPN Feature Policy" section.

- **Cache Cleaner**—The cache cleaner disables or erases all data that a user downloads and creates, or is inserted into a web browser session; it is supported with the following web browsers: Microsoft IE 5.0+, Netscape Navigator 7.1+, Mozilla 1.7+, or Firefox 1.0+ on Windows platforms, Safari 1.0+ on MacOS X, and Mozilla 1.1+ on Red Hat Linux v9. The Cache Cleaner is discussed in more depth in the "Windows Cache Cleaner" section later.

- **CSD Settings**—The CSD settings feature allows you to have CSD start up automatically after its installation on a user's computer, check for keystroke logging programs, switch between the local desktop and the Secure Desktop, restrict Windows registry access, cmd.exe access, and printing access, local browser settings, and many others. CSD Settings will be discussed in more depth in the "Secure Desktop General Settings for Windows," "Secure Desktop Settings for Windows," and "Secure Desktop Browser for Windows" sections later.

Figure 8-19 *CSD Software Screen*

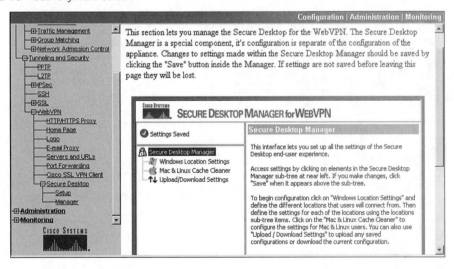

Windows Location Settings

Once you access the CSD Manager HTML/JavaScript utility, if you have Windows clients, the first thing you'll do is set up your locations by clicking the **Windows Location Settings** hyperlink in Figure 8-19. For each different group of users you have that have different policies, you'll create a separate location. Once you've created a location, you can determine how users are assigned to a location, in addition to configuring the Cache Cleaner, VPN Feature Policy, and Secure Desktop features for that location.

For example, if you have wireless LAN users who have an IP address assigned from $10.10.x.x$, which is part of the central office network, you might define a policy that disables both the Cache Cleaner and Secure Desktop function for these devices; however, for SOHO users, such as remote access WebVPN clients, you'll enable both of these features, requiring additional software on these PCs such as antivirus and personal firewall software. And finally, for remote access users who access the concentrator via Internet Café or other such locations, you might add additional policies, like a much shorter timeout period, to prevent unauthorized access.

NOTE   The Windows Location Settings feature works with only Windows-based clients.

Once you've clicked the **Windows Location Settings** hyperlink, enter the name of the location, like "Home," in the *Location Name* text box shown in Figure 8-20, and click the **Add** button.

Figure 8-20   *Adding a Windows Location*

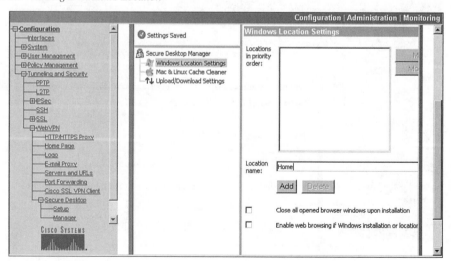

Once you have added your locations, you can move the locations up or down in the list. The order is important because CSD checks to see if a user belongs to a location by processing the locations in the order they're listed on this screen. For all locations, you have two check boxes you can select:

- **Close all opened browser windows upon installation**—Closes unsecured web browser windows once CSD has been installed on the user's desktop upon their Windows WebVPN connection to the concentrator.

- **Enable web browsing if Windows installation or location matching fails**—If the user doesn't match a listed location, enabling this check box allows Windows clients to browse the Internet minimally via a web browser. Cisco recommends enabling this option for PocketPC devices, because CSD isn't supported on this platform.

Figure 8-21 shows a list of three locations. Notice in the left JavaScript window pane that there are additional entries for the three locations you've added.

Figure 8-21   *Using Multiple Windows Locations*

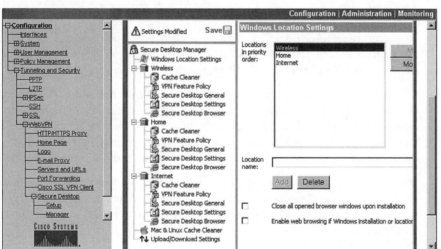

Windows Location Identification

To specify who belongs to a location, click the name of the location in the left HTML/ JavaScript window pane. In Figure 8-22, I clicked "Wireless" for local LAN users. Membership of a location can be based on information found on a user's certificate, the user's IP address, or a particular file or registry entry found on the user's Windows device. If you specify more than one type, like certificate and IP addressing information, the concentrator uses a logical "AND" to match on the criteria.

Figure 8-22 *Specifying Members of a Windows Location*

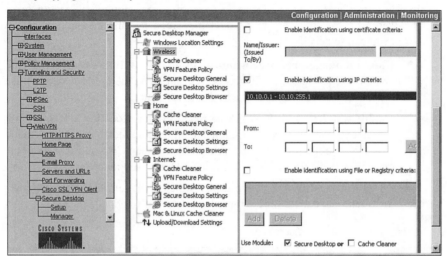

To match on a user's certificate information, click the check box labeled *Enable identification using certificate criteria*. In the first text box enter the CN on the user's certificate. Or, you can enter the CN of the issuer (Certificate Authority) in the second text box.

To match on a user's IP address, select the *Enable identification using IP criteria* check box and enter the range of IP addresses and click **Add**—you can add multiple ranges for a location. In Figure 8-22 for the Wireless location, I specified the IP addresses assigned to them via DHCP. If a client device has more than one IP address on a NIC, or multiple NICs, CSD on the desktop will use only the IP address of the first NIC detected on the PC.

To match on a user's file or registry information, click the *Enable identification using File or Registry criteria* check box. When you click the **Add** button to add an entry, a small window will pop up asking you for the file (like the location and name) or registry key information.

At the bottom of the screen is the *Use Module* section. Only one option out of the following can be selected:

- "Secure Desktop," when selected, specifies that the Secure Desktop Settings are used.
- "Cache Cleaner" specifies that the Cache Cleaner settings are used.
- If neither are selected, the VPN Feature Policy is used.

As to which you should use, you can use the following guidelines:

- For internal users, typically the VPN Feature Policy is used, where you want to ensure that users have the correct security software installed on their PCs.
- For remote access home users, either the VPN Feature Policy, Secure Desktop, or Cache Cleaner (for non-Windows systems).

- For remote access users using public PCs, either Secure Desktop or Cache Cleaner; in some cases, because of restricted access to the computer, they might not be able to use CSD.

TIP   Some older implementations of Windows, like 98, don't support CSD functionality fully; therefore, if you select the "Secure Desktop" option to the right of *Use Module*, you should configure both the Secure Desktop Settings and the Cache Cleaner, where the latter will serve as a fallback security solution.

NOTE   If you only want to configure a location where you want everyone to match, then don't specify any matching criteria; however, make sure that this location is listed at the ***bottom*** of the locations you've added, because they are processed in order (top-down).

Windows Cache Cleaner

If you selected "Cache Cleaner" from the *Use Module* section in the Identification window in Figure 8-22, you can click the **Cache Cleaner** hyperlink under the name of the location (like "Wireless"), which will take you to the screen in Figure 8-23. Normally this is used for users for whom CSD can't be installed on their desktops, like in an Internet Café, or for non-Windows 2000/XP systems. Here are your options:

- **Launch hidden URL after installation**—Specifies a hidden URL to launch so that you know that the Cache Cleaner was installed; as an example, you might place a cookie file on the user's computer and then later check for the existence of the cookie.

- **Show message at the end of successful installation**—Displays a window showing that the Cache Cleaner was installed successfully on the user's desktop.

- **Launch cleanup upon inactivity timeout**—Specifies that the idle timer should be used, and when the idle timer expires, causes cache cleaning to begin. You can then change the *Timeout after* drop-down selector to specify what the idle timer should be (the smallest is 1 minute and the largest is 60 minutes).

- **Launch cleanup upon closing of all browser instances**—Specifies that cache cleaning begins once all web browser windows are closed.

- **Disable cancellation of cleaning**—Removes the cancellation feature from the user's desktop when performing cache cleaning. I highly recommend that you leave this disabled, because this does not allow the user to cancel a cache cleaning; enabling this can create a security risk.

- **Clean the whole cache in addition to . . .**—Removes all data from the user's web browser cache upon activation, including any web browser files that existed before the user's session began. I highly recommend that you enable this; however, this feature works only with Microsoft's Internet Explorer web browser.

Figure 8-23 *Configuring Cache Cleaning for a Windows Location*

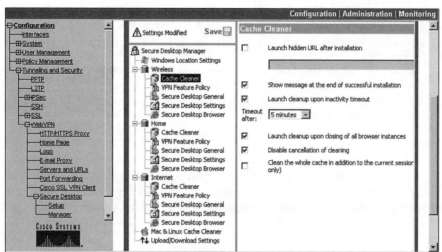

VPN Feature Policy

If you selected neither "Secure Desktop" nor "Cache Cleaner" from the *Use Module* section in the Identification window in Figure 8-22, you can click the **VPN Feature Policy** hyperlink under the name of the location, taking you to the screen in Figure 8-24. There are four features you can configure: Web Browsing, File Access, Port Forwarding, and Full Tunneling.

Here are the options you can specify for each:

- If you specify "ON" in the drop-down selector, the corresponding feature is unconditionally *allowed*.

- If you specify "OFF" in the drop-down selector, the corresponding feature is unconditionally *denied*.

- If you specify "ON if criteria are matched" in the drop-down selector, the corresponding feature is enabled if the corresponding criteria are matched. Click the **. . .** button to the right (hidden in Figure 8-24) and you'll see the criteria screen in Figure 8-25. Choose the criteria that must match and then click the **OK** button to accept them. From a category, you can CNTRL-click to select multiple options. Within a category, only one option needs to match. If you select multiple categories, at least one option in each category must match for the user to be allowed access to the corresponding feature in Figure 8-24. One additional point to make: at the bottom of the screen you can select either "Secure Desktop" or "Cache Cleaner" as the feature to use for the client; if you choose the former and CSD is not active on the client, the VPN Feature Policy fails and the user is denied access to the corresponding feature in Figure 8-24. Choosing this option might create problems for older Windows systems and non-Windows systems.

Figure 8-24 *Enabling VPN Feature Policies for Windows*

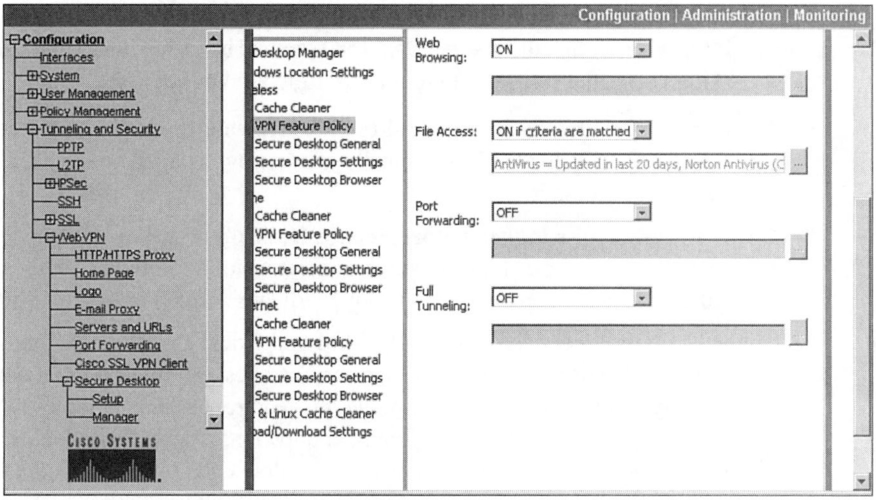

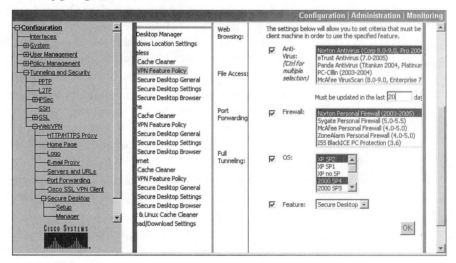

Figure 8-25 *Configuring VPN Feature Policies*

Secure Desktop General Settings for Windows

If you selected "Secure Desktop" from the *Use Module* section in the Identification window in Figure 8-22, you can click the **Secure Desktop General** hyperlink under the name of the location, taking you to the screen in Figure 8-26. Here are your options:

- **Automatically switch to Secure Desktop after installation**—When selected, specifies that CSD is loaded automatically after being installed on the user's PC, forcing the user to use it.

- **Check for keystroke logger before Secure Desktop creation**—When selected, verifies that no keystroke logging application is running on the PC before CSD is installed (the user needs Administrator privileges for this option to work).

- **Enable switching between Secure Desktop and Local Desktop**—When selected, allows users to switch between CSD and the local desktop (their normal desktop). Cisco highly recommends that you enable this feature, because it allows a user to respond to prompts from other running applications. As an example, Microsoft's AntiSpyware application might prompt you to allow CSD to be installed, in addition to other anti-spyware or antivirus software. However, by unchecking it, you are creating a more secure environment: you'll have to weigh the advantages of both choices before enabling or disabling this option.

- **Enable Vault Re-use**—When selected, allows a user to close CSD and open it later, creating a persistent desktop that's available from one session to the next. When you enable this option, users will have to enter a password to re-access CSD. Choose this option for users that use the same computer, like wireless office workers or SOHO users, or for laptop users.

- **Enable Secure Desktop inactivity timeout**—When selected, specifies an idle timeout that causes CSD to close down once the idle timer in the *Timeout After* drop-down selector parameter is reached. This parameter is used only if you also have enabled the *Enable switching between Secure Desktop and Local Desktop* parameter.

- **Open following web page after Secure Desktop closes**—When selected, causes the specified web page to open automatically upon the closing of CSD on the user's desktop.

- **Suggest application uninstall upon Secure Desktop closing**—When selected, prompts the user to uninstall CSD when it closes. For users that always use the same PC, don't enable this option; this will allow the users from this location to use the Vault feature.

- **Force Uninstall of application when Secure Desktop closes**—When selected, prompts the user to uninstall CSD when it closes; this is recommended for locations like Internet Cafés where the user doesn't own the desktop. For users (in the same location) that always use the same PC, don't enable this option; this will allow the users from this location to use the Vault feature.

Figure 8-26 *Configuring Secure Desktop General Settings*

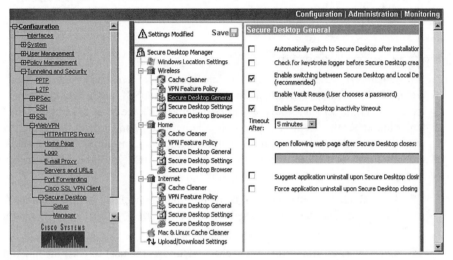

Secure Desktop Settings for Windows

If you selected "Secure Desktop" from the *Use Module* section in the Identification window in Figure 8-22, you can click the **Secure Desktop Settings** hyperlink under the name of the location, where your options are:

- **Put Secure Desktop in restricted mode**—When selected, only the originating web browser that starts CSD can be used; all other applications are denied.

- **Restrict Registry tools on Secure Desktop**—When selected, users are prevented from modifying the registry from within CSD. Cisco recommends enabling this feature to provide for optimum security.

- **Restrict DOS-CMD tools on Secure Desktop**—When selected, users are prevented from accessing a DOS command prompt. Cisco recommends enabling this feature to provide for optimum security.

- **Restrict Printing on Secure Desktop**—When selected, users are prevented from printing while CSD is active. If you have sensitive data being downloaded to the users' computers, you might want to enable this feature to prevent them from printing the sensitive information.

Secure Desktop Browser for Windows

If you selected "Secure Desktop" from the *Use Module* section in the Identification window in Figure 8-22, you can click the **Secure Desktop Browser** hyperlink under the name of the location, where your options are:

- Specifying the home page of the user's web browser

- Specifying bookmarks and folders for the user's web browser

This feature is useful for public PCs where you don't want users to be using any web pages already bookmarked in the web browser.

Configuring the Cache Cleaner for Mac & Linux Systems

Unfortunately, CSD is not available for non-Windows systems; however, the Cache Cleaner feature is. This feature is available for Windows, MacOS X, and Linux systems. To access the configuration screen for non-Windows systems, click the **Mac & Linux Cache Cleaner** hyperlink under the Secure Desktop column on the left-hand side of the screen. With this option, you can't specify a location; therefore, all your configuration options are defined globally for these devices. When you click this hyperlink, you'll be shown the screen in Figure 8-27, where you have the following options:

- **Launch cleanup upon global timeout**—When checked, specifies that the Cache Cleaner is run after the specified timeout in the *Timeout after* drop-down selector is reached.

- **Let user reset timeout**—When checked, allows the user to reset the timeout period.

- **Launch cleanup upon exiting of browser**—When checked, causes the Cache Cleaner to run when all web browser windows have closed.

- **Enabled Cancel button of cleaning**—When checked, allows the user to cancel cache cleaning. I highly recommend that you do *not* enable this feature, because it can create a security risk for sensitive data downloaded during a web session.

- **Enable web browsing if Mac or Linux installation fails**—When checked, allows the user to access the network using a web browser if the Cache Cleaner fails to install; all other remote access applications are denied, though.

- **Web Browsing, File Access, Port Forwarding**—For these three features, you can choose either "ON" to enable them or "OFF" to disable them. This is similar to configuring the same policies for Windows users, but there is not an option to specify additional matching criteria, like antivirus or personal firewall software.

Configuring Upload/Download Settings

The **Upload/Download Settings** hyperlink shown under the "Secure Desktop Manager" column allows you to back up or reload your CSD settings. This is shown at the very bottom of Figure 8-28 in the left-hand column of the CSD manager. This is a handy feature if you have configured VCA load balancing or VRRP redundancy and want to duplicate your configurations across multiple VPN 3000 concentrators easily. When you click this hyperlink, you are taken to the screen shown in Figure 8-28. Click the **Download** button to back up your CSD configuration. A new web browser window will open, displaying the configuration in an XML format. Log in to a secondary concentrator and go to this screen and paste in the configuration in the text box above the **Upload** button; click the **Upload** button to load the CSD settings.

Figure 8-27   *Configuring Cache Cleaning for Non-Windows Systems*

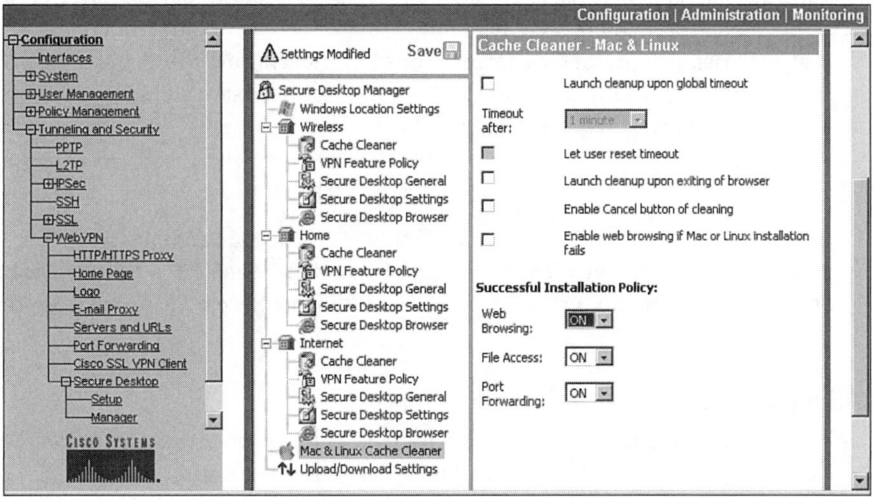

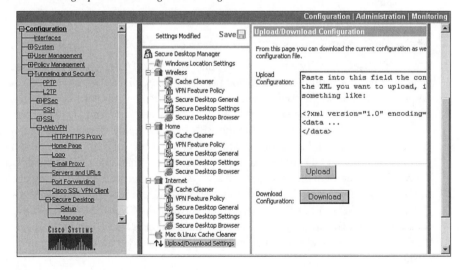

Figure 8-28   *Backing Up and Restoring CSD Settings*

Saving Settings and Enabling CSD

The configuration you create within the CSD manager on the concentrator is not saved automatically. To determine if you need to save your configuration, look for the yellow triangular warning icon indicating "Settings Modified" in the upper left-hand corner of the HTML/JavaScript window; if you see this information, the current configuration hasn't been saved. Click the **Save** floppy icon (to the right of the warning icon) to save the CSD settings to the concentrator's Flash memory.

CAUTION The **Save** button in the concentrator's CSD manager window and the **Save As Needed** button in the concentrator's GUI are *not* the same; both save different things! If you navigate to another part of the concentrator's GUI (leaving the concentrator's CSD manager application), then you'll lose your CSD settings. So make sure you save your CSD settings before leaving the CSD Manager screen!

After you've installed and configured CSD, it is not enabled automatically. You'll need to go to the **Configuration > Tunneling and Security > WebVPN > Secure Desktop > Secure Desktop Setup** screen and choose the "Enable Secure Desktop" radio button.

Using the Secure Desktop Client

To run CSD on a user's desktop optimally, Cisco recommends using Windows 2000 or XP. On these computers, you should, at a minimum, meet these specifications:

- Pentium 633MHz processor
- 128MB of RAM
- 25MB of disk space
- A supported web browser (IE 6.0, Netscape 7.1, Mozilla 1.7, or Firefox 1.0).

A WebVPN user normally will access the concentrator as if CSD wasn't being used. Before the user is prompted for a username and password, the CSD software (an ActiveX script, Javascript, or EXE program) is downloaded and installed on the user's computer. Once this has been accomplished, the user is presented with the username and password prompt, and WebVPN proceeds as normal if using the VPN Feature Policy. If you're using the Secure Desktop feature, you'll be presented with the screen shown in Figure 8-29. Based on your concentrator's CSD configuration, a web browser might open automatically to start the WebVPN user login process. You can always start this process manually by clicking the **Launch Login Page** hyperlink in the bottom right-hand corner of the screen. And assuming you've set up CSD to allow the user to switch between the CSD and local desktops, you can click the **Switch Desktop** hyperlink to go to the local desktop. When in the local desktop, the Secure Desktop is still running, and you can access it and go back to the Secure Desktop.

CSD can be run separately from the Cisco SSL VPN Client or in conjunction. When both options are configured on the concentrator, CSD is installed first, user authentication is performed, and then SVC is installed. If you have enabled desktop switching, SVC is available in both the CSD *and* on local desktops.

Figure 8-29 *Backing Up and Restoring CSD Settings*

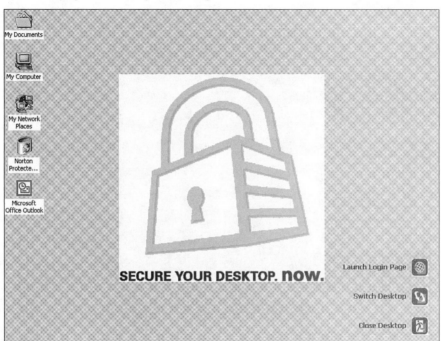

Summary

This chapter introduced you to configuring remote access sessions: PPTP L2TP/IPsec, and WebVPN. In regard to PPTP and L2TP/IPsec, I'll spend more time on how these are configured on the concentrator when I discuss the Microsoft software client in Chapter 13, "Windows Software Client."

Next up is Chapter 9, "Concentrator Site-to-Site Connections," where I show you how to use your VPN 3000 concentrator to terminate site-to-site, or LAN-to-LAN (L2L), sessions.

Concentrator Site-to-Site Connections

Chapters 7 and 8 focused on using the concentrator to terminate remote access sessions: IPsec, PPTP, L2TP/IPsec, and WebVPN. Most people assume that the concentrator's primary purpose is for remote access connectivity; however, you can also use the concentrator to set up site-to-site connections. With Cisco concentrators, site-to-site sessions commonly are referred to as LAN-to-LAN (L2L) connections. Because Cisco concentrators are fully compliant with IPsec, it is easy to use a concentrator to terminate L2L sessions with other VPN gateway devices such as Cisco routers, PIX and ASA security appliances, other VPN 3000 concentrators, and other vendors' VPN gateway products.

This chapter will focus on using a VPN 3000 concentrator to terminate L2L sessions by covering the following items:

- L2L Connectivity Example
- ISAKMP/IKE Phase 1 Preparation
- Adding Site-to-Site Connections
- Address Translation and L2L Connections

L2L Connectivity Example

To understand the components involved in an L2L session, I've created the diagram shown in Figure 9-1. This figure shows a simple example of a network using L2L sessions. In this example, a corporation has two redundant 3060 concentrators at the corporate site: ConcentratorA and ConcentratorB. These concentrators handle L2L sessions and many remote access sessions. Redundancy is set up between the concentrators. This chapter discusses L2L redundancy and in Chapter 10, "Concentrator Management," I'll discuss remote access redundancy.

The corporate network is using 172.16.0.0/16 for a network number, where this has been subnetted into many subnets. The regional offices in Orlando, Tampa, and Miami each have a 3030 concentrator. These concentrators each have an L2L session back to the redundant configuration at the corporate office. These concentrators also handle local remote access users. Because very little traffic flows between the regional offices, the network administrators decided to send all traffic through the corporate site; however, if traffic patterns change, an L2L session can easily be added between two regional sites.

Figure 9-1 *L2L Example*

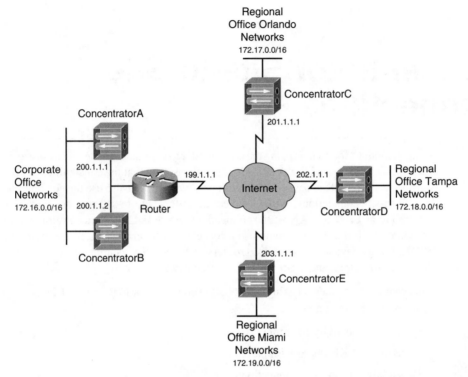

All of the VPN 3000 concentrators support IPsec L2L sessions; however, not every concentrator has the same capabilities. Table 9-1 compares the number of simultaneous L2L sessions that each of the concentrators support. Remember from Chapter 6, "Concentrator Product Information," that L2L sessions count as a session against the total number of concurrent (L2L and remote access) sessions that a concentrator supports. For example, the 3080 supports 10,000 total sessions, of which no more than 1,000 of those can be L2L sessions.

Table 9-1 *Concentrator L2L Session Restrictions*

Models	Maximum L2L Sessions
3005	100
3015	100
3020	500
3030	500
3060	1,000
3080	1,000

NOTE	The only type of L2L session that Cisco concentrators support is an IPsec L2L session.

Platform Choices for L2L Sessions

Cisco has three platform choices for L2L sessions: concentrators, routers, and PIX and ASA security appliances. Each has its advantages and disadvantages. For example, configuring L2L sessions is a simple process on a concentrator. Plus, of the three solutions, I find it much easier to troubleshoot problems with the concentrator than the other two (I'll discuss the concentrator's troubleshooting capabilities in Chapter 11, "Verifying and Troubleshooting Concentrator Connections"). However, concentrators have the following disadvantages: Limited routing functions, limited QoS support (discussed in Chapter 10), and limited address translation support (discussed in the "Address Translation and L2L Connections" section later in the chapter).

PIX security appliances, on the other hand (at least in FOS 6.3 and earlier), must be fully meshed with L2L IPsec connections. They lack QoS: a hub-and-spoke topology fails because of the Adaptive Security Algorithm (ASA) rules of traffic entering and leaving the same interface. FOS 7.0 is required on the PIX and ASA to solve these problems. One problem remains with the PIX and ASA, though: they are a very poor routing platform. The main advantages of the PIX and ASA, however, are that they are extremely flexible in their address translation policy configuration and are built as a firewall solution, and thus are very good at filtering traffic.

The best solution for L2L sessions are Cisco routers: they have the best routing capabilities for L2L sessions (I'll discuss these in Chapter 17, "Router Site-to-Site Connections") and flexible QoS capabilities. Plus, routers have better address translation abilities than concentrators, but not better than the PIXs and ASAs. The biggest advantage of the routers, though, is that they can easily scale to a large number of L2L sessions with minimal configuration, which is not true of the concentrators and PIXs and ASAs.

Therefore, if I have a complicated, redundant design, I prefer to use routers over the other two solutions. For a simple nonredundant design, I'd use a concentrator, and less preferably, a PIX or ASA. I would use the PIX (assuming it was running 6.3 or earlier) only if QoS wasn't important and the PIX was a spoke device in a hub-and-spoke design. For advanced address translation capabilities and firewall capabilities, I would consider the PIX and ASA security appliances first above the other two.

ISAKMP/IKE Phase 1 Preparation

The remainder of this chapter will discuss how to set up and modify L2L connections, and will examine the kinds of issues you'll deal with when using these connections. Before you begin adding an L2L session, you'll first need to create an ISAKMP/IKE Phase 1 transform set that you'll use for the L2L session. This section will discuss the ISAKMP/IKE Phase 1 transforms that you can use or create for your L2L connection.

Existing IKE Policies

Cisco already has some predefined Phase 1 transforms that you can use for your L2L sessions. If you recall from Chapter 7, "Concentrator Remote Access Connections with IPsec," to access the concentrator's existing Phase 1 transforms, you go to the **Configuration > Tunneling and Security > IPsec > IKE Proposals** screen.

Table 9-2 lists the L2L Phase 1 transforms that exist and are activated, by default, on the concentrators. Of course, there are other predefined transforms that are not activated by default. You can use the ones Cisco has predefined, modify these, or create your own.

Table 9-2   *Concentrator Predefined Active ISAKMP/IKE Phase 1 Transforms*

Proposal Name	Encryption Algorithm	HMAC Function	DH Key Group	Device Authentication
IKE-3DES-MD5	3DES	MD5	2	Pre-shared keys
IKE-3DES-MD5-DH1	3DES	MD5	1	Pre-shared keys
IKE-DES-MD5	DES	MD5	1	Pre-shared keys
IKE-3DES-MD5-RSA	3DES	MD5	2	RSA signatures
IKE-AES128-SHA	AES-128	SHA	2	Pre-shared keys

IKE Policy Screen

From the IKE policy screen, click the *Add* button to add a new proposal or select an existing proposal by clicking its name and click the *Modify* button to change it. This takes you to the IKE policies configuration screen shown in Figure 9-2.

I discussed the configuration of these options in chapter 7, so I'll focus only on those items important for L2L sessions. The *Authentication Mode* parameter specifies the type of device authentication that is to be used. The parameter values ending in "(XAUTH)" or "(HYBRID)" can be used by remote access clients. Therefore, your only options for parameter are these three:

- "Preshared Keys"
- "RSA Digital Certificate"
- "DSA Digital Certificate"

The only Cisco products that support DSA certificates are Cisco VPN 3000 concentrators and the PIX and ASA security appliances running 7.0 or higher. Pre-shared keys typically are used if the number of L2L peers is small; if the number of peers is large, certificates are the preferred device authentication method, because they scale better.

Figure 9-2   *IKE Policies Screen*

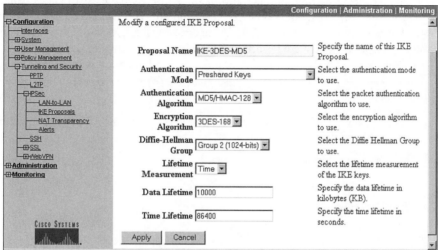

Another parameter is the *Diffie-Hellman Group* parameter. Most remote peers will support only DH group 1 and 2 keys, so be sure that your proposal supports one of these two. Cisco routers, PIX and ASA security appliances, and VPN 3000 concentrators also support group 5, which is the most secure of the three (group 7 is used by PDAs).

TIP   A matching ISAKMP/IKE Phase 1 transform set must be found between two L2L peers before an ISAKMP/IKE Phase 1 management connection is built. The default lifetime of the management connection on all of Cisco products is 86,400 seconds (1 day). If the remote peer follows the IPsec standard, this is the *only* value that doesn't have to match between the two peers when comparing management transforms; however, other vendors don't necessary follow the IPsec standards verbatim. For example, if you're building an L2L session to a CheckPoint/Nokia device, you will need to match this value between the peers; otherwise the negotiation of the transform will fail!

Adding Site-to-Site Connections

Once you have set up your IKE policies for your management connection, you are ready to create your L2L session. To add (or modify) an L2L session, go to **Configuration > Tunneling and Security > IPsec > LAN-to-LAN**. The resulting screen lists the existing L2L connections.

NOTE	Chapter 6, "Concentrator Product Information," discussed the use of Quick Configuration to put a minimal configuration on your concentrator. This method only allows you to set up remote access connectivity. Before you can add an L2L session, you must configure the concentrator's public interface by, at minimum, assigning an IP address to it. This can be done using Quick Configuration or going to **Configuration > Interfaces**.

To assist you with building and maintaining L2L sessions, the following subsections cover these topics:

- Adding L2L Sessions
- Completing L2L Sessions
- Modifying L2L Sessions

Adding L2L Sessions

The following subsections cover these topics:

- Basic L2L Configuration Parameters
- Peer Connectivity
- Device Authentication Information
- Connection Policies
- Routing Options
- Local and Remote Networks

Basic L2L Configuration Parameters

To add a new session, click the *Add* button, where you'll be taken to the screen shown in Figures 9-3, 9-4, 9-5, and 9-6 (I've broken this screen into multiple figures). The first parameter at the top of the screen in Figure 9-3 is the *Enable* parameter—clicking this check box enables this specific L2L session. This option allows you to disable a session without having to delete the session, which might be useful when you are trying to troubleshoot a problem.

Figure 9-3 *L2L Screen: Part 1*

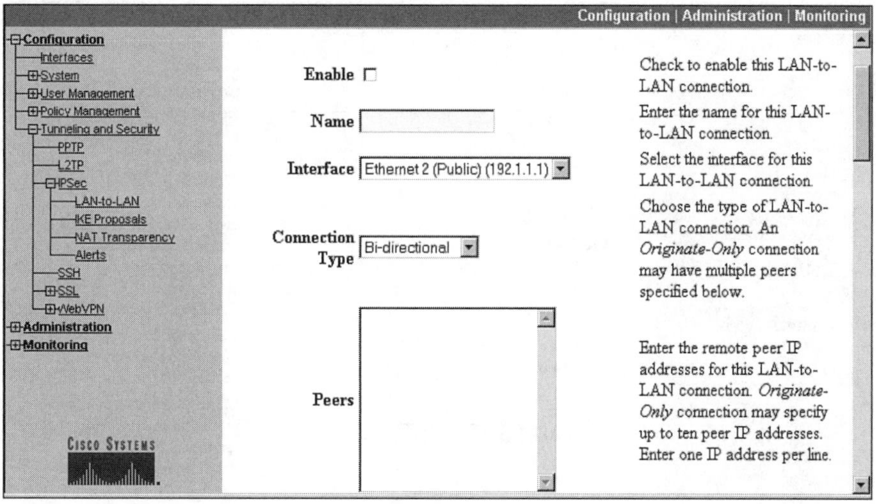

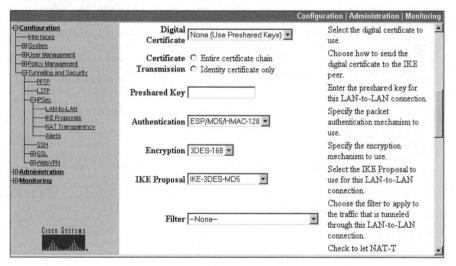

Figure 9-4 *L2L Screen: Part 2*

Figure 9-5   *L2L Screen: Part 3*

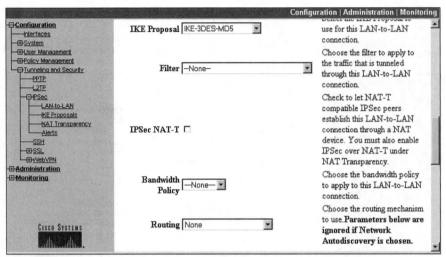

Figure 9-6   *L2L Screen: Part 4*

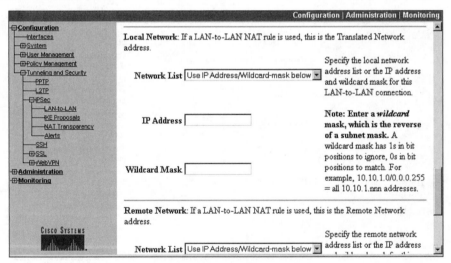

The *Name* parameter allows you to give a descriptive name (up to 32 characters) for the L2L session. Because this name is used for other related items the concentrator creates for the L2L session, such as a filter and data SA, I recommend that you keep the name of the session short (when you're done adding the connection, this name appears on the **Configuration > Tunneling and Security > IPsec > LAN-to-LAN** screen).

The *Interface* parameter specifies which interface the concentrator should use to reach the remote site. This defaults to "Public," which is probably the one you're using for the IPsec tunnel. Also, once you add an L2L session, you cannot change the interface to use for the session unless you delete the L2L session and re-add it with the correct interface.

Peer Connectivity

The *Connection Type* parameter specifies how the L2L connection will be built. There are three options:

- **"Bidirectional"**—This option should be chosen if either this concentrator or the remote peer will initiate the L2L session; it's commonly used when no redundancy is being used between the two sites.

- **"Answer-only"**—This option is used when you don't want this peer to initiate the session, but want the remote peer to do this; it's commonly chosen when redundancy is used between two sites. For example, in Figure 9-1, this would be configured on the two concentrators (ConcentratorA and ConcentratorB) at the corporate office. This is necessary to ensure that both of these concentrators don't set up two connections to a single remote site.

- **"Originate-only"**—This option is used when you want this L2L peer to initiate a session to an "Answer-only" peer; it's commonly chosen when redundancy is used between two sites. For example, in Figure 9-1, this option would be configured at the three remote sites: Orlando, Tampa, and Miami.

NOTE	I'll talk more about redundancy for L2L sessions later in the chapter in the "Routing Options" section.

The *Peer* text box allows you to enter multiple peer addresses (up to ten). For example, in Figure 9-1, the Orlando concentrator would specify the two concentrator addresses at the corporate site, 200.1.1.1 for ConcentratorA and 200.1.1.2 for ConcentratorB, for redundancy. The order in which you enter the addresses is important: put the primary L2L peer's address first and the backup L2L peer second. Doing so will cause the concentrator to contact the L2L peer at the top of the list first.

Also, if the remote peer is using a private address on its public interface, you'll need to configure the global NAT address associated with the private (local) address; in other words, if the remote peer has a private address, you need to specify the externally reachable or visible address that represents this peer (which will be translated to the private address). For example, in Figure 9-7, ConcentratorA has a private address (172.16.1.1) assigned to its public interface. A static NAT definition exists on the router that translates this to the global address of 192.1.1.2. Therefore, ConcentratorB needs to configure the global address as the peer address when establishing an L2L connection to ConcentratorA.

Figure 9-7 *L2L Connection and Private Addressing*

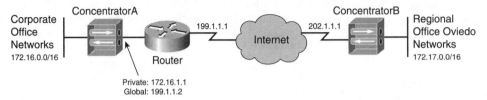

NOTE In the example in Figure 9-1, each of the remote site concentrators will configure the same two peer addresses: 200.1.1.1 and 200.1.1.2; however, if you add them in this order on the remote concentrators, ConcentratorA will handle all three L2L sessions; therefore, you'll probably want to look at the traffic sent between the three remote sites and the corporate office, and have the L2L session of the remote site that sends the most traffic terminated on one corporate concentrator, and the other two remote sites' L2L sessions terminated on the second corporate concentrator. For example, if the Orlando office generated the most amount of traffic, its primary peer at the corporate office would be 2001.1.1.1, and its backup peer would be 200.1.1.2. However, on the other two remote office concentrators, I would configure the primary peer at the corporate office as 200.1.1.2 and the backup peer as 200.1.1.1. Given this configuration, I've split the L2L sessions between the two concentrators at the corporate site; plus, if either concentrator fails at the corporate site, the remote offices already have a backup peer configured. I'll talk more about redundancy for L2L sessions later in the chapter in the "Routing Options" section.

Device Authentication Information

The next two parameters, *Digital Certificate* and *Certificate Transmission,* are shown in Figure 9-4 (this is still the same screen). These parameters are only applicable if the two L2L peers will be using certificates for device authentication during ISAKMP/IKE Phase 1. The *Digital Certificate* parameter is a drop-down selector that allows you to choose your authentication option (assuming this matches what you've chosen in your IKE proposal). The default value for this parameter is "None (Use Preshared Keys)." If you are going to use certificates for device authentication, you'll need to use the drop-down selector to choose the actual identity certificate to use for this L2L session.

The *Certificate Transmission* parameter allows you to specify what certificate information is sent to the remote peer during device authentication. Your two options are:

- **"Identity certificate only"**—Send the remote L2L peer only this concentrator's identity certificate specified in the *Digital Certificate* parameter.

- **"Entire certificate chain"**—Send the remote L2L peer the concentrator's identity certificate specified in the *Digital Certificate* parameter, and the corresponding root and subordinate CA certificates (if you're using a hierarchical PKI implementation).

If you're using pre-shared keys for device authentication during ISAKMP/IKE Phase 1, you'll need to enter the pre-shared key value in the *Preshared Key* text box. The key can be from 4–32 alphanumeric characters. Whatever key you configure on this concentrator must be configured exactly the same on the remote L2L peer.

The *Authentication* drop-down selector allows you to choose the HMAC function that should be used for the ESP data connections. If you recall from Chapter 2, "VPN Technologies," HMAC functions are used to verify a packet's integrity (the packet hasn't been tampered with) and to authenticate the origin of the packet. Your options for this parameter are "None," "ESP/MD5/HMAC-128," and "ESP/SHA/HMAC-160."

NOTE	Please note that the concentrator doesn't support AH for L2L sessions, whereas other VPN gateway products, like Cisco routers, do.

The other ESP parameter you can configure is the *Encryption* algorithm, which specifies the encryption algorithm to use for the data connections. Your options are "Null" (no encryption), "DES-56," "3DES-168," "AES-128," "AES-192," and "AES-256." The configuration of these two parameters is used to build a data transform set that will be used during ISAKMP/IKE Phase 2. Remember that what you configure on the local concentrator must match the data transform set on the remote L2L peer.

Connection Policies

The *IKE Proposal* drop-down selector allows you to choose the IKE policy that will be used to build and protect the ISAKMP/IKE Phase 1 management connection to the remote L2L peer. This is shown in Figure 9-5. The policies shown here are only the ones in the *Active Proposals* column on the **Configuration > Tunneling and Security > IPsec > IKE Proposals** screen. Remember that this management transform must match the one that is used on the remote L2L peer. I discussed the configuration of IKE policies for L2L connections earlier in the chapter in the "ISAKMP/IKE Phase 1 Preparation" section.

The *Filter* drop-down selector allows you to select an access control list (ACL) filter to filter traffic coming across the tunnel from the remote L2L peer. I discussed the creation of filters in Chapter 7, "Concentrator Remote Access Connections with IPsec." To create a filter, you must first create rules that define filtering actions; you then associate the rules to a filter.

If you recall from Chapter 3, "IPsec," and Chapter 7, "Concentrator Remote Access Connections with IPsec," NAT-T allows ESP to be tunneled through an address translation device performing PAT; the ESP packet is encapsulated in a UDP segment with a destination port number of 4,500, and then an outer IP header is added. Normally this is used to solve address translation issues with remote access clients accessing a VPN gateway. However, you might run into a situation where, for a small site, the ISP assigns a single public IP address to the small site, like that shown in Figure 9-8.

Figure 9-8 *L2L and NAT-T*

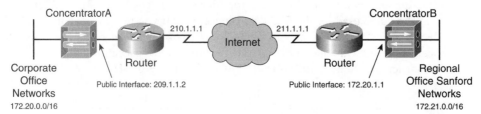

In this figure, the ISP assigned a single IP address to the Sanford office: 211.1.1.1, which is assigned to the external interface of the perimeter router. This presents a problem for the site-to-site session between the two concentrators—ConcentratorA and ConcentratorB—because the perimeter router at the Sanford site will have to perform PAT with this address to allow internal TCP and UDP traffic to access the Internet. For example, if ConcentratorA were to send traffic to 211.1.1.1, the perimeter router in Sanford would attempt to process the traffic itself.

To solve this problem of the Corporate office concentrator (ConcentratorA) accessing the Sanford concentrator (ConcentratorB), you would need to configure two static PAT translations (port address redirection, or PAR) on the Sanford perimeter router:

- One PAR rule for the ISAKMP/IKE Phase 1 management connection (UDP 500), where this traffic is redirected to 172.20.1.1

- One PAR rule for the ESP data connections

The problem with the second PAR rule on the perimeter router is that ESP is a Layer-3 protocol and PAR needs a Layer-4 protocol such as UDP or TCP. In this situation, you can use NAT-T for the ESP data connections. Recall from Chapter 7 that NAT-T uses a port number of UDP 4,500. Therefore, the second PAR rule would redirect any UDP port 4,500 traffic sent to 211.1.1.1 to 172.20.1.1. For this to work, you would need to do the following on both concentrators:

1 Enable NAT-T in the **Configuration > Tunneling and Security > IPsec > NAT Transparency** screen.

2 Select the check box for the L2L connection in the **Configuration > Tunneling and Security > IPsec > LAN-to-LAN** add/modify screen.

Given the example in Figure 9-8, ConcentratorA would specify a peer address of 211.1.1.1. ConcentratorB would specify a peer address of 209.1.1.2.

NOTE   When you have enabled and are using NAT-T, the following restrictions apply:

- Only one L2L session can use NAT-T.

- Only one Microsoft L2TP/IPsec client can use NAT-T and multiple IPsec clients can use NAT-T.

- Either one L2L session can use NAT-T *or* multiple IPsec remote access clients can use NAT-T.

Because of these restrictions, NAT-T is typically reserved for remote access use.

Also, please note that Microsoft was to provide a patch in July 2005 to remove the restriction of only one Microsoft L2TP/IPsec client using NAT-T.

Bandwidth policies allow you to limit traffic rates for sessions. There are two types of bandwidth policies: policing and reservation. Bandwidth policies can be applied to an interface, a group (remote access users), or an L2L session (which is treated as a group by the concentrator software). The *Bandwidth Policy* drop-down selector allows you to apply a bandwidth policy to the L2L session, ensuring that the L2L session receives enough bandwidth or doesn't use up all available bandwidth. I'll discuss the use and configuration of bandwidth management in more depth in Chapter 10, "Concentrator Management."

Routing Options

L2L connections support three routing options with the *Routing* parameter drop-down selector:

- "None"
- "Reverse Route Injection"
- "Network Autodiscovery"

The following sections will discuss the usage of these parameters.

None: Static Routing

If you choose "None" for the *Routing* parameter, then by default, the concentrator doesn't use any routing functions either to learn about the remote L2L peer's networks or to propagate these to internal devices. Figure 9-9 illustrates an example.

In this example, a regional office, Sarasota, has ten networks that need to reach the corporate office and the corporate office's B-class network needs to reach all networks at the Sarasota office. When you choose "None" for your *Routing* parameter on your concentrator, the corporate office will, by default, know nothing about the 192.168.x.0 networks at Sarasota.

In this situation, you will need to statically configure these networks below in the *Remote Network* section (see Figure 9-6) with a network list (I'll discuss the configuration of the network list later in the "Local and Remote Networks" section of the chapter.)

Figure 9-9 *L2L Connections and Routing*

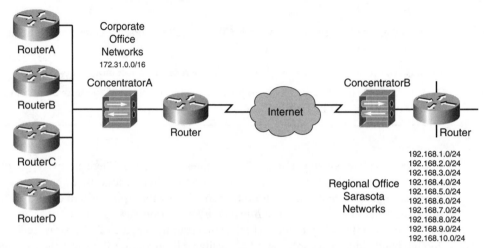

By configuring the networks locally on the corporate office concentrator, the concentrator now knows about the ten networks at Sarasota; however, using the "None" option doesn't place them in the routing and table and therefore ConcentratorA at the corporate office doesn't advertise them to the local routers and local devices. To solve this problem, you would need to configure static routes on the internal routers (RouterA, RouterB, RouterC, and RouterD) and point them to the concentrator. If there are more routers behind the four listed in Figure 9-9, you would need to redistribute the static routes into the local routing protocol to propagate the 192.168.x.0 networks throughout the corporate network.

NOTE   Because the "None" *Routing* option doesn't propagate L2L routing information, typically it is used in a spoke configuration where the concentrator doesn't need to advertise routing information, or minimal configuration is needed on routers to configure and propagate static routing information statically.

Reverse Route Injection

The "None" *Routing* option also has another problem, as illustrated in Figure 9-10. In this example, the corporate office has two concentrators for redundancy: ConcentratorA and ConcentratorB. ConcentratorC at Fort Myers is configured to use ConcentratorA as the primary concentrator and ConcentratorB as the backup. Given this situation, if you were to configure static routes at the corporate office routers to point to ConcentratorA, and this concentrator failed, then even when ConcentratorC rebuilt the connection to the backup concentrator at the corporate office, ConcentratorB, the corporate office devices still would be forwarding their traffic to the downed concentrator, ConcentratorA.

Figure 9-10 *L2L Connections, Routing, and Redundancy*

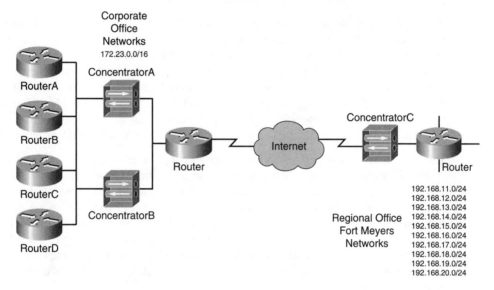

There are three possible solutions to this problem:

- NAD on the concentrators
- VRRP on the concentrators
- RRI on the concentrators

I'll discuss NAD in the next section. VRRP provides default gateway redundancy. If you choose the VRRP option to solve the problem, you must enable VRRP on both concentrators. When you do this, the internal routers would point to the virtual address to reach the tunnel, and whichever concentrator would be the master would process traffic sent to the remote site.

The main problem with VRRP is that you can't use it with the Virtual Cluster Agent (VCA) feature, which allows load balancing of remote access connections. Therefore it is typically not used when you are using the concentrator for both L2L and remote access. I'll discuss VRRP and its configuration in more depth in Chapter 10, "Concentrator Management."

Reverse Route Injection (RRI) is the second way to solve the problem in Figure 9-10. To enable RRI, set the *Routing* parameter to "Reverse Route Injection." RRI can be used when you need redundancy or load balancing for L2L or remote access sessions. In other words, for Figure 9-10, you might not know which concentrator ConcentratorC will connect to at the corporate site (nor, for that matter, which corporate site concentrator remote access clients will connect to). RRI can be used to dynamically share the concentrator's networks for IPsec sessions with devices behind it using a dynamic routing protocol. For example, in Figure 9-10, if ConcentratorC connects to ConcentratorA, ConcentratorC will advertise the 192.168.*x*.0 networks to the internal corporate office routers using a dynamic routing protocol. RRI supports both RIPv1/2 and OSPF.

If you had chosen "Reverse Route Injection" for the *Routing* parameter on the concentrator's L2L configuration screen in Figure 9-5, you would need to configure a few additional items on the concentrator. First, the L2L concentrators at both ends of the connection know nothing about the routes at the remote side. Therefore, you must manually configure these in the *Local Network* and *Remote Network* sections in Figure 9-6 of each concentrator. In the example in Figure 9-10, for ConcentratorC you would have to define 172.23.0.0/16 to be associated with the corporate site. On both ConcentratorA and ConcentratorB, you would need to configure the 192.168.x.0 networks to be associated with ConcentratorC.

This configuration brings up an interesting problem: if you configure the 192.168.*x*.0 routes on both ConcentratorA and ConcentratorB, these concentrators won't advertise the routes until something brings the tunnel up. Of course, someone at the Fort Myers office could do this. At the Fort Myers office, a default or specific route (172.23.0.0/16) would have to be set up and advertised to the Fort Myers routers so that internal users could reach the concentrator to reach the corporate office. When the tunnel would come up to either of the two corporate concentrators, RRI would allow them to advertise the 192.168.x.0 networks to the corporate users. Thus, the corporate users would be able to access any of the networks at the Fort Myers office.

However, what if someone at the corporate office was first in needing to send traffic to the Fort Myers office? How would they know which concentrator to go to in order to set up the session, because the concentrators aren't advertising the routes via RRI until the tunnel comes up?—It's a catch–22 situation. One option is to force the concentrators to advertise the routes. This feature is called hold-down routes. Hold-down routes force the concentrator to advertise the RRI routes whether or not the tunnel is up to the remote peer.

To set up hold-down routes, you would go to **Configuration > Services > IP Routing > Reverse Route Injection**, as shown in Figure 9-11.

The *Address Pool Hold-Down Routes* text box allows you to manually enter routes you always want the concentrator to advertise—whether or not they are reachable. With RRI, you would manually enter the networks in the *Remote Network* that you entered in Figure 9-6. Each route is placed on a separate line and the syntax is:

x.x.x.x/y.y.y.y

x.x.x.x is the network and y.y.y.y is a *wildcard mask*, not a subnet mask. So for the example of ConcentratorA and ConcentratorB, you would enter 192.168.11.0/0.0.0.255 for the first network, and so on, for the rest of the networks. When done, click the *Apply* button at the bottom of the screen.

Figure 9-11 *RRI and Hold-Down Routes*

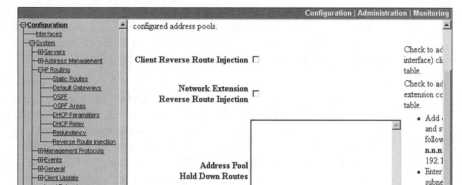

Once you do enter your hold-down router, RRI will cause the concentrator to *always* advertise the routes out of its private interface. At first this seems to fix the problem because now the corporate devices know that the two concentrators can reach the Fort Myers networks. However, this solution won't work; both concentrators are sharing the same routes, but which one should the corporate office use—ConcentratorA or ConcentratorB— if both are advertising the routes? What if your routers are set up for load balancing and split the traffic between the two concentrators? This is true even if you would try to use VRRP, because both corporate office concentrators (master and backup) would still be advertising the same routing information.

Given this example, RRI is *not* a good solution to use when there are redundant concentrators: it's a good solution when there is a single concentrator at one side and there is only *one* possible path to reach the remote site (via the concentrator). For example, RRI with hold-down routes would be a better solution for the network in Figure 9-8. In this example, there are only two concentrators that can provide connectivity. By using RRI with hold-down routes, both concentrators can advertise the remote networks you have defined locally in the L2L screen instead of configuring static routes on your internal routers.

If you are going to use RRI in single concentrator locations, you must also enable a routing protocol for your private interface. For OSPF, you would need to enable it and assign a process ID to the routing process on the **Configuration > System > IP Routing > OSPF** screen, and then for either OSPF or RIP, you would need to enable the specific routing protocol on your concentrator's private interface. I discuss how you set up routing in more depth in Chapter 10, "Concentrator Management ." I'll also discuss RRI in more depth in Chapter 14, "3002 Hardware Client," where I cover its use for remote access connections.

Network Autodiscovery (NAD)

As you saw in the last section, RRI doesn't work well (or at all) when you have redundant concentrators at a site. In such a situation, NAD is the solution of choice on the concentrators. With NAD, you do not need to manually define the local and remote subnets (statically or with network lists) that will traverse the L2L tunnel; instead, you have NAD do this dynamically.

For NAD to function, RIP must be enabled on the concentrator's private interface in the inbound and outbound direction. Once this is enabled, the concentrator will take RIP updates learned from the private interface, encrypt them, and send them across the tunnel to the remote concentrator. If a tunnel is not currently established between the two concentrators, one of the concentrators will *automatically* bring it up. This is different from the "None" and "Reverse Route Injection" routing options where user traffic must bring up the tunnel.

NOTE   NAD only supports RIP as a dynamic routing protocol; OSPF is not supported. For more information about setting up RIP on the concentrator, see Chapter 10, "Concentrator Management." Also, only concentrators support NAD, so you can't use a router or PIX as the remote end of the L2L session.

I'll look at two different situations where NAD can be useful. First I'll use Figure 9-9 as my example network. In this example, the Sarasota office has many 192.168.*x*.0 C-class networks that need to be reached at the corporate office. On both concentrators in the L2L configuration, you would set the *Routing* parameter to "Network Autodiscovery" (this parameter can be seen previously in Figure 9-5). With both concentrators, you *don't* need to specify the local and remote networks in the *Local Network* and *Remote Network* sections in Figure 9-6. Just leave these blank. Remember that NAD will bring up the tunnel and share the routes on the two sides via RIP automatically. As you can see, this was a fairly simple process to configure.

Let's look at a more complicated design like that shown previously in Figure 9-10, where the corporate office has redundant concentrators. At the corporate office, you don't want both concentrators establishing an L2L session to the Fort Myers concentrator. Therefore, you'll set the *Connection Type* parameter on each corporate concentrator to "Answer-Only" and the Fort Myers concentrator to "Originate-Only." This will cause Fort Myers to initiate the session, ensuring that there is only one L2L session between the two sites.

After you have configured the connection types properly, you'll need to enable NAD on the three concentrators by setting the *Routing* parameter to "Network Autodiscovery." Then, you will need to enable RIP in both the inbound and outbound directions of your concentrators' private interfaces. If your corporate office routers are not running RIP, then you'll need to enable it on the routers connected to ConcentratorA and ConcentratorB and redistribute the NAD RIP routes into the local routing protocol, like OSPF or EIGRP. If the local routing protocol is not RIP, you'll need to redistribute the local routes into RIP so that one of the two corporate office concentrators can advertise these to the Fort Myers concentrator. If the local routing protocol is OSPF, you can just enable OSPF on the concentrator and advertise the router OSPF routes directly to the corporate concentrator (via RIP). The corporate concentrator with the L2L to Fort Myers can then use NAD to advertise these as RIP routes to ConcentratorC.

At the Fort Myers office, you would list two remote peer addresses for the endpoints of the L2L connection, the address of each corporate office concentrator's public interface. Remember that if these are private addresses, and the corporate router is performing NAT, you would need to configure a static NAT translation on the perimeter router and then use the global (public) addresses in the configuration on ConcentratorC. You also would need to enable NAD for the *Routing* parameter. Last, on ConcentratorC, you would need to have it initiate the connection by setting the *Connection Type* to "Originate-Only," which would cause Fort Myers' concentrator to initiate the connection to the primary concentrator at the corporate site, ensuring that there would be only one connection between the two sites.

CAUTION   If you decide to use NAD, remember that both sides must be 3000 series concentrators: NAD won't work with other products. Also, NAD shares the entire routing table of each peer with the remote peer. If you don't want certain networks to be accessed by a remote peer, then you would need to configure a filter on your concentrator and apply it to the L2L session to block the unwanted traffic. (I discussed the use of filters for L2L connections earlier in the "Connection Policies" section.) Last, the concentrators must use RIP to advertise the routes to internal devices, which might present an issue if you are running a different routing protocol, like OSPF. In this situation you would have to set up redistribution to redistribute the concentrator RIP routes into the router's local routing process (like OSPF). This cannot be done on a concentrator, but can be done easily on an internal Cisco router connected to the concentrator.

Local and Remote Networks

The *Local Networks* and *Remote Networks* section of the screen in Figure 9-6 needs to be configured if you have chosen "None" or "Reverse Route Injection" for the *Routing* parameter. These two sections allow you to manually define the network or networks located at each side of the two L2L peers. This configuration isn't necessary if you are using NAD, because NAD shares the routing information between the two peers dynamically.

The *Local Networks* section allows you to define the local networks that you want to protect when traffic is sent to the networks listed in the *Remote Networks* section. If you don't list a particular network in either section, traffic to or from that network is not protected by IPsec. In both sections, you can enter:

- A single network using the *IP Address* and *Wildcard Mask* fields

- A range of contiguous networks using the *IP Address* and *Wildcard Mask* fields
- A single network, a range of contiguous networks, or a list of networks using the *Network List* drop-down selector.

If you choose the last option, you must define the network list first (I discussed this process in Chapter 7, "Concentrator Remote Access Connections with IPsec," where network lists are configured by going to **Configuration > Policy Management > Traffic Management > Network Lists**). In most cases, if I need to list more than one network, I typically use the network list option.

In addition, the network configuration that you create on one concentrator must be mirrored on the remote L2L peer. I'll use Figure 9-8 to illustrate this. For ConcentratorA, the local network would be 172.20.0.0 0.0.255.255 and the remote network would be 172.21.0.0 0.0.255.255. On ConcentratorB, the local network and remote networks would be reversed (mirrored); the local network would be 172.*21*.0.0 0.0.255.255 and the remote network would be 172.*20*.0.0 0.0.255.255. Please note that because there is just a single network at each side, you don't have to use network lists, but could configure this easily using the *IP Address* and *Wildcard Mask* fields.

NOTE   If you are using L2L NAT, discussed later in the "Address Translation and L2L Sessions," section you would enter the global translated network in the *Remote Network* section.

Completing L2L Sessions

Depending on whether you are adding or modifying an L2L session, when you are finished, you'll see one of two screens. The next section discusses these two possible alternatives. Plus, when you add a new session, the concentrator automatically creates certain components it uses to implement the L2L session; the following section will cover these components.

If you were modifying your L2L session, click the *Apply* button at the bottom of the screen: you'll be taken back to the **Configuration > Tunneling and Security > IPsec > LAN-to-LAN** screen, where you'll see the list of L2L connections configured on the concentrator.

CAUTION   As soon as you make and apply your changes to an existing L2L session, and an IPsec tunnel is currently established to the remote L2L peer, the existing tunnel is terminated and a new one is built. This could cause a brief disruption in your user traffic.

However, if you were adding a new L2L session instead of modifying an existing one, click the *Add* button at the bottom of the screen. When you do this, the session is added and you are taken to the screen shown in Figure 9-12.

Figure 9-12 *L2L Completion Screen*

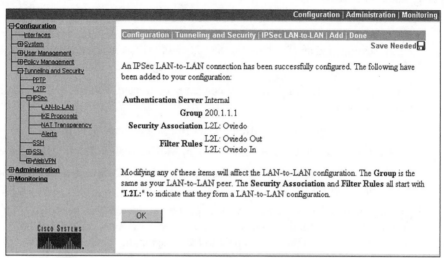

You'll notice some interesting items on this screen. First, the authentication of the remote L2L peer is done by the concentrator itself: the *Authentication Server* is set to "Internal." Also, three components for the L2L session are created automatically by the concentrator:

- A group for the L2L session (in the example in Figure 9-12, it is called "200.1.1.1," which is based on the IP address of the remote L2L peer configured on the screen shown in Figure 9-3)

- A security association for the L2L connection that defines how the two unidirectional data connections in ISAKMP/IKE Phase 2 will be protected (basically a transform set which is called "L2L: *name*," where the name is derived from the *Name* parameter in the L2L configuration in Figure 9-3)

- Two filtering rules that allow IPsec traffic between the remote L2L peer and this concentrator (the filters are named "L2L: *name*," where the name is derived from the *Name* parameter in the L2L configuration in Figure 9-3); these rules are automatically added to the filter on which the L2L connection is terminated (typically the public interface) and allows the IPsec traffic between the two peers

The following section will discuss these three items in more depth.

Click the *OK* button to return to the **Configuration > Tunneling and Security > IPsec > LAN-to-LAN** screen, where you'll see the list of L2L connections configured on the concentrator (including your new session).

Modifying L2L Sessions

As I mentioned in the last section, whenever you add an L2L session, the concentrator automatically creates the L2L session, a group for the L2L session, two filtering rules for the L2L session, and an IPsec SA for the L2L session. Likewise, any time you modify an L2L session, these components are automatically updated by the concentrator.

If you want to see the components the concentrator created, you can go to the following concentrator locations:

- The new group: **Configuration > User Management > Groups**
- The new IPsec SA: **Configuration > Policy Management > Traffic Management > SAs**
- The two new filtering rules: **Configuration > Policy Management > Traffic Management > Rules**

If you go to any of these screens, you'll see the parameters you specified from the **Configuration > Tunneling and Security > IPsec > LAN-to-LAN** *Add/Modify* screen or for other parameters that don't apply to L2L session, the default parameters for the screen(s).

Please note that you cannot delete the filtering rules, the SAs, or the group the concentrator added for the L2L session; however, you can modify the parameters for these three items in their respective screens. Also, if you delete the L2L session from the **Configuration > Tunneling and Security > IPsec > LAN-to-LAN** *Add/Modify* screen, the extra components added for the L2L connection—filters, group, and SA—are automatically deleted by the concentrator.

TIP   I highly recommend that you use only the **Configuration > Tunneling and Security > IPsec > LAN-to-LAN** *Add/Modify* screen when modifying an L2L connection, because modifying any of the other components from their respective screens could cause undesirable results. However, there are certain parameters available on screens for the groups and SAs that are not available on the LAN-to-LAN screen, such as the use of perfect forward secrecy (PFS) on the SA screen to use DH to share the encryption and hash keys for the data connections instead of using the existing management connection.

Address Translation and L2L Sessions

Because IPsec L2L sessions create a logical extension between two networks, the assumption is that the two locations have unique network numbers. Of course, if you are connecting two of your own sites together, you should have designed your network to have unique numbers. However, if you are connecting to a different company, such as a business partner, you might have overlapping addresses between the two companies or networks. In this situation, you would have to implement address translation to solve the problem.

The VPN 3000 concentrators support basic address translation abilities that you can apply to an interface and affect all traffic entering or leaving it or for L2L sessions. In this book I'll discuss only using address translation for L2L sessions because there are better solutions, such as the PIX/ASA or IOS routers, that are more flexible in creating address translation policies for traffic entering and leaving interfaces.

To help you understand address translation and the concentrator's configuration of address translation, the following sections will discuss these topics:

- Introducing concentrator address translation abilities
- Example needing L2L address translation
- Creating L2L address translation rules
- Enabling L2L address translation

Introducing Concentrator Address Translation Abilities

The address translation feature for L2L connections is commonly called LAN-to-LAN NAT (network address translation) by Cisco. L2L NAT is only necessary when you have overlapping addresses at both sides of an L2L tunnel, or you want to control what networks appear as on the two sides of an L2L tunnel. Before I begin discussing how to set up L2L NAT, I first need to discuss the address translation capabilities of the concentrators.

There are three types of address translation supported by the concentrator:

- **Static NAT**—This can be used to translate local source addresses statically before sending packets across the tunnel or remote destination addresses as packets come off of the tunnel; static NAT is most commonly used for services that must always be presented by the same address.

- **Dynamic NAT**—This can be used to translate local source addresses dynamically to unique global addresses (using a pool of addresses) before sending packets across the tunnel; dynamic NAT is typically used when dynamic PAT won't work (dynamic PAT only works with TCP and UDP connections). You cannot use dynamic NAT for packets coming from a remote L2L peer across the IPsec tunnel; the remote L2L peer has to perform this process.

- **Dynamic PAT**—This can be used to translate local source addresses dynamically to the *same* global address, differentiating each local device by ensuring that the source port number in the TCP or UDP segment is unique for each connection. You cannot use dynamic PAT for packets coming from a remote L2L peer across the IPsec tunnel; the remote L2L peer has to perform this process.

NOTE	Even though Cisco calls the address translation feature L2L NAT, this is misleading because the concentrator supports both static and dynamic NAT *and* PAT.

Example Needing L2L Address Translation

I'll now take a look at a simple example that needs address translation for an L2L connection, shown in Figure 9-13. In this example, both sites are using 10.0.0.0/8 (shown at the top of the figure). SiteA needs to access Web2 and SiteB needs to access Web1, where both servers are using the same address: 10.1.1.1. To accomplish this, we use both static and dynamic address translation. ConcentratorA will need the following address translation rules:

- For SiteA users, dynamic NAT or PAT can be used to translate 10.0.0.0/8 addresses to 172.30.0.0/16.

- The Web1 server will have a static address translation: 10.1.1.1 → 172.30.1.1.

ConcentratorB will need the following translation rules:

- For SiteB users, dynamic NAT or PAT can be used to translate 10.0.0.0/8 addresses to 172.31.0.0/16.

- The Web2 server will have a static address translation: 10.1.1.1 → 172.31.1.1.

As you can see, you must configure address translation on both concentrators.

Figure 9-13 *L2L and Overlapping Addresses*

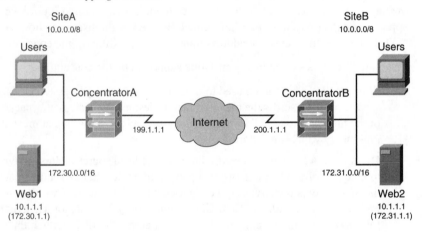

Creating L2L Address Translation Rules

There are two steps in setting up and using L2L address translation rules:

Step 1 Adding your rules

Step 2 Activating your rules

To add an address translation rule or rules, go to the **Configuration > Policy Management > NAT > LAN-to-LAN Rules** screen. To add a new rule, click the *Add* button, where you're taken to the screen shown in Figure 9-14.

Figure 9-14 *L2L Rules Screen*

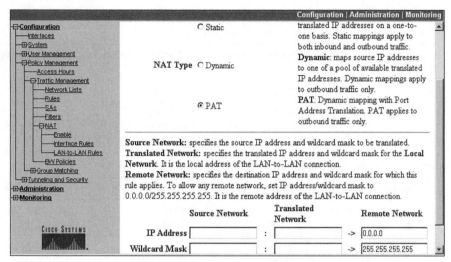

Here are the steps you'll perform in creating an address translation rule:

Step 1 Choose a translation type. There are three address translation rules you can choose from for the *NAT Type* parameter: "Static," "Dynamic" (this is NAT), and "PAT." Choose the type of translation by clicking the correct radio button and then define the rule below.

Step 2 Enter the source address(es) to be translated off of the concentrator's private interface. The *Source Network* is the local address(es) to be translated; enter an IP address and wildcard mask in this column.

Step 3 Enter the address(es) that will be used when performing address translation on the source address(es). The *Translated Network* is what the local addresses will be translated to (the global address).

Step 4 Enter the network that controls when address translation will occur, when the source addresses are sending traffic to the specified remote networks. The *Remote Network* specifies that the local addresses will be translated when they go to this network.

NOTE A wildcard mask is basically an inverse subnet mask: 0 bits are used to match on part of an IP address and 1 bit is used as a wildcard to match on anything.

For example, for my situation in Figure 9-13, you'd use Table 9-3 to configure ConcentratorA and Table 9-4 to configure ConcentratorB. In this example, I've configured a static translation on both concentrators for the web servers and a dynamic NAT translation for users off of each concentrator.

Table 9-3   *ConcentratorA LAN-to-LAN Address Translation Rules*

Rule #	NAT Type	Source Network	Translated Network	Remote Network
1	Static	10.1.1.1 0.0.0.0	172.30.1.1 0.0.0.0	172.31.0.0 0.0.255.255
2	NAT	10.0.0.0 0.255.255.255	172.30.0.0 0.0.255.255	172.31.0.0 0.0.255.255

Table 9-4   *ConcentratorB LAN-to-LAN Address Translation Rules*

Rule #	NAT Type	Source Network	Translated Network	Remote Network
1	Static	10.1.1.1 0.0.0.0	172.31.1.1 0.0.0.0	172.30.0.0 0.0.255.255
2	NAT	10.0.0.0 0.255.255.255	172.31.0.0 0.0.255.255	172.30.0.0 0.0.255.255

When you are done adding your rule, click the *Add* button at the bottom of the screen. From the *LAN-to-LAN Rules* screen, your new rule will appear. The rule is listed at the bottom of any other rules you've created.

TIP   Address translation rules are processed by the concentrator in the order in which they are listed on the *LAN-to-LAN Rules* screen. Therefore, use the *Move Up* and *Move Down* buttons to resort the order of the rules: typically you'll place the static entries at the top of the list and the dynamic ones at the bottom. However, by default, static rules have preference over dynamic ones on the concentrator. And for static rules, no prioritization is supported. The concentrator automatically processes them based on the size of the network in the translation rule: host-to-host rules are processed first, then Class-C network rules, Class-B network rules, and last, Class-A network rules.

Enabling L2L Address Translation

Once you have created your L2L address translation rules, the concentrator won't use them unless you enable them. To do this, go to the **Configuration > User Management > Traffic Management > NAT > Enable** screen. There are two check boxes on this screen:

* Interface NAT Rules Enabled
* LAN-to-LAN Tunnel NAT Rule

Click the check box to the right of *LAN-to-LAN Tunnel NAT Rule* to enable your L2L NAT translations. Click the *Apply* button to accept your changes.

Summary

This chapter showed you the basics of setting up L2L sessions on a VPN 3000 concentrator, including routing and discovery issues and address translation problems for L2L sessions. Next up is Chapter 10, "Concentrator Management," where I show you how to perform some additional configuration tasks such as routing, remote access redundancy, and bandwidth management, and some management features on the concentrator.

Concentrator Management

This chapter is unique when compared to the last three chapters on the VPN 3000 concentrator; those chapters focused on remote access and site-to-site connections. This chapter, instead, will focus on some of the additional configurations and features you might enable on your concentrator. Some important items I'll address in this chapter include bandwidth management, routing, redundancy, and administrative components, including administrative access, software upgrades, and file management.

I won't be discussing all of the screens on the concentrator in this book, because that would be a book in itself. However, what I've covered up to this point focuses on the important aspects of the concentrator. Chapter 11 will focus on using tools on the concentrator to troubleshoot VPN problems.

Bandwidth Management

The first management feature I'll focus on in this chapter is the concentrator's bandwidth management feature. Bandwidth management can be used to define bandwidth policies that affect site-to-site or remote access sessions, such as IPsec, L2TP, and PPTP connections.

Bandwidth management was first introduced in Version 3.6. One concern you might have with VPN sessions is that one group of users or a particular L2L session will use up all of your available bandwidth, leaving no bandwidth for other VPN sessions. Fortunately, bandwidth management allows you to create policies and apply them to your VPN sessions, so that you can prevent this problem.

Using bandwidth management is a two-step process:

- Creating your bandwidth management policies
- Activating your bandwidth management policies

The following two sections will discuss this two-step process.

Creating Bandwidth Policies

Cisco supports two types of bandwidth policies:

- Reservation
- Policing

Bandwidth reservation reserves a minimum amount of bandwidth for an L2L or remote access session. This policy type typically is used to ensure that certain users or L2L sessions can get a fair share of the available bandwidth, especially L2L sessions. In other words, your L2L sessions might need a certain amount of bandwidth and you don't want heavy-bandwidth remote access users, such as those with broadband access, to affect your L2L sessions adversely.

Bandwidth policing places limits on the maximum rate for tunneled traffic; traffic that exceeds the configured rates is dropped by the concentrator. This policy type typically is used when you want to ensure that a particular L2L session or group of users (like those with broadband connections) don't hog all of the bandwidth on a particular interface on which their VPN session terminates.

One of your first tasks in setting up bandwidth management is to create your bandwidth policies. Typically, you'll create three types of bandwidth policies:

- A general policy that will affect all VPN traffic entering or leaving your concentrator's public interface
- Specific policies for your remote access groups (these policies override the general interface policy)
- Specific policies for your L2L sessions (these policies override the general interface policy)

To create a bandwidth policy, go to **Configuration > Policy Management > Traffic Management > Bandwidth Polices**. This screen lists your existing policies. To add a policy, click the *Add* button, taking you to the screen in Figure 10-1.

At the top of the screen you need to enter a name for your policy in the *Policy Name* text box. I typically use descriptive names. For example, if I'm creating a general bandwidth policy for tunneled traffic on the public interface, I would call the policy "General BW Public Policy" (or something like that). Likewise, if I were creating a bandwidth policy for an L2L session, I would use the L2L session name for the policy; if the L2L session was connecting my site to the Oviedo site, I would call the policy something like "Oviedo L2L BW policy." The actual policy name can be 32 characters in length.

Below this parameter are two sections for the two types of policies:

- Bandwidth Reservation
- Bandwidth Policing

Figure 10-1 *Bandwidth Policy Creation*

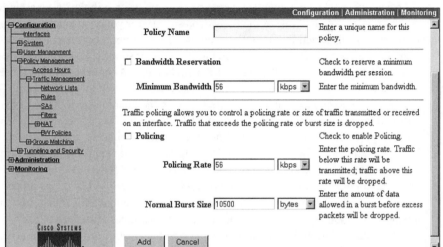

You'll notice that there is a check box to the left of each section name. This means you can configure bandwidth reservation *and* policing in the *same* policy or you could easily configure just one of the two, depending on the type of user or L2L traffic you are dealing with. The details of both are discussed in the following sections.

Bandwidth Reservation

If your policy needs bandwidth reservation, click the check box to the left of *Bandwidth Reservation*. Below this is the *Minimum Bandwidth* parameter. This parameter allows you to specify a minimum amount of bandwidth available for each VPN session that uses the policy. For an L2L session, this policy would apply to all traffic traversing the associated tunnel. For a remote access group, this policy would apply to each individual user session associated with the group. As an example of using bandwidth reservation, if you set the minimum bandwidth value to 56 Kbps and this policy was applied to a remote access group, and 20 users from this group simultaneously accessed the concentrator, each user would be guaranteed 56 Kbps of bandwidth at a minimum, or 1,120 Kbps in total bandwidth. The default value for bandwidth reservation is 56 Kbps. You can specify a traffic rate from 8,000 bps up to 100 Mbps.

CAUTION	Take care when using bandwidth reservation. As you will see in the "Activating Bandwidth Policies" section, one of the things you specify for your concentrator's interface is its maximum supported link rate. For example, if your Internet connection was a T1, then even though your concentrator's public interface might support 100 Mbps, its true link rate really would be that of the external T1: 1,544 Kbps. Assume your default bandwidth reservation policy for the public interface was 56 Kbps. Given this policy, only 27 users would be able to connect to the concentrator given the guaranteed 56 Kbps of bandwidth reserved for each user and a total capacity of 1,544 Kbps. This is true even if the users are not using their reserved bandwidth! When the first user connects, she is reserved 56Kbps, but can use more bandwidth if needed. Once the second user connects, he also is reserved 56 Kbps. At this point, 112 Kbps of bandwidth is reserved for the two users, and the two users can use the remaining bandwidth of 1,432 Kbps (1,544 − 112). This process keeps occurring for each user who establishes a remote access connection. Once the 28th user attempts to establish a connection, the concentrator assumes that given a link capacity of 1,544, this additional user can't be supported because the concentrator already has reserved 1,544 kbps of bandwidth for the first 27 users. Therefore, I would use bandwidth reservation on a very limited basis, such as for an L2L session where you need to ensure that remote access users don't use up your available bandwidth and starve your L2L sessions.

Bandwidth Policing

Bandwidth policing is more suitable for remote access users when you want to limit the amount of bandwidth they can use. Any traffic sent above the policing rate automatically is dropped by the concentrator. When using bandwidth policing for remote access users, you are ensuring that one or more users don't use up bandwidth that might be required for certain L2L sessions or other remote access groups. If you're concerned that a group of users at least receives a minimal amount of bandwidth, but doesn't starve other VPN sessions, you can combine policing with reservation.

To create a bandwidth policing policy, click the check box to the left of *Policing* in Figure 10-1. Because data traffic is bursty in nature, policing involves the configuration of two parameters:

- **Policing Rate**—This parameter limits the maximum sustained rate of traffic; this value can range from 56,000 bps to 100 Mbps.

- **Normal Burst Size**—This parameter allows a small burst of traffic before it is limited by the policing rate, but if traffic constantly exceeds this parameter, the excessive traffic is dropped; this value can be 10,500 bytes at a minimum.

The best way to look at these parameters is from a Frame Relay perspective, where the *Policing Rate* parameter is similar to the committed information rate (CIR) and the *Normal Burst Size* is similar to Frame Relay's committed burst rate (B_C). To set the burst size correctly, use the following formula: *Normal Burst Size* = (*Policing Rate* / 8) * 1.5. *Policing Rate* is measured in bits per second, whereas the Normal Burst Size is *bytes* per second, which is why the formula divides the policing rate by 8.

As an example, if you wanted to limit users to 128 Kbps of bandwidth, set the *Policing Rate* to **128 Kbps** and the *Normal Burst Size* to **24 Kbps**.

When you have finished adding your bandwidth policy, click the *Add* button at the bottom of the screen; if you're modifying an existing policy, click the *Modify* button.

Activating Bandwidth Policies

Once you have created your bandwidth policies, activate them for the policies to take effect. Bandwidth policies can be applied to one of three items:

- Interfaces
- L2L sessions
- Remote access sessions

The following sections discuss how to associate a bandwidth policy to each of the above three items.

Bandwidth Policies: Interfaces

Bandwidth management must first be enabled on the interface on which your VPN sessions will terminate; this is typically the concentrator's public interface. To use bandwidth management, the concentrator requires you first to enable bandwidth management on the interface where your VPN tunnels terminate and then to apply a general bandwidth management policy that will affect all VPN traffic terminated on this interface. As you will see in the next two sections, though, you can create specific bandwidth policies and apply them to remote access groups or L2L sessions: these override the general bandwidth policy applied to the concentrator's interface.

Per my explanation in the last section, you'll first need to create a general policy for the concentrator's interface for VPN traffic not associated with a specific bandwidth policy. Normally, this interface policy uses bandwidth policing, not reservation. Once you have created a policy for the interface, you'll need to enable bandwidth management and activate this general policy. Normally this is done on the concentrator's public interface, where most, if not all, of your VPN sessions are terminated. However, if you have a three-interface concentrator and are terminating sessions on the external and public interfaces and want to use bandwidth management on both, you'll need to create a general policy for both (if the policy requirements are different) and enable these on both interfaces.

To activate your general bandwidth policy, go to **Configuration > Interfaces** and click the hyperlink of the interface on which your VPN tunnels will terminate. Then click the

Bandwidth tab at the top of the interface screen, presenting you with the screen shown in Figure 10-2. To enable bandwidth management, click the *Bandwidth Management* check box.

Figure 10-2 *Bandwidth Policies and Interfaces*

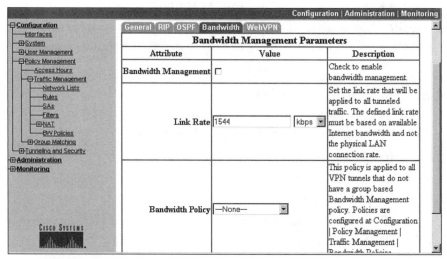

The *Link Rate* parameter specifies the true bandwidth available off of the interface. Even though the interface supports up to 100 Mbps speeds, this doesn't represent its true bandwidth. For example, if the concentrator were connected to a cable modem, then its effective available bandwidth would be between 1 and 5 Mbps. Or, if the concentrator was connected to a router, and the router had a T1 connection to the public network, the effective bandwidth would be 1,544 Kbps. The *Link Rate* parameter is used by the concentrator when you have enabled bandwidth reservation policies.

Below the *Link Rate* parameter is where you select the general bandwidth policy that should be applied to the interface. The *Bandwidth Policy* parameter is a drop-down selector that allows you to choose a policy for the interface. This policy is used for all VPN sessions terminated on this interface that are not associated with a specific bandwidth policy (one applied to a group or an L2L session). When you have finished selecting your policy, click the *Apply* button at the bottom to activate your bandwidth management changes.

NOTE Please note that bandwidth management policies apply to traffic both entering *and* leaving the concentrator's interface. To view your bandwidth management statistics, you can go to the **Monitoring > Statistics > Bandwidth** Management screen; this screen displays global statistics regarding bandwidth management. From the **Monitoring > Sessions** screen, you can view the bandwidth management statistics on a session-by-session basis by clicking the hyperlink of each individual VPN session name.

Bandwidth Policies: Remote Access Sessions

As I mentioned in the last section, the bandwidth policy applied to an interface is applied to all VPN traffic on the interface unless you override it. There are two ways of overriding the general policy: create a bandwidth policy and apply it either to a remote access group or to an L2L session. This section will discuss how you would associate a bandwidth policy with a remote access group; the following section discusses how you would do this for an L2L session.

One of the main concerns you'll have with remote access users, especially broadband users, is to ensure that their traffic doesn't consume the available bandwidth of the concentrator's effective bandwidth on its public interface. Remember that bandwidth management enforces policies in both directions on the interface, and most traffic is coming from the inside service or resource to the user. Therefore, most policies that you would create for remote access users would be bandwidth policing.

I already have discussed how to create bandwidth policies in the "Creating Bandwidth Policies" section. Once you have created a policy for a group of users, you can then apply it to the remote access group the users belong to. Do this by going to the **Configuration > User Management > Groups** screen. This was shown previously in Figure 7-2 in Chapter 7. To apply a bandwidth policy to a group, click the name of the group on this screen and then click the *Bandwidth Assignment* button (in version 3.6, this is the *Assign Bandwidth Policies* button).

You are taken to a screen where the concentrator's interfaces are listed as hyperlinks. Click the name of the interface where the remote access users for this group will terminate their VPN sessions (this is typically the public interface), which takes you to the screen shown in Figure 10-3. This screen allows you to choose the bandwidth policy that will be applied to this group. Choose the group's bandwidth policy with the *Policy* drop-down selector—the drop-down selector lists the policies you have created previously.

Figure 10-3 *Bandwidth Policies and Groups*

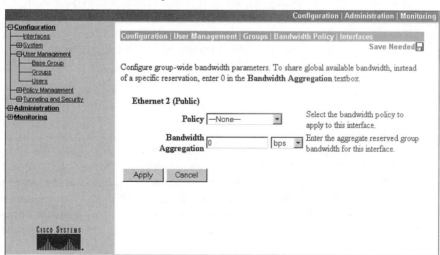

TIP   For a group (or an L2L session) to use bandwidth reservation, the general policy applied to the interface must *also* have bandwidth reservation configured. This can be accomplished by specifying a bandwidth reservation of 8,000 bps for the general policy, which is the smallest value allowed—right now, there is no way of getting around this restriction.

The second parameter you can configure on the screen in Figure 10-3 is *Bandwidth Aggregation*. I'll use an example that illustrates the usefulness of this parameter. Assume that you have a general bandwidth policy applied to the concentrator's public interface that has a reservation policy of 56 Kbps per VPN session and a reservation policy for a group, called Accounting, of 168 Kbps. The public interface has a link rate of 1,544 Kbps. A user establishes a VPN session to the concentrator and is associated with a group with no bandwidth management policy; therefore, the interface's policy is used and the user is reserved 56 Kbps, but has access to the remaining bandwidth on the interface (1,488 Kbps). Another user, from the Accounting group, then establishes a VPN connection to the concentrator and is reserved 168 Kbps of bandwidth. As more and more users of each type connect to the concentrator, they are reserved their assigned bandwidth until the concentrator reaches the rate limit of its interface; and then it drops any new connection attempts.

One of the problems in this scenario is that if enough users from groups other than Accounting connect to the concentrator, even a single user from the Accounting group might be rejected from connecting if the Accounting user's reserved rate value would cause the concentrator to exceed the rate limit of the interface. The function of the *Bandwidth Aggregation* parameter in Figure 10-3 is to reserve a specified amount of bandwidth for the group itself, ensuring that at least some users from the associated group can connect. Users using the general policy or from other groups cannot use this bandwidth; it's reserved for users of this group. For example, if the *Bandwidth Aggregation* parameter was set to 512 kbps for the Accounting group, at least three Accounting users would be guaranteed a connection to the concentrator, because this bandwidth would be reserved for the Accounting users. Then, in our example, users from any other group (including Accounting) would have access to the remaining 1,032 kbps of bandwidth.

Bandwidth Policies: L2L Sessions

Besides applying bandwidth policies to remote access groups, you can also apply them to L2L sessions. Once you have created your bandwidth policy for your L2L session, you can apply it by either going to the group screen or to the L2L screen. For the latter, go to the **Configuration > Tunneling and Security > IPsec > LAN-to-LAN** and click the *Modify* button. Then use the *Bandwidth Policy* drop-down selector to associate the policy to the L2L session.

NOTE	Please note that if you assign a bandwidth reservation policy to an L2L session, the concentrator automatically sets the *Bandwidth Aggregation* value to match the bandwidth reservation value, ensuring that the L2L connection is guaranteed its reserved bandwidth whether or not the L2L session is currently up. Also, any bandwidth policies applied to the L2L session apply to all traffic that traverses the L2L session.

Bandwidth Management and QoS

Remember that the concentrator's bandwidth management feature implements a very basic quality of service (QoS) function. One limitation of this feature is that bandwidth management is applied to all traffic entering or leaving an interface, all traffic for a group (or users in a group), or individual L2L sessions. Unfortunately, you can't implement bandwidth management at the connection level. For example, if you had an L2L session with both voice and data traffic traversing it, you couldn't have two policies applied for the two types of traffic because they would be using the same tunnel session. If you had this particular situation, and needed to have different QoS policies for the two types of traffic using the *same* tunnel session, your best solution would be to use a Cisco router.

Routing on the Concentrator

Because concentrators are used in medium-to-large networks and these networks are composed of many subnets, you'll need to set up routing on your concentrator. The concentrator supports two types of routing: static and dynamic. You can create specific static routes or default routes. In addition, the concentrator supports two dynamic routing protocols: RIP and OSPF. The remaining subsections will discuss the configuration of routing on the concentrator.

Static Routing

Global routing configurations are performed on the IP Routing screen, which is accessed by clicking **Configuration > System > IP Routing**. The concentrator supports two types of static routes: default and static. Each is discussed in turn in the following sections.

Default Route

A default route is a gateway of last resort: if a specific route is not found in the concentrator's routing table to reach a destination, the default route is used. To define a default route, click the *Default Gateways* hyperlink, which takes you to the screen in Figure 10-4.

Figure 10-4 *Default Route*

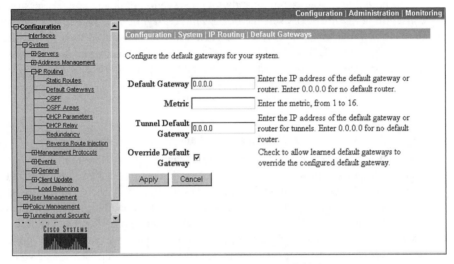

Within the screen, there are several parameters, as follows:

- The *Default Gateway* parameter allows you to assign an IP address of the next hop to reach the destination network. This is typically a router or firewall.

- The *Metric parameter* allows you to specify a metric for the default gateway. This is used when you need to create a primary and backup default route, where a metric of 1 specifies the primary default route.

- The *Tunnel Default Gateway* parameter allows you to specify a different IP address to use for the default gateway of VPN sessions—non-VPN traffic would use the default gateway specified in the *Default Gateway* parameter.

- The *Override Default Gateway* check box allows you to use a dynamically learned default gateway instead of the one hard-coded on this screen: this could be one learned via DHCP if the concentrator is a DHCP client or one learned via RIP or OSPF.

You would click the *Apply* button to accept your configuration.

Static Routes

Static routes typically are used when you aren't using a dynamic routing protocol to reach networks. To create a static route, from the IP Routing screen click the *Static Routes* hyperlink. This screen will display static routes you have configured. To create a static route, click the *Add* button, taking you to the screen in Figure 10-5.

Figure 10-5 *Static Routes*

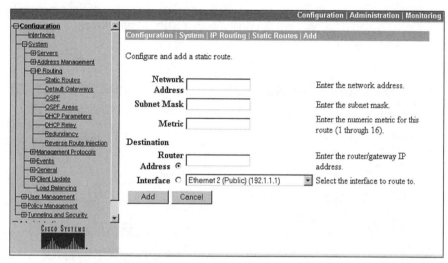

Within the screen, there are several parameters, as follows:

- The *Network Address* and *Subnet Mask* parameters allow you to enter the static route for the destination.

- The *Metric parameter,* which is required, assigns a metric to the static route: this can be from 1–16 and can be used to weight the route if you need to create more than one static route for the same destination network for redundancy.

- The *Destination parameter* can be one of two values: *Router Address* or *Interface*. If you choose the *Router Address* radio button, you'll need to enter the IP address of the next-hop address of the Layer-3 device that the concentrator will use to reach the destination network. You typically would choose this option when you know the IP address of the next hop. Otherwise, if you choose the *Interface* radio button, you'll need to use the drop-down selector to choose the interface the concentrator should use to reach the destination network. You typically would choose this option when you don't know the IP address of the next hop, because the concentrator is acquiring its addressing information dynamically via DHCP on the interface.

Last, click the *Add* button to add the static route.

RIP Routing Protocol

RIP is one of the two dynamic routing protocols that the concentrator supports. Both RIPv1 and RIPv2 are supported, in addition to a compatibility mode. The configuration of RIP is done on the concentrator's interfaces: **Configuration > Interfaces**. From here, click the hyperlink of the interface; for example, the private interface.

On the Interface screen are four tabs at the top: to enable RIP, click the *RIP* tab, which displays the screen in Figure 10-6. This is the private interface of the concentrator, for which the default configuration is that inbound RIPv1/2 updates are accepted, but no RIP updates are sent out of the interface.

Figure 10-6 *RIP Configuration*

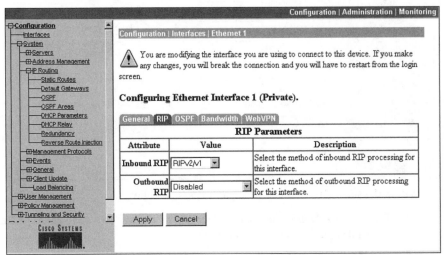

In Figure 10-6, the *Inbound RIP* parameter allows you to specify whether or not you want to learn RIP routes from neighboring RIP routers off this interface. This parameter can be set to "Disabled," "RIPv1 only," "RIPv2 only," or "RIPv2/v1." The *Outbound RIP* parameter allows you to specify whether or not you want to send RIP updates out of this interface.

NOTE	Even though RIPv2 is supported, RIPv2 authentication is not; however, other features such as variable-length subnet masks (VLSM) and multicasting are. If you create a default route on the concentrator, it is not propagated via RIP on an interface; however, static routes that you configure on the concentrator are redistributed automatically into RIP and advertised out of interfaces configured for outbound RIP. This also applies to static routes learned via reverse route injection (RRI).
	Also, inbound and outbound RIP on the public interface is denied by the public interface filter—to allow inbound and outbound RIP, you must add these rules to the public interface filter. If you have filters on other concentrator interfaces, you'll need to add RIP rules to these also.

OSPF Routing Protocol

The second dynamic routing protocol supported by the concentrator is OSPF (defined in RFC 2328). The configuration of OSPF is slightly different than RIP. First, you must enable OSPF, assign the concentrator a router ID, and define the areas the concentrator is connected to. These tasks are performed from the IP Routing screen. Second, as with RIP, you must turn on OSPF on the concentrator's interface(s).

OSPF: IP Routing Screen

The IP Routing screen has two OSPF hyperlinks:

- OSPF
- OSPF Areas

If you click the *OSPF* hyperlink, you're taken to the screen shown in Figure 10-7. To enable OSPF, click the *Enabled* check box. You must assign your concentrator a unique router ID that identifies the concentrator in the OSPF network. Normally, an IP address on one of the concentrator's interfaces is used. Once you assign the ID, you can't change it unless you first disable OSPF. The *Autonomous System* check box needs to be checked if the concentrator is going to be an autonomous system boundary router (ASBR). By enabling this, you can take RIP or static routes in the concentrator's routing table and advertise these into the OSPF process: this is *necessary* if you're using RRI. Click the *Apply* button to activate your changes.

Figure 10-7 *OSPF Routing Process Configuration*

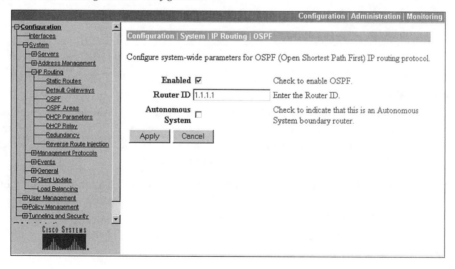

If you click the *OSPF Areas* hyperlink from the IP Routing screen, you are taken to a screen that displays the areas the concentrator is connected to. To add an area, click the *Add* button; by default, area 0 (0.0.0.0) already exists on the screen.

Figure 10-8 shows an example of adding an area by clicking the *Add* button. At the top of the screen, enter the area number in the *Area ID* text box. Below this, if the concentrator is an area border router (ABR) and you want to generate summarized LSAs, click the *Area Summary* check box. To import routes (either RIP or static) into the concentrator's OSPF process, change the *External LSA Import* drop-down selector to "External."

Figure 10-8 *OSPF Area Configuration*

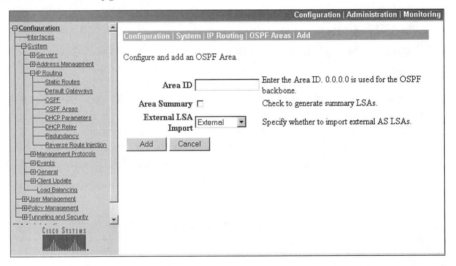

OSPF: Interfaces

Once you have configured OSPF globally, you must enable it on your concentrator's interface or interfaces where you want to learn or share OSPF routes. Go to the **Configuration > Interfaces** screen and click the hyperlink of the interface; then click the *OSPF* tab. Part of this screen is shown in Figure 10-9.

To enable OSPF on the interface, select the *OSPF Enabled* check box. The only other required parameter is the OSPF area that the interface is associated with: this value defaults to area 0 (0.0.0.0). The other parameters are optional.

Figure 10-9 *OSPF Interface Configuration*

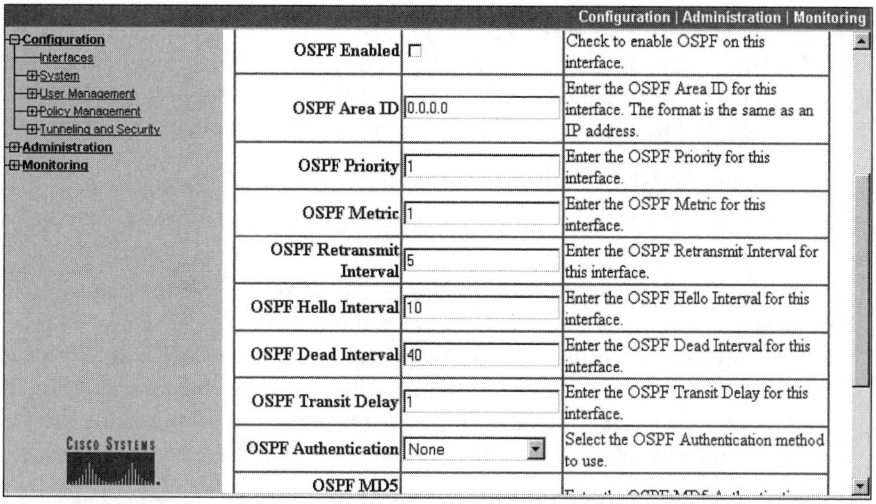

One security function you might want to enable in the screen shown in Figure 10-9 is OSPF authentication, which allows you to authenticate routing updates you receive or send. To enable this, set the *OSPF Authentication* parameter to "MD5," change the *OSPF MD5 Authentication Key ID* parameter to the correct key number, and set the *OSPF Password* to the key value used for creating the MD5 hashed output (digital signature). The key number and password will need to match what the other routers are using on the segment connected to this interface.

NOTE   Also, inbound and outbound OSPF on the public interface are denied by the public interface filter—to allow inbound and outbound OSPF, you must add these rules to the public interface filter. If you have filters on other concentrator interfaces, you'll need to add OSPF rules to these also.

Once you've configured routing on the concentrator, you can view the concentrator's routing table by going to the **Monitoring > Routing** Table.

TIP   If you're using OSPF as a routing protocol in your network and your internal Layer-3 devices are not seeing RRI routes from your concentrator, make sure that RRI has been enabled on the concentrator and that you have configured the concentrator as an ASBR for OSPF and have allowed OSPF external routes.

Chassis Redundancy

The concentrators support two general types of redundancy: intra- and inter-chassis redundancy. Intra-chassis redundancy is available on the 3015 concentrators and higher, where dual power supplies and redundant SEP cards are supported. All of the Cisco concentrators, however, support inter-chassis redundancy through one of two solutions:

- Virtual Router Redundancy Protocol (VRRP)
- Virtual Cluster Agent (VCA), sometimes referred to as Remote Access Load Balancing

Both are mutually exclusive. You can use one *or* the other; both have advantages and disadvantages. For example, VRRP, because it is a standard, can be used to provide redundancy using concentrator and nonconcentrator products (such as Cisco routers); however, VRRP does not support load balancing—only redundancy. VCA, on the other hand, allows for load balancing of incoming remote access sessions; however, VCA is supported only by the VPN 3000 concentrators and the ASA security appliances.

The following two sections will discuss how these inter-chassis redundancy features are implemented on the concentrators.

VRRP

VRRP provides inter-chassis redundancy and is an open standard; even Cisco routers support it. VRRP is typically used to provide default gateway redundancy; however, it can also be used to provide redundancy for VPN connectivity.

With VRRP, an election process is used to elect a master device responsible for handling traffic, including VPN traffic. A virtual address is then assigned by the master, and remote devices connect to this virtual address. The virtual addresses are most commonly the configured IP addresses on the interfaces of the master, but can be a virtual address. The master will process packets sent to the virtual address. One or more backup VRRP peers monitor the status of the master; if the master fails, one of the backups will be promoted to the master role and will begin processing packets sent to the virtual address.

VRRP Example

Figure 10-10 illustrates how VRRP works. In this example, there are two concentrators at the corporate site. One VRRP group is used off of each interface: Group 1. ConcentratorA is the master for each group (you can influence the election process by changing the priority of the master). Note that the virtual addresses used are those of the master concentrator.

All concentrators in the group periodically send hellos. The default polling period is once every three seconds, but this can be reduced to one second; if three hellos are missed from the master, the backup will promote itself to the master role. Based on the hello interval, this can range from 3–10 seconds.

Figure 10-10 *VRRP Example*

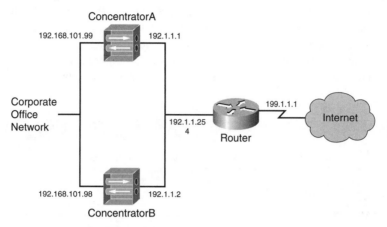

ConcentratorA

192.168.101.99   192.1.1.1

Corporate
Office
Network

192.1.1.25
4

Router

199.1.1.1

Internet

192.168.101.98   192.1.1.2

ConcentratorB

Group 1 Master: ConcentratorA
Group Private Address: 192.168.101.99
Group Public Address: 192.1.1.1

When the master fails, all VPN sessions handled by the master also fail. The backup
concentrator will take over only when it stops receiving the master's hello off of all
interfaces enabled for VRRP—a single interface failover on the master will not cause a
failover.

TIP

To ensure that inadvertent cutovers don't take place because of spanning tree (where the
concentrators are connected to switches), configure your switches using the PortFast
feature for the ports the concentrators are connected to.

L2L sessions will be rebuilt to the new master automatically when a cutover takes place;
however, remote access sessions will have to be rebuilt by the client user unless auto-
initiation for software clients or network extension mode for hardware clients is used—this
is also true of the VCA feature.

NOTE

In the example in Figure 10-10, you would probably have dual routers connected to the
Internet for redundancy and set up HSRP or VRRP between them. Then you would create
a default route on the concentrators and point them to the virtual address. The configuration
of this is beyond the scope of this book; however, I discuss this type of configuration, from
a security perspective, in my book *Cisco Router Firewall Security* from Cisco Press.

VRRP Configuration

To set up VRRP, go to the **Configuration > System > IP Routing > Redundancy** screen, as shown in Figure 10-11. To enable VRRP, click the *Enable VRRP* check box. The *Group ID* parameter assigns a number to the VRRP group—this needs to be the same on all the concentrators. Because it is rare that you would have more than one group on a LAN, you can probably accept the default value, which is 1; however, the number can range from 1–255.

Figure 10-11 *VRRP Configuration*

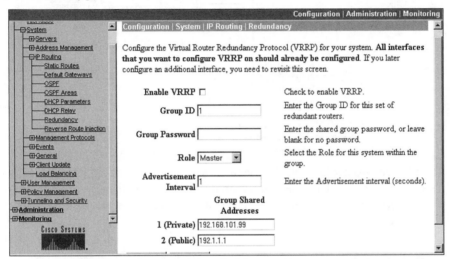

To provide additional security, you can password-authenticate VRRP messages by entering a password in the *Group Password* parameter; however, this value is sent across the wire in clear text, so it doesn't provide that much additional security! The *Role* drop-down selector allows you to choose the role the concentrator will play: "Master" and "Backup 1" through "Backup 5." The hello interval defaults to one second, but can be changed with the *Advertisement Interval* parameter; making this a higher number slows down a failover.

At the bottom of the screen are the *Group Shared Addresses*. These are the "virtual" addresses other devices will use to reach the concentrator. These addresses default to the IP addresses on the concentrator's interfaces; however, on the backup concentrators, you *must* change these to match that of the master's IP addresses on its respective interfaces. Please note that you don't have to use the physical IP addresses of the master for the virtual addresses—you can use an unused address off the concentrator's specified interface (this is a common practice).

If you have filters on the concentrator interfaces, like the public interface, you'll need to make sure you have VRRP rules on the interface filter(s) to allow the VRRP messages to be generated on the interface and received on the interface (outbound and inbound, respectively). Also, to verify that VRRP is functioning correctly between VRRP devices, go to the

Monitoring > Statistics > VRRP screen and examine its output. You should be able to see which role the concentrator is playing (for example, master) and you should see the *Advertisements Received* value incrementing when you refresh the screen periodically. If you see any of the error values increasing, you have a configuration problem.

NOTE   Because only one VRRP group can be configured on the concentrators, only one member will handle traffic sent to the virtual addresses. This means that other members will monitor the master only passively and will not pass VPN traffic. Therefore, a better solution would be to use routers, which support multiple VRRP (or HSRP) groups, which allow redundancy while at the same time allowing the use of one router in each group. This solution allows you to load balance on the router; however, the disadvantage is that concentrators are more scalable than routers when it comes to handling large numbers of remote access sessions.

VRRP Configuration Synchronization

When using VRRP for redundancy, most of the configuration of the master must be identical on the backup peers. For example, if you have remote access users connecting to you, the group and user configurations need to be replicated between the concentrators. This would be true of other VPN configurations on your concentrator. The hard way of accomplishing this would be to configure each concentrator manually and separately.

Unfortunately, there is no automatic configuration replication between concentrators. Therefore, I discuss the next-best method of accomplishing this. Many of the things discussed here will be discussed in more depth later in the "File Management" section.

The first thing you'll do is save the master's configuration. Go to the **Administration > File Management** screen on the master concentrator, which is shown later in Figure 10-15. For the file called "CONFIG," click its *View* hyperlink, displaying the current concentrator configuration. Select and copy the entire configuration and paste it into a text editor such as Windows Notepad.

In the text editor, find the following three sections: [ip 1], [ip 2], and [ip 3], as shown in Example 10-1:

Example 10-1 *Master Concentrator Configuration File: IP Addressing*

```
←output omitted→
[ip 1]
enable=1
address=192.168.101.99
mask=255.255.255.0
←output omitted→
[ip 2]
enable=1
address=192.1.1.1
mask=255.255.255.0
←output omitted→
```

Please note that for a 3005, you'll have only the first two sections because this concentrator only has two interfaces. These are the IP addresses on the master's interfaces. For the backup concentrator, these will need to be changed to represent what the backup concentrator will use. In the example in Figure 10-10, these would be 192.168.101.98 for "ip 1" and 192.1.1.2 for "ip 2".

Next, look for the [vrrpif 1.1], [vrrpif 2.1], and [vrrpif 1.1] sections in the master's configuration, as shown in Example 10-2:

Example 10-2 *Master Concentrator Configuration File: VRRP*

```
[vrrpif 1.1]
rowstatus=1
state=1
priority=255
←output omitted→
[vrrpif 2.1]
rowstatus=1
state=1
priority=255
←output omitted→
```

In each vrrpif section, change the *priority* parameter from 255 to something smaller, such as 254. Save the file as a text file (.txt extension).

Once you have completed these steps, you'll use this configuration on the backup concentrator in the VRRP group. In the example in Figure 10-10, you would log in to the *backup* concentrator and go to **Administration > File Management**. Click the *File Upload* hyperlink. For the *File on the VPN 3000 Concentrator* parameter, enter **CONFIG.BAK**. For the *Local File* parameter, use the *Browse* button to find the text file you just created. Then click the *Upload* button to upload this configuration file of the backup concentrator to Flash memory.

At this point, the backup concentrator isn't using this configuration. To use this modified configuration, you would need to click the *Swap Configuration Files* hyperlink on the **Administration > File Management** screen. Click the *OK* button to swap the CONFIG.BAK file with the CONFIG file; this will switch the two configuration files. Then reboot the concentrator by going to the reboot screen: **Administration > System Reboot**. You can then choose the following options:

- Reboot
- Reboot without saving the active configuration
- Now

Then click the *Apply* button. When the backup concentrator reboots, the file you changed will be loaded on the backup concentrator. Please note that this synchronization process also applies if you will be using VCA for redundancy, which is discussed in the next section.

NOTE	Please note that other parameters might need to be changed on the backup concentrator depending on other features you have enabled in your concentrator configuration.
	Also, you can use this handy shortcut to move other types of configurations between concentrators, such as remote access groups and their parameters.

VCA

VCA is a VPN 3000 concentrator and ASA security appliance feature that provides redundancy for remote access sessions. This feature was first introduced in 3.0 on the concentrator. VCA is part of the concentrator's operating system and requires no additional software. The next couple of sections will discuss this feature.

NOTE	VCA and VRRP are mutually exclusive: you can only use one of these redundancy features on a concentrator.

VCA Operation

Figure 10-12 illustrates how VCA works. There are three basic steps in the operation of VCA:

1 Elect a master

2 Load-balance remote access sessions

3 Verify the operation of the master

Figure 10-12 *VCA Example*

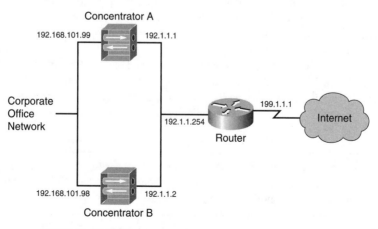

Virtual Cluster Address: 192.1.1.253

Elect a Master

With VCA, the concentrators form a cluster, with one member of the cluster performing the function of a master. The master is elected by using the one with the highest VCA priority. Each concentrator has a default priority based on its hardware model: the more powerful the concentrator, the higher the priority. The election process happens at the time the concentrators boot up and their interfaces become active. If all concentrators boot up at the same time, and they have the same priority, the one with the lowest IP address (on the public interface) is chosen as the master.

Once the master is elected, it maintains this role even if another concentrator comes online with a higher priority. Unlike other redundancy protocols such as HSRP, VCA doesn't support a preemption process. The only time a master is elected is upon the initial bootup of the concentrators or when the current master fails. For example, in Figure 10-12, if both concentrators were the same model, like 3030s, and if both booted up at the same time, ConcentratorA would be elected as master because it has a lower IP address.

Load-Balance Remote Access Sessions

The cluster itself is represented by a logical address, commonly referred to as a virtual address. This address must be an *unused* address associated with the LAN segment the concentrators' public interfaces are connected to. For example, in Figure 10-12, the public interface LAN segment is 192.1.1.0/24 and three addresses already are used. For this example, 192.1.1.253 has been chosen as the virtual address.

All remote access clients must use the virtual address when making a connection to the cluster. The master will process traffic sent to this address; so for the session from the client, the master will answer the session request; however, the master will not, by default, terminate the session on itself. Instead, the master looks at the current loads of the concentrators in the cluster and chooses the one with the least load.

Remember that load is *not* based on the amount of traffic going through the concentrator, but on the number of current sessions terminated on the concentrator. Load is calculated by taking the current number of sessions on the concentrator and dividing that number by the total number of sessions supported by the concentrator. This ensures that higher-end concentrators handle more sessions than lower-end ones, which makes sense. For example, if you had a 3005 and 3080 in a cluster, for every one connection the 3005 would handle, the 3080 would handle 100 or 50, depending on the version of software on the 3005. The current session information is periodically shared with the master.

NOTE   The number of sessions supported on a concentrator is tunable; you can make it smaller. You might want to do this in environments where you want a smaller concentrator to handle more sessions than it normally would in a cluster.

The master then sends a redirection message to the remote access client requesting the session, where the message contains the public interface IP address of the concentrator that will handle the session (which could be the master itself). Only Cisco VPN clients (software and hardware) and web browsers (WebVPN) understand this redirection message. The remote access client then tears down the initial attempt and starts the session process with the new address.

NOTE	Only the Cisco Easy VPN IPsec software and hardware clients and WebVPN clients understand the redirection message the master sends. Other VPN implementations, such as PPTP and L2TP/IPsec, still are supported on the concentrators when you are using VCA. However, they can't participate in load balancing. In this instance, you would configure these remote access clients to use the public IP addresses of the concentrators, not the virtual address of the cluster. Also, load balancing of L2L sessions is not supported with VCA. This makes sense, because VCA performs load balancing based on sessions, not amount of traffic, on a concentrator.

Verify the Operation of the Master

Once the master is elected, the backup concentrators in the cluster are responsible for ensuring that the master is still performing its role in addition to handling the setup of any redirected sessions. All the concentrators periodically generate VCA hello/keepalive messages to verify their operation and share their load information. These messages are sent to UDP port 9,023 as multicasts. Therefore, each set of interfaces of the cluster (public, private, and external) must be in the same respective broadcast domains. Optionally, these messages can be encrypted. Plus, if you have filters on the concentrators' interfaces—for example, the public interface—you'll need to ensure that you have VCA rules in the interface filter(s) to allow the VCA messages to be generated and received on the interface. VCA filtering rules have already been predefined on the concentrator: you only need to activate them for the interface filter (**Configuration > Policy Management > Traffic Management > Filters**).

VCA Configuration

To enable and configure VCA, go to **Configuration > System > Load Balancing**. Figure 10-13 shows the top of this screen and Figure 10-14 the bottom.

At the top of the screen you need to enter the virtual IP address of the cluster in the *VPN Virtual Cluster IP Address* parameter. For example, for the concentrators shown in Figure 10-12, you would enter 192.1.1.253 on both members of the cluster. Below this is the *VPN Virtual Cluster UDP Port* parameter, where the UDP port defaults to 9,023. If you change this on one concentrator in the cluster, you must change it on all the members.

Figure 10-13 *VCA Configuration: Top*

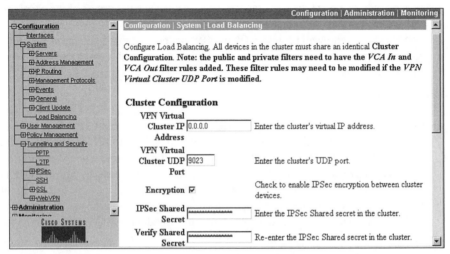

Figure 10-14 *VCA Configuration: Bottom*

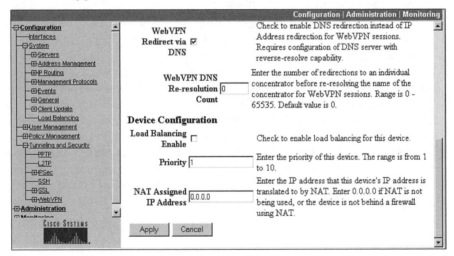

Optionally, you can encrypt the VCA messages between members of the cluster. If you check the *Encryption* check box, you'll need to enter the key for the encryption process in the *IPsec Shared Secret* and *Verify Shared Secret* parameters. This configuration needs to be the same on all peers on the cluster.

In 4.7, two new parameters were added to this screen, shown in Figure 10-14. The *WebVPN Redirect via DNS* parameter allows the master to redirect connections based on DNS names on the WebVPN client's certificate instead of its IP address. This is disabled by default; if you enable this parameter, you have the option of changing the *WebVPN DNS Re-resolution Count* parameter; this parameter specifies the maximum number of redirections to a cluster member before the IP address must be revalidated by performing a reverse DNS lookup. The default is 0, which means that no re-resolution takes place: this value can range from 0–65,535.

To enable VCA, you must click the *Load Balancing Enable* check box on each member of the cluster. This enables redirection for all supported remote access clients: Cisco VPN Client, Cisco hardware IPsec clients, and WebVPN clients. Optionally, you can change the priority of the concentrator, which affects which member will become the master. The priority can range from 1–10, where 10 is the highest. Cisco has a default value for the priority based on the concentrator model. Table 10-1 shows the default priorities. Cisco recommends that you leave the priorities at their default values if the concentrators are different models in the cluster, because, based on the default values, the higher-end (and therefore more suitable) concentrator will typically perform the additional tasks of the master.

Table 10-1 *Concentrator VCA Default Priorities*

Concentrator	Priority
3005	1
3015	3
3030	5
3060	7
3080	9

The last parameter on the screen in Figure 10-14 is the *NAT Assigned IP Address* parameter. The configuration of this parameter is necessary only if the public IP addresses the cluster members and the virtual address of the cluster are private addresses and are being NATed statically by an address translation device, such as the router in Figure 10-12. If this were true, you would put in the global (publicly visible) IP address that external remote access clients would be using to connect to the cluster in this parameter and still enter the virtual IP address of the cluster (the one associated with the physical LAN segment of the public interface) in the *VPN Virtual Cluster IP Address* parameter. If the concentrators are using public addresses, then you can leave this parameter configured for "0.0.0.0," which means that no address translation is being performed.

TIP   Remember that, just as with VRRP, the concentrators need similar configurations to support IPsec remote access sessions—in this situation, I would probably use an AAA server to maintain at least the user, and possibly group, information. Therefore, this information wouldn't need to be replicated across the members of the cluster.

VCA Verification

Once you have set up VCA on your cluster members, you'll want to ensure that load balancing is functioning correctly. First, be sure that the members of the cluster can communicate with each other. You can see this information by going to the **Monitoring > Statistics > Load Balancing** screen. From this screen you can view the following information:

- The role of the concentrator: master or secondary (backup)
- The current load of the concentrator
- The list of VCA peers of this concentrator, and their addresses, role, concentrator model, priority, cluster uptime, and other information

If you have enabled the encryption option for VCA messages, you can see the status of the connections between the concentrators by going to the **Monitoring > Sessions** screen and looking at the *Management Sessions*. You should see the IP addresses of the peers in the cluster with a corresponding connection protocol of "VCA/IPsec." If you're not seeing the information I mentioned above in the two Monitoring screens, you probably have a configuration problem on one or more of the concentrators in the cluster. Also, be sure that each concentrator in the cluster can ping other members of the cluster off each interface that is enabled and that you have added the VCA rules to all filters being used on the concentrators.

The virtual IP address cannot be pinged for testing functions. If you need to test connectivity between the remote access client and the cluster, have the client ping the IP address assigned to the master's public interface.

TIP   Because VRRP and VCA are mutually exclusive, I'm often asked which of the two should be used for redundancy. If you have two or more concentrators that primarily are terminating remote access sessions, then I would use VCA, because VCA allows you to use all members in the cluster. Just take care that any L2L sessions do not point to the virtual address of the cluster, but to one of the physical addresses of the concentrators in the cluster; otherwise the L2L session will fail to establish. If you need just temporary redundancy and you have a concentrator and a router, you can use VRRP to provide this function. However, the drawback here is that you must configure the router to support remote access connectivity—I might do this just for the most important users. If the setup primarily used L2L sessions on the concentrators, I would use VRRP, because VRRP supports redundancy for both L2L and remote access sessions.

Administration Screens

The goal of this book is to focus on VPN sessions; however, because not as many people are familiar with Cisco VPN 3000 concentrators compared to Cisco routers and security appliances, I want to spend some time focusing on some important administrative functions on the concentrator. Therefore, the last topic I'll focus on is the administrative screens (the monitoring screens I'll discuss in Chapter 11, "Verifying and Troubleshooting Concentrator Connections").

All of the administrative functions of the concentrator are found by clicking the *Administration* hyperlink at the top or left-hand side of the web browser window. You have the following options from the main Administration screen:

- **Administer Sessions**—Provides statistics for all administrative, remote access, and L2L sessions, including the ability to disconnect sessions.

- **Software Update**—Can upgrade the concentrator and remote access client software.

- **System Reboot**—Can reboot or power down the concentrator, and schedule these actions.

- **Reboot Status**—Can view any scheduled reboots of the concentrator.

- **Ping**—Tests connectivity with ICMP echoes.

- **Traceroute**—Displays the router path to reach the remote destination.

- **Monitoring Refresh**—Defines automatic screen updates for the Monitoring screens.

- **Access Rights**—Takes you to a sub-menu screen where you can maintain the administrator accounts on the concentrator, restrict management access to the concentrator, set session timeouts and limits, and specify the use of an AAA TACACS+ server for administrative authentication functions.

- **File Management**—Allows you to view, save, swap, delete, and transfer files to the concentrator's Flash memory.

- **Certificate Management**—Installs and manages your concentrator's root, identity, and SSL certificates.

The following sections will discuss some of the more important administrative items in more depth.

Administrator Access

This section will focus on managing management access to the concentrator. This can be accomplished with administrative accounts, access control lists (ACLs), access settings, centralized authentication with AAA (authentication, authorization, and accounting), and management protocols and access. The following sections will discuss these control mechanisms briefly.

Administrator Accounts

If you won't be using AAA to centralize management of your concentrators, you'll need to secure the management accounts on each concentrator. To manage your concentrator's accounts, go to the **Administration > Access Rights > Administrators** screen. This screen will list the five management accounts that the concentrators support. Depending on the concentrator software version, from 1–3 accounts will be enabled: *admin, isp,* and/or *user.* Therefore, you'll want to enable or disable the ones you want to use, and for the ones you want to use, possibly change their level of security access.

Table 10-2 lists the default accounts and their access levels. The *Authentication* parameter determines rights to access or change authentication functions, such as those in these screens: **Configuration > User Management, Configuration > Policy Management > Access Hours,** and so on. The *General* parameter defines access/change rights for most concentrator functions except for those of the other parameters. The *SNMP* parameter limits the ability to use SNMP, remotely, to manage the concentrator. The *Files* parameter determines what ability the account has to access or manipulate files in the concentrator's Flash memory; for example, saving, copying, viewing, and deleting files.

Table 10-2   *Concentrator Administrative Accounts*

Account	Authentication	General	SNMP	Files
admin	Modify Config	Modify Config	Modify Config	Read/Write Files
config	Modify Config	Modify Config	Stats Only	Read/Write Files
isp	Stats Only	Modify Config	Stats Only	Read Files
mis	Modify Config	Modify Config	Stats Only	Read Files
user	Stats Only	Stats Only	Stats Only	Read Files

Legend of valid access rights:

None: No access or rights.

Stats Only: Can access only the Monitoring screens (can't make changes to concentrator parameters).

View Config: Can access functional areas (based on the parameter that this is defined for, like *Authentication* or *General*), but can't change parameters—the account can access various Administration or Configuration screens based on the parameter, but can't change these things.

Modify Config: Can view and change parameters in the functional area—basically full rights for the functional area the parameter is enabled for.

TIP   You don't need to use the default names of the accounts on the concentrator—these can easily be changed from within the concentrator. I would highly recommend at least setting up two accounts: one with complete administrative access and one with monitoring (and possibly limited configuration rights). In both cases, I wouldn't use the names that Cisco gives to these accounts, such as *admin* or *user*—I'd change them to something more obscure. I also would change all passwords for all accounts, even those that you are not using. Also, if you want to have different accounts with the same rights, like *admin,* then typically you'll use an external AAA server using TACACS+, like Cisco Secure ACS, to define these accounts and authorizations.

Access Control Lists

By default, any device is allowed to access the concentrator off the private interface: the public interface's filter restricts management access. You can restrict management access to the concentrator by creating ACLs. You can create ACLs by going to **Administration > Access Rights > Access Control** List. As soon as you create one ACL entry, all other devices not specified by the ACL are denied management access to the concentrator automatically; therefore, make sure that *your* PC's address is the first one you add. You can enter specific IP addresses or network/subnet numbers.

Access Settings

The Access Settings screen (**Administration > Access Rights > Access Settings**) allows you to change the idle timeout of management sessions (defaults to 600 seconds), the number of allowed simultaneous management sessions (defaults to 10), and whether or not the concentrator's configuration file (in Flash) is encrypted with RC4 (defaults to encryption). I would highly recommend that you reduce the number of simultaneous management sessions to a much smaller number, like 2 or 3, since you probably won't have 10 administrators in the concentrator simultaneously.

NOTE	As soon as one administrator goes into a configuration or administration screen where he can make changes, this locks the configuration file, preventing other administrators from making changes on the concentrator; other administrators would have monitoring rights only. Also, if you use RC4 encryption to protect the configuration file from eavesdropping, just remember that only the concentrator itself can decrypt this file: so if the concentrator would fail and you would replace it with another, the encrypted configuration file wouldn't do you any good because the new concentrator wouldn't have the key to decrypt it!

AAA Servers

If you need to centralize the authentication functions for management access, the concentrator allows you to use an AAA server configured for TACACS+, like Cisco Secure ACS. Using this feature, you can define your management accounts on your AAA server. One restriction, though, is that the privilege level defined for the main management account on the concentrator (by default, this is the *admin* account) must be the same or lower than the one defined for the TACACS+ management accounts. To set the privilege level for the main management account, go to the **Administration > Access Rights > Administrators** screen and click the *Modify* button to the right of the main management account. Then change the *AAA Access Level* parameter from 0 to 15. Within your AAA server, any management account that will perform management functions on the concentrator then must at least have this privilege level; otherwise their access is denied.

To specify the use of an AAA server to authenticate management access, go to **Administration > Access Rights > AAA Servers > Authentication**. Click the *Add* button to add an AAA TACACS+ server: you'll need to enter the IP address of the AAA server and the key used to encrypt the TACACS+ messages. You have the ability to add multiple AAA servers for redundancy; if you do this, you can control which one is the primary and which ones are backup AAA servers.

CAUTION   Before you configure the concentrator for AAA TACACS+ authentication of management access, *first* configure the AAA server(s) to allow the concentrator to communicate with them. If the concentrator cannot successfully contact any configured AAA server, any new administrative access is automatically denied—you'll only be able to access the concentrator via its console port.

Management Protocols and Access

You can use several applications and protocols to manage your concentrator. Some of these are enabled by default and some are disabled: you'll want to ensure that some of these are disabled, like clear text access. Here are the management protocols supported and whether or not they are enabled by default:

- FTP: enabled
- HTTP: enabled
- TFTP: disabled
- Telnet: enabled
- SNMP: enabled
- XML: enabled
- SSH: enabled

To change or modify these management access applications, go to **Configuration > System > Management Protocols**. I would recommend that you *disable* HTTP and Telnet and only use HTTPS or SSH because these encrypt the management traffic from the administrator's desktop to the concentrator. To set this up, click the *XML* hyperlink on this page. XML allows you to enable management via HTTP or XML via HTTPS. By default, HTTPS and SSH are dropped on the public interface by this interface's filter. You could add these rules to the filter manually, but it's much easier to click the check boxes on this screen and let the concentrator automatically add them—if you already have enabled WebVPN, HTTPS will already be enabled and will be grayed out on this screen. From this screen, you can optionally restrict who is allowed to come into the public interface via HTTPS or SSH.

Only SSH 1.5 is currently supported on the concentrator. To configure SSH properties, go to **Configuration > Tunneling and Security > SSH**. You can change options such as the SSH port number (defaults to 22), the maximum number of SSH sessions, the encryption algorithm to use, and other parameters.

To configure HTTPS properties, go to **Configuration > Tunneling Protocols > SSL**. From here you can click two hyperlinks—*HTTPS* and *Protocols*—where you can enable or disable HTTPS access, change the HTTPS port number (defaults to 443), the SSL version, and the SSL encryption algorithms.

NOTE   If you recall from Chapter 8, "Concentrator Remote Access Connections with PPTP, L2TP, and WebVPN," if you are using WebVPN for remote access and you want to use HTTPS for management access on the concentrator, you'll need to go into the concentrator's public interface (**Configuration > Interfaces > Ethernet2 (Public)**) and click the *Allow Management HTTPS sessions* check box. Also click the *Redirect HTTP to HTTPS* check box to enhance your security, redirecting any HTTP access to HTTPS. Then, to access the concentrator's public interface for management access, enter either of the following URLs in your web browser's address bar:

- https://public_interface_address/admin.html
- https://public_interface_address/access.html

Concentrator Upgrades

The concentrator supports two upgrade processes: concentrator and remote access clients. This section will discuss briefly how to upgrade the software on the concentrator. Chapter 12, "Cisco VPN Software Client," will discuss the upgrade of remote access clients.

To upgrade the concentrator, first download the software from the Cisco web site and put it on your desktop. There are two software image types for the concentrator: those beginning with "3005" are for the 3005 and those beginning with "3000" are for the other concentrators. From your desktop, then log in to the concentrator and go to **Administration > Software Updates > Concentrator**. Click the *Browse* button and find the concentrator software image on your desktop and then click the *Upload* button—this begins the upgrade process.

The concentrator has two locations for storing operating system files: an active and backup location. When performing the upgrade, the image is copied to the backup location and then makes this the active location once the concentrator reboots. You'll need to reboot the concentrator to use the new image. Once you've rebooted, Cisco recommends that you clear your web browser's cache and delete all temporary Internet and history files and location bar references, because this might affect the concentrator's GUI display for the new software version.

CAUTION   When you are upgrading the concentrator, don't perform any other action on the concentrator's Flash memory, such as saving the concentrator's configuration or even viewing a file in Flash. If you do this, there is a chance you might corrupt the new image you're copying to Flash!

File Management

To view or manipulate the files in Flash on the concentrator, go to **Administration > File Management**. This screen is shown in Figure 10-15.

Figure 10-15 *File management*

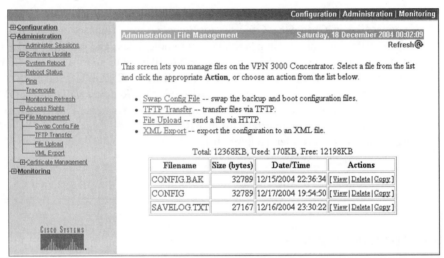

You can see that there are three files in the concentrator's Flash memory:

- CONFIG.BAK
- CONFIG
- SAVELOG.TXT

The SAVELOG.TXT is the log file that the Filterable Event Log pulls its messages from; I'll discuss this feature in the next chapter. Whenever you save the concentrator's configuration by clicking the blue floppy icon (Save Needed) in the top right-hand corner of the window, the concentrator first copies the last saved file from CONFIG to CONFIG.BAK; the concentrator then copies the current running configuration to CONFIG. This means that the concentrator maintains the last two revisions of the concentrator.

You can boot up from the configuration in CONFIG.BAK by clicking the *Swap Config File* hyperlink. This renames the two files and then boots up the newly named CONFIG (old CONFIG.BAK). This requires a reboot of the concentrator, though, to use the configuration in the swapped configuration file. This feature is useful if you made a configuration mistake and saved the mistake to Flash memory.

Also, you can upload and download files using TFTP, upload files to the concentrator using HTTP, and download the current running configuration from the concentrator using XML.

NOTE   I highly recommend that you back up the concentrator before *and* after making any changes either using TFTP or XML to ensure that if the concentrator fails, you do have a backup copy you can load on a replacement concentrator.

Summary

This chapter showed you the basics of setting up some of the additional features of the concentrator, such as bandwidth management, routing, redundancy with VRRP and VCA, management access, and other important features for using the concentrator for VPN connectivity.

Next up is Chapter 11, "Verifying and Troubleshooting Concentrator Connections," where I show you how to use various concentrator features to troubleshoot problems such as VPN connectivity issues. I'll focus on using the concentrator's monitoring screens for this function, including the Live Event Log and the Filterable Event Log (through the use of event classes).

Verifying and Troubleshooting Concentrator Connections

This chapter will discuss how to use various VPN 3000 concentrator tools to troubleshoot VPN connection problems. In the first half of the chapter I'll discuss some of the basic tools you'll use on the concentrator and in the second half I'll take a look at using these tools to solve common connectivity problems.

I won't be able to discuss every type of problem you'll see for terminating VPN sessions on the concentrator, but I'll discuss a few of the more common ones in this chapter. In Part III, "Clients," I'll discuss more problems and how to troubleshoot these problems from both the client and the concentrator ends of the connection. In this chapter, though, I'll focus on common problems and how to use various tools on the concentrator to pinpoint the cause of these problems.

Concentrator Tools

In the first half of the chapter I'll focus on the Monitoring screens of the concentrator, which up to this point haven't really been discussed. The Monitoring screens allow you to view status and statistical information about what is currently happening on the concentrator, in addition to what has happened previously.

When you click **Monitoring**, you can view the concentrator's status, the status of VPN and administrative sessions, statistics, and event logs. Each of these screens, with the exception of the Live Event Log, display read-only statistics. By default, the statistics on the screen are not updated automatically. Instead, you must click the **Refresh** icon in the top right corner of the window to update the contents on these other screens.

NOTE	You can change your screen update options by going to the **Administration > Monitoring Refresh** screen. This was discussed in the last chapter, "Concentrator Management."

When you go to the Monitoring screen, you can access the following monitoring options, which take you to different monitoring screens:

- **Routing Table**—View the current routing table entries (static and dynamic).

- **Dynamic Filters**—View the filters applied to VPN remote access user connections that were retrieved from an AAA RADIUS server during IKE Mode Config.

- **Filterable Event Log**—View the log file of events stored in the concentrator's Flash memory; these events are buffered up by the concentrator over a period of time, similar to a Cisco router's or PIX's logging buffered feature.

- **Live Event Log**—View the current events as they occur on the concentrator; these events are similar to using the debug feature on a Cisco router or PIX or ASA security appliance.

- **System Status**—View the installed software revision, the uptime, and status of the concentrator, including its front-panel LEDs.

- **Sessions**—View the current sessions on the concentrator, including VPN and administrative sessions; these can be sorted by type, amount of data transmitted, duration of the connections, or throughput of the connections.

- **Statistics**—View various statistics on the concentrator. These include VPN, administrative, Layer-2, Layer-3, and service statistics.

The following sections will discuss some of the more important monitoring screens, listed above, in more depth.

System Status

To view the status of the concentrator, go to **Monitoring > System Status**, where you'll see the screen shown in Figure 11-1. At the top of the screen, you can see the concentrator type (3005), the boot code revision (2.2), the software version (4.1.7A), how long the concentrator has been up (53 minutes, 28 seconds), the date and time the concentrator was either powered up or restarted (01/12/2005 14:06:54), and the amount of RAM (32 MB). For concentrators shipped in the last 4–5 years, you should also see the concentrator's serial number.

Below this is a picture of the front and rear of the concentrator, where the actual LED colors will be displayed depending on what is currently showing on the physical concentrator itself (this includes the meter bar on the front of the 3015 and higher concentrators). On the rear of the concentrator chassis, you can click the interfaces and power receptacle, which will display simple status statistics of these components; for example, the number of frames entering and exiting an interface, and the voltage status of the CPU and motherboard.

Even though you can't see these in Figure 11-1, below the chassis of the concentrator are two more important pieces of information: the status of the fans and temperature, and a graphic of the meter bar. For the two fans, you can see the current RPM at which the fans are running. For the temperature, you can view it in Fahrenheit and Celsius. Below this is a graphic of the meter bar found on the front of the concentrator (with the exception of the

3005). However, even with the 3005, you can view these three meter bar representations—
CPU utilization, active sessions, and data throughput—from this screen. Remember that
this screen is static, so you'll have to click the **Refresh** icon at the top of the window to
update the information you see on this screen.

Figure 11-1 *System Status Screen*

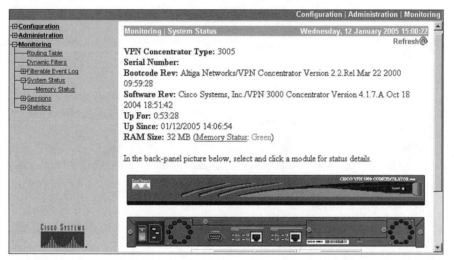

VPN Sessions

To view the sessions terminated on the concentrator, go to **Monitoring > Sessions**. You can
see the top and bottom parts of this screen in Figures 11-2 and 11-3. At the top part of the
screen, you can qualify the sessions you see by choosing a specific group name or viewing
all sessions by choosing "All," which is the default. Below this, the screen is broken into
four sections:

- Session Summary
- LAN-to-LAN Sessions
- Remote Access Sessions
- Management Sessions

The following sections will describe the above four sessions, and three additional sub-
screens you can view that summarize session statistics.

Figure 11-2 *Sessions Screen: Top Part*

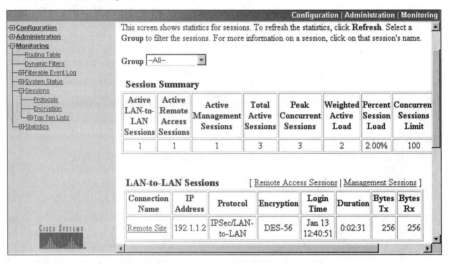

Figure 11-3 *Sessions Screen: Bottom Part*

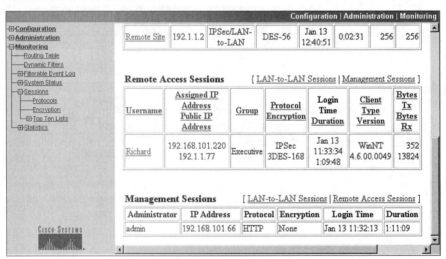

Session Summary Table

The Session Summary table at the top of Figure 11-2 displays summarized totals for the LAN-to-LAN, remote access, and management sessions terminated on the concentrator.

NOTE   Please note that these are not connections, but sessions. For example, an IPsec session has three connections: one for ISAKMP/IKE Phase 1 (management) and two for ISAKMP/IKE Phase 2 (data); the concentrator treats these as a single logical session.

There are two columns you should keep an eye on: *Peak Concurrent Sessions* (the highest number of active sessions at any point in time since the concentrator was last booted) and *Concurrent Sessions Limit* (the license limit of the concentrator for remote access sessions or what you've artificially lowered this limit to, as I mentioned in Chapter 10 in the load balancing section of the chapter). If the number of peak sessions is getting close to the license limit, you might want to think about upgrading to a larger concentrator or buying an additional one and clustering the two together. In Figure 11-2, the peak is 3 and the license limit is 100.

LAN-to-LAN Sessions Table

The LAN-to-LAN Sessions table at the bottom of Figure 11-2 shows the currently connected L2L sessions to the concentrator. In this example, there is only one called "Remote Site," where:

- The remote end has an IP address of 192.1.1.2
- DES-56 is the encryption algorithm
- The connection was built on January 13 at 12:40:51
- The connection has been up for 2 minutes, 31 seconds
- 256 bytes has been sent and received on the ISAKMP/IKE Phase 2 data connections

The "Remote Site" name is a hyperlink (this is the name of the L2L session); if you click this hyperlink, it will take you to the screen showing the detailed statistics for the three IPsec connections, shown in Figures 11-4 (top of screen) and 11-5 (bottom of screen).

At the top of the screen in Figure 11-4 is the same information found from the *LAN-to-LAN Sessions* table in Figure 11-2. Below this, you can see the bandwidth management statistics applicable to this session—you'll see this only if you have bandwidth management enabled for the interface that this session is terminated on, or for the session itself. In this example, all traffic has conformed to the bandwidth management policy.

Figure 11-4 *Session Detail Screen: Top Part*

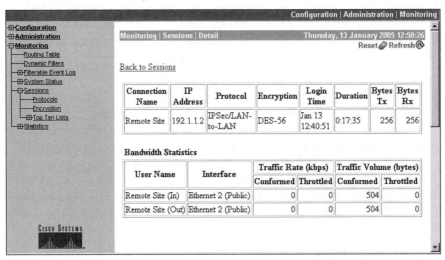

Figure 11-5 *Session Detail Screen: Bottom Part*

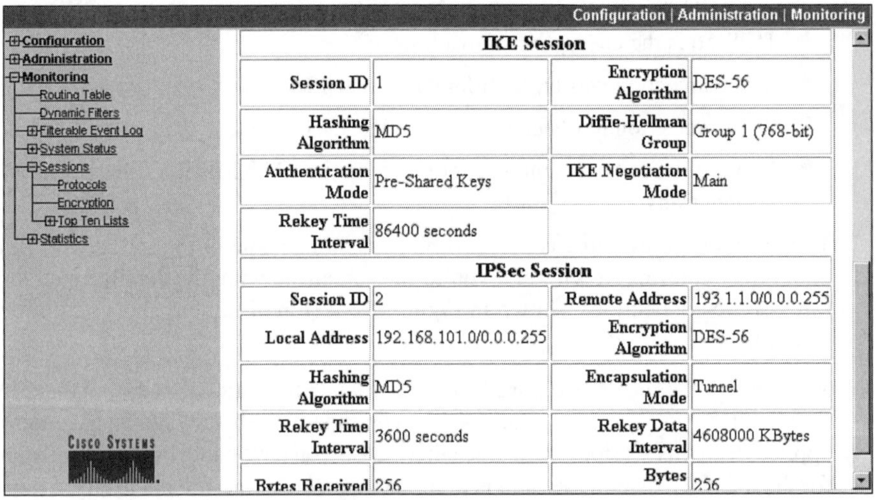

At the bottom of the screen (Figure 11-5) you can see two sections—*IKE Session* and *IPsec Session*—which display details about how each of the connections is protected and statistical information about the connections.

Remote Access Sessions Table

The top part of Figure 11-3, from **Monitoring > Sessions,** shows the summary of remote access sessions terminated on the concentrator. This would include IPsec, PPTP, L2TP/ IPsec, and WebVPN sessions. In Figure 11-3, there is currently one remote access session active, called "Richard." Sessions are always listed based on the username the user supplied during user authentication. Other information for this table entry includes:

- The user's assigned internal address is 192.168.101.220 and his NIC address is 192.1.1.77.
- The user belongs to the "Executive" group.
- The session is using IPsec and 3DES to protect the user's data.
- The user connected on January 13 at 11:33:34 and has been connected for 1 hour, 9 minutes, and 48 seconds.
- The user is using a Cisco VPN 4.6 client on a Windows NT (in this case 2000) platform.
- The user has transmitted and received 352 and 18,608 bytes, respectively.

As in the *LAN-to-LAN Session* table, you can click the name of the user, taking you to a screen with the details of the connection. This screen is similar to the one shown in Figures 11-4 and 11-5.

Management Sessions Table

The *Management Sessions* table shown at the bottom of Figure 11-3 (from **Monitoring > Sessions**) displays the administrative users that are currently logged in. In this example, one user logged in to the "admin" account from 192.168.101.66 using a web browser ("HTTP") on January 13 at 11:32:13 and has been logged in for 1 hour, 11 minutes, and 9 seconds.

TIP As mentioned in Chapter 10, I highly recommend that you change the name of the admin account to reduce the likelihood of someone attempting to break into your concentrator using this well-known account name.

NOTE You can also go to the **Administration > Administer Sessions** screen and see the same information found on the **Monitoring > Sessions** screen; however, there are two additional options available to you under the **Administer Sessions** screen:

- You can log out (disconnect) a session or sessions
- You can ping a device for a listed session

Additional **Monitoring > Sessions** Screens

There are three additional sub-screens you can go to under the **Monitoring > Sessions** screens:

- **Protocols**—Breaks out the number of sessions by protocol, such as IPsec (remote access), HTTP (administrative), and WebVPN, giving you an overall view of the types of sessions currently terminated on the concentrator.

- **Encryption**—Breaks out the number of sessions, by the type of encryption algorithm used, such as DES-56, RC4-40, AES-128, and 3DES-168 SSLv3 (WebVPN), giving you an overall view of the encryption algorithms used by the various sessions terminated on the concentrator.

- **Top Ten Lists**—Provides three additional screens that show an overview of the use of the concentrator. These can help you figure out which session is transmitting the most data or has been connected the longest:

  - **Data**—The top ten sessions sorted by the amount of data transmitted. Figure 11-6 shows an example of this screen, where the top session is the remote access session "Richard," which has transferred 24,056 bytes. This screen, for example, can be useful in determining which session is using the most total bandwidth; however, note that this is measured since the user connected, and is *not* an average rate.

  - **Duration**—The top ten sessions sorted by the length of time they were connected.

  - **Throughput**—The top ten sessions sorted on their throughput (bytes per second). You can use these measurements to see, on average, who is consuming the most bandwidth.

Figure 11-6 *Top Ten List: Data*

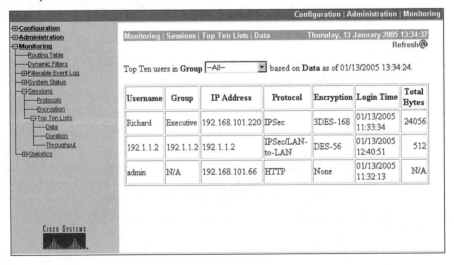

Event Logs

One of the most powerful and useful features on the concentrator is its logging and troubleshooting capabilities. You can control the granularity of how much detail you want when capturing logging events, and then you can display the events in several ways. The following sections will cover the setup and use of logging on the concentrator.

Troubleshooting: Concentrator versus Router versus PIX and ASA

Of the three products, hands-down, the VPN 3000 concentrators win when it comes to pinpointing a problem with a VPN session or concentrator process. For years I've sworn up and down that the router's debug capabilities were one of its main strengths when it came to troubleshooting problems; however, when it comes to VPN sessions, the description of the router's debug messages is very cryptic, making it sometimes impossible to figure out what the real problem is . . . and the PIX and ASA are the same in this category.

I once had a problem in which Cisco changed the IPsec code on a router and changed the default behavior for CRL checking from disabled to enabled. I was teaching a CCSP boot camp course, and when my students were doing the certificate lab with routers and site-to-site IPsec sessions, the ISAKMP/IKE Phase 1 management connection would fail. When looking at the debug output from the failed connection attempt, there was no explanation that the problem was that CRL checking was enabled on the router, and that the router couldn't download the CRL from the CA.

After poking around for about 30 minutes, I decided to move my efforts over to mimicking the configuration on a concentrator and using its logging capabilities to troubleshoot the problem. I had a feeling that the problem had something to do with certificates, so I methodically changed various configuration parameters on the concentrator until I saw the actual problem. The concentrator was trying to access the CRL but it wasn't available . . . and the concentrator's logging told me this in clear, understandable English. I then went back to the router and set CRL checking to optional, and the connection came up.

Therefore, I really prefer to use concentrators for a large number of remote access sessions and a small number of L2L sessions instead of routers and security appliances whenever possible, realizing that in certain situations I'll use a router, for advanced routing, QoS, or L2L scalability needs, or a PIX or ASA, for advanced address translation and security needs.

Date and Time for Logging Events

One of the first configuration steps you'll want to perform when setting up your concentrator for logging is to ensure that it has the correct date and time, which is obviously helpful when troubleshooting problems. You can do this manually or you can configure the use of an NTP server. The following two sections discuss both of these methods.

Manual Date and Time Configuration

To configure the date and time on your concentrator manually, go to **Configuration > System > General > Time and Date**. Here you can configure the date, time, time zone, and Daylight Saving Time values. Click the **Apply** button to accept your changes. Upon changing the time, any new events will use the time based on your new configuration.

Network Time Protocol

Setting up NTP is a two-step process:

1 Set the polling period the concentrator will use to contact the NTP server.

2 Define the necessary information for the concentrator to contact the NTP server to obtain the current time.

To set the polling period of when to contact the NTP server, go to **Configuration > System > Servers > NTP > Parameters**. The default polling period frequency is 60 minutes. This value can range from 0 (disabling NTP) to 10,080 minutes (once a week) .

To define your NTP servers, go to **Configuration > System > Servers > NTP > Hosts**. Click the **Add** button to add a new server. Enter the IP address of the NTP server and click the **Add** button. The order in which you add your servers is the order the concentrator uses when contacting them; therefore, the first server added becomes the primary time source.

CAUTION   As of 4.7, NTP Version 3, which supports authentication of NTP messages, is not supported by the concentrator, and thus the concentrator is susceptible to spoofed NTP replies. Therefore, I highly recommend that you use your own NTP server, located off the private interface of the concentrator, and that the traffic between it and the concentrator be protected. You'll also want to do this for other traffic, such as syslog, SNMP, or TFTP. In this situation, I would create a special LAN segment with only these devices on it, and would set up an IPsec L2L session between the Layer-3 device connected to this segment and the concentrator's private interface. Using this arrangement, with proper filtering on the LAN segment Layer-3 device, will reduce your exposure to spoofing, eavesdropping, or any other type of attack.

Event Classes and Logging Levels

Once you have configured your settings for the date and time, you now are ready to set up the concentrator's event classes. An event class controls the amount and detail of logging information generated for a particular type of event. Each event supports 13 levels of logging, where levels 1–6 are normal logging levels, 7–9 are debug level, and 10–13 are hex dumps. In other words, level 1 gives you the least amount of information about an event and level 13 the most.

All events have a default logging level assigned to them. You can change this globally for a logging method (for example, the Live Event log or a syslog server) or you can change each event individually—this is a much more powerful feature than a Cisco router or PIX or ASA security appliance, where you can configure only the former and not the latter.

Logging destinations supported by the concentrator include:

- **Console** (commonly called the Live Event Log)—Events are displayed in a near real-time fashion on a concentrator's Monitoring screen).

- **Log**—Events are stored in a file in Flash memory.

- **Syslog**—Sends events to a syslog server.

- **E-mail**—Sends events to an e-mail account.

- **SNMP trap**—Sends events, via traps, to an SNMP management station.

Default Logging Configuration

All logging destinations have default logging levels assigned to events. These can be changed by going to **Configuration > System > Events > General**. From this screen you can control the level of logging on a per-destination, but not per-event basis. Figure 11-7 shows the top part of this screen. Here is an explanation of the parameters you can configure on this screen:

- **Save Log on Wrap**—The 3005 event log stores 256 events while the other concentrators store 2,048 events; whenever the log file is full, the concentrator automatically overwrites older events. If you choose this option, when the log file reaches its event limit, the log file with the older events is stored in Flash memory and is called LOGxxxxx.txt, where xxxxx starts with 000001 and can reach 999999. You can access this file by going to **Administration > File Management**.

  Each of these log files requires about 334 KB of Flash memory. The concentrator will then start storing events in a new log file. If the concentrator only has 2.56 MB of space left in Flash, it will delete old log files automatically to make room for new ones. If there are no log files to delete, the save operation will fail and will generate an event about this problem. If you reboot the concentrator or if the concentrator crashes, the concentrator will save the log file, called "SAVELOG.TXT," to Flash—if this file exists, it is automatically overwritten. You can access this file by going to **Administration > File Management**.

- **Save Log Format**—This parameter specifies how to create the event entry. "Multiline" specifies that each event appears on one or more 80-character lines; "Comma Delimited" specifies that each event is on a separate line, and each field in the event is separated by a comma; "Tab Delimited" specifies that each event is on a separate line, and each field in the event is separated by a tab. The "Multiline" option should be chosen when you want to be able to read the information easily; however, one of the two last options should be chosen if you want to perform additional processing on the log files with some type of external program.

- **FTP Saved Log on Wrap**—This option allows you to have the concentrator automatically copy an event log file to an FTP server whenever the log file wraps. Notice that I said "copy" and not "delete." The log file is still in Flash memory on the concentrator. You'll need to configure the FTP access parameters, which I discuss in the "FTP Backup of Events" section of this chapter.

- **E-mail Source Address**—If you'll be sending certain events via e-mail to an e-mail account, this parameter allows you to specify what e-mail account appears in the "From:" field of the e-mail message. The e-mail account can be up to 48 characters long. If you leave it blank, and you have enabled the e-mail event log function, then the e-mail account in the "To:" field will be replicated in the "From:" field.

- **Syslog Format**—There are two formats of event messages you can choose from: "Original," which is the original format used on the concentrator, or "Cisco IOS Compatible," which should be chosen if you'll be sending events, via syslog, to a Cisco management application (this format would be similar to a log message you would see on a Cisco router or PIX or ASA security appliance).

- **Events to Log**—This option allows you to specify the default logging level to the event log file in Flash memory. Your options for logging levels are "None" (disable logging to this location), "Severity 1," "Severities 1–2," "Severities 1–3," "Severities 1–4," "Severities 1–5," and "Use Event List." If you choose "Use Event List," the events and levels you have configured in the *Event List* at the bottom of this screen are used (see the last bullet). The default logging level for this location is 1–5, which will store any of these level events to the log file; other higher numbered events are not stored.

- **Events to Console**—This option allows you to specify the default logging level to Live Event Log. This defaults to levels 1–3.

- **Events to Syslog**—This option allows you to specify the default logging level to an external syslog server. This defaults to "None," indicating that this option is disabled; if you set this, you must also define the access parameters for the syslog server. This is discussed in the "Syslog Server Configuration" section later in the chapter.

- **Events to E-mail**—This option allows you to specify that events of the specified range be sent to an e-mail recipient via an e-mail message. The default is "None"; you also must define the access parameters for the e-mail server. This is discussed in the "SMTP Server and E-mail Recipient Configuration" section later.

- **Events to Trap**—This option allows you to specify that events of the specified range be sent to an SNMP management station. The default is "None"; if you set this, you also must define the access parameters for the SNMP management station. This is discussed in the "SNMP Server Configuration for Traps" section later in the chapter.

- **Event List**—One of the problems with the above solutions for logging to a destination is that the highest level of detail you can specify is either 3 or 5, depending on the logging location. One way you can change the default logging level for an event for a location is to specify "Use Event List" for the location and then configure the event and logging level in the Event List box at the bottom of the screen in Figure 11-7 (this cannot be seen in the figure). You can change event logging based on class (type of event), event ID (the event within a class, like a particular IKE event), and the severity of an event (1–13). Each entry in the *Event List* text box must be on a separate line. The general format of an event list entry is:

```
<event_class>/<list_of_event_IDs and/or severity_numbers>
```

Entries can just be an event class name, such as "IKE" or "ALL"; just an event ID, which is the number of the event (or range of numbers) for the specified class (an event ID would be similar to a message ID, uniquely identifying a specific event within a class); just a severity level, such as SEV(1) or SEV(1-13); or a combination of these. For example, an event list entry of "IKE/1,10-13,SEV(1-7)" says that for IKE (Phase 1) event IDs 1 and 10 through 13, the event logging level should include logging levels 1 through 7. Please note that for the "ALL" class name, you cannot specify an event ID—just a severity or list of severity levels.

NOTE   One problem with the *Event List* configuration is that it changes an event logging level for any event logging destination that specifies "Use Event List." In other words, you can't have level 5 for one event for syslog and level 7 of the same event for log (log event file). If you need this type of granularity, you'll need to configure an event class, which is discussed in the "Event Class Configuration" section.

Figure 11-7 *Default Event Configuration*

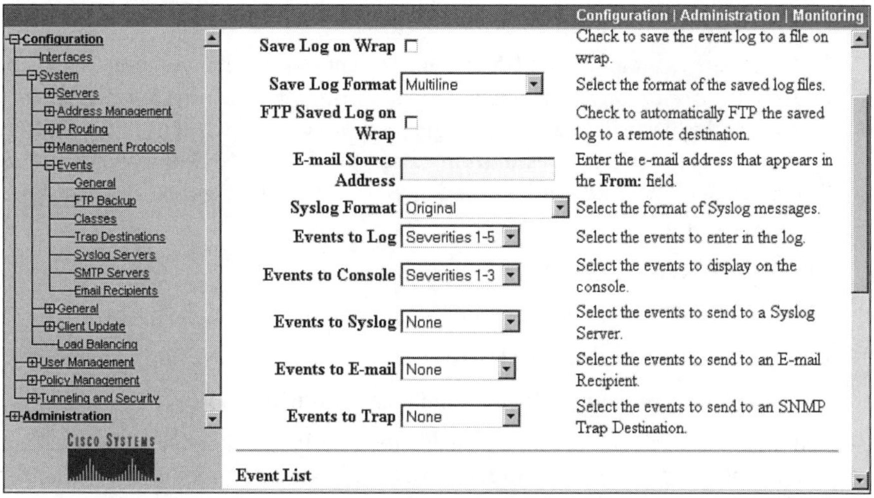

FTP Backup of Events

If you want to back up your event logs (in Flash) to an FTP server when the log file wraps, you must first select the severity level for the *Events to Trap* parameter on the **Configuration > System > Events > General** screen (see the "Default Logging Configuration" section) and then go to **Configuration > System > Events > FTP Backup** screen and enter your FTP access parameters. On this screen, you'll need to configure the following:

- The IP address of the FTP server
- Optionally, the directory location where you want the file to be stored; if you have multiple concentrators, have a separate directory for each, because the naming structure used for log file names is the same on each concentrator
- The FTP account name to authenticate to the server
- The FTP password for the account

Click the **Apply** button at the bottom of the screen to activate your changes.

CAUTION   I recommend that you use the syslog server method of saving log events versus this method, since you're probably already using syslog to save event logging information of other devices in your network. If you're using FTP, I would recommend against enabling anonymous access on the server. Configure an account for the concentrator to use. Also, I would encrypt transmissions from the concentrator to the FTP server's LAN segment using IPsec, because FTP is an insecure protocol.

SNMP Server Configuration for Traps

To send events as traps to an SNMP management station, first you must select the severity level for the *Events to Trap* parameter on the **Configuration > System > Events > General** screen (see the "Default Logging Configuration" section) and then go to the **Configuration > System > Events > Trap Destination** screen to add your SNMP management stations. When you click the **Add** button to add an SNMP management station, you'll need to specify the following:

- IP address of the SNMP management station
- The SNMP version to use: 1 or 2
- The community string for access
- The UDP port number for communications (defaults to 162)

The order in which you add your management stations is the order the concentrator uses when contacting them: therefore, the first station added becomes the default trap destination.

CAUTION   Currently, the concentrator doesn't support SNMPv3, which has support for authentication and encryption; therefore, I would encrypt transmissions from the concentrator to the SNMP management station's LAN segment using an IPsec session, because SNMPv1 and v2 are insecure protocols.

Syslog Server Configuration

To send events to a syslog server, first you must select the severity level for the *Events to Syslog* parameter on the **Configuration > System > Events > General** screen (see the "Default Logging Configuration" section) and then go to the **Configuration > System > Events > Syslog Servers** screen to add your syslog servers. When you click the **Add** button to add syslog, you'll need to specify the following:

- The IP address of the syslog server
- The UDP port number for communications (defaults to 514)
- The logging facility for the event messages (defaults to Local7)—this can be used by the syslog server to redirect the message and put it into a specific file on the server

If you add more than one syslog server, the concentrator will send messages to *each* server: the maximum number of syslog servers you can configure is five.

CAUTION   Syslog messages are not authenticated, not checked for tampering, and not verified if received; therefore, I would encrypt transmissions from the concentrator to the syslog server's LAN segment using an IPsec session.

SMTP Server and E-mail Recipient Configuration

To send events via an e-mail message, first select the severity level for the *Events to E-mail* parameter on the **Configuration > System > Events > General** screen (see the "Default Logging Configuration" section), then add an e-mail server, and last specify an e-mail recipient.

To add an e-mail server, go to the **Configuration > System > Events > SMTP Servers** screen and click the **Add** button to add an e-mail server; you'll need to specify the IP address of the e-mail server. If you add multiple e-mail servers, the first one you add becomes the primary server.

To specify the e-mail recipient of the event message, go to the **Configuration > System > Events > E-mail Recipients** screen and click the **Add** button. On this screen, enter the e-mail address and maximum severity level of events forwarded to this recipient. If you add multiple recipients, each person will receive events at the specified level.

Event Class Configuration

The event logging levels configured from the **Configuration > System > Events > General** screen sets the same logging level for all events sent to a specific logging location, such as a syslog server or the console. This is true even if you modify specific events with the *Event List* parameter on this screen. If you want to specify a specific logging level for *different* logging destinations, you need to create an event class. For example, you might want to set the logging level for IKE events to levels 1–5 for the console, but 1–9 for a syslog server; you can create an event class to accomplish this.

To create an event class, go to the **Configuration > System > Events > Classes** screen. This lists the event classes you've added. By default, one class entry exists: "MIB2TRAP," which includes SNMP MIB-II events. To add a new event class, click the **Add** button, where you're shown the screen in Figure 11-8. At the top of the screen there is a pull-down selector where you select the class name that you want to modify the logging level for. The class names and their descriptions are shown in Table 11-1. In the *Description* column, those labeled as "specific to Cisco products" apply to a Cisco feature and are not found in any standard or open implementation (almost all of the event log messages are specific to Cisco products).

NOTE   From the **Configuration > System > Events > General** screen, if you have chosen the Use Event List options for a logging destination and have defined event classes in the Event List text box, these event class configurations also will appear on the screen in Figure 11-8.

Figure 11-8 *Event Class Configuration*

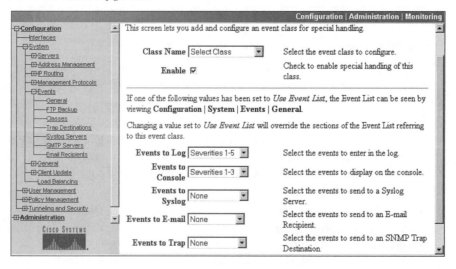

Table 11-1 *Event Class Names*

Event Class Name	Description
AUTH	Authentication functions
AUTHDBG	Authentication debugging (specific to Cisco products)
AUTHDECODE	Authentication protocol decoding (specific to Cisco products)
AUTOUPDATE	Autoupdate events
BMGT	Bandwidth management events (specific to Cisco products)
BMGTDBG	Bandwidth management debugging (specific to Cisco products)
CAPI	Cryptography events
CERT	Digital certificate events, including SCEP functions
CIFS	CIF file system access (specific to Cisco products)
CIFSDBG	CIF file system access debugging (specific to Cisco products)
CONFIG	Configuration events on the concentrator
DHCP	DHCP events
DHCPDBG	DHCP debugging (specific to Cisco products)
DHCPDECODE	DHCP decoding (specific to Cisco products)
DM	Data movement events on the concentrator's Flash memory
DNS	DNS functions
DNSDBG	DNS debug (specific to Cisco products)
DNSDECODE	DNS decoding (specific to Cisco products)
EVENT	Events occurring on the concentrator
EVENTDBG	Event debugging (specific to Cisco products)
EVENTMIB	Event MIB changes (specific to Cisco products)
EXPANSIONCARD	Events related to the SEP modules
FILTER	Events related to filtering of packets
FILTERDBG	Filter debugging (specific to Cisco products)
FSM	Finite State Machine debugging (specific to Cisco products)
FTPD	Events related to the FTP daemon process
GENERAL	NTP and other general events
GRE	GRE events
GREDBG	GRE debugging (specific to Cisco products)
GREDECODE	GRE decoding (specific to Cisco products)

continues

Table 11-1   *Event Class Names (Continued)*

Event Class Name	Description
HARDWAREMON	Monitoring of hardware components like the power voltage levels, fan RPMs, and the temperature
HTTP	HTTP access events
IKE	ISAKMP/IKE events
IKEDBG	ISAKMP/IKE debugging (specific to Cisco products)
IKEDECODE	ISAKMP/IKE decoding (specific to Cisco products)
IP	IP routing events
IPDBG	IP routing debugging (specific to Cisco products)
IPDECODE	IP packet decoding (specific to Cisco products)
IPSEC	IPsec events
IPSECDBG	IPsec debugging (specific to Cisco products)
IPSECDECODE	IPsec decoding (specific to Cisco products)
L2TP	L2TP events
L2TPDBG	L2TP debugging (specific to Cisco products)
L2TPDECODE	L2TP decoding (specific to Cisco products)
LBSSF	VCA load balancing events
MIB2TRAP	MIB-II SNMP traps
OSPF	OSPF routing events
PPP	PPP events
PPPDBG	PPP debugging (specific to Cisco products)
PPPDECODE	PPP decoding (specific to Cisco products)
PPTP	PPTP events
PPTPDBG	PPTP debugging (specific to Cisco products)
PPTPDECODE	PPTP decoding (specific to Cisco products)
PSH	Operating system command shell
POS	Embedded real-time operating system events
QUEUE	System queuing functions
REBOOT	Concentrator reboots
RM	Concentrator resource manager events
SMTP	SMTP events
SNMP	SNMP traps

Table 11-1   *Event Class Names (Continued)*

Event Class Name	Description
SSH	SSH access and events
SSL	SSL (HTTPS) access and events
SYSTEM	Buffer usage, heap usage, and other system related functions
TCP	TCP events
TELNET	Telnet access and events
TELNETDBG	Telnet debugging (specific to Cisco products)
TELNETDECODE	Telnet decoding (specific to Cisco products)
TIME	Events related to the clock on the concentrator
VRRP	VRRP events
WebVPN	SSL WebVPN session events
XML	XML events

The *Enable* check box, when checked, enables the event class. The *Events to Log* (defaults to logging levels 1–5), *Events to Console* (defaults to logging levels 1–3), *Events to Syslog* (disabled by default), *Events to E-mail* (disabled by default), and *Events to Trap* (disabled by default) parameters allow you to change the logging severity level for each destination respectively. Logging levels can be set to "None" (disabled), 1–13, or *Use Event List* (in which case the referred Event List on the **Configuration > System > Events > General** screen is used). Levels 1–6 are referred to as "Normal" by Cisco, 7–9 as "Debugging," and 10–13 as a "Hex Dump."

CAUTION   Level 1 events are the most serious events, for example, a concentrator component failing; level 13 events would be a hex dump of partial packet contents. If you set the logging level for an event above 9, this could cause additional events to trigger on the concentrator, creating additional logging information not necessarily related to the problem you're trying to troubleshoot. Cisco recommends using a logging of 6 or lower; however, I typically use 9 unless I actually need to see some of the packet contents, then I'll set it somewhere between 10–13.

TIP   For detailed troubleshooting of a specific problem, I typically use event classes to help solve the problem. Once I know what the type of problem is, I create an event class and set the logging level to 9 for the log file (*Events to Log* parameter). Once I'm done troubleshooting the problem, I'll go back into the event class and *deselect* the *Enable* check box to reset the logging back to the default level.

Live Event Log

To see events on the concentrator as they happen (on the console), you would use the Live Event Log, accessed by going to **Monitoring > Live Event Log**. The screen might take a few seconds to load. This screen, shown in Figure 11-9, requires that you have Java enabled in your web browser to see the events. This screen displays all the events in the event log, and any new events that occur (in a somewhat real time fashion), where the screen is updated once every five seconds—you can see the counter counting down from 5 to 1 at the bottom of the screen.

CAUTION If you keep this screen open, your login session will *not* time out, because the screen updates itself automatically and the concentrator sees this as activity.

Figure 11-9 *Live Event Log*

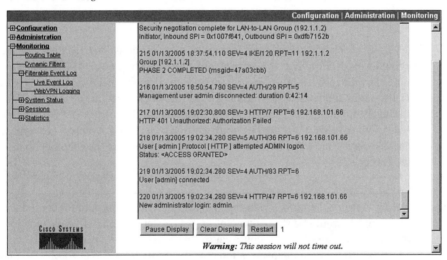

Interaction with the Live Event Log

By default, the logging level is set to 1–3 for the Live Event Log, so you'll only see important events. You can change the logging level as described in the "Default Logging Configuration" and "Event Class Configuration" sections. If you're seeing too many events in the window, you can click the **Pause Display** button at the bottom, which stops any new updates from displaying; you can click the **Resume Display** button to resume the display of new events, which also restarts the 5-second timer. If you click the **Clear Display** button at the bottom, the window display is cleared; however, the event log itself is not cleared. If you click the **Restart** button, the events in the window are cleared and the entire event log file is displayed.

TIP   The Live Event Log is similar to logging events to the console on a Cisco router; its one main advantage over a router is that it can pull the events from the event log file by clicking the **Restart** button. Unlike a router using debug, though, the concentrator's Live Event Log's main downfall is that you're seeing all events that are occurring—those that pertain to your problem and those that don't. This makes it very difficult to troubleshoot a specific problem on the concentrator using the Live Event Log. Therefore, I typically use the Filterable Event Log feature, which I'll discuss in the "Filterable Event Log" section later in the chapter.

Event Log Formatting

Each event in the event log and displayed in the Live Event Log screen consists of either eight or nine fields in the following format:

```
Sequence_#  Date  Time  Severity_Level  Event_Class/Event_ID
    Event_Count (IP_Address) Event_Description
```

Example 11-1 shows an event in the event log from Figure 11-9:

Example 11-1 *An Event from the Event Log*

```
218 01/13/2005 19:02:34.280 SEV=5 AUTH/36 RPT=6 192.168.101.66
User [ admin ] Protocol [ HTTP ] attempted ADMIN logon.
Status: <ACCESS GRANTED>
```

Here is a description of each of these fields:

- **Sequence_#**—This is the number of the event, which increments with each new event. When the concentrator boots up, resequencing starts at event 1. Please note that you can have multiple events with the same number; when the concentrator boots up, it appends events to the current log file. The largest sequence number is 65,536. In Example 11-1, the sequence number of the event is "218."

- **Date**—This is the date on which the event occurred in an "MM/DD/YYYY" format. In Example 11-1, the date is "01/13/2005."

- **Time**—This is the time at which the event occurred in an "HH:MM:SS.millisecond" format. In Example 11-1, the time is "19:02:34.280." The time is in a 24-hour format, so this event occurred at 7:02:34.280 PM.

- **Severity_Level**—This is the level of the event, which can range from 1–13. In Example 11-1, the severity level is 5.

- **Event_Class**—This is the type of event; possible event classes are listed in Table 11-1. In Example 11-1, the event class is "AUTH," indicating that the event involves some type of authentication function (in this case, it's someone trying to log in to the "admin" account on the concentrator).

- **Event_ID**—This qualifies the type of event class. In Example 11-1, the event ID is 36, indicating that this is an HTTP management connection attempt to the concentrator.

- **Event_Count**—This is the number of times that this type of event has occurred since the concentrator booted up. In Example 11-1, this particular type of event occurred six times, indicating that since the concentrator booted up, six HTTP management connection attempts were made.

- **IP_Address**—This is the IP address of the device associated with the event. Depending on the type of event, this may or may not be displayed (some events are not associated with IP connections). In Example 11-1, the person attempting the HTTP management connection is 192.168.101.66.

- **Event_Description**—The last component of the event log entry is a description of the actual event. This cannot exceed 80 characters per line, so for certain events, the description will be spread across multiple lines. In Example 11-1, there are two lines of description. For this log entry, someone was using HTTP to access the "admin" account on the concentrator and successfully supplied the correct password.

Filterable Event Log

Unlike the Live Event Log, the Filterable Event Log allows you to use filtering criteria to limit the events displayed in your window. This is very useful when troubleshooting a specific problem where you don't want to wade through many events in the event log to find the events related to your specific problem.

NOTE   To access the event log file in nonvolatile memory, you must have administrative rights to file access. These are defined in the **Administration > Access Rights > Administrators > Modify Properties** screen. This was discussed in Chapter 10, "Concentrator Management."

Filtering Options

To access the Filterable Event Log filtering functions, go to **Monitoring > Filterable Event Log**. Figure 11-10 shows a snapshot of the Filterable Event Log screen.

Figure 11-10 *Filterable Event Log*

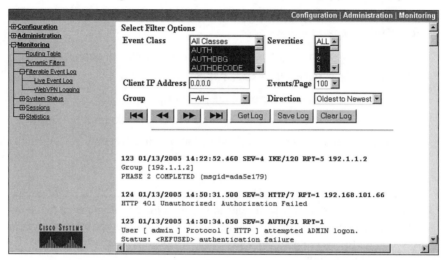

There are six filtering options in the screen:

- **Event Class**—You can choose one, multiple, or all event classes to include in your view. To select a range of contiguous classes, select the first class, hold down the SHIFT key, and then select the last class in the range. To select multiple noncontiguous event classes, select the first class, and then for each additional class, press the CTRL key and click the class name. The event class descriptions are discussed in Table 11-1.

- **Severities**—You can choose one, multiple, or all severity levels of the event class or classes you've chosen. To select more than one severity level, see the previous bullet point.

- **Client IP Address**—You can restrict events related to a specific IP address by entering the IP address in this field; to remove this restriction, re-enter 0.0.0.0 as the IP address.

- **Events/Page**—This allows you to control how many events are displayed per viewing page. The default is 100 events per page, but you can change this to "10," "25," "50," "100," "250," or "ALL."

- **Group**—You can restrict events for VPN sessions based on group membership. This drop-down selector allows you to restrict your viewing to all groups or to one specific group.

- **Direction**—You can affect the sorting of the order of the events displayed in the view by changing the direction: "Oldest to Newest" or "Newest to Oldest."

Event File Viewing and Manipulation

Once you've selected your filtering criteria, to display the filtered events, click any of the four **Page** buttons, as follows:

- ◀◀—Go to the very beginning of the event display (first screen)
- ◀◀—Go to the previous screen of the event display
- ▶▶—Go to the next screen of the event display
- ▶▶—Go to the very end of the event display (last screen)

The filtering options you have specified will remain in effect until you either change them or leave and come back to the Filterable Event Log screen.

NOTE Remember that you'll only see events in the event log file; if you need to see more detail about the events, you'll need to change the severity level for the event class or classes in question for the event log file in nonvolatile memory. This is discussed in the "Event Class Configuration" section.

Some other options available to you from this screen are these three buttons:

- **Get Log**—This opens up a new web browser window and displays the contents of the event log file based on your filtering criteria. You can then view and save the log file to your PC's hard drive. The default log file name is "vpn3000log.txt." If you right-click the **Get Log** button, a pop-up menu displays alternative choices for accessing this file.

- **Save Log**—This allows you to save the current event log file to Flash memory on the browser. The naming convention you use must follow Microsoft's DOS conventions: 8.3. If you enter a name that already exists in Flash, the file in Flash is overwritten. You can then go to **Administration > File Management** to manipulate the saved file.

- **Clear Log**—This completely erases the current event log file from the concentrator's nonvolatile memory and displays an empty event screen in the Filterable Event Log.

CAUTION If you click the **Clear Log** button, there is no undo feature: in other words, the current event log file is gone! Therefore, before using this feature, you might want to save the log file with the **Save Log File** button first.

Monitoring Statistics Screens

The last set of Monitoring screens are related to statistics gathering: **Monitoring > Statistics.** From these screens you can view various statistics of components running on the concentrator. These statistics include the following:

- **Accounting**—AAA RADIUS user accounting activity

- **Address Pools**—Address pools for remote access sessions, including allocated and available addresses

- **Administrative AAA**—Administrative access statistics for AAA TACACS+ events (if TACACS+ has been enabled for authentication of administrative access)

- **Authentication**—Remote access authentication activity via AAA RADIUS, including total number of authentications performed (accepted, rejected, timeouts, and so on)

- **Authorization**—AAA RADIUS user authorization activity

- **Bandwidth Management**—Bandwidth policy information related to traffic volume and rate

- **Compression**—Compression statistics for IPsec, L2TP, and PPTP (via MPPC) remote access sessions

- **DHCP**—Remote access sessions using DHCP, including leased addresses, duration of connection, DHCP server addresses, and so on

- **DNS**—DNS resolution information, including total requests, responses, and timeouts

- **Events**—A summarized list of logging events, summarized on event class, event number, and the total count for each event number within an event class

- **Filtering**—Number of inbound and outbound packets filtered by the concentrator on its interfaces

- **HTTP**—HTTP web-browser management statistics

- **IPsec**—ISAKMP/IKE Phase 1 and 2 summarized statistics for all sessions (remote access and L2L), including statistics about packets received and transmitted, dropped, encrypted and decrypted, and so on

- **L2TP**—L2TP summarized statistics for remote access sessions, including statistics about total number of current sessions, maximum number of sessions since the concentrator booted, failed sessions, packets received and transmitted, and the current list of authenticated users

- **Load Balancing**—VCA statistics for load balancing, including VCA role, peers, and load

- **NAT**—Address translation statistics including number of packets translated by the concentrator, number of translated sessions, and a list of the entries in the translation table

- **PPTP**—PPTP summarized statistics for remote access sessions, including statistics about total number of current sessions, maximum number of sessions since the concentrator booted, failed sessions, packets received and transmitted, and the current list of authenticated users

- **SSH**—Summarized count of current SSH sessions to the concentrator, maximum number of sessions during a peak, and a list of current accounts that have SSH sessions terminated on the concentrator

- **SSL**—Number of current and peak SSL sessions terminated on the concentrator, including encryption statistics

- **Telnet**—Summarized count of current Telnet sessions to the concentrator, maximum number of sessions during a peak, and a list of current accounts that have SSH sessions terminated on the concentrator

- **VRRP**—VRRP statistics for the configured redundancy group on the concentrator

- **MIB-II**—Statistics for the concentrator's interfaces, TCP and UDP sessions, IP packets and fragmentation, RIP configuration and updates, OSPF configuration and updates, counts of the types of ICMP packets, list of entries in the ARP table for each concentrator interface, and SNMP information for polling requests

Troubleshooting Problems

The second half of this chapter will focus on using tools on the concentrator to troubleshoot common problems, including:

- ISAKMP/IKE Phase 1 problems, such as

  — Policy mismatches

  — Authentication problems, including device pre-shared key authentication mismatches, device certificate authentication issues, and user authentication issues

- ISAKMP/IKE Phase 2 transform set mismatches

NOTE   Following chapters will discuss many more topics on troubleshooting; for example, Chapter 12, "Cisco VPN Software Client," discusses problems with MTU and address translation, and Chapter 19, "Troubleshooting Router Connections," discusses problems with fragmentation.

ISAKMP/IKE Phase 1 Problems

In this section I'll cover some common experiences with ISAKMP/IKE Phase 1 problems and how to use the concentrator's event log to troubleshoot these problems. A good number of remote access and L2L session problems I've dealt with involve either policy mismatches or authentication issues.

IKE Policy Mismatch

One of the more common problems with establishing IPsec sessions is a mismatch in the ISAKMP/IKE Phase 1 policy, what the Cisco VPN concentrators refer to as the "IKE proposals or policies." I discussed the configuration of IKE policies in Chapters 7, "Concentrator Remote Access Connections with IPsec," and 9, "Concentrator Site-to-Site Connections," under the **Configuration > Tunneling and Security > IPsec > IKE Proposals** screen.

In this example problem, I'll use an L2L session between a Cisco router and a concentrator. I've purposely set up the configuration on the concentrator so that there is *not* a matching Phase 1 policy between the two devices. Initially, the logging level was set to 5 for the event log, and the log information from the **Monitoring > Filterable Event Log** screen is shown in Example 11-2. In this example, the remote peer (192.1.1.2) is trying to establish a connection to the concentrator; however, there is an "Error processing payload" error being displayed in event 5, which doesn't illuminate the problem much.

Example 11-2 *Initial log of a Phase 1 policy mismatch*

```
5 01/16/2005 17:15:34.280 SEV=4 IKE/48 RPT=1 192.1.1.2
Error processing payload: Payload ID: 1

6 01/16/2005 17:15:44.280 SEV=4 IKE/48 RPT=2 192.1.1.2
Error processing payload: Payload ID: 1

7 01/16/2005 17:15:54.280 SEV=4 IKE/48 RPT=3 192.1.1.2
Error processing payload: Payload ID: 1

8 01/16/2005 17:16:04.280 SEV=4 IKE/48 RPT=4 192.1.1.2
Error processing payload: Payload ID: 1
```

Because the logging output in Example 11-2 didn't give me enough detailed information to troubleshoot the problem, I went to the **Configuration > System > Events > Classes** screen on the concentrator and added an event logging class, IKEDBG, and set the logging level to 9 for this event for the event log destination. I then tried to bring the IPsec session up again; this time, the events displayed are more verbose, as shown in Example 11-3. In this example, I can see the actual transforms being negotiated, such as event ID 6, which is the first proposal being negotiated. Event ID 47 states that no compatible proposals were found and thus the management connection attempt is being aborted (event ID 53).

Example 11-3 *Log of a Phase 1 Policy Mismatch with an Event Class*

```
2 01/16/2005 17:19:13.450 SEV=4 IKE/48 RPT=12 192.1.1.2
Error processing payload: Payload ID: 1


3 01/16/2005 17:19:43.670 SEV=8 IKEDBG/81 RPT=1 192.1.1.2
RECEIVED Message (msgid=0) with payloads :
HDR + SA (1) + NONE (0)
total length : 84


5 01/16/2005 17:19:43.670 SEV=9 IKEDBG/0 RPT=1 192.1.1.2
processing SA payload

6 01/16/2005 17:19:43.670 SEV=8 IKEDBG/79 RPT=1
Proposal # 1, Transform # 1, Type ISAKMP, Id IKE
Parsing received transform:
  Phase 1 failure against global IKE proposal # 1:
  Mismatched attr types for class DH Group:
    Rcv'd: Oakley Group 1
    Cfg'd: Oakley Group 2


11 01/16/2005 17:19:43.670 SEV=8 IKEDBG/79 RPT=2
  Phase 1 failure against global IKE proposal # 2:
  Mismatched attr types for class Encryption Alg:
    Rcv'd: DES-CBC
    Cfg'd: Triple-DES

←output omitted→

44 01/16/2005 17:19:43.670 SEV=8 IKEDBG/79 RPT=14
  Phase 1 failure against global IKE proposal # 14:
  Mismatched attr types for class DH Group:
    Rcv'd: Oakley Group 1
    Cfg'd: Oakley Group 2


47 01/16/2005 17:19:43.670 SEV=7 IKEDBG/0 RPT=2 192.1.1.2
All SA proposals found unacceptable

48 01/16/2005 17:19:43.670 SEV=4 IKE/48 RPT=13 192.1.1.2
Error processing payload: Payload ID: 1

49 01/16/2005 17:19:43.670 SEV=7 IKEDBG/65 RPT=1 192.1.1.2
IKE MM Responder FSM error history (struct &0x1ed3d4c)
<state>, <event>:
MM_DONE, EV_ERROR_CONT
MM_DONE, EV_ERROR
MM_START, EV_RCV_MSG
MM_START, EV_START_MM


53 01/16/2005 17:19:43.670 SEV=9 IKEDBG/0 RPT=3 192.1.1.2
IKE SA MM:801e4a41 terminating:
flags 0x01000002, refcnt 0, tuncnt 0

54 01/16/2005 17:19:43.670 SEV=9 IKEDBG/0 RPT=4
sending delete/delete with reason message
```

Authentication Problems

The following three sections will show three IPsec authentication troubleshooting examples. The first two will deal with device authentication issues with pre-shared keys and certificates, and the third will deal with user authentication for remote access sessions.

Device Authentication: Pre-Shared Keys

In this first example, the concentrator has an L2L session configured using pre-shared keys for authentication, where the pre-shared key is "cisco1"; however, the remote end is using "cisco" as the pre-shared key. Example 11-4 shows the information in the event log when the L2L session attempts to come up. This information doesn't tell me too much because it isn't in any context; but event 1 indicates an authentication problem.

Example 11-4 *Initial log of a Phase 1 group password mismatch*

```
1 01/16/2005 18:41:52.100 SEV=4 IKE/100 RPT=1 192.1.1.2
Group [192.1.1.2]
Received encrypted Oakley Main Mode packet with invalid payloads,
MsgId (0x00000000)

4 01/16/2005 18:42:02.640 SEV=5 IKE/194 RPT=6 192.1.1.2
Group [192.1.1.2]
Sending IKE Delete With Reason message: No Reason Provided.
```

I've changed the event log level for IKEDBG events to 1–9 and reattempted the session, with the results shown in Example 11-5 (I've omitted some of the output). The first event is the management connection attempt. Event 4 is a mismatch in an IKE proposal, but event 28 shows that a match in the proposal list eventually was found and a management connection is being built (event 30). Event 32 is the start of the Diffie-Hellman key exchange. The events with "VID," or "Vendor ID" in them deal with authentication. Based on this information, since the first two steps have successfully completed during Phase 1, the culprit is authentication.

Example 11-5 *Log of a Phase 1 Pre-shared Key Mismatch with an Event Class*

```
01/16/2005 18:57:01.080 SEV=8 IKEDBG/81 RPT=119 192.1.1.2
RECEIVED Message (msgid=0) with payloads :
HDR + SA (1) + NONE (0)
total length : 84

3 01/16/2005 18:57:01.080 SEV=9 IKEDBG/0 RPT=287 192.1.1.2
processing SA payload

4 01/16/2005 18:57:01.080 SEV=8 IKEDBG/79 RPT=823
Proposal # 1, Transform # 1, Type ISAKMP, Id IKE
Parsing received transform:
  Phase 1 failure against global IKE proposal # 1:
  Mismatched attr types for class DH Group:
    Rcv'd: Oakley Group 1
```

continues

Example 11-5 *Log of a Phase 1 Pre-shared Key Mismatch with an Event Class (Continued)*

```
     Cfg'd: Oakley Group 2

←output omitted→

28 01/16/2005 18:57:01.080 SEV=7 IKEDBG/28 RPT=17 192.1.1.2
IKE SA Proposal # 1, Transform # 1 acceptable
Matches global IKE entry # 4 Proposal (IKE-DES-MD5)

30 01/16/2005 18:57:01.080 SEV=9 IKEDBG/0 RPT=290 192.1.1.2
constructing ISA_SA for isakmp

31 01/16/2005 18:57:01.080 SEV=9 IKEDBG/46 RPT=73 192.1.1.2
constructing Fragmentation VID + extended capabilities payload

32 01/16/2005 18:57:01.150 SEV=8 IKEDBG/81 RPT=120 192.1.1.2
SENDING Message (msgid=0) with payloads :
HDR + SA (1) + VENDOR (13)
total length : 108

34 01/16/2005 18:57:02.630 SEV=8 IKEDBG/81 RPT=121 192.1.1.2
RECEIVED Message (msgid=0) with payloads :
HDR + KE (4) + NONCE (10) + VENDOR (13) + NONE (0)
total length : 172

36 01/16/2005 18:57:02.630 SEV=8 IKEDBG/81 RPT=122 192.1.1.2
RECEIVED Message (msgid=0) with payloads :
HDR + KE (4) + NONCE (10) + VENDOR (13) + NONE (0)
total length : 172

38 01/16/2005 18:57:02.630 SEV=9 IKEDBG/0 RPT=291 192.1.1.2
processing ke payload

39 01/16/2005 18:57:02.630 SEV=9 IKEDBG/0 RPT=292 192.1.1.2
processing ISA_KE

40 01/16/2005 18:57:02.630 SEV=9 IKEDBG/1 RPT=63 192.1.1.2
processing nonce payload

41 01/16/2005 18:57:02.630 SEV=9 IKEDBG/47 RPT=41 192.1.1.2
processing VID payload

←output omitted→

50 01/16/2005 18:57:02.700 SEV=9 IKEDBG/46 RPT=76 192.1.1.2
constructing VID payload

51 01/16/2005 18:57:02.700 SEV=9 IKEDBG/48 RPT=34 192.1.1.2
Send Altiga GW VID

52 01/16/2005 18:57:02.700 SEV=9 IKEDBG/0 RPT=294 192.1.1.2
Generating keys for Responder...
```

Example 11-5 *Log of a Phase 1 Pre-shared Key Mismatch with an Event Class (Continued)*

```
53 01/16/2005 18:57:02.710 SEV=8 IKEDBG/81 RPT=123 192.1.1.2
SENDING Message (msgid=0) with payloads :
HDR + KE (4) + NONCE (10)
total length : 224

55 01/16/2005 18:57:04.610 SEV=4 IKE/100 RPT=15 192.1.1.2
Group [192.1.1.2]
Received encrypted Oakley Main Mode packet with invalid payloads,
MsgId (0x00000000)

58 01/16/2005 18:57:04.610 SEV=8 IKEDBG/81 RPT=124 192.1.1.2
SENDING Message (msgid=0) with payloads :
HDR + NOTIFY (11) + NONE (0)
total length : 80

60 01/16/2005 18:57:15.170 SEV=7 IKEDBG/65 RPT=23 192.1.1.2
Group [192.1.1.2]
IKE MM Responder FSM error history (struct &0x1f02ee4)
<state>, <event>:
MM_DONE, EV_ERROR_CONT
MM_DONE, EV_ERROR
MM_WAIT_MSG5, EV_RESEND_MSG
MM_WAIT_MSG5, NullEvent

65 01/16/2005 18:57:15.170 SEV=9 IKEDBG/0 RPT=295 192.1.1.2
Group [192.1.1.2]
IKE SA MM:feaddc43 terminating:
flags 0x01000002, refcnt 0, tuncnt 0

←output omitted→

70 01/16/2005 18:57:15.180 SEV=5 IKE/194 RPT=22 192.1.1.2
Group [192.1.1.2]
Sending IKE Delete With Reason message: No Reason Provided.
←output omitted→
```

NOTE   Cisco devices use ISAKMP/IKE main mode during Phase 1 with one exception: Cisco VPN software clients using pre-shared keys use aggressive mode.

Device Authentication: Certificates

In this troubleshooting example, I'll take a look at an L2L session using certificates for device authentication. As you can see in Example 11-6, event 1 shows that there is problem with validating a date on a certificate (it is expired). Event 4 tells me that the peer's certificate (192.1.1.2) has expired, not the CA's.

Example 11-6 *Certificate authentication problem*

```
1 01/15/2005 19:40:44.790 SEV=3 CERT/9 RPT=1
Certificate (serial number: 11C5870A000100000007) failed validation
Reason: Invalid certificate date

3 01/15/2005 19:40:44.790 SEV=4 CERT/3 RPT=1
Certificate is invalid: X509CertExpiredErr

4 01/15/2005 19:40:44.790 SEV=4 IKE/80 RPT=1 192.1.1.2
Group [192.1.1.2]
Certificate validation failure, X509CertExpiredErr
(CN=<unavailable>, SN=11C5870A000100000007)

7 01/15/2005 19:40:44.800 SEV=5 IKE/194 RPT=25 192.1.1.2
Group [192.1.1.2]
Sending IKE Delete With Reason message: User or Root Certificate has Expired.
```

One nice thing about this troubleshooting example is that I didn't have to modify any event classes to discover the problem that was preventing the L2L session from coming up.

User Authentication: XAUTH

In this last section on troubleshooting authentication problems, I'll switch types of devices to remote access and discuss how to pinpoint problems related to IPsec users and XAUTH authentication, where the users are defined locally on the concentrator. Example 11-7 shows two examples of XAUTH failures when using the normal event logging level for the concentrator's log file. In this example, event 1 shows a connection from 192.1.1.77. Event 3 shows that the user used a username of "Richard," but put in the wrong password. This user then tried a different user name, "James," in event 5, but as you can see from the second line of this event, the username "James" doesn't exist and therefore authentication of the account was rejected.

Example 11-7 *ISAKMP/IKE Phase 1 XAUTH authentication problems*

```
1 01/15/2005 19:47:50.460 SEV=5 IKEDBG/64 RPT=25 192.1.1.77
IKE Peer included IKE fragmentation capability flags:
Main Mode:       True
Aggressive Mode: False
←output omitted→

3 01/15/2005 19:47:56.600 SEV=3 AUTH/5 RPT=2 192.1.1.77
Authentication rejected: Reason = Invalid password
handle = 34, server = Internal, user = Richard, domain = <not specified>
←output omitted→

5 01/15/2005 19:48:09.750 SEV=3 AUTH/5 RPT=3 192.1.1.77
Authentication rejected: Reason = User was not found
handle = 35, server = Internal, user = James, domain = <not specified>
```

NOTE   If your users are defined on an external authentication server instead of on the concentrator, you might not see the same level of logging as that shown in Example 11-7. If the server was an AAA server, you should be able to view accounting records to pinpoint the actual problem; this assumes you've defined an AAA accounting server globally or for the group. This was discussed in Chapter 7, "Concentrator Remote Access Connections with IPsec."

ISAKMP/IKE Phase 2 Problems

This section will examine two of the more common problems that cause ISAKMP/IKE Phase 2 to fail: mismatched Phase 2 transform sets and mismatches on the traffic that should be protected. In both cases I'll use an L2L session to illustrate the problem.

Mismatched Transform Sets

In this L2L example, a router has one transform defined for the ISAKMP/IKE Phase 2 data connection and the concentrator has a different one defined. Example 11-8 shows the results of this mismatch. In this example, event 1 displays that there is a mismatch in the proposals: this is repeated in event 14 during Phase 2. Since no matching transform is found, event 15 indicates and error and 16 that the data connections are not built, along with another description of the problem ("Proposal Mismatch").

Example 11-8 *ISAKMP/IKE Phase 2 transform set problems*

```
1 01/15/2005 20:01:42.580 SEV=3 IKE/134 RPT=2 192.1.1.2
Group [192.1.1.2]
Mismatch: Configured LAN-to-LAN proposal differs from negotiated proposal.
Verify local and remote LAN-to-LAN connection lists.

4 01/15/2005 20:01:42.580 SEV=4 IKE/119 RPT=9 192.1.1.2
Group [192.1.1.2]
PHASE 1 COMPLETED

5 01/15/2005 20:01:42.580 SEV=4 AUTH/22 RPT=9
User [192.1.1.2] Group [192.1.1.2] connected, Session Type: IPsec/LAN-to-LAN

6 01/15/2005 20:01:42.580 SEV=4 AUTH/84 RPT=7
LAN-to-LAN tunnel to headend device 192.1.1.2 connected

7 01/15/2005 20:01:42.620 SEV=5 IKE/35 RPT=6 192.1.1.2
Group [192.1.1.2]
Received remote IP Proxy Subnet data in ID Payload:
 Address 193.1.1.0, Mask 255.255.255.0, Protocol 0, Port 0

10 01/15/2005 20:01:42.620 SEV=5 IKE/34 RPT=8 192.1.1.2
Group [192.1.1.2]
Received local IP Proxy Subnet data in ID Payload:
 Address 192.168.101.0, Mask 255.255.255.0, Protocol 0, Port 0
```

continues

Example 11-8 *ISAKMP/IKE Phase 2 transform set problems (Continued)*

```
13 01/15/2005 20:01:42.620 SEV=5 IKE/66 RPT=8 192.1.1.2
Group [192.1.1.2]
IKE Remote Peer configured for SA: L2L: Remote Site

14 01/15/2005 20:01:42.620 SEV=4 IKE/0 RPT=43 192.1.1.2
Group [192.1.1.2]
All IPsec SA proposals found unacceptable!

15 01/15/2005 20:01:42.620 SEV=4 IKEDBG/97 RPT=1 192.1.1.2
Group [192.1.1.2]
QM FSM error (P2 struct &0x1dbb3c4, mess id 0xc4ae568f)!

16 01/15/2005 20:01:42.630 SEV=5 IKE/194 RPT=28 192.1.1.2
Group [192.1.1.2]
Sending IKE Delete With Reason message: Phase-2 Proposal Mismatch.
←output omitted→
```

Mismatched Protected Traffic

In this last troubleshooting example, I'll show you what can happen if the two sides of an L2L session don't mirror the traffic that is supposed to be protected. For example, I want to protect traffic between two networks: 192.168.101.0/24 (at SiteA) and 194.1.1.0/24 (at SiteB). Therefore, SiteA specifies 192.168.101.0/24 > 194.1.1.0/24, and SiteB needs to specify 194.1.1.0/24 > 192.168.101.0/24. If this is not configured correctly, the ISAKMP/IKE Phase 2 connection will fail. Example 11-9 illustrates this particular problem. Event 1 summarizes the problem by specifying that there is something different between the two peers: in this case, the concentrator's event log says that there is a mismatch in the connection lists (the traffic to be protected by the L2L *connection*). Event 13 states that the remote end (SiteB) wants to protect traffic from 193.1.1.0/24; however, as I illustrated earlier, SiteA is expecting to protect traffic to 194.1.1.0/24. Therefore the connection fails and the tunnel is terminated.

Example 11-9 *ISAKMP/IKE Phase 2 protected traffic mismatch*

```
1 01/15/2005 20:11:54.340 SEV=3 IKE/134 RPT=5 192.1.1.2
Group [192.1.1.2]
Mismatch: Configured LAN-to-LAN proposal differs from negotiated proposal.
Verify local and remote LAN-to-LAN connection lists.

4 01/15/2005 20:11:54.340 SEV=4 IKE/119 RPT=12 192.1.1.2
Group [192.1.1.2]
PHASE 1 COMPLETED

5 01/15/2005 20:11:54.340 SEV=4 AUTH/22 RPT=12
User [192.1.1.2] Group [192.1.1.2] connected, Session Type: IPsec/LAN-to-LAN

6 01/15/2005 20:11:54.340 SEV=4 AUTH/84 RPT=10
LAN-to-LAN tunnel to headend device 192.1.1.2 connected
7 01/15/2005 20:11:54.390 SEV=5 IKE/35 RPT=9 192.1.1.2
```

Example 11-9 *ISAKMP/IKE Phase 2 protected traffic mismatch (Continued)*

```
Group [192.1.1.2]
Received remote IP Proxy Subnet data in ID Payload:
 Address 193.1.1.0, Mask 255.255.255.0, Protocol 0, Port 0

10 01/15/2005 20:11:54.390 SEV=5 IKE/34 RPT=11 192.1.1.2
Group [192.1.1.2]
Received local IP Proxy Subnet data in ID Payload:
 Address 192.168.101.0, Mask 255.255.255.0, Protocol 0, Port 0

13 01/15/2005 20:11:54.390 SEV=4 IKE/61 RPT=1 192.1.1.2
Group [192.1.1.2]
Tunnel rejected: Policy not found for Src:193.1.1.0, Dst: 192.168.101.0!

15 01/15/2005 20:11:54.390 SEV=4 IKEDBG/97 RPT=3 192.1.1.2
Group [192.1.1.2]
QM FSM error (P2 struct &0x1dc3cc4, mess id 0x257b52a0)!

16 01/15/2005 20:11:54.390 SEV=5 IKE/194 RPT=31 192.1.1.2
Group [192.1.1.2]
Sending IKE Delete With Reason message: No Reason Provided.

17 01/15/2005 20:11:54.400 SEV=4 AUTH/23 RPT=10 192.1.1.2
User [192.1.1.2] Group [192.1.1.2] disconnected: duration: 0:00:00

18 01/15/2005 20:11:54.400 SEV=4 AUTH/85 RPT=10
LAN-to-LAN tunnel to headend device 192.1.1.2 disconnected: duration: 0:00:00
```

Summary

This chapter showed you the basics of using the concentrator's features to monitor and troubleshoot problems. There are four main tools you'll commonly use to monitor sessions and troubleshoot problems:

- Use the **Administration > Administer Sessions** or **Monitoring > Sessions** screen to monitor VPN and administrative sessions terminated on the concentrator.
- Use the Live Event Log to get a quick overview of a problem.
- Use the Filterable Event Log to get more details about a problem.
- If the Filterable Event Log doesn't illuminate enough information to troubleshoot a problem, configure an Event Class with a higher logging level and then use the Filterable Event Log again to pinpoint the problem.

Next up is Part III, "Clients," where I show you how to use various software and hardware clients for remote access sessions. I'll also go into more depth on troubleshooting various components of VPN sessions with remote access users.

Clients

CHAPTER 12

Cisco VPN Software Client

Part II of this book discussed how to terminate VPN sessions—L2L and remote access—on Cisco VPN 3000 concentrators. In Part III, I'll discuss three remote access clients commonly used in Cisco shops: Cisco VPN Client software, Microsoft Windows' VPN client, and Cisco VPN 3002 hardware client. In Chapter 18, "Router Remote Access Connections," I'll discuss how to use a low-end Cisco router as a client and in Chapter 22, "PIX and ASA Remote Access Connections," I'll discuss how to use a PIX 501 or 506E as one.

To start off Part III, in this chapter I'll discuss the use of the Cisco VPN Client software for Windows to terminate IPsec remote access sessions, sometimes referred to as the "Unity" client. Cisco has moved away from using the term "Unity" to describe the client, though, because it conflicts with a product in their voice product line. Even though the software client can be used to terminate IPsec VPNs on any of the Cisco Easy VPN Server products—concentrator, router, PIX, or ASA—I'll focus on terminating client sessions on the VPN 3000 concentrators. The chapter is broken into six parts:

- An introduction to the software client, including installation of the client and its files and programs
- The GUI interface of the client
- IPsec remote access sessions to an Easy VPN Server, including the use of pre-shared keys and digital certificates
- Additional client components, including Application Launcher, Windows login, auto-initiation, and the stateful firewall features
- Software updates of the client
- Troubleshooting problems with the client's included tools

Cisco VPN Client Overview

The Cisco VPN Client is a VPN remote access client that runs on Microsoft Windows PCs, Linux PCs (Intel-based), Macintoshes (Mac OS X), and Sun UltraSPARC workstations (Solaris). Of the four, the Microsoft and Macintosh clients support a graphical user interface (GUI); the other two use a command-line interface (CLI). The Cisco VPN Client uses IPsec to establish a remote access VPN session to an Easy VPN Server using Cisco Easy VPN technology. Supported servers include the VPN 3000 series concentrators,

IOS-based routers, and PIX and ASA security appliances. Other VPN connection methods, such as PPTP, L2TP/IPsec, and WebVPN, are not supported with Cisco VPN Client software. The following sections will discuss the features and installation of the VPN Client for Microsoft Windows.

NOTE	There are two basic versions of the Cisco software client for Windows: Versions 3.x and 4.x. The GUI interfaces between the two are different; however, how you perform tasks within each client is very similar. Therefore, this book will focus on using the 4.6 Windows client and I'll point out differences between the 3.x and 4.x clients as I proceed through the chapter. Because of space constraints, I will not be covering the non-Windows versions of the client. Also, Cisco used to offer two other clients, but these have been discontinued: the Cisco Secure VPN Client (discontinued in 2003) and the Cisco VPN 5000 Client (discontinued in 2002).

Cisco VPN Client Features

The Cisco VPN Client for Windows (Version 4.6) supports Windows 98, Windows NT 4.0, Windows ME, Windows 2000, and Windows XP platforms. It can be used to establish a secure IPsec session using either a dialup connection via PPP, a wireless connection, or even a LAN-based connection, such as Ethernet. Because the software implements client features, the VPN Client can have only one session active at a time.

There are many, many features that the VPN Client provides; some are based on open standards and some are proprietary to Cisco. For IPsec, it supports both main and aggressive modes for ISAKMP/IKE Phase 1; MD5 and SHA-1 HMAC functions; pre-shared keys, mutual group authentication, digital certificates, and XAUTH user authentication; DH group 1, 2, and 5 keys; and DES, 3DES, AES-128, and AES-256 (AES is new in version 3.6) encryption. To list all of the features would take about a dozen or so pages; therefore, I'll briefly cover some of the VPN Client's more important features in Table 12-1. More information on the Cisco VPN Client can be found at http://www.cisco.com/en/US/products/sw/secursw/ps2308/tsd_products_support_series_home.html.

Table 12-1   *Cisco VPN Client features*

Feature	Version	Description
Application Launcher	3.0	Launches an application when establishing an IPsec session to an Easy VPN Server
Auto-Initiation	3.6	Automatically initiates an IPsec session during bootup of the PC or when an IPsec session is dropped
Automatic Dialup Connection	3.0	Automatically dials an ISP or access server using Microsoft's or a third party's dialup software to establish an IPsec session

Table 12-1 *Cisco VPN Client features (Continued)*

Feature	Version	Description
Automatic Start Before Login and Automatic Disconnect	3.0	Allows the VPN Client to bring up an IPsec session first before the user logs in to the Windows domain; likewise, allows the VPN session to terminate if the user logs out of the domain
Automatic Updates	4.6	Allows Windows 2000 and XP clients to download and install a software update automatically; versions earlier than this only receive a notification, and then the user must manually download and install the VPN Client software update
Automatic VPN Client Configuration	3.0	Imports a pre-configured connection profile(s) during the software client installation
Browser Proxy Configuration	4.6	Allows VPN Clients with Internet Explorer installed to obtain their proxy settings automatically from an Easy VPN Server such as a concentrator
Co-Existence	4.0	Allows multiple third-party VPN software clients from Checkpoint, Intel, Microsoft, Nortel, and others to be installed along with the Cisco VPN client (only supported on Windows 2000 and XP platforms); however, only one VPN session can be up at a time
Compression	3.0	Can use LZS compression for dialup users to increase throughput
Dynamic DNS	3.6	Sends a VPN Client PC's hostname and DHCP address to a DNS server for dynamic DNS updates
Event Logging	3.0	Collects events to assist in troubleshooting
Firewall Integration	3.1	Allows the client to integrate with software-based firewall solutions such as Cisco Security Agent, Black Ice, Sygate, and others; the VPN Client comes with an integrated firewall from Zone Labs, which is a DLL program that provides a simple stateful firewall function. Please note that Cisco has enhanced this feature as software updates were introduced (like the Cisco Integrated Client, or CIC, firewall being introduced in 3.5, allowing firewall access control lists to be pushed by the concentrator to the client's firewall in 3.5, or the support for Sygate's firewalls in 4.0).
IPsec over TCP	3.5	Tunnels packets using TCP as a wrapper to work with firewall devices
IPsec over UDP	3.0	Tunnels packets using UDP as a wrapper to work with devices performing PAT

continues

Table 12-1   *Cisco VPN Client features (Continued)*

Feature	Version	Description
NAT-T	3.6	Tunnels packets using UDP as a wrapper to work with devices performing PAT
Peer Certificate DN Verification	3.6	Prevents the client from connecting to a VPN gateway that has an unexpected certificate: the VPN Client first verifies the domain name of the peer, which can be used to mitigate man-in-the-middle attacks
Set MTU Size	3.0	Automatically adjusts the MTU size for remote access VPNs during the installation of the client
Split DNS	3.6	Allows for DNS resolutions for corporate devices to be sent to corporate DNS servers and other resolutions to the ISP DNS servers
Split Tunneling	2.x	Allows packets to be sent protected to the Easy VPN Server and in clear text to other destinations
Virtual Adapter	4.0	Allows for better application compatibility support, especially for applications like H.323 that embed addressing information in IP payloads (remember that the client has two addresses: an internal, from the Easy VPN Server, and its NIC address)

Cisco VPN Client Installation

The following sections will discuss the installation of the Cisco VPN Client version 4.6 on a Windows platform. I'll discuss the requirements, the actual installation process, and how you, as an administrator, can affect the installation.

Before the Installation

To install the Windows client on your PC, you'll need to be running Windows 98 or later. Depending on the operating system, you'll need either 32MB of RAM for Windows 98, 64MB for Windows NT, ME, and 2000, or 128MB for Windows XP. You'll also need 50MB of disk space.

NOTE   The Cisco VPN 4.6 client doesn't support Windows 95 and doesn't officially support Windows Server products, including Windows NT, 2000, XP, .NET, and 2003 server platforms; however, I have successfully installed and used the client on the Windows NT and 2000 Server platforms—just don't call Cisco asking for help if you install it on a server platform and have a problem.

To download the Cisco VPN Client installation file from Cisco, you'll need a CCO account with the appropriate privileges. You can freely download the client if you've purchased a Cisco Easy VPN Server product, like a concentrator, a PIX or ASA security appliance, or an IOS-based router (with IPsec support). There are two Windows client installation files you can download from Cisco: one begins with "vpnclient-win-msi-" and the other with "vpnclient-win-is-." The MSI (Microsoft Windows Installer) file is for Windows 2000- and XP-only installations, whereas the IS (InstallShield) file is for all Windows platforms.

Before you begin the installation, you'll need to log in to your PC using an account with Administrator privileges. The client must be installed locally on the hardware; network drive installations are not supported. You also might have to have the correct service pack installed for the operating system; otherwise, the installation will give you an error message and abort the install. For example, the 4.6 client requires that Windows NT have SP6 installed.

You'll also need to gather information to build an IPsec session to an Easy VPN Server, such as the IP address of the Server and the IPsec group name and password for pre-shared keys or installing a certificate for certificate authentication.

CAUTION   Unless you're running the 4.6 or later client, you should first *uninstall* any old Cisco VPN Client before installing a new version. If you don't, the new version probably will become corrupted. If you see two lock icons in the Windows taskbar when establishing a VPN connection, then you know you didn't follow my advice and probably will experience strange problems with the software client. In this situation, try uninstalling both clients and then re-install the newer one; however, I have had problems in the past where I've had to contact TAC to assist me with this problem (when I didn't follow my own advice).

Installation Process

Once you have downloaded the necessary client file from the Cisco site, you'll need to uncompress it into a temporary directory. If you're using the InstallShield file to perform the installation, you'll need to run the "setup.exe" program to perform the installation; if you're using the MSI file, you'll need to run the "vpclient_en.exe" program. During the installation, you'll need to:

1   Accept the Cisco licensing agreement

2   Specify an installation directory; the default is "C:\Program Files\Cisco Systems\VPN Client"

3   Reboot your PC at the end

NOTE	If you'll be using hybrid or mutual authentication for your IPsec sessions, your PC will need a root certificate installed. Obtain the root certificate manually from the CA and call it "rootcert," with no extension. Place this file in the installation direction and it will be copied to the correct location on your hard drive. Optionally, you can create a pre-configured installation package that includes this; but the user still will need to install the root certificate. I discuss the installation of certificates in the "Creating Connections Using Certificates" section later in the chapter.

Installation Files

There are four files that can affect the installation process, and three that are used during normal operation of the VPN Client:

- **oem.ini**—This file is used to customize the installation.
- **vpnclient.ini**—This file is used to define global properties of the VPN Client.
- *xxx*.**pcf**—This file defines connection properties to a particular site.
- *xxx*.**png**—These files are used to display graphical information and replace the standard Cisco graphic images within the GUI.

For example, if you don't want users to be prompted for anything during the installation, and you don't want them to configure the connection profile to connect to the corporate site after the installation, you can pre-configure the above four files and put them in the same directory as the setup.exe or vpclient_en.exe file. During installation, the oem.ini file is used to control the installation process and the vpnclient.ini and any .pcf and .png files are copied into the client's installation directory. Then, when the user starts up the Cisco VPN Client software, the pre-configured vpnclient.ini, .pcf, and .png files will automatically be used. The following sections will briefly discuss some of the parameters used in these files.

oem.ini File

Example 12-1 shows a sample oem.ini file for the InstallShield process, which can be edited with a text editor. Here are some of the parameters and values found in this file:

- **Section names**—Information in brackets ("[ ]") are section names, which break up the configuration into readable areas; there are five sections: [Main], [Brand], [Default], [Dialer], and [SetMTU].
- **Comments**—Comments begin with a semicolon (";").
- **Parameters**—Parameters begin with a name, have an equal sign ("="), and then follow with the actual value.

In Example 12-1, each section and parameter are explained using comments.

Example 12-1 *Sample oem.ini File*

```
[Main]
; This section determines whether Kerberos uses TCP or UDP (UDP is
;     the default); this is only found in the InstallShield
;     installation process
DisableKerberosOverTCP = 1
;
[Brand]
; This section controls window titles during installation process
; and in the installation destination folder for the VPN Client
CompanyText = The Deal Group
ProductText = VPN Client
;     CompanyText defaults to "Cisco Systems" and ProductText
;     defaults to "VPN Client"
;
[Default]
; This section defines the default bitmaps and icons to use as well
;     as setting up a silent installation. The following parameters
;     are only found in the Install Shield installation
SilentMode = 1
;     When set to 1, specifies that the user is not prompted
;     for anything during the installation. A 0 indicates the user
;     will be prompted for information during the installation
InstallPath = C:\Program Files\Cisco Systems
;     Specifies where the VPN Client should be installed on
;     the hard drive
DefGroup = VPN Client
;     Specifies the name of the folder that will have the
;     client software installed
Reboot = 1
;     Specifies whether or not the PC should automatically
;     reboot itself at the end of the installation. Setting this
;     to 0 causes a reboot dialog window to appear. Setting it to
;     1, and if SilentMode is 1, causes the PC to automatically
;     reboot when the installation is done. Setting it to 2, and if
;     SilentMode is 2, causes the PC to not reboot upon finishing
;     the installation
;
;
[Dialer]
; This section specifies the bitmaps and icons used by the VPN
;     Client software
MainIcon = is_install.ico
;     Used by Install Shield only, it specifies shortcuts to the
;     vpngui.exe application
AppNameText = Deal Group Dialer
;     Specifies the name of the dialer application
AllowSBLLaunches = 0
;     Specifies if the client is allowed to launch a third-party
```

continues

Example 12-1 *Sample oem.ini File (Continued)*

```
;       application before logging in to Windows (1 is yes and 0 is no)
;
[Set MTU]
; This section defines settings for the Set MTU application, which
;       allows you to control the MTU settings for NICs
;
AppNameText = MTU Setter Application
;       Specifies the name of the Set MTU application
MainIcon = MtuIcon.ico
;       Specifies the icon file for the title bar for this application.
;       It can be 32x32 or 16x16 pixels with 256 colors.
AutoSetMtu = 1
;       Used by Install Shield only, it specifies the setup of the NIC
;       automatically with the value defined by SetMtuValue. Setting
;       this to 0 does do not do this, while setting it to 1 says to
;       do this
SetMtuValue = 1300
;       Used by Install Shield only, it specifies the default MTU size
;       for NICs for the Set MTU application. The default value is
;       1,300, but it can range from 64 to 1,500
VAMtu=1252
;       Allows the software to retrieve the value for the VA MTU from
;       the oem.ini file. It defaults to 1,500, but can range from 68
;       to 1,500. VA stands for Virtual Adapter and is specific to
;       Windows 2000 and XP platforms.
MTUAdjustmentOverride = 200
;       Used by InstallShield only on Windows NT-based systems, it
;       specifies the amount the NIC's MTU is reduced. This can range
;       from 0 to 1,300 bytes
```

TIP   Normally, the variables in the oem.ini file you would be setting if you didn't want the user
to play an active role in the installation are:

- SilentMode = 1 (to not prompt the user for any information)

- InstallPath = directory where you want the client installed

- DefGroup = folder where you want it installed

- Reboot = 1 (to automatically reboot at the end of the installation)

- AutoSetMTU = 1 (to automatically adjust the MTU size during the installation

- SetMtuValue = 1300 (use this value to prevent most instances of fragmentation)

- MTUAdjustmentOverride = 200 (use this value for NT-based systems)

NOTE	For MSI installations, the process is more complex. You need Microsoft ORCA installed on your administrator PC. ORCA is a Windows database table editor for creating and editing Windows Installer packages.
	Within ORCA, you must create an oem.mst transform and an oem.ini file with a text editor (the latter was previously described). The configuration of the oem.mst file is beyond the scope of this book. Because this configuration process is more complex than the InstallShield method, I prefer the use of the latter because I can update the installation files easily with a text editor. However, many large Microsoft customers use MSI because it allows for better rollback for system changes, especially those with SMS or Altiris software distribution systems.

vpnclient.ini File

The vpnclient.ini file contains the global profile settings for the VPN Client. If you have created one and placed it into the setup.exe or vpclient_en.exe directory, during installation, it is copied automatically to the software installation directory (where the vpngui.exe program is located).

Example 12-2 shows a sample vpnclient.ini file. The format is the same as the oem.ini, in that you have sections, variables, and comments. There are many more parameters than the ones you see in this example, but these are the most common (I've included additional comments to explain some of the parameters).

Example 12-2 *Sample vpnclient.ini File*

```
[Main]
RunAtLogon=1
;       Specifies that the VPN tunnel is brought up before users
;       log in to the Microsoft network. This only applies to Windows
;       NT 4.0, 2000, and XP platforms. See the "Windows Login
;       Properties" section later for configuration of this in the GUI
StatefulFirewall=0
;       The stateful firewall feature is disabled when set to 0. I
;       discuss this parameter in more depth in the "Stateful
;       Firewall" section later.
AutoInitiationEnable=0
AutoInitiationRetryInterval=1
AutoInitiationList=Corporate
;       Auto-initiation is used in wireless environments and
;       other environments to dynamically bring up a VPN tunnel.
;       This is discussed in more depth in the "Automatic
;       Initiation" section later.
EnableLog=1
;       Enables the logging functionality for debugging (this is
;       enabled by default)
ConnectOnOpen=0
;       Initiates a VPN session using the default user profile
;       (defined by the DefaultConnectionEntry parameter), when the
;       user starts the VPN Client software
```

continues

Example 12-2 *Sample vpnclient.ini File (Continued)*

```
[Corporate]
Network=192.168.101.0
Mask=255.255.255.0
Connect=1
ConnectionEntry=POD6
;      The above defines a connection profile to use with
;      auto-initiation, discussed in the 'Automatic Initiation'
;      section later.
[GUI]
; This section defines the properties in the GUI interface of the
;      client
MinimizeOnConnect=1
;      Minimizes the GUI to a system tray icon when a VPN session
;      is made. 1 means don't minimize and 0 minimize.
UseWindowSettings=1
;      Specifies to save the current window settings for the client.
ShowTooltips=0
ShowConnectHistory=1
AccessibilityOption=1
DefaultConnectionEntry=corporate
;      Specifies the default connection ".pcf" file to use to connect
;      to an Easy VPN Server. In this example, the file is
;      "corporate.pcf"
←output omitted→
; The following "Log" parameters set the default properties of the
;      client's Log application. I discuss this later in the "Log
;      Viewer" section.
LogWindowWidth=450
LogWindowHeight=500
LogWindowX=155
LogWindowY=5
[LOG.IKE]
LogLevel=1
[LOG.CM]
LogLevel=1
←output omitted→
```

TIP   One additional feature is that if you place a exclamation mark ("!") before a parameter, the user cannot change this parameter in the GUI interface of the client; the user can only view it. This feature is referred to as *GUI Locking*. This feature is also available for the connection profile files (.pcf files). Of course, a user could always use a text editor to manipulate the contents of these files. Also, I recommend that you create a template file from the client's GUI interface and then manipulate this with a text editor, because you'll be less likely to make an irreversible editing mistake using this approach.

.pcf Files

User profiles are files you create that specify the session properties to use to connect to an Easy VPN Server. Users will need one profile for each destination site they want to connect to. Each profile is stored in a separate file. The name of the file is the name of the session you give it in the GUI, like "corporate," and the file has a ".pcf" extension. These files are stored in a subdirectory called "Profiles" of the client installation.

TIP	You also can create the user profiles manually with a text editor, but I recommend that you create the files from the client's GUI. However, you might want to put a "!" before parameters, within the text file, that you don't want users to change from the GUI.

Example 12-3 shows a sample user profile called "corporate.pcf." Please note that the parameters found in a user profile will differ based on the user's platform, the type of device authentication, the type of access (LAN versus dialup), and other items. Also, if you want to distribute a .pcf file across multiple platforms, the file name cannot contain any spaces.

Example 12-3 *Sample User Profile*

```
[main]
Description=Corporate Office Connection
Host=192.1.1.1
;       This is the IP address of the Easy VPN Server
AuthType=1
;       This specifies the type of authentication: 1 is pre-shared
;       keys, 3 is RSA certificates, and 5 is mutual authentication
GroupName=Executives
;       This is the group name for pre-shared key authentication
;       that the user belongs to
GroupPwd=
enc_GroupPwd=7D34952605CE0882117EB8BF7649FFED7D50F43DDF0EEDFAE0A885A6
  F0103F0C49CC44D5B15A64A93508B81F17853FF17C79069DEDC062AD
;       This is the encrypted password for the group ("enc_GroupPWD")
EnableISPConnect=0
;       Connect to the Internet via a dialup connection (1 enables
;       this option). In this example I'm using my Ethernet NIC for
;       Internet connectivity
ISPConnectType=0
;       If set to 0, the ISPConnect parameter is used; if set to 1, the
;       ISPCommand parameter is used
ISPConnect=RoadRunner
;       This is the name of the Dial-Up Networking Phonebook Entry
;       in Microsoft Windows to use for dialup to the Internet
ISPPhonebook=C:\Documents and Settings\All Users\Application
Data\Microsoft\Network\Connections\Pbk\rasphone.pbk
ISPCommand=
Username=
;       This is the name of the user for remote access
SaveUserPassword=0
UserPassword=
enc_UserPassword=
;       This is the user's encrypted password (you should define a
;       policy for the group on the Easy VPN Server to disallow the
```

continues

Example 12-3 *Sample User Profile (Continued)*

```
;       user from saving their user password locally on their PC
NTDomain=
;       This is the name of the NT domain the user belongs to. It is
;       only necessary if the user's group authenticates via a Windows
;       NT Domain server
EnableBackup=0
BackupServer=
;       These two parameters enable a list of backup servers. Currently
;       it is disabled
EnableMSLogon=1
;       Specifies that the PC running Windows 98 or ME will log in to a
;       Microsoft Network
MSLogonType=0
;       If set to 0, the saved Windows login username and password are
;       used. If set to 1, the user is prompted for the Windows
;       username and password. This only applies to Windows 98 and ME.
EnableNat=1
;       If set to 1, transparent tunneling is used to handle IPsec
;       traffic through a PAT device
TunnelingMode=0
;       If EnableNAT is set to 1 and this is 0, then UDP encapsulation
;       is used. Otherwise, if this is set to 1, then TCP is used
TcpTunnelingPort=10000
;       This is the TCP port used for transparent tunneling with TCP
CertStore=0
CertName=
CertPath=
CertSubjectName=
CertSerialHash=00000000000000000000000000000000
SendCertChain=0
VerifyCertDN=
;       The above parameters are used to specify certificate
;       information if the device authentication type is
;       certificates
PeerTimeout=90
;       With DPD, this is the amount of seconds the VPN Client will
;       wait for a DPD response from the gateway before declaring the
;       Server dead
EnableLocalLAN=0
;       This allows the user to access the local LAN if it is set to 1.
;       Otherwise, the user cannot access the local LAN segment while a
;       VPN session is up (the group must also be set up for split
;       tunneling to allow local LAN access)
DHGroup=2
;       This specifies the Diffie-Hellman group to use: 1, 2, or 5
EnableSplitDNS=0
;       If this is set to 1, then split DNS is used: the Easy VPN
;       Server will send the DNS server address to use, as well as the
;       domain names that will be resolved with it
←output omitted→
```

CAUTION	Because of security reasons, you should not include any security parameters like a clear-text pre-shared key for the group name, a username, or a clear-text user password in pre-configured .pcf files. These parameters should be pre-configured from the GUI, which, in turn, will encrypt them. Then use this pre-configured file to distribute for the installation process.

Image Files

There are many image files the VPN Client uses to display graphical information. These files are located in the "Resources" subdirectory of the installation. You can change any of them, but you must keep the same names. The one most often changed is called "splash_screen.png," which displays an image for 2–5 seconds when the client starts. The installed file shows a Cisco logo and copyright information; some versions also display the product name and the client version. You can replace this file with a company logo if you choose.

Cisco VPN Client Interface

The Cisco VPN Client for Windows supports two interfaces: CLI and GUI. This book will focus on the GUI interface of the 4.6 client. Once you have installed the client, go to **Start > Programs > Cisco VPN Software Client > VPN Client** to access the GUI. Sometimes the application is referred to as the "VPN Dialer," after the older 3.x application name.

Operating Modes

The VPN Client has two operating modes:

- Simple Mode, shown in Figure 12-1
- Advanced Mode, shown in Figure 12-2 (this is the default mode)

Figure 12-1 *VPN Client GUI: Simple Mode*

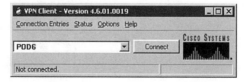

With either mode, at the top of the window in the window bar is the name of the application and version number: "VPN Client—Version 4.6.01.0019."

NOTE	You also can view the client type and version by right-clicking the VPN Client IPsec session icon (padlock) and choosing **About VPN Client**.

Figure 12-2 *VPN Client GUI: Advanced Mode*

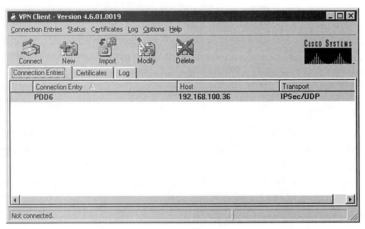

Below the window bar are the menu options. You'll notice that there is a difference between what the Simple and Advanced Modes display. Table 12-2 explains the menu options available for each mode. To toggle between the two modes, go to Options and choose **Advanced Mode** if you're currently in Simple Mode and **Simple Mode** if you're in Advanced Mode. For the most part, the remainder of this chapter will focus on the use of the Advanced Mode display.

Table 12-2 *VPN Client Mode Menu Options*

Menu Option	Simple Mode	Advanced Mode
Connection Entries	Connect to a VPN gateway and import a new session	Connect to a VPN gateway and create, add, modify, duplicate, delete, and import a session
Status	View statistics and notifications	View statistics and notifications and reset statistics
Certificates	Not available	View, import, export, enroll, verify, delete, and change password for certificates
Log	Not available	Disable logging, clear the log, change log settings, and view and search the log file
Options	Change to Advanced Mode and set the application preferences	Specify application to launch, change automatic initiation parameters, configure Window login properties, enable/disable the Cisco Integrated Client (CIC) firewall, change to Simple Mode, and set the application preferences
Help	View version information and pull up help	View version information and pull up help

TIP	Simple Mode is best if you don't want users to have access to many of the GUI options. To enforce the usage of Simple Mode by your users and to ensure that they don't use the GUI to change from Simple to Advanced Mode, be sure to set **AdvancedView=0** in the vpnclient.ini file and then precede it with an exclamation point (!)—this will gray out the option in the Options menu. Advanced Mode should be used if users must have the capability of modifying the Cisco VPN Client settings, such as adding or deleting sessions, turning on and off the stateful firewall, or using the logging function of the client.

Preferences

To change the application preferences for the VPN Client in either Simple or Advanced Mode, go to **Options > Preferences** in the menu bar. Here are the options you can enable or disable:

- **Save Window Settings**—When enabled, the application automatically will save any viewing changes you've made to the VPN Client Window upon exiting the application.

- **Hide Upon Connect**—When enabled, this minimizes the VPN Client window to the Windows taskbar when an IPsec session is established.

- **Enable Tool Tips**—When enabled, tool tips are displayed in Advanced Mode whenever you put your cursor over the toolbar buttons below the menu bar.

- **Enable Connect History Display**—When enabled, the VPN Client displays the session history of previous connections.

- **Enable Accessibility Options**—When enabled, the VPN Client doesn't display the VPN Client icon in the taskbar, but minimizes the VPN Client, enables sound and visual notifications for all dialogs and text edit boxes, and enables connecting and disconnecting of IPsec sessions (you'll need to restart the client to enable these features).

- **Enable Connect On Open**—When enabled, the VPN Client, upon starting, will connect automatically to the Easy VPN Server in the default user profile.

Advanced Mode Toolbar Buttons and Tabs

The toolbar icons displayed in the toolbar (below the menu selections in the menu bar) differ based on the tab you select. There are three GUI tabs:

- **Connection Entries**—Displays the connection entries (user profiles) that exist on the client. The buttons in the toolbar allow you to perform an action against a selected connection entry, or even create a new one. You can also use the Connection Entries option in the main menu to perform the same process. Figure 12-2 shows the VPN Client with the Connection Entries tab selected. Below the tab are the actual user profiles in the Profiles subdirectory of the VPN Client installation. In this example, there is only one entry, called "POD6." This entry connects to an Easy VPN Server with an IP address of 192.168.100.36 and uses IPsec/UDP (transparent) for its session.

- **Certificates**—Allows you to import, export, enroll, verify, view, and delete certificates using the toolbar buttons or the entries under the Certificates option in the main menu. When this tab is selected, the window below it changes to view all installed certificates.

- **Log**—Allows you to view the client's log file contents. When this tab is selected, the icons change in the toolbar to allow you to disable logging, clear the log file, change the log settings, or pull up the log in a separate window—you also can perform these functions from the Log menu option in the menu bar.

As you'll notice in Simple Mode (Figure 12-1), there are no tabs or toolbar buttons. The only thing you have access to below the menu bar is a drop-down selector of the VPN gateways you can connect to, and a **Connect** button to establish an IPsec session using the user profile that is currently being displayed).

NOTE   In the 3.x client, the three tabs don't exist in one GUI interface. Instead, they are three separate programs: VPN Dialer (Connection Entries tab in the 4.x client), Certificate Manager (Certificates tab), and the Log Viewer (Log tab). The 4.x client software combines all of these applications in one common GUI, making it easier to interface with the Cisco software.

IPsec Connections

This section will discuss how to connect to an Easy VPN Server using pre-shared keys and certificates for device authentication via Advanced Mode. As you go through this part of the chapter, note that you can connect your Cisco client to a VPN 3000 concentrator running at least Version 3.0, a PIX running 6.2.2(122) or 6.3(1), an ASA running 7.0, or an IOS router running 12.2(8)T with IPsec. For a 4.6 client, the corresponding concentrator code is 4.1.6, but 3.0 is the minimal version required on a concentrator—just realize that you'll be missing out on a lot of features using a concentrator with an older version of code than a client and vice versa—the same is true of a PIX, ASA, or router as an Easy VPN Server.

Creating Connections using Pre-Shared Keys

To create a new connection on your VPN Client, you can either:

- Click the **Connection Entries** tab and then click the **New** button in the toolbar.
- From the main menu, choose **Connection Entries > New**.

When you perform one of the two above processes, you are shown the screen in Figure 12-3. At the top of the screen you need to name the connection profile in the *Connection Entry* text box; this name must be compatible with the file-naming conventions used on your PC. In Figure 12-3, I called the profile "Corporate Office Connection." In the *Description* text box, you can enter an optional description. Below this is the *Host* text box, where you must enter the IP address of the Easy VPN Server the client will be connecting to. The next sections will discuss the four configuration tabs when adding a connection: **Authentication**, **Transport**, **Backup Servers**, and **Dial-Up**.

Figure 12-3 *Adding a Connection: Pre-shared Keys in the Authentication Tab*

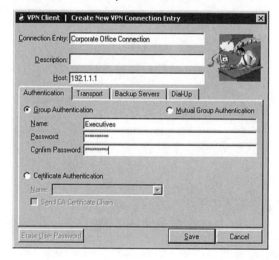

Authentication Tab

If you'll be using pre-shared keys to perform device authentication during ISAKMP/IKE Phase 1, then in the Authentication tab, you'll need to click the *Group Authentication* radio button and then enter the name of the group the user belongs to, and the pre-shared key (password) twice for verification. This information needs to match what is configured on the Easy VPN Server. In Figure 12-3, the group name I configured was "Executives." If you don't need to configure anything else in the other tabs, you can click the **Save** button to save the profile and take you back to the main GUI.

Transport Tab

If you click the **Transport** tab, you are shown the window in Figure 12-4. The top part remains the same as that in Figure 12-3; only the bottom part is different. Within the Transport tab, the top part allows you to enable transparent tunneling (this is necessary if your IPsec session will be going through an address translation device performing PAT), the middle part allows you to set up local LAN access and Dead Peer Detection (DPD), and the bottom part is for login access for Windows 98 and ME clients.

Figure 12-4 *Adding a Connection: Transport tab*

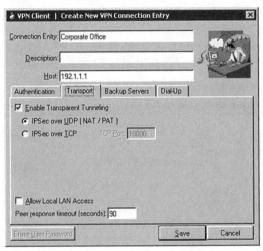

Transparent Tunneling

Transparent tunneling is enabled by default (the *Enable Transparent Tunneling* radio box is checked) and UDP is the default encapsulation method. This must be enabled on the Easy VPN Server end also. For a VPN 3000 concentrator, I discussed this in Chapter 7, "Concentrator Remote Access Connections with IPsec." If the *IPsec over UDP* radio button is selected here, either you must enable NAT-T or IPsec over UDP on the Easy VPN Server. On the VPN 3000 concentrator, you would do this as follows:

- **NAT-T**—Go to **Configuration > Tunneling and Security > IPsec > NAT Transparency** and select the *IPsec over NAT-T* check box.

- **IPsec over UDP**—Go to **Configuration > User Management > Groups**, select a group, click the **Modify** button, click the **Client Config** tab, and click the *IPsec over UDP* check box.

NAT-T and IPsec over UDP might not work with certain stateful firewalls; in that instance select the *IPsec over TCP* radio button in the client's Transport tab. You'll also need to enable this on an Easy VPN Server. On the VPN 3000 concentrator, you'll need to go to **Configuration > Tunneling and Security > IPsec > NAT Transparency** and select the *IPsec over TCP* check box; you can change the default port number from 10,000 to something else. If this has been changed on the concentrator, you'll need to match this on the client in the *TCP Port* text box.

<table>
<tr><td>**NOTE**</td><td>The client periodically sends keepalives across the data connection to ensure that it remains in the address translation table of the PAT device. On the concentrator, if both NAT-T and IPsec over UDP are enabled, NAT-T has precedence and will be used for the session. I've personally never liked how this has been designed on the VPN Client because it leads to confusion about which of the two connection methods the client is using.</td></tr>
</table>

Local LAN Access

The local LAN access feature allows you to gain access to the local LAN segment, in clear-text, when you are connected to the Easy VPN Server; however, this feature will work only if your PC has a single NIC and the Easy VPN Server has enabled this function: the split tunneling in the group configuration under the Client Config tab. You select "Allow the networks in list to bypass the tunnel" for the *Split Tunneling Policy* parameter and then for the *Split Tunneling Network List* pull-down parameter, you select "VPN Client Local LAN (Default)."

If the *Allow Local LAN Access* check box is unchecked, you will not be able to gain access to the local LAN. This might be important in situations where the local LAN devices are not in your control—for example, in an airport or hotel network. If this feature is enabled on the client and permitted on the Easy VPN Server, you'll be able to see the local LAN route or routes (up to 10 local routes) in the client's Routes table. These either are statically defined by the administrator or automatically detected by the client. This is discussed later in the "Client Connection Status" section.

Dead Peer Detection

DPD, sometimes referred to as "IKE keepalives," allows the two endpoints of an IPsec session to determine if their connected peers still are functioning. On the client side, it sends keepalives once every 90 seconds, by default. If a single response is not received within the value specified by the *Peer response timeout (seconds)* parameter, the client sends keepalives every five seconds. If it doesn't receive a reply, the client tears down the session; if the client has a list of backup Easy VPN Servers (backup servers), the client will try using this list to re-establish a session to the remote site. You can set the DPD timeout parameter from 30–480 seconds. You cannot disable this function. Therefore, it is important that this be enabled on your Easy VPN Servers.

Microsoft Network Access

For Windows 98 and Windows ME clients, you'll see an additional option at the bottom of the screen related to logging in to the Microsoft Network. The *Logon to Microsoft* parameter allows your PC to register to a private Microsoft network to browse and use network resources once the VPN Client has established an IPsec session. It is enabled by default, but you can disable it. When enabled, you can select one of two radio buttons:

- **Use default system logon credentials**—The default Windows username and password are used from the user's PC.
- **Prompt for network logon credentials**—The user will be prompted for a username and password.

Backup Servers Tab

The backup server feature allows you to define redundant Easy VPN Servers for a session, commonly called "backup servers." Click the **Backup Servers** tab when adding (or modifying) a session to specify your backup servers. This screen is shown in Figure 12-5. Click the *Enable Backup Server(s)* check box to enable this feature. Then click the **Add** button and enter an IP address or fully qualified domain name (FQDN) of a backup server. You can define up to 10 backup servers. The entry at the top of the list becomes the primary backup. To reorder your list, click the IP address/FQDN of the backup server in the window and then click the **Up** or **Down** arrow buttons on the right.

NOTE   If you've defined a backup server list on the Easy VPN Server, during IKE Mode Config in ISAKMP/IKE Phase 1, this list is pushed down to the client; the client will erase any existing list and replace it with the one received from the Easy VPN Server. I recommend using this approach because you can control and update the server list easily from a central location, as opposed to having the users update this list manually from the VPN Client GUI.

Figure 12-5 *Adding a Connection: Backup Servers Tab*

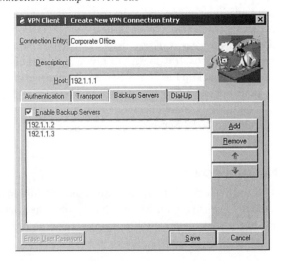

Dialup Tab

If you'll be using a dialup connection to access the Internet, you can have the VPN Client bring up the dialup connection automatically before initiating the IPsec session, as opposed to having the user manually bringing the dialup connection first. To define this process, click the **Dial-Up** tab when adding or modifying a connection entry. This window is shown in Figure 12-6. To enable the feature, click the *Connect to Internet via dial-up* check box. You have two dialup choices. In most instances you'll probably be using Microsoft's dialup software. If this is the case, click the *Microsoft Dial-Up Networking* radio button and use the drop-down selector to choose the *Phonebook Entry* (dialup profile) to use to connect to the ISP. This entry must have been defined previously on the PC.

If you're not using Microsoft's dialup software, but a third-party dialup program, you'll need to click the *Third party dial-up application* radio button, click the *Browse* button and find the dialup software, and in the *Application* parameter text box after the application, enter the name of the dialup profile to use. For example, it might look something like this:

```
C:\Program Files\Dialup Software\dialup.exe dialtheisp.profile
```

Figure 12-6 *Adding a Connection: Dial-Up tab*

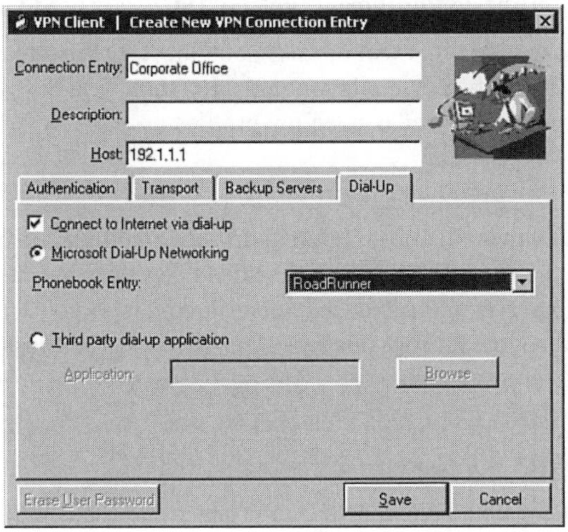

Completing the Connection

Once you've entered everything for your new connection, click the **Save** button at the bottom; this saves the connection profile as a ".pcf" file in the Profiles subdirectory of the client, using a prefix of the name given to the connection in the *Connection Entry* parameter. For example, the connection created in Figure 12-6 would have a name of "Corporate Office.pcf."

Creating Connections Using Certificates

Your second option for device authentication is to use certificates. The VPN Client supports the following CA products:

- Baltimore Technologies' UniCERT product
- Entrust Technologies' Entrust PKI product
- Netscape
- Verisign
- Microsoft Certificate Services for Windows 2000 and 2003
- Cisco IOS Router

You'll need to obtain a certificate for the VPN Client software using one of the above CAs. You have two options for obtaining certificates (assuming you're using the Cisco Certificate Store on the user's PC):

- **File-based**—obtaining a certificate manually using an out-of-band method
- **Network-based**—obtaining a certificate dynamically using an in-band method; the Simple Certificate Enrollment Protocol (SCEP) is used with this method

The following two sections will discuss obtaining a certificate and then I'll discuss management of certificates. Following this, I'll show you how to use certificates for authentication of your IPsec connection profiles.

TIP   If you only need to authenticate internal devices and there are no third-party trust issues, I recommend the use of Microsoft's Certificate Services because it comes with Windows 2000 and 2003 Server and Advanced Server products. If you'll be using SCEP, you'll need to obtain the resource kit for your version of Windows and install it from there.

Manually Obtaining a Certificate

Using the manual approach, you'll need to generate a file containing the client's PKCS #10 information and send this, out-of-band, to the CA administrator. The CA administrator will generate an X.509v3 identity certificate and send this and the CA (root) certificate back. If an RA is used, the administrator also will send a separate certificate for each RA.

Generating the PKCS #10 Information

To generate the PKCS #10 information, you need to perform one of the two following processes within the VPN Client:

- Click the **Certificates** tab in the client GUI and then click the **Enroll** button.
- Click **Certificates** in the main menu and choose the **Enroll** option.

Either of the above two options performs the same function and you'll be taken to the screen shown in Figure 12-7. Click the *File* radio button and choose the file type by using the *File encoding* drop-down selector. Your two types can be either "Binary" or "Base-64." The CA administrator will tell you which type to use, but in most instances it will be Base-64, which stores information in an ASCII-encoding file format (binary encoding uses a base-2 binary encoding scheme, which cannot be displayed). Below this, enter the location and name of the file where the PKCS #10 information should be stored. In Figure 12-7, I stored this in the Certificates subdirectory of the client's installation, but you can put it wherever you like. You can configure a certificate password that is case-sensitive. This is used to verify someone's access to the certificate on the computer via the VPN Client software. Whenever you start up a VPN session to an Easy VPN Server that uses certificates for authentication, and a certificate password has been configured, the user must enter the password to use the certificate. Once you're done entering the information on this screen, click the **Next** button.

Figure 12-7 *Manual Enrollment: Specifying the File*

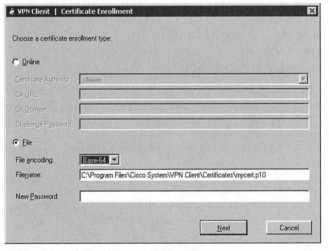

This is the PKCS #10 enrollment screen where you need to enter the identity information for the user's computer, which is shown in Figure 12-8. You can enter the same kind of information that I discussed in Chapter 7, "Concentrator Remote Access Connections with IPsec." You are required to enter the CN (Common Name). I highly recommend that you enter the user's group name in the Department or OU (Organizational Unit) field. In Figure 12-8, I put Richard's group, "Executives," in this field. By default, the Easy VPN Server uses this field to match the user to the corresponding group on the Server. If you don't specify the group name, you can use group matching on Cisco Easy VPN Servers to match the user's certificate to a particular group (again, I discussed this in Chapter 7 for the VPN 3000 concentrators). The other fields are optional.

Once you've entered your information, click the **Enroll** button. A window will pop up displaying the status of the creation of the PKCS #10 file. You'll need to send the PKCS #10 file to the CA administrator, preferably using an out-of-band method.

Figure 12-8 *Manual Enrollment: Specifying Identity Information*

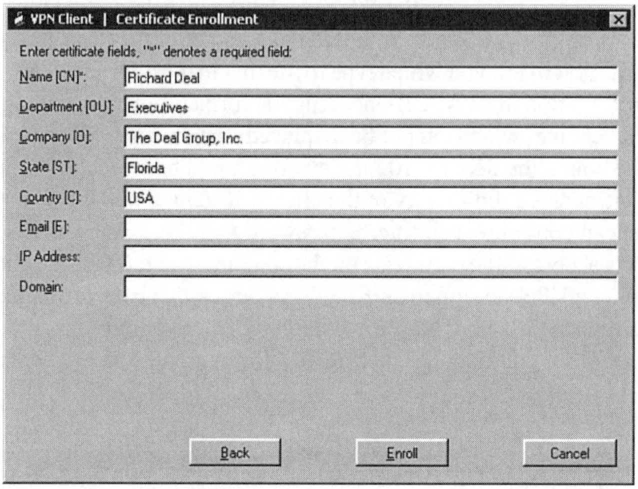

Importing the CA Certificate

The CA administrator will send you back two or more certificates. The first certificate you must install is the root, or CA's identity, certificate. To import the root certificate, use one of the following two processes:

- Click the **Certificates** tab in the client GUI and then click the **Import** button.
- Click **Certificates** in the main menu and choose **Import**.

The window in Figure 12-9 will pop up. You'll need to enter the directory path and file name where you've placed the CA's (root) certificate. Or, you can assign a password to protect your identity certificates from access via the VPN Client GUI. When done, click the **Import** button. A window should pop up saying that the certificate was installed successfully—click the **OK** button to return to the VPN Client GUI, where the Certificates tab is in the front. If you don't see the root certificate, from the main menu, choose **Certificates > Show CA/RA Certificates**, and you should now see the CA's certificate. In Figure 12-10, the "caserver" certificate is the root certificate.

Importing the Identity Certificate

After installing the root certificate, you'll perform the same process to install the client's personal identity certificate. Use one of the two options in the bullet points in the previous section to bring up the Import Certificate screen and then use the **Browse** button to find the identity certificate the CA administrator sent you, then click the **Import** button. You should then see both the CA and identity certificates in the Certificates tab on the VPN Client GUI, as shown in Figure 12-10: the "Richard Deal" certificate is the identity certificate.

Figure 12-9 *Manual Enrollment: Importing the Root Certificate*

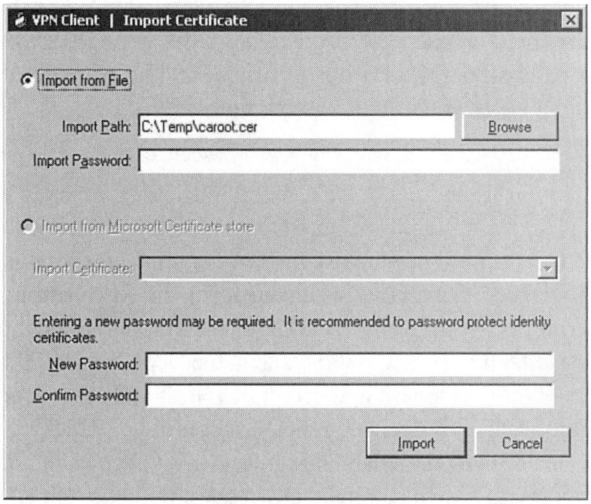

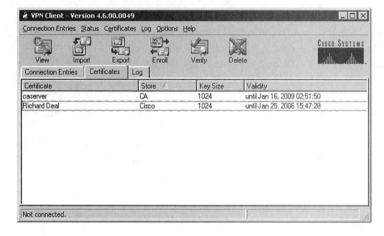

Figure 12-10 *Manual Enrollment: Seeing the Installed Certificates*

Using SCEP to Obtain a Certificate

Your other, and probably most common, option for obtaining a certificate for the VPN Client is to use SCEP. To begin, perform one of the two following processes:

- Click the **Certificates** tab in the client GUI and then click the **Enroll** button.
- Click **Certificates** in the main menu and choose **Enroll**.

Either of the above two options performs the same function and you'll be taken to the screen shown previously in Figure 12-7. Click the *Online* radio button. Make sure the *Cisco Authority* parameter says "<New>" if this is the first time you're registering with or connecting to the actual CA; or choose the name of an installed root certificate if you're obtaining another certificate from an already installed CA. For the *CA URL*, enter the full URL to access the CA. Each CA product has a different URL syntax, so you'll need to contact the CA administrator for this information. For example, if I was using Microsoft's CA product, the URL would look something like this:

```
http://IP_address_or_FQDN/certsrv/mscep/mscep.dll
```

Following this, you'll need to ask the CA administrator for the *CA Domain* parameter. If the CA has a challenge password configured to restrict the request of certificates via network enrollment (SCEP), you'll need to ask the CA administrator for this password and enter it in the *Challenge Password* text box. Once done, click the **Next** button, where you're taken to the screen shown previously in Figure 12-8. Here you'll need to enter your PKCS #10 information; make sure you enter the correct group name in the Department/OU field. Once done, click the **Enroll** button. If the enrollment is successful, you should see a window pop up with this message: "Certificate enrollment completed successfully." Clicking the **OK** button will take you to the screen shown previously in Figure 12-10. When using the network enrollment process, the VPN Client will automatically request both the root and identity certificates and install them, unlike the file-based approach where you have to do this in two separate steps.

NOTE   For additional security, some CAs are configured not to automatically grant certificates; instead, when you submit an identity certificate request to the CA, the CA administrator must log in to the CA and approve the certificate request manually—this is a common process when challenge passwords are not being used. You can determine if you have an outstanding certificate request by going to the Certificates tab in the VPN Client and looking for the CN of your certificate in the *Certificate* column and "Request" in the *Store* column. If this is the case, wait until the administrator generates you an identity certificate and then either choose **Certificates > Retry Certificate Enrollment** from the main menu options, or right-click the certificate and choose **Retry Certificate Enrollment**. The VPN Client will then attempt to download the root and identity certificates again.

Managing Certificates

You can perform many functions to manage your certificates on your VPN Client, such as view them, delete them, export them, change the password for a certificate, and so on. The following sections will briefly explore these options.

Viewing a Certificate

To view the details of a certificate, click the **Certificates** tab and then perform one of the four following processes:

- Click a certificate, go to the main menu, and choose **Certificates > View**.
- Right-click a certificate and choose **View**.

- Click a certificate and click the **View** button in the toolbar.

- Double-click a certificate.

An example identity certificate with a CN of "Richard Deal" can be seen in Figure 12-11, where the department name (used as the user's group) is "Executives." Notice that Richard's certificate is valid for one year starting on January 25, 2005.

Figure 12-11 *View a Certificate*

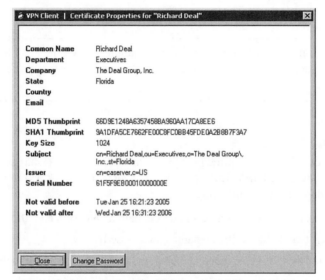

To verify if a certificate is still valid, use one of these options:

- Click the certificate name and from the main menu, go to **Certificates > Verify**.

- Click the certificate name and then click the **Verify** button in the toolbar.

- Right-click the certificate name and choose **Verify**.

A pop-up window will appear displaying the validity of the certificate. Possible messages are shown in Table 12-3.

Table 12-3   *Certificate Status*

Pop-Up Message	Explanation
Certificate is not valid yet	The beginning (start) time on the certificate has not yet been reached and the certificate is not valid yet (check the time on your computer; if it's incorrect, then fix it and re-verify the certificate).
Certificate has expired	The ending time of the certificate has been reached and the certificate is no longer valid.

continues

Table 12-3 *Certificate Status (Continued)*

Pop-Up Message	Explanation
Certificate signature is not valid	Either you don't have a root certificate installed or the root certificate has expired—in either case, download the current root certificate for the CA.
Certificate "CN on the certificate" is valid	The certificate is valid.

NOTE   Because time is important for verifying the validity of a certificate, I recommend the use of NTP to synchronize the time on your user's devices and the CA, preferably using your own time server.

Deleting a Certificate

If your certificate has expired (and you won't be renewing it), has been compromised, or you no longer need the certificate, you can delete it (and its keys) from your computer by performing one of the following:

- Click the certificate name and in the main menu go to **Certificates > Delete**.
- Right-click the certificate name and choose **Delete**.
- Click the certificate name and click the **Delete** button in the toolbar.

If the certificate has been password-protected, you'll need to supply the correct password before deleting it. Also, you'll be prompted to either click the **Delete** or **Do Not Delete** button (the latter is the default).

TIP   If you don't want your users to be playing around with any of the certificate options in the VPN Client GUI, I recommend setting the *AdvancedView* parameter in the vpnclient.ini file to "1" and then placing an exclamation point in front of this variable—this will limit the user to Simple Mode where the user doesn't have access to certificate functions.

Exporting a Certificate

If you need to move a certificate and public/private key combination to a different machine, or want to back these up, you can use the certificate export feature to copy these components. This can be accomplished by using one of the following processes:

- Clicking the certificate name and from the main menu choosing **Certificates > Export**.
- Clicking the certificate name and clicking the **Export** button in the toolbar.
- Right-clicking the certificate name and choosing **Export**.

You also can choose the option to export the entire certificate chain, which exports the identity, CA, and any RA certificates. Also, if the certificate is password-protected, you must supply the correct password. You'll be prompted for the location and name of the exported certificate, and for an optional password to protect the exported certificate.

CAUTION   If someone gains unauthorized access to a user's computer with certificates, they can use the export function to copy valid certificate information and keys to another system, and then use these to gain unauthorized access to your network. Therefore, I highly recommend you password-protect certificates. The next section discusses this.

Changing or Setting an Identity Certificate's Password

You can choose to assign a password to a certificate. If you perform this function, any type of access to the certificate requires the correctly configured password: for example, trying to export or delete a certificate, or bringing up an IPsec connection that uses a certificate. To assign a password to an identity certificate (or change it), perform one of the following processes:

- Click the certificate name and from the main menu, go to **Certificates > Change Certificate Password**.

- Right-click the certificate name and choose **Change Certificate Password**.

If the identity certificate already has a password, you must first enter the password assigned to the certificate. Once you've done this, enter the new password; you'll be prompted to confirm the new password. After this, you must always supply the new password when accessing the associated identity certificate.

Specifying Certificates in a Connection Profile

To add a new connection that will use certificates, you can either:

- Click the **Connection Entries** tab and then click the **New** icon in the toolbar.

- From the main menu, choose **Connection Entries > New**.

When you perform one of the two above processes, you'll see the screen shown previously in Figure 12-3. At the top of the screen you need to name the connection profile in the *Connection Entry* text box; this name must be compatible with the file-naming conventions used on your PC. In Figure 12-3, I called the profile "Corporate Office Connection." In the *Description* text box, you can enter an optional description. Below this is the *Host* text box, where you must enter the IP address of the Easy VPN Server the client will be connecting to.

There are two types of authentication that use certificates:

- **Certificate Authentication**—Uses certificates only for device authentication; this requires an ISAKMP/IKE Phase 1 policy that specifies RSA Digital Certificate

(XAUTH) on the VPN 3000 concentrators, PIX, ASAs and routers (both the Easy VPN Server and the client need identity certificates).

- **Mutual Group Authentication**—uses both certificates and pre-shared keys for device authentication; this requires an ISAKMP/IKE policy that specifies an RSA Digital Certificate (HYBRID) on the VPN3000 concentrators (only the Easy VPN Server needs an identity certificate, but pre-shared keys are used for additional security to authenticate the user's computer).

Click one of the two options in the screen for Figure 12-3 and then select the user's identity certificate name using the pull-down *Name* selector parameter. Click the **Save** button when done.

One optional parameter you can enable is *Send CA Certificate Chain*. By default, this is disabled; by enabling it, the VPN Client will send all CA certificates in the hierarchy of the domain, including the root certificate (these must initially be installed on the client), and the identity certificate to the authenticating Easy VPN Server. This allows the Server to trust the computers's identity certificate that has the same root certificate without the Server having to have the same subordinate CA certificate(s) installed. This option is necessary only if you have a hierarchical CA implementation and you won't be sure if the Server and the user's computer will be obtaining a certificate from the same CA in the hierarchy.

You also can modify an existing connection profile from using pre-shared keys to using certificates by doing one of the following:

- Clicking the connection name and from the main menu going to **Connection Entries > Modify**.
- Clicking the connection name and clicking the **Modify** button in the toolbar.
- Right-clicking the connection name and choosing **Modify**.

Any of these options will pull up the screen shown previously in Figure 12-3, with the Authentication tab in the forefront.

Other Connection Configuration Options

There are other connection configuration options you can configure for your VPN Client, such as setting the default connection profile; creating a shortcut startup icon on your desktop for a connection profile; modifying, deleting, and importing a connection entry; and erasing a saved password. I'll discuss some of these options in the next set of sections; the rest are easy to perform, either using the main menu options or the buttons in the Connection Entries tab.

Setting a Connection Profile as the Default

The first connection entry you add to your VPN Client becomes the default connection profile. It is highlighted using bold under the Connection Entries tab. Any connection you add after the first is displayed in a normal font (nonbold). If you select the *Enable connect on open* check box from the main menu's **Options > Preferences**, whenever you start up the VPN Client, the default connection profile is used to initiate a connection to the related Easy VPN Server.

To make a connection entry the default, either:

- Click the connection name in the Connection Entries tab and from the main menu, select **Connection Entries > Set as Default Connection Entry**.

- Right-click the connection name and select **Set as Default Connection Entry**.

Creating a Shortcut for a Connection Profile

You have the ability to create a shortcut icon on your desktop for a connection profile. By doing this, you can double-click the desktop shortcut icon, causing the VPN Client to initiate an IPsec session to the Easy VPN Server defined in the associated profile. To create a shortcut icon on your desktop for a connection profile, either:

- Click the connection name in the Connection Entries tab and from the main menu, select **Connection Entries > Create Shortcut**.

- Right-click the connection name in the Connection Entries tab and select **Create Shortcut**.

Connecting to the Easy VPN Server

Once you have created a connection profile and have configured your Easy VPN Server correctly, you're ready to establish an IPsec session from your desktop to the Server. This can be accomplished in several ways. It is different if the client is in Simple versus Advanced Mode:

- If you've created a shortcut of a connection profile on your desktop, just double-click the shortcut.

- If you've set the VPN Client preferences to enable the *Enable connect on open* parameter, the client will connect automatically using the default profile when the client starts up.

- If the client has been configured for Simple Mode, when you start the client, use the drop-down selector to choose the connection profile and click the **Connect** button (see Figure 12-1). By default, the default connection profile will be displayed for the connection entry.

- If the client has been configured for Advanced Mode, perform one of the following:

    — From the Connection Entries tab (see Figure 12-2), double-click the name of the connection profile.

- From the Connection Entries tab, click a connection name and from the main menu, select **Connection Entries > Connect**.

- From the Connection Entries tab, click a connection name and then click the **Connect** button in the toolbar.

- From the Connection Entries tab, right-click a connection name and choose **Connect**.

When using any method to establish an IPsec session to a Server, you'll see two windows pop up, as shown in Figure 12-12. The first is labeled "VPN Client I Connecting to 'Corporate Office'", and displays brief logging information of the events that are occurring. Assuming that there are no problems with the first three steps of ISAKMP/IKE Phase 1, the following will happen:

1 If you're using dialup to access the ISP, you'll be prompted for the username and password used for PPP authentication (this would occur before any ISAKMP/IKE Phase 1 tunnel attempt).

2 If you are using certificates, you'll be prompted for the password to access the certificate; even if no password has been configured, you'll still be prompted.

3 You'll need to enter the username and password to perform XAUTH authentication (this is the "VPN Client I User Authentication for 'Corporate Office'" window in Figure 12-12.

4 If the user authentication on the Easy VPN Server uses RADIUS, and the expiry authentication is enabled and your password has expired, you'll be prompted to enter and confirm a new password.

5 If the network administrator of the Easy VPN Server has configured a login banner for the group, a window will pop up on the client's desktop displaying the banner. Click the **Continue** button to proceed with the login process.

Enter the correct XAUTH username and password and click the **OK** button. The authentication information is passed to the Easy VPN Server and you'll see some more logging information appear in the "VPN Client I Connecting to 'Corporate Office'" window concerning the next steps in completing the connection. If you put in the wrong username and password, you'll be reprompted for these and a message will appear in the "VPN Client I Connecting to 'Corporate Office'" window concerning the problem, as follows:

- **Authentication failure**—You entered the wrong username and password combination.

- **Account disabled**—Your account has been disabled.

- **Error changing password**—You were prompted to change your password and did this incorrectly.

- **No dial-in permission**—You do not have the required privileges to establish a remote access session to the network.

- **Restricted login hours**—Your login hours are restricted (perhaps you cannot VPN into the network during certain times of the day) and you are denied access to the network.

If the connection is successful, the "VPN Client | Connecting to 'Corporate Office'" window will disappear.

Figure 12-12 *Connecting to a VPN Gateway*

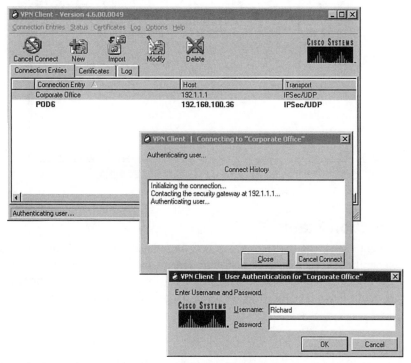

Depending on how you have the VPN Client set up, it might minimize automatically and appear as a yellow closed padlock icon in the Windows taskbar in the bottom right-hand corner of your screen. Otherwise, if you had the VPN Client open when making the connection and it was in Advanced Mode, it will remain open and you'll see the screen shown in Figure 12-13. As you can see in Figure 12-13, the connection profile "Corporate Office" has a yellow closed padlock to the left of it, indicating that there is an IPsec session to the associated Easy VPN Server.

In Figure 12-13, at the very bottom right-hand corner of the screen is a down-arrow button. Clicking this button will toggle the display of the statistics shown in the bottom taskbar of the VPN client. The statistics you can see are:

- Internal IP address assigned to the client
- The amount of time the client has been connected to the VPN gateway
- The number of bytes sent and received across the IPsec tunnel

If the network administrator of the Easy VPN Server created a login banner for the remote access group, you'll see a window pop up with the banner.

Figure 12-13 *Connected to a VPN Gateway*

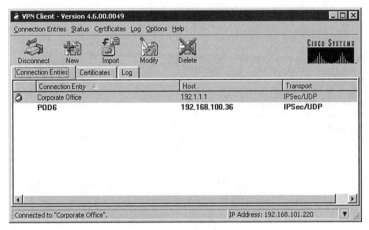

Client Connection Status

As mentioned in the last section, a yellow closed padlock icon will appear in the Windows taskbar (bottom right-hand corner of the screen) and in the Connection Entries table in the VPN Client GUI. Once a session is up, you can examine statistics for the session and view any notifications. The following two sections will discuss these processes.

Statistics

Once an IPsec session has been established to an Easy VPN Server, from your desktop you can pull up statistics about the session by performing either of the following:

- In the VPN Client GUI's main menu, go to **Status > Statistics**.

- In the Windows taskbar, right-click the yellow closed padlock icon and choose **Statistics**.

Using either method, the window shown in Figure 12-14 will pop up. There are three tabs at the top: Tunnel Details, Routing Information, and Firewall Information. The following two sections will discuss the first two tabs and the "Stateful Firewall" section later in the chapter will discuss the latter tab.

Tunnel Details Tab

When you open up the Statistics window, the Tunnel Details tab is in the foreground. You can view the following information here:

- **Address Information**—The IP address assigned to the client (192.168.101.220 in Figure 12-14) and the IP address of the Easy VPN Server (192.1.1.1).

- **Connection Information**—The connection profile used for the session ("Corporate Office") and the length of time the session has been up (1 minute and 29 seconds).

- **Bytes**—The number of bytes received (148,439) and sent (48,508) across the IPsec data connections.

- **Crypto**—The packet encryption algorithm (3DES) and hashing function (MD5) for the data connections.

- **Packets**—The number of packets encrypted (230), decrypted (167), discarded (92, because they didn't match the tunnel policy requirements), and bypassed (0, packets that were split-tunneled).

- **Transport**—The type of tunneling (transparent tunneling was enabled in this example, but NAT-T, which was enabled on the Easy VPN Server, determined that no address translation device was detected), if Local LAN access is allowed (no), and if compression has been enabled for the tunnel (no).

To reset the statistics for this screen, click the **Reset** button at the bottom—this only resets the statistics for this tab.

Figure 12-14 *Statistics Window: Tunnel Details*

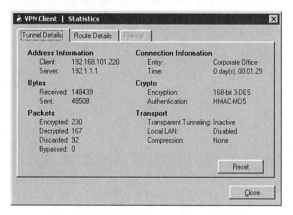

| TIP | If you're seeing packets being encrypted, but none decrypted, there is probably a routing problem at the Easy VPN Server end of the connection. It is easy to verify that you have this problem. Have the remote device at the central office ping the internal address of the VPN Client when it is connected. If this fails, you have a routing problem. Make sure that your central office devices have either static or dynamic routes to reach the Easy VPN Server and the internal addresses of the clients, and make sure that the Server is using RRI to advertise the routing information if you're using a corporate dynamic routing protocol. |

Routing Information Tab

To view the routing information for the client, in the Statistics window, click the **Route Details** tab, which is shown in Figure 12-15. The window is broken into two sections:

- **Local LAN Routes**—Displays the routes connected to the PC that it can access without going through the tunnel. You must have enabled split tunneling on the Easy VPN Server and allowed local LAN access in the VPN Client's connection profile. (In Figure 12-15, the PC has two NICs, which is why two local networks, 192.168.1.0 and 192.1.1.0, appear.)

- **Secured Routes**—Displays the routes that will be secured by the tunnel. If you see "0.0.0.0 0.0.0.0" here, then all traffic except the *Local LAN Routes* traffic will be encrypted.

Using this screen can determine if you've been allowed to use split tunneling from your desktop. In Figure 12-15, split tunneling is allowed for local LAN access only—all other traffic must traverse the IPsec tunnel.

Figure 12-15 *Statistics Window: Route Details*

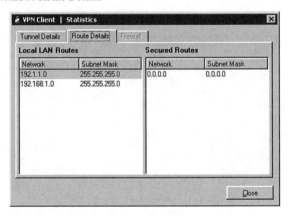

Notifications

During the initial IPsec connection process, your VPN Client software might receive notification messages from the Easy VPN Server. These appear as pop-up windows on your screen. A notification message might be something as simple as a login banner, an upgrade message from the network administrator, or configuration issues with your VPN Client. Once you have established an IPsec session, you can reexamine your notification messages by either:

- Right-clicking the yellow closed padlock icon in the Windows taskbar and choosing **Notifications**.

- From the main menu in the VPN Client GUI, choosing **Status > Notifications**.

In either case, the window in Figure 12-16 will appear. In this example, there are two notifications. The first message is the login banner message from the Easy VPN Server and the second message is the connection history message, which allows you to view the messages displayed during the connection process to the Easy VPN Server (this is the one selected in Figure 12-16).

Figure 12-16 *Notifications Window*

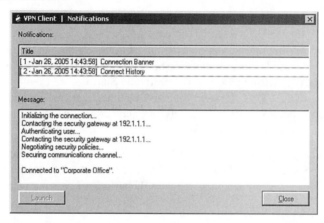

Some other types of notifications you might see (in pop-up windows or in the Notifications window) are:

- A new version of VPN Client software is available for download
- The firewall policy configured on the Easy VPN Server and the firewall configuration on your computer don't match
- The administrator of the Easy VPN Server disconnected your session
- The Easy VPN Server was shut down or rebooted
- The client's idle time was exceeded for the tunnel
- The client's maximum connect time was exceeded for the tunnel

Disconnecting the Connection

If you reboot your computer, obviously your VPN session is terminated. However, you can terminate your IPsec session manually by performing one of the following processes:

- Right-clicking the yellow closed padlock icon in the Windows taskbar and choosing **Disconnect**.
- In the toolbar of the VPN Client, clicking the **Disconnect** button.
- In the main menu of the VP Client, choosing **Connection Entries > Disconnect**.

VPN Client GUI Options

I've already discussed two of the options available from the VPN Client's Options in the main menu: Preferences and the Mode selection (Simple and Advanced). This part of the chapter will discuss the other three options: Application Launcher, Windows Login Properties, and Stateful Firewall (Always On).

Application Launcher

The Application Launcher option from the Options selection in the main menu of the VPN Client allows you to run an application before establishing a session to an Easy VPN Server. You might want to do this if you've configured Start Before Logon in the Windows Login Properties of the VPN Client and you need to authenticate to some other application before bringing the tunnel up, or you need to start another application for monitoring functions before each session is established.

By default, this option is disabled. When you go to **Options > Application Launcher** from the main menu, click the *Enable* check box to enable it and then click the **Browse** button to find the application to launch. Click the **OK** button to save your changes.

NOTE   To use the Application Launcher feature, you also must select the *Allow launching of third party applications before logon* option in the Windows Login Properties, discussed in the next section.

Windows Login Properties

The Windows Login Properties, which you can access by going to **Options > Windows Login Properties** from the main menu, allow you to specify special login functions for Windows NT 4.0, 2000, and XP platforms (for other platforms, this will not appear as a selection in the menu tree). There are three check boxes in this window that allow you to:

- **Enable start before logon**—Allows you to connect to the network via IPsec before you log on to your Windows domain. This might be necessary if the domain controller is located behind the Easy VPN Server. When this option is used, you log in to your domain after the IPsec tunnel is established.

- **Allow launching of third party applications before logon (Application Launcher, Third party dial-up application)**—Allows you to launch an application before you log in to your Windows domain.

- **Disconnect VPN connection when logging off**—Has the VPN Client automatically disconnect itself whenever you log out of the Windows domain. Of the three parameters, only this one is enabled by default. About the only time you would want to disable this feature is if your network is using Windows roaming profiles.

Automatic Initiation

Automatic initiation, commonly called auto-initiation (AI), allows computers to establish IPsec sessions automatically using the Cisco VPN Client. AI, new in Version 3.6, was developed primarily for wireless environments, but can be used in other situations. AI is disabled by default. When enabled, the VPN Client becomes active immediately whenever the following are true:

- The computer boots up or the computer comes out of a standby or hibernating state.
- The computer has an IP address assigned to a NIC that is associated with AI.

When both of these items are true, AI will use the appropriate connection profile to automatically set up a secure session to the Easy VPN Server in the associated connection profile. This is very useful in wireless LANs (WLANs) where you want to make the VPN process as transparent as possible to the user. In most WLANs conscious of security, a VPN is used to protect the wireless traffic when it is sent to the wired LAN. For example, depending on which wireless access point your computer is connected to and which DHCP server it has acquired its addressing information from, you might need to connect to a specific Easy VPN Server before you can access corporate resources. Of course, this can be problematic for users, because it will be difficult for them, in most cases, to figure out which Server they should be connected to. AI takes this guesswork out of this situation by predefining which profile the VPN Client should use based on the addressing information assigned to the local NIC.

vpnclient.ini File

Unlike the other features discussed so far with the VPN Client, AI first must be enabled by configuring parameters in the vpnclient.ini file with a text editor. Once you've done this, you can then use the VPN Client GUI to enable and disable AI, or change the retry interval for a failed session attempt. Table 12-4 lists the parameters you configure in the vpnclient.ini file.

Table 12-4 *AI Parameters in the vpnclient.ini File*

Parameter	Values	Description
AutoInitiationEnable	**0**: disable (default) **1**: enable	Enables AI
AutoInitiationRetryInterval	**1–10** minutes (1 is the default) or **5–60** seconds, depending on the interval type	Specifies the time to wait when a session attempt fails before trying again
AutoInitiationRetryIntervalType	**0**: minutes (default) **1**: seconds	Specifies the retry interval measurement in either minutes or seconds: for LAN session, I would use seconds: for dialup session, I would use minutes

continues

Table 12-4   *AI Parameters in the vpnclient.ini File (Continued)*

Parameter	Values	Description
AutoRetryLimit	A number	Specifies the number of times to try to session before failing
AutoInitiationList	A name or names separated by commas	Specifies the names of sections in the vpnclient.ini file that specify the connection profiles to use for AI
[*Section_name*]	This is one of the names specified in the AutoIntiationList parameter	Specifies the parameters to use for AI when connecting with a specified connection profile
Network and Mask	IP network number and subnet mask	These appear under the section name and specify the network number that needs to be associated with the PC's NIC to use this entry for AI
ConnectionEntry	Name of a connection profile	This is the name of the .pcf file to use for the AI connection and appears under the section name
Connect	0: do not use AI 1: use AI (default)	This enables or disables AI for the section name entry

I'll use Example 12-4 to illustrate how to set up the vpnclient.ini file for AI.

Example 12-4   *Sample vpnclient.ini File with AI*

```
[Main]
←output omitted→
AutoInitiationEnable=1
AutoInitiationRetryIntervalType=1
AutoInitationRetryInterval=30
AutoInitiationRetryLimit=20
AutoInitiationList=WLAN
[WLAN]
Network=192.168.0.0
Mask=255.255.0.0
ConnectionEntry=wirelesslan
Connect=1
←output omitted→
```

In this example, AI has been enabled in the first line under the [Main] section. The second and third lines set the interval type to seconds and the timeout to 30 seconds. The fourth line specifies the number of retries to connect when AI fails to connect initially to the Easy VPN Server or loses its current connection to the Server. The last line under the [Main] section specifies the section name that contains the parameters that determine when AI is to be used and what connection profile to use to establish a secure session. The section name is [WLAN] and if the PC's NIC has an address that begins with "192.168." (based on the IP address and subnet mask), AI will take effect. The wirelesslan.pcf file will be used by AI to establish a secure connection and the last line of [WLAN] enables this profile for AI (this is the default).

TIP   If you need to enter multiple section names, you should order them in the *AutoInitiationList* parameter based on uniqueness of the network numbers: the more specific network number sections should appear first and the least specific last. For example, if you have two sections, one with a network of 10.10.0.0 255.255.0.0 and another with 10.0.0.0 255.0.0.0, the section with 10.10.0.0 should appear first because it is more specific. The VPN Client processes sections in the *AutoInitiationList* parameter from first to last; the first match that is found for a section is used and the rest are ignored.

AI Configuration Verification

Once you have configured AI, you can verify your configuration by performing either of the following:

- From the Windows command prompt (cmd.exe), use the **vpnclient verify autoinitconfig** command.

- From the VPN Client GUI, in the main menu select **Options**: you should now see an entry for Automatic VPN Initiation under the Options menu selections.

Example 12-5 shows the use of the Windows command line to verify your AI configuration. In this example, you can see that the AI has been enabled; if there were any configuration errors, you would see them in the display output.

Example 12-5 *AI Verification: Windows Command Line*

```
C:\Program Files\Cisco Systems\VPN Client> vpnclient verify autoinitconfig
Cisco Systems VPN Client Version 4.6.00.0049
Copyright (C) 1998-2004 Cisco Systems, Inc. All Rights Reserved.
Client Type(s): Windows, WinNT
Running on: 5.0.2195 Service Pack 4
Config file directory: C:\Program Files\Cisco Systems\VPN Client\

Auto-initiation Configuration Information.
Enable:        1
Retry Interval: 60 seconds
List Entry  0:  Network:        192.168.0.0
                Mask:           255.255.0.0
                Connect Flag:   1
                Connection Entry: "wirelesslan"
```

VPN Client GUI and AI

Once you have successfully configured AI, start up the VPN Client. In the VPN Client, if you go to **Options > Automatic VPN Initiation**, you can enable or disable AI and change the retry interval. You cannot change any other parameter related to AI from the GUI; instead, you must use a text editor to manipulate the vpnclient.ini AI parameters.

AI Usage

Once your PC NIC comes up and is assigned an IP address and subnet mask, AI will compare the NIC's associated network number to the networks in its AI sections. If there is a match, AI will use the associated connection profile and bring up a secure connection to the associated Easy VPN Server automatically. You'll be prompted for your XAUTH username and password during the authentication phase.

Once you have a VPN session established, if you terminate it, AI will bring the session back up automatically. If you want to suspend the use of AI, right-click the yellow padlock icon in the Windows taskbar and choose **Suspend Auto-initiation**. This will prevent AI from re-establishing a session automatically. This only suspends the AI process for your current computer session; if you reboot your PC, AI is re-enabled automatically. To resume the use of AI, right-click the yellow padlock icon in the Windows taskbar and choose **Resume Auto-initiation**.

To disable AI, either:

- Right-click the yellow padlock icon in the Windows taskbar and choose **Disable Auto-initiation**.

- In the VPN Client main menu, go to **Options > Automatic VPN Initiation** and uncheck the *Enable automatic VPN initiation* check box.

Stateful Firewall

The Cisco VPN Client includes an integrated stateful firewall that is a .dll file provided by Zone Labs; it is commonly referred to as the Cisco Integrated Client (CIC) firewall. The feature itself is referred to as "Stateful Firewall (Always On)" and is only available on Windows clients. CIC is stateful for TCP, UDP, and ICMP packets. CIC, or some type of software firewall, should be used to provide protection for a computer when split tunneling is allowed and devices can access the PC directly without going through the tunnel. When you define split tunneling on your Easy VPN Server, you also should specify a firewall policy that the client should use.

The default behavior of the CIC stateful firewall, when enabled, is to allow all outbound traffic and deny all inbound traffic, except for the following traffic:

- For inbound traffic, if it is returning traffic for a connection originated by the computer, allow it into the computer.

- Allow inbound DHCP replies from a different port into the computer.
- Allow inbound ESP traffic into the computer. This is necessary because stateful firewalls need to examine Layers 4 and higher to determine the state of the connection and ESP is a Layer-3 protocol.

Firewall policies are defined on the Easy VPN Server and pushed to the client during IKE Mode Config (Network Admission Control, or NAC, enforcement is available in 4.7 of the VPN 3000 concentrator and allows you to define similar policies). You can define what firewall the client should be using and what policy should be used:

- **Are You There (AYT)**—The firewall must be operational on the client.
- **Central Policy Push or Central Protection Policy (CPP)**—A firewall filter is defined on the Easy VPN Server or external authorization server and pushed down to the client during IKE Mode Config, which the client's firewall will use. The filter affects only nontunneled traffic: traffic *not* traversing the tunnel (therefore split tunneling is necessary). If you want to filter traffic on the tunnel, you must define a filter on the Easy VPN Server to perform this process.

These policies and their configuration on the VPN 3000 concentrator were discussed in Chapter 7, "Concentrator Remote Access Connections with IPsec." Table 12-5 has a brief overview of the software firewalls supported by AYT and CPP. The following two sections will discuss how to enable the CIC firewall and how to view the operation of the firewall on the PC.

Table 12-5 *Supported Firewalls for AYT and CPP*

Firewall Product	Supported Policies
CIC	CPP (policies on Easy VPN Server)
Network Ice BlackICE Defender	AYT
Zone Labs ZoneAlarm and ZoneAlarm Pro	AYT and CPP (policies on the Easy VPN Server)
Zone Labs Integrity	Policy from server (policies defined on a Zone Labs Integrity server)
Sygate Personal Firewall, Personal Firewall Pro, and Security Agent	AYT
Cisco Security Agent (CSA)	AYT

Enabling the Stateful Firewall Feature

By default, the CIC firewall is disabled. To enable it, perform either of the following:

- From the main menu, choose **Options > Stateful Firewall (Always On)**.
- In the Windows taskbar, right-click the yellow padlock icon and choose **Stateful Firewall (Always On)**.

Once you do this, you can verify that the firewall is operational by pulling up the menu structure in either of the above two approaches and see a check mark to the left of the "Stateful Firewall (Always On)" option. This can be seen in Figure 12-17. If you don't see the check mark, the CIC firewall is disabled.

NOTE   Once the CIC firewall is enabled, even if you exit the VPN Client software, the CIC firewall is *still* operating, providing your computer protection. To disable the CIC firewall, start up the VPN Client and follow one of the two bullet points above.

Figure 12-17 *Enabling the CIC Firewall*

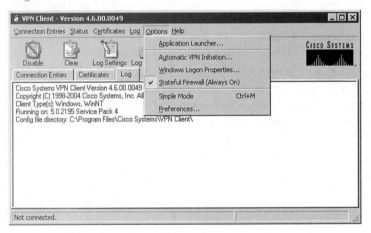

Verifying the Stateful Firewall Operation

Once you have activated the stateful firewall and established an IPsec session to the Easy VPN Server, you can view the status information about the firewall policy by going to either of the following:

- In the VPN Client GUI's main menu, go to **Status > Statistics**.
- In the Windows taskbar, right-click the yellow closed padlock icon and choose **Statistics**.

From here, click the **Firewall** tab and you'll see the screen shown in Figure 12-18.

At the top of the screen you'll see the firewall policy and the firewall type defined on the Easy VPN Server for the user's group; you'll either see AYT, CPP, or Client/Server (Zone Labs Integrity only) for the type and the actual firewall product.

Figure 12-18 *Examining the Firewall Policies*

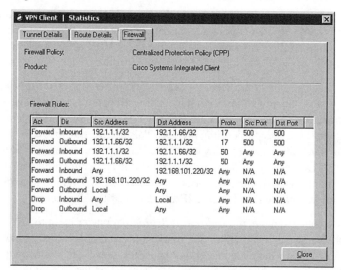

For an AYT policy, this is the only information you'll see. For CPP, however, you'll see the filtering rules pushed down to the client during IKE Mode Config, like that in Figure 12-18. Rules are processed top-down until a match is found. If no match is found, the default rule is used. If you are using the default Cisco VPN Client filter, "Firewall Filter for VPN Client (Default)," on the VPN 3000 concentrators, these rules drop any traffic that doesn't match the preceding rules (with the exception of the three bullet points at the beginning of the firewall section).

TIP   So that you don't accidentally misconfigure a filtering rule on the VPN 3000 concentrator for the firewall policy, I recommend that you copy the "Firewall Filter for VPN Client (Default)" on the concentrator and start with this as a building block for your CPP filter.

The *Action* column indicates what the firewall should do if there is a match on the filtering rule: "Forward" or "Drop." The *Dir* column indicates the direction of traffic flow: "Inbound" is into the PC and "Outbound" is leaving the PC. The *Src Address* and *Dst Address* columns indicate host addresses or networks. If you see "Local" for an address, this refers to the computer itself. The *Proto* column indicates the IP protocol; for example, 6 is TCP, 17 is UDP, and 50 is ESP. The *Src Port* and *Dst Port* columns indicate the port numbers for TCP and UDP connections.

You can expand the column headings to view all the information in a text box and you can move the column headings. However, these changes are not persistent. When you close and reopen this window, the viewing format will revert back to the default view.

Troubleshooting Firewall Connections

When you start up an IPsec session to the Easy VPN Server, the firewall policy on the Server is enforced. If your computer is not configured to follow the policy, a few things can happen. In the following scenarios, assume that a VPN 3000 concentrator is used as the Easy VPN Server.

In this first example, if the *Firewall Setting* parameter is set to "Firewall Optional" on the concentrator, and you either don't have a firewall operational, or have a different one operational than what the concentrator specifies, you'll see a notification message pop up during the IPsec session-building process. This notification message will state: "The client did not match the firewall policy configured on the central site VPN device. NetworkICE BlackICE Defender should be enabled or installed on your computer." In this example, the configured firewall on the concentrator was BlackICE. Even though the firewall policy didn't match between the two, the IPsec session still will proceed.

In this second example, if the *Firewall Setting* parameter is set to "Firewall Required" on the concentrator and you either don't have a firewall operational or have a different one operational than what the concentrator specifies, you'll see a window pop up during the connection process, stating: "Secure VPN connection terminated by Peer. Reason 435: Firewall Policy Mismatch." The VPN session is then terminated. In this instance, the concentrator refuses your session attempt unless you meet the configured firewall policy. Following this, the notification window will pop up, explaining the firewall policy requirements (an example of this is in the last paragraph).

TIP   If you're a network administrator and making changes to a group, where you want to have them use a firewall, I recommend that you use the "Firewall Optional" policy first and then send an e-mail out to everyone in the group explaining the new policy and where to download the firewall product (if it's not the CIC firewall). Unfortunately, you can't change the firewall notification message sent to the client; however, you could create a login banner explaining the access change and where to download and install the software firewall product.

VPN Client Software Updates

In this section I'll discuss how to upgrade the VPN Client software. Cisco VPN 3000 concentrators support two types of automatic client upgrades: the 3002 hardware client and the Windows VPN Client. I'll cover what you have to do on both the concentrator and VPN Client side of the connection.

Concentrator: Client Updates

There are two types of client updates or upgrades the concentrator supports: the Cisco VPN client software and the 3002 hardware client. Upgrades of both can be controlled on the concentrator. If you go to the **Configuration > System > Client Update > Entries** screen on the concentrator and click the **Add** button, you can add an update entry. This screen is shown in Figure 12-19.

Figure 12-19 *Adding Client Updates on a Concentrator*

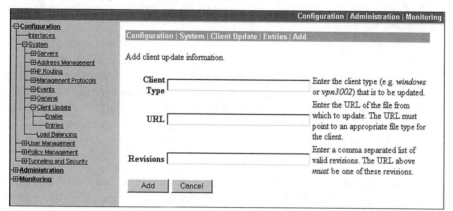

There are three parameters on the screen in Figure 12-19. The *Client Type* parameter specifies the type of client you want to upgrade. All versions of the concentrator allow you to upgrade Windows and 3002 clients. If you enter "Windows" as the parameter, this update entry applies to all Windows clients: "Win9x" applies to only Windows 95, 98, and ME; and "WinNT" applies to only Windows NT 4.0, 2000, and Windows XP. For Windows clients, your update entries should not overlap. In other words, don't specify both "Windows" and "Win9x" because this would cause the concentrator to send two update notices to the client. To specify an update for a VPN 3002 hardware client, use "vpn3002." Newer concentrator images support the upgrade of MacOS, Solaris, and Linux clients using these client types, respectively: "Mac OS X," "Solaris," and "Linux." Please note that upgrading of the non-Windows clients is a fairly new feature with the concentrators and clients.

NOTE   You must enter the *Client Type* in the exact case and spacing, or the client will ignore the update message.

The *URL* parameter specifies the location of the client update file (typically on a web server behind the VPN 3000 concentrator). For a 3002 client, the update must be a TFTP server, so you would enter something like this: tftp://192.168.1.1/vpn3002-4.1.7.Rel-k9.bin. Make sure you use the same case that Cisco specified on their web site. For all other clients (software-based), the update location must be a web server URL ("http" or "https"), like this: **http://** *IP_address/client_image*. With both types of URLs, you can include directories; and for HTTP URLs, you can include port numbers if the web server is running on a different port. You can also use a name for the server, but you must configure a DNS server on the concentrator to resolve the name to an address.

The *Revisions* parameter specifies what version or versions of software the clients should be running; if they are not running these versions, they should install the software in the *URL* parameter. You can specify multiple revision numbers; just separate them by a command and a space.

NOTE   It is important that the revision be entered in the *exact* case that appears in the image name from Cisco. In other words, the clients will see a difference between "4.1.7.Rel" and "4.1.7.rel." If the client is running 4.1.7.Rel and you enter the "r" in lower case, the client will think that this is a *different* version and download this—again and again!

If you have more than one client type, you'll add more than one update entry. Also, the above configuration applies to *all* clients of that type: you can control this on a group-by-group basis by adding an auto-update for a specific group instead of using the above process. This is done by going to **Configuration > User Management > Groups**, clicking a group name, and then clicking the **Client Update** button. The process from this point onward is the same as described above.

The last step you must perform on the concentrator is to enable the auto-update process. To do this, go to **Configuration > System > Client Update > Enable** and click the *Enable* check box to enable it.

VPN Client Preparation for Auto-Update of Windows 2000 and XP

There are a few things you have to do to prepare to use the auto-update feature for Windows 2000 and XP VPN Clients running 4.6 or later. There are two types of updates: minor (minor updates to the existing software) and major (a full update—replacing the existing software with a new version).

Web Server Configuration for Auto-Update

First, you need to download a special update file from Cisco called update-4.*x.yy.zzzz*-minor-K9.zip or update-4.*x.yy.zzzz*-major-K9.zip, where "4" is the major release and *x.yy.zzzz* is the version and revision information. Place this file in its own directory (like "windows46updates") on a web server and unzip its contents. When unzipped, you'll see the following additional files:

- **vpnclient-win-is-4.x.yy.zzzz-k9.exe**—InstallShield installation file.
- **vpnclient-win-msi-4.x.yy.zzzz-k9.exe**—MSI installation File.

- **Binary-{Major|Minor}-4.X.Yy.Zzzz.zip**—Contains the VPN Client update components (don't unzip this); this file is deleted upon installation on the client device.

- **sig.dat**—Contains a signature of the binary.zip file used by InstallShield or MSI to determine the integrity of the binary.zip file. If it's been tampered with, no installation occurs; this file is deleted upon installation on the client device.

- **binary_config.ini**—A configuration file that has the VPN Client version available on the web server; the autoupdate.exe program on the VPN Client uses this to determine if the update needs to be downloaded or not (the program looks at the *Version* parameter in this file to determine if an update is necessary. The file is deleted upon installation on the client device).

- **new_update_config.ini**—This file is used to determine what additional components need to be downloaded, like connection profiles and OEM packages (that have the oem.ini and verifying configurations); this file's name is changed to "update_config.ini" once the update is completed on the client. Please note that this file is not necessary if you're not updating or adding any .pcf, oem.ini, or verifying configurations.

Of the files in the preceding list, the only one you can create, if necessary, is the new_update_config.ini file; all of the other files are supplied by Cisco and should not be tampered with. The new_update_config.ini file can contain the contents in Table 12-6. Any files specified in this configuration file also must be copied to the installation directory on the web server; the VPN Client will download these if you specify them.

Table 12-6 *new_update_config.ini Parameters*

Parameter	Description
[Update]	First section name in the file (required).
Version=	Enter a version number of the update package—this can be any number and is used by you, the administrator, to keep track of updates. Version numbers typically start at "1" and work their way up every time there's a new update.
FileName=	This is the name of a .zip file that contains the new or updated .pcf files. This is required only if you have new connection profiles. An example would be newprofiles.zip. This needs to be placed in the web directory containing the installation files.
MaxSize=	This is the size of the above .zip file in bytes, plus 5,000.
[Oem]	This is the name of a section pertaining to a .zip file that contains a new vpnclient.ini and oem.ini files and is used only by the InstallShield update process. This section isn't necessary if you don't have these new files.

continues

Table 12-6 *new_update_config.ini Parameters (Continued)*

Parameter	Description
FileName=	This is the name of the .zip file containing the updated vpnclient.ini and oem.ini files for the InstallShield update process.
MaxSize=	This is the size of the above .zip file in bytes, plus 5000 bytes.
[Transform]	This section is needed only if you'll be doing an MSI installation; the transform in the ZIP file must be named oem.mst.
FileName=	This is the name of the .zip file containing the updated transform files for the MSI update process.
MaxSize=	This is the size of the above .zip file in bytes, plus 5000 bytes.
[Autoupdate]	This is the name of the section head for auto-update.
Required=	If set to **0**, the update is not required; if **1**, the update is required.

Concentrator Configuration for Auto-Update

Also, when you create the update entry on the concentrator, do not specify any filenames for the URL when using the VPN Client auto-update feature in 4.6 client versions; instead, specify the directory where all of the installation files for auto-update are located, like: **http://***IP_address***/windowsauto46**, where "windowsauto46" is the web server directory containing the installation files.

Client Update Process

There are two client update types: manual and automatic. The following sections will describe the two processes for the VPN Client when using the upgrade feature on the concentrator.

Manual Upgrades

With the manual process, when the client connects to the concentrator, the concentrator, during IKE Mode Config, sends an update notification to the client. If the update information is different from what the client is running, the client receives a pop-up notification window as shown in Figure 12-20. This window has a **Launch** button that, when the user clicks it, will download the image file specified in the *URL* parameter discussed previously in the "Concentrator: Client Updates" section. Once downloaded, the user will need to:

1 Manually uninstall the old client and reboot.

2 Install the new client and reboot.

This process applies to Windows 2000/XP clients running software older than 4.6 and the other non-Windows clients.

TIP   If you don't want your users to be able to download the software via the **Launch** button, don't include "http" or "https" in the URL prefix defined on the VPN 3000 concentrator.

Figure 12-20 *Manual Upgrade Process*

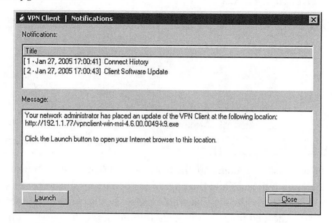

Automatic Upgrades

With a 3002 hardware client, when it receives the update notification from the Easy VPN Server, the 3002 will download the update automatically, install it, and reboot itself; upon rebooting, the 3002 will re-establish its IPsec remote access session to the concentrator.

In 4.6, the Windows 2000 and XP clients support optional automatic updates like the 3002. Unlike the manual update approach, auto-update doesn't require the remote access user to uninstall the old software first, reboot, install the new version, and then reboot. Instead, when the VPN Client makes a connection to the concentrator, the update is downloaded automatically either via the VPN tunnel or split tunneling from a web server. If the update is a major upgrade, the user will have to reboot twice, as in the manual process (the user is notified of this through pop-up windows); however, if it is a minor upgrade, the user will be notified that a reboot is not necessary. Another nice feature of Windows auto-update is that if the download is interrupted when the client disconnects, upon reconnecting to the Easy VPN Server, the download will resume where it left off.

The autoupdate.exe program (part of the VPN Client installation in 4.6) is responsible for the auto-update process. When a notification message is sent from the Easy VPN Server to the VPN Client, this program determines if any additional steps need to be taken or not. If an update is necessary, this program downloads the update files (remember that it will take some time to download these because there is probably 20+MB of file data). Once the update files from the web server have been downloaded successfully, the user is then prompted for what action should be taken through a pop-up window, as shown in Figure 12-21. The user can install the package now, install it later, or reject the downloaded update. At the top of the window is the type of update: full (major), update (minor), and profile (connection entries). Only the first type of update requires a reboot. In Figure 12-21, this is a minor upgrade.

Figure 12-21 *Auto-update Upgrade Process*

If the user accepts the update and clicks the *Install Now* button, the autoinstall.exe program installs the update files. While the upgrade is occurring, the pop-up window will display the installation status. During this whole process of downloading the installation files, log messages are recorded in the autoupdate.log file in the "updates" subdirectory of the VPN Client (this is where the client upgrade files are also downloaded to). During the installation, log messages are stored in the autoinstall.log file in the same directory.

NOTE   With a minor upgrade, if you had an IPsec session open to the concentrator, this is disconnected automatically upon finishing the upgrade. If you're using auto-initiation, the session will be re-established shortly; otherwise, you'll have to re-establish the IPsec session manually.

VPN Client Troubleshooting

The remainder of this chapter will focus on troubleshooting some common problems when using the Cisco VPN Client software. The first topic I'll discuss is the logging abilities of the software client: the Log Viewer component of the VPN Client. Then I'll discuss some common problems you'll typically come across and what to look for on your computer (or concentrator) to troubleshoot these problems:

- Authentication Problems
- ISAKMP/IKE Policy Mismatch Issues
- Address Assignment Troubleshooting
- Split Tunneling Problems

- Address Translation Problems
- Fragmentation Issues
- Microsoft Network Neighborhood Issues

Log Viewer

In the 3.x version of the VPN Client software, the Log viewer was a separate application; in 4.x, the Log application was integrated into the VPN Client software. To view the events in the log file, perform one of the following in the 4.x GUI:

- Click the **Log** tab in the middle of the window—this can be seen in Figure 12-22.
- From the main menu you can choose **Log > Log Window** to pull up this window.

The information in the Log event viewer window can be used to help in troubleshooting client problems. You can control the amount of logging information, search the logging information, and view the logging information from this window.

Figure 12-22 *Log Event Viewer*

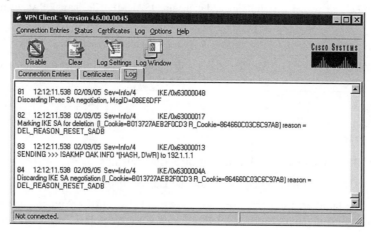

Formatting of Logging Information

Events in the Log window have the following format in two or more lines:

```
event_# time date Sev=type/level event_class/message_ID
message_description
```

Each event is assigned a unique number in sequential order. Following this is the time and date of the event, and then the type and severity level of the event. After this is the event class and message ID. Table 12-7 lists the logging event classes. For every class, there are three severity types: fault (1: system failure or unrecoverable error), warning (2–3: possible system failure or major problem), and informational (4–6: events concerning connections and processes). Most events you'll see will have a severity level of 4–6.

Table 12-7 *Logging Classes*

Class Name	Description
CERT	Obtaining, validating, and renewing certificates
CLI	Interacting with the client CLI (not GUI)
CM	Using the connection manager to establish a secure session
CVPND	Initializing client services and controlling message processes and flows by the Cisco VPN Client daemon
GUI	Configuring the client software via the GUI and initiating and monitoring VPN sessions
FIREWALL	Using the CIC firewall
IKE	Building and managing ISAKMP/IKE Phase 1 SAs
IPSEC	Building and managing ISAKMP/IKE Phase 2 SAs, including applying rules to traffic that needs to be protected
PPP	Establishing VPN sessions via PPP dialup
XAUTH	Validating user account information for user authentication during ISAKMP/IKE Phase 1

You can control the capturing of these classes and levels by performing one of the following:

- From the main menu, choose **Log > Log Settings**.
- Click the **Log** tab and then click the **Log Settings** button.

This will pull up a separate window, shown in Figure 12-23. You can change the logging level by using the drop-down selector for each logging class. Supported logging levels include:

- **"Disabled"**—Turns on the logging for the specified class.
- **"Low"**—Turns on logging for severity levels 1–3; this is the default for all classes.
- **"Medium"**—Changes logging for the specified class to include levels 1–4, which includes the informational level 4 events.
- **"High"**—Changes logging for the specified class to include levels 1–6, which is all logging levels.

After making your changes, click the **OK** button to activate and save the changes. Your changes take effect immediately for any new logging information.

TIP   When troubleshooting problems, the default logging level will, in most cases, not display enough information for you to determine the exact problem. In this case, change the log level settings for the specific event(s) to assist in the troubleshooting process. For troubleshooting IPsec session problems, you would typically set the IKE and IPSEC logging classes to "High." I've also found that sometimes I need to troubleshoot the problem from the Easy VPN Server *and* VPN Client to resolve a specific problem.

Figure 12-23 *Log Settings*

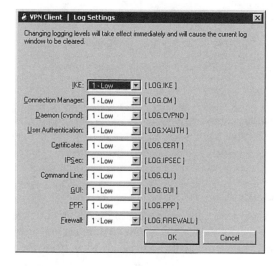

Disabling the Logging Feature

A new log file is created every time you reboot your computer. Because of the amount of logging information created and the disk space issues that this poses, you might want to disable logging globally on the client. By default, logging is enabled. You can disable this function by performing one of the following:

- From the main menu, choose **Log > Disable**
- Click the **Log** tab and click the **Disable** button above the three tabs

Searching for Logging Information

Because you might have set the logging levels to 4 or higher, it sometimes might be difficult to find a particular message or event class type within the log file. You can search the log file for a certain string in it by choosing **Log > Search Log** from the main menu. A window will pop up where you can enter the string you want to search for; then click the **Find Next** button. This causes the VPN Client to search the log file, starting at the beginning, for the terms you entered. The first time the client finds a match, it highlights the term(s). Click the **Find Next** button again to find the next occurrence.

NOTE   Searches are case-insensitive and do not support a wildcard pattern matching feature.

Clearing Logging Information

You can clear the events in the Log window by performing one of the following:

- From the main menu, choose **Log > Clear**.
- Click the Log tab and then click the **Clear** button.

NOTE   Please note that the clear logging feature clears only the logging information in this window—it does not clear the log entries in the log file on the computer's hard drive.

Authentication Problems

Now that you have a basic understanding of the client's Log viewer application, the rest of the chapter will focus on using this feature to troubleshoot problems. This section will look at troubleshooting IPsec authentication issues when using the client.

Troubleshooting XAUTH (user authentication) issues is fairly easy because the user is re-prompted for username and password if these are incorrect; this is not true if you've misconfigured the pre-shared key for the group the user belongs to. If you've misconfigured the group's pre-shared key, you'll see output in the Log viewer something like that shown in Example 12-6 (this is with the default level settings of "Low"):

Example 12-6 *Group Pre-Shared Key Authentication Problem*

```
1       13:23:46.154  02/09/05   Sev=Warning/3 IKE/0xE3000056
The received HASH payload cannot be verified
2       13:23:46.154  02/09/05   Sev=Warning/2 IKE/0xE300007D
Hash verification failed... may be configured with invalid group
        password.
3       13:23:46.154  02/09/05   Sev=Warning/2 IKE/0xE3000099
Failed to authenticate peer (Navigator:904)
4       13:23:46.154  02/09/05   Sev=Warning/2 IKE/0xE30000A5
Unexpected SW error occurred while processing Aggressive Mode
        negotiator:(Navigator:2202)
```

In Example 12-6, there are four events. Events 1 and 2 indicate a problem with pre-shared key authentication with the group, and event 3 shows that device authentication has failed.

You also can use the Log viewer to troubleshoot problems related to obtaining and using certificates. Most of these problems probably will be associated with the validity date on a certificate. If this is the case and the client's own identity certificate has expired, a window will pop up indicating that the certificate is invalid because of its date. If the peer's certificate has expired, this will appear in the normal logging activity ("Low") in the client's Log window.

TIP   When you are experiencing a problem, I recommend clearing the log first and then re-attempting the session; then, the only log messages you'll have to decipher are those that relate to this particular problem, making the troubleshooting process easier. Also, I've experienced glitches in certain client versions where changing a logging level won't take effect until you exit the VPN Client *and* restart.

ISAKMP/IKE Policy Mismatch Issues

Sometimes you'll experience a problem where the appropriate ISAKMP/IKE Phase 1 transform, called an IKE Proposal on Cisco VPN 3000 concentrators, or the ISAKMP/IKE Phase 2 transform doesn't match that found on the client. The Cisco Easy VPN clients, which include the Cisco VPN Client software, already have a list of predefined proposals and policies incorporated into their software. The Cisco Easy VPN Server must have a corresponding match for both the Phase 1 and Phase 2 transforms/policies. If a match is not found in Phase 1, no session is established. If no match is found in Phase 2, the ISAKMP/IKE Phase 1 management session will be built, but the data connection will fail—in this instance, the client will tear down the management connection also.

On the Cisco VPN Client, if there is not a matching transform/policy on the Easy VPN Server, you'll see in the message shown in Example 12-7 in the connection status pop-up window:

Example 12-7 *Mismatched ISAKMP/IKE Phase 1 Policy with the Default Logging Level*

```
Initializing the connection...
Contacting the security gateway at 192.1.1.1...
Secure VPN Connection terminated locally by the Client.
Reason 412: The remote peer is no longer responding.
Not connected.
```

The problem with the above message is that it doesn't illuminate the cause of the problem. On top of this, there are no events recorded in the Log view when the event class for "IKE" is set to "Low." In Example 12-8, I've changed the logging level for "IKE" to "Medium."

Example 12-8 *Mismatched ISAKMP/IKE Phase 1 Policy With a "Medium" Logging Level*

```
1       16:24:54.549  02/09/05  Sev=Info/4 IKE/0x63000013
SENDING >>> ISAKMP OAK AG (SA, KE, NON, ID, VID(Xauth), VID(dpd), VID(Nat-T),
  VID(Frag), VID(Unity)) to 192.1.1.1
2       16:24:59.906  02/09/05  Sev=Info/4 IKE/0x63000021
Retransmitting last packet!
3       16:24:59.906  02/09/05  Sev=Info/4 IKE/0x63000013
SENDING >>> ISAKMP OAK AG (Retransmission) to 192.1.1.1
4       16:25:04.914  02/09/05  Sev=Info/4 IKE/0x63000021
Retransmitting last packet!
5       16:25:04.914  02/09/05  Sev=Info/4 IKE/0x63000013
SENDING >>> ISAKMP OAK AG (Retransmission) to 192.1.1.1
6       16:25:09.921  02/09/05  Sev=Info/4 IKE/0x63000021
Retransmitting last packet!
7       16:25:09.921  02/09/05  Sev=Info/4 IKE/0x63000013
SENDING >>> ISAKMP OAK AG (Retransmission) to 192.1.1.1
8       16:25:14.928  02/09/05  Sev=Info/4 IKE/0x63000017
Marking IKE SA for deletion  (I_Cookie=92663B6F83385211
R_Cookie=0000000000000000) reason = DEL_REASON_PEER_NOT_RESPONDING
9       16:25:15.439  02/09/05  Sev=Info/4 IKE/0x6300004A
Discarding IKE SA negotiation (I_Cookie=92663B6F83385211
R_Cookie=0000000000000000) reason = DEL_REASON_PEER_NOT_RESPONDING
10      16:25:15.489  02/09/05  Sev=Info/4 IKE/0x63000001
IKE received signal to terminate VPN connection
```

Here you can see some additional information; for example, message #1 shows the ISAKMP policies being sent to the VPN gateway and messages #2–7 show the client resending this information. Finally, in message #8, the client gives up the session. Based on the information shown here, the appropriate ISAKMP/IKE Phase 1 policy hasn't been configured or enabled on the Easy VPN Server.

NOTE   On Cisco VPN 3000 concentrators, this shouldn't be an issue because some pre-defined policies for Cisco VPN clients are already enabled. Plus, troubleshooting the client connection on the concentrator is easier in this particular example.

Address Assignment Troubleshooting

One common problem with IPsec remote access sessions is that the Easy VPN Server administrator forgets to create an IP address pool for the group or all of the addresses in the pool are currently being used. When this happens, ISAKMP/IKE Phase 1 fails because the user device cannot obtain an internal IP address for the ESP tunnel connections.

When this occurs, you'll see the same message shown previously in Example 12-7. The only difference is that the reason code will be 427 instead of 412. There are two problems with this situation: this code doesn't tell you too much about the problem and the default logging level of the Log viewer of the client doesn't display the actual problem.

In this case you know that XAUTH works because you must supply the correct user name and password; otherwise you'll be reprompted for this information. Therefore the problem must be associated with IKE Mode Config or ISAKMP/IKE Phase 2. Example 12-9 shows the client Log with the IKE event class set to "HIGH" when this particular problem exists:

Example 12-9 *Client Addressing Problem*

```
1      15:03:39.734  02/10/05  Sev=Info/6 IKE/0x6300003B
Attempting to establish a connection with 192.1.1.1.
2      15:03:39.754  02/10/05  Sev=Info/4 IKE/0x63000013
SENDING >>> ISAKMP OAK AG (SA, KE, NON, ID, VID(Xauth), VID(dpd),
VID(Nat-T), VID(Frag), VID(Unity)) to 192.1.1.1
3      15:03:40.094  02/10/05  Sev=Info/5 IKE/0x6300002F
Received ISAKMP packet: peer = 192.1.1.1
4      15:03:40.094  02/10/05  Sev=Info/4 IKE/0x63000014
RECEIVING <<< ISAKMP OAK AG (SA, KE, NON, ID, HASH, VID(Unity),
VID(Xauth), VID(dpd), VID(Frag), VID(?), VID(?)) from 192.1.1.1
5      15:03:40.094  02/10/05  Sev=Info/5 IKE/0x63000001
Peer is a Cisco-Unity compliant peer
←output omitted→
14      15:03:40.134  02/10/05  Sev=Info/4 IKE/0x63000014
RECEIVING <<< ISAKMP OAK TRANS *(HASH, ATTR) from 192.1.1.1
15      15:03:50.559  02/10/05  Sev=Info/4 IKE/0x63000013
SENDING >>> ISAKMP OAK INFO *(HASH, NOTIFY:HEARTBEAT) to 192.1.1.1
16      15:03:50.559  02/10/05  Sev=Info/6 IKE/0x63000052
Sent a keepalive on the IKE SA
←output omitted→
26      15:03:51.541  02/10/05  Sev=Info/4 IKE/0x63000080
Delete Reason Code: 4 --> PEER_DELETE-IKE_DELETE_NO_ERROR.
27      15:03:51.541  02/10/05  Sev=Info/5 IKE/0x6300003C
Received a DELETE payload for IKE SA with Cookies:
I_Cookie=BDB5CBE8D8C747C2 R_Cookie=1E581493E9C2CBE9
28      15:03:51.541  02/10/05  Sev=Info/4 IKE/0x63000017
Marking IKE SA for deletion  (I_Cookie=BDB5CBE8D8C747C2
R_Cookie=1E581493E9C2CBE9) reason = PEER_DELETE-IKE_DELETE_NO_ERROR
29      15:03:52.061  02/10/05  Sev=Info/4 IKE/0x6300004A
Discarding IKE SA negotiation (I_Cookie=BDB5CBE8D8C747C2
R_Cookie=1E581493E9C2CBE9) reason = PEER_DELETE-IKE_DELETE_NO_ERROR
30      15:03:52.161  02/10/05  Sev=Info/4 IKE/0x63000001
IKE received signal to terminate VPN connection
```

Line 14 is where XAUTH begins (even though this isn't clear from the log output). Beginning with Line 26 you can see the VPN session being terminated. The problem with the above output is that there is nothing there (or in the pop-up window) that explains what the actual problem is. If you are able to obtain an address, you should see something like that shown in Example 12-10 in the clients' Log view:

Example 12-10 *Client Addressing When Functioning Correctly*

```
27      15:27:06.068  02/11/05  Sev=Info/5 IKE/0x63000010
MODE_CFG_REPLY: Attribute = INTERNAL_IPV4_ADDRESS: ,
value = 192.168.101.110
28      15:27:06.068  02/11/05  Sev=Info/5 IKE/0x63000010
MODE_CFG_REPLY: Attribute = INTERNAL_IPV4_NETMASK: ,
value = 255.255.255.0
```

One handy tool you can use is located at the Cisco site, called the "VPN Client Error Lookup Tool": http://www.cisco.com/en/US/products/sw/secursw/ps2308/products_tech_note09186a00801f253d.shtml. This tool is shown in Figure 12-24.

Figure 12-24 *VPN Client Error Lookup Tool*

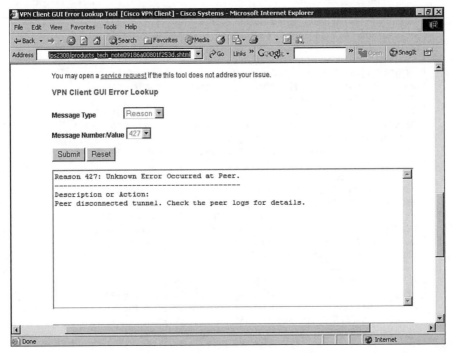

At this point, you need to pull up the type of code, such as "Reason" and the number of the code (in this instance "427"). As you can see from the results, it says to check the peer device to see what the problem is. In this example, the Easy VPN Server is a VPN 3000 concentrator. Going to the Live Event Log on the concentrator, the output in Example 12-11 can be seen:

Example 12-11 *Live Event Log: Client Addressing Problem*

```
←output omitted→
378 02/10/2005 15:32:22.530 SEV=5 IKE/132 RPT=17 192.1.1.66
Group [Splitgroup] User [Richard]
Cannot obtain an IP address for remote peer - FAILED
380 02/10/2005 15:32:22.540 SEV=5 IKE/194 RPT=26 192.1.1.66
Group [Splitgroup] User [Richard]
Sending IKE Delete With Reason message: No Reason Provided.
```

As you can see from message 378, the user ("Richard") in the "Splitgroup" group cannot obtain an IP address. In this situation, make sure that an address pool exists for the group and that there are enough addresses in the pool for all of the users that need to connect at the same time. In message 380, the notification sent to the client is "No Reason Provided," which is what the client displayed.

TIP   In many instances, you'll need to troubleshoot the VPN problem from *both* ends of the tunnel to determine what the problem is.

Split Tunneling Problems

As you recall from Chapter 2, "VPN Technologies," split tunneling is sending some traffic protected to a VPN peer and other traffic unprotected to other devices. Typically this is used when you want to protect traffic from the remote access device to the corporate office, but don't want to overload the VPN session by sending the user's Internet traffic across this session also. You can use split tunneling to solve this problem.

However, if you don't set up split tunneling correctly, your user(s) will face connectivity problems. You can do a few things on the client end of the connection to troubleshoot this problem. First, determine if the issue is related to name resolution or a connection problem. The following two sections will discuss the additional steps you can take to solve each respective problem.

Connectivity Problems

Once you have established a VPN session to the Easy VPN Server, right-click the yellow padlock icon in the Windows taskbar and choose **Statistics**. Click the **Route Details** tab, showing you the window in Figure 12-25. There are two local LAN routes for the two NICs installed on this laptop. In the right-hand column ("Secured Routes"), all traffic is to be encrypted. Based on this, split tunneling for local LAN traffic has been set up and pushed down to the client during IKE Mode Config.

As a further test, click the **Tunnel Details** tab in the window in Figure 12-25, changing the window contents to what you see in Figure 12-26. Then click the **Reset** button to reset the statistics. Next, open up a Windows command (DOS) prompt: Go to **Start > Run**, enter **cmd.exe** in the Open text box, and click the OK button. Ping a destination that is not located at the corporate site. In this example, you can see 5 under the *Packets* section for packets discarded, indicating that the destination is not across the tunnel or local LAN segments, and the client is discarding the packets.

Figure 12-25 *Route Details Window*

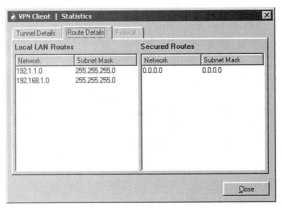

Figure 12-26 *Tunnel Details Window*

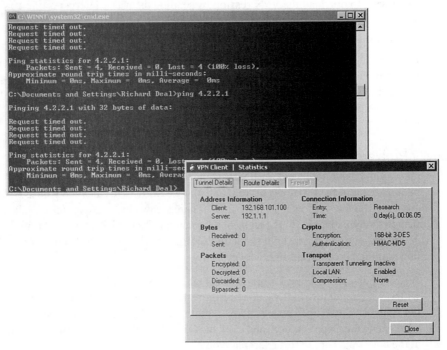

Click the **Reset** button to reset the statistics. Next, ping the inside interface of the Easy VPN Server (the one connected to the corporate network). In the client's Statistics window, you should see the received and sent bytes incrementing in the *Bytes*

section and the number of packets encrypted and decrypted incrementing in the *Packets* section.

Based on these results, you can access the corporate network, but nothing else. To allow the user to access other places, you'll need to configure split tunneling for the group or allow the user access to the Internet via the IPsec tunnel. This was discussed in Chapter 7, "Concentrator Remote Access Connections with IPsec."

Name Resolution Problems

You also might face problems with name, or DNS, resolution. Remember that for most remote access users, their ISPs assign them a DNS server address. Using an Easy VPN Server for remote access users, you also can push two DNS server addresses down to the client. Without split DNS, the client will use the assigned DNS server address(es) given to it during IKE Mode Config by the Easy VPN Server.

As an example of a problem with name resolution, you might have a DMZ with public devices on it, like a web server, e-mail server, and even a DNS server. These devices have been assigned private IP addresses, but the DMZ DNS server responds with public addresses to requesting devices; an address translation device also translates the public-to-private addresses, and vice versa, to allow for external communications to the DMZ services.

You also have an internal DNS server. Because the DMZ devices have private addresses assigned to their NICs, a DNS query to the internal DNS server comes back with a private address, allowing internal users to use the private addressing scheme to access the DMZ devices (no address translation is needed). When remote access clients access these services, you've set up split tunneling where this traffic is sent unprotected across the Internet; only corporate office internal traffic is protected by the tunnel. However, if you didn't set up split DNS, this would create connectivity problems. For remote access clients, when they performed the query to obtain the DMZ devices' IP addresses, the internal DNS server would respond with a private address, and the remote access clients need a public address (because this traffic isn't tunneled).

One option to solve the problem of incorrect name resolution might be to assign the IP address of the DMZ DNS server during IKE Mode Config to the clients; however, this server might not have internal resolutions for internal devices. Therefore, the best solution is to set up split DNS on the Easy VPN Server. Have two domains, like internal.cisco.com and external.cisco.com. Set up split DNS so that any resolutions for internal.cisco.com are resolved using the IKE Mode Config assigned DNS server and anything else resolved with the ISP's assigned DNS server. Another option is to hard-code the resolution in the user's local "host" file.

TIP	To determine if you are having resolution problems, use the nslookup.exe program (included with Windows) to perform DNS resolutions from the Windows command line. Based on the lookup results, you can determine what DNS server the client is using for the resolution, and the name-to-address resolution. Example 12-12 shows the use of this program. In this example, 4.2.2.1 is one of Verizon's DNS servers (a DNS server assigned by the user's ISP).

Example 12-12 nslookup *Program Example*

```
C:\> nslookup www.cisco.com
Server:  vnsc-pri.sys.gtei.net
Address:  4.2.2.1

Non-authoritative answer:
Name:    www.cisco.com
Address:  198.133.219.25
```

Address Translation Problems

One of the more common problems with remote access sessions deals with issues related to address translation. In many instances, a remote access user will be connecting via a public network—for example, at a hotel or airport—or will have a router for a SOHO session. In most of these instances, the user's sessions are being translated with PAT. As I discussed in Chapter 3, "IPsec," ESP is a Layer-3 protocol and doesn't work with PAT, which requires a Layer-4 transport. You can solve this problem by using NAT-T, IPsec over UDP, or IPsec over TCP; the former two encapsulate ESP in a UDP segment and the latter in a TCP segment. You really don't want to do either unless it's necessary, because the encapsulation process adds additional overhead to the connection.

Address translation issues can be difficult to troubleshoot. On a VPN Client device, it looks as if the connection is made and you see the closed yellow padlock icon in the taskbar. In reality, only the ISAKMP/IKE Phase 1 connection has completed, and the Phase 2 connection has completed but will not function. If the user was using a PIX security appliance for a connection to the ISP, the address translation table would look like that found in Example 12-13. As you can see from this example, only the ISAKMP/IKE Phase 1 port 500 connection has been established.

Example 12-13 *PIX Firewall Translation Table with PAT Problem*

```
pixfirewall# show xlate
1 in use, 1 most used
PAT Global 192.1.1.3(1) Local 191.1.1.66(500)
```

If you're using Dead Peer Detection (DPD, which is enabled by default), these are transported across the management connection, so the client and gateway assume the session is functioning correctly; however, if you would try, from the client, to ping the internal (private) interface of the Easy VPN Server, the ping would fail.

To solve address translation problems involving PAT, you need to use either NAT-T, IPsec over UDP, or IPsec over TCP; this will need to be configured on *both* the client and Easy VPN Server. On the client, you need to modify the properties of the remote access session. This window was shown previously in Figure 12-4. Make sure the *Enable Transport Tunneling* check box is checked (this is the default) and either the *IPsec over UDP (NAT/PAT)* or the *IPsec over TCP* radio box is checked. You'll then need to configure the Easy VPN Server. I discussed this process for the VPN 3000 concentrators in Chapter 7, "Concentrator Remote Access Connections with IPsec." On the concentrator, NAT-T and IPsec over TCP are configured globally while IPsec over UDP is configured within the group. On the client, if you choose *IPsec over UDP (NAT/PAT)* and you have both NAT-T and IPsec over UDP enabled on the Easy VPN Server, NAT-T takes precedence.

Example 12-14 shows an example of a PIX security appliance's translation table where NAT-T is used for the remote access session by the client and the PIX is the client's connection to the ISP, where PAT is being used for address translation. As you can see in this example, the first PAT translation is for the ISAKMP/IKE Phase 1 connection (port 500) and the second translation for NAT-T (UDP port 4,500), the encapsulated data connections.

Example 12-14 *PIX Firewall Translation Table with PAT and NAT-T*

```
pixfirewall# show xlate
2 in use, 4 most used
PAT Global 192.1.1.3(2) Local 191.1.1.66(500)
PAT Global 192.1.1.3(1024) Local 191.1.1.66(4500)
```

Fragmentation Issues

As mentioned in the last section, using NAT-T, IPsec over UDP, and IPsec over TCP adds additional overhead to an IPsec session. In many instances, the packets will have to be fragmented to be transmitted across the wire. Here's a quick illustration of this when using L2TP over IPsec over UDP: the L2TP header is 12 bytes (includes the PPP header), the UDP header is 8 bytes, and the IP header is 20 bytes. And if data sequencing is used (this is enabled on Cisco devices, by default), you'll need an additional 4–40 bytes. Adding these up totals 40 or more bytes for the encapsulation process; therefore, if you're transmitting this across an Ethernet medium, you might need 1,500 + 40 = 1,540 bytes. In this situation, the VPN device needs to fragment the packet to send it out the interface. The first fragment will contain 40 bytes of the L2TP encapsulation plus 1,460 bytes of the data, and the second fragment will contain the last 20 bytes of the IP header and the 40 remaining bytes of data (the L2TP header is only found in the first fragment).

Problems that Fragmentation Creates

There are a few problems that fragmentation can create:

- Slower throughput
- Data sometimes transmitted
- Data never transmitted

One of the most common results of fragmentation is slower throughput. I've seen many administrators complain about throughput once they've set up a VPN implementation. At first they blame it on the encryption and decryption process; but in most cases, fragmentation is causing the problem. For example, if an IOS router has to handle the fragmentation and reassembly process, it must do this at the process level, which is very CPU-intensive. In many cases, I've seen throughput drop down to 10–50 percent when fragmentation is occurring.

Another problem with fragmentation is that an intermediate device might need to perform the fragmentation to send the traffic across an intermediate link with a smaller MTU size, but the intermediate device isn't capable of handling fragmentation. In this instance, you'll see one of two scenarios. In the first one, sometimes things will work and sometimes they won't. Take an example of sending e-mail in this situation. If it's a small message (about 5–10 lines), it probably will be sent without fragmentation needed; but if you send an e-mail with an attachment, fragmentation probably will be needed and in this particular situation, it will fail. Or if you're always sending large data files, these will always fail because the intermediate device can't fragment the large packets. Typically, if you can ping a destination across a VPN, like an e-mail server, but can't send large e-mail messages to it, you're probably experiencing a fragmentation problem.

Misdiagnosing VPN Problems

One of the most common questions I'm asked is how much throughput a company will lose when deploying a VPN implementation such as IPsec. It really depends on a few factors, like how the information is transported between the two VPN peers. In a worse case example, you might have to deal with NAT-T, IPsec over UDP, or IPsec over TCP overhead in addition to PPPoE. Or you might have to deal with L2TP over IPsec over PPPoE, which is even worse! In most cases, though, you'll lose about 200 bytes. However, I commonly see administrators implement a VPN solution and then scratch their heads and give up when their throughput drops by 50–90 percent. In most cases, this is not the packet overhead or the encryption/decryption processing that is causing the connection to slow down. The problem usually is fragmentation: either the remote side is fragmenting packets even before they hit the LAN or there is an intermediate device that won't perform any required fragmentation, and thus drops the packets. Diagnosing this problem is not very simple, but by tuning the MTU size for the users' connections, they probably won't even notice any difference between a connection to the corporate site in clear text and one going across a properly tuned VPN.

Looking for Fragmentation Problems

Before you begin implementing any solutions concerning fragmentation, first you should discover if you are having problems associated with fragmentation. On a VPN 3000 concentrator, you can go to the **Monitoring > Statistics > MIB-II Stats > IP screen**. Look at the bottom of the screen at the *Fragments Needing Reassembly* statistic. If this is incrementing, you have a device sending packets that are fragmented to the concentrator. Unfortunately, this won't tell you which client the fragments are coming from.

To determine if your Windows-based computer is performing the fragmentation, use the **netstat -s** command, shown in Example 12-15. Look at the bottom three lines under the *IP Statistics* section to determine if your remote access computer is creating fragments. In this example, five packets were fragmented into a total of 10 fragments.

Example 12-15 *Using the* **netstat** *Program to Find Client Fragmentation*

```
C:\> netstat -s
IP Statistics
  Packets Received                   = 91140
  Received Header Errors             = 0
  Received Address Errors            = 548
  Datagrams Forwarded                = 0
  Unknown Protocols Received         = 0
  Received Packets Discarded         = 0
  Received Packets Delivered         = 90709
  Output Requests                    = 92228
←output omitted→
  Reassembly Required                = 0
  Reassembly Successful              = 0
  Reassembly Failures                = 0
  Datagrams Successfully Fragmented  = 5
  Datagrams Failing Fragmentation    = 0
  Fragments Created                  = 10
←output omitted→
```

Of course, it might not be your remote access computer that's causing the problem, but an intermediate device. If your device's packets reach an intermediate device and the next-hop segment has a smaller MTU size, fragmentation is needed; however, the intermediate device might have disabled fragmentation, causing the packet to be dropped. Normally the intermediate device should send back an ICMP Destination Unreachable message with the "Don't Fragment" flag set. Some intelligent end system devices can then dynamically change their MTU size to meet the smaller MTU requirements. However, this doesn't always work correctly in the real world. Therefore, you might need to determine the smaller MTU size and change your device's configuration properly. To discover the router that has the MTU issue, sometimes referred to as the *blackhole router*, use the Windows **ping** command with the **-f** (sets the "do not fragment" flag) and the **–1** (specifies the payload size of the ICMP packet) parameters:

```
ping -f -n #_of_echos -1 payload_size_in_bytes destination_IP_address
```

Because Ethernet has an MTU size of 1,500 bytes and the Ethernet header is 8 bytes and the IP header is 20 bytes, set the payload size to 1,472 in the **ping** command initially. This will help determine if an intermediate router is having MTU issues with the size of packets you're sending through it. You might want to start with a smaller payload size to determine if the ICMP echos are successfully getting through, and then slowly increase the size to determine what the actual MTU size should be for your session. Example 12-16 shows an example of using the **ping** command on a Windows computer. The first ping test shows that no fragmentation occurred with a payload size of 1,472 bytes; however, as soon as I set the payload to 1,473 bytes (which will need to be fragmented), I received an ICMP message back in relation to this.

Example 12-16 *Using the* **ping** *Program to Find an Optimal MTU Size*

```
C:\> ping -f -n 1 -l 1472 192.1.1.1
 Pinging 192.1.1.1 with 1472 bytes of data:
 Reply from 192.1.1.1: bytes=1472 time<10ms TTL=128
 Ping statistics for 192.1.1.1:
     Packets: Sent = 1, Received = 1, Lost = 0 (0% loss),
 Approximate round trip times in milli-seconds:
     Minimum = 0ms, Maximum = 0ms, Average = 0ms
 C:\> ping -f -n 1 -l 1473 192.1.1.1
 Pinging 192.1.1.1 with 1473 bytes of data:
 Packet needs to be fragmented but DF set.
 Ping statistics for 192.1.1.1:
     Packets: Sent = 1, Received = 0, Lost = 1 (100% loss),
 Approximate round trip times in milli-seconds:
     Minimum = 0ms, Maximum =  0ms, Average =  0ms
```

The problem with using **ping** to find an optional size is that you have to tweak the payload size continually to discover the optimal size. If you have Windows NT or higher, you can use the Network Monitor program to view the optimal size, as shown in Example 12-17. In this example I used **ping -f –l 1000** to create the output you see. In the output, the optimal size is 576 bytes—using this will not cause any fragmentation across the current path to 192.1.1.1.

Example 12-17 *Using the Network Monitor Program to Find an Optimal MTU Size*

```
+ FRAME: Base frame properties
 + ETHERNET: ETYPE = 0x0800 : Protocol = IP:  DOD Internet Protocol
 + IP: ID = 0x4401; Proto = ICMP; Len: 56
   ICMP: Destination Unreachable: 192.1.1.1   See frame 3
       ICMP: Packet Type = Destination Unreachable
       ICMP: Unreachable Code = Fragmentation Needed, DF Flag Set
       ICMP: Checksum = 0xA05B
       ICMP: Next Hop MTU = 576 (0x240)
       ICMP: Data: Number of data bytes remaining = 28 (0x001C)
     + ICMP: Description of original IP frame
```

On top of this, the size you find is optimal only for the current path the ICMP messages are traversing. This means that for a different Easy VPN Server, the size might be different; or if the traffic takes a different path to the same destination, your first optimal value still might cause fragmentation issues.

Fragmentation Solutions

There are two basic solutions you can use to solve fragmentation problems:

* Use Path MTU (PMTU) discovery
* Hard-code the MTU size for the adapter to a size that will always work

The preferable method is to use PMTU, which uses ICMP to discover the correct MTU setting for the current destination and automatically adjusts the MTU size. However, not all Windows systems support this or have it enabled. For XP and 2003, this is enabled by default. If you have Windows 2000, follow these steps to enable it:

1 Start the editor for the registry (**regedit.exe**).

2 Find this registry key: HKEY_LOCAL_MACHINE\SYSTEM\CurrentControlSet\Services\tcpip\ parameters.

3 Choose **Edit > New > DWORD Value**.

4 Change the name of the value to "EnablePMTUBHDetect," (without the quotes).

5 Right-click the name of the value and choose **Modify**.

6 Set the value to **1** and select the *Decimal* base radio button.

7 Click the **OK** button.

8 Exit the registry editor and reboot your computer for the results to take effect.

Your second option is to change the MTU size manually for your adapter. You can do this the hard way using Windows' registry editor (described here: http://support.microsoft.com/ default.aspx?scid=kb;en-us;Q314825) or the easy way by using the Cisco SetMTU program. This program is included in the installation of the Cisco VPN Client software. During the installation of the 4.x client, the MTU size is adjusted automatically to 1,300 bytes for all NICs installed on the client's desktop. In 3.x, you must run this program manually to set the MTU size.

To access the SetMTU program, from the Windows desktop go to **Start > Programs > Cisco Systems VPN Client > SetMTU**, which displays the window shown in Figure 12-27. You can adjust the MTU size manually here. For LAN-based connections, typically 1,300 bytes will remove the likelihood of experiencing fragmentation problems; for dialup connections, typically 576 bytes will do the trick.

TIP   Please note that for the 4.x client, all adapters have their MTU adjusted to 1,300 bytes. However, many times this isn't very efficient: Cisco assumes the worse case of doing something like NAT-T with IPsec with PPPoE or L2TP over IPsec with PPPoE. Also, for WAN adapters, you'll want to adjust this to a typically much smaller value, like 576 bytes.

Therefore, if your computer doesn't support PMTU, use the **ping** command to find a more exact size for your client. Of course, if your client is continuously making connections from different destinations, I would use the 1,300- or 576-byte configuration depending on the adapter; otherwise, I would fine-tune the MTU size until I find the optimal one.

Figure 12-27 *SetMTU Program*

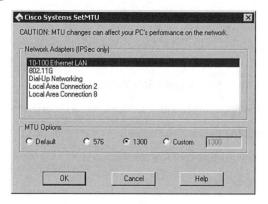

NOTE   I'll discuss fragmentation problems in more depth in Chapter 19, "Troubleshooting Router Connections."

Microsoft Network Neighborhood Issues

Besides address translation and fragmentation issues, the third biggest problem I commonly see network administrators deal with is Windows Network Neighborhood browsing and access issues when an IPsec session has been established. Some common problems might be that you can't ping a destination by its name, log in to a domain, browse the Network Neighborhood, or map a network drive. I'll discuss each of these problems, with their corresponding solutions, in the following subsections:

Cannot Log in to a Windows Domain

If you are having problems with logging in to a Windows domain, it probably is because you've misconfigured the Cisco VPN Client. Depending on the Windows platform you have, you'll do one of two things:

- For Windows 95/98/ME: The client doesn't initially log in to the domain upon bootup. On the desktop, right-click the **Network Neighborhood** icon and select **Properties**; make sure that the Client for Microsoft Networks and File and Print Sharing are displayed. Then, on the VPN Client, click a connection profile and from the main menu choose **Options > Windows Logon Properties**. Make sure *Enable start before logon* is checked. If not, select it and exit the client. Log out of Windows and log back in and reconnect—it is not necessary to reboot your PC.

- For Windows NT/2000/XP: the client is prompted during bootup to log in to a domain. This is a catch-22 because the IPsec session hasn't been established. If you try to start up the IPsec session, you'll get this error message: "No Domain Controller could be found." Follow the instructions in the above bulleted item to ensure that *Enable start before logon* is checked for the connection profile in the VPN Client.

Cannot Ping Network Resources

First make sure that you ping the destination by its IP address: this indicates that you have network connectivity; if you are unable to, the problem is not a name resolution problem. If you can ping the destination by its address, but not by its name, the problem is associated with name resolution. Be sure that the client is assigned a DNS and/or WINS server address. On a VPN 3000 concentrator, this is configured on a group-by-group basis. If all groups use the same resolution servers, configure this in the base group and let the specific groups inherit this. If there is still a problem, see the following section.

To see if your client is assigned a DNS and/or WINS server during IKE Mode Config, set the *IKE* log level to "High" and then start up the IPsec session to the Easy VPN Server. Example 12-18 shows the output from the Log viewer. In this example, a DNS server was assigned, but a WINS server wasn't. Also, if you're using split DNS, make sure this was set up correctly on the Easy VPN Server.

Example 12-18 *Determining if a DNS/WINS Server Address(es) Were Assigned to the Client*

```
←output omitted→
27    15:27:06.068  02/11/05  Sev=Info/5 IKE/0x63000010
MODE_CFG_REPLY: Attribute = INTERNAL_IPV4_ADDRESS: ,
value = 192.168.101.110
28    15:27:06.068  02/11/05  Sev=Info/5 IKE/0x63000010
MODE_CFG_REPLY: Attribute = INTERNAL_IPV4_NETMASK: ,
value = 255.255.255.0
29    15:27:06.068  02/11/05  Sev=Info/5 IKE/0x63000010
MODE_CFG_REPLY: Attribute = INTERNAL_IPV4_DNS(1): ,
value = 192.168.101.99
←output omitted→
38    15:27:06.088  02/11/05  Sev=Info/4 IKE/0x63000055
Received a key request from Driver: Local IP = 192.168.101.110,
GW IP = 192.1.1.1, Remote IP = 0.0.0.0
```

Cannot Browse the Network or Map a Network Drive

One limitation of IPsec is that it requires IP as a transport. With Microsoft Networking, you might be configured to transport NetBIOS over NetBEUI, which can't be transported across an IPsec tunnel. This is a common problem I see when administrators are converting from Microsoft's L2TP/IPsec or PPTP clients to the Cisco client; Microsoft uses PPP as a transport, which can carry NetBEUI. Cisco uses IP, which won't.

If you have this problem, double-click the *Network Neighborhood* icon on the desktop and verify that the corporate resources are appearing. If they are not, then it is probably a WINS resolution problem; in that case, see the previous section. If you're using an LMHOSTS file for resolution, use the names listed in this file; you can view these by executing **nbtstat -c** from the Windows command prompt. Also make sure that NetBIOS over TCP is enabled for your network adapter!

NOTE   Browsing the Network Neighborhood is a Microsoft browsing function and has nothing to do with the Cisco VPN Client—make sure that you have logged in to the Microsoft network first and are getting a WINS or DNS server address from the Easy VPN Server. Also make sure that no ACL is blocking the traffic between the Easy VPN Server and the corporate service.

Summary

This chapter introduced you to the Cisco VPN Client for Windows. Installing, configuring, and managing it is fairly easy. And with 4.6 and the auto-update feature, managing it becomes even easier. In the last part of the chapter I devoted quite a few pages to common problems you'll see when setting up remote access sessions. The most common of these problems are: address translation, fragmentation, and Microsoft Network access. Using the client Log event viewer and Windows command tools makes most troubleshooting tasks a simple process.

Next up is Chapter 13, "Windows Software Client," where I show you how to configure Microsoft's Windows Software Client for remote access connectivity to the VPN 3000 concentrators.

Windows Software Client

The last chapter discussed the use of the Cisco VPN Client to establish remote access IPsec sessions to a Cisco VPN gateway (Easy VPN Server) product, such as a concentrator, IOS router, or PIX firewall. Because many companies have policies that center on Microsoft products, you might have to use a Microsoft client to establish connections to a Microsoft VPN gateway. Likewise, your users might have to establish VPN connections to a Cisco gateway and a Microsoft gateway, requiring you to use both client products. This chapter will focus on using Microsoft's VPN client to establish PPTP or L2TP/IPsec connections to a VPN gateway.

NOTE   Even though Microsoft's Windows VPN client is obviously not a Cisco product, and this book is about Cisco VPNs, as a consultant I'm constantly asked questions about how to set up PPTP or L2TP over IPsec (L2TP/IPsec) sessions from a Microsoft client to a Cisco VPN gateway. Therefore I've decided to include this chapter in the book to help those people who must deal with this type of connectivity issue. This chapter, however, will focus only on the use of the client with the Windows 2000, XP, and 2003 operating systems, even though Microsoft has a different client that will run on older operating systems.

To help you with using Microsoft's VPN client, the following sections cover these topics:

- Windows Client
- Configuring the Windows VPN Client
- Configuring the VPN 3000 Concentrator
- Microsoft Client Connections
- Troubleshooting VPN Connections

Windows Client

Originally, the Microsoft Windows client software was developed for Remote Access Server (RAS) environments. Normally, you think of a remote access VPN as a solution that protects traffic from the user desktop to the VPN gateway at the corporate site, but

Microsoft added flexibility into the design with PPTP and L2TP/IPsec to allow an intermediate device, typically an RAS, to perform this process on behalf of the client. In this situation, the client would dial into the RAS with a clear-text PPP connection, authenticate via PPP, and then request the RAS to set up a PPTP or L2TP/IPsec encrypted connection to the corporate RAS. Using this process offloads the protection process to the RAS instead of to an underpowered user PC.

Today, of course, most PCs and laptops should have no problem handling the processing required to protect traffic for a VPN. Therefore, in today's networks, most PPTP or L2TP/ IPsec sessions start with the remote access user and terminate at the remote corporate office VPN gateway (see Chapter 4, "PPTP and L2TP," for more information on the connection and operation process of these protocols).

Understanding Features of the Windows Client

The current Windows client supports L2TP over IPsec (L2TP/IPsec) for VPN sessions, but also supports PPTP. With the L2TP/IPsec client, you can use either pre-shared keys or digital certificates for authentication. If you recall from Chapter 4, both protocols rely on PPP to perform authentication, provide protection services, and transport data.

Because of the encryption strength of 3DES, it is recommended to use L2TP/IPsec rather than either L2TP or PPTP with MPPE's encryption. Whereas 3DES supports 168-bit encryption, the highest that MPPE supports is RC-4's 128-bit encryption; and where MPPE provides only data confidentiality (encryption), IPsec provides data confidentiality, data origin authentication (using a hashing function), data integrity (using a hashing function), and anti-replay protection. Another concern with PPTP is that of security issues surrounding the use of MSCHAPv1 and v2 for authentication. Therefore, this chapter will focus on the use of L2TP over IPsec.

Cisco VPN Client versus
Microsoft's L2TP/IPsec Client

Obviously both clients support IPsec; however, even though they support IPsec, this basically means that they follow the first three steps in ISAKMP/IKE Phase 1 (negotiate the IKE parameters, use DH, and perform device authentication with either pre-shared keys or certificates) and ISAKMP/IKE Phase 2. As I pointed out in Chapter 7, "Concentrator Remote Access Connections with IPsec," Cisco has added some additional functionality to ISAKMP/IKE Phase 1 which is not part of the IPsec standards. For example, Cisco supports the following for their software and hardware clients: split-tunneling (supported only in XP by the L2TP/IPsec client) and split DNS, client type and version limiting, backup server lists, IPsec over TCP, client and network extension modes, reverse route injection, load balancing, and firewall policies, to name a few. When using a Microsoft L2TP/IPsec client, you don't have access to these features when terminating the client on a Cisco VPN gateway. In other words, using Cisco VPN products, for both the gateway *and* client devices, gives you much more centralized control over policies on the gateway device. Another disadvantage of Microsoft's client is that two levels of encryption will be used for data—IPsec and MPPE—adding additional overhead.

However, this is not to say that you should never use Microsoft's client. It does have some advantages related to the use of L2TP over IPsec. For example, because PPP is used, you can run multiple protocols across the connection, such as IP and IPX (Cisco VPN 3000 concentrators, though, only support IP). Plus, the client comes pre-installed on Windows 2000 and higher computers, so no extra software needs to be installed. You can even create a special installation package that installs all IPsec policies and VPN connection profiles. And before the release of Cisco VPN Client 4.6, upgrading the Cisco software client was not very easy.

Verifying that the Windows Client is Operational

With Windows 2000 and later, the Windows VPN client should be installed automatically when you install the operating system. However, if you have installed another VPN client product, the Microsoft VPN client might be deactivated (Starting with Cisco VPN 3.6 client software, Cisco and Microsoft's clients can co-exist with each other). To determine if the Microsoft VPN client is running, perform the following:

1   Go to **Start > (Programs) > Administrative Tools > Component Services**.

2   Double-click **Services (Local)** under the **Tree** tab.

3   Find the **IPsec Policy Agent** and make sure that it is set to "Automatic" (in XP, it's called **IPSEC Services**); if not, right-click it and select **Properties**. Set the Startup Type to **Automatic**. See Figure 13-1 for an example of this screen.

4   If it's not started, start it up by right-clicking **IPsec Policy Agent** and selecting *Start*.

By setting the service to automatic, every time you reboot your computer, the L2TP/IPsec client will be operational.

TIP   If you need to use both a Cisco VPN Client and Microsoft's L2TP/IPsec remote access products, you'll minimally need to use the Cisco 3.6 client version, which allows more than one VPN client to be used on the same platform. After installing the Cisco client, follow the guidelines in this section to verify that the L2TP/IPsec client is still active. In 3.5 and earlier versions of the Cisco client, the Cisco installation software automatically disables the Microsoft L2TP/IPsec client.

If you don't have the L2TP/IPsec client installed, go to http://www.microsoft.com/windows2000/techinfo/howitworks/communications/remoteaccess/l2tpclientfaq.asp.

You'll find the installation file (msl2tp.exe), and release notes and an administrator guide that you can download; Windows versions earlier than 2000 require the download of this file. Plus, with some Windows platforms, such as 2000, the L2TP over IPsec functionality in the client did not support NAT-T, which can create connectivity issues in environments using address translation; however, Microsoft has issued a patch to their VPN client that adds this functionality. Use the Windows Update utility on Microsoft's site to add this feature to your client.

Once you install this update, you'll need to reboot your computer. You must also have Version 1.4 of the Microsoft Dial-Up Networking software installed on your computer, which is required if you have Windows 95 (http://www.microsoft.com/downloads/release.asp?ReleaseID=29411&area=search&ordinal=1). You might need to install other service packs or updates as required by the operating system. For example, with Windows NT, you need Service Pack 6. Downloading the above-mentioned release notes will assist you with this process.

TIP   Because of the complexities in getting the right software loaded on the PC, you might want to put all of these on an internal web server or on a CD-ROM and have the user install the software from one of these locations.

Figure 13-1 *Windows Component Services Window*

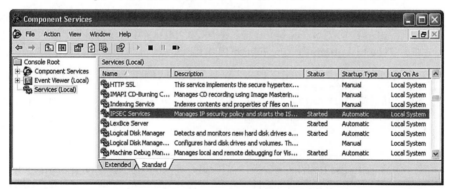

Configuring the Windows VPN Client

Once the Windows L2TP/IPsec client is running, you are ready to create a connection profile to protect traffic from the client to the corporate office. Creating a connection profile is done in four steps:

> **1** Obtaining certificates (optional—obtaining certificates on Microsoft Windows desktops is beyond the scope of this book; please consult your local Microsoft

administrator for more details): for Windows 2000 and earlier, you will need certificates to use L2TP/IPsec—pre-shared keys are not supported

2 Creating a security policy

3 Requiring the use of IPsec for L2TP

4 Creating a VPN connection

The following sections will discuss the last three steps in more depth.

Creating a Security Policy

Before you can create a VPN connection, you'll want to create a security policy. The security policy is used to define the method of authentication, such as pre-shared keys or certificates, and how the connection is protected. Here are the steps to create a security policy that your VPN connection will use:

1 Go to **Start > (Programs) > Administrative Tools > Local Security Policy** and click **IP Security Policies on Local Machine** under the **Security Settings** heading, shown in Figure 13-2.

2 Right-click **IP Security Policies on Local Machine** and choose **Create IP Security Policy**.

3 The IP Security Policy Wizard will begin. Click the **Next** button to go to the next screen.

4 You are taken to the IP Security Policy Name window. Enter the name of the security policy; for example, "Corporate Network Policy." Give it something descriptive that defines what the policy will be used for. Optionally, you can enter a multi-lined detailed description of the policy. Click the **Next** button when done.

5 You are taken to the Requests for Secure Communication window. This window allows you to activate the default response rule to use when the remote VPN gateway requests a security policy that doesn't match any that have been defined. There is only a check box on this screen labeled *Activate the default response rule*—it is recommended to keep this checked. Click the **Next** button when done.

6 You are taken to the Default Response Rule Authentication Method window, shown in Figure 13-3. Here you define the type of authentication to use with the VPN gateway: Windows 2000 with Kerberos v5, certificates (if you've installed them), or pre-shared keys. In this example, I entered a pre-shared key of "cisco." This also will need to be configured on the VPN gateway. Please note that only through the use of certificates can you use groups on Cisco products, where the OU (Organizational Unit)/Department field contents represent the group name. If you use pre-shared

keys, the users will be associated with the *Base Group* on Cisco concentrators. This is because there is no field in the L2TP/IPsec client which represents a group name when using pre-shared keys. Click the **Next** button to continue with the wizard.

7   Last, you are taken to the Completing the IP Security Policy Wizard window. There is only a check box on this screen, labeled *Edit Properties*, which is checked. If you click the **Finish** button, the wizard will complete, but you'll be taken to the Properties window for the policy you just created.

Figure 13-2   *Local Security Settings Window*

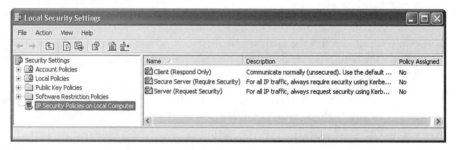

Figure 13-3   *Authentication Method*

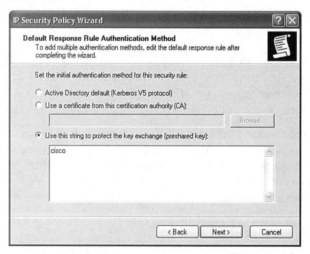

Edit Properties Windows: Rules Tab

Assuming you left the *Edit Properties* check box checked on the Completing the IP Security Policy Wizard window, you'll be taken to the Properties window shown in Figure 13-4 (you can also reach this screen by right-clicking the name of the policy in the right-hand column of the Local Security Settings window). The **Rules** tab will be in the foreground. In the *IP Security Rules* section, you'll see one default rule, called "<Dynamic>." From this screen you can modify the existing rule or create new rules. These rules define how traffic is to be protected based on the destination network to which you are sending it. Normally, you would not need to create more than one rule; however, you might want to edit the default one ("<Dynamic>"). Click the **Edit** button to do this.

Figure 13-4 *Security Policy Properties Window: Rules*

Here you'll see the Edit Rule Properties window shown in Figure 13-5, which displays the security policies, in order, that will be sent from the client to the VPN gateway to protect the IPsec data connections (ISAKMP/IKE Phase 2). You can add new rules, edit existing ones, delete rules, or reorder them, because they are sent in a top-down order to the VPN gateway and processed in this fashion. For sessions to Cisco gateway products, you should use ESP with encryption (3DES or DES) and an HMAC function (SHA or MD5). In the "Configuring the VPN 3000 Concentrator" section later in the chapter, I'll discuss how to set these up on the VPN 3000 concentrators. When adding or editing a rule's properties, you also can specify the lifetime of the data connection. The first policy listed uses ESP with SHA-1 and 3DES, with a data connection lifetime of 3,600 seconds).

From the Edit Rule Properties window, if you click the **Authentication Methods** tab, you'll see the window shown in Figure 13-6. You can see the pre-shared key authentication method I defined when adding the security policy. You can add multiple authentication methods, and they are processed in the order listed.

Figure 13-5 *Edit Rule Properties Window: Security Methods*

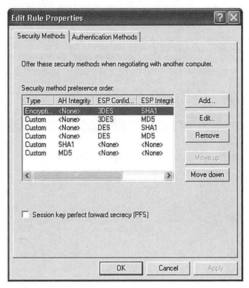

NOTE   Only Windows XP systems and higher support pre-shared keys for device authentication; all other Windows systems must use certificates!

Figure 13-6 *Edit Rule Properties Window: Authentication Methods*

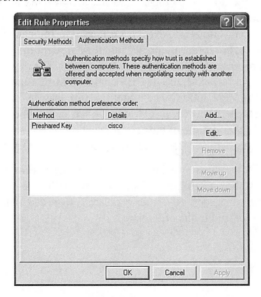

Edit Properties Windows: General Tab

In the Properties window shown in Figure 13-4, if you click the **General** tab, you'll be shown the window in Figure 13-7. If you click the **Advanced** button, you'll be taken to the window shown in Figure 13-8. You can enable PFS for the ISAKMP/IKE Phase 2 data connections (disabled by default) and change the default lifetime of the ISAKMP/IKE Phase 1 connection, which is 480 minutes (8 hours), but you can modify these.

Figure 13-7 *Security Policy Properties Window: General*

Figure 13-8 *Key Exchange Settings Window*

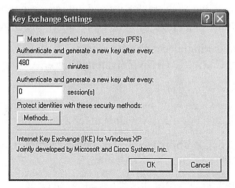

At the bottom of the window is a **Methods** button, which when clicked, displays the window in Figure 13-9. This is a list of pre-defined ISAKMP/IKE Phase 1 policies to use. At least one of these has to match one on the VPN gateway. You can change the integrity algorithm (SHA-1 or MD5), the encryption algorithm (3DES or DES), and the DH group to use (2 or 1). The first policy listed uses SHA-1, 3DES, and DH group 2 keys.

Figure 13-9 *Key Exchange Security Methods Window*

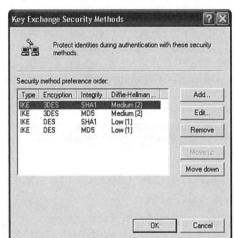

Policy Assignment

Once you have created your VPN connection policy, you must activate it for the policy to be used by any VPN connections. Right-click the policy name in the Local Security Settings window shown in Figure 13-2 and select **Assign**. In the far right-hand column, the *Policy Assignment* should change from "No" to "Yes."

Requiring the Use of L2TP

To enable your Windows computer to use L2TP instead of L2TP/IPsec (not recommended since MPPE is used for encryption) on Windows 2000 or XP, you must edit your Windows registry. Begin by going to **Start > Run** and entering **regedit** in the Open text box; then click the *OK* button. This opens up the editor for the registry. Then perform the following:

1 Go to the following place in the registry:
   HKEY_LOCAL_MACHINE\System\CurrentControlSet\Services\Rasman\Parameters

2 In the register value window on the right-hand side, right-click and choose **New > DWORD** Value. For the new value, enter a name of "ProhibitIpSec."

3 Then right-click **ProhibitIpSec** and choose *Modify.* In the *Value data* text box, set the value to "1." Then click the **OK** button.

4 Reboot your computer for this change to take effect.

CAUTION   Before you begin modifying the Windows registry, I highly recommend that you back it up *first!* Failure to do this can render the operating system inoperable if you incorrectly edit the registry.

Figure 13-10 shows an example of the registry after this change has been made. If you follow these steps, your Windows 2000 or XP computer will use L2TP *without* IPsec. However, since most of the Cisco products only support L2TP/IPsec, you should only perform the above when, possibly, connecting to a non-Cisco VPN gateway.

Figure 13-10 *Registry Change for Using L2TP/IPsec*

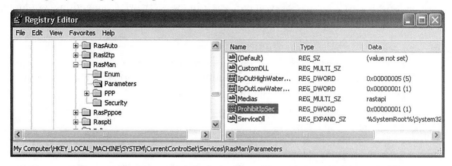

Creating a Microsoft VPN Connection

Once you have created your Windows client policy, you are now ready to create your remote access VPN session. The following sections will discuss how this is done.

Initial Connection Setup

Here are the steps to add a new remote access VPN session on your Windows computer:

1 On a Windows 2000 system, go to: **Start > Settings > Network and Dial-up Connections > Make New Connection**. On a Windows XP system, go to: **Start > My Network Places** and click **View network connections**, and then click **Create a new connection**.

2 You'll be presented with the New Connection Wizard window. Click the **Next** button.

3 For the *Network Connection Type* options, choose "Connect to the network at my workplace," which allows for the setup of dialup or VPN connections to your corporate office. Click the **Next** button.

4 On this screen there are two options: "Dial-up connection" and "Virtual Private Network connection." Click the radio button for the latter and then click the **Next** button.

5 In the Connection Name window, give the connection profile a descriptive name, such as "VPN Corporate Office Connection." Then click the **Next** button.

6 In the VPN Server Selection window, enter the IP address of the VPN gateway, such as a VPN 3000 concentrator, and click the **Next** button.

7   In the Completing the New Connection Wizard window, there is an optional check box to add a shortcut icon for this connection to your desktop. Click the **Finish** button to add the new connection profile.

When you are done, the profile will automatically start up, where you either can change the properties of the connection profile or connect to the VPN gateway via your profile. Once you have added your profile, you can see it in the Network Connections window under the *Virtual Private Network* section, as shown in Figure 13-11.

NOTE   The above steps are based on using Windows XP Professional, so there might be some slight differences with other Windows operating systems.

Figure 13-11 *Network Connections Window*

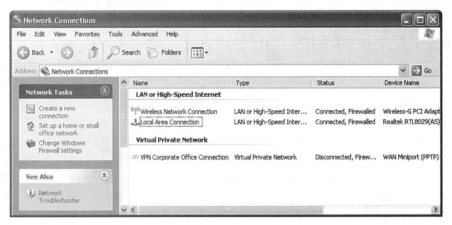

Connection Properties

Once you've added the connection profile, you'll need to modify its properties before using it. To do this, from the Network Connections window, right-click the VPN connection profile you've added and click **Properties**.

General Tab

You'll see the window shown in Figure 13-12, with the **General** tab in the foreground. From this tab you can change the IP address of the VPN gateway (at the top of the window), specify a dialup profile to use to connect to the ISP, and then use the VPN profile to connect to the VPN gateway (in the middle of the window), and allow a PC icon to display in the taskbar when a VPN connection is up (at the bottom of the window).

Figure 13-12 *Connection Properties Window: General Tab*

Options Tab

Clicking the **Options** tab takes you to the window shown in Figure 13-13. At the top are *Dialing Options*: you can have the connection profile manager display the status of the connection while the connection attempt is made, have the connection profile manager always prompt for a username and password (don't use the saved one), and include the Windows domain name in the login credentials. In the middle of the window are *Redialing* options, which specify the actions to take when a VPN connection is not set up successfully.

Security Tab

Clicking the **Security** tab takes you to the window shown in Figure 13-14. If you use the *Typical* settings, you can require the use of a secured password (some form of CHAP) or use a smartcard for authentication, use the Windows logon name and password (including any domain name) for authentication, and require data encryption between the client and gateway (if this is selected and encryption can't be successfully negotiated, the connection is dropped by the client).

Figure 13-13 *Connection Properties Window: Options Tab*

Figure 13-14 *Connection Properties Window: Security Tab*

If you click the **Advanced (custom settings)** radio button and click the **Settings** button (grayed-out in Figure 13-14), you can customize the settings: This is the option you need to choose when connecting to a Cisco VPN 3000 concentrator! This screen is shown in Figure 13-15. Select the data encryption option, leave it as "Require Encryption," because this is the most secure, and change the authentication method to what you've configured on the VPN gateway; in this example, I've chosen only MSCHAPv2; however, most customers will use EAP because EAP supports the most flexible number of authentication choices. Click the **OK** button to close the window.

Figure 13-15 *Advanced Security Settings Window*

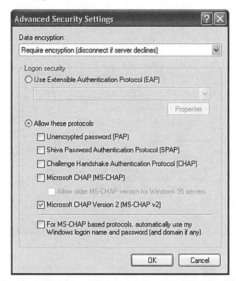

At the bottom of the window in Figure 13-14 is the **IPsec Settings** button. Clicking this takes you to the window in Figure 13-16. Here you can enter the pre-shared key that will be used during device authentication in ISAKMP/IKE Phase 1. This can be used to override the local policy configuration, which probably is necessary if you need to create multiple connection profiles for multiple VPN gateways. Click the **OK** button to accept your changes and return to the window in Figure 13-14.

Figure 13-16 *IPsec Pre-shared Key Configuration*

Network Tab

Clicking the **Network** tab in Figure 13-14 takes you to the window shown in Figure 13-17. At the top of the window you can choose the type of VPN: "Automatic," "PPTP VPN," or "L2TP IPsec VPN." If your client doesn't support L2TP/IPsec, you won't see the latter option, but just plain "L2TP VPN." I recommend that you choose L2TP/IPsec manually, because it is more secure than PPTP.

Figure 13-17 *Connection Properties Window: Networking Tab*

CAUTION   If you have set the *ProhibitIpSec* parameter in the registry to 1, then choosing "L2TP IPsec VPN" is misleading, because this selection causes your connection profile to use L2TP without IPsec!

In Figure 13-17, clicking the **Settings** button below the type selection will pop up a PPP Settings window where you can:

- **Enable LCP extensions**—enabled by default; LCP extensions are used by PPP to establish a session

- **Enable software compression**—enabled by default; for LAN connections, like cable modem or PPP over Ethernet, disable this!

- **Negotiate multi-link for single link connections**—disabled by default

---

TIP   Be sure that for LAN connections, you disable the *Enable software compression* option in the PPP Settings window; otherwise, your VPN throughput will suffer dramatically.

Below the types of VPN selections in Figure 13-17 is the list of the networking protocols and features enabled. You might want to configure your TCP/IP settings for the VPN connection by double-clicking the "Internet Protocol (TCP/IP)." The screen you see here is the same you would see if configuring a physical adapter. Be sure the *Obtain an IP address automatically* radio box is selected. Unfortunately, split DNS is not supported, so if you need to resolve DNS names located at the corporate office where these devices are using private addresses, then you must ensure that the *Obtain DNS server address automatically* radio box is also selected.

At the bottom of this same window is an **Advanced** button; clicking this pulls up the Advanced TCP/IP Settings window where three tabs are shown:

- **General**—allows you to define routing options.
- **DNS**—allows you to define DNS options, like appending name suffixes together, dynamic DNS, and so on.
- **WINS**—allows you to add multiple WINS server addresses, including the prioritization of their usage, enable LMHOSTS lookup, and enable or disable NetBIOS over TCP/IP (enabled by default).

The only tab I'll talk about is the **General** tab, because this can create connectivity problems if not properly configured (the other two tabs are self-explanatory). There is only one option in this window: a check box for *Use default gateway on remote network,* which specifies the VPN gateway as the default route when a VPN connection is established, overriding any other default route on your PC. This is enabled by default.

When you choose this option, the VPN default route is used for all traffic sent by your computer. In other words, all traffic is sent to the VPN gateway. Unfortunately, split-tunneling is not supported by Microsoft's client (if you used the Cisco VPN Client, then you wouldn't have this problem because you could enable split-tunneling). There are two ways you can solve your routing issues in this instance:

- Use the default route feature, causing all of your computer's traffic to be routed first to the VPN gateway, and then to its destination. In many instances this can place an undue burden on the VPN gateway. Example 13-1 shows the routing table of a computer with this option enabled. As you can see from this example, the internally assigned address from the VPN gateway is the default route, which means that all traffic must be sent across the VPN tunnel before going to its ultimate destination. The problem with this approach is that all traffic—corporate office and Internet—must be sent to the VPN gateway. The only exception to this is local LAN traffic.
- Disable the default route feature. Upon doing this, your computer no longer will know how to reach destinations across the L2TP/IPsec tunnel at the corporate office.

NOTE   In Windows XP, the L2TP/IPsec client does support split-tunneling population via DHCP: this was a new feature added in VPN 3000 Concentrator's Version 4.0 software. Even though it doesn't have the same level of absolute enforcement as the Cisco VPN client, it is available and a more preferable solution than the two above bullet points.

Example 13-1 *IP Configuration and Routing*

```
C:\> ipconfig
Windows IP Configuration

Ethernet adapter Local Area Network:
        Connection-specific DNS Suffix . :
        IP Address. . . . . . . . . . .: 192.1.1.67
        Subnet Mask . . . . . . . . . .: 255.255.255.0
        Default Gateway . . . . . . . .:

PPP adapter VPN Corporate Office Connection:
        Connection-specific DNS Suffix . :
        IP Address. . . . . . . . . . .: 192.168.101.120
        Subnet Mask . . . . . . . . . .: 255.255.255.0
        Default Gateway . . . . . . . .: 192.168.101.120
C:\> route print
←output omitted→
Active Routes:
Network Dest        Netmask          Gateway        Interface   Metric
      0.0.0.0          0.0.0.0  192.168.101.120  192.168.101.120       1
    192.1.1.0  255.255.255.0        192.1.1.67       192.1.1.67      30
←output omitted→
```

To solve the latter problem in the previous bulleted list, you'll need to create static routes on your computer with the **route** command. For example, assume that there are two networks at the corporate office your computer needs to access across the L2TP/IPsec connection: 192.168.101.0/24 and 192.168.102.0/24. You'll need to create two static routes. However, for the next-hop address, you'll have to put the VPN gateway assigned address (the internal one), which is dynamically assigned to the client. This causes the computer to route traffic for the specified networks across the VPN connection. For example, if the VPN gateway assigned you an internal address of 192.168.101.120 (determined by using the **ipconfig** command), your two static routes would be like that shown in Example 13-2:

Example 13-2 *Static Route Configuration*

```
C:\> route add 192.168.101.0 mask 255.255.255.0 192.168.101.120
C:\> route add 192.168.102.0 mask 255.255.255.0 192.168.101.120
```

The problem with this approach is that because your computer always acquires its address dynamically, each time you establish a VPN connection, you would have to re-enter the static routes manually with the correct internally assigned address. If this creates problems, then configure an internal address on the client statically in the Network Settings for the VPN connection profile on the computer and then, on the concentrator, in the user's group under the *PPTP/L2TP* tab, check the *Use Client Address* check box. By using this option, you can create the static routes with the **-d** option, which makes them persistent routes: they'll stay in the computer's configuration even if you reboot the computer. Using this solution reduces the burden on the computer and VPN gateway because all traffic doesn't have to be protected and forwarded to the gateway. In this example, only 192.168.101.0/24 and 192.168.102.0/24 traffic is protected and forwarded to the VPN gateway.

NOTE   The above solution is not valid for laptops that will be connected directly to the corporate network sometimes and at other times connected via an L2TP/IPsec session.

Advanced Tab

Clicking the **Advanced** tab in Figure 13-14 takes you to the window in Figure 13-18. In the *Windows Firewall* section at the top (Windows XP SP2 and higher only), clicking the **Settings** button pulls up the Windows Firewall window, which allows you to configure firewall rules for the VPN connection (if this is necessary). Below the *Windows Firewall* section is the *Internet Connection Sharing* section, where you can define sharing properties for allowing other network users to use your VPN session.

TIP   If a corporate office network administrator needs to access your machine remotely for troubleshooting purposes, click the **Exceptions** tab in the Windows Firewall window and check the *Remote Desktop* check box.

Figure 13-18 *Connection Properties Window: Advanced Tab*

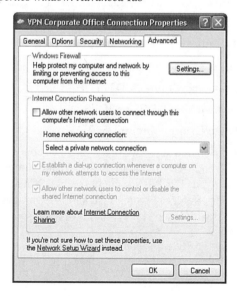

Configuring the VPN 3000 Concentrator

Now that I've explained how to configure the Microsoft client, I'll focus on things you need to configure on Cisco VPN 3000 concentrators to support Windows client access. I covered many of these screens in Chapter 8, "Concentrator Remote Access Connections with PPTP, L2TP, and WebVPN," so I'll briefly explain the items that you must create or change to support Microsoft connections in the following sections. Here are the basic items you need to configure or add to your concentrator's configuration:

- IKE Proposals
- IPsec SAs
- Group Configuration: Specific and/or Base Group
- Address Management
- User Configuration

IKE Proposals

First, on your concentrator you need to ensure that you either have created or activated an IKE proposal that will work with the Microsoft L2TP/IPsec client (assuming that you're not using plain L2TP or PPTP). On the concentrator, go to **Configuration > Tunneling and Security > IPsec > IKE Proposals**.

Proposal names beginning with "CiscoVPNClient" will *not* work with Microsoft's L2TP/IPsec client—the Microsoft client doesn't understand the concept of groups and XAUTH. Therefore, you need to choose a proposal that doesn't do XAUTH authentication, like those beginning with "IKE."

IKE proposals that will work include these properties:

- **Authentication mode**—Pre-shared keys and RSA and DSA certificates
- **Authentication algorithm**—MD5 or SHA1
- **Encryption algorithm**—DES or 3DES
- **Diffie-Hellman Group**—Group 1 or 2

If you'll be using pre-shared keys, two of the included concentrator proposals that will work are IKE-DES-MD5 and IKE-3DES-MD5—just make sure you haven't deactivated these security policies for your L2TP/IPsec client (see the "Creating a Security Policy" section earlier in the chapter). Refer to Figures 7-18 and 7-19 in Chapter 7, "Concentrator Remote Access Connections with IPsec" for examples of these screens.

NOTE	I've experienced a lot of headaches with customizing Microsoft's L2TP/IPsec client. In many instances, I've had to use an IKE Policy that had only DES for encryption, DH group 1 keys, and either MD5 or SHA for an HMAC function because of the quirks in Microsoft's software.

IPsec SAs

Next, on the VPN 3000 concentrator, create an IPsec SA transform that will be used to protect the ISAKMP/IKE Phase 2 data connections for the Windows client. To do this, go to **Configuration > Policy Management > Traffic Management > SAs**. Click the **Add** button to add a new SA, and then enter the following for the SA parameters:

- **SA Name**—"ESP-L2TP-Transport," or something similar
- **Authentication Algorithm**—ESP with MD5 or SHA
- **Encryption Algorithm**—DES or 3DES
- **Encapsulation Mode**—Transport
- **Perfect Forward Secrecy**—Disabled (this can be enabled if you enabled it on the Windows client)
- **Lifetime Measurement**—Time
- **IKE Peer**—0.0.0.0
- **Negotiation Mode**—Main
- **Digital Certificate**—Either the name of the certificate to use, if certificates will be used for authentication, or "None (Use Preshared Keys)"
- **IKE Proposal**—The name of the IKE proposal you created in the last section.

Click the **Add** button to add your new SA. Figures 13-19 and 13-20 show an example IPsec SA that is used by L2TP/IPsec clients.

NOTE	I'd like to point out two important pieces of information regarding the setup of your data SA for L2TP/IPsec clients. First, the encapsulation mode must be set to *transport* mode, not tunnel. Second, I've experienced with some Windows platforms that in some cases, no matter what IKE Proposal you choose from this screen, the only one that the L2TP/IPsec client will use is one with DES and either MD5 or SHA. Even if you don't specify it here, this IKE Proposal must be activated in the IKE Proposal screen on the concentrator—this never made any sense to me because the concentrator basically ignores what you have configured on this screen for the IKE Proposal!

Figure 13-19 *SA Configuration: Top of Screen*

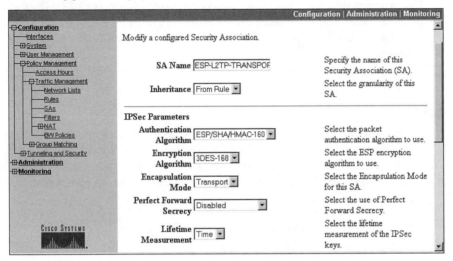

Figure 13-20 *SA Configuration: Bottom of Screen*

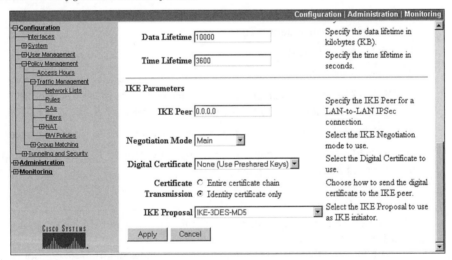

Group Configuration

If your L2TP/IPsec clients are using pre-shared keys, the concept of a group is nonexistent; therefore, you'll need to configure these clients' remote access properties in the concentrator's Base Group. Otherwise, if the clients are using certificates, whatever name appears in the OU (Organizational Unit) field is the name of the group you'll need to configure on the concentrator; then configure this group for these users.

NOTE   You can also use the certificate/group matching feature of the concentrator to examine other certificate fields, and based on the matching rules you create, put a user into a specific, or even a default, group.

In this section, assume that pre-shared keys are being used and that you'll need to configure the Base Group (the configuration is the same for the Base Group versus a specific group). To configure the Base Group, go to **Configuration > User Management > Base Group** and then perform the following:

1   Click the **General** Tab and choose the *Tunneling Protocols* you want these users to use, such as L2TP over IPsec, L2TP, or PPTP, depending on the security protocol(s) your Microsoft clients will be using. Deselect the ones you won't be using. If the clients will be sending the Windows domain name with their authentication, and the concentrator will be performing internal authentication, select the check box for *Strip Realm.*

2   Click the **IPsec** tab. For the *IPsec SA* parameter, use the pull-down selector and choose the name of the SA you created in the last section, such as "ESP-L2TP-Transport." If you'll be defining the users on the concentrator, then select "Internal" for the *Authentication* parameter. In most cases, you'll probably use "NT Domain" or "Kerberos Active Directory," because these are Microsoft users; if this is the case, then you'll need to add these servers to the concentrator by going to **Configuration > System > Servers > Authentication**. If you're using pre-shared keys for device authentication, set the *Default Preshared Key* parameter under the **IPsec** tab to match the pre-shared key the L2TP/IPsec clients will use.

3   Click the **PPTP/L2TP** tab. If clients will be using their own internally assigned address (which I wouldn't recommend), click the *Use Client Address* check box. If you'll be using PPTP, select the correct protocols for the *PPTP Authentication Protocols* parameter. To ensure that encryption is used for PTTP, select "Required" for *PPTP Encryption* and both 40-bit and 128-bit encryption if you're not sure which of the two clients will use. By using encryption, PPTP will only use MS-CHAPv1 or v2 for authentication (this is also true of L2TP). For L2TP or L2TP/IPsec clients, choose the correct *L2TP Authentication Protocols* and the correct *L2TP Encryption* algorithms.

The screens and their contents discussed above are found throughout Chapter 7, "Concentrator Remote Access Connections with IPsec," and Chapter 8, "Concentrator Remote Access Connections with PPTP, L2TP, and WebVPN."

CAUTION If you are using pre-shared keys, then because all clients are placed in the Base Group, they all must use the same pre-shared key, which might introduce security risks. A better approach would be to use certificates for authentication. Your IPsec SA and IKE proposal would have to reflect this configuration, though.

Address Management

If the concentrator will be assigning addresses to the Windows client for the VPN connection, you'll need to create an address pool. For the Base Group (pre-shared key authentication), go to **Configuration > System > Address Management > Address Pools**. Click the **Add** button to add a new address pool. In the *Range Start* text box, enter the beginning IP address in the pool; in the *Range End* text box, enter the ending address in the pool; and in the *Subnet Mask* text box, enter the subnet mask associated with the pool of addresses. Click the **Add** button when done.

For certificate authentication, if you choose to use specific groups, you can create an address pool per group. First, create the group from the **Configuration > User Management > Groups** screen and configure the group. Once you have configured it (as discussed in the last section), from the specific group listing screen, click the name of the group, and then click the **Address Pools** button. Click the **Add** button to add a new address pool for the group, and follow the instructions in the last paragraph.

NOTE Please note that you can also use an external DHCP or AAA server to assign addresses to the Windows clients, as discussed in Chapter 7. If clients always need to have the same IP address assigned to them, instead of manually assigning it on the client, I would use AAA RADIUS for authentication and have the AAA server assign the address to the client.

User Configuration

If you'll be defining the PPTP, L2TP, or L2TP/IPsec users locally on the concentrator, go to **Configuration > User Management > Users** and click the **Add** button. Refer to Chapters 7 and 8, for snapshots of the following screens. Under the **Identity** tab, enter the name of the users along with their passwords. For the *Group* parameter, specify the name of the group the users belong to (for pre-shared key authentication, this must be the Base Group). If you always want to assign the same IP address to a user, enter the IP address and subnet mask under this tab (I recommend *not* letting the users assign their own addresses on the client). There are also **General, IPsec,** and **PPTP/L2TP** tabs, where you can override the properties of group the users belong to: otherwise, the users' accounts will inherit the configuration properties from the group name you specified under the **Identity** tab. Click the **Add** button at the bottom of the screen to add the users.

Microsoft Client Connections

Now that you have configured the Microsoft client(s) and VPN 3000 concentrator, the client can now establish a connection to the concentrator. The following sections will discuss how to establish a connection from the client to the concentrator. The network shown in Figure 13-21 illustrates the process.

Figure 13-21 *L2TP/IPsec Client and VPN 3000 Concentrator Example*

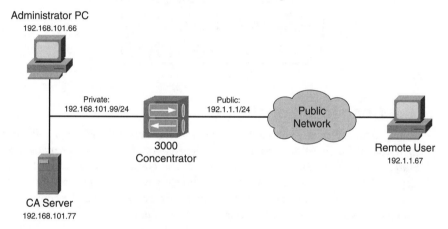

Connecting to a VPN Gateway

On the Microsoft computer, open the Network Connections window in one of the following ways:

- On Windows 2000, go to **Start > Settings > Network and Dialup Connections,** right-click and choose **Explore**.

- On Windows XP, go to **Start > My Network Places > View network connections**.

In this window there should be a section entitled *Virtual Private Network,* listing the VPN connections you have set up from the "Creating a Microsoft VPN Connection" section earlier in the chapter. Their statuses should say "Disconnected." Either double-click the name of the VPN connection profile or right-click the name and choose **Connect**. You should see the Connection window, shown in Figure 13-22.

Enter your username and password and click the **Connect** button. Assuming that you enabled the *Display progress while connecting* parameter for the connection profile, a window will pop up displaying the status of the building of the connection. Likewise, if you enabled the *Show icon in the notification area when connected*, you should see a PC icon in the taskbar once the connection is completed.

Figure 13-22 *Microsoft VPN Client Connection Window*

Verifying the Connection on the PC

To see status information about the connection, right-click the PC icon in the taskbar or right-click the connection profile name in the Network Connections window and choose **Status**. There are two tabs at the top of the screen: **General** and **Details**. The **General** tab displays how long the session has been up, how many bytes were sent and received, how many packets were compressed, and how many errors were sent and received. Clicking the **Details** tab, you can see how the connection is configured, as shown in Figure 13-23.

Figure 13-23 *Microsoft VPN Client Status Detail Window*

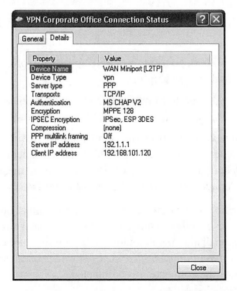

In this example, MS-CHAPv2 was used for authentication and MPPE RC-128 bit encryption for L2TP. For the IPsec data SA, 3DES is used for encryption. The address assigned to the client by the VPN gateway is 192.168.101.120. At this point, the client should be able to ping anything behind the concentrator, like 192.168.101.99, 192.168.101.66, and 192.168.101.77.

To disconnect the VPN session, right-click the PC icon in the taskbar or right-click the connection profile name in the Network Connections window and choose **Disconnect**.

Verifying the Connection on the Concentrator

Once the PPTP, L2TP, or L2TP/IPsec client makes a connection to the concentrator, you should be able to see the connection status on the concentrator by going to **Monitor > Sessions**, shown in Figure 13-24. As you can see from this figure, the user called "l2tp" has terminated a VPN connection on the concentrator and was assigned an IP address of 192.168.101.120. This connection is associated with the Base Group and is protected by L2TP/IPsec 3DES.

Figure 13-24 *Session Overview Screen*

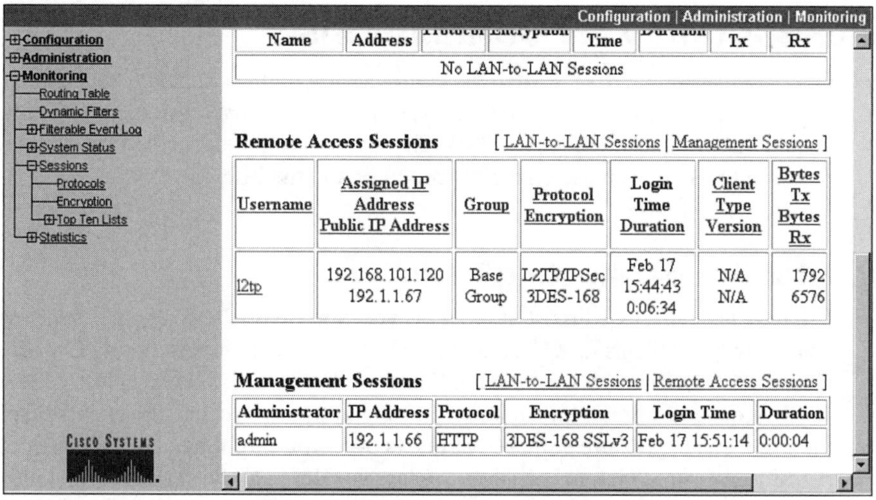

Clicking the name of the user takes you to the screen in Figure 13-25. Here you can see how the connection is protected by IKE (DES, SHA, pre-shared keys, and DH group 1), IPsec (3DES, SHA, and transport mode), and L2TP (RC4-128 and MS-CHAPv2).

Figure 13-25 *Session Detail Screen*

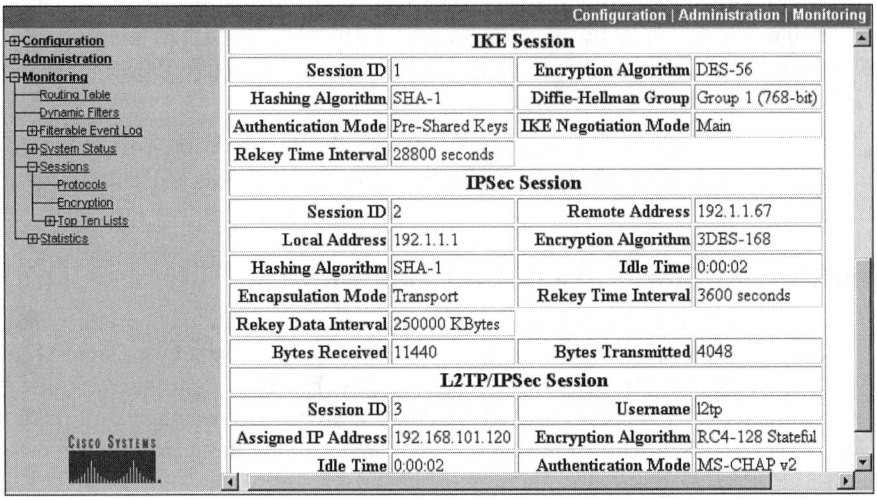

Troubleshooting VPN Connections

Of course, once you have created the configuration on the client and concentrator, there's no guarantee it will work the first time you try to bring up a session. I've already talked about a few troubleshooting processes related to routing previously in the chapter. Now I'll focus on tools you can use on the concentrator and the Microsoft client.

Concentrator Troubleshooting Tools

I already have discussed most of the tools you can use on the concentrator to troubleshoot connectivity problems (see Chapter 11, "Verifying and Troubleshooting Concentrator Connections"). First, I would use the Filterable Event Log, since it is less CPU-intensive for the concentrator, and it supports filtering actions. Because the events displayed in the log file typically are captured at levels 3–5, you might need to add an event class (**Configuration > System > Events > Classes**). Here are the classes that would apply to Microsoft clients:

- **AUTH**—Authentication functions (such as PAP or MS-CHAP) with PPP
- **CERT**—Device authentication with certificates when using L2TP/IPsec
- **IKE**—ISAKMP/IKE Phase 1 problems
- **IPSEC**—ISAKMP/IKE Phase 2 problems

- **L2TP**—L2TP problems
- **PPP**—L2TP's and PPTP's use of PPP (like MPPE)
- **PPTP**—PPTP problems

Use the Filterable Event Log to get an idea as to what the problem might be and then add the required event class(es). Then go back to the Filterable Event Log to pinpoint the problem.

TIP   When done troubleshooting, be sure to delete the event classes you added; otherwise you'll be capturing more logging information than necessary.

Microsoft Client Troubleshooting Tools

In most cases, you'll be able to troubleshoot the problem from the concentrator's end; however, in those instances when you can't, or if you're not connecting to a VPN 3000 concentrator, there are quite a few things you can do from the Microsoft client end of the connection to pinpoint the problem. The following sections will discuss some of the things you can do to help troubleshoot VPN connection problems on a Microsoft platform. The tools I focus on are used on a Windows XP system; however, many of them will work on Windows 2000 and earlier systems.

IP Security Monitor Snap-In

The IP Security Monitor snap-in application for MMC allows you to view your security policy settings, and the policies being used for any existing L2TP/IPsec connections. To add the IP Security Monitor Snap-in to MMC, follow these instructions:

1 Go to **Start > Run** and enter **mmc**; then click the **OK** button.

2 Go to **File > Add/Remove Snap-in**.

3 In the **Standalone** tab, click the **Add** button.

4 Find **IP Security Monitor**, click it, and then click the Add button.

5 Click the **Close** button in the Add Standalone Snap-in window and the **OK** button in the Add/Remove Snap-in window.

Once you have an L2TP/IPsec connection established, you can go to MMC with this snap-in and see how the connection is protected in ISAKMP/IKE Phase 1 (under **IP Security Monitor > *Computer Name* > Main Mode > Security Associations**) and ISAKMP/IKE Phase 2 (under **IP Security Monitor > *Computer Name* > Quick Mode > Security**

Associations). Figure 13-26 shows where I double-clicked the L2TP/IPsec entry in the latter location. As you can see, L2TP (port 1,701) is being used over IPsec (ESP 3DES and SHA-1 with a lifetime of 3,600 seconds).

TIP   You might want to save the MMC console as a special file: then from the MMC application, you can load this, which will include all of the other snap-ins you have added previously.

Figure 13-26 *MMC and IP Security Monitor*

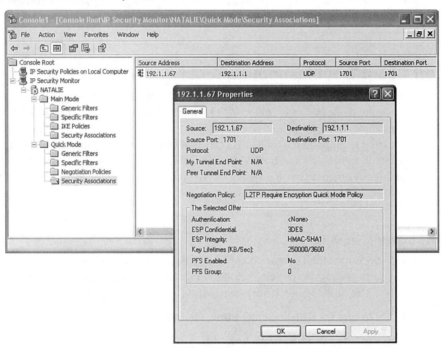

IPsecCMD

Another tool you can use is the **ipseccmd** command in Windows XP; however, this first requires you to download a set of support tools from Microsoft and install them. These tools are a part of the Windows XP Service Pack 2 Support Tools package. This command (and other tools) is found by going to: http://www.microsoft.com/downloads/details.aspx?FamilyID= 49ae8576-9bb9-4126-9761-ba8011fabf38&DisplayLang=en.Link verified. Once you have downloaded and installed them, you can open a Windows command prompt to use this command.

There are several parameters for the **ipseccmd** command; however, I'll only focus on two: **show sas** and **show stats**. Example 13-3 shows an example of the **ipseccmd show sas** command. This displays the current ISAKMP/IKE Phase 1 and Phase 2 SAs established to remote peers. Please note that you can see the same type of information from the IP Security Monitor snap-in. The **ipseccmd show stats** command displays statistics related to IPsec SAs, including the number of connections set up, the number of attempts that failed, packet statistics (number of packets authenticated and decrypted), and many more statistics.

Example 13-3 *The* **ipseccmd show sas** *Command*

```
C:\> ipseccmd show sas
Main Mode SAs
- - - - - - - - - - - - - - - - - - - - - - - - - - - -
Main Mode SA #1:
 From 192.1.1.67
  To   192.1.1.1
 Policy Id : {8D7E56B0-6A03-4BAE-8A51-243A4DDC443F}
 Offer Used :
         DES SHA1  DH Group 1
         Quickmode limit : 0, Lifetime 0Kbytes/28800seconds
 Auth Used : Preshared Key
 Initiator cookie 01799ad050d44371
 Responder cookie 1aeffc5ad47e220b
 Source UDP Encap port : 500  Dest UDP Encap port: 500

Quick Mode SAs
- - - - - - - - - - - - - - - - - - - - - - - - - - - -
Quick Mode SA #1:
 Filter Id : {2F998F9A-8393-440E-8BF0-1FE43D6532B1}
  Transport Filter
  From 192.1.1.67
   To  192.1.1.1
 Protocol : 17  Src Port : 1701  Des Port : 1701
 Direction : Outbound
 Policy Id : {3369FE53-D30F-43AA-A285-FAC9266E97C4}
 Offer Used :
         Algo #1 : Encryption 3DES SHA1 (24bytes/0rounds)
                   (20secbytes/0secrounds)
                   MySpi 2425637736 PeerSpi 1065420224
         PFS : False, Lifetime 250000Kbytes/3600seconds
 Initiator cookie 01799ad050d44371
 Responder cookie 1aeffc5ad47e220b

The command completed successfully.
```

Audit Logging

The Event Viewer application in Microsoft Windows allows you to see events related to system and application activities. By default, IPsec events are not recorded in the Event Viewer; however, you can enable these to help troubleshoot problems. To do this, perform the following:

1   Go to **Start > Run** and enter **regedit** in the open box and click the **OK** button. In the Windows registry, go to **HKEY_Local_MACHINE\System\CurrentControlSet\ Services\IPsec** (before changing the registry, make sure you first back it up!).

2 Right-click in the right-hand window pane and choose **New > DWORD Value**. Change its name to "DiagnosticMode."

3 Double-click **DiagnosticMode** and in the *Value data* field, enter "1." Click the **OK** button to accept your change.

4 Reboot your computer. Once your computer has rebooted, the registry change will take effect.

Next, you need to enable audit logging for logon events and policy changes. To do this, follow these instructions:

1 Go to **Start > (Programs) > Administrative Tools > Local Security Policy** (this window was shown previously in Figure 13-2).

2 Double-click **Local Policies** and then double-click **Audit Policy**.

3 Double-click **Audit logon events** and check the check boxes for *Success* and *Failure*; then click the **OK** button.

4 Double-click **Audit object access** and check the check boxes for *Success* and *Failure*; then click the **OK** button.

Now you can view events in the Event Viewer related to IPsec when connections are established. To see your events, go to **Start > (Programs) > Administrative Tools > Event Viewer**. Double-click **Security** to view all of the security events in the right-hand window. Those related to the auditing functions you've just enabled will be labeled "Success Audit" and "Failure Audit." To view an event, just double-click it. Example 13-4 shows an example of the former for the successful setup of an L2TP/IPsec connection.

Example 13-4 *Event Viewer: Successful L2TP/IPsec Session Setup*

```
IKE security association established.
 Mode:
Data Protection Mode (Quick Mode)

 Peer Identity:
Preshared key ID.
Peer IP Address: 192.1.1.1

 Filter:
Source IP Address 192.1.1.67
Source IP Address Mask 255.255.255.255
Destination IP Address 192.1.1.1
Destination IP Address Mask 255.255.255.255
Protocol 17
Source Port 1701
Destination Port 1701
```

Example 13-4 *Event Viewer: Successful L2TP/IPsec Session Setup (Continued)*

```
IKE Local Addr 192.1.1.67
IKE Peer Addr 192.1.1.1

 Parameters:
ESP Algorithm Triple DES CBC
HMAC Algorithm SHA
AH Algorithm None
Encapsulation Transport Mode
InboundSpi 2425637736 (0x90944b68)
OutBoundSpi 1065420224 (0x3f8105c0)
Lifetime (sec) 3600
Lifetime (kb) 250000

For more information, see Help and Support Center at http://go.microsoft.com/fwlink/
events.asp.
```

Example 13-5 shows an example of the latter for the failure of a setup of an L2TP/IPsec session. In this example, the negotiation of the ISAKMP/IKE Phase 1 policies failed (see the first line).

Example 13-5 *Event Viewer: Failed L2TP/IPsec Session Setup*

```
IKE security association negotiation failed.
 Mode:
Data Protection Mode (Quick Mode)

 Filter:
Source IP Address 192.1.1.67
Source IP Address Mask 255.255.255.255
Destination IP Address 192.1.1.1
Destination IP Address Mask 255.255.255.255
Protocol 17
Source Port 1701
Destination Port 1701
IKE Local Addr 192.1.1.67
IKE Peer Addr 192.1.1.1

 Peer Identity:
Preshared key ID.
Peer IP Address: 192.1.1.1

 Failure Point:
Me

 Failure Reason:
IKE SA deleted by peer before establishment completed
←output omitted→
```

TIP	Of all the troubleshooting methods to use on Microsoft computers related to VPN sessions, the Event Viewer is probably the easiest one to use.

Oakley Logging

The last tool I'll talk about is related to tracking down specific ISAKMP/IKE Phase 1 and 2 problems. One of the problems with the Event Viewer is that the information you see about the success or failure of an event is summarized. In some instances, you need to be able to access the details of the setup of a VPN session (like using the **debug** command on a Cisco router or PIX or ASA security appliance).

By default, this type of functionality is disabled on Microsoft systems. To enable it, perform the following:

1 Go to **Start > Run** and enter **regedit** in the open box and click the **OK** button. In the Windows registry, go to HKEY_Local_MACHINE\System\CurrentControlSet\ Services\PolicyAgent (backup with Windows registry first!).

2 Right-click **PolicyAgent** and choose **New > Key**. Change the name of the key to "Oakley."

3 Double-click **Oakley** and in the right-hand window, right-click and choose **New > DWORD Value**. Change the name of the value to "EnableLogging."

4 Right-click **EnableLogging** and set its value to "Hex" and "1." Click the **OK** button to accept the change.

Once you've done this, you can either reboot your computer for the change to take effect or, from the Windows command prompt, enter **net stop policyagent** and **net start policyagent**: this stops and starts all IPsec-related services on the computer. At this point, any functions related to IPsec will be recorded in a log file at the following location: *windir*\debug\oakley.log where *windir* is where the Windows operating system is stored, like "C:\windows" or "C:\WINNT". Anytime you restart the policy agent (like rebooting your PC), the old oakley.log file is copied to oakley.log.sav and a new oakley.log file is created. The log file is limited to 50,000 log entries (which is about 6 MB). The contents of the file are very verbose, so you should be able to find the problem of establishing an IPsec session if it relates to either ISAKMP/IKE Phase 1 or 2 in the messages listed in this file: Establishing one IPsec session takes about seven Microsoft Word pages to list all of the messages!

Summary

This chapter introduced you to the setup and configuration of a Windows-based PC to use the PPTP, L2TP, and L2TP/IPsec protocols to secure connections to a VPN gateway. Because of the limited use of centralized policy control, I prefer to use Cisco VPN clients, like the Cisco VPN software client, the 3002 hardware client, the PIX 501 and 506E security appliances, and the 800, UBR900, and 1700 series routers as remote access clients. However, if you need to support both types of clients, the Cisco VPN gateway products can easily accommodate this need.

Next up is Chapter 14, "3002 Hardware Client," where I show you how to use the Cisco 3002 hardware client to set up secure connections with SOHO sites to a VPN 3000 concentrator at the corporate site.

CHAPTER 14

3002 Hardware Client

The last two chapters focused on the Cisco VPN Client and Microsoft's L2TP/IPsec client. Both of these clients are software clients, where VPN software is installed on a PC. Software clients allow a single user to secure a session to a remote VPN gateway. But software clients don't scale well, especially in environments where more than one person at a location needs to establish a secure session to a remote destination. In this case, it would be better to use a centralized device, like a remote access hardware appliance or a site-to-site gateway device.

This chapter will focus on using one of the Cisco hardware clients: the VPN 3002 hardware client. I'll discuss the 3002's features and deployment options, your initial access to the 3002, connection and authentication options, and administrative tasks. Chapters 18, "Router Remote Access Connections," and 22, "PIX and ASA Remote Access Connections," will discuss two other Cisco hardware clients: low-end routers and PIXs.

Overview of the 3002 Hardware Client

The 3002 is a hardware version of the Cisco VPN software client. Like the software client, it is easy to use, but provides much more scalability where a large number of SOHO sites need to connect to a central site. It is easy to deploy and support; most IPsec functionality is hidden from the user who has to deploy and manage it, just as is the case with the Cisco VPN Client software. The 3002 fully supports Cisco Easy VPN Remote technologies and is used as a remote access device, protecting traffic for users behind it.

Because the 3002 is an Easy VPN Remote, you can centralize policies on an Easy VPN Server and push them down to the 3002. The 3002 supports two modes for protecting users' traffic to a central site: client and network extension modes (these will be discussed later in the "Connection Modes" section). The following sections will discuss the features, models, and deployment options for the 3002.

3002 Features

The 3002 is easy to deploy and support. It already is a DHCP client on its public interface, acquiring addressing information dynamically from the ISP (the 3002 also supports PPPoE on its public interface in addition to static IP addressing). It has a static IP address on its private interface and is a DHCP server on the private interface, giving out addressing information to internal devices. It supports a Quick Configuration process similar to the VPN 3000 concentrators, making it easy to set it up to connect to an Easy VPN Server. Here are some of the 3002's many features:

- It is fully IPsec-compliant and supports the following IPsec functions: Automatic configuration of ISAKMP/IKE Phase 1 Policies and Phase 2 transforms—you don't need to configure these on the client; authentication with pre-shared keys and digital certificates; DH groups 1, 2, and 5; ESP in tunnel mode, NAT-T, IPsec over UDP, and IPsec over TCP; DES, 3DES, AES-128, and AES-256 encryption algorithms; and SHA-1 and MD5 HMAC functions.

> **Note**   Due to limited room for storing transforms on the 3002, it does not support AES-192 for encryption.

- It supports Path MTU discovery and manual MTU adjustment to reduce the likelihood of IPsec fragmentation.
- It can be upgraded from policies defined by an Easy VPN Server and pushed down to the 3002 during IKE Phase 1 in the IKE Mode Config step, allowing the 3002 to automatically download a new software image from a TFTP server and then reboot itself.
- It supports client and network extension modes. In client mode, the 3002 is assigned a single internal address and PATs all user's addresses to the internally assigned address from the concentrator; this makes all devices at the SOHO appear as one logical device from the corporate office's perspective. In network extension mode, the 3002 simulates an L2L tunnel, where no address translation is performed on the SOHO devices' addresses, making them appear as an extension of the corporate office network.
- It provides authentication credentials to bring up the IPsec tunnel (default or unit authentication), or one (interactive unit authentication) or more users (user authentication) can provide this information.
- It is fully compliant with the load balancing features of the VPN 3000 concentrators and ASA security appliances via VCA, and supports a backup server list for redundancy.
- It supports up to 253 devices behind its private interface.

3002 Models

There are two 3002 models, as shown in Figure 14-1 (rear of the chassis).

Figure 14-1 *3002 Models*

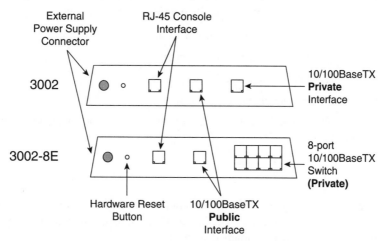

In the figure, both models have an external power supply, a hardware reset button, an RJ-45 console interface (uses a roll-over cable), and a 10/100BaseTX public interface. The only difference between the two models is that the 3002 has a single 10/100BaseTX private interface and the 3002-8E has an 8-port 10/100BaseTX auto-sensing private interface. The front of the 3002 chassis has three LEDs. Table 14-1 explains the status of the LEDs.

Table 14-1   *3002 Front Chassis LEDs*

LED	Color	Description
PWR	Off	3002 is powered off
	Green	3002 is powered on
SYS	Green	3002 is operational
	Flashing green	3002 is negotiating on its public interface using DHCP or PPPoE
	Flashing amber	3002 is performing diagnostic tests
	Solid amber	3002 has failed diagnostic tests
VPN	Off	No VPN tunnel has been established
	Amber	Establishing a VPN tunnel has failed
	Green	A VPN tunnel is established

Deployment of the 3002

Normally small remote offices or SOHO environments use remote access solutions to provide secure connections to a central site. Deploying a VPN gateway for an L2L connection is typically not necessary and cost-prohibitive. Therefore, there are four choices for VPN solutions in small remote office or SOHO environments:

- Software clients installed on users' desktops
- A small VPN-enabled router appliance
- A small VPN-enabled security appliance
- A 3002 hardware client appliance

The following sections will discuss the advantages and disadvantages of using software and hardware clients.

Software Client Option

The main advantage that VPN software client solutions have over hardware solutions is that software clients are typically free, like the Cisco VPN Client and Microsoft's L2TP/IPsec client. However, they have many disadvantages:

- They scale poorly if you need to support a large number of them.
- They require more management and administration on a network administrator's part.
- They have limited operating system support (only Microsoft Windows 98 and higher, Linux/Intel, Solaris/UltraSparc, and MAC OS X are supported) for the Cisco software client.

The software client commonly is used for the home user and, more commonly, mobile users.

Hardware Client Option

Hardware clients can handle the limitations that software clients have:

- They can handle protection of traffic for multiple computers, thereby offloading the administration and maintenance to a smaller number of devices—this is ideal for small branch offices or SOHO environments.
- They can protect any traffic the PC users send to the corporate office (typically limited to IP).
- They can provide additional features that PCs lack, such as stateful firewall functions, address translation, quality of service, and so on.
- The user can't mess up the VPN configuration because this is located on the secured hardware appliance (in this situation, two or three service calls to fix a user's software client configuration typically can pay for the cost of a VPN-enabled hardware appliance.
- You might not have control of the users' desktops, and therefore a hardware client solution is a better fit in this scenario.

If a VPN-enabled hardware appliance is a better fit for many sites in your network, you now need to decide which type of hardware appliance to use: security appliances (like the PIX 501 or 506E), routers (like the Cisco IOS 830s, UBR900s, and 1700s), or VPN 3002s. Table 14-2 displays when each type of hardware appliance should be deployed.

Table 14-2 *VPN-Enabled Hardware Appliance Comparison*

Device	Best for these purposes
IOS Router	Need a non-Ethernet interface connection to the ISP, such as ISDN, xDSL, or serial Need enhanced QoS Need voice support
PIX	Need a hardware-based stateful firewall Implements split tunneling Need complex address translation policies, especially with protocols that have problems with address translation (For non-Ethernet ISP connections, you'll still need a router)
3002	Need ease of implementation, upgrades, and support Requires little training since the GUI interface is the same as the VPN 3000 concentrators (For non-Ethernet ISP connections, you'll still need a router)

TIP In most cases, if I needed to support voice connections or I needed a non-Ethernet-based ISP connection, I would use a router; for enhanced throughput, I'd get a 1700 series router with the VPN encryption module. If I needed to allow for split tunneling at the remote access site, or had need of complex address-translation policies, I would use a small-end PIX security appliance. If I had none of these concerns, then I would prefer to use a 3002 hardware client, because, of the three solutions, it is the easiest to install, upgrade, and maintain.

Initial Access to the 3002

The 3002 hardware client supports both a command-line interface (CLI), which is menu-driven, and a graphical user interface (GUI). Both are discussed in this part of the chapter. The 3002 has the following default configuration:

- DHCP client on its public interface
- Static IP address of 192.168.10.1 on its private interface
- DHCP server on its private interface

So, unlike with the VPN 3000 concentrators, you don't need to use the CLI to initially configure the 3002. Because the 3002 has an IP address on its private interface, you just need to set up your PC to acquire its addressing information via DHCP and then use a web browser and point it to 192.168.10.1.

Command-Line Interface

The menu-drive CLI is used primarily for troubleshooting of the 3002 when you cannot access the 3002 via a web browser; otherwise, the web-based GUI is used to manage and troubleshoot the 3002. Accessing the CLI of the 3002 typically is done via the console port with a Cisco rollover cable. When you access the CLI, you'll be prompted to log in to the 3002. The default username and password are just like those for the 3000 concentrators: "admin" for both.

Example 14-1 shows a simple login process. As you can see from the CLI output, the interface looks the same as the CLI on the 3000 concentrators; how you move around the CLI is the same as on the concentrators (See Chapter 6, "Concentrator Product Information" for more information about using the concentrator's CLI). However, because the 3002 is a client, you will not see all the options you see on the concentrator's CLI—and vice versa.

Example 14-1 *3002 CLI Login and Main Menu*

```
Login: admin
Password: admin

              Welcome to
            Cisco Systems
        VPN 3002 Hardware Client
          Command Line Interface
Copyright (C) 1998-2004 Cisco Systems, Inc.

1) Configuration
2) Administration
3) Monitoring
4) Save changes to Config file
5) Help Information
6) Exit


Main ->
```

Graphical User Interface

With few exceptions, you'll be using a web browser to manage the 3002. Because the 3002 already is set up with an IP address on its private interface (192.168.10.1) and is acting as a DHCP server on this interface, you only need to connect a PC to this interface and set it to acquire its addressing via DHCP. Then point your web browser to the 3002 like this: **http://192.168.10.1.** You'll be presented with the login screen shown in Figure 14-2.

Figure 14-2   *3002 Web Access*

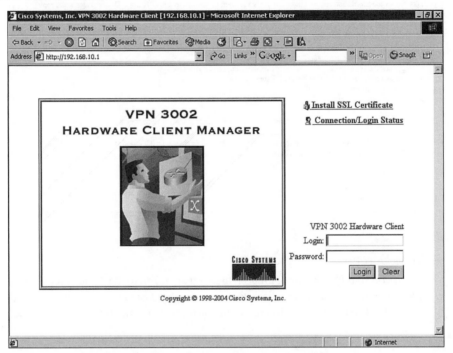

The only difference between this login screen and the concentrators' is that there is an extra hyperlink: Connection/Login Status, which I'll be talking about in the "Connection and Authentication Options" section later in the chapter. Enter the account and password and click the **Login** button to log in to the 3002.

Quick Configuration of the 3002

The first time you log in to the 3002, you have access to the Quick Configuration mode, which, like the corresponding process on the concentrator, allows you to put a base configuration on the 3002. This configuration allows the 3002 to set up an IPsec session to an Easy VPN Server. The first screen you see is shown in Figure 14-3. Here you have an option to start the Quick Configuration process by clicking the **Click here to start Quick Configuration** hyperlink or to skip this process and proceed to the main menu by clicking the **Click here to go to the Main Menu** hyperlink.

Figure 14-3 *3002 Initial Web-Based Login*

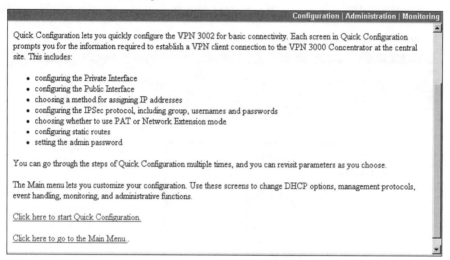

Configuration | Administration | Monitoring

Quick Configuration lets you quickly configure the VPN 3002 for basic connectivity. Each screen in Quick Configuration prompts you for the information required to establish a VPN client connection to the VPN 3000 Concentrator at the central site. This includes:

- configuring the Private Interface
- configuring the Public Interface
- choosing a method for assigning IP addresses
- configuring the IPSec protocol, including group, usernames and passwords
- choosing whether to use PAT or Network Extension mode
- configuring static routes
- setting the admin password

You can go through the steps of Quick Configuration multiple times, and you can revisit parameters as you choose.

The Main menu lets you customize your configuration. Use these screens to change DHCP options, management protocols, event handling, monitoring, and administrative functions.

Click here to start Quick Configuration.

Click here to go to the Main Menu.

Time Screen

When you start Quick Configuration, first you are taken to the Time and Date screen where you can enter the date, time, time zone, and Daylight Saving Time information, shown in Figure 14-4. When you are done entering the information on this screen, click the **Continue** button.

NOTE   During Quick Configuration, you can exit it immediately by clicking the **Main** hyperlink in the top right corner or the three operational area hyperlinks below this: **Configuration, Administration,** or **Monitoring.** One different twist, compared to the concentrators, is that you don't have to proceed, screen by screen, to access a particular Quick Configuration screen; instead, you can click the name of the Quick Configuration screen (these are hyperlinks) below the "Configuration | Administration | Monitoring" bar: **Time, Upload Config, Private Intf, Public Intf, IPsec, PAT, DNS, Static Routes, Admin,** and **Done.** If you want to save your current parameter changes on the screens you have updated and exit Quick Configuration mode, click the **Done** hyperlink on this screen bar. When you do this, you'll be taken to the 3002's Main screen.

Figure 14-4 *Quick Configuration: Time Screen*

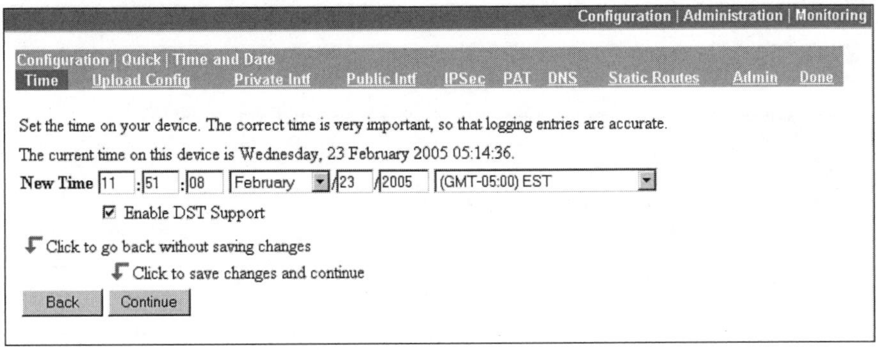

Upload Config Screen

The Upload Config screen is the next screen in sequence during the Quick Configuration process, shown in Figure 14-5. This screen allows you to import an already created configuration file for the 3002 and have the 3002 activate this configuration. This commonly is used when the 3002 is sent directly from Cisco or the reseller to the SOHO, where the employees at the SOHO have little understanding of configuring networking products. You can create a 3002 configuration file at the corporate office and e-mail this attachment to someone who will perform this task at the SOHO. You'll lead them through the first few screens and then have them click the **Yes** button on this screen and then the **Browse** button (on the next screen). Have them find the 3002 configuration file on their PC and click the **Upload** button to load the 3002's configuration file. Once this is done, have them click the **Done** hyperlink in the above taskbar to save and activate the changes. Once this is done, the 3002 will be using the configuration file you e-mailed the SOHO user. If you're not using this process, then just click the **No** button to continue the Quick Configuration process.

TIP   Notice that as you complete a screen, such as Time, that there is a check mark next to it in the above taskbar: this allows you to keep track of the screens you have completed in Quick Configuration mode.

Figure 14-5 *Quick Configuration: Upload Config Screen*

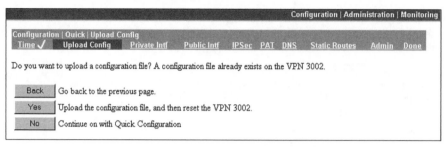

Private Intf Screen

On the Private Intf screen, shown in Figure 14-6, you can change the IP addressing for the private interface, and its DHCP server configuration. The default is to use the existing IP address (192.168.10.1) and the existing DHCP server configuration. To change the private interface address or the DHCP server settings, click **Yes** for changing the private interface's IP address and the appropriate radio button for the DHCP server settings. After you have clicked the **Continue** button and you have chosen **Yes** for either the interface or DHCP server settings, you'll see the screen in Figure 14-7—if you don't change the options on the screen in Figure 14-6, you're taken to the next screen, Public Intf.

Figure 14-6 *Quick Configuration: Private Intf Screen, Part 1*

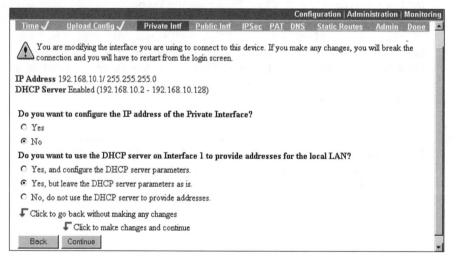

Figure 14-7 *Quick Configuration: Private Intf Screen, Part 2*

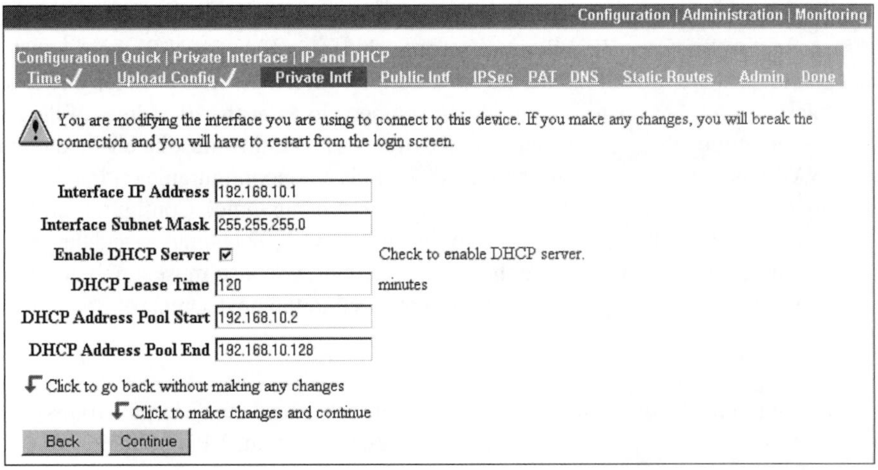

Public Intf Screen

After configuring the private interface, you are taken to the Public Intf screen, shown in Figure 14-8. At the top of the screen you can give the hardware client a name. In Figure 14-8, I used "hw3002" (the name is required if you'll be using certificates). The default addressing configuration is to acquire the IP addressing information for the public interface via DHCP, but you can acquire it using PPPoE or by defining it statically (as I did in Figure 14-8). Click the **Continue** button to proceed to the next screen.

Figure 14-8 *Quick Configuration: Public Intf Screen*

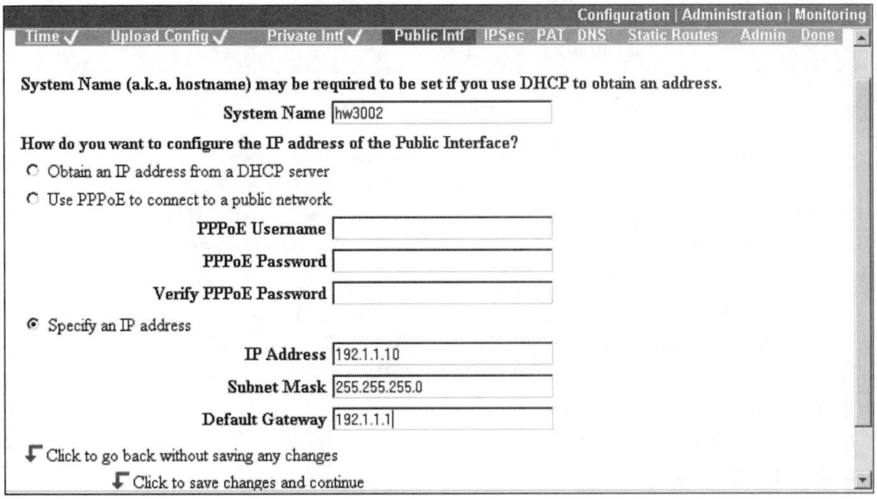

IPsec Screen

The IPsec screen, shown in Figure 14-9, allows you to specify the properties to use to connect to the Easy VPN Server. Because this is an Easy VPN Remote, most of the parameters are hidden from you, for example, ISAKMP/IKE policies and IPsec SA transform sets. At the top of the screen you need to enter the IP address of the Easy VPN Server. Optionally, you can select *IPsec over TCP*, but this must be enabled on the Server (NAT-T is enabled by default on the 3002 and is a nonconfigurable option). If you want to use certificates, you must have set this up before using Quick Configuration; otherwise, in the *Group* text box enter the name of the group the 3002 belongs to and the corresponding pre-shared group key. Because the 3002 is a client, you also must supply a username and password. Click the **Continue** button to proceed to the next screen.

TIP   I recommend that you place hardware and software clients in different groups on your Easy VPN Server, giving you more flexibility in assigning your VPN policies.

NOTE   Please note that the 3002 is a remote access IPsec client, and as such, it can have only a single IPsec tunnel established at a time. If a SOHO network needs more than one tunnel established, the 3002 is not the best possible product. In this situation, I would look at a low-end PIX or IOS router products instead and set up L2L sessions.

Figure 14-9 *Quick Configuration: IPsec Screen*

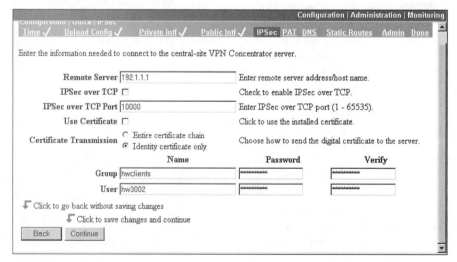

PAT Screen

The name "PAT" for this screen is somewhat misleading: it should read "Client and Network Extension Modes," because the connection mode is what you can enable on this screen. By default, if you leave the IP address of 192.168.10.1 on the private interface, your 3002 will operate *only* in client mode. By changing the address on the private interface, you can enable network extension mode (this is discussed later in the "Connection Modes" section). With PAT (Port Address Translation) enabled, the 3002 operates in client mode. When disabled, it operates in network extension mode. In the screen in Figure 14-10, you can see there is no option for disabling PAT, indicating that the IP address on the private interface hasn't been changed from 192.168.10.1. At this point, if you wanted to use network extension mode, you would click the **Private Intf** hyperlink at the top of the screen and change the IP address from 192.168.10.1 to something else; then return to this screen by clicking the **PAT** hyperlink at the top of the screen. Click the **Continue** button from this screen to proceed with Quick Configuration.

Figure 14-10 *Quick Configuration: PAT Screen*

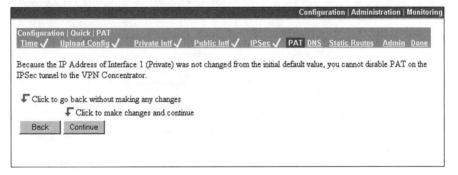

DNS Screen

The DNS screen allows you to specify the IP address of a DNS server to use for DNS resolutions and the domain name the 3002 belongs to (the domain name is required if the 3002 will be using certificates). This screen is shown in Figure 14-11. Click the **Continue** button to proceed with Quick Configuration.

Static Routes Screen

The Static Routes screen allows you to add default and static routes, shown in Figure 14-12. If you statically define an address and default route for the public interface from Figure 14-8, you'll see a default route here. In most cases, because this is a SOHO device, you won't have additional LAN segments behind the 3002, so adding additional static routes won't be necessary. And unlike the VPN 3000 concentrators, the 3002 doesn't support any dynamic routing protocol. Click the correct button to add or delete a static route. When done, click the **Continue** button to proceed with Quick Configuration.

Figure 14-11 *Quick Configuration: DNS Screen*

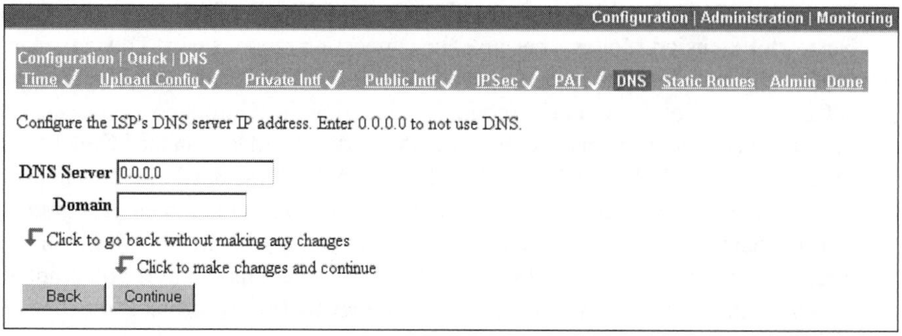

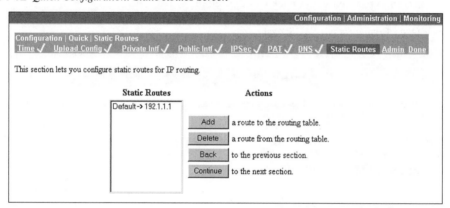

Figure 14-12 *Quick Configuration: Static Routes Screen*

NOTE   If you'll be using network extension mode, only the directly connected LAN subnet of the 3002's private interface is advertised, via RRI, to the corporate office; therefore, other LAN subnets behind the 3002 won't be able to receive traffic from the corporate office.

Admin Screen

The Admin screen allows you to change the password for the administrator account (admin). Cisco and I highly recommend this because the password defaults to "admin," the same as the administrator account name. This screen is the last one in the Quick Configuration process. By clicking either the **Continue** button at the bottom or the **Done** hyperlink above, the configuration is activated on the 3002 and automatically saved to Flash memory.

Figure 14-13 *Quick Configuration: Admin Screen*

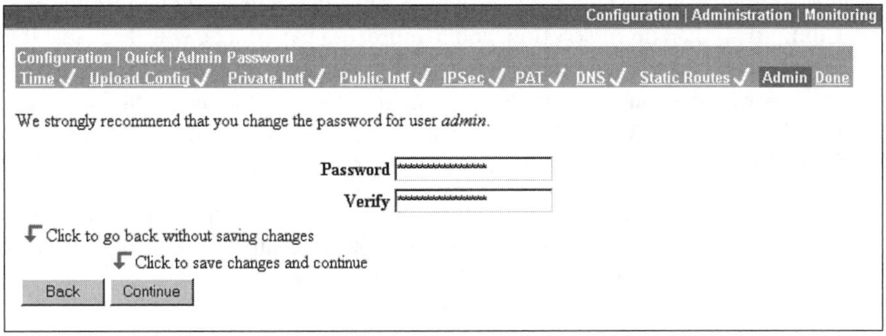

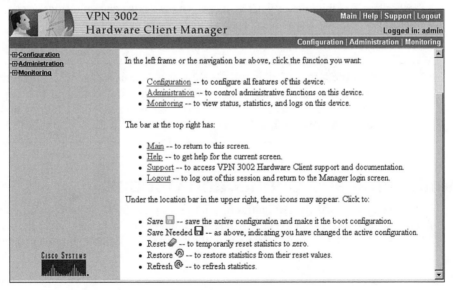

TIP After you've completed Quick Configuration, unlike a VPN 3000 concentrator, you can still use it to make changes on the 3002. To access Quick Configuration, go to **Configuration > Quick Configuration.**

Overview of the Main GUI

Upon finishing Quick Configuration or logging in to a 3002 with a base configuration, you'll see the main GUI screen shown in Figure 14-14.

Figure 14-14 *Main Menu Screen*

As you can see from this screen, the look and feel is the same as in the VPN 3000 concentrator's web-based GUI. However, once you burrow down through the various **Configuration, Administration,** and **Monitoring** hyperlinks, you'll see that the 3002 is a remote access *client* (your menu options will reflect this). However, for those administrators familiar with the concentrator's web-based interface, interacting with the 3002 is a simple task. Please refer to Chapter 6, "Concentrator Product Information," for an overview of the main menu of the 3000 concentrator, which is the same as the menu for the 3002.

In this book, I'll focus on the Configuration and Administration sections of the 3002. The 3002's Monitoring section is similar to the 3000 concentrator's Monitoring section. Under the Monitoring section, you can perform such tasks as:

- View the Filterable Event Log and the Live Event Log (you can even affect the level of logging, just as on a concentrator, by going to **Configuration > System > Events > Classes** and adding or changing a class's logging level for a logging destination).

- Examine the current routing table.

- Examine the current system status, and any connected IPsec tunnel to an Easy VPN Server.

- See the users that currently have authenticated when Individual User Authentication (UA) is employed (please see the "Connection and Authentication Options" section later for more information).

- View various statistics, including those related to IPsec, HTTP, Telnet, DNS, SSL, DHCP, SSH, PPPoE, NAT, and MIB-II information.

Because the layout and use of the Monitoring section information is very similar to that on the concentrators, and because I've covered the screens that are the same or similar to those in Part II of this book, I'll not go into any more depth concerning these screens except when called for throughout this chapter.

NOTE   Most items you need to configure on the 3002 can be done using Quick Configuration—the same things can be done from the main menu's Configuration section, in addition to some things that are beyond the scope of this book (with a few exceptions I'll bring up later in the "Connection Modes" section).

Authentication and Connection Options

Once you have used Quick Configuration to set up the 3002 or have modified its configuration, you'll want to verify that an IPsec tunnel can be brought up to the configured VPN gateway. The following sections will discuss three possible options you can use to perform authentication: Unit Authentication, Interactive Unit Authentication, and Individual User Authentication. If the 3002 will be connecting to a VPN 3000 concentrator, you also must enable the correct policy on the concentrator. Under the "Building the IPsec Tunnel" subheading, I also will discuss three possible options of performing authentication for use of the IPsec tunnel when Interactive Unit or Individual User Authentication is enabled.

Unit Authentication

The default authentication method on the 3002 is called Unit Authentication, sometimes referred to as the default method. With the default method, the XAUTH remote access username and password are configured on the 3002 itself; therefore, no users behind the 3002 have to perform any type of authentication to either bring up the IPsec tunnel or to use an existing tunnel.

With the default method, there are three ways of bringing up the IPsec tunnel to the VPN gateway: one brings up the tunnel automatically and two require user intervention to bring up the tunnel. Here are the three connection options (these only apply to client mode connections, because network extension mode automatically brings up the tunnel):

- **Automatically**—A user behind the 3002 sends traffic destined beyond the 3002. Even if the traffic is not meant for the corporate site, the 3002 still will bring up the tunnel to determine what the split tunneling policy is.
- **Manually**—With this approach there are two options:
  - A user behind the 3002 opens up a web browser connection to the private interface of the 3002, and in the web browser window clicks the **Connection/Login Status** hyperlink and then clicks the **Connect Now** button.
  - A user behind the 3002 opens up a web browser connection to the private interface of the 3002 and logs in to one of the three accounts: admin, config, or monitor. Only the first one is enabled, by default. To enable the other two, go to **Administration > Access Rights > Administrators** after logging in to the admin account. For user access, I would enable only the monitor account, because it has read-only privileges on the 3002; mostly, it's restricted to the Monitoring menu structure. Once logged in, the user goes to the **Monitoring > System Status** screen and clicks the **Connect Now** button to bring up the tunnel. Of the two manual options, this is the least preferred because you are letting SOHO users log in to the 3002, which might present a security risk.

For testing purposes, as an administrator, you'll probably go to the **Monitoring > System Status** screen to bring up the tunnel. When no tunnel is up, you'll see the screen shown in Figure 14-15.

Figure 14-15 *System Status Screen: No Tunnel*

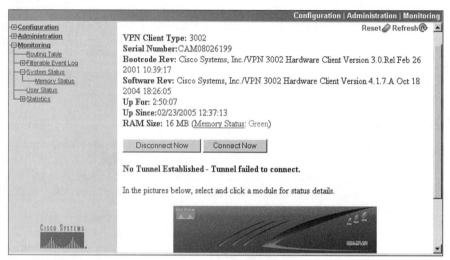

Click the **Connect Now** button to bring up the IPsec tunnel to the configured Easy VPN Server; this will take a few seconds. Once the tunnel is up, an updated System Status screen will appear, shown in Figure 14-16. The internal address assigned to the 3002 by the Easy VPN Server is 192.168.101.130 and below this is statistical information for the IKE and IPsec SAs. There are two IPsec SAs; however, the second one won't show up here until traffic traverses the connection from the Easy VPN Server to the 3002.

Figure 14-16 *System Status Screen: IPsec Tunnel*

Configuration | Administration | Monitoring

RAM Size: 16 MB (Memory Status: Green)

[Disconnect Now]   [Connect Now]

Assigned IP Address: 192.168.101.130
Tunnel Established to: 192.1.1.1
Duration: 0:00:01
Tunnel Type: IPSec
Security Associations:

Type	Remote Address	Encryption	Authentication	Octets In	Octets Out	Packets In	Packets Out	Other
IKE	192.1.1.1	3DES/MD5	Pre-Shared Key	1068	1793	6	7	Aggressive Mode, DH Group2
IPSec	192.1.1.1	3DES	HMAC/MD5	0	0	0	0	

In the pictures below, select and click a module for status details.

Additional Authentication Options

The main problem with Unit Authentication is that if the 3002 is ever compromised or stolen (it's fairly small), the remote access username and password are stored in Flash memory—the hacker or thief can then use this to establish an encrypted connection into your network. Cisco has two other solutions with the hardware clients to deal with this problem:

- Interactive Unit Authentication (Interactive UA)
- Individual User Authentication (Individual UA)

The following two sections discuss these methods.

Interactive Unit Authentication

With Interactive UA, the remote access username and password is *not* stored on the 3002's Flash memory; instead, one user behind the 3002 must supply this information to bring up the tunnel. This information is used by the 3002 to perform XAUTH during ISAKMP/IKE Phase 1. Once the tunnel is up, every user behind the 3002 can use the tunnel without any further authentication.

There are a few limitations of Interactive UA:

- If you use a single username and password, all users behind the 3002 will need this, since there is no guarantee which user will need to bring up the tunnel; you could create separate usernames and passwords for each person to solve this problem, but this might create an administrative burden.
- When a tunnel isn't up, it will take a few seconds for a user to figure this out and perform the authentication to bring it up.
- Once the tunnel is up, any user can use the tunnel; this can present problems in SOHO networks that use wireless LANs that might have rogue devices connected to them; this is also true of Unit Authentication.

Individual User Authentication

Individual UA solves the issues in the previous bulleted list. With Individual UA, once the tunnel is up, every user that wants to use the tunnel *also* must authenticate. This authentication is not part of XAUTH but is an additional authentication function. The hardware client passes this information over the ISAKMP/IKE Phase 1 connection and the Easy VPN Server performs the authentication and passes back the results to the hardware client.

NOTE   Individual UA can be combined with either Unit Authentication or Interactive UA.

The hardware client keeps track of authenticated users based on both their IP and MAC addresses; if these change, the user is forced to re-authenticate. An idle timer is associated with the user: if the user doesn't send traffic across the tunnel during this idle period, at the end of the idle period, the user is cleared from the hardware client's authentication cache and is forced to re-authenticate the next time the user needs access to the IPsec tunnel. This process provides better control over who uses the tunnel.

The next section will discuss how to configure Interactive UA and Individual UA. Following this, I will discuss how users can authenticate to bring up and use the IPsec tunnel. Last, I'll discuss how you can monitor the Interactive UA and Individual UA processes.

Configuring the VPN 3000 Concentrator

One of the interesting things about Interactive and Individual UA is that they are *not* configured on the 3002 client; instead, this policy is configured on the Easy VPN Server device, such as a concentrator. This policy is then pushed down to the hardware client during IKE Mode Config. Even if the hardware client has the remote access username and password stored in Flash memory, if the policy pushed down to the hardware client is not Unit Authentication, the hardware client erases the XAUTH username and password in its configuration automatically.

If you're configuring Interactive or Individual UA for a hardware client on a VPN 3000 concentrator, this is performed from the HW Client tab under the group configuration (**Configuration > User Management > Groups**). Figure 14-17 shows an example of this screen.

Figure 14-17 *3000 Concentrator: HW Client Group Tab*

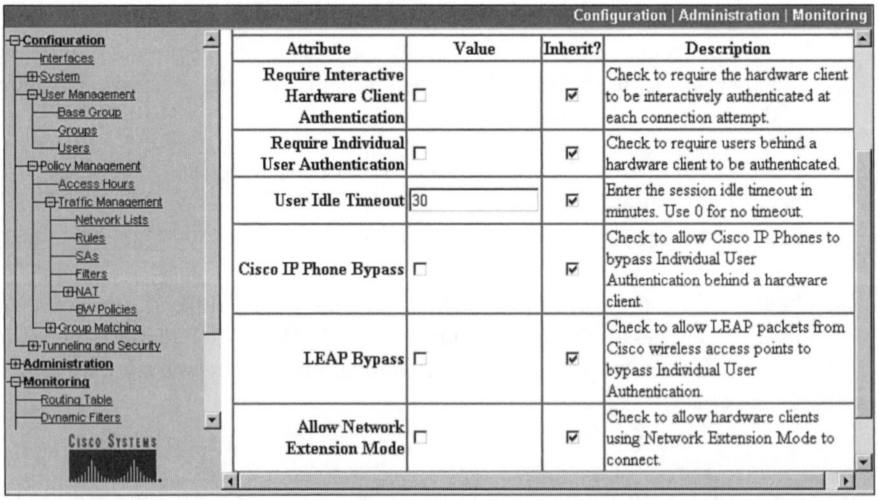

At the top of the screen are two check boxes—*Require Interactive Hardware Authentication* and *Require Individual User Authentication*—which enable Interactive and Individual UA, respectively. If both are checked, then both are used, where one user must authenticate to bring up the tunnel and then every user must authenticate to use the tunnel.

Below this you can change the idle timer for authenticated hardware clients (UA and Interactive UA) and users (Individual UA)—it defaults to 30 minutes. Changing the timer to 0 disables the idle timeout, which is not recommended.

Two other optional parameters are *Cisco IP Phone Bypass* and *Leap Bypass*. These are necessary when you have Cisco IP Phones or wireless devices using LEAP (Lightweight Extension Authentication Protocol) behind the hardware client, because the IP Phones and LEAP don't understand the authentication process that needs to take place (LEAP is used by wireless devices for authentication).

NOTE   If you have Cisco IP Phones or wireless clients using LEAP, then you must use either UA or Individual UA—Interactive UA is not supported. Plus, you'll need to use network extension mode, which causes the 3002 to automatically bring an IPsec tunnel up once the 3002 boots up.

If you have Cisco IP Phones behind the 3002 that might need to contact the corporate office via the IPsec tunnel before a user can perform the authentication, click the check box labeled *Cisco IP Phone Bypass*. Likewise, if you have wireless clients that will be using LEAP for authentication, you need to check the *Leap Bypass* check box: this allows LEAP packets to traverse the IPsec tunnel without being authenticated. However, once LEAP authentication is performed, the user still must authenticate to send normal packets across the tunnel. LEAP bypass will work only if the wireless access point (AP) is a Cisco Aironet AP running the Cisco Discovery Protocol (CDP).

CAUTION   Using either bypass method presents a security risk because unauthenticated packets are allowed to traverse the tunnel.

Building the IPsec Tunnel

Once you have defined your Interactive or Individual UA policy for the group containing the hardware clients, there are three ways authentication can take place:

- You enable the monitor account on the 3002 and have the users log in to this account via a web browser and the private interface of the 3002, go to the **Monitoring > System Status** screen, and click the **Connect Now** button. The top of the screen shows that Interactive UA is being used. Enter the correct username and password (see Figure 14-18) and click the **Continue** button. If successful, you should see a screen like that shown previously in Figure 14-16.

- A user opens a web browser connection to the private interface of the 3002, and clicks the **Connection/Login Status** hyperlink. If a tunnel is not yet up, then the **Connect Now** button will be visible; click it and enter the correct username and password that represents the 3002 for XAUTH. If a tunnel is up, you'll see something like that in Figure 14-19 when Interactive UA is enabled.

- A user opens a web browser connection and points it to any web server beyond the 3002. This will cause the 3002 to intercept the web connection request and display a web page indicating that a tunnel is not up (possibly) and that the user must authenticate. If you look at the web browser URL in the address text box, it will look something like this: **http://192.168.10.1/connstatus.html?url=http://192.168.101.99/**. The 192.168.10.1 address is the 3002's private interface. The "http://192.168.101.99" is the URL the user originally tried to access before it was intercepted by the 3002. Click the **Connect Now** button and supply the correct username and password to be used for XAUTH. Click the **Continue** button and if XAUTH authentication is successful, you'll see a screen like that shown previously in Figure 14-19. In a few seconds, the web browser will be redirected back to the URL the user originally was trying to access at the corporate site.

TIP   Because the web browser redirection method works only for web browser connections, if a user attempts to make a connection to the corporate office using another application, this will fail. Therefore, I recommend that you do two things on the user's desktop. First, set the user's web browser default home page to an IP address of a web server at the corporate site; second, put the web browser in the user's startup menus, which will cause the web browser to begin when the desktop boots up, causing the web browser's redirection process and any necessary authentication that needs to be performed.

Figure 14-18 *3002* **Monitoring > System Status** *Interactive UA*

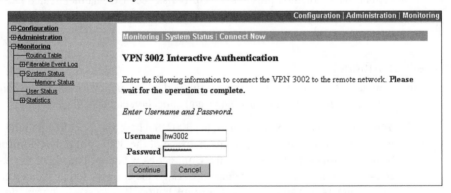

Figure 14-19 *Connection/Login Status with a Tunnel Up*

In the previous bulleted list, I assumed that you were using Interactive UA. The process is very similar if you are using Individual UA. I'll use an example where a user clicks the **Connection/Login Status** hyperlink on the 3002's login screen. If no tunnel is up (assuming you're using an Interactive UA), one user must provide the XAUTH credentials to bring up the tunnel. From the **Connection/Login Status** screen, click the **Connect Now** button and provide the username and password given to you that's associated with the group the 3002 belongs to. If successful, you'll see the screen shown in Figure 14-20. On this screen, the tunnel is up, but you must perform Individual UA to use it.

Figure 14-20 *Connection/Login Status with Individual UA Before Logging In*

Next, click the **Login Now** button, reenter your user name and password, and click the **Continue** button. Once authenticated, you should see a screen like that shown in Figure 14-21, with the message of "You are logged in" followed by your username, IP address, and MAC address, when you logged in, and for how long you were logged in.

If the tunnel is already up, when you click the **Connection/Login Status** hyperlink on the main 3002 login screen, you're taken immediately to the screen in Figure 14-20, where you must perform Individual UA. Please note that the process for performing this from the **Monitoring > System Status** screen and using the web browser redirection method are basically the same.

Figure 14-21 *Connection/Login Status with Individual UA After Logging In*

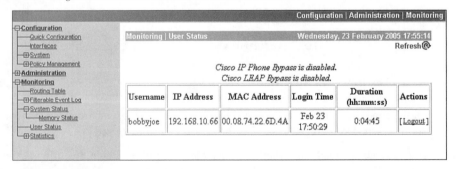

Verifying the Connection

On the 3002 and VPN 3000 concentrator, there is no difference, from a monitoring perspective, if you are using UA or Interactive UA. The devices treat them as a normal IPsec remote access session using XAUTH for user authentication. However, this is not true of Individual UA. On a 3002, you can see the list of authenticated users by going to **Monitoring > User Status**, shown in Figure 14-22.

On a VPN 3000 concentrator, go to **Monitoring > Sessions** and scroll down to the Remote Access Sessions section. Click the name of the user that was used for XAUTH to bring up the tunnel from the 3002. After seeing the session summary and the IKE and IPsec connection details, you will see a section entitled Authenticated Users, listing the users who currently are authenticated via Individual UA who can use the existing tunnel.

Figure 14-22 *Viewing Authenticated Individual UA Users on the 3002*

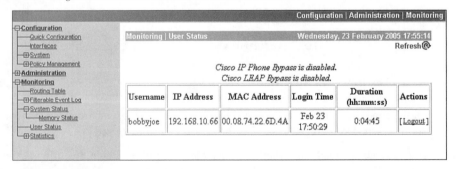

Connection Modes

The Cisco hardware clients, including the 3002, support two connection modes to an Easy VPN Server: client mode and network extension mode. Both of these modes were discussed in Chapter 3, "IPsec." The following sections will discuss the two modes and how to enable them.

Client Mode

The top part of Figure 3-3 from Chapter 3 shows an example of client mode. As a quick review, in client mode, the Easy VPN Server assigns the remote access hardware client a single, internal IP address. For devices behind the hardware client to access the corporate site across the tunnel, the hardware client performs PAT on the inside packets to the internal IP address assigned to it by the Server. From the corporate office's perspective, it looks as if a single device is connected to the network, when in reality, it could be a few hundred (with the 3002, the limit is 253 devices off of the private interface).

NOTE   The default behavior of the 3002 is to use client mode; in other words, it's already set up to PAT addresses going across the tunnel.

Network Extension Mode

The bottom part of Figure 3-3 shows an example of network extension mode. Network extension mode simulates an L2L tunnel. Please note that it is *not*, however, an L2L session. The hardware client, like the 3002, is still a client and connects to the Easy VPN Server, where in ISAKMP/IKE Phase 1, XAUTH and IKE Mode Config occur (which is not the case with a true L2L tunnel session). The main difference is that the remote access client will share the network number and subnet mask of its private interface, during ISAKMP/IKE Phase 1, with the Server via reverse route injection (RRI).

The main limitation of client mode is that the central office cannot initiate a connection to a device behind the hardware client because PAT is being used. With network extension mode, no address translation occurs; typically, the network number off of the private interface of the hardware client is a unique subnet of a network used from the corporate office. Using this mode, a device at the central office can access a device at the SOHO easily. This might be necessary for management, file-sharing, or VoIP purposes.

NOTE   In network extension mode, only the directly connected network of the private interface is advertised to the Easy VPN Server. If you had more than one network behind the hardware client, these additional networks would be unknown to the VPN gateway. Therefore, if you had multiple subnets behind your hardware client, you would have to use client mode or use a different VPN device that supported L2L sessions.

The configuration of network extension mode involves three configuration steps: two on the 3002 and one on the Easy VPN Server. The following sections will discuss the setup of these items on both the 3002 and VPN 3000 concentrators.

Network extension mode version L2L sessions

You might ask, Why not use an L2L session instead of using network extension mode? If you recall from Chapter 3, "IPsec," an L2L session goes through three basic steps in ISAKMP/IKE Phase 1: Negotiate the Phase 1 policies, use DH to share keying information, and perform device authentication. Network extension mode requires a hardware client device, which means additional steps will occur: XAUTH, IKE Mode Config, and RRI, the latter being discussed later in the "Routing and Reverse Route Injection" section.

Using a hardware client, you have more control over policy configuration and enforcement than you would over an L2L session. Plus, if the Easy VPN Server is a VPN 3000 concentrator, the higher-end concentrators support more remote access sessions than they do L2L sessions. Therefore, if I was using a 3020 or higher at the central site, I would prefer setting up remote access sessions to be able to support more total VPN sessions.

Given this information, this does not mean that you should always use hardware clients with network extension mode instead of L2L sessions. L2L sessions have their place. For example, one limitation of a hardware client is that since it is a client, it can have only one tunnel up at a time. With L2L sessions, you can more easily mesh your network to reduce latency, which might be important for delay-sensitive traffic, like voice or video.

Also, remote access clients typically have addresses assigned to them dynamically via their connected ISP. This means that you cannot use GRE tunnels to propagate dynamic routing protocol information (unless using DMVPN), which provides better scalability in larger networks. With remote access clients, routing typically is done statically (please note that only IOS routers, out of all the Cisco products, support GRE tunnels).

And last, if there is more than one network connected to the hardware client using network extension mode, only the network number attached to its private interface is advertised to the central office VPN gateway; the others are not, which presents reachability issues.

3002 Network Extension Mode Configuration

By default, the 3002 uses client mode for its connection to an Easy VPN Server. There are two configuration steps you need to perform on the 3002 to enable network extension mode:

Step 1   Change the IP address on the private interface to something different than 192.168.10.1.

Step 2   Disable PAT.

Either you can perform these steps from Quick Configuration mode (go to **Configuration > Quick Configuration**), which I discussed in the "Quick Configuration" section earlier in the chapter, or do them from the main menu Configuration section.

Within Quick Configuration, you need to click to the **Private Intf** hyperlink first and change the private interface IP address to something different from 192.168.10.1 (Figures 14-6 and 14-7) and then click the **PAT** hyperlink and select the *No, use Network Extension mode* option (Figure 14-10 shows an example where the IP address wasn't changed from 192.168.10.1). Click the **Done** hyperlink when you're finished with Quick Configuration mode.

If you are going to do it using the latter method, to perform the first step, go to **Configuration > Interfaces** and click the hyperlink labeled **Ethernet 1 (Private)**. Change the IP address and, possibly, subnet mask, and click the **Apply** button. Once you have done this, then go to **Configuration > Policy Management > Traffic Management > PAT > Enable** and uncheck the check box labeled *PAT Enabled*. Click the **Apply** button to accept your change.

Concentrator Network Extension Mode Configuration

The last step you must perform is on the Easy VPN Server, such as a VPN 3000 concentrator. On a concentrator, this is performed under the group configuration (**Configuration > User Management > Groups**). Select the group name and click the **Modify** button; then click the **HW Client** tab. If you refer back to Figure 14-17, the last option under this tab is *Allow Network Extension Mode*; click the check box for this option and click the **Apply** button at the bottom. Now, if any hardware client in the group is set up for network extension mode, the connection mode will be allowed.

NOTE   It is important to point out that if you don't enable network extension mode on the VPN 3000 concentrator, the 3002 can only use client mode; and if you have disabled PAT, then devices behind the 3002's private interface won't be able to access the central site via the IPsec tunnel.

Network Extension Mode Verification

There are a few ways that you can verify if your IPsec tunnel to the VPN 3000 concentrator is using network extension mode. First, on the 3002, go to **Monitoring > System Status**. Examine Figure 14-16. If you see the line *Assigned IP Address* and an internal IP address assigned by the Easy VPN Server, then you're operating in client mode. You won't see this line when operating in network extension mode.

On the VPN 3000 concentrator, go to **Monitoring > Sessions** and scroll down to the Remote Access Sessions section, like that shown in Figure 14-23. Examine the *Assigned IP Address Public IP Address* column. With a session using client mode, you'll see the assigned IP address from the address pool the concentrator is using (or from an AAA or DHCP server if the address pool is defined externally); with network extension mode, you'll see the network number of the hardware client's private interface. In Figure 14-23, this is 192.168.10.0.

Figure 14-23 *Verifying Network Extension Mode on a Concentrator*

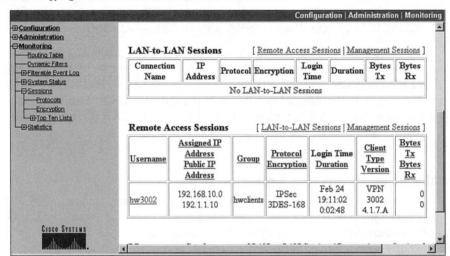

If there is a problem connecting using network extension mode, the 3002's Event Log is not too illuminating about this particular problem; however, if you look at the concentrator's Event Log, you'll see something like that shown in Example 14-2. In this example, a 3002 with an address of 192.1.1.10 is trying to make a connection. Event 823 indicates that device and XAUTH authentication are successful. Event 826, however, displays that the group the 3002 belongs to is not configured for network extension mode, but the 3002 is trying to use it (PAT is disabled). Given this, the ISAKMP/IKE Phase 1 connection will fail.

Example 14-2 *Network Extension Mode Misconfiguration*

```
817 02/26/2005 15:49:05.310 SEV=5 IKEDBG/64 RPT=45 192.1.1.10
IKE Peer included IKE fragmentation capability flags:
Main Mode:        True
Aggressive Mode:  True

819 02/26/2005 15:49:05.800 SEV=5 IKE/172 RPT=45 192.1.1.10
Group [hwclients]
Automatic NAT Detection Status:
   Remote end is NOT behind a NAT device
   This   end is NOT behind a NAT device

823 02/26/2005 15:49:06.120 SEV=4 IKE/52 RPT=43 192.1.1.10
Group [hwclients] User [hw3002]
User (hw3002) authenticated.
```

Example 14-2 *Network Extension Mode Misconfiguration (Continued)*

```
824 02/26/2005 15:49:06.150 SEV=5 IKE/184 RPT=43 192.1.1.10
Group [hwclients] User [hw3002]
Client Type: VPN 3002
Client Application Version: 4.1.7.A

826 02/26/2005 15:49:06.150 SEV=4 IKE/174 RPT=34 192.1.1.10
Group [hwclients] User [hw3002]
Hardware Client connection rejected!
Network Extension Mode is not allowed for this group!
```

If the negotiation of network extension mode is successful, instead of seeing event 826 in Example 14-2, you would see the event in Example 14-3. In this example, you can see the client type and version. Of course, this message has nothing to do with network extension mode, but this is what you will see if policies are successfully negotiated.

Example 14-3 *Successful Negotiation of Network Extension Mode*

```
1679 02/26/2005 15:54:59.910 SEV=5 IKE/184 RPT=114 192.1.1.10
Group [hwclients] User [hw3002]
Client Type: VPN 3002
Client Application Version: 4.1.7.A
```

NOTE   To use network extension mode, the 3002's IP address cannot be 192.168.10.1. However, this does not mean you have to change the network addressing scheme; you can easily change the IP address to 192.168.10.2, which would fulfill the address change requirements. In Figure 14-23, the 3002 has this address on its private interface. However, each hardware client needs a *unique* network number for its private interface.

Routing and Reverse Route Injection

One of the problems with remote access clients connecting to a central office using client mode or network extension mode is that if there are two Easy VPN Servers, like that shown in Figure 14-24, then which of the Servers should central office devices use to reach the client? This is especially problematic if you're using VCA load balancing or VRRP redundancy. Which of the Servers is the client connected to? And even if you would find out this information, it might change based on the next session the client builds to the central office.

Figure 14-24 *Remote Access Clients, Central Site Redundancy, and Routing Issues*

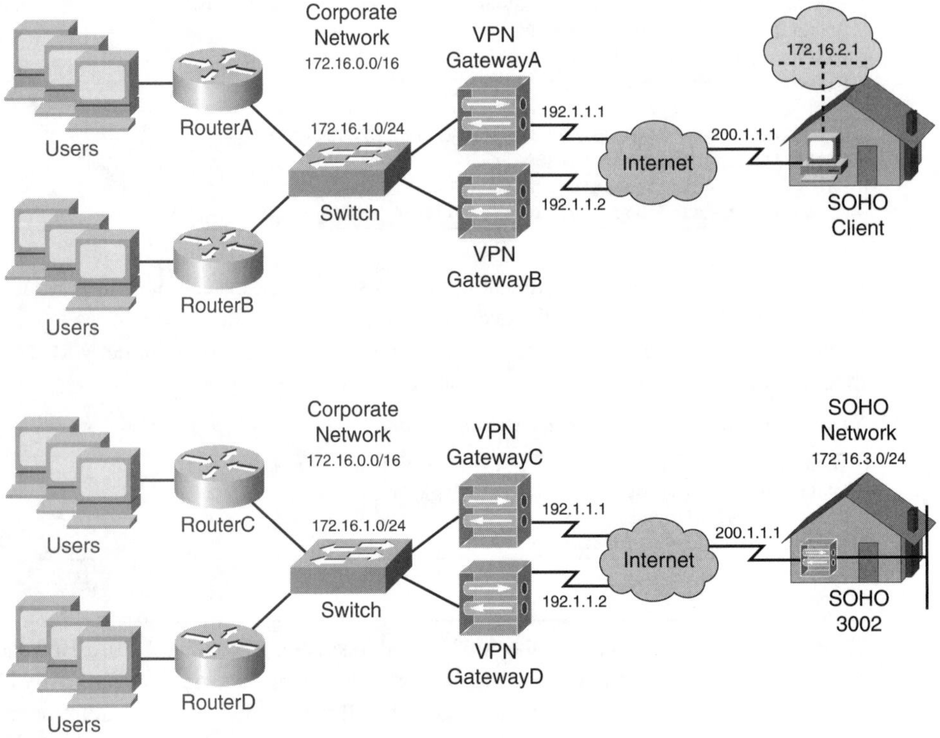

Routing Features

The only way to deal with this reachability problem is to:

- Use a dynamic routing protocol on the VPN gateways and have the gateways advertise this information to the central site layer-3 devices; this is necessary if an AAA RADIUS or DHCP server will be assigning addresses to the clients using client mode or the client is using network extension mode

- Use static routing on the layer-3 devices to point to the correct concentrator; this will only work for client mode connections where each concentrator has its own pool of addresses it assigns to clients

Assuming you're using the first bullet point as your solution. No matter what Easy VPN Server a remote access client is connected to, the Servers will propagate the updated routing information to the internal layer-3 devices so that corporate office devices can reach the remote access clients.

One of the interesting things about this process is that remote access clients don't advertise routing information via a routing protocol. Instead, either the internally assigned IP address (client mode) or the network number of the private interface (network extension mode) is shared with the Easy VPN Server. Only the Server understands this and associates these numbers with the IPsec SAs—this information doesn't even appear in the Server's routing table.

However, Cisco Easy VPN Servers support a process called reverse route injection (RRI) to place the client's routing information in the Easy VPN Server's local routing table as a static route and allow the static routes to be redistributed via a local routing protocol out of the Server's other interfaces. With the VPN 3000 concentrators, the static routes can be redistributed using RIPv1, RIPv2, or OSPF.

RRI Configuration

Configuring RRI is an Easy VPN Server configuration task: the remote access clients have no clue, nor do they care, that this process is occurring. On the VPN 3000 concentrators, this configuration is done in two steps:

Step 1   Enable RRI.

Step 2   Configure the dynamic routing protocol.

I already discussed Step 2 in Chapter 10, "Concentrator Management." You need to configure the routing protocol, if it happens to be OSPF, and enable the routing protocol on the private, and possibly external, interface of the concentrator. In this section, I'll only discuss the first step: Enabling RRI.

To enable RRI on your VPN 3000 concentrator, go to the **Configuration > System > IP Routing > Reverse Route Injection** screen, shown in Figure 14-25. If you use both types, select both check boxes: *Client Reverse Route Injection* and *Network Extension Reverse Route Injection*. If you don't select an RRI type, that type doesn't show up as a static route in the concentrator's local routing table and thus can't be redistributed to other central office devices. The *Address Pool Hold Down Routes* allows you to list routes the concentrator will *always* advertise as reachable: this option can be used if a client always connects to the same concentrator no matter what, and you always want the concentrator to advertise the route, especially with RIP, to reduce convergence time when an IPsec tunnel is being built or rebuilt by the client. Once you've configured the information on the screen, click the **Apply** button to save your changes.

Once you have configured RRI, you can verify that it's working by examining the concentrator's local routing table: **Monitoring > Routing Table**. For clients using network extension mode, you should see their private interface network numbers show up as static routes in the routing table; for clients using client mode, you should see their internal IP addresses show up as static host routes.

Figure 14-25 *RRI Configuration on a Concentrator*

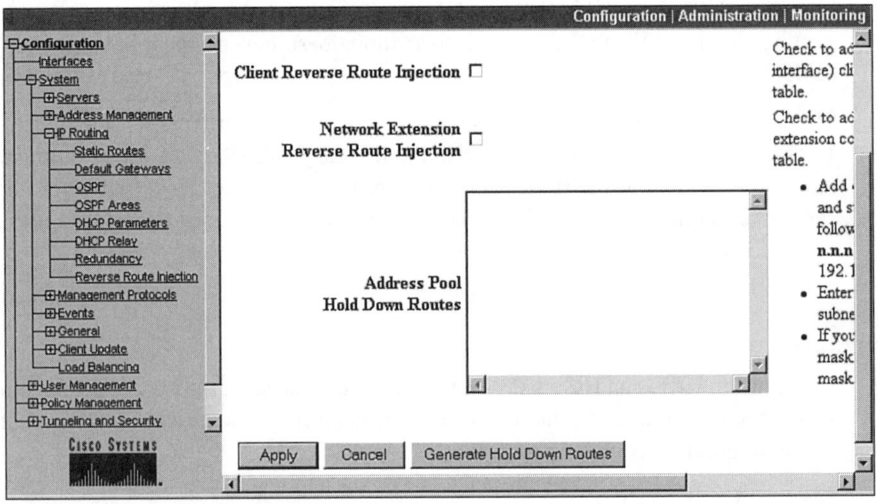

Administrative Tasks

The Administrative section available on the 3002 is similar to that of the 3000 concentrators. As a quick overview, you can perform the following administrative tasks on the 3002 from the Administration screens:

- Update the 3002's software image.

- Reboot or shutdown the 3002.

- Test connectivity with ping and traceroute.

- Manage the 3002's files in Flash memory.

- Administer the three accounts on the 3002: admin, config, and monitor (only the first is enabled, by default).

- Change the idle timeout for management sessions and encrypt the 3002's configuration file.

- Import, enroll, and manage certificates.

As you can see from this list, these are similar to the 3000 concentrator's administrative tasks; plus, how you perform them is essentially the same. Therefore, instead of repeating the information covered in Chapter 10, I'll discuss only two topics in this section that are important for management functions of the 3002: how to access the 3002 from its public interface and how to upgrade it.

Accessing the 3002 from its Public Interface

Because the 3002 is a SOHO device, you'll need to be able to access it periodically from the central site for management purposes. This can be accomplished in one of two ways:

across an IPsec tunnel to the private interface of the 3002 or to the 3002's public interface. The problem with the former method is that the IPsec tunnel might not be coming up, which means you'll need to perform the latter; and by default, management access to the public interface of the 3002 is disabled.

Only encrypted management access is allowed on the public interface, which makes sense because you don't want to manage the 3002 across a public network in clear text. Both HTTPS (SSL) and SSH are supported and are enabled as followed:

- To enable HTTPS access on the public interface, go to the **Configuration > System > Management Protocols > HTTP/HTTPS** screen on the 3002 and make sure that both the *Enable HTTPS* and the *Enable HTTPS on Public* check boxes are checked: the former should be, by default, but the latter isn't. Click the **Apply** button to accept the change—when you do this, your current web browser management session is terminated and you'll need to log back in to the 3002.

- To enable SSH access (for CLI access) on the public interface, go to the **Configuration > System > Management Protocols > SSH** screen on the 3002 and make sure that both the *Enable SSH* and the *Enable SSH on Public* check boxes are checked. The former should be, by default, but the latter isn't. Encryption algorithms supported are 3DES, RC-4, and DES; you can choose which one or ones you want to use. Click the **Apply** button to accept the change(s). Unlike HTTPS access, your web browser management session is not terminated upon accepting your changes.

NOTE   As of 4.1.7 software on the 3002, only SSHv1.5 is supported.

Upgrading the 3002

You can upgrade the 3002 manually on the 3002 or automatically during ISAKMP/IKE Phase 1 based on update parameters you have configured on an Easy VPN Server, such as a VPN 3000 concentrator. The following two sections will discuss both processes.

Manual Upgrade

Manually upgrading a 3002 is as simple as upgrading a VPN 3000 concentrator. Log in to the 3002 under the admin account and go to the **Administration > Software Update** screen. Click the **Browse** button to find the 3002 binary image. Be sure the image name begins with "vpn3002-"; a VPN 3000 concentrator image will *not* run on the 3002! Then click the **Upload** button to pull the image from your desktop, via the web management connection, to the Flash memory of the 3002.

It takes a few minutes to erase the current operating system in Flash and download the new one. Upon completion, you'll need to reboot the 3002. Click the **Click here to go to the reboot options** hyperlink. On the reboot screen, click the *Reboot* radio button, the **Save**

the active configuration at time of reboot and the *Now* radio button. Then click the **Apply** button to reboot the 3002. Once the 3002 comes back up, log in and go to **Monitoring > System Status** and make sure the new software version appears in the display.

Auto-Update

One of the features I like about the 3002 is that you can define upgrade policies on the Easy VPN Servers and have these pushed down to the 3002 during ISAKMP/IKE Phase 1. The 3002 will compare its version and the Server's recommended version automatically; if they are different, the 3002 will download the new image, install it, and automatically reboot itself. Using this feature, you can be assured that your 3002s are running the correct software image.

The actual setup for the auto-update process is done on the Easy VPN Server, as on the VPN 3000 concentrators. I covered this in Chapter 12, "Cisco VPN Software Client," as it pertains to the Cisco software client. Here, I'll discuss what you need to do to upgrade the 3002 using a VPN 3000 concentrator.

Adding Client Update Entries

There are two ways to add client update entries on a VPN 3000 concentrator: system-wide and on a group-by-group basis. Your main concern with auto-update is that if too many 3002s try to perform the upgrade simultaneously, this could create connection problems with the TFTP server where the upgrade image is located. Therefore, I prefer to use the latter approach.

TIP   To limit the number of updates that can be performed simultaneously, create multiple groups for your hardware clients, placing 10–20 of them in each group. You might want to place them in groups based on their geographic location.

To add client updates to a group, go to the group screen (**Configuration > User Management > Groups**), click the name of a group, and then click the **Client Update** button. This screen will list the update entries you have created. Click the **Add** button to add an update entry, showing you the screen in Figure 14-26.

The *Client Type* parameter specifies the type of client you want to upgrade. To specify an update for a VPN 3002 hardware client, use "vpn3002." You must enter the *Client Type* in the exact case and spacing, or the 3002 client will ignore the update message. The *URL* parameter specifies the location of the client update file. For a 3002 client, the update must be on a TFTP server, so you would enter something like this: tftp://192.168.101.66/ vpn3002-4.1.7.D-k9.bin. Be sure to use the same case that Cisco specified on their site for the name of the VPN 3002 image file. Also, the TFTP site can be across the IPsec tunnel at the central site (this is the preferred approach). The *Revisions* parameter specifies what version or versions of software the remote access clients should be running; if they are not running these versions, they then should install the software in the *URL* parameter. You can specify multiple revision numbers; just separate them by a comma and a space.

Figure 14-26 *Creating a 3002 Auto-Update Entry*

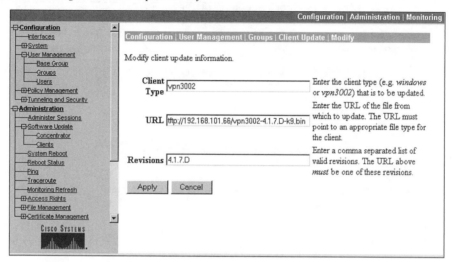

NOTE   It is important that the revision be entered in the exact case that appears in the image name from Cisco. In other words, the clients will see a difference between "4.1.7.D" and "4.1.7.d." If the client is running 4.1.7.D and you enter the "d" in lower case, the 3002 client will think that this is a *different* version and will download this again and again at every session attempt!

NOTE   To use the system-wide auto-update configuration approach, go to the **Configuration > System > Client Update > Entries** screen and follow the same steps listed above.

Enabling Client Updates

Next, you need to ensure that the auto-update process is enabled on the concentrator. To do this, go to **Configuration > System > Client Update > Enable** and make sure the *Enable* check box is checked. Example 14-4 shows an example of a 3002's Event Log where it makes a connection to a concentrator, notices that a new software revision is available, and then downloads it. Notice that the first download attempt failed (entry 167) because ISAKMP/IKE Phase 2 hadn't completed and the TFTP server was located at the central office behind the VPN 3000 concentrator. Once the Phase 2 connections came up, the 3002 was able to successfully download the file and reboot itself to use the new image.

Example 14-4 *3002 Auto-Update Event Log Example*

```
129 02/26/2005 14:25:40.960 SEV=4 IKE/41 RPT=6 192.1.1.1
IKE Initiator: New Phase 1, Intf 2, IKE Peer 192.1.1.1
local Proxy Address 192.1.1.10, remote Proxy Address 192.1.1.1,
SA (ESP-3DES-MD5)

132 02/26/2005 14:25:41.430 SEV=5 IKEDBG/64 RPT=4 192.1.1.1
IKE Peer included IKE fragmentation capability flags:
Main Mode:       True
Aggressive Mode: True
←output omitted→

140 02/26/2005 14:25:42.850 SEV=3 AUTH/24 RPT=3
Tunnel to headend device hwclients connected

141 02/26/2005 14:25:42.860 SEV=4 IKE/119 RPT=3 192.1.1.1
Group [hwclients]
PHASE 1 COMPLETED
←output omitted→

152 02/26/2005 14:25:42.950 SEV=4 AUTOUPDATE/6 RPT=2
Current version 4.1.7.D does not match 4.1.7.A.Rel.

154 02/26/2005 14:25:42.950 SEV=4 AUTOUPDATE/7 RPT=2
Updating firmware to 4.1.7.A.Rel from 4.1.7.D.

155 02/26/2005 14:25:42.950 SEV=4 AUTOUPDATE/12 RPT=4
Update firmware will now begin using file vpn3002-4.1.7.A-k9.bin on
server 192.168.101.66 [C0A86542].

166 02/26/2005 14:26:10.000 SEV=4 IKE/120 RPT=5 192.1.1.1
Group [hwclients]
PHASE 2 COMPLETED (msgid=0f2c27c3)

167 02/26/2005 14:26:19.890 SEV=4 AUTOUPDATE/16 RPT=4
Update download failed. Retry number 1 will be attempted
in 20 seconds.

168 02/26/2005 14:26:39.890 SEV=4 AUTOUPDATE/12 RPT=5
Update firmware will now begin using file vpn3002-4.1.7.A-k9.bin on
server 192.168.101.66 [C0A86542].

170 02/26/2005 14:30:55.260 SEV=4 AUTOUPDATE/18 RPT=1
Updated image was successfully downloaded. The unit will now reboot
for the image to take effect.

172 02/26/2005 14:30:55.260 SEV=1 REBOOT/1 RPT=1
Reboot scheduled immediately.
```

NOTE	Once an upgrade of a 3002 is done, the next time you log in to the 3002 using a web browser, you'll be prompted to clear your web browser's cache, because the web content of the 3002's GUI may have changed.

Pushing Updates to Clients

If a 3002 is already connected when you add an auto-update entry for the group (or system-wide), the 3002 will not learn about this until its ISAKMP/IKE Phase 1 connection expires and is renegotiated. You can force the auto-update process to take place by logging in to the concentrator and going to the **Administration > Software Updates > Clients** screen. From the drop-down group name selector, choose the name of the group that has 3002s in it that you want to upgrade. Then click the **Upgrade Clients Now** button. The concentrator will send an ISAKMP/IKE notification message down to the connected 3002 clients. The 3002 clients will then compare the revision listed in the notification message with what they are running. If there is a difference, the 3002 will disconnect from the concentrator and reconnect, and then begin the download process.

TIP	I highly recommend that you first test your upgrade process out with a test group that has only a small number of 3002s in it, and verify that the upgrade took place, and took place only once! Do this by disconnecting and reconnecting a 3002 client and be sure that it gets the AUTOUPDATE message in the Event Log. Then, send an auto-update notification message again down to the 3002 using the above process. If the 3002 does the update again, then you've probably messed up the *Revision* parameter on the Client Update Entry screen. To simplify the search of the 3002's Event Log, use the Filterable Event Log and use the *Event Class* drop-down selector and click "AUTOUPDATE." Then click the last page button ("|>>") to go to the end of the file. Examine the messages and look for updates using the same image. If auto-update is enabled on the concentrator and the 3002 has the most up-to-date image, then in the 3002's Event Log, you should see a string of these messages for each time the 3002 connects to the concentrator: "Current version w.x.y.z is up to date."

Summary

This chapter showed you the basics of using the Cisco 3002 hardware client to establish IPsec connectivity to a central site Easy VPN Server. Because of its similarity in management to the VPN 3000 concentrators, many administrators prefer these devices over small-end routers or firewalls for SOHO VPN hardware appliances. I prefer to use the 3002 when split tunneling is not being used and I have more than one person at the SOHO site. I've deployed quite a few of these and because of their simplicity and easy maintenance, they are one of my favorite VPN SOHO appliances.

Next up is Part IV, "IOS Routers," where I show you how to use routers for L2L and remote access sessions (gateways and remote access clients).

IOS Routers

CHAPTER 15

Router Product Information

Part IV will discuss the use of Cisco IOS-based routers to initiate and terminate VPN sessions. Cisco routers are very flexible and can be used for site-to-site (LAN-to-LAN or L2L) sessions, VPN gateways, and remote access clients. I'll focus primarily on how to configure Cisco routers using the IOS CLI interface; however, other GUI-based products, such as Security Device Manager (SDM) and CiscoWorks VMS Router Management Center (MC), can be used to configure VPNs on routers.

In this chapter, however, I'll introduce you to the Cisco router product line that supports VPN capabilities. I'll discuss some typical VPN deployment scenarios used with Cisco routers, and some of the advantages they have over other Cisco VPN products.

Router Deployment Scenarios

Cisco VPN capabilities have their roots in Cisco IOS-based routers, where VPNs were first introduced in the Cisco router line. Cisco routers support many VPN solutions including IPsec, PPTP, L2TP, and WebVPN (in the newest IOS versions). Because of their flexibility, routers can be used in many different situations. This section will focus on how routers can be used with L2L and remote access VPNs in your network, including the router's special advantages over other Cisco VPN products.

L2L and Remote Access Connections

Cisco routers support L2L and remote access connections. As mentioned in Chapter 8, "Concentrator Remote Access Connections with PPTP, L2TP, and WebVPN," I prefer to use Cisco routers for L2L sessions, but concentrators for remote access sessions. Routers support enhanced routing, quality of service (QoS), and L2L scalability capabilities over Cisco PIX and ASA security appliances and VPN 3000 concentrators. However, concentrators scale better for remote access sessions and are easy to set up.

Figure 15-1 shows an example in which routers are being used to terminate VPN sessions. At the Central Office, a VPN-enabled router is used to terminate an L2L session from the Regional Office, and remote access sessions from the Cable Modem, DSL, and dial-up users, and the SOHO 1 and SOHO 2 sites. Because the number of remote access devices is small, it is more cost-effective to let the Central Office router terminate these versus buying an extra product such as a VPN 3000 series concentrator. Plus, because SOHO 2 has a server that the Central Office needs to access, the session can be set up using either remote access with network extension mode or as an L2L session.

Figure 15-1 *Using Routers for VPN Solutions*

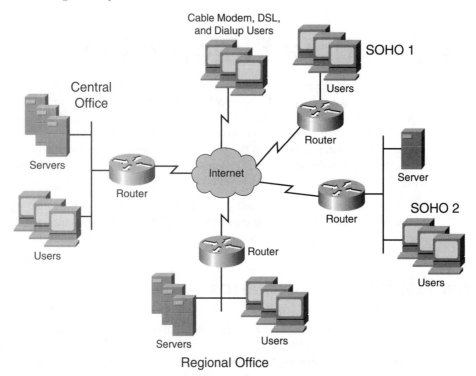

Special Capabilities of Routers

As I mentioned in Chapter 8, I prefer (and Cisco recommends) to use routers for L2L sessions. I'm constantly asked why routers are better for this role than the VPN 3000 concentrators and the PIX and ASA security appliances. There are four main features the Cisco IOS-based routing products have over Cisco 3000 concentrators and PIX/ASA security appliances when it comes to VPN implementations: data transport, routing scalability, media translation, and quality of service (QoS). The next four sections will discuss these features in more depth.

Data Transport

Two limitations of IPsec for VPNs are that IPsec doesn't support IP multicasting and it doesn't support non-IP protocols such as IPX or AppleTalk. With a VPN 3000 concentrator or PIX or ASA security appliance, there's nothing you can do about these problems;

however, Cisco routers can easily get around these two problems by encapsulating multicast or non-IP protocols using a GRE tunnel, and have the GRE tunnel go across a unicast IPsec session—in other words, a tunnel (GRE) within a tunnel (IPsec). Using this approach, you can send IP multicast and broadcast traffic, including routing protocol and non-IP protocols, across an IPsec tunnel. See Chapter 1, "Overview of VPNs," for more information on GRE.

Routing Scalability

When I need to interconnect a large number of large sites, where each site has many networks connected to it, routers perform this task better than the other two products. With Cisco routers, I can use a feature called Dynamic Multipoint VPNs (DMVPNs) which simplifies the interconnection/meshing process and the routing function of learning about the destinations at each end of the tunnel (with a minimal configuration).

One problem with VPN 3000 concentrators is that you either do this manually with network lists and RRI, or automatically, with Network Auto Discovery. The problem with the latter approach is that it only works with RIP, and it requires that the two endpoints be concentrators. Cisco routers, on the other hand, support many IP routing protocols, such as RIP, IGRP, OSPF, IS-IS, EIGRP, and BGP.

With PIX and ASA security appliances, routing protocols are not supported across VPN tunnels (at least not until version 7.0) and therefore the routing must be done manually, which doesn't scale well when connecting a large number of sites, with each site having a large number of networks. As an example, if you need to connect three sites together, where each site has 100 networks, on each site's PIX or ASA, you would need to configure 200 networks for the 100 networks at each remote site. As you add more sites and more networks, managing the routing process becomes *unmanageable.*

Media Translation

A third advantage of Cisco routers is that they support a wide variety of media types, such as Ethernet, ATM, ISDN, DSL, Frame Relay, point-to-point serial links, and many others. Cisco VPN 3000 concentrators and PIX and ASA security appliances support only Ethernet-based connections. Therefore, if you only need one Layer-3 device at a small site, it makes no sense to buy two products to handle multiple functions such as terminating VPNs and firewalling, in addition to connecting to an ISP with a non-Ethernet connection. Instead, you could use a router to handle all of these functions.

Quality of Service

The fourth advantage that routers have over VPN 3000 concentrators and PIX and ASA security appliances is their support for sophisticated QoS features. For example, suppose you had implemented VoIP throughout your network in Figure 15-1. A Call Manager device is located at the Central Office and a hub-and-spoke design is used to interconnect the various users and sites (with the Central Office being the hub). Given this situation, you need to prioritize your VoIP traffic over your data traffic to ensure that phone communications receive the necessary bandwidth and minimal delay.

The problem of using a VPN 3000 concentrator for this process is that its bandwidth management features are applied to a VPN termination point, like a remote access user or an L2L session; it cannot prioritize the traffic that traverses the tunnel, like VoIP over data traffic. In 6.3 and earlier of the PIX operating system, there is no support for QoS (in Version 7, there is support for low-latency queuing (LLQ), which is used primarily for VoIP applications.

Cisco routers, when compared to the other Cisco VPN products, are feature-rich with QoS capabilities, and they do the following:

- Use and control resources efficiently
- Adapt QoS based on needs of specific groups, users, and/or applications
- Allow VoIP, mission-critical resources, and bandwidth-intensive applications to co-exist

With the Cisco QoS features, you can classify your traffic manually or dynamically based on issues such as bandwidth, delay, jitter, and data loss requirements. The Cisco router QoS capabilities allow you to avoid congestion problems, or, in a worse case, at least deal with congestion problems so that they don't create additional problems for VoIP and mission-critical resources.

Cisco QoS features implement some or all of the following functions to handle your QoS needs:

- **Classifying traffic**—Sort traffic into different groups.
- **Marking traffic**—Place marking information in a packet to indicate its class (priority).
- **Policing traffic**—Compare received packets and determine whether they are following expected patterns concerning bandwidth, jitter, delay, packet loss, and so on, or are breaking a QoS policy (packets breaking a QoS policy are typically dropped but can be marked instead).
- **Queuing packets**—Examine the classification of packets to determine how it should be placed in an egress queue before being transmitted out of the router.
- **Scheduling**—Determine how queued traffic should be processed from the egress queue.
- **Shaping traffic**—Send traffic out at a constant rate to remove the jitter from a traffic stream and enforce a bandwidth limit, which is important for VoIP and multimedia applications.

Cisco supports the following classification features:

- Policy-based routing (PBR)
- Priority queuing

- Custom queuing
- Committed access rate (CAR)
- Class-based policing
- Network-based application recognition (NBAR)

Cisco supports the following queuing implementations:

- First-in-first-out (FIFO)
- Class-based weighted-fair queuing (CB-WFQ)
- Custom queuing (CQ)
- Class-based low latency queuing (CB-LLQ)
- IP RTP prioritization (for multimedia applications)
- Weighted round-robin queuing (WRRQ)
- Priority queuing (PQ)

WFQ is the default for WAN interfaces that are E1 or smaller. WRRQ is used, by default, on the egress interfaces of Catalyst Layer-3 switches. It uses a queuing policy similar to PQ, except that it guarantees that no queue will ever be starved. LLQ is ideal for networks that need to transport both voice and data. It combines PQ and CB-WFQ.

Cisco supports the following congestion avoidance features:

- Tail dropping
- Weighted random early detection (WRED)

Of the two, WRED is the more sophisticated because it uses the markings in packets to determine what should be dropped, to avoid any congestion problems.

NOTE   This chapter will not cover any IOS QoS mechanism in depth. For a quick overview of IOS QoS mechanisms, please read Chapter 9 of my book entitled *CCNP BCMSN Exam Cram 2 (642-811), Second Edition* by Que Publishing (ISBN: 0789729911).

Router Product Overview

Of the Cisco VPN solutions, their IOS-based routing platforms provide the most options to choose from. Because the Cisco product line for routers changes quite often, I've decided that in this chapter, I'll focus not on any particular router model, but will provide a brief comparison between the various models.

Table 15-1 shows a comparison of the various router models. Please note that some routers support hardware encryption via an add-on encryption card or module, and that there might be a few modules or cards to choose from for a particular router platform (the table lists the fastest encrypting module for each platform).

Table 15-1 *Router Product Comparison*

Router Model	Location	VPN Sessions	VPN Throughput (in Mbps)
SOHO 90 series[1]	SOHO	8	3DES: 1
830 series	SOHO	10	3DES: 7; AES: 2
850 series	SOHO or small branch office	5	3DES and AES: 8
870 series	SOHO or small branch office	10	3DES and AES: 30
1700 w/VPN module	Small branch office	100	3DES: 15
1841 w/AIM-VPN BP II Plus	Small to medium branch office	800	3DES and AES: 95
2600XM w/AIM-VPN/ BP II module	Medium branch office	800	3DES: 22; AES: 22
2691 w/AIM-VPN/EP II module	Medium branch office	800	3DES: 150; AES: 150
2621, 3640, or 3660 with hardware card	Medium branch office		3DES: 32 Mbps
2800s w/AIM-VPN/EP II-Plus	Enterprise branch office	1,500	3DES and AES: 145
3725 w/AIM-VPN/EP II module	Enterprise branch office	800	3DES: 186; AES: 186
3745 w/AIM-VPN/HP II module	Enterprise branch office	2,000	3DES: 190; AES: 190
3825 w/AIM-VPN/ EP II-Plus	Enterprise branch or regional office	2,000	3DES and AES: 175
3845 w/AIM-VPN/ HP II-Plus	Enterprise branch or regional office	2,500	3DES and AES: 185
7100 w/SM-VAM	Enterprise branch or regional office	3,000	3DES: 145; AES: N/A
7200 w/one ISA module	Enterprise branch or regional office	2,000	3DES: 90; AES: N/A
7200VXR w/one SA-VAM2+ module	Enterprise edge	5,000	3DES: 260; AES: 280
7300 w/one SA-VAM2+	Enterprise edge	5,000	3DES: 370; AES: 370
7400 w/one SA-VAM	Enterprise edge	5,000	3DES: 145; AES: N/A
7600 or Catalyst 6500 w/one VPN Service Module (VPNSM)[2]	Enterprise data center	8,000	3DES: 1,900; AES: N/A

[1] The SOHO 90s do not support QoS except for those platforms that have an ATM interface.

[2] You can install up to 10 VPNSMs into a 7600 or 6500 to achieve up to 19 Gbps of VPN throughput.

NOTE	The VPN throughputs listed in Table 15-1 are reflective of the router *only* doing VPN functions. Adding other features such as context-based access control (CBAC), IDS, address translation, and others will change the performance. The exceptions to this are the 1800, 2800, and 3800 ISR series of routers, which process traffic at rated interface speeds. Therefore, I highly recommend that you call Cisco TAC before using an existing product or purchasing a product for a VPN implementation. Discuss with them what you need to run on the router and about the kind of throughput you can expect to get based on the information you share with them.

Cisco Secure Socket Layer Services Module (SSLSM)

Besides selling a VPN Services Module for the Catalyst 6500 switch and 7600 router, Cisco also sells the SSLSM, which accelerates the performance for SSL web-based applications. It can be integrated with the Cisco Content Switching Module (CSM) to offload security functions to the SSLSM, increasing your web applications' performance and scalability. Some of the features that the SSLSM supports are certificate optimization, deterministic throughput, persistent connections, and server SSL offloading.

With certificate optimization feature, certificates can be managed by the SSLSM instead of on individual servers. Thus, the SSLSM can use a single certificate for all web servers it is offloading for. With the deterministic performance feature, the SSLSM provides the fastest SSL session setup and encryption throughput times in the industry. It can set up 2,500 connections per second per module, encrypt 300 Mbps per module (with a limit of 4 modules per chassis), and maintain 50,000 simultaneous SSL sessions. With the persistent connections feature, the SSLSM maintains persistence even if the SSL client gets a new session identifier from a Cisco CSM. And with the server SSL offloading feature, the SSLSM handles all SSL processes while the end web applications receive clear text traffic, reducing the overhead on the web servers.

Please note that coverage of this product is beyond the scope of this book.

Summary

This chapter introduced you to Cisco router products that support VPN capabilities. I wanted to give you an overall idea as to where Cisco routers play a role in implementing VPNs, and what kind of router you should use when creating your VPN design. Routers are best used when you need a one-box solution, combining features such as security, QoS, routing, WAN interfaces, and voice support, or if you have many L2L sessions you need to support. Therefore, you might already have a router-based network and want to add VPN functionality to it. You might easily be able to do this with the existing equipment you have, or at a minimal outlay of cost for equipment and software. Plus, out of all of the Cisco VPN offerings, the VPNSM can provide 19 Gbps VPN throughput from a single chassis, which is quite a lot of sessions!

Next up is Chapter 16, "Router ISAKMP/IKE Phase 1 Connectivity," where I discuss how to configure a router to establish a Phase 1 management connection as well as many of its advanced Phase 1 capabilities, like being able to perform the functions of a certificate authority (CA).

CHAPTER 16

Router ISAKMP/IKE Phase 1 Connectivity

This chapter is the first chapter on configuring routers for VPN implementations, where I'll focus on setting up ISAKMP/IKE Phase 1 to establish a management connection to a remote IPsec peer (site-to-site or remote access). I assume that you have a basic understanding of the Cisco IOS.

In this chapter, I'll discuss the commands that are used to create an ISAKMP/IKE Phase 1 policy for your management connection and the three types of supported device authentication: pre-shared keys, RSA encrypted nonces, and RSA signatures. I'll also briefly discuss how to manage and monitor your management connections. I'll wrap up the chapter discussing a new feature of the IOS, where you can have a Cisco IOS router perform the functions of a certificate authority (CA) or registration authority (RA).

NOTE Even though I'll briefly discuss some **show** and **debug** commands in this chapter, I'll reserve most of this discussion for Chapter 19, "Troubleshooting Router Connections."

IPsec Preparation

As with any type of VPN implementation, one of the first steps you'll go through is preparation. This is important for IOS-based routers because the configuration is more complex than setting up a GUI product like the Cisco VPN 3000 concentrators. The next few sections will briefly cover some basic information you'll need to gather, basic configuration tasks you'll perform on your routers, and additional ACL statements you'll need to add to perimeter routers to build IPsec sessions.

Gathering Information

The first step you'll take for your preparation is to gather information that will help you implement your IPsec sessions. If you recall from Chapter 3, "IPsec," two sets of connections are built: a management connection in ISAKMP/IKE Phase 1 and two unidirectional data connections in Phase 2. Each set of connections has protection properties you need to define. For example, with the Phase 1 connection, you'll need to minimally define the following:

- Device authentication type: pre-shared keys, RSA encrypted nonces, or RSA signatures (digital certificates)
- HMAC function: MD5 or SHA-1
- Encryption algorithm: DES, 3DES, or AES
- Diffie-Hellman (DH) group: 1, 2, or 5
- Lifetime of the connection: defaults to 86,400 seconds

For the Phase 2 connection, you'll need to define the following:

- What traffic is to be protected: crypto ACL
- To whom the protected traffic should be forwarded: IPsec peer
- How the traffic is to be protected: transform set
- What traffic should be protected to which peer: crypto map entry
- If Perfect Forward Secrecy (PFS) should be used to share new keying information for the data connections: DH groups 1, 2, or 5
- How long the data connection is valid: defaults to 3,600 seconds

Of course, the above items are the minimum items you'll need to identify and configure. In this chapter, though, I'll focus only on the first set of bullet points.

Allowing IPsec Traffic

One of the tasks you'll need to perform is to allow IPsec traffic into your network on your perimeter routers and firewalls. For a perimeter router, at a minimum you'll need to add the following entries into your ACL (assuming it's a numbered ACL and your perimeter router is using ACLs for filtering):

```
Router(config)# access-list ACL_# permit udp host remote_peer_IP
                host local_router's_IP eq 500
Router(config)# access-list ACL_# permit ahp host remote_peer_IP
                host local_router's_IP
Router(config)# access-list ACL_# permit esp host remote_peer_IP
                host local_router's_IP
Router(config)# access-list ACL_# permit udp host remote_peer_IP
                host local_router's_IP eq 4500
```

The first ACL statement allows the management connection to the router. With your ACL statements for L2L sessions, you want to be as specific as possible with the remote peer's IP address and the local router's IP address; with remote access sessions you might not know the source address, so you would typically use the keyword **any** for the source address and wildcard mask (this applies to the other ACL statements as well). The second statement is probably not necessary because AH doesn't work with any type of packet manipulation, such as address translation and QoS, and therefore isn't used commonly when sending protected traffic across a public network. The third statement allows the two data connections into the router. If you need to use NAT Traversal (NAT-T) because of PAT being performed or because of a firewall breaking ESP traffic, then instead of configuring the third ACL statement, you would configure the fourth. Remember that NAT-T encapsulates ESP in a UDP segment with a destination port number of 4,500.

NOTE	Remember that many remote access IPsec clients, like Cisco clients, have NAT-T enabled by default. Also, if you'll be using IPsec over UDP or IPsec over TCP for your data connections, you'll also need to allow this traffic in your ACLs on your perimeter devices.

ISAKMP/IKE Phase 1 Policies

One of the first steps you'll take in setting up IPsec—L2L or remote access—is to define your ISAKMP policies for your ISAKMP/IKE Phase 1 management connection. The following subsections will discuss how to create your policies and the following section will define how to configure the device authentication information you've chosen for your Phase 1 policies.

Enabling ISAKMP

If you have a router with the IPsec feature, ISAKMP/IKE is enabled by default. To enable or disable it, use the following command:

```
Router(config)# [no] crypto isakmp enable
```

You need to disable ISAKMP/IKE only if the remote peers do not support it, in which case you'll have to configure *all* parameters and keys for the data connection manually instead of having ISAKMP/IKE negotiate the parameters and create keying material dynamically; however, this is rarely done.

Creating Policies

An ISAKMP/IKE policy defines how the management connection is to be created, authenticated, and protected. You can have more than one policy on your router. You might need to do this if your router has multiple peers and each peer has different abilities or policy configurations. If you own the entire network and all the routers are Cisco routers, typically you would have a single policy that would encompass any management connection to any of your peering Cisco routers.

A single ISAKMP/IKE policy contains the following parameters: prioritization or sequence number, encryption algorithm, hashing function, authentication method, DH key group, and connection lifetime. Here are the commands to create a policy for the management connection:

```
Router(config)# crypto isakmp policy priority
Router(config-isakmp)# encryption {des | 3des | aes}
Router(config-isakmp)# hash {sha | md5}
Router(config-isakmp)# authentication {rsa-sig | rsa-encr | pre-share}
Router(config-isakmp)# group {1 | 2 | 5}
Router(config-isakmp)# lifetime seconds
Router(config-isakmp)# exit
```

The **crypto isakmp policy** command creates a unique ISAKMP/IKE management connection policy on the router, where each policy requires a separate number. Numbers can range between 1–10,000. Executing this command takes you to a subcommand mode where you enter the configuration for the policy. The **encryption** command specifies which encryption algorithm to use; the **hash** command specifies the HMAC function to use; the **authentication** command specifies the method to use for device authentication (you'll also need to configure the actual authentication information that you have decided to use, discussed in the "ISAKMP/IKE Phase 1 Device Authentication" section later); the **group** command specifies the DH key group to use; and the **lifetime** command specifies the lifetime of the management connection. If you don't specify a particular parameter in a policy, it has a default value, as follows:

- Encryption algorithm: DES
- HMAC function: SHA-1
- Authentication method: RSA signatures (certificates)
- DH group: 1
- Lifetime: 86,400 seconds

Likewise, a default, unnumbered ISAKMP/IKE policy exists on the router with the above configured values; so if these are sufficient, you don't need to configure an ISAKMP/IKE policy on your router. However, if you do create a policy, the pre-configured router policy always has the lowest priority. Also, you can use the **default** command within the ISAKMP policy to set a parameter back to the Cisco default value for the specified policy:

```
Router(config)# crypto isakmp policy priority
Router(config-isakmp)# default {encryption | hash | authentication |
                        group | lifetime}
Router(config-isakmp)# exit
```

TIP   The lower the policy number, the higher the priority for the ISAKMP policy, affecting which policy will be used between a peer. Therefore, give the *most* secure policy the lowest number (like **1**) and the *least* secure policy the highest number (like **10000**). The next section of this chapter discusses how a policy is chosen between two peers.

To view your ISAKMP policies, use the **show crypto isakmp policy** command shown in Example 16-1; this example has one configured policy (10) and the default policy.

Example 16-1 *The* **show crypto isakmp policy** *Command*

```
Router# show crypto isakmp policy
Global IKE policy
Protection suite of priority 10
        encryption algorithm:   AES - Advanced Encryption Standard
                            (128 bit keys).
        hash algorithm:         Message Digest 5
        authentication method:  Pre-Shared Key
        Diffie-Hellman group:   #2 (1024 bit)
        lifetime:               86400 seconds, no volume limit
Default protection suite
        encryption algorithm:   DES - Data Encryption Standard
                            (56 bit keys).
        hash algorithm:         Secure Hash Standard
        authentication method:  Rivest-Shamir-Adleman Signature
        Diffie-Hellman group:   #1 (768 bit)
        lifetime:               86400 seconds, no volume limit
```

Negotiating Policies with Peers

For two peers to establish an IPsec management connection, at least one configured ISAKMP/IKE policy on each peer must match. The peer that initiates the connection sends its entire list of management connection policies to the remote peer. The remote peer then looks for a match by comparing the sender's highest priority policy (lowest number, in the case of Cisco), against the local policies. These are processed based on the sequence numbers, from the lowest number to the highest. If no match is found, the remote peer compares the sender's second highest priority policy to its local list of policies (from the lowest to the highest), and so on until a match is found. Based on this process, the initiator of the connection has influence over which policy is used. Once a match is found, DH is performed and then the device authentication method that was negotiated. If no match is found, the negotiation *fails* and the management connection is not built.

NOTE   For a match to occur between two Phase 1 policies, the encryption algorithm, hashing function, DH group, and authentication method must match; if the lifetimes don't match, the shorter lifetime value between the two peers should be used. However, in real life, I've experienced problems with this process between Cisco and non-Cisco equipment where I also had to match the lifetime values for the policy negotiation to succeed.

Let's look at an example of policies on two devices in Examples 16-2 and 16-3, where I'll assume RouterA initiates the connection to RouterB. RouterA sends its two policies to RouterB. RouterB then compares its highest priority policy (1) to RouterA's 1, which doesn't match. RouterB then compares its policy 2 to RouterA's policy 1. In this instance, all of the values match except the lifetime; therefore, the policy is used with the lesser lifetime (3,600 seconds). Even if RouterB initiated the connection to RouterA, the same outcome would occur.

Example 16-2 *Phase 1 Policies on RouterA*

```
RouterA(config)# crypto isakmp policy 1
RouterA(config-isakmp)# authentication pre-share
RouterA(config-isakmp)# encryption 3des
RouterA(config-isakmp)# group 2
RouterA(config-isakmp)# lifetime 3600
RouterA(config-isakmp)# exit
RouterA(config)# crypto isakmp policy 2
RouterA(config-isakmp)# authentication pre-share
RouterA(config-isakmp)# hash md5
RouterA(config-isakmp)# exit
```

Example 16-3 *Phase 1 Policies on RouterB*

```
RouterB(config)# crypto isakmp policy 1
RouterB(config-isakmp)# authentication pre-share
RouterB(config-isakmp)# hash md5
RouterB(config-isakmp)# exit
RouterB(config)# crypto isakmp policy 2
RouterB(config-isakmp)# authentication pre-share
RouterB(config-isakmp)# encryption 3des
RouterB(config-isakmp)# group 2
RouterB(config-isakmp)# lifetime 86400
RouterB(config-isakmp)# exit
```

Enabling IKE Dead Peer Detection

Another feature that is commonly used for Cisco IPsec sessions is Dead Peer Detection (DPD). DPD allows Cisco IPsec peers to discover a dead peer using a keepalive mechanism across the management connection. DPD can work in one of two modes:

- **periodic**—the peer always sends periodic keepalives to ensure that the remote peer is still alive.

- **on-demand**—the peer sends a message based on traffic patterns between the peers, where the local peer has a question about the liveliness of the remote peer. This is triggered only when the local peer has no traffic to send and is not receiving traffic from the remote peer; otherwise, a remote peer will be found to be dead upon re-keying for the management or data connections.

NOTE   Like ISAKMP/IKE Phase 1 policies, the use of DPD, when configured, is negotiated between the two peers; if one peer doesn't support it or has it enabled, then DPD is not used. I highly recommend the use of DPD because it speeds up the process of discovering a dead peer and setting up a tunnel to a backup peer (if this has been configured).

To configure DPD, use the following command:

```
Router(config)# crypto isakmp keepalive seconds [retries]
                      [periodic | on-demand]
```

The first time value that you enter is the number of seconds between DPD messages. The *retries* parameter specifies the number of seconds between DPD retries when a response is not received for an initial DPD query. If you don't specify the DPD mode, it defaults to **on-demand**. The **crypto isakmp keepalive** command is useful only if you have multiple peers defined for redundancy and the primary peer fails; DPD will be able to detect this and will allow the router to bring up the connection to a backup peer.

NOTE   There is no **show** command to see the configuration of DPD (with the exception of **show running-config**); to see DPD in operation, you have to use the **debug crypto isakmp** command, which I discuss in Chapter 19, "Troubleshooting Router Connections").

TIP   You can use the **debug crypto isakmp** command to troubleshoot Phase 1 problems. I'll discuss this command in more depth in Chapter 19.

ISAKMP/IKE Phase 1 Device Authentication

Because the configuration of device authentication can be complex, at least when it comes to RSA encrypted nonces and especially digital certificates, I've separated the configuration process for authentication from the ISAKMP/IKE Phase 1 policy configuration and will cover it in its own section.

Note that Cisco routers support three methods of authenticating IPsec devices (peers): Pre-shared keys, RSA encrypted nonces, and RSA signatures (digital certificates). The following sections will discuss the configuration of these authentication methods.

ISAKMP/IKE Identity Type

Before I discuss the three ways of configuring device authentication, I first need to discuss the use of a router's identity type. The ISAKMP/IKE identity type specifies how each peer sends its identity to the remote peer; it will send either its IP address or its host name. This is used only when pre-shared (symmetric) keys or RSA encrypted nonces (asymmetric pre-shared keys) are used. This information is used by the remote peer to determine what pre-shared key information should be used to perform the device authentication.

The default is to have the router send its IP address. This works well if the local device has only one IP address that it will always use to initiate or terminate IPsec sessions. However, in certain cases this will cause problems if the local device can use more than one IP address (thus, more than one interface) to communicate to the remote device. In this case, I recommend that you use the router's host name for the identity type.

To specify the identity type, use the following command:

```
Router(config)# crypto isakmp identity {address | hostname}
```

address is the default type; so if your router will always use the same IP address to reach the remote peer, you don't need to configure this command. I recommend that if you use the **hostname** parameter, you should configure a static resolution table on your router for the name to the multiple IP addresses associated with the peer; if you don't do this, and DNS resolution fails, authentication also will fail and no IPsec tunnel will be built. To build a static DNS table, use the following command:

```
Router(config)# ip host hostname address1 [address2...address8]
```

You can list up to eight IP addresses per host name.

NOTE   Please note that the **crypto isakmp identity** command is a global command; you can't change the identity type on a peer-by-peer basis. Therefore, if you set it to **hostname** on one device, all of the other IPsec peer devices must be configured the same.

Pre-Shared Keys

Of the three methods of device authentication, configuring what Cisco calls "pre-shared keys" is the easiest. With pre-shared keys, the same key (symmetric) is used on both peers to perform the device authentication. Pre-shared keys, symmetric or asymmetric, commonly are used when you have a small number of devices with which you need to establish IPsec tunnels. When you add more and more IPsec devices to the network, however, pre-shared keys scale poorly and thus digital certificates are used to solve the device authentication scalability issues. The one advantage that pre-shared keys have over certificates, especially symmetric pre-shared keys, is that they are simple to set up on the two IPsec peers.

Configuring Pre-shared Keys

To configure a symmetric pre-shared key for device authentication on a router, use one of the following two commands, based on the identity type used on the router:

```
Router(config)# crypto isakmp {0 | 6} key keystring
                          address peer_address [subnet_mask] [no-xauth]
Router(config)# crypto isakmp {0 | 6} key keystring
                          hostname peer_hostname [no-xauth]
```

The **0** indicates that the key following the **key** parameter is unencrypted and a **6** indicates that it already is encrypted (in the router's configuration). If the identity type is **address**, use the first command. In this situation, the *keystring* value is the pre-shared key, and must match what is configured on the remote peer. If you don't specify a subnet mask, it defaults to a host mask: 255.255.255.255. With the ability to configure a subnet mask, you can wildcard a key to be used for multiple peers, like this:

```
Router(config)# crypto isakmp 0 key cisco123abc address
                    0.0.0.0 0.0.0.0
```

CAUTION   I highly recommend that you configure a different key for each peer; otherwise, if you wildcard keys and one device becomes compromised, the attacker now knows the authentication key for all of the devices covered by the masking process.

Remember that the **crypto isakmp key** command is used for non-remote access device authentication. As you'll see in Chapter 18, "Router Remote Access Connections," a different process is used for remote access users. However, this presents a problem if you have both L2L and remote access sessions terminated on your router. In this situation, the router will assume that XAUTH (user authentication) will be performed for *both* connection types. Of course, this will create problems for L2L sessions. Therefore, I always recommend that you add the **no-xauth** parameter to your pre-shared key configuration even if you don't currently have remote access sessions. If you add them later, you don't have to worry about your L2L sessions failing because they're trying to use XAUTH also.

NOTE   In older IOS versions, support for encrypting the pre-shared key on the router does not exist, and thus the **0** and **6** parameters in the **crypto isakmp key** command are omitted.

Protecting Pre-Shared Keys

By default, when you are entering your pre-shared symmetric or asymmetric (see the next section) keys, they are saved in clear text. In IOS 12.3(2)T, you have the option of encrypting these keys. One limitation, however, is that you must have an IOS image with AES encryption. Here are the commands you'll need to configure on your router to encrypt your unencrypted pre-shared keys:

```
Router(config)# key config-key password-encrypt
New key:
Confirm key:
Router(config)# password encryption aes
```

The **key config-key password-encrypt** command will prompt you for the encryption key to use to encrypt the pre-shared keys; this key must be eight alphanumeric characters in length at a minimum. The **password encryption aes** command performs the actual encryption of your router's pre-shared keys.

CAUTION   If you want to remove the encryption option with the **no key config-key password-encrypt** command, the encrypted pre-shared are not automatically decrypted in your router's configuration; instead, all encrypted pre-shared keys become unusable, meaning that you'll have to re-enter them manually.

Viewing your Pre-Shared Keys

Once you have created your pre-shared keys, you can view them with the **show crypto isakmp key** command. An example of this command is shown in Example 16-4. In this example, the actual pre-shared keys have been encrypted using the process discussed in the previous section. If the pre-shared key wasn't encrypted, you would see it in clear text under the *Preshared Key* column.

Example 16-4 *Phase 1 Keys*

```
Router# show crypto isakmp key
Keyring            Hostname/Address              Preshared Key
default            192.1.1.1                        (encrypted)
```

RSA Encrypted Nonces

One problem with symmetric pre-shared keys is that both sides need to use the same key to perform authentication, which means that either you should configure the pre-shared key out-of-band on both peers, like a console port, or use an encrypted CLI session, such as SSH. Plus, if someone can learn somehow what the symmetric key is, that person can pretend to be either peer when establishing a session to the other peer. RSA encrypted nonces limit the exposure in this situation to a single peer, because each peer has its own keying information using asymmetric keys (public and private).

With RSA encrypted nonces, you create a public/private key combination on each peer and encode your local peer's public key manually on the remote peer and the remote peer's public key on the local peer. One advantage of asymmetric keying for authentication, as I discussed in Chapter 2, "VPN Technologies," is that the private key creates the authentication information and only the related public key verifies it; the private key is never shared with anyone. In this situation, an attacker actually would have to break into your router, versus eavesdropping on a connection, to see the private key that creates the authentication information.

Using RSA encrypted nonces typically is a two step-process:

Step 1   Generate the RSA encrypted nonces on each peer (public and private keys), where you can create separate public/private keys for each remote peer.

Step 2   Share your public key with your peer and vice versa; then configure the peer's public key on your peer.

The following three sections will discuss these two steps. I'll also discuss how you can remove configured keys.

Generating RSA Encrypted Nonces (Key Pairs)

The first step you need to perform is to create your RSA encrypted nonces, commonly called key pairs—a router's public and private key combination. To create encrypted nonces, first you need to configure a host name and domain name on your router with the following two commands:

```
Router(config)# hostname router_name
Router(config)# ip domain-name domain_name
```

If you don't configure these commands at a minimum, the **crypto key generate rsa** command will give you an error message prompting you to configure both commands. The RSA algorithm needs these two components as input to the algorithm for generating the public/private keys, and also to name the key pair.

NOTE   Even though the router has a host name of "Router," the **crypto key generate rsa** command requires you to change it to something different.

Once you have configured the above commands, execute this command to generate your public/private keys:

```
Router(config)# crypto key generate rsa [general-keys | usage-keys]
```

The **general-keys** parameter generates a single public/private key combination used for signature purposes and **usage-keys** generates two key pairs: one for signatures and one for encryption. For authentication functions, you can use the **general-keys** parameter, which is the default if not specified. When you execute the command, you'll be prompted for a modulus value ranging from 360–2,048 bits. You can't choose any value at random; it has to be a modulus factor.

NOTE   I've noticed in more recent IOS versions that the default is **usage-keys** instead of **general-keys** with the **crypto key generate rsa** command; this doesn't really matter in that for device authentication purposes, you're only interested in the public/private signature keys that are created.

Example 16-5 shows an example of using the **crypto key generate rsa** command. With this command, I chose the largest size modulus (the most secure) on a 3640 router—it took almost two minutes to generate the keys. With smaller routers, like the end-of-life 2500s, it takes longer than an hour. Therefore, I recommend that you use a smaller modulus for smaller routers.

Example 16-5 *Generating RSA Keys*

```
Router(config)# hostname r3640
Router(config)# ip domain-name cisco.com
r3640(config)# crypto key generate rsa
The name for the keys will be: r3640.cisco.com
Choose the size of the key modulus in the range of 360 to 2048 for
  your General Purpose Keys. Choosing a key modulus greater than 512
  may take a few minutes.
How many bits in the modulus [512]: 2048
% Generating 2048 bit RSA keys ...[OK]
r3640(config)#
```

Once you have created your keys, you can view your router's public keys with the **show crypto key mypubkey rsa** command, shown in Example 16-6. With this command you can only view the current router's keys, not a peer's keys.

Example 16-6 *Viewing a Router's RSA Keys*

```
r3640# show crypto key mypubkey rsa
% Key pair was generated at: 06:13:07 UTC Mar 1 2002
Key name: r3640.cisco.com
 Usage: General Purpose Key
 Key is not exportable.
 Key Data:
  30820122 300D0609 2A864886 F70D0101 01050003 82010F00 3082010A
←output omitted→
  23CA4ACE 63F1D296 1B020301 0001
% Key pair was generated at: 06:13:10 UTC Mar 1 2005
Key name: r3640.cisco.com.server
 Usage: Encryption Key
 Key is not exportable.
 Key Data:
  307C300D 06092A86 4886F70D 01010105 00036B00 30680261 00BFB7C0
←output omitted→
  BAE69169 713DCF99 B1020301 0001
```

NOTE   To save your public and private keys, execute the **copy running-config startup-config** command. Please note that if you back up your router's configuration to a remote device, such as a TFTP or SCP server, the router's private keying information is *not* backed up to the external server. I'll discuss how this can be done in the "Importing and Exporting RSA Keys and Certificates" section later in the chapter.

Multiple RSA Key Pairs

As of IOS 12.2(8)T, you can create multiple RSA key pairs on a single router; with this approach, you can use different keys for different peers with RSA encrypted nonces or for digital certificates discussed later in the "Digital Certificates and Router Enrollment" section. And because you can have multiple RSA key pairs, each key pair's policy can match that of the remote peer or certificate service.

Each RSA key pair on your router has a unique label. Without specifying any label for a key pair, as illustrated previously in Example 16-6, the label will default to the FQDN of the router (r3640.cisco.com). To create a different key pair on your router, use the following syntax:

```
Router(config)# crypto key generate rsa [general-keys | usage-keys]
                     key_pair_label
```

TIP When using different keys for different peers, I like to use a key pair label that describes the peer, like the name of the peer; when used for certificates, I like to use the name of the CA listed in the **crypto ca trustpoint** command discussed later in the chapter. Using this approach makes it easier to see where the keys are being used.

Configuring a Peer's Public Key

Once you have generated your public/private keys on both devices, you'll exchange public keys between the peers (use the **show crypto key mypubkey rsa** command to view your router's public key. You'll now need to configure the remote peer's public key on your router.

Based on the identity type you have defined with the **crypto isakmp identity** command, you'll configure it in one of two ways:

```
Router(config)# crypto key pubkey-chain rsa
Router(config-pubkey-c)# named-key peer_name [encryption |
                               signature]
Router(config-pubkey-k)# key-string key_string
Router(config-pubkey-k)# quit
```

or:

```
Router(config)# crypto key pubkey-chain rsa
Router(config-pubkey-c)# addressed-key peer_IP_address [encryption |
                               signature]
Router(config-pubkey-k)# key-string key_string
Router(config-pubkey-k)# quit
```

If the identity type is based on host names, use the **named-key** parameter followed by the name of the peer; otherwise, use the **addressed-key** parameter followed by the IP address of the peer. If you don't specify the key type, it defaults to **signature**.

The **key-string** subcommand allows you to enter the actual hexadecimal key for the remote peer. This can be entered on multiple lines. When finished entering the peer's key, on a blank command line enter the **quit** command, which tells the router you have finished entering the key with the **key-string** command.

TIP   When entering a peer's public key, I highly recommend that you don't type it in; instead, copy it on the peer and paste it into a file. Using a secure or out-of-band method, take the key to the PC you'll use to configure your router. Then use the key in this file and copy and paste it into your router. By doing this, you'll reduce the likelihood of mistyping the key; one wrong character when entering the key will invalidate the key when authentication is performed.

Once you have configured your peers' public keys on your router, you can view them with the following command:

```
Router# show crypto key pubkey-chain rsa
                    {name peer_name | address peer_IP_address}
```

Without the **name** or **address** parameter, you won't see the peers' public keys, just the peers that you have set up on your router with public keys, like those shown in Example 16-7. If you enter the identity type followed by the peer's identity, like that shown in Example 16-8, you'll see that specific peer's public key.

Example 16-7 *Viewing a List of Peers Configured for RSA Keying*

```
r3640# show crypto key pubkey-chain rsa
Codes: M - Manually configured, C - Extracted from certificate

Code Usage        IP-Address/VRF      Keyring         Name
M    General      192.1.1.1           default
```

Example 16-8 *Viewing a Peer's Public Key*

```
r3640# show crypto key pubkey-chain rsa address 192.1.1.1
Key address:        192.1.1.1
 Usage: General Purpose Key
 Source: Manually entered
 Data:
  30820122 300D0609 2A864886 F70D0101 01050003 82010F00 3082010A
←output omitted→
  23CA4ACE 63F1D296 1B020301 0001
```

Removing RSA Keys

If a peer generates new keys, you'll need to enter that peer's new public key on your router—you'll need to remove the old key for the peer and then re-add it. To do this, first execute the **crypto key pubkey-chain rsa** command. Then use the **no named-key** or **no addressed-key** command to remove the peer (based on how you added the key), which will remove the peer and the key; then re-add the peer's key as I explained at the beginning of the section. Example 16-9 shows an example of this for the peer listed in Examples 16-7 and 16-8.

Example 16-9 *Removing a Peer's Public Key*

```
r3640(config)# crypto key pubkey-chain rsa
r3640(config-pubkey-chain)# no addressed-key 192.1.1.1
```

Of course, you might need to generate and use new keys on your router. You might need to do this because your keys have been compromised, or because a change in security policy dictates a change in the modulus value used to generate the keys. To remove your router's own public/private keys, use this command:

```
Router(config)# crypto key zeroize rsa [key_pair_label]
```

Without specifying a key pair label for a specific key pair, all the router's personal public/private keys are deleted. If the router has more than one set of keys, you can specify which is deleted by examining the list of keys from the output of the **show crypto key mypubkey rsa** command and entering the name of the key.

NOTE   If the router's key is specified manually somewhere else in the router's configuration, you won't be able to delete it until you remove its reference. For example, certificates use public/private keys; therefore, if the router has a certificate, you'd first have to delete the router's certificate, and then the router's keys associated with the certificate.

Digital Certificates and Router Enrollment

Unlike symmetric or asymmetric (RSA encrypted nonces) pre-shared keys, digital certificate information is *not* pre-shared with other peers. Like RSA encrypted nonces, a private key is used to create authentication information (signature) and a public key is used to verify the signature; however, this information is located on a certificate and is not pre-shared with a peer. Thus, digital certificates scale better than either of the two pre-shared methods.

In this section I'll discuss the use of certificates on routers and how they're used for authentication. The first two sections will discuss how to obtain a certificate with SCEP (in-band) and manually (out-of-band). Following this, I'll discuss how to export and import certificate and keying information for backup and redundancy purposes.

Enrolling for a Certificate using SCEP

Between manual enrollment and the Simple Certificate Enrollment Protocol (SCEP), SCEP is used most often to set up certificate services on a router. To use SCEP, though, your router cannot use public keys greater than 2,048 bits and you must use ISAKMP/IKE and IPsec to set up the management and data connections dynamically.

No matter whether you're using SCEP or the manual approach, typically you'll go through the following steps to get certificates on a router:

Step 1 Verify that certificates can fit into NVRAM (optional).

Step 2 Configure a host name and domain name (required).

Step 3 Generate an RSA key pair (required).

Step 4 Define a Certificate Authority or CA (required).

Step 5 Download and authenticate the CA's certificate (required).

Step 6 Request the router's identity certificate (required).

Step 7 Save the CA and identity certificates (required).

Step 8 Verify the certificate operation (optional).

The following subsections will discuss each of these tasks.

Step 1: Verify that Certificates Can Fit into NVRAM

When using certificates for device authentication, the following information is, by default, stored in NVRAM of the router: the router's identity certificate, the router's private and public keys used to create and validate the signature on the router's PKCS #10 information, the CA's certificate, root certificates obtained from the CA, if any, two Registration Authority (RA) certificates, if the CA supports an RA, and one or more CRLs.

NOTE Use the **show running-config** command to determine how much NVRAM your router is currently using.

Because this can represent a large amount of information, NVRAM might be too small to store this information, which is possible on smaller, older router models. If this is the case, you have the option of having the router download this information from the CA with the exception of the following information: the router's public and private keys and the signature on the CA certificate—this information will be stored locally in NVRAM and all other certificate information will be downloaded to the router when it boots up and will be stored in RAM. This process is called query mode. To turn on the query mode of the router, use this command:

```
Router(config)# crypto ca certificate query
```

To turn off query mode later, use the **no crypto ca certificate query** after the router has downloaded all certificate information and then execute **copy running-config startup-config** to save the downloaded certificate information to NVRAM. If you currently are not using query mode and want to enable it, use the above command to remove all certificate information stored in NVRAM and then save the router's configuration (**copy running config startup-config**).

Steps 2 and 3: Names and RSA Key Pairs

A private key is needed on the router to generate the signature for the router's identity information (PKCS #10) and a public key is necessary to validate the signature for the PKCS #10 information. I've already discussed this configuration in the "Generating RSA Encrypted Nonces (Key Pairs)" section, where you use the **hostname** command to assign a name to the router, the **ip domain-name** command to assign a domain name, and the **crypto key generate rsa** command to create the router's public/private keys. Remember that if you want to create a separate RSA key pair for this certificate compared to other certificates your router has, you'll need to add a key pair label to the end of the command (see the "Multiple RSA Key Pairs" section earlier).

Step 4: Define a CA

Once you have generated your RSA key pair, you can then define the CA your router will be using for IPsec device authentication. This is done with the commands shown in the following code listing:

```
Router(config)# crypto {ca | pki} trustpoint CA_name
Router(ca-trustpoint)# enrollment url CA_URL
Router(ca-trustpoint)# enrollment http-proxy proxy_IP_address
                       proxy_port_#
Router(ca-trustpoint)# enrollment mode ra
Router(ca-trustpoint)# enrollment retry period minutes
Router(ca-trustpoint)# enrollment retry count number
Router(ca-trustpoint)# crl {query URL | optional}
Router(ca-trustpoint)# ocsp url OCSP_server_URL
Router(ca-trustpoint)# revocation-check method1 [method2 [method3]]
Router(ca-trustpoint)# query certificate
Router(ca-trustpoint)# primary
Router(ca-trustpoint)# source interface name_and_number_of_interface
Router(ca-trustpoint)# default command
Router(ca-trustpoint)# exit
```

The **crypto ca trustpoint** specifies CA properties to use to interact with the CA: you can use either the **ca** or **pki** parameter to signify the configuration type. The *CA_name* you specify is typically the FQDN of the CA—your CA administrator will give you this value. When executing this command, you are taken into a subcommand mode where you can enter the properties for interacting with the CA.

The **enrollment url** command specifies the URL to interact with the CA when requesting certificates; again, your CA administrator will give you this information. These are the only two required commands to interact with the CA; the remaining commands are optional. If your CA is behind a web proxy, you'll need to configure your router to interact with the proxy with the **enrollment http-proxy** command, specifying the IP address (or FQDN) of the proxy and the port number to use when contacting the proxy.

The **enrollment mode ra** command specifies whether or not the CA provides for an RA(s); you don't need to configure this command because IOS routers will determine automatically whether the CA is using an RA(s) or not. If the router determines that RAs are being used, this command will appear automatically in the router's configuration.

The **enrollment retry period** command specifies the length of time that the router will wait for a certificate from the CA before requesting it again. The default is one minute. The **enrollment retry count** command specifies how many times the router will continue contacting the CA for a certificate request before giving up; the default configuration specifies that the router will try continually without ever giving up.

NOTE   If your CA is an IOS router CA, the URL you specify in the **enrollment url** command needs to be as follows: **enrollment url http://***IP_address_or_FQDN_of_router_CA*; no CGI-BIN script or additional information is necessary. For more information on using a router as a CA, see the "Routers as Certificate Authorities" section later in the chapter.

The **crl** command specifies configuration options for using CRLs. The **query** parameter specifies an LDAP or HTTP server where the CRL is located and is in the format of "**{ldap|http}**://*IP_address/other_URL_info.*" The **optional** parameter specifies that CRLs might or might not be used by your CA and thus your router will accept a peer's certificate if a CRL cannot be located. If you know that your CA uses CRLs, don't configure this command; otherwise you inadvertently might use a revoked certificate, because CRL checking is optional with this command enabled.

The Online Certificate Status Protocol (OCSP) allows devices to use this process, instead of CRLs, to check the status of certificates. This feature is new in IOS 12.3(2)T. OCSP has a few advantages over CRLs. First, it runs across HTTP instead of the possibility of LDAP; second, it provides more frequent updates to the edge devices than CRLs provide (CRLs do this only periodically); and third, OCSP allows you to configure a central OCSP server to collect and update CRLs from multiple CAs, simplifying and speeding up the CRL checking process by an edge device.

The **ocsp url** command specifies the OCSP's location of revoked certificates; if the CA's certificate has this location already on it and you configure the **ocsp url** command, the configured command overrides the information on the CA's certificate. The **revocation-check** command specifies the method or order of methods to use to check the revocation status of a certificate. There are three defined method parameters: **crl**, **ocsp**, and **none**. **crl** specifies that certificate checking is performed by a CRL—this is the default option; **oscp** specifies that checking is performed by an OCSP server; and **none** specifies that no certificate checking is performed (this command replaces the **crl optional** command in the latest IOS releases).

The **query certificate** command specifies that any certificate information for this particular trustpoint is not stored in NVRAM—the advantage of this command over the **crypto ca certificate query** command is that the latter is global and affects all CAs defined on the router, whereas the former affects only the current trustpoint's configuration. The **primary** command specifies that this particular trustpoint is assigned the primary CA role on the router; this command is necessary only if you have more than one CA configured and you want one to be the primary one. The **source interface** command, new in IOS 12.2(15)T, specifies the source interface to use for traffic to be sent to the CA. This command typically is used when the exit interface of the router has a private (or IP address, but the router does have another interface with a public address and wants this address to be used. If you omit this command, the router uses the interface chosen based on its routing table selection.

The **default** command, followed by another trustpoint command, sets the specified trustpoint command back to the default value. This is useful if you want to undo a trustpoint configuration command. Other optional commands can be configured under the trustpoint (in the trustpoint subcommand mode), however, I'll discuss these in later sections.

NOTE   In IOS versions before 12.2(8)T, the command to specify the CA is **crypto ca identity**; this has be supplanted by the **crypto ca trustpoint** command. This is also true of the **crypto ca trusted-root**, which allows you to specify a root CA in a hierarchical CA setup.

Step 5: Download and Authenticate the CA's Certificate

Once you have defined the interaction between the router and the CA, you are ready to download and authenticate the CA's self-signed certificate by using this command:

```
Router(config)# crypto {ca | pki} authenticate CA_name
```

You need to configure the same CA name that you configured in the **crypto ca trustpoint** command in the last section. Example 16-10 illustrates this process. The name of the CA is "caserver." Upon downloading the CA certificate, you'll be prompted to accept it; before accepting it, first validate the CA's signature on the self-signed certificate. It's important that you do this, because this is the weakest link in the security process of using certificates. At this point, a man-in-the-middle attack could be occurring and you could be receiving a hostile or invalid CA certificate.

Example 16-10 *Downloading and Authenticating the CA's Certificate*

```
r3640(config)# crypto ca authenticate caserver
Certificate has the following attributes:
Fingerprint MD5: CE9956AA C02D15DF A2309A9C E059BD47
Fingerprint SHA1: 475A5DBA 0283DB43 305E9CF7 A208C8B8 E894C379
% Do you accept this certificate? [yes/no]: yes
Trustpoint CA certificate accepted.
```

Step 6: Request the Router's Identity Certificate

Before you can request the router's identity certificate, first you must have downloaded and verified the CA's certificate in Step 5. This is necessary so that the router can use the CA certificate to validate any certificate received (from the same CA's domain), including the router's own identity certificate. Likewise, you already must have generated an RSA key pair which is used to sign and verify the identity certificate request. When you have completed these steps, you are now ready to create the PKCS #10 information that will be sent to the CA, via SCEP, with this command:

```
Router(config)# crypto {ca | pki} enroll CA_name
```

The CA name you list must be the same name configured in the **crypto ca authenticate** and **crypto ca trustpoint** commands. First you'll be prompted for a challenge password. This password serves two purposes: it is used by the CA to control who can request a new certificate and by the CA administrator to revoke a valid certificate. You also have the option of including the router's serial number or IP address in the identity certificate. Once you answer **yes** to request a certificate, the router puts together the PKCS #10 information and sends this to the CA via HTTP. Once the request has been approved and the identity certificate generated, your router will download the identity certificate automatically. Example 16-11 illustrates how to use SCEP to request an identity certificate for your router.

Example 16-11 *Obtaining the Router's Identity Certificate*

```
r3640(config)# crypto ca enroll caserver
% Start certificate enrollment ..
% Create a challenge password. You will need to verbally provide this
    password to the CA Administrator in order to revoke your
    certificate. For security reasons your password will not be saved
    in the configuration. Please make a note of it.
Password: cisco123abc
Re-enter password: cisco123abc
% The fully-qualified domain name in the certificate will be:
                        r3640.cisco.com
% The subject name in the certificate will be: r3640.cisco.com
% Include the router serial number in the subject name? [yes/no]: no
% Include an IP address in the subject name? [no]: no
Request certificate from CA? [yes/no]: yes
% Certificate request sent to Certificate Authority
% The certificate request fingerprint will be displayed.
% The 'show crypto pki certificate' command will also show the
    fingerprint.
```

Example 16-11 *Obtaining the Router's Identity Certificate (Continued)*

```
05:32:29: CRYPTO_PKI:  Certificate Request Fingerprint MD5:
   F9A3574C 09BAC68D 491D0FDA 1EBCE0BC
05:32:29: CRYPTO_PKI:  Certificate Request Fingerprint SHA1:
   898BDC0B 69F74320 8EECF1FF FD86503F 3DC366BB
05:32:34: %PKI-6-CERTRET: Certificate received from Certificate
   Authority
```

Step 7: Save the CA and Identity Certificates

Assuming you have enough NVRAM to store your router's certificate components, the last step is to save these components to NVRAM with the **copy running-config startup-config** command. If the router reboots before the requested identity certificate was installed and saved, you'll need to re-execute the **crypto ca enroll** command; the same is true for downloading and authenticating the CA certificate: **crypto ca authenticate**. Both of these commands are not saved in the router's NVRAM.

Step 8: Verify the Certificate Operation

Once you have an identity certificate on the router, the last step is to verify the certificate operation process. To view the CA or CAs you have configured on your router, use the **show crypto {ca | pki} trustpoint**. The output of this command, shown in Example 16-12, displays some of the information found on the CA certificate, in addition to how the trustpoint is configured on the router.

Example 16-12 *The* **show cyrpto ca trustpoints** *Command*

```
r3640# show crypto ca trustpoints
Trustpoint caserver:
    Subject Name:
    cn=caserver
    c=US
          Serial Number: 6EBD53BA55C2D29841E0A0D48E40CF96
    Certificate configured.
    SCEP URL: http://192.1.1.77:80/certsrv/mscep/mscep.dll
```

To view any certificates the router has, use the **show crypto {ca | pki} certificates** command, shown in Example 16-13. The first certificate is the router's identity certificate and the second one is the CA's.

Example 16-13 *The* **show crypto ca certificates** *Command*

```
r3640# show crypto ca certificates
Certificate
  Status: Available
  Certificate Serial Number: 11320A3500010000001A
  Certificate Usage: General Purpose
  Issuer:
    cn=caserver
    c=US
```

continues

Example 16-13 *The* **show crypto ca certificates** *Command (Continued)*

```
  Subject:
    Name: r3640.cisco.com
    hostname=r3640.cisco.com
  CRL Distribution Points:
    http://i7500/CertEnroll/caserver(1).crl
  Validity Date:
    start date: 03:41:05 UTC Feb 26 2005
    end   date: 03:51:05 UTC Feb 26 2006
  Associated Trustpoints: caserver

CA Certificate
  Status: Available
  Certificate Serial Number: 6EBD53BA55C2D29841E0A0D48E40CF96
  Certificate Usage: Signature
  Issuer:
    cn=caserver
    c=US
  Subject:
    cn=caserver
    c=US
←output omitted→
```

To request the current CRL for the CA or configured LDAP server, execute the following command:

```
Router(config)# crypto ca crl request CA_name
```

Be sure to use the name of the CA configured in the **crypto ca trustpoint** command when requesting the current CRL. This command typically is used if certificates have been revoked on the CA, but you suspect your router doesn't have the most up-to-date CRL. To view the status of the CRL, use the **show crypto {ca | pki} crls** command; an example of this is shown in Example 16-14.

Example 16-14 *The* **show crypto ca crls** *Command*

```
r3640# show crypto ca crls
CRL Issuer Name:
    cn=caserver,c=US
    LastUpdate: 01:18:27 UTC Feb 25 2005
    NextUpdate: 13:38:27 UTC Mar 4 2005
    Retrieved from CRL Distribution Point:
      http://i7500/CertEnroll/caserver(1).crl
```

TIP   You can use the **debug crypto pki** command to troubleshoot problems related to the request and use of certificates

Deleting Certificates

There are many reasons you might want to delete a certificate, including the following:

- You need to generate an RSA key pair with a longer (or shorter) modulus.
- Your current certificate has expired.
- Your private key has been compromised.
- You no longer are using the certificate for authentication functions.

To delete a certificate, such as your router's identity certificate, first view the certificate with the **show crypto ca certificates** command and look for the serial number of the certificate to be revoked. Then execute the following two commands:

```
Router(config)# crypto ca certificate chain CA_name
Router(config-cert-cha)# no certificate certificate-serial-number
```

With the first command, you must specify the name of the trustpoint configured in the **crypto ca trustpoint** command. This takes you into a subcommand mode where you remove the certificate by specifying the serial number of the certificate to be deleted with the **no certificate** command.

Once a certificate is deleted, you can remove its associated RSA key pair with the **crypto key zeroize rsa** command, discussed earlier in the "Removing RSA Keys" section. Also, if you no longer will be using certificates for authentication functions and wish to remove all certificate information on your router, use the following command:

```
Router(config)# no crypto ca trustpoint CA_name
```

This command allows you to remove not only the configuration of the trustpoint (the associated trustpoint commands), but the CA certificate, any RA certificates, any CRLs, and the router's identity certificate(s).

Enrolling for a Certificate Manually

If your CA doesn't support or use SCEP, you'll need to obtain certificates for your router using manual enrollment. Manual enrollment can be accomplished using TFTP or cut-and-paste if you're running IOS 12.2(13)T or later.

NOTE   Cisco doesn't recommend using SCEP to obtain one certificate and TFTP or cut-and-paste to obtain the other certificate when retrieving the CA and identity certificates; this might create problems when trying to retrieve the second certificate from the CA.

Configuring Manual Enrollment Using TFTP

Configuring manual enrollment using TFTP is very similar to configuring certificate enrollment using SCEP: you'll need to go through the same eight steps discussed in the "Enrolling for a Certificate using SCEP" section. However, there are obviously a few differences. Steps 1–3 are the same: verify NVRAM usage, configure the router's host and domain names, and generate the RSA keys.

Step 4, defining a CA, is slightly different. First, make sure the router can reach a TFTP server and has write access to the TFTP server's directory structure. Next, configure the trustpoint with the **crypto ca trustpoint** command. This command was discussed previously in the "Step 4: Define a CA" section. The main difference is the **enrollment url** command, which needs to specify a URL with a TFTP file type and the location of the TFTP server:

```
Router(config)# crypto ca trustpoint CA_name
Router(ca-trustpoint)# enrollment url
                        tftp://server_name_or_address/file_name
```

For example, you might enter something like **enrollment url tftp://caserver/directory/ cacert**. In most cases, the TFTP server will be the same device that's the CA if you're setting up your own CA. Otherwise, you'll use a local TFTP server. The file specified is the CA's certificate and must be in a base-64 encoding scheme. Also, the router will append ".ca" as an extension to the file name; so in this example, the file on the TFTP server is "cacert.ca." If you omit a file name, the name will default to the router's FQDN plus the ".ca" extension, like "r3640.cisco.com.ca." The other trustpoint commands discussed previously in the "Step 4: Define a CA" section also can be configured as necessary.

Next, perform Step 5 as discussed previously in the "Step 5: Download and Authenticate the CA's Certificate" section by executing the **crypto ca authenticate** command to download and authenticate the CA's certificate (from the TFTP server). You'll need to verify the CA's signature and accept it if valid.

Following this, request the router's certificate by executing the **crypto ca enroll** command, discussed previously in the "Step 6: Request the Router's Identity Certificate" section. In this case, the command creates the router's PKCS #10 information and sends it to the TFTP server, which Example 16-15 illustrates. The name of the file on the TFTP server will be the file name listed in the **enrollment url** command followed by ".req" as an extension, as you can see from Example 16-15. Give this file to the CA administrator, which then will be used by the CA to create an identity certificate for your router.

Example 16-15 *Sending the Router's PKCS #10 Information to the TFTP Server*

```
r3640(config)# crypto ca enroll caserver
% Start certificate enrollment ..
% The fully-qualified domain name in the certificate will be:
   r3640.cisco.com
% The subject name in the certificate will be: r3640.cisco.com
% Include the router serial number in the subject name? [yes/no]: no
% Include an IP address in the subject name? [no]: no
Send Certificate Request to file system? [yes/no]: yes
% Certificate request sent to file system
% The certificate request fingerprint will be displayed.
% The 'show crypto pki certificate' command will also show the
   fingerprint.
```

Example 16-15 *Sending the Router's PKCS #10 Information to the TFTP Server (Continued)*

```
!Writing file to tftp://192.1.1.77/cacert.req!
09:20:42: CRYPTO_PKI:  Certificate Request Fingerprint MD5: E5CC32D1
     AB29F816 94BC76A8 ADC525EE
09:20:42: CRYPTO_PKI:  Certificate Request Fingerprint SHA1: A5006A64
     5E0BA531 97878ED0 A84AA3A8 8F6B9C82
```

Once the CA administrator has generated an identity certificate for your router, it needs to be saved with a ".crt" extension and with the same filename specified in the **enrollment url** command. This file must be stored in a base-64 encoding scheme (PKCS #10) as the CA certificate was previously, and placed in the same directory on the TFTP server as the CA's certificate. Then you can import the identity certificate with the **crypto ca import** command:

```
Router(config)# crypto ca import CA_name certificate
```

You must specify the name of the CA configured as a trustpoint with the **crypto ca trustpoint** command. Example 16-16 illustrates the use of this command. As you can see in this example, the router's identity certificate is named "cacert.crt" on the TFTP server.

Example 16-16 *Importing the Router's Identity Certificate via TFTP*

```
r3640(config)# crypto ca import caserver certificate
% The fully-qualified domain name in the certificate will be:
     r3640.cisco.com
Retrieve Certificate from file system? [yes/no]: yes
% Request to retrieve Certificate queued
Reading file from tftp://192.1.1.77/cacert.crt
Loading cacert.crt from 192.1.1.77 (via Ethernet0/0): !
[OK - 1118 bytes]
09:31:07: %PKI-6-CERTRET: Certificate received from Certificate
     Authority
```

TIP   Because of naming complications on multiple routers, I recommend that you have a separate certificate directory on the TFTP server for each router. This reduces the likelihood of another router pulling in your certificate, since there is no authentication or access control with TFTP. Plus, the same file name is used for the CA and identity certificate, like "caserver"; what's unique is the extension: ".ca" for the CA certificate and ".crt" for the identity certificate.

Finally, save your router's certificate information with the **copy running-config startup-config** command, view the trustpoint with the **show crypto ca trustpoint** command, and view your router's certificate information with the **show crypto ca certificates** command (steps 7 and 8).

Configuring Manual Enrollment Using Cut-and-Paste

If using SCEP and a TFTP server is not an option, you can use the old-fashioned copy-and-paste process with manual enrollment. Steps 1–3 are the same as the other two processes for obtaining a certificate. Step 4, defining a CA, is slightly different than the other two, however. As with the other two, configure the trustpoint with the **crypto ca trustpoint** command. This command was discussed previously in the "Step 4: Define a CA" section. The main difference is the **enrollment terminal** command, which specifies that cut-and-paste will be used to obtain the CA's certificate.

```
Router(config)# crypto ca trustpoint CA_name
Router(ca-trustpoint)# enrollment terminal
```

The other trustpoint commands discussed previously in the "Step 4: Define a CA" section can also be configured as necessary.

Once you have defined the CA, in Step 5 you'll execute the **crypto ca authenticate** command to obtain the CA's certificate. In the other two processes, this was achieved using SCEP or TFTP. With cut-and-paste, you'll need to open the file the CA administrator gave you containing the CA's certificate, copy the contents including the beginning and ending lines starting with the dashes ("-----"), and paste it into the router's configuration when prompted. Example 16-17 illustrates this process. Once you have pasted the CA certificate into the router, type in **quit** on a blank line to terminate the cut-and-paste process and to have the router import the CA's certificate.

Example 16-17 *Importing the CA's Certificate with Cut-and-Paste*

```
r3640(config)# crypto ca authenticate caserver
Enter the base 64 encoded CA certificate.
End with a blank line or the word "quit" on a line by itself
-----BEGIN CERTIFICATE-----
MIIChTCCAe6gAwIBAgIQbr1TulXC0phB4KDUjkDP1jANBgkqhkiG9w0BAQUFADAg
MQswCQYDVQQGEwJVUzERMA8GA1UEAxMIY2FzZXJ2ZXIwHhcNMDQwMTE2MDc0MjAw
←output omitted→
BX3p1Wxz+tSEQwrChIzbHcFAUP1Gq0dpBQ==
-----END CERTIFICATE-----
quit
Certificate has the following attributes:
Fingerprint MD5: CE9956AA C02D15DF A2309A9C E059BD47
Fingerprint SHA1: 475A5DBA 0283DB43 305E9CF7 A208C8B8 E894C379
% Do you accept this certificate? [yes/no]: yes
Trustpoint CA certificate accepted.
% Certificate successfully imported
```

Next, you need to create your PKCS #10 information for your router's identity certificate with the **crypto ca enroll** command, as shown in Example 16-18. The execution of this command is similar to the other two processes; however, you have the option of displaying the PKCS #10 information to the router's terminal screen, which you want to answer **yes**. At the line that states *Certificate Request follows*, select the information here, copy it, store it in a file, and send it to the administrator of the CA, who will use it to create an identity certificate for your router.

Example 16-18 *Creating the Router's PKCS #10 Information for the Cut-and-Paste Process*

```
r3640(config)# crypto ca enroll caserver
% Start certificate enrollment ..
% The fully-qualified domain name in the certificate will be:
    r3640.cisco.com
% The subject name in the certificate will be: r3640.cisco.com
% Include the router serial number in the subject name? [yes/no]: no
% Include an IP address in the subject name? [no]: no
Display Certificate Request to terminal? [yes/no]: yes
Certificate Request follows:
MIH7MIGmAgEAMCAxHjAcBgkqhkiG9w0BCQIWD3IzNjQwLmNpc2NvLmNvbTBcMA0G
CSqGSIb3DQEBAQUAA0sAMEgCQQCobLU/S3ExRpMEJrkDLGMxHInlrwH33C7PpLli
hehmSFlWgTx1GSTTAxVkQdpYJ09NQ76CFGQ6Bpi7BDCI8hZrAgMBAAGgITAfBgkq
hkiG9w0BCQ4xEjAQMA4GA1UdDwEB/wQEAwIFoDANBgkqhkiG9w0BAQQFAANBACNW
JHzO5brezlfI4db5RdLjgh7Wd5zmv84gfQwxtL0GPXJ0SRzK4/1L6le15jefrEu2
Tkag3YiQUZURfJB1smA=
---End - This line not part of the certificate request---
Redisplay enrollment request? [yes/no]: no
r3640(config)#
```

Once the administrator has created a certificate for your router and sent this to you, you can then import the certificate into your router using the **crypto ca import** command discussed in the last section, which is shown in Example 16-19. After pasting in the certificate, on a blank line type in **quit**, signifying that this is the end of the cut-and-paste process. The router will validate the certificate and import it. And as with the other two certificate enrollment processes, be sure to save your router's certificate and configuration information to NVRAM and view your certificate information to validate it.

Example 16-19 *Importing the Router's Identity Certificate Using Cut-and-Paste*

```
r3640(config)# crypto ca import caserver certificate
% The fully-qualified domain name in the certificate will be:
    r3640.cisco.com
Enter the base 64 encoded certificate.
End with a blank line or the word "quit" on a line by itself
-----BEGIN CERTIFICATE-----
MIIC/TCCAmagAwIBAgIKEgiafQABAAAAGzANBgkqhkiG9w0BAQUFADAgMQswCQYD
VQQGEwJVUzERMA8GA1UEAxMIY2FzZXJ2ZXIwHhcNMDUwMzE3MDAzNTIyWhcNMDYw
←output omitted→
+vtDsziATo59EAjGmV8ofqr+oxpuOCM4cCN0BL3babe70dqtbMYLGyN+p6/K1jqA
-----END CERTIFICATE-----
quit
% Router Certificate successfully imported
```

Autoenrollment for Certificates

In IOS 12.2(8)T, Cisco introduced the certificate autoenrollment feature, which allows you to set up your router so that it will request a certificate from a CA using the parameters in your configuration, eliminating any type of administrator intervention on the router when requesting a certificate from a CA. This process is triggered when a trustpoint CA has been configured, but a corresponding CA certificate doesn't exist on the router; plus, when the router's certificate expires, the router automatically will request a new certificate as needed. Of course, the administrator of the CA still might need to approve your router's certificate request via autoenrollment; however, you don't have to do anything to initiate the process from the router side.

Autoenrollment Trustpoint Configuration

The configuration of autoenrollment is very similar to the configuration of enrollment for certificates using SCEP. As with SCEP, you need to verify your NVRAM usage, configure a name and domain name on the router, and generate an RSA key pair. Once you've done this, you now need to configure your trustpoint. The commands discussed in the "Enrolling for a Certificate using SCEP" section earlier apply to this configuration, because SCEP is being used; however, there are some additional commands you need to configure, shown here:

```
Router(config)# crypto ca trustpoint CA_name
Router(ca-trustpoint)# enrollment url CA_URL
Router(ca-trustpoint)# subject-name [x.500_name]
Router(ca-trustpoint)# ip-address
                       {interface_name_or_IP_address | none}
Router(ca-trustpoint)# serial-number [none]
Router(ca-trustpoint)# password password_value
Router(ca-trustpoint)# rsakeypair key_label [key_size
                       [encryption_key_size]]
Router(ca-trustpoint)# auto-enroll [regenerate]
```

The **subject-name** command specifies the X.500 field values that will appear on the certificate; if you omit this, it defaults to the FQDN of the router only for the Common Name. The **ip-address** command specifies the IP address or router interface name (which would include that interface's IP address) to be included on the certificate; specify the **none** parameter if you don't want an IP address on the identity certificate. The **serial-number** command specifies that the router's serial number should be included in the certificate request; use the **none** parameter to exclude this from the certificate request. The **password** command specifies the password to use for revoking passwords, called the challenge password.

The **rsakeypair** command specifies which RSA key pair to use for the certificate; the *key_label* parameter specifies the name of an existing key pair or of a new key pair, the *key_size* parameter specifies the modulus for the signature keys and the *encryption_key_size* specifies the modulus for the encryption keys. If you omit this command, the FQDN default key pair is used. If you specify the keying information, once autoenrollment starts, if the specified key label doesn't exist, autoenrollment will create the RSA key pair automatically; you can view the new key pair with the **show crypto key mypubkey rsa** command. For more information on multiple key pairs, see the "Multiple RSA Key Pairs" section earlier.

NOTE   One thing to note is that if you don't configure a specific value that typically is prompted
         for by the router, you'll still be prompted for these items; therefore, be sure that you
         configure all command values (even if you set it to **none**) so that autoenrollment occurs
         without any operator intervention.

The last step you need to perform in the trustpoint configuration is to enable autoenrollment
with the **auto-enroll** command. The **regenerate** parameter specifies that a new RSA key
pair should be created for the certificate even if a named key pair already exists. This
ensures that when a router's certificate expires and it needs to request a new one, new keys
are used instead of the ones from the old certificate.

Autoenrollment and the CA Certificate

When you're done with the trustpoint configuration with autoenrollment, within a few
seconds the IOS will tell you that autoenrollment won't work until you obtain the CA's
certificate and authenticate it. This can be done using one of the following two methods:

- Using SCEP to obtain the CA certificate
- Manually adding the CA certificate from the CLI

To use SCEP to obtain the CA's certificate, execute the **crypto ca authenticate** command
with the name of the CA, discussed previously in the "Step 5: Download and Authenticate
the CA's Certificate" section. The second option is to add the CA's certificate manually,
using the **crypto ca certificate chain** and **certificate ca** commands. Because SCEP already
is required to use autoenrollment, I won't discuss the latter approach.

Wait a few minutes for the autoenrollment process to start and obtain the router's identity
certificate. If you're impatient, save your router's configuration and reboot it; upon
rebooting, it will obtain its identity certificate.

Autoenrollment Example

Now that you understand the basic configuration for autoenrollment, I'll look at a simple
configuration in Example 16-20 that illustrates how to set up autoenrollment. After the
trustpoint configuration, the IOS warns you that you must next download and authenticate
the CA certificate, which I did with the **crypto ca authenticate** command. Once this was
done, about a minute later the autoenrollment process started with the information I
configured under the trustpoint. At the end, the router automatically saved its certificates
(and configuration) to NVRAM. Once done, you'll want to use the **show crypto ca
certificates** and **show crypto ca trustpoints** command to verify that autoenroll did indeed
acquire an identity certificate for your router.

Example 16-20 *Sample Configuration Using Autoenrollment*

```
r3640(config)# crypto ca trustpoint caserver
r3640(ca-trustpoint)# enrollment url
                      http://192.1.1.77/certsrv/mscep/mscep.dll
r3640(ca-trustpoint)# ip-address none
r3640(ca-trustpoint)# password dontrevokeme
r3640(ca-trustpoint)# rsakeypair caserver 512
r3640(ca-trustpoint)# auto-enroll regenerate
r3640(ca-trustpoint)# exit
% You must authenticate the Certificate Authority before
you can enroll with it.
r3640(config)# crypto ca authenticate caserver
Certificate has the following attributes:
Fingerprint MD5: CE9956AA C02D15DF A2309A9C E059BD47
Fingerprint SHA1: 475A5DBA 0283DB43 305E9CF7 A208C8B8 E894C379
% Do you accept this certificate? [yes/no]: yes
Trustpoint CA certificate accepted.
% Start certificate enrollment ..
% The subject name in the certificate will be: CN=r3640.cisco.com,
    OU=corporate, O=cisco
% The fully-qualified domain name in the certificate will be:
    r3640.cisco.com
% The subject name in the certificate will be: r3640.cisco.com
% Certificate request sent to Certificate Authority
% The certificate request fingerprint will be displayed.
% The 'show crypto pki certificate' command will also show the
    fingerprint.
05:23:29: %CRYPTO-6-AUTOGEN: Generated new 512 bit key pair
05:23:30: CRYPTO_PKI:  Certificate Request Fingerprint MD5:
    85D91350 640EA994 0645C9C9 5D86563E
05:23:30: CRYPTO_PKI:  Certificate Request Fingerprint SHA1:
    677272CE B3E44144 AF143210 025C8AA3 36C155E1
05:23:33: %PKI-6-CERTRET: Certificate received from Certificate
    Authority
05:23:33: %PKI-6-AUTOSAVE: Running configuration saved to NVRAM
```

Certificate Attribute-Based Access Control

The certificate attribute-based access control (CABAC) feature, introduced in IOS 12.2(15)T, allows you to perform an additional step in authenticating a certificate. With CABAC, you can have the router look at specific certificate fields on a certificate and the values associated with them when determining whether or not you'll accept the certificate.

CABAC allows you to look at one or more fields on a certificate for an acceptable value(s). The kinds of tests you can perform are: equal to, not equal to, contains, doesn't contain, is less than, and is greater than or equal to, for the contents of a field. If you specify more than one test, all tests on all the specified fields must be true for a match to occur and an action to take place. Another nice feature is that you can specify a field multiple times within CABAC if you are looking for a number of permitted values.

For example, maybe you have a network with a router that handles site-to-site sessions with only a few remote access sessions for administrative functions, where the remote access authentication is handled by an AAA server such as Cisco Secure ACS (CSACS). You also have a VPN 3030 concentrator that handles user remote access IPsec sessions, where the 3030 also uses CSACS to authenticate the users. Both the router and 3030 use certificates for device authentication. However, you don't want the users to establish IPsec remote access sessions to the router, which they could, by default, because both the router and 3030 use certificates from the same CA for device authentication and the same source (CSACS) for user authentication (XAUTH). In this instance, you can use CABAC to match on the OU field that the network administrators belong to, in addition to the site-to-site connection devices, and thereby exclude all other remote access users.

NOTE   The memory and processing required to perform CABAC is minimal and adds very little overhead to the router and certificate verification process.

CABAC Configuration

Configuring CABAC is a two-step process:

1 Creating the matching rules for certificates to be allowed

2 Applying the matching rules to a trustpoint

To create your match rules, you need to create a certificate map with your rules embedded within the map:

```
Router(config)# crypto ca certificate map map_name sequence_#
Router(ca-certificate-map)# field_name operator match_value
```

The **crypto ca certificate map** command is similar to configuring a crypto map for IPsec (discussed in the next chapter). The map can have multiple entries in it, where each entry has a unique sequence number. Sequence numbers can range from 1–65,535, where entries are processed in numerical order. The entries are grouped together into a single map by specifying the same *map_name* for each statement. Normally, I use the name of the CA that this will be applied against, but you can use whatever map name you choose (just so it is unique among all certificate map names on the router).

After executing the **crypto ca certificate map** command, you are taken into a subcommand mode where you can enter your matching criteria. The first value you enter on a command line is the name of the field on the certificate you're going to match against: **subject-name, issuer-name, unstructured-subject-name, alt-subject-name, name, valid-start**, and **expires-on**. The second value you enter is the operator, which can be one of the following:

- **eq**—equal to (valid for the name and date fields only)
- **ne**—not equal to (valid for the name and date fields only)

- **co**—contains the specified value (valid only for the name fields)
- **nc**—does not contain the specified value (valid only for the name fields)
- **lt**—less than (valid only for the date fields)
- **ge**—greater than or equal to (valid only for the date fields)

The last parameter, *match_value,* specifies what value you are matching against.

Once you have created your certificate mappings, you need to apply them to the trustpoint CA that handles the certificate functions in question:

```
Router(config)# crypto ca trustpoint CA_name
Router(ca-trustpoint)# match certificate map_name
```

This is done by going into the trustpoint configuration with the **crypto ca trustpoint** command for the CA that you want to apply the map to. The **match certificate** command specifies the certificate map configuration you created with the **crypto ca certificate map** command. At this point, any new IPsec sessions brought up will first be validated using the certificate map.

NOTE   The entries in the certificate map are processed in numerical order. Matching on names (strings) is *case-insensitive*. As soon as a match is found for an entry, no further processing occurs. When a match occurs (all specific matchings in the entry must match), the peer's certificate will then be validated by checking the authenticity of it with the CA's signature, checking the validity date of the certificate, and checking the revocation status (the last is optional). If a match isn't found in the certificate map, the certificate is automatically considered invalid and device authentication fails.

CABAC Configuration Example

Now that you have a basic understanding of the commands used for CABAC, I'll look at an example that illustrates its use. I'll use the example I referred to earlier about limiting IPsec access to the router to just the site-to-site sessions and the remote access network administrators, all of which are using certificates for device authentication. Example 16-21 shows the configuration of the router. The first entry (10) allows only a certificate that was issued by "caserver" where the Common Name (CN) is "r3620a.cisco.com" and the Organizational Unit (OU) field is "corporate"; this matches on one of the two routers for L2L sessions. Entry 20 matches on the second L2L peer. Entry 30 only looks for matches on certificates issued by "caserver" where the OU field is "netadmins," which represents the group name of the network administrator group. As you can see in this example, if there is not a match on these three entries, the remote peer will fail device authentication with certificates.

Example 16-21 *Sample CABAC Configuration*

```
r3640(config)# crypto ca certificate map certsallowed 10
r3640(ca-certificate-map)# issuer-name co caserver
r3640(ca-certificate-map)# subject-name co cn=r3620a.cisco.com
r3640(ca-certificate-map)# subject-name co ou=corporate
r3640(ca-certificate-map)# exit
r3640(config)# crypto ca certificate map certsallowed 20
r3640(ca-certificate-map)# issuer-name co caserver
r3640(ca-certificate-map)# subject-name co cn=r3620b.cisco.com
r3640(ca-certificate-map)# subject-name co ou=corporate
r3640(config)# crypto ca certificate map certsallowed 30
r3640(ca-certificate-map)# issuer-name co caserver
r3640(ca-certificate-map)# subject-name co ou=netadmins
r3640(ca-certificate-map)# exit
r3640(config)# crypto ca trustpoint caserver
r3640(ca-trustpoint)# match certificate certsallowed
```

CRL and Expired Certificate Access Control Lists

Another way of controlling authentication with certificates is to use the CRL and expired certificate Access Control List (ACL) feature, new in IOS 12.3(4)T. If you are using CRLs and a peer's serial number is listed in the CRL, by default, your router will invalidate the peer's certificate, causing authentication to fail. Likewise, if your router's date is beyond the expiration date on a peer's certificate, your router will invalidate the peer's certificate, causing authentication to fail.

With the certificate ACL feature, you can create exceptions to these cases. This is useful, for instance, if your router's battery for its clock dies and always comes up with an incorrect date such as 1993 or 2002. Even using NTP, the router's NTP process only allows incremental changes in the time, so it might take a long time for the router to synchronize its time with the NTP server. In this situation, if a peer's certificate says the validation dates are from November 30, 2004 to November 30, 2006 and the current day is November 19, 2005, the certificate is obviously valid; however, when your router, with the bad clock battery, boots up, it might have a date of March 1, 2003. Obviously the router would think the peer's certificate is invalid, when in reality it is valid. The real remedy to this problem is to replace the router's clock battery. In the interim, though, you can use the certificate ACL feature to allow the router to accept the certificate based on an "invalid" date.

Certificate ACL Configuration

Configuring the certificate ACL feature is a two-step process similar to CABAC:

1 Creating the matching rules for certificates to be allowed

2 Applying the matching rules to a trustpoint with the type of exception allowed

To create your match rules, you need to create a certificate map with your rules embedded within the map using the **crypto ca certificate map** (discussed in the last section). Once you create your map and its corresponding entries, you must enable them, which is done under the corresponding trustpoint CA:

```
Router(config)# crypto ca trustpoint CA_name
Router(ca-trustpoint)# match certificate map_name
                       [allow expired-certificate |
                       skip revocation-check |
                       skip authorization-check]
```

The **allow expired-certificate** parameter causes the router to not invalidate a certificate match found in the certificate map based on its date. The **skip revocation-check** parameter causes the router to ignore a serial number found in a CRL for matching certificates found in the certificate map. The **skip authorization-check** parameter specifies that the AAA check of a certificate is skipped when certificates with an AAA server are configured.

Expired Certificate ACL Configuration

I'll now illustrate the usefulness of the certificate ACL feature. In this example, assume that the clock battery on a 3640 has died and you have ordered a replacement. In the meantime, every time you cold-boot your router, it comes up with the wrong time and you have to change the time of the router manually to something close to what the NTP server is advertising to speed up the time-synchronization process. This has become a hassle because this router (at a remote site) periodically loses power and reboots. Using an Uninterrupted Power Supply would help simplify the problem, but the budget at the remote office didn't allow for it. This whole process has created a headache for you, because to administer the router, typically you do it through an IPsec L2L session from the corporate office; but in this case, the remote office's 3640 is invalidating the corporate office's certificate because the 3640 router's time always states March 1, 2002 when it boots up.

As a temporary fix to this problem, you've decided to exempt the corporate office's 7200 router certificate from expiration (on the remote office's 3640 router). Example 16-22 shows an example of what the remote office's 3640 router configuration would look like. In this example, the 7200's certificate (r7200.cisco.com) will be exempted from the expiration check when the 3640 at the remote office validates the 7200's certificate. Of course, once you replace the clock battery on the 3640, I would remove this configuration on the router.

Example 16-22 *Sample Expiry ACL Configuration*

```
r3640(config)# crypto ca certificate map certsallowed 10
r3640(ca-certificate-map)# issuer-name co caserver
r3640(ca-certificate-map)# subject-name co cn=r7200.cisco.com
r3640(ca-certificate-map)# subject-name co ou=corporate
r3640(ca-certificate-map)# exit
r3640(config)# crypto ca trustpoint caserver
r3640(ca-trustpoint)# match certificate exemptcorprouter
                      allow expired-certificate
```

Importing and Exporting RSA Keys and Certificates

One of the issues with RSA keys, which are used to sign and validate certificates, is that, by default, they cannot be saved anywhere except for NVRAM. This can present problems if the router fails and must be replaced, or if you buy a newer model router to replace an old one: you can't use the same certificate because you can't copy the RSA private key to the new router. In this situation, you would have to generate a new RSA key pair on the new router and acquire a new certificate.

Cisco realizes that this can create problems in certain situations. For example, in a failover configuration, two routers should have the same certificate and keys, otherwise the failover won't be seamless. Likewise, if you accidentally remove the wrong RSA key pair on a router, you would have to revoke the router's current certificate and generate new keys and a certificate request to allow for certificate authentication to proceed. Therefore, Cisco has developed a way that allows you to export and import RSA keys in IOS 12.2(15)T, specifically the private keys. This process applies to authentication methods that use RSA encrypted nonces or RSA signature—anything that uses an RSA key pair.

TIP   SSH also uses RSA key pairs for encryption. You can use the method described in this section to place the same RSA key pair on all routers and then allow your management station(s) to use the same public key to encrypt traffic to the routers, simplifying the management of RSA key pairs. Generate an RSA key pair to one router and export it to all other routers; then take the public key and configure it on the SSH client.

Creating an Exportable RSA Key Pair

By default, when you use the **crypto key generate rsa** command, the RSA key pair(s) created are *not* exportable. Plus, once a key pair is created, you cannot change whether or not it can be exportable. The only way to make an RSA key pair exportable is to define this when you create the key pair with the **exportable** parameter:

```
Router(config)# crypto key generate rsa {general-keys | usage-keys}
                        [label RSA_key_label] exportable
```

You can verify whether or not an RSA key pair is exportable by executing the **show crypto key mypubkey rsa** command on your router. Example 16-23 shows an example of two key pairs: one exportable and one not.

Example 16-23 *Nonexportable and Exportable RSA Key Pairs*

```
r3640# show crypto key mypubkey rsa
% Key pair was generated at: 10:49:01 EDT Mar 15 2005
Key name: r3640.cisco.com
 Usage: General Purpose Key
 Key is not exportable.
```

continues

Example 16-23 *Nonexportable and Exportable RSA Key Pairs (Continued)*

```
 Key Data:
  305C300D 06092A86 4886F70D 01010105 00034B00 30480241 00A86CB5
  3F4B7131 46930426 B9032C63 311C89E5 AF01F7DC 2ECFA4B9 6285E866
  48595681 3C751924 D3031564 41DA5827 4F4D43BE 8214643A 0698BB04
  3088F216 6B020301 0001
% Key pair was generated at: 14:24:54 EDT Mar 17 2005
Key name: caservercert
 Usage: General Purpose Key
 Key is exportable.
 Key Data:
  305C300D 06092A86 4886F70D 01010105 00034B00 30480241 00C158F6
  72F69C0D D0A8064E EAA88CE8 38A852CA C3927EEA 00CC8C62 8D8C26C4
  38634CBE 5DF98751 B6F1194F DE80D659 6D5D3ADA EF6A708D 2EC77F46
  CBCDF7C1 35020301 0001
```

Using a Configured RSA Key Pair for a Certificate

To associate the key pair with a certificate you'll be creating for your router, you would configure the following, which I've discussed in various sections throughout this chapter:

```
Router(config)# crypto ca trustpoint CA_name
Router(ca-trustpoint)# enrollment url CA_URL
Router(ca-trustpoint)# rsakeypair RSA_key_label
Router(ca-trustpoint)# exit
Router(config)# crypto ca authenticate CA_name
Router(config)# crypto ca enroll CA_name
Router(config)# exit
Router# copy running-config startup-config
```

The important thing about this code is that you specify the exportable key pair label name in the CA trustpoint configuration *before* requesting your router's identity certificate.

Exporting the RSA Key Pair and Certificates

To back up your RSA key pair, in addition to the CA and identity certificates, use the following command on the router that has the exportable keys:

```
Router(config)# crypto {ca | pki} export CA_name pkcs12
                destination_URL passphrase
```

You must specify the name of the CA trustpoint where you obtained your identity certificate. The *destination_URL* parameter specifies to where you want the keys exported. This can include the following locations: Flash memory, FTP, NVRAM, RCP, SCP, TFTP, XMODEM, and YMODEM. The *passphrase* parameter is used to encrypt the PKCS #12 file that will have the exported keys. You must use the same passphrase value when importing the keys so as to decrypt them. This process protects the keys from unauthorized access. The passphrase can be any combination of characters, numbers, and special characters with the exception of "?" (the question mark).

| NOTE | The passphrase you enter for exporting and importing is not saved on the router—if you forget the phrase, you will not be able to import an encrypted PKCS #12 with your router's key pair. |

| CAUTION | When setting up exportable keys and certificates, anyone who has level 15 access on the router can export this information, which might create a security issue. If you are concerned about this, configure AAA on your router with accounting enabled for command execution; then you can determine who exported any keying material and when they did it. I discuss the use of AAA in my *Cisco Router Firewall Security* book with Cisco Press. |

Importing the RSA Key Pair and Certificates

To import an RSA key pair, CA certificate, and identity certificate into a router, use the following command:

```
Router(config)# crypto {ca | pki} import CA_name pkcs12
                       source_URL passphrase
```

You'll need to use the same passphrase to decrypt the RSA key pair in the PKCS #12 file. Once you do this, you will still need to configure the router with the correct commands to interact with the CA, if necessary. You could easily copy the configuration of the original router and select and paste the correct router CA commands into the new router.

Backing up RSA Information Example

To help illustrate this process, I'll use a simple example shown in Examples 16-24 and 16-25. The first example shows the creation of the exportable keys, the process of acquiring certificates, and the exporting of the RSA information. In this example, I gave the RSA key pair label the name of the CA I'll use for certificates. You can use whatever key label you want; however, I typically use the name of the CA that the key pair will be associated with. The second example shows the import process on a second router. Of course, you'll need to complete the configuration on the second router to match that of the first, to use the imported RSA keys and certificates.

Example 16-24 *RSA Key Pair Export Example*

```
r3640A(config)# crypto key generate rsa general-keys label caserver
                         exportable
The name for the keys will be: caserver
Choose the size of the key modulus in the range of 360 to 2048 for
  your General Purpose Keys. Choosing a key modulus greater than 512
  may take a few minutes.
```

continues

Example 16-24 *RSA Key Pair Export Example (Continued)*

```
How many bits in the modulus [512]:
% Generating 512 bit RSA keys ...[OK]
r3640A(config)# crypto ca trustpoint caserver
r3640A(ca-trustpoint)# enrollment url
                       http://192.1.1.77/certsrv/mscep/mscep.dll
r3640A(ca-trustpoint)# rsakeypair caserver
r3640A(ca-trustpoint)# exit
r3640A(config)# crypto ca authenticate caserver
←output omitted→
r3640A(config)# crypto ca enroll caserver
←output omitted→
r3640A(config)# crypto ca export caserver pkcs12
                       tftp://192.1.1.77/r3640A.pkcs12 cisco123
←output omitted→
!Writing pkcs12 file to tftp://192.1.1.77/r3640A.pkcs12
CRYPTO_PKI: Exported PKCS12 file successfully.
04:01:56: %PKI-6-PKCS12EXPORT_SUCCESS: PKCS #12 Successfully
       Exported.
```

Example 16-25 *RSA Key Pair Import Example*

```
r3620B(config)# crypto ca import caserver pkcs12
                       tftp://192.1.1.77/r3640A.pkcs12 cisco123
←output omitted→
Loading r3640.pkcs12 from 192.1.1.77 (via Ethernet0/0): !
[OK - 2307 bytes]
CRYPTO_PKI: Imported PKCS12 file successfully.
.Mar 18 19:37:58.987: %CRYPTO-6-PKCS12IMPORT_SUCCESS:
```

Monitoring and Managing Management Connections

In the next two sections I'll discuss some **show**, **clear**, and **debug** commands you can use to view and manage your ISAKMP/IKE Phase 1 management connections. This chapter introduces these commands and Chapter 19, "Troubleshooting Router Connections," will provide an in-depth coverage of these commands as they relate to troubleshooting IPsec sessions.

Viewing ISAKMP/IKE Phase 1 Connections

When a management connection is being built, it will go through various states. The current state of this connection can be seen with this command:

```
Router# show crypto isakmp sa [detail]
```

Example 16-26 illustrates the use of this command. In this example, only one management connection exists. The *state* column indicates what state the connection is in. Table 16-1 explains the various states a connection can be in.

Example 16-26 *Viewing Management Connections*

```
r3640# show crypto isakmp sa
dst            src            state        conn-id slot status
192.1.1.40     192.1.1.20     QM_IDLE            1     0 ACTIVE
```

Table 16-1   *Management Connection States*

State	Explanation
MM_NO_STATE	When using main mode, the ISAKMP SA is in an infancy state and has not completed; you'll typically see this appear when a management connection fails to establish.
MM_SA_SETUP	When using main mode, the policy parameters have been negotiated between the peers successfully.
MM_KEY_EXCH	When using main mode, the peers have performed DH and created a shared secret key, but device authentication hasn't occurred yet.
MM_KEY_AUTH	When using main mode, the peers have passed authentication and will transition to a QM_IDLE state.
AG_NO_STATE	When using aggressive mode, the ISAKMP SA is in an infancy state and has not completed; you'll typically see this appear when a management connection fails to establish.
AG_INIT_EXCH	The first exchange in aggressive mode has completed, but device authentication hasn't been performed yet.
AG_AUTH	When using aggressive mode, the peers have passed authentication and will transition to a QM_IDLE state.
QM_IDLE	The management connection has been built and can be used during ISAKMP/IKE Phase 2 to build data connections. This is commonly referred to as *quiescent* mode.

You can view more details about the management connections by adding the **detail** parameter to the **show crypto isakmp sa** command, as illustrated in Example 16-27. Here you can see information like the type of encryption algorithm used ("aes"), the HMAC function used ("md5"), the authentication method ("psk," which stands for pre-shared keys), the DH key group ("2"), and the remaining lifetime of the connection (a little over 11 hours). Also, at the bottom, you can see if encryption is being performed in software or hardware: in this example, it's being done in software.

Example 16-27 *Viewing Details of Management Connections*

```
r3640# show crypto isakmp sa detail
Codes: C - IKE configuration mode, D - Dead Peer Detection
       K - Keepalives, N - NAT-traversal
       X - IKE Extended Authentication
       psk - Preshared key, rsig - RSA signature
       renc - RSA encryption
```

continues

Example 16-27 *Viewing Details of Management Connections (Continued)*

```
C-id Local      Remote    I-VRF Status Encr Hash Auth DH Lifetime Cap
1    192.1.1.40 192.1.1.20      ACTIVE aes  md5  psk  2  23:02:47
          Connection-id:Engine-id =  1:1(software)
```

Managing ISAKMP/IKE Phase 1 Connections

To tear down a management connection, use the following **clear** command:

```
Router# clear crypto isakmp [conn_ID]
```

If you don't enter a specific connection ID, all management connections are torn down—Connection IDs can be found in the **show crytpo isakmp sa** command.

If you are having problems establishing a management connection, you can use the **debug crypto isakmp** command. I'll discuss this command in much more depth in Chapter 19, "Troubleshooting Router Connections."

Routers as Certificate Authorities

As of IOS 12.3(4)T, Cisco routers can perform the function of a CA; RA functionality was added in a later IOS release. As a CA, routers can accept certificate requests using SCEP (which means that they have to run an HTTP server) and manual enrollment with cut-and-paste of the PKCS #10 information.

The CA server feature was added mostly for small shops that wanted to use an existing router for certificate services instead of purchasing a stand-alone product. However, the Cisco CA server feature does have limitations; it isn't a full-blown CA product. Here are some of its restrictions:

- When acting as an RA, the CA must be an IOS router.
- Only a central design with one CA is supported.
- As a CA, time services (NTP) must be running on the router or the router must have a hardware clock; otherwise, the CA process will not start on the router.

Like getting a certificate on a router, there are many steps involved in setting up and managing a router acting as a CA:

1 Generating and exporting an RSA key information (optional)

2 Enabling the CA (required)

3 Defining additional CA parameters (optional)

4 Handling enrollment requests (required)

5 Revoking identity certificates (optional)

6 Configuring a server to run in RA mode (optional)

7 Backing up a CA (optional, but highly recommended)

8 Restoring a CA (optional)

9 Removing CA services (optional)

Of the nine steps, note that only Steps 2 and 4 are required. The following sections will discuss these steps, and will show a simple example of a router configured as a CA.

Battle of the CAs

One of the questions I'm constantly asked as a consultant is which CA product a company should use. For an in-house CA, I always sided with the CA product that comes bundled with Microsoft 2000 and 2003 Server/Advanced Server products. SCEP is an add-on from the Windows resource kit. I always liked using this product because it was simple to set up and manage and it came with the operating system. However, Microsoft's application has a downside. If you experience problems obtaining certificates from it, troubleshooting these problems from within Windows is not an easy proposition. When it works, it works great, and when it doesn't work, you want to pull your hair out in frustration in finding the problem.

When Cisco introduced the CA functionality on a Cisco router, I immediately downloaded it on one of my 3640s and played around with the code. I really liked the flexibility in its configuration, and the ability to see detailed debugging information with interactions between other certificate-requesting devices. Even so, the Cisco CA solution has a problem, too. If you want to handle lots of certificates, the certificates will have to be stored on an external box; this slows down the validation part of certificates when a peer requests your certificate from the router CA and then has to, in turn, go to an external server to download the requested certificate. However, for small- to-medium-sized networks, I would highly recommend that you investigate the use of a Cisco router as a CA when looking for a CA product.

Step 1: Generating and Exporting RSA Key Information

The router, as a CA, needs an RSA key pair to create a signature on the root (its own) certificate and to validate it. You do not have to create the key pair manually, because the keys will be generated automatically during the configuration of the CA; however, if you use the automatic approach, you make the following concessions:

- The keys will be nonexportable unless you're running IOS 12.3(11)T, where the auto-archiving feature will solve this problem and back up your RSA information.

- The key length defaults to 1,024 bits.

CAUTION If the router automatically generates the keys, the keys will be marked as nonexportable (unless using auto-archiving), making it impossible to move the CA from one router to another if the CA fails. Therefore, if you are not running IOS 12.3(11)T with auto-archiving, I highly recommend that you create the key pair manually and mark them as exportable.

There are two basic ways of generating the RSA key pair on your CA router: manually or dynamically. With the latter, I recommend using the auto-archive option. The next two sections will discuss manual RSA keying and the "Step 2: Enabling the CA" section will discuss auto-archiving.

Manual RSA Key Generation for the CA

To manually generate your RSA keys for your router CA, use the following command:

```
Router(config)# crypto key generate rsa general-keys label CA_name
                exportable
```

The label you associate with the keys must *match* the name of the CA trustpoint (the router). Also, be sure to specify the keys as exportable.

NOTE The *CA_name* key label should not exceed 13 characters, because this is used as the CA's name and this name, when the router is a CA, has that restriction.

Next, you need to export your keys using the following command:

```
Router(config)# crypto key export rsa CA_name pem
                {terminal | url URL} {des | 3des} passphrase
```

For the key label, you must specify the name of the CA from the **crypto key generate rsa** command. The **pem** parameter specifies that this is a backup process. Two files will be created: one for the public key and one for the private. The **terminal/url** parameters specify where to back it up; most commonly it is first backed up to NVRAM or Flash memory for simplicity's sake and then moved to a more secure location. You must tell the router which encryption algorithm to use to encrypt the two files, and the passphrase used for the encryption process.

CAUTION Don't forget what you configured as the passphrase when exporting the CA's RSA key pair; otherwise you'll never be able to re-import your keys to restore your router CA if it fails! If this happens, you'll have to create new keys and a new root certificate, install the root certificate on all devices, and then create identity certificates for each device and install these. I definitely would not want to re-implement a certificate solution over something as simple as forgetting the passphrase for the PEM files!

To import your RSA keys into a router, use the following command:

```
Router(config)# crypto key import rsa CA_name pem
                        {terminal | url URL} {des | 3des}
                        [exportable] passphrase
```

TIP   Here's a trick I learned to protect the CA's keys. First, export the keys, then reimport them but use a different key label; when importing them, *don't* specify them as **exportable**. If you use this process, the keys you imported are re-imported but can no longer be exported. Then place the keys you exported in a safe place. This way, no one who has access to the router will be able to export the keys and use them to create a rogue CA. You can also use the **crypto key export rsa** and **crypto key import rsa** commands in this fashion for non-CA routers, which will prevent anyone with a level-15 access from re-exporting the keys.

Example 16-28 illustrates this process. The numbered references to the right of certain commands are explained below the example.

Example 16-28 *Protecting the CA's Keys*

```
routerca(config)# crypto key generate rsa general-keys        (1)
                        label routerca exportable
The name for the keys will be: routerca
Choose the size of the key modulus in the range of 360 to 2048 for
  your General Purpose Keys. Choosing a key modulus greater than 512
  may take a few minutes.
How many bits in the modulus [512]: 1024
% Generating 1024 bit RSA keys ...[OK]
routerca(config)# crypto key export rsa routerca pem          (2)
                        url nvram:routerca 3des cisco123
% Key name: routerca
   Usage: General Purpose Key
Exporting public key...
Destination filename [routerca.pub]?
Writing file to nvram:routerca.pub
Exporting private key...
Destination filename [routerca.prv]?
Writing file to nvram:routerca.prv
routerca(config)# crypto key import rsa routerca2 pem         (3)
                        url nvram:routerca cisco123
% Importing public key or certificate PEM file...
Source filename [routerca.pub]?
Reading file from nvram:routerca.pub
% Importing private key PEM file...
Source filename [routerca.prv]?
Reading file from nvram:routerca.prv% Key pair import succeeded.
routerca(config)# exit
routerca# show crypto key mypubkey rsa                        (4)
% Key pair was generated at: 20:30:59 EDT Mar 18 2005
```

continues

Example 16-28 *Protecting the CA's Keys (Continued)*

```
Key name: routerca
 Usage: General Purpose Key
 Key is exportable.
 Key Data:
  30819F30 0D06092A 864886F7 0D010101 05000381 8D003081 89028181
 ←output omitted→
% Key pair was generated at: 20:31:02 EDT Mar 18 2005
Key name: routerca.server
 Usage: Encryption Key
 Key is not exportable.
 Key Data:
  307C300D 06092A86 4886F70D 01010105 00036B00 30680261 00B637AD
 ←output omitted→
% Key pair was generated at: 20:36:47 EDT Mar 18 2005
Key name: routerca2
 Usage: General Purpose Key
 Key is not exportable.
 Key Data:
  30819F30 0D06092A 864886F7 0D010101 05000381 8D003081 89028181
 ←output omitted→
routerca# configure terminal
routerca(config)# crypto key zeroize rsa routerca                    (5)
% Keys to be removed are named named 'routerca'.
% All router certs issued using these keys will also be removed.
Do you really want to remove these keys? [yes/no]: yes
routerca(config)# exit
routerca# dir nvram:                                                 (6)
Directory of nvram:/
←output omitted→
    2  -rw-        272              <no date>  routerca.pub
    3  -rw-        963              <no date>  routerca.prv
129016 bytes total (124616 bytes free)
routerca# copy nvram:routerca.pub tftp://192.1.1.77/routerca.pub   (7)
←output omitted→
!!
272 bytes copied in 0.100 secs (2720 bytes/sec)
routerca# copy nvram:routerca.prv tftp://192.1.1.77/routerca.prv   (8)
←output omitted→
!!
963 bytes copied in 0.100 secs (9630 bytes/sec)
routerca# delete nvram:routerca.pub                                 (9)
Delete filename [routerca.pub]?
Delete nvram:routerca.pub? [confirm]
routerca# delete nvram:routerca.prv
Delete filename [routerca.prv]?
Delete nvram:routerca.prv? [confirm]
```

Here's an explanation of the numbered references in Example 16-28:

1 I'm generating the RSA key pair as exportable. The key label name, "routerca,"
   doesn't have to match the name of the CA because of the process I'm using. The re-
   imported key label, however, does have to match.

2 I'm exporting the key pair to NVRAM, encrypting with 3DES and an encryption key of "cisco123"—don't forget the passphrase key, because this will be your only way of reimporting the RSA key pair into another device, including the router itself! Two files are created in NVRAM: routerca.pub (public key for the key label routerca) and routerca.prv (private key).

3 I'm re-importing the key pair back into the router; however, because I'm not specifying it as exportable, no one will be able to export the re-imported keys. Just remember that your new CA will have to be called what the new key label is; in this example, that would be "routerca2."

4 The key labels and public keys configured on the router are displayed: routerca is exportable and the re-imported key pair, routerca2, isn't.

5 I'm deleting the exportable key pair.

6 I'm displaying the two exported keys in the router's NVRAM.

7 I'm backing up the router's public key to a TFTP server.

8 I'm backing up the router's private key to a TFTP server; you'll want to move both of these keys to a more secure location because TFTP lacks security (and remember the encryption passphrase!).

9 I'm deleting the exported PEM key files in the router's NVRAM.

Step 2: Enabling the CA

Whether you're using manually generated RSA keys or auto archiving, you must enable the CA process on the router. The next two sections describe this process.

Using Manual RSA Keys

If you have defined your RSA keys manually, use the following process to bring up the CA and use the configured key pair:

```
Router(config)# ip http server
Router(config)# crypto pki server CA_name
Router(cs-server)# issuer-name CA_string
Router(cs-server)# lifetime ca-certificate time_in_days
Router(cs-server)# database url root_URL
Router(cs-server)# no shutdown
Router(cs-server)# exit
```

The **ip http server** command allows you to use SCEP for end-clients to obtain certificates. The **crypto pki server** command creates the CA process on the router. It is important to use the RSA key pair label you specified (when generating the RSA key pair) as the CA name; this tells the router which key pair label to use for signing and validating the self-signed certificate.

The **issuer-name** command specifies the name that will appear on the CA's certificate for the Common Name (CN) and on all identity certificates under the Issuer section. If this is omitted, the *CA_name* parameter is used from the **crypto pki server** command. Once the router CA is brought up initially and the CA certificate created, you cannot change this value without deleting the CA and re-adding it. The *CA_string* parameter specifies what should appear in the X.509 CA certificate fields. An example *CA_string* would look something like this: **issuer-name CN = routerca.cisco.com, L = San Jose, C = USA**.

The **lifetime ca-certificate** command specifies the lifetime of the CA's certificate. The time is specified in days and if you omit it, the time defaults to three years. The lifetime can range from 1–1,825 days. Once you create the CA's certificate you cannot change its lifetime length without deleting and re-adding the router CA process (which invalidates any currently created identity certificates).

The **database url** command specifies the location where all database entries (certificate information) for the router CA and its clients will be stored. The default location, if this command is not configured, is in NVRAM. If the router needs to manage a large number of certificates that contain detailed information, I would recommend placing this on a remote device, such as an SCP server, or a large Flash image, like a PCMCIA Flash card. TFTP or FTP will work for external storage, but it lacks a real protection mechanism (confidentiality, authentication, except for FTP, and data integrity). In this case, you might want to use a transport IPsec session (point-to-point) between the router CA and the storage server. If you change the value for the **database url** command, you'll need to move the current database contents from the original location to the new location.

TIP   Assuming that your router CA will handle only a small number of certificates, you might want to put these in Flash memory on the router (**database url flash:**) or on a PCMCIA Flash card (**databse url slot***X***:**, where *X* is the slot number). For a very large number of identity certificates, I would recommend storing them on an SCP server first, or if this is not available, a TFTP server where the connection between the router CA and the TFTP server is protected using a transport IPsec session and is firewalled.

The **no shutdown** command enables the router CA process and will generate the CA's certificate when initially performed. If the *CA_name* doesn't match an existing key pair, the router will generate an RSA key pair automatically using 1,024-bit keys, as shown in Example 16-29.

Example 16-29 *Starting the CA with no Specified RSA Key Pair*

```
routerca(config)# crypto pki server routerca
routerca(cs-server)# no shutdown
% Generating 1024 bit RSA keys ...[OK]
% Ready to generate the CA certificate.
% Some server settings cannot be changed after CA certificate generation.
```

Example 16-29 *Starting the CA with no Specified RSA Key Pair (Continued)*

```
Are you sure you want to do this? [yes/no]: yes
% Exporting Certificate Server signing certificate and keys...
% Please enter a passphrase to protect the private key.
Password: cisco123
% Certificate Server enabled.
```

CAUTION   If you use the approach shown in Example 16-29, the keys *cannot* be exported; so I highly recommend you do not do this! If you make this mistake, delete the CA (see the "Step 8: Removing a CA" section later) and then either use the manual key creation approach or auto-archiving (see the next section).

The CA's self-signed certificate is automatically created and can be viewed with the **show crypto ca certificates** command shown in Example 16-30. Notice that the issuer and subject CN names are the same.

Example 16-30 *Viewing the CA's Certificate*

```
routerca# show crypto ca certificates
CA Certificate
  Status: Available
  Certificate Serial Number: 01
  Certificate Usage: Signature
  Issuer:
    cn=routerca2
  Subject:
    cn=routerca2
  Validity Date:
    start date: 01:32:12 EDT Mar 19 2005
    end   date: 01:32:12 EDT Mar 18 2008
  Associated Trustpoints: routerca2
```

If you configured the **database url** command and the URL is not reachable when the router CA is creating its root certificate, you'll see the output in Example 16-31. You'll need to fix the problem and attempt the **no shutdown** command again.

Example 16-31 *CA Database Not Located in NVRAM*

```
routerca(config)# crypto pki server routerca
routerca(cs-server)# database url ftp://192.1.1.77
routerca(cs-server)# no shutdown
% Once you start the server, you can no longer change some of
% the configuration.
Are you sure you want to do this? [yes/no]: yes
Translating "192.1.1.77"
% Failed to generate CA certificate - 0xFFFFFFFF
% The Certificate Server has been disabled.
```

Using Auto-Archiving

In IOS 12.3(11)T, Cisco introduced the auto-archiving feature. This process is used to eliminate the complicated process of creating and exporting a key pair manually and then calling the CA service by the same name used by the key pair.

When using auto-archiving, the router automatically will create an RSA key pair (1,024 bits in length) and export the keying information into a PKCS #12 or PEM file in NVRAM. To configure auto-archiving, use these commands:

```
Router(config)# ip http server
Router(config)# crypto pki server CA_name
Router(cs-server)# issuer-name CA_string
Router(cs-server)# lifetime ca-certificate time_in_days
Router(cs-server)# database url root_URL
Router(cs-server)# database archive {pkcs12 | pem}
                       [password passphrase]
Router(cs-server)# no shutdown
Router(cs-server)# exit
```

As with the manual process, you must enable the HTTP server for SCEP and then specify the trustpoint you're creating. You can generate an RSA key pair manually and specify the key label for the *CA_name*; this is necessary only if you don't want to use the default of 1,024 bits for the keys, but another value. If this is necessary, be sure to create the keys as exportable with the **crypto key generate rsa** command. The **issuer-name** and **lifetime ca-certificate** commands were discussed in the last section.

Within the CA configuration, the **database archive** command specifies that auto-archiving will be used. The two file formats you have to choose from are PKCS #12 or PEM. If you don't specify the passphrase to encrypt the exported information, you'll be prompted for this. Execute the **no shutdown** command to generate the keying information (if the keys don't already exist) and the CA's certificate with the name of the certificate specified in **crypto pki server** command.

NOTE   If you don't execute the **database archive** command, auto-archiving *still* will take place, where the default file format will be PKCS #12—you'll be prompted for the encryption password. The auto-archiving process occurs only once, when the CA is initially started. When done, you should back up the files in NVRAM that the auto-archiving process created!

Example 16-32 illustrates bringing up a CA with auto-archiving. If I had omitted the **database archive** command before bringing up the database (**no shutdown**), auto-archiving still would take place. In this example, I had not pre-created any RSA keys. After the CA came up, looking in NVRAM revealed three new files: routerca.ser, routerca.crl, and routerca.p12. The first file (.ser), the enrollment database, contains identity certificates issued by the router CA; the second file (.crl) contains the CRL; and the last file (.p12 or .pem) contains the encrypted public/private keys. You should copy all three of these files to a secure location.

Example 16-32 *Bringing up a CA with Auto-Archiving*

```
routerca(config)# crypto pki server routerca
routerca(cs-server)# database archive pkcs12 password cisco123
routerca(cs-server)# no shutdown
% Generating 1024 bit RSA keys ...[OK]
% Ready to generate the CA certificate.
% Some server settings cannot be changed after CA certificate generation.
Are you sure you want to do this? [yes/no]: yes
% Exporting Certificate Server signing certificate and keys...
% Certificate Server enabled.
routerca(cs-server)# end
routerca# dir nvram:
Directory of nvram:/
←output omitted→
    2  -rw-          32                 <no date>  routerca.ser
    3  -rw-         218                 <no date>  routerca.crl
    4  -rw-        1515                 <no date>  routerca.p12
129016 bytes total (122570 bytes free)
```

CAUTION   Once the CA is brought up and the CA certificate created, you cannot change anything on the CA certificate unless you completely delete the CA on the router. This also is true of some CA commands discussed in the next section! Therefore, because this would affect any identity certificates the CA generated, you would have to start from scratch if you deleted the CA and changed its certificated information.

Step 3: Defining Additional CA Parameters

Optionally, you can define parameters for the CA that affects its functionality. Here are the commands to define these parameters:

```
Router(config)# crypto pki server CA_name
Router(cs-server)# database level {minimal | names | complete}
Router(cs-server)# database username username password password
Router(cs-server)# lifetime certificate time_in_days
Router(cs-server)# lifetime crl time_in_hours
Router(cs-server)# lifetime enrollment-request time_in_hours
Router(cs-server)# cdp-url URL_of_CRL
Router(cs-server)# grant {none | auto | ra-auto}
Router(cs-server)# [no] shutdown
Router(cs-server)# exit
```

The **database level** command specifies what kind of information is stored in the certificate enrollment database for identity certificates. Your options are as follows:

- **minimal**—Stores only enough information to ensure that newly generated certificates are unique.

- **names**—Only the serial number and subject name of each certificate is stored in the enrollment database (this option makes it easy to find and revoke particular certificates).

- **complete**—The complete contents of each issued identity certificate are stored in the database (this option mimics what a real CA would do, but the downside is that it requires more storage for the certificate information).

If you don't configure this command, the default is **minimal.**

The **database username** command allows you to restrict access to the database file (*CA_name*.ser). By specifying a username and an associated password, only the specified users with the specified passwords can access the enrollment database to add/revoke identity certificates. If you have different types of administrators accessing the CA—one to manage the router and one to manage certificate services—you should configure this command to lock out the router management people from being able to manipulate the ".ser" file.

The **lifetime certificate** command specifies the lifetime, in days, of any generated identity certificate. If you omit this parameter, it defaults to one year. The lifetime can range from 1–1,825 days. If you change this value, the new lifetime will affect only newly created identity certificates. The **lifetime crl** command specifies the valid lifetime length, in hours, of a CRL the CA generates. The default lifetime is one week (168 hours), but can be extended to 336 hours. This value affects any newly created CRLs by the router CA (the CRL is stored in the *CA_name*.crl file). The **lifetime enrollment-request** command specifies how long, in hours, an open enrollment request is allowed to stay in the enrollment database. This value affects identity certificates that are not automatically created by the CA when the client is using SCEP. The default lifetime is one week, but it can be extended to 1,000 hours.

The **cdp-url** command specifies the CRL distribution point (CDP) to be used in identity certificates issued by the CA. When this doesn't appear on a certificate, the client will use SCEP to directly retrieve the CRL from the CA (stored in the *CA_name*.crl file). This command allows you to hardcode the CRL location on any newly issued identity certificate, offloading the CRL process to a different device. However, if the remote CRL is not reachable, a client always can use SCEP to obtain the CRL directly from the CA. Because of possible client constrictions, it is highly recommended to put the CRL on an HTTP server instead of another type. In this case, the **cdp-url** command would look something like this:

```
Router(cs-server)# cdp-url http://IP_address_or_name_of_CRL_server/
                   directory_location/CA_name.crl
```

When executing this command, any newly issued identity certificates will have this listed as its CRL Distribution Point on the identity certificate—existing certificates either will have the old URL or none at all, depending on the previous CDP configuration on the router CA.

The **grant** command specifies whether manual authorization of a requested identity certificate is required (**none**) or that the router CA automatically will grant an identity certificate request (**auto**). The default is **none**. The third parameter is **ra-auto**, which allows auto-enrollment requests from an RA. For this option to work, the RA's X.509 certificate must include the following: "cn=ioscs RA" or "ou=ioscs RA."

CAUTION	If your router CA is connected to the Internet, I highly recommend that you do ***not*** set the **grant** command to **auto** or **auto-ra**, since this allows almost anybody to request a certificate. Even if you use a pre-shared key for this process, it is possible for an authorized person to keep on requesting certificates for the same device, wasting storage resources on the router or remote server. If you use the **grant auto** command, I recommend setting a password lifetime that is very short—this way, the client requests a certificate via SCEP using the password, then this password expires shortly and no one else can use the same password. See the next section, "Step 4: Handling Enrollment Requests" for more information on the **crypto pki server password generate** command.

The **shutdown** command disables the router CA without removing its configuration commands and certificate information. To re-enable it, use **no shutdown**.

Once the CA is up, you can verify its configuration and operation with the **show crypto pki server** command, shown in Example 16-33. In this example, the CA is enabled and the CA's certificate is valid until 2008. The next CRL will be generated on March 28, 2005 and the certificate database is set to a minimal level and is stored in NVRAM.

Example 16-33 *Viewing the Status of the Router CA*

```
routerca# show crypto pki server
Certificate Server routerca:
    Status: enabled
    Issuer name: CN=routerca
    CA cert fingerprint: DC978D21 375DA8DE 2F28FF16 B45C2103
    Granting mode is: manual
    Last certificate issued serial number: 0x1
    CA certificate expiration timer: 11:54:32 EDT Mar 20 2008
    CRL NextUpdate timer: 11:54:33 EDT Mar 28 2005
    Current storage dir: nvram:
    Database Level: Minimum - no cert data written to storage
```

When you reboot your router, if you see either of the following two messages, this probably indicates a temporary problem where the router hasn't fully parsed the startup configuration file to configure the CA process:

- % Failed to find Certificate Server's trustpoint at startup
- % Failed to find Certificate Server's cert

Once the router has loaded and executed its configuration file, use the **show crypto pki server** command to verify its status.

Step 4: Handling Enrollment Requests

Now that you have your router CA up and operational, it's ready to handle enrollment requests for identity certificates.

The management commands that handle the enrollment process are not Configuration mode commands, but Privilege EXEC commands:

```
Router# crypto pki server CA_name info requests
Router# crypto pki server CA_name remove {all | reqID}
Router# crypto pki server CA_name grant {all | reqID}
Router# crypto pki server CA_name reject {all | reqID}
Router# crypto pki server CA_name password generate [minutes]
Router# crypto pki server CA_name request pkcs10
          {URL | terminal} [pem]
```

The following subsections will discuss these commands.

Viewing Enrollment Requests

To view identity certificate enrollment requests, use the **crypto pki server** CA_name **info requests** command. Example 16-34 illustrates the use of this command, where one certificate request (reqID #1) is pending approval/authorization. Table 16-2 lists the states a certificate request can be in.

Example 16-34 *Listing Certificate Requests in the Enrollment Database*

```
routerca# crypto pki server routerca info requests
Enrollment Request Database:
Subordinate CA certificate requests:
ReqID  State       Fingerprint                     SubjectName
-------------------------------------------------------------
←output omitted→
Router certificates requests:
ReqID  State       Fingerprint                     SubjectName
-------------------------------------------------------------
1      pending     F089C0A84FC27545E01BE806978D898A hostname=r3620.
cisco.com
```

Table 16-2 *Router CA States*

State	Description
Authorized	The CA authorized the request
Denied	The CA denied the request (probably because of policy reasons)
Granted	The CA granted the request and generated an identity certificate (if using SCEP, this is sent automatically to the requesting device)
Initial	The CA received the request
Malformed	The client request was invalid because of some cryptographic reason (like an invalid signature)
Pending	The request must be manually accepted or rejected by an administrator of the CA

When a user either sends a certificate request via SCEP or a router administrator enters the user's request manually on the router CA, the enrollment request is added to the router CA's enrollment database in an *initial* state. Each enrollment request is assigned a unique request

ID (ReqID) number. If using SCEP, the end user will receive a *pending* reply, if **grant none** has been configured for the CA. If **grant auto** is configured and the correct password is supplied to the user, the user will see a *granted* reply; otherwise, the certificate request is *denied*. If the router CA is configured with **grant none**, an administrator will need to log in to the CA and either approve the certificate request (*granted*) or deny it (*denied*).

NOTE	All SCEP enrollment requests are treated as new certificate enrollment requests, even if the requestor specifies the same subject name or public key pair as what was in a previous request — in other words, the router CA doesn't perform an extended database lookup — the router CA ignores any the old request by the same requestor.

TIP	You can use the **debug crypto pki server** command to troubleshoot enrollment problems for certificate requests using SCEP.

Removing Requests from the Enrollment Database

To remove an enrollment request from the CA's database, use the **crypto pki server** *CA_name* **remove** command. If you specify the **all** parameter, all enrollment requests are removed; in most cases, you'll use the *reqID* of the request to remove a single request. Please note that this is *not* the same as rejecting a request. Also, if you have configured a username/password for the CA database (**database username** command), you'll be prompted for this before the command can be executed successfully.

TIP	Typically, when requesting clients submit their certificate request, the CA places the request in the enrollment database in a pending state. Normally, these clients will recheck the CA for a limited time to see if the request was granted, at which point they give up. On a Cisco router as a client, you can execute the **crypto ca enroll** command to resend the request and retrieve the newly created identity certificate. However, on other clients, a new request sometimes is generated, leaving the old request in the database. Using the **crypto pki server remove** command allows you to remove the old entry.

Granting Enrollment Requests

To grant a pending enrollment request, use the **crypto pki server** *CA_name* **grant** command; specifying the **all** parameter grants all pending certificate requests while specifying the *reqID* of the single request only grants that specific request. Also, if you've configured a username/password for the CA database (**database username** command), you'll be prompted for this before the command can be executed successfully.

The actual identity certificate created for the requesting device is then stored in the location specified by the **database url** command. Two files will be created using this nomenclature:

- *certificate_serial_#*.crt
- *certificate_serial_#*.cnm

The .crt file contains the actual identity certificate and the .cnm file contains a brief description of the certificate: the subject name, host name, and the expiration date. Once a certificate is downloaded from the CA, the router CA removes the enrollment entry from its database. Certificate requests not granted within the lifetime value specified in the **lifetime enrollment-request** command will expire and will be removed from the enrollment database automatically.

Rejecting Certificate Requests

If a certificate request is not valid, you can reject it with the **crypto pki server** *CA_name* **reject** command. In most instances, you'll only reject a specific request by adding the *reqID* to the command. Also, if you have configured a username/password for the CA database (**database username** command), you'll be prompted for this before the command can be executed.

Controlling Certificate Requests with Passwords

When using SCEP, as mentioned earlier, I recommend password-protecting certificate requests. To create a password for certificate requests, use the **crypto pki server** *CA_name* **password generate** command. This causes a random password to be created that is used to validate SCEP requests (the challenge password). Also, if you have configured a username/ password for the CA database (**database username** command), you'll be prompted for this before the command can be executed successfully. By default, the generated password is valid for 60 minutes unless you specify otherwise (1–1,440 minutes). If you create a password and then use the command to create another password, the first one is removed and replaced with the second one. Example 16-35 illustrates the use of this command:

Example 16-35 *Creating a Challenge Password for SCEP*

```
routerca# crypto pki server routerca password generate
% New password is B71725E963B49FAB, valid for 60 minutes
```

Manually Entering a Certificate Enrollment

If the client doesn't support SCEP, you can perform a manual enrollment process, creating a PKCS #10 file on the client and then importing it into the router CA. To import the client's PKCS #10 file on the router CA, use the **crypto pki server** *CA_name* **request pkcs10** command. You can specify either a URL with the location of the requesting client's PKCS #10 file or specify the **terminal** parameter and cut-and-paste the PKCS #10 file into the router CA. If you specify the **pem** (privacy-enhanced mail) option, PEM headers are added automatically to the certificate when it is granted. Example 16-36 illustrates the process of pulling in a PKCS #10 file (.req) extension and granting request, and generating the certificate (.crt file).

Example 16-36 *Manually Importing a PKCS #10 File and Granting a Certificate*

```
routerca# crypto pki server mycs request pkcs10
                     tftp://192.1.1.77/r3620
% Retrieving Base64 encoded or PEM formatted PKCS10 enrollment
    request...
Reading file from tftp://192.1.1.77/router5.req
Loading router5.req from 192.1.1.77 (via Ethernet0/0): !
[OK - 582 bytes]
% Enrollment request pending, reqId=1
routerca# crypto pki server mycs grant 1
% Writing out the granted certificate...
!Writing file to tftp://192.1.1.77/router5.crt!
```

Step 5: Revoking Identity Certificates

If an identity certificate is no longer being used, has been compromised, or if there has been a change of policy, you can revoke it with the following command:

```
Router# crypto pki server CA_name revoke certificate_serial_#
```

The certificate serial number is the same as the *reqID* number in decimal; you can enter the serial number in hexadecimal by preceding the hexadecimal number by "0x." Also, if you have configured a username/password for the CA database (**database username** command), you'll be prompted for this before the command can be executed.

A new CRL is created whenever the previous CRL is revoked or updated (a new revoked certificate is added); however, it is not issued to the URL in the **cdp-url** command until the time period in the **lifetime-crl** command is reached. To see the list of revoked certificates, and the CRL, use the following command:

```
Router# crypto pki server CA_name info crl
```

Example 16-37 illustrates the use of this command. In this example, there is only one revoked certificate.

Example 16-37 *Viewing the Router CA's CRL*

```
routerca# crypto pki server routerca info crl
Certificate Revocation List:
    Issuer: cn=routerca
    This Update: 20:16:34 EDT Mar 21 2005
    Next Update: 20:16:34 EDT Mar 28 2005
    Number of CRL entries: 1
    CRL size: 240 bytes
Revoked Certificates:
    Serial Number: 0x02
    Revocation Date: 20:16:34 EDT Mar 21 2005
```

TIP   When you revoke a certificate, remember to delete the corresponding .cnm and .crt files for the serial number, since the **crypto pki server** *CA_name* **revoke** command doesn't perform this task for you.

Step 6: Configuring a Server to Run in RA Mode

Once you have configured a router as a CA, you might want to consider configuring another router as an RA and then delegate the enrollment request process to that device. The RA is responsible for recording or verifying certificate information that the CA will need to issue a certificate, and to validate existing certificates. Please note that the RA cannot itself generate new certificates; only the CA can do this. By offloading much of the enrollment process to the RA, in addition to validating certificates, the only two tasks the CA has to perform are to sign certificates and maintain the CRL.

RA Configuration and Operation

You can configure a router to run in RA mode; however, the limitation of this process is that the CA must also be an IOS router. When operating as an RA and when the RA receives an enrollment request (manual or SCEP), the RA can grant or reject the request based on policy information. If the request is granted, however, the certificate request is forwarded to the CA, which will generate the identity certificate and return it to the RA; the requestor can then recontact the RA to obtain its new identity certificate. Once you've set up the CA, setting up an RA is a two-step process: (1) enroll with the CA and (2) define the RA.

To enroll with the CA, you would perform the steps that you normally would to obtain an identity certificate. You would define a trustpoint; however, you won't actually download the CA certificate with the **crypto ca authenticate** command and an identity certificate with the **crypto ca enroll** command. Instead, you'll set up the router as an RA, which will perform this process automatically:

```
Router(config)# crypto key generate rsa
Router(config)# crypto {ca | pki} trustpoint CA_name
Router(ca-trustpoint)# enrollment url CA_URL
Router(ca-trustpoint)# subject-name X.500_name
Router(ca-trustpoint)# exit
Router(config)# crypto pki server RA_name
Router(cs-server)# mode ra
Router(cs-server)# grant ra-auto
Router(cs-server)# no shutdown
```

The **subject-name** command must include either "cn=ioscs RA" or "ou=ioscs RA" for the CA to recognize it as an RA. Also, when creating the RA server with the **crypto pki server** command, you must enter the name of the RA, *not* the CA. The **grant ra-auto** command allows automatic approval of SCEP certificate requests. As mentioned in the "Step 3: Defining Additional CA Parameters" section earlier, I highly recommend *not* using this option but to manually approve certificates (**grant none**), which is the default.

Once the RA has its certificate from the CA and is operational, it can view and handle certificate requests sent to it using the **crypto pki server** *CA_name* **info requests** and **crypto pki server** *CA_name* **grant** *reqID* commands. Please note that the RA cannot revoke certificates: only the CA can perform that task.

Example of Setting Up an RA

As you can see from the previous section, setting up an RA is a simple process. Example 16-38 illustrates the setup of an RA. When the **no shutdown** command is executed, an RSA key pair is generated automatically, the CA certificate is downloaded, the RA requests an identity certificate, and the CA grants it (automatically with a SCEP challenge password, in this instance). The **show crypto pki server** command shows that the router is running in RA server mode.

Example 16-38 *Setting Up an RA Router*

```
Routerraconfig)# crypto pki trustpoint routerca
Routerra(ca-trustpoint)# enrollment url http://192.1.1.40
Routerra(ca-trustpoint)# subject-name cn=routerfa, ou=ioscs RA,
                         o=cisco, c=us
Routerra(ca-trustpoint)# exit
Routerra(config)# crypto pki server routerra
Routerra(cs-server)# mode ra
Routerra(cs-server)# no shutdown
% Generating 1024 bit RSA keys ...[OK]
Certificate has the following attributes:
Fingerprint MD5: 32661452 0DDA3CE5 8723B469 09AB9E85
Fingerprint SHA1: 9785BBCD 6C67D27C C950E8D0 718C7A14 C0FE9C38
% Do you accept this certificate? [yes/no]: yes
Trustpoint CA certificate accepted.
% Ready to request the CA certificate.
% Some server settings cannot be changed after the CA certificate has
been requested.
Are you sure you want to do this? [yes/no]: yes
%
% Start certificate enrollment ..
% Create a challenge password. You will need to verbally provide this
    password to the CA administrator in order to revoke your
    certificate. For security reasons your password will not be saved
    in the configuration. Please make a note of it.
Password: cisco123
Re-enter password: cisco123
% The subject name in the certificate will include: cn=routerca,
    ou=ioscs RA, o=cisco, c=us
% The subject name in the certificate will include: routerra.cisco.com
% Include the router serial number in the subject name? [yes/no]: no
% Include an IP address in the subject name? [no]: no
Request certificate from CA? [yes/no]: yes
% Certificate request sent to Certificate Authority
% The certificate request fingerprint will be displayed.
% The 'show crypto pki certificate' command will also show the fingerprint.
```

continues

Example 16-38 *Setting Up an RA Router (Continued)*

```
% Enrollment in progress...
Mar 22 22:32:40.197: CRYPTO_PKI:  Certificate Request Fingerprint
  MD5: 82B41A76 AF4EC87D AAF093CD 41ACDB20
Mar 22 22:32:40.201: CRYPTO_PKI:  Certificate Request Fingerprint
  SHA1: 897CDF40 C6563EAA 0FED05F7 0115FD3A F137CADF
Mar 22 22:34:00.366: %PKI-6-CERTRET: Certificate received from
  Certificate Authority
routerra(cs-server)# end
routerra# show crypto pki server
Certificate Server routerfa:
    Status: enabled
    Issuer name: CN=routerca
    CA cert fingerprint: 32661452 0DDA3CE5 8723B469 09AB9E92
    Server configured in RA mode
    RA cert fingerprint: C65F5724 0E63B3CC BE7AE016 BE0D34D1
    Granting mode is: manual
    Current storage dir: nvram:
    Database Level: Minimum - no cert data written to storage
```

Step 7: Backing up a CA

Once you've set up your CA, you should back up its files. In Example 16-39, I chose the option of storing files in the router's NVRAM.

Example 16-39 *CA Files to Back Up*

```
routerca# dir nvram:
Directory of nvram:/
←output omitted→
    2  -rw-         32           <no date>  routerca.ser
    3  -rw-        261           <no date>  routerca.crl
    4  -rw-       1515           <no date>  routerca.p12
    6  -rw-        515           <no date>  routerca#6101CA.cer
    7  -rw-        508           <no date>  2.crt
    8  -rw-         80           <no date>  2.cnm
    9  -rw-        508           <no date>  3.crt
   10  -rw-         80           <no date>  3.cnm
←output omitted→
```

Here are the files you should regularly back up:

- **.ser file**—contains the certificate serial numbers.

- **.crl file**—contains the current CRL.

- **.p12 or .pem file**—contains the CA's RSA key pair.

- **.cer file**—contains the CA's certificate.

- **.crt files**—contains identity certificates (this assumes you are storing these either in the router's NVRAM or Flash memory; if you are storing them on the router, then you'll probably have these in Flash memory).

- **.cnm files**—contains descriptions of identity certificates (this assumes you are storing these either in the router's NVRAM or Flash memory; if you are storing them on the router, then you'll probably have these in Flash memory).

- **running-config**—the running configuration of the CA.

Step 8: Restoring a CA

If your CA configuration becomes corrupted or the CA itself dies, you can restore the CA from the files you backed up on the previous section (you should be doing this religiously!).

CAUTION   Remember that each time your router CA generates an identity certificate, you'll need to back up the corresponding .crt and .cnm files! And a good backup strategy is to make sure that these files are at a physically *different* location than the current CA, just in case there is a catastrophic disaster and the location of where the CA is situated is completely destroyed by a fire or by some other disaster. If the .ser, .crl, .p12/.pem, or .cer files are lost, you will *not* be able to restore the CA. Likewise, you need the password that encrypted the .p12/.pem file!

The first step is to take the saved running configuration of the failed CA and paste in only the commands that are not CA- and certificate-related, such as IP addressing, routing, security, and so on. Next, you need to copy in the files you backed up in "Step 7: Backing up a CA" (with the exception of the running configuration). Example 16-40 illustrates the copying process, where I'm restoring the .cer, the .crl, the .ser, and each identity certificate (I only listed the first one, serial number 2).

Example 16-40 *Restoring the Files to a New CA*

```
routerca# copy tftp://192.1.1.77/routerca#6101CA.cer nvram:
←output omitted→
515 bytes copied in 0.180 secs (2861 bytes/sec)
routerca# copy tftp://192.1.1.77/routerca.crl nvram:
←output omitted→
261 bytes copied in 0.176 secs (1483 bytes/sec)
routerca# copy tftp://192.1.1.77/routerca.ser nvram:
←output omitted→
32 bytes copied in 0.180 secs (178 bytes/sec)
routerca# copy tftp://192.1.1.77/2.crt nvram:
←output omitted→
508 bytes copied in 0.188 secs (2702 bytes/sec)
routerca# copy tftp://192.1.1.77/2.cnm nvram:
←output omitted→
80 bytes copied in 0.188 secs (426 bytes/sec)
←output omitted→
```

Please note that in this example, originally I had stored the identity certificate files (.crt and .cnm) in NVRAM; in most cases they'd be restored to Flash memory or not on the router at all—the files are located external to the router. Once you have copied the files into NVRAM, you now need to import your RSA key pair, as shown in Example 16-41. Remember that you must know the encryption key ("cisco123" in this example) to import the keys.

Example 16-41 *Importing the Saved RSA Key Pair*

```
routerca# configure terminal
routerca(config)# crypto pki import routerca pkcs12
                       tftp://192.1.1.77/routerca.p12 cisco123
←output omitted→
CRYPTO_PKI: Imported PKCS12 file successfully.
01:53:03: %PKI-6-PKCS12IMPORT_SUCCESS: PKCS #12 Successfully Imported
```

After importing the key pair, you can configure the CA and bring it up, as shown in Example 16-42. Please note that before bringing up the CA (**no shutdown**), enter all of the CA's configuration commands from the backed-up CA configuration. Remember that some things cannot be changed with the CA after you bring it up. If you make this mistake, remove the CA (see the next section), reimport the keys, and redo the CA configuration. Use the **show crypto pki server** command to verify the operational status of the CA, its configuration, and its certificate signature. As you can see from this process, restoring a CA is not hard; however, it will be impossible if you don't back up the correct files on the CA!

Example 16-42 *Configuring and Bringing Up the New CA*

```
routerca(config)# crypto pki server routerca
routerca(config)#
! Enter the other CA configuration commands before bringing
!    up the CA!
routerca(cs-server)# no shutdown
% Certificate Server enabled.
routerca(cs-server)# end
routerca# show crypto pki server
Certificate Server routerca:
    Status: enabled
    Issuer name: CN=routerca
    CA cert fingerprint: DC978D21 375DA8DE 2F28FF16 B45C2103
    Granting mode is: manual
    Last certificate issued serial number: 0x4
    CA certificate expiration timer: 11:54:32 EDT Mar 20 2008
    CRL NextUpdate timer: 11:21:10 EDT Mar 29 2005
    Current storage dir: nvram:
    Database Level: Minimum - no cert data written to storage
```

Step 9: Removing CA Services

Normally, you won't delete a CA (remove its services) unless you want to remove it from service or replace it with another system. When deleting the CA services on a router, the

CA trustpoint, the CA certificate, and the CA RSA key pair are automatically deleted. To perform this process, use this command:

```
Router(config)# no crypto pki server CA_name
```

Example 16-43 shows an example of removing the CA services on a router. You'll be prompted to verify that you really want to do this and acknowledge that the trustpoint configuration, the CA certificate, and the RSA key pair will be deleted.

Example 16-43 *Removing CA Services on a Router*

```
routerca(config)# no crypto pki server routerca
% This will stop the Certificate Server process and delete the server
  configuration
Are you sure you want to do this? [yes/no]: yes
% Do you also want to remove the associated trustpoint and
  signing certificate and key? [yes/no]: yes
No enrollment sessions are currently active.
% Certificate Server Process stopped
```

CAUTION   If you'll be moving CA services to another router, be sure that you follow the guidelines in "Step 7: Backing up a CA" before removing the CA from your router! Otherwise you'll have to start from scratch and re-create all your devices' identity certificates, which is not a task I would envy.

Summary

This chapter showed you the basics of setting up ISAKMP/IKE Phase 1. The defining of the policy statements on a router is straightforward. With three types of device authentication to choose from, pre-shared keys is the simplest to configure but scales the least; certificates are the hardest to implement, but scale the best. And with the ability of a Cisco router to function as a CA, you can deploy certificate services easily using existing equipment.

Next up is Chapter 17, "Router Site-to-Site Connections," where I show you how to configure your router to establish various types of site-to-site sessions with remote peers, covering topics such as static and dynamic crypto maps, the Tunnel Endpoint Discovery (TED) protocol, dynamic multipoint VPNs (DMVPNs), and many others.

Router Site-to-Site Connections

Where the last chapter focused on ISAKMP/IKE Phase 1, this chapter will focus on ISAKMP/
IKE Phase 2 and what you have to do on a router to set up IPsec site-to-site or LAN-to-LAN
(L2L) sessions. As mentioned in Chapter 15, "Router Product Information," routers
typically are the best solution for L2L sessions because they support advanced QoS, routing,
and L2L scalability features. Some of the topics I discuss here are applicable to remote
access connections for an Easy VPN Server, such as static and dynamic crypto maps, address
translation, and many others, which you'll see in the next chapter as well. Throughout the
chapter I'll go through many examples that illustrate the different types of configurations
I discuss. However, I'll reserve an in-depth discussion of troubleshooting commands, such
as **show** and **debug**, for Chapter 19, "Troubleshooting Router Connections."

ISAKMP/IKE Phase 2 Configuration

Once ISAKMP/IKE Phase 1 completes (negotiates the Phase 1 policies, performs DH, and
authenticates the peer), the management connection is established. The management
connection is then used to build the two unidirectional data connections during ISAKMP/
IKE Phase 2. In its simplest form, there are three components that need to be configured for
L2L sessions for ISAKMP/IKE Phase 2:

- Define the traffic that needs to be protected (crypto ACL).
- Define how that traffic is to be protected (transform set).
- Define to whom the traffic should be forwarded (crypto map).

If the remote L2L peer acquires its address dynamically, and you want to allow the remote
peer to build an L2L session to your router, you'll have to build a dynamic crypto map with
an entry for this peer. If you're using certificates for device authentication, you can use a
new feature in the IOS called distinguished named-based crypto maps. This feature allows
you to have more control over what certificate you'll accept from a particular peer. The
following section will discuss the three bullets above and these two additional, yet optional,
configuration tasks.

Defining Protected Traffic: Crypto ACLs

One method of defining what traffic needs to be protected is to create a crypto ACL. A crypto ACL is basically an ACL with **permit** or **deny** statements in it, where a **permit** statement specifies the traffic is to be protected and a **deny** statement specifies the traffic doesn't need to be protected. Named or numbered ACLs can be used. The crypto ACL created on one peer should be mirrored on the other peer; this ensures that traffic that is to be protected locally by your router is processed correctly by the remote peer.

TIP   In most instances, if you don't mirror crypto ACLs on the two peers, the ISAKMP/IKE Phase 2 connection will fail.

For example, if I want to protect traffic between two networks—192.168.1.0/24 connected to RouterA and 192.168.2.0/24 connected to RouterB—I would use the configuration shown in Example 17-1 (I assume you are familiar with ACLs on IOS routers). The names or numbers of the ACLs on the two peers don't need to match; however, I've found that when a router is connected to many different peers, possibly in a partially or fully meshed environment, using the same ACL name for each peer-to-peer session makes it easier to manage. Notice that in the two ACL **permit** statements, the addressing information is mirrored (reversed).

Example 17-1 *Mirroring Crypto ACLs*

```
! RouterA's configuration
RouterA(config)# ip access-list extended mirrored
RouterA(config-ext-nacl)# permit 192.168.1.0 0.0.0.255
                          192.168.2.0 0.0.0.255
! RouterB's configuration
RouterB(config)# ip access-list extended mirrored
RouterB(config-ext-nacl)# permit 192.168.2.0 0.0.0.255
                          192.168.1.0 0.0.0.255
```

Cisco highly discourages the use of the keyword **any** in a crypto ACL, because this can create connectivity problems. For example, if you want multicast traffic to enter the router's external interface where IPsec is applied, this will cause the router to drop the traffic unless it is protected by IPsec. This is also true of other kinds of traffic, like ICMP messages. If you do use the keyword **any** in a **permit** statement, be sure to precede the statement with specific **deny** statements for traffic that shouldn't be protected.

TIP   I recommend using named IP ACLs, using the name of the remote site or peer. This makes it easy to determine which ACL is to be used with which site (peer).

As you will see in the "Building a Static Crypto Map Entry" section later, the crypto ACL is activated in a crypto map entry, which is associated with an interface. If you have multiple sites, you'll need multiple entries in your crypto map where each entry has a unique crypto ACL. If there is an overlap between crypto ACLs in different entries, the crypto ACL in the highest priority crypto map entry will be used to protect traffic to a destination; based on this process, there is a chance, given the order (priority) of the crypto map entries, that an overlapping entry could be used to verify returning traffic, which could cause the router to drop it. The IOS is not smart enough to generate a message indicating that you have overlapping ACLs; you'll have to ensure this.

When the router processes the crypto ACL, it looks for a match in the first **permit** statement. If the packet matches this, the packet will be protected as it leaves the router; if no match is found, the traffic leaves the router as is. For packets coming from an external network in the router, if it matches a **permit** statement in a crypto ACL, the router validates the traffic based on the IPsec SA that's established for the unidirectional data connection from the remote peer to the local router. If the packet is unprotected (but matches a **permit** statement in the crypto ACL), it is automatically dropped. If there is no match with a **permit** statement, the router processes the packet normally. Like normal ACLs, you can view your crypto ACLs with the **show [ip] access-lists** command.

NOTE	Assuming that your router is a perimeter router, is filtering inbound traffic from the outside world, and is also terminating VPN sessions, you'll probably experience problems with data getting through the ACL check if you're new to Cisco IPsec router configurations. When a VPN connection is terminated on a Cisco router with an inbound ACL, the ACL is checked first—I assume you are permitting the ISAKMP/IKE Phase 1 connection (UDP 500) and the ESP, AH, and/or NAT-T (UDP 4,500) connections. If the packet passes this check, the router then verifies the protection and decrypts it. Most people are unaware that the IOS then runs the unprotected packet through the ACL check again! Therefore, whatever statements you include in your crypto ACL(s), you also need to include in the perimeter ACL allowing the inbound, unprotected traffic. Otherwise, the IPsec-protected packets will be allowed in, but once they're processed, they'll be dropped.

As you will see later in the chapter, there are other options besides the use of crypto ACLs to define what traffic needs to be protected; however, this was the first implementation of Cisco L2L sessions, so I've discussed it first.

Defining Protection Methods: Transform Sets

Where the crypto ACL defines what data traffic should be protected, a transform set defines how the data traffic is going to be protected—the security protocols and algorithms/functions. For the ISAKMP/IKE Phase 2 negotiation to be successful for the data SAs, there has to be at least one matching transform between the two IPsec peers. If all peers have the same capabilities, then you typically define a single transform; however, if you have multiple peers with different capabilities, you typically define multiple transform sets.

To create a transform set, use the following command(s):

```
Router(config)# crypto ipsec transform-set transform_set_name
                           transform1 [transform2 [transform3 [transform4]]]
Router(cfg-crypto-tran)# mode [tunnel | transport]
```

Each transform set needs a unique name and can contain up to four transforms. A transform defines how traffic will be protected. Table 17-1 defines the transforms that can be defined. You can have only one transform from each type. For example, you can't define both **esp-des** and **esp-3des** in the same set.

Table 17-1   *IPsec SA Transforms*

Transform Type	Transform Parameter
AH	**ah-md5-hmac**
	ah-sha-hmac
ESP authentication	**esp-md5-hmac**
	esp-sha-hmac
ESP encryption	**esp-null**
	esp-des
	esp-3des
	esp-seal
	esp-aes 128
	esp-aes 192
	esp-aes-256
Compression	**comp-lzs**

SEAL is a new encryption type introduced in IOS 12.3(7)T. It uses a 160-bit encryption key and has less of an impact on the router's CPU cycles compared to the other algorithms. However, SEAL does have three limitations:

- It is not supported by hardware encryption modules and thus is better suited to smaller-end routers like the 830 series.

- It must be used with an authentication transform because SEAL encryption has a difficult time detecting tampered packets.

- It must be used with dynamic ISAKMP/IKE for the Phase 2 SAs; manual SAs are not supported.

<table>
<tr><td>**TIP**</td><td>Only enable compression in a transform set if the connection uses dialup to the remote peer; for any connection faster than this, you'll lose significant throughput by having the router perform both encryption and compression. Therefore, the most likely place you would use this transform in a transform set is for remote access users that dial into an ISP—not L2L sessions.</td></tr>
</table>

Once you have entered the **crypto ipsec transform-set** command, you are taken into a subcommand mode where you can enter the connection type. The default mode is tunnel, which is used for L2L and remote access sessions; transport mode is used for point-to-point sessions—for example, between a router and a syslog or TFTP server. One exception to this is the use of dynamic multipoint VPNs, which I discuss in the "Scalability" section at the end of the chapter.

To view the transform sets on your router, use the **show crypto ipsec transform-set** command.

<table>
<tr><td>**NOTE**</td><td>If you change a transform set's configuration, it will affect only newly established SAs. Existing SAs will not use this until the lifetime of the connection expires and the SAs are re-negotiated or the SAs are torn down manually (cleared) and forced to be rebuilt (the **clear crypto sa** or **clear crypto ipsec sa** commands).</td></tr>
</table>

Building a Static Crypto Map Entry

The function of a crypto map is to bring all the necessary information together to build an IPsec session—management and data connections—to remote peers. Each crypto map on a router has a unique crypto map name. Normally, one crypto map is necessary on a router because only one map can be activated on an interface. Therefore, if you have to protect traffic on two or more interfaces on your router and you need different policies for this traffic, you would need more than one crypto map; otherwise, if the policies are the same, you can apply the same crypto map to multiple interfaces.

There are two types of crypto maps:

- Static crypto map
- Dynamic crypto map

Static crypto maps normally are used for L2L sessions and dynamic crypto maps for remote access; however, as you'll see later, dynamic crypto maps also can be used for L2L sessions where some information about the remote peer cannot be determined until the negotiation process begins. The following sections will discuss more about crypto maps, entries in crypto maps, using ISAKMP/IKE to build IPsec data connections or manually specifying information, activating a crypto map, viewing a crypto map, and examining a simple example of creating a static crypto map.

Crypto Map Entries

A crypto map is made up of one or more entries. The function of an entry in a crypto map is to specify what traffic (crypto ACL) should be protected, how the traffic should be protected (transform set), where the protected traffic should be sent (remote peer), what address to use on the router to send protected traffic, how the ISAKMP/IKE Phase 1 and 2 connections are built (dynamically or manually), the lifetime of the data connections, and other information.

The entries in a crypto map help the router determine which policies should be used when negotiating security associations with a remote peer. Each crypto map entry is assigned a unique sequence number which determines how the router will process the entries when looking for a compatible entry. The lower the sequence number, the higher the priority. If your router will be initiating an L2L session, it must use a static crypto map entry; however, if your router is accepting a session request from a remote peer, it can use either a static or dynamic entry to determine how the connection will be built and protected. When routers are performing the negotiation process, a compatible crypto map entry must be found on both peers, where the entry contains, at a minimum, a mirrored crypto ACL, a matching identity of the peer, and a common transform set.

If any of the following conditions exist, you'll need more than one entry in your crypto map:

- Different traffic flows are to be handled by different peers (like having multiple sites you're connected to).

- You want to have a different policy applied to different types of traffic being sent to the same or different peers.

- When you are not using ISAKMP/IKE to build a session to a remote peer, you cannot have more than one **permit** statement in a crypto ACL; for multiple traffic flows, you would have to create a separate crypto ACL for each flow and thus would need a separate crypto map entry for each crypto ACL.

Using ISAKMP/IKE

When building a static crypto map entry for an L2L session, 99 percent of the time you'll use ISAKMP/IKE to build the session. To create a static crypto map entry using ISAKMP/IKE, use the following configuration:

```
Router(config)# crypto map map_name seq_# ipsec-isakmp
Router(config-crypto-m)# match address ACL_name_or_#
Router(config-crypto-m)# set peer {hostname | IP_address}
Router(config-crypto-m)# set transform-set transform_set_name1
                         [transform-set-name2...transform-set-name6]
Router(config-crypto-m)# set pfs [group1 | group2 | group5]
Router(config-crypto-m)# set security-association level per-host
Router(config-crypto-m)# set security-association lifetime
                         {seconds seconds | kilobytes kilobytes}
Router(config-crypto-m)# set security-association idle-time seconds
Router(config-crypto-m)# exit
```

The **crypto map** command creates a static map entry. You must give the static crypto map a unique name, followed by the sequence number for the entry, which can range from 1–65,535. Remember that the lower the number, the higher the priority of the statement. Upon executing this command, you are taken into a subcommand mode where you can configure the commands pertinent to this entry.

The **match address** command specifies the number or name of the crypto ACL that has the traffic to be protected. For a static crypto map entry, this is a required command.

NOTE   If the **match address** command references a nonexistent crypto ACL, the router will drop all unprotected traffic sent to it, because a nonexistent ACL *permits* all traffic by default.

The **set peer** command specifies who the router will connect to for the traffic specified in the crypto ACL. You can specify either the FQDN, the name, or the IP address of the peer. If specifying the name or FQDN, the router can resolve it by using a static host table (**ip host**) or DNS. For redundancy, you can add multiple **set peer** commands to a crypto map entry; however, only one peer connection is built. Based on how you enter the **set peer** commands, the first instance becomes the primary, the second the secondary, and so on. If the primary cannot be reached, the second **set peer** command is used to establish the session. For a static crypto map entry, this is a required command.

The **set transform-set** command specifies the name of the transform set or sets (**crypto ipsec transform-set**) that can be used to protect traffic to the peer in the **set peer** command. You can list up to six transform set names. Normally, you'll know how the traffic to the peer is to be protected and therefore you will configure a single transform set name; but if you don't know, you can list multiple transform set names. The order in which you enter them is important, because this is the order the remote peer will use; therefore, list the most secure transform set name first and the least secure last. For a static crypto map entry, this is a required command.

The **set pfs** command is optional. It specifies that Perfect Forward Secrecy (PFS) should be used to share keying information for the data connections, via DH, instead of using the existing management connection. If this command is not configured, PFS is not used. Using PFS, you can specify either group 1, 2, or 5 keys, with group 5 being the most secure. If you specify this option, the (re-)negotiation of the data connection will take a little bit longer, but the sharing of the encryption and HMAC keys will be more secure.

By default, all traffic specified in the crypto ACL is protected by one SA pair between the local and remote peer. You can override this behavior with the **set security-association level per-host** command, which specifies that each host pairing between the local and remote side will be represented by a different SA pair. For example, if you had ten hosts at one site and ten at another, theoretically you could have 100 SA pairs between the two L2L routers. The one advantage of using this command is that you'll have different tunnels for the different peering relationships, where you can control both the priority of the packets (after encryption) and enable encryption. However, if you have many devices at each site, this can easily exhaust the resources on your router and, as such, should be used with care. This command is applicable only to static crypto map entries and is optional.

There are two sets of commands to change the lifetime of a data SA. The **set security-association lifetime** command is used within a crypto map entry and changes the lifetime of only the SA associated with that entry. You also can change this value globally with this command:

```
Router(config)# crypto ipsec security-association lifetime
               {seconds seconds | kilobytes kilobytes}
```

The above command affects all IPsec data SAs; however, the **set security-association lifetime** command allows you to override the global values for a specific crypto map entry. The default global lifetime of an SA is 3,600 seconds or 4,608,000 KB of transmitted user data (this equates to about 10 Mbps of traffic in an hour). Whenever the SA's lifetime reaches within 30 seconds of the **seconds** parameter *or* 256 KB of the **kilobytes** parameter, a new SA is negotiated; this process is used to ensure that there is no time lag between tearing down and rebuilding an SA between peers. To view your globally configured lifetime values, use the **show crypto ipsec security-association lifetime** command.

With the above commands, even if no traffic is transmitted between the peers, the SA is considered active and will not be removed until the lifetime expires. Inactive SAs waste memory and CPU resources on the router. With hundreds of peers, this can create a serious resource problem on a router. In IOS 12.2(15)T, Cisco introduced idle timers for data SAs. Like the absolute timer in the previous paragraph, idle timers can be configured globally and per crypto map entry. When the idle timer is reached (no traffic is transmitted across the SA for the duration of the idle timer), the SA is deleted automatically by the router.

```
Router(config)# crypto ipsec security-association idle-time seconds
```

You can override the global idle timeout with the **set security-association idle-time** command. The idle time can range from 60–86,400 seconds. By default, the idle timeout mechanism is disabled on the router.

TIP　For routers that have to handle a large number of L2L and remote access connections, I highly recommend that you configure the SA idle timeout feature to remove idle SA connections so that your router can deal more effectively with active SAs. However, this should be used only between Cisco routers. When connecting to a non-Cisco router, remember that you might have to match the absolute data SA lifetime values for Phase 2 negotiations to succeed.

Not Using ISAKMP/IKE

While using ISAKMP/IKE, when the router receives traffic that needs to be protected for the first time, it needs to build a management connection and two data connections. This negotiation might take a few seconds, and this delay might cause problems for certain kinds of delay-sensitive applications. To overcome this problem, you can create manual SA entries in a crypto map. With a manual SA, ISAKMP/IKE is not used and therefore no connections are built dynamically. Instead, you specify all the criteria for the data SAs on both peers (no management connection is needed and thus is not built). Once you've done this, as soon as your router receives traffic that needs to be protected, it uses the information about the manual SA configuration to protect and forward the traffic, introducing no extra delay. Please note that because you are defining all criteria for the data SAs on both peers, including encryption and HMAC keys and the SA identifiers, you no longer need an ISAKMP/IKE Phase 1 management connection.

There are a few downsides, though, to using manual SAs:

- You must specify *all* SA information manually on both peers.

- You cannot use certificates for device authentication, because this requires the use of ISAKMP/IKE.

- The encryption and HMAC keys are not negotiated dynamically, increasing the likelihood that someone eventually will be able to crack the keys.

- The SAs never time out and are always up.

- Anti-replay services are not available.

- Crypto ACLs can have only a single **permit** statement in them; if you need multiple **permit** statements, you'll need to create a separate crypto ACL for each one and then create a separate crypto map entry for each crypto ACL, in effect creating a separate SA for each crypto ACL **permit** statement.

To create a manual SA entry in a crypto map entry, use the following configuration:

```
Router(config)# crypto map map_name seq_# ipsec-manual
Router(config-crypto-m)# match address ACL_name_or_#
Router(config-crypto-m)# set peer {hostname | IP_address}
Router(config-crypto-m)# set transform-set transform_set_name
Router(config-crypto-m)# set session-key inbound ah SPI_# HMAC_key
Router(config-crypto-m)# set session-key outbound ah SPI_# HMAC_key
Router(config-crypto-m)# set session-key inbound esp SPI_#
                         cipher encryption_key [authenticator HMAC_key]
Router(config-crypto-m)# set session-key outbound esp SPI_#
                         cipher encryption_key [authenticator HMAC_key]
```

The **ipsec-manual** parameter in the **crypto map** command specifies that the entry will contain a manually created SA. The **match address** command specifies what traffic is to be protected. Remember that this ACL can have only one permit statement. The **set peer** command specifies which peer this traffic will be forwarded to; with a manual entry, you can list only a single peer. If you want to change the peer, you must delete the old peer first before adding the new one. The **set transform-set** command specifies the transform set to use; unlike with a dynamic entry, you can specify only a single transform set.

Up until this point, the commands mostly are the same as those for an ISAKMP/IKE entry; however, the **set session-key** commands are new. These commands specify the SPI values to use for the SAs and the keys for the encryption and HMAC functions. Remember that there are two data SAs to define (hence, the **inbound** and **outbound** parameters). If you'll be using AH, use the first two **set session-key** commands. You'll need a unique SPI value for each connection (the connection identifier).

An SPI value can range from 256–4,294,967,295. One restriction for SAs is that you can use the same SA only for each security protocol/destination/direction pair. If you used AH and ESP to a particular destination, you would need four SPI values: two for inbound and outbound AH and two for inbound and outbound ESP. As an example, if you were only using ESP, you could use 256 for an inbound SA and 257 for an outbound SA. In this situation, you'd need to configure the reverse on the remote peer: 256 for the outbound SA and 257 for the inbound SA. The encryption and HMAC keys are a string of 8-, 16-, or 20-byte hexadecimal characters. If you enter a key length longer than the above three, it is truncated to the lower number. Also, encryption keys must be at least 8 bytes, MD5 keys 16 bytes, and SHA keys 20 bytes. Remember that when you configure a key for an SA, it must match the key used for the SA by the other peer; also, these keys never expire and must be changed manually on both peers to meet any policy requirements regarding keys.

Activating a Crypto Map

Once you've built your static crypto map, it does not protect traffic until you activate it. Activating it is done on a physical interface where traffic will exit to the remote peer:

```
Router(config)# interface type [slot_#/]port_#
Router(config-if)# crypto map map_name
```

The **crypto map** command applies the crypto map to the router's interface. In newer versions of the IOS, if ISAKMP/IKE isn't enabled, it is enabled with the execution of this command.

By default, the IP address of the interface that the crypto map is applied to is used for the tunnel or transport connections. You can override this with the following command:

```
Router(config)# crypto map map_name local-address
                     interface_name_and_number
```

Normally this is done when you have two interfaces you can use to reach a remote peer and have the same crypto map applied to both interfaces. In this situation, you want to the remote peer to see your router as having a single IP address, no matter which interface the local router uses to send IPsec packets to the remote peer. Normally, a loopback interface is created, placing a publicly reachable address on it; of course you could put a private address on it, but then you might have to use NAT-T to get through an address translation device.

Viewing a Crypto Map

Once you've created your crypto map and, possibly, activated it, you can view its configuration with the following command:

```
Router# show crypto map [interface interface | tag map_name]
```

Example 17-2 illustrates the use of this command. The crypto map is called "mymap" and has one entry in it (sequence number 10). This entry defines one peer (192.1.1.20), one crypto ACL (called "r3620," which permits traffic between two C-class networks), the default lifetimes, no PFS, and one transform set (called "RTRBtrans"). The crypto map is activated on Ethernet0/0.

Example 17-2 *The* **show crypto map** *Command*

```
RTRA# show crypto map
Crypto Map "mymap" 10 ipsec-isakmp
        Peer = 193.1.1.20
        Extended IP access list RTRB
            access-list RTRB permit ip 192.168.1.0 0.0.0.255
                                       192.168.2.0 0.0.0.255
        Current peer: 193.1.1.20
        Security association lifetime: 4608000 kilobytes/3600 seconds
        PFS (Y/N): N
        Transform sets={
                RTRBtrans,
        }
        Interfaces using crypto map mymap:
                Ethernet0/0
```

Configuring an Example Using Static Map Entries

Now that you have an understanding of configuring static crypto maps, I'll illustrate their use through an example configuration. The network I'll use to illustrate this configuration is shown in Figure 17-1 and the code in Examples 17-3 for RTRA and 17-4 for RTRB, with comments explaining RTRA's configuration—RTRB's is similar. Traffic between 192.168.1.0/24 and 192.168.2.0/24 is being protected by this configuration.

Figure 17-1 *Simple Configuration Example Using Static Crypto Map Entries*

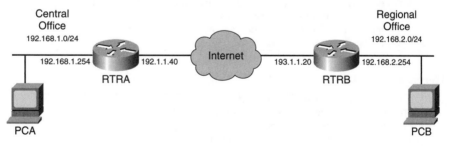

Example 17-3 *Static Crypto Map Example: RTRA*

```
! Enabling ISAKMP and defining the management connection policy
RTRA(config)# crypto isakmp enable
RTRA(config)# crypto isakmp identity address
RTRA(config)# crypto isakmp policy 10
RTRA(config-isakmp)# encryption aes 128
RTRA(config-isakmp)# hash md5
```

continues

Example 17-3 *Static Crypto Map Example: RTRA (Continued)*

```
RTRA(config-isakmp)# authentication pre-share
RTRA(config-isakmp)# group 2
RTRA(config-isakmp)# exit
! Using pre-shared keys for authentication
RTRA(config)# crypto isakmp key cisco123 address
                          193.1.1.20 255.255.255.255 no-xauth
! This is the crypto ACL
RTRA(config)# ip access-list extended RTRB
RTRA(config-ext-nacl)# permit ip 192.168.1.0 0.0.0.255
                              192.168.2.0 0.0.0.255
RTRA(config-ext-nacl)# exit
! The static route specifies how to reach the remote networks
RTRA(config)# ip route 192.168.2.0 255.255.255.0 192.1.1.20
! Defining the transform set
RTRA(config)# crypto ipsec transform-set RTRB esp-aes esp-md5-hmac
RTRA(cfg-crypto-tran)# exit
! Creating the crypto map entry for RTRB using ISAKMP/IKE
RTRA(config)# crypto map mymap 10 ipsec-isakmp
RTRA(config-crypto-m)# set peer 193.1.1.20
RTRA(config-crypto-m)# set transform-set RTRB
RTRA(config-crypto-m)# match address RTRB
RTRA(config-crypto-m)# exit
! Creating the perimeter ACL, allowing only IPSec traffic
! Note that you need to add an entry for the unprotected traffic too
RTRA(config)# ip access-list extended perimeter
RTRA(config-ext-nacl)# permit udp host 193.1.1.20
                                host 192.1.1.40 eq 500
RTRA(config-ext-nacl)# permit esp host 193.1.1.20 host 192.1.1.40
RTRA(config-ext-nacl)# permit ip 192.168.2.0 0.0.0.255
                              192.168.1.0 0.0.0.255
RTRA(config-ext-nacl)# deny ip any any
RTRA(config-ext-nacl)# exit
! Activating the inbound ACL and crypto map on the external interface
RTRA(config)# interface Ethernet0/0
RTRA(config-if)# ip address 192.1.1.40 255.255.255.0
RTRA(config-if)# crypto map mymap
```

Example 17-4 *Static Crypto Map Example: RTRB*

```
RTRB(config)# crypto isakmp enable
RTRB(config)# crypto isakmp identity address
RTRB(config)# crypto isakmp policy 10
RTRB(config-isakmp)# encryption aes 128
RTRB(config-isakmp)# hash md5
RTRB(config-isakmp)# authentication pre-share
RTRB(config-isakmp)# group 2
RTRB(config-isakmp)# exit
RTRB(config)# crypto isakmp key cisco123 address
                      192.1.1.40 255.255.255.255 no-xauth
RTRB(config)# ip access-list extended RTRA
RTRB(config-ext-nacl)# permit ip 192.168.2.0 0.0.0.255
                              192.168.1.0 0.0.0.255
```

Example 17-4 *Static Crypto Map Example: RTRB (Continued)*

```
RTRB(config-ext-nacl)# exit
RTRB(config)# ip route 192.168.1.0 255.255.255.0 193.1.1.1
RTRB(config)# crypto ipsec transform-set RTRA esp-aes esp-md5-hmac
RTRB(cfg-crypto-tran)# exit
RTRB(config)# crypto map mymap 10 ipsec-isakmp
RTRB(config-crypto-m)# set peer 192.1.1.40
RTRB(config-crypto-m)# set transform-set RTRA
RTRB(config-crypto-m)# match address RTRA
RTRB(config-crypto-m)# exit
RTRB(config)# ip access-list extended perimeter
RTRB(config-ext-nacl)# permit udp host 192.1.1.40
                                 host 193.1.1.20 eq 500
RTRB(config-ext-nacl)# permit esp host 192.1.1.40 host 193.1.1.20
RTRB(config-ext-nacl)# permit ip 192.168.1.0 0.0.0.255
                                 192.168.2.0 0.0.0.255
RTRB(config-ext-nacl)# deny ip any any
RTRB(config-ext-nacl)# exit
RTRB(config)# interface Ethernet0/0
RTRB(config-if)# ip address 193.1.1.20 255.255.255.0
RTRB(config-if)# ip access-group perimeter in
RTRB(config-if)# crypto map mymap
```

NOTE   When examining Examples 17-3 and 17-4, notice that the interface ACL allows the traffic between the two sites. This is necessary since the external ACL is processed twice: on the protected IPsec traffic and then again once the traffic is verified and decrypted. Of course, you could also use certificates, which would be the most secure authentication solution.

Building Dynamic Crypto Maps

One problem with static crypto map entries is that you must specify the IP address of the remote peer. This can be difficult if the local or remote router is acquiring its addressing information dynamically. In this instance, you can use dynamic crypto maps to solve your connectivity problem. Normally dynamic crypto maps are used for remote access IPsec sessions; however, you can use them for L2L sessions also. In this chapter I'll focus on the latter. The next chapter will focus on the former.

NOTE   One problem with peers obtaining their addresses dynamically is that if you're using pre-shared symmetric or asymmetric keys, you cannot use the IP address of the peer as its identity; instead, you'll need to use its name, typically a FQDN, or, less preferably, a wild-carded pre-shared key, which is less secure.

A dynamic crypto map is, by and large, a static map entry without all the required configuration parameters. With a static crypto map entry, you must at a minimum enter the peer's name or address (**set peer**), the traffic to be protected (**match address**), and how the traffic is to be protected (**set transform-set**). However, in many instances, you won't know this information until the remote peer actually connects to you. With dynamic crypto maps, the missing configuration parameters are filled in dynamically when negotiating the IPsec parameters. This allows your router to accept connections from a remote peer without having to configure everything statically.

Some limitations of using dynamic crypto maps include:

- You must use ISAKMP/IKE to perform the negotiation.

- One peer must have a static configuration (typically the spoke or remote access device) and one must have a dynamic configuration (typically the hub or VPN gateway device).

- Only one peer (the one with the static configuration) can initiate the IPsec tunnel.

Because of the last bullet point, dynamic crypto maps typically are not used for L2L sessions because either side might initiate traffic.

To help you with the configuration of dynamic crypto maps, the following sections cover these topics:

- Creating a Dynamic Crypto Map

- Using a Dynamic Crypto Map

- Configuring an Example Using a Dynamic Crypto Map

- Configuring Tunnel Endpoint Discovery with Dynamic Crypto Maps

Creating a Dynamic Crypto Map

Creating a dynamic crypto map is similar to creating a static one. Here are the basic commands associated with this process:

```
Router(config)# crypto dynamic-map dynamic_map_name sequence_#
Router(config-crypto-m)# match address ACL_name_or_#
Router(config-crypto-m)# set peer {hostname | IP_address}
Router(config-crypto-m)# set transform-set transform_set_name1
                         [transform-set-name2...transform-set-name6]
Router(config-crypto-m)# set pfs [group1 | group2 | group5]
Router(config-crypto-m)# set security-association level per-host
Router(config-crypto-m)# set security-association lifetime
                         {seconds seconds | kilobytes kilobytes}
Router(config-crypto-m)# set security-association idle-time seconds
Router(config-crypto-m)# exit
```

To create a dynamic crypto map, use the **crypto dynamic-map** command. You must give the dynamic map a unique name. Within the dynamic crypto map you can have multiple entries, where each entry is given a unique sequence number. The sequence number can range from 1–65,535, where 1 has the highest priority and is processed first during the IPsec negotiation. The rest of the commands were discussed previously in the "Using ISAKMP/IKE" section.

With dynamic crypto map entries, there is only *one* required command: **set transform-set**. The rest of the commands are optional. If you don't configure the **match address** command, the router will accept any crypto ACL the remote peer proposes during the Phase 2 negotiation. The peer's identity typically is not known, so configuring the **set peer** command is uncommon in a dynamic crypto map entry.

TIP   If you have multiple L2L peers that acquire their addressing information dynamically, I recommend configuring a separate crypto ACL for each and then a separate entry in the dynamic crypto map for each peer, specifying minimally the transform set and the crypto ACL. Therefore, if there is a mismatch in the crypto ACL between the remote and local router, the IPsec connection won't come up—this tells you that there is a possible problem with the mirrored crypto ACLs, and allows you to control what traffic should be protected.

To view the entries in your dynamic crypto map, use this command:

```
Router# show crypto dynamic-map [tag dynamic_map_name]
```

The output of this command is similar to that of the **show crypto map** command. Example 17-5 illustrates the use of this command. In this example, a crypto ACL and transform set are defined; everything else is left to its default value.

Example 17-5 *The* **show crypto dynamic-map** *command*

```
RTRA# show crypto dynamic-map
Crypto Map Template"dynmap" 10
        Extended IP access list RTRB
            access-list RTRB permit ip 192.168.1.0 0.0.0.255
                                       192.168.2.0 0.0.0.255
        Security association lifetime: 4608000 kilobytes/3600 seconds
        PFS (Y/N): N
        Transform sets={
                RTRB,
        }
```

Using a Dynamic Crypto Map

Once you've created your dynamic crypto map, you must activate it. Unlike a static crypto map configuration, you don't apply it to the router's interface. Because only a single crypto map (which must be a static map) can be applied to a router's interface, Cisco has you embed a dynamic crypto map as an entry within a static map configuration; this allows you to configure static L2L, dynamic L2L, and remote access IPsec VPNs on the same router.

TIP	Because you need to embed the dynamic crypto map as an entry in a static crypto map, and because the dynamic crypto map typically lacks a lot of configuration information that is filled in during the IPsec negotiation process, you typically give the dynamic crypto map entry reference a high sequence number within the static map; this ensures that the static entries are used before any dynamic ones.

When a router uses a dynamic crypto map to establish an IPsec session with a remote peer, a temporary static crypto map entry is created in the static map with the IPsec-negotiated information. When the session expires, the temporary crypto map entry is removed.

To embed a dynamic crypto map and its entries within a static map, use the following command:

```
Router(config)# crypto map static_map_name seq_# ipsec-isakmp
                    dynamic dynamic_map_name
```

Notice that you add the **dynamic** parameter along with the dynamic map name to the static crypto map entry. Also, be sure to give the dynamic crypto map a sequence number higher than all of the static entries, ensuring that it won't be used by an L2L session where you know all the parameters involved.

Configuring an Example Using a Dynamic Crypto Map

I'll now illustrate an example using dynamic crypto maps. I'll use Figure 17-1 and the previous example from the "Configuring an Example Using Static Map Entries" section. In this example, assume RTRB is acquiring its address dynamically via DHCP. The dynamic crypto map configuration is done on RTRA. Example 17-6 shows RTRA's configuration, including appropriate comments. One important item to point out is that because RTRB's IP address is unknown, a wildcard must be used for the pre-shared key, which might be of concern. If so, then either use a hostname as the identity type with pre-shared keys or, more preferably, use certificates. Also, notice that I only configured a transform set and a crypto ACL for the dynamic map ("dynmap"). The static map ("statmap") only has one entry in it; but that entry has a very high sequence number. This makes it easy to add static entries with lower numbers (higher preference).

Example 17-6 *Dynamic Crypto Map Example: RTRA*

```
! Enabling ISAKMP and defining the management connection policy
RTRA(config)# crypto isakmp enable
RTRA(config)# crypto isakmp identity address
RTRA(config)# crypto isakmp policy 10
RTRA(config-isakmp)# encryption aes 128
RTRA(config-isakmp)# hash md5
RTRA(config-isakmp)# authentication pre-share
RTRA(config-isakmp)# group 2
RTRA(config-isakmp)# exit
! Using pre-shared keys for authentication
```

Example 17-6 *Dynamic Crypto Map Example: RTRA (Continued)*

```
! Because the IP address of RTRB is unknown, you must
!     wildcard the key
RTRA(config)# crypto isakmp key cisco123 address
                            0.0.0.0 0.0.0.0 no-xauth
! This is the crypto ACL
RTRA(config)# ip access-list extended RTRB
RTRA(config-ext-nacl)# permit ip 192.168.1.0 0.0.0.255
                               192.168.2.0 0.0.0.255
RTRA(config-ext-nacl)# exit
! The static route specifies how to reach the remote networks
RTRA(config)# ip route 192.168.2.0 255.255.255.0 192.1.1.20
! Defining the transform set
RTRA(config)# crypto ipsec transform-set RTRBtrans
                          esp-aes esp-md5-hmac
RTRA(cfg-crypto-tran)# exit
! Creating a dynamic crypto map for RTRB
RTRA(config)# crypto dynamic-map dynmap 10
RTRA(config-crypto-map)# set transform-set RTRBtrans
RTRA(config-crypto-map)# match address RTRB
RTRA(config-crypto-map)# exit
! Creating the crypto map entry for the dynamic crypto map
RTRA(config)# crypto map statmap 65000 ipsec-isakmp dynamic dynmap
! Creating the perimeter ACL, allowing only IPSec traffic
! Note that you need to add an entry for the unprotected traffic too
RTRA(config)# ip access-list extended perimeter
RTRA(config-ext-nacl)# permit udp host 193.1.1.20
                                host 192.1.1.40 eq 500
RTRA(config-ext-nacl)# permit esp host 193.1.1.20 host 192.1.1.40
RTRA(config-ext-nacl)# permit ip 192.168.2.0 0.0.0.255
                               192.168.1.0 0.0.0.255
RTRA(config-ext-nacl)# deny ip any any
RTRA(config-ext-nacl)# exit
! Activating the inbound ACL and crypto map on the external interface
RTRA(config)# interface Ethernet0/0
RTRA(config-if)# ip address 192.1.1.40 255.255.255.0
RTRA(config-if)# crypto map statmap
```

RTRB's configuration (Example 17-7) is very similar to that previously done in Example 17-3 with a static crypto map. Since RTRB knows RTRA's address, a specific pre-shared key with a corresponding address is used and a static crypto map is used.

Example 17-7 *Dynamic Crypto Map Example: RTRB*

```
RTRB(config)# crypto isakmp enable
RTRB(config)# crypto isakmp identity address
RTRB(config)# crypto isakmp policy 10
RTRB(config-isakmp)# encryption aes 128
RTRB(config-isakmp)# hash md5
RTRB(config-isakmp)# authentication pre-share
RTRB(config-isakmp)# group 2
RTRB(config-isakmp)# exit
```

continues

Example 17-7 *Dynamic Crypto Map Example: RTRB (Continued)*

```
! Since the peer's address is known, a specific address
!        is given for the key
RTRB(config)# crypto isakmp key cisco123 address
                            192.1.1.40 255.255.255.255 no-xauth
RTRB(config)# ip access-list extended RTRA
RTRB(config-ext-nacl)# permit ip 192.168.2.0 0.0.0.255
                              192.168.1.0 0.0.0.255
RTRB(config-ext-nacl)# exit
RTRB(config)# ip route 192.168.1.0 255.255.255.0 193.1.1.1
RTRB(config)# crypto ipsec transform-set RTRAtrans
                            esp-aes esp-md5-hmac
RTRB(cfg-crypto-tran)# exit
RTRB(config)# crypto map mymap 10 ipsec-isakmp
RTRB(config-crypto-m)# set peer 192.1.1.40
RTRB(config-crypto-m)# set transform-set RTRAtrans
RTRB(config-crypto-m)# match address RTRA
RTRB(config-crypto-m)# exit
RTRB(config)# ip access-list extended perimeter
RTRB(config-ext-nacl)# permit udp host 192.1.1.40
                                host 193.1.1.20 eq 500
RTRB(config-ext-nacl)# permit esp host 192.1.1.40 host 193.1.1.20
RTRB(config-ext-nacl)# permit ip 192.168.1.0 0.0.0.255
                              192.168.2.0 0.0.0.255
RTRB(config-ext-nacl)# deny ip any any
RTRB(config-ext-nacl)# exit
! Getting an address via DHCP
RTRB(config)# interface Ethernet0/0
RTRB(config-if)# ip address dhcp
RTRB(config-if)# ip access-group perimeter in
RTRB(config-if)# crypto map mymap
```

Configuring Tunnel Endpoint Discovery with Dynamic Crypto Maps

Using static crypto maps presents one problem: as you add more and more peers to your configuration, management becomes a real burden. Dynamic crypto maps, as I described in the last section, are restricted in that only one of the two peers can initiate the connection (the one with the strictly static map configuration).

Tunnel Endpoint Discovery (TED) is a Cisco-proprietary feature developed to deal with these problems. TED allows routers to discover IPsec endpoints and their configurations automatically, reducing the amount of configuration you have to perform on your routers.

TED Process

I'll use Figure 17-1, shown previously, to illustrate how TED works.

1 Assume that PCB sends a packet to PCA. RTRB receives the packet and doesn't currently have an IPsec SA established, but the packet does match a **permit** statement in a crypto ACL. RTRB drops the packet, but sends a TED probe to determine who

the remote peer is to RTRA. The TED probe contains the IP address of RTRB and is sent across the network in clear text.

2   When RTRA receives the TED probe, it drops it because it isn't protected, but sends back a TED reply with the IP address of itself in the reply packet.

3   After RTRB receives the reply, it now knows the IP address of RTRA and can initiate an ISAKMP/IKE Phase 1 connection.

If you had 100 peers and used a static crypto map configuration and wanted to fully mesh the network, each router would need 99 entries in a static crypto map. And as you added more and more peers, this quickly would become unmanageable. Likewise, dynamic crypto maps work only in a hub-and-spoke design; fully meshing them is impossible because either peer might need to initiate a connection, which presents a dilemma as to which peer should have the static configuration and which peer the dynamic configuration.

With TED, only a single dynamic crypto map with the TED feature needs to be created because the peers will be discovered dynamically. Therefore, static crypto maps are not needed. TED has the following restrictions, however:

- It is Cisco-proprietary and will work only with IOS routers.
- It works only with dynamic crypto maps.
- Because the peer IP addresses are embedded in the payloads of TED discovery probes, this causes TED to fail when performing address translation.
- TED simplifies the configuration of the routers by providing a discovery process; it does not provide any scalability advantages as to managing many connections with many L2L peers.
- It increases the amount of time to set up an IPsec session because a discovery phase must take place first.
- The routers' IP addresses must be in the same subnet (one hop away), limiting TED's usefulness to private WAN networks; plus the destinations that you want to reach must be in your router's routing table.
- The crypto ACL used for TED in the crypto map can specify only the IP protocol (**ip** parameter) in TEDv1 and v2; other protocols, such as TCP, UDP, ICMP, and others, cannot be specified; TEDv3 removes this restriction.

TED Configuration

To configure TED, first you must create a dynamic crypto map. These commands were discussed in the "Creating a Dynamic Crypto Map" section. There are two required commands you must configure for the dynamic crypto map entry: **set transform-set** (defines how to protect the traffic) and **match address** (defines what traffic is to be protected).

Once you've built your dynamic crypto map, you need to reference it in a static crypto map using the following command:

```
Router(config)# crypto map static_map_name seq_# ipsec-isakmp
                      dynamic dynamic_map_name discover
```

Notice that this command is almost like the one in the "Using a Dynamic Crypto Map" section, which specifies a dynamic crypto map. The only difference with this command is the **discover** parameter, which enables TED.

TED Example

Setting up TED is fairly straightforward. The network shown in Figure 17-2 illustrates the configuration of TED. Because TED doesn't work across networks with multiple hops, like the Internet, assume that RTRA and RTRB are connected via a dedicated serial connection, but this could easily be Frame Relay or ATM.

Example 17-8 shows RTRA's configuration and 17-9 shows RTRB's configuration. The configuration of the two routers is very similar. I'll point out a few interesting things about this configuration. First, because pre-shared keys are used and the IP addresses of the peers are unknown, I've wildcarded the key. Of course, in this instance, you could easily hard-code the addresses; but if you had 200 or 300 peers, this would not be practical. Instead, in this situation, I'd recommend the use of certificates. I used static routes so that the two routers can learn the remote destinations; however, in a large WAN deployment, you'd probably use a dynamic routing protocol. If this is the case, you'd have to change the perimeter ACL to allow routing traffic to enter your router.

Figure 17-2 *Simple WAN Network Using TED*

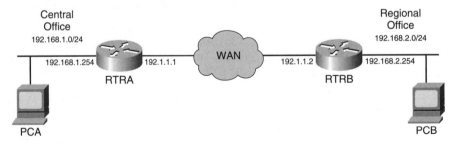

Example 17-8 *TED Configuration on RTRA*

```
! Enabling ISAKMP and defining the management connection policy
RTRA(config)# crypto isakmp enable
RTRA(config)# crypto isakmp identity address
RTRA(config)# crypto isakmp policy 10
RTRA(config-isakmp)# encryption aes 128
RTRA(config-isakmp)# hash md5
RTRA(config-isakmp)# authentication pre-share
RTRA(config-isakmp)# group 2
RTRA(config-isakmp)# exit
```

Example 17-8 *TED Configuration on RTRA (Continued)*

```
! Using pre-shared keys for authentication
! Because the IP address of TED peer is unknown, you must
!      wildcard the key
RTRA(config)# crypto isakmp key cisco123 address
                              0.0.0.0 0.0.0.0 no-xauth
! This is the crypto ACL
RTRA(config)# ip access-list extended RTRB
RTRA(config-ext-nacl)# permit ip 192.168.1.0 0.0.0.255
                              192.168.2.0 0.0.0.255
RTRA(config-ext-nacl)# exit
! The static route specifies how to reach the remote networks
RTRA(config)# ip route 0.0.0.0 0.0.0.0 192.1.1.2
! Defining the transform set
RTRA(config)# crypto ipsec transform-set RTRB esp-aes esp-md5-hmac
RTRA(cfg-crypto-tran)# exit
! Creating a dynamic crypto map for TED usage
RTRA(config)# crypto dynamic-map dynmap 10
RTRA(config-crypto-map)# set transform-set RTRB
RTRA(config-crypto-map)# match address RTRB
RTRA(config-crypto-map)# exit
! Creating the TED crypto map entry for the dynamic crypto map
RTRA(config)# crypto map statmap 65000 ipsec-isakmp
                              dynamic dynmap discover
! Creating the perimeter ACL, allowing only IPSec traffic
! Note that you need to add an entry for the unprotected traffic too
! Also, I removed the ACL entry for NAT-T, since address translation
!      doesn't work with the TED discovery process
RTRA(config)# ip access-list extended perimeter
! I removed the NAT-T ACL entry since the routers are directly
!      connected to each other
RTRA(config-ext-nacl)# permit udp host 192.1.1.2
                              host 192.1.1.1 eq 500
RTRA(config-ext-nacl)# permit esp host 192.1.1.2 host 192.1.1.1
RTRA(config-ext-nacl)# permit ip 192.168.2.0 0.0.0.255
                              192.168.1.0 0.0.0.255
RTRA(config-ext-nacl)# deny ip any any
RTRA(config-ext-nacl)# exit
! Activating the inbound ACL and crypto map on the external interface
RTRA(config)# interface Serial0/0
RTRA(config-if)# ip address 192.1.1.1 255.255.255.0
RTRA(config-if)# crypto map statmap
```

Example 17-9 *TED Configuration on RTRB*

```
RTRB(config)# crypto isakmp enable
RTRB(config)# crypto isakmp identity address
RTRB(config)# crypto isakmp policy 10
RTRB(config-isakmp)# encryption aes 128
RTRB(config-isakmp)# hash md5
RTRB(config-isakmp)# authentication pre-share
RTRB(config-isakmp)# group 2
RTRB(config-isakmp)# exit
```

continues

Example 17-9 *TED Configuration on RTRB (Continued)*

```
RTRB(config)# crypto isakmp key cisco123 address
                            0.0.0.0 0.0.0.0 no-xauth
RTRB(config)# ip access-list extended RTRA
RTRB(config-ext-nacl)# permit ip 192.168.2.0 0.0.0.255
                                  192.168.1.0 0.0.0.255
RTRB(config-ext-nacl)# exit
RTRB(config)# ip route 0.0.0.0 0.0.0.0 192.1.1.1
RTRB(config)# crypto ipsec transform-set RTRA esp-aes esp-md5-hmac
RTRB(cfg-crypto-tran)# exit
RTRB(config)# crypto dynamic-map dynmap 10
RTRB(config-crypto-map)# set transform-set RTRB
RTRB(config-crypto-map)# match address RTRB
RTRB(config-crypto-map)# exit
RTRB(config)# crypto map statmap 65000 ipsec-isakmp
                            dynamic dynmap discover
RTRB(config)# ip access-list extended perimeter
RTRB(config-ext-nacl)# permit udp host 192.1.1.1
                                  host 192.1.1.2 eq 500
RTRB(config-ext-nacl)# permit esp host 192.1.1.1 host 192.1.1.2
RTRB(config-ext-nacl)# permit ip 192.168.1.0 0.0.0.255
                                  192.168.2.0 0.0.0.255
RTRB(config-ext-nacl)# deny ip any any
RTRB(config-ext-nacl)# exit
RTRB(config)# interface Serial0/0
RTRB(config-if)# ip address 192.1.1.2 255.255.255.0
RTRB(config-if)# ip access-group perimeter in
RTRB(config-if)# crypto map statmap
```

Distinguished Name-Based Crypto Maps

The Distinguished Name-Based crypto map feature, introduced in IOS 12.2(4)T, allows you to restrict access on IPsec interfaces based on information in a user's certificate, especially those certificates that have Distinguished Names (DNs). Without this feature, a router will accept any certificate from an authenticated source; with this feature, you can control which peers you'll allow by examining additional information in the peer's certificate. As an example, you might have an Internet and Extranet connection on your router and you're using certificates for IPsec device authentication. Your SOHO and mobile users use the Internet for making connections to the corporate office while your third-party company uses the Extranet. Your concern is that you want only the third-party company to use the Extranet connection, and not the Internet connection, when establishing IPsec sessions to you. DN-Based crypto maps allow you to implement this type of policy.

Setting Up DN-Based Crypto Maps

Setting up DN-based crypto maps is fairly simple. First, you need to define the criteria to match on in a certificate. Your choices are matching on certificate field information, like the

CN, OU, O, and other certificate fields or the hostname of a peer. To configure DN matching, use these commands:

```
Router(config)# crypto identity DN_policy_name
Router(config-identity)# description descriptive_text
Router(crypto-identity)# dn name=string [,name=string...]
```

The **crypto identity** command creates the policy matching rules. The **description** command allows you to assign a brief description that describes the policy-matching criteria. The **dn** subcommand specifies which fields and values on a certificate to examine for a match. For example, if you want to match on "ou=Developers, o=Cisco" to match a certificate containing these two fields, you can enter multiple **dn** commands within a policy configuration.

To configure hostname matching, use these commands:

```
Router(config)# crypto identity DN_policy_name
Router(config-identity)# description descriptive_text
Router(crypto-identity)# fqdn hostname_or_FQDN
```

The **fqdn** command allows you to enter a FQDN or the domain name that will appear on a certificate, such as "fatcat.cisco.com" or "cisco.com." To view your configured policies, use the **show crypto identity** command.

One you've defined your matching criteria, you have to activate your rules. This is done by applying the matching criteria to a crypto map entry, like this for a static crypto map entry:

```
Router(config)# crypto map map_name seq_# ipsec-isakmp
Router(config-crypto-map)# set identity DN_policy_name
```

or like this for a dynamic crypto map entry:

```
Router(config)# crypto dynamic-map map_name seq_#
Router(config-crypto-map)# set identity DN_policy_name
```

You need to do this process for *each* crypto map entry for a crypto map activated on a particular interface. Once you've configured this feature, if you see the following message for peers with nonmatching criteria, you know that your policy configuration is working:

```
<time>: %CRYPTO-4-IKE_QUICKMODE_BAD_CERT: encrypted connection
        attempted with a peer without the configured certificate
        attributes.
```

Illustrating the Use of DN-Based Crypto Maps

Now that you have a basic understanding for configuring DN-based crypto maps, I'll illustrate the process in Example 17-10. In this example, a router has two external interfaces: one to the Internet and one to an Extranet partner. The router is accepting remote access sessions, using certificates for device authentication. The problem you've been experiencing is that in many instances, the Extranet people are coming through the Internet to reach your company instead of using the directly connected Extranet connection; this is causing bandwidth issues for your Internet connection and you want to halt this practice. Example 17-10 omits some of the basic configuration, such as the ISAKMP/IKE Phase 1 policy, the certificate configuration, perimeter ACL, and so on. Instead, I'll focus on the DN-based crypto map configuration. In this example, I created two policies: "myidentpolicy" and "extidentpolicy." I've also created two dynamic crypto maps with a single entry each, one for each policy. I then created two separate static crypto maps and referenced a dynamic crypto map in them.

Example 17-10 *DN-Based Crypto Map Example*

```
! Transform set for all remote peers
RTRA(config)# crypto ipsec transform-set remote esp-aes esp-sha-hmac
RTRA(cfg-crypto-tran)# exit
! Creating a certificate matching policy for my company
RTRA(config)# crypto identity myidentpolicy
RTRA(config-identity)# description Certificate policy for My Company
RTRA(crypto-identity)# dn o=mycompany
RTRA(crypto-identity)# exit
! Creating a certificate matching policy for the Extranet
RTRA(config)# crypto identity extidentpolicy
RTRA(config-identity)# description Certificate policy for Extranet
RTRA(crypto-identity)# dn o=theircompany
RTRA(crypto-identity)# exit
! Creating a dynamic crypto map for my company's peers
RTRA(config)# crypto dynamic-map mydynmap 10
RTRA(config-crypto-map)# set transform-set remote
RTRA(config-crypto-map)# set identity myidentpolicy
RTRA(config-crypto-map)# exit
!Creating a dynamic crypto map for Extranet peers
RTRA(config)# crypto dynamic-map extdynmap 10
RTRA(config-crypto-map)# set transform-set remote
RTRA(config-crypto-map)# set identity extidentpolicy
RTRA(config-crypto-map)# exit
! Creating the crypto map entry for my company's dynamic crypto map
RTRA(config)# crypto map mystatmap 65000 ipsec-isakmp
                         dynamic mydynmap
! Creating a different crypto map and crypto map entry for Extranet's
    dynamic crypto map
RTRA(config)# crypto map extstatmap 65000 ipsec-isakmp
                         dynamic extdynmap
! Applying my company's static map to the Internet interface
RTRA(config)# interface Ethernet0/0
RTRA(config-if)# description Internet Connection
RTRA(config-if)# ip address 192.1.1.40 255.255.255.0
RTRA(config-if)# crypto map mystatmap
RTRA(config-if)# exit
! Applying the Extranet's static map to the Extranet interface
RTRA(config)# interface Ethernet0/1
RTRA(config-if)# description Extranet Connection
RTRA(config-if)# ip address 192.1.1.40 255.255.255.0
RTRA(config-if)# crypto map extstatmap
```

Viewing and Managing Connections

Now that I've discussed how to build some basic types of L2L connections, I'll focus on how to view and manage these connections using some basic **show, clear**, and **debug** commands in the following two sections.

Viewing IPsec Data SAs

To view your ISAKMP/IKE Phase 2 data SAs, use the following **show** command:

```
Router# show crypto ipsec sa [map crypto_map_name | address |
                             identity | interface interface_type_and_#]
                             [detail]
```

If you don't enter any optional parameters, all data SAs are displayed. The **address** parameter sorts the SAs based on the peers' IP addresses. The **identity** parameter displays a summarized view. You can qualify what data SAs are displayed with additional parameters: the **map** parameter allows you to restrict the SAs displayed to the crypto map specified, whereas the **interface** parameter restricts the displayed SAs to those terminated on the specified interface. The **detail** parameter also will display send and receive error counter statistics.

Example 17-11 illustrates the use of this command. In this example, the *local ident* and *remote ident* specifies the traffic to be protected based on the crypto ACL. The *current peer* specifies the remote peer's address. The first two *#pkts* lines specify the number of IPsec packets encapsulated and deencapsulated, encrypted and decrypted, hashed and verified. Below this are the inbound and outbound SAs. Because only ESP is used for the data connections, only two SAs are seen (*inbound esp sas* and *outbound esp sas*). In both cases, the SAs are protected by AES-128 and MD5. AH and PCP (compression) are not used and thus no SAs for these exist.

Example 17-11 *Using the* **show crypto ipsec sa** *Command*

```
r3640# show crypto ipsec sa
interface: Ethernet0/0
    Crypto map tag: mymap, local addr 192.1.1.40
    protected vrf: (none)
    local  ident (addr/mask/prot/port): (192.168.1.0/255.255.255.0/0/0)
    remote ident (addr/mask/prot/port): (192.168.2.0/255.255.255.0/0/0)
    current_peer 192.1.1.20 port 500
      PERMIT, flags={origin_is_acl,}
     #pkts encaps: 5, #pkts encrypt: 5, #pkts digest: 5
     #pkts decaps: 5, #pkts decrypt: 5, #pkts verify: 5
     #pkts compressed: 0, #pkts decompressed: 0
     #pkts not compressed: 0, #pkts compr. failed: 0
     #pkts not decompressed: 0, #pkts decompress failed: 0
     #send errors 0, #recv errors 0

      local crypto endpt.: 192.1.1.40, remote crypto endpt.: 192.1.1.20
      path mtu 1500, ip mtu 1500
      current outbound spi: 0xED39B285(3979981445)

      inbound esp sas:
       spi: 0x5B5A20FC(1532633340)
         transform: esp-aes esp-md5-hmac ,
         in use settings ={Tunnel, }
         conn id: 3001, flow_id: SW:1, crypto map: mymap
         sa timing: remaining key lifetime (k/sec): (4458063/3572)
```

continues

Example 17-11 *Using the* **show crypto ipsec sa** *Command (Continued)*

```
         IV size: 16 bytes
         replay detection support: Y
         Status: ACTIVE
   inbound ah sas:
   inbound pcp sas:
   outbound esp sas:
    spi: 0xED39B285(3979981445)
       transform: esp-aes esp-md5-hmac ,
       in use settings ={Tunnel, }
       conn id: 3002, flow_id: SW:2, crypto map: mymap
       sa timing: remaining key lifetime (k/sec): (4458063/3570)
       IV size: 16 bytes
       replay detection support: Y
       Status: ACTIVE
   outbound ah sas:
   outbound pcp sas:
```

Managing IPsec Data SAs

Whenever you make changes to things such as crypto ACLs, transform sets, and other information related to an entry or entries in a crypto map, any existing data SAs built with this information are not updated automatically; you either have to wait for the data SA to expire, or tear them down manually to be rebuilt with the updated information. To tear down a data SA or SAs manually, use the following command:

```
Router# clear crypto sa [peer IP_address | map crypto_map_name |
                        spi IP_address protocol SPI_# | counters]
```

If you don't specify any optional parameters, all data SAs are cleared on the router. To clear data SAs used with a specific remote peer, enter the **peer** parameter. To clear all data SAs associated with a particular crypto map, use the map parameter. To remove a specific SA based on a peer's IP address, data encapsulation protocol (AH or ESP), and SPI number, use the **spi** parameter. The **counters** parameter resets the statistical counters displayed in the **show crypto ipsec sa** command, like the *#pkts* information shown previously in Example 17-11.

The main **debug** command used to troubleshoot the setup of data SAs is **debug crypto ipsec**—I'll discuss this command in more depth in Chapter 19, "Troubleshooting Router Connections."

Issues with Site-to-Site Connections

As you can see from the previous section, setting up L2L sessions on a router is a little more difficult than setting them up on a concentrator; but the configuration process is still fairly straightforward. However, there can be a handful of issues that you'll need to deal with when setting up and using L2L sessions, including:

- Migration to an IPsec-based design
- Filtering of IPsec traffic

- Address translation usage
- Non-unicast traffic
- Configuration simplification
- IPsec Redundancy
- Scalability

The following sections will cover each of these issues and explain solutions you can use to help you with your IPsec implementation.

Migration to an IPsec-Based Design

One issue you might have when implementing a large number of IPsec L2L sessions is that data won't transfer if only one peer is configured with IPsec, or if IPsec is misconfigured. To alleviate these problems, Cisco introduced the IPsec Passive Mode feature in IOS 12.2(13)T. IPsec Passive Mode allows a router to accept both encrypted and unencrypted traffic that matches a crypto ACL. Routers will attempt to negotiate a protected session, if specified. If they are successful, they'll protect the traffic before sending it; otherwise, they'll forward the traffic unencrypted.

IPsec Passive Mode Process

When a router configured for IPsec Passive Mode receives a packet that needs to be sent to a peer using IPsec to protect it, the router will try to establish an SA to the peer. The router waits 10 seconds for a tunnel to be established. Within the 10 seconds, the router will drop any packets that need to be forwarded to the remote peer if it cannot buffer them up while waiting for an SA to be established; after 10 seconds, if no SA can be established, packets will be forwarded to the remote peer in clear text. When the latter happens, the router will generate a warning message indicating that IPsec Passive Mode is being used:

```
Unencrypted traffic is sent to X.X.X.X because crypto optional
    is configured
```

$X.X.X.X$ is the IP address of the remote peer. If an SA can be established, the SA is used to protect the packet before forwarding it to the remote peer. If the router receives unprotected traffic from the remote peer, the following message is displayed:

```
Unencrypted traffic is received from X.X.X.X because crypto optional
    is configured
```

Both messages are rate-limited to ensure that they don't waste resources on the router; by default, they are generated once a minute no matter how many instances of the two processes have occurred.

TIP   Look for the above messages in your router's log output. These messages tell you of peers that either haven't been configured or have been configured incorrectly.

IPsec Passive Mode Configuration

You can configure two commands to enable and tune IPsec Passive Mode. To enable it, use the following command:

```
Router(config)# crypto ipsec optional
```

Once it is enabled, the following message is displayed every 10 minutes in the router's logs, reminding you that IPsec Passive Mode is enabled:

```
Security warning: crypto ipsec optional is configured
```

There is no way to disable this log message.

When the router has to forward traffic in clear text to a destination because an SA cannot be established, the router will continually try to bring up the SA. By default, this time interval is once every 300 seconds (5 minutes), but can be changed with the following command:

```
Router(config)# crypto ipsec optional retry seconds
```

CAUTION Because a router will accept unprotected traffic that matches a crypto ACL when IPsec Passive Mode is enabled, or forward traffic that should be protected in an unprotected fashion, I typically do not use this feature because of security issues that can arise. For example, if you enable this feature and forget to disable it, traffic could be passing between peers unprotected. Therefore, if you must use this to maintain connectivity, remember to disable the feature when everything is upgraded, configured, and working correctly!

Filtering of IPsec Traffic

As mentioned earlier in the "Defining Protected Traffic: Crypto ACLs" section, when IPsec traffic is received on a router's interface where a crypto map and an interface ACL have been activated, the protected traffic is processed by the ACL, processed by the crypto map and decrypted, and then the clear-text traffic is processed again by the ACL. The main problem with this approach is that:

- The ACL is processed twice, putting a larger burden on the router.
- There is no easy mechanism of filtering traffic for a particular SA without creating extensive crypto ACLs and duplicating this within an external ACL.

In IOS 12.3(8)T Cisco introduced the Crypto Access Check on Clear-Text Packets feature (I'll abbreviate this to CACCTP). CACCTP allows you to solve both of these problems; however, the feature currently doesn't work on the VPN Service Module for the Catalyst 6500 switches and 7600 routers.

CACCTP Feature

With the CACCTP feature, the router no longer runs the decrypted packets through a second ACL check with the external interface's ACL. This is also true of outbound packets; clear-text packets won't be checked against an outgoing ACL before the crypto map is applied. Only inbound encrypted packets are checked against the inbound external ACL and outbound encrypted packets are checked against the outbound external ACL. This feature makes it easier to configure your ACLs and reduces the overhead of double-processing on the router.

This feature is similar to the IPsec bypass feature that PIX and ASA security appliances support. However, one concern you may have is what traffic actually is allowed to traverse the data SAs. For example, you might have a crypto ACL that specifies that all traffic between 192.168.1.0/24 and 192.168.2.0/24 should be protected; however, you don't want traffic from 192.168.1.10 sending anything to 192.168.2.20. You could do this easily by creating a crypto ACL that has a **deny** statement first for the host-to-host matching, and then a **permit** statement for the two networks. However, I have experienced problems in various IOS versions where if a packet can match against more than one statement in a crypto ACL, the crypto ACL fails to function correctly. Therefore, to solve this problem, CACCTP allows you to apply an ACL to a data SA, restricting the traffic that can flow across it.

NOTE	If you don't configure CACCTP, any traffic specified in the crypto ACL is allowed to be sent across and received from the corresponding data SAs.

CACCTP Configuration

To implement CACCTP, you first need to ensure that IPsec traffic is allowed inbound and outbound on any external interface ACLs: ISAKMP (UDP port 500); ESP (protocol 50); AH, if it's being used (protocol 51); and, possibly, NAT-T (UDP port 4,500).

When you upgrade your router to IOS 12.3(8)T, your router no longer will perform double-ACL processing; therefore, you can go ahead and remove any entries in your external ACL that you used for double-ACL processing. Or, if you need to filter traffic traversing a data SA that your crypto ACL would permit, by default, you can use the following configuration for a crypto map entry:

```
Router(config)# crypto map map_name seq_# {ipsec-isakmp | ipsec-manual}
Router(config-crypto-map)# set ip access-group
                            {ACL_# | ACL_name} {in | out}
```

The **set ip access-group** command allows you to specify a named or numbered ACL that you want to be applied to data SAs built with the crypto map; you can apply the ACL inbound or outbound on the data SAs. For that matter, you can use the command twice with different ACLs, filtering traffic on both unidirectional data connections for the IPsec session to the remote peer. The **in** parameter specifies that after an inbound packet has been decrypted, it will then have the corresponding SA ACL checked against it; the **out** parameter specifies that before the packet is protected, it is first verified with the corresponding SA ACL. The **show [ip] access-list** command can be used to verify your CACCTP ACLs and the **show crypto map** command can be used to verify that CACCTP has been enabled for a particular crypto map entry.

NOTE   Even though the above command illustration shows the use of a static crypto map, you can *also* apply CACCTP to dynamic crypto map entries. Also, if you downgrade your router to a version earlier than 12.3(8)T, double ACL filtering once again will be performed. So you'll need to duplicate the crypto ACL entries in your external ACLs again when downgrading.

Example Configuring CACCTP

To help illustrate the use of CACCTP, I'll use Figure 17-1 and the previous configuration in Example 17-3, which set up a simple L2L session between RTRA and RTRB using a static crypto map entry. In this example, the two routers are running 12.3(8)T; therefore double ACL checking is not used. Also, I want to restrict access between the two sites by denying 192.168.1.10 to access 192.168.2.20 via Telnet and HTTP; all other traffic should be permitted across the IPsec tunnel. Instead of repeating the entire configuration for the two routers, I'll just focus on the changes that need to be made to set up this configuration (see Example 17-12).

Example 17-12 *Using CACCTP*

```
RTRA(config)# ip access-list extended perimeter
! Removing the crypto ACL entry from the external ACL
RTRA(config-ext-nacl)# no permit ip 192.168.1.0 0.0.0.255
                                   192.168.2.0 0.0.0.255
RTRA(config-ext-nacl)# exit
! Building the SA filtering ACL
RTRA(config)# ip access-list extended RTRB_ACL
RTRA(config-ext-nacl)# deny tcp host 192.168.1.10
                                host 192.168.2.20 eq 23
RTRA(config-ext-nacl)# deny tcp host 192.168.1.10
                                host 192.168.2.20 eq 80
RTRA(config-ext-nacl)# permit ip any any
RTRA(config-ext-nacl)# exit
RTRA(config)# crypto map mymap 10 ipsec-isakmp
! Applying the SA filtering ACL for teh peer connection
RTRA(config-crypto-map)# set ip access-group RTRB_ACL out
RTRA(config-crypto-m)# end
! Clearing any data SAs so that they use the new policy
RTRA# clear crypto sa peer 193.1.1.20
```

First, I'm removing the crypto ACL entry from the perimeter ACL that was required prior to 12.3(8)T for double-ACL processing. Second, I'm creating an ACL to deny Telnet and HTTP traffic from 192.168.1.10 to 192.168.2.20, but allowing everything else. Third, I'm applying this setting to the crypto map entry for the L2L session. Last, I'm clearing the current data SAs so that the new policy will be used.

Address Translation and Stateful Firewalls

As mentioned in Chapter 3, "IPsec," address translation devices performing NAT or PAT break AH connectivity, whereas devices performing PAT break ESP. Likewise, stateful firewalls typically support only TCP and UDP as protocols, not ESP and AH. I'll discuss two router issues when dealing with address translation and two corresponding solutions to these problems:

- Moving traffic through address translation devices or firewalls: NAT Transparency (NAT-T)
- Moving traffic through a router performing address translation function: ESP through NAT

NAT Transparency

As discussed in Chapter 3, Cisco developed three solutions to move traffic through a PAT device or a stateful firewall: NAT-T, IPsec over UDP, and IPsec over TCP. Cisco VPN 3000 concentrators support all three types; however, Cisco routers support only NAT-T. NAT-T encapsulates an ESP packet in a UDP payload, which can traverse an address translation device performing NAT or PAT easily.

TIP   NAT-T does have one main limitation: IKE matching on IP addresses for pre-shared keys must match on the translated address for a pre-shared key match to be found; in this instance, you might want to use hostnames or FQDNs for the specification of pre-shared keys or use digital certificates.

NAT-T on a Router

NAT-T was introduced in IOS 12.2(13)T. Assuming you have this version or higher installed on your router, NAT-T is enabled automatically. Once ISAKMP/IKE Phase 1 completes and before ISAKMP/IKE Phase 2 begins, the two peers will exchange a vendor identification string packet indicating that NAT-T is supported. Once this is done, a detection process takes place to determine if address translation is occurring between the two peers. This is done by creating a packet with a hash (where the packet includes the local address of the local peer) and transmitting to the remote peer; the remote peer will then validate the hash.

If the hash is invalid, the remote peer will notify the local peer that NAT-T needs to be used; the included local address is also compared with the IP address in the outside IP header. If the hash is valid, the remote peer will repeat the test in the backward direction to the remote peer.

NAT Keepalives

There is no required configuration of NAT-T. If you have IOS 12.2(13)T installed, your router can already use it. The only concern is that if the data SAs are idle for a period of time, the translation entry in the translation table of the address translation device could expire, causing a subsequent sending of data across the SA to fail. To solve this problem, Cisco added the NAT keepalive feature in IOS 12.2(13)T. This feature has a router send an unencrypted UDP packet with a one-byte payload to the remote peer periodically; this causes the translation device to reset the idle timer for the entry in its address translation table. To enable NAT keepalives, use the following command:

```
Router(config)# crypto isakmp nat keepalive seconds
```

The number of seconds can range from 5–3,600. When picking a value, you want to make sure that it is smaller than the UDP session idle timer for the address translation device. For example, if a Cisco router was performing address translation, the default idle timer for UDP sessions is 600 seconds; for a PIX firewall, it defaults to 10,800 seconds (3 hours). If a Cisco router was performing a stateful firewall function, an idle UDP entry would remain in the state table for up to 30 seconds before expiring; a PIX firewall maintains an idle UDP session for two minutes, by default. The **show crypto ipsec sa** command will display the NAT keepalive timer, if configured.

TIP   Because of all of these varying factors for maintaining UDP connections by an address translation or stateful firewall device, I recommend that you set the NAT keepalive interval to something between 10–20 seconds. I've seen some cases with CheckPoint firewalls where I've had to use a keepalive value of 10 seconds. Also, remember to enable Dead Peer Detection (DPD) for the management connection to ensure that it does not remain idle and therefore removed from a connection table in a stateful firewall. I discussed the configuration of DPD in the last chapter, "Router ISAKMP/IKE Phase 1 Connectivity."

ESP Through NAT

The second issue related to the use of ESP is that your router might be set up as an address translation device performing PAT and might need to translate packets. In this situation, the router itself typically is not the VPN termination point, but some other device behind it, like a VPN 3000 concentrator or a client, is. The issue here is that ESP doesn't contain port numbers and would not be translated going through the router; thus the remote endpoint wouldn't know how to return traffic because address translation hadn't been performed.

ESP Through NAT Phase 1 Feature

Cisco has two phases for implementing the ESP through NAT feature. Beginning with IOS 12.2(13)T, Cisco introduced the ESP Through NAT Phase 1 feature. Phase 1 allows a router performing PAT to handle ESP connections through it. The configuration of it is done through a static translation:

```
Router(config)# ip nat [inside | outside] source static
                       local_IP_address global_IP_address
```

The *local_IP_address* is what the device is actually using and the *global_IP_address* is what it will be translated to.

NOTE   The details of the configuration of address translation on a router are beyond the scope of this book. For more information on this topic, see my *Cisco Router Firewall Security* book, published by Cisco Press (ISBN: 1587051753).

ESP Through NAT Phase 2 Feature

Beginning with IOS 12.2(15)T, Cisco introduced the ESP through NAT Phase 2 feature. The main problems that ESP through NAT Phase 1 doesn't address are:

- For ISAKMP/IKE Phase 1 management connections, some devices require that both the source and destination port be 500, where an address translation device might change the source port from 500 to something else.

- ESP through NAT Phase 1 requires the use of static translations. This isn't a problem with L2L sessions because you should easily be able to figure out the IP address of the local L2L peer; however, for remote access clients that acquire their addresses dynamically behind the router, Phase 1 doesn't provide a scalable solution.

ESP through NAT Phase 2 can deal with both of these issues.

Preserving Port 500

If you have a router performing PAT translation, you can disable PAT translation on source or destination ports in ISAKMP/IKE management connections (leaving them as 500), with the following configuration:

```
Router(config)# ip nat service list standard_ACL_#_or_name
                       ike preserve-port
```

The standard ACL you specify includes the IP addresses (untranslated) that should not have their source or destination UDP ports for the ISAKMP/IKE Phase 1 management connections changed from 500 to something else. When configured, the router uses an internal method of differentiating multiple ISAKMP/IKE Phase 1 management connections.

NOTE   Normally, preserving a source port number of 500 for ISAKMP/IKE Phase 1 management connections is necessary only for those devices that require it. Cisco devices can use any port number for initiating the management connection, but will always use 500 for the destination port. Therefore, if all your IPsec devices are Cisco devices, you won't need to configure the Preserving Port 500 feature.

ESP SPI Matching

The ESP SPI matching feature allows you to move ESP packets through an IOS router performing PAT without having to encapsulate the ESP packets in a UDP payload. With this feature, you can use either static or dynamic translations on your address translation router. To implement ESP SPI matching, you'll need to configure this feature on the address translation router and both IPsec endpoints, which means that your endpoints are probably Cisco routers. When enabled, SPI matching has the address translation device use the SPI value to uniquely identify different ESP SAs. To enable ESP SPI matching on the address translation router, configure the following command along with the rest of your address translation commands:

```
Router(config)# ip nat service list standard_ACL_#_or_name
                esp spi-match
```

In the standard ACL, you need to specify the IPsec endpoints that will be involved in the SPI matching process. If you're not sure of the IP addresses of the devices, because they might be remote access clients, you might need to be promiscuous in listing the addresses in question.

For the IPsec endpoints, you'll need to configure the following command:

```
Router(config)# crypto ipsec nat-transparency spi-matching
```

By using this command, you are disabling the use of NAT-T.

TIP   The advantage of using SPI matching, when possible, is that you're not adding overhead to the process by having to use ESP encapsulated within UDP. However, if you cannot get this to work through your address translation device, reset the two endpoint routers with these two commands: **no crypto ipsec nat-transparency spi-matching** and **crypto ipsec nat-transparency udp-encapsulation**. I've personally experienced problems on multiple IOS images with the SPI matching feature and thus am somewhat leery about using it. But if you are concerned about the UDP encapsulation overhead, first try to implement SPI matching; and if that doesn't work, then use NAT-T.

Non-Unicast Traffic

One of the problems with IPsec is that it only supports unicast traffic; multicasts and broadcasts will not traverse a data SA. The most common solution to this problem is to encapsulate a multicast or broadcast packet into a unicast packet, which IPsec can deal with. Cisco refers to this process as Generic Route Encapsulation (GRE) tunneling. I discussed this topic briefly in Chapter 1, "Overview of VPNs." GRE is a Layer-3 transport protocol that allows you to encapsulate other protocols, such as IP, IPX, AppleTalk, and others, in a different IP unicast packet.

Originally, GRE was developed to move non-IP traffic across an IP backbone. It was never meant to be part of a VPN solution because it lacked security. However, someone at Cisco figured out that GRE can be used along with IPsec. GRE handles the transport of broadcast, multicast, and non-IP packets, and IPsec provides the protection in a unicast framework.

GRE Tunneling Overview

GRE encapsulates an original entire packet within another packet. Cisco implements this feature by creating a tunnel (virtual/logical) interface to handle this process. This tunnel interface is not tied to any physical interface or protocols, but is used to handle the encapsulation process. Figure 17-3 illustrates this process.

Figure 17-3 *GRE Example*

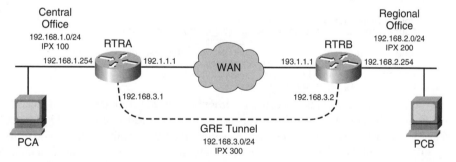

In this example, there are three reachability issues:

- Both networks run IP and IPX.
- Both networks would like to run a dynamic routing protocol to learn about the networks on the two sites.
- Traffic needs to be protected between the two sites.

To solve the first two problems, a GRE tunnel is set up between the two sites. As in an IPsec session, a GRE tunnel is a logical connection. As you can see from Figure 17-3, a logical network (IP 192.168.3.0/24 and IPX 300) provides the logical connection between the two routers. You easily could add additional Layer-3 protocols to this configuration by configuring the tunnel interface with the Layer-3 protocol information. For IP routing, you would need to include the 192.168.3.0/24 network in the IP routing process with a **network** statement. The GRE tunnel is unique in that not just broadcast, multicast, and non-IP traffic would traverse this tunnel, but also unicast IP traffic. Finally, to protect the traffic, you would specify that the GRE packets themselves be protected. In other words, your crypto ACL would have to specify only the GRE packets between RTRA and RTRB, making the configuration of the crypto ACL fairly simple. And if you didn't want traffic to traverse the GRE tunnel, you could easily apply an ACL to the GRE tunnel interface to filter it.

GRE Tunnel Configuration

Setting up a GRE tunnel is one of the simpler things to do on a Cisco router. The following are configured to set up a tunnel:

- Defining the tunnel interface: **interface tunnel** (required)
- Source IP address of the tunneled packet: **tunnel source** (required)
- Destination IP address of the tunneled packet: **tunnel destination** (required)
- Encapsulation method of the tunnel: **tunnel mode** (optional)
- Keepalives: **keepalive** (optional)

There are other GRE tunnel commands, but these are the ones you would configure for sending GRE tunneled traffic through an IPsec tunnel. Here is the syntax of these commands:

```
Router(config)# interface tunnel port_#
Router(config-if)# tunnel source {IP_address_on_router|
                    interface_name_on_router}
Router(config-if)# tunnel destination {IP_address_of_dst_router |
                    name_of_dst_router}
Router(config-if)# keepalive [seconds [retries]]
Router(config-if)# tunnel mode mode
```

To create the tunnel interface, use the **interface tunnel** command. When creating the tunnel, the tunnel automatically comes up: the **no shutdown** command is not necessary. The **tunnel** source command specifies which IP address on the router should be used in the IP header of the GRE packet; you can specify the IP address or name of an interface on the local router. The **tunnel destination** command specifies the IP address or name of the destination router where the tunnel will terminate (this address appears in the destination IP address field of the GRE header). Note that the source and destination addresses are addresses of loopback or physical router interfaces, not the tunnel interface(s) themselves. Of the GRE tunnel configuration, these are the only three required commands.

The **keepalive** command, which allows you to send keepalives across a GRE tunnel (encapsulated in a GRE packet), was introduced in IOS 12.2(8)T and incorporated into 12.0(23)S. Using this feature, you can determine if a tunnel endpoint is reachable, and if not, use another path to the destination, if available. You can configure this from one or both sides of the tunnel. In a hub-and-spoke configuration, where you have redundancy at the hub, this configuration typically is done on the spoke devices. By default, keepalives are disabled. If you enter the **keepalive** command without any parameters, the number of seconds between keepalives defaults to 10 (can be 1–32,767) and the retry interval defaults to 3 (can be 1–255). Once configured, you can verify that keepalives are being sent and received with the **show interfaces** command.

TIP   To ensure that a small number of dropped keepalives doesn't bring a tunnel down in a nonredundant configuration, make sure you increase the number of retries for keepalives. However, this can cause increased latency if you have a redundant configuration. I typically set the periodic interval to 5 seconds and the retry interval to 6 if there is no redundancy. When redundancy exists, I usually set the periodic interval to 5 seconds and the retry count to 3, meaning that in the worse case, it would take 15 seconds to cut over to a redundant path.

The **tunnel mode** command specifies the encapsulation method to use for the tunnel; if you omit the mode, it defaults to GRE (**gre ip**). The term GRE can be somewhat misleading because this type of tunnel supports multiple encapsulation types, one of which is GRE. In most instances, especially if you need to carry multiple protocols such as IP and IPX, you'd use this mode. I'll discuss one other mode, **gre multipoint**, and some other GRE tunnel commands, when I discuss DMVPNs later in the "Scalability" section.

NOTE   Please note that you cannot have two GRE tunnels with the same encapsulation mode and same source/destination address pairings; if this is necessary, you would need to use a different source interface on the router, such as a loopback interface, that has a different IP address.

GRE Tunnel and OSPF Example Protected with IPsec

Now that you have a basic understanding of setting up a GRE tunnel, I'll illustrate an example where OSPF is to be used between two sites for an IPsec tunnel (shown previously in Figure 17-3).

TIP   When tunneling GRE traffic across an IPsec VPN, I highly recommend that you configure the GRE tunnel first and verify that traffic flows across it to the remote peer. Once you know this works, then use IPsec to protect the GRE tunneled traffic.

Examples 17-13 and 17-14 show the GRE and OSPF configuration of the two routers. You need IP addressing on the GRE tunnel interface to pass IP traffic across it. In my example, I used the 192.168.3.x address for the two peers. However, you easily could have used the

IP unnumbered feature (I don't like using the latter feature because of issues it can create when troubleshooting problems). Notice that for the source IP address of the GRE tunnel, I'm using the external interface address of the router. I also didn't configure GRE keep-alives on the tunnel because OSPF hellos are generated every 10 seconds; this should bring the tunnel up and keep it up. If I was using static routers, I would then use the **keepalive** command. With the OSPF configuration, the OSPF backbone is located at the corporate office and the GRE tunnel link and other networks at RTRB are in area 1.

Example 17-13 *RTRA's GRE and OSPF Configuration*

```
RTRA(config)# interface Tunnel0
RTRA(config-if)# ip address 192.168.3.1 255.255.255.0
RTRA(config-if)# tunnel source 192.1.1.1
RTRA(config-if)# tunnel destination 193.1.1.1
RTRA(config-if)# exit
RTRA(config)# interface Ethernet0/1
RTRA(config-if)# ip address 192.168.1.254 255.255.255.0
RTRA(config-if)# no shutdown
RTRA(config)# interface Ethernet0/0
RTRA(config-if)# ip address 192.1.1.1 255.255.255.0
RTRA(config-if)# ip access-group perimeter in
RTRA(config-if)# no shutdown
RTRA(config-if)# exit
RTRA(config)# router ospf 1
RTRA(config-router)# network 192.168.1.0 0.0.0.255 area 0
RTRA(config-router)# network 192.168.3.0 0.0.0.255 area 1
RTRA(config-router)# exit
RTRA(config)# ip route 0.0.0.0 0.0.0.0 192.1.1.2
RTRA(config)# ip access-list extended perimeter
RTRA(config-ext-nacl)# permit udp host 193.1.1.1 host 192.1.1.1 eq 500
RTRA(config-ext-nacl)# permit esp host 193.1.1.1 host 192.1.1.1
RTRA(config-ext-nacl)# permit gre host 193.1.1.1 host 192.1.1.1
RTRA(config-ext-nacl)# deny ip any any
```

Example 17-14 *RTRB's GRE and OSPF Configuration*

```
RTRB(config)# interface Tunnel0
RTRB(config-if)# ip address 192.168.3.2 255.255.255.0
RTRB(config-if)# tunnel source 193.1.1.1
RTRB(config-if)# tunnel destination 192.1.1.1
RTRB(config-if)# exit
RTRB(config)# interface Ethernet0/1
RTRB(config-if)# ip address 192.168.2.254 255.255.255.0
RTRB(config-if)# no shutdown
RTRB(config)# interface Ethernet0/0
RTRB(config-if)# ip address 193.1.1.1 255.255.255.0
RTRB(config-if)# ip access-group perimeter in
RTRB(config-if)# no shutdown
RTRB(config-if)# exit
RTRB(config)# router ospf 1
RTRB(config-router)# network 192.168.2.0 0.0.0.255 area 1
RTRB(config-router)# network 192.168.3.0 0.0.0.255 area 1
```

Example 17-14 *RTRB's GRE and OSPF Configuration (Continued)*

```
RTRB(config-router)# exit
RTRB(config)# ip route 0.0.0.0 0.0.0.0 193.1.1.2
RTRB(config)# ip access-list extended perimeter
RTRB(config-ext-nacl)# permit udp host 192.1.1.1 host 193.1.1.1 eq 500
RTRB(config-ext-nacl)# permit esp host 192.1.1.1 host 193.1.1.1
RTRB(config-ext-nacl)# permit gre host 192.1.1.1 host 193.1.1.1
RTRB(config-ext-nacl)# deny ip any any
```

An extended ACL has been configured to filter inbound traffic on the routers. Notice that I've allowed IPsec traffic and the GRE tunnel traffic; the latter is necessary to test the tunnel. Once I get IPsec up and running, I'll remove the ACL statement for the GRE tunnel traffic. If you are running an IOS version earlier than 12.3(8)T Cisco (before the CACCTP feature), you'll need to keep this statement in the ACL because the ACL is processed twice.

When you are done configuring the two routers with OSPF and the GRE tunnel, verify that you have connectivity between the two by using the **ping** and the **show ip route** commands; if things are working correctly, you should see OSPF routes from the neighboring router from the tunnel interface. Example 17-15 shows an example of RTRB's routing table.

NOTE   Please note that OSPF will not help you in finding the tunnel endpoints, but only the networks behind the two GRE routers.

Example 17-15 *RTRB's Routing Table*

```
RTRB# show ip route
←output omitted→
C    192.1.1.0/24 is directly connected, Ethernet0/0
     192.168.1.0/32 is subnetted, 1 subnets
O IA    192.168.1.254 [110/11112] via 192.168.3.1, 00:04:53, Tunnel0
C    192.168.2.0/24 is directly connected, Ethernet0/1
C    192.168.3.0/24 is directly connected, Tunnel0
S*   0.0.0.0/0 [1/0] via 193.1.1.2
```

Once you have the GRE tunnel working, you're ready to set up IPsec. Examples 17-16 and 17-17 show the configuration for IPsec for routers RTRA and RTRB, respectively. I've created an ISAKMP/IKE Phase 1 policy on each router using pre-shared keys for authentication. I've created a crypto ACL, called "cryptoACL," which specifies that only the GRE tunnel traffic should be protected. This has one advantage: if you're not running 12.3(8)T, the double ACL process only includes GRE between two hosts instead of a range of networks like that shown previously in Examples 17-3 and 17-4.

Example 17-16 *RTRA's IPsec Configuration for a GRE Tunnel*

```
RTRA(config)# crypto isakmp policy 10
RTRA(config-isakmp)# encryption aes 128
RTRA(config-isakmp)# hash sha
RTRA(config-isakmp)# authentication pre-share
RTRA(config-isakmp)# group 2
RTRA(config-isakmp)# exit
RTRA(config)# crypto isakmp key cisco123 address 193.1.1.1 no-xauth
RTRA(config)# ip access-list extended cryptoACL
RTRA(config-ext-nacl)# permit gre host 192.1.1.1 host 193.1.1.1
RTRA(config-ext-nacl)# exit
RTRA(config)# crypto ipsec transform-set RTRtran esp-aes esp-sha-hmac
RTRA(cfg-crypto-trans)# mode transport
RTRA(cfg-crypto-trans)# exit
RTRA(config)# crypto map mymap 10 ipsec-isakmp
RTRA(config-crypto-map)# set peer 193.1.1.1
RTRA(config-crypto-map)# set transform-set RTRtran
RTRA(config-crypto-map)# match address cryptoACL
RTRA(config-crypto-map)# exit
RTRA(config)# interface Ethernet0/0
RTRA(config-if)# crypto map mymap
RTRA(config-if)# exit
RTRA(config)# ip access-list extended perimeter
! Only remove the GRE ACL entry if your IOS is 12.3(8)T or greater
RTRA(config-ext-nacl)# no permit gre host 193.1.1.1 host 192.1.1.1
```

Example 17-17 *RTRB's IPsec Configuration for a GRE Tunnel*

```
RTRB(config)# crypto isakmp policy 10
RTRB(config-isakmp)# encryption aes 128
RTRB(config-isakmp)# hash sha
RTRB(config-isakmp)# authentication pre-share
RTRB(config-isakmp)# group 2
RTRB(config-isakmp)# exit
RTRB(config)# crypto isakmp key cisco123 address 192.1.1.1 no-xauth
RTRB(config)# ip access-list extended cryptoACL
RTRB(config-ext-nacl)# permit gre host 193.1.1.1 host 192.1.1.1
RTRB(config-ext-nacl)# exit
RTRB(config)# crypto ipsec transform-set RTRtran esp-aes esp-sha-hmac
RTRB(cfg-crypto-trans)# mode transport
RTRB(cfg-crypto-trans)# exit
RTRB(config)# crypto map mymap 10 ipsec-isakmp
RTRB(config-crypto-map)# set peer 192.1.1.1
RTRB(config-crypto-map)# set transform-set RTRtran
RTRB(config-crypto-map)# match address cryptoACL
RTRB(config-crypto-map)# exit
RTRB(config)# interface Ethernet0/0
RTRB(config-if)# crypto map mymap
RTRB(config-if)# exit
RTRB(config)# ip access-list extended perimeter
RTRB(config-ext-nacl)# no permit gre host 192.1.1.1 host 193.1.1.1
```

In the preceding examples, note that both routers are using a data transform set that uses AES 128 encryption and the SHA-1 HMAC function. One of the interesting things about the transform is that it is *not using tunnel mode, but transport* mode, because it is a point-to-point connection for the GRE traffic.

NOTE	If you use tunnel mode in a transform for a GRE/IPsec connection, the connection won't work.

The crypto map on each peer includes the destination peer's external interface address, the transform, and the crypto ACL (if you look back to Examples 17-13 and 17-14, you'll notice that the "perimeter" ACL allows IPsec traffic between these two IP addresses). The crypto map is then activated on the routers' external interfaces. The last thing I did, assuming that these routers were running 12.3(8)T or later, was to remove the "perimeter" ACL entry related to the GRE traffic; at this point, the traffic is coming into the interface in an ESP packet, so this entry is no longer necessary. To control traffic traversing the data SAs, use the CACCTP feature discussed earlier in the "Filtering of IPsec Traffic" section.

NOTE	Before IOS 12.2(13)T, you had to apply the crypto map to both the GRE tunnel interface (Tunnel0 in Examples 17-13 and 17-14) and the physical interface. With IOS 12.2(13)T, this is no longer necessary. Given that this example used 12.3(8)T or later, I've only applied the crypto map to the routers' physical interfaces. You still can apply it to both, but Cisco recommends against this practice. So when you upgrade your routers to 12.2(13)T or higher, be sure to remove the crypto map application on your GRE tunnel interfaces.

Configuration Simplification

L2L configurations can be complex to set up. Cisco has simplified this process with two features: IPsec Profiles and Virtual Tunnel Interfaces. These features will be discussed in the next two sections.

IPsec Profiles

IPsec profiles, introduced in IOS 12.2(13)T, are used to abstract information from a crypto map entry and place it into a profile. The profile is then referenced within a crypto map entry. Profiles can contain transform sets, PFS group information, the identity type, and the lifetime of the SA. This makes the configuration of crypto map entries easier when remote peers have similar connection properties.

To create an IPsec profile, use the following commands:

```
Router(config)# crypto ipsec profile profile_name
Router(ipsec-profile)# set transform-set transform_set_name1
                       [transform-set-name2...transform-set-name6]
Router(ipsec-profile)# set pfs DH_group_#
Router(ipsec-profile)# set identity DN_policy_name
Router(ipsec-profile)# set security-association level per-host
Router(ipsec-profile)# set security-association lifetime
                       {seconds seconds | kilobytes kilobytes}
Router(ipsec-profile)# set security-association idle-time seconds
```

The only required command in a profile is the **set transform-set** command. These commands were discussed previously in the "Using ISAKMP/IKE" and "Setting Up DN-Based Crypto Maps" sections. To view your IPsec profiles, use the **show crypto ipsec profiles** command.

Then, in your crypto map entry, reference the profile. Here's the configuration to perform this process:

```
Router(config)# crypto map map_name seq_# ipsec-isakmp
Router(config-crypto-m)# set profile profile_name
```

IPsec Virtual Tunnel Interfaces

The IPsec virtual tunnel interface (VTI) feature, introduced in IOS 12.3(14)T, simplifies the configuration of GRE tunnels that need to be protected by IPsec. In the last section, I discussed the use of GRE tunnels and crypto maps. IPsec virtual tunnel interfaces reduce the configuration by eliminating the need to create static mapping of IPsec sessions to a particular physical interface (where the crypto map is applied). VTIs are similar to a GRE tunnel (but not the same).

The actual encryption process occurs in the tunnel. The traffic is encrypted when forwarded to the tunnel interface, which includes both unicast and multicast traffic. Either static or dynamic routing will forward packets to the tunnel interface, and static or dynamic routing can be used to identify destinations off of the tunnel. Here's how an IPsec VTI works:

Step 1   Packets arrive on an internal interface of the router.

Step 2   The routing table routes the packets to the virtual tunnel interface.

Step 3   The tunneled packets are protected based on the configured IPsec profile.

Step 4   The tunneled packets are routed to a router's exit interface and forwarded to the destination.

IPsec VTI Configuration

Here are the basic commands you would configure to set up an IPsec virtual tunnel interface:

```
Router(config)# crypto ipsec profile profile_name
Router(ipsec-profile)# set transform-set transform_set_name1
                       [transform-set-name2...transform-set-name6]
Router(ipsec-profile)# exit
```

```
Router(config)# interface tunnel port_#
Router(config-if)# ip address IP_address subnet_mask
Router(config-if)# tunnel source {IP_address_on_router |
                    local_interface_name}
Router(config-if)# tunnel destination {IP_address_of_dst_router |
                    name_of_dst_router}
Router(config-if)# keepalive [seconds [retries]]
Router(config-if)# tunnel mode ipsec ipv4
Router(config-if)# tunnel protection ipsec profile profile_name
```

As you can see from the above commands, IPsec virtual tunnel interfaces require you to
configure an IPsec profile with, at a minimum, a transform set, followed by the creation
of a tunnel. The tunnel commands are the same as those for a GRE tunnel, with two
exceptions:

- The **tunnel mode ipsec ipv4** command specifies that this is not a GRE encapsulation
  process, but an IPsec encapsulation process with IPv4 packets.

- The **tunnel protection ipsec profile** command specifies an IPsec profile to use for the
  configuration.

NOTE   Because you can't configure a crypto ACL for an IPsec profile, all traffic that traverses the
tunnel will be protected. In other words, a default *logical* crypto ACL of **permit ip any any**
is used. Normally, this would create problems for traffic that is to enter or leave a physical
interface; however, this is a handy feature because the IPsec process is tied to the tunnel
interface, and not a physical interface. In other words, the **permit ip any any** logical crypto
ACL is applied only to the tunneled traffic. You can easily apply filtering policies to the
tunnel to affect whether or not traffic is allowed to traverse it. You also can apply other
policies, such as address translation, CBAC, and QoS, for tunneled traffic.

IPsec VTI Example

To help illustrate how easy it is to set up an IPsec VTI configuration, I'll use the network
shown previously in Figure 17-3. Examples 17-18 and 17-19 display the configuration
of the two routers. As you can see from these configurations, this is *a lot* easier than
configuring a GRE tunnel with IPsec — or, for that matter, a normal static or dynamic crypto
map configuration. In this example, I used static routes to define the networks at the two
ends; however, you just as easily could have configured a dynamic routing protocol such as
OSPF or EIGRP.

Example 17-18 *RTRA's IPsec VTI Configuration*

```
RTRA(config)# crypto isakmp policy 10
RTRA(config-isakmp)# encryption aes 128
RTRA(config-isakmp)# hash sha
RTRA(config-isakmp)# authentication pre-share
RTRA(config-isakmp)# group 2
RTRA(config-isakmp)# exit
```

continues

Example 17-18 *RTRA's IPsec VTI Configuration (Continued)*

```
RTRA(config)# crypto isakmp key cisco123 address
                       193.1.1.1 255.255.255.255 no-xauth
RTRA(config)# crypto ipsec transform-set RTRtran esp-aes esp-sha-hmac
RTRA(cfg-crypto-trans)# exit
RTRA(config)# crypto ipsec profile VTI
RTRA(ipsec-profile)# set transform-set RTRtran
RTRA(ipsec-profile)# exit
RTRA(config)# interface tunnel 0
RTRA(config-if)# ip address 192.168.3.1 255.255.255.0
RTRA(config-if)# tunnel source 192.1.1.1
RTRA(config-if)# tunnel destination 193.1.1.1
RTRA(config-if)# tunnel mode ipsec ipv4
RTRA(config-if)# tunnel protection ipsec VTI
RTRA(config)# interface Ethernet0/0
RTRA(config-if)# ip address 192.1.1.1 255.255.255.0
RTRA(config-if)# exit
RTRA(config)# interface Ethernet 1/0
RTRA(config-if)# ip address 192.168.1.1 255.255.255.0
RTRA(config-if)# exit
RTRA(config)# ip route 192.168.2.0 255.255.255.0 tunnel0
```

Example 17-19 *RTRB's IPsec VTI Configuration*

```
RTRB(config)# crypto isakmp policy 10
RTRB(config-isakmp)# encryption aes 128
RTRB(config-isakmp)# hash sha
RTRB(config-isakmp)# authentication pre-share
RTRB(config-isakmp)# group 2
RTRB(config-isakmp)# exit
RTRB(config)# crypto isakmp key cisco123 address
                       192.1.1.1 255.255.255.255 no-xauth
RTRB(config)# crypto ipsec transform-set RTRtran esp-aes esp-sha-hmac
RTRB(cfg-crypto-trans)# exit
RTRB(config)# crypto ipsec profile VTI
RTRB(ipsec-profile)# set transform-set RTRtran
RTRB(ipsec-profile)# exit
RTRB(config)# interface tunnel 0
RTRB(config-if)# ip address 192.168.3.2 255.255.255.0
RTRB(config-if)# tunnel source 193.1.1.1
RTRB(config-if)# tunnel destination 192.1.1.1
RTRB(config-if)# tunnel mode ipsec ipv4
RTRB(config-if)# tunnel protection ipsec VTI
RTRB(config)# interface Ethernet0/0
RTRB(config-if)# ip address 193.1.1.1 255.255.255.0
RTRB(config-if)# exit
RTRB(config)# interface Ethernet 1/0
RTRB(config-if)# ip address 192.168.2.1 255.255.255.0
RTRB(config-if)# exit
RTRB(config)# ip route 192.168.1.0 255.255.255.0 tunnel0
```

Use the **show interface tunnel 0, show crypto session** (see Example 17-20), and **show ip route** commands to verify your configuration.

Example 17-20 *Verifying RTRA's Tunnel Status*

```
RTRA# show crypto session
Crypto session current status
Interface: Tunnel0
Session status: UP-ACTIVE
Peer: 193.1.1.1 port 500
IKE SA: local 192.1.1.1/500 remote 193.1.1.1/500
Active
IPSEC FLOW: permit ip 0.0.0.0/0.0.0.0 0.0.0.0/0.0.0.0
Active SAs: 4, origin: crypto map
```

IPsec Redundancy

The next two sections will discuss some options for redundancy for your IPsec implementation. These options include Hot Standby Router Protocol (HSRP) with Reverse Route Injection (RRI) and IPsec stateful failover. Both use HSRP to implement redundancy; however, HSRP with RRI provides for chassis failover, and IPsec stateful failover provides a transparent failover.

NOTE   When I discuss the use of HSRP below, I assume that you are already familiar with the protocol's operation and configuration on IOS devices for default gateway redundancy; I'll only expand on its use for providing redundancy for IPsec sessions.

HSRP with RRI

The first IPsec redundancy feature introduced in the IOS was HSRP with RRI in IOS 12.1(9)E and 12.2(8)T. With this feature, HSRP and RRI work together to provide chassis redundancy. With this type of redundancy, if one router fails, a redundant router can assume its role and rebuild the downed connections; therefore, some user data connections will fail while IPsec sessions are being rebuilt.

RRI was initially developed to provide redundancy for remote access solutions; however, on Cisco routers, with HSRP, it also can be used to provide redundancy for L2L sessions. It can be configured for both static and dynamic crypto maps. When used with dynamic crypto maps, the router will create a static route for each subnet or host protected by the remote peer—the remote peer shares this information with the peer having the dynamic crypto map during ISAKMP/IKE Phase 1. With static crypto maps, the router will create a static route for each destination listed in the crypto ACL for the remote peer. When the RRI static routes are created, they are redistributed automatically into any local routing protocol configured on the router.

NOTE   With static crypto maps, RRI static routes exist even if an IPsec session hasn't yet been established.

HSRP originally was developed as a default gateway redundancy mechanism, but Cisco has enhanced it in many ways to provide other types of redundancy, including IPsec. When used for IPsec redundancy, the HSRP standby IP address (virtual address) is used as the local IPsec identity (the endpoint of the tunnel). By using this address, if the primary HSRP router fails and a secondary promotes itself to the primary role, the same IP address is used to terminate the tunnel; therefore, the remote IPsec peers do not need to know about an address for each redundant peer, but only the virtual address. As mentioned earlier, when the failover takes place, the peers will have to rebuild the IPsec sessions. In other words, this solution does not provide for stateful redundancy; there is no replication of IPsec information between members of an HSRP group.

NOTE   One limitation of RRI is that routing information is exchanged *only* when an IPsec session is built or rebuilt; therefore, if routes appear or disappear while the tunnel is up, the remote peer will not learn this information. Also, HSRP with RRI doesn't provide stateful failover. When the active router fails, all IPsec sessions are lost and will have to be rebuilt to a standby router.

HSRP with RRI Configuration

HSRP with RRI can be used with dynamic or static crypto maps. If you're using a dynamic crypto map, the assumption is that you have a hub-and-spoke design, like that shown in Figure 17-4.

Figure 17-4 *HSRP with RRI Example*

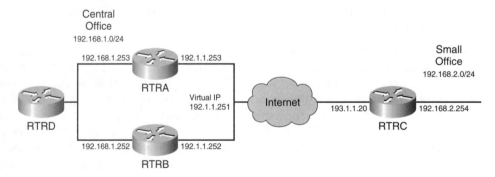

When creating the dynamic crypto map, you'll need at least to specify a transform set and the use of RRI:

```
Router(config)# crypto dynamic dynamic_map_name seq_#
Router(config-crypto-m)# set transform-set transform_name
Router(config-crypto-m)# reverse-route
Router(config-crypto-m)# exit
Router(config)# crypto map static_map_name seq_#
                       dynamic dynamic_map_name
```

With a static crypto map, you'll need to minimally configure the following:

```
Router(config)# crypto map static_map_name seq_# ipsec-isakmp
Router(config-crypto-m)# set peer IP_address_or_name
Router(config-crypto-m)# match address crypto_ACL_#_or_name
Router(config-crypto-m)# set transform-set transform_name
Router(config-crypto-m)# reverse-route
```

With a static crypto map, routing information is not learned via the crypto ACL statement, but learned dynamically via the remote peer when the IPsec tunnel is built.

To set up HSRP, you at least need to perform the following:

```
Router(config)# interface type [slot_#/]port_#
Router(config-if)# standby name HSRP_group_name
Router(config-if)# standby ip virtual_IP_address
Router(config-if)# standby timers hello_seconds dead_seconds
Router(config-if)# standby track interface_name
Router(config-if)# standby preempt
Router(config-if)# standby delay minimum [minimum_delay]
                           reload [reload_delay]
Router(config-if)# crypto map static_map_name redundancy
                           [HSRP_group_name]
```

The HSRP configuration on the external interface of the router requires the configuration of the **standby name** command and the **standby ip** command. Other HSRP commands can be configured, but these two commands are the minimum that is required. The **standby timers** command sets the hello and dead intervals. The **standby track** command allows you to track the status of an another interface; if this tracked interface fails, the router will demote itself to a standby role. The **standby preempt** command allows a router to assume the primary role when it can perform that role; this command should be configured only on the *primary* HSRP router.

When the active HSRP router fails or is stopped, a standby router promotes itself to the active role. If preemption is not configured, when the old active router comes back online, there is a slight chance that it will assume the active role, even though there is an active router. This can happen if you don't have PortFast enabled on connected switches and STP is running. In this instance, both routers don't see each other's hello messages and move to an active HSRP state. The minimum delay, which defaults to 1 second, specifies the length of time to delay HSRP group initialization. The reload delay, which defaults to 5 seconds, specifies the number of seconds the router should delay HSRP group initialization when it either has booted up or has been reloaded. Cisco recommends keeping the minimum delay value at its default, but configuring the reload delay value to 120 seconds.

NOTE	Both routers must be in the same subnet and broadcast domain on their interface where the crypto map is applied: if they aren't, they won't see each other's keepalives, and therefore both will be in an active state and both will build sessions to a remote peer, which will cause connectivity problems.

The HSRP configuration then needs to be applied to the crypto map on the interface with the **crypto map** command, specifying the **redundancy** parameter and the HSRP group name. If you add or change the HSRP group name or virtual address on the external interface, you'll need to reapply the crypto map. If you delete the virtual address on the interface, any existing IPsec sessions are dropped and rebuilt, but using the actual IP address on the interface. To verify your configuration, use the **show crypto map** command. To verify HSRP operations, use the **show standby** commands.

TIP	I typically configure the **standby timers** command to decrease the convergence time when there is a problem with the primary HSRP router. The default timers are a hello period of 3 seconds and a hold-down period of 10 seconds. Normally I set these to 1 and 4, respectively. Also, I typically don't configure the **standby preempt** command for HSRP with RRI, because this will cause a brief break in connectivity whenever there is a failure and a fix of the failure.

CAUTION	The HSRP priorities need to be the same on the two routers. When they are different, the one with the higher priority becomes the active router. In this situation, if the two routers have IP addresses in a different chronological order between them, the active router can go up and down continuously through the HSRP states. When I use the term "chronological," I'm referring to one router having the higher IP address on the external interface than the standby one, but a lower IP address on the internal interface than the standby router (or vice versa).

HSRP with RRI Example

The network shown previously in Figure 17-4 illustrates an example of configuring HSRP with RRI. Assume that the addresses of the remote peers are unknown until they connect, so dynamic crypto maps are necessary at the corporate site. Example 17-21 shows RTRA's configuration.

Example 17-21 *HSRP with RRI Example: RTRA's Configuration*

```
RTRA(config)# crypto isakmp policy 10
RTRA(config-isakmp)# encryption aes
RTRA(config-isakmp)# hash md5
RTRA(config-isakmp)# authentication pre-share
RTRA(config-isakmp)# group 2
RTRA(config-isakmp)# exit
RTRA(config)# crypto isakmp key cisco123 address
                         0.0.0.0 0.0.0.0 no-xauth
RTRA(config)# crypto isakmp keepalive 10
RTRA(config)# crypto isakmp nat keepalive 20
RTRA(config)# crypto ipsec transform-set RTRtrans esp-aes esp-sha-hmac
RTRA(cfg-crypto-trans)# exit
RTRA(config)# crypto dynamic-map dynmap 10
RTRA(config-crypto-map)# set transform-set RTRtrans
RTRA(config-crypto-map)# reverse-route
RTRA(config-crypto-map)# exit
RTRA(config)# crypto map statmap 65000 ipsec-isakmp dynamic dynmap
RTRA(config-crypto-map)# exit
RTRA(config)# router ospf 1
RTRA(config-router)# redistribute static subnets
RTRA(config-router)# network 192.168.1.0 0.0.0.255 area 0
RTRA(config-router)# exit
RTRA(config)# ip access-list extended perimeter
RTRA(config-ext-nacl)# permit udp any host 192.1.1.251 eq 500
RTRA(config-ext-nacl)# permit esp any host 192.1.1.251
RTRA(config-ext-nacl)# permit udp any host 192.1.1.251 eq 4500
RTRA(config-ext-nacl)# permit udp host 192.1.1.252 eq 1985
                          host 224.0.0.2 eq 1985
RTRA(config-ext-nacl)# deny ip any any
RTRA(config)# interface Ethernet0/0
RTRA(config-if)# description Connection to Internet
RTRA(config-if)# ip address 192.1.1.253 255.255.255.0
RTRA(config-if)# ip access-group perimeter in
RTRA(config-if)# standby ip 192.1.1.251
RTRA(config-if)# standby timers 1 4
RTRA(config-if)# standby name RRI
RTRA(config-if)# standby track Ethernet1/0
RTRA(config-if)# crypto map statmap redundancy RRI
RTRA(config-if)# exit
RTRA(config)# interface Ethernet1/0
RTRA(config-if)# description Connection to Internal network
RTRA(config-if)# ip address 192.168.1.253 255.255.255.0
RTRA(config-if)# no shutdown
RTRA(config-if)# exit
```

First, in the preceding example, notice that pre-shared keys are used; because the remote
site address isn't known, I've had to wildcard the keys. In this particular situation, I
probably would have used either a name identity type or, more preferably, certificates (the
latter provides for better and more secure device authentication). Below this I've configured
keepalives for ISAKMP and NAT (if NAT-T is used) to ensure that if there is a break in
the IPsec session, it is torn down, allowing RTRC to re-establish the IPsec session to the
same address (but a different router). Because the remote address isn't known, RTRA has

configured a dynamic crypto map with a transform set and RRI; this then is referenced as an entry in a static crypto map. If the remote site addresses were known, you could have done this easily with a static crypto map configuration at the corporate office routers.

The OSPF configuration redistributes the static routes into the OSPF process (including the RRI routes). Normally, you would set up a route map to restrict the redistribution process. The "perimeter" ACL allows ISAKMP, ESP, and NAT-T traffic to the virtual IP address used by HSRP. Also, notice the entry for UDP that has a source and destination port of 1985: this is to allow RTRB to communicate with RTRA via HSRP hello messages.

On RTRA's Internet interface, HSRP is configured (please note that I'm assuming the two routers are connected via a Cisco switch, with PortFast configured; enable the **spanning-tree portfast** command on every switch port that connects to an HSRP-enabled router interface). The HSRP timers are set to a small number to reduce convergence with RTRA fails. The virtual IP address is 192.1.1.251. The crypto map is applied to the interface referencing the HSRP configuration, enabling HSRP with RRI.

RTRB's configuration, the backup router, is very similar to RTRA's. Instead of repeating it, here are the changes you would need to make for RTRB's configuration:

- In the extended "perimeter" ACL, the HSRP ACL entry should reference RTRA's IP address: 192.168.1.253.

- The IP addresses on the internal and external interfaces are 192.168.1.252 and 192.1.1.252, respectively.

RTRC's configuration, the small office router, is shown in Example 17-22. I'll point out the important things in this configuration. Notice that the pre-shared key specifies the virtual IP address at the corporate site. Below this, I've matched the ISAKMP and NAT timers configured on the corporate routers. Because this router is initiating the connection to the corporate site, I've configured a crypto ACL specifying the traffic to be protected: the local and remote networks. After the transform configuration I'm building a static crypto map. For RRI to work, it needs to be configured on both endpoints of the IPsec tunnel.

Example 17-22 *HSRP with RRI Example: RTRC's Configuration*

```
RTRC(config# crypto isakmp policy 10
RTRC(config-isakmp)# encryption aes 128
RTRC(config-isakmp)# hash md5
RTRC(config-isakmp)# authentication pre-share
RTRC(config-isakmp)# group 2
RTRC(config-isakmp)# exit
RTRC(config# crypto isakmp key cisco123 address
                      192.1.1.251 no-xauth
RTRC(config# crypto isakmp keepalive 10
RTRC(config# crypto isakmp nat keepalive 20
RTRC(config# ip access-list extended cryptoACL
RTRC(config-ext-nacl)# permit ip 192.168.2.0 0.0.0.255
                      192.168.1.0 0.0.0.255
RTRC(config-ext-nacl)# exit
RTRC(config# crypto ipsec transform-set RTRtrans esp-aes esp-sha-hmac
```

Example 17-22 *HSRP with RRI Example: RTRC's Configuration (Continued)*

```
RTRC(cfg-crypto-trans)# exit
RTRC(config# crypto map statmap 10 ipsec-isakmp
RTRC(config-crypto-map)# set peer 192.1.1.251
RTRC(config-crypto-map)# set transform-set RTRtrans
RTRC(config-crypto-map)# match address cryptoACL
RTRC(config-crypto-map)# reverse-route
RTRC(config-crypto-map)# exit
RTRC(config# interface Ethernet0
RTRC(config-if)# description Internet Connection
RTRC(config-if)# ip address 193.1.1.17 255.255.255.0
RTRC(config-if)# crypto map statmap
RTRC(config-if)# no shutdown
RTRC(config-if)# exit
RTRC(config# interface FastEthernet0
RTRC(config-if)# ip address 192.168.2.1 255.255.255.0
RTRC(config-if)# no shutdown
```

When a device at the small office tries to access the corporate office's 192.168.1.0/24 network, RTRC will bring up an IPsec tunnel to 192.1.1.251, which is the corporate office router currently in an active HSRP state. When this completes, Example 17-23 shows you the routing information in RTRA's table (the active HSRP) router: notice the RRI static route from RTRC. Example 17-24 shows the redistributed static route from RTRA in RTRD's routing table.

Example 17-23 *HSRP with RRI Example: RTRA's Routing Table*

```
RTRA# show ip route
←output omitted→
C    192.1.1.0/24 is directly connected, Ethernet0/0
C    192.168.1.0/24 is directly connected, Ethernet1/0
S    192.168.2.0/24 [1/0] via 192.1.1.17
```

Example 17-24 *HSRP with RRI Example: RTRD's Routing Table*

```
RTRD# show ip route
←output omitted→
C    192.168.1.0/24 is directly connected, Ethernet0
O E2 192.168.2.0/24 [110/20] via 192.168.1.253, 00:43:31, Ethernet0
```

Stateful Failover for IPsec

The main problem with HSRP with RRI is that it is not a stateful solution; it takes time for the standby HSRP router to detect a failure and more time for the remote router to determine that a problem exists and to attempt to reconnect. During that time lapse, no traffic can be transmitted between the two sites. The stateful failover for IPsec feature, new as of IOS 12.3(11)T, allows all necessary ISAKMP/IKE and IPsec SA information to be replicated between a primary and backup router; therefore, if the primary fails, the backup can take over processing of the SAs and thus a failover is, for the most part, transparent to the remote VPN devices (L2L or remote access). Like HSRP with RRI, stateful failover for IPsec works with HSRP, but also uses stateful switchover (SSO) to provide transparent failover redundancy. HSRP provides IP redundancy and SSO provides ISAKMP/IKE and IPsec SA redundancy.

Stateful failover for IPsec will work with both L2L and remote access sessions. The main difference between the handling of these sessions is that remote access has two additional components: XAUTH (user authentication) and IKE Mode Config (addressing and policy information pushed down to the remote access clients). For stateful failover over IPsec to provide redundancy for remote access sessions, you need to ensure that both failover routers use the same addressing pools when assigning clients addressing information. The following sections will discuss the restrictions of stateful failover, how it's used, and how it's configured, including an example configuration.

Stateful Failover for IPsec Restrictions and Limitations

Stateful failover for IPsec has the following restrictions and limitations:

- It is currently supported on only the 3700, 3800, 7200, and 7300 router platforms. Cisco will add to this list; to see the current supported platforms, go to http://www.cisco.com/go/fn and look for the stateful failover feature for IPsec.

- In the failover configuration, both routers must be identical: same router model, same interfaces in the same slots, same RAM and CPU type, same VPN hardware acceleration card (if used), and same software version. If using a VPN accelerator card, only the VAM, VAM2, and AIM-VPN/HPII modules are supported.

- The routers cannot be connected via a crossover cable; it must be via a switch or hub connection. This means you cannot use a WAN medium for the router connections.

- Only failover is supported; load balancing is not.

- Only IPsec failover is supported; L2TP over IPsec, PPTP, and WebVPN are not. Currently only pre-shared keys are supported (certificates are not). IKE keepalives are also not supported; if used, this will cause the remote peer to tear down a connection the standby router assumes control over. However, DPD is supported. Likewise, IPsec idle timers are not supported.

- Failover is not supported with the State Synchronization Protocol (SSP).

Stateful Failover for IPsec Deployment

Cisco recommends that stateful failover for IPsec be deployed using one of two methods: single-interface and dual-interface design. Figure 17-5 illustrates the two deployment methods, where RTRA and RTRB will implement the stateful failover for IPsec feature, as follows:

- In the single-interface design, the same interface is used to handle both encrypted and unencrypted traffic. This design typically is used when internal users access the Internet directly and also when needing to send protected traffic to remote sites or users. Normally, the two failover routers are placed in a DMZ-like configuration, as shown in the top part of Figure 17-5, but they also can sit behind or in front of the firewall. The HSRP and SSO configuration is done on the same interface. RRI is required to advertise the routes to internal devices.

- In the dual-interface design, traffic flows through the two failover routers. RRI typically is not used in this situation because a default route is set up in the internal network pointing to these two routers. However, if you are not using a default static route, but a dynamic routing protocol, you'll need to use RRI. HSRP is used on the internal interface with the internal static route pointing to the internal virtual IP address. HSRP is used on both the internal and external interfaces; interface tracking is used to determine if an interface fails on the primary failover router. The standby router will assume IPsec connection responsibilities. This design provides for better security of SSO communications when exchanging state information, because you can use the internal interface for communications instead of the external one as in the single-interface design. As in the single-interface design, the routers can sit behind or in front of a firewall design.

Figure 17-5 *Stateful Failover for IPsec Deployment*

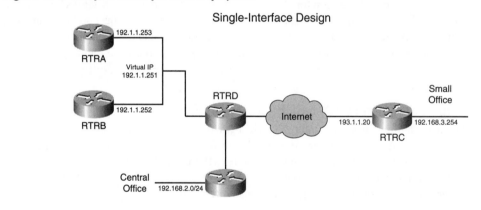

Single-Interface Design

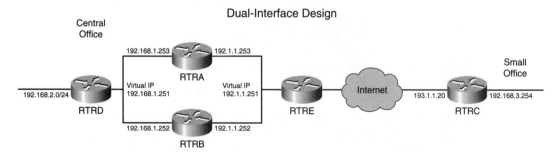

Dual-Interface Design

Steps for Configuring Stateful Failover for IPsec

Setting up stateful failover involves these steps:

Step 1 Configure HSRP (required).

Step 2 Configure SSO (required).

Step 3 Configure RRI (depends).

Step 4 Enable stateful failover for IPsec (required).

Step 5 Protect SSO traffic (optional).

Step 6 Tune stateful failover (optional).

Step 7 Manage and monitor stateful failover (optional).

The next few sections will discuss each of these in more depth, followed by a configuration example.

NOTE The configuration information for HSRP, stateful failover, and the ISAKMP/IKE and IPsec configuration is *not* synchronized between the failover routers; you must do this manually. Failover only provides synchronization of the IPsec tunnels that are built, including information about how they are protected and the keys used to protect them.

Step 1: Configuration of HSRP for Stateful Failover

The first step in setting up stateful failover for IPsec is to configure HSRP. HSRP provides a virtual IP address for IP redundancy. Because HSRP uses hello messages to communicate with other routers in the same HSRP group, it's important that you allow HSRP through any ACL on the routers' interface(s), and ensure that the STP PortFast feature is enabled on any directly connected switch port.

You'll need to configure the following on both routers in the failover group:

```
Router(config)# interface type [slot_#/]port_#
Router(config-if)# standby name HSRP_group_name
Router(config-if)# standby ip virtual_IP_address
Router(config-if)# standby timers hello_seconds dead_seconds
Router(config-if)# standby track interface_name
Router(config-if)# standby preempt
Router(config-if)# standby delay minimum [minimum_delay]
                        reload [reload_delay]
```

I discussed the **standby** commands previously in the "HSRP with RRI Configuration" section. For each HSRP group, the virtual IP address on the routers must be the same. Also, in a dual-interface deployment, the configuration of interface tracking is recommended. And unlike HSRP with RRI, you can use preemption without any issues of lost connectivity when preemption takes place.

TIP	In HSRP with stateful failover for IPsec, when the active router is demoted to a standby role, it automatically will reboot itself to ensure that it synchronizes itself correctly with the new active router. Because of this, it is imperative that you use PortFast to ensure that STP issues don't cause your routers to change roles and reboot continually.

Step 2: Configuration of SSO for Stateful Failover

SSO is used to transfer the necessary ISAKMP/IKE and IPsec information to maintain protected sessions between the active and standby routers. Before setting up SSO, be sure that you first complete the setup of HSRP. Here are the commands to set up SSO:

```
Router(config)# redundancy inter-device
Router(config-red-interdevice)# scheme standby HSRP_group_name
Router(config-red-interdevice)# exit
Router(config)# ipc zone default
Router(config-ipczone)# association assoc_ID_#
Router(config-ipczone)# no shutdown
Router(config-ipc-assoc)# protocol sctp
Router(config-ipc-protocol-sctp)# local-port local_port_#
Router(config-ipc-protocol-sctp-l)# local-ip local_IP_address
Router(config-ipc-protocol-sctp-l)# exit
Router(config-ipc-protocol-sctp)# remote-port remote_port_#
Router(config-ipc-protocol-sctp-r)# remote_ip remote_IP_address
Router(config-ipc-protocol-sctp-r)# exit
Router(config-ipc-protocol-sctp)# retransmit-timeout
                        min_msec max_msec
Router(config-ipc-protocol-sctp)# path-retransmit max_path_retries
Router(config-ipc-protocol-sctp)# assoc-retransmit
                        max_association_retries
```

Setting up SSO can be complex, as you can see from the above list of commands. The **redundancy-inter-device** command allows you to enable and protect SSO traffic.

The **scheme standby** command specifies the HSRP group to use for redundancy. It needs to match the name specified by the **standby name** command (the HSRP virtual IP address is not used by SSO). Type **exit** to leave the subcommand mode.

The **ipc zone default** command configures the SSO inter-device communication protocol and Inter-Process Communication (IPC), and enters the IPC zone subcommand mode. The **association** command creates an association between the two devices. The association ID number can range from 1–255, where the value must be the same on the two failover routers. The **no shutdown** command enables the IPC process. The **protocol sctp** command specifies that the Stream Control Transmission Protocol (SCTP) is to be used to transport SSO messages; this is the only protocol currently supported, and it takes you into a different subcommand mode.

Within the SCTP subcommand mode, you need to specify the communication parameters that SCTP will use. There are no defaults as to which IP addresses should be used for communications, nor ports. The **local-port** command specifies the local port number to use on this peer for SCTP communications; the port number can range from 1–65,535. The

local-ip command is a subcommand of the **local-port** command. You can specify up to two IP addresses to use as the local source of SCTP communications. The **remote-port** command specifies the port number to use on the remote failover device for SCTP, which can range from 1–65,535, and the **remote-ip** subcommand specifies the IP address to connect to on the remote failover peer (you can specify up to two addresses for the remote peer).

NOTE   The local IP and port numbers on one peer must match the remote IP and port numbers on the other peer, and vice versa. Normally, you would either use a dedicated connection between the two routers for SCTP communication or the internal interfaces of the two routers. Also, make sure that the SCTP addresses and ports are allowed through the router's interface ACL.

Cisco recommends that you configure the **retransmit-timeout, path-retransmit,** and **assoc-retransmit** commands to limit the likelihood of losing SCTP communication between the failover peers. The **retransmit-timeout** (RTO) command specifies the number of milliseconds that SCTP waits before transmitting information. The minimal interval defaults to 300 milliseconds and the maximum defaults to 1,000 (1 second). Both values can range from 300–60,000 milliseconds. Whatever timeouts you specify, they should be greater than the round-trip delay between the two peers. You can use the following algorithm to configure the delay values correctly: estimated round trip time = ((152 * 8) / link speed in bits) * 2. The 152 represents a 20-byte IP header, a 32-byte SCTP header, and a 100-byte payload. The 8 converts the bytes to bits. The **path-retransmit** (PTO) command specifies the number of consecutive retransmissions of SCTP packets before considering that the current path to the peer is bad. The default is 4 retries, but can be changed to 2–10. If you've specified a second remote IP address, this will be used once this limit is reached. With an RTO of 1 second and a PTO of 4, it would take 4 seconds for a secondary remote IP address to be used when communications are lost using the primary remote IP address. The **assoc-retransmit** command specifies the number of consecutive retransmissions of SCTP packets before the router considers the association to have failed. The default is 4, but can range from 2–10.

TIP   You can use the **debug redundancy** command to troubleshoot SSO communication problems.

Step 3: Configuration of RRI for Stateful Failover

If you are not using a default route pointing to an internal virtual HSRP address for internal devices to access the failover routers, but are using a dynamic routing protocol, you'll need to configure RRI. RRI can be used for both static and dynamic crypto maps. Its configuration was discussed previously in the "HSRP with RRI Configuration" section.

Step 4: Enabling Stateful Failover

There are two ways of enabling stateful failover depending on how you have set up IPsec. When not using IPsec VTI tunnels (or DMVPN, discussed later in the "L2L Scalability" section), you would use the following configuration:

```
Router(config)# crypto map map_name redundancy HSRP_group_name
                stateful
```

The only difference between this command and enabling redundancy for HSRP with RRI is that you add the **stateful** parameter to enable stateful failover for IPsec. Please note that you must have defined a virtual IP address for the HSRP group before enabling SSO.

If you're using VTIs for your connectivity, you would enable stateful failover as follows:

```
Router(config)# crypto ipsec profile profile_name
Router(ipsec-profile)# redundancy HSRP_group_name stateful
Router(ipsec-profile)# exit
Router(config)# interface tunnel port_#
Router(config-if)# tunnel source {IP_address_on_router}
Router(config-if)# tunnel destination {IP_address_of_dst_router}
Router(config-if)# tunnel mode ipsec ipv4
Router(config-if)# tunnel protection ipsec profile profile_name
```

Please note that the preceding commands are only for stateful failover—you will still need the other commands necessary for IPsec VTI connections. Also, for the **tunnel source** command, you can't use an interface name—you must use an *IP address*.

Step 5: Protecting SSO Traffic

If you're concerned about someone eavesdropping on the SSO traffic transmitted between the two failover routers, you can protect it. This is done by setting up an IPsec transport session between the two routers.

CAUTION   Remember that all information related to an SA, including encryption and HMAC keys, needs to be synchronized between the two failover routers. If you don't configure SSO protection, these are sent in clear text! Protecting SSO traffic is not necessary, however, especially if you're using a dedicated link between the two routers for the SSO communications.

To protect SSO traffic, configure the following:

```
Router(config)# crypto isakmp key pre_shared_key address
                remote_IP no-xauth
Router(config)# crypto ipsec profile SSO_profile_name
```

```
Router(ipsec-profile)# set transform-set transform_name
Router(ipsec-profile)# exit
Router(config)# redundancy inter-device
Router(config-red-interdevice)# security ipsec SSO_profile_name
Router(config-red-interdevice)# exit
```

First, you'll need to configure an ISAKMP/IKE Phase 1 policy that matches on the two failover routers, and that uses pre-shared keys. You'll then need to configure a pre-shared key on each router, matching the remote IP address found in the **remote-ip** command discussed in Step 2. Next, create an IPsec profile with a matching transform set on the two failover peers. Then, in the **redundancy inter-device** subcommand mode, specify the IPsec profile to use to build the IPsec tunnel to the remote peer with the **security ipsec** command.

Step 6: Tuning Stateful Failover

Also, you can tune SSO and change the interval by which the active router forwards anti-replay updates to the standby router. For inbound SAs, by default, the active router sends an anti-replay update every 1000 packets; for outbound SAs, this is done once every 100,000 packets. To change the update interval, use the following command:

```
Router(config)# crypto map map_name redundancy replay-interval
                     inbound #_of_packets outbound #_of_packets
```

Step 7: Managing and Monitoring Stateful Failover

Once you have configured stateful failover for IPsec, you can use various commands to view the status of your configuration and to clear connections. Use the following commands to view the operation of stateful failover:

- **show redundancy**—Shows the current state of SSO; once the two routers have negotiated the SSO process, one device should be "ACTIVE" and the other "STANDBY HOT." Here are the parameters you can use to qualify this command:
  - **clients**—displays a redundancy-aware application list
  - **counters**—displays counters for SSO operations
  - **debug-log**—displays a log of up to 256 SSO debug entries
  - **handover**—displays details of any pending handovers from active to standby
  - **history**—displays a history of past handover events
  - **states**—displays the SSO state of a router (disabled, initialization, standby, or active)
  - **inter-device**—displays the SSO operational state and statistics

- **show crypto isakmp sa [active | standby]**—Shows the ISAKMP/IKE Phase 1 management SAs; you can qualify the command with two parameters, where **active** displays only the active SAs and **standby** displays only the SAs in an "STDBY" (standby) state.

- **show crypto ipsec sa [active | standby]**—Shows the ISAKMP/IKE Phase 2 data SAs; you can qualify this command with two parameters, which perform the same function as described in the last bullet point.

- **show crypto session [active | standby]**—Shows the current IPsec sessions (Phase 1 and Phase 2) to the remote peers; you can qualify this command with two parameters, which perform the same function as described in the last bullet point.

- **show crypto ha**—Shows the virtual IP addresses used by the ISAKMP/IKE Phase 1 and Phase 2 connections.

Example 17-25 shows the output of the **show redundancy states** command. In this example, this router is the currently active router for SSO.

Example 17-25 *The* **show redundancy states** *Command*

```
Router# show redundancy states
       my state = 13 -ACTIVE
     peer state = 8  -STANDBY HOT
           Mode = Duplex
        Unit ID = 0
←output omitted→
```

To clear connections or sessions, use the following commands:

- **clear crypto isakmp sa** *connection_ID_#* **[active | standby]**—Deletes the ISAKMP/IKE Phase 1 connections (you can optionally specify SAs in a particular state, in addition to a particular SA); please note that if you do this on a standby router, it will rebuild the standby SAs immediately, making it seem as though the standby SAs had not been cleared.

- **clear crypto sa [active | standby]**—Deletes the ISAKMP/IKE Phase 2 connections (you can specify SAs in a particular state, and a particular peer); please note that if you do this on a standby router, it will rebuild the standby SAs immediately, making it seem as though the standby SAs had not been cleared.

- **clear crypto session [active | standby]**—Deletes all the IPsec Phase 1 and 2 connections (you can optionally specify SAs in a particular state, and a particular peer); please note that if you do this on a standby router, it will rebuild the standby SAs immediately, making it seem as though the standby SAs had not been cleared.

To troubleshoot SSO operations, use the following commands:

- **debug crypto ha**—Displays high availability (SSO) messages sent between the active and standby routers.

- **debug crypto isakmp ha** [**detail** | **update**]—Displays high availability information shared between two routers concerning the synchronization of ISAKMP/IKE Phase 1 connections.

- **debug crypto ipsec ha** [**detail** | **update**]—Displays high availability information shared between two routers concerning the synchronization of ISAKMP/IKE Phase 2 connections; the **detail** parameter displays all debugging details, whereas the **update** parameter only displays updates for Phase 2 synchronization of connections (such as adding or removing a data connection).

Example Configuration of IPsec Stateful Failover

Now that I've gone through the various commands to set up and maintain IPsec stateful failover, I'll now illustrate an example that uses L2L sessions with a dual-interface SSO design shown previously in the bottom part of Figure 17-5. Example 17-26 and 17-27 show RTRA's and RTRB's configurations, respectively. Both routers are using a default route pointing to RTRE and a static route for 192.168.2.0/24 to RTRD. The HSRP group "SSO-in," for the inside interface of the two routers, is used for the stateful failover communications; plus, this communication is protected by an IPsec profile, "sso-secure."

Example 17-26 *SSO Example: RTRA's Configuration*

```
RTRA(config)# ip route 0.0.0.0 0.0.0.0 192.1.1.254
RTRA(config)# ip route 192.168.2.0 255.255.255.0 192.168.1.250
RTRA(config)# redundancy inter-device
RTRA(config-red-interdevice)# scheme standby SSO-in
RTRA(config-red-interdevice)# security ipsec sso-secure
RTRA(config-red-interdevice)# exit
RTRA(config)# ipc zone default
RTRA(config-ipczone)# association 1
RTRA(config-ipczone)# no shutdown
RTRA(config-ipczone)# protocol sctp
RTRA(config-ipc-protocol-sctp)# local-port 5555
RTRA(config-ipc-protocol-sctp-l)# local-ip 192.1.1.253
Router(config-ipc-protocol-sctp-l)# exit
Router(config-ipc-protocol-sctp)# remote-port 5555
RTRA(config-ipc-protocol-sctp-r)# remote-ip 192.1.1.252
RTRA(config-ipc-protocol-sctp-r)# exit
RTRA(config-ipc-protocol-sctp)# exit
RTRA(config-ipczone)# exit
RTRA(config)# crypto isakmp policy 1
RTRA(config-isakmp)# encryption aes
RTRA(config-isakmp)# hash sha
RTRA(config-isakmp)# group 2
RTRA(config-isakmp)# authentication pre-share
RTRA(config-isakmp)# exit
RTRA(config)# crypto isakmp key cisco123 address 0.0.0.0 0.0.0.0
                         no-xauth
RTRA(config)# ip access-list extended protecttraffic
RTRA(config-ext-nacl)# permit ip 192.168.2.0 0.0.0.255
                            192.168.3.0 0.0.0.255
```

Example 17-26 *SSO Example: RTRA's Configuration (Continued)*

```
RTRA(config-ext-nacl)# exit
RTRA(config)# crypto ipsec transform-set trans2 esp-md5-hmac esp-aes
RTRA(cfg-crypto-trans)# exit
RTRA(config)# crypto ipsec profile sso-secure
RTRA(ipsec-profile)# set transform-set trans2
RTRA(ipsec-profile)# exit
RTRA(config)# crypto map mymap redundancy replay-interval
                         inbound 800 outbound 10000
RTRA(config)# crypto map mymap 10 ipsec-isakmp
RTRA(config-crypto-map)# set peer 193.1.1.20
RTRA(config-crypto-map)# set transform-set trans2
RTRA(config-crypto-map)# match address protecttraffic
RTRA(config-crypto-map)# exit
RTRA(config)# interface Ethernet0/0
RTRA(config-if)# description Connection to RTRE
RTRA(config-if)# ip address 192.1.1.253 255.255.255.0
RTRA(config-if)# standby 1 ip 192.1.1.251
RTRA(config-if)# standby 1 preempt
RTRA(config-if)# standby 1 name SSO-out
RTRA(config-if)# standby 1 track Ethernet1/0
RTRA(config-if)# standby delay reload 120
RTRA(config-if)# crypto map mymap redundancy SSO-out stateful
RTRA(config-if)# exit
RTRA(config)# interface Ethernet1/0
RTRA(config-if)# description Connection to RTRD
RTRA(config-if)# ip address 192.168.1.253 255.255.255.0
RTRA(config-if)# standby 2 ip 192.168.1.251
RTRA(config-if)# standby 2 preempt
RTRA(config-if)# standby 2 name SSO-in
RTRA(config-if)# standby delay reload 120
RTRA(config-if)# standby 2 track Ethernet0/0
```

Example 17-27 *SSO Example: RTRB's Configuration*

```
RTRB(config)# ip route 0.0.0.0 0.0.0.0 192.1.1.254
RTRB(config)# ip route 192.168.2.0 255.255.255.0 192.168.1.250
RTRB(config)# redundancy inter-device
RTRB(config-red-interdevice)# scheme standby SSO-in
RTRB(config-red-interdevice)# security ipsec sso-secure
RTRB(config-red-interdevice)# exit
RTRB(config)# ipc zone default
RTRB(config-ipczone)# association 1
RTRB(config-ipczone)# no shutdown
RTRB(config-ipczone)# protocol sctp
RTRB(config-ipc-protocol-sctp)# local-port 5555
RTRB(config-ipc-protocol-sctp-l)# local-ip 192.168.1.252
RTRB(config-ipc-protocol-sctp-l)# exit
RTRB(config-ipc-protocol-sctp)# remote-port 5555
RTRB(config-ipc-protocol-sctp-r)# remote-ip 192.168.1.253
RTRB(config-ipc-protocol-sctp-r)# exit
RTRB(config-ipc-protocol-sctp)# exit
RTRB(config-ipczone)# exit
```

continues

Example 17-27 *SSO Example: RTRB's Configuration (Continued)*

```
RTRB(config)# crypto isakmp policy 1
RTRB(config-isakmp)# encryption aes
RTRB(config-isakmp)# hash sha
RTRB(config-isakmp)# group 2
RTRB(config-isakmp)# authentication pre-share
RTRB(config-isakmp)# exit
RTRB(config)# crypto isakmp key cisco123 address 0.0.0.0 0.0.0.0
                        no-xauth
RTRB(config)# ip access-list extended protecttraffic
RTRB(config-ext-nacl)# permit ip host 192.168.3.0 0.0.0.255
                                      192.168.2.0 0.0.0.255
RTRB(config-ext-nacl)# exit
RTRB(config)# crypto ipsec transform-set trans2 esp-md5-hmac esp-aes
RTRB(cfg-crypto-trans)# exit
RTRB(config)# crypto ipsec profile sso-secure
RTRB(ipsec-profile)# set transform-set trans2
RTRB(ipsec-profile)# exit
RTRB(config)# crypto map mymap redundancy replay-interval
                          inbound 800 outbound 10000
RTRB(config)# crypto map mymap 10 ipsec-isakmp
RTRB(config-crypto-map)# set peer 193.1.1.20
RTRB(config-crypto-map)# set transform-set trans2
RTRB(config-crypto-map)# match address protecttraffic
RTRB(config-crypto-map)# exit
RTRB(config)# interface Ethernet0/0
RTRB(config-if)# description Connection to RTRE
RTRB(config-if)# ip address 192.1.1.252 255.255.255.0
RTRB(config-if)# standby 1 ip 192.1.1.251
RTRB(config-if)# standby 1 preempt
RTRB(config-if)# standby 1 name SSO-out
RTRB(config-if)# standby 1 track Ethernet1/0
RTRB(config-if)# standby delay reload 120
RTRB(config-if)# crypto map mymap redundancy SSO-out stateful
RTRB(config-if)# exit
RTRB(config)# interface Ethernet1/0
RTRB(config-if)# description Connection to RTRD
RTRB(config-if)# ip address 192.168.1.252 255.255.255.0
RTRB(config-if)# standby 2 ip 192.168.1.251
RTRB(config-if)# standby 2 preempt
RTRB(config-if)# standby 2 name SSO-in
RTRB(config-if)# standby delay reload 120
RTRB(config-if)# standby 2 track Ethernet0/0
```

In the preceding examples, IPC communications are set up using the physical addresses of the inside interfaces of the two routers and a source and destination port number of 5,555. ISAKMP/IKE policy 10 defines the protection for the management connections that will be built, with a wildcarded pre-shared key. A crypto ACL called "protecttraffic" specifies that packets between 192.168.2.0/24 and 192.168.3.0/24 will be protected and the transform set "trans2" specifies that these packets will be protected with ESP MD5 and AES. The anti-replay intervals have been changed from their default values with the **crypto map redundancy replay-interval** command. A static crypto map called "mymap" has been created to build the L2L session to (or from) RTRC. E0/0 is the outside interface and interface tracking is enabled for the inside interface; this ensures that if the inside interface of the active router fails, SSO failover will occur to the standby router.

Note that the virtual IP address in the preceding examples is 192.1.1.251, which is what RTRC needs to use when connecting to the SSO failover-configured routers. An HSRP reload delay has been configured for two minutes to ensure that when a reload occurs on the active router, there is enough time for the standby router to promote itself. The **crypto map redundancy stateful** command enables the static crypto map in addition to the SSO functionality on the routers' interfaces. The inside interfaces also are set up for HSRP with interface tracking. When setting up RTRC, the peer's IP address in the static crypto map entry needs to be the HSRP virtual IP address for the external interfaces of RTRA and RTRB: 192.1.1.251. Otherwise, the configuration of RTRC is straightforward. If RTRC was obtaining its address dynamically, you could easily set up a dynamic crypto map on RTRA and RTRB to handle this. This also would be true for remote access connections.

NOTE	If you'll be using certificates for authentication, make sure you create RSA keys as exportable on one peer, in addition to the certificate information. With SSO Failover, you need to obtain only one certificate on one of the failover peers; however, you'll need to export this to the standby router. I explained this in the last chapter.

L2L Scalability

One concern administrators have in enterprise networks is to provide scalability for their IPsec L2L solutions. Imagine that you have 300 sites that you need to mesh partially or fully. The most common implementation would be to implement a hub-and-spoke design to interconnect the sites. However, there might be situations where, because of delay issues, spoke-to-spoke connections are sometimes necessary. Based on the information I've discussed so far, adding and managing the hub-and-spoke and spoke-to-spoke connections would not be a simple task. For every new connection you'd need to implement, you'd need to configure the L2L session on the two routing peers manually and set up routing, either static or dynamic, for traffic traversing the IPsec connection.

Of course, to help with the situation of a large L2L network, you could set up GRE tunnels to share routing information between sites, somewhat simplifying the routing configuration; but you just added the task of building and managing the GRE tunnels themselves. Plus, the tunnel endpoints must be known (no dynamic IP addressing) to create the GRE tunnels. With 300 devices using a hub-and-spoke and spoke-to-spoke mixed topology, you easily might have to set up 300–400 sessions, with crypto ACLs, GRE tunnels, and crypto map entries!

Dynamic Multipoint VPNs (DMVPNs) can deal with these issues easily to provide a scalable L2L network with IPsec. DMVPN uses multipoint GRE (mGRE) tunnels along with the Next Hop Resolution Protocol (NHRP) to implement scalability. The following sections will discuss how DMVPN works, the disadvantages of not using it, how to configure it, and how to use it in a nonredundant and redundant design.

DMVPN Overview

DMVPN requires that a hub-and-spoke design be used. This does not mean that spokes can't set up connections to other spokes, but a hub router is required to register addresses, via NHRP, from spokes. Then, if a spoke needs to set up a connection to another spoke, it can send an NHRP query to the hub to find the spoke responsible for a particular network and then set up an IPsec session directly between the two spokes dynamically. Because of this arrangement, when spokes boot up, they will set up an IPsec session to the hub device automatically and register their IP addressing information via NHRP. Note that the hub doesn't need to know anything about the spokes; it will learn which traffic needs to be protected when a peer spoke connects. This allows the spoke devices to acquire their addressing dynamically (like via DHCP or PPPoE). However, spokes must define who the hub is, and the traffic that needs to be protected; GRE is used to transport data and routing traffic.

Traffic flowing between two DMVPN routers is sent via a GRE tunnel. For the hub, this is a multipoint tunnel, resulting in a single GRE tunnel interface supporting multiple connections from spoke devices. For spoke devices, if spoke-to-spoke connectivity is needed, multipoint GRE tunnels also are used; if only spoke-to-hub connectivity is necessary, then a point-to-point GRE tunnel configuration can be used on the spoke. Because GRE tunnels are used, broadcast and multicast packets (which include routing protocols), can be transported between the DMVPN routers. Before DMVPN, GRE tunneled traffic was process-switched; however, today CEF-enabled routers can use Cisco Express Forwarding (CEF) to switch GRE traffic at high rates.

IPsec is used to protect just the GRE packets between IPsec peers, which means that any traffic traversing the tunnel also is protected. Because GRE is a point-to-point connection, it is most common to use ESP in transport mode to protect the GRE tunneled packets (tunnel mode can be used, but this adds additional overhead to the packets). Because only GRE traffic needs to be protected, the crypto ACL configuration is simplified on the spoke device—only the GRE traffic needs to be specified in the crypto ACL. Once the tunnel is up, the hub and spokes use a dynamic routing protocol to learn about where to reach destinations. For a spoke, if a destination is located at another spoke, it will use NHRP to learn this and can, if configured correctly, set up a connection directly to the remote spoke.

Given the information I've discussed so far, DMVPNs provide the following advantages:

- The hub router doesn't need separate GRE tunnel interfaces and crypto map entries for each spoke device, greatly simplifying its IPsec configuration.
- The hub router doesn't need to know the details of the spoke devices; therefore, adding a spoke router means that you don't need to add additional configurations to the hub router.

- The spoke router can acquire its external interface addressing information dynamically, even though GRE tunnels are being used—NHRP will handle address registration with the hub router.

- A dynamic routing protocol is used to learn which networks are at which hub or spoke, eliminating the need for complex crypto ACLs and static routing configurations.

TIP   If there is an address translation device between the hub and spokes, where the external addresses of either device are being translated to a different address before reaching the public network, DMVPN will *not* necessarily work. Address translation devices are not typically smart enough to figure out that addresses being registered via NHRP messages also must be translated; therefore, in many cases DMVPN won't work. In most cases this shouldn't be a problem, because the routers participating in DMVPN are connected directly to the ISP and thus are in front of an address translation device. If they are behind an address translation device, you will probably need to assign these routers publicly reachable addresses; and on your translation device, set up a static translation for mapping this address to the same address, or set it up for address translation exemption.

If the address translation device is a Cisco IOS router and is running either IOS 12.3(9)a or 12.3(11)T, you can get DMVPN to work through the Cisco translation router if you've set up static translations for the DMVPN router(s) behind the address translation router.

A Network Not Using DMVPN

To understand the advantages that DMVPNs provide, I'll first start out by showing an example network (see Figure 17-6) that needs to support a large number of L2L sessions and the traditional approach used to build the connectivity. In this figure, "X" represents a spoke, like 5 for Spoke5 and 192.168.5.0/24. In this network, assume that DMVPN is not available, and thus an IPsec and GRE solution is necessary to connect the sites together.

Figure 17-6 *Hub-and-Spoke Network*

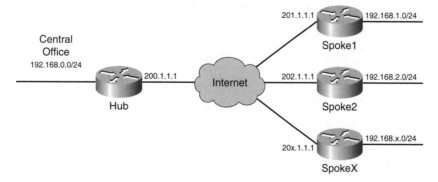

The hub configuration is shown in Example 17-28, where "*x*" represents a spoke router/ network. The first part of the hub configuration is not unusual: the ISAKMP/IKE Phase 1 policy, the pre-shared key, the crypto ACL, the transform set, and the crypto map entries. You'll need a separate crypto ACL for each L2L session, specifying only the GRE traffic in transport mode. You'll also need a separate crypto map entry for each L2L session. Likewise, each L2L session will need a separate GRE tunnel interface with unique addressing—you could use the **ip unnumbered** command to reduce your addressing requirements, but this could make troubleshooting difficult at a later time. The tunnel source is E0 and the destination is the remote peer (this is what is specified in the crypto ACL for protected traffic). In this example, the crypto map is applied only to the physical interface instead of to both the physical and tunnel interfaces, so I'm assuming the hub is running IOS 12.2(13)T or later. At the end of the configuration is the OSPF routing configuration for routing; you easily could have used EIGRP instead (in the latter instance, I would configure the **no auto-summary** command to disable summarization).

Example 17-28 *Hub Router Without DMVPN*

```
hub(config)# crypto isakmp policy 1
hub(config-isakmp)# authentication pre-share
hub(config-isakmp)# encryption aes
hub(config-isakmp)# exit
hub(config)# crypto isakmp key cisco123 address 0.0.0.0 0.0.0.0
                            no-xauth
hub(config)# access-list 101 permit gre host 200.1.1.1
                                    host 201.1.1.1
hub(config)# access-list <x+100> permit gre host 200.1.1.1
                                    host <200+x>.1.1.1
hub(config)# crypto ipsec transform-set trans2 esp-aes esp-sha-hmac
hub(cfg-crypto-trans)# mode transport
hub(cfg-crypto-trans)# exit
hub(config)# crypto map mymap local-address Ethernet0
hub(config)# crypto map mymap 10 ipsec-isakmp
hub(config-crypto-map)# set peer 201.1.1.1
hub(config-crypto-map)# set transform-set trans2
hub(config-crypto-map)# match address 101
hub(config-crypto-map)# exit
hub(config)# crypto map mymap <x*10> ipsec-isakmp
hub(config-crypto-map)# set peer <200+x>.1.1.1
hub(config-crypto-map)# set transform-set trans2
hub(config-crypto-map)# match address <x+100>
hub(config-crypto-map)# exit
hub(config)# interface Tunnel1
hub(config-if)# description Connection to Spoke1
hub(config-if)# bandwidth 1000
hub(config-if)# ip address 10.0.0.1 255.255.255.252
hub(config-if)# ip mtu 1440
hub(config-if)# delay 1000
hub(config-if)# tunnel source Ethernet0
hub(config-if)# tunnel destination 201.1.1.1
hub(config-if)# exit
hub(config)# interface Tunnel<x>
```

Example 17-28 *Hub Router Without DMVPN (Continued)*

```
hub(config-if)# description Connection to SpokeX
hub(config-if)# bandwidth 1000
hub(config-if)# ip address 10.0.0.<4*x-1> 255.255.255.252
hub(config-if)# ip mtu 1440
hub(config-if)# delay 1000
hub(config-if)# tunnel source Ethernet0
hub(config-if)# tunnel destination <200+x>.1.1.1
hub(config-if)# exit
hub(config)# interface Ethernet0
hub(config-if)# description Internet Connection
hub(config-if)# ip address 200.1.1.1 255.255.255.0
hub(config-if)# crypto map mymap
hub(config-if)# exit
hub(config)# interface Ethernet1
hub(config-if)# description Local LAN
hub(config-if)# ip address 192.168.0.1 255.255.255.0
hub(config-if)# exit
hub(config)# router ospf 1
hub(config-router)# network 10.0.0.0 0.0.0.255 area 1
hub(config-router)# network 192.168.0.0 0.0.0.255 area 0
hub(config-router)# exit
```

TIP   In this example, I've placed all of the spokes in area 1 and the central office network in area 0. You easily could have put the spoke connections in area 0 and the spoke networks in separate areas; however, I like my backbone being stable with few or no changes. Therefore, I prefer the approach of putting all spoke connections and networks in a separate area if the spokes are small networks. If the spokes are large networks, I prefer to put the spoke connections in the backbone and the spoke networks in separate areas. You also could do a combination of the two, but this would require that you would need a separate tunnel interface for each type (and a separate NHRP network identifier when using DMVPN).

Example 17-29 shows the configuration of the spoke devices, where "*x*" represents the spoke router number. If you would examine the routing tables of a particular spoke, it should see OSPF routes for the hub and all of the other spokes with a next-hop address of the hub's GRE tunnel interface for the respective spoke router.

Example 17-29 *Spoke Routers Without DMVPN*

```
spokeX(config)# crypto isakmp policy 1
spokeX(config-isakmp)# authentication pre-share
spokeX(config-isakmp)# encryption aes
spokeX(config-isakmp)# exit
spokeX(config)# crypto isakmp key cisco123 address
                        0.0.0.0 0.0.0.0 no-xauth
spokeX(config)# crypto ipsec transform-set trans2 esp-aes
                        esp-sha-hmac
spokeX(cfg-crypto-trans)# mode transport
```

continues

Example 17-29 *Spoke Routers Without DMVPN (Continued)*

```
spokeX(cfg-crypto-trans)# exit
spokeX(config)# crypto map mymap local-address Ethernet0
spokeX(config)# crypto map mymap 10 ipsec-isakmp
spokeX(config-crypto-map)# set peer 172.17.0.1
spokeX(config-crypto-map)# set transform-set trans2
spokeX(config-crypto-map)# match address 101
spokeX(config-crypto-map)# exit
spokeX(config)# interface Tunnel0
spokeX(config-if)# bandwidth 1000
spokeX(config-if)# ip address 10.0.0.<4*x-2> 255.255.255.252
spokeX(config-if)# ip mtu 1440
spokeX(config-if)# delay 1000
spokeX(config-if)# tunnel source Ethernet0
spokeX(config-if)# tunnel destination 200.1.1.1
spokeX(config-if)# exit
spokeX(config)# interface Ethernet0
spokeX(config-if)# description Internet Connection
spokeX(config-if)# ip address <200+x>.1.1.1 255.255.255.0
spokeX(config-if)# crypto map mymap
spokeX(config-if)# exit
spokeX(config)# interface Ethernet1
spokeX(config-if)# description Local LAN
spokeX(config-if)# ip address 192.168.<x>.1 255.255.255.0
spokeX(config-if)# exit
spokeX(config)# router ospf 1
spokeX(config-router)# network 10.0.0.0 0.0.0.255 area 1
spokeX(config-router)# network 192.168.<n>.0 0.0.0.255 area 1
spokeX(config-router)# exit
spokeX(config)# access-list 101 permit gre host <200+x>.1.1.1
                                       host 200.1.1.1
```

TIP   For a small number of routers, using DMVPN isn't necessary. However, if you will be adding spokes to your network continually, using DMVPN is preferred over the examples shown in 17-28 and 17-29. Therefore, I always use DMVPN when I can, even for a small number of initial routers.

DMVPN Configuration

As you can see from the last section, the more spokes you add, the more configuration you need to do on both the hub and new spoke routers. DMVPN is not that different from setting up an L2L session using IPsec and GRE tunnels. You'll need to perform three types of configuration to set up DMVPN: the hub, the spokes, and dynamic routing.

DMVPN Hub Configuration

DMVPN will need the following commands on the hub router(s):

```
hub(config)# crypto ipsec profile profile_name
hub(ipsec-profile)# set transform-set transform_set_name1
                    [transform-set-name2...transform-set-name6]
```

```
hub(ipsec-profile)# exit
hub(config)# interface tunnel tunnel_#
hub(config-if)# ip mtu 1436
hub(config-if)# tunnel mode gre multipoint
hub(config-if)# tunnel key key_#
hub(config-if)# tunnel protection ipsec profile profile_name
hub(config-if)# ip nhrp network-id network_identifier
hub(config-if)# ip nhrp authentication string
hub(config-if)# ip nhrp map multicast dynamic
hub(config-if)# ip nhrp holdtime seconds
```

The **crypto ipsec profile** command creates an IPsec profile to protect the GRE tunnel traffic. It is activated on the tunnel interface with the **tunnel protection ipsec profile** command. Only a transform set needs to be defined for the profile. When using the **tunnel protection ipsec profile** command, applying a static crypto map to the hub router's physical interface is no longer necessary.

To prevent fragmentation problems, set the MTU size on the GRE interface to 1,436 bytes with the **ip mtu** command. Because spokes will terminate their tunnel connections on the same hub tunnel interface, you need to specify the connection mode as multipoint with the **tunnel mode gre multipoint** command. If more than one tunnel interface will exist on the hub, you'll need to specify a tunnel key for each tunnel interface with the **tunnel key** command: based on the key the spoke uses, the router will know which GRE tunnel interface to process the traffic.

The **ip nhrp network-id** command specifies a network identifier for the broadcast domain the hub and spokes belong to. If there is more than one broadcast domain, you'll need more than one tunnel interface and NHRP network identifier. The **ip nhrp authentication** command specifies a key to use for authentication: this must match for all NHRP routers associated with the same network identifier.

Of course, because the spoke devices might be acquiring their addresses dynamically, you can't manually map the GRE tunnel connections with NHRP. Instead, the hub router must learn these addresses when the spokes boot up and connect to the hub; this is enabled with the **ip nhrp map multicast dynamic** command. This command allows the registration of multicast addresses for routing protocols like RIPv2, EIGRP, and OSPF. Without this command, you would need to map the routing protocol multicast address(es) manually for each remote spoke, which would be a headache. With the **ip nhrp map multicast dynamic** command, because the hub knows nothing about the spokes, the spoke routers must initiate the connection to the hub. Cisco ensures this by forcing the spoke routers to build the session when they boot up, or if they ever lose their connectivity. The **ip nhrp holdtime** command specifies how long a hub router will tell a spoke to keep an NHRP reply. The default is 7,200 seconds (two hours). If your spoke routers are acquiring their addresses dynamically, you might want to make this a smaller value, like 300 seconds.

NOTE   Because all spokes terminate their connections on the same tunnel interface on the hub, the IP addressing for the GRE tunnel interfaces must have addresses from the *same* subnet.

DMVPN Spoke Configuration

DMVPN will need the following commands on the spoke routers:

```
spoke(config)# crypto ipsec profile profile_name
spoke(ipsec-profile)# set transform-set transform_set_name1
                          [transform-set-name2...transform-set-name6]
spoke(ipsec-profile)# exit
spoke(config)# interface tunnel tunnel_#
spoke(config-if)# ip mtu 1436
spoke(config-if)# tunnel mode gre multipoint
spoke(config-if)# tunnel key key_#
spoke(config-if)# tunnel protection ipsec profile profile_name
spoke(config-if)# ip nhrp network-id network_identifier
spoke(config-if)# ip nhrp authentication string
spoke(config-if)# ip nhrp map hub_GRE_IP_address
                          hub_external_interface_IP_address
spoke(config-if)# ip nhrp map multicast
                          hub_external_interface_IP_address
spoke(config-if)# ip nhrp nhs hub_GRE_IP_address
spoke(config-if)# ip nhrp holdtime seconds
```

The configuration of the spokes is similar to that of the hub. With IOS 12.2(13)T, I highly recommend that you use IPsec profiles, because this greatly simplifies your IPsec configuration (see the Note at the end of this section for IPsec legacy IOS versions).

If the spoke will be setting up connections to other spokes, you must use the **tunnel mode gre multipoint** command; omitting this command will restrict the spoke to setting up connections to *only* the hub router. On the tunnel interface, you'll need to map the hub's IP address manually, on the GRE tunnel interface with the hub's external interface address, with this **ip nhrp map** command. For routing protocols that use multicasts (RIPv2, OSPF, and EIGRP), you also must use the **ip nhrp map multicast** command to map the routing protocols' multicast address with the hub router. This is necessary only if the GRE interface has been configured as a multipoint interface. Last, you need to tell the spoke who the next-hop server (NHS) is with the **ip nhrp nhs** command; this is the IP address on the hub's GRE interface. This command specifies who the spoke should register its addressing information with.

NOTE   This section doesn't cover the complete configuration, because I've already discussed many of the commands in this chapter. The next section will pull all of this together in an example. Also, static crypto maps can be used instead of IPsec profiles if the spokes don't support IPsec profiles, which requires IOS 12.2(13)T; however, using IPsec profiles greatly simplifies the configuration. In the crypto map entry for the hub, you'll need to define the transform set to use to protect the traffic and the peer to connect to (the hub's IP address on its external interface). For the crypto ACL, if the spoke has a static IP address on its external interface, then specify that as the source address for GRE traffic; otherwise, you'll need to use the keyword **any** for the source because this is unknown based on what the ISP assigns you. However, the **set security-association level per-host** command qualifies the proxy setup between the spoke and hub. Instead of using the keyword **any** in the exchange with the hub as to what traffic is protected, the **set** command restricts the protected traffic from any to the actual address on the spoke's interface where the crypto map is activated. Here's a sample configuration for the static crypto map :

```
spoke(config)# crypto map map_name seq_# ipsec-isakmp
spoke(ipsec-profile)# set transform-set transform_set_name1
                              [transform-set-name2...transform-set-name6]
spoke(ipsec-profile)# set peer hub_external_interface_IP_address
spoke(ipsec-profile)# match address ACL_name_or_#
spoke(ipsec-profile)# set security-association level per-host
spoke(ipsec-profile)# exit
```

You'll need to activate the crypto map on the spoke's external interface.

DMVPN Routing Configuration

Because routing updates need to enter and leave the same interface to go from one spoke router to another spoke via the GRE tunnel interface on the hub, you'll have to disable split horizon on the hub for EIGRP, IGRP (no longer supported by Cisco), or RIP. To disable split horizon for EIGRP, perform the following:

```
hub(config)# interface tunnel tunnel_#
hub(config-if)# no ip split-horizon eigrp AS_#
hub(config-if)# no ip next-hop-self eigrp AS_#
```

On the tunnel interface, use the **no ip split-horizon eigrp** command to disable split horizon, allowing routes from one spoke to propagate to another via the hub router. By default, the hub router will advertise itself as the next hop when sending any routes to the spokes. If you want a spoke to set up an IPsec GRE connection to another spoke, you must disable this behavior with the **no ip next-hop-self eigrp** command; otherwise, the spokes will always send traffic to the hub to reach another spoke device.

NOTE

If you want spokes to set up connections to other spokes, you must configure the **no ip next-hop-self eigrp** command on the hub router. Up until 12.3(2), this will work only if the routers are configured for process switching. Later IOS versions support CEF. Given this restriction, I typically used OSPF or RIPv2 in older IOS versions.

To disable split horizon for RIP or IGRP, configure this for the tunnel interface:

```
hub(config)# interface tunnel tunnel_#
hub(config-if)# no ip split-horizon
```

Unlike EIGRP, you don't need to disable the next-hop process: with RIP, the next-hop address of an advertised route from the spoke will be the spoke when the hub forwards the advertisement to other spokes.

If you're running OSPF on the hub router, you'll need to configure the following:

```
hub(config) interface tunnel tunnel_#
hub(config-if)# ip ospf network broadcast
hub(config-if)# ip ospf priority #_>_1
```

OSPF doesn't have problems with split horizon; however, you must tell the hub router that the GRE interface is multipoint with the **ip ospf network broadcast** command: this allows spokes to send updates to the hub, which will forward them to the other spokes. The hub must also be elected as the designated router (DR) for the logical segment connecting the hub and spokes (remember that the tunnel interfaces are in the same broadcast domain). To enforce this, set the OSPF priority for the hub router to something greater than one.

TIP   I would also recommend that you set the OSPF priority to 0 for the spoke routers, ensuring that they never become a DR. This is important when you configure redundancy with multiple hub routers and want only the hub routers to perform the DR and backup DR (BDR) roles.

NOTE   The configured dynamic routing protocol runs only between the hub and spokes: it doesn't run directly between spokes. Therefore, if one spoke wants to send traffic to a destination at a different spoke, the source spoke must send an NHRP query to the advertising router (hub) for the route in its routing table. The hub will send back the spoke connected to the network and the source spoke can set up a connection directly to the destination spoke.

A Network Using DMVPN on Hubs and Spokes

I'll now illustrate an example using DMVPN on both hubs and spokes, where spokes can set up connections to other spokes. I'll use previous examples from Figure 17-6 and Examples 17-25 and 17-26; however, I'll convert the hub-and-spoke configurations from these examples to use DMVPN.

Example 17-30 shows the hub's new configuration. This example uses pre-shared keys for authentication, wildcarding the source address. If this is a concern, I would recommend you use certificates for device authentication. I've configured DPD so that any dropped connections from a spoke allow the hub to remove them, enabling the spoke to reconnect in a reasonable period of time. Notice that the transform set below the pre-shared key configuration is using transport mode; this is because only the GRE traffic between the hub and spokes needs to be protected. Below this, I created an IPsec profile called "dmvpnprofile" that uses this transform set.

Example 17-30 *Hub Router with DMVPN*

```
hub(config)# crypto isakmp policy 1
hub(config-isakmp)# authentication pre-share
hub(config-isakmp)# encryption aes
hub(config-isakmp)# exit
hub(config)# crypto isakmp key cisco123 address 0.0.0.0 0.0.0.0
                          no-xauth
hub(config)# crypto isakmp keepalive 20 3
hub(config)# crypto ipsec transform-set trans2 esp-aes esp-sha-hmac
hub(cfg-crypto-trans)# mode transport
hub(cfg-crypto-trans)# exit
hub(config)# crypto ipsec profile dmvpnprofile
hub(ipsec-profile)# set transform-set trans2
hub(ipsec-profile)# exit
hub(config)# interface tunnel0
hub(config-if)# description Connection to Spokes
hub(config-if)# bandwidth 1000
hub(config-if)# ip address 10.0.0.1 255.255.255.0
hub(config-if)# ip mtu 1436
hub(config-if)# delay 1000
hub(config-if)# ip ospf network broadcast
hub(config-if)# ip ospf priority 2
hub(config-if)# ip nhrp authentication cisco123
hub(config-if)# ip nhrp map multicast dynamic
hub(config-if)# ip nhrp network-id 100000
hub(config-if)# ip nhrp holdtime 600
hub(config-if)# tunnel source Ethernet0
hub(config-if)# tunnel mode gre multipoint
hub(config-if)# tunnel key 100000
hub(config-if)# tunnel protection ipsec profile dmvpnprofile
hub(config-if)# exit
hub(config)# interface Ethernet0
hub(config-if)# description Internet Connection
hub(config-if)# ip address 200.1.1.1 255.255.255.0
hub(config-if)# exit
hub(config)# interface Ethernet1
hub(config-if)# description Local LAN
hub(config-if)# ip address 192.168.0.1 255.255.255.0
hub(config-if)# exit
hub(config)# router ospf 1
hub(config-router)# network 10.0.0.0 0.0.0.255 area 1
hub(config-router)# network 192.168.0.0 0.0.0.255 area 0
hub(config-router)# exit
```

In the preceding example, on the only GRE tunnel interface, I've assigned an IP address of
10.0.0.1/24—this is different from the non-DMVPN solution, which required a different
tunnel interface for each spoke, and thus different subnets. In this example, all spokes are in
the 10.0.0.0/24 subnet. Since the routing protocol is OSPF, I set the OSPF priority to 2 to
ensure that the hub becomes the DR, and I set the medium type to broadcast. For the NHRP
configuration, I've specified the map type as "multicast dynamic" to accept the registrations
from the spokes. For the GRE configuration, I've set the tunnel type to "gre multipoint" to
terminate multiple tunnel connections on the hub. I've also enabled the IPsec profile.

The spoke routers' configuration is shown in Example 17-31. Looking through the
example, you can see that it is very similar to that of the hub's. Just replace the "*x*" with the
spoke router number throughout the configuration example. Notice that the pre-shared key
for device authentication is wildcarded—this is necessary because a spoke router, besides
connecting to the hub, might be setting up dynamic IPsec sessions to other spokes; again,
you can use certificates if you are concerned about using wildcarded pre-shared keys.

Example 17-31 *Spoke Routers with DMVPN*

```
spokeX(config)# crypto isakmp policy 1
spokeX(config-isakmp)# authentication pre-share
spokeX(config-isakmp)# encryption aes
spokeX(config-isakmp)# exit
spokeX(config)# crypto isakmp key cisco123 address
                        0.0.0.0 0.0.0.0 no-xauth
spokeX(config)# crypto isakmp keepalive 20 3
spokeX(config)# crypto ipsec transform-set trans2 esp-aes
                        esp-sha-hmac
spokeX(cfg-crypto-trans)# mode transport
spokeX(cfg-crypto-trans)# exit
spokeX(config)# crypto ipsec profile dmvpnprofile
spokeX(ipsec-profile)# set transform-set trans2
spokeX(ipsec-profile)# exit
spokeX(config)# interface tunnel0
spokeX(config-if)# description Connection to hub
spokeX(config-if)# bandwidth 1000
spokeX(config-if)# ip address 10.0.0.<x+1> 255.255.255.0
spokeX(config-if)# ip mtu 1436
spokeX(config-if)# delay 1000
spokeX(config-if)# ip ospf network broadcast
spokeX(config-if)# ip ospf priority 0
spokeX(config-if)# ip nhrp authentication cisco123
spokeX(config-if)# ip nhrp map multicast 200.1.1.1
spokeX(config-if)# ip nhrp map 10.0.0.1 200.1.1.1
spokeX(config-if)# ip nhrp nhs 10.0.0.1
spokeX(config-if)# ip nhrp network-id 100000
spokeX(config-if)# ip nhrp holdtime 300
spokeX(config-if)# tunnel source Ethernet0
spokeX(config-if)# tunnel mode gre multipoint
spokeX(config-if)# tunnel key 100000
spokeX(config-if)# tunnel protection ipsec profile dmvpnprofile
spokeX(config-if)# exit
spokeX(config)# interface Ethernet0
spokeX(config-if)# description Connection to Internet
spokeX(config-if)# ip address dhcp hostname Spoke<x>
spokeX(config-if)# exit
spokeX(config)# interface Ethernet1
spokeX(config-if)# description Local LAN
spokeX(config-if)# ip address 192.168.<x>.1 255.255.255.0
spokeX(config-if)# exit
spokeX(config)# router ospf 1
spokeX(config-router)# network 10.0.0.0 0.0.0.255 area 1
spokeX(config-router)# network 192.168.<n>.0 0.0.0.255 area 1
spokeX(config-router)# exit
```

On the GRE tunnel interface of the spoke routers, there are some differences compared to what is configured on the hub router. First, I've set the OSPF priority to 0, ensuring that a spoke will never become a DR; this is necessary because only the hub router by default has direct connections to all routers in the DMVPN network. Below this I've mapped multicasting addresses to the hub's external interface, in addition to telling the spoke that 10.0.0.1 (the hub's GRE tunnel interface address) is reachable via the hub's external interface. I've also indicated that the NHS is 10.0.0.1: the GRE interface of the hub. When the spoke boots up, it will register its addressing information with the NHS at this address. And because the spoke might set up connections directly to other spokes, I've configured the tunnel interface on the spokes in GRE multipoint mode.

TIP	If you don't want to allow spokes to set up connections to other spokes, leave the mode default to GRE point-to-point. In this case, you'll need to configure the tunnel destination command on the GRE tunnel interface, specifying the hub's external IP address for the destination.

Another interesting difference is that for Ethernet0, the external interface of the spoke, I've configured it for dynamic address acquisition. Of course, if your router has a static address for the interface, you would configure this manually. In either situation, on the tunnel interface, I've specified the tunnel source address as Ethernet0, so it doesn't matter whether the address is defined statically on the interface or acquired dynamically.

To understand what takes place when the spokes boot up and connect to the hub router in Figure 17-6, let's look at some **show** commands on the routers. Assume that Spoke1 and Spoke2 have connected to the hub. Example 17-32 shows the routing table, the NHRP registration table, and the current IPsec SAs on the hub. In the routing table, you can see the two routes for Spoke1's and Spoke2's local LAN segments. In the NHRP table, you can see the two registered tunnel addresses of the spokes. The **show crypto session** command displays the two SAs built from the spokes to the hub.

Example 17-32 *Hub's Operation After Spokes Boot Up*

```
hub# show ip route
←output omitted→
     10.0.0.0/24 is subnetted, 1 subnets
C       10.0.0.0 is directly connected, Tunnel0
C    192.168.0.0/24 is directly connected, Loopback1
C    192.1.1.0/24 is directly connected, Ethernet0/0
     192.168.1.0/32 is subnetted, 1 subnets
O       192.168.1.1 [110/101] via 10.0.0.2, 00:04:32, Tunnel0
     192.168.2.0/32 is subnetted, 1 subnets
O       192.168.2.1 [110/101] via 10.0.0.3, 00:04:32, Tunnel0
hub# show ip nhrp
10.0.0.2/32 via 10.0.0.2, Tunnel0 created 00:05:24, expire 00:04:33
```

continues

Example 17-32 *Hub's Operation After Spokes Boot Up (Continued)*

```
    Type: dynamic, Flags: authoritative unique registered used
    NBMA address: 201.1.1.1
10.0.0.3/32 via 10.0.0.3, Tunnel0 created 00:05:33, expire 00:04:26
    Type: dynamic, Flags: authoritative unique registered used
    NBMA address: 202.1.1.1
hub# show crypto session
Crypto session current status
Interface: Tunnel0
Session status: UP-ACTIVE
Peer: 201.1.1.1 port 500
   IKE SA: local 200.1.1.1/500 remote 201.1.1.1/500 Active
   IPSEC FLOW: permit 47 host 200.1.1.1 host 201.1.1.1
        Active SAs: 2, origin: crypto map
Interface: Tunnel0
Session status: UP-ACTIVE
Peer: 202.1.1.1 port 500
   IKE SA: local 200.1.1.1/500 remote 202.1.1.1/500 Active
   IPSEC FLOW: permit 47 host 200.1.1.1 host 202.1.1.1
        Active SAs: 2, origin: crypto map
```

Example 17-33 shows Spoke1's operation after it has booted up. In its routing table you
can see the hub's local LAN segment in area 0 and Spoke2's local LAN segment in area 1
(the same area that Spoke1 is in). You can see the NHRP information, of which it currently
only knows about the hub, which we configured manually. Only one IPsec session has been
established, and it's to the hub router.

Example 17-33 *Spoke1's Operation After it Boots Up*

```
spoke1# show ip route
←output omitted→
     10.0.0.0/24 is subnetted, 1 subnets
C       10.0.0.0 is directly connected, Tunnel0
     192.168.0.0/32 is subnetted, 1 subnets
O IA    192.168.0.1 [110/101] via 10.0.0.1, 00:05:44, Tunnel0
C    192.1.1.0/24 is directly connected, Ethernet0
C    192.168.1.0/24 is directly connected, Loopback0
     192.168.2.0/32 is subnetted, 1 subnets
O       192.168.2.1 [110/101] via 10.0.0.3, 00:05:44, Tunnel0
S*   0.0.0.0/0 [1/0] via 201.1.1.2
spoke1# show ip nhrp
10.0.0.1/32 via 10.0.0.1, Tunnel0 created 00:20:01, never expire
   Type: static, Flags: authoritative used
   NBMA address: 200.1.1.1
spoke1# show crypto session
Crypto session current status
Interface: Tunnel0
Session status: UP-ACTIVE
Peer: 200.1.1.1 port 500
   IKE SA: local 201.1.1.1/500 remote 200.1.1.1/500 Active
   IPSEC FLOW: permit 47 host 201.1.1.1 host 200.1.1.1
        Active SAs: 2, origin: crypto map
Interface: Tunnel0
Session status: UP-ACTIVE
```

At this point, if someone from Spoke1's LAN segment would access a device at Spoke2's LAN segment, Spoke1 would perform the following:

Step 1   Look at its routing table and determine that the next hop is 10.0.0.3 (Spoke2).

Step 2   Because it doesn't know about 10.0.0.3, Spoke1 would forward an NHRP resolution request to the NHS (the hub).

Step 3   The NHS would respond with Spoke2's physical external interface address.

Step 4   Spoke1 would establish an IPsec session directly with Spoke2.

Step 5   Spoke1 would send the traffic directly to Spoke2 across the new IPsec session.

When done, Example 17-34 shows the NHRP and IPsec results on Spoke1. Notice that the NHRP resolution table contains Spoke2 (10.0.0.3–202.1.1.1) and that there is an IPsec session connected to Spoke2.

Example 17-34 *Spoke1's Operation When Connecting to Another Spoke*

```
spoke1# show ip nhrp
10.0.0.1/32 via 10.0.0.1, Tunnel0 created 00:21:46, never expire
  Type: static, Flags: authoritative used
  NBMA address: 200.1.1.1
10.0.0.3/32 via 10.0.0.3, Tunnel0 created 00:00:10, expire 00:04:18
  Type: dynamic, Flags: router
  NBMA address: 202.1.1.1
spoke1# show crypto session
Crypto session current status
Interface: Tunnel0
Session status: UP-ACTIVE
Peer: 200.1.1.1 port 500
  IKE SA: local 201.1.1.1/500 remote 200.1.1.1/500 Active
  IPSEC FLOW: permit 47 host 201.1.1.1 host 200.1.1.1
      Active SAs: 2, origin: crypto map
Interface: Tunnel0
Session status: UP-ACTIVE
Peer: 202.1.1.1 port 500
  IKE SA: local 201.1.1.1/500 remote 202.1.1.1/500 Active
  IPSEC FLOW: permit 47 host 201.1.1.1 host 202.1.1.1
      Active SAs: 2, origin: crypto map
```

DMVPN and Hub Redundancy

One of the problems with the DMVPN example shown in Examples 17-30 and 17-31 is that if the hub fails, the spokes lose connectivity to both the corporate office and the other spokes (the hub is the NHRP server and is needed to resolve addresses to reach other spokes). Because of this concern, there are two redundancy designs you can implement:

- Single-DMVPN design with dual hubs
- Dual-DMVPN design with dual hubs

The following two sections will discuss each solution.

NOTE   One problem with HSRP with RRI and Stateful IPsec Failover is that both use HSRP as part
of their implementation for redundancy, and this requires that the devices be connected on
the same medium. In many cases, this is not feasible. In these situations, you can implement
either a single-DMVPN or dual-DMVPN design with dual hubs. These two solutions don't
provide a stateful failover implementation, but they do provide chassis redundancy as well
as possible load balancing.

Single-DMVPN Design with Dual Hubs

In a single-DMVPN design with dual hubs, a single DMVPN network is used with two
hubs as NHSs for the single subnet infrastructure. All hubs and spokes have a single GRE
tunnel, as shown in Figure 17-7, with a single subnet. The advantage of this design is that
it is simple to set up compared to a dual-DMVPN/dual-hub design. However, its main
disadvantage is that you have less control over routing across the DMVPN network because
the spokes have a single interface connected to both hubs; therefore, you can't configure
things like metrics, cost, delay, or bandwidth to favor one hub over another. If you need to
configure a preference of one hub over another, you must do it with the features of your
routing protocol. In this case, Cisco recommends using EIGRP or RIP over other protocols,
or you could use policy routing (which is what I would recommend).

Figure 17-7 *Single-DMVPN Design With Dual Hubs*

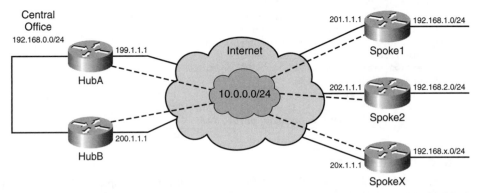

Figure 17-7 illustrates how to configure a single-DMVPN design with dual hubs.
Example 17-35 shows the configuration of HubA: this is same configuration used
previously in Example 17-30, except that the hub's external IP address is different.

Example 17-35 *Single-DMVPN Design With Dual Hubs: HubA's Configuration*

```
hubA(config)# crypto isakmp policy 1
hubA(config-isakmp)# authentication pre-share
hubA(config-isakmp)# encryption aes
```

Example 17-35 *Single-DMVPN Design With Dual Hubs: HubA's Configuration (Continued)*

```
hubA(config-isakmp)# exit
hubA(config)# crypto isakmp key cisco123 address 0.0.0.0 0.0.0.0
                    no-xauth
hubA(config)# crypto isakmp keepalive 20 3
hubA(config)# crypto ipsec transform-set trans2 esp-aes esp-sha-hmac
hubA(cfg-crypto-trans)# mode transport
hubA(cfg-crypto-trans)# exit
hubA(config)# crypto ipsec profile dmvpnprofile
hubA(ipsec-profile)# set transform-set trans2
hubA(ipsec-profile)# exit
hubA(config)# interface tunnel0
hubA(config-if)# description Connection to Spokes
hubA(config-if)# bandwidth 1000
hubA(config-if)# ip address 10.0.0.1 255.255.255.0
hubA(config-if)# ip mtu 1436
hubA(config-if)# delay 1000
hubA(config-if)# ip ospf network broadcast
hubA(config-if)# ip ospf priority 2
hubA(config-if)# ip nhrp authentication cisco123
hubA(config-if)# ip nhrp map multicast dynamic
hubA(config-if)# ip nhrp network-id 100000
hubA(config-if)# ip nhrp holdtime 600
hubA(config-if)# tunnel source Ethernet0
hubA(config-if)# tunnel mode gre multipoint
hubA(config-if)# tunnel key 100000
hubA(config-if)# tunnel protection ipsec profile dmvpnprofile
hubA(config-if)# exit
hubA(config)# interface Ethernet0
hubA(config-if)# description Internet Connection
hubA(config-if)# ip address 199.1.1.1 255.255.255.0
hubA(config-if)# exit
hubA(config)# interface Ethernet1
hubA(config-if)# description Local LAN
hubA(config-if)# ip address 192.168.0.1 255.255.255.0
hubA(config-if)# exit
hubA(config)# router ospf 1
hubA(config-router)# network 10.0.0.0 0.0.0.255 area 1
hubA(config-router)# network 192.168.0.0 0.0.0.255 area 0
hubA(config-router)# exit
```

Example 17-36 shows HubB's configuration, which is similar to HubA's.

Example 17-36 *Single-DMVPN Design with Dual Hubs: HubB's Configuration*

```
hubB(config)# crypto isakmp policy 1
hubB(config-isakmp)# authentication pre-share
hubB(config-isakmp)# encryption aes
hubB(config-isakmp)# exit
hubB(config)# crypto isakmp key cisco123 address 0.0.0.0 0.0.0.0
                    no-xauth
hubB(config)# crypto isakmp keepalive 20 3
hubB(config)# crypto ipsec transform-set trans2 esp-aes esp-sha-hmac
```

continues

Example 17-36 *Single-DMVPN Design with Dual Hubs: HubB's Configuration (Continued)*

```
hubB(cfg-crypto-trans)# mode transport
hubB(cfg-crypto-trans)# exit
hubB(config)# crypto ipsec profile dmvpnprofile
hubB(ipsec-profile)# set transform-set trans2
hubB(ipsec-profile)# exit
hubB(config)# interface tunnel0
hubB(config-if)# description Connection to Spokes
hubB(config-if)# bandwidth 900
hubB(config-if)# ip address 10.0.0.2 255.255.255.0
hubB(config-if)# ip mtu 1436
hubB(config-if)# delay 1000
hubB(config-if)# ip ospf network broadcast
hubB(config-if)# ip ospf priority 1
hubB(config-if)# ip nhrp authentication cisco123
hubB(config-if)# ip nhrp map 10.0.0.1 199.1.1.1
hubB(config-if)# ip nhrp map multicast dynamic
hubB(config-if)# ip nhrp nhs 10.0.0.1
hubB(config-if)# ip nhrp network-id 100000
hubB(config-if)# ip nhrp holdtime 600
hubB(config-if)# tunnel source Ethernet0
hubB(config-if)# tunnel mode gre multipoint
hubB(config-if)# tunnel key 100000
hubB(config-if)# tunnel protection ipsec profile dmvpnprofile
hubB(config-if)# exit
hubB(config)# interface Ethernet0
hubB(config-if)# description Internet Connection
hubB(config-if)# ip address 200.1.1.1 255.255.255.0
hubB(config-if)# exit
hubB(config)# interface Ethernet1
hubB(config-if)# description Local LAN
hubB(config-if)# ip address 192.168.0.2 255.255.255.0
hubB(config-if)# exit
hubB(config)# router ospf 1
hubB(config-router)# network 10.0.0.0 0.0.0.255 area 1
hubB(config-router)# network 192.168.0.0 0.0.0.255 area 0
hubB(config-router)# exit
```

There are a few things to point out, though, about HubB's configuration concerning its GRE tunnel interface:

- Notice that the bandwidth parameter is set to 900 instead of 1,000; this ensures that the central office routers prefer HubA over HubB to reach the spokes. With OSPF, you also could have used the **ip ospf cost** command. If running EIGRP, changing the bandwidth is sufficient because this is one of the parameters in the computation of the route metric. If you don't change the routing metric for HubB, the spokes will see two equal-cost paths to reach destinations through the hubs; and if per-packet load balancing is enabled, this could create out-of-order packets, which, in some situations, might cause problems with applications.

- HubB's OSPF priority is set to 1 to ensure that it becomes the BDR and HubA the DR.

- HubB must register with HubA; therefore, the **ip nhrp map** commands are needed in addition to the **ip nhrp nhs** command.

Other than the differences in the preceding list, the configuration is the same as HubA.

Example 17-37 shows the configuration of the spoke routers. The main changes are on the tunnel interface. First, notice that the hubs and the spokes all have unique IP addresses in the same subnet on the GRE tunnel interface. Next, the OSPF priority is set to 0, ensuring that only HubA and HubB perform the functions of the DR/BDR. Unlike the single-DMVPN single-hub design, you'll need to configure two sets of NHRP mappings and NHS servers on the spokes: one for HubA and one for HubB. To prevent the spokes from load balancing traffic to the two hubs, as an additional precaution I've assigned an administrative distance of 111 (the default for OSPF is 110) for all route advertisements coming from 10.0.0.2 (HubB), thereby preferring HubA to reach destinations at the central office. With this change and either the bandwidth or cost change on the HubB, HubA is preferred for all destinations over HubB, but HubB still provides redundancy for HubA. Other than this, the configuration of the spoke routers is the same as that in a single-DMVPN single-hub design.

Example 17-37 *Single-DMVPN Design with Dual Hubs: Spoke Configuration*

```
spokeX(config)# crypto isakmp policy 1
spokeX(config-isakmp)# authentication pre-share
spokeX(config-isakmp)# encryption aes
spokeX(config-isakmp)# exit
spokeX(config)# crypto isakmp key cisco123 address
                        0.0.0.0 0.0.0.0 no-xauth
spokeX(config)# crypto isakmp keepalive 20 3
spokeX(config)# crypto ipsec transform-set trans2 esp-aes
                        esp-sha-hmac
spokeX(cfg-crypto-trans)# mode transport
spokeX(cfg-crypto-trans)# exit
spokeX(config)# crypto ipsec profile dmvpnprofile
spokeX(ipsec-profile)# set transform-set trans2
spokeX(ipsec-profile)# exit
spokeX(config)# interface tunnel0
spokeX(config-if)# description Connection to hubs
spokeX(config-if)# bandwidth 1000
spokeX(config-if)# ip address 10.0.0.<x+10> 255.255.255.0
spokeX(config-if)# ip mtu 1436
spokeX(config-if)# delay 1000
spokeX(config-if)# ip ospf network broadcast
spokeX(config-if)# ip ospf priority 0
spokeX(config-if)# ip nhrp authentication cisco123
spokeX(config-if)# ip nhrp map multicast 199.1.1.1
spokeX(config-if)# ip nhrp map 10.0.0.1 199.1.1.1
spokeX(config-if)# ip nhrp map multicast 200.1.1.1
spokeX(config-if)# ip nhrp map 10.0.0.2 200.1.1.1
spokeX(config-if)# ip nhrp nhs 10.0.0.1
spokeX(config-if)# ip nhrp nhs 10.0.0.2
```

continues

Example 17-37 *Single-DMVPN Design with Dual Hubs: Spoke Configuration (Continued)*

```
spokeX(config-if)# ip nhrp network-id 100000
spokeX(config-if)# ip nhrp holdtime 300
spokeX(config-if)# tunnel source Ethernet0
spokeX(config-if)# tunnel destination 199.1.1.1
spokeX(config-if)# tunnel mode gre multipoint
spokeX(config-if)# tunnel key 100000
spokeX(config-if)# tunnel protection ipsec profile dmvpnprofile
spokeX(config-if)# exit
spokeX(config)# interface Ethernet0
spokeX(config-if)# description Connection to Internet
spokeX(config-if)# ip address dhcp hostname Spoke<x>
spokeX(config-if)# exit
spokeX(config)# interface Ethernet1
spokeX(config-if)# description Local LAN
spokeX(config-if)# ip address 192.168.<x>.1 255.255.255.0
spokeX(config-if)# exit
spokeX(config)# access-list 1 permit any
spokeX(config)# router ospf 1
spokeX(config-router)# network 10.0.0.0 0.0.0.255 area 1
spokeX(config-router)# network 192.168.<n>.0 0.0.0.255 area 1
spokeX(config-router)# distance 111 10.0.0.2 0.0.0.0 1
spokeX(config-router)# exit
```

Dual-DMVPN Design with Dual Hubs

The dual-DMVPN design with dual hubs requires more configuration on your part, but provides better routing control for destinations across the DMVPN cloud. Figure 17-8 illustrates this design. Unlike the Single-DMVPN/dual-hub design, this design deploys dual DMVPN networks: these are basically two subnets, where each hub router is responsible for their respective subnet. The spokes will have two GRE tunnel interfaces connected to both of these subnets.

Figure 17-8 *Dual-DMVPN Design with Dual Hubs*

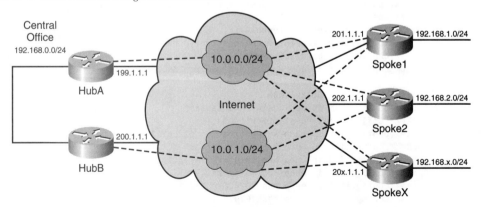

Dual-DMVPN and Dual-Hub Design Issues

One issue with the dual-DMVPN/dual-hub design deals with the configuration of the GRE tunnel interfaces on the spokes. You can use either point-to-point GRE (p-pGRE) or multipoint GRE (mGRE) interfaces. With p-pGRE interfaces, each tunnel interface can use the same tunnel source, because each p-p interface represents a different subnet. However, this can create a problem with mGRE interfaces; with these interfaces, when ISAKMP initiates, the ISAKMP connection only knows about the source and destination addresses. The problem with the source address is that it can be associated with more than one mGRE interface. In this situation, any inbound multicast packets, like those from routing protocols, might be forwarded to the wrong MGRE interface, thereby breaking the dynamic routing protocol you're running. GRE itself doesn't have this problem because you can use the **tunnel key** command to differentiate between multiple mGRE interfaces on the same router. Currently, Cisco requires unique source IP addresses for mGRE tunnels, but plans to remove this restriction in a later IOS. Until then, either use p-pGRE connections or have two public IP addresses on each of your spokes' external interfaces, where one is used for one hub and the other for the redundant hub.

The very first time I implemented this feature, I was scratching my head when looking at the routing tables in the spokes, which were missing many routes via the hubs. I took a while to figure out that the mGRE interfaces on the spokes were causing the problem. I fixed this by using p-pGRE interfaces on the spokes, suffering the additional delay when a spoke would have to send traffic via a hub to a second spoke. However, I was able to manipulate the spokes' routing tables so that half would prefer HubA and the other half HubB, taking advantage of bandwidth to both hubs.

Figure 17-8 illustrates the configuration of a dual-DVMPN/dual-hub design. Example 17-38 shows HubA's configuration; this is the same configuration used by HubA in the single-DMVPN/dual-hub design shown previously in Example 17-35.

Example 17-38 *Dual-DMVPN Design with Dual Hubs: HubA's Configuration*

```
hubA(config)# crypto isakmp policy 1
hubA(config-isakmp)# authentication pre-share
hubA(config-isakmp)# encryption aes
hubA(config-isakmp)# exit
hubA(config)# crypto isakmp key cisco123 address 0.0.0.0 0.0.0.0
                      no-xauth
hubA(config)# crypto isakmp keepalive 20 3
hubA(config)# crypto ipsec transform-set trans2 esp-aes esp-sha-hmac
hubA(cfg-crypto-trans)# mode transport
hubA(cfg-crypto-trans)# exit
hubA(config)# crypto ipsec profile dmvpnprofile
hubA(ipsec-profile)# set transform-set trans2
hubA(ipsec-profile)# exit
hubA(config)# interface tunnel0
```

continues

Example 17-38 *Dual-DMVPN Design with Dual Hubs: HubA's Configuration (Continued)*

```
hubA(config-if)# description Connection to Spokes
hubA(config-if)# bandwidth 1000
hubA(config-if)# ip address 10.0.0.1 255.255.255.0
hubA(config-if)# ip mtu 1436
hubA(config-if)# delay 1000
hubA(config-if)# ip ospf network broadcast
hubA(config-if)# ip ospf priority 2
hubA(config-if)# ip nhrp authentication cisco123
hubA(config-if)# ip nhrp map multicast dynamic
hubA(config-if)# ip nhrp network-id 100000
hubA(config-if)# ip nhrp holdtime 600
hubA(config-if)# tunnel source Ethernet0
hubA(config-if)# tunnel mode gre multipoint
hubA(config-if)# tunnel key 100000
hubA(config-if)# tunnel protection ipsec profile dmvpnprofile
hubA(config-if)# exit
hubA(config)# interface Ethernet0
hubA(config-if)# description Internet Connection
hubA(config-if)# ip address 199.1.1.1 255.255.255.0
hubA(config-if)# exit
hubA(config)# interface Ethernet1
hubA(config-if)# description Local LAN
hubA(config-if)# ip address 192.168.0.1 255.255.255.0
hubA(config-if)# exit
hubA(config)# router ospf 1
hubA(config-router)# network 10.0.0.0 0.0.0.255 area 1
hubA(config-router)# network 192.168.0.0 0.0.0.255 area 0
hubA(config-router)# exit
```

Example 17-39 shows HubB's configuration. Its configuration is almost identical to HubA's shown in Example 17-38 except for these three items on its tunnel interface:

- Its subnet is different (10.0.1.0/24 for HubB compared to 10.0.0.0/24 for HubA).

- The NHRP network ID is different (100001), making this a separate DMVPN network.

- The GRE tunnel ID is different, allowing the spoke to differentiate between packets coming from the two hub devices.

Other than these three things, the configuration of HubB is similar to HubA.

Example 17-39 *Dual-DMVPN Design with Dual Hubs: HubB's Configuration*

```
hubB(config)# crypto isakmp policy 1
hubB(config-isakmp)# authentication pre-share
hubB(config-isakmp)# encryption aes
hubB(config-isakmp)# exit
hubB(config)# crypto isakmp key cisco123 address 0.0.0.0 0.0.0.0
                        no-xauth
hubB(config)# crypto isakmp keepalive 20 3
hubB(config)# crypto ipsec transform-set trans2 esp-aes esp-sha-hmac
```

Example 17-39 *Dual-DMVPN Design with Dual Hubs: HubB's Configuration (Continued)*

```
hubB(cfg-crypto-trans)# mode transport
hubB(cfg-crypto-trans)# exit
hubB(config)# crypto ipsec profile dmvpnprofile
hubB(ipsec-profile)# set transform-set trans2
hubB(ipsec-profile)# exit
hubB(config)# interface tunnel0
hubB(config-if)# description Connection to Spokes
hubB(config-if)# bandwidth 1000
hubB(config-if)# ip address 10.0.1.1 255.255.255.0
hubB(config-if)# ip mtu 1436
hubB(config-if)# delay 1000
hubB(config-if)# ip ospf network broadcast
hubB(config-if)# ip ospf priority 2
hubB(config-if)# ip nhrp authentication cisco123
hubB(config-if)# ip nhrp map multicast dynamic
hubB(config-if)# ip nhrp network-id 100001
hubB(config-if)# ip nhrp holdtime 600
hubB(config-if)# tunnel source Ethernet0
hubB(config-if)# tunnel mode gre multipoint
hubB(config-if)# tunnel key 100001
hubB(config-if)# tunnel protection ipsec profile dmvpnprofile
hubB(config-if)# exit
hubB(config)# interface Ethernet0
hubB(config-if)# description Internet Connection
hubB(config-if)# ip address 200.1.1.1 255.255.255.0
hubB(config-if)# exit
hubB(config)# interface Ethernet1
hubB(config-if)# description Local LAN
hubB(config-if)# ip address 192.168.0.2 255.255.255.0
hubB(config-if)# exit
hubB(config)# router ospf 1
hubB(config-router)# network 10.0.0.0 0.0.0.255 area 1
hubB(config-router)# network 192.168.0.0 0.0.0.255 area 0
hubB(config-router)# exit
```

Example 17-40 shows the configuration of the spoke routers. Notice that there are two GRE tunnel interfaces, both of which are configured for point-to-point (**tunnel mode gre ip**). Each tunnel interface has its own unique subnet, NHRP ID, NHS server (HubA for Tunnel0 versus HubB for Tunnel1), and its own GRE tunnel ID.

Example 17-40 *Dual-DMVPN Design with Dual Hubs: Spoke Configuration*

```
spokeX(config)# crypto isakmp policy 1
spokeX(config-isakmp)# authentication pre-share
spokeX(config-isakmp)# encryption aes
spokeX(config-isakmp)# exit
spokeX(config)# crypto isakmp key cisco123 address
                       0.0.0.0 0.0.0.0 no-xauth
spokeX(config)# crypto isakmp keepalive 20 3
spokeX(config)# crypto ipsec transform-set trans2 esp-aes
                       esp-sha-hmac
```

continues

Example 17-40 *Dual-DMVPN Design with Dual Hubs: Spoke Configuration (Continued)*

```
spokeX(cfg-crypto-trans)# mode transport
spokeX(cfg-crypto-trans)# exit
spokeX(config)# crypto ipsec profile dmvpnprofile
spokeX(ipsec-profile)# set transform-set trans2
spokeX(ipsec-profile)# exit
spokeX(config)# interface tunnel0
spokeX(config-if)# description Connection to hubA
spokeX(config-if)# bandwidth 1000
spokeX(config-if)# ip address 10.0.0.<x+1> 255.255.255.0
spokeX(config-if)# ip mtu 1436
spokeX(config-if)# delay 1000
spokeX(config-if)# ip ospf network broadcast
spokeX(config-if)# ip ospf priority 0
spokeX(config-if)# ip nhrp authentication cisco123
spokeX(config-if)# ip nhrp map multicast 199.1.1.1
spokeX(config-if)# ip nhrp map 10.0.0.1 199.1.1.1
spokeX(config-if)# ip nhrp nhs 10.0.0.1
spokeX(config-if)# ip nhrp network-id 100000
spokeX(config-if)# ip nhrp holdtime 300
spokeX(config-if)# tunnel source Ethernet0
spokeX(config-if)# tunnel destination 199.1.1.1
spokeX(config-if)# tunnel mode gre ip
spokeX(config-if)# tunnel key 100000
spokeX(config-if)# tunnel protection ipsec profile dmvpnprofile
spokeX(config-if)# exit
spokeX(config)# interface tunnel1
spokeX(config-if)# description Connection to hubB
spokeX(config-if)# bandwidth 1000
spokeX(config-if)# ip address 10.0.1.<x+1> 255.255.255.0
spokeX(config-if)# ip mtu 1436
spokeX(config-if)# delay 1000
spokeX(config-if)# ip ospf network broadcast
spokeX(config-if)# ip ospf priority 0
spokeX(config-if)# ip nhrp authentication cisco123
spokeX(config-if)# ip nhrp map multicast 200.1.1.1
spokeX(config-if)# ip nhrp map 10.0.1.1 200.1.1.1
spokeX(config-if)# ip nhrp nhs 10.0.1.1
spokeX(config-if)# ip nhrp network-id 100001
spokeX(config-if)# ip nhrp holdtime 300
spokeX(config-if)# tunnel source Ethernet0
spokeX(config-if)# tunnel destination 200.1.1.1
spokeX(config-if)# tunnel mode gre ip
spokeX(config-if)# tunnel key 100001
spokeX(config-if)# tunnel protection ipsec profile dmvpnprofile
spokeX(config-if)# exit
spokeX(config)# interface Ethernet0
spokeX(config-if)# description Connection to Internet
spokeX(config-if)# ip address dhcp hostname Spoke<x>
spokeX(config-if)# exit
spokeX(config)# interface Ethernet1
spokeX(config-if)# description Local LAN
spokeX(config-if)# ip address 192.168.<x>.1 255.255.255.0
```

Example 17-40 *Dual-DMVPN Design with Dual Hubs: Spoke Configuration (Continued)*

```
spokeX(config-if)# exit
spokeX(config)# router ospf 1
spokeX(config-router)# network 10.0.0.0 0.0.0.255 area 1
spokeX(config-router)# network 192.168.<n>.0 0.0.0.255 area 1
spokeX(config-router)# exit
```

To ensure that you don't have asymmetric routing problems, on one hub, configure a better (lower) bandwidth value for the tunnel interface than the other hub when running OSPF (or you can use the **ip ospf cost** command to accomplish the same thing). If using EIGRP, I would recommend changing the **delay** parameter so that one hub is preferred over the other. On the spokes, I would use the **distance** command for the routing protocol as described in the last section.

The drawback of the p-pGRE configuration is that for a spoke to reach another spoke, it must send its traffic to one of the hubs first. If you need to overcome this problem, your spoke router will need two public IP addresses on its external interface. Then on the first tunnel interface you would use the **tunnel source** command with the first public address and then on the second tunnel interface use the **tunnel source** command with the second IP address. Last, change the tunnel mode on both tunnels to mGRE with the **tunnel mode gre multipoint** command. Obviously, the main drawback of this approach is that each of your spokes needs *two* public IP addresses, which might not be feasible.

Summary

This chapter showed you the basics of setting up L2L sessions on routers. I've focused primarily on the ISAKMP/IKE Phase 2 components for building these connections. The order of the chapter has led you through the features as they became available in the Cisco IOS: static crypto maps, dynamic crypto maps, TED, GRE across IPsec, and DMVPN.

Next up is Chapter 18, "Router Remote Access Connections," where I show you how to configure your router to be an Easy VPN Server or Remote (Client).

Router Remote Access Connections

In this chapter I'll focus on using a Cisco router for remote access sessions. I'll discuss how you can use a router as a VPN gateway (Easy VPN Server), terminating remote access sessions from client devices, like the Cisco VPN Client software and VPN 3002 hardware clients. Because routers commonly are used for LAN-to-LAN (L2L) sessions, they're typically not used as Easy VPN Servers; however, for a small number of remote access clients, it is common to use an existing router for this function instead of purchasing a stand-alone remote access device like a VPN 3000 concentrator. I'll discuss how to terminate both L2L and remote access sessions on the same router.

I'll also discuss how you can use a router as an Easy VPN Server and how to set up a small-end router as a remote access client, called an Easy VPN Remote. Routers commonly are used as Remotes for small office, home office (SOHO) networks when you need complex QoS policies or have Internet connections that are non-Ethernet-based, such as ISDN, xDSL, or serial. At the end of the chapter I'll discuss a new remote access feature supported by Cisco Routers: WebVPN. Starting in late releases of 12.3T, a Cisco router can be used to terminate WebVPN sessions.

NOTE Because of page constraints, I'll focus only on IPsec and WebVPN remote access VPNs in this chapter; PPTP and L2TP/IPsec are not covered.

Easy VPN Server

Easy VPN is a Cisco feature that allows you to deploy IPsec remote access devices easily using Cisco VPN Client software; their 800, 900, and 1700 series routers; the VPN 3002 hardware client; and the 501 and 506E PIX security appliances. Policies are defined on the Easy VPN Server and pushed down to the Easy VPN Remotes during IKE Mode Config.

However, as you'll see in this section, the configuration of the Easy VPN Server function from the router's CLI is not a simple endeavor, which is why I prefer using the VPN 3000 concentrators over Cisco routers or PIXs for Easy VPN Servers. Given that the configuration of an Easy VPN Server is more difficult than a concentrator, you might wonder why you should even bother with a router. Well, if you already have a perimeter router with extra capacity and need to support only a small number of remote access users, it doesn't make any sense to spend money to buy a VPN 3000 concentrator: instead, just use the existing router to perform this function.

NOTE Please note that the Cisco Security Device Manager (SDM) software makes it easy to set up a router as an Easy VPN Server or Remote, hiding the commands and their syntax behind a user-friendly GUI interface. The discussion of SDM is beyond the scope of this book.

The Easy VPN Server function was introduced in IOS 12.2(8)T, and Cisco has added features to it constantly to match support with other Cisco Easy VPN Server products. Routers, when functioning as Easy VPN Servers, do *not* support the following options:

- RSA encrypted nonces or DSS certificates for device authentication
- DH group 1 keys
- AH for data encapsulation
- Transport mode for data connections
- Manual keying for data connections (ISAKMP/IKE is required)
- PFS for data connections: as of IOS 12.3(4)T, PFS support has been added
- IPsec over TCP and IPsec over UDP: standards-based NAT-T, however, is supported

To help you set up a router as an Easy VPN Server, the following sections cover these topics:

- Easy VPN Server Configuration
- VPN Group Monitoring
- Easy VPN Server Configuration Example

Easy VPN Server Configuration

Many of the tasks that are configured for L2L sessions, as discussed in Chapter 17, "Router Site-to-Site Connections," also are configured for IPsec remote access sessions, including ISAKMP/IKE Phase 1 policies, transform sets, dynamic crypto maps, and static crypto maps. Because I've already discussed these commands in Chapters 16 and 17, I'll only focus on the Easy VPN Server commands in the following sections. After this, I'll put all of these components together (from this and the previous two chapters) in an Easy VPN Server example.

Defining AAA

AAA (authentication, authorization, and accounting) is used to restrict traffic to or through a router. Easy VPN uses AAA to implement group policies and authorization and also for XAUTH (user) authentication. This section will focus on only the basics of AAA in regard to its use with an Easy VPN Server: for more detailed information on using AAA on a Cisco router, read my book entitled *Cisco Router Firewall Security* published by Cisco Press (ISBN 1587051753).

The group and user information used by an Easy VPN Server to restrict IPsec access and authenticate users can be defined locally on the router or on an AAA server using RADIUS as a communication protocol. For a small number of users and a single router terminating the IPsec remote access sessions, I would define the group and user information locally on the router; if you have more than one router at a location where users will terminate their remote access sessions, I would centralize the configuration and management of group and user information by using an AAA RADIUS server such as Cisco Secure Access Control Server (CSACS).

The commands used to set up AAA for an Easy VPN Server include the following:

```
Router(config)# aaa new-model
Router(config)# aaa authentication login authentication_list_name
                method1 [method2...]
Router(config)# username user's_name {password | secret} password
Router(config)# radius-server host AAA_IP_address [auth-port port_#]
                [acct-port port_#] key AAA_key_string
Router(config)# aaa authorization network authorization_list_name
                method1 [method2...]
```

The **aaa new-model** command enables AAA on a router. The **aaa authentication login** command sets up authentication of usernames and passwords for XAUTH. The *list_name* parameter needs to match the same parameter in the **crypto map** *map_name* **client authentication list** *list_name* command, discussed later in the "Creating a Static Crypto Map and XAUTH" section.

The two methods you can list in **aaa authentication login** command are **local** or **group radius**. Methods define how authentication will be done. If you specify **local**, you must define the usernames and passwords on the router manually, using the **username** command. Using the **secret** parameter with this latter command will encrypt the user's password on the router automatically. If you specify **group radius**, an AAA RADIUS server is used to authenticate the user's username and password. You'll need to define the AAA RADIUS server with the **radius-server** command. If you don't specify the authentication/authorization (**auth-port**) or accounting (**acct-port**) ports, they default to 1,645 and 1,646, respectively, which is what CSACS uses; other implementations sometimes use 1,812 and 1,813, respectively. The **key** parameter specifies the encryption key used to encrypt any passwords sent between the router and AAA RADIUS server—this must match the key used on the AAA RADIUS server. You also can specify two methods for redundancy, such as **local group radius** or **group radius local**. The router will process the methods in the order listed.

The **aaa authorization network** command specifies that AAA will be used to handle the IPsec remote access group functions. In this command, the *authorization_list_name* parameter needs to match the list name configured in with the **crypto map** *static_map_name* **isakmp authorization list** command (discussed in the "Creating a Static Crypto Map and XAUTH" section later in the chapter). Like the **aaa authentication login** command, you can specify up to two methods to determine how group authorization will be done: **local** or **group radius**. If you choose **local**, you must define the group locally on the router, including its properties; if you choose **group radius**, the group must be defined on the AAA RADIUS server.

NOTE   Currently only an AAA server supporting the RADIUS communication protocol is supported for user and group functions on an Easy VPN Server: TACACS+ is not.

Creating Groups

If you have chosen the **local** authorization method in the **aaa authorization network** command, you must define your groups locally on the router. You can use the following commands to create a group on the Easy VPN Server for your users:

```
Router(config)# ip local pool pool_name first_IP_address
             last_IP_address
Router(config)# crypto isakmp client configuration address-pool
             local pool_name
Router(config)# crypto isamkp client configuration group
             {group_name | default}
Router(config-isakmp-group)# key pre_shared_key
Router(config-isakmp-group)# pool pool_name
Router(config-isakmp-group)# domain domain_name
Router(config-isakmp-group)# dns 1st_DNS_server [2nd_DNS_server]
Router(config-isakmp-group)# split-dns domain_name
Router(config-isakmp-group)# wins 1st_WINS_server [2nd_WINS_server]
Router(config-isakmp-group)# include-local-lan
Router(config-isakmp-group)# acl ACL_name_or_#
Router(config-isakmp-group)# firewall are-u-there
Router(config-isakmp-group)# backup-gateway {IP_address | hostname}
Router(config-isakmp-group)# save-password
Router(config-isakmp-group)# pfs
Router(config-isakmp-group)# max-logins #_of_simultaneous_logins
Router(config-isakmp-group)# max-users #_of_users
Router(config-isakmp-group)# access-restrict interface_name
Router(config-isakmp-group)# group-lock
Router(config-isakmp-group)# exit
```

The **ip local pool** command specifies an address pool to use to assign internal addresses to remote access users. You must assign a name to the pool, and a beginning and ending address for the pool.

The **crypto isakmp client configuration address-pool** command allows you to associate an address pool created by the **ip local pool** command with remote access usage. If a particular remote access group doesn't specify an address pool, this pool is used. Using this command allows multiple groups to share the same address pool; however, you can create different pools for different groups with the **pool** subcommand for a group (discussed later in this section).

The **crypto isakmp client configuration group** command creates your users' groups locally on a router. This is necessary if you specified the **local** method for the **aaa authorization network** command. To create a specific group, just use the name of the group with the **crypto isakmp client configuration group** command. You can create a default group by using the **default** parameter instead of a group name: if users don't specify what group they belong to, the default group will then be used. After you execute the **crypto isakmp client configuration group** command, you are taken into a subcommand mode where you can enter the group's properties.

The **key** command creates a pre-shared key to be used for the group's authentication. The user must specify the group name and this key to authenticate with the group. If you don't configure the **key** command, digital certificates are used for device authentication.

TIP   If you'll be using digital certificates for remote access device authentication, the name of the group must be in the Organizational Unit (OU)/Department field.

The **pool** command specifies the pool of addresses that will be used to assign internal addresses to clients for this specific group. The name specified with this command must match the name configured in the **ip local pool** command. You can assign only one address pool to a group.

NOTE   If you forget to assign an address pool to the group or create a global address pool, clients attempting to build a remote access session to the router will fail.

The **domain** command specifies the domain name to assign to the client, like "cisco.com" or "ciscopress.com." This overrides the domain name already manually or dynamically assigned on the remote access client. The **dns** command allows you to assign up to two DNS servers to the client; just specify the IP addresses, separated by a space, after the **dns** command. The assignment of these to the client overrides any DNS servers currently configured on the client.

The split DNS feature was added in IOS 12.3(4)T. This allows some DNS queries to be forwarded to the DNS servers specified in the **dns** command and other DNS queries to be handled by the DNS servers either manually defined or dynamically acquired on the client (like from the ISP's DHCP assignment). Split DNS is enabled with the **split-dns** command. For domains that you want users to resolve using the DNS servers listed in the **dns** command, list those domains with the **split-dns** command. If you have multiple domains you want these servers to resolve, list them in separate **split-dns** commands. For domains not listed in the **split-dns** commands, the user's locally defined DNS servers will be used to perform the resolution.

If you use WINS in a Microsoft-centric environment, you can use the **wins** command to assign up to two WINS server addresses to the remote access client: these addresses will override any locally configured WINS server addresses on the client.

The **include-local-lan** command allows clients of the group to access the local LAN segment in clear text, while all other traffic must be sent protected to the Easy VPN Server. This feature is new in IOS 12.3(2)T. With Cisco VPN Client software, you also must enable this feature on the client to allow clear-text local LAN access.

The **acl** command allows you to set up more complex split-tunnel configurations. With this command, you reference the name or number of an extended IP ACL that specifies what is to be protected. **permit** commands specify traffic to be protected by the tunnel; **deny** commands or the implicit deny specifies traffic to be sent in clear text by the client.

Example 18-1 illustrates an ACL that will be used for split tunneling. The configuration of the ACL can be somewhat confusing, since you would think that the source address would be the client and the destination is the place the client is trying to reach; however, this is not true. The ACL is configured from the *router's* perspective. In Example 18-1, any client traffic (listed as the destination address in the ACL), when sent to 192.168.0.0/24 (the source address in the ACL), will be protected. All other traffic is sent in clear text.

Example 18-1 *Split Tunneling ACL Example*

```
Router(config)# ip access-list extended splitengineering
Router(config-ext-nacl)# remark Protect this traffic
Router(config-ext-nacl)# permit ip 192.168.0.0 0.0.0.255 any
Router(config-ext-nacl)# remark Send all other traffic in clear-text
Router(config-ext-nacl)# deny ip any any
```

TIP   Remember that when setting up your split tunneling ACL on your router, the source address in the ACL is what the client is trying to reach and the destination address represents the client itself. In Example 18-1, you could easily have replaced the keyword **any** for the destination address with the range of addresses in the client address pool for the group using this split tunneling ACL.

As of IOS 12.3(2)T, Cisco routers, as Easy VPN Servers, support the Are You There (AYT) firewall feature, which allows you to have the Cisco VPN Client software (Windows-only) poll periodically for the operation of a supported firewall. I discussed the AYT feature in Chapter 7, "Concentrator Remote Access Connections with IPsec." This feature is enabled with the **firewall are-u-there** command. Unlike the concentrators, you cannot specify which firewall the group should be running; nor does the router, acting as a server, support Central Policy Push (CPP). The AYT feature on Cisco routers currently supports Black ICE or Zone Alarm personal firewalls.

NOTE   You should enable the AYT feature for an Easy VPN Server group only if that group contains the Cisco VPN Client for Windows clients; otherwise, other IPsec software clients will have their remote access sessions dropped.

As of 12.3(4)T, the router can push down a list of up to 10 backup Easy VPN Servers to a connecting Easy VPN Remote. The backup servers are configured with the **backup-gateway** command. Each backup server must be listed with a *separate* **backup-gateway** command, where in each command you can list either the IP address of the Easy VPN Server or its FQDN.

By default, Easy VPN Remote devices cannot save their username's XAUTH password locally. In IOS 12.3(2)T, you can enable this function with the **save-password** command. When enabled, after the client connects and receives this policy during IKE Mode Config, on a subsequent connection to the Server, the client is allowed to store the password locally when prompted for its XAUTH credentials. Please note that this feature will not work with one-time passwords, such as those derived from token cards.

CAUTION   Using the save password feature could present a security risk if the client's device becomes compromised. Therefore its use should be evaluated carefully before enabling it; however, it is commonly used on hardware clients like the VPN 3002 and low-end PIXs and routers when configured for unit, or the default, authentication method.

The **pfs** command, new in IOS 12.3(4)T, allows the use of Perfect Forward Secrecy (PFS) by clients. If you recall from Chapter 3, "IPsec," PFS is an alternative to sharing keying information for the two unidirectional data connections instead of the existing management connection. PFS is more secure because it uses DH, which supports larger key sizes than DES, 3DES, or AES. The DH key group used will be the same one negotiated by the Server and Remote during ISAKMP/IKE Phase 1.

The **max-logins** and **max-users** commands allow you to implement a simple form of call admission control (CAC). Both of these commands were introduced in IOS 12.3(4)T. They allow you to place limits on the maximum number of simultaneous logins and user sessions for a particular group. This might be necessary on lower-end routers where you don't want users from one group using up all of the IPsec sessions that the router supports.

With IPsec remote access CAC, you place connection limits on a group-by-group basis. The **max-logins** command specifies the maximum number of simultaneous logins allowed for the group (logins occurring at the same time); this ensures that if too many incoming session requests occur at the same time for a group, the router will handle only the ones up to the maximum value specified by this command. You can specify from 1–10 simultaneous logins. The **max-users** command places a limit on the maximum number of connected user sessions for a group, thereby ensuring that one group doesn't use up all of the router's IPsec sessions and starves other groups on the router. This is important for smaller-end routers functioning as Easy VPN Servers. You can specify limits from 1–5,000 users for a group.

You can use the **access-restrict** command to restrict the interface(s) that users from the group can terminate VPN sessions on. This command has meaning only when you have applied a crypto map for the remote access users to more than one interface on the router, or have more than one crypto map applied to interfaces on the router, but only want the users to use one of the interfaces for their remote access connections. The name of the interface you specify with this command restricts the Easy VPN Remotes of the associated group to terminating their connections on only that interface. When enabled, if a user from the group attempts to set up an IPsec session to another interface, the router drops the connection attempt. You can define multiple interfaces for a group, but each interface must be defined with a separate **access-restrict** command.

The group lock feature, new in IOS 12.2(13)T, allows you to perform an extra authentication check during XAUTH. With this feature enabled, the user must enter user name, group name, and user password during XAUTH to authenticate. The user and group names can be entered in any of the following formats: "*user's name/group name,*" "*user's name\group name,*" "*user's name%group name,*" or "*user's name@group name.*" The group name entered during XAUTH is compared by the Server with the group name sent for pre-shared key device authentication. If they don't match, the Server denies the connection. To enable this feature, use the **group-lock** command for the group.

NOTE   Group locking only works with pre-shared key authentication. If you enable this command for users who use digital certificates, XAUTH authentication will fail.

Implementing Call Admission Control for IKE

I discussed two generic forms of CAC for groups in the last section: the **max-logins** and **max-users** subcommands. However, both of these require an initial management connection dialog to be established between the Remote and Server, which can tie up resources on the router. In 12.3(8)T, Cisco introduced CAC for IKE to help deal with this problem. Actually, CAC for IKE can be used for both L2L and remote access sessions; however, it is best suited with remote access scenarios where you have many users who connect at random times.

CAC for IKE supports two methods of limiting the number of ISAKMP/IKE Phase 1 SAs being established to or from a router:

- Setting an absolute limit to the number of IKE SAs with the **crypto call admission limit** command—once the configured limit is reached, all new IKE Phase 1 SA requests are dropped.

- Setting a resource limit with the **call admission limit** command—new IKE SA requests are dropped once the specified percentage of system resources is reached. A global resource monitor keeps track of the CPU cycles and memory buffers on the router, which CAC polls when a new IKE Phase 1 connection is requested.

To define an absolute limit for the number of ISAKMP/IKE Phase 1 SAs the router will accept or build, use the following command:

```
Router(config)# crypto call admission limit ike sa #_of_IKE_SAs
```

The number of ISAKMP/IKE Phase 1 SAs you specify must be greater than one and should be less than what the router physically supports for VPN sessions. If you specify a number that is lower than the current number of existing management SAs on the router, the router will display a warning message, but won't remove any of the existing SAs: only new ISAKMP/IKE Phase 1 SAs will be rejected.

To define a resource limit for new ISAKMP/IKE Phase 1 SAs, use the following command:

```
Router(config)# call admission limit percentage
```

The percentage can range from 1–100. Once the limit is reached, no new ISAKMP/IKE Phase 1 SAs are allowed. If you're not sure what you should set this value to, Cisco recommends you set it to 90 percent to start with and examine the effect this has on the router and ISAKMP/IKE Phase 1 connection attempts.

NOTE   The configurations of the **crypto call admission limit ike sa** and **call admission limit** commands are independent of each other; you can configure one or both.

You can use two **show** commands to verify the configuration and operation of CAC for IKE:

- **show call admission statistics**
- **show crypto call admission statistics**

Example 18-2 illustrates the use of the **show call admission statistics** command. Table 18-1 explains the fields in the output of this command.

Example 18-2   *The* **show call admission statistics** *Command*

```
Router# show call admission statistics
Total call admission charges: 0, limit 90
Total calls rejected 0, accepted 11
Load metric: charge 0, unscaled 0%
```

Table 18-1 *Information Found in the* **show call admission statistics** *Command*

Field	Description
Total call admission charges	This is the percentage of system resources used on the router; once this reaches the system resource limit configured in the **call admission limit** command, new ISAKMP/IKE Phase 1 SAs are rejected.
Limit	This is the maximum percentage of system resources specified by the **call admission limit** command.
Total calls rejected	This is the number of ISAKMP/IKE Phase 1 SAs that were rejected because the resource limit was reached.
Accepted	This is the number of ISAKMP/IKE Phase 1 SAs that were accepted because the resource limit wasn't reached.
Unscaled	This is unrelated to ISAKMP/IKE Phase 1 connections.

Example 18-3 illustrates the use of the **show crypto call admission statistics** command. This command provides more details than the **show call admission statistics** command; here you can see the resource limit (95 percent), the maximum number of allowed SAs (500), and a breakdown of SAs for total, incoming, outgoing, and rejected. In Example 18-3, there were 11 incoming ISAKMP/IKE Phase 1 requests, and all were accepted.

Example 18-3 *The* **show crypto call admission statistics** *Command*

```
Router# show crypto call admission statistics
        Crypto Call Admission Control Statistics
System Resource Limit:     95 Max IKE SAs:   500
Total IKE SA Count:        0 active:          0 negotiating:   0
Incoming IKE Requests:    11 accepted:       11 rejected:      0
Outgoing IKE Requests:     0 accepted:        0 rejected:      0
Rejected IKE Requests:     0 rsrc low:        0 SA limit:      0
```

Use the **clear crypto call admission statistics** command to clear the counters that track the number of rejected and accepted ISAKMP/IKE Phase 1 SAs.

Creating a Dynamic Crypto Map Entry

Because an Easy VPN Server doesn't know the IP address of an Easy VPN Remote until the Remote connects, a dynamic crypto map is needed to handle the building of the remote access session. I discussed dynamic crypto maps in Chapter 17, "Router Site-to-Site Connections," so I won't go into a lot of details about their configuration; instead, I'll only focus on those commands that are important for Easy VPN Remote sessions:

```
Router(config)# crypto dynamic-map dynamic_map_name sequence_#
Router(config-crypto-m)# set transform-set transform_set_name1
            [transform-set-name2...transform-set-name6]
Router(config-crypto-m)# set security-association lifetime
            {seconds seconds | kilobytes kilobytes}
Router(config-crypto-m)# set security-association idle-time seconds
Router(cofnig-crypto-m)# reverse-route
Router(config-crypto-m)# exit
```

I've already talked about all of these commands in Chapter 17 with the exception of **reverse-route**. The only required command is the **set transform-set** command, which specifies how the data connections will be protected.

The **reverse-route** command enables Reverse Route Injection (RRI). When you enable this command, the client's internal IP address (client mode) or the client's private/inside interface network number (network extension mode) is entered as a static route in the router's routing table. You can then take these static routes and redistribute them via a dynamic routing protocol with the **redistribute static** command within the dynamic routing protocol. This process is necessary if you have multiple Easy VPN Servers and you don't know which Server a Remote will connect to. Using this process allows internal routers and other devices behind the Easy VPN Servers to learn dynamically which Easy VPN Server has which clients connected to it. The RRI process was discussed in depth in Chapter 3, "IPsec."

Creating a Static Crypto Map and XAUTH

Once you have created your dynamic crypto map entry for your Easy VPN Remote users, you need to set up XAUTH and your static crypto map. First you must create a static crypto map and reference the dynamic crypto map as an entry within the static map:

```
Router(config)# crypto map static_map_name seq_# ipsec-isakmp
               dynamic dynamic_map_name
```

I discussed this process in depth in Chapter 17, "Router Site-to-Site Connections."

NOTE   If you have both L2L and remote access sessions being terminated on an Easy VPN Server, be sure that the dynamic crypto map entry in the static map has the highest sequence number, thus giving it the lowest priority; this ensures that static entries are used by L2L sessions.

Next, you'll configure the following commands:

```
Router(config)# crypto map static_map_name isakmp authorization
               list authorization_list_name
Router(config)# crypto map static_map_name client authentication
               list authentication_list_name
Router(config)# crypto map static_map_name client configuration
               address [initiate | respond]
Router(config)# crypto isakmp xauth timeout seconds
```

The **crypto map** *static_map_name* **isakmp authorization list** command specifies the **aaa authorization network** command to use to find the remote access group(s) configuration: the router looks for matching *authorization_list_name* values. If the method list is defined as **local** in the **aaa authorization network** command, the router looks for the group attributes locally; if you have specified **group radius**, the router looks for the group configuration on an AAA server.

The **crypto map** *static_map_name* **client authentication list** specifies the **aaa authentication login** command to use to authenticate users. The latter command tells the router to look for the user accounts on an AAA RADIUS server (a method list of **group radius**) or on the router itself (a method list of **local** specifies that the user accounts and passwords are defined locally with the **username** command).

The **crypto map** *static_map_name* **client configuration address** command specifies whether the Server initiates IKE Mode Config (**initiate** parameter) or the Remote initiates it (**respond** parameter). The Cisco VPN Client software and Easy VPN Remote hardware clients initiate IKE Mode config. The old Cisco Secure 1.1 VPN and Microsoft's L2TP/IPsec clients don't. Therefore, in most cases you'll need to configure just the **respond** parameter. If you have a mixture of both types of clients, enter the command twice: with one command specify the **respond** parameter and the other the **initiate** parameter.

By default, users have 60 seconds to enter their usernames and passwords during XAUTH. You can change this value with the **crypto isakmp xauth timeout** command. The time can range from 5–90 seconds. I recommend setting this value to 30 seconds or less unless you're using one-time passwords (OTP) and the passwords are quite lengthy.

VPN Group Monitoring

You can use two commands to monitor remote access groups and their sessions (new in IOS 12.3(4)T):

- **show crypto session group**—Shows the groups on the router that are currently active and the number of active users for that group. See Example 18-4.

- **show crypto session summary**—Shows the groups on the router that are currently active and the users that have authenticated via each group. See Example 18-5.

Example 18-4   *The* **show crypto session group** *Command*

```
Router# show crypto session group
 Group:    Connections
 engineering:   0
 sales:     0
 admin:     2
```

Example 18-5   *The* **show crypto session summary** *Command*

```
Router# show crypto session summary
 Group admin has 2 connections
 User    (Logins)
 rdeal    (1)
 nillarionova (1)
```

Easy VPN Server Configuration Example

Now that you understand the configuration of the Easy VPN Server functionality on a router, I'll illustrate the complete configuration by looking at an example network shown in Figure 18-1. Assume that the Cisco VPN Client 4.x software is used by the remote access users.

Figure 18-1 *Easy VPN Server Example Network*

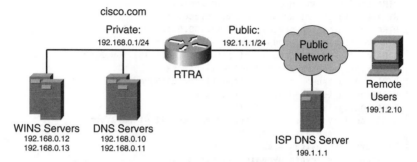

The Easy VPN Server's configuration is shown in Example 18-6. Numbered references to the right of configuration commands are discussed is the list following Example 18-6.

Example 18-6 *Easy VPN Server Example Configuration*

```
RTRA(config)# aaa new-model                                          (1)
RTRA(config)# aaa authentication login vpnclient local
RTRA(config)# aaa authorization network localgroups local
RTRA(config)# username rdeal secret rdeal123
RTRA(config)# username nillarionova secret nilla123
RTRA(config)# username smarcinek secret smarc123
RTRA(config)# username edeal secret edeal123
RTRA(config)# ! ←output omitted→
RTRA(config)# crypto isakmp policy 10                                (2)
RTRA(config-isakmp)# encryption aes 128
RTRA(config-isakmp)# hash sha
RTRA(config-isakmp)# authentication pre-share
RTRA(config-isakmp)# group 2
RTRA(config-isakmp)# exit
RTRA(config)# crypto isakmp keepalive 20 3
RTRA(config)# ip local pool enginepool 192.168.0.200               (3)
             192.168.0.219
RTRA(config)# ip local pool adminpool 192.168.0.220 192.168.0.239
RTRA(config)# ip access-list extended splitremote                 (4)
RTRA(config-ext-nacl)# permit ip 192.168.0.0 0.0.0.255 any
RTRA(config-ext-nacl)# exit
RTRA(config)# crypto isakmp client configuration group            (5)
             engineering
RTRA(config-isakmp-group)# key engine123
RTRA(config-isakmp-group)# pool enginepool
RTRA(config-isakmp-group)# domain cisco.com
RTRA(config-isakmp-group)# dns 192.168.0.10 192.168.0.11
```

continues

Example 18-6 *Easy VPN Server Example Configuration (Continued)*

```
RTRA(config-isakmp-group)# wins 192.168.0.12 192.168.0.13
RTRA(config-isakmp-group)# include-local-lan
RTRA(config-isakmp-group)# firewall are-u-there
RTRA(config-isakmp-group)# max-logins 1
RTRA(config-isakmp-group)# exit
RTRA(config)# crypto isakmp client configuration group admin
RTRA(config-isakmp-group)# key admin123
RTRA(config-isakmp-group)# pool adminpool
RTRA(config-isakmp-group)# domain cisco.com
RTRA(config-isakmp-group)# dns 192.168.0.10 192.168.0.11
RTRA(config-isakmp-group)# split-dns cisco.com
RTRA(config-isakmp-group)# wins 192.168.0.12 192.168.0.13
RTRA(config-isakmp-group)# acl splitremote
RTRA(config-isakmp-group)# firewall are-u-there
RTRA(config-isakmp-group)# max-logins 1
RTRA(config-isakmp-group)# exit
RTRA(config)# crypto ipsec transform-set clienttransform            (6)
             esp-aes esp-sha-hmac
RTRA(cfg-crypto-tran)# exit
RTRA(config)# crypto dynamic-map dynmap 10                           (7)
RTRA(config-crypto-m)# set transform-set clienttransform
RTRA(config-crypto-m)# exit
RTRA(config)# crypto map mymap client authentication                (8)
             list vpnclient
RTRA(config)# crypto map mymap isakmp authorization                 (9)
             list localgroups
RTRA(config)# crypto map mymap client configuration                 (10)
             address respond
RTRA(config)# crypto map mymap 1000 ipsec-isakmp dynamic dynmap      (11)
RTRA(config)# interface Ethernet0/0
RTRA(config-if)# description Local LAN
RTRA(config-if)# ip address 192.168.0.1 255.255.255.0
RTRA(config-if)# exit
RTRA(config)# interface Ethernet0/1
RTRA(config-if)# description Internet Connection
RTRA(config-if)# ip address 192.1.1.1 255.255.255.0
RTRA(config-if)# crypto map mymap                                   (12)
```

1 The beginning part of Example 18-6 enables AAA and specifies that the Easy VPN Remotes' usernames and passwords (**aaa authentication login** and **username** commands), and the groups (**aaa authorization network** commands) are defined locally.

2 A compatible ISAKMP/IKE Phase 1 policy for the VPN Client software is defined and DPD is enabled.

3 Two local address pools are defined (**ip local pool** commands) and are referenced in their respective groups (**pool** commands).

4 This extended ACL is used for split tunneling by the admin group.

5 Two groups are defined—engineering and admin—with the **crypto isakmp client configuration group** commands. Both groups use pre-shared keys for device

authentication; assign a domain name, DNS server, and WINS servers; require a supported PC firewall application; and restrict access to one simultaneous login. The engineering group allows clear-text access to the local LAN, but all other traffic must be tunneled to the Easy VPN Server. The admin group sets up split DNS (**split-dns** command), with DNS queries for only cisco.com being sent to the central office DNS server and all other DNS queries being forwarded to the ISP DNS server. The admin group also sets up split tunneling (**acl** and **ip access-list** commands), where only traffic sent to 192.168.0.0/24 is protected and all other traffic is sent in clear text.

6 One transform set is defined for the Remote data connections (**crypto ipsec transform-set**).

7 A dynamic crypto map is created for the remote access users. RRI is not configured because there is only one Easy VPN Server and redundancy is not necessary. If there were other routers behind RTRA, because the address pools are associated with RTRA's private interface, no additional routing configuration would be required; however, if you used IP addresses that were not associated with a physical interface of RTRA, the internal routers would need static routes pointing to RTRA to reach these "internal" addresses. Make sure that proxy ARP is enabled on RTRA's internal interface.

8 A static crypto map called "mymap" is created. XAUTH authentication is enabled (**crypto map mymap client authentication list**) and references the **aaa authentication login** command to determine where to find the user accounts.

9 The remote access groups are associated with the crypto map (**crypto map mymap isakmp authorization list**), telling the router where to find the group attributes. This command references the **aaa authorization network** statements that tell the router that the groups are defined locally.

10 Because the Remotes are Cisco 4.x clients and they'll initiate IKE Mode Config, I've configured the Server to respond to IKE Mode Config queries (**crypto map mymap client configuration address respond**).

11 The dynamic crypto map is referenced in a static crypto map (**crypto map mymap 1000 ipsec-isakmp dynamic dynmap**).

12 The static crypto map is applied to Ethernet 0/1 (**crypto map mymap**).

As you can see from this example, the configuration is not that complex, even though the configuration is more complicated than an L2L router session.

Routers as Easy VPN Servers

Even though routers support the Easy VPN Server function, they're actually my last choice as a platform for terminating IPsec remote access sessions. One of the limitations the router suffers as a Server is that it cannot assign the two following policies to the Remotes: individual user authentication (Individual UA) and interactive unit authentication

(Interactive UA). If you recall from Chapter 14, "3002 Hardware Client," Interactive UA allows the XAUTH username and password to be entered dynamically by a single user to bring up the tunnel instead of storing this on the Remote, which might be a security concern. And with Individual UA, each individual user must authenticate, either to bring up the tunnel to the central office, or to use the existing tunnel. These features unfortunately don't exist on Easy VPN Server routers, but I expect them to be added at some point; currently both the VPN 3000 concentrators and PIX and ASA security appliances support these features.

About the only time I'll use a router as an Easy VPN Server is when I already have a router in place supporting IPsec L2L sessions, I only need to support a small number of remote access users, and I currently don't have a VPN 3000 concentrator or PIX or ASA security appliance at the central site. In this situation, it makes no sense to buy an extra device to support a small number of remote access users.

Easy VPN Remote

Besides supporting the Easy VPN Server function, certain routers also can be Easy VPN Remotes. These routers include the 800, ubr900, and 1700 series routers. This was introduced in IOS 12.2(4)YA and 12.2(13)T. As you saw in the last section, setting up an Easy VPN Server on a router from the CLI is not the simplest process in the world. Because of this complication and because administrators at remote offices might not be very Cisco-savvy at configuring IPsec sessions, Cisco has simplified the configuration for Easy VPN Remote devices. In other words, there are very few commands you need to configure to set up a router as an Easy VPN Remote.

Cisco accomplishes this by using the same process used with the Cisco VPN Client software: hiding all of the IPsec details from the user. Policies are defined on an Easy VPN Server and pushed down to the Remote during IKE Mode Config. These advantages allow you to deploy a large number of Remotes quickly and easily.

NOTE   Even though Cisco officially supports Remote functionality on the 800, ubr900, and 1700 series routers, the Remote commands work on other routers. I've successfully set up 3620 and 3640 routers as Remotes. However, don't expect any help from the Cisco TAC if you have a problem with an unsupported Remote router client.

Easy VPN Remote Connection Modes

Cisco Easy VPN Remote routers are more similar to Cisco 3002 hardware clients. Both support client and network extension modes, as shown in Figure 18-2. If you recall from Chapter 3, in client mode, the Easy VPN Remote is assigned a single internal IP address;

all devices behind the Remote have PAT performed on them by the Remote to send their traffic across the IPsec tunnel.

Figure 18-2 *Easy VPN Remote with Client and Network Extension Modes*

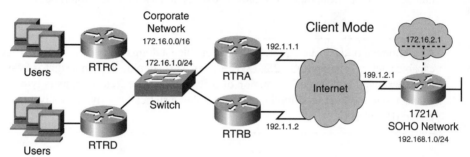

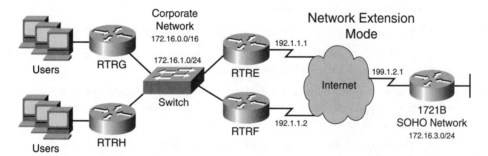

The main limitation of client mode is that devices behind the Easy VPN Server can't initiate connections to devices behind the client-mode Remote; in this case, you would use network extension mode. Because of the word "easy" in Easy VPN, you don't have to set up NAT or PAT on the Remote device. Cisco Easy VPN software will do this automatically. The only requirement is that the Remote act as a DHCP server for its internal devices. Cisco does make some assumptions about the NAT/PAT configuration, though, as follows:

- The NAT inside interface is Ethernet0 on the 800 and UBR900 and FastEthernet0 on the 1700 series routers.

- The NAT outside interface is the interface where the Easy VPN Remote configuration is applied.

- You must let the router create the NAT/PAT commands: if you already have NAT/PAT commands on the router, you'll need to remove them before beginning your Easy VPN Remote configuration.

| TIP | Because the Remote, in client mode, is using PAT, all remotes theoretically could use the same IP network number for their inside interfaces, thereby conserving IP addressing space. |

Network extension simulates an L2L session, allowing devices behind the Server to establish connections to devices behind the Remote; no internal IP address is assigned to the Remote device. Each Remote device's inside interface will need a unique network number (different from other Remotes' networks in network extension mode).

NOTE As mentioned in the last chapter, NAT-T is enabled automatically on all Cisco IPsec-capable routers running IOS 12.2(13)T or later. This shouldn't be an issue for Easy VPN Remote routers with an earlier version of software, because Remote routers typically are connected to the Internet directly, and have either a statically or dynamically acquired public IP Address.

Given the advantages I've discussed so far with Easy VPN Remotes, it's important that I also mention their disadvantages:

- You cannot create an NAT/PAT configuration manually on the Remote.
- If you change the IP address of the inside interface of the Remote, any existing tunnel is terminated and rebuilt automatically.
- The Remote is a client and therefore cannot have more than one IPsec tunnel up at a time; if you need more than one tunnel up, you'll have to configure the router using L2L IPsec sessions.
- The initial release of Easy VPN Remote on Cisco routers doesn't support digital certificates (even through Servers do), DH group 5 keys, PFS, and AES; with the exception of certificates, the current IOS versions support the rest.

Easy VPN Remote Configuration

Configuring an Easy VPN Remote involves these steps:

Step 1 Configure a DHCP server pool (this is required if the Remote is operating in client mode, where the Remote will assign addressing information to inside users).

Step 2 Set up the Easy VPN Remote configuration.

Step 3 Connect to the Easy VPN Server.

Step 4 Configure User Authentication.

Step 5 Verify the Easy VPN Remote configuration.

The following sections will discuss each of these steps.

Step 1: Configure a DHCP Server Pool

If you'll be using client mode on your Easy VPN Remote router, you must set it up as a DHCP server and assign IP addressing information to internal devices. I won't discuss all the DHCP commands you can set up on your Remote, but just the main ones:

```
Router(config)# ip dhcp pool pool_name
Router(dhcp-config)# network IP_network [subnet_mask | /prefix_length ]
Router(dhcp-config)# default-router this_router's_address
Router(dhcp-config)# domain-name domain_name
Router(dhcp-config)# dns-server 1st_DNS_server 2nd_DNS_server
Router(dhcp-config)# netbios-name-server 1st_WINS_server
                2nd_WINS_server
Router(dhcp-config)# lease {days [hours [minutes]] | infinite}
Router(dhcp-config)# exit
Router(config)# ip dhcp excluded-address IP_address
```

On the client mode Remote, use the **ip dhcp pool** command to create your DHCP server configuration; this takes you into a subcommand mode. The **network** command specifies the IP network number (with the exception of the network number and directed broadcast address) to use for assigning addresses to requesting clients. If you omit the subnet mask or prefix, it defaults to the class mask of the network number. The **default-router** command defines the default gateway address and should specify the IP address of the router's private/internal interface. The **domain-name** command defines the domain name, the **dns-server** command can specify up to two DNS servers, the **netbios-name-server** command can specify up to two WINS servers, and the **lease** command specifies the length of the lease of any assigned addressing information to internal devices.

The **ip dhcp excluded-address** command specifies an address that should not be included in the address pool. At a minimum, this should include the IP address of the router's internal interface. Enter this command separately for each address you want to exclude.

You can use the following commands to verify your Remote's configuration:

- **show ip dhcp pool**—Displays the addresses in the address pool.
- **show ip dhcp binding**—Displays the addresses assigned to requesting clients.

For Windows-based PCs connected to the internal interface of the router, set them up for DHCP and then use the **ipconfig /all** command to verify that they are obtaining IP addressing information from the Remote.

Step 2: Set up the Easy VPN Remote Configuration

Setting up the Easy VPN Remote configuration on the Remote is an easy process and can involve the following commands:

```
Router(config)# crypto ipsec client ezvpn profile_name
Router(config-crypto-ezvpn)# group group_name key group_password_key
Router(config-crypto-ezvpn)# peer IP_address_of_the_Server
Router(config-crypto-ezvpn)# mode {client | network-extension}
Router(config-crypto-ezvpn)# exit
Router(config)# interface type port_#
Router(config-if)# crypto ipsec client ezvpn profile_name
                [outside | inside]
```

The **crypto ipsec client ezvpn** global command creates a connection profile that is used to connect to an Easy VPN Server; the profile name is locally significant. This command takes you into a subcommand mode. The **group** command specifies the group the Remote belongs to on the Server, and the pre-shared key for the group. The **peer** command specifies the Easy VPN Server to which the remote will be connecting. Until IOS 12.3(4)T, you could configure only one Server; from this release onward, you can enter this command multiple times for multiple Servers. The **mode** command specifies the connection mode the Remote will use: client or network extension mode.

NOTE   If the Remote will be connecting to a VPN 3000 concentrator in network extension mode, you need to enable this in the group under the HW Client tab.

Once you have configured the connection profile for the Remote, you need to activate it on the router's interface facing the Server (the interface connected to the public network). This is done with the **crypto ipsec client ezvpn interface** command. For client mode connections, this interface becomes the "outside," and will be the default, when the Remote automatically sets up its NAT/PAT configuration. You can override the location of the interface with the **outside** and **inside** parameters. You can have up to four outside interfaces (one tunnel per interface). These parameters are necessary only when you have more than two interfaces on your router, as might be the case with a 1700 series router.

Step 3: Connect to the Easy VPN Server

On the Easy VPN Remote routers, there are two methods of bringing up a connection: manually or automatically. The default connection mode is automatic, where any outbound traffic will trigger the router to bring up the IPsec tunnel to the configured Easy VPN Server. To change it to manual, enter your connection profile and configure the **connect manual** command:

```
Router(config)# crypto ipsec client ezvpn profile_name
Router(config-crypto-ezvpn)# connect [auto | manual]
```

Then from either User or Privilege EXEC mode, use the following command to bring up the IPsec tunnel to the Easy VPN Server:

```
Router> crypto ipsec client ezvpn profile_name
```

On the ubr900 cable access routers, instead of using the CLI to bring up the connection, users behind the ubr900 can use a web browser. However, this process is not enabled by default. To allow users connected to a ubr900 router to use a web browser to bring up a connection, configure the following:

```
Router(config)# ip http server
Router(config)# ip http ezvpn
```

The first command enables the HTTP web server on the router and the second allows a user to access the ubr900 using a web browser to bring up the IPsec session.

NOTE   The web browser method of bringing up IPsec sessions is currently available only on the ubr900 cable modems.

Step 4: Configure User Authentication

If the Easy VPN Server has not been configured with the "save the password" function for the group that the Remote router belongs to, you must supply this to the router before the IPsec session can be established. To do this, use the following command at User or Privilege EXEC mode:

```
Router> crypto ipsec client ezvpn xauth [profile_name]
```

You'll be prompted to enter the XAUTH username and password for the router's authentication credentials. If you don't specify the profile name, the router assumes that the username and password will be used with the tunnel you're bringing up. Example 18-7 illustrates this process. In this example the router attempted to bring up a connection, but the Server is asking the Remote for XAUTH credentials. The XAUTH credentials for this router are a username of "1751A" and a password of "cisco123." If someone doesn't supply the username and password through the use of the **crypto ipsec client ezvpn xauth** command, the Remote will repeat the request (the first two messages in Example 18-7) every 10 seconds.

Example 18-7 *Manually Supplying the XAUTH Credentials*

```
1751A>
20:27:39: EZVPN: Pending XAuth Request, Please enter the following command:
20:27:39: EZVPN: crypto ipsec client ezvpn xauth
1751A> crypto ipsec client ezvpn xauth
Enter Username and Password: 1751A
Password: cisco123
```

The problem with the above approach is that every time the Remote needs to bring up an IPsec tunnel to the Server, someone has to log in to the router and provide the user credentials. This would be true if you hadn't enabled the **save-password** command for the Remote's group on the Server, assuming that a router is a Server. Instead of having to supply the XAUTH credentials manually every time the Remote needs to bring up an IPsec tunnel to the Server, you can configure and store this on the Remote. This feature is new in IOS 12.3(4)T.

First, you must configure this option for the group that the Remote belongs to. Because of security concerns, I recommend that you place hardware clients such as the 3002, PIXs, and routers in their own group that is separate from software clients. Then for the hardware client group(s), enable the "save the XAUTH credentials locally" feature on the Easy VPN Server.

CAUTION   Because both the device and user authentication credentials are stored locally on the Remote, it is imperative that you secure the router locally—if someone steals the router, they can bring up a VPN session to a Server without having to enter any authentication credentials.

Second, on the Easy VPN Remote router, you'll need to configure and save the XAUTH credentials. Use the **username** command within the Remote's connection profile:

```
Router(config)# crypto ipsec client ezvpn config_name
Router(config-crypto-ezvpn)# username username password password
```

NOTE   If the Easy VPN Server doesn't have the save-the-password parameter enabled, or disables it at a later time, when the Easy VPN Remote router makes a connection, it will learn this new policy and erase the username and password configured for the Easy VPN connection profile.

TIP   Also, I've only been able to use the **username** in the crypto-ezvpn subcommand mode on an 800 series router: I've not been able to get this to work on 1700 series routers. To get around this problem on a 1700 router, configure the Server to allow the 1700 to save its password locally and then use the **crypto ipsec client ezvpn xauth** command shown in Example 18-7, where you'll enter the username and password manually. Because the Server allows this to be stored locally, what you enter in the **crypto** command will be saved on the router automatically; just be sure to save the router's configuration with the **copy running-config startup-config** command.

Step 5: Verify the Easy VPN Remote Configuration

The following commands will help you manage and troubleshoot IPsec tunnels on your Easy VPN Remote router:

- **show crypto ipsec client ezvpn**—Displays the current state of the Remote's tunnel, if any, including policy information pushed down from the Server during IKE Mode Config.

- **show ip nat statistics**—Displays the address translation configuration and table used by a Remote router running in client mode.

- **debug crypto ipsec client ezvpn**—Helps troubleshoot the setup and operation of Easy VPN Remote connections; Example 18-8 illustrates the use of this command, where a connection is established successfully to a Server.

- **clear crypto ipsec client ezvpn**—Tears down any IPsec tunnel currently established to an Easy VPN Server.

Example 18-8 *Debugging an Easy VPN Remote Connection*

```
1751A# debug crypto ipsec client ezvpn
EzVPN debugging is on
1751A#
1d17h: EZVPN: New State: READY
1d17h: EZVPN: Current State: READY
1d17h: EZVPN: Event: MODE_CONFIG_REPLY
1d17h: ezvpn_mode_config
1d17h: ezvpn_parse_mode_config_msg
1d17h: EZVPN: Attributes sent in message:
1d17h:     DNS Primary: 172.16.1.25
1d17h:     DNS Secondary: 172.16.1.26
1d17h:     NBMS/WINS Primary: 172.16.1.27
1d17h:     NBMS/WINS Secondary: 172.16.1.28
1d17h:     Default Domain: cisco.com
1d17h: EZVPN: New State: SS_OPEN
1d17h: EZVPN: Current State: SS_OPEN
3d17h: EZVPN: Event: SOCKET_READY
```

Easy VPN Remote Configuration Example

I'll now show you how to set up an Easy VPN Remote by illustrating its configuration in an example. I'll build upon the Server example in Example 18-6. The new updated configuration includes the commands in Example 18-9; I'll show only the new commands added to this configuration. There is a new group called "hwclients" for the Remote hardware clients, including Cisco routers. Assume the Easy VPN Remote router is an 831. A username of "r831" has been added for the Server router for XAUTH. In this instance, client mode will be used, so an address pool has been created and referenced in the new group. Notice that split DNS has been set up, and split tunneling. Below this, I'm allowing the hardware clients to store the XAUTH username and password locally.

Example 18-9 *Easy VPN Server Example Configuration for an Easy VPN Remote Router*

```
RTRA(config)# aaa authorization network localgroups local
RTRA(config)# username r831 secret cisco123
RTRA(config)# ip local pool hwclientspool 192.168.0.240 192.1.1.249
RTRA(config)# crypto isakmp client configuration group hwclients
RTRA(config-isakmp-group)# key cisco123
RTRA(config-isakmp-group)# pool hwclientspool
```

continues

Example 18-9 *Easy VPN Server Example Configuration for an Easy VPN Remote Router (Continued)*

```
RTRA(config-isakmp-group)# domain cisco.com
RTRA(config-isakmp-group)# dns 192.168.0.10 192.168.0.11
RTRA(config-isakmp-group)# wins 192.168.0.12 192.168.0.13
RTRA(config-isakmp-group)# max-logins 1
RTRA(config-isakmp-group)# split-dns cisco.com
RTRA(config-isakmp-group)# acl splitremote
RTRA(config-isakmp-group)# save-password
RTRA(config-isakmp-group)# exit
RTRA(config)# crypto map mymap isakmp authorization list localgroups
```

The Easy VPN Remote configuration of the 831 router is shown in Example 18-10. The top part of the configuration has the 831 Remote acting as a DHCP server—this is necessary because client mode is being used for the remote access session. Notice that the router's local LAN interface is excluded from the DHCP server pool. Below this, an Easy VPN connection profile called "hwclients" is created. The 831 belongs to the group called "hwclients" and connects using client mode. The Server is 192.1.1.1 and an IPsec tunnel will be brought up automatically as needed, where the username and password for 831 is stored locally (the group policy on the Server allows this). Last, the connection profile is activated on the interface connected to the Internet.

Example 18-10 *Easy VPN Remote Example Configuration*

```
r831(config)# ip dhcp pool REMOTE
r831(dhcp-config)# network 192.168.1.0 255.255.255.0
r831(dhcp-config)# default-router 192.168.1.1
r831(dhcp-config)# domain-name cisco.com
r831(dhcp-config)# dns-server 199.1.1.1
r831(dhcp-config)# lease 1 0 0
r831(dhcp-config)# exit
r831(config)# ip dhcp excluded-address 192.168.1.1
r831(config)# crypto ipsec client ezvpn hwclients
r831(config-crypto-ezvpn)# group hwclients key cisco123
r831(config-crypto-ezvpn)# mode client
r831(config-crypto-ezvpn)# peer 192.1.1.1
r831(config-crypto-ezvpn)# connect auto
r831(config-crypto-ezvpn)# username r831 password cisco123
r831(config-crypto-ezvpn)# exit
r831(config)# interface Ethernet0
r831(config-if)# description Internet Connection
r831(config-if)# ip address 199.1.2.1 255.255.255.0
r831(config-if)# crypto ipsec client ezvpn hwclients
r831(config-if)# exit
r831(config)# interface FastEthernet0
r831(config-if)# description Local LAN Connection
r831(config-if)# ip address 192.168.1.1 255.255.255.0
```

IPsec Remote Access and L2L Sessions on the Same Router

Figure 18-3 shows an example network that has both remote access and L2L sessions. In this example, the remote office network is acquiring its address dynamically, via DHCP, from its connected ISP, which also is true of the remote access clients. Because the central office router doesn't know the remote office router's IP address, you would have to configure the pre-shared key for the router as 0.0.0.0 0.0.0.0 with no XAUTH. However, doing this would cause XAUTH to not work for the remote access clients. One solution would be to use certificates instead of pre-shared keys; for small networks, though, this might not be cost-effective or practical.

Figure 18-3 *Remote Access and L2L Connections*

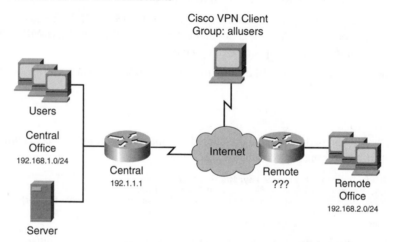

With IOS 12.2(15)T, however, you now can use ISAKMP/IKE profiles to match on other properties to determine how to do authentication during ISAKMP/IKE Phase 1, such as a client's group name, a peer's IP address, a fully qualified domain name, and other information than just the IP address of the peer. You also can define other properties to use for the ISAKMP/IKE Phase 1 connection.

CAUTION   Because of a bug in 12.2(15)T, the wildcarding of pre-shared keys doesn't work. This has been fixed in 12.3(3) and 12.3(2)T. Therefore, to use this feature, be sure you are running one of these two IOS versions or a later version.

The following sections will cover these topics:

- Central Office Router Configuration
- Remote Access and L2L Example Configuration

Central Office Router Configuration

When a central office router needs to terminate remote access and L2L sessions with pre-shared keys, and one or more of the L2L peers acquires its address dynamically, you can create an ISAKMP/IKE profile and use it with peers that match the components of the profile.

There are a few components you need to configure on your router to allow pre-shared keys for this particular situation above and beyond your normal configuration for L2L and remote access clients:

- A keyring, which specifies the pre-shared key to use for a peer or peers
- An ISAKMP/IKE profile for L2L peer(s)
- An ISAKMP/IKE profile for remote access clients
- A dynamic crypto map entry that specifies the ISAKMP/IKE Phase 1 profile for the remote access clients and another entry that specifies the ISAKMP/IKE Phase 1 profile for the L2L peers with dynamic IP addressing

The following sections will discuss the configuration of the above components.

Keyrings

A keyring is used to define a pre-shared key that one or more L2L peers will use. Use the following commands to configure a keyring:

```
Router(config)# crypto keyring keyring_name
Router(conf-keyring)# description description
Router(conf-keyring)# pre-shared-key address address [subnet_mask]
         key key
Router(conf-keyring)# exit
```

The **crypto keyring** command creates the keyring—each keyring must have a unique name. This command takes you into a subcommand mode. The **description** command assigns a brief description to the keyring. The **pre-shared-key address** command assigns a pre-shared key to the keyring. For L2L peers that acquire addresses dynamically, the IP address and subnet mask should be "0.0.0.0 0.0.0.0."

L2L ISAKMP/IKE Profiles

An ISAKMP/IKE profile specifies certain properties that should be used by certain peers for establishing an ISAKMP/IKE Phase 1 connection. ISAKMP/IKE policies still need to be defined, but with the addition of profiles, you can control when certain components should be used for a peer, such as wildcarded pre-shared keys for L2L peers and group pre-shared keys for remote access groups.

You'll need to configure at least one ISAKMP/IKE profile for the L2L peers that acquire their addresses dynamically. Here is the configuration to accomplish this:

```
Router(config)# crypto isakmp profile ISAKMP_profile_name
Router(conf-isa-prof)# description description
Router(conf-isa-prof)# match identity address IP_address
Router(conf-isa-prof)# match identity host FQDN domain_name
Router(conf-isa-prof)# match identity host domain FQDN
Router(conf-isa-prof)# self-identity {address | fqdn}
Router(conf-isa-prof)# keyring keyring_name
Router(conf-isa-prof)# keepalive seconds
Router(conf-isa-prof)# exit
```

The **crypto isakmp profile** command creates the ISAKMP/IKE profile for Phase 1 connections. Each profile needs a unique name. This command takes you into a subcommand mode. The **description** command assigns a description to the profile.

The **match identity** commands specify how to match on a peer that should use this profile. The **address** parameter allows you to specify an address of a peer: if you specify 0.0.0.0, this matches on all peers. The **host** parameter allows you to match on a fully qualified domain name, like "router.cisco.com." The **host domain** parameter allows you to match on a domain name of a peer, like "cisco.com."

The **self-identity** command allows you to specify how the local router will identify itself to the remote router, by an IP address or a FQDN; if you omit this command, it defaults to the globally configured identity type configured with the **crypto isakmp identity** command, which was discussed in Chapter 16, "Router ISAKMP/IKE Phase 1 Connectivity."

The **keyring** command specifies the keyring (i.e., the pre-shared key) to use for peers that match the **match identity** commands in the ISAKMP/IKE profile. The **keepalive** command specifies the keepalive interval for dead peer detection (DPD).

NOTE   You can use ISAKMP/IKE profiles with DMVPN configurations. When you are creating your IPsec profile with the **crypto ipsec profile** command, in the subcommand mode, use the **set isakmp-profile** command to reference your ISAKMP/IKE Phase 1 profile.

Remote Access ISAKMP/IKE Profiles

For every remote access group you have, you'll need to create a separate ISAKMP/IKE profile—one for each group. Here are the commands to create a profile for a remote access group:

```
Router(conf)# crypto isakmp profile ISAKMP_profile_name
Router(conf-isa-prof)# description description
Router(conf-isa-prof)# match identity group group_name
Router(conf-isa-prof)# match identity host FQDN domain_name
Router(conf-isa-prof)# match identity host domain FQDN
Router(conf-isa-prof)# self-identity {address | fqdn}
Router(conf-isa-prof)# client authentication list
                AAA_authentication_list_name
```

```
Router(conf-isa-prof)# isakmp authorization list group_name
Router(conf-isa-prof)# client configuration address
                 {respond | initiate}
Router(conf-isa-prof)# keepalive seconds
Router(conf-isa-prof)# exit
```

Some of the ISAKMP/IKE profile commands are the same as those used for L2L peers, so I'll focus only on the ones unique to remote access groups. The **match identity group** command allows you to associate the specified remote access group with this particular profile. Optionally, you can further subqualify matches with FQDN or domain names. The **client authentication list** command associates this profile with the **aaa authentication login** command the router should use for XAUTH authentication. The **isakmp authorization list** command specifies the **aaa authorization network** command that is used by remote access groups that match this profile: this command gives you the flexibility to have different groups on different AAA servers, or one group on an AAA server and one group defined locally The **client configuration address** command specifies whether the central office router should initiate IKE Mode Config or respond to initiations from the remote access users. For the Cisco VPN Client and other Easy VPN Remotes, set this to **respond**; for other clients, set it to **initiate**.

Dynamic Crypto Maps and Profiles

To use the ISAKMP/IKE profiles you have created, you need to reference them in a crypto map entry. For remote access users or L2L peers with dynamically acquired addresses, this is in a dynamic crypto map entry:

```
Router(config)# crypto dynamic-map dynamic_map_name seq_#
Router(config-crypto-map)# set transform-set transform_set_name
Router(config-crypto-map)# set isakmp-profile ISAKMP_profile_name
```

In the dynamic crypto map entry, only two commands are required:

- The **set transform-set** command specifies the transform set or sets that should be used to protect the data connections between the router and the remote peer.

- The **set isakmp-profile** command specifies the ISAKMP/IKE profile that should be used to build and manage the management connection to the remote peer.

NOTE   Each profile needs to be in a *different* dynamic crypto map entry. The profile you place in an entry *does* matter. The remote access group ISAKMP/IKE profiles should be placed in dynamic crypto map entries with a higher priority (lower sequence number) than the L2L profiles. If you reverse the order, the remote access users would match against the wildcarded pre-shared key in the keyring and thus fail XAUTH.

Remote Access and L2L Example Configuration

To understand how to configure both remote access and L2L peers (with dynamically acquired addresses) on the same router, I'll show you an example configuration based on the network in Figure 18-3. Example 18-11 shows the central office router's configuration that accepts the L2L and remote access sessions.

Example 18-11 *Central Office Router with L2L and Remote Access Peers*

```
Central(config)# username user secret userpassword
Central(config)#! ←other usernames omitted→
Central(config)# aaa new-model
Central(config)# aaa authentication login remoteaccess local
Central(config)# aaa authorization network allusers local
Central(config)# crypto isakmp policy 10
Central(config-isakmp)# encryption 3des
Central(config-isakmp)# hash sha
Central(config-isakmp)# authentication pre-share
Central(config-isakmp)# group 2
Central(config-isakmp)# exit
Central(config)# ip local pool clientpool 192.168.1.240 192.168.1.254
Central(config)# crypto isakmp client configuration group allusers
Central(config-isakmp-group)# key allusers123
Central(config-isakmp-group)# dns 192.168.1.2
Central(config-isakmp-group)# wins 192.168.1.3
Central(config-isakmp-group)# domain cisco.com
Central(config-isakmp-group)# pool clientpool
Central(config-isakmp-group)# exit
Central(config)# crypto isakmp profile allusersprofile
Central(conf-isa-prof)# description Remote access users profile
Central(conf-isa-prof)# match identity group allusers
Central(conf-isa-prof)# client authentication list remoteaccess
Central(conf-isa-prof)# isakmp authorization list allusers
Central(conf-isa-prof)# client configuration address respond
Central(conf-isa-prof)# keepalive 20 3
Central(conf-isa-prof)# exit
Central(config)# crypto keyring L2Lkeyring
Central(conf-keyring)# description Pre-shared key for L2L peers
          with dynamic addressing
Central(conf-keyring)# pre-shared-key address 0.0.0.0 0.0.0.0
          key cisco123
Central(conf-keyring)# exit
Central(config)# crypto isakmp profile L2Lprofile
Central(conf-isa-prof)# description All L2L peers
Central(conf-isa-prof)# keyring L2Lkeyring
Central(conf-isa-prof)# match identity address 0.0.0.0
Central(conf-isa-prof)# keepalive 20 3
Central(conf-isa-prof)# exit
Central(config)# crypto ipsec transform-set transset esp-3des
          esp-sha-hmac
Central(cfg-crypto-tran)# exit
Central(config)# crypto dynamic-map dynmap 5
Central(config-crypto-m)# set transform-set transset
```

continues

Example 18-11 *Central Office Router with L2L and Remote Access Peers (Continued)*

```
Central(config-crypto-m)# set isakmp-profile allusersprofile
Central(config-crypto-m)# exit
Central(config)# crypto dynamic-map dynmap 10
Central(config-crypto-m)# set transform-set transset
Central(config-crypto-m)# set isakmp-profile L2Lprofile
Central(config-crypto-m)# exit
Central(config)# crypto map staticmap 10 ipsec-isakmp dynamic dynmap
Central(config)# interface Ethernet0/0
Central(config-if)# description Internet interface
Central(config-if)# ip address 192.1.1.1 255.255.255.0
Central(config-if)# crypto map staticmap
Central(config-if)# exit
Central(config)# interface Ethernet0/1
Central(config-if)# description Local LAN interface
Central(config-if)# ip address 192.168.1.1 255.255.255.0
```

In this example, XAUTH authentication is performed locally on the router using the **username** commands. One group, called "allusers," is configured. Both the VPN Client software clients and the remote office router use the same ISAKMP/IKE Phase 1 policy to build the management connection, policy 10, which uses pre-shared keys for device authentication.

The remote access group "allusers" is assigned addresses from the "clientpool" address pool. The pre-shared key is "allusers123." An ISAKMP/IKE profile is defined for the group, called "allusers," which specifies that any user from the "allusers" group (the **match identity group allusers** command) will use this profile to supplement the building of the management connection. XAUTH authentication is done with the **aaa authentication login remote access** command and authorization with the **aaa authorization network allusers** command.

A keyring is created for the remote office router, which is acquiring its IP address dynamically. A pre-shared key of "cisco123" is defined for all L2L routers. This key is then referenced in the ISAKMP/IKE "L2Lprofile" for the L2L routers. The **match identity address 0.0.0.0** command matches on all devices.

A transform set is defined that both the remote office router and the remote access group will use. There are two dynamic crypto map entries. Notice that entry 5, the first one, references the remote access ISAKMP/IKE profile: "allusersprofile." It is important that this appears before the L2L profile because the matching is based on a group name. If you would re-order the two entries in the dynamic crypto map, because the L2L profile matches on all addresses (the **match identity address 0.0.0.0** command), this would also include the remote access users, thereby not invoking XAUTH to perform user authentication. Toward the end of the configuration, the dynamic crypto map is referenced in a static crypto map and the static crypto map is activated on the central office router's Internet interface.

The remote office router is configured as normal, as shown in Example 18-12.

Example 18-12 *Remote Office Router's Configuration*

```
Remote(config)# crypto isakmp policy 10
Remote(config-isakmp)# encryption 3des
Remote(config-isakmp)# authentication pre-share
Remote(config-isakmp)# hash sha
Remote(config-isakmp)# group 2
Remote(config-isakmp)# exit
Remote(config)# crypto isakmp key cisco123 address 192.1.1.1
Remote(config)# crypto ipsec transform-set transset esp-3des
          esp-sha-hmac
Remote(cfg-crypto-tran)# exit
Remote(config)# access-list 100 permit ip 192.168.2.0 0.0.0.255
          192.168.1.0 0.0.0.255
Remote(config)# crypto map staticmap 10 ipsec-isakmp
Remote(config-crypto-map)# set peer 192.1.1.1
Remote(config-crypto-map)# set transform-set transset
Remote(config-crypto-map)# match address 100
Remote(config-crypto-map)# exit
Remote(config)# interface Ethernet0/0
Remote(config-if)# description Internet interface
Remote(config-if)# ip address dhcp
Remote(config-if)# crypto map staticmap
Remote(config-if)# exit
Remote(config)# interface Ethernet0/1
Remote(config-if)# description Local LAN interface
Remote(config-if)# ip address 192.168.2.1 255.255.255.0
```

WebVPN

In 12.3(14)T Cisco introduced SSL VPN functionality, called WebVPN, on Cisco IOS-based routers. This feature allows you to set up a router to terminate user-based SSL VPNs. Cisco took much of the WebVPN technology that exists in the VPN 3000 concentrators and ported it to the IOS routers. In other words, an IOS-based router, with WebVPN implemented, is by and large a secure web proxy.

The user desktop requirements are essentially the same as those for WebVPN sessions terminating on concentrators:

- Supported SSL-enabled browser: Internet Explorer, Netscape, Mozilla, or FireFox
- Sun Microsystems Java Runtime (for the Port Forwarding, or thin client, feature only)
- Optionally a supported e-mail client: Microsoft Outlook, Netscape Mail, or Eudora

However, Cisco VPN 3000 concentrators support more SSL VPN features than Cisco routers; for example, WebVPN-enabled routers have the following limitations, and others, when compared to the concentrators:

- Only SSLv3 is supported: TLS is not supported.

- The Cisco Secure Desktop and Cisco SSL VPN Client are not yet supported; therefore, a WebVPN router can only terminate clientless and thin client connections.

- URLs referenced by Macromedia Flash are not supported for secure retrieval.

What the user sees when accessing the WebVPN device—concentrator, ASA, or router—is the same, requiring no additional user training. Therefore, you might start deploying the Cisco WebVPN solution using routers, and then migrate to the use of VPN 3000 concentrators, which are more scalable when it comes to WebVPN services, and also support more SSL VPN features. The transition between using a router and a concentrator to terminate WebVPN services is transparent to the user because the user still sees the same information when accessing the WebVPN device, authenticating via a user account, and then using services via the WebVPN web home page and toolbar (this is true with the clientless and thin client implementation).

I discussed how to use WebVPN from the user-side in Chapter 8, "Concentrator Remote Access Connections with PPTP, L2TP, and WebVPN." Therefore, this chapter focuses only on how to set up a router as a WebVPN server, not how to use WebVPN services as a user. See Chapter 8 for using WebVPN services as a user.

WebVPN Setup

The setup and maintenance/monitoring of WebVPN connections on IOS routers is not difficult. The following steps summarize this process:

Step 1 Configuring Prerequisites: AAA, DNS, and Certificates (required)

Step 2 Configuring WebVPN (required)

Step 3 Creating URL and Port Forwarding Entries for the Home Page (optional, but recommended)

Step 4 Maintaining, monitoring, and troubleshooting WebVPN connections (optional)

In the following sections, I'll discuss the commands necessary to perform the above steps.

Step 1: Configuring Prerequisites

Before you begin configuring WebVPN on your router, you'll need to perform some prerequisite configuration tasks that are necessary for WebVPN. These include:

- Setting up AAA for authenticating WebVPN users

- Setting up DNS to resolve URL name information

- Obtaining an SSL certificate for the router

The following paragraphs will explain these tasks in more depth.

AAA Configuration

When users access your WebVPN-enabled router, they must authenticate for the SSL VPN to be established. The username and password can be located locally on the router or defined on an AAA server using either the TACACS+ or RADIUS security protocols. I discussed how to set up AAA previously in the "Defining AAA" subsection of the "Easy VPN Server Configuration" earlier. Here's a brief review of the commands:

```
Router(config)# aaa new-model
Router(config)# aaa authentication login list_name method1
          [method2...]
Router(config)# username user's_name {password|secret} password
Router(config)# tacacs-server host AAA_IP_address key AAA_key_string
Router(config)# radius-server host AAA_IP_address [auth-port port_#]
          [acct-port port_#] key AAA_key_string
```

If you specify **local** as the authentication method for the **aaa authentication login** command, the router will look for usernames defined by the **username** command on the router. If you specify **group tacacs+** or **group radius** as the method, you'll need to configure an AAA server (the **tacacs-server** and **radius-server** commands, respectively).

DNS Configuration

DNS is necessary for two WebVPN purposes:

- To generate an RSA key pair for protecting SSL connections
- To resolve names in URLs (remember that the router is acting as a web proxy)

To set up DNS, configure the following on your WebVPN-enabled router:

```
Router(config)# hostname router_name
Router(config)# ip domain-name domain_name
Router(config)# ip name-server DNS_server_IP1 [...DNS_server_IP6]
```

The **hostname** and **ip domain-name** commands are necessary for generating RSA keys on your router that will be used for the SSL certificate. The **ip name-server** command allows you to specify up to six DNS servers that the router can use to resolve FQDNs.

SSL Certificate Configuration

To use SSL, your WebVPN-enabled router needs a certificate: the keys on the certificate are used for protecting data between the user's desktop and the router. There are two ways you can get a certificate on the router:

- Obtain a certificate from a CA
- Create a self-signed certificate

If you're going to use a CA for certificate services, note that I described this process in Chapter 16, "Router ISAKMP/IKE Phase 1 Connectivity" in the "Digital Certificates and Router Enrollment" section. If the number of WebVPN users is small, using an external CA is probably overkill. In this situation, I would install a self-signed certificate on the router.

In this section I'll focus on creating a self-signed certificate, which involves the following commands:

```
Router(config)# crypto {ca | pki} trustpoint trustpoint_name
Router(ca-trustpoint)# enrollment selfsigned
Router(ca-trustpoint)# subject-name X.500_certificate_components
Router(ca-trustpoint)# rsakeypair RSA_key_label modulus
Router(ca-trustpoint)# exit
Router(ca-trustpoint)# crypto pki enroll CA_name
```

As you can see from the above commands, this process is similar to obtaining a certificate from a CA. The **crypto {ca | pki} trustpoint** command specifies a trustpoint; for a self-signed certificate, the router itself is a trustpoint: therefore, the name given doesn't matter. However, Cisco typically recommends using "SSLVPN," because this is the default trustpoint that WebVPN uses.

The **enrollment selfsigned** command specifies that the router will get a certificate from itself. The **subject-name** command specifies the components to be placed on the certificate, like the CN, OU, and O values. The **rsakeypair** command specifies a key label to use for the RSA keys and the modulus to use when creating the signature and encryption keys. When you generate your self-signed certificate with the **crypto pki enroll** command, the router will then generate the RSA key pair and the self-signed certificate.

CAUTION   Specify only one modulus value for the RSA key pair. This will create general purpose keys; if you specify two modulus values, usage keys are created. Upon doing this for usage keys, any SSL connection to the WebVPN-enabled router will fail.

Example 18-13 illustrates the process of creating the RSA key pair and self-signed certificate. Once done, you can use the **show crypto key mypubkey rsa** command to view the two key pairs created and the **show crypto ca certificates** command to view the self-signed certificate that was generated.

Example 18-13 *Generating a Self-Signed Certificate*

```
r3640(config)# crypto pki trustpoint SSLVPN
r3460(ca-trustpoint)# enrollment selfsigned
r3460(ca-trustpoint)# subject-name CN=SSLVPN OU=Cisco O=Cisco
r3460(ca-trustpoint)# rsakeypair SSLVPN 512
r3460(ca-trustpoint)# exit
r3460(config)# crypto pki enroll SSLVPN
*Mar 1 00:11:43.519: %CRYPTO-6-AUTOGEN: Generated new 512 bit
 key pair
*Mar 1 00:11:44.135: %SSH-5-ENABLED: SSH 1.99 has been enabled
% Include the router serial number in the subject name? [yes/no]: no
% Include an IP address in the subject name? [no]: no
Generate Self Signed Router Certificate? [yes/no]: yes
Router Self Signed Certificate successfully created
```

TIP   When using a CA, remember to make the RSA key exportable and then export the keypair and certificate with this command: **crypto pki export** *CA_name* **pkcs12** *destination_URL passphrase*. Exporting and importing keys was discussed in Chapter 16. You'll want to do this in case the WebVPN router fails and your users must access a backup router and you want to use the same certificate. Please note that this process is not necessary for self-signed certificates, only CA-based identity certificates.

Step 2: Configuring WebVPN

Once you either have installed an identity certificate from a CA or generated a self-signed certificate, you're ready to set up WebVPN on your router using the following commands:

```
Router(config)# webvpn enable [gateway-addr IP_address]
Router(config)# webvpn
Router(config-webvpn)# ssl trustpoint trustpoint_name
Router(config-webvpn)# ssl encryption [3des-sha1] [des-sha-1]
              [rc4-md5]
Router(config-webvpn)# title "home_page_title"
Router(config-webvpn)# title-color color_value
Router(config-webvpn)# text-color [black | white]
Router(config-webvpn)# secondary-color color_value
Router(config-webvpn)# secondary-text-color [black | white]
Router(config-webvpn)# login-message "login_string"
Router(config-webvpn)# logo [file filename | none]
Router(config-webvpn)# idle-timeout [never | seconds]
Router(config-webvpn)# exit
```

The **webvpn enable** command enables the WebVPN services on your router. Optionally, you can specify an IP address on the router that will terminate WebVPN connections; if you omit this, the router will accept WebVPN sessions on any of its configured IP addresses. Normally I configure this for the router's external or loopback IP address.

TIP   If you have HTTPS services already running on the router, along with WebVPN, you must specify the **gateway-addr** parameter; otherwise, WebVPN users will connect to the HTTPS service on the router instead of WebVPN. You can determine if the router is running any HTTPS services by executing the **show tcp brief all** command, which displays all of the TCP services currently running on the router. If you see port 443 listed, the router is running an HTTPS server and you must specify the **gateway-addr** parameter. For the address specified by this parameter, the router will process only WebVPN services; other addresses on the router can use the router's internal HTTPS service. Therefore, for example, if you need to manage the router using SDM and terminate WebVPN sessions on the same interface, you might want to assign two IP addresses (primary and secondary) to the router's interface; then use the **gateway-addr** command to specify the address used by WebVPN users.

The **webvpn** command enters the WebVPN subcommand mode where you can configure the parameters for client interaction and for the WebVPN home page. The **ssl trustpoint** command specifies the trustpoint that has the certificate the WebVPN-enabled router should use. For self-signed certificates, if you specified the trustpoint name as "SSLVPN," it is not necessary to specify the trustpoint in the subcommand mode. The **ssl encryption** command specifies the packet encryption and authentication algorithm(s) to use. By default, the algorithms specified in the above command are enabled in the order specified. With the **ssl encryption** command, you can change the order of the algorithms or the algorithms to use.

The **title** command allows you to create a title for the WebVPN home page that appears once a user authenticates. The title can be up to 255 characters; if you omit the title, it defaults to "WebVPN Service." You must enclose the title in quotes (" ") if there is more than one word in the title. The **title-color** specifies the color the title bar should be; by default, it's purple. You can enter the color by specifying red, green, and blue (separated by commas), which is an RGB value; you also can use an HTML color value that begins with a "#" or the name of the color. The value is limited to 32 characters. The **text-color** command specifies the color the text in the title bars should be on the WebVPN home page. This can be black or white, where the default is white (Cisco documentation incorrectly states this as black).

TIP   I commonly use this sight to access RGB color coding schemes: http://www.hyper-solutions.org/rgb.html. But you can easily do a search for "RGB table" or "RGB color" to find other tables.

The **secondary-color** command specifies the color that the secondary title bars should be on the WebVPN home page. The color value is entered in the same format at the title bar color. If you omit this color, it defaults to purple. The **secondary-text-color** command specifies the color of the text in the secondary title bars; if you omit this command, the color defaults to black (Cisco documentation incorrectly states this as white).

The **login-message** command specifies a heading that appears above the username and password prompt when performing user authentication. The login message can be up to 255 characters in length and defaults to "Please enter your username and password." You must enclose the login message in quotes (" ") if there is more than one word in the message.

The **logo** command specifies the logo image that should be displayed on the WebVPN login and home pages. The default is the Cisco logo. If you want to use a custom logo, the file format must be either GIF, JPG, or PNG and must be smaller than 100 KB. The name of the file must also have fewer than 255 characters. Normally, this file is placed somewhere in Flash memory on the router. If you specify a file name that the router can't locate, the router will display an error message.

NOTE	Remember that logos are *not* automatically resized; therefore, you'll need to make sure your logo images are small to begin with.

The **idle-timeout** command specifies the number of seconds to maintain idle WebVPN sessions. The default idle timeout is 1,800 seconds (30 minutes), but can range from 180–86,400 seconds. If you specify **never** or 0 for the seconds, then idle WebVPN sessions will never time out (this is not recommended).

NOTE	The **webvpn enable** and **webvpn** commands are the only two necessary to enable WebVPN on your router, assuming that the trustpoint is called "SSLVPN."

Step 3: Creating URL and Port Forwarding Entries for the Home Page

Once users have authenticated, they are taken to the WebVPN home page, which Cisco commonly refers to as the "Portal Page." From this screen you can list URLs and port forwarding applications to which the users have access. By default, no URLs or port forwarding entries are listed on the portal page.

NOTE	Cisco has hinted that they might allow you to restrict access to URL and port listings based on a group's configuration on the WebVPN router, similar to the concentrators; however, this feature isn't present in 12.3(14)T.

Portal Page URLs

To define a URL or list of URLs that appear on the portal page, use the following configuration:

```
Router(config)# webvpn
Router(config-webvpn)# url-list URL_list_name
Router(config-webvpn-url)# heading "URL_heading_name"
Router(config-webvpn-url)# url-text URL_name url-value URL_value
```

The **url-list** command specifies a group of related URLs that will appear on the portal page. The list name you specify groups the URLs under a common heading and doesn't actually appear on the portal page. The **heading** command specifies the actual heading that will appear above the URLs on the home page. Each group of URLs under a different list can have a different heading. If the heading contains more than one word, then you must enclose it in quotation marks (" "). The **url-text** command specifies the URLs that will appear under the heading in the list. The *url_name* parameter specifies the hyperlink text that will appear on the portal page, presenting the hyperlink specified in the **url-value** parameter. For example, if you configured **url-text "Sales Link" url-value http://www.sales.cisco.com**, the portal page would display "Sales Link" as a hyperlink the user could click, taking them to http://www.sales.cisco.com. Please note that you can enter multiple URLs for a list—just enter them in separate **url-text** commands. If you have multiple URL entries for a listing, they'll be displayed in a two-column format on the portal page.

Portal Page Port Forwarding

To define a port forwarding application(s) that appears on the portal page, use the following configuration:

```
Router(config)# webvpn
Router(config-webvpn)# port-forward list list_name
            local-port local_port_#
            remote-server server_IP_address
            remote-port remote_port_#
```

The **port-forward** command in the WebVPN subcommand mode creates port-forwarding entries. The **list** parameter allows you to group port-forwarding entries under this name on the portal page. The local port number specifies what the WebVPN applet will use to change the default port number of the application to ensure that it goes across the SSL tunnel. This port number must currently be unused on the user's PC; normally using a port number greater than 60,000 will work. The remote server's IP address is the IP address that the WebVPN router should forward the traffic to and the remote port number is what the user application normally connects to.

NOTE   If you recall from Chapter 8, "Concentrator Remote Access Connections with L2TP, PPTP, and WebVPN," the JavaScript code is downloaded to the user's web browser and adds entries in the hosts file to allow the port-redirection process to take place. The user needs to terminate the WebVPN session gracefully to undo the changes made within this file on the user's desktop. To access port-forwarding applications from the port page, the user must click the "Start Application Access" hyperlink, which appears above any configured URLs. Once this has been done, the user can then start the normal application.

Step 4: Maintaining, Monitoring, and Troubleshooting WebVPN Connections

There are three commands you can use to manage your WebVPN sessions:

- **show webvpn session**
- **show webvpn statistics**
- **debug webvpn**

The **show webvpn session** command, shown in Example 18-14, displays connected SSL VPN sessions to the WebVPN router. In this example, only one user, "richard," has connected from 192.168.1.100, and he has four protected connections currently open to the WebVPN router. Currently, "richard" has been idle for more than eight minutes.

Example 18-14 *Viewing WebVPN Sessions*

```
r3640# show webvpn session
WebVPN domain name: cisco.com
Client Login Name      Client IP Address   Number of Connections
richard          192.168.1.100     4
  Created 00:11:01, Last-used 00:08:17
  Client Port: 3516
  Client Port: 3520
  Client Port: 3521
  Client Port: 3538
```

The **show webvpn statistics** command, shown in Example 18-15, displays a summary of the WebVPN activity on the router. In Example 18-15, one user is currently connected with four protected connections. No one has yet failed authentication to the WebVPN router, but six have successfully connected, authenticated, and then disconnected.

Example 18-15 *Viewing WebVPN Statistics*

```
r3640# show webvpn statistics
Active user sessions: 1
Active user TCP connections: 4
Authentication failures: 0
Terminated user sessions: 6
```

The **debug webvpn** command can be used for low-level troubleshooting and supports the following additional parameters: **aaa, cookie, dns, http, port-forward, webservice**.

WebVPN Configuration Example

Now that you have a basic understanding of the commands used to set up and manage WebVPN on a router, I'll illustrate the configuration process by going through an example configuration, shown in Example 18-16.

Example 18-16 *Example WebVPN Router Configuration*

```
r3640(config)# aaa new-model
r3640(config)# aaa authentication login consoleaaa none
r3640(config)# line con 0
r3640(config-line)# login authentication consoleaaa
r3640(config-line)# exit
r3640(config)# aaa authentication login default local
r3640(config)# username richard secret password
r3640(config)# ! ←other user accounts omitted→
r3640(config)# ip domain-name cisco.com
```

continues

Example 18-16 *Example WebVPN Router Configuration (Continued)*

```
r3640(config)# ip name-server 192.168.1.2
r3640(config)# crypto pki trustpoint SSLVPN
r3460(ca-trustpoint)# enrollment selfsigned
r3460(ca-trustpoint)# subject-name CN=SSLVPN OU=Cisco O=Cisco
r3460(ca-trustpoint)# rsakeypair SSLVPN 512
r3460(ca-trustpoint)# exit
r3460(config)# crypto pki enroll SSLVPN
*Mar 1 00:11:43.519: %CRYPTO-6-AUTOGEN: Generated new 512 bit
 key pair
*Mar 1 00:11:44.135: %SSH-5-ENABLED: SSH 1.99 has been enabled
% Include the router serial number in the subject name? [yes/no]: no
% Include an IP address in the subject name? [no]: no
Generate Self Signed Router Certificate? [yes/no]: yes
r3640 Self Signed Certificate successfully created
r3640(config)# webvpn enable gateway-addr 192.1.1.1
r3640(config)# webvpn
r3640(config-webvpn)# ssl trustpoint SSLVPN
r3640(config-webvpn)# title "Cisco Portal Page"
r3640(config-webvpn)# text-color black
r3640(config-webvpn)# secondary-text-color black
r3640(config-webvpn)# login-message "You must enter your user name
             and password before proceeding"
r3640(config-webvpn)# logo file flash:company.gif
r3640(config-webvpn)# idle-timeout 300
r3640(config-webvpn)# url-list saleslist
r3640(config-webvpn-url)# heading "Sales URLs"
r3640(config-webvpn-url)# url-text SALE_SRV_1 url-value
             http://www1.sales.cisco.com
r3640(config-webvpn-url)# url-text SALE_SRV_2 url-value
             http://www2.sales.cisco.com
r3640(config-webvpn-url)# exit
r3640(config-webvpn-url)# url-list mktlist
r3640(config-webvpn-url)# heading "Marketing URLs"
r3640(config-webvpn-url)# url-text Marketing_Server url-value
             http://www.marketing.cisco.com
r3640(config-webvpn-url)# exit
r3640(config-webvpn)# port-forward list telnet local-port 60001
             remote-server 192.168.1.3 remote-port 23
```

The top part of the configuration enables AAA and ensures that the default list is not used on the console—on the console, no authentication is required. The domain name of "cisco.com" is assigned to the router and a DNS server that is internal to the company: 192.168.1.2. Below this, a trustpoint called "SSLVPN" is defined, where the router creates a self-signed certificate. WebVPN is enabled on the router, but only for the external interface: 192.1.1.1.

Within the WebVPN configuration, the trustpoint is defined ("SSLVPN"), which tells the router what certificate to use. The title for the portal page, and the login message on the login page are changed from their default values. The idle timeout for SSL sessions is changed from three minutes to five minutes. Two groupings of URLs are defined for the portal page: "Sales URLs and Marketing URLs." Last, port forwarding is set up for Telnet. In this instance, when a user clicks the "Start Application Access" hyperlink, the port-forwarding window opens. It lists the actual IP address and port number the user should telnet to, to access Telnet on the remote server. In this example, if the user telnets to 127.0.0.1 on port 60001, the WebVPN JavaScript redirects this to the actual Telnet server (192.168.1.3) on port 23.

NOTE   As you can see from this section on WebVPNs, the Cisco initial implementation of SSL VPNs on Cisco routers is very minimal (similar to that of a VPN 3000 concentrator running 4.1). If you need more enhanced features, or need to support a large number of users, then I would seriously look at using a VPN 3000 concentrator or an ASA security appliance instead of a router.

Summary

This chapter showed you the basics of setting up a router for remote access services, including Easy VPN Server, Easy VPN Remote, and WebVPN. Normally, routers are not used as Easy VPN Servers, because the configuration is complex and the VPN 3000 concentrators and PIX and ASA security appliances support more enhanced remote access capabilities. However, there are many cases where routers are used as Easy VPN Remote devices, especially in cases where non-Ethernet Internet connections or enhanced QoS are required. The last part of the chapter dealt with a new feature on routers: WebVPN. With this feature, you can set up very basic SSL VPNs to Cisco routers.

Next up is Chapter 19, "Troubleshooting Router Connections," where I show you how to use **show** and **debug** commands to troubleshoot router VPN sessions.

Troubleshooting Router Connections

This chapter will focus on how to troubleshoot IPsec sessions on Cisco routers. I've broken the chapter into two areas on troubleshooting: ISAKMP/IKE Phase 1 and Phase 2 issues. I'll show you how ISAKMP/IKE Phase 1 and 2 connections are built using **debug** commands and what to look for when there is a problem with either of these phases. I'll also discuss a new feature in the IOS called VPN Monitoring, which allows you to determine problems with IPsec sessions more easily. The last part of the chapter will deal with one main issue with any type of VPN implementation: fragmentation.

NOTE This chapter by no means covers all possible problems you'll experience with IPsec sessions on Cisco routers. However, I hope to provide you with the necessary background so that troubleshooting IPsec sessions is a simpler process. I could easily talk about troubleshooting IPsec sessions on routers for over 200 pages, but because of all of the other topics in this book, I'll keep my discussion to a reasonable number of pages. Plus, the solutions I discuss here, such as how to troubleshoot fragmentations problems, can be applied easily to other Cisco VPN products.

ISAKMP/IKE Phase 1 Connections

In the first part of this chapter I'll focus on troubleshooting ISAKMP/IKE Phase 1 connections. If you recall from Chapter 3, "IPsec," the management connections built during Phase 1 are used to pass IPsec management traffic; no data traverses these connections. These connections are important, however, because they are used to build the data connections for Phase 2.

I've broken this part of the chapter into three areas. In the first part, I discuss the commands used to troubleshoot ISAKMP/IKE Phase 1 connections; the two sections following this are specific to L2L and remote access implementations, respectively.

Overview of the Phase 1 Commands

You can use the following router commands to troubleshoot ISAKMP/IKE Phase 1 connections:

- **show crypto isakmp sa**—Displays the status of all management connections.

- **debug crypto isakmp**—Displays the steps taken to build a management connection and data connections via the management connection.

- **debug crypto pki {messages | transactions}:**—Displays the interaction between the router and CA for certificate enrollment and authentication functions.

- **debug crypto engine**—Displays events related to encrypting and decrypting packets, and applies to both Phase 1 and Phase 2 connections.

- **clear crypto isakmp** [*SA_ID_#*]—Deletes all of the specified management SAs.

The show crypto isakmp sa Command

Example 19-1 illustrates the use of the **show crypto isakmp sa** command. I discussed this command in Chapter 16, "Router ISAKMP/IKE Phase 1 Connectivity." Table 16-1 in that chapter explained the states. If you recall, QM_IDLE indicates the successful setup of the connection to the associated peer. If you're seeing MM_NO_STATE or AG_NO_STATE, this indicates that there is a problem with the initial setup of the connection.

Example 19-1 *The* **show crypto isakmp sa** *Command*

```
spoke1# show crypto isakmp sa
dst            src            state       conn-id slot
192.1.1.40     192.1.1.42     QM_IDLE           2    0
```

The two most common problems that might cause a management connection from being set up are:

- You forgot to activate the crypto map or profile on the remote peer router's interface.

- There is no matching ISAKMP/IKE Phase 1 policy on the remote peer.

If you see a state of MM_KEY_EXCH or AG_INIT_EXCH, probably device authentication failed. For pre-shared keys or RSA encrypted nonces, make sure you've configured the pre-shared keys correctly. For certificates, make sure:

- The certificates haven't expired.

- The date and time are correct on the two peers.

- The certificates haven't been revoked.

TIP   You can use the **debug crypto isakmp** command for more detailed troubleshooting of the building of the management connection based on the output of the **show crypto isakmp sa** command.

The debug crypto isakmp Command

In most instances, you'll use the **debug crypto isakmp** command to assist in detailed troubleshooting of building ISAKMP/IKE Phase 1 management connections. Deciphering the output of this command is not simple. The following two sections will take a look at a few examples of L2L and remote access sessions being built.

L2L Sessions

To understand how a session is set up successfully, view the output from the **debug crypto isakmp** command in Example 19-2. In this example, the output is from a simple L2L configuration where the router is accepting a session from a remote peer. I've added steps to the right of some of the output, like "(1)." This is explained after the example.

Example 19-2 *Successfully Building an IPsec L2L Session*

```
ISAKMP (0:0): received packet from 192.1.1.42 dport 500 sport      (1)
      500 Global (N) NEW SA
ISAKMP: Created a peer struct for 192.1.1.42, peer port 500
ISAKMP: Locking peer struct 0x64DB0004, IKE refcount 1 for
      crypto_isakmp_process_block
ISAKMP: local port 500, remote port 500 insert sa successfully
      sa = 651706A4
ISAKMP:(0:0:N/A:0):Input = IKE_MESG_FROM_PEER, IKE_MM_EXCH
ISAKMP:(0:0:N/A:0):Old State = IKE_READY  New State =
      IKE_R_MM1
ISAKMP:(0:0:N/A:0): processing SA payload. message ID = 0
←output omitted→
ISAKMP:(0:0:N/A:0):Looking for a matching key for 192.1.1.42       (2)
      in default
ISAKMP:(0:0:N/A:0): : success
ISAKMP:(0:0:N/A:0):found peer pre-shared key matching
      192.1.1.42
ISAKMP:(0:0:N/A:0): local preshared key found
ISAKMP : Scanning profiles for xauth ...
ISAKMP:(0:0:N/A:0):Checking ISAKMP transform 1 against             (3)
      priority 1 policy
ISAKMP:       encryption AES-CBC
ISAKMP:       keylength of 128
ISAKMP:       hash SHA
ISAKMP:       default group 1
ISAKMP:       auth pre-share
ISAKMP:       life type in seconds
ISAKMP:       life duration (VPI) of  0x0 0x1 0x51 0x80
ISAKMP:(0:0:N/A:0):atts are acceptable. Next payload is 0          (4)
←output omitted→
ISAKMP:(0:1:SW:1): sending packet to 192.1.1.42 my_port 500
      peer_port 500 (R) MM_SA_SETUP
ISAKMP (0:134217729): received packet from 192.1.1.42 dport 500    (5)
      sport 500 Global (R) MM_SA_SETUP
ISAKMP:(0:1:SW:1):Input = IKE_MESG_FROM_PEER, IKE_MM_EXCH
ISAKMP:(0:1:SW:1):Old State = IKE_R_MM2  New State = IKE_R_MM3
```

continues

Example 19-2 *Successfully Building an IPsec L2L Session (Continued)*

```
ISAKMP:(0:1:SW:1): processing KE payload. message ID = 0
ISAKMP:(0:1:SW:1): processing NONCE payload. message ID = 0
ISAKMP:(0:0:N/A:0):Looking for a matching key for 192.1.1.42
    in default
ISAKMP:(0:0:N/A:0): : success
ISAKMP:(0:1:SW:1):found peer pre-shared key matching 192.1.1.42
ISAKMP:(0:1:SW:1):SKEYID state generated                        (6)
ISAKMP:(0:1:SW:1): processing vendor id payload
ISAKMP:(0:1:SW:1): vendor ID is Unity
ISAKMP:(0:1:SW:1): processing vendor id payload
ISAKMP:(0:1:SW:1): vendor ID is DPD
ISAKMP:(0:1:SW:1): processing vendor id payload
ISAKMP:(0:1:SW:1): speaking to another IOS box!
ISAKMP:(0:1:SW:1):Input = IKE_MESG_INTERNAL, IKE_PROCESS_MAIN_MODE
ISAKMP:(0:1:SW:1):Old State = IKE_R_MM3  New State = IKE_R_MM3
ISAKMP:(0:1:SW:1): sending packet to 192.1.1.42 my_port 500 peer_
    port 500 (R) MM_KEY_EXCH
ISAKMP:(0:1:SW:1):Input = IKE_MESG_INTERNAL,
    IKE_PROCESS_COMPLETE
ISAKMP:(0:1:SW:1):Old State = IKE_R_MM3  New State = IKE_R_MM4
ISAKMP (0:134217729): received packet from 192.1.1.42 dport 500   (7)
    sport 500 Global (R) MM_KEY_EXCH
ISAKMP:(0:1:SW:1):Input = IKE_MESG_FROM_PEER, IKE_MM_EXCH
ISAKMP:(0:1:SW:1):Old State = IKE_R_MM4  New State = IKE_R_MM5
ISAKMP:(0:1:SW:1): processing ID payload. message ID = 0
ISAKMP (0:134217729): ID payload
        next-payload : 8
        type         : 1
        address      : 192.1.1.42
        protocol     : 17
        port         : 500
        length       : 12
ISAKMP:(0:1:SW:1):: peer matches *none* of the profiles
ISAKMP:(0:1:SW:1): processing HASH payload. message ID = 0
ISAKMP:received payload type 17
ISAKMP:(0:1:SW:1): processing NOTIFY INITIAL_CONTACT protocol 1
    spi 0, message ID = 0, sa = 651706A4
ISAKMP:(0:1:SW:1):SA authentication status:                      (8)
        authenticated
ISAKMP:(0:1:SW:1): Process initial contact, bring down existing
    phase 1 and 2 SA's with local 192.1.1.40
    remote 192.1.1.42 remote port 500
ISAKMP:(0:1:SW:1):SA authentication status:
        authenticated
ISAKMP:(0:1:SW:1):SA has been authenticated with 192.1.1.42
ISAKMP: Trying to insert a peer 192.1.1.40/192.1.1.42/500/,
    and inserted successfully 64DB0004.
ISAKMP:(0:1:SW:1):IKE_DPD is enabled, initializing timers
ISAKMP:(0:1:SW:1):Input = IKE_MESG_INTERNAL, IKE_PROCESS_MAIN_MODE
ISAKMP:(0:1:SW:1):Old State = IKE_R_MM5  New State = IKE_R_MM5
ISAKMP:(0:1:SW:1):SA is doing pre-shared key authentication
    using id type ID_IPV4_ADDR
```

Example 19-2 *Successfully Building an IPsec L2L Session (Continued)*

```
←output omitted→
ISAKMP:(0:1:SW:1):Input = IKE_MESG_INTERNAL,
    IKE_PROCESS_COMPLETE
ISAKMP:(0:1:SW:1):Old State = IKE_R_MM5  New State =
    IKE_P1_COMPLETE
ISAKMP:(0:1:SW:1):Input = IKE_MESG_INTERNAL, IKE_PHASE1_COMPLETE  (9)
ISAKMP:(0:1:SW:1):Old State = IKE_P1_COMPLETE  New State =
    IKE_P1_COMPLETE
ISAKMP (0:134217729): received packet from 192.1.1.42 dport 500  (10)
    sport 500 Global (R) QM_IDLE
ISAKMP: set new node 482536716 to QM_IDLE
ISAKMP:(0:1:SW:1): processing HASH payload. message ID =
    482536716
ISAKMP:(0:1:SW:1): processing SA payload. message ID = 482536716
ISAKMP:(0:1:SW:1):Checking IPsec proposal 1                       (11)
ISAKMP: transform 1, ESP_AES
ISAKMP:    attributes in transform:
ISAKMP:        encaps is 1 (Tunnel)
ISAKMP:        SA life type in seconds
ISAKMP:        SA life duration (basic) of 3600
ISAKMP:        SA life type in kilobytes
ISAKMP:        SA life duration (VPI) of  0x0 0x46 0x50 0x0
ISAKMP:        authenticator is HMAC-SHA
ISAKMP:        key length is 128
ISAKMP:(0:1:SW:1):atts are acceptable.                            (12)
←output omitted→
ISAKMP:(0:1:SW:1): Creating IPsec SAs                             (13)
        inbound SA from 192.1.1.42 to 192.1.1.40 (f/i)  0/ 0
        (proxy 192.168.3.0 to 192.168.2.0)
        has spi 0x705B8268 and conn_id 0 and flags 2
        lifetime of 3600 seconds
        lifetime of 4608000 kilobytes
        has client flags 0x0
        outbound SA from 192.1.1.40 to 192.1.1.42 (f/i) 0/0
        (proxy 192.168.2.0 to 192.168.3.0)
        has spi 1221163868 and conn_id 0 and flags A
        lifetime of 3600 seconds
        lifetime of 4608000 kilobytes
        has client flags 0x0
ISAKMP:(0:1:SW:1): sending packet to 192.1.1.42 my_port 500
    peer_port 500 (R) QM_IDLE
ISAKMP:(0:1:SW:1):Node 482536716, Input = IKE_MESG_FROM_IPSEC,
    IKE_SPI_REPLY
ISAKMP:(0:1:SW:1):Old State = IKE_QM_SPI_STARVE  New State =
    IKE_QM_R_QM2
ISAKMP: Locking peer struct 0x64DB0004, IPSEC refcount 2 for
    from create_transforms
ISAKMP: Unlocking IPSEC struct 0x64DB0004 from create_
    transforms, count 1
ISAKMP (0:134217729): received packet from 192.1.1.42 dport 500
    sport 500 Global (R) QM_IDLE
```

continues

Example 19-2 *Successfully Building an IPsec L2L Session (Continued)*

```
ISAKMP:(0:1:SW:1):deleting node 482536716 error FALSE reason
    "QM done (await)"
ISAKMP:(0:1:SW:1):Node 482536716, Input = IKE_MESG_FROM_PEER,
    IKE_QM_EXCH
ISAKMP:(0:1:SW:1):Old State = IKE_QM_R_QM2  New State = IKE_QM_  (14)
    PHASE2_COMPLETE
```

Here's a brief description of these steps (the output is very verbose, so I've omitted some of it):

1 Main mode exchange is beginning; no policies have been shared yet and the routers are still in an MM_NO_STATE.

2 The router first verifies that there is a pre-shared key that matches an address of the remote peer (no authentication is done at this point).

3 The comparison of ISAKMP/IKE policies begins here.

4 This message indicates that a matching policy has been found.

5 This is where authentication begins with pre-shared keys; remember that authentication occurs on both routers, and thus you'll see two sets of corresponding authentication processes.

6 The router generates an authentication nonce to send to the remote peer.

7 The router receives the nonce for authentication from the remote peer.

8 The received nonce is validated and the peer is authenticated.

9 Phase 1 is complete.

10 Phase 2 (quick mode) begins.

11 The router looks for a matching data transform for the data connections.

12 A matching data transform is found for the data connections.

13 The SAs for the data connections are built.

14 Phase 2 completes.

Now that you have an understanding of the debug output that you'll see when an L2L IPsec session is established successfully with a peer, I'll look at some examples of output from the **debug crypto isakmp** command where problems exist that prevent the management connection from being established successfully.

If there is a mismatch in the ISAKMP/IKE Phase 1 policies between the peers, your debug output will look like that in Example 19-3. Likewise, in the output of the **show crypto isakmp sa** command, the state will be MM_NO_STATE. I've omitted a lot of the output from the **debug crypto isakmp** command and kept the most important parts.

Example 19-3 *Mismatch ISAKMP/IKE Phase 1 Policies*

```
←output omitted→
ISAKMP:(0:0:N/A:0):Checking ISAKMP transform 1 against priority   (1)
    1 policy
ISAKMP:       encryption AES-CBC
ISAKMP:       keylength of 128
ISAKMP:       hash SHA
ISAKMP:       default group 1
ISAKMP:       auth pre-share
ISAKMP:       life type in seconds
ISAKMP:       life duration (VPI) of  0x0 0x1 0x51 0x80
ISAKMP:(0:0:N/A:0):Hash algorithm offered does not match policy!
ISAKMP:(0:0:N/A:0):atts are not acceptable. Next payload is 0      (2)
ISAKMP:(0:0:N/A:0):Checking ISAKMP transform 1 against priority   (3)
      65535 policy
ISAKMP:       encryption AES-CBC
ISAKMP:       keylength of 128
ISAKMP:       hash SHA
ISAKMP:       default group 1
ISAKMP:       auth pre-share
ISAKMP:       life type in seconds
ISAKMP:       life duration (VPI) of  0x0 0x1 0x51 0x80
ISAKMP:(0:0:N/A:0):Encryption algorithm offered does not
    match policy!
ISAKMP:(0:0:N/A:0):atts are not acceptable. Next payload is 0      (4)
ISAKMP:(0:0:N/A:0):no offers accepted!
ISAKMP:(0:0:N/A:0): phase 1 SA policy not acceptable!
    (local 192.1.1.40 remote 192.1.1.42)
ISAKMP:(0:0:N/A:0):incrementing error counter on sa: construct_
    fail_ag_init
ISAKMP:(0:0:N/A:0): sending packet to 192.1.1.42 my_port 500
    peer_port 500 (R) MM_NO_STATE
ISAKMP:(0:0:N/A:0):peer does not do paranoid keepalives.
ISAKMP:(0:0:N/A:0):deleting SA reason "Phase1 SA policy          (5)
    proposal not accepted" state (R) MM_NO_STATE
    (peer 192.1.1.42)
←output omitted→
```

Here's an explanation of the debug information in Example 19-3:

1 The router is checking the remote peer's policy 1 against the local policy 1.

2 There is no match in the first policy comparison.

3 The router is checking the remote peer's policy 1 against the router's local default policy.

4 Again, there is no match with the peer's policy.

5 The management connection is being terminated because there is no matching policy between the peers (MM_NO_STATE).

If there is a mismatch in a key used for pre-shared key authentication, the output of the **debug crypto isakmp** command will look like that found in Example 19-4.

Example 19-4 *Mismatched Pre-Shared Key Illustration*

```
←output omitted→
ISAKMP:(0:0:N/A:0):atts are acceptable. Next payload is 0          (1)
ISAKMP:(0:1:SW:1): processing vendor id payload
ISAKMP:(0:1:SW:1): vendor ID seems Unity/DPD but major
      245 mismatch
ISAKMP (0:134217729): vendor ID is NAT-T v7
ISAKMP:(0:1:SW:1): processing vendor id payload
ISAKMP:(0:1:SW:1): vendor ID seems Unity/DPD but major
      157 mismatch
ISAKMP:(0:1:SW:1): vendor ID is NAT-T v3
ISAKMP:(0:1:SW:1): processing vendor id payload
ISAKMP:(0:1:SW:1): vendor ID seems Unity/DPD but major
      123 mismatch
ISAKMP:(0:1:SW:1): vendor ID is NAT-T v2
ISAKMP:(0:1:SW:1):Input = IKE_MESG_INTERNAL, IKE_PROCESS_
      MAIN_MODE
ISAKMP:(0:1:SW:1):Old State = IKE_R_MM1  New State = IKE_R_MM1
ISAKMP:(0:1:SW:1): constructed NAT-T vendor-07 ID
ISAKMP:(0:1:SW:1): sending packet to 192.1.1.42 my_port 500
      peer_port 500 (R) MM_SA_SETUP
ISAKMP:(0:1:SW:1):Input = IKE_MESG_INTERNAL, IKE_
      PROCESS_COMPLETE
ISAKMP:(0:1:SW:1):Old State = IKE_R_MM1  New State = IKE_R_MM2
ISAKMP (0:134217729): received packet from 192.1.1.42 dport 500   (2)
      sport 500 Global (R) MM_SA_SETUP
ISAKMP:(0:1:SW:1):Input = IKE_MESG_FROM_PEER, IKE_MM_EXCH
ISAKMP:(0:1:SW:1):Old State = IKE_R_MM2  New State = IKE_R_MM3
ISAKMP:(0:1:SW:1): processing KE payload. message ID = 0
ISAKMP:(0:1:SW:1): processing NONCE payload. message ID = 0
ISAKMP:(0:0:N/A:0):Looking for a matching key for 192.1.1.42 in   (3)
      default
ISAKMP:(0:0:N/A:0): : success
ISAKMP:(0:1:SW:1):found peer pre-shared key matching 192.1.1.42
ISAKMP:(0:1:SW:1):SKEYID state generated                          (4)
←output omitted→
ISAKMP:(0:1:SW:1): sending packet to 192.1.1.42 my_port 500       (5)
      peer_port 500 (R) MM_KEY_EXCH
ISAKMP:(0:1:SW:1):Input = IKE_MESG_INTERNAL, IKE_PROCESS_COMPLETE
ISAKMP:(0:1:SW:1):Old State = IKE_R_MM3  New State = IKE_R_MM4
ISAKMP (0:134217729): received packet from 192.1.1.42 dport 500
      sport 500 Global (R) MM_KEY_EXCH
ISAKMP: reserved not zero on ID payload!                          (6)
%CRYPTO-4-IKMP_BAD_MESSAGE: IKE message from 192.1.1.42
      failed its sanity check or is malformed
ISAKMP:(0:1:SW:1):incrementing error counter on sa: PAYLOAD_
      MALFORMED
←output omitted→
```

Here's an explanation of the abbreviated output:

1 A matching Phase 1 policy is found.

2 Pre-shared key authentication begins by receiving the nonce (created with the pre-shared key) from the remote peer.

3 A matching **crypto isakmp key** command is found for the remote peer (the IP address of the peer).

4 The router generates a nonce to validate the authentication.

5 This router sends its nonce information to the remote peer.

6 Verification of the nonce fails and the keying is retried multiple times.

7 The retry threshold is reached and the peers give up building the management connection.

When you look at the output of the **show crypto isakmp sa** command, the state will be MM_KEY_EXCH. The key message to look for in the output is the highlighted one in the debug output from Example 19-4, which typically indicates an authentication failure.

TIP   One of the problems I've seen with the output of Cisco **debug** commands is that the nomenclature and verbiage has a tendency of changing from one IOS release to another (my debug output was from a 3640 router running IOS 12.3(14)T). Therefore, you have to scrutinize the output carefully to determine the exact problem. In certain cases, you might want to look at the debug output from a connection that works from the same IOS revision that you're using and compare that to a connection that fails. You can use the successful connection output as a baseline when comparing this debug output to the debug output from a failed connection attempt to pinpoint the problem.

Remote Access Sessions

The router debug output from setting up a remote access session can be very verbose—about 20 pages in length! Remember that remote access sessions, using Easy VPN, go through more steps in setting up a session than an L2L session. Example 19-5 shows the output of the **debug crypto isakmp** command, where I've omitted much of the output to keep it brief.

Example 19-5 *Successfully Building an IPsec Remote Access Session to an Easy VPN Server*

```
ISAKMP (0:0): received packet from 192.168.1.100 dport 500
    sport 500 Global (N) NEW SA
←output omitted→
ISAKMP (0:0): ID payload                                    (1)
        next-payload : 13
        type         : 11
```

continues

Example 19-5 *Successfully Building an IPsec Remote Access Session to an Easy VPN Server (Continued)*

```
              group id    : admin
              protocol    : 17
              port        : 500
              length      : 13
←output omitted→
ISAKMP:(0:0:N/A:0): Authentication by
      xauth preshared
ISAKMP:(0:0:N/A:0):Checking ISAKMP                                   (2)
      transform 1 against priority 10 policy
ISAKMP:      encryption AES-CBC
ISAKMP:      hash SHA
ISAKMP:      default group 2
ISAKMP:      auth XAUTHInitPreShared
ISAKMP:      life type in seconds
ISAKMP:      life duration (VPI) of  0x0 0x20 0xC4 0x9B
ISAKMP:      keylength of 256
ISAKMP:(0:0:N/A:0):Hash algorithm offered does not match policy!
ISAKMP:(0:0:N/A:0):atts are not acceptable. Next payload is 3
←output omitted→
ISAKMP:(0:0:N/A:0):Checking ISAKMP transform 6 against priority
      10 policy
ISAKMP:      encryption AES-CBC
ISAKMP:      hash MD5
ISAKMP:      default group 2
ISAKMP:      auth XAUTHInitPreShared
ISAKMP:      life type in seconds
ISAKMP:      life duration (VPI) of  0x0 0x20 0xC4 0x9B
ISAKMP:      keylength of 128
ISAKMP:(0:0:N/A:0):atts are acceptable.                              (3)
ISAKMP:(0:2:SW:1): processing KE payload. message ID = 0
ISAKMP:(0:2:SW:1): processing NONCE payload. message ID = 0
←output omitted→
ISAKMP:(0:2:SW:1):SKEYID state generated
ISAKMP:(0:2:SW:1):SA is doing pre-shared key authentication         (4)
      plus XAUTH using id type ID_IPV4_ADDR
ISAKMP (0:134217730): ID payload next-payload : 10
        type         : 1
        address      : 192.1.1.40
        protocol     : 17
←output omitted→
ISAKMP (0:134217730): received packet from 192.168.1.100
      dport 500 sport 500 Global (R) AG_INIT_EXCH
ISAKMP:(0:2:SW:1): processing HASH payload. message ID = 0
ISAKMP:(0:2:SW:1): processing NOTIFY INITIAL_CONTACT protocol 1
        spi 0, message ID = 0, sa = 652680F0
ISAKMP:(0:2:SW:1):SA authentication status:                         (5)
        authenticated
←output omitted→
ISAKMP:(0:2:SW:1):SA has been authenticated with 192.168.1.100
←output omitted→
ISAKMP:(0:2:SW:1):IKE_DPD is enabled, initializing timers           (6)
←output omitted→
```

Example 19-5 *Successfully Building an IPsec Remote Access Session to an Easy VPN Server (Continued)*

```
ISAKMP:(0:2:SW:1):Need XAUTH                                         (7)
ISAKMP: set new node -753458994 to CONF_XAUTH
ISAKMP/xauth: request attribute XAUTH_USER_NAME_V2
ISAKMP/xauth: request attribute XAUTH_USER_PASSWORD_V2
ISAKMP:(0:2:SW:1): initiating peer config to 192.168.1.100.
    ID= -753458994
ISAKMP:(0:2:SW:1): sending packet to 192.168.1.100 my_port 500
    peer_port 500 (R) CONF_XAUTH
←output omitted→
ISAKMP (0:134217730): received packet from 192.168.1.100            (8)
    dport 500 sport 500 Global (R) CONF_XAUTH
ISAKMP:(0:2:SW:1):processing transaction payload from
    192.168.1.100. message ID = -753458994
ISAKMP: Config payload REPLY
ISAKMP/xauth: reply attribute XAUTH_USER_NAME_V2
ISAKMP/xauth: reply attribute XAUTH_USER_PASSWORD_V2
ISAKMP:(0:2:SW:1):deleting node -753458994 error FALSE reason
    "Done with xauth request/reply exchange"
←output omitted→
ISAKMP: Config payload ACK
ISAKMP:(0:2:SW:1):       (blank) XAUTH ACK Processed                (9)
ISAKMP:(0:2:SW:1):deleting node 147119650 error FALSE reason
    "Transaction mode done"
ISAKMP:(0:2:SW:1):Input = IKE_MESG_FROM_PEER, IKE_CFG_ACK
ISAKMP:(0:2:SW:1):Old State = IKE_XAUTH_SET_SENT  New State =
    IKE_P1_COMPLETE
←output omitted→
*Mar  1 05:06:03.199: ISAKMP (0:134217730): received packet        (10)
    from 192.168.1.100 dport 500 sport 500 Global (R) QM_IDLE
*Mar  1 05:06:03.203: ISAKMP: set new node -1691114311 to QM_IDLE
*Mar  1 05:06:03.203: ISAKMP:(0:2:SW:1):processing transaction
    payload from 192.168.1.100. message ID = -1691114311
*Mar  1 05:06:03.203: ISAKMP: Config payload REQUEST
←output omitted→
ISAKMP/author: Author request for group admin successfully
    sent to AAA
←output omitted→
ISAKMP:(0:2:SW:1):allocating address 192.168.0.222                 (11)
ISAKMP: Sending private address: 192.168.0.222
ISAKMP: Sending subnet mask: 255.255.255.0
ISAKMP: Sending IP4_DNS server address: 192.168.0.10
ISAKMP: Sending IP4_NBNS server address: 192.168.0.12
ISAKMP: Sending ADDRESS_EXPIRY seconds left to use the address:
    86395
ISAKMP (0/134217730): Unknown Attr: UNKNOWN (0x7000)
ISAKMP: Sending save password reply value 0
Sending DEFAULT_DOMAIN default domain name: cisco.com
ISAKMP: Sending split include name splitremote network
    192.168.0.0 mask 255.255.255.0 protocol 0, src port 0,
    dst port 0
ISAKMP: Sending SPLIT_DNS domain name: cisco.com
```

continues

Example 19-5 *Successfully Building an IPsec Remote Access Session to an Easy VPN Server (Continued)*

```
←output omitted→
ISAKMP:(0:2:SW:1):Input = IKE_MESG_INTERNAL, IKE_PHASE1_COMPLETE (12)
ISAKMP:(0:2:SW:1):Old State = IKE_P1_COMPLETE  New State = IKE_
    P1_COMPLETE
ISAKMP (0:134217730): received packet                            (13)
    from 192.168.1.100 dport 500 sport 500 Global (R) QM_IDLE
←output omitted→
ISAKMP:(0:2:SW:1): processing SA payload.
ISAKMP:(0:2:SW:1):Checking IPsec proposal 1
ISAKMP: transform 1, ESP_AES
ISAKMP:   attributes in transform:
ISAKMP:      authenticator is HMAC-MD5
ISAKMP:      key length is 256
ISAKMP:      encaps is 1 (Tunnel)
ISAKMP:      SA life type in seconds
ISAKMP:      SA life duration (VPI) of  0x0 0x20 0xC4 0x9B
ISAKMP:(0:2:SW:1):atts are acceptable.                          (14)
←output omitted→
ISAKMP:(0:2:SW:1): Creating IPsec SAs                           (15)
        inbound SA from 192.168.1.100 to 192.1.1.40 (f/i) 0/ 0
        (proxy 192.168.0.222 to 0.0.0.0)
        has spi 0x213909D3 and conn_id 0 and flags 2
        lifetime of 2147483 seconds
        has client flags 0x0
        outbound SA from 192.1.1.40 to 192.168.1.100 (f/i) 0/0
        (proxy 0.0.0.0 to 192.168.0.222)
        has spi 2072708995 and conn_id 0 and flags A
        lifetime of 2147483 seconds
        has client flags 0x0
←output omitted→
*Mar  1 05:06:03.367: ISAKMP:(0:2:SW:1):Old State = IKE_QM_R_   (16)
    QM2  New State = IKE_QM_ PHASE2_COMPLETE
←output omitted→
```

Here's an explanation of the debug output from Example 19-5:

1 The Easy VPN Remote (client) establishes a connection to an Easy VPN Server (the router) and specifies that it wants to access the "admin" group.

2 The first policy for Phase 1 didn't match the Remote's list of policies.

3 After a few comparisons of Phase 1 policies, a match was found.

4 Group authentication begins for the "admin" group using pre-shared keys.

5 The group authentication is successful.

6 DPD is enabled.

7 XAUTH has been enabled on the Easy VPN Server and the Server prompts the user for a username and password.

8 The Server receives the username and password from the Remote.

9   User authentication is successful; if it wasn't successful, you would see a debug line with *retransmitting Phase 2 CONF_XAUTH* in it, where the Server is retransmitting the XAUTH username and password query.

10 The Remote initiates IKE Mode Config.

11 The Remote is assigned his policies, of which one is his IP address: 192.168.0.222. If the user can't be assigned an IP address, you'll see the following debug message: *deleting SA reason "Failed to allocate ip address."*

12 This completes ISAKMP/IKE Phase 1.

13 In Phase 2, a matching data transform is searched.

14 A matching data transform is found.

15 The two IPsec SAs (inbound and outbound) are created for the data connections.

16 Phase 2 has completed.

The debug crypto pki Command

The **debug crypto pki** command is used to troubleshoot the interaction between a CA and a router. You must specify one of two parameters: **messages** or **transactions**. The **messages** parameter basically prints a dump of the message contents sent between the router and CA and is of use only to Cisco personnel. The **transactions** parameter, however, is useful, because it displays the events that occur. Example 19-6 illustrates the use of this command. In this example, an administrator is requesting the root certificate (the **crypto ca authenticate** command) and then the identity certificate (the **crypto ca enroll** command) for his router. As you can see from the URI, the CA server is a Microsoft product. I've used this command to troubleshoot date/time issues when validating a certificate the router receives from the CA.

Example 19-6 *Troubleshooting the Certificate Enrollment Process*

```
RTRA(config)# crypto ca authenticate caserver
Certificate has the following attributes:
Fingerprint:A5DE3C51 AD8B0207 B60BED6D 9356FB00
00:44:00:CRYPTO_PKI:Sending CA Certificate Request:
GET /certsrv/mscep/mscep.dll/pkiclient.exe?operation=GetCACert&
    message=caserver HTTP/1.0
00:44:00:CRYPTO_PKI:http connection opened
00:44:01:CRYPTO_PKI:HTTP response header:
  HTTP/1.1 200 OK
  Server:Microsoft-IIS/5.0
  Date:Fri, 17 Apr 2005 19:50:59 GMT
  Content-Length:2693
  Content-Type:application/x-x509-ca-ra-cert
  Content-Type indicates we have received CA and RA certificates.
00:42:01:CRYPTO_PKI:WARNING:A certificate chain could not be
    constructed while selecting certificate status
```

continues

Example 19-6 *Troubleshooting the Certificate Enrollment Process (Continued)*

```
00:42:01:CRYPTO_PKI:WARNING:A certificate chain could not be
      constructed while selecting certificate status
00:42:01:CRYPTO_PKI:Name:CN = caserverRA, O = Cisco System, C = US
00:42:01:CRYPTO_PKI:Name:CN = caserverRA, O = Cisco System, C = US
00:42:01:CRYPTO_PKI:transaction GetCACert completed
00:42:01:CRYPTO_PKI:CA certificate received.
% Do you accept this certificate? [yes/no]:yes
Router(config)# crypto ca enroll caserver
% Start certificate enrollment ..
% Create a challenge password. You will need to verbally provide this
    password to the CA Administrator in order to revoke your certificate.
    For security reasons your password will not be saved in the configuration.
    Please make a note of it.
Password:
Re-enter password:
% The subject name in the certificate will be:Router.cisco.com
% Include the router serial number in the subject name? [yes/no]: no
% Include an IP address in the subject name? [yes/no]:no
Request certificate from CA? [yes/no]:yes
% Certificate request sent to Certificate Authority
% The certificate request fingerprint will be displayed.
% The 'show crypto ca certificate' command will also show the fingerprint.
  Fingerprint: 2CFC6265 77BA6496 3AEFCB50 29BC2BF2
00:43:39:CRYPTO_PKI:transaction PKCSReq completed
00:43:39:CRYPTO_PKI:status:
00:43:39:CRYPTO_PKI:http connection opened
00:43:39:CRYPTO_PKI: received msg of 1924 bytes
00:43:39:CRYPTO_PKI:HTTP response header:
  HTTP/1.1 200 OK
  Server:Microsoft-IIS/5.0
  Date:Fri, Apr Nov 2005 19:51:28 GMT
  Content-Length:1778
  Content-Type:application/x-pki-message
00:45:29:CRYPTO_PKI:signed attr:pki-message-type:
00:45:29:13 01 33
00:45:29:CRYPTO_PKI:signed attr:pki-status:
00:45:29:13 01 30
00:45:29:CRYPTO_PKI:signed attr:pki-recipient-nonce:
00:45:29:04 10 B4 C8 2A 12 9C 8A 2A 4A E1 E5 15 DE 22 C2 B4 FD
00:45:29:CRYPTO_PKI:signed attr:pki-transaction-id:
00:45:29:13 20 34 45 45 41 44 42 36 33 38 43 33 42 42 45 44 45 39 46
00:45:29:34 38 44 33 45 36 39 33 45 33 43 37 45 39
00:45:29:CRYPTO_PKI:status = 100:certificate is granted
00:45:29:CRYPTO__PKI:All enrollment requests completed.
00:45:29:%CRYPTO-6-CERTRET:Certificate received from
      Certificate Authority
```

The debug crypto engine Command

The **debug crypto engine** command displays messages about performing encryption processes on the router—not just information about encrypting data packets, but all encryption processes. Actually, this command is applicable to both Phase 1 and 2 connections. Example 19-7 illustrates the use of this command.

Example 19-7 *Using the* **debug crypto engine** *Command*

```
*Mar  1 04:03:17.338: %CRYPTO-6-ISAKMP_ON_OFF: ISAKMP is ON
*Mar  1 04:03:17.454: CryptoEngine0: generate alg parameter
*Mar  1 04:03:17.554: CRYPTO_ENGINE: Dh phase 1 status: 0          (1)
*Mar  1 04:03:17.682: CryptoEngine0: generate alg parameter
*Mar  1 04:03:17.810: CryptoEngine0: create ISAKMP SKEYID          (2)
       for conn id 14
*Mar  1 04:03:17.818: CryptoEngine0: generate hmac context
       for conn id 14
*Mar  1 04:03:17.838: CryptoEngine0: generate hmac context
       for conn id 14
*Mar  1 04:03:17.842: CryptoEngine0: clear dh number for           (3)
       conn id 1
*Mar  1 04:03:17.850: CryptoEngine0: generate hmac context
       for conn id 14
*Mar  1 04:03:17.878: CryptoEngine0: generate hmac context
       for conn id 14
*Mar  1 04:03:17.878: CryptoEngine0: validate proposal             (4)
*Mar  1 04:03:17.878: CryptoEngine0: validate proposal request
*Mar  1 04:03:17.882: CryptoEngine0: generate hmac context
       for conn id 14
*Mar  1 04:03:17.882: CryptoEngine0: ipsec allocate flow           (5)
```

Here is an explanation of the important messages in the debug output from Example 19-7 output:

1 Diffie-Hellman (DH) is successful based on this and the next message.

2 Device authentication begins and the pre-shared key is encrypted using nonces.

3 DH is no longer necessary and the temporary DH connection is removed.

4 A matching transform is searched for the ISAKMP/IKE Phase 2 data connections.

5 The two data connections are successfully built.

Here are some items to look for if you can't complete a session attempt to a remote IPsec peer:

- If there is a mismatch in the ISAKMP/IKE Phase 1 policy, you'll see no output from this command.

- If there is a problem with device authentication, the output will stop at the first line that states *CryptoEngine0: generate hmac context for conn id*.

- If the two peers can't find a matching data transform for the Phase 2 connection, you won't see the messages that have *ipsec allocate flow* in them; instead, you'll see a message like this: *%CRYPTO-6-IKMP_MODE_FAILURE: Processing of Quick mode failed with peer at 192.1.1.40*.

TIP	Actually, reading the output of this command is easier than the **debug crypto isakmp** command; many times I'll start with this command first when troubleshooting Phase 1 or 2 connections instead of other **debug** commands.

ISAKMP/IKE Phase 2 Connections

In this section I'll discuss some router commands you can use to troubleshoot ISAKMP/IKE Phase 2 connections. I'll begin by describing briefly the commands you can use and then, in later sections, discuss some of these commands in more depth.

Overview of the Phase 2 Commands

If you're experiencing problems with establishing IPsec data connections with an IPsec peer, there are several commands you can use to help pinpoint the problem. Here's a brief summary of these commands:

- **show crypto engine connections active**—Displays each data SA that was built and the amount of traffic traversing each.

- **show crypto ipsec sa**—Displays the data SAs established between two IPsec peers, and the components used to protect the connections and statistical information.

- **debug crypto isakmp**—Displays the steps taken to build a management connection and data connections via the management connection (see "The **debug crypto isakmp** Command" section previously in the chapter).

- **debug crypto engine**—Displays events related to encrypting and decrypting packets and applies to both Phase 1 and Phase 2 (see "The **debug crypto engine** Command" section previously in the chapter).

- **debug crypto ipsec**—Displays the actual creation of the two unidirectional data SAs between two peers.

- **clear crypto sa [counters | map** *map_name* **| peer** *IP_address|* **spi** *IP_address* {**ah | esp**} *SPI_#]*—Clears the statistics (**counters**), all data SAs associated with a crypto map (**map**), all data SAs associated with a peer (**peer**), or a particular data SA to a particular peer.

The following sections will discuss some of these commands in more depth.

The show crypto engine connection active Command

The **show crypto engine connection active** command displays the active SAs (management and data connections) terminated on the router, and the number of data packets encrypted and decrypted for each SA. Example 19-8 illustrates the use of this command.

Example 19-8 *Using the* **show crypto engine connection active** *Command*

```
r3640a# show crypto engine connection active
  ID Interface    IP-Address   State Algorithm          Encrypt  Decrypt
   1 Ethernet0/0  192.1.1.40   set   HMAC_SHA+AES_CBC       0        0
2001 Ethernet0/0  192.1.1.40   set   AES+SHA                0        5
2002 Ethernet0/0  192.1.1.40   set   AES+SHA                5        0
```

The first entry (ID #1) is the management connection and the following two entries (ID #2001 and #2002) are the two data connections. A state of "set" indicates that the connections have been fully established.

The show crypto ipsec sa Command

The **show crypto ipsec sa** command displays the crypto map entry information used to build data connections and any existing data connections to remote peers. Example 19-9 illustrates the use of this command. At the top of the display, you can see that the crypto map called "mymap" has been activated on ethernet0/0. The *local ident* and *remote ident* entries display the traffic that is to be protected (traffic between 192.168.2.0/24 and 192.168.3.0/24). The *#pkts encaps* and *#pkts decaps* displays the number of packets encapsulated or de-encapsulated using IPsec (AH or ESP); likewise, you can see the number of packets encrypted and decrypted, and the number of packets where a hash function was created or verified. Given that there are nonzero numbers in these fields, a connection is currently established to the remote peer (192.1.1.42).

Example 19-9 *Using the* **show crypto ipsec sa** *Command*

```
r3640a# show crypto ipsec sa
interface: Ethernet0/0
    Crypto map tag: mymap, local addr 192.1.1.40
    protected vrf: (none)
    local  ident (addr/mask/prot/port): (192.168.2.0/255.255.255.0/0/0)
    remote ident (addr/mask/prot/port): (192.168.3.0/255.255.255.0/0/0)
    current_peer 192.1.1.42 port 500
      PERMIT, flags={origin_is_acl,}
     #pkts encaps: 5, #pkts encrypt: 5, #pkts digest: 5
     #pkts decaps: 5, #pkts decrypt: 5, #pkts verify: 5
     #pkts compressed: 0, #pkts decompressed: 0
     #pkts not compressed: 0, #pkts compr. failed: 0
     #pkts not decompressed: 0, #pkts decompress failed: 0
     #send errors 0, #recv errors 0
      local crypto endpt.: 192.1.1.40, remote crypto endpt.: 192.1.1.42
      path mtu 1500, ip mtu 1500
      current outbound spi: 0x79B5B3BD(2041951165)

      inbound esp sas:
       spi: 0x4D1107A7(1292961703)
         transform: esp-aes esp-sha-hmac ,
         in use settings ={Tunnel, }
         conn id: 2001, flow_id: SW:1, crypto map: mymap
         sa timing: remaining key lifetime (k/sec): (4456557/2479)
         IV size: 16 bytes
```

continues

Example 19-9 *Using the* **show crypto ipsec sa** *Command (Continued)*

```
         replay detection support: Y
         Status: ACTIVE
    inbound ah sas:
    inbound pcp sas:
    outbound esp sas:
      spi: 0x79B5B3BD(2041951165)
        transform: esp-aes esp-sha-hmac ,
        in use settings ={Tunnel, }
        conn id: 2002, flow_id: SW:2, crypto map: mymap
        sa timing: remaining key lifetime (k/sec): (4456557/2472)
        IV size: 16 bytes
        replay detection support: Y
        Status: ACTIVE
    outbound ah sas:
    outbound pcp sas:
```

The SAs are displayed in separate sections. In this example, only ESP is used, so you can see the SPI values, transforms, and other connection particulars in the *inbound esp sas* and *outbound esp sas* sections of the output. If you don't see anything under these sections, then no data connections have been established. Common problems that might cause this situation are:

- Mismatch in transforms

- Mismatch in crypto ACLs

- Mismatch in addresses the two peers will use for IPsec communications

Further troubleshooting can be done with the **debug crypto ipsec** command.

The debug crypto ipsec Command

If you're experiencing problems establishing the two IPsec data connections between peers, the most common IOS command to troubleshoot the problem is **debug crypto ipsec**. Example 19-10 illustrates the use of this command where the two data connections between two peers are established successfully. In this example, the router is accepting an L2L connection request from a remote peer. The referenced numbers to the right are explained below the example.

Example 19-10 *Successfully Established IPsec Data SAs*

```
IPSEC(key_engine): got a queue event with 1 kei messages
IPSEC(validate_proposal_request): proposal part #1,                    (1)
  (key eng. msg.) INBOUND local= 192.1.1.40, remote= 192.1.1.42,
    local_proxy= 192.168.2.0/255.255.255.0/0/0 (type=4),
    remote_proxy= 192.168.3.0/255.255.255.0/0/0 (type=4),
    protocol= ESP, transform= esp-aes esp-sha-hmac  (Tunnel),
    lifedur= 0s and 0kb,
    spi= 0x0(0), conn_id= 0, keysize= 128, flags= 0x2
  Crypto mapdb : proxy_match                                           (2)
        src addr     : 192.168.2.0
        dst addr     : 192.168.3.0
        protocol     : 0
```

Example 19-10 *Successfully Established IPsec Data SAs (Continued)*

```
                 src port     : 0
                 dst port     : 0
IPSEC(key_engine): got a queue event with 1 kei messages
IPSEC(spi_response): getting spi 3754627978 for SA             (3)
        from 192.1.1.40 to 192.1.1.42 for prot 3
IPSEC(key_engine): got a queue event with 2 kei messages
IPSEC(initialize_sas): ,
  (key eng. msg.) INBOUND local= 192.1.1.40, remote= 192.1.1.42,
    local_proxy= 192.168.2.0/255.255.255.0/0/0 (type=4),
    remote_proxy= 192.168.3.0/255.255.255.0/0/0 (type=4),
    protocol= ESP, transform= esp-aes esp-sha-hmac  (Tunnel),
    lifedur= 3600s and 4608000kb,
    spi= 0xDFCB138A(3754627978), conn_id= 0, keysize= 128,
    flags= 0x2
IPSEC(initialize_sas): ,                                        (4)
  (key eng. msg.) OUTBOUND local= 192.1.1.40, remote= 192.1.1.42,
    local_proxy= 192.168.2.0/255.255.255.0/0/0 (type=4),
    remote_proxy= 192.168.3.0/255.255.255.0/0/0 (type=4),
    protocol= ESP, transform= esp-aes esp-sha-hmac  (Tunnel),
    lifedur= 3600s and 4608000kb,
    spi= 0x3DC7A592(1036494226), conn_id= 0, keysize= 128,
    flags= 0xA
  Crypto mapdb : proxy_match
        src addr     : 192.168.2.0
        dst addr     : 192.168.3.0
        protocol     : 0
        src port     : 0
        dst port     : 0
IPSEC(crypto_ipsec_sa_find_ident_head): reconnecting with the
        same proxies and 192.1.1.42
IPSEC: Flow_switching Allocated flow for sibling 80000003
IPSEC(policy_db_add_ident): src 192.168.2.0, dest 192.168.3.0,
        dest_port 0
IPSEC(create_sa): sa created,                                   (5)
  (sa) sa_dest= 192.1.1.40, sa_proto= 50,
    sa_spi= 0xDFCB138A(3754627978),
    sa_trans= esp-aes esp-sha-hmac , sa_conn_id= 2002
IPSEC(create_sa): sa created,                                   (6)
  (sa) sa_dest= 192.1.1.42, sa_proto= 50,
    sa_spi= 0x3DC7A592(1036494226),
    sa_trans= esp-aes esp-sha-hmac , sa_conn_id= 2001
IPSEC(key_engine): got a queue event with 1 kei messages
IPSEC(key_engine_enable_outbound): rec'd enable notify         (7)
    from ISAKMP
IPSEC(key_engine_enable_outbound): enable SA with spi 1036494226/50
```

Here's a brief explanation of the output from Example 19-10:

1 A transform was sent from the remote peer to the local router to protect the data SA in the inbound direction. If you look back to Example 19-5, reference 13 in the output from the **debug crypto isakmp** command, you can see the negotiation of the transforms being done for the data connection. At this point, the data SA is being built.

> **2** The traffic to be proxied is verified (the mirrored crypto ACL): traffic between 192.168.2.0 and 192.168.3.0.
>
> **3** An SPI is assigned to the inbound data SA and it is initialized.
>
> **4** The outbound data SA is being initialized to the remote peer.
>
> **5** The inbound data SA is created.
>
> **6** The outbound data SA is created.
>
> **7** The remote peer is ready to send data on the local router's outbound data SA.

Mismatched Data Transforms

As you can see from the output in Example 19-10, the debug output is fairly straightforward to interpret. Of course, not all data SAs are built successfully. For example, if you don't have a matching transform for the data connections, you'll see the output in Example 19-11 from the **debug crypto isakmp** and the **debug crypto ipsec** commands. The first message is from the latter **debug** command and the last two messages are from the former command. Use the **show crypto ipsec transform-set** command on the two Cisco IOS routers to determine what transforms have already been created.

Example 19-11 *Mismatched IPsec data transforms*

```
IPsec (validate_proposal): transform proposal
   (port 3, trans 2, hmac_alg 2) not supported
ISAKMP (0:2) : atts not acceptable. Next payload is 0
ISAKMP (0:2) SA not acceptable
```

Mismatched Crypto ACLs

If the crypto ACLs are not mirrored on the two peers, you'll see debug output from the **debug crypto ipsec** and **debug crypto isakmp** commands shown in Example 19-12. The *proxy identities not supported* message indicates that the crypto ACLs (if routers, PIXs, or ASAs) or network lists (if concentrators) do not match (are not mirrored) on the two IPsec peers.

Example 19-12 *Mismatched Crypto ACLs: Not Mirrored*

```
IPsec(validate_transform_proposal): proxy identities not supported
ISAKMP: IPsec policy invalidated proposal
ISAKMP (0:2): SA not acceptable!
```

Another set of messages you might see appear in Example 19-13. In this example, one side has host-specific ACL entries (192.168.1.1/32 and 192.168.2.1/32) and the other side has network-specific ACL entries (192.168.1.0/24 and 192.168.2.0/24). This misconfiguration is commonly called an *invalid proxy ID*. Based on the IOS version, you also might see *%CRYPTO-4-RECVD_PKT_INV_IDENTITY* for an error message when there is a non-mirrored ACL condition.

Example 19-13 *Mismatched Crypto ACLs: Network Versus Host Match*

```
IPSEC(validate_proposal_request): proposal part #1, (key eng. msg.)
    dest= 193.1.1.1, src= 192.1.1.1,
    dest_proxy= 192.168.1.1/255.255.255.255/0/0 (type=4),
    src_proxy= 192.168.2.1/255.255.255.255/0/0 (type=4)
```

Incorrect Peer Address

A less common problem I've seen is where the IP address of the peer has been misconfigured on one of the two ends. For example, if a router has two interfaces it can use to reach a remote peer, and has a crypto map applied to both, whichever interface the router uses to connect to the remote peer is the IP address it would use as its local address. However, if the remote peer doesn't define both IP addresses, but only for one of the interfaces, an error will occur, as shown in Example 19-14, when the local peer uses the unconfigured IP address (on the remote peer).

Example 19-14 *Invalid Peer Address*

```
IPSEC(validate_proposal): invalid local address 192.1.1.2
ISAKMP (0:3): atts not acceptable. Next payload is 0
ISAKMP (0:3): SA not acceptable!
```

To solve this problem, on the router with multiple interfaces, use the **crypto map** *static_map_name* **local-address** *local_interface_name* command to specify which interface address should be used as the local address; most commonly this is a loopback interface. Another reason that the error in Example 19-14 might occur is if you've applied a crypto map to the wrong interface or forgotten to enable the crypto map at all. Therefore, be sure you have applied the crypto map to the correct interface on your router.

Matching on the Incorrect Crypto Map Entry

Another uncommon problem you might experience is if there are overlapping crypto ACLs on a router, where a match is found for a peer for the *wrong* crypto ACL. This can be very difficult to pinpoint. For example, a router might have two crypto ACLs with overlapping entries like that found in Example 19-15. In this example, crypto ACLs 101 and 102 overlap.

Example 19-15 *Overlapping Crypto ACL Entries Example*

```
RTRA(config)# access-list 101 permit ip 192.168.1.0 0.0.0.255
                    192.168.2.0 0.0.0.255
RTRA(config)# access-list 102 permit ip host 192.168.1.1
                    host 192.168.2.1
RTRA(config)# crypto map mymap 10 ipsec-isakmp
RTRA(config-crypto-m)# match address 101
RTRA(config-crypto-m)# set peer 192.1.1.1
RTRA(config-crypto-m)# set transform-set trans1
```

continues

Example 19-15 *Overlapping Crypto ACL Entries Example (Continued)*

```
RTRA(config-crypto-m)# exit
RTRA(config)# crypto map mymap 20 ipsec-isakmp
RTRA(config-crypto-m)# match address 102
RTRA(config-crypto-m)# set peer 192.1.1.2
RTRA(config-crypto-m)# set transform-set trans1
RTRA(config-crypto-m)# exit
```

If RTRA has an IPsec tunnel to 192.1.1.2, but not to 192.1.1.1, and 192.1.1.2 forwards a packet from 192.168.2.1 to 192.168.1.1, it will match the crypto ACL in the first entry, thus causing the error shown in Example 19-16. To solve this problem, put the crypto map entry with the more specific crypto ACL entry or entries before the less specific one; in other words, give the 192.1.1.2 peer a lower crypto map entry number than peer 192.1.1.1.

Example 19-16 *Overlapping Crypto ACL Error*

```
IPSEC(validate_proposal_request): proposal part #1,
   (key eng. msg.) dest= 200.1.1.1, src= 192.1.1.2,
     dest_proxy= 192.168.1.1/255.255.255.255/0/0 (type=1),
     src_proxy= 192.168.2.1/255.255.255.255/0/0 (type=1),
     protocol= ESP, transform= esp-3des esp-md5-hmac ,
     lifedur= 0s and 0kb,
     spi= 0x0(0), conn_id= 0, keysize= 0, flags= 0x4
IPSEC(validate_transform_proposal): peer address 192.1.1.1 not found
```

New IPsec Troubleshooting Features

There are two new IPsec troubleshooting features you can use in the IOS:

- IPsec VPN Monitoring: IOS 12.3(4)T
- Invalid Security Parameter Index Recovery: IOS 12.3(2)T

The following three sections will discuss both of these features.

IPsec VPN Monitoring Feature

IPsec VPN monitoring is a feature new in IOS 12.3(4)T. This feature allows you to monitor VPN sessions to provide for enhanced troubleshooting. These enhancements include:

- Adding a description to IKE peers so that it becomes easier to identify the peer other than using their IP address or FQDN.
- Clearing a crypto session: before IOS 12.3(4)T, you had to clear both the Phase 1 and 2 connections to a peer individually to tear down the crypto session; in IOS 12.3(4)T, you can tear down both sets of connections with a single command.

The following two sections will discuss these enhancements.

Configuring IKE Peer Descriptions

To configure IKE peer descriptions, use the following configuration:

```
Router(config)# crypto isakmp peer {address peer_IP_address |
                       hostname peer_hostname}
Router(config-isakmp-peer)# description description
```

You first must specify the identity of the peer (based on the configuration of the **crypto isakmp identity** command), which takes you into a subcommand mode. The **description** command allows you to assign a 80-character description, including spaces, for the remote peer. This description will then appear in the output of various **show** commands.

NOTE   If multiple remote peers sit behind the same PAT device, you cannot use address as an identity type for a description, since they'll all have the same IP address.

Seeing Peer Descriptions in **show** Commands

There are two **show** commands that take advantage of the use of descriptions:

- **show crypto isakmp peer** [*IP_address_of_peer*]—Briefly displays the IPsec peer connections and descriptions. Example 19-17 illustrates the use of this command, where the local peer (192.1.1.40) is connected to the remote peer 192.1.1.42. A description of "Connection to SiteA" was assigned to this peer.

- **show crypto session** [**local** *local_IP_address*] [**remote** *remote_IP_address*] [**detail**]— Displays status information for active crypto map sessions. Example 19-18 illustrates the use of this command without the **detail** parameter and 19-19 with it. In Example 19-18, you can see the peer the router is connected to (192.1.1.42) and that the management and two data connections were built. Table 19-1 explains the statuses that can appear in the output of this command. If no flow exists, this could be because a dynamic crypto map is being used. Example 19-19, with the detail parameter, shows more information, including the description and the number of packets encrypted and decrypted.

Example 19-17 *Using the* **show crypto isakmp peer** *Command*

```
RTRA# show crypto isakmp peer
Peer: 192.1.1.42 Port: 500 Local: 192.1.1.40
 Description: Connection to SiteA
 Phase1 id: 192.1.1.42
```

Example 19-18 *Using the* **show crypto session** *Command*

```
RTRA# show crypto session
Crypto session current status
Interface: Ethernet0/0
Session status: UP-ACTIVE
Peer: 192.1.1.42 port 500
   IKE SA: local 192.1.1.40/500 remote 192.1.1.42/500 Active
   IPSEC FLOW: permit ip 192.168.2.0/255.255.255.0
                         192.168.3.0/255.255.255.0
         Active SAs: 2, origin: crypto map
```

Example 19-19 *Using the* **show crypto session detail** *Command*

```
RTRA# show crypto session detail
Crypto session current status
Code: C - IKE Configuration mode, D - Dead Peer Detection
K - Keepalives, N - NAT-traversal, X - IKE Extended Authentication
Interface: Ethernet0/0
Session status: UP-ACTIVE
Peer: 192.1.1.42 port 500 fvrf: (none) ivrf: (none)
      Desc: Connection to SiteA
      Phase1_id: 192.1.1.42
  IKE SA: local 192.1.1.40/500 remote 192.1.1.42/500 Active
          Capabilities:D connid:2 lifetime:23:48:48
  IPSEC FLOW: permit ip 192.168.2.0/255.255.255.0
                       192.168.3.0/255.255.255.0
        Active SAs: 2, origin: crypto map
        Inbound:  #pkts dec'ed 9 drop 0 life (KB/Sec) 4479991/2929
        Outbound: #pkts enc'ed 9 drop 0 life (KB/Sec) 4479991/2929
```

Table 19-1 *Status of VPN Sessions*

IKE SA	IPsec SAs	VPN Tunnel Status
Exists, active	Exists (flow exists)	UP-ACTIVE
Exists, active	None (flow exists)	UP-IDLE
Exists, active	None (no flow exists)	UP-IDLE
Exists, inactive	Exists (flow exists)	UP-NO-IKE
Exists, inactive	None (flow exists)	DOWN-NEGOTIATING
Exists, inactive	None (no flow)	DOWN-NEGOTIATING
None	Exists (flow exists)	UP-NO-IKE
None	None (flow exists)	DOWN
None	None (no flow exists)	DOWN

TIP   I prefer to use the **show crypto isakmp peer** command over the **show crypto isakmp sa** command because the former gives me a brief description of the connection. I also prefer to use the **show crypto session** command over the **show crypto ipsec sa** command because the former easily summarizes the important information in a short display. The latter display is too verbose for me for a quick determination of whether either the Phase 1 or 2 SAs have been established.

Clearing Crypto Sessions

Another new feature introduced with the IKE description feature is the ability to delete all IKE and IPsec SAs associated with all peers or a specific peer. Before this enhancement, you had to delete the management and data SAs individually. Use the following command to delete all SAs associated with a peer or peers:

```
Router# clear crypto session
                      [local local_IP_address [port local-port]]
                      [remote ip-address [port remote-port]]
```

When you execute this command, the session(s) torn down will have "DOWN-NEGOTIATING" as the status in the output of the **show crypto session** command, indicating that the SAs are either completely down or in the process of being brought back up.

Invalid Security Parameter Index Recovery Feature

The invalid security parameter index (SPI) recovery feature was introduced in IOS 12.3(2)T and integrated into 12.2(18)SXE. This feature allows the router to recover from an invalid security parameter index error (displayed as *Invalid SPI* in the output of the **debug crypto ipsec** command. With this feature, the IPsec peers can resynchronize their SA databases and successfully bring up the data connections. The following two sections will discuss more information about how an invalid SPI condition can occur and how to enable the feature.

Invalid SPI Condition and the Invalid SPI Recovery Feature

An invalid SPI condition can occur if one IPsec peer dies (is shut down, is rebooted, has its interface reset, loses its management connection to a peer, and so on) and has an existing IPsec session to a remote peer. The remote peer still might try to use the SA even though a new one is built (with a new SA). The old SPI value from the old SA is no longer in the local peer, and the peer will respond with an "INVALID SPI NOTIFY" message to the remote peer, indicating that the data SA that the remote peer is trying to use is no longer available. The local peer's default action is to continue dropping traffic from the invalid SA (commonly referred to as a "black hole").

Upon receiving the "INVALID SPI NOTIFY" message, the default behavior of the local peer is to drop traffic. With the recovery feature enabled on both routers, the remote router will understand that an abnormal condition occurred with the local peer and that the remote peer should delete the existing SAs and establish new ones.

NOTE   Dead Peer Detection (DPD) can also detect this problem; however, DPD might take longer to detect it, depending on the keepalive interval. The Invalid SPI Recovery feature is more similar to the Initial Contact supported by Easy VPN devices.

Invalid SPI Recovery Configuration

To enable the invalid SPI recovery feature, use the following command:

```
Router(config)# crypto isakmp invalid-spi-recovery
```

This should be configured on all IOS routers that have peer relationships. Once enabled, you can use the **debug crypto ipsec** and **show crypto ipsec sa** commands to verify that the feature is enabled. When an invalid SPI condition exists, you'll see a message similar to Example 19-20, where the destination and source addresses are replaced by the peer addresses. In this example, a data SA using ESP was determined to be invalid.

Example 19-20 *Message from an Invalid SPI Condition*

```
%CRYPTO-4-RECVD_PKT_INV_SPI: decaps: rec'd IPSEC packet has
    invalid spi for destaddr=x.x.x.x, prot=50,
    spi=0x1214F0D(18960141), srcaddr=y.y.y.y
```

TIP   To test the configuration of the invalid SPI recovery feature, from the local peer, bring up an IPsec session to a remote peer (if one doesn't exist). On the local peer, execute the **debug crypto ipsec** command. Clear the Phase 1 and 2 SAs on the remote peer. From the local peer, send traffic to the remote peer. A small number of packets might be dropped, but on the remote peer you should see the message in Example 19-20 and on the local peer you should see the old data SAs torn down from the debug output and new ones built.

CAUTION   A denial of service (DoS) attack can occur if the invalid SPI recovery is enabled. The feature has a built-in mechanism to reduce the likelihood of this occurring, but there is still a chance that a DoS can occur; therefore, Cisco has disabled this feature by default, requiring you to enable it manually.

Fragmentation Problems

IP supports a maximum length of 65,536 bytes for an IP packet; however, most data-link layer protocols support a much smaller length, called a maximum transmission unit (MTU). Based on the supported MTU, it might be necessary to break up (fragment) an IP packet to transmit it across a particular data-link layer media type. The destination then would have to reassemble the fragments back into the original complete IP packet.

The problem with fragmentation is that it requires additional CPU and memory resources on devices performing fragmentation. This is not to say that the actual source and destination will perform the fragmentation. For example, assume that the source and destination are on a Token Ring network with an MTU size of 4K. However, between these two networks is an Ethernet network. To transmit the 4KB data payloads across a 1500-byte Ethernet MTU, an intermediate device connected to the Token Ring and Ethernet networks would have to fragment the original packet. If the intermediate device supports fragmentation, additional resources (CPU and memory) are required to perform fragmentation on the original payload, and on the destination device, to reassemble the fragments back into a complete payload. In some instances, the intermediate device won't perform fragmentation and might drop the packet; in other cases, the intermediate device might notify the source of the correct MTU size to use.

When using a VPN to protect data between two VPN peers, additional overhead is added to the original data, which might require that fragmentation occur. Table 19-2 lists fields that might have to be added to the protected data to support a VPN connection. Please note that multiple protocols might be necessary, increasing the size of the original packet. For example, if you're using an L2L DVMPN IPsec connection between two Cisco routers where you've implemented a GRE tunnel, you'll have this additional overhead: ESP, GRE, and the outer IP header. If you have an IPsec software client connecting to a VPN gateway where the traffic is going through an address translation device, you'll have this additional overhead: ESP, UDP header for NAT-T, and the outer IP header for the tunnel mode connection.

Table 19-2 *VPN Overhead*

Protocol	Additional Bytes
ESP (encryption and hash)	56
AH	24+
GRE	24
NAT-T/IPsec over UDP (UDP part)	8
IPsec over TCP (TCP part)	20
L2TP	12
PPTP	48
Outer IP header in IPsec tunnel mode or PPTP/L2TP	20
PPPoE	8

Given that this book is about VPNs, my concern is that I need to get protected traffic between two devices and I definitely don't want fragmentation occurring, because this places extra overhead on the source (or intermediate) and destination devices and runs the risk of breaking the VPN session. The remainder of this chapter will focus on problems that fragmentation can create and how you can deal with them on a Cisco IOS router. Please note that much of what I talk about here applies also to the VPN concentrator, PIX and ASA security appliances, and Cisco client products.

Issues with Fragmentation

When the source sends a packet to a destination, it will place a value in the control flags field of the IP header that affects fragmentation of the packet by intermediate devices. The control flag is three bits long, but only the first two are used in fragmentation. If the second bit is set to 0, the packet is allowed to be fragmented; if set to 1, the packet is not allowed to be fragmented. The second bit is commonly called the "don't fragment" (DF) bit. The third bit specifies when fragmentation occurs, whether or not this fragmented packet is the last fragment (set to 0) or there are more fragments (set to 1) that make up the packet.

There are several issues that can create problems when fragmentation is required.

- First, additional overhead in CPU cycles and memory is required by the two devices performing fragmentation and reassembly. If the destination is a Cisco router, the router automatically will set aside 18KB of RAM as a buffer for a fragmented packet.

This is inefficient in most cases because the fragments of a packet, when reassembled, don't require a full 18KB—however, the destination router doesn't know this. On top of this, if the traffic is VPN-related, the VPN destination endpoint is hit twice as hard because it has to verify the packet and decrypt it. On a device that performs VPN functions in hardware, it is not unusual that your throughput with a VPN connection that needs fragmentation could drop by 50–90 percent! On Cisco routers, the fragmentation process occurs with process switching, the slowest form of switching on a router; therefore, even if you have a hardware card for encrypting or decrypting VPN packets, it won't matter because the fragmentation process occurs in software. And imagine if the destination was a broadband user with a software client; their throughput would be horrible!

- A second issue with fragmentation is that if one fragment is dropped on the way to the destination, the packet can't be reassembled and therefore the entire packet must be fragmented and sent again. This creates additional throughput problems, especially in situations where the traffic in question is being rate-limited and the source is sending traffic above the allowable limit.

- A third issue is that packet filtering and stateful firewalls might have difficulty processing the fragments. When fragmentation occurs, the first fragment contains an outer IP header, the inner header, like TCP, UDP, ESP, and so on, and part of the payload. Subsequent fragments of the original packet will contain an outer IP header and the continuation of the payload. The problem with this process is that certain firewalls need to see the inner header information in every packet to make intelligent filtering decisions; and if it's missing, they inadvertently may drop all fragments except for the first one.

- A fourth issue is that in the IP header, the source of the packet might set the third control bit to "don't fragment," which means that if an intermediate device receives the packet and must fragment it, the intermediate device won't. Instead, the intermediate device will drop the packet.

Headaches of Fragmentation

Probably the biggest problem I run into as a VPN consultant deals with fragmentation issues. I constantly get calls from clients complaining about the dramatic difference in throughput before (great) and after a VPN solution is implemented (horrible). Or sometimes a client will tell me that when they send e-mail without attachments, it works across the VPN; and with attachments it doesn't. In this latter example, the problem typically is where the device is setting the DF bit and fragmentation is needed; and when sending e-mail without an attachment, fragmentation is not necessary, but with the attachment, it is. Whenever I hear of something similar to either of these two situations, the first thing I look at is whether or not fragmentation is occurring. The next section discusses a simple way to discover if you're experiencing fragmentation issues.

Fragmentation Discovery

Because most networks use Ethernet, a default MTU value of 1,500 bytes typically is used for IP packets. To determine if fragmentation is occurring, or is needed but can't be done (DF bit is set), first bring your VPN session up and try pinging a device located at the other end (assuming that ping is allowed across the VPN tunnel). If this is successful, try accessing an application on the same device; for example, if it's a Microsoft Exchange server, open Outlook and try to download your e-mail. If this doesn't work, and assuming you have name resolution (DNS and WINS) configured correctly, the culprit could be fragmentation.

As a second test, you can use the **ping** command; this will work with almost any operating system, including the Privilege EXEC extended **ping** on IOS devices. From a Windows device, use the following:

```
c:\> ping -f -l packet_size_in_bytes destination_IP_address
```

The **-f** option specifies that the packet should not be fragmented. The **-l** option specifies the length of the packet. First try using ping with a packet size of 1,500. You'll get a message like "Packet needs to be fragmented but DF set" if fragmentation is required but can't be performed.

In the case of a Cisco router, execute **debug ip icmp** and use the extended **ping** command. If you see *ICMP: dst (x.x.x.x) frag. needed and DF set, unreachable sent to y.y.y.y*", where *x.x.x.x* is a destination device and *y.y.y.y* is your router, then an intermediate device is telling you that fragmentation is needed, but because you set the DF bit in the echo request, an intermediate device couldn't fragment it to forward it to the next hop. In this case, gradually decrease the MTU size of the pings until you find one that works.

NOTE When you do a ping, remember that the size you specify in the ping option doesn't include the IP, ICMP, and Ethernet headers. These headers total 42 bytes, which you'll need to accommodate when you compute the correct MTU size.

Also, the IOS's extended ping can do a ping that sweeps sizes with the DF bit set, which can also help you pinpoint the correct MTU size. Using the extended **ping** command is done from Privilege EXEC mode on a router.

Solutions to Fragmentation Issues

There are a variety of solutions available to you to solve fragmentation issues. The following sections will discuss each of these, including their advantages and disadvantages.

Static MTU Setting

One of the most common solutions is to configure a static MTU size for IP packets on your devices. For example, if you're using the Cisco VPN Client software on a Windows platform, it comes with a utility that automatically adjusts the MTU size for adapters on your PC: 576 bytes for dialup connections and 1,300 bytes for LAN connections. In both cases, Cisco assumes the worse case situation where the client needs to use IPsec over TCP or NAT-T for the transport. The Cisco MTU utility allows you to configure a custom setting to increase the MTU size to maximize your throughput; if you use this utility to change the MTU size, you'll need to reboot your PC for the setting to take effect. This program was discussed in Chapter 12, "Cisco VPN Software Client."

NOTE   Of course, one problem with this solution is that your adapter now will always use the specified MTU for all traffic, not just the VPN traffic, which will reduce your throughput for nonprotected connections.

On Cisco routers, you use the **ip mtu** command to adjust the MTU size on an interface (typically this is a GRE tunnel interface since routers commonly are used for L2L sessions):

```
Router(config)# interface type [slot_#/]port_#
Router(config-if)# ip mtu MTU_size_in_bytes
```

For IPsec GRE transport mode connections (DMVPN), use an MTU size of 1,440 on the GRE tunnel interface; for IPsec GRE tunnel mode connections, use 1,420. Once you've configured this, on the router's tunnel interface, if any packets from a source device are received that need to be tunneled and have the DF bit, the router will automatically send an ICMP type 3 "host unreachable," code 4, "fragmentation needed" message to the packet originator. This allows the source, at least when using ping, to see that fragmentation is needed and can't be performed.

NOTE   Please note that manually setting the MTU on the router tells the router, acting as a VPN gateway, to fragment received packets *before* protecting them and sending them across the tunnel. This is preferable over having the router protect the traffic and then fragment it; however, the router *is* fragmenting the packets. This solution should be used to ensure that router-initiated traffic is not fragmented. You should still adjust the MTU size on your edge devices to ensure that they don't cause the router to have to perform fragmentation of packets destined across the VPN session.

CAUTION   Changing the MTU size on any router interface will cause all tunnels terminated on that interface to be torn down. So you might want to plan this during a time of inactivity.

TCP Maximum Segment Size (MSS)

Using a static MTU configuration, as I mentioned in the above section, isn't necessarily the best solution, because the NIC will use this for both protected and nonprotected traffic, which is inefficient for nonprotected traffic; plus, you have to do this manually for all your edge devices. A more preferable solution would limit the number of devices that this configuration has to be performed on.

In most instances, fragmentation occurs with TCP traffic because TCP is normally used to transport large amounts of data. TCP supports a feature called TCP maximum segment size (MSS) that allows the two devices to negotiate a suitable size for TCP traffic. The MSS value is configured statically on each device and represents the buffer size to use for an expected packet. When two devices establish TCP connections they will compare the local MSS value with the local MTU value during the three-way handshake; whichever is lower is sent to the remote peer. The two peers then will use the lower of the two exchanged values.

The problem of this approach is that you have to manually configure an appropriate TCP MSS size on the two end hosts (or adjust the IP MTU size), which is probably not practical in most situations where you have hundreds or thousands of devices that build or use VPN sessions. To deal with this problem, Cisco added the TCP MSS feature in IOS 12.2(4)T. With this feature, the router can modify the TCP MSS value sent in the original TCP SYN segment from a device to a value that you, as an administrator, know will work for a VPN session. By and large, the router is performing a proxy for this exchange. To configure this feature, use the following configuration:

```
Router(config)# interface type [slot_#/]port_#
Router(config-if)# ip tcp adjust-mss MSS_size_in_bytes
```

This configuration should be performed on the interface where VPN sessions are terminated, like the router's public or GRE tunnel interface. Remember to accommodate for all of the VPN or additional overhead that will be added to the packet, where you also might need to compensate for links beyond the router that have a smaller MTU size.

NOTE   Remember that this feature only works with TCP; other IP protocols will have to use another solution to solve IP fragmentation problems. Also, even if you set the **ip mtu** on the router, it does not affect what the two end hosts negotiate during the TCP three-way handshake with TCP MSS.

Path MTU Discovery (PMTUD)

The main problem with TCP MSS is that you, as an administrator, have to know what value to configure on your router to prevent fragmentation from occurring. This can be a problem if more than one path exists between you and the remote VPN location, and when you do your initial query, you find the second- or third-smallest MTU, instead of the smallest, based on the routing decision used during your initial query. Given this situation, you could, and probably would, still experience fragmentation problems depending on how your packets were routed.

How PMTUD Works

PMTUD (RFC 1191) was developed to discover the smallest segment between two end devices dynamically. Because TCP is usually the protocol that experiences fragmentation problems, PMTUD only supports TCP. When a device sends a TCP segment with MSS information and the DF bit set and this is received by a device with an MTU that requires fragmentation for the next hop, the device responds back to the source with an ICMP destination unreachable message and a code of "fragmentation needed and DF set." When the source receives this, PMTUD allows the source to lower the MTU size and retry. The source will keep doing this until the TCP data is transmitted successfully. Upon a successful transmission, the source typically will create a static host route (/32) in its routing table along with the corresponding MTU size so that it doesn't have to repeat this process for the destination.

As mentioned at the beginning of this section, one problem with TCP MSS is that if you don't find the smallest MTU path for all possible paths to a destination, fragmentation still can occur. To prevent this, PMTUD is performed continually on all packets sent between the source and destination; and every time the source receives a "can't fragment" ICMP message, the source will resend the information with lower and lower MTU sizes until it works, and then will update the host routing entry with the updated MTU information.

NOTE   PMTUD is done in both directions of a connection, because the packets could be traveling different paths based on the flow of packets; in other words, when an asymmetric routing condition exists.

Issues with PMTUD

PMTUD can encounter three issues that can cause it not to function:

- An intermediate router can drop the packet and not respond with an ICMP message; this is not very common on the Internet, but could be common inside a network where routers are configured to not respond with ICMP unreachable messages.

- An intermediate router can respond with an ICMP unreachable message, but on the return flow, a firewall blocks this message; this is probably a more common occurrence than the preceding issue.

- The ICMP unreachable message makes its way all the way back to the source, but the source ignores the fragmentation message; this is the most uncommon of the three issues.

If you experience the first issue, either you could clear the DF bit in the IP header that the source placed there, or manually adjust the TCP MSS size. To clear the DF bit, an intermediate router would have to change this value from 1 to 0 (typically a router in your network before the packet leaves the network). Here's a simple code configuration that will do this on an IOS-based router:

```
Router(config)# access-list ACL_# permit tcp any any
Router(config)# route-map route_map_name permit seq_#
Router(config-route-map)# match ip address ACL_#
Router(config-route-map)# set ip df 0
Router(config-route-map)# exit
Router(config)# interface type [slot_#/]port_#
Router(config-if)# ip policy route-map route_map_name
```

The above configuration commonly is referred to as policy routing. To clear the DF bit using this feature, your router needs to be running IOS 12.1(6) or later. For L2L sessions, this commonly is performed on the GRE tunnel interface or for remote access or standard L2L sessions, on the public interface of the router.

PMTUD and GRE Tunnels

By default, a router doesn't perform PMTUD on GRE tunnel packets that it generates itself. To enable PMTUD on GRE tunnel interfaces and to have the router participate in the MTU tuning process for source/destination devices for traffic traversing the tunnel, configure the following:

```
Router(config)# interface tunnel tunnel_#
Router(config-if)# tunnel path-mtu-discovery
                        [age-timer {minutes | infinite}]
                        [min-mtu MTU_size]
```

The **tunnel path-mtu-discovery** command enables PMTUD for a router's GRE tunnel interface. The optional **age-timer** parameter specifies the number of minutes after which the tunnel interface resets the maximum MTU size discovered, minus 24 bytes for the GRE header. If you specify **infinite** for the timer, the timer is not used. The **min-mtu** parameter specifies the minimum number of bytes the MTU value should be.

NOTE   If you still are experiencing fragmentation issues and dropped packets, optionally, you can manually adjust the MTU size with the **ip mtu** tunnel interface command; in this case, the router will fragment the packet before protecting it. This command can be used in conjunction of PMTUD and/or TCP MSS.

Summary

This chapter showed you the basics of troubleshooting IPsec VPNs on Cisco routers. It is by no means an all-encompassing coverage of troubleshooting VPN problems; however, I've tried to discuss some of the most common problems you'll experience and how to pinpoint those problems using **show** and **debug** commands on Cisco routers.

Next up is Part IV, "PIX Firewalls," where I show you how to set up VPN features on Cisco PIX and ASA appliances.

PIX Firewalls

CHAPTER 20

PIX and ASA Product Information

In Part V, I'll discuss the use of Cisco PIX and ASA security appliances to initiate and terminate VPN sessions. PIXs and ASAs are very flexible and can be used for site-to-site (LAN-to-LAN or L2L) sessions, VPN gateways, and remote access clients. I'll cover topics on how to configure the PIX security appliances using the new 7.0 Finesse Operating System (FOS) and its predecessor, 6.x (the ASA only supports version 7.0).

In this chapter, however, I'll introduce you to the Cisco PIX and ASA security appliance solutions, focusing on VPN deployment scenarios and their VPN capabilities. I'll also discuss some of the advantages that Cisco PIXs and ASAs have over other Cisco products when being used for VPN solutions.

PIX Deployment Scenarios

The Cisco PIX and ASA VPN capabilities have their roots in Cisco IOS VPN technologies. VPNs were first introduced in the Cisco IOS router product line and then added to the PIXs in an early 5.x release. Like the routers and the concentrators, Cisco PIXs support many VPN solutions including IPsec, PPTP, and L2TP. Because of their flexibility, they can be used in many different situations. The ASA was introduced in the spring of 2005. The ASA is a unique hybrid security appliance, having abilities from the PIX, VPN 3000, and IDS 4200 sensors. This section will focus on how PIX and ASA security appliances can be used to enhance a VPN solution in your network.

Specifically, the section will cover the following:

- L2L and Remote Access Connections
- The Special Capabilities of PIXs and ASAs

L2L and Remote Access Connections

PIXs and ASAs support L2L and remote access connections. For remote access solutions, the PIXs and ASAs can be Easy VPN Servers and the PIX 501 and 506E can be Easy VPN Remotes (clients). As I mentioned in Chapter 9, "Concentrator Site-to-Site Connections,"

I prefer to use Cisco routers for L2L sessions and concentrators for remote access connections. With the introduction of the ASA security appliances, they also can terminate SSL VPNs, with similar SSL capabilities compared to the VPN 3000 concentrators.

Routers support enhanced routing and QoS capabilities over Cisco PIX and ASA security appliances and VPN 3000 concentrators. Plus, VPN 3000 concentrators scale better for remote access connections and are easy to set up. However, the Cisco PIX and ASA security appliances, first and foremost, provide better-integrated and more comprehensive security services than routers and concentrators. Therefore, if you need to enhance your VPN solution with security and firewall functions and place it in one box, or if you need enhanced address translation services for VPNs that terminate on a VPN device, the PIX or ASA is a much better choice than a router or a concentrator.

Special Capabilities of PIXs and ASAs

As I mentioned in Chapter 6, I prefer to use PIXs or ASAs in a VPN solution when I need advanced address translation capabilities in addition to advanced firewall and security services. There are three main features the PIX and ASA security appliances have over Cisco VPN 3000 concentrators and IOS-based routers when it comes to VPN implementations: address translation, stateful firewall services, and redundancy.

Address Translation

The PIX was originally developed by Network Translation as an address translation device back in 1994. From the beginning, the PIX has had its roots in address translation. The concentrator's address translation capabilities are very minimal and Cisco routers' capabilities are based primarily on address translation involving two logical locations: inside and outside. However, the PIX's address translation capabilities can handle multiple interfaces easily, with different translation policies for different interfaces. Policy address translation is one of its main strengths. Many times I've attempted to configure complex address translation policies, such as bidirection NAT on a multi-interfaced router, and then shortly gave up and easily configured the same policies on a PIX.

Stateful Firewall Services

With the introduction of FOS 6.x and 7.0, the PIX and ASA security appliances provide one of the best, if not the best, integrated stateful firewall services in the market, including support for both IPv4 and IPv6. Besides performing stateful firewall functions, they support superb application layer inspection and filtering capabilities, including detailed inspection of application layer information such as HTTP, FTP, SMTP, ESMTP, multimedia applications, voice, and many others. They support advanced guard and detection features to protect against TCP flood attacks, DNS spoofing, fragmentation attacks, web server attacks, and e-mail attacks. The PIX and ASA also can be used to detect and block instant messaging applications, peer-to-peer file sharing programs, and other applications that tunnel traffic through web services, such as AOL's Instant Messenger, KaZaA, and GoToMyPC.

Redundancy

Cisco PIXs support stateful failover for redundancy of connections. Before FOS 7.0, though, this did not include redundancy for VPN sessions; nor did it allow both PIXs, in a failover configuration, to process traffic. With the introduction of FOS 7.0, both PIXs or ASAs in a failover configuration can actively process traffic; this is referred to as *Active/ Active* failover. Cisco routers don't support this type of redundancy, but the VPN 3000 concentrators do with VCA. However, with VCA, any remote access connections dropped by a failed concentrator must be rebuilt by the remote access clients via the master of the cluster, so temporary loss of connectivity will occur.

With 7.0 of the FOS software, if one of the PIXs (or ASAs) in a failover configuration fails, all of the necessary VPN information already exists on the other redundant PIX, and the redundant PIX can immediately begin processing traffic for the VPN traffic. This solution provides a true stateful failover configuration not only for VPN traffic, but for any traffic flowing through the PIXs.

NOTE	Active/Active failover is load balancing based on the VCA code in VPN 3000 concentrators, and active/standby failover provides stateful failover for VPN sessions.

Failover times between PIXs or ASAs have been reduced to subsecond times when serial-based failover is used and three seconds when LAN-based failover is used. Another great feature in FOS 7.0 is zero-downtime software upgrades. You can upgrade the PIX or ASA without having to reboot it, which can be very important for mission-critical VPN applications.

PIX and ASA Feature and Product Overview

In the next two sections, I'll discuss briefly some of the VPN features and VPN capabilities of the PIX and ASA security appliances. This information can help you in determining if the PIX or ASA is the right product platform for you, and which PIX or ASA appliance you should choose for a VPN implementation.

PIX and ASA VPN Features

Cisco PIX and ASA security appliances support many VPN features. They are fully IPsec-compliant and support both L2L and remote access services, where they can perform both Easy VPN Server and Remote functions. The features listed below include features that have existed in older FOS versions, and those that are new in FOS 7.0.

- All PIXs and ASAs support AES, DES, and 3DES encryption algorithms (with AES added in FOS 6.3) and MD5 and SHA hashing functions; DH groups 1, 2, and 5 are supported, with FOS 7.0 adding support for DH group 7.

- As an Easy VPN Remote, the PIX can use client and network extension modes with RRI, and can perform device, interactive user, and individual user authentication (like the 3002 hardware client); ASAs cannot be Easy VPN Remotes, but they can be Easy VPN Servers.

- VPN client security posture enforcement allows the PIX and ASA to perform NAC for VPN clients, restricting clients' access based on their operating system and type, and installed security product software (like antivirus and personal firewall software)—new in FOS 7.0.

- Like the VPN 3000 concentrators, the PIXs and ASAs can perform automatic software updates for the 3002 hardware clients and Cisco VPN software clients—new in FOS 7.0.

- The PIX and ASA can act as a hub in a hub-and-spoke topology—new in FOS 7.0, where traffic can be inspected and policies enforced before allowing traffic to flow between the spokes via the hub PIX or ASA—new in FOS 7.0.

- The PIX has supported NAT-T since FOS 6.2; however, FOS 7.0 has added support for IPsec over TCP and Cisco IPsec over UDP.

- The PIX and ASA can route OSPF traffic across VPN tunnels and can inject RRI routes into an OSPF routing process—new in FOS 7.0.

- In FOS 7.0, support has been added to enroll for certificates manually. Other features are the export of private keys, support for hierarchical CA implementations, the increase of RSA key sizes to 4,096 bits, support for DSA-based X.509 certificates, and use of an IOS router acting as a CA.

- The ASA supports the termination of SSL VPNs from SSL clients. Currently, the PIX does not support this feature; the ASA's SSL VPN capabilities are more comparable to the VPN 3000 concentrators than to Cisco routers.

As you can see from the preceding list, many VPN improvements have been added in FOS 7.0.

NOTE	Up until 6.3, all of the PIXs supported the same FOS, and with a few exceptions of features, all had the same capabilities. When FOS 7.0 was introduced, it was initially available only on the 515/515E and higher PIXs, with possible support for the 501 and 506E to be added later.

Pre- and Post-FOS 7.0

In FOS 6.3 and earlier, I typically shied away from using the PIX as a VPN solution because of the many VPN features that it lacked (the ASA only supports FOS 7.0 and later). Probably my biggest issue with the pre-7.0 FOS was that traffic that entered a PIX's interface could not leave the same interface. This meant that the PIX could not be a VPN hub device in a VPN hub-and-spoke topology. Nor could you have a policy that dictated that remote access clients had split tunneling disabled, if you wanted their traffic to come to the PIX first and then go back out to the Internet. You had to use split tunneling to allow this on the PIX. Of course, Cisco has remedied this in FOS 7.0.

Another limitation of the pre-7.0 FOS was that it didn't support any QOS. With 7.0, the PIX and ASA now support QoS services that allow it to classify and police traffic, and use low latency queuing (LLQ) and priority queuing (PQ)—the IOS routers still support more advanced QoS functions, but in many situations, the PIX's QoS features are more than sufficient to deal with delay-sensitive or bursty traffic. Before FOS 7.0, redundancy features were somewhat lacking, since there was no stateful failover for VPNs nor support for both PIXs in the failover configuration to process traffic; 7.0 remedied this situation.

Cisco has more than made up for the pre-FOS 6.3 VPN shortcomings in features with the introduction of FOS 7.0, putting it on par with the Cisco IOS-based routers and VPN 3000 concentrators, and in certain categories surpassing these products. Likewise, the ASA hybrid security appliance allows you to use these features, and other security features, bundled into one high-performance platform.

PIX Models

The PIX security appliances come in several models: 501, 506E, 515E, 525, and 535. The 501 and 506E commonly are used in SOHO or small offices, the 515E in medium networks, the 525 in enterprise networks, and the 535 by very large enterprise or ISP networks. The 501 and 506E support only software-based encryption. The higher-end PIXs can do both software- and hardware-based encryption. Hardware encryption is accomplished through the VPN Accelerator Card (VAC). There are two versions of the card:

- VAC: hardware encryption using DES and/or 3DES
- VAC+: hardware encryption of DES, 3DES, and/or AES, including faster processing than the VAC

Table 20-1 has a brief comparison of the PIX models and their capabilities. Please note that VPN throughput figures are based on using the VAC+ instead of the VAC (Cisco no longer sells the VAC). Also, the maximum number of VPN peers of the 515E, 525, and 535 are based on the use of the VAC or VAC+.

Table 20-1   *PIX Security Appliances*

Specification	501	506E	515E	525	535
Firewall throughput in Mbps	60	100	190	330	1,650
Failover/redundancy support	N	N	Y	Y	Y
3DES throughput in Mbps (software/VAC+)	3	15	20/130	70/145	50/425
AES-128 throughput in Mbps (software/VAC+)	4.5	30	45/130	65/135	110/495
AES-256 throughput in Mbps (software/VAC+)	3.4	25	35/130	50/135	90/425
Maximum VPN peers	10	25	2,000[1]	2,000[1]	2,000[1]

[1] The 515E, 525, and 535 appliances support 2,000 VPN sessions with the VAC+ card installed; without this card, only 1,000 VPN sessions are supported.

ASA Models

The ASA security appliances come in several models: 5510, 5520, and 5540. The ASAs are feature-rich; here is a very brief list of these features:

- High-performance firewall services
- Intrusion prevention system (IPS)
- Network antivirus, trojan horse, and worm detection and deterrence
- SSL (WebVPN), L2L, and remote access VPNs

The ASA security appliances by and large combine the functionality of the PIX security appliances, IPS 4200 series sensors, and VPN 3000 series concentrators in a single chassis. Table 20-2 has a quick overview of the VPN performance specifications of the ASA security appliances.

Table 20-2 *ASA Security Appliances*

Specification	5510	5520	5540
Firewall throughput in Mbps	300	450	650
Failover/redundancy support, including VPNs	Active/Standby	Active/Standby, Active/Active, VCA	Active/Standby, Active/Active, VCA
3DES/AES throughput in Mbps	170	225	325
Maximum IPsec peers	50/150[1]	300/750[1]	500/2,000/5,000[1]
Maximum WebVPN peers	50/150[1]	300/750[1]	500/1,250/2,500[1]

[1] Support for additional VPN sessions on a particular ASA model can be upgraded by purchasing the proper upgrade license.

Summary

This chapter introduced you to the PIX and ASA security appliance family. I've attempted to give you a brief introduction to the PIXs and ASAs so that you have an understanding of their capabilities—strengths and weaknesses—and therefore can properly choose the correct solution, and the correct PIX or ASA, when designing a VPN implementation.

Next up is Chapter 21, "PIX and ASA Site-to-Site Connections," where I show you how to create L2L sessions on these devices.

PIX and ASA Site-to-Site Connections

In this chapter I'll discuss how to configure IPsec LAN-to-LAN (L2L) sessions on the PIX and ASA security appliances. The first part of the chapter focuses on the components you'll need to configure the management connection, much of which applies to remote access sessions, and the second part will focus on configuring the components of the data connections. At the end of the chapter I'll illustrate an example of an L2L session between PIXs/ASAs.

In April 2005, Cisco introduced a new version of the Finesse Operating System (FOS) for the PIX security appliances, called 7.0. Currently this is supported only on the 515/515E PIXs and higher. Likewise, in May 2005, Cisco introduced the new Adapter Security Appliance (ASA) devices, which support PIX, VPN concentrator, router, and IDS features all in one box. Fortunately, much of the code and commands found in the 7.0 PIX security appliances are the same as those found in the ASA devices. However, the 501 and 506/506E PIXs only support the FOS 6.3 software. Because the 7.0 software is new, and the 6.x software is still in wide use, I'll point out differences in the configurations of both operating systems throughout the chapter where appropriate.

NOTE In version 7.0, the PIX/ASA supports VPN only in single mode, commonly called routed mode. VPNs are not supported when your PIX/ASA is configured for multiple security contexts (multi-mode) or in an Active/Active stateful failover configuration. In FOS 6.3 and earlier, the stateful failover feature of the PIXs did not provide stateful failover for VPN sessions; in FOS 7.0, this enhancement has been added. The configuration of failover and stateful failover on the PIX/ASA, however, is beyond the scope of this book. Topics such as tunnel groups, which were added in FOS 7.0, I'll address in Chapter 22, "PIX and ASA Remote Access Connections," where it is more appropriate.

ISAKMP/IKE Phase 1 Management Connection

In this first part of the chapter, I'll focus on the components necessary to allow IPsec traffic into the PIX/ASA and to build a management connection to a remote peer. Much of what I discuss here is applicable to both L2L and remote access sessions.

Allowing IPsec Traffic

Your first task is to allow IPsec session traffic into your PIX/ASA. Unlike Cisco routers, PIX/ASA devices behave differently when traffic is flowing through them. With these security appliances, interfaces are assigned security levels, and based on security level configurations, traffic is not allowed to flow from a lower to a higher level, by default. In most cases, your IPsec session traffic will be terminated on the device's outside interface, which is, from the FOS's perspective, the least secure.

You can use two methods to allow VPN traffic into or through the PIX from a less- to more-secure interface:

- Access control lists (ACLs)
- ACL bypassing

The following two sections will discuss both options. After this, I'll discuss one issue with moving traffic between interfaces that have the same security level.

Using ACLs to Allow IPsec Traffic

If you decide you'll use ACLs to allow IPsec traffic into your PIX/ASA, your ACL configuration will look something like the following:

```
appliance(config)# access-list ACL_name_or_# permit udp
                       remote_peer_IP_address subnet_mask
                       local_IP_address subnet_mask eq 500
appliance(config)# access-list ACL_name_or_# permit esp
                       remote_peer_IP_address subnet_mask
                       local_IP_address subnet_mask
appliance(config)# access-list ACL_name_or_# permit udp
                       remote_peer_IP_address subnet_mask
                       local_IP_address subnet_mask eq 4500
appliance(config)# access-list ACL_name_or_# permit tcp
                       remote_peer_IP_address subnet_mask
                       local_IP_address subnet_mask eq port_#
appliance(config)# access-list ACL_name_or_# permit protocol
                       remote_protected traffic subnet_mask
                       local_protected traffic subnet_mask
                       [protocol_information]
```

The first ACL statement allows the management connection to be built. The second, third, and fourth statements are for the data connections. The second statement assumes that ESP traffic can reach the PIX/ASA without having to go through a PAT device. The third statement is for ESP traffic that is being encapsulated using NAT-T. New in FOS 7.0 is the ability of encapsulating ESP traffic in TCP, which statement four would allow. You can list up to ten TCP ports for IPsec over TCP, but the default is port 10,000; you'll need to list all ports you've configured the PIX/ASA to use, if any, in separate ACL statements.

The last ACL statement in the preceding syntax allows the tunneled packets to pass the ACL check. As mentioned in Chapter 17, "Router Site-to-Site Connections," routers process IPsec packets twice on the ACL (depending on the IOS version): once when they're protected and again after the router has verified the protection and decrypted them (in their clear-text form). PIX/ASA devices do the same thing. You'll need to list, probably in multiple ACL statements, the traffic that is allowed *through* the tunnel.

One other thing to point out about the ACL configuration is that in FOS 6.3, both AH and ESP are supported; however, in the initial release of FOS 7.0, only ESP is supported. If you are running 6.3 or earlier, and need to use AH, use protocol number 51 in the protocol field of the ACL statement.

TIP Whenever possible, be specific about the remote and local addressing information in the PIX/ASA's ACL, because you want only certain types of IPsec traffic to enter your security appliance.

You'll then need to activate the ACL on the PIX/ASA's interface where the traffic will be entering:

```
appliance(config)# access-group ACL_name_or_# in
                         interface logical_interface_name
```

Using ACL Bypassing to Allow IPsec Traffic

The second and less configuration-intensive solution (than configuring ACLs) is to use the ACL bypass feature for IPsec, which is configured with this command:

```
appliance(config)# sysopt connection permit-ipsec
```

This command performs the same function as manual configuration of the ACL statements, in the preceding section.

NOTE Many administrators like to use this command because it's simple to configure; however, I don't like it for two reasons. First, any and all IPsec traffic is allowed into the PIX/ASA, which might not be legitimate IPsec traffic. Second, sometimes I don't have control of the remote peer and the traffic allowed to traverse the tunnel. To simplify things, the remote administrator and I agree on protecting traffic between two networks; however, I might need to exclude some of that traffic. In this instance, I would prefer to use an ACL to perform this function. Remember that in FOS 6.3 and earlier, an ACL could be applied only inbound on an interface. In 7.0, however, you can have an ACL applied inbound or outbound on the same interface. With 7.0, you might want to use the ACL bypassing option to allow the traffic into the router, but then use an ACL applied outbound on the other interfaces of the PIX/ASA to restrict where the tunneled packets can go.

Transmitting IPsec Traffic Between Multiple Interfaces with the Same Security Level

In FOS 6.x and earlier, one restriction the PIX had was that if traffic entered an interface, it could not exit an interface with the same security level; in other words, traffic could not traverse interfaces of the same security level. This, for most purposes, prevented you from setting up a PIX as a hub device in a hub-and-spoke design, or, for remote access sessions, required you to enable split tunneling to allow a user to access both the corporate site and the Internet. As an example, for hub devices in L2L sessions, or when split tunneling was disabled for remote access sessions, traffic would have to enter the outside interface of the PIX and then would have to exit the same interface (entering and leaving interfaces with the same security level). The PIX would not allow this process to occur.

In 7.0, the PIX/ASA allows you to enable this process by configuring the following command:

```
appliance(config)# same-security-traffic permit
                   {intra-interface | inter-interface}
```

The **intra-interface** parameter allows traffic to enter and leave the same interface while the **inter-interface** parameter allows traffic to enter and leave two different interfaces with the same security level. With VPNs, the first parameter is the one used for hub devices in an L2L session, and as an Easy VPN Server or VPN gateway for remote access sessions where split tunneling is disabled.

Setting Up ISAKMP

ISAKMP/IKE typically is used to build IPsec sessions; however, you can do this manually, but then you would have to make the following concessions:

- You cannot use certificates for device authentication
- Anti-replay services are not used
- The encryption and hashing keys must be configured manually
- The IPsec SAs will never time out
- All SA configurations must be configured manually in all crypto map entries on all peers

Because of these concessions, most administrators opt to use ISAKMP/IKE to build and maintain IPsec sessions. However, you must enable ISAKMP/IKE on your PIX/ASA with the following command:

```
appliance(config)# crypto isakmp enable logical_interface_name
```

For each interface that will have IPsec sessions terminated on it, you'll need to repeat the command with the correct logical interface name. This is all that is necessary to enable ISAKMP/IKE; however, there are other options you can configure, as the next few sections will explain.

Address Translation Issues

As mentioned in Chapter 3, "IPsec," ESP packets typically cannot be forwarded through an address translation device performing PAT. To solve this problem, an IPsec device can encapsulate the ESP packet either in a UDP or TCP segment. Of the three approaches I discussed in Chapter 3, the PIX/ASA support two solutions: NAT-T and IPsec over TCP.

NAT-T was added in FOS 6.3, using a detection method to discover if UDP encapsulation is necessary. By default NAT-T is disabled, but can be enabled with this command:

```
appliance(config)# isakmp nat-traversal [keepalive_seconds]
```

By default, a keepalive is generated every 20 seconds to ensure that the associated address translation entry stays in the translation table of the address translation device the packets will be traversing. You can change this by specifying a value from 10–3,600 seconds. You'll probably want to set this to a small value, like 10–20 seconds, to ensure that an idle data connection isn't timed out of any address translation device's translation table inadvertently.

IPsec over TCP support was added in FOS 7.0. This feature typically is used when the protected traffic has to move through a stateful firewall, and the firewall doesn't support UDP (which NAT-T uses). To enable IPsec over TCP, use the following command:

```
appliance(config)# isakmp ipsec-over-tcp [port port1...port10]
```

If you don't specify a port number for the connection, it defaults to port 10,000. However, you can specify a different port number and up to a total of 10 ports. In many instances, some ISP firewalls will block UDP port 4,500 and TCP port 10,000. You can get around this by specifying a TCP port that you don't use, but that the ISP will allow through, such as 8080 (some ISPs do this to residential customers, wanting more money for what they refer to as a "business-class" service).

NOTE   IPsec over TCP will not work with proxy-based firewalls; also, if you've enabled both NAT-T and IPsec over TCP, IPsec over TCP takes precedence over NAT-T.

Disconnect Notifications

By default, if you reset a PIX/ASA's interface, reboot the PIX/ASA, or clear the IPsec sessions, the PIX/ASA will not notify the remote IPsec peer(s) that the SA(s) are no longer available, which could cause connectivity issues. In FOS 7.0, Cisco added the disconnect notification feature, which has the local PIX/ASA send an ISAKMP disconnect message to all IPsec peers connected to it. To enable this feature, use the following command:

```
appliance(config)# isakmp disconnect-notify
```

Using this command definitely is useful when you have two PIX/ASA devices at a site and the remote peers know about both devices. In this situation, when the PIX/ASA must drop an SA(s) associated with an IPsec interface, it will notify the remote peers, which then can proceed to rebuild their sessions to the other PIX/ASA device at the same site.

Main Mode Restriction

The PIX/ASA support both main and aggressive modes in setting up the management connection, where main mode is the default. Aggressive mode is faster in setting up the connection; however, it transmits the identity information of the two peers in clear text, making it less secure. If you always want the PIX to use main mode, you can disable aggressive mode with the following command:

```
appliance(config)# isakmp am-disable
```

Please note that this command was introduced in FOS 7.0.

Configuring Management Connection Policies

Once you've taken care of the ISAKMP preliminary configurations, you're ready to define your ISAKMP policies. ISAKMP policies define how the management connection is to be protected and built. On Cisco routers, you would use the **crypto isakmp policy** command and define the policies in a subcommand mode, where each policy is given a unique number. The number denotes the priority of the policy, with lower numbers having higher priorities. When peers exchange policies, they process them based on the order in which they're sent (for example, lower-numbered ones are sent first).

Configuring Phase 1 policies on a PIX/ASA is similar to doing them on a router, except that all of the policy configuration components of a policy are done from global configuration mode:

```
appliance(config)# isakmp policy priority encryption {aes | aes-192 |
                     aes-256 | des | 3des }
appliance(config)# isakmp policy priority hash {md5 | sha}
appliance(config)# isakmp policy priority authentication
                     {pre-share | rsa-sig | dsa-sig}
appliance(config)# isakmp policy priority group {1 | 2 | 5 | 7}
appliance(config)# isakmp policy priority lifetime seconds
```

If you don't configure any policies, there is a default policy that the PIX, in FOS 6.3, will use: DES, SHA, RSA-SIG, DH group 1, and a lifetime of 86,400 seconds; however, once you configure a policy, the default never is used. For 7.0 there is no default ISAKMP policy.

For a specific policy, if you want to use a default value for a parameter, it is not necessary to configure it. For example, to use SHA-1 for a hash function, you don't need to configure this manually for a policy; this is the default value for every policy.

To perform AES encryption, you need FOS 6.3 or later; and to perform it in hardware, you need the VAC+ card. And, unlike Cisco routers, RSA encrypted nonces are not supported for device authentication; however, in FOS 7.0, DSA certificates are now supported. Plus, to use DH group 5 keys, you need FOS 6.3, and for group 7 keys (PDA devices) you need FOS 7.0. For the management connection lifetime, you can specify a value from 120–2,147,483,647 seconds.

NOTE   You can create up to 20 ISAKMP policies on your PIX/ASA; different policies are required if you have different peers with different capabilities, and you want to take advantage of the strongest security measures whenever the remote peer supports them.

To view your configured ISAKMP policies in 6.3, use the **show isakmp policy** command. The output of this command is very similar to the IOS router's **show crypto isakmp policy** command, discussed in Chapter 16, "Router ISAKMP/IKE Phase 1 Connectivity." In 7.0, use the **show running-config isakmp** command.

Configuring Device Authentication

The PIX/ASA devices support two types of device authentication:

- Pre-shared keys: symmetric
- Certificates: RSA and DSA (DSA is new in FOS 7.0)

The next section will discuss identity types used for device authentication, and the following two sections will discuss the configuration of the authentication methods in the preceding list.

Device Identity Type

During the ISAKMP/IKE negotiations, the IPsec peers identify themselves to each other. To configure which identity type should be used, use the following command:

```
appliance(config)# isakmp identity {address | hostname |
                       key-id ID_string | auto}
```

The **address** parameter specifies that the IP address of the PIX/ASA should be used for the identity; the **hostname** parameter specifies that the FQDN (hostname plus domain name) should be used; and the **key-id** parameter specifies that the configured ID value should be used. The **auto** parameter is new in 7.0. It specifies that the IP address should be used if pre-shared keys are used for device authentication; otherwise, the DN (distinguished name) fields in the certificate should be used. In 6.3, the identity type defaults to **address**, whereas in 7.0, it defaults to **auto**.

NOTE   The identity type must match on the two peers for authentication to proceed. And because the **isakmp identity** command is a global configuration command, all devices connected to your PIX/ASA also must use the same identity type.

Pre-Shared Key Authentication

The most common method of setting up device authentication on a PIX/ASA, at least with a small number of IPsec devices, is to use pre-shared keys.

For 6.3 L2L sessions, configuring pre-shared keys is done with the following command:

```
appliance(config)# isakmp key keystring address peer_IP_address
                   [netmask subnet_mask] [no-xauth]
                   [no-config-mode]
```

The pre-shared key can be an alphanumeric key up to 128 characters in length. You can wildcard the peer's address with a subnet mask, allowing multiple peers to share the same key, but Cisco doesn't recommend this practice unless the peers are acquiring their addressing information dynamically. The **no-xauth** and **no-config-mode** parameters were added in FOS 6.3. The **no-xauth** parameter specifies that user authentication should not be performed when this key is used (L2L connections) and the **no-config-mode** parameter specifies that IKE Mode config should not be performed (non-Cisco remote access clients).

For 7.0 L2L sessions, each L2L peer is associated with a tunnel group and the pre-shared key is configured in a subcommand mode:

```
appliance(config)# tunnel-group peer_IP_address type ipsec-l2l
appliance(config)# tunnel-group peer_IP_adress ipsec-attributes
appliance(config-ipsec)# pre-shared-key key_value
```

I'll save a more in-depth discussion of tunnel groups for the next chapter, "PIX and ASA Remote Access Connections," where it is more appropriate.

Certificate Authentication (CA)

Your second choice for device authentication is certificates. Cisco supports the following CA products on their PIX/ASA devices:

- Verisign
- Entrust
- Baltimore Technologies
- Microsoft Windows 2000/2003 Certificate Services (only a central design)
- Cisco IOS CS (7.0)
- Netscape (7.0)
- RSA (7.0)

The configuration of the PIX/ASA to obtain and use certificates is not very similar in 6.3 versus 7.0. In 7.0, the configuration is by and large the same that is performed on a Cisco IOS router. In both cases, though, you'll need to perform the following steps:

Step 1   Define a name and a domain name.

Step 2   Generate a public/private key pair.

Step 3 Specify a trustpoint.

Step 4 Obtain the root certificate.

Step 5 Create the PIX/ASA's PKCS #10 information and obtain an identity certificate.

Step 6 Verify and save your certificates and configuration information.

The following sections will discuss how to obtain, verify, and save certificate information if you are using a PIX running FOS 6.3 or earlier or a PIX/ASA running FOS 7.0 or later.

CA Configuration for 6.3

FOS 6.3 and earlier only supports SCEP to obtain certificates. The following commands outline what you need to do to obtain certificates for your 6.3 and earlier PIX:

```
pix(config)# hostname name
pix(config)# domain-name domain_name
pix(config)# ca generate rsa key {512 | 768 | 1024 | 2048}
pix(config)# show ca mypubkey rsa
pix(config)# ca identity CA_name [CA_ipaddress | hostname
                        [:ca_script_location]
                        [ldap_ip address|hostname]]
pix(config)# show ca identity
pix(config)# ca configure CA_name {ca | ra}
                        retry_period retry_count [crloptional]
pix(config)# show ca configure
pix(config)# ca authenticate CA_name [fingerprint]
pix(config)# ca subject-name CA_name X.500_string
pix(config)# ca enroll CA_name challenge_password [serial]
                        [ipaddress]
pix(config)# show ca certificate
pix(config)# ca crl request
pix(config)# show ca crl
pix(config)# ca save all
pix(config)# write memory
```

The **hostname** and **domain-name** commands are necessary to generate an RSA public/ private key pair. The **ca generate rsa key** command generates the public/private keys that will be used to sign and authenticate the PKCS #10 information sent to the CA via SCEP. The **show ca mypubkey rsa** command displays the PIX's public keys that have been configured.

The **ca identity** command specifies how the PIX should interact with the CA; you need to specify at least a name for the CA (typically a FQDN). If the name is not the same as the FQDN of the CA, you either need to specify one that is, or the IP address of the CA. In many instances, the CA product will require you to use a specific name for the CA. Also, you typically need to specify the script location that contains the SCEP software on the CA. The default location is "/cgi-bin/pkiclient.exe," which will not work with most CA products. For example, a Microsoft CA would require that you specify "/certsrv/mscep/mscep.dll."

The **show ca identity** command displays the configuration of the **ca identity** command. You can specify an LDAP IP address or hostname if the CA is publishing its CRL to an

LDAP server. The **ca configure** command, which is optional, allows you to specify parameters that affect the interaction with the CA or RA. The retry period specifies the amount of seconds that need to expire before recontacting a CA to obtain certificate information; the retry count specifies the maximum number of times to retry obtaining certificate information (this defaults to 0, meaning an infinite number of times); and **crloptional** indicates that using a CRL to validate a certificate is optional. The **show ca configure** command displays the configuration of the **ca configure** command.

The **ca authentication** command downloads the root certificate from the CA. If you don't know the fingerprint (signature) of the CA, you'll be prompted to verify this before accepting the root certificate; otherwise, if you've already obtained this from the CA, you can configure this command and have the PIX verify the root's signature automatically.

The **ca subject-name** command, which is optional, allows you to specify the X.500 information that should appear on the PIX's identity certificate, such as the OU (department), O (company), ST (state), C (country), and EA (e-mail address). Here's an example of the format of an X.500 string: "OU=mydept, O=dealgroup, ST=FL, C=USA, EA=rdeal2@cfl. rr.com," without the quotes. This command is new in FOS 6.3.

The **ca enroll** command obtains an identity certificate for the PIX via SCEP. The challenge password you enter is required. You should remember this because the CA administrator will require it if you need to revoke your certificate; also, this password can be used to automate the identity certificate enrollment process. You can optionally put the PIX's serial number or IP address on the identity certificate.

Once you have obtained the root and identity certificates, you can view them with the **show ca certificate** command. By default, the PIX will download the CRL periodically; however, if you suspect that your PIX doesn't have the most recent CRL, you can download it with the **ca crl request** command. You can view the CRL with the **show ca crl** command.

Upon completion, you need to save your configuration and certificate information. The **ca save all** command saves the public/private keys and certificate information to Flash memory. The **write memory** command saves the configuration commands necessary to interoperate with the CA, like **ca identity** and **ca configure**.

Example 21-1 illustrates how to prepare your PIX for certificates using FOS 6.3.

Example 21-1 *Using FOS 6.3 to Obtain Certificates*

```
pixfirewall(config)# hostname pix63
pix63(config)# domain-name thedealgroup.com
pix63(config)# ca generate rsa key 512
Keypair generation process begin.
Success.
pix63(config)# ca identity caserver
                    192.1.1.77:/certsrv/mscep/mscep.dll
pix63(config)# ca authenticate caserver
Certificate has the following attributes:
Fingerprint: ce9956aa c02d15df a2309a9c e059bd47
```

Example 21-1 *Using FOS 6.3 to Obtain Certificates (Continued)*

```
pix63(config)# ca subject-name caserver OU=mydept,
                              O=dealgroup, ST=FL, C=USA
pix63(config)# ca enroll caserver itsasecret
% Start certificate enrollment ..
% The subject name in the certificate will be: pix63.thedealgroup.com
% Certificate request sent to Certificate Authority
% The certificate request fingerprint will be displayed.
    Fingerprint:  33c1af83 7c8a2665 2c74e153 8cbd1a96
The certificate has been granted by CA!
pix63(config)# ca save all
pix63(config)# write memory
```

If you no longer want to use certificates, or need to change the modulus of your public/private keys and create new certificates, first you'll need to delete the old certificate and then the associated RSA public/private keys. To remove certificates and keys, use the following commands in the specified order:

```
pix(config)# clear ca identity CA_name
pix(config)# ca zeroize rsa
```

NOTE   Because certificates have a beginning and ending validation date, it is important that your PIX/ASA device has the correct time on it. This can be set manually with the **clock set** configuration command, but it is preferred to set it using NTP. The configuration of NTP on the PIX/ASA is beyond the scope of this book.

CA Configuration for 7.0

FOS 7.0 for the PIX and ASA supports both manual and SCEP enrollment. The configuration process is very similar to that of an IOS router, and doesn't look anything like what I described in the previous section for a PIX running FOS 6.3 or earlier. Because it is so similar to a Cisco router, I'll illustrate only two examples of the enrollment process: SCEP and manual (with cut-and-paste). You can refer to Chapter 16, "Router ISAKMP/IKE Phase 1 Connectivity," for a more detailed explanation of the commands.

NOTE   The commands used to configure a trustpoint and obtain certificates in FOS 6.3 also work with 7.0; but Cisco is moving toward a more IOS-style command convention in 7.0 and eventually will phase out the 6.3 **ca** commands.

Example 21-2 illustrates how to obtain the root and identity certificates via SCEP on a PIX/ASA running FOS 7.0. As you can see from the example, this is almost the same as doing it on a router. When generating a public/private key pair, you can specify either **rsa** or **dsa**, depending on your CA and its use of keys. Also, unlike on a router, if you don't specify the modulus in the command, it defaults to 512 (an IOS router will prompt you for the modulus). In this example, I created the key pair with a label, which I'll reference in the trustpoint configuration. The trustpoint configuration is very similar to a router's, using the **crypto ca trustpoint** command. Obtaining the root and identity certificates is mostly the same as a router with the **crypto ca authenticate** and **crypto ca enroll** commands. To view your certificates, use the **show crypto ca certificate** command. And as with a router, to save the certificate, keys, and configuration information, use the **write memory** or the **copy running-config startup-config** command; the **ca save all** command is no longer supported in FOS 7.0.

NOTE   You don't have to use a label for the RSA key pair, just like with IOS routers; however, I prefer to do this so that I can have different key pairs for different certificates, if needed. If you generate keys without a label, you don't need the **keypair** command in the trustpoint configuration. Also, you can use the **crypto key zeroize {rsa | dsa}** command to remove a specific RSA/DSA key label or all RSA/DSA keys. To remove certificates and CA interoperability, use the **no crypto ca trustpoint** command.

Example 21-2 *Using 7.0 on a PIX/ASA to Obtain Certificates via SCEP*

```
appliance(config)# hostname pix70
pix70(config)# domain-name thedealgroup.com
pix70(config)# crypto key generate rsa label certkeys modulus 512
INFO: The name for the keys will be: certkeys
Keypair generation process begin. Please wait...
pix70(config)# show crypto key mypubkey rsa
←output omitted→
pix70(config)# crypto ca trustpoint caserver
pix70(config-ca-trustpoint)# enrollment url
                      http://192.1.1.77/certsrv/mscep/mscep.dll
pix70(config-ca-trustpoint)# crl optional
pix70(config-ca-trustpoint)# enrollment retry period 1
pix70(config-ca-trustpoint)# enrollment retry count 10
pix70(config-ca-trustpoint)# subject-name CN=pix70.thedealgroup.com
pix70(config-ca-trustpoint)# keypair certkeys
pix70(config-ca-trustpoint)# exit
pix70(config)# crypto ca authenticate caserver
INFO: Certificate has the following attributes:
Fingerprint:    ce9956aa c02d15df a2309a9c e059bd47
Do you accept this certificate? [yes/no]: yes
Trustpoint CA certificate accepted.
pix70(config)# crypto ca enroll caserver
% Start certificate enrollment ..
% Create a challenge password. You will need to verbally provide
   this password to the CA Administrator in order to revoke your
   certificate. For security reasons your password will not be
   saved in the configuration. Please make a note of it.
```

Example 21-2 *Using 7.0 on a PIX/ASA to Obtain Certificates via SCEP (Continued)*

```
Password: itsasecret
Re-enter password: itsasecret
% The subject name in the certificate will be:
   CN=pix70.thedealgroup.com
% The fully-qualified domain name in the certificate will be:
   pix70.thedealgroup.com
% Include the device serial number in the subject name? [yes/no]: no
Request certificate from CA? [yes/no]: yes
% Certificate request sent to Certificate Authority
The certificate has been granted by CA!
pix70(config)# show crypto ca certificate
←output omitted→
pix70(config)# write memory
```

Here is an explanation of the trustpoint configuration commands:

- **enrollment {terminal | url** *URL*}—Specifies the enrollment mode (manual or SCEP).

- **crl {required | optional | nocheck}**—Specifies whether or not CRLs are used.

- **fqdn** *FQDN_of_appliance*—Specifies the fully qualified domain name to use for the enrollment certificate instead of the values from the **hostname** and **domain-name** commands.

- **email** *email_address*—specifies the e-mail address to use for the enrollment certificate.

- **subject-name** *X.500_values*—specifies the X.500 values, such as CN, OU, O, and others, to use for the enrollment certificate.

- **serial-number**—Specifies that the serial number of the appliance should be used during the enrollment process.

- **ip-address** *IP_address*—Specifies the IP address to use during the enrollment process.

- **password** *passphrase*—Specifies the challenge password to use during SCEP registration or, once a certificate is obtained, to revoke it.

- **keypair** *key_label_name*—Specifies the RSA/DSA key pair to use during the certificate enrollment process.

- **id-cert-issuer**—Specifies whether the appliance will accept peer certificates issued by the CA associated with the configured trustpoint (by default, yes).

- **accept-subordinates**—Specifies whether the appliance will accept certificates from subordinate CAs during ISAKMP/IKE Phase 1, when the subordinate CA certificates are not installed on the appliance (by default, yes).

- **support-user-cert-validation**—Specifies whether the appliance will validate remote peer certificates with the currently configured CA (by default, yes).

Example 21-3 illustrates how to use the manual approach: generating the PKCS #10 information on your PIX/ASA and then importing the certificates the CA sends you. Up until the **crypto ca trustpoint** command, the configuration is the same as in Example 21-2. In the trustpoint configuration, the only main difference is the **enrollment** command, which specifies that the terminal (**terminal** parameter) will be used instead of SCEP (**url** parameter). At this point, you don't have to import the root certificate first, but can go ahead and start the enrollment process by generating your PIX/ASA's PKCS #10 information (**crypto ca enroll** command). In Example 21-3, however, I already had the root certificate, so I went and imported it here. Using the **crypto ca authenticate** command allows you to cut and paste the root certificate into your PIX/ASA; after cutting and pasting the root certificate into the terminal session to your PIX/ASA, on a blank line type in the **quit** command and then press the <ENTER> key to import the root certificate. The **crypto ca enroll** command creates your PKCS #10 information, which you need to send to the CA. The CA administrator will use this to create the PIX/ASA's X.509 identity certificate and send this back to you. The **crypto ca import** command allows you to import the identity certificate from the terminal (using cut-and-paste). The **show crypto ca certificate** command displays the certificates on the PIX/ASA. Last, I saved the PIX/ASA's configuration, keying, and certificate information.

Example 21-3 *Using 7.0 on a PIX/ASA to Obtain Certificates via Cut-and-Paste*

```
pixfirewall(config)# hostname pix70
pix70(config)# domain-name thedealgroup.com
pix70(config)# crypto key generate rsa label certkeys modulus 512
INFO: The name for the keys will be: certkeys
Keypair generation process begin. Please wait...
pix70(config)# crypto ca trustpoint caserver
pix70(config-ca-trustpoint)# enrollment terminal
pix70(config-ca-trustpoint)# crl optional
pix70(config-ca-trustpoint)# subject-name CN=pix70.thedealgroup.com
pix70(config-ca-trustpoint)# keypair certkeys
pix70(config-ca-trustpoint)# exit
pix70(config)# crypto ca authenticate caserver
Enter the base 64 encoded CA certificate.
End with a blank line or the word "quit" on a line by itself
-----BEGIN CERTIFICATE-----
MIIChTCCAe6gAwIBAgIQbr1TulXC0phB4KDUjkDPljANBgkqhkiG9w0BAQUFADAg
←output omitted→
BX3p1Wxz+tSEQwrChIzbHcFAUP1Gq0dpBQ==
-----END CERTIFICATE-----
quit
INFO: Certificate has the following attributes:
Fingerprint:     ce9956aa c02d15df a2309a9c e059bd47
Do you accept this certificate? [yes/no]: yes
Trustpoint CA certificate accepted.
% Certificate successfully imported
pix70(config)# crypto ca enroll caserver
% Start certificate enrollment ..
% The subject name in the certificate will be: CN=pix70.thedealgroup.com
```

Example 21-3 *Using 7.0 on a PIX/ASA to Obtain Certificates via Cut-and-Paste (Continued)*

```
% The fully-qualified domain name in the certificate will be:
     pix70.thedealgroup.com
% Include the device serial number in the subject name? [yes/no]: no
Display Certificate Request to terminal? [yes/no]: yes
Certificate Request follows:
MIIBQzCB7gIBADBIMR8wHQYDVQQDExZwaXg3MC50aGVkZWFsZ3JvdXAuY29tMSUw
IwYJKoZIhvcNAQkCFhZwaXg3MC50aGVkZWFsZ3JvdXAuY29tMFwwDQYJKoZIhvcN
AQEBBQADSwAwSAJBALKJho6w+fJtIG8Vok6lGaoGqwWPvsg0/p0TALlVzCPwkYBy
2vVN9m8T5XI4PQTvoAUv6cUtvvkGi/dxyspVm60CAwEAAaBBMD8GCSqGSIb3DQEJ
DjEyMDAwCwYDVR0PBAQDAgWgMCEGA1UdEQQaMBiCFnBpeDcwLnRoZWRlYWxncm91
cC5jb20wDQYJKoZIhvcNAQEEBQADQQCvTroxRLG3C2NU3gv/deUggTDnSj2IFz4q
NhlWinSioX1D05q66YXjueKz+iNSSeNoKtvU9vUo0eNY4xovjtS+
---End - This line not part of the certificate request---
Redisplay enrollment request? [yes/no]: no
pix70(config)# crypto ca import caserver certificate
% The fully-qualified domain name in the certificate will be:
     pix70.thedealgroup.com
Enter the base 64 encoded certificate.
End with a blank line or the word "quit" on a line by itself
-----BEGIN CERTIFICATE-----
MIIDRTCCAq6gAwIBAgIKYQoE8AABAAAAIzANBgkqhkiG9w0BAQUFADAgMQswCQYD
←output omitted→
U9wt0p0NCoZhb6iAPTW37APBnUiihTiUTw==
-----END CERTIFICATE-----
quit
INFO: Certificate successfully imported
pix70(config)# show crypto ca certificate
←output omitted→
pix70(config)# copy running-config startup-config
```

NOTE   You can back up your identity certificate and keys with the **crypto ca export** command, which backs up the information in a PKCS #12 format. The information is password-protected and displayed on the terminal. You can then cut and paste this information into a file in a safe place. This can then be re-imported on the PIX/ASA later if you need to recover your PIX/ASA's certificate information.

Certificate Validation

In FOS 6.3 and later, you can specify which components have to be on a peer's certificate before the PIX/ASA will validate it. This feature adds an additional layer of security for preventing a man-in-the-middle attack. With certificate verification, you can specify the distinguished name (DN) value the certificate must contain (the various fields and their values on the peer's identity certificate).

The fields and values that you require are defined with the following command in FOS 6.3:

```
appliance(config)# ca verifycertdn X.500_string
```

In FOS 7.0, this command is preceded by "crypto": **crypto ca verifycertdn**.

If you wanted to accept only certificates that had a CN that contained "corp," an OU that is "engineering," an O that is "dealgroup," an ST that is "FL," and a C that is "US," you would use this command in 7.0:

```
appliance(config)# crypto ca verifycertdn cn*corp, ou=engineering,
                        o=dealgroup, st=FL, c=US
```

The "*" between the field name and a parameter states that the field should contain the following value. For "*corp," this string could be included in words such as "incorporate," "engcorp," and "corporate," where all three values contain "corp." Normally this command is used with a public CA, where other companies also are using the same CA, but you want to restrict the PIX/ASA to accepting certificates only from devices within your organization or a trusted third-party company.

NOTE   Please note that you can enter the [**crypto**] **ca verifycertdn** command only once, which must encompass all certificates that your PIX/ASA will accept. Also, in 7.0, when you execute the **ca verifycertdn** command, you get a warning to use the **crypto ca verifycertdn** command; however, I found that in the initial release of 7.0, this command doesn't exist! On top of that, no matter what you enter for the **ca verifycertdn** command, in 7.0 it looks like it takes the command, gives the warning, but when you execute the **show running-config** command, it doesn't appear in the output! Based on this, apparently this feature isn't quite working in the initial release of FOS 7.0, which contradicts Cisco documentation.

7.0 and CRL Configuration Options

In FOS 7.0, Cisco added enhancements to the use of CRLs, similar to what the concentrators could do for quite some time. By default, a PIX/ASA will locate the CRL by using the URL on the CA's (root) certificate. Of course, this can present a problem if you're concerned about redundancy where you have a CA and multiple RAs, and the CA fails; no device will be able to obtain the CRL. Likewise, using the CA to download a CRL puts an additional processing burden on the CA. You can place the CRL in other locations, most commonly in an LDAP directory structure; but by default, the PIX/ASA doesn't know about the additional location. In 7.0, you have the flexibility to define when a CRL is used and where the CRL should be obtained. Here is the basic configuration to perform this task:

```
appliance(config)# crypto ca trustpoint CA_name
appliance(config-ca-trustpoint)# crl configure
appliance(config-ca-crl)# default
appliance(config-ca-crl)# policy {cdp | static | both}
appliance(config-ca-crl)# url {1-5} URL
appliance(config-ca-crl)# protocol {http | ldap | scep}
appliance(config-ca-crl)# ldap-defaults server_name_or_IP_address
                        [port_#]
appliance(config-ca-crl)# ldap-dn admin_X.500_DN password
appliance(config-ca-crl)# cache-time minutes
appliance(config-ca-crl)# [no] enforcenextupdate
```

```
appliance(config-ca-crl)# exit
appliance(config-ca-trustpoint)# exit
appliance(config)# crypto ca crl request CA_name
appliance(config)# show crypto ca crls
```

The **crypto ca trustpoint** command takes you into the trustpoint subcommand mode. The **crl configure** command then takes you into the CRL subcommand mode. The **default** command resets the CRL configuration on the appliance back to the defaults. The **policy** command specifies where the PIX/ASA should obtain its CRL:

- **cdp**—From the CRL distribution point (CDP) on the CA's certificate.

- **static**—From URLs you define statically.

- **both**—From the CDP, if it's reachable, otherwise the static definitions.

For static URL definitions, use the **url** command to define CRL locations. You can specify up to 5 CRL locations using a URL syntax, where each location must have a number associated with it (**1–5**). The number is used by the PIX/ASA to prioritize the entries, with 1 being the highest.

In the preceding code, the **protocol** command specifies the protocol to use to retrieve the CRL. For LDAP interactions, the **ldap-defaults** command specifies the name or IP address of the LDAP server and optionally the port number to use; the **ldap-dn** command specifies the X.500 DN settings and password to use, if the LDAP server requires authentication. The DN information is in this type of format: "CN=value,OU=value,O=value."

The **cache-time** command specifies, in minutes, how long a CRL is to be cached locally before the PIX/ASA downloads a new one. The default is 60 minutes, but the value can range from 1–1,440 minutes. However, if the "NextUpdate" field in the CRL is not specified, the PIX/ASA never will cache the CRL, but always will obtain it when needed. On the PIX/ASA, you can require this field in the CRL with the **enforcenextupdate** command, which is the default. Using the **no** parameter with this command disables this requirement.

ISAKMP/IKE Phase 2 Data Connections

This part of the chapter will discuss the components you need to configure for the Phase 2 data connections in an IPsec L2L session for your PIX/ASA security appliance. This includes specifying what traffic to protect and how it should be protected. If you've configured L2L sessions on routers, the process and commands described here will be nothing new to you.

NOTE   Please note that even though Cisco has added many IPsec enhancements in 7.0, the PIX/ASA still lags behind routers when it comes to deploying scalable L2L IPsec sessions. For instance, 7.0 doesn't support advanced QoS, GRE tunnels, or DMVPN. Therefore, I typically use the PIX/ASA with a small number of L2L sessions where I need advanced address translation configurations, or want to enhance the security of the IPsec implementation.

Specifying Traffic to Protect

ACLs are used to specify what traffic is to be protected for an IPsec session to a particular peer, commonly called a crypto ACL:

```
appliance(config)# access-list ACL_name_or_# {permit | deny}
                       protocol_name_or_#
                       src_IP src_subnet_mask [protocol_info]
                       dst_IP dst_subnet_mask [protocol_info]
```

Any ACL command in the grouping that has a **permit** statement specifies traffic to be protected, whereas a **deny** or implicit deny statement specifies traffic that doesn't have to be protected. Unlike on an IOS router, PIX/ASA ACLs use a subnet mask to match on a range of addresses, whereas routers use a wildcard (inverted) mask. The source IP address/network specifies locations connected to the local PIX/ASA and the destination IP address/network specifies locations connected to the remote peer.

CAUTION As with IOS routers, you should be very careful about using the keyword **any** (0.0.0.0/0) for the source or destination address in a crypto ACL, because this includes broadcast and multicast addresses and can cause certain data transmissions to fail. Therefore, you should be as specific as possible concerning what traffic is to be protected.

Defining How to Protect Traffic

As with IOS routers, a transform set is used to specify how traffic is to be protected. How this is configured is similar to configuration for a Cisco IOS router. Here are the commands to create a transform set on a PIX/ASA:

```
appliance(config)# crypto ipsec transform-set transform_set_name
                       transform1 [transform2 [transform3]]
appliance(config)# [no] crypto ipsec transform-set transform_set_name
                       mode transport
```

Each transform set must have a unique name. Within each set, you define between one to three transforms: one for AH authentication, one for ESP authentication, and one for ESP encryption. Here are the valid transform names: **ah-md5-hmac**, **ah-sha-hmac**, **esp-md5-hmac**, **esp-sha-hmac**, **esp-des**, **esp-3des**, **esp-aes** (128-bit), **esp-aes-192**, **esp-aes-256**, and **esp-null** (no encryption). The default connection mode of the transform is tunnel. This can be changed with the **mode** parameter after you already have created a transform set (this is different from a router, where the mode is configured in the transform set's subcommand mode). You can use the **show crypto ipsec transform-set** command in 6.3 to view your configured transform sets. In 7.0, use the **show running-config crypto** command.

NOTE	Here are some important items concerning the use of transform sets on PIX/ASA security appliances:

- AES encryption was added in FOS 6.3.

- AH transforms are not supported in FOS 7.0.

- A transform of DES and SHA no longer is supported in any current versions of the FOS software.

Building Crypto Maps

As with IOS routers, the function of a crypto map is to bring all the necessary information together to build an IPsec session to a remote peer. And like IOS routers, security appliances support two types of crypto maps:

- **Static**—Used for L2L sessions where the remote peer information is known.

- **Dynamic**—Used for L2L sessions where most of the remote peer information is unknown, or for remote access sessions.

The following two sections will discuss the configuration of both of these, which is very similar to the configuration of crypto maps on IOS routers.

Static Crypto Maps

Static crypto maps are used for L2L sessions where the peer's IP address and the traffic to be protected is known. For each destination and session, a separate crypto map entry is used. There are two types of static crypto map entries: ISAKMP and manual. ISAKMP entries use ISAKMP/IKE to build a management connection, generate keying information for the management connection, build the data connections, generate keying information for the data connections, and refresh the keying information periodically for both sets of connections. Manual crypto map entries do not use ISAKMP/IKE. With these types of entries, no management connection is needed and you specify the connection information manually for the two unidirectional data connections, including any encryption and HMAC keys.

Creating a static crypto map entry that uses ISAKMP/IKE to build the IPsec session involves the following commands:

```
appliance(config)# crypto map map_name seq_# ipsec-isakmp
appliance(config)# crypto map map_name seq_# match address ACL_name
appliance(config)# crypto map map_name seq_# set peer IP_address
appliance(config)# crypto map map_name seq_# set transform-set
                        trans_name1 [trans_name2...trans_name6]
appliance(config)# crypto map map_name seq_# set security-association
                        lifetime {seconds seconds |
                        kilobytes kilobytes}
```

```
appliance(config)# crypto map map_name seq_# set pfs
                     [group1 | group2 | group5 | group7]
appliance(config)# crypto map map_name seq_# set connection-type
                     {answer-only | originate-only |
                      bidirectional}
appliance(config)# crypto map map_name seq_# set inheritance
                     {data | rule}
appliance(config)# crypto map map_name seq_# set nat-t-disable
appliance(config)# crypto map map_name seq_# set phase1mode
                     {main | aggressive [group1 | group2 | group5 |
                      group7]}
appliance(config)# crypto map map_name seq_# set reverse-route
appliance(config)# crypto map map_name seq_# set trustpoint
                     CA_name [chain]
```

The **crypto map** command creates a static crypto map. All entries in the map must use the same crypto map name, where each entry is given a unique sequence number within the crypto map. An entry represents a session to a remote peer. An entry might have multiple parameters associated with it, where the map name and sequence number are the same for the entry's parameters. As with Cisco routers, the lower the sequence number, the higher the priority, where sequence numbers can range from 1–10,000.

NOTE Unlike with Cisco routers, there is no subcommand mode for the parameters for a particular entry; all **crypto map** commands on the PIX/ASA are global commands.

In the preceding code, note that the **ipsec-isakmp** parameter specifies that ISAKMP/IKE will be used to build and manage the Phase 1 and 2 connections (required).

The **match address** parameter specifies the ACL name of the traffic to be protected (required). The **set peer** command specifies the IP address or name (FQDN) of the remote peer (required). In 6.3, you can specify up to 6 peers by executing this command six times; with 7.0, this has been expanded to 10 peers. By specifying multiple peers, the first peer configured becomes the primary and the second and other peers are backup peers. The **set transform-set** parameter specifies the transform set name to use to protect the traffic to the remote peer (required); you can specify up to six transform sets, where the order you enter them is the order in which they're processed. Therefore, put the most secure one first.

All the remaining parameters in the previous code are optional. The **set security-association lifetime** parameter changes the default lifetime of the data connections. In seconds, the default is 28,800 seconds and the amount of traffic transmitted is 4,608,000KB. This value overrides the global value that is configured with the **crypto ipsec security-association lifetime** command (preface this command with **show** to see the configured global lifetime values).

The **set pfs** command enables Perfect Forward Secrecy (PFS), which uses Diffie-Hellman (DH) to share the keys instead of the existing management connection. Group 5 keys were added in FOS 6.3 and Group 7 in 7.0. Of the four types, Group 5 is the most secure.

The remainder commands in the previous command list were added in FOS 7.0. The **set connection-type** parameter specifies which end will initiate the IPsec session. For a hub device, you would set it to **answer-only** for each peer entry and for a spoke device, **originate-only**; if you don't care which side initiates the session, use **bidirectional**. However, if the originating end is acquiring its address dynamically, the originating end would specify **originate-only** and the remote end **answer-only**.

The **set inheritance** parameter controls how many SAs are created per peer; the default is **rule**, which creates one SA in each direction to the peer—**data** creates a separate set of SAs per address pair, where the addresses are devices (not the appliances) transmitting actual user data. Using the latter parameter can generate a lot of SAs and overhead on the appliances and should be used only with very security-sensitive applications with short lifetimes associated with them. This parameter can be used only by the initiator of the IPsec session.

NAT-T was introduced in FOS 6.3 and is enabled by default; the **set nat-t-disable** parameter allows you to disable it for a peer (entry). The **set phase1 mode** parameter specifies the mode to use when initiating an IPsec session with a peer. The default is main mode. If you specify aggressive mode, you can override the DH key group to use; otherwise DH key group 2 is used. The **set reverse-route** parameter enables RRI, where the appliance will place static routes in its routing table for the remote networks and then automatically advertise these, via OSPF, to any connected private network. Normally this is used with remote access clients but can be used with L2L sessions, assuming you've configured OSPF on your PIX and internal routing devices.

Last, note that the **set trustpoint** parameter specifies the CA to use for the particular peer. It is used only when the appliance initiates a session. This is necessary only if you are using more than one CA. The **chain** parameter specifies that the complete CA chain of certificates, in a hierarchical implementation, is sent to the remote peer (this is disabled by default). The responder side can implement this feature, but this requires the configuration of a tunnel group, which I'll discuss in Chapter 22, "PIX and ASA Remote Access Connections."

In FOS 6.3, you can use the **show crypto map** command to view the static crypto maps configured on your PIX/ASA. In 7.0, use the **show running-config crypto** command to see your **crypto map** and other **crypto** commands.

NOTE	A manual crypto map entry is used for a remote peer when there are ISAKMP/IKE compatibility issues with the two peers. This feature was added in FOS 6.3 and then removed in FOS 7.0. Because of this, I won't cover manual crypto map entries for PIX/ASA security appliances.

Dynamic Crypto Maps

Dynamic crypto maps typically are used for remote access sessions; however, they also can be used for L2L sessions where the remote peer's information won't be known until it connects (for example, when the remote peer is assigned an IP address dynamically by the ISP). Dynamic crypto maps can be used only on a peer that will be accepting, not initiating, connections from peers; and in any configuration, one peer can use a dynamic crypto map, but the other peer must use a static crypto map.

Dynamic crypto maps and their configurations are very similar to those of IOS-based routers. A dynamic crypto map has multiple entries: typically one for L2L sessions and one for remote access users (or perhaps just one). The dynamic crypto map is then referenced within a static crypto map as an entry in the static map. When a remote peer builds a connection to your appliance and the dynamic map is used to build the session, the information about the session is placed in the static map as a temporary entry, and then removed upon termination of the connection.

Here are the PIX/ASA commands to create a dynamic crypto map:

```
appliance(config)# crypto dynamic-map map_name seq_# match
                     address ACL_name
appliance(config)# crypto dynamic-map map_name seq_# set
                     peer IP_address
appliance(config)# crypto dynamic-map map_name seq_# set
                     transform-set trans_name1
                     [trans_name2...trans_name6]
appliance(config)# crypto dynamic-map map_name seq_# set
                     security-association lifetime
                     {seconds seconds | kilobytes kilobytes}
appliance(config)# crypto dynamic-map map_name seq_# set pfs
                     [group1 | group2 | group5 | group7]
appliance(config)# crypto dynamic-map map_name seq_# set
                     nat-t-disable
appliance(config)# crypto dynamic-map map_name seq_# set
                     reverse-route
```

As you can see from the above commands, configuring a dynamic crypto map is similar to configuring a static one. Each dynamic crypto map needs to have a unique dynamic crypto map name. In FOS 6.3, you can use the **show crypto dynamic-map** command to view the dynamic crypto maps configured on your PIX/ASA.

TIP   It is possible to use the same map name for a dynamic and static map, but this creates confusion for the novice administrator implementing a VPN. Typically I put the term "stat" in the name of the static map and "dyn" in the dynamic crypto map, like "statmap" and "dynmap," respectively.

Only one command parameter is required for the dynamic crypto map entry: **set transform-set**. All of the other parameters are optional and were discussed in the previous section.

Once you've created your dynamic crypto map, like an IOS-based router, you need to reference it as an entry within your static crypto map:

```
appliance(config)# crypto map static_map_name seq_# ipsec-isakmp
                     dynamic dynamic_map_name
```

NOTE   The sequence number for the reference should be the highest number (lowest priority) of all of the entries in your static map: you want your known peers to use the specific static entries and unknown peers to use the dynamic crypto map reference.

Activating a Crypto Map

Once you have created your static crypto map (and possible dynamic crypto map references), the static map won't be used until you activate it on the appliance's interface(s):

```
appliance(config)# crypto map static_map_name
                     interface interface_name
```

The name of the interface is the logical interface name on the PIX/ASA, like "outside" or "inside" and **not** the physical interface name, like "ethernet0" or "ethernet1."

Data Connection Management Commands

There are various appliance commands you can use to monitor and maintain your IPsec sessions. Here are the **show** commands you can use:

- **show isakmp sa**—Displays the management connections.
- **show crypto ipsec sa**—Displays the data connections.

I'll discuss these commands and their output in more depth in Chapter 23, "Troubleshooting PIX and ASA Connections."

You can use the following commands to clear IPsec connections and sessions:

```
appliance(config)# crypto map map_name interface interface_name
appliance(config)# clear [crypto] isakmp sa
appliance(config)# clear [crypto] ipsec sa
                     [{peer IP_address | map map_name |
                     entry dest_IP protocol SPI_value}
```

The **crypto map interface** command will reinitialize the SA and security policy databases. The **clear isakmp sa** command tears down all of the Phase 1 management connections. The **clear ipsec sa** command deletes one or more Phase 2 data SAs. In FOS 7.0, the additional **clear** commands were added:

- **clear configure crypto**—Deletes all IPsec commands: crypto maps, IPsec, and ISAKMP configurations.
- **clear configure crypto ca trustpoint**—Deletes all certificate trustpoint configurations.

- **clear configure crypto dynamic-map**—Deletes all dynamic crypto map configurations.
- **clear configure iskamp**—Deletes all ISAKMP commands.
- **clear configure isakmp policy**—Deletes a specific ISAKMP policy or all policies.

Differences between FOS 6.3 and 7.0

FOS 7.0 adds many features that the 6.3 and earlier FOS versions lacked; however, for the PIX novice who just started getting used to FOS 6.3 and then upgraded to 7.0, you'll see that the commands have not always been preserved from the older to the newer version. For example, if I want to view the Phase 1 management connections, in FOS 6.3 it's **show iskamp policy**; but in FOS 7.0 it's **show running-config isakmp**. Or if I want to configure a pre-shared key in 6.3, it's **isakmp key**. In contrast, in FOS 7.0 it's configured in a tunnel group with the **pre-shared-key** command.

These configuration differences make it very confusing for a novice, and also frustrating for an expert with PIXs, like myself: I'm constantly using the old-style 6.3 syntax on 7.0 appliances, and it's going to take me a while to become accustomed to the new syntax. On top of that, even though the 7.0 CLI is much more similar to an IOS CLI than version 6.3, there is still not a synchronization of the commands between the two platforms. For example, to delete management connections on a 7.0 appliance, you would use **clear [crypto] isakmp sa**; but on an IOS router you would use **clear crypto isakmp**, omitting the **sa**. I had hoped that Cisco would rectify this on the security appliances in 7.0, making it easy for IOS router experts, but alas, Cisco hasn't quite reached this point.

L2L Connection Examples

Now that you have a basic understanding of the commands used to build L2L IPsec sessions on a PIX/ASA appliance, I'll show you a couple of examples that illustrate the configurations. The first example will be based on FOS 6.3 for the PIX appliances and the second example on 7.0. I'll use the same situation in both examples, shown in Figure 21-1. In the figure, one PIX functions as a hub and two PIXs as spokes connecting to the central site via the hub PIX.

Figure 21-1 *L2L Simple Hub-and-Spoke Design*

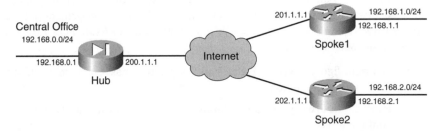

FOS 6.3 L2L Example

Examples 21-4, 21-5, and 21-6 illustrate the configuration of the hub and two-spoke PIXs using FOS 6.3. Each example contains reference numbers, which are explained following the specific example.

Example 21-4 *Hub Configuration in FOS 6.3*

```
hub(config)# ip address outside 200.1.1.1 255.255.255.0
hub(config)# ip address inside 192.168.0.1 255.255.255.0
hub(config)# route outside 0.0.0.0 0.0.0.0 200.1.1.2 1
hub(config)# access-list nonat permit ip                          (1)
                    192.168.0.0 255.255.255.0
                    192.168.1.0 255.255.255.0
hub(config)# access-list nonat permit ip
                    192.168.0.0 255.255.255.0
                    192.168.2.0 255.255.255.0
hub(config)# nat (inside) 0 access-list nonat
hub(config)# sysopt connection permit-ipsec                       (2)
hub(config)# isakmp enable outside                                (3)
hub(config)# isakmp identity address
hub(config)# isakmp policy 10 authentication pre-share
hub(config)# isakmp policy 10 encryption aes
hub(config)# isakmp policy 10 hash sha
hub(config)# isakmp policy 10 group 2
hub(config)# isakmp keepalive 20 3
hub(config)# isakmp key cisco123 address 201.1.1.1               (4)
                    netmask 255.255.255.255
                    no-xauth no-config-mode
hub(config)# isakmp key cisco123 address 202.1.1.1
                    netmask 255.255.255.255
                    no-xauth no-config-mode
hub(config)# access-list 101 permit ip                           (5)
                    192.168.0.0 255.255.255.0
                    192.168.1.0 255.255.255.0
hub(config)# access-list 102 permit ip
                    192.168.0.0 255.255.255.0
                    192.168.2.0 255.255.255.0
hub(config)# crypto ipsec transform-set mytrans                  (6)
                    esp-aes esp-sha-hmac
hub(config)# crypto map mymap 20 ipsec-isakmp                    (7)
hub(config)# crypto map mymap 20 match address 101
hub(config)# crypto map mymap 20 set peer 201.1.1.1
hub(config)# crypto map mymap 20 set transform-set mytrans
hub(config)# crypto map mymap 30 ipsec-isakmp                    (8)
hub(config)# crypto map mymap 30 match address 102
hub(config)# crypto map mymap 30 set peer 202.1.1.1
hub(config)# crypto map mymap 30 set transform-set mytrans
hub(config)# crypto map mymap interface outside                  (9)
```

Here's a brief explanation of the hub's configuration in Example 21-4:

1 I'm disabling address translation between the local network (192.168.0.0/24) and the two remote networks (192.168.1.0/24 and 192.168.2.0/24).

2 IPsec traffic is being bypassed from the ACL check.

3 This is the Phase 1 configuration, with ISAKMP being enabled on the outside interface and one ISAKMP policy defined to protect the management connection to the two spokes.

4 The pre-shared keys are defined for the two spoke routers.

5 Two crypto ACLs are created for the two respective spokes: 101 is for spoke1 and 102 is for spoke2.

6 A transform set is defined to protect the data SAs.

7 A crypto map entry is defined for spoke1.

8 A crypto map entry is defined for spoke2.

9 The crypto map is activated on the hub's outside interface.

As you can see from Example 21-4, configuring the PIX for L2L sessions is somewhat similar to configuring IOS routers. The configuration of the two spokes in Examples 21-5 and 21-6 is very similar to the hub configuration.

Example 21-5 *Spoke1 Configuration in FOS 6.3*

```
spoke1(config)# ip address outside 201.1.1.1 255.255.255.0
spoke1(config)# ip address inside 192.168.1.1 255.255.255.0
spoke1(config)# route outside 0.0.0.0 0.0.0.0 201.1.1.2 1
spoke1(config)# access-list nonat permit ip 192.168.1.0 255.255.255.0
                                            192.168.0.0 255.255.255.0
spoke1(config)# nat (inside) 0 access-list nonat
spoke1(config)# sysopt connection permit-ipsec
spoke1(config)# isakmp enable outside
spoke1(config)# isakmp identity address
spoke1(config)# isakmp policy 10 authentication pre-share
spoke1(config)# isakmp policy 10 encryption aes
spoke1(config)# isakmp policy 10 hash sha
spoke1(config)# isakmp policy 10 group 2
spoke1(config)# isakmp key cisco123 address 200.1.1.1
                           netmask 255.255.255.255
                           no-xauth no-config-mode
spoke1(config)# isakmp keepalive 20 3
spoke1(config)# access-list 101 permit ip 192.168.1.0 255.255.255.0
                                          192.168.0.0 255.255.255.0
spoke1(config)# crypto ipsec transform-set mytrans
                        esp-aes esp-sha-hmac
spoke1(config)# crypto map mymap 10 ipsec-isakmp
spoke1(config)# crypto map mymap 10 match address 101
spoke1(config)# crypto map mymap 10 set peer 200.1.1.1
spoke1(config)# crypto map mymap 10 set transform-set mytrans
spoke1(config)# crypto map mymap interface outside
```

Example 21-6 *Spoke2 Configuration in FOS 6.3*

```
spoke2(config)# ip address outside 202.1.1.1 255.255.255.0
spoke2(config)# ip address inside 192.168.2.1 255.255.255.0
spoke2(config)# route outside 0.0.0.0 0.0.0.0 202.1.1.2 1
spoke2(config)# access-list nonat permit ip 192.168.2.0 255.255.255.0
                                           192.168.0.0 255.255.255.0
spoke2(config)# nat (inside) 0 access-list nonat
spoke2(config)# sysopt connection permit-ipsec
spoke2(config)# isakmp enable outside
spoke2(config)# isakmp identity address
spoke2(config)# isakmp policy 10 authentication pre-share
spoke2(config)# isakmp policy 10 encryption aes
spoke2(config)# isakmp policy 10 hash sha
spoke2(config)# isakmp policy 10 group 2
spoke2(config)# isakmp key cisco123 address 200.1.1.1
                          netmask 255.255.255.255
                          no-xauth no-config-mode
spoke2(config)# isakmp keepalive 20 3
spoke2(config)# access-list 101 permit ip 192.168.2.0 255.255.255.0
                                          192.168.0.0 255.255.255.0
spoke2(config)# crypto ipsec transform-set mytrans
                          esp-aes esp-sha-hmac
spoke2(config)# crypto map mymap 10 ipsec-isakmp
spoke2(config)# crypto map mymap 10 match address 102
spoke2(config)# crypto map mymap 10 set peer 200.1.1.1
spoke2(config)# crypto map mymap 10 set transform-set mytrans
spoke2(config)# crypto map mymap interface outside
```

FOS 7.0 L2L Example

The main problem with the last example is that the two spokes, if they need to send traffic to each other, cannot do this through the hub. If you recall earlier from the "Transmitting IPsec Traffic Between Multiple Interfaces with the Same Security Level" section, traffic cannot be transmitted between the spokes via the hub because traffic enters the hub on the outside interface and leaves it on the same interface, which is not allowed in FOS 6.3 and earlier. In this situation, you would have to build an L2L session directly between the two spokes to overcome this problem.

FOS 7.0 resolves this issue. Using the same network in Figure 21-1, I'll redo the configuration of the three PIXs. In this example, the FOS level on the spokes doesn't matter: only the hub needs to be running 7.0. Example 21-7 illustrates the hub's configuration. Within the configuration are references which are explained following the example.

Example 21-7 *Hub Configuration in FOS 7.0*

```
hub(config)# interface Ethernet0
hub(config-if)# nameif outside
hub(config-if)# security-level 0
hub(config-if)# ip address 200.1.1.1 255.255.255.0
hub(config-if)# exit
```

continues

Example 21-7 *Hub Configuration in FOS 7.0 (Continued)*

```
hub(config)# interface Ethernet1
hub(config-if)# nameif inside
hub(config-if)# security-level 100
hub(config-if)# ip address 192.168.0.1 255.255.255.0
hub(config-if)# exit
hub(config)# route outside 0.0.0.0 0.0.0.0 200.1.1.2 1
hub(config)# same-security-traffic permit intra-interface          (1)
hub(config)# sysopt connection permit-ipsec
hub(config)# isakmp enable outside
hub(config)# isakmp policy 10 authentication pre-share
hub(config)# isakmp policy 10 encryption aes
hub(config)# isakmp policy 10 hash sha
hub(config)# isakmp policy 10 group 2
hub(config)# isakmp policy 10 lifetime 86400
hub(config)# access-list nonat extended permit ip                  (2)
                  192.168.0.0 255.255.255.0
                  192.168.1.0 255.255.255.0
hub(config)# access-list nonat extended permit ip
                  192.168.0.0 255.255.255.0
                  192.168.2.0 255.255.255.0
hub(config)# nat (inside) 0 access-list nonat
hub(config)# tunnel-group 192.1.1.40 type ipsec-l2l               (3)
hub(config)# tunnel-group 192.1.1.40 ipsec-attributes
hub(config-ipsec)# pre-shared-key cisco123
hub(config-ipsec)# isakmp keepalive threshold 20 retry 3
hub(config-ipsec)# exit
hub(config)# tunnel-group 192.1.1.42 type ipsec-l2l
hub(config)# tunnel-group 192.1.1.42 ipsec-attributes
hub(config-ipsec)# pre-shared-key cisco123
hub(config-ipsec)# isakmp keepalive threshold 20 retry 3
hub(config-ipsec)# exit
hub(config)# access-list 101 extended permit ip                   (4)
                  192.168.0.0 255.255.255.0
                  192.168.1.0 255.255.255.0
hub(config)# access-list 101 extended permit ip
                  192.168.2.0 255.255.255.0
                  192.168.1.0 255.255.255.0
hub(config)# access-list 102 extended permit ip
                  192.168.0.0 255.255.255.0
                  192.168.2.0 255.255.255.0
hub(config)# access-list 102 extended permit ip
                  192.168.1.0 255.255.255.0
                  192.168.2.0 255.255.255.0
hub(config)# crypto ipsec transform-set mytrans
                  esp-aes esp-sha-hmac
hub(config)# crypto map mymap 10 match address 101
hub(config)# crypto map mymap 10 set peer 192.1.1.40
hub(config)# crypto map mymap 10 set transform-set mytrans
hub(config)# crypto map mymap 20 match address 102
hub(config)# crypto map mymap 20 set peer 192.1.1.42
hub(config)# crypto map mymap 20 set transform-set mytrans
hub(config)# crypto map mymap interface outside
```

Here's an explanation of the references in Example 21-7:

1 This command allows traffic from one tunnel on the interface to travel to another tunnel on the same interface.

2 NAT is disabled for all traffic from the hub to the spokes; since the spoke-to-hub-to-spoke traffic is entering and leaving the same interface, address translation is not performed on it, by default.

3 Tunnel groups are used to assign the pre-shared keys and ISAKMP DPD timers for each spoke.

4 The crypto ACLs for each spoke contain an additional statement to allow spoke-to-hub-to-spoke traffic to be protected; traffic between 192.168.1.0 to 192.168.2.0 and vice versa is allowed.

As you can see from the rest of Example 21-7's configuration, it's mostly the same as the 6.3 configuration in Example 21-4. For the spokes, only one item needs to be added on each spoke from the configurations in Examples 21-5 and 21-6. For spoke1, an additional ACL statement is needed in the crypto ACL to allow the spoke1-to-hub-to-spoke2 traffic: **access-list 101 permit ip 192.168.1.0 255.255.255.0 192.168.2.0 255.255.255.0**. On spoke2, the crypto ACL statement would look like this: **access-list 101 permit ip 192.168.2.0 255.255.255.0 192.168.1.0 255.255.255.0**.

Summary

This chapter showed you the basics of setting up ISAKMP/IKE Phase 1 policies and configurations on Cisco PIX and ASA security appliances and on L2L IPsec sessions. As you can see from this chapter, when compared to Chapter 16 and 17 on IOS routers, Cisco security appliances have less capabilities when it comes to features with ISAKMP/IKE Phase 1 connectivity and scalable L2L IPsec sessions.

Next up is Chapter 22, "PIX and ASA Remote Access Connections," where I show you how to set up a PIX/ASA as an Easy VPN Server and a PIX as an Easy VPN Remote.

PIX and ASA Remote Access Connections

Where the last chapter focused on IPsec L2L sessions with Cisco security appliances, this chapter will focus on their IPsec Easy VPN Server and Remote features. Both PIXs and ASA security appliances can perform the role of an Easy VPN Server, acting as a VPN gateway for client (Remote) devices; however, only the PIX 501 and 506/506E security appliances currently can perform the role of an Easy VPN Remote or hardware client. Cisco plans to release a low-end ASA appliance later that will also support this functionality.

Easy VPN Server Support for 6.*x*

Since the release of FOS 6.2, the PIX security appliances, from the 501 all the way up to the 535, can perform the function of an Easy VPN Server; and with the addition of the ASA appliances, they, too, can perform this function. Normally, I prefer to use a VPN 3000 concentrator to support a large number of remote access users; however, if you already have a PIX/ASA appliance in place and need to support only a small number of clients, you can use your existing PIX/ASA for this function. This is preferable to a router if your PIX supports a VAC+ encryption card to perform hardware encryption and your router lacks this, or if you need advanced address translation capabilities or security functions or features, which the router might lack.

The configuration of an Easy VPN Server is different if you're running FOS 6.3 or earlier when compared to 7.0. Because of the differences, I've split up the configuration explanation into the following two sections: one for 6.3 (this section) and one for 7.0 (the following main section).

Easy VPN Server Configuration for 6.*x*

Starting in FOS 6.2 and in later FOS releases, the PIX and ASA (7.0) appliances support the Easy VPN Server function, which allows them to terminate IPsec sessions from Easy VPN Remote devices, including the Cisco VPN Client software, the 3002 hardware client, the 800, ubr900, and 1700 routers, and the PIX 501 and 506E security appliances. As with the routers and concentrators performing the Easy VPN Server function, groups are used to apply policies to the Remotes connecting the Server.

Configuring an Easy VPN Server is broken into these components:

Step 1 Create an address pool for remote access devices' internal addresses with the **ip local pool** command (this is required only for client mode connections—network extension mode connections do not require this).

Step 2 Define group policies for remote access users with the **vpngroup** command.

Step 3 Disable address translation for the users' internal addresses with the **nat** (*interface*) **0 access-list** *ACL_name* command (discussed in Chapter 21).

Step 4 Enable XAUTH with the **crypto map** *map_name* **client authentication** command.

Step 5 Create ISAKMP policies with the **isakmp policy** command (discussed in the last chapter).

Step 6 Define a compatible tunnel-mode transform set with the **crypto ipsec transform-set** command (discussed in the last chapter).

Step 7 Create a dynamic crypto map with the **crypto dynamic-map** command (discussed in the last chapter).

Step 8 Create a static crypto map and enable it with the **crypto map** command (discussed in the last chapter).

Step 9 Enable IKE Mod Config for the static crypto map that has the dynamic crypto map reference with the **crypto map** *map_name* **client configuration** command.

Step 10 Allow IPsec traffic with an ACL or the **sysopt connection permit-ipsec** command (discussed in the last chapter).

As you can see from the above steps, many of the things you have to configure I've already discussed in the last chapter, "PIX and ASA Site-to-Site Connections." Therefore, I'll focus primarily on Steps 1, 2, 4, and 9 in my discussions throughout this section. With hardware clients connecting to the PIX Server, additional items may be configured, like the type of connection (client versus network-extension mode) and the type of authentication (default, device, and user).

Address Pool Configuration for 6.*x*

An address pool is needed on the PIX Server to assign logical internal addresses to connecting Remote clients. The same command used on an IOS router to define an address pool is used on the PIX appliance:

```
pix(config)# ip local pool pool_name IP_first-IP_last
             [mask subnet_mask]
```

You can have different pools of addresses for different remote access groups. Each pool needs a unique name, which can contain up to 63 characters. Within a pool, you specify the IP addresses by listing the first address in the pool, followed by a dash ("–"), and then the last address in the pool, like this: **192.168.0.201-192.168.0.249**. Optionally, you can specify a subnet mask value to ensure that the network number and directed broadcast addresses are not assigned to Remotes.

NOTE   Remember that any type of masking configuration on a PIX/ASA is a subnet mask, not a wildcard mask.

Group Configuration for 6.*x*

Groups are used to assign policies to the Remotes. The groups and policies are defined on the PIX and pushed down to the Remotes during IKE Mode/Client Config. The **vpngroup** *group_name* command is used to assign policies to a group. The group name should be descriptive of the group, like "marketing" or "sales," and should contain no more than 63 characters.

TIP   The group names are *case-sensitive* and must be configured the same way on the Remotes; otherwise, authentication will fail!

Here are the commands you can use to create a group:

```
pix(config)# vpngroup group_name password preshared_key
pix(config)# vpngroup group_name address-pool pool_name
pix(config)# vpngroup group_name authentication-server AAA_tag
pix(config)# vpngroup group_name backup-server {{IP_1 [IP2...IP10]} |
              clear-client-cfg}
pix(config)# vpngroup group_name default-domain domain_name
pix(config)# vpngroup group_name dns-server DNS_IP_1 [DNS_IP_2]
pix(config)# vpngroup group_name split-dns domain_name1
              [domain_name2 ... domain_8]
pix(config)# vpngroup group_name wins-server WINS_IP_1 [WINS_IP_2]
pix(config)# vpngroup group_name pfs
pix(config)# vpngroup group_name split-tunnel access_list_name
pix(config)# vpngroup group_name idle-time idle_seconds
pix(config)# vpngroup group_name max-time max_seconds
pix(config)# vpngroup group_name secure-unit-authentication
pix(config)# vpngroup group_name user-authentication
pix(config)# vpngroup group_name device-pass-through
pix(config)# vpngroup group_name user-idle-timeout hh:mm:ss
pix(config)# show vpngroup [group_name]
```

The **password** parameter specifies a pre-shared key to use for device authentication during ISAKMP/IKE Phase 1. The key can be up to 127 characters in length and is case-sensitive. When using pre-shared keys, aggressive mode is used. In FOS 6.3 and later, if you omit the pre-shared key, certificates and main mode are used instead. In this case, the OU (Organizational Unit)/Department field is used as the group name.

NOTE	The **isakmp key address** and **vpngroup password** commands both specify a pre-shared key to use for device authentication during ISAMP/IKE Phase 1. Cisco recommends that you use the **vpngroup password** command for Remote authentication if you will have more than one remote access group on your PIX. If you have only one group, you could just as easily use the **isakmp key address** command instead.

The **address-pool** parameter assigns an address pool (configured with the ip **local pool** command) to the associated group. You can assign only one address pool per group.

The **authentication-server** parameter specifies which AAA group tag to use to perform XAUTH. This parameter is new in 6.3. It allows you to use a different AAA designation for each group configured on the PIX; if all your groups use the same AAA designation, this command isn't necessary. But, for example, if you had two groups, marketing and sales, you could define the marketing accounts (usernames) on the PIX (in 6.3 and later) and the sales accounts on a Cisco Secure ACS AAA server.

The **backup-server** parameter allows you to assign up to ten backup Easy VPN Servers to the Remote for redundancy. This parameter is new in 6.3. The **clear-client-cfg** parameter allows you to erase any configured backup servers on the Remote device.

The **default-domain** parameter assigns a domain name to the Remotes authenticating to the group. The **dns-server** parameter allows you to assign up to two DNS servers to the group. The **split-dns** parameter, new in 6.3, allows the Remotes to use the DNS servers in the **dns-server** parameter for the domain names listed (up to eight) in the **split-dns** command; otherwise, the Remote's locally configured DNS servers are used to resolve names. The **wins-server** parameter allows you to assign up to two WINS server addresses to the Remote, overriding any locally configured WINS server addresses.

The **pfs** parameter, new in 6.3, allows Remote devices to use PFS to exchange the keying information (via DH) instead of using the protected management connection. Before enabling this, be sure all Remotes in the group support this feature.

The **split-tunnel** parameter specifies an ACL that defines which traffic is to be protected (**permit** statements in the ACL) and which traffic doesn't need to be protected (**deny** or the implicit deny statements in the ACL).

NOTE	If you don't configure split tunneling, all Remote traffic must be sent to the PIX in a protected fashion. In 6.*x* and earlier, that means the Remote won't be able to access the Internet because all traffic must be sent to the PIX and the PIX can't send the Internet traffic back out the same interface. In 7.0, this has been rectified; therefore, in 6.3 and earlier, it is very common to use split tunneling on the PIX when it is an Easy VPN Server.

CAUTION	If you allow Remotes to use split tunneling, be sure they have some kind of firewall feature configured to protect themselves from nontunneled traffic.

The **idle-time** parameter specifies the number of seconds to wait before terminating an idle Remote session. The default is 1,800 seconds (30 minutes), but you can specify a value from 60–86,400 seconds. The **max-time** parameter specifies the maximum number of seconds a Remote is allowed to have a session up. The default is infinite, but you can restrict this by specifying a value from 60–31,536,000 seconds. The timers specified in these commands take precedence over the timers configured with the **isakmp policy lifetime** command for the management connection and the **crypto map set security-association lifetime seconds** or **crypto ipsec security-association lifetime seconds** commands for the data connections.

The commands from here on out in the above code section apply only to Remote hardware clients and are new in FOS 6.3. The **secure-unit-authentication** (SUA) parameter enables what the VPN 3000 concentrators refer to as interactive unit authentication (Interactive UA); the password for the XAUTH user account is not saved on the hardware client (Remote). Instead, a user behind the Remote must supply this to bring up the tunnel. Once the tunnel is up, all users behind the Remote can use the tunnel. Note that the SUA feature is configured on the Server, not the Remote.

The **user-authentication** parameter enables individual user authentication for users behind the Remote (hardware client). The first user must supply XAUTH credentials to bring up the tunnel and each user that wants to use the tunnel also must authenticate. When either SUA or individual user authentication are configured and pushed down to the Remote during IKE Mode Config, any XAUTH password that has been hard-configured on the Remote is erased.

One problem with individual user authentication is that certain types of devices, such as IP Phones, can't perform HTML-based XAUTH authentication, which would prevent them from using the tunnel. The **device-pass-through** parameter exempts devices that can't perform authentication themselves; however, the actual list of exempted clients must be configured on the Remote, assuming it's a PIX, with the **vpnclient mac-exempt** command. The **user-idle-timeout** parameter is used when individual user authentication is enabled. It specifies when the tunnel is brought down when there is no user activity.

Last in the previous list of commands, the **show vpngroup** command displays the **vpngroup** commands you've configured on your PIX. You can restrict the output to just one group by specifying the name of that group.

XAUTH User Authentication Configuration for 6.*x*

The user accounts used for XAUTH (user authentication) can be defined locally on the PIX or on an AAA server that supports either TACACS+ or RADIUS. If you want to use local authentication and are going to create the user accounts on the PIX for XAUTH, you'll first need to make sure you are running FOS 6.3, and then you'll use the following configuration:

```
pix(config)# aaa-server LOCAL protocol local
pix(config)# username name password password
pix(config)# crypto map static_map_name client authentication LOCAL
```

The **aaa-server LOCAL** command is not necessary because it is pre-configured on a 6.3 PIX: this command specifies that the user accounts specified by the local **username** commands will be used. Any passwords configured with the **username** command are automatically encrypted by the PIX. The **show username** command displays all of the **username** commands configured on the PIX. The **crypto map client authentication** command specifies the static crypto map for which XAUTH user authentication will be enabled; this crypto map contains a reference to the dynamic crypto map for the remote access users. The **LOCAL** parameter at the end of the command points to the **aaa-server** command to use for XAUTH.

Note that if you don't have any user accounts created when executing the **crypto map client authentication** command, you'll see this message on the PIX: "Warning: local database is empty! Use 'username' command to define local users." If you already have user accounts defined when executing the command, but then subsequently delete them, you'll see this message on the PIX: "Warning: Local user database is empty and there are still commands using LOCAL for authentication."

If you are running 6.2, you can't use local authentication on the Server, but must define the user accounts on an AAA server that supports either TACACS+ or RADIUS as a communications protocol. In this case, you would use the following PIX commands:

```
pix(config)# aaa-server group_tag protocol {radius | tacacs+}
pix(config)# aaa-server group_tag (if_name)
            host AAA_server_IP encryption_key
pix(config)# crypto map static_map_name client [token]
            authentication group_tag
```

The preceding commands will work with both 6.2 and 6.3. The first **aaa-server** command specifies the protocol the PIX should use when communicating with the AAA server: either TACACS+ or RADIUS. The *group_tag* parameter in the AAA configuration is used to group related AAA commands together. The second **aaa-server** command specifies the interface the AAA server resides off of (you must give the logical interface name, like "inside"), the IP address of the AAA server, and the encryption key used either to encrypt the AAA payload for TACACS+ communications or any password information for RADIUS communications. The encryption key must match the key used on the AAA server for communications to the local PIX. The **crypto map client authentication** command then activates XAUTH authentication for the static crypto map. Optionally, the **token** parameter specifies that a token card server associated with the AAA server will be used to handle the authentication.

IKE Mode Config Activation for 6.*x*

To enable IKE Mode Config on your PIX so that you can apply group policies to IPsec remote access devices, use the following command:

```
pix(config)# crypto map static_map_name client
                configuration {initiate | respond}
```

The **respond** parameter is used most commonly, where the remote access client will initiate the IKE Mode Config process; this is necessary for Cisco client devices. For the old 2.5 Cisco software client or non-Cisco IPsec clients (Microsoft's L2TP client), use the **initiate** parameter, which causes the Server PIX to initiate IKE Mode Config. If you have both types of clients, configure the command twice, using each parameter separately.

NOTE	You still have to create an ISAKMP/IKE Phase 1 policy, configure a transform set supported by the remote access devices, associate the transform set with a dynamic crypto map entry, possibly enable RRI, create a static crypto map entry that references the dynamic crypto map, and then enable the static crypto map; however, I discussed these commands in Chapter 21.

Easy VPN Server Example for 6.*x*

Now that you have a basic understanding of the extra commands required to configure a 6.2 or 6.3 PIX as an Easy VPN Server, I'll look at an example to illustrate the use of these commands, using the network shown in Figure 22-1. In this situation, only a small number of remote access users need to set up IPsec sessions, so I'll use pre-shared keys for device authentication; however, since an AAA server is already in the network, I'll use the user accounts defined there instead of replicating this information locally on the PIX.

Figure 22-1 *6.x PIX Easy VPN Server Example*

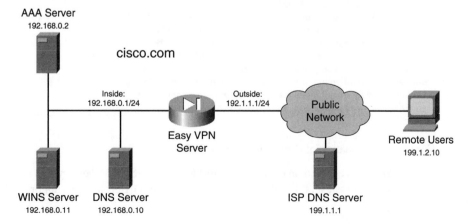

Example 22-1 illustrates the PIX Server configuration, where I'll assume the PIX is running FOS 6.3. There are two basic requirements in this example: split tunneling is required because the remote access users need access to both the LAN segment behind the PIX and the Internet, and split-DNS should be used. Remote access users will be assigned an internal address from 192.168.0.240–192.168.0.254. The reference numbers to the right of various command sections are explained below Example 22-1.

Example 22-1 *6.3 PIX Easy VPN Server Configuration*

```
server(config)# isakmp enable outside                                   (1)
server(config)# isakmp policy 10 encryption aes
server(config)# isakmp policy 10 hash sha
server(config)# isakmp policy 10 group 5
server(config)# isakmp policy 10 authentication pre-share
server(config)# access-list NONATREMOTE permit ip                       (2)
                192.168.0.0 255.255.255.0
                192.168.0.0 255.255.255.0
server(config)# nat (inside) 0 access-list NONATREMOTE
server(config)# crypto ipsec transform-set mytrans                      (3)
                esp-aes esp-sha-hmac
server(config)# crypto dynamic-map dynmap 10                            (4)
                set transform-set mytrans
server(config)# crypto map statmap 999 ipsec-isakmp
                dynamic dynmap
server(config)# crypto map statmap interface outside
server(config)# sysopt connection permit-ipsec
server(config)# aaa-server AAASERVER protocol radius                    (5)
server(config)# aaa-server AAASERVER (inside) host 192.168.0.2
                cisco123
server(config)# crypto map statmap client authentication AAASERVER
server(config)# crypto map statmap client configuration                (6)
                address respond
server(config)# ip local pool remotepool
                192.168.0.240-192.168.0.254
server(config)# access-list splittunnelACL permit ip                   (7)
                192.168.0.0 255.255.255.0
                192.168.0.0 255.255.255.0
server(config)# vpngroup smallgroup address-pool remotepool            (8)
server(config)# vpngroup smallgroup password 123cisco
server(config)# vpngroup smallgroup dns-server 192.168.0.10
server(config)# vpngroup smallgroup default-domain cisco.com
server(config)# vpngroup smallgroup split-dns cisco.com
server(config)# vpngroup smallgroup wins-server 192.168.0.11
server(config)# vpngroup smallgroup split-tunnel splittunnelACL
server(config)# vpngroup idle-time 600
```

Here is an explanation of the sections found in Example 22-1:

1 ISAKMP is enabled on the outside interface and an ISAKMP policy is created for the remote access users. For the 2.5 Cisco client, only DH group 1 is supported. If you

also terminated L2L sessions on this PIX and were using pre-shared keys, when configuring the pre-shared key for each L2L peer, you would use the **no-xauth** and **no-config-mode** parameters to disable XAUTH and IKE Mode Config, respectively, for the L2L peers.

2 The **access-list** and **nat** commands disable address translation between the local LAN (source addresses in the ACL) and the remote access user's internal addresses (destination addresses in the ACL).

3 A supported transform set for the remote access users is defined.

4 A dynamic crypto map entry is created for the remote access users, specifying the transform set to use to protect the users' data SAs. This is then referenced in the static crypto map applied to the Server's outside interface; remember that if you have both L2L and remote access sessions terminated on the Server, use a high-sequence number for the dynamic crypto map entry in the static map, giving it a lower priority than the static map entries for L2L peers. The **sysopt** command then exempts the IPsec traffic by being processed by any ACL applied to the PIX's outside interface.

5 An AAA server, which contains the user accounts, is identified and XAUTH is associated with the static crypto map and the AAA server; notice that the AAA protocol used between the PIX and the AAA server is RADIUS.

6 IKE Mode Config is enabled on the Server, with the assumption that this is a Cisco client; for non-Cisco clients or the 2.5 Cisco client, you would use the **initiate** parameter instead of the **respond** parameter. Also, an address pool containing the remote access users' internal addresses is defined with the **ip local pool** command.

7 An ACL is defined to allow for split tunneling. All traffic between 192.168.0.0/24 devices will be protected from the remote access clients to the local LAN segment and all other traffic from the remote access clients is sent in clear text. The first 192.168.0.0/24 reference, the source addresses, is for the local LAN traffic (the inside interface of the Server) and the second 192.168.0.0/24 reference, the destination addresses, is for the internal addresses of the Remotes.

8 One group, called "smallgroup," is created. This group specifies the address pool to use ("remotepool"), the pre-shared key to use for device authentication ("123cisco"; if you were using certificates, this command would be omitted), the DNS servers, domain name, and split DNS, the WINS server, the split tunneling ACL to use ("splittunnelACL"), and an idle timeout (600 seconds).

As you can see from this example, the configuration in 6.3 is somewhat similar to configuring an Easy VPN Server on an IOS router. The only thing you might want to do is ensure that the Remotes have a personal firewall installed because split tunneling is enabled; unfortunately, you can't enforce that kind of group policy on the PIX/ASA until Version 7.0.

Easy VPN Remote Support for 6.*x*

Starting in FOS 6.2 and 6.3, a PIX 501 or 506/506E can perform the function of an Easy VPN Remote, initiating client connections to an Easy VPN Server, like a VPN 3000 concentrator, a Cisco IOS router, or another PIX or ASA security appliance. If you recall from Chapter 14, "3002 Hardware Client," and Chapter 18, "Router Remote Access Connections," the 3002 and 800, ubr900, and 1700 routers are also hardware clients. One advantage of setting up a low-end PIX as a Remote is that minimal configuration is needed on the PIX to establish an IPsec session to an Easy VPN Server; policies are centralized on the Server and pushed down to the Remote during IKE Mode Config, and individual users behind the PIX do not need to load an IPsec software client on their desktops.

TIP	A low-end PIX is an ideal hardware client for SOHO environments where you have a cable or DSL modem connection and need to use split tunneling; the PIX provides many security features to deal with the traffic that is not protected. It's my preferred hardware client in this situation. Also, the low-end PIXs can perform Server functions to handle a small number of Remote connections, which is ideal for the 2–3 users that need to work from home.

The PIX Remote supports many of the features of the Cisco VPN Client software and the VPN 3002, including:

- Pre-shared key and certificate device authentication
- Client and network extension modes
- Split tunneling and split DNS
- Backup server lists (6.3)
- AES encryption (6.3) and DH group 5 (6.3)
- Unit authentication (6.2), individual user authentication (6.3), and secure unit authentication (6.3), which is similar to Interactive Unit Authentication on the 3002

The following two sections will discuss the commands to configure a low-end PIX as a Remote and also an example configuration.

NOTE	Version 7.0 is not supported on the 501 and 506/506E PIX firewalls; only on the PIX 515/515E, 525, and 535. Therefore, it is not currently possible to configure a PIX (or ASA) running 7.0 as an Easy VPN Remote device.

6.*x* Easy VPN Remote Configuration

Like a low-end IOS router Remote device, configuring a low-end PIX Remote is straightforward and requires few commands. Use the following commands to set up the PIX Remote to connect to the Easy VPN Server:

```
pix(config)# vpnclient vpngroup group_name password preshared_key
pix(config)# vpnclient username XAUTH_username
             password XAUTH_password
pix(config)# vpnclient server Server_IP_address_1
             [Server_IP_address_2 ...Server IP address_11]
pix(config)# vpnclient mode {client-mode | network-extension-mode}
pix(config)# vpnclient mac-exempt MAC_addr_1 MAC_mask_1
             [MAC_addr_2 MAC_mask_2]
pix(config)# vpnclient management tunnel IP_address_1 subnet_mask
             [IP_address_2 subnet_mask]
pix(config)# management-access interface_name
pix(config)# vpnclient nem-st-autoconnect
pix(config)# vpnclient enable
pix(config)# vpnclient connect
pix(config)# vpnclient disconnect
```

The **vpnclient vpngroup password** command is used if the group on the Server is using pre-shared keys for device authentication; if you are using certificates, this command is omitted (requires FOS 6.3). Group names cannot exceed 63 characters and cannot contain any spaces; the pre-shared key cannot exceed 127 characters. For user authentication/ XAUTH (assuming it is enabled on the Server, which it probably is), if device, or unit, authentication is being used, you must define the Remote's username and password with the **vpnclient username** command. Neither the username nor the password can exceed 127 characters.

The **vpnclient server** command specifies one or more Server addresses the Remote should use to connect to the central site. The first address is the primary address, which can be followed by up to ten backup Server addresses (in 6.3, only). If the Server has a defined backup list, the PIX Remote will replace its list of backup servers with that given to it by the Server during IKE Mode Config. When connecting to a Server, if a Server is not reachable within five seconds, the Remote will try the next server in the list.

The **vpnclient mode** command specifies whether the PIX should use client or network-extension mode for the connection to the Server. When you configure client mode, your PIX must be a DHCP server for its inside interface, handing out addressing information to the connected SOHO devices. With client mode, the PIX also will perform PAT automatically on the SOHO IP addresses to the internal address assigned by the Server, for all local LAN traffic that needs to be protected across the tunnel to the central site. If you have IP Phones behind the PIX Remote, you must use network extension mode for the connection type. And if you've enabled either user authentication or IUA/SUA for the group the PIX Remote belongs to, on the Remote, you'll need to exclude any MAC addresses of IP phones and printers that need to initiate or send traffic across the tunnel, which is accomplished with the **vpnclient mac-exempt** command. However, this command requires FOS 6.3 on your PIX Remote. You can list two MAC addresses and masks. To match on all Cisco IP Phones, you would specify the following MAC address and mask: **0003.E300.0000 FFFF.FF00.0000** (all Cisco IP Phones' MAC addresses begin with "0003.E3").

NOTE   If your PIX Remote is connecting to a VPN 3000 concentrator and you'll be using network extension mode, this policy must be enabled on the concentrator also; this is not true if the Easy VPN Server is an IOS router or a PIX/ASA appliance.

If you use network extension mode, you can manage your PIX Remote from the central site across the tunnel. To do this, you need to configure two commands: **vpnclient management tunnel** and **management-access**. The first command specifies IP addresses that are allowed to manage the Remote, via the tunnel, from the Server's network. The second command specifies which interface should be used to terminate the management connections; for tunnel connections, this should be "inside." To manage the PIX Remote, you can then use Telnet, SSH, HTTPS (PDM), SNMP polls, and ping to access the IP address of the configured management interface in the **management-access** command.

The **vpnclient nem-st-autoconnect** command specifies that the Remote should automatically bring up an IPsec session, when using network extension mode, to the Server whenever the split-tunneling policy has been enabled on the Server and pushed to the Remote. This command is necessary only for network extension mode; in client mode, all traffic is sent to the Server and thus there is little likelihood of the IPsec tunnel timing out to the Server. In network extension mode, this is more likely when split tunneling is enabled and more traffic is going to other places on the Internet than to the Server site.

The **vpnclient enable** command allows an IPsec session to be initiated to the configured Server(s). To bring a tunnel up manually, use the **vpnclient connect** command; user traffic, however, will do this automatically, so this command typically is used for testing purposes. To terminate a tunnel, use either the **no vpnclient connect** or the **vpnclient disconnect** command.

NOTE   Just as with routers functioning as Remote devices, you don't need to configure ISAKMP policies, crypto ACLs, transform sets, and crypto maps on the PIX Remote. Also, to remove the VPN client configuration on your PIX Remote completely, use the **clear vpnclient** command, which removes *all* of the **vpnclient** commands.

Using Certificates for Remote Access

In 6.3 the Easy VPN Remote and Server functions on PIX security appliances support X.509 digital certificates via ISAKMP/IKE main mode for device authentication. In 6.2, only pre-shared keys were supported via aggressive mode. If you omit the **vpnclient**

vpngroup command from the last section on configuring a PIX Remote, digital certificates will be used for device authentication.

How you obtain a certificate on a PIX Remote is the same as if it were terminating an L2L session. This was discussed in the last chapter. However, when a PIX is configured as a Remote, it will *not* check a CRL to see if the Server's certificate has been revoked, which could be used in a man-in-the-middle attack! Because of this security concern, Cisco has added a command you can configure on the Remote to examine certain fields on the certificate to determine if the Remote will accept the Server's certificate:

```
pix(config)# ca verifycertdn X.500_string
```

The X.500 string is a list of fields and values that must appear on the Server's identity certificate. On the Server, view the personal identity certificate to determine which fields you want to validate on the Remote. For example, this command, "**ca verifycertdn cn*server, ou=perimeter, o=cisco, st=ca, c=us**", would match on a CN containing "server" and on the rest of the certificate fields exactly matching the above parameters.

NOTE   Remember to put the group name of the PIX Remote in the OU/Department field of its identity certificate so that the Easy VPN Server knows what policies to apply to the Remote.

Verifying Your 6.*x* Remote Configuration and Connection

The **show vpnclient** command, shown in Example 22-2, displays the Easy VPN Remote's configuration and any policy information downloaded from the Server. To see more details about the configuration of the Remote, add the **detail** parameter to the preceding command.

Example 22-2 *Remote Configuration Verification*

```
Remote# show vpnclient
LOCAL CONFIGURATION
vpnclient server 192.1.1.1
vpnclient mode network-extension-mode
vpnclient vpngroup client-access password ********
vpnclient username RemotePIX password ********
vpnclient management tunnel 192.168.0.0 255.255.255.0
vpnclient enable

DOWNLOADED DYNAMIC POLICY
Current Server          : 192.1.1.1
Default Domain          : cisco.com
PFS Enabled       : No
Secure Unit Authentication Enabled : No
User Authentication Enabled    : No
Backup Servers          : None
```

Example 22-3 illustrates the use of the **detail** parameter. The beginning output is the same as the **show vpnclient** command; however, two additional sections are added: STORED POLICY displays any policies the Remote has received from the Server that it has saved locally and the RELATED CONFIGURATION section has the related commands the Remote created *dynamically* to build an IPsec tunnel to the Server. Reference numbers in parentheses are listed to the right of the output, which is explained after the example.

Example 22-3 *Remote Configuration Verification Details*

```
Remote# show vpnclient detail
LOCAL CONFIGURATION
vpnclient server 192.1.1.1
vpnclient mode network-extension-mode
vpnclient vpngroup client-access password ********
vpnclient username userX password ********
vpnclient management tunnel 192.168.0.0 255.255.255.0
vpnclient enable

DOWNLOADED DYNAMIC POLICY
Current Server              : 192.1.1.1
Default Domain              : cisco.com
PFS Enabled                 : No
Secure Unit Authentication Enabled : No
User Authentication Enabled    : No
Backup Servers              : None

STORED POLICY
Secure Unit Authentication Enabled : No
Split Networks              : None
Backup Servers              : None

RELATED CONFIGURATION
sysopt connection permit-ipsec                                    (1)
←output omitted→
nat (inside) 0 access-list _vpnc_acl                              (2)
←output omitted→
access-list _vpnc_acl permit ip 192.168.1.0 255.255.255.0 any
access-list _vpnc_acl permit ip host 192.168.1.1
              192.168.0.0 255.255.255.0
←output omitted→
crypto ipsec transform-set _vpnc_tset_1 esp-aes-256 esp-sha-hmac  (3)
crypto ipsec transform-set _vpnc_tset_2 esp-aes-256 esp-md5-hmac
←output omitted→
crypto ipsec transform-set _vpnc_tset_11 esp-null esp-sha-hmac
crypto map _vpnc_cm 10 ipsec-isakmp                               (4)
crypto map _vpnc_cm 10 match address _vpnc_acl
crypto map _vpnc_cm 10 set peer 192.1.1.1
crypto map _vpnc_cm 10 set transform-set _vpnc_tset_1 _vpnc_tset_2 _
  vpnc_tset_3 _vpnc_tset_4 _vpnc_tset_5 _vpnc_test_6 _vpnc_tset_7 _
  vpnc_tset_8 _vpnc_tset_9 _vpnc_tset_10 _vpnc_tset_11
crypto map _vpnc_cm interface outside
isakmp enable outside                                            (5)
isakmp key ******** address 192.1.1.1 netmask 255.255.255.255
```

Example 22-3 *Remote Configuration Verification Details (Continued)*

```
isakmp keepalive 10 5
isakmp nat-traversal 20
isakmp policy 65001 authentication xauth-pre-share
isakmp policy 65001 encryption aes-256
isakmp policy 65001 hash sha
isakmp policy 65001 group 2
isakmp policy 65001 lifetime 86400
←output omitted→
isakmp policy 65018 authentication pre-share
isakmp policy 65018 encryption des
isakmp policy 65018 hash md5
isakmp policy 65018 group 2
isakmp policy 65018 lifetime 86400
```

Here is an explanation of the references in Example 22-3:

1 IPsec traffic is exempted from ACL checking from the Remote's outside interface.

2 Any traffic from the Remote's local network, 192.168.1.0/24, including the Remote's inside interface address, 192.168.1.1, is exempt from address translation for the tunnel; in this example, the Remote is using network extension mode.

3 Eleven transform sets are created automatically to protect the data connection: one of these has to match a transform set on the Easy VPN Server.

4 A static crypto map entry is created automatically for the Server connection; you can see that the "vpnc_acl" ACL is used to specify traffic to protect and the 11 transform sets created are referenced in the crypto map entry.

5 ISAKMP is enabled and a pre-shared key is created dynamically for the Server; 18 different ISAKMP policies are created for possible use in protecting the management connection to the Server, where at least one of these has to exist on the Server for the management connection to be built.

6.*x* Easy VPN Remote Example Configuration

To show you how easy it is to set up a PIX as an Easy VPN Remote, I'll illustrate an example configuration. Figure 22-2 displays the network I'll use and Example 22-4 shows the Remote's configuration. In this example, the Remote belongs to a group called "hwclients," which uses pre-shared keys. The XAUTH username and password are defined, as is the Easy VPN Server address. The connection mode is network extension, where management access is allowed from the central site to the inside interface of the Remote. If a split tunneling policy is enabled for the "hwclients" group on the Server, the **vpnclient nem-st-autoconnect** command ensures that an IPsec tunnel remains up between the Remote and the Server. Last, I enabled Easy VPN on the Remote and then manually brought up the tunnel to test the connection.

Figure 22-2 *6.x PIX Easy VPN Remote Example*

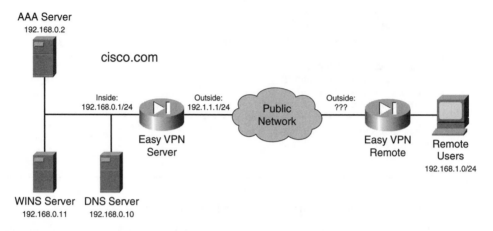

Example 22-4 *PIX Remote Configuration Example*

```
Remote(config)# vpnclient vpngroup hwclients password secretpass
Remote(config)# vpnclient username RemotePIX password PIXpass
Remote(config)# vpnclient server 192.1.1.1
Remote(config)# vpnclient mode network-extension
Remote(config)# vpnclient management tunnel 192.168.0.0 255.255.255.0
Remote(config)# management-access inside
Remote(config)# vpnclient nem-st-autoconnect
Remote(config)# vpnclient enable
Remote(config)# vpnclient connect
```

You can use the **debug crypto isakmp** command on the Remote or Server to troubleshoot the establishment of the management connection, and the **debug crypto ipsec** command for the data connections. Plus, you can use the **show vpnclient detail** command to display the Remote's configuration, policies downloaded from the Server, and all commands the Remote created dynamically to allow for the IPsec session to be built to the Server. The two **debug** commands are discussed in more depth in Chapter 23, "Troubleshooting PIX and ASA Connections."

Easy VPN Server Support for 7.0

Continued support for Easy VPN Server is provided in FOS 7.0. Many, many new enhancements have been made to the Server function, putting the PIX and ASA more in line with the IPsec capabilities of the VPN 3000 concentrators. However, the configuration of an Easy VPN Server is very different than what I discussed earlier for 6.x.

This part of the chapter will focus on the configuration of a PIX/ASA as an Easy VPN Server. The following are tasks you need to perform on the 7.0 security appliance to set it up as a Server:

- Enabling ISAKMP, including policies (discussed in the last chapter)
- Defining IP address pools (discussed previously in the "Address Pool Configuration for 6.x" section)
- Creating tunnel groups (this is new in 7.0)
- Specifying where user accounts are located, locally on the PIX/ASA or on an AAA server (discussed previously in the "XAUTH User Authentication Configuration for 6.x" section)
- Creating user accounts, if specified locally
- Defining IPsec transform sets for data connections (discussed in the last chapter)
- Creating a dynamic crypto map for remote access users (discussed in the last chapter)
- Referencing the dynamic crypto map as an entry in a static crypto map (discussed in the last chapter)
- Activating the static crypto map on the PIX/ASA's interface

Because I described many of the above tasks previously in this and the last chapter, the next few sections will focus on configurations unique to FOS 7.0, including:

- Understanding Tunnel Groups
- Defining Group Policies
- Creating Tunnel Groups
- Creating User Accounts for XAUTH

Following these sections, I'll also discuss issues with remote access sessions and solutions that are provided in FOS 7.0, and an example that will illustrate the configuration of an Easy VPN Server running FOS 7.0.

Understanding Tunnel Groups

The main IPsec change from 6.3 to 7.0 is the introduction of the tunnel group feature. Tunnel groups allow you to define VPN session policies associated with a particular session or group of sessions, like a related group of remote access users or L2L sessions. Tunnel groups are used to simplify the configuration and management of your IPsec sessions. By default, two tunnel groups already are created on your PIX/ASA: "DefaultL2LGroup" for L2L sessions and "DefaultRAGroup" for remote access sessions. A tunnel group might include parameters such as general policy information and information to build IPsec sessions.

A group policy is used to define attributes associated with a user or group of users. It is associated with a tunnel group. A default group policy, called "DfltGrpPolicy," exists on the security appliance for users who are not associated with a specific remote access group (similar to the Base Group on a VPN 3000 concentrator).

The use of tunnel groups involves three configuration steps:

Step 1 Define group policies.

Step 2 Create tunnel groups.

Step 3 Create user accounts for XAUTH.

The above three tasks replace the function of the **vpngroup** command in FOS 6.*x*. Tunnel groups must be configured locally on a PIX/ASA. The following three sections will discuss each of these steps in more depth.

Defining Group Policies

Group policies define attributes you want to assign to remote access clients during IKE Mode Config that belong to a particular remote access group. These policies either can be defined locally or on an AAA RADIUS server. Creating policies locally is done with the **group-policy** command. Once policies are created, you then must associate them with a tunnel group, which specifies the group name the remote access users will use. This section discusses how you create group policies, and the next section discusses how you associate the policies to a tunnel group that is used for the remote access clients.

Group Policy Locations

Your group policies for your remote access users can be defined locally or on an AAA RADIUS server. To define the location of a group's policies, use the following command:

```
security(config)# group-policy group_policy_name {internal
          [from group_policy_name]| external
          server-group server_tag password
          server_password
```

The **group-policy** command can be used to specify the location of the group policy information. **internal** specifies that the policies are defined on the PIX/ASA itself and **external** on an AAA RADIUS server. If you specify **internal**, you can even specify for the group policy, whatever other group policy it should use to get its default policies from (similar to the VPN 3000 concentrators' Base Group feature). The *server_tag* parameter specifies which AAA RADIUS server to use by looking for the same tag in the **aaa-server** commands and the password for the access; TACACS+ is not supported.

Default Group Policies

There is a default group policy, called "DfltGrpPolicy" on the appliance, which supports the following default policies (you can treat this as the Base Group found on a VPN 3000 concentrator). These can be viewed with the **show running-config all group-policy DfltGrpPolicy** command, shown here:

- Default domain name: none
- DNS server addresses: none
- Split DNS: disabled
- WINS server addresses: none
- Access hour restrictions: none
- Simultaneous login restrictions: 3
- Tunnel session idle timeout: 30 minutes
- Maximum session connection timeout: none
- Filter applied to tunneled traffic: none
- Supported tunneling protocol: IPsec and WebVPN
- Allowing a user to store the XAUTH password locally: disabled
- Re-authenticate users upon expiration of the tunnel: disabled
- Locking a user into a group: disabled
- Restricting client types and version: disabled
- Compression of tunneled traffic: none
- Using PFS: no
- Login banner: none
- Backup server list: use the client-defined list
- Using IPsec over UDP: disabled
- For IPsec over UDP, the default port number: 10,000
- Split tunneling policy: disabled (tunnel all traffic)
- Split tunneling network list: none
- Software client firewall policy: none
- Secure unit authentication for hardware clients: disabled
- User authentication for hardware clients: disabled
- User authentication idle timeout: none
- IP phone bypass feature for user authentication: disabled
- LEAP bypass feature for user authentication: disabled
- Network extension mode for hardware clients: disabled

Default and Specific Group Policy Attribute Configuration

You can change the values for the default group policy or define local policies for specific internal groups with the **group policy attributes** command. The configuration of the policy attributes is shown here:

```
security(config)# group-policy {DfltGrpPolicy | group_policy_name}
            attributes
security(config-group-policy)# domain-name domain_name
security(config-group-policy)# dns-server value IP_address
            [IP_address]
security(config-group-policy)# split-dns domain_name1 domain_name2
            ... domain_nameX
security(config-group-policy)# wins-server value IP_address
            [IP_address]
security(config-group-policy)# dhcp-network-scope IP_network_#
security(config-group-policy)# vpn-access-hours value time_range_name
security(config-group-policy)# vpn-simultaneous-logins number
security(config-group-policy)# vpn-idle-timeout minutes
security(config-group-policy)# vpn-session-timeout minutes
security(config-group-policy)# vpn-filter value ACL_name
security(config-group-policy)# vpn-tunnel-protocol [ipsec] [webvpn]
security(config-group-policy)# password-storage {enable | disable}
security(config-group-policy)# re-xauth {enable | disable}
security(config-group-policy)# group-lock value tunnel_group_name
security(config-group-policy)# client-access-rule priority
            {permit | deny} type type version none
security(config-group-policy)# ip-comp {enable | disable}
security(config-group-policy)# pfs {enable | disable}
security(config-group-policy)# banner value string
security(config-group-policy)# backup-servers {server1 server2 ...
            server10 | clear-client-config |
            keep-client-config}
security(config-group-policy)# ipsec-udp {enable | disable}
security(config-group-policy)# ipsec-udp-port port
security(config-group-policy)# split-tunnel-policy {tunnelall |
            tunnelspecified | excludespecified}
security(config-group-policy)# split-tunnel-network-list
            value ACL_name
security(config-group-policy)# client-firewall {none | {{opt | req}
            firewall_type} policy {AYT |
            CPP acl-in ACL_name acl-out ACL_name}}
security(config-group-policy)# secure-unit-authentication
            {enable | disable}
security(config-group-policy)# user-authentication-idle-timeout
            minutes
security(config-group-policy)# ip-phone-bypass {enable | disable}
security(config-group-policy)# leap-bypass {enable | disable}
security(config-group-policy)# nem {enable | disable}
```

The above configuration applies only if the group policy type is defined as **internal** from the previous section. Using the **attributes** parameter with the **group-policy** command takes you into a subcommand mode where you can change the policies for the default group policy or a specific group policy.

NOTE   These are policies for the group or groups—not the group itself. I discuss the use of groups in the next section.

The **domain-name** command allows you to specify a domain name to assign to a remote access device. The domain name can be up to 63 characters in length. The **dns-server value** command allows you to specify up to two DNS servers for the remote access clients. The use of these servers overrides the client's locally configured DNS servers unless you set up split DNS with the **split-dns** command. You can define as many domain names as you like for the **split-dns** command; however, the entire string cannot exceed 255 characters. Any domain names listed here will cause the client to use the DNS servers in the **dns-server value** command; other domain names will be resolved using the DNS server configured locally on the client. The **wins-server value** command allows you to specify up to two WINS server addresses to assign remote access clients. The **dhcp-network-scope** command is used only when the appliance will obtain a user's internal IP address from a DHCP server. This command specifies the network number the DHCP server should pull a dynamic IP address from. I discuss the assignment of internal IP addresses to clients in the next section.

The **vpn-access-hours value** command specifies a time range configuration to use to restrict a remote access device's VPN access, based on a time of day, day of week, or a specific day when connecting to the Easy VPN Server. The time range configured with the **time-range** command is the same as how you would configure this on IOS-based routers. The following commands configure a time range:

```
security(config)# time-range time_range_name
security(config-time-range)# absolute [start hh:mm date]
        [end hh:mm date]
security(config-time-range)# periodic day_of_the_week time to
        [day_of_the_week] hh:mm
```

The name of the time range cannot exceed 64 characters. Upon executing the **time-range** command, you are taken into a subcommand mode. The **absolute** command specifies a specific, one-time-only period when access is allowed. The time is entered in an hours and minutes format based on a 24-hour time period, like 23:00 for 11 PM. The date is entered by entering the day of the month, followed by the name of the month, and then a 4-digit year, like "23 May 2005." If you don't enter a starting time, the current time is used; if you don't enter an ending time, the time period is infinite. For remote access, this typically is used to give a group temporary access to the Easy VPN Server, which, upon the end time, access is then denied. This type of configuration would be common for temporary consultants or extranet partners.

The **periodic** subcommand is used more commonly in situations that occur periodically because it allows you to specify recurring time intervals when access is allowed. For the *day_of_week* parameter, you can use "Monday," "Tuesday," "Wednesday," "Thursday," "Friday," "Saturday," "Sunday," "daily" (Monday through Sunday), "weekdays" (Monday through Friday), and "weekend" (Saturday and Sunday); you also can specify more than one day for the *day_of_week* parameter. The time is specified in an hour and minute format based on a 24-hour period. If you omit the second *day_of_week* parameter, it defaults to the first value. For example, **periodic weekdays 07:00 to 18:00** would allow access from 7 AM to 6 PM Monday through Friday, but deny access any other time.

To ensure that the security appliance has the correct time when restricting VPN access usage, I highly recommend that you use an internal NTP master clock. This is especially true if the appliance is using certificates for device authentication.

The **vpn-simultaneous-logins** group policy command limits the number of simultaneous logins allowed for any single user. The default is 3, but this can range from 0–2,147,483,647. Normally you don't want Remotes to share usernames and passwords, so this should be a low value. The **vpn-idle-timeout** command controls how long an idle Remote session is allowed before it is terminated; this defaults to 30 minutes but can range from 1–35,791, 394 minutes. The **vpn-session-timeout** command specifies a maximum number of minutes the Remote can connect to the Server before the Server disconnects the Remote, even if traffic is being transmitted between the two devices. There is no limit, by default, but you can specify a value from 1–35,791,394 minutes.

Once a tunnel is established from the Remote to the Server, the Server will allow all traffic that is tunneled to it to exit the tunnel. You can restrict traffic across the tunnel by using the **vpn-filter** value command, where you need to specify a named ACL on the Server. The **vpn-tunnel-protocol** command can be used to restrict what remote access protocol or protocols (IPsec or WebVPN) can be used by remote access users associated with the policy; the default is IPsec (only the ASA currently supports WebVPN).

The **password-storage** command specifies the policy concerning the storage of the XAUTH password on the Remote. By default this is disabled. It is recommended to keep it disabled for software clients, but must be enabled for hardware clients where the default authentication method is unit authentication (the username and password are stored on the hardware client). If you need to support both software and hardware clients, in this situation create two policies: for the software clients, leave it disabled and for the hardware clients, enable it. The **re-xauth** command controls whether or not users must re-authenticate when IKE rekeying occurs (the management connection is rebuilt). By default this is disabled; if the rekeying interval is short, you'd probably want to keep this disabled. Also, for SUA and user authentication, this might cause the tunnel to fail if no user is there to perform the authentication. Plus, if you are using network extension mode and have IP phones at the remote site, you probably don't want to use this feature.

The **group-lock** command forces users who belong to a specific group to connect only to the specified group (the *tunnel_group_name*). This is disabled, by default, which allows a user to connect to any group if they know the pre-shared key for that group (assuming pre-shared key authentication is being used).

The **client-access-rule** command allows you to restrict the termination of remote access sessions on the appliance, based on the type of client and the client's software version. The *priority* value ranks the rules, where 1 is the highest priority and is processed first by the Server. The *type* value is the type of VPN client, like "VPN 3002." You can't choose any type; instead, the value you enter (including the quotes, if the client type is more than one word) must match exactly as it is displayed in the output of the **show vpn-sessiondb remote** command. This also is true of the client version in the *version* parameter. You can wildcard the version with an "*," like "4.*" (matches all 4.*x* versions); or "*" (by itself matches on any version). For example, **client-access-rule 1 deny type WinNT version *** prevents all software clients running on Windows NT from connecting to the appliance, whereas **client-access-rule 2 permit type "Cisco VPN Client" version 4**.* would allow all other software client connections, assuming that they were running some 4.*x* version of software. You can create only 25 of these rules per group policy. Also, for clients that don't send the type or version, you can specify "n/a" for each of these values.

The **ip-comp** command allows for compression of IP packets using LZS compression. This should be used only by remote access groups with only software-based users using dialup connections; for broadband users, enabling this can affect their throughput negatively in most situations if the user has enabled compression inadvertently. Therefore, enable this policy attribute only when it is associated with a group of dialup-only users. The **pfs** command enables the use of DH for sharing keys when building the data SAs during ISAKMP/IKE Phase 2; by default this is disabled. The **banner value** command specifies a banner that should be displayed once the Remote connects. By default, no banner is displayed. The banner can be up to 510 characters in length. You can't type the banner across multiple command lines in the **banner value** command; however, you can insert carriage returns into the banner by specifying "\n" in the banner message (this counts as two characters).

The **backup-servers** command specifies a list of up to 10 backup Easy VPN Server addresses to push down to the Remote; the Remote then will erase any list it has and use this list. The default value is the **keep-client-config** parameter, which specifies that the client should use its locally configured backup server list. Specifying the **clear-client-config** parameter has the client remove its configured backup server list.

IPsec over UDP is enabled with the **ipsec-udp** command (it's disabled by default). As with the VPN 3000 concentrators, this is enabled on a group-by-group basis, whereas IPsec over TCP and NAT-T are enabled globally with the **isakmp** command (discussed in the last chapter). If you enable IPsec over UDP, you must enable it manually on the Cisco VPN Client software and VPN 3002 hardware appliance—Cisco router and PIX Remotes currently don't support IPsec over UDP. The default port number for IPsec over UDP is 10,000, but this can range from 4,001–49, 151, except for 4,500, which is used by NAT-T. Remember that IPsec over UDP is proprietary to Cisco and will work only with certain Cisco devices.

The **split-tunnel-policy** command allows you to specify whether or not split tunneling is enabled; by default, all traffic must be tunneled (the **tunnelall** parameter). If you configure the **tunnelspecified** parameter, traffic matching **permit** statements in the ACL defined in the **split-tunnel-network-list** command are tunneled and traffic matching the **deny** statements is sent in clear text. If you configure the **excludespecified** parameter, traffic that matches **permit** statements in the ACL defined in the **split-tunnel-network-list** command is sent in clear text and traffic matching the **deny** statements is protected.

The **client-firewall** command is used to define the firewall policy the remote user (Cisco Windows VPN Client software) must use when connecting to the Server. The syntax of the command is slightly different based on the firewall that you want the user to use, so here's a list of the firewall commands based on the firewall that you want users to use:

```
hostname(config-group-policy)# client-firewall none
hostname(config-group-policy)# client-firewall opt | req custom
            vendor-id num product-id num policy AYT |
            {CPP acl-in ACL_name acl-out ACL_name}
            [description string]
hostname(config-group-policy)# client-firewall opt | req
            {zonelabs-zonealarm | zonelabs-zonealarmpro |
            zonelabs-zonealarmorpro} policy AYT |
            {CPP acl-in ACL_name acl-out ACL_name}
hostname(config-group-policy)# client-firewall opt | req
            cisco-integrated acl-in ACL_name
            acl-out ACL_name
hostname(config-group-policy)# client-firewall opt | req
            {sygate-personal | sygate-personal-pro |
            sygate-security-agent | networkice-blackice |
            cisco-security-agent}
```

I discussed the configuration of client firewall policies on the concentrator in Chapter 7, "Concentrator Remote Access Connections with IPsec." The only difference between configuring it on the concentrator and the security appliance is that the security appliance uses a CLI. There are three firewall types: **none** (the default), **opt** (optional), and **req** (required). If you specify the latter two, you must specify the firewall software that the user must have installed and running. The two policies a firewall might support are Are You There (AYT) and CPP (Custom Policy Push or Protection). For CPP, you must specify the name of an ACL you've already created on the appliance that will be used to filter traffic entering the client (**acl-in**) and another ACL that will be used to filter traffic leaving the client (**acl-out**). This is different from the VPN 3000 concentrator, where in a filter you can have both inbound and outbound rules: on the PIX/ASA, you must have a separate ACL for each. The CIC client (**cisco-integrated**) supports only CPP; Sygate, NetworkICE, and CSA only support AYT; and Zone Labs firewalls support both.

The rest of the commands discussed in the **group policy attributes** subcommand mode apply to only two hardware clients. The **secure-unit-authentication** command enables SUA (referred to as Interactive Unit Authentication on the VPN 3002 hardware client), where only a single user must authenticate to bring up the tunnel and then all users can use the tunnel; this is disabled by default (unit, or the default/device, authentication is used). When enabled, the hardware client will not store the XAUTH password on the box; also, you must specify an authentication server group tag to use, which could be "LOCAL," for the tunnel group, which tells the appliance where to find the user accounts (this is discussed in the next section).

The **user-authentication** command specifies that all users must authenticate to either bring up or to use an existing tunnel to the Server. This, too, is disabled by default. If you enable it, you can override the default idle timeout for authenticated users, which defaults to 30 minutes, with the **user-authentication-idle-timeout** command. This value can range from 1–35, 791, 394 minutes. Please note that this command affects a user's access only through the tunnel, not the lifetime of the tunnel itself, which is negotiated during ISAKMP/IKE Phase 1.

The **ip-phone-bypass** and **leap-bypass** commands allow IP phones, and wireless devices using LEAP authentication, to bypass user authentication when enabled for a group, which is necessary in this situation. Both of these will not work properly if the Easy VPN Server is configured for SUA and no one else has brought up the tunnel first. LEAP bypass is necessary only if the LEAP authentication needs to be performed across the IPsec tunnel to the network connected behind the Server.

The **nem** command is used to enable network extension mode; by default, client mode is used for groups containing hardware clients. This mode should be used when you have devices at the Remote that the central office needs to establish connections to, such as a file server or IP phones.

NOTE   To set a group's policy value back to its default, use the attribute command followed by the **none** keyword, like **vpn-idle-timeout none**.

Creating Tunnel Groups

There are two default tunnel groups on your security appliance: "DefaultRAGroup" for remote access users and "DefaultL2LGroup" for site-to-site sessions. You can modify the properties of these default tunnel groups, but cannot delete them; however, you can create additional tunnel groups if necessary. The configuration of tunnel groups is different between remote access and L2L sessions. The next two sections will discuss each remote access tunnel group's properties and the third section will discuss L2L tunnel group properties.

Remote Access Tunnel Group General Properties

Creating a tunnel group for remote access sessions requires either configuring the existing default remote access tunnel group (similar to the Base Group on a VPN 3000 concentrator) or creating specific tunnel groups. The configuration of a tunnel group for remote access sessions involves the configuration of two sets of properties: General and IPsec. The following commands discuss how to configure a remote access tunnel group's general properties:

```
security(config)# tunnel-group group_name type ipsec-ra
security(config)# tunnel-group {DefaultRAGroup | group_name}
          general-attributes
security(config-general)# address-pool [(interface name)]
          address_pool1 [...address_pool6]
security(config-general)# dhcp-server hostname1 [...hostname10]
security(config-general)# authentication-server-group
          {LOCAL | AAA_server_tag}
```

```
security(config-general)# authorization-server-group
              {LOCAL | AAA_server_tag}
security(config-general)# accounting-server-group
              {LOCAL | AAA_server_tag}
security(config-general)# default-group-policy {DfltGrpPolicy |
              group_policy_name}
security(config-general)# strip-realm
security(config-general)# strip-group
security(config-general)# exit
```

The **tunnel-group type** command specifies the type of the tunnel: the **ipsec-ra** parameter indicates that the tunnel type is for remote access client sessions. The group name for the tunnel group clumps together the **tunnel-group** commands. The **tunnel-group general-attributes** command specifies general attributes for the remote access tunnel of the specified group name, which can include the default group (DefaultRAGroup). This command takes you into a subcommand mode where you can configure the general properties for the remote access group.

The **address-pool** command specifies the address pool or pools created by the **ip local pool** command that should be used by the group. I discussed the **ip local pool** command earlier in the "Address Pool Configuration for 6.x" section. You can qualify which logical interface name on the appliance the pool should be used with—this is necessary only if clients might terminate their VPN tunnel on more than one interface on the appliance. If you don't specify an interface name, the address pool(s) can be used for any interface the client terminates its VPN tunnel on. You can define up to six different address pools for a single group.

The configuration of local pools, as shown in the following code, is necessary when the **vpn-addr-assign** command specifies the **local** parameter:

```
security(config)# vpn-addr-assign {aaa | dhcp | local}
```

There are no defaults to this global command, so you must specify where remote access users will obtain their addressing from. If you specify **aaa**, you'll need to define the addresses on the AAA RADIUS server in each user's account; this is discussed further in this section. If you specify **dhcp**, you must use the **dhcp-server** command to define the IP address or name of the DHCP server or servers that have the user's addressing information; you can define up to 10 DHCP servers.

If you're using an AAA server to store the user accounts and addressing information, you must use the **authentication-server-group** command to specify the AAA group tag that defines the protocol and AAA servers that contain this information (this references the **aaa-server** commands on the appliance). If you specify **LOCAL** (the default, if unspecified), the appliance will look for the user accounts on the PIX/ASA itself by searching for **username** commands, discussed later in the "Creating User Accounts for XAUTH" section of this chapter.

If you've defined your group policies on the PIX/ASA appliance with the **group-policy** commands, you don't need to configure AAA authorization in the tunnel group (it defaults to **LOCAL**); otherwise, if the group policies are on an AAA RADIUS server, you need to specify the AAA group tag to use to download the group policies (this references the **aaa-server** commands that tell the appliance what protocol and server or servers to use). This is configured with the **authorization-server-group** command.

For AAA authentication and authorization functions, you can create accounting records on your AAA server, like when a user brought up a tunnel and authenticated. To perform this function, configure the **accounting-server-group** command, and the required AAA group tag that references the AAA server or servers that will store the accounting records. There is no option for storing these records locally on the PIX/ASA, or for sending them as syslog messages to a syslog server.

NOTE   If you're using AAA, in most cases, the AAA group tag is the same for authentication, authorization, and accounting; however, you can have different sets of servers handling the three separate functions. The configuration of AAA on the security appliance is beyond the scope of this book.

The **default-group-policy** command references the name of the group policy (configured with the **group-policy** commands discussed in the last section) that should be used for this group. You can specify the default policy (DfltGrpPolicy) or specify a specific group policy you created. If you forget to define a policy, the default group policy is used. Only one policy can be applied to a group.

The **strip-realm**, when configured, causes the appliance to strip off any realm qualifier in the user's XAUTH information. With many systems, the user might send something like *username@realm;* this command would strip off the "@realm" portion of the username. This would be required when authentication is occurring externally on an AAA server and the AAA server doesn't support this capability. The **strip-group** command performs the same function, removing any group name that is appended to the user's name in this format: *username@group*. By default, both of these are disabled.

Remote Access Tunnel Group IPsec Properties

Once you've defined your general properties for your tunnel group, you're ready to define its ISAKMP/IKE/IPsec properties. This is done with the following configuration:

```
security(config)# tunnel-group group_name ipsec-attributes
security(config-ipsec)# pre-shared-key key
security(config-ipsec)# peer-id-validate {req | cert | nocheck}
security(config-ipsec)# chain
security(config-ipsec)# trustpoint trustpoint_name
security(config-ipsec)# authorization-dn-attributes
                {primary_attribute [secondary_attribute] |
                use-entire-name}
security(config-ipsec)# authorization-required
security(config-ipsec)# radius-with-expiry
security(config-ipsec)# client-update type type url url_string
                rev-nums revision_numbers
security(config-ipsec)# isakmp keepalive threshold number retry number
```

The **tunnel-group ipsec-attributes** command defines ISAKMP/IKE/IPsec attributes for your remote access group. Executing this command takes you into a subcommand mode where you can define your properties. If the remote access group is using pre-shared keys, use the **pre-shared-key** command to define the key. The key can be between 1–128 characters in length. If you're going to use certificates, omit the configuration of this command.

When using certificates in your network, you can configure a certificate policy on your appliance with the **peer-id-validate** command. If you specify the **req** parameter, the peer must use a certificate. The **cert** parameter specifies that if the appliance has a certificate and an ISAKMP policy with certificates enabled, and the peer has and wants to use certificates, the appliance will use certificates for device authentication. The **nocheck** parameter specifies that the appliance should not check for the use of certificates. If you don't configure a pre-shared key for the group with the **pre-shared-key** command, the default value for this command is **req**. Remember that if you'll be using certificates, you'll need an ISAKMP/IKE Phase 1 policy that includes certificates for device authentication.

If you are using a hierarchical implementation with certificates and want to send the appliance's subordinate root certificate and the certificates for the other higher-level root certificates, use the **chain** command; by default, the appliance will send only the root certificate of the CA that generated the appliance's identity certificate. If your appliance has two identity certificates from two different roots, you can specify which identity certificate to use for the remote access group by using the **trustpoint** command followed by the name of the trustpoint that generated the appliance's identity certificate.

You also can specify which field to use on the certificate for user authorization. By default, this is only the CN field on the certificate, but can be changed with the **authorization-dn-attributes** command. Attributes you can specify are CN (common name), OU (organizational unit), O (organization), L (locality), SP (state/province), C (country), UID (user ID), T (title), SN (surname), N (name), I (initials), GN (given name), DNQ (DN qualifier), EA (e-mail address), SER (serial number), and GENQ (generational qualifier). You can specify up to two attributes. The **use-entire-name** parameter specifies that the appliance should use the entire subject DN information to derive the user name credentials. The default value for the primary attribute is DN and the secondary attribute is OU.

The **authorization-required** command specifies that a user must be authorized before allowing the user to connect (this is disabled, by default). If your appliance will be using MS-CHAPv2 to negotiate a password update with a user during authentication, you need to configure the **radius-with-expiry** command. This is necessary only if the remote client is using Cisco VPN Client software and the user account is stored on an AAA RADIUS server; Microsoft's L2TP/IPsec client is not presently supported.

The **client-update** command specifies which clients should be running which version of software; if the client is not running the specified software version, it tells the client where to download the correct version. The **type** parameter refers to the type of client, which can be **Win9X** (Windows 95, 98, and ME), **WinNT** (Windows NT 4.0, 2000, and XP), **Windows** (all Windows platforms), and **vpn3002** (3002 hardware client). The **url** parameter specifies the URL location to download the file if the client isn't running the specified client version. The client version is specified by the **rev-nums** parameter, like 4.6.1 or 4.1.7.Rel. This process also is discussed in Chapters 12, "Cisco VPN Software Client," and 14, "3002 Hardware Client." For a VPN 3002 hardware client, the URL must use TFTP for the download; for the Windows client, use HTTP or HTTPS. Within a tunnel group, you can specify up to four client update entries by executing the **client-update** command four times with different update entries.

NOTE	The VPN 3002 supports automatic updates. It will download the correct software version automatically, install it, and reboot itself. Only the 4.6 version of the Cisco VPN Client for Windows supports this feature for software clients; prior versions of the VPN Client require the user to download the software update, uninstall the software client, reboot the PC, install the new client, and re-reboot the PC.

The **isakmp keepalive threshold** command defines the values for dead peer detection (DPD). The default threshold is to send an ISAKMP/IKE keepalive every 300 seconds for remote access groups and every 10 seconds for L2L groups, but this can range from 10–3,600 seconds. If a response is not received for a keepalive, the appliance will retry in 2 seconds, but this value can range from 2–10 seconds.

L2L Tunnel Groups

FOS 6.*x* had one problem with IPsec VPNs: if you wanted to terminate both L2L and remote access sessions on a PIX, remote access users using pre-shared keys could be confused with L2L peers with dynamic addresses and wildcarded pre-shared keys, and treated as an L2L peer, causing session failures because the client was expecting XAUTH and IKE Mode Config. Version 7.0 uses tunnel groups to deal with this issue.

I've already discussed how to set up tunnel groups and group policies for remote access users. With L2L sessions, you also can use tunnel groups to define properties for the L2L peers, as shown in the following configuration code:

```
security(config)# tunnel-group peer_name_or_IP_address type ipsec-l2l
security(config)# tunnel-group {DefaultL2LAGroup | group_name}
               general-attributes
security(config-general)# accounting-server-group
               {LOCAL | AAA_server_tag}
security(config-general)# exit
security(config)# tunnel-group peer_name_or_IP_address
               ipsec-attributes
security(config-ipsec)# pre-shared-key key
security(config-ipsec)# peer-id-validate {req | cert | nocheck}
security(config-ipsec)# chain
security(config-ipsec)# trustpoint trustpoint_name
security(config-ipsec)# isakmp keepalive threshold number retry number
```

The **tunnel-group** command specifies the L2L peer that is connecting to the appliance. If the ISAKMP identity type is IP address (configured with the **isakmp identity** command), then you specify the IP address of the peer; if the type is hostname, you specify the name of the remote peer. For peers that obtain their addresses dynamically, you would use the default L2L group (DefaultL2LGroup). The tunnel type must be configured as **ipsec-l2l**. The only general attribute that is applicable for L2L sessions is AAA accounting. For IPsec attributes, only the **pre-shared-key, peer-id-validate, chain, trustpoint**, and **isakmp keepalive threshold** commands are applicable: these commands were discussed in the last section.

Creating User Accounts for XAUTH

On FOS 7.0 Easy VPN Servers, if you have defined a group policy for remote access users that specifies that their accounts are stored on the security appliance, you'll need to create the accounts and, possibly, specific user policies for your users. These specific user policies can override the group policies. For example, the group policy might specify that users in the group can connect to the appliance only during business hours; however, for a specific user or users you can override the group policy and define a different restriction, or ignore the restriction.

To create users locally, use the following command:

```
security(config)# username user's_name password password
               [privilege privilege_level]
```

The **username** command creates a user's account; whatever password you configure on the appliance will be encrypted by the appliance automatically and cannot be seen once configured. The appliance supports 16 privilege levels: 0–15, where 0 restricts the user to very few appliance commands and 15 allows access to all commands. If you don't specify the privilege level, it defaults to 2.

CAUTION   If AAA is enabled on your appliance, if you've defined both management and XAUTH accounts locally, and if you are using these accounts for management access to the PIX, the XAUTH accounts can be used to access the PIX. Based on this issue, you can use an AAA server for the XAUTH accounts and then specify on the AAA server that local login access (to the ASA) is not allowed. If this is not an option, set the privilege level to 0 for the XAUTH accounts, restricting what the user can execute on the appliance.

When you add a user locally, it does not have any attributes associated with it and is associated with a group only when the user brings up a remote access session and either provides the group name with the pre-shared key or the group name is obtained from the user's certificate. With 7.0, you now have the ability to define attributes specific to a user with the following commands:

```
security(config)# username user's_name attributes
security(config-username)# vpn-group-policy group_policy_name
security(config-username)# vpn-framed-ip-address IP_address
security(config-username)# vpn-access-hours value time_range_name
security(config-username)# vpn-simultaneous-logins number
security(config-username)# vpn-idle-timeout minutes
security(config-username)# vpn-session-timeout minutes
security(config-username)# vpn-filter value ACL_name
security(config-username)# vpn-tunnel-protocol [ipsec] [webvpn]
security(config-username)# group-lock value tunnel_group_name
security(config-username)# password-storage {enable | disable}
```

The **username attributes** command takes you into a subcommand mode where the attributes you specify in this mode apply only to this user; plus, any attributes you define here automatically override any group attributes assigned to the user based on the user's group membership.

The **vpn-group-policy** command specifies the name of the group policy configured in the **group-policy** command that should be applied to the user, allowing the user to inherit the policies from the specified policy. If you don't configure this command, the user inherits no properties by default, but obtains these once the user connects and specifies the group name, if any, that user should be associated with. This command is commonly used for remote access clients that don't or can't specify a group name for their membership.

The **vpn-framed-ip-address** command allows you to assign a specific IP address to a user instead of assigning an address dynamically from a locally configured pool, a DHCP server, or an AAA server. This is useful if you have per-user policies based on ACLs behind the security appliance, and the user always must use the same IP address.

I discussed the rest of the commands previously in the "Default and Specific Group Policy Attribute Configuration" section. If you don't configure any attributes for the user, the user will use the attribute defined by the group policy that user is associated with, after being authenticated.

Once you've created your users and, possibly, specific user policies, you can view them with the **show running-config all username** command.

TIP   For the one or two remote access hardware clients that are set up for default unit authentication, where you must store the XAUTH username and password locally on the hardware client, instead of creating a separate group for this small number of hardware clients, you could set up their usernames with the **password-storage enable** command. By doing this, you still could put the hardware clients in the same group as remote access users, but allow the use of default unit authentication.

Issues with Remote Access Sessions and Solutions in 7.0

In this last section covering the 7.0 software and Easy VPN Servers, I'll discuss some issues related to remote access users, including problems and solutions related to the following:

- Simultaneously supporting both remote access and L2L sessions
- Using more than one Server to handle remote access sessions
- Restricting the total number of VPN sessions

Simultaneously Supporting Remote Access and L2L Sessions

One problem that has always existed on the PIX in FOS 6.*x* and earlier versions was supporting both remote access and L2L sessions simultaneously. Even when using certificates, there still might be a problem where:

- Certain remote access users are associated with an L2L session
- An L2L session is associated with a default remote access group

To overcome this problem, one solution is to create certificate map rules and then associate these rules with a particular tunnel group (assuming you're using certificates for device authentication). Certificate map rules allow you to look at X.500 information on a certificate, and based on matching criteria you specify, such as certain CN and/or OU values, you can associate the device of that certificate with a specific tunnel group; this ensures that remote access users are associated with remote access tunnel groups and L2L peers with L2L tunnel groups.

Using the certificate map rules feature involves two steps: configuring the certificate mapping rules and then associating them with a tunnel group. The following two sections will discuss each of these steps, followed by an example configuration.

Configuring Certificate Mapping Rules

Certificate mapping rules allow you to specify which fields on a certificate you want to examine and which values should be found in those fields. Creating a certificate mapping rule involves the following commands:

```
security(config)# crypto ca certificate map rule_#
security(config-ca-cert-map)# issuer {eq | ne | co | nc} value
security(config-ca-cert-map)# subject-name [attr tag]
               {eq | ne |co | nc} string
```

The **crypto ca certificate map** command is used to create mapping rules. You can create multiple rules, where each rule is given a different number from 1–65,535. Rules are processed in numerical order. Executing this command takes you into a subcommand mode. The **issuer** command allows you to look at the issuer field on the identity certificate for a match—this can be used if you have two identity certificates from two different CAs and want to specify the correct IPsec tunnel group (and thus CA) to use for device authentication. You can match a value in the issuer field using the following values:

- **eq**—equal to the specified value
- **ne**—not equal to the specified value
- **co**—contains the specified value
- **nc**—does not contain the specified value

For example, **issuer eq caserver** in the rule specifies that the issuer on the certificate must match "caserver." The match type parameter also is used in the **subject-name** command. This command specifies which contents of the certificate will be associated with the rule. If you don't specify the **attr** parameter, the entire identity certificate information is used when looking for match in the *string;* otherwise, if you use this parameter, you can examine a specific field on the certificate: **DNQ** (DN qualifier), **GENQ** (generational qualifier), **I** (initials), **GN** (given name), **N** (name), **SN** (surname), **IP** (IP address), **SER** (serial number), **UNAME** (unstructured name), **EA** (e-mail address), **T** (title), **O** (organization name), **L** (locality), **SP** (state/province), **C** (country), **OU** (organizational unit), and **CN** (common name).

As an example of matching on identity information on a certificate, if you configured **subject-name attr cn eq "richard deal,"** this command would cause an identity certificate with the common name of "richard deal" to be associated with this rule; in addition, when the rule is associated with a tunnel group, the user of this certificate then could be placed in the correct tunnel group. This might be necessary for this user if the user was originally in the sales group and then moved to marketing, where you currently are using the OU field for the group name; however, when the user moved to the new group, instead of creating a new certificate for the user, you could create the appropriate certificate matching rule and then associate the rule with the user's new group.

Associating Certificate Mapping Rules with a Tunnel Group

Once you've created your certificate mapping rules, you can then use them by associating the rules with a tunnel group. First, you must specify which type of matching will be used to associate a user to a group with this command:

```
security(config)# tunnel-group-map enable
              {ike-id | ou | peer-ip | rules}
```

If you don't configure this command, the default matching is **ou**, which causes the appliance to use the OU field in a certificate when associating the remote access user or L2L peer to a group. If you want to use your certificate matching rules, you must configure the above command with the **rules** parameter. The **ike-id** parameter specifies group matching when certificates are being used—this is not done by the OU value on the certificate, but instead on the ID information shared during ISAKMP/IKE Phase 1. The **peer-ip** parameter specifies that the IP address of the peer is used to associate a peer to a particular tunnel group.

If you're using the certificate matching rules, you can then use the following command to associate a match for a particular rule to a specific tunnel group:

```
security(config)# tunnel-group-map rule_# default-group
              tunnel_group_name
```

This command associates a specific matching rule for a specific group.

Illustrating the Use of Certificate Mapping Rules

Example 22-5 illustrates the use of certificate mapping rules. In this example, Alina was originally in the sales group, had an OU value of "sales" on her certificate, and correctly was associated with the sales group; however, she was moved over to marketing and needs to use the policies associated with this group. The configuration in Example 22-5 accomplishes this, assuming the CN field on Alina's certificate is "alina deal." Otherwise, the OU field is used to associate users to the marketing or sales group. Also, one L2L peer, asapeer, who has a CN of "asapeer.cisco.com," is being associated to an L2L IPsec tunnel group called "asapeer."

Example 22-5 *Using Certificate Mapping Rules*

```
asa(config)# crypto ca certificate map 1
asa(config-ca-cert-map)# subject-name attr co cn "alina deal"
asa(config-ca-cert-map)# exit
asa(config)# crypto ca certificate map 2
asa(config-ca-cert-map)# subject-name attr eq ou marketing
```

continues

Example 22-5 *Using Certificate Mapping Rules (Continued)*

```
asa(config-ca-cert-map)# exit
asa(config)# crypto ca certificate map 3
asa(config-ca-cert-map)# subject-name attr eq ou sales
asa(config-ca-cert-map)# exit
asa(config)# crypto ca certificate map 4
asa(config-ca-cert-map)# subject-name attr co cn asapeer.cisco.com
asa(config-ca-cert-map)# exit
asa(config)# tunnel-group-map enable rules
asa(config)# tunnel-group-map 1 default-group marketing
asa(config)# tunnel-group-map 2 default-group marketing
asa(config)# tunnel-group-map 3 default-group sales
asa(config)# tunnel-group-map 4 default-group asapeer
```

NOTE   If you are using certificate mapping with an appliance terminating both remote access and
L2L sessions, you can use the above feature easily to look at certificate information for L2L
peers and put them into the correct L2L group, and remote access users in the correct remote
access group; however, certificate mapping could involve a lot of configuration on your part
to associate the right device or user to the correct tunnel group on the appliance. Therefore,
I typically try to use this as a last resort when associating a peer with the correct tunnel group.

Using More than One Server to Handle Remote Access Sessions

With the introduction of FOS 7.0 and the ASA security appliances (5520s and 5540s), you
now can use the load balancing feature (VCA) that only the VPN 3000 series concentrators
originally supported. Unfortunately, this feature is not supported on the PIX security
appliances; but one nice bonus is that the load balancing feature is fully compatible with
the VPN 3000 concentrators and can be included in the same VCA cluster.

As you recall from Chapter 10, "Concentrator Management," VCA requires that you set up
a virtual IP address that the Easy VPN Remotes connect to. The master of the cluster handles
this initial connection, examines the load across the members of the cluster, and sends back
a physical address of the member with the least load. The Remote then connects to the
physical address. If a member of the cluster fails, the Remote should be able to discover this
quickly using DPD, reconnect to the virtual address, and thus be redirected to another
member of the cluster.

Setting up VCA on an ASA involves the following commands:

```
asa(config)# vpn load-balancing
asa(config-load-balancing)# cluster ip address virtual_IP_address
asa(config-load-balancing)# cluster port port_#
asa(config-load-balancing)# cluster encryption
asa(config-load-balancing)# cluster key shared_secret_key
asa(config-load-balancing)# interface {lbprivate | lbpublic}
                 logical_interface_name
asa(config-load-balancing)# nat IP_address
asa(config-load-balancing)# priority priority_#
asa(config-load-balancing)# participate
```

The **vpn load-balancing** command configures VCA, taking you into a subcommand mode to complete the configuration. The **cluster ip address** command specifies the virtual IP address of the cluster—this is what the Remotes will use for the Easy VPN Server address. The default port number of load balancing is UDP 9,023; this can be changed with the **cluster port** command. If you change the port number on one member in the cluster, you must match this on all members of the cluster. VCA messages sent between cluster members are not encrypted by default. The **cluster encryption** command enables the encryption of VCA messages and the **cluster key** command configures the encryption key to encrypt the messages (this must match what's configured on the other members). The **interface** command specifies which logical interface on the ASA should be associated with the public interface (**lbpublic**) and which with the private (**lbprivate**). The **nat** command is necessary only if an address translation device sits between the cluster and the Remotes. This command specifies the global address that represents the address of the ASA on its public interface. When performing redirection, the master will send the global address to the Remote, which the Remote will use to connect to the cluster member. The **priority** command is used to affect which cluster member is chosen as the master: the higher the number the more likely the member will be chosen. The priority can range from 1–10. If you don't configure it, the 5520 has a default priority of 5 and the 5540 a priority of 7. Last, you must enable load balancing with the **participate** command.

To view your load balancing configuration, use the **show running-config vpn load-balancing** command; to view the runtime statistics of the operation of load balancing, use the **show vpn load-balancing** command.

Setting up load balancing, as you can see, is simple. I'll use Figure 22-3 to illustrate its configuration. Examples 22-6 and 22-7 show the configurations of the two ASAs. In this example, Remotes need to connect to 192.1.1.3, which, by default, ASA1 will handle because it has a higher priority.

Figure 22-3 *ASA and Load Balancing*

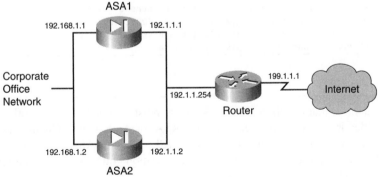

Virtual Cluster Address: 192.1.1.3

Example 22-6 *Load Balancing on ASA1*

```
asa1(config)# interface GigabitEthernet 0/1
asa1(config-if)# ip address 192.1.1.1 255.255.255.0
asa1(config-if)# nameif public
asa1(config-if)# security-level 0
asa1(config-if)# exit
asa1(config)# interface GigabitEthernet 0/2
asa1(config-if)# ip address 192.168.1.1 255.255.255.0
asa1(config-if)# nameif private
asa1(config-if)# security-level 100
asa1(config-if)# exit
asa1(config)# vpn load-balancing
asa1(config-load-balancing)# interface lbpublic public
asa1(config-load-balancing)# interface lbprivate private
asa1(config-load-balancing)# cluster ip address 192.1.1.3
asa1(config-load-balancing)# cluster key 123cisco
asa1(config-load-balancing)# cluster encryption
asa1(config-load-balancing)# priority 10
asa1(config-load-balancing)# participate
```

Example 22-7 *Load Balancing on ASA2*

```
asa2(config)# interface GigabitEthernet 0/1
asa2(config-if)# ip address 192.1.1.2 255.255.255.0
asa2(config-if)# nameif public
asa1(config-if)# security-level 0
asa2(config-if)# exit
asa2(config)# interface GigabitEthernet 0/2
asa2(config-if)# ip address 192.168.1.2 255.255.255.0
asa2(config-if)# nameif private
asa1(config-if)# security-level 100
asa2(config-if)# exit
asa2(config)# vpn load-balancing
asa2(config-load-balancing)# interface lbpublic public
asa2(config-load-balancing)# interface lbprivate private
asa2(config-load-balancing)# cluster ip address 192.1.1.3
asa2(config-load-balancing)# cluster key 123cisco
asa2(config-load-balancing)# cluster encryption
asa2(config-load-balancing)# participate
```

NOTE   Remember that members of a VCA cluster must be able to see each other off of all
enabled interfaces. This means that the ASA must allow the VCA messages (UDP port
9,023) on any interface that contains an ACL. Also, the ASA must have an active 3DES/
AES license; if it doesn't, any VCA configuration you've set up on the ASA is ignored
by the ASA.

To use a PIX/ASA or not?

If I had to implement an Easy VPN Server or an L2L session and I had a choice between a PIX running FOS 6.*x* and another device, such as a concentrator for remote access or a router for L2L, I would very rarely choose the PIX because of its limitations. Some people like the 6.*x* software because setting up VPNs is simple; but the FOS 6.*x* software had too many limitations that typically wouldn't provide the functionality I or my customers needed. However, with the introduction of 7.0, Cisco has greatly enhanced the capabilities of the PIX/ASA. Actually, if I had to choose between a router and a PIX/ASA for an Easy VPN Server, today I would easily choose the PIX/ASA because of their advanced capabilities, especially the ASA with its support of features like WebVPN and load balancing. And if I needed a one-box solution, with firewall, remote access VPN, and intrusion prevention in one box, I definitely would consider the PIX/ASA over a VPN concentrator or an IOS router.

Restricting the Total Number of VPN Sessions

One problem you might face with your appliance is dealing with the large number of IPsec sessions terminating on it. With the ASAs, this is more of a concern on the 5510 and, possibly, the 5520, because of their VPN session license limits. This can be problematic if one group of remote access users is using up all of the VPN sessions allowed by the appliance, leaving none for other groups or for L2L sessions. One solution to this is to disconnect the users with the **vpn-sessiondb logoff** command:

```
security# vpn-sessiondb logoff {remote | l2l | webvpn | email-proxy |
          protocol protocol_name | name username |
          ipaddress IP_address | tunnel-group
          tunnel_group_name | index indexnumber | all}
```

As you can see from the above command, you can terminate all remote access users with the **remote** parameter, all L2L users with the **l2l** parameter, a specific user with the **name** parameter, a user based on their IP address with the **ipaddress** parameter, all members of a particular tunnel group with the **tunnel-group** parameter, and others.

Also, if your appliance is overloaded, you can specify a lower limit of VPN sessions the appliance will accept. This is configured with the following command:

```
security(config)# vpn-sessiondb max-session-limit #_of_sessions
```

Illustrating an Easy VPN Server Configuration Example for 7.0

To better understand how tunnel groups and group policies are used to terminate Easy VPN Remote sessions on your security appliance acting as an Easy VPN Server, I'll now show you a simple configuration example. In this example, I'll use a PIX 515E running Version 7.0 as the Server and the network shown previously in Figure 22-1. This is basically the same example I illustrated earlier in the "6.*x* Easy VPN Remote Example Configuration"; however, this example will show you how to configure the Server running 7.0.

Example 22-8 shows the configuration of the Server. Reference numbers to the right of the configuration commands are explained below the example.

Example 22-8 *Network with a 515E and 7.0 as an Easy VPN Server*

```
Server(config)# interface ethernet0
Server(config-if)# ip address 192.1.1.1 255.255.0.0
Server(config-if)# nameif outside
Server(config-if)# exit
Server(config)# interface ethernet1
Server(config-if)# ip address 192.168.0.1 255.255.0.0
Server(config-if)# nameif inside
Server(config-if)# exit
Server(config)# isakmp policy 1 authentication pre-share          (1)
Server(config)# isakmp policy 1 encryption 3des
Server(config)# isakmp policy 1 hash sha
Server(config)# isakmp policy 1 group 2
Server(config)# isakmp policy 1 lifetime 3600
Server(config)# isakmp enable outside
Server(config)# access-list split-tunnel permit                   (2)
            192.168.0.0 255.255.255.0
            192.168.0.0 255.255.255.0
Server(config)# group-policy salespolicy internal                 (3)
Server(config)# group-policy salespolicy attributes
Server(config-group-policy)# domain-name cisco.com
Server(config-group-policy)# dns-server value 192.168.0.10
Server(config-group-policy)# split-dns cisco.com
Server(config-group-policy)# wins-server value 192.168.0.11
Server(config-group-policy)# vpn-session-timeout 15
Server(config-group-policy)# split-tunnel-policy tunnelspecified
Server(config-group-policy)# split-tunnel-network-list
            value split-tunnel
Server(config-group-policy)# client-firewall req
            sygate-personal-pro
Server(config-group-policy)# exit
Server(config)# ip local pool salespool                           (4)
            192.168.0.200-192.168.0.254
Server(config)# username salesuser password sales123              (5)
Server(config)# tunnel-group salesgroup type ipsec-ra             (6)
Server(config)# tunnel-group salesgroup general-attributes
Server(config-general)# address-pool salespool
Server(config-general)# exit
Server(config)# tunnel-group salesgroup ipsec-attributes
Server(config-ipsec)# pre-shared-key salesgroup123
Server(config-ipsec)# isakmp keepalive threshold 20 retry 10
Server(config-ipsec)# exit
Server(config)# crypto ipsec transform set trans1                 (7)
            esp-3des esp-md5-hmac
Server(config)# crypto dynamic-map dyn1 1 set                     (8)
            transform-set trans1
Server(config)# crypto dynamic-map dyn1 1 set reverse-route
Server(config)# crypto map mymap 999 ipsec-isakmp dynamic dyn1
Server(config)# crypto map mymap interface outside
Server(config)# sysopt connection permit-ipsec
```

Here's an explanation of the references in the above example:

1 An ISAKMP/IKE Phase 1 policy is defined for pre-shared keys and ISAKMP is enabled on the PIX's outside interface.

2 A split tunneling ACL is configured: only the traffic sent to and from the Remotes to the cisco.com site is protected.

3 A policy called "salespolicy" is defined with the split tunneling policy, and with other parameters, including the requirement of Sygate's firewall with the AYT feature.

4 An address pool is created to be used in the assignment of internal addresses to the Remotes.

5 A user is defined and will inherit its attributes from the group it authenticates to.

6 A remote access group is created and associated with the address pool in reference (4) along with a pre-shared key of "salesgroup123."

7 A transform set is defined to protect the data SAs.

8 A dynamic and static crypto map are enabled, in addition to being activated on the outside interface; IPsec traffic is also exempted from ACL processing on the outside interface.

As you can see from this example, the configuration is more complex than an Easy VPN PIX Server running 6.2 or 6.3 code; however, you have much more flexibility and management in defining and associating polices for the Remote devices.

NOTE   The ASAs support the ability to terminate WebVPN sessions; however, the PIXs do not. The configuration of WebVPN is very similar to the configuration of it on Cisco routers, which was discussed in Chapter 18, "Router Remote Access Connections." Therefore, I've omitted the discussion of WebVPN from this chapter.

Summary

This chapter showed you the basics of setting up your security appliance as an Easy VPN Server using both the older PIX FOS (6.x) and the newer 7.0 (PIXs and ASAs). And in 7.0, support for WebVPN was added for the ASAs. In 6.x, the PIX 501 and 506E can also be Remotes.

Next up is Chapter 23, "Troubleshooting PIX and ASA Connections," where I show you how to use basic security appliance commands to troubleshoot the setup of VPN sessions.

CHAPTER 23

Troubleshooting PIX and ASA Connections

This chapter will focus on how to troubleshoot IPsec sessions on Cisco PIX and ASA security appliances. The layout of this chapter is similar to that found in Chapter 19, "Troubleshooting Router Connections." I've broken the chapter into two areas on troubleshooting: ISAKMP/IKE Phase 1 and ISAKMP/IKE Phase 2 issues. With these two areas, I'll show you how ISAKMP/IKE Phase 1 and 2 connections are built, and what to look for when there is a problem with either of these phases.

This chapter by no means covers all possible problems you'll experience with IPsec sessions on Cisco security appliances. However, I hope to provide you with the basic background knowledge so that troubleshooting IPsec sessions on the appliances is a simpler process.

ISAKMP/IKE Phase 1 Connections

In the first part of this chapter I'll focus on troubleshooting ISAKMP/IKE Phase 1 connections. If you recall from Chapter 3, "IPsec," the management connection built during Phase 1 is used to pass IPsec management traffic; no user data traverses this connection. This connection is important, however, because it is used to build the two data connections for Phase 2. I've broken this part of the chapter into three areas:

- An overview of the ISAKMP/IKE Phase 1 troubleshooting commands
- Examining your management connections
- Examining the building of L2L and remote access management connections
- Troubleshooting Easy VPN connections on a Remote

Overview of the Phase 1 Commands

You can use several commands to troubleshoot ISAKMP/IKE Phase 1 connections on the security appliances, including the following:

- **show isakmp sa [detail]**—Displays the status of any management connections.
- **show [crypto] isakmp stats**—Displays the statistics of the management connections (FOS 7.0 only).

- **show [crypto] isakmp ipsec-over-tcp stats**—Displays the statistics of any IPsec over TCP connections the management connection is managing (FOS 7.0 only).

- **debug crypto isakmp**—Displays the steps taken to build a management connection and data connections via the management connection.

- **debug crypto vpnclient**—Displays the interaction between the appliance, acting as an Easy VPN Remote, and the Easy VPN Server (FOS 6.3 only).

- **debug crypto ca [messages | transactions]**—Displays the interaction between the appliance and CA for certificate enrollment and authentication functions; the optional parameters are new in FOS 7.0. The 7.0 version of this command produces similar output compared to the **debug crypto pki** command discussed in Chapter 19; therefore, I won't cover it in this chapter.

- **debug crypto engine**—Displays events related to the encryption/decryption problems on the appliance.

- **clear [crypto] isakmp sa** [*SA_ID_#*]—Deletes all the management SAs or a specific management connection by specifying the SA ID number.

As you can see from the above list, not all commands are supported in all FOS versions. The following sections will discuss some of the more important commands, related to troubleshooting connectivity processes, in more depth.

NOTE   Before FOS 7.0, I found the output of **debug** commands less administrator-friendly than the debug output from IOS routers. In FOS 6.3 and earlier, I tended to try to troubleshoot IPsec problems from the remote peer and would look at the PIX's debug output only when I was still having problems trying to pinpoint the problem. However, Cisco has rectified most of my concerns in regard to this in FOS 7.0. In FOS 7.0, the debug output is much more similar to the debug output of IOS-based routers.

The show isakmp sa Command

Example 23-1 illustrates the use of the **show isakmp sa** command with an appliance running FOS 6.3. The output of this command is very similar to the **show crypto isakmp sa** command in Chapter 16, "Router ISAKMP/IKE Phase 1 Connectivity." Table 16-1 in that chapter explains the states. If you recall, QM_IDLE indicates the successful setup of the connection to the associated peer. If you're seeing MM_NO_STATE or AG_NO_STATE, this indicates that there is a problem with the initial setup of the connection. The two most common problems that might cause this are:

- You forgot to activate the crypto map or profile on the remote peer router's interface.

- There is no matching ISAKMP/IKE Phase 1 policy on the remote peer.

If you see a state of MM_KEY_EXCH or AG_INIT_EXCH, then probably the culprit is failed device authentication. For pre-shared keys, be sure you've configured the keys correctly. For certificates, verify that they haven't expired, that the date and time are correct on the peers, and that they haven't been revoked.

TIP   You can use the **debug [crypto] isakmp sa** command for more detailed troubleshooting based on the output of the **show crypto isakmp sa** command.

Example 23-1 *The* **show crypto isakmp sa** *Command in 6.3*

```
pix63(config)# show isakmp sa
Total    : 1
Embryonic : 0
         dst              src          state     pending     created
     192.1.1.101       192.1.1.40      QM_IDLE         0           0
```

In FOS 7.0, the output of the command is different, as shown in Example 23-2. Instead of seeing "QM_IDLE" when the management connection has completed, you'll see either "MM_Active" or "AG_Active," depending on whether main mode or aggressive mode was used to build the management connection, respectively.

Example 23-2 *The* **show crypto isakmp sa** *Command in 7.0*

```
pix70(config-general)# show isakmp sa
   Active SA: 1
    Rekey SA: 0 (A tunnel will report 1 Active and 1 Rekey SA during rekey)
Total IKE SA: 1

1   IKE Peer: 192.1.1.40
    Type    : L2L            Role     : responder
    Rekey   : no             State    : MM_ACTIVE
```

The debug crypto isakmp Command

In most instances, you'll use the **debug crypto isakmp** command to assist in detailed troubleshooting of building ISAKMP/IKE Phase 1 management connections as well as Phase 2 data connections the management connection builds. Deciphering the output of this command is not that simple. The following two sections will take a look at a few examples of L2L and remote access sessions.

NOTE   Because the output of the **debug** commands in FOS 6.3 and earlier is somewhat similar to that of Cisco routers, the following sections will focus on the use of the commands in FOS 7.0.

L2L Sessions

To understand how an L2L session is successfully set up, view the output from the **debug crypto isakmp** command in Example 23-3. In this example, the output is from a simple L2L configuration where the appliance is accepting a session setup request from a remote L2L peer. I've added steps to the right of some of the output, which are explained below the example.

Example 23-3 *Successful Building of the Management Connection in FOS 7.0*

```
[IKEv1 DEBUG]: IP = 192.1.1.40, processing SA payload              (1)
[IKEv1 DEBUG]: IP = 192.1.1.40, Oakley proposal is acceptable
←output omitted→
[IKEv1 DEBUG]: IP = 192.1.1.40, Received NAT-Traversal ver 03 VID (2)
←output omitted→
[IKEv1 DEBUG]: IP = 192.1.1.40, processing IKE SA                 (3)
[IKEv1 DEBUG]: IP = 192.1.1.40, IKE SA Proposal # 1,              (4)
    Transform # 1 acceptable  Matches global IKE entry # 2
[IKEv1 DEBUG]: IP = 192.1.1.40, constructing ISA_SA for isakmp    (5)
←output omitted→
[IKEv1 DEBUG]: IP = 192.1.1.40, processing ke payload
[IKEv1 DEBUG]: IP = 192.1.1.40, processing ISA_KE
[IKEv1 DEBUG]: IP = 192.1.1.40, processing nonce payload
[IKEv1 DEBUG]: IP = 192.1.1.40, processing VID payload
[IKEv1 DEBUG]: IP = 192.1.1.40, Received Cisco Unity client VID
[IKEv1 DEBUG]: IP = 192.1.1.40, processing VID payload
[IKEv1 DEBUG]: IP = 192.1.1.40, Received DPD VID
[IKEv1 DEBUG]: IP = 192.1.1.40, processing VID payload
[IKEv1 DEBUG]: IP = 192.1.1.40, Processing IOS/PIX Vendor ID payload
      (version: 1.0.0, capabilities: 0000077f)
[IKEv1 DEBUG]: IP = 192.1.1.40, processing VID payload
[IKEv1 DEBUG]: IP = 192.1.1.40, Received xauth V6 VID
[IKEv1 DEBUG]: IP = 192.1.1.40, constructing ke payload
[IKEv1 DEBUG]: IP = 192.1.1.40, constructing nonce payload
[IKEv1 DEBUG]: IP = 192.1.1.40, constructing Cisco Unity VID payload
[IKEv1 DEBUG]: IP = 192.1.1.40, constructing xauth V6 VID payload
[IKEv1 DEBUG]: IP = 192.1.1.40, Send IOS VID
[IKEv1 DEBUG]: IP = 192.1.1.40, Constructing ASA spoofing IOS Vendor
ID payload (version: 1.0.0, capabilities: 20000001)
[IKEv1 DEBUG]: IP = 192.1.1.40, constructing VID payload
[IKEv1 DEBUG]: IP = 192.1.1.40, Send Altiga/Cisco
    VPN3000/Cisco ASA GW VID
[IKEv1]: IP = 192.1.1.40, Connection landed on tunnel_group        (6)
    192.1.1.40
[IKEv1 DEBUG]: Group = 192.1.1.40, IP = 192.1.1.40, Generating keys
    for Responder...
[IKEv1]: IP = 192.1.1.40, IKE DECODE SENDING Message (msgid=0) with
    payloads : HDR + KE (4) + NONCE (10) + VENDOR (13) + VENDOR (13)
    + VENDOR (13) + VENDOR (13) + NONE (0) total length : 256
[IKEv1]: IP = 192.1.1.40, IKE DECODE RECEIVED Message (msgid=0) with
    payloads : HDR + ID (5) + HASH (8) + IOS KEEPALIVE (14) +
    NOTIFY (11) + NONE (0) total length : 112
[IKEv1 DEBUG]: Group = 192.1.1.40, IP = 192.1.1.40, Processing ID (7)
[IKEv1 DECODE]: ID_IPV4_ADDR ID received 192.1.1.40
```

Example 23-3 *Successful Building of the Management Connection in FOS 7.0 (Continued)*

```
[IKEv1 DEBUG]: Group = 192.1.1.40, IP = 192.1.1.40, processing hash
[IKEv1 DEBUG]: Group = 192.1.1.40, IP = 192.1.1.40, computing hash
[IKEv1 DEBUG]: IP = 192.1.1.40, Processing IOS keep alive payload:
    proposal=30/10 sec.
[IKEv1 DEBUG]: IP = 192.1.1.40, Starting IOS keepalive monitor:
    80 sec.
[IKEv1 DEBUG]: Group = 192.1.1.40, IP = 192.1.1.40, Processing
    Notify payload
[IKEv1]: IP = 192.1.1.40, Connection landed on tunnel_group
    192.1.1.40
[IKEv1 DEBUG]: Group = 192.1.1.40, IP = 192.1.1.40, constructing ID
[IKEv1 DEBUG]: Group = 192.1.1.40, IP = 192.1.1.40, construct hash
    payload
[IKEv1 DEBUG]: Group = 192.1.1.40, IP = 192.1.1.40, computing hash
[IKEv1 DEBUG]: IP = 192.1.1.40, Constructing IOS keep alive     (8)
    payload: proposal=32767/32767 sec.
[IKEv1 DEBUG]: Group = 192.1.1.40, IP = 192.1.1.40,
    constructing dpd vid payload
←output omitted→
[IKEv1]: Group = 192.1.1.40, IP = 192.1.1.40, PHASE 1 COMPLETED   (9)
[IKEv1]: IP = 192.1.1.40, Keep-alive type for this connection: DPD
[IKEv1 DEBUG]: Group = 192.1.1.40, IP = 192.1.1.40, Starting
    phase 1 rekey timer: 82080000 (ms)
[IKEv1 DECODE]: IP = 192.1.1.40, IKE Responder starting QM:
    msg id = 4a9a7c8b
[IKEv1]: IP = 192.1.1.40, IKE DECODE RECEIVED Message            (10)
    (msgid=4a9a7c8b) with payloads : HDR + HASH (8) + SA (1) +
    NONCE (10) + ID (5) + ID (5) + NONE (0) total length : 172
←output omitted→
[IKEv1 DECODE]: ID_IPV4_ADDR_SUBNET ID received--               (11)
    192.168.0.0--255.255.255.0
[IKEv1]: Group = 192.1.1.40, IP = 192.1.1.40, Received remote IP
    Proxy Subnet data in ID Payload:    Address 192.168.0.0,
    Mask 255.255.255.0, Protocol 0, Port 0
[IKEv1 DEBUG]: Group = 192.1.1.40, IP = 192.1.1.40, Processing ID
[IKEv1 DECODE]: ID_IPV4_ADDR_SUBNET ID received--
    192.168.2.0--255.255.255.0
[IKEv1]: Group = 192.1.1.40, IP = 192.1.1.40, Received local IP Proxy
    Subnet data in ID Payload:    Address 192.168.2.0,
    Mask 255.255.255.0, Protocol 0, Port 0
[IKEv1]: QM IsRekeyed old sa not found by addr
[IKEv1]: Group = 192.1.1.40, IP = 192.1.1.40, Static Crypto Map  (12)
    check, checking map = mymap, seq = 10...
[IKEv1]: Group = 192.1.1.40, IP = 192.1.1.40, Static Crypto Map
    check, map mymap, seq = 10 is a successful match
[IKEv1]: Group = 192.1.1.40, IP = 192.1.1.40, IKE Remote Peer
    configured for SA: mymap
[IKEv1]: Group = 192.1.1.40, IP = 192.1.1.40, processing IPSEC SA
[IKEv1 DEBUG]: Group = 192.1.1.40, IP = 192.1.1.40, IPsec SA      (13)
    Proposal # 1, Transform # 1 acceptable  Matches global IPsec
    SA entry # 10
```

continues

Example 23-3 *Successful Building of the Management Connection in FOS 7.0 (Continued)*

```
[IKEv1]: Group = 192.1.1.40, IP = 192.1.1.40, IKE: requesting SPI!
[IKEv1 DEBUG]: IKE got SPI from key engine: SPI = 0xcc3dcb5a
←output omitted→
[IKEv1 DEBUG]: Group = 192.1.1.40, IP = 192.1.1.40, Transmitting (14)
    Proxy Id: Remote subnet: 192.168.0.0  Mask 255.255.255.0
    Protocol 0  Port 0   Local subnet:  192.168.2.0
    mask 255.255.255.0 Protocol 0  Port 0
←output omitted→
[IKEv1 DEBUG]: Group = 192.1.1.40, IP = 192.1.1.40, loading all  (15)
    IPSEC SAs
[IKEv1 DEBUG]: Group = 192.1.1.40, IP = 192.1.1.40, Generating
    Quick Mode Key!
[IKEv1 DEBUG]: Group = 192.1.1.40, IP = 192.1.1.40, Generating
    Quick Mode Key!
[IKEv1]: Group = 192.1.1.40, IP = 192.1.1.40, Security         (16)
    negotiation complete for LAN-to-LAN Group (192.1.1.40)
    Responder, Inbound SPI = 0xcc3dcb5a, Outbound SPI = 0x382e1cb2
[IKEv1 DEBUG]: IKE got a KEY_ADD msg for SA: SPI = 0x382e1cb2
[IKEv1 DEBUG]: pitcher: rcv KEY_UPDATE, spi 0xcc3dcb5a
[IKEv1]: Group = 192.1.1.40, IP = 192.1.1.40, Starting P2 Rekey timer
    to expire in 3420 seconds
[IKEv1]: Group = 192.1.1.40, IP = 192.1.1.40, PHASE 2 COMPLETED  (17)
    (msgid=4a9a7c8b)
[IKEv1 DEBUG]: Group = 192.1.1.40, IP = 192.1.1.40, Sending     (18)
    keep-alive of type DPD R-U-THERE (seq number 0x3252ed2c)
```

Here's a brief description of the references in Example 23-3 (the output **the debug crypto isakmp** command is very verbose, so I've omitted some of it):

1 Main mode exchange is beginning; no policies have been shared yet and the peers are still in an MM_NO_STATE.

2 The remote peer is testing for the use of NAT-T.

3 The comparison of ISAKMP/IKE policies begins here.

4 This message indicates that a matching policy has been found.

5 The management connection is being built.

6 The peer is associated with the "192.1.1.40" L2L tunnel group and the encryption and hash keys are being generated.

7 This is where authentication begins with pre-shared keys: remember that authentication occurs on both peers, and thus you'll see two sets of corresponding authentication processes.

8 DPD is being negotiated.

9 Phase 1 is complete.

10 Phase 2 (quick mode) begins.

11 The remote subnet (192.168.0.0/24) is received and compared to the local subnet (192.168.2.0/24).

12 A matching static crypto entry is looked for and found.

13 The appliance finds a matching data transform for the data connections.

14 A check is performed for mirrored crypto ACLs.

15 Keys are generated for the data SAs.

16 SPIs are assigned to the data SAs.

17 Phase 2 completes.

18 A DPD keepalive is being sent to the remote peer on the management connection.

CAUTION Also in 7.0, you control the debugging level by specifying a number from 1–255 after the **debug** command: this affects the amount of output you see from the **debug** command. A level of **1** will give you little information, if any, and **255** will show partial packet contents (the most in-depth). Therefore, you'll want to specify a number like **100** or **150** for the debug level to give you a reasonable amount of output to troubleshoot problems. Also, if you enter the **debug** command without specifying a level number, it defaults to level 1; therefore, if you don't see any output from your **debug** command, this is the first thing I would check: use the **show debug** command to determine what debug functions you've enabled and for what output level they've been configured.

If there is a mismatch in the ISAKMP/IKE Phase 1 policy, between the peers, your debug output will look like that in Example 23-4.

Example 23-4 *Mismatch ISAKMP/IKE Phase 1 Policies in 7.0*

```
[IKEv1 DEBUG]: IP = 192.1.1.40, processing SA payload
[IKEv1]: IP = 192.1.1.40, IKE DECODE SENDING Message (msgid=0)
    with payloads : HDR + NOTIFY (11) + NONE (0) total length : 100
[IKEv1 DEBUG]: IP = 192.1.1.40, All SA proposals found unacceptable
[IKEv1]: IP = 192.1.1.40, Error processing payload: Payload ID: 1
[IKEv1 DEBUG]: IP = 192.1.1.40, IKE MM Responder FSM error
    history (struct &0x19f49a0)  <state>, <event>:  MM_DONE,
    EV_ERROR-->MM_START, EV_RCV_MSG-->MM_START, EV_
    START_MM-->MM_START, EV_START_MM
[IKEv1 DEBUG]: IP = 192.1.1.40, IKE SA MM:2d31c23f terminating:
    flags 0x01000002, refcnt 0, tuncnt 0
[IKEv1 DEBUG]: sending delete/delete with reason message
```

TIP   I've found out, the hard way, in certain FOS releases that even if the ISAKMP policies match on the two peers, you still could get the dreaded "All SA proposals found unacceptable" message. Apparently, certain combinations of policies, especially for the two data connections, will not work, even though you can configure them on the appliance, like AES-128 and SHA. Playing around, I've found out that in most instances, any encryption algorithm and MD5 will work; but only certain encryption algorithms and SHA will work. Therefore, before you waste your time troubleshooting this problem with either a Phase 1 or, more likely, Phase 2 connection, first I would try a proposal that supported MD5 with your selected encryption algorithm.

If there is a mismatch in a key used for pre-shared key authentication, the output of the **debug crypto isakmp** command will look like that found in Example 23-5.

Example 23-5 *Mismatched Pre-shared Key Illustration in 7.0*

```
[IKEv1 DEBUG]: IP = 192.1.1.40, processing SA payload
[IKEv1 DEBUG]: IP = 192.1.1.40, Oakley proposal is acceptable
←output omitted→
[IKEv1 DEBUG]: IP = 192.1.1.40, IKE SA Proposal # 1,
    Transform # 1 acceptable  Matches global IKE entry # 3
←output omitted→
[IKEv1]: Group = 192.1.1.40, IP = 192.1.1.40, Received
    encrypted Oakley Main Mode packet with invalid payloads,
    MessID = 0
[IKEv1]: IP = 192.1.1.40, IKE DECODE SENDING Message (msgid=0)
    with payloads : HDR + NOTIFY (11) + NONE (0) total length : 136
[IKEv1]: Group = 192.1.1.40, IP = 192.1.1.40, ERROR, had problems
    decrypting packet, probably due to mismatched pre-shared key.
    Aborting
[IKEv1]: Group = 192.1.1.40, IP = 192.1.1.40, Duplicate Phase 1
    packet detected.  Retransmitting last packet.
←output omitted→
Jun 29 17:39:09 [IKEv1 DEBUG]: sending delete/delete with reason message
←output omitted→
```

TIP   One of the problems I've seen with the output of the FOS debug commands is that the nomenclature and verbiage has a tendency of changing from one FOS release to another. This is very apparent if you compare the 6.3 output to that of 7.0. Therefore, you have to scrutinize the output carefully to determine the exact problem. In certain cases, you might want to look at the debug output from a connection that works from the same FOS revision that you're using on a connection that is failing. You can use the successful connection output as a baseline when comparing this debug output to the debug output from a failed connection attempt. I've also found the FOS 7.0 debug output more user-friendly in deciphering its messages than with the 6.x and earlier releases.

Remote Access Sessions

The debug output from setting up a remote access session can be very verbose—about 20 pages in length! Example 23-6 shows the output of the **debug crypto isakmp** command from a 7.0 Easy VPN Server, where I've omitted much of the output to keep it brief. I explain the numbered references below the example output.

Example 23-6 *Establishing a Remote Access Connection to an Easy VPN Server Running 7.0*

```
[IKEv1 DEBUG]: IP = 192.1.1.77, processing SA payload          (1)
←output omitted→
 [IKEv1 DEBUG]: IP = 192.1.1.77, IKE Peer included IKE
    fragmentation capability flags:  Main Mode:        True
    Aggressive Mode:  False
[IKEv1 DEBUG]: IP = 192.1.1.77, processing VID payload
[IKEv1 DEBUG]: IP = 192.1.1.77, Received Cisco Unity client VID  (2)
[IKEv1]: IP = 192.1.1.77, Connection landed on tunnel_
    group salesgroup
[IKEv1 DEBUG]: Group = salesgroup, IP = 192.1.1.77, processing
    IKE SA
[IKEv1 DEBUG]: Group = salesgroup, IP = 192.1.1.77, IKE SA       (3)
    Proposal # 1, Transform # 5 acceptable  Matches global
    IKE entry # 1
[IKEv1 DEBUG]: Group = salesgroup, IP = 192.1.1.77, constructing
    ISA_SA for isakmp
 [IKEv1 DEBUG]: Group = salesgroup, IP = 192.1.1.77, constructing
    nonce payload
←output omitted→
[IKEv1 DEBUG]: Processing MODE_CFG Reply attributes.             (4)
[IKEv1 DEBUG]: Group = salesgroup, Username = salesuser,
    IP = 192.1.1.77, IKEGetUserAttributes: primary DNS = 4.2.2.1
[IKEv1 DEBUG]: Group = salesgroup, Username = salesuser,
    IP = 192.1.1.77, IKEGetUserAttributes: secondary DNS = cleared
[IKEv1 DEBUG]: Group = salesgroup, Username = salesuser,
    IP = 192.1.1.77, IKEGetUserAttributes: primary WINS = cleared
[IKEv1 DEBUG]: Group = salesgroup, Username = salesuser,
    IP = 192.1.1.77, IKEGetUserAttributes: secondary WINS = cleared
[IKEv1 DEBUG]: Group = salesgroup, Username = salesuser,
    IP = 192.1.1.77, IKEGetUserAttributes: IP Compression = disabled
[IKEv1 DEBUG]: Group = salesgroup, Username = salesuser,
    IP = 192.1.1.77, IKEGetUserAttributes: Split Tunneling
    Policy = Disabled
[IKEv1]: Group = salesgroup, Username = salesuser,              (5)
    IP = 192.1.1.77, User (salesuser) authenticated.
←output omitted→
 [IKEv1 DEBUG]: Processing cfg Request attributes               (6)
[IKEv1 DEBUG]: MODE_CFG: Received request for IPV4 address!
[IKEv1 DEBUG]: MODE_CFG: Received request for IPV4 net mask!
[IKEv1 DEBUG]: MODE_CFG: Received request for DNS server address!
[IKEv1 DEBUG]: MODE_CFG: Received request for WINS server address!
[IKEv1]: Group = salesgroup, Username = salesuser,
    IP = 192.1.1.77, Received unsupported transaction mode
    attribute: 5
[IKEv1 DEBUG]: MODE_CFG: Received request for Banner!
```

continues

Example 23-6 *Establishing a Remote Access Connection to an Easy VPN Server Running 7.0 (Continued)*

```
[IKEv1 DEBUG]: MODE_CFG: Received request for Save PW setting!
[IKEv1 DEBUG]: MODE_CFG: Received request for Default Domain Name!
[IKEv1 DEBUG]: MODE_CFG: Received request for Split Tunnel List!
[IKEv1 DEBUG]: MODE_CFG: Received request for Split DNS!
[IKEv1 DEBUG]: MODE_CFG: Received request for PFS setting!
[IKEv1]: Group = salesgroup, Username = salesuser,
    IP = 192.1.1.77, Received unknown transaction mode attribute: 28683
[IKEv1 DEBUG]: MODE_CFG: Received request for backup ip-sec peer
    list!
[IKEv1 DEBUG]: MODE_CFG: Received request for Application          (7)
    Version!
[IKEv1]: Group = salesgroup, Username = salesuser,
    IP = 192.1.1.77, Client Type: WinNT  Client Application
    Version: 4.6.01.0019
[IKEv1 DEBUG]: MODE_CFG: Received request for FWTYPE!
[IKEv1 DEBUG]: MODE_CFG: Received request for DHCP hostname for
    DDNS is: i7500!
[IKEv1 DEBUG]: MODE_CFG: Received request for UDP Port!
[IKEv1 DEBUG]: Group = salesgroup, Username = salesuser,          (8)
    IP = 192.1.1.77, constructing blank hash
[IKEv1 DEBUG]: Group = salesgroup, Username = salesuser,
    IP = 192.1.1.77, constructing qm hash
[IKEv1]: IP = 192.1.1.77, IKE DECODE SENDING Message
    (msgid=e9f26b16) with payloads : HDR + HASH (8) + ATTR (14)
    + NONE (0) total length : 170
[IKEv1 DECODE]: IP = 192.1.1.77, IKE Responder starting QM:
    msg id = d9fcc34b
[IKEv1 DEBUG]: Group = salesgroup, Username = salesuser,
    IP = 192.1.1.77, Delay Quick Mode processing, Cert/Trans
    Exch/RM DSID in progress
[IKEv1 DEBUG]: Group = salesgroup, Username = salesuser,
    IP = 192.1.1.77, Resume Quick Mode processing, Cert/Trans
    Exch/RM DSID completed
[IKEv1]: Group = salesgroup, Username = salesuser,                (9)
    IP = 192.1.1.77, PHASE 1 COMPLETED
←output omitted→
[IKEv1 DEBUG]: Group = salesgroup, Username = salesuser,          (10)
    IP = 192.1.1.77, constructing blank hash
[IKEv1 DEBUG]: Group = salesgroup, Username = salesuser,
    IP = 192.1.1.77, constructing qm hash
[IKEv1]: IP = 192.1.1.77, IKE DECODE SENDING Message
    (msgid=3b776e14) with payloads : HDR + HASH (8) +
    NOTIFY (11) + NONE (0) total length : 92
[IKEv1]: IP = 192.1.1.77, IKE DECODE RECEIVED Message
    (msgid=d9fcc34b) with payloads : HDR + HASH (8) + SA (1)
    + NONCE (10) + ID (5) + ID (5) + NONE (0) total length : 1026
[IKEv1 DEBUG]: Group = salesgroup, Username = salesuser,
    IP = 192.1.1.77, processing hash
[IKEv1 DEBUG]: Group = salesgroup, Username = salesuser,
    IP = 192.1.1.77, processing SA payload
[IKEv1 DEBUG]: Group = salesgroup, Username = salesuser,
    IP = 192.1.1.77, processing nonce payload
```

Example 23-6 *Establishing a Remote Access Connection to an Easy VPN Server Running 7.0 (Continued)*

```
[IKEv1 DEBUG]: Group = salesgroup, Username = salesuser,
    IP = 192.1.1.77, Processing ID
[IKEv1 DECODE]: ID_IPV4_ADDR ID received 192.168.2.200          (11)
[IKEv1]: Group = salesgroup, Username = salesuser,
    IP = 192.1.1.77, Received remote Proxy Host data in ID
    Payload:  Address 192.168.2.200, Protocol 0, Port 0
[IKEv1 DEBUG]: Group = salesgroup, Username = salesuser,
    IP = 192.1.1.77, Processing ID
[IKEv1 DECODE]: ID_IPV4_ADDR_SUBNET ID received--
    0.0.0.0--0.0.0.0
[IKEv1]: Group = salesgroup, Username = salesuser,
    IP = 192.1.1.77, Received local IP Proxy Subnet data in ID
    Payload:   Address 0.0.0.0, Mask 0.0.0.0, Protocol 0, Port 0
[IKEv1]: QM IsRekeyed old sa not found by addr                  (12)
[IKEv1]: Group = salesgroup, Username = salesuser,             (13)
    IP = 192.1.1.77, Static Crypto Map check, checking
    map = mymap, seq = 10...
[IKEv1]: Group = salesgroup, Username = salesuser,
    IP = 192.1.1.77, Static Crypto Map check, map = mymap,
    seq = 10, ACL does not match proxy IDs src:192.168.2.200
    dst:0.0.0.0
[IKEv1]: Group = salesgroup, Username = salesuser,             (14)
    IP = 192.1.1.77, IKE Remote Peer configured for SA: dynmap
[IKEv1]: Group = salesgroup, Username = salesuser,
    IP = 192.1.1.77, processing IPSEC SA
[IKEv1 DEBUG]: Group = salesgroup, Username = salesuser,       (15)
    IP = 192.1.1.77, IPsec SA Proposal # 11, Transform # 1
    acceptable  Matches global IPsec SA entry # 1
←output omitted→
[IKEv1]: Group = salesgroup, Username = salesuser,             (16)
    IP = 192.1.1.77, Overriding Initiator's IPsec rekeying
    duration from 2147483 to 28800 seconds
←output omitted→
[IKEv1]: Group = salesgroup, Username = salesuser,             (17)
    IP = 192.1.1.77, Security negotiation complete for
    User (salesuser)  Responder, Inbound SPI = 0x46ffd888,
    Outbound SPI = 0xfc4dd2f3
[IKEv1 DEBUG]: IKE got a KEY_ADD msg for SA: SPI = 0xfc4dd2f3
[IKEv1 DEBUG]: pitcher: rcv KEY_UPDATE, spi 0x46ffd888
←output omitted→
[IKEv1]: Group = salesgroup, Username = salesuser,             (18)
    IP = 192.1.1.77, Adding static route for client address:
    192.168.2.200
[IKEv1]: Group = salesgroup, Username = salesuser,             (19)
    IP = 192.1.1.77, PHASE 2 COMPLETED (msgid=d9fcc34b)
←output omitted→
[IKEv1 DEBUG]: Group = salesgroup, Username = salesuser,       (20)
    IP = 192.1.1.77, Received keep-alive of type DPD R-U-THERE
    (seq number 0xa780a31f)
[IKEv1 DEBUG]: Group = salesgroup, Username = salesuser,
    IP = 192.1.1.77, Sending keep-alive of type DPD R-U-THERE-ACK
    (seq number 0xa780a31f)
←output omitted→
```

Here's an explanation of the debug output from Example 23-6:

1 The Remote (192.1.1.77) initiates a session to the appliance (acting as a Server).

2 The Remote sends its identity type to the Server, along with the group it wants to connect to ("salesgroup").

3 A matching Phase 1 policy is found: policy 5 of the Remote matches the first policy of the Server).

4 The Remote initiates IKE Mode Config and the appliance is determining which parameters it has configured for the associated group.

5 The group authentication is successful, as is the XAUTH authentication via the user account "salesuser"; notice that this message appears here rather than before IKE Mode Config, because the appliance needs to verify whether or not the user is allowed access to the group.

6 The Remote sends an IKE Mode Config request for the policies defined for the salesgroup group.

7 During IKE Mode Config, the appliance learns the client type and version.

8 The Server sends back the IKE Mode Config parameters.

9 This completes ISAKMP/IKE Phase 1.

10 Quick mode begins with an exchange of policies.

11 The internal address of the client is 192.168.2.200 and the proxy message it sends indicates that all of its traffic is to be protected (the group policy is split tunneling disabled).

12 A check is performed to make sure that the client isn't reconnecting (the Initial Contact feature for Easy VPN); in this example, the client is initiating a new connection.

13 The appliance compares the proxy information with its first crypto map entry (which is a static one) and finds that it doesn't match this entry (the proxy information doesn't match).

14 The appliance compares the proxy information with its second crypto map entry, which is a dynamic crypto map for remote access users.

15 A matching data transform is found.

16 There is a difference in the data SA lifetime values between the two devices: the lower one (28,800 seconds) is negotiated.

17 The two IPsec data SAs (inbound and outbound) are created and SPIs are assigned.

18 Because RRI is enabled, a static route for the Remote's internal address (192.168.2.200) is added to the Server's local routing table.

19 Phase 2 has completed.

20 Because DPD was negotiated in Phase 1, DPD now takes place; in this instance, the Remote is initiating DPD (however, both sides of the tunnel will do this periodically based on their local keepalive counters).

The debug crypto vpnclient Command

For 6.x PIXs configured as Easy VPN Remotes, you can use the **debug crypto vpnclient** command to troubleshoot client-specific configuration and connection setup issues. Example 23-7 illustrates the use of this command, where the client is using network extension mode. Below the example, I explain the numbered references found in the example.

Example 23-7 *Establishing a Remote Access Connection from an Easy VPN Remote Running 6.3*

```
VPNC CFG: transform set unconfig attempt done                        (1)
VPNC CLI: no isakmp keepalive 10 5
VPNC CLI: no isakmp nat-traversal 20
VPNC CFG: IKE unconfig successful
VPNC CLI: no crypto map _vpnc_cm
VPNC CFG: crypto map deletion attempt done
VPNC CFG: crypto unconfig successful
VPNC CLI: no global (outside) 65001
VPNC CLI: no nat (inside) 0 access-list _vpnc_acl
VPNC CFG: nat unconfig attempt failed
VPNC CLI: no http 192.168.3.1 255.255.255.0 inside
VPNC CLI: no http server enable
VPNC CLI: no access-list _vpnc_acl
VPNC CFG: ACL deletion attempt failed
VPNC CLI: no crypto map _vpnc_cm interface outside
VPNC CFG: crypto map de/attach failed
VPNC CFG: transform sets configured                                  (2)
VPNC CFG: crypto config successful
VPNC CLI: isakmp keepalive 10 5
VPNC CLI: isakmp nat-traversal 20
VPNC CFG: IKE config successful
VPNC CLI: http 192.168.3.1 255.255.255.0 inside
VPNC CLI: http server enable
VPNC CLI: aaa-server _vpnc_nwp_server protocol tacacs+
VPNC CLI: aaa-server _vpnc_nwp_server (outside) host 192.1.1.100
VPNC CLI: access-list _vpnc_nwp_acl permit ip any any
VPNC CLI: aaa authentication match _vpnc_nwp_acl outbound
    vpnc_nwp_server
VPNC CLI: no access-list _vpnc_acl
VPNC CFG: ACL deletion attempt failed
VPNC CLI: access-list _vpnc_acl permit ip host 192.1.1.101           (3)
    host 192.1.1.100
VPNC CLI: crypto map _vpnc_cm 10 match address _vpnc_acl
VPNC CFG: crypto map acl update successful
VPNC CLI: no crypto map _vpnc_cm interface outside
VPNC CLI: crypto map _vpnc_cm interface outside
```

continues

Example 23-7 *Establishing a Remote Access Connection from an Easy VPN Remote Running 6.3 (Continued)*

```
VPNC INF: IKE trigger request done                                   (4)
VPNC INF: Constructing policy download req
VPNC INF: Packing attributes for policy request
VPNC INF: Attributes being requested
VPNC ATT: INTERNAL_IP4_DNS: 4.2.2.1
VPNC ATT: ALT_PFS: 0
VPNC INF: Received application version 'Cisco Systems, Inc           (5)
    PIX-515 Version 7.0(1) built by builders on
    Thu 31-Mar-05 14:37'
VPNC ATT: ALT_CFG_SEC_UNIT: 0
VPNC ATT: ALT_CFG_USER_AUTH: 0
VPNC CLI: no aaa authentication match _vpnc_nwp_acl outbound _
    vpnc_nwp_server
VPNC CLI: no access-list _vpnc_nwp_acl permit ip any any
VPNC CLI: no aaa-server _vpnc_nwp_server
VPNC CLI: no access-list _vpnc_acl
VPNC CLI: access-list _vpnc_acl permit ip                            (6)
    192.168.3.0 255.255.255.0 any
VPNC CLI: access-list _vpnc_acl permit ip
    host 192.1.1.101 any
VPNC CLI: access-list _vpnc_acl permit ip
    host 192.1.1.101 host 192.1.1.100
VPNC CFG: _vpnc_acl no ST define done
VPNC CLI: crypto map _vpnc_cm 10 match address _vpnc_acl
VPNC CFG: crypto map acl update successful
VPNC CLI: no crypto map _vpnc_cm interface outside
VPNC CLI: crypto map _vpnc_cm interface outside
VPNC CLI: no global (outside) 65001                                  (7)
VPNC CLI: no nat (inside) 0 access-list _vpnc_acl
VPNC CFG: nat unconfig attempt failed
VPNC CLI: nat (inside) 0 access-list _vpnc_acl
VPNC INF: IKE trigger request done                                   (8)
←output omitted→
```

Here is an explanation of the numbered references in Example 23-7:

1 This is the first time the VPN Remote functionality was enabled on the PIX, so the PIX is first removing any VPN commands that could cause any type of conflict.

2 After attempting to remove all VPN-related commands, the Remote then configures the necessary VPN commands.

3 An ACL is built to allow communications between this PIX (192.1.1.101) and the Easy VPN Server (192.1.1.100).

4 The PIX Remote initiates its connection to the Server and sends its policies.

5 The Server is a PIX 515 running FOS 7.0.

6 Based on the split tunneling policy passed to it by the Server, the client PIX builds an appropriate crypto ACL.

7 Based on the split tunneling policy, the appropriate address translation policy is configured.

8 The tunnel is now established to the Server.

TIP   Unfortunately, the **debug crypto vpnclient** command is not that useful for troubleshooting the setup of an IPsec session. If something is misconfigured on the Remote or Server, you'll see something like that in Example 23-8 repeated over and over; however, as you'll notice in the output, there is nothing that indicates what the problem is. In this example, the Remote was configured for network extension mode, but the group on the Server didn't have this policy defined. For example, with the output of the **debug crypto isakmp** command on the Server, you would see a message like this: "[IKEv1]: Group = salesgroup, Username = salesuser, IP = 192.1.1.101, Hardware Client connection rejected! Network Extension Mode is not allowed for this group!" Unfortunately, the debug output from the same command on a 6.3 Remote isn't as verbose, making the troubleshooting of this problem more difficult, if not impossible, from the Remote end using the **debug crypto vpnclient** command.

Example 23-8 *A Failed Remote Access Connection from an Easy VPN Remote Running 6.3*

```
VPNC INF: Constructing policy download req
VPNC INF: Packing attributes for policy request
VPNC INF: Attributes being requested
VPNC CLI: no access-list _vpnc_acl
VPNC CLI: access-list _vpnc_acl permit ip host 192.1.1.101 host 192.1.1.100
VPNC CLI: crypto map _vpnc_cm 10 match address _vpnc_acl
VPNC CFG: crypto map acl update successful
VPNC CLI: no crypto map _vpnc_cm interface outside
VPNC CLI: crypto map _vpnc_cm interface outside
VPNC INF: IKE trigger request done
```

ISAKMP/IKE Phase 2 Connections

In this section I'll discuss some security appliance commands you can use to troubleshoot ISAKMP/IKE Phase 2 connections. I'll begin by briefly describing the commands you can use and then, in later sections, I'll discuss some of these commands in more depth.

Overview of the Phase 2 Commands

If you're experiencing problems with establishing IPsec data connections with an IPsec peer, you could use several PIX/ASA commands to help pinpoint the problem. Here's a brief summary of these commands:

- **show crypto engine [verify]**—Displays the usage statistics for the appliance's crypto engine (FOS 6.x only); the verify parameter runs the Known Answer Test (KAT), which checks the integrity of the cryptography engine used by the appliance.

- **show crypto interface** [**counters**]—Displays the VAC/VAC+ card installed in the appliance and, optionally, traffic statistics for the card (FOS 6.x only).

- **show crypto accelerator statistics**—Displays the VAC/VAC+ card installed in the appliance and, optionally, traffic statistics for the card (FOS 7.0 only).

- **show crypto protocol statistics** {**ikev1** | **ipsec**}—Displays general traffic statistics about the management or data connections (FOS 7.0 only).

- **show** [**crypto**] **ipsec sa**—Displays the data SAs established between two IPsec peers, and the components used to protect the connection and packet statistical information.

- **debug crypto isakmp**—Displays the steps taken to build a management connection and data connections via the management connection (see "The **debug crypto isakmp** Command" section previously in the chapter).

- **debug crypto ipsec**—Displays the actual creation of the two unidirectional data SAs between two peers.

- **clear crypto** [**ipsec**] **sa** [**counters** | **map** *map_name* | **peer** *IP_address*| **entry** *IP_address* {**ah** | **esp**} *SPI_#*]—Clears the statistics (**counters**), all data SAs associated with a crypto map (**map**), all data SAs associated with a peer (**peer**), or a particular data SA to a particular peer (**entry**).

The following sections will discuss some of the above troubleshooting commands in more depth; these commands discussed below are the more common ones used to troubleshoot data SA problems.

The show crypto ipsec sa Command

The **show crypto ipsec sa** command displays the crypto map entry information used to build data connections, and any existing data connections to remote peers. There are two forms of the command, depending on which FOS version your appliance is running.

In FOS 6.x and earlier, the following syntax applies:

```
pix63# show crypto [ipsec] sa [map map_name | address| identity]
```

Without any specified parameters, the crypto map information used to create the data SAs is displayed, in addition to traffic statistics, and the inbound and outbound connections and their SPI numbers. The **map** parameter allows you to display only the SAs associated with the specified crypto map name. The **address** parameter sorts the output based on the IP address of the SA. The **identity** parameter sorts the display by SA flows.

In FOS 7.0, the following syntax can be used:

```
pix70# show crypto [ipsec] sa [entry | identity | map map_name |
                  peer peer_IP_address ] [detail]
```

As you can see from the syntax of this command, it is similar to the 6.x version. The **entry** parameter performs the same function as the address parameter in the 6.x command; it sorts the SAs based on IP addresses. The **identity** parameter sorts the display by SA flows. The

map parameter displays only the SAs associated with the specified crypto map. The **peer** parameter allows you to display only the SAs established to the specified peer. The **detail** parameter displays more detailed information about the SAs, including error information.

In the case of either of these two commands, the output produced, shown in Example 23-9, is very similar to a router's output from the same command. The output in Example 23-9 is from a security appliance running 7.0, even though the 6.x output is almost the same. The crypto map called "mymap" has an entry associated with a remote peer, 192.1.1.40. The *local ident* and *remote ident* entries display the traffic that is to be protected (traffic between 192.168.2.0/24 and 192.168.0.0/24). The *#pkts encaps* and *#pkts decaps* display the number of packets encapsulated/deencapsulated using IPsec (AH and/or ESP); likewise, you can see the number of packets encrypted and decrypted, and the number of packets where a hash function was created or verified. Given that there are nonzero numbers in these fields, a connection is currently established to the remote peer (192.1.1.40).

Example 23-9 *Using the* **show crypto ipsec sa** *Command*

```
pix70(config)# show crypto ipsec sa
interface: outside
    Crypto map tag: mymap, local addr: 192.1.1.100
      local ident (addr/mask/prot/port): (192.168.2.0/255.255.255.0/0/0)
      remote ident (addr/mask/prot/port): (192.168.0.0/255.255.255.0/0/0)
      current_peer: 192.1.1.40

      #pkts encaps: 4, #pkts encrypt: 4, #pkts digest: 4
      #pkts decaps: 4, #pkts decrypt: 4, #pkts verify: 4
      #pkts compressed: 0, #pkts decompressed: 0
      #pkts not compressed: 4, #pkts comp failed: 0, #pkts decomp failed: 0
      #send errors: 0, #recv errors: 0

      local crypto endpt.: 192.1.1.100, remote crypto endpt.: 192.1.1.40
      path mtu 1500, ipsec overhead 76, media mtu 1500
      current outbound spi: 2ED644AD

    inbound esp sas:
      spi: 0x76DFE868 (1994385512)
         transform: esp-aes esp-sha-hmac
         in use settings ={L2L, Tunnel, }
         slot: 0, conn_id: 1, crypto-map: mymap
         sa timing: remaining key lifetime (kB/sec): (4274999/3586)
         IV size: 16 bytes
         replay detection support: Y
    outbound esp sas:
      spi: 0x2ED644AD (785794221)
         transform: esp-aes esp-sha-hmac
         in use settings ={L2L, Tunnel, }
         slot: 0, conn_id: 1, crypto-map: mymap
         sa timing: remaining key lifetime (kB/sec): (4274999/3584)
         IV size: 16 bytes
         replay detection support: Y
```

The SAs are displayed in separate sections in Example 23-9. In this example, only ESP is used, so you can see the SPI values, transforms, tunnel type, and other connection particulars in the *inbound esp sas* and *outbound esp sas* sections of the output. If you don't see anything under these subsections, no data connections have been established. Common problems that might cause this situation are:

- Mismatch in transforms

- Mismatch in crypto ACLs

- Mismatch in addresses that the two peers will use for IPsec communications

Further troubleshooting can be done with the **debug crypto ipsec** command. I'll discuss that in the next section.

The debug crypto ipsec Command

If you're experiencing problems establishing the two IPsec data connections between peers, the most common appliance commands to troubleshoot this problem are the **debug crypto isakmp** and the **debug crypto ipsec** commands. I discussed the former command earlier in "The **debug crypto isakmp** Command" section. The **debug crypto ipsec** command is supported by both 6.x and 7.0; the only difference is that in 7.0, you need to specify a debug level from 1–255, where 255 displays partial packet contents. Normally I set it to **150**, which gives me enough information to troubleshoot a problem. With 6.3 and earlier, there is no option of specifying a debug level, as is the case with Cisco routers.

Example 23-10 illustrates the use of this command in 6.3, where the two data connections between two peers are established successfully. In this example, an appliance is accepting an L2L connection request from a remote peer. The local appliance's address is 192.1.1.101 with a local subnet of 192.168.3.0/24. Below the example is an explanation of the debug output reference numbers.

Example 23-10 *Successful IPsec Data SAs Established on a 6.3 Appliance*

```
IPSEC(key_engine): got a queue event...
IPSEC(key_engine_delete_sas): rec'd delete notify from ISAKMP      (1)
IPSEC(key_engine_delete_sas): delete all SAs shared with
     192.1.1.40
IPSEC(validate_proposal_request): proposal part #1,               (2)
   (key eng. msg.) dest= 192.1.1.101, src= 192.1.1.40,
    dest_proxy= 192.168.3.0/255.255.255.0/0/0 (type=4),
    src_proxy= 192.168.0.0/255.255.255.0/0/0 (type=4),
    protocol= ESP, transform= esp-aes esp-md5-hmac ,
    lifedur= 0s and 0kb,
    spi= 0x0(0), conn_id= 0, keysize= 128, flags= 0x4
IPSEC(key_engine): got a queue event...
IPSEC(spi_response): getting spi 0xffc3de48(4291026504) for SA    (3)
        from 192.1.1.40 to 192.1.1.101 for prot 3
IPSEC(key_engine): got a queue event...
```

Example 23-10 *Successful IPsec Data SAs Established on a 6.3 Appliance (Continued)*

```
IPSEC(initialize_sas): ,                                        (4)
  (key eng. msg.) dest= 192.1.1.101, src= 192.1.1.40,
    dest_proxy= 192.168.3.0/255.255.255.0/0/0 (type=4),
    src_proxy= 192.168.0.0/255.255.255.0/0/0 (type=4),
    protocol= ESP, transform= esp-aes esp-md5-hmac ,
    lifedur= 3600s and 4608000kb,
    spi= 0xffc3de48(4291026504), conn_id= 2, keysize= 128,
    flags= 0x4
IPSEC(initialize_sas): ,                                        (5)
  (key eng. msg.) src= 192.1.1.101, dest= 192.1.1.40,
    src_proxy= 192.168.3.0/255.255.255.0/0/0 (type=4),
    dest_proxy= 192.168.0.0/255.255.255.0/0/0 (type=4),
    protocol= ESP, transform= esp-aes esp-md5-hmac ,
    lifedur= 3600s and 4608000kb,
    spi= 0x378ef8b8(932116664), conn_id= 1, keysize= 128,
    flags= 0x4
```

Here's a brief explanation of the numbered references in the output from Example 23-10:

1 Any existing data SAs are being deleted before the new ones are added between the two peers: 192.1.1.101 is the local appliance and 192.1.1.40 is the remote peer.

2 A matching transform set (ESP with AES-128 and MD5) and crypto ACL are found; in this example, the remote peer initiated the connection, requesting that traffic from 192.168.0.0/24 to 192.168.3.0/24 be protected. This can be determined by the "validate proposal request" message.

3 The remote peer assigns an SPI for the SA from the remote peer to the local appliance.

4 The SA from the local appliance to the remote peer is initialized and assigned an SPI value.

5 The SA from the remote peer to the local appliance is initialized.

As you can see from this output, it is much less verbose than what you would see with the **debug crypto isakmp** command; this makes sense because only the particulars of the building of the data connection are displayed, whereas with the **debug crypto isakmp** command, you see everything that ISAKMP/IKE builds, which includes both the management *and* data connections.

The following sections will cover some common problems with establishing data connections, including:

- Mismatched Data Transforms
- Mismatched Crypto ACLs
- Matching on the Incorrect Crypto Map Entry

Mismatched Data Transforms

As you can see from the output in Example 23-10, the debug output from the **debug crypto ipsec** command is fairly straightforward to interpret. Of course, not all data SAs are built successfully. For example, if you don't have a matching transform for the data connections, you'll see the output in Example 23-11 from the **debug crypto isakmp** and the **debug crypto ipsec** commands. The first part is from the former **debug** command (begins with "ISKAMP") and the last part is from the latter command (begins with "IPSEC"). Use the **show crypto ipsec transform-set** command on the local appliance to determine which transforms have been created already, and the **show crypto map** command to see which transform set has been associated with the remote peer's crypto map entry.

Example 23-11 *Mismatched IPsec Data Transforms*

```
←output omitted→
ISAKMP (0): processing SA payload. message ID = 2686916944
ISAKMP : Checking IPsec proposal 1
ISAKMP: transform 1, ESP_AES
ISAKMP:    attributes in transform:
ISAKMP:        encaps is 1
ISAKMP:        SA life type in seconds
ISAKMP:        SA life duration (basic) of 3600
ISAKMP:        SA life type in kilobytes
ISAKMP:        SA life duration (VPI) of  0x0 0x46 0x50 0x0
ISAKMP:        authenticator is HMAC-SHA
ISAKMP:        key length is 128IPSEC(validate_proposal):
    transform proposal (prot 3, trans 12, hmac_alg 2) not supported
ISAKMP (0): atts not acceptable. Next payload is 0
ISAKMP (0): SA not acceptable!
←output omitted→
IPSEC(key_engine): got a queue event...
IPSEC(key_engine_delete_sas): rec'd delete notify from ISAKMP
IPSEC(key_engine_delete_sas): delete all SAs shared with 192.1.1.40
IPSEC(validate_proposal): transform proposal (prot 3, trans 12,
    hmac_alg 2) not supported
```

At the beginning of Example 23-11, you can see the output from the **debug crypto isakmp** command. The first two highlighted lines display that there is a problem with an ESP proposal that the remote peer wants to use: ESP with AES-128 and SHA. The last part of the output shows that the transform proposed by the remote peer wasn't accepted because of a conflict in the HMAC function defined on both peers. Obviously, the local peer wants to use MD5, but the remote peer has been configured with only one transform that has SHA.

Mismatched Crypto ACLs

If the crypto ACLs are not mirrored on the two peers, you'll see debug output from the **debug crypto ipsec** and **debug crypto isakmp** commands shown in Example 23-12. The *proxy identities not supported* message indicates that the crypto ACLs (if routers or PIXs), or network lists (if concentrators), do not match (are not mirrored) on the two IPsec peers.

This misconfiguration is commonly called an "invalid proxy ID." When this error occurs, examine the crypto ACLs (or network lists, if the peer's a concentrator) to see where the ACL entries are not mirrored.

TIP   From practical experience, I've learned that in certain cases you'll get the mismatched crypto ACL error even if you have the entries mirrored on the same side, but the crypto ACL entries happen to be in a *different* order on the two peers. Therefore, I recommend mirroring each statement and also matching up the statements in the same order.

Example 23-12 *Mismatched Crypto ACLs: Not Mirrored*

```
←output omitted→
ISAKMP (0): processing SA payload. message ID = 2620452987
ISAKMP : Checking IPsec proposal 1
ISAKMP: transform 1, ESP_AES
ISAKMP:    attributes in transform:
ISAKMP:        encaps is 1
ISAKMP:        SA life type in seconds
ISAKMP:        SA life duration (basic) of 3600
ISAKMP:        SA life type in kilobytes
ISAKMP:        SA life duration (VPI) of  0x0 0x46 0x50 0x0
ISAKMP:        authenticator is HMAC-MD5
ISAKMP:        key length is 128
ISAKMP (0): atts are acceptable.IPSEC(validate_proposal_request):
    proposal part #1,
  (key eng. msg.) dest= 192.1.1.101, src= 192.1.1.40,
    dest_proxy= 192.168.3.0/255.255.255.0/0/0 (type=4),
    src_proxy= 192.168.1.0/255.255.255.0/0/0 (type=4),
    protocol= ESP, transform= esp-aes esp-md5-hmac ,
    lifedur= 0s and 0kb,
    spi= 0x0(0), conn_id= 0, keysize= 128, flags= 0x4
IPSEC(validate_transform_proposal): proxy identities not supported
IPSEC(validate_proposal_request): proposal part #1,
  (key eng. msg.) dest= 192.1.1.101, src= 192.1.1.40,
    dest_proxy= 192.168.1.0/255.255.255.0/0/0 (type=4),
    src_proxy= 192.168.3.0/255.255.255.0/0/0 (type=4),
    protocol= ESP, transform= esp-aes esp-md5-hmac ,
    lifedur= 0s and 0kb,
    spi= 0x0(0), conn_id= 0, keysize= 128, flags= 0x4
IPSEC(validate_transform_proposal): proxy identities not supported
ISAKMP: IPsec policy invalidated proposal
ISAKMP (0): SA not acceptable!
←output omitted→
```

Matching on the Incorrect Crypto Map Entry

Another uncommon problem you might experience is if there are overlapping crypto ACLs, where a match is found for a peer for the wrong crypto ACL in a wrong crypto map entry. For example, an appliance might have two crypto ACLs with overlapping entries like that found in Example 23-13. In this example, crypto ACLs 101 and 102 overlap. If the security appliance has an IPsec tunnel to 192.1.1.2, but not 192.1.1.1, and 192.1.1.2 forwards a packet from 192.168.2.1 to 192.168.1.1, it will match the crypto ACL in the first entry, thus causing the error similar to the one shown previously in Example 23-12. To solve this problem, put the crypto map entry with the more specific crypto ACL entry or entries before the less specific one; in other words, give the former a lower entry number.

Example 23-13 *Overlapping Crypto ACL Entries Example*

```
security(config)# access-list 101 permit ip 192.168.0.0 0.0.0.255
                        192.168.3.0 0.0.0.255
security(config)# access-list 102 permit udp host 192.168.0.10
                        host 192.168.3.25 eq 69
security(config)# crypto map mymap 10 ipsec-isakmp
security(config)# crypto map mymap 10 match address 101
security(config)# crypto map mymap 10 set peer 192.1.1.1
security(config)# crypto map mymap 10 set transform-set trans1
security(config)# crypto map mymap 20 ipsec-isakmp
security(config)# crypto map mymap 20 match address 102
security(config)# crypto map mymap 20 set peer 168.3.25
security(config)# crypto map mymap 20 set transform-set trans2
```

In some older FOS versions of the PIXs, you might see an "ACL = deny; no sa created" message, which also could indicate that you have a proxy mismatch:

- A nonmatching mirrored crypto ACL condition exists.
- The same ACL is being used with a **nat 0 access-list** command and a crypto ACL.
- A match on the wrong crypto map entry with overlapping crypto ACLs occurred.

I've never seen the message in the first bullet point; I've always seen the messages displayed (or something very similar) in Example 23-12. With a crypto ACL mismatch, you'll see one of the following:

- The connection fails (with a proxy ID mismatch).
- An asymmetric tunnel startup condition, where the tunnel will come up when started from one peer, but not from the other.
- An asymmetric transfer condition, where data will flow across the tunnel depending on which peer brought up the tunnel, but not in the reverse direction.

With the last two bullet points, you might commonly see error statements about packets being dropped that should be protected: you can also view the output of the **show crypto ipsec sa** command and look for packet errors or drops.

A bug in earlier FOS versions prevented you, in certain situations, from using the same ACL for address translation with the **nat 0 access-list** command and as a crypto ACL. Cisco highly encourages its customers to not use the same ACL for crypto and address translation functions; doing so might cause the proxy process, and thus the data connections, to fail.

The most common problem with overlapping crypto ACLs is when two entries in your crypto map match on the same ACL reference, but in two different ACLs. At first this might sound impossible, but it is quite plausible based on your security policy. For example, you might have an L2L session between two appliances, protecting traffic between 192.168.0.0/24 and 192.168.3.0/24. However, on the remote peer, you have a second crypto map entry that's a transport connection, protecting syslog traffic from a remote appliance (192.168.0.10) to a local TFTP server (192.168.3.25). In this situation, if the crypto map entry that represented this connection appeared *after* the L2L connection, it would never match and thus never would be used. Depending on how the TFTP server was set up, the syslog messages from the appliance might or might not be dropped. Reordering the crypto map entries would fix this problem. In Example 23-13, renumber crypto map entry 20 to something like 5.

TIP	The crypto map entry with the more specific ACL should have a lower number than an overlapping crypto map entry with a less specific ACL.

Overlapping Crypto ACL Entries

Troubleshooting an overlapping crypto ACL entry problem is not simple, since it requires an understanding of how the crypto map entries are used. When you experience this problem, unfortunately, no output from **debug** commands will actually pinpoint this problem, because the IPsec tunnel is successfully established (or used) to the wrong peer. The first time I experienced this problem was when I had a very similar problem as I described in the last paragraph: I couldn't understand why the PIX's syslog messages weren't showing up on the syslog server. When I broke out a protocol analyzer and realized that syslog messages were showing up in clear text at the TFTP server, and the TFTP server was dropping them because they weren't protected, I then began to realize that something wasn't quite right with my configuration on the PIX. I had configured the PIX to protect the TFTP traffic using ESP AES-256 and SHA, but the L2L traffic only needed to be protected with AES-128 and MD5. So I created two crypto map entries for each, with the L2L traffic being entry 10 and the TFTP server, using transport mode, being entry 20. Once I found my configuration mistake, I reordered the crypto map entries and my problem was solved. However, it took me the better part of a morning to discover my configuration mistake.

Summary

This chapter showed you the basics of troubleshooting IPsec sessions on Cisco security appliances. The commands and processes used are very similar to those on IOS-based routers, reducing your learning curve if you already have experience with IPsec tunnels on IOS-based routers. Remember that in FOS 7.0, the **debug** commands have a level qualifier which affects the amount of debug output the command generates.

This chapter completes the configuration and troubleshooting part of this book. Next up is Part VI, "Case Study," where I pull many of the important elements together from this book and apply them to an example company's VPN implementation.

Case Study

CHAPTER 24

Case Study

This chapter is different from the rest of the chapters in this book. From the beginning of this book, each chapter has focused on VPNs and various VPN implementation types, and how these are configured on Cisco VPN 3000 concentrators, software and hardware clients, IOS-based routers, and PIX and ASA security appliances. Throughout the book I've tried to include many configuration examples, illustrating common scenarios and possible problems you might face while implementing VPNs.

This chapter doesn't introduce any new material. Instead, this chapter will focus on the use of the concepts and features discussed in this book and implement many of them in a case study environment. In other words, I'll create a fictitious company with various Cisco VPN-capable products and bring together much of the VPN knowledge I've discussed so far and apply it to my fictitious company. Using a case study, you can see more easily where certain VPN solutions make more sense than other solutions.

Throughout this case study, I'll discuss why I'm using certain VPN implementations over others and, within a certain product, why I'm using one particular feature instead of another. The configurations I'll put together focus primarily on the implementation of VPNs. I'll discuss other non-VPN items that are important to the design, but in most cases the configuration of those items is beyond the scope of this book.

Company Profile

The network shown in Figures 24-1 and 24-2 illustrates this case study. The company in this network has a corporate office, a handful of regional sites, a few dozen branch offices, and hundreds of remote access users that connect via the Internet. The following sections will discuss the necessary requirements for these components.

NOTE The detailed IP addressing scheme is not displayed in the two figures; this will be revealed throughout the case study. Also, I've shown redundant components only as they relate to the VPN functions of the VPN design; other redundant components, such as redundant stateful firewalls, redundant application and file services, and others, are not shown, but are implied. Likewise, I'll focus primarily on the VPN configuration and management of the VPN devices, even though other configurations will be necessary, especially on the perimeter routers.

Figure 24-1 *Company Internet Connections*

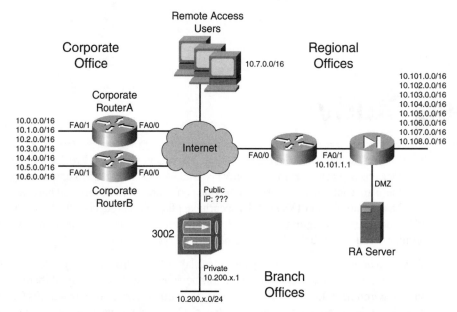

The following sections will discuss the different components contained within the figures.

Corporate Office

Of the entire network, the corporate office has the more complex design. The corporate office's VPN design can be broken into these main VPN areas:

- Authentication devices, including AAA, RADIUS, and CA services
- Perimeter routers for L2L sessions to the regional offices
- Concentrators on the DMZ2 segment for Internet remote access users and branch office Easy VPN Remote clients
- Campus concentrators for internal wireless users

The following subsections will discuss each of these areas in more depth.

Authentication Devices

In this network, two types of authentication devices are employed for VPN services:

- CA (Certificate Authority) and RA (Registration Authority) servers
- AAA RADIUS servers

Figure 24-2 *Company Campus Network*

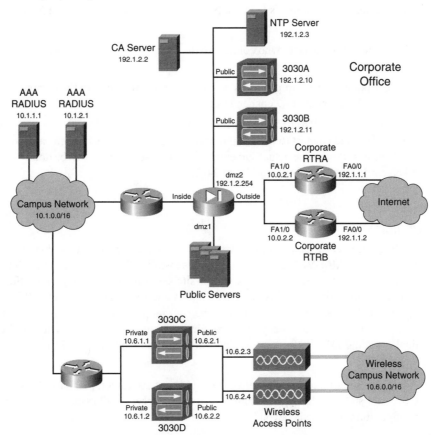

Certificates are used for device authentication, given the large number of devices and the need for scalability and flexibility. A flat CA design is used, with a CA and two RAs. If you recall from Chapter 2, "VPN Technologies," a CA provides all certificate services, whereas an RA can be used to validate existing certificates; it provides a backup for the CA. The CA is connected to the DMZ2 segment at the corporate office's network, and two RAs exist at two different regional offices' DMZ segments to provide redundancy. The RA shown in Figure 24-1 at the regional office appears at only two of the regional offices. The CA product is Microsoft's certificate services running on a Windows 2003 server.

TIP   Because the CA plays a fundamental and critical role in the VPN implementation, it should be backed up (or imaged) periodically and religiously. Even though RAs provide this function, RAs cannot issue new certificates nor revoke existing certificates. If you don't follow this simple tip and the CA fails, get ready to spend *a lot* of time rebuilding your CA and issuing *new* certificates to all of your devices!

There are two AAA RADIUS servers in the corporate office's campus server farm, which is connected to the campus's network backbone. These servers hold the XAUTH user profiles for:

- Remote access users who connect to the campus network via the 3030A and 3030B concentrators

- Corporate office campus users who connect, via wireless, to the campus network via the 3030C and 3030D concentrators

There are two AAA RADIUS servers for redundancy, ensuring that the users can authenticate via XAUTH and connect to the campus network. Users are issued token cards to generate one-time passwords. The actual authentication for these accounts will be done by a back-end token card server not shown in Figure 24-2.

Perimeter Routers

At the perimeter of the campus network are two Cisco 3845 routers, connected to the Internet, with AIM-VPN/HP II-Plus modules installed. They're running 12.3(14)T. Their main function is to terminate VPN site-to-site sessions from the regional offices and provide routing functions between the campus and regional offices. DMVPN is used to provide for both of these functions. The routing protocol used across the network is OSPF. Because redundancy and throughput is critical, two routers are used with a dual-hub/dual-DMVPN design, which I discussed in Chapter 17, "Router Site-to-Site Connections."

Additional security features should be enabled on these routers, such as ACLs for filtering, CBAC for stateful filtering, disabling unnecessary services, QoS, and others; however, the configuration of these is beyond the scope of this book.

DMZ2 Concentrators

On the DMZ2 segment are two 3030 concentrators running version 4.7. They are responsible for terminating remote access sessions from software (Internet users) and hardware clients (branch offices). They use a VPN-on-a-stick approach, where only their public interfaces are used. This design is used when you want to take the protected traffic, verify and decrypt it, and forward it to a firewall before it reaches the campus network, but you don't want to use two interfaces on your firewall to handle these functions. Because the private interface isn't used on the concentrators, you'll need to perform some extra steps on the concentrators to ensure that protected and unprotected traffic can enter and leave the public interface filter. Redundancy is a concern, so VCA will be used.

NOTE	Using a VPN-on-a-stick approach is not very common. In most scenarios, you would want to use both the private and public interfaces on the concentrators. In this situation, both sets of interfaces would connect to two different interfaces on your perimeter firewall. In Figure 24-2, this would require the firewall to have five interfaces. In my fictitious company, I'm assuming that it is impossible to add an additional interface to the perimeter firewall, and therefore I need to use a VPN-on-a-stick design.

All users' accounts for remote access are defined on the AAA RADIUS servers in the server farm of the corporate office campus network. The token card servers, which are used by both AAA servers, are located on the campus server farm with the two campus AAA servers. The DMZ2 concentrators will assign internal addresses from 10.7.0.0/17 to the remote access clients that are operating in client mode. Here are the addresses that will be assigned to the three remote access groups:

- Sales: 10.7.0.1–10.7.15.254
  - 3030A: 10.7.0.1–10.7.7.254
  - 3030B: 10.7.8.1–10.7.15.254
- Administrators: 10.7.16.1–10.7.31.254
  - 3030A: 10.7.16.1–10.7.23.254
  - 3030B: 10.7.24.1–10.7.31.254
- Programmers: 10.7.32.1–10.7.47.254
  - 3030A: 10.7.32.1–10.7.39.254
  - 3030B: 10.7.40.1–10.7.47.254

The 10.7.128.0/17 network (the other half of this A-class subnet) is used for the internal wireless users at the campus backbone. As you'll see in the "Campus Concentrators" section shortly, all remote access users have an internal address of 10.7.0.0/16 assigned to them, which makes it easier to assign internal filtering policies to this traffic, if necessary.

Perimeter Firewalls

Even though Figure 24-2 shows one perimeter firewall, like a PIX or ASA security appliance, at the corporate office network, this network actually uses two firewalls for redundancy. However, because of space constraints in Figure 24-2, only one firewall is shown. The primary functions of the firewalls are:

- Stateful filtering
- Address translation

For example, the internal campus network devices are using private addresses, so the perimeter firewall will need to perform address translation for these devices. The perimeter firewalls also will need to be configured to allow tunneled traffic to the concentrators from the Internet and clear-text traffic to the concentrators from the inside network with filtering statements. Likewise, traffic to the DMZ2 NTP and CA servers needs to be allowed.

Campus Concentrators

Two concentrators, running 4.7, are used inside the campus to secure the wireless LANs that are scattered throughout the campus network. The basic design has all wireless traffic from the access points placed into a VLAN (or VLANs) that the two internal concentrators (3030C and 3030D) are connected to with their public interfaces. Their private interfaces are connected to the campus network. AAA servers in the campus server farm reference the token card servers at the same location for XAUTH password functions. There are currently 1,000 users that connect to the campus backbone via wireless, which is why the 3030 was chosen as a product. The IP addresses used on NICs in the wireless part of the network are from 10.6.0.0/8. Two concentrators are used to provide for redundancy. The wireless users will use Cisco VPN Client software to protect traffic across the wireless network. The auto-initiation feature will be used to make the software client as transparent as possible on their users' desktops. The concentrators will assign addresses from 10.7.128.0/17 as internal addresses to the wireless clients. Here are the address assignments for the three wireless groups:

- Sales: 10.7.128.1–10.7.43.254
  - 3030C: 10.7.128.1–10.7.135.254
  - 3030D: 10.7.136.1–10.7.143.254
- Administrators: 10.7.144.1–10.7.159.254
  - 3030C: 10.7.144.1–10.7.151.254
  - 3030D: 10.7.152.1–10.7.159.254
- Programmers: 10.7.160.1–10.7.175.254
  - 3030C: 10.7.160.1–10.7.167.254
  - 3030D: 10.7.168.1–10.7.175.254

Regional Offices

There are eight regional offices in this network, even though Figure 24-1 illustrates just the perimeter of one regional office. Each regional office is very similar, with a perimeter router and firewall. The perimeter routers are 3825s with AIM-VPN/EP II-Plus modules, running IOS 12.3(14)T. The regional perimeter routers use DMVPN to connect to the two DMVPN hubs (perimeter routers) at the corporate office. All traffic meant for the corporate office is sent via this connection. DMVPN was chosen for this design because there is a lot of inter-regional office traffic and I want to minimize the amount of VPN configurations needed on the perimeter routers. Using DMVPN allows a regional office router to set up an IPsec tunnel directly to another regional office router without any additional configuration on my part. Because some of the traffic at the regional offices goes to noncompany sites, a stateful firewall and other services are used to provide additional protection. At two of the regional sites an RA is placed on the DMZ segment to provide for certificate services redundancy of the CA at the corporate office's DMZ2 segment.

Branch Offices

There are a few dozen branch offices. Each of these offices has 4–30 employees. Because I want to simplify my management for these offices, I've decided to use a 3002 hardware client running 4.7 and disable split tunneling. This requires all branch office traffic to go to the DMZ2 concentrators at the corporate site, allowing me to centralize my security functions for the branch offices. Remote network management might be implemented in the future; therefore, I'll use network extension mode for the 3002 hardware client connections.

I easily could have enabled split tunneling for the branch offices, but then I'd have had to put a small-end PIX (501 or 506E) at these locations to provide for additional security services. If bandwidth at the central office was a concern, I definitely would consider the latter approach, because enabling split tunneling would reduce the amount of bandwidth I'd need at the central office. Plus, this company might have a policy that required all Internet traffic to be examined before leaving the network. In this situation, I would disable split tunneling for all remote access (software and hardware) users and have their traffic examined at the corporate site by a URL filtering product such as WebSense or N2H2's Sentian. Because of the amount of traffic at the regional sites, I would place a separate filtering server at each of these locations and allow them to reach the Internet directly without having to go to the corporate site first.

Also, if bandwidth were a concern, I would set up a bandwidth policy for the group of 3002s that would give them a reserved bandwidth value and an upper, policed value; whereas the remote access users would have a general policed bandwidth policy applied to them.

Remote Access Users

For salespeople who travel a lot and the many users who either telecommute or need to work part of the time at home, I've decided to use Cisco VPN Client software, version 4.6, as a solution on Windows 2000 and XP computers. For home users, if I'm concerned about management and maintenance, I might decide to put a hardware client at their location, such as a PIX 501 or a VPN 3002; however, if cost is more of a concern, using the software client is the best approach.

In the current network, there are about 800 users from the Internet that connect to the DMZ2 concentrators at the corporate office periodically, and this number is expected to almost double in the next couple of years, which is why 3030s were chosen for the solution. There are three basic groups of users: sales, administrators, and programmers. Inside the campus network, these people (the wired network) have the following addressing structures, respectively: 10.3.0.0/16, 10.4.0.0/16, 10.5.0.0/16.

Case Study Configuration

Now that I've defined the policies for this network, I'll explain the configuration for the following VPN-enabled devices:

- DMVPN routers
- VPN 3030 concentrators
- VPN 3002 hardware clients
- Cisco VPN software clients

I've broken up the configuration explanation into the following sections:

- **Perimeter router configuration**—Discusses the DMVPN configuration on both the dual corporate routers and the regional routers.

- **Internet remote access configuration**—Discusses the configuration of the DMZ2 concentrators, the 3002 hardware clients, and the Cisco VPN Client for Internet users.

- **Main campus wireless configuration**—Discusses the configuration of the campus concentrators for wireless users and the setup of the Cisco VPN Client software for the wireless users.

Perimeter Router Configuration

A dual-DMVPN design with dual hubs is used to interconnect the corporate office and regional sites via IPsec site-to-site sessions. Certificates are used for device authentication. The following sections will discuss the configuration of each device.

Basic VPN Configurations on the Routers

All of the routers will require certain commands that will be similar in their configuration. These commands will perform the following:

- Allowing VPN traffic
- Enabling ISAKMP

- Defining ISAKMP policies

- Configuring DPD

- Obtaining and using certificates

- Defining IPsec transform sets and profiles

This section will discuss the configurations that are common to all the perimeter routers. Example 24-1 shows this base configuration:

Example 24-1 *Base Perimeter Router Configuration*

```
perim(config)# access-list 100 remark insert other ACLs here
perim(config)# access-list 100 permit udp any any eq 500
perim(config)# access-list 100 permit udp any any eq 4500
perim(config)# access-list 100 permit esp any any
perim(config)# access-list 100 permit tcp any host 192.1.2.2 eq 80
perim(config)# access-list 100 permit tcp any host 192.1.2.3 eq 123
perim(config)# access-list 100 permit udp any host 192.1.2.3 eq 123
perim(config)# access-list 100 remark insert other ACLs here
perim(config)# interface fastethernet0/0
perim(config-if)# ip access-group 100 in
perim(config-if)# exit
perim(config)# ntp server 192.1.2.3 key 99 source fastethernet0/1
perim(config)# ntp authenticate
perim(config)# ntp authentication-key 99 md5 55ab8971F
perim(config)# ntp trusted-key 99
perim(config)# ntp update-calendar
perim(config)# access-list 1 permit 192.1.2.3 0.0.0.0
perim(config)# ntp access-group peer 1
perim(config)# crypto isakmp policy 1
perim(config-isakmp)# authentication rsa-sig
perim(config-isakmp)# hash sha
perim(config-isakmp)# encryption aes 256
perim(config-isakmp)# group 5
perim(config-isakmp)# lifetime 3600
perim(config-isakmp)# exit
perim(config)# crypto isakmp keepalive 15 3
perim(config)# ip domain-name company.com
perim(config)# crypto key generate rsa general-keys label certkeys
The name for the keys will be: perim.company.com
Choose the size of the key modulus in the range of 360 to 2048 for
 your General Purpose Keys. Choosing a key modulus greater than 512
 may take a few minutes.
How many bits in the modulus [512]: 2048
% Generating 2048 bit RSA keys ...[OK]
perim(config)# crypto pki trustpoint caserver
perim(ca-trustpoint)# enrollment url
            http://192.1.2.2/certsrv/mscep/mscep.dll
perim(ca-trustpoint)# enrollment mode ra
perim(ca-trustpoint)# enrollment retry period 5
perim(ca-trustpoint)# enrollment retry count 5
perim(ca-trustpoint)# rsakeypair certkeys
perim(ca-trustpoint)# exit
```

continues

Example 24-1 *Base Perimeter Router Configuration (Continued)*

```
perim(config)# crypto ca authenticate caserver
Certificate has the following attributes:
Fingerprint MD5: CE9956AA C02D15DF A2309A9C E059BD47
Fingerprint SHA1: 475A5DBA 0283DB43 305E9CF7 A208C8B8 E894C379
% Do you accept this certificate? [yes/no]: yes
Trustpoint CA certificate accepted.
perim(config)# crypto ca enroll caserver
% Start certificate enrollment ..
% Create a challenge password. You will need to verbally provide this
  password to the CA Administrator in order to revoke your
  certificate. For security reasons your password will not be saved
  in the configuration. Please make a note of it.
Password: cisco123abc789xyz
Re-enter password: cisco123abc789xyz
% The fully-qualified domain name in the certificate will be:
            perim.company.com
% The subject name in the certificate will be: perim.company.com
% Include the router serial number in the subject name? [yes/no]: no
% Include an IP address in the subject name? [no]: no
Request certificate from CA? [yes/no]: yes
% Certificate request sent to Certificate Authority
% The certificate request fingerprint will be displayed.
% The 'show crypto pki certificate' command will also show the
  fingerprint.
05:32:29: CRYPTO_PKI: Certificate Request Fingerprint MD5:
  F9A3574C 09BAC68D 491D0FDA 1EBCE0BC
05:32:29: CRYPTO_PKI: Certificate Request Fingerprint SHA1:
  898BDC0B 69F74320 8EECF1FF FD86503F 3DC366BB
05:32:34: %PKI-6-CERTRET: Certificate received from Certificate
  Authority
perim(config)# crypto ipsec transform-set trans1 esp-aes-256
            esp-sha-hmac
perim(cfg-crypto-trans)# mode transport
perim(cfg-crypto-trans)# exit
perim(config)# crypto ipsec profile dmvpnprofile
perim(ipsec-profile)# set transform-set trans1
perim(ipsec-profile)# exit
perim(config# copy running-config startup-config
```

The first part of Example 24-1 sets up the ACL used to filter traffic from the Internet. Notice that I've included only the commands necessary to allow IPsec traffic, including access to the CA and NTP servers; you'll still need to add ACL statements before or after this to allow or deny other types of traffic (see my book entitled *Cisco Router Firewall Security* with Cisco Press for more information about this). This ACL is applied inbound on the Internet interface.

NOTE   Because certificates are being used, you'll need to allow TCP port 80 traffic to the CA on the corporate perimeter routers and the same at the two regional sites that have the RAs; if you forget to do this, Internet devices will not be able to obtain their own or other devices' certificates. Also, at the two regional sites with the RAs, you'll need to change the ACL statement with the 192.1.2.2 address to the address that the RA is using; and for the regional offices that don't have RAs, you'll omit this ACL statement from their configuration.

In 12.3(8)T, you don't need an ACL statement to allow the tunneled traffic: the Crypto Access Check on Clear-Text Packets feature removes the double-ACL processing. However, in IOS versions earlier than this, your perimeter ACL must allow the clear-text traffic between the various sites.

Below the ACL configuration is a set of commands to use NTP to synchronize the time with the NTP server on the DMZ2 segment. The use of NTP is important because certificates are being used. Again, if you have multiple NTP servers, this configuration for a regional office router might be slightly different based on the NTP server the router is using.

TIP   You can create an NTP server easily by buying a GPS and attaching it to a Linux/Unix or Windows 2003 server. You can get a reasonable GPS for under $200 US. And instead of putting it on a separate standalone server, you might want to consider even putting this on the CA server itself. I would not rely on using an external NTP server because you would be opening yourself up to the possibility of a denial-of-service (DoS) attack, where an attacker pretends to be a valid time source and sends you a time that is either before or after a certificate's validation date, invalidating that particular certificate and thus causing authentication to fail.

For the regional office routers, you do not need the ACL statements for the NTP server, because this device is at the corporate office (these are the two ACL statements with the 192.1.2.3 addresses). However, for redundancy, you might want to have other NTP servers in your design, some of which are located at various regional offices.

Below the NTP configuration is an ISAKMP policy that's mirrored on all perimeter routers. Notice that it uses certificates (**rsa-sig**) for device authentication. Also, I've changed the lifetime of the management connection to one hour to match that of the data SAs. After one hour, both sets of connections are torn down and rebuilt. Following this, the **crypto isakmp keepalive** command enables DPD.

Because certificates are to be used, the router needs a name and domain name. Once these are configured, the **crypto key generate rsa** command generates the RSA public/private keys. I used a key label with the keys because the router might have another key pair created and being used for other purposes already; in this example, I want to use 2048-bit RSA keys for the certificates, no matter whatever any existing key pair is using.

TIP   You might want to create exportable keys (and exportable certificates) to ease a recovery process if a perimeter router fails. However, it isn't a requirement in my situation. In my fictitious company, if a perimeter router failed, I'd have to generate new keys and acquire a new identity certificate for the replacement router.

The name of the CA is "caserver" and it has an IP address of 192.1.2.2. Because RAs are being used, I configured the mode as RA. I've also referenced the RSA key pair label to use "certkeys," when creating the identity certificate. The **crypto ca authenticate** command obtains the root certificate and the **crypto ca enroll** command obtains the router's identity certificate.

I've only defined one transform set, "trans1," for the DMVPN routers, using ESP with AES 256 as an encryption algorithm and SHA as a hashing function. Notice that because I'm using DMVPN, which uses GRE tunnels, the ESP mode is transport mode (point-to-point tunnel). Last, since DMVPN doesn't use crypto maps, I've created an IPsec profile that references the transform set I've created. This will be referenced on the GRE tunnel interfaces when I set up DMVPN in the "Corporate Office Router Configuration" and "Regional Office Router Configuration" sections.

NOTE   Even though I'm using Fast Ethernet interfaces for the Internet connections, this is only an example; based on bandwidth and available connection options, this might be an ATM interface, an HSSI interface, or an IMA interface.

Corporate Office Router Configurations

Examples 24-2 and 24-3 show the two corporate office routers' configurations. Because DMVPN is being used, I've set up a GRE tunnel interface on both routers and have ensured that the bandwidth metric is the same. This allows the regional routers to load balance traffic on a destination-by-destination basis to the corporate networks, if they chose. The subnet for this DMVPN network is 10.0.0.0/24. OSPF is the routing protocol used in this network and I want to ensure that in this DMVPN network, corpA becomes the designated router (DR). NHRP is set up to implement the dynamic registration and discovery process for DMVPN. Both the NHRP network and GRE tunnel need unique IDs in each of their domains—I used the same number to simplify the configuration. Notice that the tunnel mode for GRE is multipoint, which allows the spoke router to accept multiple tunnel connections on the same logical interface. Last, I specify the IPsec profile, "dmvpnprofile," to use to protect traffic on the GRE tunnel. At the bottom of the configuration, I've set up the interfaces and the OSPF configuration. For OSPF, the GRE tunnel connections and local sites are in the same area, area 0—the remote sites' networks are configured in separate areas because of their size.

Example 24-2 *Dual-DMVPN Design with Dual Hubs: Corporate Router's, corpA's Configuration*

```
corpA(config)# interface tunnel0
corpA(config-if)# description Connection to regional routers
corpA(config-if)# bandwidth 1000
corpA(config-if)# ip address 10.0.0.1 255.255.255.0
corpA(config-if)# ip mtu 1436
corpA(config-if)# tunnel path-mtu-discovery
corpA(config-if)# delay 1000
corpA(config-if)# ip ospf network broadcast
corpA(config-if)# ip ospf priority 2
corpA(config-if)# ip nhrp authentication cisco123
corpA(config-if)# ip nhrp map multicast dynamic
corpA(config-if)# ip nhrp network-id 100000
corpA(config-if)# ip nhrp holdtime 600
corpA(config-if)# tunnel source fastethernet0/0
corpA(config-if)# tunnel mode gre multipoint
corpA(config-if)# tunnel key 100000
corpA(config-if)# tunnel protection ipsec profile dmvpnprofile
corpA(config-if)# exit
corpA(config)# interface fastthernet0/0
corpA(config-if)# description Internet Connection
corpA(config-if)# ip address 192.1.1.1 255.255.255.0
corpA(config-if)# exit
corpA(config)# interface fastethernet0/1
corpA(config-if)# description Local LAN
corpA(config-if)# ip address 10.0.2.1 255.255.255.0
corpA(config-if)# exit
corpA(config)# router ospf 1
corpA(config-router)# network 10.0.0.0 0.0.0.255 area 0
corpA(config-router)# network 10.0.2.0.0 0.0.0.255 area 0
corpA(config-router)# exit
```

Example 24-3 shows corpB's configuration. Its configuration is almost identical to corpA's shown in Example 24-2, except for these three things on its tunnel interface:

- Its NHRP subnet is different (10.0.1.0/24 for corpA compared to 10.0.0.0/24 for corpB).

- The NHRP network ID is different (100001), making this a separate DMVPN network.

- The GRE tunnel ID is different, allowing the spoke to differentiate between packets coming from the two hub devices.

Other than these three things, the configuration of the corpB router is similar to that of corpA.

Example 24-3 *Dual-DMVPN Design with Dual Hubs: Corporate Router's, corpB's, Configuration*

```
corpB(config)# interface tunnel0
corpB(config-if)# description Connection to regional routers
corpB(config-if)# bandwidth 1000
corpB(config-if)# ip address 10.0.1.1 255.255.255.0
corpB(config-if)# ip mtu 1436
corpB(config-if)# tunnel path-mtu-discovery
corpB(config-if)# delay 1000
corpB(config-if)# ip ospf network broadcast
```

continues

Example 24-3 *Dual-DMVPN Design with Dual Hubs: Corporate Router's, corpB's, Configuration (Continued)*

```
corpB(config-if)# ip ospf priority 2
corpB(config-if)# ip nhrp authentication cisco123
corpB(config-if)# ip nhrp map multicast dynamic
corpB(config-if)# ip nhrp network-id 100001
corpB(config-if)# ip nhrp holdtime 600
corpB(config-if)# tunnel source fastethernet0/0
corpB(config-if)# tunnel mode gre multipoint
corpB(config-if)# tunnel key 100001
corpB(config-if)# tunnel protection ipsec profile dmvpnprofile
corpB(config-if)# exit
corpB(config)# interface fastethernet0/0
corpB(config-if)# description Internet Connection
corpB(config-if)# ip address 192.1.1.2 255.255.255.0
corpB(config-if)# exit
corpB(config)# interface Ethernet1
corpB(config-if)# description Local LAN
corpB(config-if)# ip address 10.0.2.2 255.255.255.0
corpB(config-if)# exit
corpB(config)# router ospf 1
corpB(config-router)# network 10.0.1.0 0.0.0.255 area 1
corpB(config-router)# network 10.0.2.0 0.0.0.255 area 0
corpB(config-router)# exit
```

Regional Office Router Configuration

Example 24-4 shows the configuration of the regional routers. Notice that there are two GRE tunnel interfaces, both of which are configured for multipoint mode (**tunnel mode gre multipoint**). Each tunnel interface has its own unique subnet (10.0.0.0/24 and 10.0.1.0/24), NHRP ID, NHS server (corpA for tunnel0 versus corpB for tunnel1), and its own GRE tunnel ID. For the OSPF configuration, the two tunnel subnets are in area 0 and the local LAN segment is in area 100 + the region number. Using this design, each regional office is its own area, and any routing problems that occur at a regional office are contained, assuming that route summarization has been configured on the regional perimeter routers, which are area border routers (ABRs).

Example 24-4 *Dual-DMVPN Design with Dual Hubs: Spoke Configuration*

```
regionX(config)# interface tunnel0
region(config-if)# description Connection to corpA
regionX(config-if)# bandwidth 1000
regionX(config-if)# ip address 10.0.0.<x+1> 255.255.255.0
regionX(config-if)# ip mtu 1436
regionX(config-if)# delay 1000
regionX(config-if)# ip ospf network broadcast
regionX(config-if)# ip ospf priority 0
regionX(config-if)# ip nhrp authentication cisco123
regionX(config-if)# ip nhrp map multicast 192.1.1.1
regionX(config-if)# ip nhrp map 10.0.0.1 192.1.1.1
regionX(config-if)# ip nhrp nhs 10.0.0.1
regionX(config-if)# ip nhrp network-id 100000
regionX(config-if)# ip nhrp holdtime 300
```

Example 24-4 *Dual-DMVPN Design with Dual Hubs: Spoke Configuration (Continued)*

```
regionX(config-if)# tunnel source fastethernet0/0
regionX(config-if)# tunnel destination 192.1.1.1
regionX(config-if)# tunnel mode gre multipoint
regionX(config-if)# tunnel key 100000
regionX(config-if)# tunnel protection ipsec profile dmvpnprofile
regionX(config-if)# exit
regionX(config)# interface tunnel1
regionX(config-if)# description Connection to corpB
regionX(config-if)# bandwidth 2000
regionX(config-if)# ip address 10.0.1.<x+1> 255.255.255.0
regionX(config-if)# ip mtu 1436
regionX(config-if)# tunnel path-mtu-discovery
regionX(config-if)# delay 1000
regionX(config-if)# ip ospf network broadcast
regionX(config-if)# ip ospf priority 0
regionX(config-if)# ip nhrp authentication cisco123
regionX(config-if)# ip nhrp map multicast 192.1.1.2
regionX(config-if)# ip nhrp map 10.0.1.1 192.1.1.2
regionX(config-if)# ip nhrp nhs 10.0.1.1
regionX(config-if)# ip nhrp network-id 100001
regionX(config-if)# ip nhrp holdtime 300
regionX(config-if)# tunnel source fastethernet0/0
regionX(config-if)# tunnel destination 192.1.1.2
regionX(config-if)# tunnel mode gre multipoint
regionX(config-if)# tunnel key 100001
regionX(config-if)# tunnel protection ipsec profile dmvpnprofile
regionX(config-if)# exit
regionX(config)# interface FastEthernet0/0
regionX(config-if)# description Connection to Internet
regionX(config-if)# ip address 192.1.x.1 255.255.255.0
regionX(config-if)# exit
regionX(config)# interface FastEthernet0/1
regionX(config-if)# description Local LAN
regionX(config-if)# ip address 10.10x.1.1 255.255.255.0
regionX(config-if)# exit
regionX(config)# router ospf 1
regionX(config-router)# network 10.0.0.0 0.0.0.255 area 0
regionX(config-router)# network 10.10x.1.0 0.0.0.255 area X+100
regionX(config-router)# exit
```

TIP   In the configuration in Example 24-4, the bandwidth metric for the two GRE tunnel interfaces is different: tunnel0 uses 1000 and tunnel1 uses 2000. Based on this, the regional office will prefer the corpA router. However, you probably don't want all of your routers using the same corporate router; so on half of them, switch the bandwidth metrics on the two tunnel interfaces. By doing so, half your regional office routers will use corpA and the other half corpB. Optionally, you can set the metrics the same, which will then cause a regional router to use per-destination load balancing to the two corporate office routers; however, the downside of this is that a misconfiguration on your part could lead to a routing loop when spokes bring up connections to other spokes.

NOTE   If you recall from Chapter 17, "Router Site-to-Site Connections," the spoke routers will need *two* public IP addresses if they will be setting up spoke-to-spoke connections, where the tunnel source address for each interface will need to reference a different public IP address.

Internet Remote Access Configuration

In this next section I'll discuss how to set up the Easy VPN Servers and Remotes to provide a secure remote access solution using the Internet to connect the software and hardware clients to the corporate network. I've broken this part into three sections:

- The corporate office's DMZ2 concentrators' configuration
- The branch office's VPN 3002 hardware clients' configuration
- The remote access users' software client configuration

DMZ2 Concentrators

The configuration of the two DMZ2 concentrators is mostly the same, with the exception of the IP addressing information. Therefore, I'll discuss the configuration of one of the concentrators, 3030A. Part of the configuration will require the use of the CLI, but most of it will involve the GUI.

DMZ2 CLI Quick Configuration

First, boot up the 3030A and log in to its console using **admin** and **admin** as the username and password. When performing quick configuration, accept all the defaults. Because the private interface is not being used, also accept the defaults for it (0.0.0.0 for the address and 255.255.255.255 for the subnet mask). When you see the screen where it asks you to modify the IP address of either the public or private interface, save the changes, and exit (enter **h** to take you to the main menu). I'll bypass quick configuration and do everything from the main menus of the CLI.

DMZ2 IP Addressing

To assign the IP address to the public interface and allow HTTPS management access, perform the following from the concentrator's CLI:

Step 1   Enter **1**, Configuration.

Step 2   Enter **2**, Interface Configuration.

Step 3 Enter **2**, Configure Ethernet #2 (Public).

Step 4 Enter **1**, Interface Setting (Disable, DHCP or Static IP).

Step 5 Enter **3**, Enable using Static IP Addressing.

Step 6 Enter **192.1.2.10.**

Step 7 Enter **255.255.255.0.**

Step 8 Enter **10**, Set Interface WebVPN Parameters.

Step 9 Enter **1**, Enable/Disable HTTP and HTTPS Management.

Step 10 Enter **1**, Enable HTTP and HTTPS Management.

Step 11 Enter **h** to return to the main menu.

Step 12 Enter **1**, Configuration.

Step 13 Enter **1**, Interface Configuration.

Step 14 Enter **1**, Configure Ethernet #1 (Private).

Step 15 Enter **1**, Interface Setting (Disable, DHCP, or Static IP).

Step 16 Enter **1**, Disable.

Step 17 Enter **h** to return to the main menu.

NOTE   You must disable the private interface when implementing a VPN-on-a-stick, otherwise the public interface won't come up.

DMZ2 Default Route

Now you need to set up a default route so that from the campus network, you can reach and manage the 3030A using a web browser:

Step 1 Enter **1**, Configuration.

Step 2 Enter **2**, System Management.

Step 3 Enter **3**, IP Routing (static routes, OSPF, etc.).

Step 4 Enter **2**, Default Gateways.

Step 5 Enter **1**, Set Default Gateway.

Step 6 Enter **192.1.2.254**.

Step 7 Enter **h** to return to the main menu.

Step 8   Enter **4**, Save changes to Config file.

Step 9   Enter **6**, Exit.

DMZ2 Access the Concentrator using a Web Browser

Now that you've put a very basic configuration on the 3030A, you should be able to access from the campus using a web browser, assuming you've configured your stateful firewall (192.1.2.254) correctly.

Step 1   From your PC in the campus network, open a web browser and enter **https://192.1.2.10/admin** in the web browser's address bar.

Step 2   Accept the certificate by clicking the **OK** button.

Step 3   Enter **admin** and **admin** for the username and password and click the **Login** button.

Step 4   Click the **Click here to go to the Main Menu** hyperlink to go to the main menu and skip quick configuration.

DMZ2 Basic Administration

Now that you've logged in to the 3030A, you're ready to use your web browser to complete the concentrator's configuration. This and the following sections discuss some common and necessary steps you would perform to complete this process:

Step 1   Go to **Configuration > System > General > Identification**; in the *System Name* field, enter **3030A**; click the **Apply** button.

Step 2   Go to **Configuration > System > Servers > NTP Servers > Hosts**; click the **Add** button; enter **192.1.2.3**; click the **Add** button.

Step 3   Go to **Configuration > System > Servers > DNS Servers**; in the *Domain* field, enter the domain name (**company.com**); click the **Apply** button.

Step 4   Go to **Administration > Access Rights > Administrators**; click the **Modify** button for the admin account; change the password for the account in both password fields; click the **Apply** button.

Step 5   Go to **Configuration > System > Address Management > Assignment**; click the *Use Address Pools* check box; click the **Apply** button.

NOTE   At some point in time, don't forget to change the password for the concentrator's admin account!

DMZ2 Certificate Enrollment

Because certificates are used for device authentication, you'll need to install a root and identity certificate on the 3030A. I'll use SCEP for this process, where the CA is a Microsoft 2003 server with certificate services and SCEP installed:

Step 1 Go to **Administration > Certificate Management**; click the **Click here to install a CA certificate** hyperlink; click the **SCEP (Simple Certificate Enrollment Protocol)** hyperlink.

Step 2 In the *URL* field, enter the URL of the CA, like **http://192.1.2.2/certsrv/ mscep/mscep.dll** for Microsoft's Certificate Authority; in the *CA Descriptor* field, enter the name of the CA (I used **caserver**, but you'll need to obtain this information from the CA administrator); click the **Retrieve** button.

Step 3 From the **Administration > Certificate Management** screen, click the **Click here to enroll with a Certificate Authority** hyperlink; click the **Enroll via SCEP at caserver** hyperlink (the name of the CA appears in the hyperlink).

Step 4 In the *Common Name* field, enter **3030A**; in the *Organizational Unit* field, enter **dmz2**; in the *Organization* field, enter the company name; in the challenge password field, enter a password that will be used to revoke the certificate, if needed, like **boson123456**; change the *Key Size* to **RSA 2048 bits**; click the **Enroll** button (this may take some time, based on the large key size, so be patient).

Step 5 Click the **Go to Certificate Management** hyperlink and examine your 3030A's identity certificate.

DMZ2 ISAKMP/IKE Configuration

Once you have both certificates, you'll need to set up ISAKMP/IKE:

Step 1 Because some of the clients might have to go through an address translation device, you'll need to enable NAT-T: Go to **Configuration > Tunneling and Security > IPsec > NAT Transparency**; click the *IPsec over NAT-T* check box; click the **Apply** button.

Step 2 Set up an ISAKMP/IKE Phase 1 proposal for certificates: Go to **Configuration > Tunneling and Security > IPsec > IKE Proposals.**

Step 3 In the *Active Proposals* column, deactivate all possible proposals except for "CiscoVPNClient-AES128-SHA" by clicking the name of the proposal and then clicking the **Deactivate** button.

Step 4 Click the **CiscoVPNClient-AES128-SHA** proposal name under the *Active Proposals* column and click the **Copy** button; enter **CiscoVPNClient-AES128-SHA-RSA** for the *Proposal Name*; for the *Authentication Mode* drop-down selector, choose **RSA Digital Certificate (XAUTH)** and click the **Apply** button.

Step 5 Under the *Inactive Proposals* column, select the **CiscoVPNClient-AES128-SHA-RSA** proposal name and click the **<<Activate** button.

Step 6 Click the **CiscoVPNClient-AES128-SHA** proposal name under the *Active Proposals* column and click the **Deactivate** button.

In the above sequence, I want to have only the "CiscoVPNClient-AES-128-SHA-RSA" proposal activated, which forces all IPsec clients to use the one I configured for certificates.

DMZ2 Data SA Configuration

Next, you'll need to set up a data SA to use the ISAKMP/IKE proposal:

Step 1 Go to **Configuration > Policy Management > Traffic Management > SAs**; click the **Add** button.

Step 2 For the *SA Name* parameter, enter **ESP-AES128-SHA-RSA**; under the *IPsec* parameters section, change the *Authentication Algorithm* to **ESP/SHA/HMAC-160**; change the *Encryption Algorithm* to **AES-128**; change the *Time Lifetime* parameter to **3600** seconds.

Step 3 Under the *IKE Parameters* section, for the *Digital Certificate* parameter, use the drop-down selector and select **3030A**; For the *IKE Proposal* parameter, use the drop-down selector and select **CiscoVPNClient-AES128-SHA-RSA**; then click the **Apply** button.

DMZ2 VPN-On-A-Stick, Rules, and Filters

I'm using a VPN-on-a-stick implementation with the DMZ2 corporate office concentrators. A VPN-on-a-stick uses a single interface for both protected and unprotected traffic. Because I'm using only the public interface on the DMZ2 concentrators, certain kinds of traffic are being dropped that I will need to allow, including OSPF routing updates, VCA messages, and the local campus traffic that wants to access remote access clients. There already are existing rules for the first two, but you'll need to add a set of rules for the local campus traffic. Once you have created the necessary rules, you'll need to activate these for the public interface filter. Here are the steps you'll need to perform:

Step 1 Go to **Configuration > Policy Management > Traffic Management > Rules** and click the **Add** button.

Step 2   In the *Rule Name* parameter, enter **Campus 10.0.0.0/8 In**; for the *Direction* drop-down selector, choose **Inbound**; for the *Action* drop-down selector, choose **Forward**; in the *Source Address* section, enter **10.0.0.0** for the *IP Address* parameter and **0.255.255.255** for the *Wildcard-mask* parameter; in the *Destination Address* section, enter **10.0.0.0** for the *IP Address* parameter and **0.255.255.255** for the *Wildcard-mask* parameter; click the **Add** button (this creates a rule that will allow traffic from and between 10.0.0.0/8, the corporate network, to enter the interface and reach the remote access clients.

Step 3   In the *Rule Name* parameter, enter **Remote Access 10.0.0.0/8 Out**; for the *Direction* drop-down selector, choose **Outbound**; for the *Action* drop-down selector, choose **Forward**; in the *Source Address* section, enter **10.0.0.0** for the *IP Address* parameter and **0.255.255.255** for the *Wildcard-mask* parameter; in the *Destination Address* section, enter **0.0.0.0** for the *IP Address* parameter and **255.255.255.255** for the *Wildcard-mask* parameter; click the **Add** button (this allows all traffic from the remote access clients with an internal address of 10.0.0.0/8 to leave the interface and go anywhere once their packets are verified and decrypted).

Step 4   In the *Rule Name* parameter, enter **Campus 192.1.2.0/24 In**; for the *Direction* drop-down selector, choose **Inbound**; for the *Action* drop-down selector, choose **Forward**; in the *Source Address* section, enter **192.1.2.0** for the *IP Address* parameter and **0.0.0.255** for the *Wildcard-mask* parameter; in the *Destination Address* section, enter **10.0.0.0** for the *IP Address* parameter and **0.255.255.255** for the *Wildcard-mask* parameter; click the **Add** button (this creates a rule that will allow traffic from 192.1.2.0/24 to 10.0.0.0/8—the remote access clients—to enter the interface).

Step 5   Next you'll need to assign these rules to the public interface filter: Go to **Configuration > Policy Management > Traffic Management > Filters**; click the **Public (Default)** filter and then click the **Assign Rules to Filter** button.

Step 6   Under the *Available Rules* column, select the following rules individually and click the **<<Add** button: **OSPF In (forward/in), OSPF Out (forward/out), VCA In (forward/in), VCA Out (forward/out), Campus 10.0.0.0/8 In (forward in), Remote Access 10.0.0.0/8 Out (forward out)**, and **Campus 192.1.2.0/24 In (forward in)**; click the **Done** button.

Step 7   Go to **Configuration > Interfaces**; click the **Ethernet 2 (Public)** hyperlink; make sure that the *Filter* parameter is set to **2. Public (Default)**. Click the **Apply** button.

DMZ2 AAA

As mentioned earlier in the chapter, the user accounts will be defined on AAA RADIUS servers located in the corporate office's server farm. If you want to store accounting information about remote access connections, also define your AAA RADIUS servers as both authentication and accounting servers:

Step 1 Because I skipped quick configuration, no internal server exists to allow for the remote access groups to be defined locally. To do this, go to **Configuration > System > Servers > Authentication**; click the **Add** button; for the *Server Type* drop-down selector, choose **Internal Server**; click the **Add** button.

Step 2 Next, add the two RADIUS servers: go to **Configuration > System > Servers > Authentication**; click the **Add** button; for the *Server Type* drop-down selector, choose **RADIUS** or **RADIUS with Expiry**, depending on whether or not your AAA server supports changing of users' passwords when accounts expire; in the *Authentication Server* parameter, enter the IP address of the first AAA server, **10.1.1.1**; if it's a Cisco Secure ACS server, leave the port number as 0, which defaults to UDP port 1645, otherwise you might have to change the port number to 1812 in the *Server Port* field depending on your server's RADIUS implementation; in the *Server Secret* and *Verify* fields, enter the encryption key for RADIUS communications (this must match what is configured on the AAA server; click the **Add** button.

Step 3 From the **Configuration > System > Servers > Authentication** screen, select the newly added AAA RADIUS server and click the **Test** button; enter a username and password that exists on the AAA server and click the **OK** button; if you set everything up correctly on the concentrator and AAA RADIUS server, the authentication should be successful.

Step 4 Repeat the last two steps for the second AAA RADIUS server in the server farm on the campus backbone, **10.1.2.1**.

Step 5 Go to the **Configuration > System > Servers > Accounting** screen and add the same two sets of AAA RADIUS servers again, but this time list them as places to store AAA accounting records; click the **Add** button; in the *Accounting Server* field, enter **10.1.1.1**; in the Server Port field, change it to either 1,646 or 1,813 depending on what your AAA server uses for receiving accounting records; enter the same encryption key used when adding the server as an authentication server; click the **Add** button.

Step 6 Repeat the last step for the second AAA RADIUS server, **10.1.2.1**.

DMZ2 Base Group Configuration

Now that the basic configuration is done, you're ready to set up your group configuration. I'll start with the base group first. If you recall from earlier in the chapter, there are three groups of Internet users—sales, administrators, and programmers—and one group of hardware clients for the branch offices. For the most part, the configuration of these groups is the same, with some minor differences. Therefore, I'll start with the Base group configuration first and define all of the parameters that are the same among all groups:

Step 1   Go to **Configuration > User Management > Base Group**.

Step 2   Under the General tab, set the primary and secondary DNS servers to **10.1.1.3** and **10.1.1.4**, respectively (these servers are located in the campus server farm along with the AAA RADIUS servers); set the primary and secondary WINS servers to **10.1.1.5** and **10.1.1.6** respectively; for the *Tunneling Protocols* parameter, uncheck **PPTP**, **L2TP**, and **WebVPN**—only IPsec should be allowed.

Step 3   Under the IPsec tab, use the drop-down selector to change the *IPsec SA* parameter to **ESP-AES128-SHA-RSA**; change the *IKE Peer Identity Validation* drop-down selector to **Required**, which forces the use of certificates for authentication; use the drop-down selector to change the *Authentication* parameter to either **RADIUS** or **RADIUS with Expiry**.

Step 4   Under the Client FW tab, set the *Firewall Setting* parameter to **Required**; set the *Firewall* parameter to **Cisco Integrated Client**; set the *Firewall Policy* parameter to **Policy Pushed (CPP)** (the firewall policy will need to be disabled for the hardware client group); in the drop-down selector, choose **Firewall Filter for VPN Client (Default)**.

Step 5   Click the **Apply** button at the bottom of the screen.

DMZ2 Specific Hardware Client Group Configuration

Once you've configured the base group, you're ready to set up the specific groups. I'll start first with the hardware clients used by the branch offices. Perform the following to create and set up the branch office group:

Step 1   Go to **Configuration > User Management > Groups** and click the **Add Group** button.

Step 2   Under the Identity tab, set the *Group Name* attribute to **Branch Office**; set the password to **cisco123** or something like this and re-enter it (you are required to do this even if you'll only be using certificates).

Step 3   Under the Client Config tab, set the check the *Allow Password Storage on Client* parameter to allow the 3002s to store their username and password locally.

Step 4   Under the Client FW tab, set the *Firewall Setting* parameter to **No Firewall**.

Step 5   Under the Hw Client tab, check the check box for the *Allow Network Extension Mode* parameter.

Step 6   Click the **Add** button.

DMZ2 Specific Software Client Group Configuration

Once I've created the branch office group, I'm ready to create the specific groups for the remote access users: sales, administration, and programming. Each group is by and large the same, except that I want to apply a filter to them to restrict each group's access, as follows:

- All groups should be able to access: 10.0.0.0/16 (the L2L connections) and 10.1.0.0/16 (the campus backbone).
- The sales group should be able to access 10.3.0.0/16.
- The administration group should be able to access 10.4.0.0/16.
- The programming group should be able to access 10.5.0.0/16.
- All other access should be blocked.

The actual filtering will be done by the stateful firewall; however, to enforce these rules, the remote access users must be assigned addresses that will allow the stateful firewall to implement its filtering policies easily. Therefore, the following address pools will be used to assign internal addresses to the Internet clients:

- Sales: 10.7.0.1–10.7.15.254
  - 3030A: 10.7.0.1–10.7.7.254
  - 3030B: 10.7.8.1–10.7.15.254
- Administrators: 10.7.16.1–10.7.31.254
  - 3030A: 10.7.16.1–10.7.23.254
  - 3030B: 10.7.24.1–10.7.31.254
- Programmers: 10.7.32.1–10.7.47.254
  - 3030A: 10.7.32.1–10.7.39.254
  - 3030B: 10.7.40.1–10.7.47.254

Here is the configuration to set this up:

Step 1   Go to **Configuration > User Management > Group** and click the **Add Group** button; under the Identity tab, set the *Group Name* parameter to **Sales**; set the password to something like **cisco123** or something harder to guess (even though pre-shared keys aren't used in this design, they're required when adding a group); click the **Add** button.

Step 2   On the Group screen, select the **Sales** group and click the **Address Pools** button; click the **Add** button; for the *Range Start* parameter, enter **10.7.0.1** for the 3030A concentrator; for the *Range End* parameter enter **10.7.7.254** for the 3030A concentrator; for the *Subnet Mask* parameter, enter **255.255.248.0**; click the **Add** button; click the **Done** button.

Step 3   Go to **Configuration > User Management > Group** and click the **Add Group** button; under the Identity tab, set the *Group Name* parameter to **Administrators**; set the password to something like **cisco123** or something harder to guess (even though pre-shared keys aren't used in this design, they're required when adding a group); click the **Add** button.

Step 4   On the Group screen, select the **Administrators** group and click the **Address Pools** button; click the **Add** button; for the *Range Start* parameter, enter **10.7.16.1** for the 3030A concentrator; for the *Range End* parameter enter **10.7.23.254** for the 3030A concentrator; for the *Subnet Mask* parameter, enter **255.255.248.0**; click the **Add** button; click the **Done** button.

Step 5   Go to **Configuration > User Management > Group** and click the **Add Group** button; under the Identity tab, set the *Group Name* parameter to **Programmers**; set the password to something like **cisco123** or something harder to guess (even though pre-shared keys aren't used in this design, they're required when adding a group); click the **Add** button.

Step 6   On the Group screen, select the **Programmers** group and click the **Address Pools** button; click the **Add** button; for the *Range Start* parameter, enter **10.7.32.1** for the 3030A concentrator; for the *Range End* parameter enter **10.7.39.254** for the 3030A concentrator; for the *Subnet Mask* parameter, enter **255.255.248.0**; click the **Add** button; click the **Done** button.

NOTE   For the 3030B, be sure to use the other sets of addresses for the group assignment.

DMZ2 VCA

For IPsec remote access redundancy, I'll implement VCA to allow for both load balancing and redundancy. I've already allowed VCA messages to be transmitted and received on the public interface in the "VPN-On-A-Stick, Rules, and Filters" section. Only VCA needs to be enabled. Here are the steps to do this:

Step 1   Go to **Configuration > System > Load Balancing**; enter **192.1.2.12** for the *VPN Virtual Cluster IP Address* parameter; for the *IPsec Shared Secret* and *Verify Shared Secret*, enter the same encryption password, like **cisco123**; check the check box for the *Load Balancing Enable* parameter; click the **Apply** button.

Note   You'll need to use the 192.1.2.12 address for the Easy VPN Server address on your clients.

Step 2   When using VCA, you'll need to enable RRI and OSPF to allow the stateful firewalls to know which concentrator the appropriate hardware/software client is connected to. To enable RRI, go to **Configuration >**

System > IP Routing > Reverse Route Injection; click the check boxes for both the *Client Reverse Route Injection* and *Network Extension Reverse Route Injection* parameters; click the **Apply** button.

Step 3   Go to **Configuration > System > IP Routing > OSPF**; click the *Enabled* check box; enter **192.1.1.10** on 3030A (or **192.1.1.11** on 3030B) for the *Router ID* parameter; click the **Apply** button.

Step 4   Go to **Configuration > System > IP Routing > OSPF Areas**; click the **Add** button; in the *Area ID* parameter, enter **0.0.0.7** for the area ID; click the **Add** button.

Tip   You'll want to put the RRI routing information, that is, the concentrators, in a different area than the backbone (0.0.0.0) to reduce the effect of address updates from the concentrators disturbing the backbone OSPF devices; therefore, the DMZ2 interface on the stateful firewall will need to be in OSPF area 0.0.0.7.

Step 5   Go to **Configuration > Interfaces**; click the **Ethernet 2 (Public)** hyperlink; click the **OSPF** tab; select the *OSPF Enable* check box; in the OSPF Area ID parameter, enter **0.0.0.7**; click the **Apply** button.

TIP   Based on the internal IP addressing used for the remote access software client groups, you could configure static routes on your stateful firewall to point to the correct concentrator instead of using RRI with OSPF:

- 3030A: 10.7.0.0/21, 10.7.16.0/21, and 10.7.32.0/21

- 3030B: 10.7.8.0/21, 10.7.24.0/21, and 10.7.40.1/21

Based on this implementation the concentrator doesn't need to advertise host-specific routes, reducing the size of the routing table for the stateful firewall(s); however, you'll still need to enable OSPF and RRI on the concentrator to advertise the 3002s' network RRI routes. In this situation, be sure that client RRI is disabled on *both* concentrators!

NOTE   Once you've configured 3030A, you'll need to configure the 3030B. The configuration is essentially the same, with the exception of the IP addressing of the interfaces, the IP address groups for the internal addresses of the remote access users, the certificate CN field, and the OSPF routing ID.

Branch Office 3002 Hardware Clients

The 3002s will need to be configured for each branch office. Because certificates are being used, you'll need to perform the following steps:

- Perform quick configuration.
- Acquire certificates for the 3002.
- Change the IPsec session from pre-shared keys to certificates.

The following sections will discuss this configuration for the 3002s at the branch offices.

NOTE   You might want to pre-configure the 3002s at the corporate office network and then drop-ship them at the branch offices. Then, all the branch office needs to do is to cable up the 3002 and turn it on.

3002 Quick Configuration

Here are the steps to access and configure the 3002 at a branch office:

Step 1   Connect your PC to the 3002's private interface; set up your PC's IP address to 192.168.10.2; open a web browser to **http://192.168.10.1**; log in as **admin** and **admin**; click the **Login** button.

Step 2   Click the **Click here to start Quick Configuration** hyperlink.

Step 3   On the Time screen, make sure the date and time are correct and click the **Continue** button.

Step 4   On the Upload Config screen, click the **No** button to continue with quick configuration.

Step 5   On the Private Intf screen, choose the **Yes** option for *Do you want to configure the IP address of the Private Interface?* For the *Do you want to use the DHCP server on Interface 1 to provide addresses for the local LAN?* question, choose **Yes, and configure the DHCP server parameters**; click the **Continue** button.

Step 6   For the *Interface IP Address* parameter, enter **10.200.*x*.**," where *x* is the branch number; for the *DHCP Address Pool Start* parameter, enter **10.200.*x*.100** and for the DHCP Address Pool End parameter, enter **10.200.*x*.250**; click the **Continue** button.

Step 7   You'll lose your access to the 3002; set up your PC's IP address to 10.200.*x*.2; open up a web browser to **http://10.200.*x*.1**; log in as **admin** and **admin**; click the **Login** button.

Step 8   Click the **Click here to start Quick Configuration** hyperlink; click the **Public Intf** hyperlink at the top of the web page; in the *System Name* field, enter **BranchOffice*X***, where *X* is the branch office number;

depending on how your 3002 will obtain its address, either set it up as a DHCP client, as a PPoE client, or statically configure the IP address; click the **Continue** button.

Step 9 On the IPsec screen, enter the virtual IP address of **192.1.2.12** for the *Remote Server* parameter; in the group name field, enter **Branch Office** and in the password field, enter the password for this group; in the *Username* and *Password* field, enter the XAUTH username of the 3002 (I typically use something like "3002br1," which needs to be configured on the AAA RADIUS Servers in the corporate office server farm); click the **Continue** button.

Note   You can't add a certificate during quick configuration on the VPN 3002s, so I'll temporarily go through quick configuration using pre-shared keys, obtain a certificate, and then change the configuration to use certificates for device authentication.

Step 10 On the PAT screen, choose the radio button labeled *No, use Network Extension mode*; click the **Continue** button.

Step 11 On the DNS screen, enter a domain name of **company.com** (your company name); click the **Continue** button; click the **Continue** button on the Static Routes screen; on the Admin screen, change the administrator account's password; click the **Continue** button, taking you back to the Main access window.

3002 Certificate Enrollment

To obtain a certificate for the 3002, perform the following steps:

Step 1 From the main access screen, go to **Administration > Certificate Management**.

Step 2 Obtain a root certificate: click the **Click here to install a CA certificate** hyperlink; click the **SCEP (Simple Certificate Enrollment Protocol)** hyperlink; in the *URL* field, enter the URL of the CA, like **http:// 192.1.2.2/certsrv/mscep/mscep.dll**; in the *CA Descriptor* field, enter the name of the CA, like **caserver** (this will be different for every CA); click the **Retrieve** button.

Step 3 From the **Administration > Certificate Management** screen, click the **Click here to enroll with a Certificate Authority** hyperlink; click the **Enroll via SCEP at caserver** hyperlink (the name of the CA appears in the hyperlink).

Step 4   In the *Common Name* field, enter **3002brX**, where *X* is the branch office number; in the *Organizational Unit* field, enter **Branch Office**, the name of the group on the DMZ2 concentrators; in the *Organization* field, enter the company name; in the challenge password field, enter a password that will be used to revoke the certificate, if needed, like **boson123456**; change the *Key Size* to **RSA 2048 bits**; click the **Enroll** button (this may take some time, based on the large key size, so be patient).

Step 5   Click the **Go to Certificate Management** hyperlink and examine your 3030A's identity certificate.

CAUTION   Unfortunately, the 3002s currently don't support NTP. Therefore, you'll want to check the date and time on the 3002s to periodically ensure that they are correct.

3002 Quick Configuration Again

Once you've installed the 3002's root and identity certificate, you can go back to quick configuration and change the device authentication to certificates:

Step 1   Go to **Configuration > Quick Configuration**.

Step 2   Click the **IPsec** hyperlink; check the check box labeled *Use Certificate*.

Step 3   Click the **Continue** button; click the **Done** hyperlink at the top of the page.

Step 4   Go to **Monitoring > System Status** and make sure the IPsec tunnel comes up you've installed the 3002's identity certificate.

Remote Access User Configuration

Once the 3002s are configured, the last part of the VPN Internet connectivity is to configure the Cisco VPN Client software on the Internet users' desktops. I'll assume that the users are using either Windows 2000 or XP and that the client will be the 4.6 version, which I'll assume is already installed on the users' desktops. Here are the steps you'll need to perform to prepare the users' configuration:

Step 1   From your desktop, go to **Start > Programs > Cisco Systems VPN Client > VPN Client**.

Step 2   Install your certificates first: click the **Certificates** tab; click the **Enroll** button.

Step 3   Click the *Online* radio button; in the *CA URL* field, enter **http://192.1.2.2/certsrv/mscep/mscep.dll**; in the *CA Domain* parameter, enter **caserver**; for the *Challenge Password*, enter the value given to you by the CA administrator, if one exists, or one that you'll use to revoke the certificate; click the **Next** button.

Step 4 In the *Name* field, enter the user's XAUTH username; in the *Department* field, enter the name of the group (either **Sales**, **Administrators**, or **Programmers**); in the *Company* field, enter the name of the company; in the *ST* field, enter the name of the state; in the *Country* field, enter the name of the country; click the **Enroll** button; verify your certificate by double-clicking it.

Step 5 Next, add the connection profile to connect to the concentrator cluster on the DMZ2 segment; click the **Connection Entries** tab; click the *New* button; in the *Connection Entry* field, enter **Corporate Office**; in the *Host* field, enter the virtual address of the cluster (**192.1.2.12**); click the *Certificate Authentication* radio button; make sure the identity certificate with the user's CN value appears; click the **Save** button.

Step 6 From the main menu, click **Options > Stateful Firewall (Always On)**; from the main menu click **Options** and make sure that a check mark appears next to "Stateful Firewall (Always On)."

Step 7 Test the new profile by selecting it and clicking the **Connect** button; enter the username and password: for token cards, you'll need to generate the one-time password (OTP) first and then enter the password.

TIP Before enabling the use of token cards on the AAA RADIUS server, first I would test it with a static password defined for the users' accounts. Once this works on a handful of accounts, I would migrate to the use of token cards by the users.

NOTE You'll want to install an NTP client on your user's computers and have it use the NTP server on the DMZ2 segment (this is beyond the scope of this book).

Main Campus Wireless Configuration

I've decided to use IPsec over the wireless transmission between the campus users' desktops and the campus network for added security, as you can see from Figure 24-2. The setup of the concentrators and software clients is similar to that done for the Internet remote access setup. However, there are some differences. For instance, I'll be using both interfaces on the two redundant concentrators and I'll enable auto-initiation on the software clients. Plus, the VPN Client needs to bring up the connection first before the users log in to the Microsoft domain/directory structure. The following sections will discuss the configuration of both of these platforms.

Wireless Concentrators

There are two concentrators handling the wireless access users. The users connect to an access point—there are many—and are assigned a DHCP address from a DHCP server (for their wireless NICs). This is an address from 10.6.0.0/16; however, to access any campus resource, the users also must establish an IPsec tunnel to one of the two concentrators— 3030C or 3030D—to access resources on the campus backbone or other locations, like the Internet or other offices. The following sections will discuss the configuration of the concentrators.

Wireless CLI Quick Configuration

First, boot up the 3030C and log in to its console using **admin** and **admin** as the username and password. When using quick configuration from the CLI, perform the following:

Step 1 Accept all the defaults until you get to the private interface configuration prompt, *Quick Ethernet 1 -> [0.0.0.0]*. Then enter **10.6.1.1** for 3030C (or **10.6.1.2** for 3030D).

Step 2 When prompted for the subnet mask of the private interface, enter **255.255.255.0**.

Step 3 Accept the defaults for the speed, duplexing, and MTU; then choose option **3**, *Save changes to Config file*, and exit the CLI; the rest of the configuration can now be done using a web browser; therefore, enter **h** to remain to the main menu and log out.

Wireless Base Configuration

Now you can use a web browser to complete the configuration of the wireless campus concentrator by following these steps:

Step 1 From your PC in the campus network, open a web browser and enter **http://10.6.1.1/admin** in the address bar.

Step 2 Enter **admin** and **admin** for the username and password and click the **Login** button.

Step 3 Click the **Click here to go to the Main Menu** hyperlink to go to the main menu and skip quick configuration.

Step 4 Go to **Configuration > System > General > Identification**; in the *System Name* field, enter **3030C**; click the **Apply** button.

Step 5 Go to **Configuration > System > Servers > NTP Servers > Hosts**; click the **Add** button; enter **192.1.2.3**; click the **Add** button.

Step 6 Go to **Configuration > System > Servers > DNS Servers**; in the *Domain* field, enter the domain name (**company.com**); click the **Apply** button.

Step 7   Go to **Administration > Access Rights > Administrators**; click the **Modify** button for the admin account; change the password for the account in both password fields; click the **Apply** button.

Step 8   Go to **Configuration > System > Address Management > Assignment**; click the *Use Address Pools* check box; click the **Apply** button.

Step 9   Go to **Configuration > Interfaces**; click the **Ethernet 2 (Public)** hyperlink; select the *Static IP Addressing* radio button; in the *IP Address* parameter, enter **10.6.2.1** for the 3030C or **10.6.2.2** for the 3030D concentrator; make sure the *Subnet Mask* parameter is **255.255.255.0**; click the **Apply** button.

Step 10 Go to **Configuration > System > IP Routing > Default Gateways**; enter the IP address of the Layer-3 device connected to the campus backbone, like **10.6.1.254**.

NOTE   At some point in time, remember to change the password for the admin account on the "wireless" concentrators!

TIP   You'll probably want to use HSRP or VRRP to provide default gateway redundancy for your concentrators; otherwise, you'll need to configure a dynamic routing protocol, like OSPF, on the concentrators and connected Layer-3 devices.

Wireless Certificate Enrollment

Because certificates are used for device authentication, you'll need to install a root and identity certificate on the 3030C (and 3030D). This is almost the identical process I described earlier for the 3030A and 3030B:

Step 1   Go to **Administration > Certificate Management**; click the **Click here to install a CA certificate** hyperlink; click the **SCEP (Simple Certificate Enrollment Protocol)** hyperlink.

Step 2   In the *URL* field, enter the URL of the CA, like **http://192.1.2.2/certsrv/ mscep/mscep.dll**; in the *CA Descriptor* field, enter the name of the CA, like **caserver**; click the **Retrieve** button.

Step 3   From the **Administration > Certificate Management** screen, click the **Click here to enroll with a Certificate Authority** hyperlink; click the **Enroll via SCEP at caserver** hyperlink (the name of the CA appears in the hyperlink).

Step 4 In the *Common Name* field, enter **3030C**; in the *Organizational Unit* field, enter **wireless**; in the *Organization* field, enter the company name; in the challenge password field, enter a password that will be used to revoke the certificate, if needed, like **boson123456**; change the *Key Size* to **RSA 2048 bits**; click the **Enroll** button (this may take some time, based on the large key size, so be patient).

Step 5 Click the **Go to Certificate Management** hyperlink and examine your 3030C's identity certificate.

NOTE The only difference between this and the 3030D's certificate enrollment process is the CN value on the identity certificate.

Wireless ISAKMP/IKE Configuration

Once you have a certificate on the 3030C and 3030D, you'll need to set up ISAKMP/IKE. Unlike the Internet connectivity for remote access users, your wireless users don't need NAT-T, so it won't be enabled. However, an ISAKMP/IKE policy that uses certificates still needs to be set up:

Step 1 Set up an ISAKMP/IKE Phase 1 proposal for certificates: Go to **Configuration > Tunneling and Security > IPsec > IKE Proposals**.

Step 2 In the *Active Proposals* column, deactivate all possible proposals except for CiscoVPNClient-AES128-SHA by clicking the name of the proposal and then clicking the **Deactivate** button.

Step 3 Click the **CiscoVPNClient-AES128-SHA** proposal name under the *Active Proposals* column and click the **Copy** button; enter **CiscoVPNClient-AES128-SHA-RSA** for the *Proposal Name*; for the *Authentication Mode* drop-down selector, choose **RSA Digital Certificate (XAUTH)** and click the **Apply** button.

Step 4 Under the *Inactive Proposals* column, select the "**CiscoVPNClient-AES128-SHA-RSA**" proposal name and click the **<<Activate** button.

Step 5 Select the **CiscoVPNClient-AES128-SHA** proposal name under the *Active Proposals* column and click the **Deactivate** button.

In the above sequence, I want to have only the "CiscoVPNClient-AES-128-SHA-RSA" proposal activated. This forces all IPsec wireless clients to use the one I configured for certificates.

Wireless Data SA Configuration

Next, you'll need to set up a data SA to use the ISAKMP/IKE proposal, like so:

Step 1 Go to **Configuration > Policy Management > Traffic Management > SAs**; click the **Add** button.

Step 2   For the *SA Name* parameter, enter **ESP-AES128-SHA-RSA**; under the
IPsec parameters section, change the *Authentication Algorithm* to **ESP/
SHA/HMAC-160**; change the *Encryption Algorithm* to **AES-128**;
change the *Time Lifetime* parameter to **3600** seconds.

Step 3   Under the *IKE Parameters* section, for the *Digital Certificate* parameter,
use the drop-down selector and select **3030C** (or **3030D** for the other
concentrator); For the *IKE Proposal* parameter, use the drop-down
selector and select **CiscoVPNClient-AES128-SHA-RSA**; then click
the **Apply** button.

Wireless AAA

As mentioned earlier in the chapter, the user accounts will be defined on AAA
RADIUS servers located on the campus server farm segment. If you want to store
accounting information about wireless remote access sessions, also define your AAA
RADIUS servers as both authentication and accounting servers by using the following
steps:

Step 1   Because I skipped quick configuration, no internal server exists to allow
for the groups to be defined locally. To do this, go to **Configuration >
System > Servers > Authentication**; click the **Add** button; for the *Server
Type* drop-down selector, choose **Internal Server**; click the **Add** button.

Step 2   Next add the two RADIUS servers: go to **Configuration > System >
Servers > Authentication**; click the **Add** button; for the *Server Type*
drop-down selector, choose **RADIUS** or **RADIUS with Expiry**,
depending on whether or not your AAA server supports changing of
users' passwords when accounts expire; in the *Authentication Server*
parameter, enter the IP address of the first AAA server, **10.1.1.1**; if it's a
Cisco Secure ACS server, leave the port number as 0, which defaults to
UDP port 1645, otherwise you might have to change the port number
of 1812 in the Server *Port field depending on your server's RADIUS
implementation*; in the *Server Secret* and *Verify* fields, enter the
encryption key for RADIUS communications (this must match what
is configured on the AAA server); click the **Add** button.

Step 3   From the **Configuration > System > Servers > Authentication** screen,
select the newly added AAA RADIUS server and click the **Test** button;
enter a username and password that exists on the AAA server and click
the **OK** button; if you set everything up correctly on the concentrator and
AAA RADIUS server, the authentication should be successful.

Step 4   Repeat the last two steps for the second AAA RADIUS server on the
DMZ2 segment, **10.1.2.1**.

Step 5 Go to the **Configuration > System > Servers > Accounting** screen and add the same two sets of DMZ2 AAA RADIUS servers again, but this time list them as places to store AAA accounting records; click the **Add** button; in the *Accounting Server* field, enter **10.1.1.1**; in the Server Port field, change it to either 1646 or 1813 depending on what your AAA server uses for receiving accounting records; enter the same encryption key used when adding the server as an authentication server; click the **Add** button.

Step 6 Repeat the last step for the second AAA RADIUS server, **10.1.2.1**.

Wireless Base Group Configuration

Now that the basic configuration is done, you're ready to set up your group configuration. I'll start with the base group first. If you recall from earlier in the chapter, there are three groups of users: sales, administrators, and programmers. Unlike the Internet remote access devices, I don't have to worry about any hardware clients—just the desktop software clients. For the most part, the configuration of these groups is the same, with some minor differences. Therefore, I'll start with the base group configuration first and define all of the parameters that are the same among all groups:

Step 1 Go to **Configuration > User Management > Base Group**.

Step 2 Under the General tab, set the primary and secondary DNS servers to **10.1.1.3** and **10.1.1.4**, respectively (these servers are located in the campus server farm along with the AAA RADIUS servers); set the primary and secondary WINS servers to **10.1.1.5** and **10.1.1.6**, respectively; for the *Tunneling Protocols* parameter, uncheck **PPTP**, **L2TP**, and **WebVPN**—only IPsec should be allowed.

Step 3 Under the IPsec tab, use the drop-down selector to change the *IPsec SA* parameter to **ESP-AES128-SHA-RSA**; change the *IKE Peer Identity Validation* drop-down selector to **Required**, which forces the use of certificates for authentication; use the drop-down selector to change the *Authentication* parameter to either **RADIUS** or **RADIUS with Expiry**.

Step 4 Under the Client FW tab, set the *Firewall Setting* parameter to **Required**; set the *Firewall* parameter to **Cisco Integrated Client**; set the *Firewall Policy* parameter to **Policy Pushed (CPP)**; in the drop-down selector, choose **Firewall Filter for VPN Client (Default)**.

Step 5 Click the **Apply** button at the bottom of the screen.

Wireless Specific Software Client Group Configuration

Once I've configured the base group policies, I'm ready to create the specific groups for the wireless users: sales, administration, and programming. These are the same three groups I defined on the DMZ2 concentrators. The following address pools will be used to assign internal addresses to the clients:

- Sales: 10.7.128.1–10.7.43.254
  - 3030C: 10.7.128.1–10.7.135.254
  - 3030D: 10.7.136.1–10.7.143.254
- Administrators: 10.7.144.1–10.7.159.254
  - 3030C: 10.7.144.1–10.7.151.254
  - 3030D: 10.7.152.1–10.7.159.254
- Programmers: 10.7.160.1–10.7.175.254
  - 3030C: 10.7.160.1–10.7.167.254
  - 3030D: 10.7.168.1–10.7.175.254

Based on this addressing implementation, I could easily apply additional filtering policies inside the campus network Layer-3 devices to restrict access to various locations. Here is the configuration to set this address configuration policy on the campus concentrators:

Step 1   Go to **Configuration > User Management > Group** and click the **Add Group** button; under the Identity tab, set the *Group Name* parameter to **Sales**; set the password to something like **cisco123** or something harder to guess (even though pre-shared keys aren't used in this design, they're required when adding a group); click the **Add** button.

Step 2   On the Group screen, click the **Sales** group and click the **Address Pools** button; click the **Add** button; for the *Range Start* parameter, enter **10.7.128.1** for the 3030C concentrator; for the *Range End* parameter enter **10.7.135.254** for the 3030C concentrator; for the *Subnet Mask* parameter, enter **255.255.248.0**; click the **Add** button; click the **Done** button.

Step 3   Go to **Configuration > User Management > Group** and click the **Add Group** button; under the Identity tab, set the *Group Name* parameter to **Administrators**; set the password to something like **cisco123** or something harder to guess (even though pre-shared keys aren't used in this design, they're required when adding a group); click the **Add** button.

Step 4   On the Group screen, click the **Administrators** group and click the **Address Pools** button; click the **Add** button; for the *Range Start* parameter, enter **10.7.144.1** for the 3030C concentrator; for the *Range End* parameter enter **10.7.151.254** for the 3030C concentrator; for the *Subnet Mask* parameter, enter **255.255.248.0**; click the **Add** button; click the **Done** button.

Step 5   Go to **Configuration > User Management > Group** and click the **Add Group** button; under the Identity tab, set the *Group Name* parameter to **Programmers**; set the password to something like **cisco123** or something harder to guess (even though pre-shared keys aren't used in this design, they're required when adding a group); click the **Add** button.

Step 6 On the Group screen, click the **Programmers** group and click the **Address Pools** button; click the **Add** button; for the *Range Start* parameter, enter **10.7.160.1** for the 3030C concentrator; for the *Range End* parameter enter **10.7.167.254** for the 3030C concentrator; for the *Subnet Mask* parameter, enter **255.255.248.0**; click the **Add** button; click the **Done** button.

NOTE   For the 3030D, be sure to use the other sets of addresses for the group assignment listed in the above bullet points.

Wireless VCA

I'll implement VCA on the 3030C and 3030D to allow for both load balancing and redundancy. Here are the steps to do this:

Step 1 You need to allow VCA messages on the public interface: Go to **Configuration > Policy Management > Traffic Management > Filters**; select the **Public (Default)** filter and click the **Assigns Rules to Filter** button; under the *Available Rules* column, select **VCA In (forward/in)** and click the **<<Add** button; under the *Available Rules* column, select **VCA Out (forward/out)** and click the **<<Add** button; click the **Done** button; repeat the same process for the physical interface filter.

Step 2 Go to **Configuration > System > Load Balancing**; enter **10.6.2.5** for the *VPN Virtual Cluster IP Address* parameter; for the *IPsec Shared Secret* and *Verify Shared Secret*, enter the same encryption password, like **cisco123**; check the check box for the *Load Balancing Enable* parameter; click the **Apply** button.

Note   You'll need to use the **10.6.2.5** address for the Easy VPN Server address on your clients.

Step 3 When using VCA, you'll need to enable RRI and OSPF to allow the stateful firewalls to know which concentrator the appropriate hardware/software client is connected to. To enable RRI, go to **Configuration > System > IP Routing > Reverse Route Injection**; click the check boxes for only the *Client Reverse Route Injection* parameter (Network Extension mode isn't used and therefore is not necessary); click the **Apply** button.

Step 4   Go to **Configuration > System > IP Routing > OSPF**; click the *Enabled* check box; enter **10.6.1.1** on 3030C (or **10.6.1.2** on 3030D) for the *Router ID* parameter; click the **Apply** button.

Step 5   Go to **Configuration > System > IP Routing > OSPF Areas**; click the **Add** button; in the *Area ID* parameter, enter **7.7.7.128** for the area ID; click the **Add** button.

Tip   You'll want to put the RRI routing information, that is, the concentrators, in a different area than the backbone (0.0.0.0) to reduce the effect of address updates from the concentrators disturbing the backbone OSPF devices; therefore, the DMZ2 interface on the stateful firewall will need to be in OSPF area 0.0.7.128.

Step 6   Go to **Configuration > Interfaces**; click the **Ethernet 2 (Private)** hyperlink; click the **OSPF** tab; select the *OSPF Enable* check box; in the OSPF Area ID parameter, enter **0.0.7.128**; click the **Apply** button.

TIP   Based on the internal IP addressing used for the wireless software client groups, you could configure static routes on your Layer-3 campus device to point to the correct concentrator:

- 3030C: 10.7.128.0/21, 10.7.144.0/21, and 10.7.160.0/21

- 3030D: 10.7.136.0/21, 10.7.152.0/21, and 10.7.4168.1/21

Based on this implementation, the concentrator doesn't need to advertise host-specific routes, reducing the size of the routing table for the stateful firewall(s); and because there are no 3002s, you don't need to advertise any network extension mode network numbers. If you decide to implement this solution, be sure that client RRI is disabled on both concentrators.

NOTE   Once you've configured 3030C, you'll need to configure the 3030D. The configuration is essentially the same, with the exception of the IP addressing of the interfaces, the IP address groups for the internal addresses of the wireless users, the certificate CN field, and the OSPF routing ID.

Wireless User Configuration

The last part of the discussion on wireless campus connectivity is how to configure the Cisco VPN Client software on the wireless users' desktops. I'll assume that the users either are using Windows 2000 or XP and that the client will be the 4.6 version, which I'll assume is installed already on the users' desktops. Here are the steps you'll need to perform to prepare the users' configuration:

Step 1 From your desktop, go to **Start > Programs > Cisco Systems VPN Client > VPN Client**.

Step 2 Install your certificates first: click the **Certificates** tab; click the **Enroll** button.

Step 3 Click the *Online* radio button; in the *CA URL* field, enter **http:// 192.1.2.2/certsrv/mscep/mscep.dll**; in the *CA Domain* parameter, enter **caserver**; for the *Challenge Password*, enter the value given to you by the CA administrator, if one exists, or one that you'll use to revoke the certificate; click the **Next** button.

Step 4 In the *Name* field, enter the user's XAUTH username; in the *Department* field, enter the name of the group (either **Sales**, **Administrators**, or **Programmers**); in the *Company* field, enter the name of the company; in the *ST*, field, enter the name of the state; in the *Country* field, enter the name of the country; click the **Enroll** button; verify your certificate by double-clicking it.

Step 5 Next, add the connection profile to connect to the concentrator cluster on the wireless segment: click the **Connection Entries** tab; click the **New** button; in the *Connection Entry* field, enter **Corporate Wireless**; in the *Host* field, enter the virtual address of the cluster (**10.6.2.5**); click the *Certificate Authentication* radio button; make sure the identity certificate with the user's CN value appears; click the **Save** button.

Step 6 From the main menu, click **Options > Stateful Firewall (Always On)**; from the main menu click **Options** and make sure that a check mark appears next to "Stateful Firewall (Always On)."

Step 7 From the main menu, click **Options > Windows Logon Properties**; click the check box labeled *Enable start before logon*, which allows the VPN Client to start up before the user logs in to a Microsoft domain or directory structure; click the **OK** button.

Step 8 Test the new profile by selecting it and clicking the **Connect** button; enter the username and password. For token cards, you'll need to generate the OTP first and then enter the password.

Step 9 Once the connection works, you can now change the vpnclient.ini file to allow for auto-initiation: open the vpnclient.ini file with a text editor and place the entries in Example 24-5 at the end of the "[Main]" section; at the bottom of the vpnclient.ini file, add section information listed in Example 24-6 (for the *ConnectionEntry* parameter in this example, use the name of the group previously defined in Step 5); close the VPN Client, if open, and when re-opened, verify that you see the *Automatic VPN Initiation* option from the *Options* menu.

Note   Notice that in Example 24-6, the section for the WLAN profile specifies an address and mask of 0.0.0.0/0, which means that any address assigned to the wireless client will cause auto-initiation to take place.

Step 10 Based on a 30-second retry interval, the wireless client should bring up a tunnel to the 3030 cluster within 30 seconds.

Example 24-5 vpnclient.ini *File for Wireless Users' Auto-Initiation*

```
[Main]
←output omitted→
AutoInitiationEnable=1
AutoInitiationRetryIntervalType=1
AutoInitationRetryInterval=30
AutoInitiationRetryLimit=20
AutoInitiationList=WLAN
```

Example 24-6 vpnclient.ini *File for Wireless User's Connection Profile Information*

```
[WLAN]
Network=0.0.0.0
Mask=0.0.0.0
ConnectionEntry=Sales
Connect=1
```

TIP   To simplify the client configuration, I would pre-configure the vpnclient.ini with the auto-initiation parameters and the .pcf files for the connection profiles and then test them. Once I had auto-initiation working for each profile, I would then place these in the client installation package and install the client software. Once installed, the only thing you would need to do is to go through the certificate enrollment process to obtain a certificate.

Summary

This case study showed you the use of the many VPN features discussed in this book. This is by no means the only possible solution to the given scenario; however, the goal of this chapter was to show you how to implement Cisco VPN features in an integrated fashion. As you will learn, each networking situation has its own set of unique problems and issues and its own set of possible solutions.

A Last Bit of Advice

As you can see from this case study, even though the network is medium-sized, the configuration is quite involved. Therefore, I would highly recommend that you implement one VPN component at a time, making the setup and troubleshooting process easier. For example, I would probably set up the L2L DMVPN configuration first, and then focus on the remote access. And as a final note in this book, VPNs are probably one of the most complicated technologies you'll deal with in the security field. I've learned a long time ago that I don't know everything and am always being introduced to problems I've never seen before. Therefore, having a very good foundation in the understanding of VPNs is very important (I can't stress this last point enough), which is why the first part of the book was devoted to VPN technologies and why each part of the book contained a troubleshooting chapter. With a good foundation, you should be able to design a solid, secure VPN solution and troubleshoot any problems that may crop up. And last, good luck with your VPN endeavors! Cheers!

INDEX

Numerics

3DES (Triple DES), 51, 93

A

E

F

H

I

Q

R

S

U

V

W–Z

Cisco Press

SAVE UP TO 30%

Become a member and save at **ciscopress.com**!

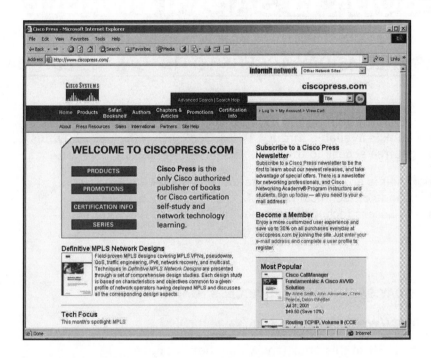

Complete a **user profile** at ciscopress.com today to become a member and benefit from **discounts up to 30% on every purchase** at ciscopress.com, as well as a more customized user experience. Your membership will also allow you access to the entire Informit network of sites.

Don't forget to subscribe to the monthly Cisco Press newsletter to be the first to learn about new releases and special promotions. You can also sign up to get your first **30 days FREE on Safari Bookshelf** and preview Cisco Press content. Safari Bookshelf lets you access Cisco Press books online and build your own customized, searchable electronic reference library.

Visit **www.ciscopress.com/register** to sign up and start saving today!

The profile information we collect is used in aggregate to provide us with better insight into your technology interests and to create a better user experience for you. You must be logged into ciscopress.com to receive your discount. Discount is on Cisco Press products only; shipping and handling are not included.

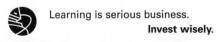

Learning is serious business.
Invest wisely.

Safari®
BOOKS ONLINE
ENABLED

THIS BOOK IS SAFARI ENABLED

INCLUDES FREE 45-DAY ACCESS TO THE ONLINE EDITION

The Safari® Enabled icon on the cover of your favorite technology book means the book is available through Safari Bookshelf. When you buy this book, you get free access to the online edition for 45 days.

Safari Bookshelf is an electronic reference library that lets you easily search thousands of technical books, find code samples, download chapters, and access technical information whenever and wherever you need it.

TO GAIN 45-DAY SAFARI ENABLED ACCESS TO THIS BOOK:

- Go to **http://www.ciscopress.com/safarienabled**

- Enter the ISBN of this book (shown on the back cover, above the bar code)

- Log in or Sign up (site membership is required to register your book)

- Enter the coupon code found in the front of this book before the "Contents at a Glance" page

If you have difficulty registering on Safari Bookshelf or accessing the online edition, please e-mail customer-service@safaribooksonline.com.